# Dewey Decimal Classification and Relative Index

# Dewey Decimal Classification and Relative Index

Devised by Melvil Dewey

## EDITION 23

Edited by

Joan S. Mitchell, Editor in Chief

Julianne Beall, Assistant Editor

Rebecca Green, Assistant Editor

Giles Martin, Assistant Editor

Michael Panzer, Assistant Editor

## VOLUME 2
### Schedules 000–599

OCLC

OCLC Online Computer Library Center, Inc.

Dublin, Ohio

2011

Library of Congress Cataloging-in-Publication Data
**Dewey, Melvil, 1851-1931.**
   Dewey decimal classification and relative index / devised by Melvil Dewey. — Ed. 23 / edited by Joan S. Mitchell, Editor in Chief ; Julianne Beall, Assistant Editor ; Rebecca Green, Assistant Editor ; Giles Martin, Assistant Editor ; Michael Panzer, Assistant Editor.
   v. cm.
   Includes bibliographical references and index.
   Contents: v. 1. Manual. Tables — v. 2. Schedules 000-599 — v. 3. Schedules 600-999 — v. 4. Relative index.
   ISBN-13: 978-1-910608-81-4 (set : alk. paper)
   ISBN-10: 1-910608-81-5 (set : alk. paper)
   ISBN-13: 978-1-910608-80-7 (vol. 1 : alk. paper)
   ISBN-10: 1-910608-80-7 (vol. 1 : alk. paper)
   [etc.]
   1. Classification, Dewey decimal. I. Mitchell, Joan S. II. Beall, Julianne, 1946- III. Green, Rebecca, 1952- IV. Martin, Giles. V. Panzer, Michael. VI. Title.
   Z696.D52 2011
   025.4'31—dc22                      2011001112

OCLC Online Computer Library Center, Inc.
6565 Kilgour Place
Dublin, OH 43017-3395 USA
www.oclc.org/dewey

The paper used in this publication meets the requirements of ANSI/NISO Z39.48-1992 (Permanence of Paper).

ISBN-13: (set) 978-1-910608-81-4; v. 1 978-1-910608-80-7;
v. 2 978-1-910608-76-0; v. 3 978-1-910608-79-1; v. 4 978-1-910608-78-4

ISBN-10: (set) 1-910608-81-5; v. 1 1-910608-80-7; v. 2 1-910608-76-9;
v. 3 1-910608-79-3; v. 4 1-910608-78-5

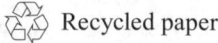 Recycled paper

# Summaries

## First Summary
## *The Ten Main Classes*

000  **Computer science, information & general works**
100  **Philosophy & psychology**
200  **Religion**
300  **Social sciences**
400  **Language**
500  **Science**
600  **Technology**
700  **Arts & recreation**
800  **Literature**
900  **History & geography**

*Consult schedules for complete and exact headings*

# Second Summary
## *The Hundred Divisions*

000 Computer science, knowledge & systems
010 Bibliographies
020 Library & information sciences
030 Encyclopedias & books of facts
040 [Unassigned]
050 Magazines, journals & serials
060 Associations, organizations & museums
070 News media, journalism & publishing
080 Quotations
090 Manuscripts & rare books

100 Philosophy
110 Metaphysics
120 Epistemology
130 Parapsychology & occultism
140 Philosophical schools of thought
150 Psychology
160 Philosophical logic
170 Ethics
180 Ancient, medieval & eastern philosophy
190 Modern western philosophy

200 Religion
210 Philosophy & theory of religion
220 The Bible
230 Christianity
240 Christian practice & observance
250 Christian pastoral practice & religious orders
260 Christian organization, social work & worship
270 History of Christianity
280 Christian denominations
290 Other religions

300 Social sciences, sociology & anthropology
310 Statistics
320 Political science
330 Economics
340 Law
350 Public administration & military science
360 Social problems & social services
370 Education
380 Commerce, communications & transportation
390 Customs, etiquette & folklore

400 Language
410 Linguistics
420 English & Old English languages
430 German & related languages
440 French & related languages
450 Italian, Romanian & related languages
460 Spanish, Portuguese, Galician
470 Latin & Italic languages
480 Classical & modern Greek languages
490 Other languages

500 Science
510 Mathematics
520 Astronomy
530 Physics
540 Chemistry
550 Earth sciences & geology
560 Fossils & prehistoric life
570 Biology
580 Plants (Botany)
590 Animals (Zoology)

600 Technology
610 Medicine & health
620 Engineering
630 Agriculture
640 Home & family management
650 Management & public relations
660 Chemical engineering
670 Manufacturing
680 Manufacture for specific uses
690 Construction of buildings

700 Arts
710 Area planning & landscape architecture
720 Architecture
730 Sculpture, ceramics & metalwork
740 Graphic arts & decorative arts
750 Painting
760 Printmaking & prints
770 Photography, computer art, film, video
780 Music
790 Sports, games & entertainment

800 Literature, rhetoric & criticism
810 American literature in English
820 English & Old English literatures
830 German & related literatures
840 French & related literatures
850 Italian, Romanian & related literatures
860 Spanish, Portuguese, Galician literatures
870 Latin & Italic literatures
880 Classical & modern Greek literatures
890 Other literatures

900 History
910 Geography & travel
920 Biography & genealogy
930 History of ancient world (to ca. 499)
940 History of Europe
950 History of Asia
960 History of Africa
970 History of North America
980 History of South America
990 History of other areas

*Consult schedules for complete and exact headings*

# Third Summary
## *The Thousand Sections*

000 Computer science, information & general works
001 Knowledge
002 The book
003 Systems
004 Computer science
005 Computer programming, programs & data
006 Special computer methods
007 [Unassigned]
008 [Unassigned]
009 [Unassigned]

010 **Bibliography**
011 Bibliographies & catalogs
012 Bibliographies & catalogs of individuals
013 [Unassigned]
014 Of anonymous & pseudonymous works
015 Of works from specific places
016 Of works on specific subjects
017 General subject catalogs
018 [Unassigned]
019 [Unassigned]

020 **Library & information sciences**
021 Library relationships
022 Administration of physical plant
023 Personnel management
024 [Unassigned]
025 Library operations
026 Libraries for specific subjects
027 General libraries
028 Reading & use of other information media
029 [Unassigned]

030 **General encyclopedic works**
031 Encyclopedias in American English
032 Encyclopedias in English
033 In other Germanic languages
034 Encyclopedias in French, Occitan & Catalan
035 In Italian, Romanian & related languages
036 Encyclopedias in Spanish, Portuguese & Galician
037 Encyclopedias in Slavic languages
038 Encyclopedias in Scandinavian languages
039 Encyclopedias in other languages

040 **[Unassigned]**
041 [Unassigned]
042 [Unassigned]
043 [Unassigned]
044 [Unassigned]
045 [Unassigned]
046 [Unassigned]
047 [Unassigned]
048 [Unassigned]
049 [Unassigned]

050 **General serial publications**
051 Serials in American English
052 Serials in English
053 Serials in other Germanic languages
054 Serials in French, Occitan & Catalan
055 In Italian, Romanian & related languages
056 Serials in Spanish, Portuguese & Galician
057 Serials in Slavic languages
058 Serials in Scandinavian languages
059 Serials in other languages

060 **General organizations & museum science**
061 Organizations in North America
062 Organizations in British Isles
063 Organizations in Germany; in central Europe
064 Organizations in France & Monaco
065 In Italy, San Marino, Vatican City, Malta
066 In Spain, Andorra, Gibraltar, Portugal
067 Organizations in Russia; in eastern Europe
068 Organizations in other geographic areas
069 Museum science

070 **News media, journalism & publishing**
071 Newspapers in North America
072 Newspapers in British Isles
073 Newspapers in Germany; in central Europe
074 Newspapers in France & Monaco
075 In Italy, San Marino, Vatican City, Malta
076 In Spain, Andorra, Gibraltar, Portugal
077 Newspapers in Russia; in eastern Europe
078 Newspapers in Scandinavia
079 Newspapers in other geographic areas

080 **General collections**
081 Collections in American English
082 Collections in English
083 Collections in other Germanic languages
084 Collections in French, Occitan & Catalan
085 In Italian, Romanian & related languages
086 Collections in Spanish, Portuguese & Galician
087 Collections in Slavic languages
088 Collections in Scandinavian languages
089 Collections in other languages

090 **Manuscripts & rare books**
091 Manuscripts
092 Block books
093 Incunabula
094 Printed books
095 Books notable for bindings
096 Books notable for illustrations
097 Books notable for ownership or origin
098 Prohibited works, forgeries & hoaxes
099 Books notable for format

*Consult schedules for complete and exact headings*

# Philosophy & psychology

**100 Philosophy & psychology**
101 Theory of philosophy
102 Miscellany
103 Dictionaries & encyclopedias
104 [Unassigned]
105 Serial publications
106 Organizations & management
107 Education, research & related topics
108 Groups of people
109 Historical & collected biography

**110 Metaphysics**
111 Ontology
112 [Unassigned]
113 Cosmology
114 Space
115 Time
116 Change
117 Structure
118 Force & energy
119 Number & quantity

**120 Epistemology, causation & humankind**
121 Epistemology
122 Causation
123 Determinism & indeterminism
124 Teleology
125 [Unassigned]
126 The self
127 The unconscious & the subconscious
128 Humankind
129 Origin & destiny of individual souls

**130 Parapsychology & occultism**
131 Parapsychological & occult methods
132 [Unassigned]
133 Specific topics in parapsychology & occultism
134 [Unassigned]
135 Dreams & mysteries
136 [Unassigned]
137 Divinatory graphology
138 Physiognomy
139 Phrenology

**140 Specific philosophical schools**
141 Idealism & related systems
142 Critical philosophy
143 Bergsonism & intuitionism
144 Humanism & related systems
145 Sensationalism
146 Naturalism & related systems
147 Pantheism & related systems
148 Eclecticism, liberalism & traditionalism
149 Other philosophical systems

**150 Psychology**
151 [Unassigned]
152 Perception, movement, emotions & drives
153 Mental processes & intelligence
154 Subconscious & altered states
155 Differential & developmental psychology
156 Comparative psychology
157 [Unassigned]
158 Applied psychology
159 [Unassigned]

**160 Philosophical logic**
161 Induction
162 Deduction
163 [Unassigned]
164 [Unassigned]
165 Fallacies & sources of error
166 Syllogisms
167 Hypotheses
168 Argument & persuasion
169 Analogy

**170 Ethics**
171 Ethical systems
172 Political ethics
173 Ethics of family relationships
174 Occupational ethics
175 Ethics of recreation & leisure
176 Ethics of sex & reproduction
177 Ethics of social relations
178 Ethics of consumption
179 Other ethical norms

**180 Ancient, medieval & eastern philosophy**
181 Eastern philosophy
182 Pre-Socratic Greek philosophies
183 Socratic & related philosophies
184 Platonic philosophy
185 Aristotelian philosophy
186 Skeptic & Neoplatonic philosophies
187 Epicurean philosophy
188 Stoic philosophy
189 Medieval western philosophy

**190 Modern western philosophy**
191 Philosophy of United States & Canada
192 Philosophy of British Isles
193 Philosophy of Germany & Austria
194 Philosophy of France
195 Philosophy of Italy
196 Philosophy of Spain & Portugal
197 Philosophy of Russia
198 Philosophy of Scandinavia
199 Philosophy in other geographic areas

*Consult schedules for complete and exact headings*

# Religion

| | | | |
|---|---|---|---|
| **200** | **Religion** | **250** | **Christian orders & local church** |
| 201 | Religious mythology & social theology | 251 | Preaching |
| 202 | Doctrines | 252 | Texts of sermons |
| 203 | Public worship & other practices | 253 | Pastoral office & work |
| 204 | Religious experience, life & practice | 254 | Parish administration |
| 205 | Religious ethics | 255 | Religious congregations & orders |
| 206 | Leaders & organization | 256 | [Unassigned] |
| 207 | Missions & religious education | 257 | [Unassigned] |
| 208 | Sources | 258 | [Unassigned] |
| 209 | Sects & reform movements | 259 | Pastoral care of families & groups of people |

| | | | |
|---|---|---|---|
| **210** | **Philosophy & theory of religion** | **260** | **Social & ecclesiastical theology** |
| 211 | Concepts of God | 261 | Social theology |
| 212 | Existence, knowability & attributes of God | 262 | Ecclesiology |
| 213 | Creation | 263 | Days, times & places of observance |
| 214 | Theodicy | 264 | Public worship |
| 215 | Science & religion | 265 | Sacraments, other rites & acts |
| 216 | [Unassigned] | 266 | Missions |
| 217 | [Unassigned] | 267 | Associations for religious work |
| 218 | Humankind | 268 | Religious education |
| 219 | [Unassigned] | 269 | Spiritual renewal |

| | | | |
|---|---|---|---|
| **220** | **Bible** | **270** | **History, geography, biography of Christianity** |
| 221 | Old Testament (Tanakh) | 271 | Religious orders in church history |
| 222 | Historical books of Old Testament | 272 | Persecutions in church history |
| 223 | Poetic books of Old Testament | 273 | Doctrinal controversies & heresies |
| 224 | Prophetic books of Old Testament | 274 | History of Christianity in Europe |
| 225 | New Testament | 275 | History of Christianity in Asia |
| 226 | Gospels & Acts | 276 | History of Christianity in Africa |
| 227 | Epistles | 277 | History of Christianity in North America |
| 228 | Revelation (Apocalypse) | 278 | History of Christianity in South America |
| 229 | Apocrypha & pseudepigrapha | 279 | History of Christianity in other areas |

| | | | |
|---|---|---|---|
| **230** | **Christianity** | **280** | **Christian denominations & sects** |
| 231 | God | 281 | Early church & Eastern churches |
| 232 | Jesus Christ & his family | 282 | Roman Catholic Church |
| 233 | Humankind | 283 | Anglican churches |
| 234 | Salvation & grace | 284 | Protestants of Continental origin |
| 235 | Spiritual beings | 285 | Presbyterian, Reformed & Congregational |
| 236 | Eschatology | 286 | Baptist, Disciples of Christ & Adventist |
| 237 | [Unassigned] | 287 | Methodist & related churches |
| 238 | Creeds & catechisms | 288 | [Unassigned] |
| 239 | Apologetics & polemics | 289 | Other denominations & sects |

| | | | |
|---|---|---|---|
| **240** | **Christian moral & devotional theology** | **290** | **Other religions** |
| 241 | Christian ethics | 291 | [Unassigned] |
| 242 | Devotional literature | 292 | Greek & Roman religion |
| 243 | Evangelistic writings for individuals | 293 | Germanic religion |
| 244 | [Unassigned] | 294 | Religions of Indic origin |
| 245 | [Unassigned] | 295 | Zoroastrianism |
| 246 | Use of art in Christianity | 296 | Judaism |
| 247 | Church furnishings & articles | 297 | Islam, Babism & Bahai Faith |
| 248 | Christian experience, practice & life | 298 | (Optional number) |
| 249 | Christian observances in family life | 299 | Religions not provided for elsewhere |

*Consult schedules for complete and exact headings*

# Social sciences

**300  Social sciences**
301  Sociology & anthropology
302  Social interaction
303  Social processes
304  Factors affecting social behavior
305  Groups of people
306  Culture & institutions
307  Communities
308  [Unassigned]
309  [Unassigned]

**310  Collections of general statistics**
311  [Unassigned]
312  [Unassigned]
313  [Unassigned]
314  General statistics of Europe
315  General statistics of Asia
316  General statistics of Africa
317  General statistics of North America
318  General statistics of South America
319  General statistics of other areas

**320  Political science**
321  Systems of governments & states
322  Relation of state to organized groups
323  Civil & political rights
324  The political process
325  International migration & colonization
326  Slavery & emancipation
327  International relations
328  The legislative process
329  [Unassigned]

**330  Economics**
331  Labor economics
332  Financial economics
333  Economics of land & energy
334  Cooperatives
335  Socialism & related systems
336  Public finance
337  International economics
338  Production
339  Macroeconomics & related topics

**340  Law**
341  Law of nations
342  Constitutional & administrative law
343  Military, tax, trade & industrial law
344  Labor, social, education & cultural law
345  Criminal law
346  Private law
347  Procedure & courts
348  Laws, regulations & cases
349  Law of specific jurisdictions & areas

**350  Public administration & military science**
351  Public administration
352  General considerations of public administration
353  Specific fields of public administration
354  Administration of economy & environment
355  Military science
356  Infantry forces & warfare
357  Mounted forces & warfare
358  Air & other specialized forces
359  Sea forces & warfare

**360  Social problems & services; associations**
361  Social problems & services
362  Social problems of groups of people
363  Other social problems & services
364  Criminology
365  Penal & related institutions
366  Secret associations & societies
367  General clubs
368  Insurance
369  Associations

**370  Education**
371  Schools & their activities; special education
372  Primary education
373  Secondary education
374  Adult education
375  Curricula
376  [Unassigned]
377  [Unassigned]
378  Higher education
379  Public policy issues in education

**380  Commerce, communications & transportation**
381  Commerce
382  International commerce
383  Postal communication
384  Communications
385  Railroad transportation
386  Inland waterway & ferry transportation
387  Water, air & space transportation
388  Transportation
389  Metrology & standardization

**390  Customs, etiquette & folklore**
391  Costume & personal appearance
392  Customs of life cycle & domestic life
393  Death customs
394  General customs
395  Etiquette (Manners)
396  [Unassigned]
397  [Unassigned]
398  Folklore
399  Customs of war & diplomacy

*Consult schedules for complete and exact headings*

# Language

*Consult schedules for complete and exact headings*

# Science

| | | | | |
|---|---|---|---|---|
| **500** | **Natural sciences & mathematics** | | **550** | **Earth sciences** |
| 501 | Philosophy & theory | | 551 | Geology, hydrology & meteorology |
| 502 | Miscellany | | 552 | Petrology |
| 503 | Dictionaries & encyclopedias | | 553 | Economic geology |
| 504 | [Unassigned] | | 554 | Earth sciences of Europe |
| 505 | Serial publications | | 555 | Earth sciences of Asia |
| 506 | Organizations & management | | 556 | Earth sciences of Africa |
| 507 | Education, research & related topics | | 557 | Earth sciences of North America |
| 508 | Natural history | | 558 | Earth sciences of South America |
| 509 | History, geographic treatment, biography | | 559 | Earth sciences of other areas |
| | | | | |
| **510** | **Mathematics** | | **560** | **Paleontology** |
| 511 | General principles of mathematics | | 561 | Paleobotany; fossil microorganisms |
| 512 | Algebra | | 562 | Fossil invertebrates |
| 513 | Arithmetic | | 563 | Fossil marine & seashore invertebrates |
| 514 | Topology | | 564 | Fossil mollusks & molluscoids |
| 515 | Analysis | | 565 | Fossil arthropods |
| 516 | Geometry | | 566 | Fossil chordates |
| 517 | [Unassigned] | | 567 | Fossil cold-blooded vertebrates |
| 518 | Numerical analysis | | 568 | Fossil birds |
| 519 | Probabilities & applied mathematics | | 569 | Fossil mammals |
| | | | | |
| **520** | **Astronomy & allied sciences** | | **570** | **Biology** |
| 521 | Celestial mechanics | | 571 | Physiology & related subjects |
| 522 | Techniques, equipment & materials | | 572 | Biochemistry |
| 523 | Specific celestial bodies & phenomena | | 573 | Specific physiological systems in animals |
| 524 | [Unassigned] | | 574 | [Unassigned] |
| 525 | Earth (Astronomical geography) | | 575 | Specific parts of & systems in plants |
| 526 | Mathematical geography | | 576 | Genetics & evolution |
| 527 | Celestial navigation | | 577 | Ecology |
| 528 | Ephemerides | | 578 | Natural history of organisms |
| 529 | Chronology | | 579 | Microorganisms, fungi & algae |
| | | | | |
| **530** | **Physics** | | **580** | **Plants (Botany)** |
| 531 | Classical mechanics | | 581 | Specific topics in natural history |
| 532 | Fluid mechanics | | 582 | Plants noted for characteristics & flowers |
| 533 | Gas mechanics | | 583 | Dicotyledons |
| 534 | Sound & related vibrations | | 584 | Monocotyledons |
| 535 | Light & related radiation | | 585 | Gymnosperms |
| 536 | Heat | | 586 | Seedless plants |
| 537 | Electricity & electronics | | 587 | Vascular seedless plants |
| 538 | Magnetism | | 588 | Bryophytes |
| 539 | Modern physics | | 589 | [Unassigned] |
| | | | | |
| **540** | **Chemistry & allied sciences** | | **590** | **Animals (Zoology)** |
| 541 | Physical chemistry | | 591 | Specific topics in natural history |
| 542 | Techniques, equipment & materials | | 592 | Invertebrates |
| 543 | Analytical chemistry | | 593 | Marine & seashore invertebrates |
| 544 | [Unassigned] | | 594 | Mollusks & molluscoids |
| 545 | [Unassigned] | | 595 | Arthropods |
| 546 | Inorganic chemistry | | 596 | Chordates |
| 547 | Organic chemistry | | 597 | Cold-blooded vertebrates |
| 548 | Crystallography | | 598 | Birds |
| 549 | Mineralogy | | 599 | Mammals |

*Consult schedules for complete and exact headings*

# Technology

**600 Technology**
601 Philosophy & theory
602 Miscellany
603 Dictionaries & encyclopedias
604 Special topics
605 Serial publications
606 Organizations
607 Education, research & related topics
608 Patents
609 History, geographic treatment, biography

**610 Medicine & health**
611 Human anatomy, cytology & histology
612 Human physiology
613 Personal health & safety
614 Incidence & prevention of disease
615 Pharmacology & therapeutics
616 Diseases
617 Surgery & related medical specialties
618 Gynecology, obstetrics, pediatrics & geriatrics
619 [Unassigned]

**620 Engineering & allied operations**
621 Applied physics
622 Mining & related operations
623 Military & nautical engineering
624 Civil engineering
625 Engineering of railroads & roads
626 [Unassigned]
627 Hydraulic engineering
628 Sanitary engineering
629 Other branches of engineering

**630 Agriculture & related technologies**
631 Techniques, equipment & materials
632 Plant injuries, diseases & pests
633 Field & plantation crops
634 Orchards, fruits & forestry
635 Garden crops (Horticulture)
636 Animal husbandry
637 Processing dairy & related products
638 Insect culture
639 Hunting, fishing & conservation

**640 Home & family management**
641 Food & drink
642 Meals & table service
643 Housing & household equipment
644 Household utilities
645 Household furnishings
646 Sewing, clothing & personal living
647 Management of public households
648 Housekeeping
649 Child rearing & home care of people

**650 Management & auxiliary services**
651 Office services
652 Processes of written communication
653 Shorthand
654 [Unassigned]
655 [Unassigned]
656 [Unassigned]
657 Accounting
658 General management
659 Advertising & public relations

**660 Chemical engineering**
661 Industrial chemicals
662 Explosives, fuels & related products
663 Beverage technology
664 Food technology
665 Industrial oils, fats, waxes & gases
666 Ceramic & allied technologies
667 Cleaning, color & coating technologies
668 Technology of other organic products
669 Metallurgy

**670 Manufacturing**
671 Metalworking & primary metal products
672 Iron, steel & other iron alloys
673 Nonferrous metals
674 Lumber processing, wood products & cork
675 Leather & fur processing
676 Pulp & paper technology
677 Textiles
678 Elastomers & elastomer products
679 Other products of specific materials

**680 Manufacture for specific uses**
681 Precision instruments & other devices
682 Small forge work (Blacksmithing)
683 Hardware & household appliances
684 Furnishings & home workshops
685 Leather, fur goods & related products
686 Printing & related activities
687 Clothing & accessories
688 Other final products & packaging
689 [Unassigned]

**690 Construction of buildings**
691 Building materials
692 Auxiliary construction practices
693 Specific materials & purposes
694 Wood construction
695 Roof covering
696 Utilities
697 Heating, ventilating & air-conditioning
698 Detail finishing
699 [Unassigned]

*Consult schedules for complete and exact headings*

# Arts & recreation

**700 The arts; fine & decorative arts**
701 Philosophy of fine & decorative arts
702 Miscellany of fine & decorative arts
703 Dictionaries of fine & decorative arts
704 Special topics in fine & decorative arts
705 Serial publications of fine & decorative arts
706 Organizations & management
707 Education, research & related topics
708 Galleries, museums & private collections
709 History, geographic treatment & biography

**710 Area planning & landscape architecture**
711 Area planning
712 Landscape architecture
713 Landscape architecture of trafficways
714 Water features
715 Woody plants
716 Herbaceous plants
717 Structures in landscape architecture
718 Landscape design of cemeteries
719 Natural landscapes

**720 Architecture**
721 Architectural materials & structural elements
722 Architecture to ca. 300
723 Architecture from ca. 300 to 1399
724 Architecture from 1400
725 Public structures
726 Buildings for religious purposes
727 Buildings for education & research
728 Residential & related buildings
729 Design & decoration

**730 Sculpture & related arts**
731 Processes, forms & subjects of sculpture
732 Sculpture to ca. 500
733 Greek, Etruscan & Roman sculpture
734 Sculpture from ca. 500 to 1399
735 Sculpture from 1400
736 Carving & carvings
737 Numismatics & sigillography
738 Ceramic arts
739 Art metalwork

**740 Graphic arts & decorative arts**
741 Drawing & drawings
742 Perspective
743 Drawing & drawings by subject
744 [Unassigned]
745 Decorative arts
746 Textile arts
747 Interior decoration
748 Glass
749 Furniture & accessories

**750 Painting & paintings**
751 Techniques, equipment, materials & forms
752 Color
753 Symbolism, allegory, mythology & legend
754 Genre paintings
755 Religion
756 [Unassigned]
757 Human figures
758 Other subjects
759 History, geographic treatment, biography

**760 Printmaking & prints**
761 Relief processes (Block printing)
762 [Unassigned]
763 Lithographic processes
764 Chromolithography & serigraphy
765 Metal engraving
766 Mezzotinting, aquatinting & related processes
767 Etching & drypoint
768 [Unassigned]
769 Prints

**770 Photography, computer art, film, video**
771 Techniques, equipment & materials
772 Metallic salt processes
773 Pigment processes of printing
774 Holography
775 [Unassigned]
776 Computer art (Digital art)
777 Cinematography and videography
778 Fields & kinds of photography
779 Photographic images

**780 Music**
781 General principles & musical forms
782 Vocal music
783 Music for single voices
784 Instruments & instrumental ensembles
785 Ensembles with one instrument per part
786 Keyboard & other instruments
787 Stringed instruments
788 Wind instruments
789 (Optional number)

**790 Recreational & performing arts**
791 Public performances
792 Stage presentations
793 Indoor games & amusements
794 Indoor games of skill
795 Games of chance
796 Athletic & outdoor sports & games
797 Aquatic & air sports
798 Equestrian sports & animal racing
799 Fishing, hunting & shooting

*Consult schedules for complete and exact headings*

# Literature

**800  Literature & rhetoric**
801  Philosophy & theory
802  Miscellany
803  Dictionaries & encyclopedias
804  [Unassigned]
805  Serial publications
806  Organizations & management
807  Education, research & related topics
808  Rhetoric & collections of literature
809  History, description & criticism

**810  American literature in English**
811  American poetry in English
812  American drama in English
813  American fiction in English
814  American essays in English
815  American speeches in English
816  American letters in English
817  American humor & satire in English
818  American miscellaneous writings
819  (Optional number)

**820  English & Old English literatures**
821  English poetry
822  English drama
823  English fiction
824  English essays
825  English speeches
826  English letters
827  English humor & satire
828  English miscellaneous writings
829  Old English (Anglo-Saxon)

**830  German & related literatures**
831  German poetry
832  German drama
833  German fiction
834  German essays
835  German speeches
836  German letters
837  German humor & satire
838  German miscellaneous writings
839  Other Germanic literatures

**840  French & related literatures**
841  French poetry
842  French drama
843  French fiction
844  French essays
845  French speeches
846  French letters
847  French humor & satire
848  French miscellaneous writings
849  Occitan & Catalan literatures

**850  Italian, Romanian & related literatures**
851  Italian poetry
852  Italian drama
853  Italian fiction
854  Italian essays
855  Italian speeches
856  Italian letters
857  Italian humor & satire
858  Italian miscellaneous writings
859  Romanian & related literatures

**860  Spanish, Portuguese, Galician literatures**
861  Spanish poetry
862  Spanish drama
863  Spanish fiction
864  Spanish essays
865  Spanish speeches
866  Spanish letters
867  Spanish humor & satire
868  Spanish miscellaneous writings
869  Portuguese & Galician literature

**870  Latin & Italic literatures**
871  Latin poetry
872  Latin dramatic poetry & drama
873  Latin epic poetry & fiction
874  Latin lyric poetry
875  Latin speeches
876  Latin letters
877  Latin humor & satire
878  Latin miscellaneous writings
879  Literatures of other Italic languages

**880  Classical Greek & related literatures**
881  Classical Greek poetry
882  Classical Greek dramatic poetry & drama
883  Classical Greek epic poetry & fiction
884  Classical Greek lyric poetry
885  Classical Greek speeches
886  Classical Greek letters
887  Classical Greek humor & satire
888  Classical Greek miscellaneous writings
889  Modern Greek literature

**890  Literatures of other languages**
891  East Indo-European & Celtic literatures
892  Afro-Asiatic literatures
893  Non-Semitic Afro-Asiatic literatures
894  Altaic, Uralic, Hyperborean & Dravidian
895  Literatures of East & Southeast Asia
896  African literatures
897  North American native literatures
898  South American native literatures
899  Austronesian & other literatures

*Consult schedules for complete and exact headings*

# History & geography

**900  History & geography**
901  Philosophy & theory
902  Miscellany
903  Dictionaries & encyclopedias
904  Collected accounts of events
905  Serial publications
906  Organizations & management
907  Education, research & related topics
908  Groups of people
909  World history

**910  Geography & travel**
911  Historical geography
912  Atlases, maps, charts & plans
913  Geography of & travel in ancient world
914  Geography of & travel in Europe
915  Geography of & travel in Asia
916  Geography of & travel in Africa
917  Geography of & travel in North America
918  Geography of & travel in South America
919  Geography of & travel in other areas

**920  Biography, genealogy & insignia**
921  (Optional number)
922  (Optional number)
923  (Optional number)
924  (Optional number)
925  (Optional number)
926  (Optional number)
927  (Optional number)
928  (Optional number)
929  Genealogy, names & insignia

**930  History of ancient world to ca. 499**
931  China to 420
932  Egypt to 640
933  Palestine to 70
934  South Asia to 647
935  Mesopotamia & Iranian Plateau to 637
936  Europe north & west of Italy to ca. 499
937  Italy & adjacent territories to 476
938  Greece to 323
939  Other parts of ancient world to ca. 640

**940  History of Europe**
941  British Isles
942  England & Wales
943  Germany & central Europe
944  France & Monaco
945  Italy, San Marino, Vatican City, Malta
946  Spain, Andorra, Gibraltar, Portugal
947  Russia & eastern Europe
948  Scandinavia
949  Other parts of Europe

**950  History of Asia**
951  China & adjacent areas
952  Japan
953  Arabian Peninsula & adjacent areas
954  India & south Asia
955  Iran
956  Middle East (Near East)
957  Siberia (Asiatic Russia)
958  Central Asia
959  Southeast Asia

**960  History of Africa**
961  Tunisia & Libya
962  Egypt & Sudan
963  Ethiopia & Eritrea
964  Morocco & adjacent areas
965  Algeria
966  West Africa & offshore islands
967  Central Africa & offshore islands
968  Republic of South Africa & southern Africa
969  South Indian Ocean islands

**970  History of North America**
971  Canada
972  Mexico, Central America, West Indies, Bermuda
973  United States
974  Northeastern United States
975  Southeastern United States
976  South central United States
977  North central United States
978  Western United States
979  Great Basin & Pacific Slope region

**980  History of South America**
981  Brazil
982  Argentina
983  Chile
984  Bolivia
985  Peru
986  Colombia & Ecuador
987  Venezuela
988  Guiana
989  Paraguay & Uruguay

**990  History of other areas**
991  [Unassigned]
992  [Unassigned]
993  New Zealand
994  Australia
995  New Guinea & Melanesia
996  Polynesia & other Pacific Ocean islands
997  Atlantic Ocean islands
998  Arctic islands & Antarctica
999  Extraterrestrial worlds

*Consult schedules for complete and exact headings*

# Schedules

# 000

---

## 000     Computer science, information, general works

| | |
|---|---|
| 050 | **General serial publications** |
| .9 | History, geographic treatment, biography |
| 051 | **General serial publications in American English** |
| 052 | **General serial publications in English** |
| 053 | **General serial publications in other Germanic languages** |
| 054 | **General serial publications in French, Occitan, Catalan** |
| 055 | **General serial publications in Italian, Dalmatian, Romanian, Rhaetian, Sardinian, Corsican** |
| 056 | **General serial publications in Spanish, Portuguese, Galician** |
| 057 | **General serial publications in Slavic languages** |
| 058 | **General serial publications in Scandinavian languages** |
| 059 | **General serial publications in other languages** |
| | |
| 060 | **General organizations and museology** |
| .1–.9 | Standard subdivisions and special topics of general organizations |
| 061 | **General organizations in North America** |
| 062 | **General organizations in British Isles** |
| 063 | **General organizations in Germany and neighboring central European countries** |
| 064 | **General organizations in France and Monaco** |
| 065 | **General organizations in Italy, San Marino, Vatican City, Malta** |
| 066 | **General organizations in Spain, Andorra, Gibraltar, Portugal** |
| 067 | **General organizations in Russia and neighboring east European countries** |
| 068 | **General organizations in other geographic areas** |
| 069 | **Museology (Museum science)** |
| | |
| 070 | **Documentary media, educational media, news media; journalism; publishing** |
| .01–.09 | Standard subdivisions |
| .1–.9 | [Documentary media, educational media, news media; journalism; publishing] |
| 071 | **Journalism and newspapers in North America** |
| 072 | **Journalism and newspapers in British Isles** |
| 073 | **Journalism and newspapers in Germany and neighboring central European countries** |
| 074 | **Journalism and newspapers in France and Monaco** |
| 075 | **Journalism and newspapers in Italy, San Marino, Vatican City, Malta** |
| 076 | **Journalism and newspapers in Spain, Andorra, Gibraltar, Portugal** |
| 077 | **Journalism and newspapers in Russia and neighboring east European countries** |
| 078 | **Journalism and newspapers in Scandinavia** |
| 079 | **Journalism and newspapers in other geographic areas** |
| | |
| 080 | **General collections** |
| .9 | History, geographic treatment, biography |
| 081 | **General collections in American English** |
| 082 | **General collections in English** |
| 083 | **General collections in other Germanic languages** |
| 084 | **General collections in French, Occitan, Catalan** |
| 085 | **General collections in Italian, Dalmatian, Romanian, Rhaetian, Sardinian, Corsican** |
| 086 | **General collections in Spanish, Portuguese, Galician** |
| 087 | **General collections in Slavic languages** |
| 088 | **General collections in Scandinavian languages** |
| 089 | **General collections in other languages** |

| | |
|---|---|
| 090 | **Manuscripts, rare books, other rare printed materials** |
| 091 | **Manuscripts** |
| 092 | **Block books** |
| 093 | **Incunabula** |
| 094 | **Printed books** |
| 095 | **Books notable for bindings** |
| 096 | **Books notable for illustrations and materials** |
| 097 | **Books notable for ownership or origin** |
| 098 | **Prohibited works, forgeries, hoaxes** |
| 099 | **Books notable for format** |

# 001 Knowledge

Description and critical appraisal of intellectual activity in general

Including interdisciplinary works on consultants

Class here discussion of ideas from many fields; interdisciplinary approach to knowledge

Class epistemology in 121. Class a compilation of knowledge in a specific form with the form, e.g., encyclopedias 030

> *For consultants or use of consultants in a specific subject, see the subject, e.g., library consultants 023.2, engineering consultants 620, use of consultants in management 658.46*

> *See Manual at 500 vs. 001*

.01  Theory of knowledge

Do not use for philosophy of knowledge, philosophical works on theory of knowledge; class in 121

.1  **Intellectual life**

Nature and value

> *For scholarship and learning, see 001.2*

> *See also 900 for broad description of intellectual situation and condition*

.2  **Scholarship and learning**

Intellectual activity directed toward increase of knowledge

Class methods of study and teaching in 371.3. Class a specific branch of scholarship and learning with the branch, e.g., scholarship in the humanities 001.3, in history 900

> *For research, see 001.4*

> *See Manual at 500 vs. 001*

.3  **Humanities**

Including relative value of science versus the humanities

Class here government policy on humanities

**.4**      **Research**

Class here action research, evaluation research, works discussing what research is

Class research in a specific subject with the subject, plus notation 072 from Table 1, e.g., research in linguistics 410.72; class results of research in a specific subject with the subject without notation 072 from Table 1, e.g., results of research in linguistics 410 (*not* 410.72)

*See Manual at 500 vs. 001*

.42      Research methods

Class here qualitative research, quantitative research, scientific method

Class operations research in 003; class computer modeling and simulation in 003.3

*For descriptive and experimental methods, see 001.43*

.422      Statistical methods

*See also 310 for collections of general statistical data; also notation 021 from Table 1 for statistics on a specific subject*

*See Manual at 519.5, T1—015195 vs. 001.422, T1—0727*

.422 6      Presentation of statistical data

Class here graphic presentation

.43      Descriptive and experimental methods

[.432]      Historical research

Case studies relocated to 001.433; interdisciplinary works on historical research relocated to 907.2

.433      Descriptive research

Including case studies [*formerly* 001.432]; sampling techniques; surveys, questionnaires, field work, observation, interviews

Class here data collection

*For analysis of statistical data, see 001.422; for presentation of statistical data, see 001.4226*

*See also 310.723 for methods of collecting general social statistical data*

.434      Experimental method

**.44**      Support of and incentives for research

Standard subdivisions are added for either or both topics in heading

Class here awards, bursaries, certificates, competitions, contests, fellowships and scholarships, financial support, grants, honors, medals, prizes

Class student finance in higher education in 378.3. Class support of and incentives for research in a specific subject with the subject, plus notation 079 from Table 1, e.g., research awards in mechanical engineering 621.079

*See also 929.81 for orders and decorations*

**.9**      **Controversial knowledge**

Including well-established phenomena for which explanations are controversial; the end of the world

Class here interdisciplinary works on controversial knowledge, parapsychology, occultism

*For parapsychology and occultism, see 130. For controversial knowledge concerning a specific subject, see the subject, e.g., paranatural and legendary phenomena as subjects of folklore 398.4, Piltdown man hoax 569.9, controversial medical remedies 615.856, an alleged conspiracy to assassinate John F. Kennedy 973.922*

*See Manual at 001.9 and 130*

**.94**      Mysteries

Reported phenomena not explained, not fully verified

Including Atlantis, Bermuda Triangle, pyramid power

Class here nonastronomical extraterrestrial influences on earth

*See also 900 for Atlantis as a subject of archaeology*

**.942**      Unidentified flying objects (UFOs)

Variant name: flying saucers

Class here human-alien encounters

**.944**      Monsters and related phenomena

Including abominable snowman, Loch Ness monster

*See also 590 for animals whose reality is not controversial*

**.95**      Deceptions and hoaxes

Class a hoax that influenced history with the hoax in 900, e.g., False Dmitri 947.045

**.96**      Errors, delusions, superstitions

## 002    The book

Including interdisciplinary works on chapbooks [*formerly* 398.5]

Class here historical bibliography, interdisciplinary works on the book

Class comprehensive works on historical and analytical bibliography in 010.42

> *For book publishing, see 070.5; for rare books, see 090; for social aspects of the book, see 302.232; for book arts, see 686. For chapbooks with content limited to a specific subject, see the subject, e.g., murder 364.1523, anonymous jokes from oral tradition 398.7, 18th-century English fiction 823.5*

[.021 6]         Lists, inventories, catalogs

Do not use; class in 010

.029         Commercial miscellany

Do not use for trade catalogs and directories; class in 010

.074         Museums, collections, exhibits

Class catalogs and lists in 010

## 003    Systems

Class here operations research; systems theory, analysis, design, optimization; models (simulations) applied to real-world systems

Unless other instructions are given, class a subject with aspects in two or more subdivisions of 003 in the number coming last, e.g., control of discrete-time linear systems 003.830115 (*not* 003.5 or 003.74)

Class simulation in education in 371.397; class use of systems analysis and operations research in management in 658.4032. Class systems in a specific subject with the subject, plus notation 011 from Table 1, e.g., systems theory in the social sciences 300.11

> *See also 004.21 for analysis and design of computer-based systems; also 511.8 for mathematical models not applied to real-world systems; also 519.7 for mathematical programming not applied to real-world systems*
>
> *See Manual at 510, T1—0151 vs. 003, T1—011*

[.028 5]         Computer applications

Do not use; class in 003.3

### .1    System identification

Determining a mathematical model for a system by observing its input-output relationships

### .2    Forecasting and forecasts

Class here interdisciplinary works on forecasting

> *For forecasting by parapsychological and occult means, see 133.3; for social forecasting, see 303.49. For forecasting in a particular kind of system, see the system in 003.7–003.8, e.g., forecasting in stochastic systems 003.760112*

.209　　　　　History, geographic treatment, biography of forecasting as a discipline

*For forecasting and forecasts for specific areas, see 303.491–303.499*

## .3　　Computer modeling and simulation

Standard subdivisions are added for either or both topics in heading

Class here computer applications in systems, computer implementation of mathematical models of systems, interdisciplinary works on computer modeling and simulation

Add to base number 003.3 the numbers following 00 in 004–006, e.g., computer simulation languages 003.3513

*For computer modeling and simulation applied to a specific subject, see the subject, plus notation 0113 from Table 1, e.g., computer modeling in economics 330.0113*

## .5　　Theory of communication and control

In living and nonliving systems

Including bionics

Class here cybernetics, interdisciplinary works on control and stability of systems

Class social aspects of and interdisciplinary works on communication in systems in 302.2

*For artificial intelligence, see 006.3; for control theory in automation engineering, see 629.8312. For control and stability of systems in a specific subject, see the subject, plus notation 0115 from Table 1, e.g., control and stability of systems in general engineering 620.00115*

.52　　　　　Perception theory

Class computer vision in 006.37; class psychology of human perception in 153.7; class perception in animals in 573.87

*See also 006.4 for computer pattern recognition*

.54　　　　　Information theory

Theory concerning measurement of quantities of information; accuracy in transmission of messages subject to noise (unwanted, usually random, signals), distortion, and transmission failure; and methods of coding for efficient, accurate transmission

Class here coding theory

Class information theory in communications engineering in 621.3822, without using notation 01154 from Table 1; class coding for purpose of limiting access to information (cryptography) in 652.8. Class information theory in communications engineering of a specific kind of communications with the kind, without using notation 01154 from Table 1, e.g., radio 621.384; class information theory in any other specific subject with the subject, plus notation 01154 from Table 1, e.g., information theory in economics 330.01154

.56 Decision theory

> *See also 153.83 for decision theory in psychology; also 511.65 for decision theory in combinatorial analysis; also 658.40301 for decision theory in management*

**.7 Kinds of systems**

Systems distinguished by type or equations used to model them

Including deterministic, hierarchical, lumped-parameter, self-organizing, small-scale systems

> *For systems distinguished in relation to time, see 003.8*

.71 Large-scale systems

> Limited to works emphasizing that the systems are large

.72 Networks

> Class here network theory

> *For purely mathematical treatment of networks without reference to real-world systems, see 511.5*

.74 Linear systems

.75 Nonlinear systems

.76 Stochastic systems

.78 Distributed-parameter systems

**.8 Systems distinguished in relation to time**

Including continuous-time, instantaneous (zero-memory), time-invariant, time-varying systems

.83 Discrete-time systems

.85 Dynamic systems

> Systems in which response depends upon past values of excitation as well as current excitation

.857 Chaotic systems

> Class here chaotic behavior in systems

---

\> ## 004–006 Computer science; computer programming, programs, data; special computer methods

Unless other instructions are given, class a subject with aspects in two or more subdivisions of 004–006 in the number coming last, e.g., external storage for personal computers 004.56 (*not* 004.16), data security in client-server computing 005.8 (*not* 004.36), natural language processing in full-text database management systems 006.35 (*not* 005.759)

Class comprehensive works in 004

## 004     Computer science

Class here data processing; selection and use of computer hardware; electronic computers; electronic digital computers; computer systems (computers, their peripheral devices, their operating systems); cyberinfrastructure; central processing units; computer reliability; interactive, online processing; mobile computing; comprehensive works on hardware and programs in electronic data processing

Class computer modeling and simulation in 003.3. Class computer applications in a specific subject with the subject, plus notation 0285 from Table 1, e.g., computer applications in banking 332.10285

> *For computer programming, programs, data, see 005; for special computer methods, see 006; for engineering, manufacture, repair of computers, see 621.39. For a specific aspect of mobile computing, see the aspect, e.g., handheld computing devices 004.167, wireless communications 004.6, mobile operating systems for handheld computing devices 005.446*

> *See also 025.04 for automated information storage and retrieval; also 303.4834 for computers as a cause of social change; also 343.0999 for computer law; also 364.168 for financial and business computer crimes; also 371.334 for computer-assisted instruction (CAI); also 658.05 for data processing in management; also 794.8 for computer games*

> *See Manual at 004–006 vs. 621.39; also at 004 vs. 005; also at 510, T1—0151 vs. 004–006, T1—0285*

### SUMMARY

| | |
|---|---|
| 004.01–.09 | **Standard subdivisions** |
| .1 | **General works on specific types of computers** |
| .2 | **Systems analysis and design, computer architecture, performance evaluation** |
| .3 | **Processing modes** |
| .5 | **Storage** |
| .6 | **Interfacing and communications** |
| .7 | **Peripherals** |
| .9 | **Nonelectronic data processing** |

**.015 1**      Mathematical principles

Class here computer mathematics

*See Manual at 004.0151 vs. 511.1, 511.35*

**.019**      Psychological principles

Class here human-computer interaction, human factors, usability

Apply notation 019 from Table 1 as modified here throughout 004–006, e.g., human factors in user interfaces 005.437019

**.028**      Auxiliary techniques and procedures; apparatus, equipment, materials

**[.028 7]**      Testing and measurement

Do not use; class in 004.24

**.1**      **General works on specific types of computers**

Class here specific types of processors, computer systems based on specific types of computers

Class specific types of computers, processors, computer systems distinguished by their processing modes in 004.3; class programmable calculators in 510.28541

*See Manual at 004.1; also at 004.1 vs. 004.24; also at 004.1 vs. 004.3*

Embedded computer systems relocated to 006.22

---

>      004.11–004.16   Digital computers

Multifunctional digital devices are classed with their predominant function, e.g., personal digital assistants (PDAs), which often include mobile phone and portable media player capabilities in addition to their baseline computing capabilities, with handheld computing devices 004.167. However, a work that focuses on a specific function other than the predominant function is classed with the specific function, e.g., audio recording using a personal computer 006.5

Class comprehensive works in 004

*See Manual at 004.11–004.16*

**.11**      *Supercomputers

Class massively parallel supercomputers in 004.35

**.12**      *Mainframe computers

Class here large-scale digital computers

*For supercomputers, see 004.11; for midrange computers, see 004.14*

**.125**      Specific mainframe computers

Arrange alphabetically by name of computer or processor, e.g., IBM System z9®

**.14**      *Midrange computers

Class here minicomputers, server class computers

Class comprehensive works on midrange and personal computers in 004.16

**.145**      Specific midrange computers

Arrange alphabetically by name of computer or processor, e.g., Dell PowerEdge® 1955

**.16**      *Personal computers

Former heading: Microcomputers

Class here specific types of personal computers; comprehensive works on midrange and personal computers

*For midrange computers, see 004.14*

---

*Use notation 019 from Table 1 as modified at 004.019

.165        Specific personal computers

> Arrange alphabetically by name of computer or processor, e.g., Apple iMac®
>
> Specific handheld computing devices relocated to 004.1675

.167        *Handheld computing devices

> Class here specific types of handheld computing devices

.167 5        Specific handheld computing devices [*formerly* 004.165]

> Arrange alphabetically by name of computer or processor, e.g., BlackBerry®

.19        *Hybrid and analog computers

> Standard subdivisions are added for either or both topics in heading
>
> *For nonelectronic analog computers, see 004.9*

## .2    *Systems analysis and design, computer architecture, performance evaluation

.21        *Systems analysis and design

> Standard subdivisions are added for either or both topics in heading
>
> Class here analysis of a user's problem preparatory to developing a computer system to solve it
>
> Class communications network design and architecture in 004.65
>
> *For software systems analysis and design, see 005.12; for database design and architecture, see 005.74*
>
> *See also 003 for interdisciplinary works on systems analysis and design; also 658.4032 for management use of systems analysis*
>
> *See Manual at 004.21 vs. 004.22, 621.392*

.22        *Computer architecture

> *See Manual at 004.21 vs. 004.22, 621.392*

.24        *Performance evaluation

> Class here performance measurement and evaluation to aid in designing or improving the performance of a computer system
>
> Class performance evaluation as a consideration in purchasing a specific item with the item in 004, plus notation 029 from Table 1, e.g., evaluating personal computers for purchase 004.16029
>
> *See also 004.0685 for management techniques to ensure quality control in data processing*
>
> *See Manual at 004.1 vs. 004.24*

---

*Use notation 019 from Table 1 as modified at 004.019

.25     Systems analysis and design, computer architecture, performance evaluation of specific types of electronic computers

Add to base number 004.25 the numbers following 004.1 in 004.11–004.19, e.g., architecture of personal computers 004.256

*For systems analysis and design, computer architecture, performance evaluation of specific types of computers distinguished by processing mode, see 004.3*

**.3     \*Processing modes**

Including batch, offline, pipeline processing; CISC (complex instruction set computing), RISC (reduced instruction set computing); multiprogramming, time-sharing

Class here computers, processors, computer systems distinguished by their processing modes; centralized processing

Class comprehensive works on multiprogramming, on time-sharing in 005.434

*See Manual at 004.1 vs. 004.3*

.33     \*Real-time processing

Limited to processing defined by predictability constraints and timing deadlines

Including systems analysis and design, computer architecture, performance evaluation of real-time computers

Class interactive, online, real-time data processing covering immediate processing of input or an immediate response to a user's action in 004

.35     \*Multiprocessing

Including systems analysis and design, computer architecture, performance evaluation; array processing, associative processing, dataflow computation

Class here cluster computing, massively parallel supercomputers, parallel processing

Class comprehensive works on associative processing and memory in 004.5; class programming for multiprocessor computers in 005.275

.357    Specific multiprocessor computers

Including systems analysis and design, computer architecture, performance evaluation of specific multiprocessor computers

Arrange alphabetically by name of computer or processor, e.g., Inmos Transputer®

*Use notation 019 from Table 1 as modified at 004.019

.36     *Distributed processing

Including systems analysis and design, computer architecture, performance evaluation

Class here client-server computing, web servers, grid computing

Class web services in 006.78

*See also 004.6 for computer communications networks; also 005.758 for distributed databases*

**.5**     **\*Storage**

Including hardware aspects of virtual memory; comprehensive works on associative (content-addressable) memory and associative processing

Class comprehensive works on virtual memory in 005.435

*For associative processing, see 004.35*

.53     *Internal storage (Main memory)

Including metal-oxide-semiconductor (MOS), semiconductor bipolar, thin-film memory; random-access memory (RAM); read-only memory (ROM)

Class CD-ROM (compact disc read-only memory) in 004.565

*See also 005.18 for microprogramming and microprograms*

.56     *External storage (Auxiliary storage)

Including punched cards

.563     *Magnetic storage

Including floppy disks, floppy disk drives; magnetic tapes, e.g., cartridges, cassettes, reel-to-reel tapes; tape drives

Class here hard disks, hard disk drives; magnetic bubble memory

.565     *Optical storage

Including CD-ROM (compact disc read-only memory), DVD, WORM (write once read many) discs and drives

.568     *Semiconductor storage

Class here solid-state storage; flash drives, memory cards

---

*Use notation 019 from Table 1 as modified at 004.019

.6     **\*Interfacing and communications**

Standard subdivisions are added for either or both topics in heading

Class here data communications; internetworking, interoperability; wired communications, wireless communications; interdisciplinary works on computer communications

Class data, programs, programming in interfacing and communications in 005.7; class security measures in interfacing and communications in 005.8

*For interdisciplinary works on telecommunication, see 384; for social aspects of computer communications, see 302.231; for economic and related aspects of providing computer communications to the public, see 384.3*

*See also 004.36 for distributed processing*

*See Manual at 004.6 vs. 005.71; also at 004.6 vs. 384.3; also at 004.6 vs. 621.382, 621.3981*

[.602 18]     Standards

Do not use; class in 004.62

.61     Interfacing and communications for specific types of electronic computers

[.610 1–.610 9]     Standard subdivisions

Do not use; class in 004.601–004.609

.611–.616     **\*Digital computers**

Add to base number 004.61 the numbers following 004.1 in 004.11–004.16, e.g., interfacing and communications for personal computers 004.616

.618     **\*Computers distinguished by processing modes**

Add to base number 004.618 the numbers following 004.3 in 004.33–004.36, e.g., parallel processing computers 004.6185

.619     **\*Hybrid and analog computers**

Standard subdivisions are added for either or both topics in heading

.62     **\*Interfacing and communications protocols**

Standard subdivisions are added for either or both topics in heading

Variant name for protocols: standards

Class protocols for specific aspects of interfacing and communications with the aspect, e.g., protocols for error-correcting codes 005.717

[.620 218]     Standards

Do not use; class in 004.62

---

\*Use notation 019 from Table 1 as modified at 004.019

.64      *Kinds of hardware

Including baseband and broadband equipment, modems, optical-fiber cable, peripheral control units

Class peripheral control units controlling a specific kind of peripheral with the peripheral, e.g., printer controllers 004.77

---

>      004.65–004.68   Computer communications networks

Class comprehensive works in 004.6

.65      *Communications network architecture

Class here systems analysis, design, topology (configuration) of computer communications networks

.652      *Peer-to-peer (P2P) architecture

Class here peer-to-peer (P2P) networks

*For client-server computing, see 004.36*

.654      *Service-oriented architecture

.66      *Data transmission modes and data switching methods

Including circuit and packet switching, multiplexing

.67      *Wide-area networks

Class here metropolitan-area networks

.670 917 32      Urban regions

Do not use for metropolitan-area networks; class in 004.67

.678      *Internet

Including extranets, virtual private networks

Class here World Wide Web

Class a specific regional or national network with the area served, e.g., BiblioRedes (Chilean network) 004.6780983

*For Internet, World Wide Web as information systems, see 025.042*

*See Manual at 004.678 vs. 006.7, 025.042, 384.33*

Interdisciplinary works on World Wide Web relocated to 025.042

.678 2      Cloud computing

*For a specific aspect of cloud computing, see the aspect, e.g., grid computing 004.36, web services 006.78*

---

*Use notation 019 from Table 1 as modified at 004.019

| .68 | *Local-area networks |
|---|---|

Including baseband and broadband local-area networks, high-speed local networks

Class here personal-area networks

| .682 | *Intranets |
|---|---|

| .69 | Specific kinds of computer communications |
|---|---|

Class computer communications in multimedia systems with the system, e.g., online social networks 006.754

| [.690 1–.690 9] | Standard subdivisions |
|---|---|

Do not use; class in 004.601–004.609

| .692 | *Electronic mail |
|---|---|

Class here instant messaging; point-to-point communications

Class e-mail lists in 004.693

| .693 | *Discussion groups |
|---|---|

Class here chat groups, electronic bulletin boards, e-mail lists, newsgroups; broadcast communications

Class electronic mail in 004.692

| .695 | *Internet telephony |
|---|---|

| [.696] | Videotex |
|---|---|

Number discontinued; class in 004.69

| .7 | **\*Peripherals** |
|---|---|

Including peripherals for analog, digital, hybrid computers; peripherals for computers distinguished by processing modes

Class peripheral storage in 004.56; class ergonomic engineering of computer peripherals in 621.3984

*See also 004.64 for communications devices*

| .75 | *Peripherals combining input and output functions |
|---|---|

Class here computer terminals

Class tape and disk devices in 004.56

| .76 | *Input peripherals |
|---|---|

Including keyboards

Class input devices that utilize pattern recognition methods in 006.4. Class a special-purpose input device with the purpose, e.g., graphics input devices 006.62, game paddles 688.748

*See also 005.72 for data entry*

---

*Use notation 019 from Table 1 as modified at 004.019

**.77**       *Output peripherals

Including monitors (video display screens), printers

Class output peripherals that utilize computer sound synthesis in 006.5; class computer graphics output devices in 006.62

*See also 005.43 for monitors (software control programs); also 005.18 for monitors (firmware control programs)*

**.9**       **\*Nonelectronic data processing**

Automatic and nonautomatic

Including nonelectronic analog computers; nonelectronic punched-card data processing, e.g., pre-computer use of Hollerith cards

Class comprehensive works on analog computers in 004.19

# 005       \*Computer programming, programs, data

Class here software compatibility, portability, reliability, reusability

Class computer programming, programs, data for special computer methods in 006; class comprehensive works on hardware and programs in electronic data processing in 004

*See Manual at 004–006 vs. 621.39; also at 004 vs. 005; also at 510, T1—0151 vs. 004–006, T1—0285*

## SUMMARY

|  |  |
|---|---|
| 005.019 | **Psychological principles** |
| .1 | **Programming** |
| .2 | **Programming for specific types of computers, for specific operating systems, for specific user interfaces** |
| .3 | **Programs** |
| .4 | **Systems programming and programs** |
| .5 | **General purpose application programs** |
| .7 | **Data in computer systems** |
| .8 | **Data security** |

**.019**       Psychological principles

Class here usability

---

**>**       **005.1–005.5  Computer programming and programs**

Class comprehensive works in 005

*Use notation 019 from Table 1 as modified at 004.019

**.1**     **\*Programming**

Class here application frameworks, application programming, computer algorithms, integrated development environments, software engineering

Class algorithms discussed solely from a theoretical perspective, without regard to computer implementation, in 518.1. Class a specific application of programming within computer science with the application in 005.4–005.8 or 006, e.g., programming of computer graphics 006.66

*For programming for specific types of computers, for specific operating systems, for specific user interfaces, see 005.2*

*See Manual at 005.1–005.2 vs. 005.42; also at 005.1 vs. 005.3*

### SUMMARY

| | | |
|---|---|---|
| 005.101–.109 | Standard subdivisions | |
| .11 | Special programming techniques | |
| .12 | Software systems analysis and design | |
| .13 | Programming languages | |
| .14 | Verification, testing, measurement, debugging | |
| .15 | Preparation of program documentation | |
| .16 | Program maintenance | |
| .18 | Microprogramming and microprograms | |

**.101**     Philosophy and theory

Do not use notation 01 from Table 1 here or with subdivisions of 005.1–005.2 for general discussions of logic in programming

*See also 005.131 for the symbolic (mathematical) logic of programming languages*

*See Manual at 005.101*

**.102**     Miscellany

**.102 8**     Auxiliary techniques and procedures; apparatus, equipment, materials

Class special techniques in 005.11

**[.102 87]**     Testing and measurement

Do not use; class in 005.14

**[.102 88]**     Maintenance and repair

Do not use; class in 005.16

**.11**     †\*Special programming techniques

Class real-time programming in 005.273; class parallel programming in 005.275. Class special programming techniques applied to a specific phase of programming with the phase, e.g., works on functional program design 005.12, works on functional programming with a specific programming language 005.133

---

\*Use notation 019 from Table 1 as modified at 004.019

†Do not use notation 01 from Table 1 for general discussion of logic in programming; see Manual at 005.101

| .112 | †*Modular programming |
| .113 | †*Structured programming |
| .114 | †*Functional programming |
| .115 | †*Logic programming |
| .116 | †*Constraint programming |
| .117 | †*Object-oriented programming |
| .118 | †*Visual programming |

.12      †*Software systems analysis and design

> Standard subdivisions are added for either or both topics in heading

> Class here analysis of a user's problem preparatory to developing a software system to solve it

.120 28       Auxiliary techniques and procedures; apparatus, equipment, materials

> Including use of flow-charting and flow charts as aids in program design

> *See also 005.15028 for preparation of flow charts as program documentation*

.13      †*Programming languages

> Including application generators, nonprocedural (declarative) languages, text editors specially designed to assist in coding programs

> Class here coding of programs

> Class comprehensive works on text editors in 005.52

> *See also 005.434 for job control languages*

[.130 151]       Mathematical principles

> Do not use; class in 005.131

.131      †*Symbolic logic (Mathematical logic)

> Class here mathematical principles of programming languages, e.g., automata, formal languages, grammars, recursive functions applied to programming languages

> Class mathematical principles of programming in 005.10151. Class the mathematical principles of programming languages applied to the development of a programming language translator with the translator in 005.45, plus notation 015113 from Table 1, e.g., theory of formal languages applied to development of compilers 005.453015113

> *See also 005.1 for general works about logic in programming*

---

*Use notation 019 from Table 1 as modified at 004.019
†Do not use notation 01 from Table 1 for general discussion of logic in programming; see Manual at
  005.101

.133 Specific programming languages

Class here comprehensive works on programming with specific programming languages

Arrange alphabetically by name of programming language, e.g., C++

Class specific microprogramming languages in 005.18

*For specific machine and assembly languages, see 005.2*

*See also 005.45 for programming language translators for specific programming languages*

.136 †*Machine and assembly languages

Class specific machine and assembly languages in 005.2

*For assemblers, see 005.456*

.14 †*Verification, testing, measurement, debugging

Including software metrics

Class a specific application of software metrics with the application, plus notation 0285514 from Table 1, e.g., software metrics applied to parallel programming 005.2750285514

.15 †*Preparation of program documentation

Including development of online help

Class here preparation of software documentation

*See also 005.12 for preparation of program design specifications and other technical documentation as an aid in program design; also 005.3 for program documentation itself; also 808.066005 for technical writing in preparation of program documentation*

*See Manual at 005.15 vs. 808.066005*

.16 †*Program maintenance

Class here software maintenance

.18 †*Microprogramming and microprograms

Microprogramming means writing programs in which each instruction specifies a minute operation of the computer

Including firmware viewed as microprograms, firmware development, microassembly languages, microcode

Class firmware viewed as hardware in 004; class programming for personal computers in 005.26; class programs for personal computers in 005.36

*Use notation 019 from Table 1 as modified at 004.019
†Do not use notation 01 from Table 1 for general discussion of logic in programming; see Manual at 005.101

**.2**     **Programming for specific types of computers, for specific operating systems, for specific user interfaces**

> Class here specific machine and assembly languages
>
> *See Manual at 005.1 vs. 005.3; also at 005.1–005.2 vs. 005.42*

.21     †\*Programming for supercomputers

.22     †\*Programming for mainframe computers

> Add to base number 005.22 the numbers following 005.26 in 005.262–005.269, e.g., programming for the IBM System/390® 005.225

.24     †\*Programming for midrange computers

> Class here programming for minicomputers, server class computers
>
> Add to base number 005.24 the numbers following 005.26 in 005.262–005.269, e.g., programming for the Dell PowerEdge®1955 005.245
>
> Class comprehensive works on programming for midrange and personal computers in 005.26

.25     †\*Programming for handheld computing devices

> Class here programming for specific types of handheld computing devices
>
> Add to base number 005.25 the numbers following 005.26 in 005.262–005.269, e.g., programming for Palm OS® 005.258

.26     †\*Programming for personal computers

> Class here programming for specific types of personal computers; comprehensive works on programming for midrange and personal computers
>
> *For programming for midrange computers, see 005.24; for programming for handheld computing devices, see 005.25*

.262     Programming in specific programming languages

> Arrange alphabetically by name of programming language, e.g., C++

.265     Programming for specific computers

> Class here programming for specific processors, for computer systems based on specific computers
>
> Arrange alphabetically by name of computer, e.g., Apple iMac®
>
> *See Manual at 005.268 vs. 005.265, 005.269*

---

\*Use notation 019 from Table 1 as modified at 004.019

†Do not use notation 01 from Table 1 for general discussion of logic in programming; see Manual at 005.101

.268    Programming for specific operating systems

Writing programs that run on specific operating systems

Arrange alphabetically by name of operating system, e.g., Linux®

Class programming for a specific operating system where the operating system is the only operating system that runs on a specific computer in 005.265

*See Manual at 005.268 vs. 005.265, 005.269*

.269    Programming for specific user interfaces

Writing programs that run on specific user interfaces other than the native interface of the operating system

Arrange alphabetically by name of user interface, e.g., Microsoft Windows®

Class programming for the native interface of an operating system (interface bound inseparably with the operating system) in 005.268

*See Manual at 005.268 vs. 005.265, 005.269; also at 005.269 and 005.284, 005.3684, 005.384*

.27     †*Programming for processing modes

.273    †*Programming for real-time computer systems

Add to base number 005.273 the numbers following 005.26 in 005.262–005.269, e.g., programming in Ada for real-time computers 005.2732

.275    †*Programming for multiprocessor computers

Class here concurrent, parallel programming

Add to base number 005.275 the numbers following 005.26 in 005.262–005.269, e.g., programming in Java 005.2752

.276    †*Programming for distributed computing

Add to base number 005.276 the numbers following 005.26 in 005.262–005.269, e.g., programming for Unix® client-server computing 005.2768

*See also 006.76 for Internet programming, web programming*

.28     Programming for specific operating systems and for specific user interfaces

Not limited by type of computer

.282    Programming for specific operating systems

Arrange alphabetically by name of operating system, e.g., Unix®

---

*Use notation 019 from Table 1 as modified at 004.019

†Do not use notation 01 from Table 1 for general discussion of logic in programming; see Manual at 005.101

.284      Programming for specific user interfaces

Writing programs that run on specific user interfaces other than the native interface of the operating system

Arrange alphabetically by name of user interface, e.g., Motif®

Class programming for the native interface of an operating system (interface bound inseparably with the operating system) in 005.282

*See Manual at 005.269 and 005.284, 005.3684, 005.384*

.29      †*Programming for hybrid and analog computers

**.3**      **\*Programs**

Software, firmware, middleware

Class here application programs, collections of programs, software documentation, software packages, comprehensive works on software and firmware, on applications and systems programs

Class programs for a specific application in computer science with the application in 005–006, e.g., programs for computer graphics 006.68; class collections of programs of a specific kind with the kind, e.g., collections of general purpose application software 005.5; class online help in specific kinds of programs with the kind, e.g., online help in programs for personal computers 005.36

*For firmware, see 005.18; for systems programs, see 005.43*

*See also 005.15 for preparation of program documentation*

*See Manual at 005.3; also at 005.1 vs. 005.3; also at 005.3, 005.5 vs. 005.43–005.45*

### SUMMARY

|  |  |
|---|---|
| **005.302** | **Miscellany** |
| **.31** | **Programs for supercomputers** |
| **.32** | **Programs for mainframe computers** |
| **.34** | **Programs for midrange computers** |
| **.36** | **Programs for personal computers** |
| **.37** | **Programs for specific processing modes** |
| **.38** | **Programs for specific operating systems and for specific user interfaces** |
| **.39** | **Programs for hybrid and analog computers** |

.302 18      Standards

*See also 005.10218 for standards for programming; also 005.150218 for standards for preparation of software documentation*

---

*Use notation 019 from Table 1 as modified at 004.019

†Do not use notation 01 from Table 1 for general discussion of logic in programming; see Manual at 005.101

.302 87        Testing and measurement

Do not use for software metrics, quality assurance, reliability, testing, verification; class in 005.14

Class here usability testing, software evaluation as an aid in selection

[.302 88]        Maintenance and repair

Do not use; class in 005.16

.302 9        Commercial miscellany

*See Manual at 011.39 vs. 005.3029, 016.0053, 025.0422*

---

>        005.31–005.36 Programs for digital computers

Class comprehensive works in 005.3

.31        *Programs for supercomputers

.32        *Programs for mainframe computers

Add to base number 005.32 the numbers following 005.36 in 005.362–005.368, e.g., programs for IBM System/390® 005.325

.34        *Programs for midrange computers

Class here programs for minicomputers, server class computers

Add to base number 005.34 the numbers following 005.36 in 005.362–005.368, e.g., programs in Java® 005.342

Class comprehensive works on programs for midrange and personal computers in 005.36

.36        *Programs for personal computers

Including programs for handheld computing devices

Class here programs for specific types of personal computers; comprehensive works on programs for midrange and personal computers

*For programs for midrange computers, see 005.34*

.362        Programs in specific programming languages

Limited to programs and works about programs where the material being classified emphasizes the programming language

Arrange alphabetically by name of programming language, e.g., BASIC

---

*Use notation 019 from Table 1 as modified at 004.019

.365            Programs for specific computers

Class here programs for specific processors, programs for computer systems based on specific computers

Arrange alphabetically by name of computer or processor, e.g., Apple iMac®

*See Manual at 005.3682 vs. 005.365, 005.3684*

.368            Programs for specific operating systems and for specific user interfaces

.368 2          Programs for specific operating systems

Arrange alphabetically by name of operating system, e.g., MS-DOS®

Class programs for a specific operating system where the operating system is the only operating system that runs on a specific computer in 005.365

*See Manual at 005.3682 vs. 005.365, 005.3684*

.368 4          Programs for specific user interfaces

Programs that run on specific user interfaces other than the native interface of the operating system

Arrange alphabetically by name of user interface, e.g., Microsoft Windows® programs

Class programs that run on the native interface of an operating system (interface bound inseparably with the operating system) in 005.3682

*See Manual at 005.269 and 005.284, 005.3684, 005.384; also at 005.3682 vs. 005.365, 005.3684*

.37            Programs for specific processing modes

.373            *Programs for real-time computer systems

.375            *Programs for multiprocessor computers

.376            *Programs for distributed computing

Class here client-server applications, web server programs, groupware

Add to base number 005.376 the numbers following 005.36 in 005.362–005.368, e.g., programs in Java® 005.3762

.38            Programs for specific operating systems and for specific user interfaces

Not limited by type of computer

.382            Programs for specific operating systems

Arrange alphabetically by name of operating system, e.g., Unix®

**.384**      Programs for specific user interfaces

> Programs that run on specific user interfaces other than the native interface of the operating system
>
> Arrange alphabetically by name of user interface, e.g., Motif®
>
> Class programs that run on the native interface of an operating system (interface bound inseparably with the operating system) in 005.382
>
> *See Manual at 005.269 and 005.284, 005.3684, 005.384*

**.39**      *Programs for hybrid and analog computers

> Standard subdivisions are added for either or both topics in heading

**.4**      **\*Systems programming and programs**

> Class programming and programs for interfacing and data communications in 005.71; class programming and programs for internal management of data files and databases in 005.74
>
> *See Manual at 005.1 vs. 005.3*

### SUMMARY

| | |
|---|---|
| **005.42** | **Systems programming** |
| **.43** | **Systems programs** |
| **.44** | **Operating systems for specific types of computers** |
| **.45** | **Programming language translators** |

**.42**      *Systems programming

> Writing systems programs
>
> Class here programming to produce operating systems
>
> Class programming for specific aspects of operating systems with the aspect, e.g., programming for communications 005.711; class programming for other specific kinds of systems programs with the kind, e.g., programming for compilers 005.453
>
> > *See also 005.43 for systems programming (system administration using expertise in systems software to keep a computer system functioning effectively)*
> >
> > *See Manual at 005.1–005.2 vs. 005.42*

**.422**      Systems programming for specific types of computers, for specific operating systems, for specific user interfaces

> Add to base number 005.422 the numbers following 005.2 in 005.21–005.29, e.g., systems programming for Unix-based systems 005.42282

**.428**      *Programming of user interfaces

> Add to base number 005.428 the numbers following 005.2 in 005.21–005.29, e.g., programming of user interfaces for Unix-based systems 005.42882

---

*Use notation 019 from Table 1 as modified at 004.019

.43            *Systems programs

Class here operating systems, system administration (using expertise in systems programs to keep computer systems functioning efficiently), systems software, utility programs

Class programming for operating systems in 005.42; class text editors in 005.52. Class a specific application of systems programs with the application, e.g., programming language translators 005.45, computer interfacing and device drivers 005.71, computer security 005.8

*For operating systems for specific types of computers, see 005.44*

*See Manual at 005.3, 005.5 vs. 005.43–005.45*

.432           Specific operating systems

Not limited by type of computer

Arrange alphabetically by name of operating system, e.g., Unix®

.434           *Process management

Including process management programming, job control languages

Class here comprehensive works on multiprogramming (multitasking)

Add to base number 005.434 the numbers following 005.3 in 005.31–005.39, e.g., multitasking for Apple iMac® 005.43465

Class job control languages for a specific type of computer with the type, e.g., job control languages for mainframe computers 005.4342

*For hardware aspects of multiprogramming, see 004.3*

.435           *Memory management programs

Including memory management programming, comprehensive works on virtual memory

Add to base number 005.435 the numbers following 005.3 in 005.31–005.39, e.g., memory managers for Apple iMac® 005.43565

*For hardware aspects of virtual memory, see 004.5*

.436           *File system management programs

Including file system management programming

Add to base number 005.436 the numbers following 005.3 in 005.31–005.39, e.g., file system management programs for Apple iMac® 005.43665

*For data backup and recovery, see 005.86*

*See Manual at 005.74 vs. 005.436*

---

*Use notation 019 from Table 1 as modified at 004.019

.437      *User interfaces

Class here graphical user interfaces, windowing programs

Add to base number 005.437 the numbers following 005.3 in 005.31–005.39, e.g., KDE® 005.4376; however, for specific user interfaces not limited by type of computer, see 005.438

.438      Specific user interfaces

Not limited by type of computer

Arrange alphabetically by name of user interface, e.g., Motif®

.44      Operating systems for specific types of computers

Add to base number 005.44 the numbers following 005.3 in 005.31–005.39, e.g., operating systems for web servers 005.4476

Class specific systems functions of operating systems for specific types of computers in 005.434–005.436

*See Manual at 005.3, 005.5 vs. 005.43–005.45*

.45      *Programming language translators

Class here code generators, macro processors, parsers, translators for specific programming languages

Class translators for microprogramming languages in 005.18

*See also 418.02028553 for programs to translate natural languages into other natural languages*

*See Manual at 005.3, 005.5 vs. 005.43–005.45*

.452      *Interpreters

.453      *Compilers

.456      *Assemblers

.5      **\*General purpose application programs**

Programs and integrated software packages that can be used in a wide range of applications

Class here integrated programs, specific programs with interdisciplinary applications

Arrange alphabetically by name of program or software package, e.g., OpenOffice.org®

Class database software in 005.74

*See Manual at 005.1 vs. 005.3; also at 005.3, 005.5 vs. 005.43–005.45*

*\*Use notation 019 from Table 1 as modified at 004.019

.52      *Word processing

         Including grammar checkers, spelling checkers, style checkers

         Class here desktop publishing software, text editors, text processing

         Arrange alphabetically by name of program or software package, e.g., Corel WordPerfect®

         Class works on desktop publishing that emphasize typography in 686.22

.54      *Electronic spreadsheets

         Arrange alphabetically by name of program or software package, e.g., Microsoft Excel®

.55      *Statistical programs

         Class here statistical software

         Arrange alphabetically by name of program or software package, e.g., SAS/STAT®

.57      *Personal information management programs

         Software that typically includes an address book, a calendar or diary, electronic mail software, a meeting scheduler, and a time or task manager

         Arrange alphabetically by name of program or software package, e.g., Microsoft Outlook®

.58      *Presentation software

         Class here business presentation software

         Arrange alphabetically by name of program or software package, e.g., Microsoft PowerPoint®

.7      **\*Data in computer systems**

         *For data security, see 005.8*

         *See Manual at 005.1 vs. 005.3*

### SUMMARY

| | |
|---|---|
| **005.71** | **Data communications** |
| **.72** | **Data preparation and representation** |
| **.73** | **Data structures** |
| **.74** | **Data files and databases** |
| **.75** | **Specific types of data files and databases** |

.71      *Data communications

         Class here computer communications; device drivers, interfacing, interprocess communications

            *See also 004.6 for hardware for interfacing and data communications; also 005.437 for user interfaces*

            *See Manual at 004.6 vs. 005.71*

*Use notation 019 from Table 1 as modified at 004.019

.711        *Programming

> *For programming for specific types of computers, see 005.712*

.712        Programming for specific types of computers, for specific operating systems, for specific user interfaces

> Add to base number 005.712 the numbers following 005.2 in 005.21–005.29, e.g., programming personal computers for data communications 005.7126

.713        *Programs

> Add to base number 005.713 the numbers following 005.3 in 005.31–005.39, e.g., communications programs for personal computers 005.7136

.717        *Error-correcting codes [*formerly* 005.72]

> *See also 005.72 for data validation*

.72        *Data preparation and representation

> Class here file formats [*formerly* 005.741]; conversion to machine-readable form, data entry and validation; document formats, record formats
>
> Class computer input devices in 004.76; class data validation in file processing in 005.74
>
> > *For data representation through data structures, see 005.73; for data representation through file organization, see 005.741; for data encryption and ciphers, see 005.82; for markup languages, see 006.74*
> >
> > *See also 006.7 for information architecture, web page design, web site development*
>
> Error-correcting codes relocated to 005.717

.722        *Character sets

> Including ASCII, Unicode

.726        *Programs

> Including portable document software

.73        *Data structures

*Use notation 019 from Table 1 as modified at 004.019

.74      *Data files and databases

*Access*

Standard subdivisions are added for either or both topics in heading

Including data validation in file processing

Class here data file processing, data file and database management

Class comprehensive works on data validation in 005.72; class interdisciplinary works on computer and information science aspects of databases in 025.04. Class data files and databases with regard to their subject content with the subject, e.g., encyclopedic databases 030, nonbibliographic medical databases 610

> For specific types of data files and databases, see 005.75

> See Manual at 005.74 vs. 005.436; also at 025.04, 025.06 vs. 005.74

Data mining relocated to 006.312

.740 151 13      Mathematical logic

> Class here logic databases, deductive databases [*both formerly* 006.33]

.740 285      Computer applications

.740 285 467 8      Internet

> Class here comprehensive works on web databases

>> For web databases as information storage and retrieval systems, see 025.0422

.740 6      Organizations and management

.740 68      Management

> Do not use notation 068 from Table 1 for file management or database management (computer programs that enable operation of files or databases); class in 005.74

> Class here management of organizations concerned with databases, e.g., firms that create them

.741      *File organization and access methods

Standard subdivisions are added for either or both topics in heading

Including hashing, merging, search algorithms, search trees, sort algorithms, sorting

Data file formats relocated to 005.72

.742      *Data dictionaries and directories

Standard subdivisions are added for either or both topics in heading

---

*Use notation 019 from Table 1 as modified at 004.019

.743      *Database design and architecture

         Standard subdivisions are added for either or both topics in heading

         Class here data modeling, data models

.745      *Data warehousing

         Class here transaction processing systems

.746      *Data compression

         Variant names: data compaction, file compression

         *For the compression of sound files, see 006.5; for the compression of graphic files, see 006.6*

.75      Specific types of data files and databases

         Including centralized files and databases; flat-file databases

.753      *Temporal, spatial, constraint databases

———————

>      005.754–005.757 Databases based on specific data models

         Class distributed versions of databases in 005.758; class comprehensive works on databases in 005.74; class comprehensive works on data models in 005.743

.754      *Network databases

         Database management systems that conform to the standards developed by CODASYL (Conference on Data Systems Languages)

.755      *Hierarchical databases

.756      *Relational databases

         Class here object-relational databases [*formerly* 005.757]

.756 5      Specific relational database management systems

         Arrange alphabetically by name of database management system, e.g., Oracle®

.757      *Object-oriented databases

         Object-relational databases relocated to 005.756

.757 5      Specific object-oriented database management systems

         Arrange alphabetically by name of database management system, e.g., Objectivity/DB®

.758      *Distributed data files and databases

         Class here data files and databases used in client/server computing

         *See also 004.36 for distributed processing*

*Use notation 019 from Table 1 as modified at 004.019

.758 5                    Specific distributed database management systems

                          Arrange alphabetically by name of database management system, e.g.,
                          IBM DB2®

.759            *Full-text database management systems

                          Database management systems designed to manage records consisting
                          largely or exclusively of free-form text

                          Including hypertext databases, specific full-text database management
                          systems

**.8**          **\*Data security**

                          Including digital rights management, electronic signatures

                          Class here access control, computer network security, firewalls;
                          interdisciplinary works on computer security

                          Class electronic signatures involving encryption in 005.82

                          *For a specific aspect of computer security, see the aspect, e.g., management
                          of computer security 658.478*

.82             *Data encryption

                          Including digital signatures (electronic signatures involving cryptography)

                          Class here ciphers

                          Class comprehensive works on electronic signatures in 005.8; class
                          interdisciplinary works on cryptography in 652.8

.84             *Malware

                          Including computer viruses, spyware, Trojan horses, worms

.86             *Data backup and recovery

                          Standard subdivisions are added for data backup and recovery together, for
                          data backup alone

**006**     **\*Special computer methods**

                          Not otherwise provided for

                          Class here programs, programming, selection and use of hardware in relation to
                          special computer methods

                          *See also 003.3 for computer modeling and simulation; also notation 0113 from
                          Table 1 for computer modeling and simulation in a specific subject; also 004.6
                          for computer communications; also 005.74 for file and database management;
                          also 005.8 for data security; also 629.89 for special methods in automatic
                          control engineering*

                          *See Manual at 004–006 vs. 621.39; also at 005.1 vs. 005.3; also at 510,
                          T1—0151 vs. 004–006, T1—0285*

*Use notation 019 from Table 1 as modified at 004.019

## SUMMARY

**.2       *Special-purpose systems**

> Including automatic data collection

**.22       *Embedded computer systems [*formerly* 004.1]**

> *For a specific aspect of embedded computer systems, see the aspect, e.g., systems analysis and design of embedded computer systems 004.21, software for embedded systems 005.3*

**.24       *Automatic identification and data capture (AIDC)**

> Including magnetic stripe encoding

> Class here interdisciplinary works on automatic identification and data capture

> *For optical character recognition, see 006.424; for speaker recognition, see 006.454; for biometric identification, see 570.15195. For specific applications of automatic identification and data capture, see the application, plus notation 0285624 from Table 1, e.g., inventory control in business 658.7870285624*

**.242       *Bar coding [*formerly* 006.42]**

> *For use of bar coding in materials management, see 658.7802856242*

**.245       *Radio frequency identification**

> Class real-time locating systems that use radio frequency identification in 910.2856245

**.246       *Smart cards**

**.3       *Artificial intelligence**

> Class here computational intelligence, intelligent agents, multi-agent systems, question-answering systems, comprehensive works on artificial intelligence and cognitive science

> Class robotics in 629.892

> *For cognitive science, see 153*

> *See also 005.115 for logic programming; also 006.4 for pattern recognition not used as a tool of artificial intelligence*

> *See Manual at 006.3 vs. 153*

---

*Use notation 019 from Table 1 as modified at 004.019

| | |
|---|---|
| .31 | *Machine learning |

        Including genetic algorithms

           *For machine learning in knowledge-based systems, see 006.331*

| | |
|---|---|
| .312 | *Data mining [*formerly also* 005.74] |
| .32 | *Neural nets (Neural networks) |

        Including perceptrons

        Class here connectionism, neural computers

| | |
|---|---|
| .33 | *Knowledge-based systems |

        Class here expert systems

        Logic databases, deductive databases relocated to 005.74015113

| | |
|---|---|
| .331 | *Knowledge acquisition |
| .332 | *Knowledge representation |

        Class here knowledge engineering

| | |
|---|---|
| .333 | *Deduction, problem solving, reasoning |
| [.336–.338] | Programming, programming languages, programs for knowledge-based systems |

        Numbers discontinued; class in 006.33

| | |
|---|---|
| .35 | *Natural language processing |

        Class here computational linguistics [*formerly* 410.285]

           *See Manual at 006.35 vs. 410.285*

| | |
|---|---|
| .37 | *Computer vision |

           *See also 006.42 for optical pattern recognition*

           *See Manual at 006.37 vs. 006.42, 621.367, 621.391, 621.399*

| | |
|---|---|
| **.4** | **\*Computer pattern recognition** |

        Class pattern recognition as a tool of artificial intelligence in 006.3

| | |
|---|---|
| .42 | *Optical pattern recognition |

        Class here comprehensive works on optical pattern recognition and computer graphics

        Class optical engineering aspects of optical pattern recognition in 621.367

           *For perceptrons, see 006.32; for computer graphics, see 006.6*

           *See also 006.37 for computer vision*

           *See Manual at 006.37 vs. 006.42, 621.367, 621.391, 621.399*

        Interdisciplinary works on bar coding relocated to 006.242

*Use notation 019 from Table 1 as modified at 004.019

.424 *Optical character recognition (OCR)

.425 *Handwriting recognition

.45 *Acoustical pattern recognition

.454 *Speech recognition

Including speaker recognition

Class here comprehensive works on speech recognition and speech synthesis

*For speech synthesis, see 006.54*

**.5 *Digital audio**

Class here computer sound synthesis

Class digital audio engineering in 621.3893; class computer audio art in 776

*See Manual at 776 vs. 006.5–006.7*

.54 *Speech synthesis

**.6 *Computer graphics**

Class here image manipulation

Class multimedia systems, interactive video, comprehensive works on computer graphics and computer sound synthesis in 006.7; class computer graphic art in 776; class use of computers in video production in 777.0285

*See Manual at 776 vs. 006.5–006.7*

.62 *Hardware

Including digitizer tablets, graphics terminals, plotters, scanners

Class here equipment specifically designed for computer graphics and works treating use of equipment for computer graphics even if the equipment was not specifically designed for that purpose

Class works that treat equally the use of equipment for graphics and nongraphics tasks in 004

.66 *Programming

*For programming for specific types of computers, for specific operating systems, for specific user interfaces, see 006.67*

.663 *Programming languages for computer graphics

.663 3 Specific programming languages

Arrange alphabetically by name of programming language, e.g., C++

.67 Programming for specific types of computers, for specific operating systems, for specific user interfaces

Add to base number 006.67 the numbers following 005.2 in 005.21–005.29, e.g., graphics programming for IBM PC® 006.6765

*Use notation 019 from Table 1 as modified at 004.019

38

| | |
|---|---|
| .68 | *Programs |

> Add to base number 006.68 the numbers following 005.3 in 005.31–005.39, e.g., graphics programs that run on MS-DOS® 006.68682

| | |
|---|---|
| .69 | *Special topics in computer graphics |
| .693 | *Three-dimensional graphics |

> Including ray tracing

| | |
|---|---|
| .696 | *Digital video |

> Including morphing

> Class here computer animation

> Class interactive video in 006.7; class digital television in 621.38807; class digital video hardware in 777.3; class digital video effects in 777.9

>> *For a specific product of computer animation techniques, see the product, e.g., animated films 791.437*

| | |
|---|---|
| **.7** | ***Multimedia systems** |

> Including interactive video

> Class here hypermedia, hypertext; information architecture, web page design, web site development; comprehensive works on computer graphics and digital audio, interactive multimedia

> Class web databases in 005.7402854678; class hypertext databases in 005.759; class multimedia computer art in 776.7; class use of computers in video production in 777.0285; class interdisciplinary works on Internet in 004.678; class interdisciplinary works on World Wide Web in 025.042; class interdisciplinary works on web publishing in 070.57973

>> *For digital audio, see 006.5; for computer graphics, see 006.6*

>> *See also 384.35 for interactive videotex*

>> *See Manual at 004.678 vs. 006.7, 025.042, 384.33; also at 776 vs. 006.5–006.7*

| | |
|---|---|
| .72 | *Hardware |
| .74 | *Markup languages |

> Class here general document markup languages, style sheet languages

> Arrange alphabetically by name of language, e.g., Cascading Style Sheets (CSS), XML

| | |
|---|---|
| .75 | Specific types of multimedia systems |

> Including wikis

| | |
|---|---|
| .752 | *Blogs |
| .754 | *Online social networks |

> Class interdisciplinary works on online social networks in 302.30285

---

*Use notation 019 from Table 1 as modified at 004.019

.76        *Programming

Class here Internet programming, web application frameworks, web programming

*For programming for specific types of computers, for specific operating systems, for specific user interfaces, see 006.77*

.77        Programming for specific types of computers, for specific operating systems, for specific user interfaces

Add to base number 006.77 the numbers following 005.2 in 005.21–005.29, e.g., writing multimedia programs for Linux® 006.7768

.78        Programs

Including rich Internet applications (RIAs), web services

Class here multimedia authoring programs, software; multimedia software

Add to base number 006.78 the numbers following 005.3 in 005.31–005.39, e.g., multimedia authoring software that runs on Apple iMac® 006.7865

Class web servers in 004.36

.8        **Augmented and virtual reality**

A combination of computer software and hardware that adds computer-generated information to the visual presentation of a real environment or that gives an illusion of being in an artificial environment or a remote real environment, and gives the user an ability to manipulate objects in that environment. The illusion is created by visual, auditory, and other sensory data provided by the computer system to the user

Standard subdivisions are added for either or both topics in heading

**[007]        [Unassigned]**

Most recently used in Edition 16

**[008]        [Never assigned]**

**[009]        [Never assigned]**

**010        Bibliography**

History, identification, description of printed, written, audiovisual, electronic resources

Class catalogs and lists of art works with the subject, plus notation 074 from Table 1, e.g., a catalog of the prints in the Library of Congress 769.074753

*See also 028.1 for reviews*

*Use notation 019 from Table 1 as modified at 004.019

## SUMMARY

[.28]     Auxiliary techniques and procedures; apparatus, equipment, materials

Do not use; class in 010.44

**.4**     **Special topics of bibliography**

.42     Analytical bibliography (Descriptive bibliography)

Analysis of the structure of books and their bibliographic description

Class here comprehensive works on historical and analytical bibliography

Class descriptive cataloging in 025.32

*For historical bibliography, see 002*

*See also 070.5 for book publishing*

.44     Systematic bibliography

Preparation and compilation of bibliographies

Class systematic bibliography applied to a specific kind of bibliography with the kind, plus notation 028 from Table 1, e.g., preparation and compilation of biobibliographies 012.028

## 011     Bibliographies and catalogs

Standard subdivisions are added for either or both topics in heading

Class here general collections of brief bibliographic abstracts; bibliographies and catalogs not provided for elsewhere

Class bibliography, bibliographies as a subject in 010; class bibliographies and catalogs of material in a specific form other than books in 011.3; class catalogs as a subject in 025.31; class comprehensive works on collections of abstracts, general collections of abstracts giving substantive information on the subject in 080; class interdisciplinary works on bibliographic catalogs in 025.31

*For bibliographies and catalogs of individuals, of anonymous and pseudonymous works, of works from specific places, of works on specific subjects, of works held in specific collections or offered for sale, see 012–017*

*See Manual at 011–017*

## SUMMARY

.001    Philosophy and theory

.002    Miscellany

.002 9    Commercial miscellany

> Do not use for auction catalogs; class in 017.3. Do not use for sales catalogs; class in 017.4

.003–.007    Standard subdivisions

.008    Groups of people

> Do not use for bibliographies and catalogs of works by groups of authors; class in 011.8

[.008 3]    Young people

> Do not use; class in 011.62

.008 7    Gifted people

> Do not use for people with disabilities and illnesses; class in 011.63

.009    History, geographic treatment, biography

.009 01–.009 05    Historical periods

> Do not use for bibliographies and catalogs of works published in specific historical periods; class in 011.09

.009 1–.009 9    Geographic treatment and biography

> Do not use for bibliographies and catalogs of works from specific places; class in 015

.02    *Bibliographies and catalogs of reference works

> *For bibliographies and catalogs of general encyclopedic works, see 016.03; for bibliographies and catalogs of general collected biographies, see 016.92*

*Do not use notation 091–099 from Table 1 for bibliographies and catalogs of works from specific places; class in 015

.03       \*Bibliographies and catalogs of free materials

          Class bibliographies and catalogs of free reference works in 011.02

.09       General bibliographies and catalogs of works published in specific historical periods

          Add to base number 011.09 the numbers following —090 in notation 0903–0905 from Table 1, e.g., 16th century publications 011.0931

          Class bibliographies and catalogs of reference works published in specific historical periods in 011.02; class bibliographies and catalogs of free materials published in specific historical periods in 011.03; class bibliographies and catalogs of works from specific places in 015

          *For bibliographies and catalogs of incunabula, see 011.42*

---

> ### 011.1–011.8 General bibliographies and catalogs

          Lists of works not held in a specific collection or group of collections; not offered for sale by specific organizations or at auction; not restricted to specific subjects, to individuals, to anonymous or pseudonymous works, or to specific places of publication

          Unless other instructions are given, class a subject with aspects in two or more subdivisions of 011.1–011.8 in the number coming last, e.g., Russian-language newspapers on microfilm 011.36 (*not* 011.29171 or 011.35)

          Class comprehensive general bibliographies and catalogs in 011

          *For comprehensive bibliographies and catalogs of reference works, see 011.02; for comprehensive bibliographies and catalogs of free material, see 011.03; for comprehensive bibliographies and catalogs of works published in specific periods, see 011.09*

.1       **\*Universal bibliographies and catalogs**

.2       **\*General bibliographies and catalogs of works published in specific languages**

          Add to base number 011.2 notation 2–9 from Table 6, e.g., general bibliographies of Russian-language works 011.29171

.3       **General bibliographies and catalogs of works published in specific forms**

          Class general bibliographies and catalogs of books, of works in written or printed form in 011; class bibliographies and catalogs of music scores in 016.78026; class bibliographies and catalogs of cartographic materials in 016.912

[.301–.309]       Standard subdivisions

          Do not use; class in 011.001–011.009

.31       \*Manuscripts

---

\*Do not use notation 091–099 from Table 1 for bibliographies and catalogs of works from specific places; class in 015

.32      *Paperbacks

.33      *Pamphlets

.34      *Serial publications

> Class here general indexes to serial publications
>
> *For newspapers, see 011.35*
>
> *See also 011.48 for works in series*

.35      *Newspapers

.36      *Microforms

> Microreproductions of written and printed media

.37      *Audiovisual and visual media

> Standard subdivisions are added for audiovisual and visual media together, for audiovisual media alone
>
> Including filmstrips, slides
>
> Class microforms in 011.36
>
> *For sound recordings, see 011.38*

.372      *Motion pictures

> Class comprehensive works on motion pictures and videorecordings in 011.37
>
> *For bibliographies and catalogs of dramatic and entertainment motion pictures, see 016.79143*

.373      *Video recordings

> Class here videodiscs, videotapes
>
> Class bibliographies and catalogs of dramatic and entertainment video recordings in 016.79145

.376      *Pictures and related illustrations

> Standard subdivisions are added for either or both topics in heading

.38      *Sound recordings

> Class here cassettes, compact discs
>
> Class sound films in 011.37
>
> *For sound recordings of music, see 016.780266*

.384      *Audiobooks (Talking books)

> Class here comprehensive works on audiobooks and braille publications
>
> *For braille publications, see 011.63*

---

*Do not use notation 091–099 from Table 1 for bibliographies and catalogs of works from specific places; class in 015

| .39 | *Electronic resources |
|---|---|

Including CD-ROMs, electronic books

Class here electronic publications

Class bibliographies and catalogs of computer programs and software in 016.0053

*For bibliographies and catalogs of web sites, see 025.0422*

*See Manual at 011.39 vs. 005.3029, 016.0053, 025.0422*

**.4 *General bibliographies and catalogs of works exhibiting specific bibliographic characteristics other than form**

*See also 011.3 for works published in specific forms*

| .42 | *Incunabula |
|---|---|
| .44 | *Rare books |

*For incunabula, see 011.42*

| .47 | *Reprints |
|---|---|
| .48 | *Works in series |

*See also 011.34 for serial publications*

**.5 *General bibliographies and catalogs of works issued by specific kinds of publishers**

Class general bibliographies and catalogs of specific publishers in 015

| .52 | *Publications of international organizations |
|---|---|
| .53 | *Government publications |
| .532 | *Government publications issued by legislative bodies and their committees |

Standard subdivisions are added for legislative bodies, their committees, or both

| .534 | *Government publications issued by executive agencies |
|---|---|
| .54 | *Publications of university and college presses |

Standard subdivisions are added for either or both topics in heading

*See also 011.75 for theses and dissertations*

| .55 | *Publications of private presses |
|---|---|

Presses printing in limited quantities or for limited distribution

| .56 | *Underground publications (Clandestine publications) |
|---|---|

**.6 *General bibliographies and catalogs of works for young people and people with disabilities; for specific types of libraries**

*Do not use notation 091–099 from Table 1 for bibliographies and catalogs of works from specific places; class in 015

| | |
|---|---|
| .62 | *Works for young people |
| | Class here works for children |
| .624 | *Works for specific sexes |
| .624 1 | *Works for young males |
| | Including young men twelve to twenty |
| .624 2 | *Works for young females |
| | Including young women twelve to twenty |
| .625 | *Works for young people twelve to twenty |
| | Class works for males twelve to twenty in 011.6241; class works for females twelve to twenty in 011.6242 |
| .63 | *Works for people with disabilities and illnesses |
| | Including braille, large-print publications |
| | Class here works for people with physical disabilities |
| | Class audiobooks for people with physical disabilities, comprehensive works on audiobooks and braille publications in 011.384 |
| .67 | *Works for specific types of libraries |
| | Including bibliographies and catalogs of books for public libraries |
| **.7** | **\*General bibliographies and catalogs of works having specific kinds of content** |
| | Including directories, textbooks, translations |
| | *For reference works, see 011.02; for general encyclopedic works, see 016.03* |
| .73 | *Best books |
| | Class best books for young people and people with disabilities; for specific types of libraries in 011.6 |
| .75 | *Theses and dissertations |
| | Standard subdivisions are added for either or both topics in heading |

*Do not use notation 091–099 from Table 1 for bibliographies and catalogs of works from specific places; class in 015

.8     **General bibliographies and catalogs of works by groups of authors**

Do not use for material emphasizing special interests of groups of people, e.g., bibliographies of works on women emphasizing the status of women are classed in 016.30542 (*not* 011.82), catalogs of works by clergy emphasizing religion are classed in 016.2 (*not* 011.882)

Class here general bibliographies and catalogs of works by minorities

Add to base number 011.8 the numbers following —08 in notation 081–089 from Table 1, e.g., bibliographies of works by women 011.82, catalog of works by clergy 011.882

*For bibliographies and catalogs of individuals, see 012*

> **012–017 Bibliographies and catalogs of individuals, of anonymous and pseudonymous works, of works from specific places, of works on specific subjects, of works held in specific collections or offered for sale**

Standard subdivisions are added for bibliographies, catalogs, or both

Unless other instructions are given, observe the following table of preference, e.g., pseudonymous scientific works published in France 016.5 (*not* 014 or 015.44):

| | |
|---|---|
| Bibliographies and catalogs of works on specific subjects | 016 |
| Bibliographies and catalogs of individuals | 012 |
| Bibliographies and catalogs of anonymous and pseudonymous works | 014 |
| Bibliographies and catalogs of works from specific places | 015 |
| General bibliographies and catalogs of works held in specific collections or offered for sale | 017 |

Class bibliography, bibliographies as a subject in 010; class general bibliographies and catalogs in 011; class catalogs as a subject, interdisciplinary works on bibliographic catalogs in 025.31

*See Manual at 011–017*

012    **Bibliographies and catalogs of individuals**

Works by or about people not clearly associated with a specific subject

Class here biobibliographies

*For biobibliographies of people associated with a specific subject, see the biography of the subject, e.g., biobibliographies of psychologists 150.92*

[013]    **[Unassigned]**

Most recently used in Edition 21

**014**     **Bibliographies and catalogs of anonymous and pseudonymous works**

> Add to base number 014 the numbers following 03 in 031–039 (but not notation 02 for books of miscellaneous facts), e.g., bibliographies of anonymous and pseudonymous works in Russian 014.71

**015**     **Bibliographies and catalogs of works from specific places**

> Works issued in specific regions, continents, countries, localities, or by specific publishers
>
> Class here bibliographies and catalogs of authors resident in specific regions, continents, countries, localities
>
> Add to base number 015 notation 1–9 from Table 2, e.g., works issued in China 015.51; then add 0* and to the result add the numbers following 011 in 011.1–011.7, e.g., catalogs of manuscripts from China 015.51031, catalogs of manuscripts from China held in German libraries 015.510310943
>
> Class bibliographies and catalogs of works of specific kinds of people resident in specific places in 011.8

**016**     **Bibliographies and catalogs of works on specific subjects**

> Class here annotated subject bibliographies with descriptive annotations that do not give substantive information about the subject; indexes
>
> Add to base number 016 notation 001–999, e.g., bibliographies of computer programs and software 016.0053, of general encyclopedic works 016.03, of philosophy 016.1, of novels 016.80883, of general collected biographies 016.92
>
> Add to the various subdivisions of 016 notation 01–09 from Table 1 as required for works listed in the bibliographies and catalogs, but not for the bibliographies and catalogs being classed, e.g., bibliographies of serial publications on philosophy 016.105, but serially published bibliographies on philosophy that include monographs 016.1 (*not* 016.105)
>
> Class bibliographies and catalogs of belles-lettres in more than two languages in 016.8088. Class biobibliographies of people associated with a specific subject with the biography of the subject, e.g., biobibliographies of psychologists 150.92; class bibliographies with abstracts giving substantive information about the subject with the subject, e.g., bibliographies with substantive abstracts about chemistry 540
>
>> *See also 011 for general bibliographies and catalogs arranged by subject; also 011.3 for general bibliographies and catalogs of works published in specific forms; also 011.42 for bibliographies and catalogs of incunabula; also 011.44 for bibliographies and catalogs of rare books; also 017 for general bibliographies and catalogs of works held in specific collections or offered for sale and general catalogs of serial publications; also 050 for general indexes of specific serial publications not limited by subject*
>>
>> *See Manual at 016 vs. 026, T1—07; also at 011.39 vs. 005.3029, 016.0053, 025.0422*
>
> (Option: Class with the specific subject, plus notation 016 from Table 1, e.g., bibliographies of medicine 610.16)

---

*Add 00 for standard subdivisions; see instructions at beginning of Table 1

# 017 General bibliographies and catalogs of works held in specific collections or offered for sale

Lists of works held in a specific collection or group of collections, or offered for sale by specific organizations other than publishers or at auction, and not restricted to specific subjects, to individuals, to anonymous and pseudonymous works, or to specific places of publication

Class here catalogs arranged by author, main entry, date, or register number [*formerly* 018], dictionary catalogs [*formerly* 019]; classified, alphabetic catalogs; general catalogs of serial publications and their indexes, union catalogs, catalogs not provided for elsewhere

Add to notation for each term identified by * the numbers following 011 in 011.1–011.7, e.g., classified sales catalogs of periodicals 017.434

> *See also 011 for general bibliographies and catalogs; also 016 for bibliographies and catalogs on specific subjects*

Comprehensive works on catalogs relocated to 025.31

## .1 *†Bibliographies and catalogs of nonprivate libraries

Class here alphabetic subject catalogs of nonprivate libraries [*formerly* 017.5], catalogs arranged by author, main entry, date, or register number of nonprivate libraries [*formerly* 018.1], dictionary catalogs of nonprivate libraries [*formerly* 019.1], classified subject catalogs of nonprivate libraries

## .2 *†Bibliographies and catalogs of private and family libraries

Standard subdivisions are added for either or both topics in heading

Class here alphabetic subject catalogs of private and family libraries [*formerly* 017.6], catalogs arranged by author, main entry, date, or register number of private and family libraries [*formerly* 018.2], dictionary catalogs of private and family libraries [*formerly* 019.2], classified subject catalogs of private and family libraries

## .3 *†Auction catalogs

Class here alphabetic subject auction catalogs [*formerly* 017.7], auction catalogs arranged by author, main entry, date, or register number [*formerly* 018.3], dictionary auction catalogs [*formerly* 019.3], classified auction catalogs

## .4 *†Sales catalogs

Class here alphabetic subject sales catalogs [*formerly* 017.8], sales catalogs arranged by author, main entry, date, or register number [*formerly* 018.4], dictionary sales catalogs [*formerly* 019.4], classified sales catalog

> *For auction catalogs, see 017.3*

## [.5] Alphabetic subject catalogs of nonprivate libraries

Relocated to 017.1

---

*Add as instructed under 017
†Do not use notation 091–099 from Table 1 for bibliographies and catalogs of works from specific places; class in 015

[.6]    **Alphabetic subject catalogs of private and family libraries**

Relocated to 017.2

[.7]    **Alphabetic subject auction catalogs**

Relocated to 017.3

[.8]    **Alphabetic subject sales catalogs**

Relocated to 017.4

**[018]    Catalogs arranged by author, main entry, date, or register number**

Relocated to 017

[.1]    **Catalogs arranged by author, main entry, date, or register number of nonprivate libraries**

Relocated to 017.1

[.2]    **Catalogs arranged by author, main entry, date, or register number of private and family libraries**

Relocated to 017.2

[.3]    **Auction catalogs arranged by author, main entry, date, or register number**

Relocated to 017.3

[.4]    **Sales catalogs arranged by author, main entry, date, or register number**

Relocated to 017.4

**[019]    Dictionary catalogs**

Relocated to 017

[.1]    **Dictionary catalogs of nonprivate libraries**

Relocated to 017.1

[.2]    **Dictionary catalogs of private and family libraries**

Relocated to 017.2

[.3]    **Dictionary auction catalogs**

Relocated to 017.3

[.4]    **Dictionary sales catalogs**

Relocated to 017.4

# 020 Library and information sciences

Standard subdivisions are added for either or both topics in heading

Class here archival science

Unless other instructions are given, observe the following table of preference, e.g., administration of cataloging in academic libraries 025.3068 (*not* 025.1977 or 027.7):

| | |
|---|---|
| Reading and use of other information media | 028 |
| Operations of libraries, archives, information centers (*except* 025.1) | 025 |
| Administration of physical plant | 022 |
| Personnel management | 023 |
| Administration | 025.1 |
| Relationships of libraries, archives, information centers | 021 |
| Libraries, archives, information centers devoted to specific subjects | 026 |
| General libraries, archives, information centers | 027 |

Class information theory in 003.54; class government policy on libraries in 021.8; class government policy on information in 338.926

*For bibliography, see 010*

*See also 651.5 for records management as a managerial service*

## SUMMARY

| | |
|---|---|
| 020.1–.9 | **Standard subdivisions** |
| 021 | **Relationships of libraries, archives, information centers** |
| 022 | **Administration of physical plant** |
| 023 | **Personnel management (Human resource management)** |
| 025 | **Operations of libraries, archives, information centers** |
| 026 | **Libraries, archives, information centers devoted to specific subjects** |
| 027 | **General libraries, archives, information centers** |
| 028 | **Reading and use of other information media** |

[.601]    International organizations

Do not use; class in 020.621

[.603–.609]    National, state, provincial, local organizations

Do not use; class in 020.622–020.624

.62    Permanent organizations

.621    International organizations

Including International Federation of Library Associations and Institutions

.622    National organizations

Add to base number 020.622 notation 3–9 from Table 2, e.g., Indian Library Association 020.62254, American Society for Information Science and Technology 020.62273

.623    Regional, state, provincial organizations

| .623 2 | Regional organizations |
|---|---|

Add to base number 020.6232 notation 3–9 from Table 2, e.g., New England Library Association 020.623274

| .623 4 | State and provincial organizations |
|---|---|

Add to base number 020.6234 notation 3–9 from Table 2, e.g., Ontario Library Association 020.6234713

| .624 | Local organizations |
|---|---|

Add to base number 020.624 notation 3–9 from Table 2, e.g., New York Library Club 020.6247471

| [.68] | Management |
|---|---|

Do not use; class in 025.1

| [.682] | Plant management |
|---|---|

Do not use; class in 022

| [.683] | Personnel management (Human resource management) |
|---|---|

Do not use; class in 023

**.9 History, geographic treatment, biography**

Class here comparative librarianship; history, geographic treatment, biography of librarianship

Class history and biography of libraries in 027.009; class geographic treatment of libraries in 027.01–027.09

# 021 Relationships of libraries, archives, information centers

Standard subdivisions are added for any or all topics in heading

Including role as storage centers

*See also 025.56 for orientation and instructional manuals for users; also 027 for comprehensive works on libraries, archives, information centers*

**.2 Relationships with the community**

| .24 | Educational role |
|---|---|

*For relationships with other educational institutions, see 021.3*

| .26 | Cultural role |
|---|---|

Including sponsorship of community cultural programs

| .28 | Informational role |
|---|---|

Including clearinghouse for information on community action programs

**.3 Relationships with other educational institutions**

Including relationships with museums

**.6 Cooperation and networks**

Including centralization of systems

| | | |
|---|---|---|
| **.64** | | Cooperation |

Including bibliographic centers

Class cooperation in a specific activity with the activity, e.g., cooperative cataloging 025.35

*For networks, see 021.65*

**.642** Cooperation through union catalogs

*See also 017–019 for specific union catalogs*

**.65** Networks

Class here systems, consortia

Class networks, systems, consortia for a specific kind of institution in 026–027. Class networks, systems, consortia for a specific function with the function, e.g., interlibrary loan networks 025.62

*See also 025.0028546 for computer networks in libraries*

**.7** **Promotion of libraries, archives, information centers**

Standard subdivisions are added for any or all topics in heading

Including friends of the library organizations

Class here public relations

Class advertising in 659.1902

**.8** **Relationships with government**

Regardless of governmental level

Including library-government aspects of exchanges, gifts, deposits; political aspects

Class here government policy on libraries

Class government policy on information in 338.926

*See also 025.26 for acquisition through exchange, gift, deposit*

**.82** Commissions and governing boards

Standard subdivisions are added for either or both topics in heading

**.83** Financial support

*See also 025.11 for financial administration*

**022** **Administration of physical plant**

Including bookmobiles

Class here library quarters in buildings devoted primarily to other activities, e.g., physical plant of school libraries; maintenance of physical plant

*See also 025.82 for physical security of collections*

**.1** **Location and site**

.3     **Buildings**

Class here planning for buildings

*See also 727.8 for library architecture*

.31     Buildings for specific kinds of institutions

Add to base number 022.31 the numbers following 027 in 027.1–027.8, e.g., college library buildings 022.317

.4     **Stacks and shelving**

Standard subdivisions are added for either or both topics in heading

*See also 025.81 for closed versus open stacks*

.7     **Lighting for library buildings**

Class interdisciplinary works on lighting for library buildings in 621.32278

.8     **Heating, ventilation, air conditioning**

Class interdisciplinary works on heating, ventilation and air conditioning of library buildings in 697

.9     **Equipment, furniture, furnishings**

Class comprehensive works on computers in libraries, archives, information centers in 025.00285

*For stacks and shelving, see 022.4*

*See also 025.56 for signs*

# 023     Personnel management (Human resource management)

---

\>     **023.2–023.4   Types of positions**

Class here titles and job descriptions for specific types of positions

Class comprehensive works in 023

.2     **Professional positions**

Including librarians, consultants, systems analysts

Class administrative positions in 023.4

.3     **Technician positions**

Including library aides, assistants, clerks, paraprofessionals, technicians

Class administrative positions in 023.4

.4     **Administrative positions**

.7     **Job description**

Class a job description for a specific type of position with the position in 023.2–023.4

**.8**     **Management of in-service training**

Class comprehensive works on in-service training in 020.7155; class management of in-service training for specific types of positions in 023.2–023.4

**.9**     **Elements of personnel management**

Including recruitment, selection, supervision, employer-employee relations, performance evaluation, wage and salary administration; staff manuals, rules, codes

Class elements of personnel management applied to specific types of positions in 023.2–023.4

*For in-service training, see 023.8*

# [024]     [Unassigned]

Most recently used in Edition 18

# 025     Operations of libraries, archives, information centers

Standard subdivisions are added for any or all topics in heading

Class here documentation (the systematic collection, organization, storage, retrieval, and dissemination of recorded information)

Class comprehensive works on operations in specific kinds of institutions in 026–027

### SUMMARY

| | |
|---|---|
| 025.001–.009 | **Standard subdivisions** |
| .02–.06 | **[Technical services, information storage and retrieval systems]** |
| .1 | **Administration** |
| .2 | **Acquisitions and collection development** |
| .3 | **Bibliographic analysis and control** |
| .4 | **Subject analysis and control** |
| .5 | **Services for users** |
| .6 | **Circulation services** |
| .7 | **Physical preparation for storage and use** |
| .8 | **Maintenance and preservation of collections** |

**.001–.009**     Standard subdivisions

**.02**     Technical services

Class here commercial and noncommercial processing centers

Class a specific technical service with the service, e.g., acquisitions 025.2

.04        Information storage and retrieval systems

Including recall, precision, relevance

Class here search and retrieval in information storage and retrieval systems; front-end systems; comprehensive works on online catalogs integrated with information storage and retrieval systems, on automated storage, search, retrieval of information; interdisciplinary works on databases

Class aspects of information storage for specific types of retrieval systems with the aspect for the type of system, e.g., mark-up languages for web retrieval systems 006.74, record formats for bibliographic retrieval systems 025.316

> *For computer science aspects of information storage and retrieval systems, of databases, see 005.74; for information storage and retrieval systems, bibliographies of web sites, digital libraries devoted to specific subjects, see 025.06. For a specific kind of information storage and retrieval system, see the kind, e.g., online catalogs 025.3132*

> *See also 658.4038011 for management use of information storage and retrieval systems*

> *See Manual at 025.04, 025.06 vs. 005.74*

.042       World Wide Web

Class here interdisciplinary works on World Wide Web [*formerly* 004.678]; digital libraries, Internet viewed as an information storage and retrieval system, Internet literacy

Class interdisciplinary works on Internet in 004.678

> *For specific aspects of World Wide Web, see the aspect, e.g., computer science aspects of World Wide Web 004.678*

> *See Manual at 004.678 vs. 006.7, 025.042, 384.33*

.042 2     Web sites

Class here directories of web sites, portals

Works on web sites hosting a search engine plus other resources that treat the site comprehensively are classed here, that focus on the search engine in 025.04252

> *See Manual at 011.39 vs. 005.3029, 016.0053, 025.0422*

.042 5     Search and retrieval

Standard subdivisions are added for either or both topics in heading

Including recall, precision, relevance

Class here Internet searching

.042 52    Search engines

> *See also 658.872 for search engine optimization*

.042 7     Semantic web

World Wide Web structured for semantic computing

.06          Information storage and retrieval systems devoted to specific subjects

Class here bibliographies of web sites devoted to specific subjects, digital libraries devoted to specific subjects, documentation of specific subjects

*See Manual at 025.04, 025.06 vs. 005.74*

[.060 001–.060 009]          Standard subdivisions

Do not use; class in 025.0401–025.0409

.060 01–.069 99          Specific subjects

Add to base number 025.06 notation 001–999, e.g., MEDLINE 025.0661

.069 1          Geography and travel

Number built according to instructions under 025.06001–025.06999

Class geographic information systems (GIS) in 910.285

### .1      Administration

Class administration of a specific function with the function, plus notation 068 from Table 1, e.g., administration of cataloging 025.3068

*For administration of physical plant, see 022; for personnel management, see 023*

.11          Finance

Including comprehensive works on user fees

Class government financial support in 021.83

*For user fees for a specific service, see the service, plus notation 0681 from Table 1, e.g., fees for automated information search and retrieval 025.040681*

.12          Duplication services (Reprography)

Including library procedures to comply with copyright legislation

Class here photocopying (photoduplication) services, printing services

Class publishing by libraries, archives, information centers in 070.594; class interdisciplinary works on photocopying in 686.4

*See also 346.0482 for copyright law; also 686.2 for technology of printing*

.17          Administration of collections of special materials

Class here nonbook materials, comprehensive works on treatment of special materials

Add to base number 025.17 the numbers following 025.34 in 025.341–025.349, e.g., administration of a map collection 025.176, comprehensive treatment of serials 025.1732

*For a specific kind of treatment of special materials, see the kind, e.g., acquisition of and collection development for materials in special forms 025.28*

**.3**      **Bibliographic analysis and control**

Including cataloging in publication, International Standard Book Numbers (ISBNs)

Class here standards for bibliographic analysis and control; comprehensive works on cataloging and classification, on indexing, on information storage

*For subject analysis and control, see 025.4. For information storage using a specific system, see the system, e.g., information storage through coordinate indexing 025.47*

*See also 025.04 for comprehensive works on information storage and retrieval systems*

### SUMMARY

| | |
|---|---|
| 025.302 85 | **Computer applications** |
| .31 | **The catalog** |
| .32 | **Descriptive cataloging** |
| .34 | **Cataloging, classification, indexing of special materials** |
| .35 | **Cooperative cataloging, classification, indexing** |
| .39 | **Recataloging, reclassification, reindexing** |

[.302 18]       Standards

Do not use; class in 025.3

.302 85       Computer applications

.302 855 72       Data preparation and representation

Class machine-readable record formats in 025.316; class data entry, conversion to machine-readable form in 025.317

.302 855 74       Data files and databases

Class here comprehensive works on data files and databases used for cataloging and indexing

*For data files and databases used for a specific purpose, see the purpose, e.g., online catalogs 025.3132*

.302 855 741       File organization and access methods

Class computer sorting of records in 025.3177

.31       *The catalog

.313       *Form

Including card catalogs

.313 2       *Online catalogs

Class comprehensive works on online catalogs integrated with information storage and retrieval systems in 025.04

---

*Do not use notation 0218 from Table 1; class in base number

.315    *Structure

Including classified, divided, unified catalogs

.316    *Machine-readable record formats

Class here communication and internal formats for machine-readable cataloging records, for metadata; Machine-Readable Cataloging (MARC); comprehensive works on machine-readable formats for catalog records, on machine-readable formats for catalog and index records

*For display formats, see 025.313; for input formats, see 025.317. For formats for a specific kind of record, see the kind in 025.32–025.49, plus notation 0285572 from Table 1, e.g., name authority formats 025.32220285572, serials formats 025.34320285572, subject authority formats 025.49000285572*

.317    *Conversion and maintenance

Including preparing, correcting, updating manual and machine-readable catalog records

Class retrospective conversion combined with recataloging and reclassification in 025.39

.317 3    *Retrospective conversion

.317 7    *Filing

Including computer sorting of cataloging records

Class here filing rules

.32    *Descriptive cataloging

Class here descriptive cataloging codes, e.g., Resource Description and Access

Class descriptive cataloging of special materials in 025.34; class cooperative descriptive cataloging in 025.35; class recataloging in 025.39

.322    *Choice of entry and form of heading

Including corporate headings, personal name headings, uniform titles

Class here author-title indexing

.322 2    *Authority files

Class here name, title authorities; comprehensive works on authority files

*For subject authorities, see 025.49*

.324    *Bibliographic description

Class here codes for bibliographic description

.34    *Cataloging, classification, indexing of special materials

Class here nonbook materials

Class comprehensive works on treatment of special materials in 025.17

*Do not use notation 0218 from Table 1; class in base number

| .341 | *Manuscripts, archival materials, rarities |
|---|---|
| .341 2 | *Manuscripts |
| .341 4 | *Archival materials |

Class here arrangement, description, processing

Class manuscripts in 025.3412

| .341 6 | *Rarities |
|---|---|

Class rare manuscripts in 025.3412; class archival materials in 025.3414

| .342 | *Clippings, broadsides, pamphlets |
|---|---|

Class here contents of vertical files, printed ephemera

| .343 | *Serials, government publications, report literature |
|---|---|
| .343 2 | *Serials |

Including CONSER (Cooperative Conversion of Serials) Project, International Serials Data Program (ISDP), International Standard Serial Numbers (ISSNs)

| .343 4 | *Government publications |
|---|---|

Class government serials in 025.3432

| .343 6 | *Report literature |
|---|---|

Class serial report literature in 025.3432; class government reports in 025.3434

| .344 | *Electronic resources |
|---|---|

Class here CD-ROM (compact disc read-only memory), computer software, interactive multimedia, web sites

| .346 | *Maps, atlases, globes |
|---|---|

Standard subdivisions are added for any or all topics in heading

| .347 | *Pictures and materials for projection |
|---|---|

Class here comprehensive works on audiovisual materials

*For multimedia, see 025.344; for maps, atlases, globes, see 025.346; for sound recordings and music scores, see 025.348; for other special materials, see 025.349*

| .347 1 | *Pictures and prints |
|---|---|
| .347 3 | *Motion pictures, slides, video recordings |
| .348 | *Sound recordings and music scores |

*Do not use notation 0218 from Table 1; class in base number

| | |
|---|---|
| .348 2 | *Sound recordings |

Class here cassettes, compact discs

Class sound films and video recordings in 025.3473

| | |
|---|---|
| .348 8 | *Music scores |
| .349 | *Other special materials |

Including large-type publications, realia

| | |
|---|---|
| .349 2 | *Publications in raised characters |

Including braille

| | |
|---|---|
| .349 4 | *Microforms |
| .349 6 | *Games, media kits, models, toys |

Standard subdivisions are added for any or all topics in heading

Including flashcards

| | |
|---|---|
| .35 | *Cooperative cataloging, classification, indexing |

Including cooperative development of name and subject authority files

Class cooperative cataloging, classification, indexing of special materials in 025.34

| | |
|---|---|
| .39 | *Recataloging, reclassification, reindexing |

Standard subdivisions are added for any or all topics in heading

Class recataloging, reclassification, reindexing of special materials in 025.34

| | |
|---|---|
| [.393] | Recataloging |

Number discontinued; class in 025.39

| | |
|---|---|
| [.396] | Reclassification |

Number discontinued; class in 025.39

| | |
|---|---|
| **.4** | **Subject analysis and control** |

Class here standards for subject analysis and control

| | |
|---|---|
| [.402 18] | Standards |

Do not use; class in 025.4

| | |
|---|---|
| .402 8 | Auxiliary techniques and procedures; apparatus, equipment, materials |

Abstracting relocated to 025.41

| | |
|---|---|
| .41 | *Abstracting [*formerly* 025.4028] |

Class here comprehensive works on abstracting and subject indexing

Class composition of abstracts in 808.062

*For subject indexing, see 025.47*

*Do not use notation 0218 from Table 1; class in base number

| | |
|---|---|
| .410 285 | Computer applications |
| .410 285 635 | Natural language processing |

> Class here automatic abstracting, automatic text summarization

.42 *Classification and shelflisting

> Standard subdivisions are added for classification and shelflisting together, for classification alone

> Class use of classification for search and navigation in information storage and retrieval systems in 025.04; class classification of special materials in 025.34; class cooperative classification in 025.35; class reclassification in 025.39

> *For general classification systems, see 025.43; for classification of specific subjects, see 025.46*

.428 *Shelflisting

> *See also 025.3 for International Standard Book Numbers (ISBNs)*

.43 *General classification systems

> Class parts of general classification systems applied to a specific subject with the subject in 025.46, e.g., Library of Congress Classification Class L Education 025.4637

.431 *Dewey Decimal Classification

.432 *Universal Decimal Classification

.433 *Library of Congress Classification

.434 *Bliss Bibliographic Classification

.435 *Colon Classification

.46 Classification of specific subjects

[.460 001–.460 009] Standard subdivisions

> Do not use; class in 025.4201–025.4209

.460 01–.469 99 *Specific subjects

> Add to base number 025.46 notation 001–999, e.g., classification of education 025.4637

---

*Do not use notation 0218 from Table 1; class in base number

.47      *Subject indexing [*formerly* 025.48] and cataloging

Standard subdivisions are added for either or both topics in heading

Class here precoordinate indexing [*formerly* 025.482], coordinate and postcoordinate indexing [*both formerly* 025.484]; general controlled subject vocabularies (subject authority files, subject headings, thesauri) [*all formerly* 025.49]; comprehensive works on subject indexing and cataloging using natural language and controlled vocabulary

Class subject cataloging and indexing of special materials in 025.34; class cooperative subject cataloging and indexing in 025.35; class recataloging and reindexing in 025.39. Class parts of general controlled subject vocabularies (subject authority files, subject headings, thesauri) applied to a specific subject with the subject, e.g., Library of Congress Subject Headings for law 025.4934

*For classification, see 025.42; for subject cataloging and indexing based on natural language, see 025.48; for subject cataloging and indexing of specific subjects, see 025.49*

.472–.479      *General subject cataloging and indexing schemes in specific languages

Add to base number 025.47 notation 2–9 from Table 6, e.g., list of Italian subject headings 025.4751

A bilingual or multilingual scheme is classed with the language coming last in Table 6, e.g., a general thesaurus in English, French, Spanish, Russian, Arabic, and Chinese 025.47951

.48      *Subject cataloging and indexing based on natural language

Class comprehensive works on natural language and controlled vocabulary subject indexing and cataloging in 025.47; class subject cataloging and indexing of specific subjects based on natural language in 025.49

Comprehensive works on subject indexing relocated to 025.47

[.482]      Precoordinate indexing

Relocated to 025.47

[.484]      Coordinate and postcoordinate indexing

Relocated to 025.47

.486      *Full-text indexing

Class here keyword indexing

.487      *Tagging

Variant names: collaborative indexing, folksonomies, social classification, social indexing

---

*Do not use notation 0218 from Table 1; class in base number

.49      Subject cataloging and indexing of specific subjects

> Class general subject cataloging and indexing using controlled vocabulary in 025.47; class general subject cataloging and indexing based on natural language in 025.48

> General controlled subject vocabularies (subject authority files, subject headings, thesauri) relocated to 025.47

[.490 001–.490 009]      Standard subdivisions

> Do not use; class in 025.4701–025.4709

.490 01–.499 99      Specific subjects

> Add to base number 025.49 notation 001–999, e.g., subject headings in science 025.495

## .5      Services for users

> Works intended for staff or users

> Class library services to special groups and organizations in 027.6

> *For a specific service not provided for here, see the service, e.g., photocopying services 025.12*

.52      Reference and information services

> Standard subdivisions are added for either or both topics in heading

> Class here information and referral services, services that involve the use or assistance in the use of information tools but not the creation of them, virtual reference services

> Class the use of books and other media as sources of information in 028.7; class comprehensive works on the creation and use of information storage and retrieval systems in 025.04; class comprehensive works on the creation and use of specific tools for bibliographic control in 025.3

.523      Cooperative information services

.524      Information search and retrieval

> Using multiple kinds of information sources, e.g., the library catalog, reference books, automated information storage and retrieval systems

> Class here search strategy

> Class information search and retrieval using a specific system with the system, e.g., searching an information storage and retrieval system devoted to medicine 025.0661

> *See also 025.04 for information storage and retrieval systems*

.525      Selective dissemination of information (SDI)

> Class here current awareness services

| | |
|---|---|
| .527 | Reference and information services in specific types of institutions |

Add to base number 025.527 the numbers following 02 in 026–027, e.g., reference and information services in college and university libraries 025.52777; however, for reference and information services to special groups and organizations, see 027.6

Class specific aspects of reference and information service in specific types of institutions in 025.523–025.525

| | |
|---|---|
| .54 | Reader advisory services to individuals and groups |

*See also 028.8 for use of books and other media as sources of recreation and self-development*

| | |
|---|---|
| .56 | Orientation and bibliographic instruction for users |

Including signs, regulations for use, user manuals

Add to base number 025.56 the numbers following 02 in 026–027, e.g., orientation to public libraries 025.5674; however, for orientation and bibliographic instruction for special groups and organizations, see 027.6 Subdivisions are added for either or both topics in heading

| | |
|---|---|
| .58 | Library use studies |

Add to base number 025.58 the numbers following 02 in 026–027, e.g., use of government libraries 025.5875; however, for use studies of libraries for special groups and organizations, see 027.6

Class studies of use of a specific system and service with the system or service, e.g., catalog use studies 025.313, studies of use of interlibrary loans 025.62

| | |
|---|---|
| **.6** | **Circulation services** |

Including reserve collections

Class here document delivery

Class circulation services for special groups and organizations in 027.6

| | |
|---|---|
| .62 | Interlibrary loans |
| **.7** | **Physical preparation for storage and use** |

Including binding, labeling, pocketing

Class conservation and preservation in 025.84

Repair and restoration relocated to 025.84

| | |
|---|---|
| **.8** | **Maintenance and preservation of collections** |
| .81 | Physical arrangement and access to collections |

Including closed and open stacks, integrated shelving of materials in different formats

| | |
|---|---|
| .82 | Security against theft and other hazards |

Including disaster preparedness, taking of inventory

.84 Preservation

Including deacidification

Class here repair and restoration [*both formerly* 025.7]; conservation, digital preservation

---

> ## 026–027 Specific kinds of institutions

Class here specific libraries, archives, information centers, and their collections; systems and networks for specific kinds of institutions; comprehensive works on operations in specific kinds of institutions

Class comprehensive works in 027. Class a specific operation in a specific kind of institution with the operation, e.g., reference and information services in college libraries 025.52777

## 026 Libraries, archives, information centers devoted to specific subjects

Class here information organizations and library departments and collections in specific subjects; comprehensive works on special libraries

*For special libraries not devoted to specific subjects, see the kind of library in 027.6, e.g., general museum libraries 027.68, general libraries in newspaper offices 027.69*

*See Manual at 016 vs. 026, T1—07*

.000 1–.000 5 Standard subdivisions

.000 6 Organizations

[.000 68] Management

Do not use; class in 025.19

.000 7–.000 9 Standard subdivisions

.001–.999 Specific subjects

Add to base number 026 notation 001–999, e.g., medical libraries 026.61; however, do not add notation 068 from Table 1 for organizations and management; class in 025.19

## 027 General libraries, archives, information centers

Standard subdivisions are added for any or all topics in heading

In the subdivisions of this number, the term libraries is used as a short way of saying libraries, archives, information centers, media centers

Class here comprehensive works on libraries, on archives, on information centers, on libraries and information centers devoted to special materials

*For libraries, archives, information centers devoted to specific subjects, see 026*

## SUMMARY

.001–.005  Standard subdivisions

.006  Organizations

[.006 8]  Management

    Do not use; class in 025.1

[.006 82]  Plant management

    Do not use; class in 022

[.006 83]  Personnel management (Human resource management)

    Do not use; class in 023

.007  Education, research, related topics

.008  Groups of people

    Do not use for minorities; class in 027.63

[.008 3]  Young people

    Do not use; class in 027.625

[.008 35]  Young people twelve to twenty

    Do not use; class in 027.626

[.008 46]  People in late adulthood

    Do not use; class in 027.622

[.008 694]  People with social disadvantages

    Do not use; class in 027.6

.008 7  People with disabilities and illnesses, gifted people

    Do not use for people with disabilities; class in 027.663

.009  History and biography

    Do not use for geographic treatment; class in 027.01–027.09

.01–.09  *Geographic treatment

    Add to base number 027.0 notation 1–9 from Table 2, e.g., libraries in France 027.044

*Do not use notation 068 from Table 1; class in 025.19

**.1** **\*Private and family libraries**

> Collections not open to general use
>
> Standard subdivisions are added for either or both topics in heading

.109      History and biography

> Do not use for geographic treatment; class in 027.11–027.19

.11–.19      \*Geographic treatment

> Add to base number 027.1 notation 1–9 from Table 2, e.g., family libraries in the United Kingdom 027.141

**.2** **\*Proprietary libraries**

> Semiprivate libraries requiring subscription or membership fees for general use

.209      History and biography

> Do not use for geographic treatment; class in 027.21–027.29

.21–.29      \*Geographic treatment

> Add to base number 027.2 notation 1–9 from Table 2, e.g., proprietary libraries in Leeds 027.242819

**.3** **\*Rental libraries**

> Libraries whose materials are available for use on a commercial basis

.309      History and biography

> Do not use for geographic treatment; class in 027.31–027.39

.31–.39      \*Geographic treatment

> Add to base number 027.3 notation 1–9 from Table 2, e.g., rental libraries in United States 027.373

**.4** **\*Public libraries**

> Class here public library branches
>
> Class public library units for special groups and organizations in 027.6

[.409 3–.409 9]      Specific continents, countries, localities

> Do not use; class in 027.43–027.49

.42      \*Library outreach programs

> Class here library extension, the use of bookmobiles (mobile libraries) in public librarianship

[.420 93–.420 99]      Specific continents, countries, localities

> Do not use; class in 027.43–027.49

---

\*Do not use notation 068 from Table 1; class in 025.19

.43–.49     *Specific continents, countries, localities

> Add to base number 027.4 notation 3–9 from Table 2, e.g., public libraries in France 027.444

## .5     *Government libraries

> National, state, provincial, local
>
> Including overseas information libraries [*formerly* 027.65]
>
> *For legislative reference bureaus, see 027.65*

.508        Government libraries for groups of people [*formerly also* 027.65]

.509        History, geographic treatment, biography

.509 3–.509 9     Specific continents, countries, localities

> Class specific institutions in 027.53–027.59

.53–.59     *Specific institutions

> Add to base number 027.5 notation 3–9 from Table 2 for area served, e.g., Library of Congress 027.573

## .6     *Libraries for special groups and organizations

> Class here library and information services to special groups and organizations, to the socially disadvantaged
>
> Unless other instructions are given, class a subject with aspects in two or more subdivisions of 027.6 in the number coming last, e.g., libraries for children with disabilities 027.663 (*not* 027.625)
>
> Class libraries for special groups and organizations devoted to specific subjects in 026
>
> *For libraries for educational institutions, see 027.7–027.8*

.62         *Libraries for specific age groups

.622            *Libraries for people in late adulthood

.625            *Libraries for children

> To age eleven

.625 1              Storytelling

.626            *Libraries for young people aged twelve to twenty

.63         *Libraries for minorities

.65         *Legislative reference bureaus

> Class here parliamentary libraries
>
> Overseas information libraries relocated to 027.5; government libraries for groups of people relocated to 027.508

---

*Do not use notation 068 from Table 1; class in 025.19

[.652]           Legislative reference bureaus

> Number discontinued; class in 027.65

.66       *Welfare institution libraries

.662        *Hospital libraries

> Class here comprehensive works on patients' and medical libraries
>
> *For medical libraries, see 026.61*

.663        *Libraries for people with disabilities

> Including libraries for people with visual impairments
>
> Class here mainstreaming (the provision of library and information services through regular channels to individuals with special needs)

.665        *Prison libraries

.67       *Libraries for religious organizations

.68       *Libraries for nonprofit organizations

> Including libraries of learned societies, museum libraries, United Nations Library
>
> *For welfare institution libraries, see 027.66; for libraries for religious organizations, see 027.67*

.69       *Libraries for business and industrial organizations

> Standard subdivisions are added for either or both topics in heading
>
> Including reference collections in newspaper offices used in the writing or editing of articles

---

>      **027.7–027.8 Libraries for educational institutions**

> Class here instructional media centers
>
> Class comprehensive works in 027.7

.7      **\*College and university libraries**

> Standard subdivisions are added for either or both topics in heading
>
> Including comprehensive works on instructional materials centers
>
> Class here comprehensive works on libraries for educational institutions, college and university library branches
>
> *For libraries and instructional materials centers in primary and secondary schools, see 027.8*

.709 3–.709 9     Specific continents, countries, localities

> Class specific institutions in 027.73–027.79

*Do not use notation 068 from Table 1; class in 025.19

.73–.79     *Specific institutions

> Add to base number 027.7 notation 3–9 from Table 2, e.g., Perkins Library of Duke University 027.7756563

**.8     *School libraries**

> Including school resource centers

.809 3–.809 9     Specific continents, countries, localities

> Class specific institutions in 027.823–027.829

.82     Specific levels and specific libraries

> Class libraries in religious schools of specific levels, in specific religious schools in 027.83

.822     Specific levels

> Class specific libraries of specific levels in 027.823–027.829

.822 2     *Primary level

.822 3     *Secondary level

.823–.829     *Specific libraries

> Add to base number 027.82 notation 3–9 from Table 2, e.g., Phillips Exeter Academy Library 027.827426

.83     *Libraries in religious schools

# 028     Reading and use of other information media

[.083]     Young people

> Do not use; class in 028.5

**.1     Reviews**

> Class here general collections of book reviews

> Class reviews of computer programs in 005.3029; class techniques of reviewing in 808.066028. Class reviews of works on a specific subject with the subject, e.g., reviews of works on chemistry 540, reviews of entertainment films 791.43, critical appraisal of literature 800

.108     Reviews for and by groups of people

.108 3     Reviews by young people

> Do not use for reviews of works for young people; class in 028.162

.108 7     Reviews by people with disabilities and illnesses; reviews for and by gifted people

> Do not use for reviews of works for people with disabilities; class in 028.163

---

*Do not use notation 068 from Table 1; class in 025.19

.12 Reviews of reference works

> Class reviews of reference works published in specific forms in 028.13; class reviews of reference works for specific kinds of users in 028.16. Class reviews of a specific kind of reference works with the kind, e.g., reviews of encyclopedias 030

.13 Reviews of works published in specific forms

> Add to base number 028.13 the numbers following 011.3 in 011.31–011.39, e.g., reviews of documentary, educational, and entertainment films 028.137

> Class general collections of book reviews in 028.1; class reviews of works published in specific forms for specific kinds of users in 028.16

.16 Reviews of works for specific kinds of users

> Add to base number 028.16 the numbers following 011.6 in 011.62–011.67, e.g., reviews of works for young people 028.162

**.5 Reading and use of other information media by young people**

> Standard subdivisions are added for either or both topics in heading

> *See also 028.162 for reviews of materials for young people*

.53 Reading and use of other information media by specific age groups

> Add to base number 028.53 the numbers following —083 in notation 0832–0835 from Table 1, e.g., reading and use of other information media by children six to eleven 028.534
> Subdivisions are added for either or both topics in heading

.55 Reading interests and habits of young people

> Standard subdivisions are added for either or both topics in heading

> Class reading interests and habits of young people of specific age groups in 028.53

**.7 Use of books and other information media as sources of information**

> Standard subdivisions are added for either or both topics in heading

> Class here use of reference works

[.708 3] Young people

> Do not use; class in 028.5

**.8 Use of books and other information media as sources of recreation and self-development**

> Standard subdivisions are added for either or both topics in heading

[.808 3] Young people

> Do not use; class in 028.5

**.9 Reading interests and habits**

[.908 3] Young people

> Do not use; class in 028.55

**[029]** **[Unassigned]**

Most recently used in Edition 18

# 030 General encyclopedic works

Class here almanacs with general information; books of miscellaneous, curious, unusual facts; encyclopedia yearbooks

.9 **History, geographic treatment, biography**

Class history, geographic treatment, biography of encyclopedic works in specific languages and language families in 031–039

---

> **031–039 General encyclopedic works in specific languages and language families**

By language in which originally written

Class here specific encyclopedias and books of miscellaneous facts, works about them

Except for modifications shown under specific entries, add to each subdivision identified by * as follows:

01      Philosophy and theory
02      Books of miscellaneous facts
        Do not use for other types of miscellany; class in base number for the language
        Class here almanacs with general information, books of curious and unusual facts
03–09   Standard subdivisions

Class comprehensive works, encyclopedic works originally written in two or more languages or language families in which no language or language family is predominant in 030. Class encyclopedic works originally written in two or more languages or language families in which one language or language family is predominant with the predominant language or language family, e.g., encyclopedic work written in Portuguese with some articles in Spanish 036.9

(Option A: To give local emphasis and a shorter number to encyclopedias in a specific language, place them first by use of a letter or other symbol, e.g., Arabic-language encyclopedias 03A [preceding 031]. Option B is described under 031)

# 031 *General encyclopedic works in American English

English-language encyclopedias and books of miscellaneous facts originating in Western Hemisphere

(Option B: To give local emphasis and a shorter number to encyclopedias in a specific language other than English, class them in this number; in that case class American English-language encyclopedias in 032. Option A is described under 031–039)

# 032 *General encyclopedic works in English

*For general encyclopedic works in American English, see 031*

---

*Add as instructed under 031–039

# 033 General encyclopedic works in other Germanic languages

Class here comprehensive works on Germanic-language encyclopedias

*For English-language encyclopedias, see 032; for Scandinavian-language encyclopedias, see 038*

**.1–.8 General encyclopedic works in German and German dialects**

Add to base number 033 the numbers following —3 in notation 31–38 from Table 6, e.g., Swiss-German-dialect encyclopedias 033.5; then add further as instructed under 031–039, e.g., Swiss-German-dialect books of miscellaneous facts 033.502

**.9 General encyclopedic works in Yiddish and Low Germanic languages**

Add to base number 033.9 the numbers following —39 in notation 391–394 from Table 6, e.g., Dutch-language encyclopedias 033.931; then add further as instructed under 031–039, e.g., Dutch-language books of miscellaneous facts 033.93102

# 034 General encyclopedic works in French, Occitan, Catalan

Add to base number 034 the numbers following —4 in notation 41–49 from Table 6, e.g., French-language encyclopedias 034.1; then add further as instructed under 031–039, e.g., French-language almanacs 034.102

# 035 General encyclopedic works in Italian, Dalmatian, Romanian, Rhaetian, Sardinian, Corsican

Add to base number 035 the numbers following —5 in notation 51–59 from Table 6, e.g., Italian-language encyclopedias 035.1; then add further as instructed under 031–039, e.g., Italian-language books of miscellaneous facts 035.102

# 036 General encyclopedic works in Spanish, Portuguese, Galician

Add to base number 036 the numbers following —6 in notation 61–69 from Table 6, e.g., Portuguese-language encyclopedias 036.9; then add further as instructed under 031–039, e.g., Portuguese-language books of miscellaneous facts 036.902

# 037 General encyclopedic works in Slavic languages

**.1 *General encyclopedic works in Russian**

**.8 General encyclopedic works in other Slavic languages**

*For Ukrainian-language and Belarusian-language encyclopedias, see 037.9*

.81 General encyclopedic works in Bulgarian and Macedonian

.811 *General encyclopedic works in Bulgarian

.819 *General encyclopedic works in Macedonian

*Add as instructed under 031–039

.82       *General encyclopedic works in Serbian

> Class here general encyclopedic works in Serbo-Croatian

> General encyclopedic works in Croatian relocated to 037.83; general encyclopedic works in Bosnian relocated to 037.839

.83       *General encyclopedic works in Croatian [*formerly* 037.82] and Bosnian

> Subdivisions are added for Croatian and Bosnian together, for Croatian alone

.839       *General encyclopedic works in Bosnian [*formerly* 037.82]

.84       *General encyclopedic works in Slovenian

.85       *General encyclopedic works in Polish

.86       *General encyclopedic works in Czech

.87       *General encyclopedic works in Slovak

.88       *General encyclopedic works in Wendish (Sorbian, Lusatian)

**.9**       **General encyclopedic works in Ukrainian and Belarusian**

.91       *General encyclopedic works in Ukrainian

.99       *General encyclopedic works in Belarusian

## 038   General encyclopedic works in Scandinavian languages

> Add to base number 038 the numbers following —39 in notation 396–398 from Table 6, e.g., Swedish-language encyclopedias 038.7; then add further as instructed under 031–039, e.g., Swedish-language books of miscellaneous facts 038.702

## 039   General encyclopedic works in other languages

> Add to base number 039 notation 7–9 from Table 6, e.g., Chinese-language encyclopedias 039.951; then add further as instructed under 031–039, e.g., Chinese-language books of miscellaneous facts 039.95102

## [040]   [Unassigned]

> Most recently used in Edition 16

## [041]   [Unassigned]

> Most recently used in Edition 16

## [042]   [Unassigned]

> Most recently used in Edition 16

## [043]   [Unassigned]

> Most recently used in Edition 16

## [044]   [Unassigned]

> Most recently used in Edition 16

*Add as instructed under 031–039

**[045]** **[Unassigned]**

Most recently used in Edition 16

**[046]** **[Unassigned]**

Most recently used in Edition 16

**[047]** **[Unassigned]**

Most recently used in Edition 16

**[048]** **[Unassigned]**

Most recently used in Edition 16

**[049]** **[Unassigned]**

Most recently used in Edition 16

**050** **General serial publications**

Class here periodicals; indexes to general serial publications

Class books of miscellaneous facts (even if published annually, e.g., almanacs), encyclopedia yearbooks in 030; class administrative reports and proceedings of general organizations in 060. Class indexes that focus on a specific subject in general serial publications with the subject in 016, e.g., an index to information on medicine in general serial publications 016.61

*For newspapers, see 070*

*See also 011.34 for bibliographies of general serial publications; also 011.7 for bibliographies of directories; also 017–019 for catalogs of general serial publications*

**.9** **History, geographic treatment, biography**

Class history, geographic treatment, biography of serial publications in specific languages and language families in 051–059

> ## 051–059   General serial publications in specific languages and language families

By language in which originally written

Class here specific serial publications and works about them

Class comprehensive works, serials originally written in two or more languages or language families in which no language or language family is predominant in 050. Class serials originally written in two or more languages or language families in which one language or language family is predominant with the predominant language or language family, e.g., serial written in Portuguese with some articles in Spanish 056.9

(Option A: To give local emphasis and a shorter number to serial publications in a specific language, place them first by use of a letter or other symbol, e.g., Hindi-language serial publications 05H [preceding 051]

(Option B: Arrange serial publications alphabetically under 050

(Option C is described under 051)

## 051   General serial publications in American English

English-language serial publications of Western Hemisphere

(Option C: To give local emphasis and a shorter number to serial publications in a specific language other than English, class them in this number; in that case class American English-language serial publications in 052. Options A and B are described under 051–059)

## 052   General serial publications in English

*For general serial publications in American English, see 051*

## 053   General serial publications in other Germanic languages

Class here comprehensive works on general serial publications in Germanic languages

*For English-language serial publications, see 052; for Scandinavian-language serial publications, see 058*

### .1–.8   General serial publications in German and German dialects

Add to base number 053 the numbers following —3 in notation 31–38 from Table 6, e.g., Swiss-German-dialect serial publications 053.5

### .9   General serial publications in Yiddish and Low Germanic languages

Add to base number 053.9 the numbers following — 39 in notation 391–394 from Table 6, e.g., Dutch-language serial publications 053.931

## 054   General serial publications in French, Occitan, Catalan

Add to base number 054 the numbers following —4 in notation 41–49 from Table 6, e.g., French-language serial publications 054.1

**055**     **General serial publications in Italian, Dalmatian, Romanian, Rhaetian, Sardinian, Corsican**

Add to base number 055 the numbers following —5 in notation 51–59 from Table 6, e.g., Italian-language serial publications 055.1

**056**     **General serial publications in Spanish, Portuguese, Galician**

Add to base number 056 the numbers following —6 in notation 61–69 from Table 6, e.g., Portuguese-language serial publications 056.9

**057**     **General serial publications in Slavic languages**

Add to base number 057 the numbers following 037 in 037.1–037.9 for language only, e.g., Polish-language serial publications 057.85

**058**     **General serial publications in Scandinavian languages**

Add to base number 058 the numbers following —39 in notation 396–398 from Table 6, e.g., Swedish-language serial publications 058.7

**059**     **General serial publications in other languages**

Add to base number 059 notation 7–9 from Table 6, e.g., Chinese-language serial publications 059.951

# 060     General organizations and museology

General organizations: academies, associations, conferences, congresses, foundations, societies whose activity is not limited to a specific field

Including history, charters, regulations, membership lists, administrative reports and proceedings

Class here interdisciplinary works on organizations; interdisciplinary works on licensing, certification, accreditation by nongovernmental organizations

Class history, charters, regulations, membership lists, administrative reports and proceedings of a specific organization in 061–068; class interdisciplinary works on licensing, certification, accreditation by governmental and nongovernmental bodies in 352.84

> *For interdisciplinary works on intergovernmental organizations, see 341.2. For organizations devoted to a specific subject, see the subject, plus notation 06 from Table 1, e.g., organizations devoted to computer science 004.06*

> *See Manual at T1—025 vs. T1—029*

(Option A: To give local emphasis and a shorter number to organizations in a specific country, place them first by use of a letter or other symbol, e.g., organizations in Pakistan 06P [preceding 061]. Option B is described under 061)

**.4**     **Special topics of general organizations**

.42     General rules of order (Parliamentary procedure)

Including Robert's Rules of Order

> *For rules and procedures of legislative bodies, see 328.1*

> *See also 658.456 for conduct of meetings of business organizations*

**.9** **History and biography**

Do not use for geographic treatment of general organizations; class in 061–068

> **061–068 General organizations**

Class comprehensive works in 060

# 061 General organizations in North America

*For organizations in Middle America, see 068.72*

(Option B: To give local emphasis and a shorter number to organizations in a specific country other than the United States and Canada, class them in this number; in that case class organizations in North America in 068.7. Option A is described under 060)

**.1** **General organizations in Canada**

Add to base number 061.1 the numbers following —71 in notation 711–719 from Table 2, e.g., organizations in British Columbia 061.11

**.3–.9** **General organizations in United States**

Add to base number 061 the numbers following —7 in notation 73–79 from Table 2, e.g., general organizations in Ohio 061.71

*For organizations in Hawaii, see 068.969*

# 062 General organizations in British Isles

Class here general organizations in England

**.1–.8** **General organizations in England**

Add to base number 062 the numbers following —42 in notation 421–428 from Table 2, e.g., organizations in London 062.1

**.9** **General organizations in Scotland, Ireland, Wales**

Add to base number 062.9 the numbers following —4 in notation 41–42 from Table 2, e.g., organizations in Scotland and Ireland 062.91

# 063 General organizations in Germany and neighboring central European countries

Standard subdivisions are added for Germany and neighboring central European countries together, for Germany alone

Class here general organizations in central Europe

Add to base number 063 the numbers following —43 in notation 431–439 from Table 2, e.g., organizations in Poland 063.8

# 064 General organizations in France and Monaco

Standard subdivisions are added for France and Monaco together, for France alone

Add to base number 064 the numbers following —44 in notation 441–449 from Table 2, e.g., organizations in Paris metropolitan area 064.36

**065 General organizations in Italy, San Marino, Vatican City, Malta**

> Standard subdivisions are added for Italy, San Marino, Vatican City, Malta together; for Italy alone
>
> Add to base number 065 the numbers following —45 in notation 451–459 from Table 2, e.g., organizations in Rome 065.632

**066 General organizations in Spain, Andorra, Gibraltar, Portugal**

> Standard subdivisions are added for Spain, Andorra, Gibraltar, Portugal together; for Spain alone
>
> Add to base number 066 the numbers following —46 in notation 461–469 from Table 2, e.g., organizations in Portugal 066.9

**067 General organizations in Russia and neighboring east European countries**

> Standard subdivisions are added for Russia and neighboring east European countries together, for Russia alone
>
> Add to base number 067 the numbers following —47 in notation 471–479 from Table 2, e.g., organizations in Moscow 067.31
>
> *For organizations in Balkan Peninsula, see 068.496; for organizations in Commonwealth of Independent States in Asia, see 068.57–068.58*

**068 General organizations in other geographic areas**

> Add to base number 068 notation 1–9 from Table 2, e.g., comprehensive works on general organizations in Europe 068.4, in Balkan Peninsula 068.496, in Middle America 068.72, in Hawaii 068.969

**069 Museology (Museum science)**

> Class here government policy on museums
>
> *For museum activities and services limited to a specific subject, see the subject, plus notation 075 from Table 1, e.g., activities and services of a clock museum 681.113075*

.028 8      Maintenance and repair

> Do not use for maintenance and repair of museum objects; class in 069.53

.068      Management

[.068 2]      Plant management

> Do not use; class in 069.2

[.068 3]      Personnel management

> Do not use; class in 069.63

[.068 5]      Organization of production

> Do not use; class in 069.1

| [.068 7] | Management of materials |
|---|---|

                              Do not use; class in 069.5

.07              Education, research, related topics

.074             Museums, collections, exhibits

                              Limited to museums, collections, exhibits about museology

                              Class comprehensive works on museums in 069; class comprehensive works on collections and exhibits in 069.5

.075             Museum activities and services

                              Limited to museums about and collecting objects related to museology

                              Class comprehensive works on museum services to patrons in 069.1; class comprehensive works on collecting and preparing museum objects in 069.4

.09              History, geographic treatment, biography

                              Class here specific museums not limited to a specific subject

                              Class history, geographic treatment, biography of museum buildings in 069.209. Class museums devoted to a specific subject with the subject, plus notation 074 from Table 1, e.g., natural history museums 508.074

**.1**        **Museum services to patrons**

                          Class here organization of production

.108 7         People with disabilities and illnesses, gifted people

                              Do not use for museum services to people with disabilities; class in 069.17

.13              Circulation services

                        Lending and renting materials

                           *See also 069.56 for lending and rental collections*

.132             Museum objects

.134             Representations of museum objects

                        Including pictures, slides, films; aids to use of representations

.15              Instruction services

                      Including lectures, classes, field trips

.16              Recreational services

                      Including musical programs, theatrical presentations

.17              Special services to people with disabilities

**.2**        **Management and use of physical plant**

                      Standard subdivisions are added for either or both topics in heading

                      *For equipment, furniture, furnishings, see 069.3*

.21      Location and site

       Standard subdivisions are added for either or both topics in heading

.22      Planning for buildings

       *See also 727.6 for museum architecture*

.24      Special rooms

.29      Utilities and related facilities

       Standard subdivisions are added for utilities and related facilities together, for utilities alone

       Including communication systems, lighting, plumbing, heating, ventilating, air-conditioning

**.3**      **Equipment, furniture, furnishings**

.31      Exhibit cases, screens, pedestals

.32      Audiovisual apparatus

.33      Furniture

**.4**      **Collecting and preparing museum objects**

       Including equipment, materials, methods

       Class here management of collecting and preparing museum objects, interdisciplinary works on collecting objects

       Class comprehensive works on management of museum materials, on collecting or preparing museum objects and collections of museum objects, interdisciplinary works on collecting and collections in 069.5. Class collecting a specific kind of object or objects that pertain to a specific subject with the subject, plus notation 075 from Table 1, e.g., collecting fossils 560.75

**.5**      **Collections and exhibits of museum objects**

       Standard subdivisions are added for either or both topics in heading

       Class here comprehensive works on management of museum materials, on collecting or preparing museum objects and collections of museum objects; interdisciplinary works on collecting and collections together, on collections alone

       *For collecting and preparing museum objects and for interdisciplinary works on collecting, see 069.4. For collections of a specific kind of object or objects that pertain to a specific subject, see the subject, plus notation 074 from Table 1, e.g., collections of fossils 560.74*

[.502 88]      Maintenance and repair

       Do not use; class in 069.53

.502 89      Safety measures

       *See also 069.54 for prevention of thefts and identification of forgeries*

>     069.51–069.54  General activities of collections and exhibits

       Class general activities applied to special collections in 069.55–069.57; class comprehensive works in 069.5

.51     Selection, acquisition, disposal

.52     Registration, recording, indexing

       Standard subdivisions are added for any or all topics in heading

       Class here museum documentation

.53     Maintenance, conservation, preservation, restoration, display, arrangement, storage, transportation

       Including museum labels

       Class historic preservation in 363.69

.54     Prevention of thefts and identification of forgeries

>     069.55–069.57  Special collections

       Including classification, arrangement, housing

       Class comprehensive works in 069.5

.55     Study collections

.56     Lending and rental collections

       Standard subdivisions are added for either or both topics in heading

       *See also 069.13 for circulation services*

.57     Collections of secondary materials

       Including brochures, films, motion pictures, photographs, pictures, prints, slides representing museum objects

**.6**     **Personnel management, regulations for patrons, relations with other organizations**

.62     Regulations for patrons

       Including regulations for members, for visitors

.63     Personnel management

       Including in-service training, staff manuals

.68     Relations with other organizations

       Class public relations for museums in 659.29069

# 070 Documentary media, educational media, news media; journalism; publishing

Standard subdivisions are added for documentary media, educational media, news media, journalism, publishing together; for journalism and newspapers alone; for newspapers alone

## SUMMARY

| | |
|---|---|
| 070.01–.09 | **Standard subdivisions** |
| .1–.9 | **[Documentary media, educational media, news media; journalism; publishing]** |
| 071 | **Journalism and newspapers in North America** |
| 072 | **Journalism and newspapers in British Isles** |
| 073 | **Journalism and newspapers in Germany and neighboring central European countries** |
| 074 | **Journalism and newspapers in France and Monaco** |
| 075 | **Journalism and newspapers in Italy, San Marino, Vatican City, Malta** |
| 076 | **Journalism and newspapers in Spain, Andorra, Gibraltar, Portugal** |
| 077 | **Journalism and newspapers in Russia and neighboring east European countries** |
| 078 | **Journalism and newspapers in Scandinavia** |
| 079 | **Journalism and newspapers in other geographic areas** |

.01–.08 Standard subdivisions

.09 History, geographic treatment, biography

> Do not use for history and biography of journalism and newspapers; class in 070.9. Do not use for geographic treatment of journalism and newspapers; class in 071–079

## SUMMARY

| | |
|---|---|
| 070.1 | **Documentary media, educational media, news media** |
| .4 | **Journalism** |
| .5 | **Publishing** |
| .9 | **History and biography of journalism and newspapers** |

.1 **Documentary media, educational media, news media**

> Class here comprehensive works on journalism and production of specific documentary, educational, news media

> Class interdisciplinary works on mass media in 302.23. Class documentary, educational, news works themselves and discussion of them with the kind of general work or the subject, e.g., general periodicals 050, recorded television programs on investing 332.6

> *For specific topics of journalism in specific media, see 070.4; for expository writing and editorial techniques, see 808.066*

.17 Print media

> Class the book in 002

.172 Newspapers

Limited to comprehensive works on newspaper journalism

Class comprehensive works on newspapers in 070; class newspaper publishing in 070.5722. Class a newspaper on a specific subject with the subject, plus notation 05 from Table 1, e.g., a newspaper on computers 004.05

*See also 011.35 for bibliographies of newspapers*

[.172 09] History, geographic treatment, biography

Do not use for history and biography; class in 070.9. Do not use for geographic treatment of specific general newspapers; class in 071–079

.175 Serial publications

Including newsletters

Class a serial publication on a specific subject with the subject, plus notation 05 from Table 1, e.g., science journals 505

*For newspapers, see 070.172*

.175 09 History, geographic treatment, biography

Do not use for specific general serial publications; class in 051–059

.18 Motion pictures

Including documentary films, educational films

Class photography aspects in 777; class comprehensive works about documentary, educational, news and dramatic or entertainment films in 791.43; class interdisciplinary works on motion pictures in 384.8

*See also 371.33523 for instructional use of motion pictures*

.19 Broadcast media

Class radio and television news programs in 070.43

*See also 070.57973 for Internet publications*

.194 Radio

Class comprehensive works on documentary, educational, news and dramatic or entertainment radio programs in 791.44; class interdisciplinary works on radio in 384.54

*See also 371.3331 for use of radio in teaching*

.195 Television

Class photographic aspects in 777; class comprehensive works on documentary, educational, news and dramatic or entertainment television programs in 791.45; class interdisciplinary works about television in 384.55

*See also 371.3358 for use of television in teaching*

**.4** **Journalism**

Class here specific topics of journalism in specific media

Unless other instructions are given, observe the following table of preference, e.g., photojournalism in war news 070.49 (*not* 070.4333):

| | |
|---|---|
| Features and special topics | 070.44 |
| Pictorial journalism | 070.49 |
| News gathering and reporting | 070.43 |
| Editing | 070.41 |
| Journalism directed to specific groups of people | 070.48 |

Class journalists whose careers span many activities in 070.92; class freedom of the press in 323.445; class press control in 363.31; class journalistic composition and editorial mechanics in 808.06607; class comprehensive works on journalism and information media in 070; class comprehensive works on journalism of specific media in 070.1. Class journalism of a specific general serial publication with the language of the publication in 051–059, e.g., journalism of a French periodical 054.1; class journalism of a specific newspaper with the place of publication of the newspaper in 071–079, e.g., journalism of an Arab-language newspaper published in Paris 074.361; class journalism of serial publications on a specific subject with the subject in 001–999, plus notation 05 from Table 1, e.g., journalism of science journals 505

*For student journalism, see 371.897*

*See also 070.5722 for newspaper publishing; also 174.907 for ethics of journalism*

### SUMMARY

| | | |
|---|---|---|
| | 070.408 | **Journalism for and by groups of people** |
| | .41 | **Editing** |
| | .43 | **Reporting and news gathering** |
| | .44 | **Features and specific subjects** |
| | .48 | **Journalism directed to specific groups** |
| | .49 | **Pictorial journalism** |

.408        Journalism for and by groups of people

.408 1        Journalism by people by gender or sex

> Do not use for journalism for people by gender or sex; class in 070.483

.408 11        Journalism by men

> Do not use for journalism for men; class in 070.48346

.408 2        Journalism by women

> Do not use for journalism for women; class in 070.48347

.408 3        Journalism by young people

> Do not use for journalism for young people; class in 070.4832

.408 341        Journalism by boys six to eleven

> Do not use for journalism for boys six to eleven; class in 070.48326

| | |
|---|---|
| .408 342 | Journalism by girls six to eleven |
| | Do not use for journalism for girls six to eleven; class in 070.48327 |
| .408 35 | Journalism by young people twelve to twenty |
| | Do not use for journalism for young people twelve to twenty; class in 070.4833 |
| .408 351 | Journalism by males twelve to twenty |
| | Do not use for journalism for males twelve to twenty; class in 070.48336 |
| .408 352 | Journalism by females twelve to twenty |
| | Do not use for journalism for females twelve to twenty; class in 070.48337 |
| .408 8 | Journalism by occupational and religious groups |
| | Do not use for journalism for religious groups; class in 070.482. Do not use for journalism for occupational groups; class in 070.486 |
| .408 9 | Journalism by ethnic and national groups |
| | Do not use for journalism for ethnic and national groups; class in 070.484 |
| [.409] | History, geographic treatment, biography |
| | Do not use for history and biography; class in 070.9. Do not use for geographic treatment; class in 071–079 |

.41 **Editing**

Class here editorial policy (selection, presentation, display of news; advocacy of specific points of view)

Class editorials in 070.442; class comprehensive works on editing and news gathering or reporting in 070.4

*See also 808.06607 for editorial mechanics, e.g., copy editing, Associated Press stylebook*

.43 **Reporting and news gathering**

Standard subdivisions are added for reporting and news gathering together, for reporting alone

Class here newsreels, radio news programs, television news programs, other news programs

Class comprehensive works on editorial policy and news gathering or reporting in 070.4

.431 News sources

.433 Reporting local, international, war news

Class reporting on a specific subject with the subject in 070.449, e.g., reporting on world-wide energy resources 070.44933379

| | |
|---|---|
| .433 2 | International news |

> Class here foreign news
>
> Class foreign war news in 070.4333

| | |
|---|---|
| .433 3 | War news |

> Class reporting on a specific war with the war in 070.4499, e.g., reporting on World War II 070.44994053

| | |
|---|---|
| .435 | News agencies |

> Class here electronic news services, wire services

| | |
|---|---|
| .44 | Features and specific subjects |

> Class here newspaper columns; techniques and procedures for information-gathering, writing, editing for features and specific subjects

| | |
|---|---|
| .442 | Interpretation and opinion |

> Standard subdivisions are added for either or both topics in heading
>
> Including newspaper editorials, radio comment
>
> Class editorial policy in 070.41. Class journalistic aspects of interpretation and opinion on a specific subject with the subject in 070.449, e.g., journalistic aspects of health columns 070.449613

| | |
|---|---|
| .444 | Miscellaneous information, advice, amusement |

> Including humor, general personal advice columns
>
> Class journalistic aspects of information, advice, amusement on a specific subject with the subject in 070.449, e.g., advice on health 070.449613
>
> *See also 741.56 for artistic aspects of comic strips*

| | |
|---|---|
| .444 092 | Biography |

> Class here biographies of journalists specializing in humor, of journalists known for general personal advice columns
>
> Class biographies of cartoonists in 741.569. Class biographies of a humorous writer with the writer in 800, e.g., a contemporary British writer of humorous essays 824.914

| | |
|---|---|
| .449 | Specific subjects |

> Class here journalists specializing in specific subjects, e.g., health columnists 070.449613092
>
> Add to base number 070.449 notation 001–999, e.g., works about journalistic aspects of health columns 070.449613; however; for war news as a general type of news, see 070.4333
>
> Class reports, criticisms, opinions on a specific subject with the subject, e.g., health columns 613
>
> *See also 070.433 for reporting of local and foreign news as general types of news; also 070.444 for miscellaneous information, advice, amusements as types of journalism*

| | |
|---|---|
| .48 | Journalism directed to special groups |

Class school journalism in 371.897

| | |
|---|---|
| .482 | Religious groups |
| .483 | Groups by age and sex |
| .483 2 | Young people |

Class here children from birth to eleven

*For young people twelve to twenty, see 070.4833*

| | |
|---|---|
| .483 26 | Boys |
| .483 27 | Girls |
| .483 3 | Young people twelve to twenty |
| .483 36 | Males twelve to twenty |
| .483 37 | Females twelve to twenty |
| .483 4 | Adults |

Class here young adults twenty-one and above, comprehensive works on young adults

*For young adults twelve to twenty, see 070.4833*

| | |
|---|---|
| .483 46 | Men |
| .483 47 | Women |
| .484 | Foreign-language and nondominant ethnic and national groups |
| .486 | Occupational and employee groups |

Standard subdivisions are added for either or both topics in heading

General journalism for occupational and employee groups

Including house organs

| | |
|---|---|
| .49 | Pictorial journalism |

Class here photojournalism

| | |
|---|---|
| **.5** | **Publishing** |

Class here book publishing; publishers regardless of their field of activity; book clubs, e.g., Book-of-the-Month Club®; comprehensive works on publishing and printing

Unless other instructions are given, class a subject with aspects in two or more subdivisions of 070.5 in the number coming first, e.g., commercial map publishers 070.5793 (*not* 070.592)

Class works on desktop publishing that emphasize typography in 686.22

*For printing, see 686.2*

| | |
|---|---|
| .502 9 | Commercial miscellany |

Class publishers' catalogs in 015

| | |
|---|---|
| .509 3–.509 9 | Specific continents, countries, localities |

Class here specific publishers, using the area number for the publisher's main office, e.g., U.S. Government Printing Office 070.509753, University of California Press 070.50979467

| | |
|---|---|
| .51 | Selection and editing of manuscripts |

Class editorial techniques in 808.02

| | |
|---|---|
| .52 | Relations with authors |

Including literary agents

Class interdisciplinary works on composition, preparation of manuscript, publishing in 808.02

| | |
|---|---|
| .57 | Kinds of publications |

Class specific publishers regardless of kind of publication in 070.5093–070.5099

| | |
|---|---|
| .572 | Serial publications |

Class comprehensive works on journalism and publishing of serial publications in 070.175. Class a serial version of a specific kind of publication with the kind in 070.579, e.g., a serial Braille publication 070.5792

| | |
|---|---|
| .572 2 | Newspapers |
| .573 | Specific kinds of books |

Including electronic books, limited editions, paperbacks, subscription books

Class serials in book form in 070.572

| | |
|---|---|
| [.573 01–.573 09] | Standard subdivisions |

Do not use; class in 070.501–070.509

| | |
|---|---|
| .579 | Special kinds of publications |

Including comprehensive works on audio publications

Class a specific kind of audio publication with the kind, e.g., audio music publication 070.5794

| | |
|---|---|
| .579 2 | Braille and other raised characters |

Standard subdivisions are added for Braille and other raised characters together, for Braille alone

| | |
|---|---|
| .579 3 | Maps |
| .579 4 | Music |

Class here recorded music

Class comprehensive works on audio publications in 070.579

| | |
|---|---|
| .579 5 | Microforms |

.579 7          Electronic publications (Digital publications)

                 Including CD-ROM (compact disc read-only memory)

                 Class an electronic version of a specific kind of publication with the kind, e.g., electronic books 070.573, electronic maps 070.5793

.579 73         Web publications

                 Class here Internet publishing

.59           Kinds of publishers

                 Class specific publishers regardless of kind in 070.5093–070.5099

.592          Commercial publishers

.593          Private publishers

                 Class here self-publishing

                 Class works on desktop publishing that emphasize typography in 686.22

.594          Institutional publishers

                 Including archive, church, information center, library, museum, society, university publishers

                 Class here nonprofit organizations

.595          Governmental and intergovernmental publishers

                 Standard subdivisions are added for either or both topics in heading

                 *See also 070.509753 for U.S. Government Printing Office*

**.9**         **History and biography of journalism and newspapers**

                 Class history of specific topics of journalism in 070.41–070.49

[.91]         Areas, regions, places in general

                 Do not use; class in 079.1

.92          Biography regardless of area, region, place

                 Class people associated with a specific aspect of journalism with the aspect in 070.41–070.49, plus notation 092 from Table 1, e.g., foreign correspondents 070.4332092

[.93–.99]     Specific continents, countries, localities

                 Do not use; class in 071–079

> ## 071–079 Geographic treatment of journalism and newspapers

Class here specific general newspapers regardless of language, indexes to them, other works about them

For a specific continent, country, or locality, add subdivisions for journalism, newspapers, or both

When adding from Table 2 for a specific newspaper, use the number for the primary area served by the newspaper; for example, a newspaper published in a city but carrying news about and having many subscribers in the surrounding region should be given the Table 2 number for the region, e.g., Los Angeles Times 071.79493

Class geography of specific topics of journalism in 070.41–070.49, e.g., journalism directed toward ethnic minorities in United States 070.4840973; class biography of journalism and newspapers regardless of area in 070.92; class comprehensive works in 070

(Option A: To give local emphasis and a shorter number to newspapers and journalism in a specific country, place them first by use of a letter or other symbol, e.g., newspapers and journalism in New Zealand 07N [preceding 071]

(Option B: Arrange newspapers alphabetically under 070

(Option C is described under 071)

## 071 *Journalism and newspapers in North America

*For journalism and newspapers in Middle America, see 079.72*

(Option C: To give local emphasis and a shorter number to journalism and newspapers in a specific country other than the United States and Canada, class them in this number; in that case class journalism and newspapers in North America in 079.7. Options A and B are described under 071–079)

### .1 *Journalism and newspapers in Canada

Add to base number 071.1 the numbers following —71 in notation 711–719 from Table 2, e.g., journalism and newspapers in British Columbia 071.11

### .3–.9 *Journalism and newspapers in the United States

Add to base number 071 the numbers following —7 in notation 73–79 from Table 2, e.g., New York Times 071.471

*For journalism and newspapers in Hawaii, see 079.969*

## 072 *Journalism and newspapers in British Isles

Class here journalism and newspapers in British Isles

### .1–.8 *Journalism and newspapers in England

Add to base number 072 the numbers following —42 in notation 421–428 from Table 2, e.g., Times of London 072.1

---

*Subdivisions are added for journalism, newspapers, or both

**.9** **\*Journalism and newspapers in Scotland, Ireland, Wales**

> Add to base number 072.9 the numbers following —4 in notation 41–42 from Table 2, e.g., newspapers in Scotland and Ireland 072.91

**073** **\*Journalism and newspapers in Germany and neighboring central European countries**

> Standard subdivisions are added for Germany and neighboring central European countries together, for Germany alone

> Class here journalism and newspapers in central Europe

> Add to base number 073 the numbers following —43 in notation 431–439 from Table 2, e.g., journalism and newspapers in Austria 073.6

**074** **\*Journalism and newspapers in France and Monaco**

> Standard subdivisions are added for France and Monaco together, for France alone

> Add to base number 074 the numbers following —44 in notation 441–449 from Table 2, e.g., journalism and newspapers in Paris metropolitan area 074.36

**075** **\*Journalism and newspapers in Italy, San Marino, Vatican City, Malta**

> Standard subdivisions are added for Italy, San Marino, Vatican City, Malta together; for Italy alone

> Add to base number 075 the numbers following —45 in notation 451–459 from Table 2, e.g., journalism and newspapers in Rome 075.632

**076** **\*Journalism and newspapers in Spain, Andorra, Gibraltar, Portugal**

> Standard subdivisions are added for Spain, Andorra, Gibraltar, Portugal together; for Spain alone

> Add to base number 076 the numbers following —46 in notation 461–469 from Table 2, e.g., journalism and newspapers in Portugal 076.9

**077** **\*Journalism and newspapers in Russia and neighboring east European countries**

> Standard subdivisions are added for Russia and neighboring east European countries together, for Russia alone

> Class here journalism and newspapers in eastern Europe

> Add to base number 077 the numbers following —47 in notation 471–479 from Table 2, e.g., journalism and newspapers in Moscow 077.31

> *For journalism and newspapers in Balkan Peninsula, see 079.496; for journalism and newspapers in Commonwealth of Independent States in Asia, see 079.57–079.58*

---

\*Subdivisions are added for journalism, newspapers, or both

**078** **\*Journalism and newspapers in Scandinavia**

Add to base number 078 the numbers following —48 in notation 481–489 from Table 2, e.g., journalism and newspapers in Sweden 078.5

**079** **\*Journalism and newspapers in other geographic areas**

Add to base number 079 notation 1–9 from Table 2, e.g., comprehensive works on general newspapers in Europe 079.4, in Balkan Peninsula 079.496, in Middle America 079.72, in Hawaii 079.969

# 080 General collections

Class here abstracts, addresses, lectures, essays, interviews, graffiti, quotations

Class collections of brief bibliographic abstracts in 011; class essays as literary form, collections gathered for their literary quality in 800

> *See Manual at 080 vs. 800*

**.9** **History, geographic treatment, biography**

Class history, geographic treatment, biography of collections in specific languages and language families in 081–089

---

> **081–089 General collections in specific languages and language families**

Class comprehensive works in 080

> *See Manual at 081–089*

(Option A: To give local emphasis and a shorter number to collections in a specific language, place them first by use of a letter or symbol, e.g., collections in Urdu 08U [preceding 081]

(Option B: Arrange collections alphabetically under 080)

(Option C is described under 081)

**081** **General collections in American English**

English-language collections of Western Hemisphere

(Option C: To give local emphasis and a shorter number to collections in a specific language other than English, class them in this number; in that case class American English-language collections in 082. Options A and B are described under 081–089)

**082** **General collections in English**

> *For general collections in American English, see 081*

---

\*Subdivisions are added for journalism, newspapers, or both

# 083 General collections in other Germanic languages

Class here comprehensive works on Germanic-language collections

*For English-language collections, see 082; for Scandinavian-language collections, see 088; for Old-English-language (Anglo-Saxon-language) collections, see 089*

**.1–.8 General collections in German and German dialects**

Add to base number 083 the numbers following —3 in notation 31–38 from Table 6, e.g., Swiss-German-dialect collections 083.5

**.9 General collections in Yiddish and Low Germanic languages**

Add to base number 083.9 the numbers following —39 in notation 391–394 from Table 6, e.g., Dutch-language collections 083.931

# 084 General collections in French, Occitan, Catalan

Add to base number 084 the numbers following —4 in notation 41–49 from Table 6, e.g., French-language collections 084.1

# 085 General collections in Italian, Dalmatian, Romanian, Rhaetian, Sardinian, Corsican

Add to base number 085 the numbers following —5 in notation 51–59 from Table 6, e.g., Italian-language collections 085.1

# 086 General collections in Spanish, Portuguese, Galician

Add to base number 086 the numbers following —6 in notation 61–69 from Table 6, e.g., Portuguese-language collections 086.9

# 087 General collections in Slavic languages

Add to base number 087 the numbers following 037 in 037.1–037.9 for language only, e.g., Polish-language collections 087.85

# 088 General collections in Scandinavian languages

Add to base number 088 the numbers following —39 in notation 396–398 from Table 6, e.g., Swedish-language collections 088.7

# 089 General collections in other languages

Including Old English (Anglo-Saxon)

Add to base number 089 notation 7–9 from Table 6, e.g., Chinese-language collections 089.951

# 090 Manuscripts, rare books, other rare printed materials

Including rare broadsides

Class interdisciplinary works on books in 002. Class a manuscript or rare work on a specific subject with the subject, e.g., a book of hours 242; class an artistic aspect of a manuscript or rare book with the aspect, e.g., illumination 745.67

*See also 011.31 for bibliographies of both manuscripts and rare books; also 011.44 for bibliographies of rare books only*

## 091 Manuscripts

*See also 011.31 for bibliographies of manuscripts*

## 092 Block books

## 093 Incunabula

Books printed before 1501

*See also 011.42 for bibliographies of incunabula*

## 094 Printed books

### .2 Early printed books

To 1700

*For block books, see 092; for incunabula, see 093*

### .4 Special editions

Including first editions, limited editions, typographic masterpieces

## 095 Books notable for bindings

*See also 686.3 for bookbinding*

## 096 Books notable for illustrations and materials

### .1 Books notable for illustrations

Class illustrated manuscripts in 091

### .2 Books notable for materials

Including leaves of vellum and silk, letters of silver and gold

## 097 Books notable for ownership or origin

Standard subdivisions are added for either or both topics in heading

## 098 Prohibited works, forgeries, hoaxes

### .1 Prohibited works

### .11 Prohibited by religious authorities

.12        Prohibited by civil authorities

**.3        Forgeries and hoaxes**

Standard subdivisions are added for either or both topics in heading

# 099        Books notable for format

Including books of unusual shapes, miniature editions

## 100 Philosophy, parapsychology and occultism, psychology

Works that discuss the discipline of philosophy itself; works that discuss several of philosophy's major questions and branches; comprehensive works on philosophy broad enough to include nonwestern or medieval as well as modern western philosophy are classed in 100 itself or 101–109

Class comprehensive works on Christian philosophy, on modern philosophy, on western philosophy, on modern western philosophy, on European philosophy in 190. Class philosophy of a specific subject with the subject, plus notation 01 from Table 1, e.g., philosophy of history 901

*See Manual at T1—01; also at 200 vs. 100*

### SUMMARY

| | |
|---|---|
| 140 | Specific philosophical schools and viewpoints |
| 141 | Idealism and related systems and doctrines |
| 142 | Critical philosophy |
| 143 | Bergsonism and intuitionism |
| 144 | Humanism and related systems and doctrines |
| 145 | Sensationalism |
| 146 | Naturalism and related systems and doctrines |
| 147 | Pantheism and related systems and doctrines |
| 148 | Dogmatism, eclecticism, liberalism, syncretism, traditionalism |
| 149 | Other philosophical systems and doctrines |
| | |
| 150 | Psychology |
| .1–.9 | Standard subdivisions, systems, viewpoints |
| 152 | Sensory perception, movement, emotions, physiological drives |
| 153 | Conscious mental processes and intelligence |
| 154 | Subconscious and altered states and processes |
| 155 | Differential and developmental psychology |
| 156 | Comparative psychology |
| 158 | Applied psychology |
| | |
| 160 | Philosophical logic |
| 161 | Induction |
| 162 | Deduction |
| 165 | Fallacies and sources of error |
| 166 | Syllogisms |
| 167 | Hypotheses |
| 168 | Argument and persuasion |
| 169 | Analogy |
| | |
| 170 | Ethics (Moral philosophy) |
| .1–.9 | Standard subdivisions and special topics of ethics |
| 171 | Ethical systems |
| 172 | Political ethics |
| 173 | Ethics of family relationships |
| 174 | Occupational ethics |
| 175 | Ethics of recreation, leisure, public performances, communication |
| 176 | Ethics of sex and reproduction |
| 177 | Ethics of social relations |
| 178 | Ethics of consumption |
| 179 | Other ethical norms |
| | |
| 180 | Ancient, medieval, eastern philosophy |
| .01–.09 | Standard subdivisions of ancient, medieval, eastern philosophy |
| .1–.9 | Standard subdivisions of ancient philosophy |
| 181 | Eastern philosophy |
| 182 | Pre-Socratic Greek philosophies |
| 183 | Sophistic, Socratic, related Greek philosophies |
| 184 | Platonic philosophy |
| 185 | Aristotelian philosophy |
| 186 | Skeptic and Neoplatonic philosophies |
| 187 | Epicurean philosophy |
| 188 | Stoic philosophy |
| 189 | Medieval western philosophy |
| | |
| 190 | Modern western and other noneastern philosophy |
| 191 | Philosophy of United States and Canada |
| 192 | Philosophy of British Isles |
| 193 | Philosophy of Germany and Austria |
| 194 | Philosophy of France |
| 195 | Philosophy of Italy |
| 196 | Philosophy of Spain and Portugal |
| 197 | Philosophy of Russia |
| 198 | Philosophy of Scandinavia and Finland |
| 199 | Philosophy in other geographic areas |

**101** **Theory of philosophy**

> Class here works on the concept of philosophy, on the nature of the philosophical task, on the method of philosophy
>
> Class schools of philosophical thought in 140; class ancient, medieval, eastern schools in 180

**102** **Miscellany of philosophy**

**103** **Dictionaries, encyclopedias, concordances of philosophy**

**[104]** **[Unassigned]**

> Most recently used in Edition 16

**105** **Serial publications of philosophy**

**106** **Organizations and management of philosophy**

**107** **Education, research, related topics of philosophy**

**108** **Groups of people**

**109** **History and collected biography**

> Do not use for geographic treatment; class in 180–190
>
> Not limited by period or place

   **.2** **Collected biography**

> Do not use for individual persons; class in 180–190

   **[.22]** Collected biography

> Do not use; class in 109.2

# 110 Metaphysics

> *For epistemology, causation, humankind, see 120*

**111** **Ontology**

   **.1** **Existence, essence, substance, accidents**

   **.2** **Universals**

   **.5** **Nonbeing, nothingness**

   **.6** **Finite and infinite**

> Including the absolute

   **.8** **Properties of being**

> Class comprehensive works on truth in 121

.82      Unity

Including identity, part-whole relationships

*See also 126 for personal identity*

.84      Good and evil

*For ethics, see 170*

.85      Beauty

Class here interdisciplinary works on aesthetics

*For aesthetics of a specific subject, see the subject, e.g., aesthetics of the fine arts 701.17*

## [112]     [Unassigned]

Most recently used in Edition 18

## 113     Cosmology (Philosophy of nature)

Including cosmic harmony, origin of universe (cosmogony)

Class cosmology as a topic in astronomy in 523.1

*For specific topics of cosmology not provided for here, see 114–119*

### .8     Philosophy of life

Origin and nature of life

Class origin and nature of human life in 128

## 114     Space

Class here relation of space and matter

Class matter in 117

## 115     Time

Including eternity, space and time, space-time, relation of time and motion

*For space, see 114*

## 116     Change

Including becoming, cycles, evolution, motion, process

Class relation of time and motion in 115

## 117     Structure

Including matter, form, order, chaos

Class relation of space and matter in 114

## 118     Force and energy

Standard subdivisions are added for either or both topics in heading

## 119     Number and quantity

# 120 Epistemology, causation, humankind

## SUMMARY

## 121 Epistemology (Theory of knowledge)

Class here coherence, correspondence theories of truth; comprehensive works on truth

Class knowledge and its extension in 001

*For truth as a classical property of being, see 111.8; for truth in logic, see 160*

**.2 Possibility and limits of knowledge**

Standard subdivisions are added for either or both topics in heading

Including solipsism and problem of other minds

**.3 Origin, sources, means of knowledge**

Standard subdivisions are added for any or all topics in heading

Including intuition, reason

Class reason as a human attribute in 128.33

**.34 Perception**

*For sensation, see 121.35*

**.35 Sensation**

Including vision

Class here sense knowledge

**.4 Structure of knowledge**

Subjective and objective components

Including concepts, ideas

**.5 Doubt and denial**

Standard subdivisions are added for either or both topics in heading

Class comprehensive works on doubt, denial, certainty, probability in 121.63

**.6 Nature of inquiry**

Including belief

Class faith in 121.7

.63        Certainty and probability

Standard subdivisions are added for either or both topics in heading

Class here comprehensive works on doubt, denial, certainty, probability

*For doubt and denial, see 121.5*

.65        Evidence and criteria

Standard subdivisions are added for either or both topics in heading

.68        Meaning, interpretation, hermeneutics

Standard subdivisions are added for meaning, interpretation, hermeneutics together, for meaning alone

Including reference, semantics, semiotics

Class here interdisciplinary works on philosophy of language

Class philosophy of language in linguistics in 401

> *See also 149.94 for general semantics as a school of linguistic philosophy; also 401.4 for semiotics in linguistics; also 401.43 for semantics in linguistics*

.686        Philosophical hermeneutics

Class here interpretation

.7        **Faith**

Class belief in 121.6; class religious faith in 200

.8        **Worth and theory of values (Axiology)**

Standard subdivisions are added for any or all topics in heading

Class ethical values in 170

# 122    Causation

Class here chance versus cause

*For determinism and indeterminism, see 123; for teleology, see 124*

# 123    Determinism and indeterminism

Standard subdivisions are added for either or both topics in heading

Including contingency

.3        **Chance**

Class chance versus cause in 122

.5        **Freedom**

Including free will

.7        **Necessity**

**124 Teleology**

Class here final cause

**[125] [Unassigned]**

Most recently used in Edition 18

**126 The self**

Limited to topics named below

Class here consciousness of self as person, personal identity, personality, personhood

Class the unconscious and the subconscious in 127; class comprehensive works on consciousness in 128.2

*See also 111.82 for identity*

**127 The unconscious and the subconscious**

Standard subdivisions are added for either or both topics in heading

**128 Humankind**

Class here philosophical anthropology; comprehensive works on philosophy of human life, on philosophy and psychology of human life

*For the self, see 126; for psychology, see 150*

*See also 599.9 for physical anthropology*

**.1 Soul**

*For origin and destiny of individual souls, see 129*

**.2 Mind**

Including intentionality, mind-body relationship

Class here comprehensive works on consciousness

*For consciousness of self as person, see 126*

**.3 Attributes and faculties**

Standard subdivisions are added for either or both topics in heading

Including imagination, intellect, memory, will

*For perception, see 121.34; for sensation, see 121.35; for free will, see 123.5*

.33 Reason and rationality

Standard subdivisions are added for either or both topics in heading

Class reason as an instrument of knowledge in 121.3

*For science of reasoning (logic), see 160*

*See also 149.7 for rationalism*

.37          Emotion

        Class love in 128.46

**.4          Human action and experience**

        Standard subdivisions are added for either or both topics in heading

        Nature, conditions, origin

        Class here comprehensive works on philosophical counseling

> *For collections of texts for philosophical counseling clients on a specific subject, see the subject, e.g., a general collection of philosophical texts for philosophical counseling clients 100; for philosophical counseling focusing on specific issues or types of issues, see the issue or type of issue, e.g., philosophical counseling focusing on ethics issues 170*

.46          Love

> *For ethics of love, see 177.7*

**.5          Human death**

        Class interdisciplinary works on death in 306.9

**.6          Body**

# 129     Origin and destiny of individual souls

        Including immortality, incarnation, reincarnation, transmigration

        Class personal accounts of previous incarnations in 133.90135; class interdisciplinary works on reincarnation in 202.37

# 130     Parapsychology and occultism

        Standard subdivisions are added for either or both topics in heading

        Class here paranormal phenomena, frauds in occultism

        Class phenomena of religious experience in 200; class interdisciplinary works on controversial knowledge and paranormal phenomena in 001.9

> *See Manual at 001.9 and 130; also at 130 vs. 200*

### SUMMARY

.112            Forecasting and forecasts

> Do not use for comprehensive works on parapsychological and occult forecasting and forecasts; class in 133.3

> Class a specific type of forecasting or forecast with the type, without adding notation 0112 from Table 1, e.g., astrological methods of forecasting 133.5

## 131    Parapsychological and occult methods for achieving well-being, happiness, success

> Standard subdivisions are added for any or all topics in heading

> Class interdisciplinary works limited to psychological and parapsychological or occult techniques for achieving personal well-being, happiness, success in 158; class interdisciplinary works on successful living, on management of personal and family living in 646.7. Class a specific method of parapsychology and occultism for achieving well-being with the method in 133–139, e.g., spells and charms 133.44

## [132]    [Unassigned]

> Most recently used in Edition 16

## 133    Specific topics in parapsychology and occultism

> *For parapsychological and occult methods of achieving well-being, happiness, success, see 131; for Rosicrucianism, Hermeticism, cabala, see 135.4*

### SUMMARY

| | |
|---|---|
| 133.1 | **Apparitions** |
| .2 | **Parapsychological and occult aspects of specific things** |
| .3 | **Divinatory arts** |
| .4 | **Demonology and witchcraft** |
| .5 | **Astrology** |
| .6 | **Palmistry** |
| .8 | **Psychic phenomena** |
| .9 | **Spiritualism** |

[.01–.09]    Standard subdivisions

> Do not use; class in 130.1–130.9

.1        Apparitions

> Class here ghosts

> Class folkloristic ghost stories in 398.25; class ghosts as a subject of folklore in 398.47; class literary accounts of ghosts in 808.80375; class interdisciplinary works on spirits (discarnate beings) in 133.9

.109        History, geographic treatment, biography

> Class here works that treat two or more haunted places during a specific historical period or in a specific geographic area, e.g., haunted places in Cornwall 133.1094237

> *For specific haunted places, see 133.129*

.12        Haunted places

[.120 9]    History, geographic treatment, biography

Do not use; class in 133.109

.122    Specific types of haunted places

Including haunted churches, forests, graveyards, houses

Class specific haunted places regardless of type in 133.129

.129    Specific haunted places

Limited to works that treat only one single haunted place

Add to base number 133.129 notation 3–9 from Table 2, e.g., the Tower of London 133.1294215, old Monterey's Hotel del Monte 133.1297947

Class works that treat two or more haunted places during a specific historical period or in a specific geographic area in 133.109

.14    Specific kinds of apparitions

Including animal ghosts, hobgoblins, phantasms of the living

Class haunted places regardless of kind of apparition in 133.12; class materialization of spirits as a mediumistic phenomenon in 133.92

.142    Poltergeists

**.2    Parapsychological and occult aspects of specific things**

Specific things used for more than one purpose, in more than one branch of parapsychology and occultism

*For a specific parapsychological or occult use of a specific thing, see the use in 131–139, e.g., fortune-telling by crystals 133.322, fortune-telling by cards 133.3242; for a specific thing in a specific branch of parapsychology and occultism, see the branch in 131–139, e.g., use of candles in witchcraft 133.43028, astrological aspects of planets 133.53*

*See also 001.94 for pyramid power; also 135.3 for parapsychological aspects of dreams*

.25    Natural things

.250 02–.250 08    Physical sciences, space sciences, groups of people

Add to base number 133.25 the numbers following 5 in 500.2–500.8, e.g., occult use of a collection of natural things from various physical sciences for multiple purposes, such as healing, personality analysis, fortune-telling 133.25002

.250 1–.250 9    Standard subdivisions and natural history

Add to base number 133.25 the numbers following 5 in 501–509, e.g., occult use of seasons for multiple purposes, such as healing, personality analysis, fortune-telling 133.25082

.251–.259    Mathematics, astronomy, physics, chemistry, earth sciences, paleontology, biology, plants, animals

Add to base number 133.25 the numbers following 5 in 510–590, e.g., occult use of crystals for multiple purposes, such as healing, personality analysis, fortune-telling 133.2548

**.3**      **Divinatory arts**

Including fortune-telling by bones, dice, pendulum

Class here works on the symbolism of divinatory arts and objects, comprehensive works on divination as an aspect of parapsychology and religion, comprehensive works on occult methods of foretelling the future

Class use of extrasensory perception for divination in 133.82–133.86; class interdisciplinary works on forecasting in 003.2

*For astrology, see 133.5; for palmistry, see 133.6; for dream books, see 135.3; for divinatory graphology, see 137; for physiognomy, see 138; for divination as a religious practice, see 203.2*

*See also 303.49 for social forecasting*

.309 2        Biography

Class here persons known chiefly for their predictions rather than their methods of predicting, e.g., Nostradamus (Michel de Notredame)

.32      Fortune-telling by crystals and stones; dowsing; fortune-telling by cards, tea leaves and coffee grounds, oracles and sibyls

.322        Fortune-telling by crystals and stones

Standard subdivisions are added for crystals and stones together, for crystals alone

.323        Dowsing

Location of living and inert substances through human sensitivity to latent radiation and use of divining rods, pendulums, other devices

Class here radiesthesia

---

>      133.323 2–133.323 7  Location of specific substances

Class comprehensive works in 133.323

.323 2        Location of water

.323 3        Location of metals

.323 7        Location of petroleum and gases

.324        Fortune-telling by cards, tea leaves and coffee grounds, oracles and sibyls

.324 2        Fortune-telling by cards (Cartomancy)

.324 24         Fortune-telling by tarot

.324 4        Fortune-telling by tea leaves and coffee grounds

Standard subdivisions are added for either or both topics in heading

.324 8        Fortune-telling by oracles and sibyls

Standard subdivisions are added for either or both topics in heading

.33 Symbolic divination

> Including divination with I Ching, names, runes

> *For fortune-telling by cards, see 133.3242*

.333 Geomancy

.333 7 Feng shui

.334 Divinatory signs and omens

> Standard subdivisions are added for either or both topics in heading

.335 Numerology

.335 4 Fortune-telling by numbers

> Including fortune-telling by birthdays

> *See also 133.5 for astrology*

.335 9 Symbolism of specific numbers

**.4** **Demonology and witchcraft**

> Class here black arts

> *For divinatory arts, see 133.3*

> *See also 299.675 for voodoo as a religion*

> *See Manual at 130 vs. 200*

.42 Demonology

> *See also 202.16 for religious beliefs about demons*

> *See Manual at 130 vs. 200*

.422 Satanism (Devil worship)

> *See also 299 for Satanism regarded as a religion*

> *See Manual at 130 vs. 200*

.423 Evil spirits

> Including incubi, succubi, vampires, werewolves

.425 The evil eye

.426 Demoniac possession

.427 Exorcism of demons

.43        Magic and witchcraft

> Standard subdivisions are added for either or both topics in heading

> Class here magicians' manuals, e.g., grimoire; witch hunting; interdisciplinary works on witchcraft

>> *For spells, curses, charms, see 133.44; for witchcraft as a religious practice, see 203.3; for religions based on modern revivals of witchcraft, see 299.94*

>> *See Manual at 130 vs. 200*

.430 9        History, geographic treatment, biography

> Class here history of witch crazes

.44        Spells, curses, charms

> Including amulets, mascots, talismans

.442        Love spells and charms

> Standard subdivisions are added for either or both topics in heading

.443        Good luck spells and charms

> Standard subdivisions are added for either or both topics in heading

.446        Therapeutic spells and charms

> Standard subdivisions are added for either or both topics in heading

**.5**        **Astrology**

> Class here works on the symbolism of astrology

[.501 12]        Forecasting and forecasts

> Do not use; class in 133.5

.508 82        Specific religious groups

> Do not use for types or schools of astrology originating in or associated with a specific religious group; class in 133.594

> Class here astrology in general with respect to specific religious groups

.508 9        Specific ethnic and national groups

> Do not use for types or schools of astrology originating in or associated with a specific ethnic or national group; class in 133.593

> Class here astrology in general with respect to specific ethnic and national groups

.509        History, geographic treatment, biography

.509 3–.509 9        Specific continents, countries, localities; extraterrestrial worlds

> Do not use for types or schools of astrology originating in or associated with a specific area; class in 133.592

> Class here astrology in general in a specific area

> 133.52–133.58 Specific aspects of western astrology

Class specific aspects of nonwestern astrology in 133.59; class comprehensive works in 133.5

.52 Signs of the zodiac

Class planets in 133.53

| | | |
|---|---|---|
| .526 | First six signs | |
| .526 2 | | Aries |
| .526 3 | | Taurus |
| .526 4 | | Gemini |
| .526 5 | | Cancer |
| .526 6 | | Leo |
| .526 7 | | Virgo |
| .527 | Second six signs | |
| .527 2 | | Libra |
| .527 3 | | Scorpio |
| .527 4 | | Sagittarius |
| .527 5 | | Capricorn |
| .527 6 | | Aquarius |
| .527 7 | | Pisces |

.53 Planets, sun, moon

Standard subdivisions are added for planets, sun, moon together; for planets alone

Class here positions of planets

.530 4 Special topics of planets, sun, moon

.530 42 Houses

Class houses in relation to the zodiac in 133.52

.530 44 Aspects

.531 Sun

.532 Moon

.533 Mercury

.534 Venus

.535 Mars

.536 Jupiter

.537 Saturn

| .538 | Uranus |
|---|---|
| .539 | Neptune, Pluto, asteroids, related bodies |

Former heading: Trans-uranian planets, and asteroids

| .539 1 | Neptune |
|---|---|
| .539 2 | Pluto |
| .539 8 | Asteroids |

Including Chiron

| .54 | Horoscopes |
|---|---|

Class works that emphasize parts or aspects of horoscopes with the part or aspect, e.g., houses 133.53042; class horoscopes for persons associated with a particular part or aspect of the horoscope with the part or aspect, e.g., horoscopes for Gemini 133.5264

| [.540 112] | Forecasting and forecasts |
|---|---|

Do not use; class in 133.54

| .540 4 | Special topics of horoscopes |
|---|---|
| .540 42 | Daily guides and birthday books |
| .542 | Casting horoscopes |
| .548 | Horoscopes of individuals |

Class horoscopes of individuals connected with specific topics in 133.58

| .55 | Astrological ephemerides |
|---|---|
| .56 | Horary astrology |
| .58 | Application of astrology to specific topics |

Add to base number 133.58 notation 001–999, e.g., medical astrology 133.5861, astrological guides to dating 133.5864677, astrological analysis and prediction about the United States and its leaders 133.58973; however, do not add notation 0112 from Table 1 for forecasts and forecasting

| .59 | Types or schools of astrology originating in or associated with a specific area; originating in or associated with a specific ethnic or national group; originating in or associated with a specific religion |
|---|---|

Class here nonwestern types or schools of astrology

Unless other instructions are given, class a subject with aspects in two or more subdivisions of 133.59 in the number coming last, e.g., Hindu astrology in India 133.594450954 (*not* 133.59254)

| .592 | Types or schools of astrology originating in or associated with a specific area |
|---|---|

Add to base number 133.592 notation 3–9 from Table 2, e.g., Chinese astrology 133.59251

.593            Types or schools of astrology originating in or associated with a specific ethnic or national group

> Add to base number 133.593 notation 1–9 from Table 5, e.g., Aztec astrology 133.59397452

> Class types or schools of astrology originating in or associated with an ethnic or national group in areas where the group predominates in 133.592

.594            Types or schools of astrology originating in or associated with a specific religious group

> Add to base number 133.594 the numbers following 29 in 292–299, e.g., Hindu astrology 133.59445

**.6          Palmistry**

[.601 12]            Forecasting and forecasts

> Do not use; class in 133.6

**.8          Psychic phenomena**

> Class here psi phenomena, psychic communication, psychic talents and gifts; comprehensive works treating extrasensory perception (ESP), spiritualism, and ghosts together

> Class comprehensive works on divination in 133.3

> *For ghosts, see 133.1; for spiritualism, see 133.9*

[.801 12]            Forecasting and forecasts

> Do not use; class in 133.8

---

>               133.82–133.86  Extrasensory perception

> Class extrasensory perception of animals in 133.89; class comprehensive works on extrasensory perception in 133.8

.82            Telepathy

.84            Clairvoyance

[.840 112]            Forecasting and forecasts

> Do not use; class in 133.84

.85            Clairaudience

[.850 112]            Forecasting and forecasts

> Do not use; class in 133.85

.86            Precognition

[.860 112]            Forecasting and forecasts

> Do not use; class in 133.86

.88            Psychokinesis

> *For levitation as a mediumistic phenomenon, see 133.92*

.89        Animal magnetism, hypnosis, extrasensory perception of animals, aura

Class interdisciplinary works on animal magnetism in 154.72; class interdisciplinary works on hypnotism in 154.7

*For use of hypnosis for past-life recall, see 133.90135*

.892        Aura

Including Kirlian photography of aura

Class human aura when scientifically considered in 612.0142

*See also 778.3 for photographic aspects of Kirlian photography*

**.9**        **Spiritualism**

The phenomena and systems of ideas connected with belief in communication with spirits (discarnate beings)

Class here communication with extraterrestrial spirits, necromancy, interdisciplinary works on spirits (discarnate beings)

*For ghosts, see 133.1*

*See also 202.13 for spiritualism as a religious doctrine; also 289.9 for spiritualist Christian sects; also 292–299 for other spiritualist sects and religions*

*See Manual at 130 vs. 200*

.901        Philosophy and theory; personal survival, nature of spiritual world and life after death; reincarnation

Notation 01 from Table 1 as modified below

.901 3        Personal survival, nature of spiritual world and life after death

Class philosophical discussions of personal survival and life after death in 129

.901 35        Reincarnation

Including use of hypnosis for past-life recall

Class here personal recollections of previous incarnations, transmigrations

Class interdisciplinary works on reincarnation in 202.37

.91        Mediumship

Nature and practice

Class here channeling, psychic experiences of individual mediums

*For specific mediumistic phenomena, see 133.92*

.92        Specific mediumistic phenomena

Including ectoplasm, levitation, materialization and dematerialization, rapping, spirit photography, table tipping, transportation

*For psychic messages, see 133.93*

.93 Psychic messages

Method and content of communications purporting to come from discarnate entities

Including psychic messages on specific nonreligious topics not provided for in 130–139, e.g., unidentified flying objects (UFOs)

*For psychic messages on religious subjects, see 200. For messages on a specific subject in paranormal phenomena, see the subject, e.g., messages concerning nature of spiritual world and life after death 133.9013*

.932 Specific methods

Including automatic writing and utterance; use of audiotapes

.932 5 Ouija board

.95 Astral projection (Out-of-body experience)

# [134] [Unassigned]

Most recently used in Edition 16

# 135 Dreams and mysteries

Class mysteries of magic and witchcraft in 133.43; class interdisciplinary works on mysteries in the sense of reported phenomena not explained, not fully verified in 001.94

## .3 Dreams

Including dream books

Class interdisciplinary works on psychological and parapsychological aspects of dreams in 154.63

## .4 Rosicrucianism, Hermetism, cabala

*See also 133.32424 for tarot*

.43 Rosicrucianism

.45 Hermetism

.47 Cabala

*See also 296.16 for cabala in Judaism*

# [136] [Unassigned]

Most recently used in Edition 16

# 137 Divinatory graphology

Class interdisciplinary works on graphology and use of graphology in analyzing character in 155.282

## 138 Physiognomy

Class here comprehensive works on determination of character or divination from analysis of physical features

*For palmistry, see 133.6; for phrenology, see 139*

## 139 Phrenology

Determination of mental capacities from skull structures

# 140 Specific philosophical schools and viewpoints

Including the concept of ideology, of a world view, of a system of beliefs

Class development, description, critical appraisal, collected writings, biographical treatment of individual philosophers regardless of viewpoint in 180–190; class comprehensive works on modern western and ancient, medieval, eastern viewpoints in 100; class comprehensive works on modern western viewpoints in 190. Class a specific topic or branch of philosophy treated from a specific philosophical viewpoint with the topic or branch, e.g., existentialist ontology 111, realist epistemology 121; class ideologies concerning a specific discipline with the discipline, e.g., political ideologies 320.5

*For ancient, medieval, eastern schools, see 180*

*See also 171 for systems and schools of ethics*

### SUMMARY

| | |
|---|---|
| 141 | **Idealism and related systems and doctrines** |
| 142 | **Critical philosophy** |
| 143 | **Bergsonism and intuitionism** |
| 144 | **Humanism and related systems and doctrines** |
| 145 | **Sensationalism** |
| 146 | **Naturalism and related systems and doctrines** |
| 147 | **Pantheism and related systems and doctrines** |
| 148 | **Dogmatism, eclecticism, liberalism, syncretism, traditionalism** |
| 149 | **Other philosophical systems and doctrines** |

## 141 Idealism and related systems and doctrines

Standard subdivisions are added for idealism and related systems and doctrines together, for idealism alone

Including panpsychism, spiritualism, subjectivism, voluntarism

### .2 Modern Platonism and Neoplatonism

Standard subdivisions are added for either or both topics in heading

Class comprehensive works on Platonism in 184; class comprehensive works on Neoplatonism in 186.4

### .3 Transcendentalism

### .4 Individualism

### .5 Personalism

### .6 Romanticism

## 142    Critical philosophy

> Class critical realism in 149.2

**.3**    **Kantianism**

> Class here Neo-Kantianism

**.7**    **Phenomenology**

.78    Existentialism

## 143    Bergsonism and intuitionism

## 144    Humanism and related systems and doctrines

> Standard subdivisions are added for humanism and related systems and doctrines together, for humanism alone

**.3**    **Pragmatism**

**.5**    **Instrumentalism**

**.6**    **Utilitarianism**

## 145    Sensationalism

> Class here ideology as the system based on analysis of ideas into their sensory elements
>
> Class works that discuss ideology, not as a specific philosophical school, but as systems of beliefs in general in 140

## 146    Naturalism and related systems and doctrines

> Standard subdivisions are added for naturalism and related systems and doctrines together, for naturalism alone
>
> Including dynamism, energism

**.3**    **Materialism**

.32    Dialectical materialism

> *For dialectical materialism as a philosophical foundation of Marxism, see 335.4112*

**.4**    **Positivism and related systems**

> Standard subdivisions are added for positivism and related systems together, for positivism alone
>
> Variant name for positivism: comtism
>
> Class here comprehensive works on the analytical movement
>
> *For linguistic analysis, see 149.94*

.42    Logical positivism (Logical empiricism)

.44    Empiricism

**.5** **Atomism**

Including logical atomism

**.6** **Mechanism**

**.7** **Evolutionism and process philosophy**

# 147 Pantheism and related systems and doctrines

Standard subdivisions are added for pantheism and related systems and doctrines together, for pantheism alone

Including animism, occasionalism, panentheism, parallelism, vitalism

**.3** **Monism**

**.4** **Dualism and pluralism**

Standard subdivisions are added for either or both topics in heading

# 148 Dogmatism, eclecticism, liberalism, syncretism, traditionalism

# 149 Other philosophical systems and doctrines

Including constructivism, objectivism, relativism

**.1** **Conceptualism and nominalism**

Standard subdivisions are added for either or both topics in heading

**.2** **Realism**

Class here neorealism, critical realism

**.3** **Mysticism**

Class occult mysticism in 130; class religious mysticism in 204.22

**.5** **Optimism**

Class here meliorism

**.6** **Pessimism**

**.7** **Rationalism and related systems and doctrines**

Standard subdivisions are added for rationalism and related systems and doctrines together, for rationalism alone

Including innatism, intellectualism, nativism

**.72** Agnosticism

**.73** Skepticism

**.8** **Nihilism**

Class here fatalism

*For existentialism, see 142.78*

**.9        Miscellaneous systems and doctrines**

Limited to systems and doctrines provided for below

[.901–.909]      Standard subdivisions

Do not use; class in 149.01–149.09

.91        Neo-Aristotelianism, neo-scholasticism, neo-Thomism

Standard subdivisions are added for any or all topics in heading

Class ancient Aristotelianism in 185; class medieval scholasticism, medieval Thomism in 189.4

.94        Linguistic philosophies

Including ordinary language philosophy

Class here general semantics as a school of linguistic philosophy (e.g., the school of Alfred Korzybski)

Class semantics, semiotics as philosophical topics in 121.68; class comprehensive works on the analytical movement in 146.4

*See also 302.2 for interdisciplinary works on semiotics; also 401 for philosophy of language*

[.96]        Structuralism

Relocated to 149.97

.97        Structuralism [*formerly* 149.96], poststructuralism, postmodernism

Class here deconstruction

Class structuralism, poststructuralism, postmodernism in relation to a specific discipline with the discipline, e.g., in relation to literary criticism 801.95

# 150        Psychology

Unless other instructions are given, observe the following table of preference, e.g., emotions of children 155.4124 (*not* 152.4):

| | |
|---|---|
| Aptitude tests | 153.94 |
| Comparative psychology | 156 |
| Subconscious and altered states and processes | 154 |
| Differential and developmental psychology | 155 |
| Sensory perception, movement, emotions, physiological drives | 152 |
| Conscious mental processes and intelligence 153.94) | |
| Applied psychology | 158 |

Class testing for aptitude in a specific subject in 153.94; class social psychology in 302

*For abnormal and clinical psychologies, see 616.89. For psychological principles (other than principles of aptitude testing) of a specific subject, see the subject, plus notation 019 from Table 1, e.g., psychological principles of advertising 659.1019*

*See Manual at 302–307 vs. 150, T1—019*

## SUMMARY

| | |
|---|---|
| 150.1–.9 | Standard subdivisions, systems, viewpoints |
| 152 | Sensory perception, movement, emotions, physiological drives |
| 153 | Conscious mental processes and intelligence |
| 154 | Subconscious and altered states and processes |
| 155 | Differential and developmental psychology |
| 156 | Comparative psychology |
| 158 | Applied psychology |

**.1**      **Philosophy and theory; systems, viewpoints**

Notation 01 from Table 1 as modified below

Do not use for schools of psychology; class in 150.19

**.19**      Systems, schools, viewpoints

Standard subdivisions are added for any or all topics in heading

*See Manual at 152–158 vs. 150.19*

**.192**      Existential, faculty, phenomenological, rational schools

**.193**      Functionalism

Including dynamic, holistic, hormic, organismic psychologies

**.194**      Reductionism

**.194 3**      Behaviorism

**.194 32**      Watsonian behaviorism

**.194 34**      Neobehaviorism (Pragmatic reductionism)

Including systems of Guthrie, Hull, Skinner, Tolman

**.194 4**      Reflexology (Associationism)

Including systems of Pavlov, Bekhterev, Thorndike

*For associative learning, see 153.1526*

**.195**      Psychoanalytic systems

*See Manual at 616.89 vs. 150.195*

**.195 2**      Freudian system

**.195 3**      Adlerian system

**.195 4**      Jungian system

**.195 7**      Neopsychoanalytic systems

Including systems of Horney, Fromm, Sullivan

**.198**      Other systems

**.198 2**      Gestalt psychology

**.198 4**      Field theory

| | | |
|---|---|---|
| .198 5 | | Personal construct psychology |
| | | Class here personal construct theory |
| .198 6 | | Humanistic psychology |
| | | *For transpersonal psychology, see 150.1987* |
| .198 7 | | Transpersonal psychology |
| | | Class comprehensive works on humanistic psychology in 150.1986 |
| .198 8 | | Positive psychology |

**.2** **Miscellany**

.287 Testing and measurement

Class comprehensive works on intelligence testing and personality testing in 153.93

*See also 174.915 for ethics of psychological testing*

**.7** **Education, research, related topics**

.724 Experimental research

*See also 174.915 for the ethics of research in psychology*

**.8** **Groups of people**

Do not use for psychology of groups of people; class in 155

**.9** **History, geographic treatment, biography**

.93–.99 Specific continents, countries, localities; extraterrestrial worlds

Do not use for national psychology of specific countries; class in 155.89

**[151]** **[Unassigned]**

Most recently used in Edition 16

---

> ## 152–158 Specific topics in psychology

Class comprehensive works in 150

*See Manual at 152–158 vs. 150.19*

## 152 Sensory perception, movement, emotions, physiological drives

Class here sensory perception, movement, emotions, physiological drives of adults in general [*formerly* 155.6]; comprehensive works on psychology and neurophysiology of sensory perception, movement, emotions, physiological drives

Class sensory perception, movement, emotions, physiological drives of adults by marital status and relationships in 155.64; class sensory perception, movement, emotions, physiological drives of people in specific stages of adulthood in 155.65–155.67

> *For neurophysiology of sensory perception, movement, emotions, physiological drives, see 612.8*
>
> *See Manual at 612.8 vs. 152*

### SUMMARY

| | |
|---|---|
| 152.1 | **Sensory perception** |
| .3 | **Movements and motor functions** |
| .4 | **Emotions** |
| .5 | **Physiological drives** |
| .8 | **Threshold, discrimination, reaction-time studies** |

### .1 Sensory perception

Class here receptive processes and functions, discrimination, thresholds

> *For threshold and discrimination studies, see 152.82*
>
> *See Manual at 153.7 vs. 152.1*

.14 Visual perception

.142 Spatial perception

Class comprehensive works on spatial perception in 153.752

.142 2 Visual acuity

.142 3 Pattern perception

Including form perception

.142 5 Movement perception

Class comprehensive works on movement perception in 153.754

.143 Brightness perception

.145 Color perception

.148 Optical illusions

Including afterimages

Class here interdisciplinary works on optical illusions

> *For a specific aspect or use of optical illusions, see the aspect or use, e.g., physiological aspects 612.84, use of optical illusions in art 701*

.15 Auditory perception

| | | |
|---|---|---|
| .152 | Pitch perception | |
| .154 | Volume perception | |
| .157 | Timbre perception (Tone discrimination) | |
| .158 | Localization | |
| .16 | Chemical sensory perception | |
| .166 | Perception of smells | |
| .167 | Perception of tastes | |
| .18 | Other types of sensory perception | |
| .182 | Cutaneous perception | |
| | Class here tactile perception, touch | |
| .182 2 | Thermal perception | |
| .182 3 | Pressure perception | |
| | Including perception of vibration | |
| .182 4 | Pain perception | |
| .188 | Proprioceptive and visceral perceptions | |
| | Class here biofeedback | |
| .188 2 | Proprioceptive perception | |
| | Including vestibular perception | |
| | Class here kinesthetic perception | |
| .188 6 | Visceral perceptions | |
| | Including fatigue, hunger, thirst, well-being | |
| .189 | Synesthesia | |

**.3**      **Movements and motor functions**

Standard subdivisions are added for either or both topics in heading

*For reaction-time studies, see 152.83*

.32      Involuntary movements

Class here automatic movements

*For habits and habit formation, see 152.33*

.322      Reflexes

Class comprehensive works on reflexology as a psychological system in 150.1944

.322 3      Innate reflexes

.322 4      Conditioned reflexes

| | |
|---|---|
| .324 | Instinctive movements |

> *For innate reflexes, see 152.3223*

| | |
|---|---|
| .33 | Habits and habit formation |

Standard subdivisions are added for either or both topics in heading

Class here comprehensive works on habits

> *For conscious mental habits, see 153*

> *See also 362.29 for substance abuse*

| | |
|---|---|
| .334 | Motor learning |
| .335 | Handedness and laterality |

Standard subdivisions are added for either or both topics in heading

| | |
|---|---|
| .35 | Voluntary movements |
| .38 | Special motor functions |
| .382 | Locomotion |
| .384 | Expressive movements |

Noncognitive aspects

Class meaning of movements (as in body language) and cognitive aspects in 153.69

| | |
|---|---|
| .384 2 | Vocal expressions |
| .384 5 | Graphic expressions |
| .385 | Coordination |

**.4 Emotions**

Including aversion, hate; embarrassment; hope; grief, sadness

Class here affects, attitudes, feelings, moods, sentiments; emotional intelligence

Class character traits such as bashfulness in 155.232; class loneliness in 155.92; class grief associated with bereavement by death in 155.937; class depression in 616.8527; class comprehensive works on emotions and cognition in 153

| | |
|---|---|
| .41 | Love and affection |

Standard subdivisions are added for either or both topics in heading

Including empathy

| | |
|---|---|
| .42 | Pleasure, enjoyment, happiness, joy, ecstasy |

Standard subdivisions are added for any or all topics in heading

| | |
|---|---|
| .43 | Wit and humor |

Standard subdivisions are added for either or both topics in heading

| | |
|---|---|
| .44 | Guilt and shame |

Standard subdivisions are added for either or both topics in heading

| .46 | Fear, anxiety, worry |
| --- | --- |

Standard subdivisions are added for any or all topics in heading

| .47 | Anger |
| --- | --- |

Including frustration

Class here aggressive moods and feelings

Class comprehensive works on psychology of aggression in 155.232

| .48 | Jealousy and envy |
| --- | --- |

Standard subdivisions are added for either or both topics in heading

| **.5** | **Physiological drives** |
| --- | --- |

Class motivation, comprehensive works on drives in 153.8

| **.8** | **Threshold, discrimination, reaction-time studies** |
| --- | --- |
| .82 | Threshold and discrimination studies |

Standard subdivisions are added for either or both topics in heading

| .83 | Reaction-time studies |
| --- | --- |

# 153 Conscious mental processes and intelligence

Standard subdivisions are added for conscious mental processes and intelligence together, for conscious mental processes alone

Class here conscious mental processes and intelligence of adults in general [*formerly* 155.6], cognition, cognitive psychology, cognitive science, intellectual processes, comprehensive works on emotions and cognition

Class conscious mental processes and intelligence of adults by marital status and relationships in 155.64; class conscious mental processes and intelligence of people in specific stages of adulthood in 155.65–155.67; class comprehensive works on artificial intelligence and cognitive science in 006.3

*For emotions, emotional intelligence, see 152.4*

*See also 121 for epistemology; also 128.2 for mind-body problem in philosophy*

*See Manual at 006.3 vs. 153; also at 153 vs. 153.4*

### SUMMARY

| | |
| --- | --- |
| 153.1 | **Memory and learning** |
| .2 | **Formation and association of ideas** |
| .3 | **Imagination, imagery, creativity** |
| .4 | **Thought, thinking, reasoning, intuition, value, judgment** |
| .6 | **Communication** |
| .7 | **Perceptual processes** |
| .8 | **Will (Volition)** |
| .9 | **Intelligence and aptitudes** |

| [.028 7] | Testing and measurement |
| --- | --- |

Do not use; class in 153.93

| **.1** | **Memory and learning** |
| --- | --- |

| | |
|---|---|
| .12 | Memory |

Class memory with respect to a specific topic with the topic, e.g., memory and dreams 154.63

*For types of memory, see 153.13; for mnemonics, see 153.14*

| | |
|---|---|
| .122 | Retention |
| .123 | Recall and reproduction |

Standard subdivisions are added for either or both topics in heading

| | |
|---|---|
| .124 | Recognition |
| .125 | Forgetting |
| .13 | Types of memory |
| [.130 1–.130 9] | Standard subdivisions |

Do not use; class in 153.1201–153.1209

| | |
|---|---|
| .132 | Visual memory |
| .133 | Auditory memory |
| .134 | Visual-auditory memory |
| .14 | Mnemonics |
| .15 | Learning |

Class application of learning psychology to education in 370.15

| | |
|---|---|
| .152 | Methods of learning |
| .152 2 | Rote learning, learning by repetition |

Standard subdivisions are added for either or both topics in heading

| | |
|---|---|
| .152 3 | Learning by imitation |
| .152 4 | Trial-and-error learning |
| .152 6 | Associative learning |

Including Pavlovian conditioning (classical conditioning), operant conditioning

Class comprehensive works on associationism in 150.1944

| | |
|---|---|
| .152 8 | Discrimination learning |
| .153 | Factors in learning |
| .153 2 | Attention and concentration |

Standard subdivisions are added for either or both topics in heading

| | |
|---|---|
| .153 3 | Interest and enthusiasm |

Standard subdivisions are added for either or both topics in heading

| | |
|---|---|
| .153 4 | Motivation |
| .154 | Transfer of learning |

| | |
|---|---|
| .158 | Learning curves |

**.2**      **Formation and association of ideas**

| | |
|---|---|
| .22 | Association of ideas |
| .23 | Concepts and concept formation |

       Standard subdivisions are added for either or both topics in heading

       *For abstraction, see 153.24*

| | |
|---|---|
| .24 | Abstraction |

**.3**      **Imagination, imagery, creativity**

       Standard subdivisions are added for imagination, imagery, creativity together; for imagination alone

       Class here daydreams, fantasies, reveries considered as aspects of the imagination

       Class comprehensive works on daydreams, fantasies, reveries in 154.3

| | |
|---|---|
| .32 | Imagery |

       Including visualization

| | |
|---|---|
| .35 | Creativity |

       Class here interdisciplinary works on creativity

       *For creativity in a specific field, see the field, plus notation 019 from Table 1, e.g., creativity in the arts 700.19*

**.4**      **Thought, thinking, reasoning, intuition, value, judgment**

       *For formation and association of ideas, see 153.2*

       *See Manual at 153 vs. 153.4*

| | |
|---|---|
| [.402 87] | Testing and measurement |

       Do not use; class in 153.93

| | |
|---|---|
| .42 | Thought and thinking |

       Standard subdivisions are added for either or both topics in heading

       *For reasoning, see 153.43*

| | |
|---|---|
| .43 | Reasoning |

       Class here problem solving

       Class logical processes of reasoning and problem solving in 160

| | |
|---|---|
| .432 | Inductive reasoning |

       Including inference

| | |
|---|---|
| .433 | Deductive reasoning |
| .44 | Intuition |
| .45 | Value |

| .46 | Judgment |
|---|---|

*For moral judgment, see 155.232*

**.6 Communication**

Class here individual aspects of interpersonal communication

Class sociolinguistics in 306.44; class psychology of language and language processing (psycholinguistics) in 401.9; class psychology of reading in 418.4019; class social psychology of, interdisciplinary works on communication in 302.2

| .68 | Listening |
|---|---|

Class speech perception in 401.9

| .69 | Nonverbal communication |
|---|---|

Class here meaning of movements, body language; cognitive processes involved in interpreting movements

**.7 Perceptual processes**

Perceptual apprehension and understanding

*For extrasensory perception, see 133.82–133.86; for sensory perception, see 152.1*

*See Manual at 153.7 vs. 152.1*

| .73 | Basic elements |
|---|---|

Including apperception

Class basic elements of a specific type of perception in 153.75

*See also 155.2844 for thematic apperception tests*

| .733 | Attention |
|---|---|

Including listening, looking

| .736 | Subliminal perception |
|---|---|

| .74 | Errors (Normal illusions) |
|---|---|

| .75 | Types of perception |
|---|---|

Class social perception, social risk perception in 302.12

| [.750 1–.750 9] | Standard subdivisions |
|---|---|

Do not use; class in 153.701–153.709

| .752 | Spatial perception |
|---|---|

Including size perception

Class visual spatial perception in 152.142

| .753 | Time and rhythm perception |
|---|---|

Standard subdivisions are added for time and rhythm perception together, for time perception alone

| .754 | Movement perception |
|---|---|

Class visual perception of movement in 152.1425

| .758 | Face perception |
|---|---|

## .8 Will (Volition)

Including self-control

Class here intentionality, motivation; comprehensive works on drives

*For physiological drives, see 152.5*

| .83 | Choice and decision |
|---|---|

Standard subdivisions are added for either or both topics in heading

| .85 | Modification of will |
|---|---|

Class here behavior modification and attitude change when reference is to bending the will or changing conscious intent

*See also 155.25 for modification of character and personality*

| .852 | Persuasion |
|---|---|
| .853 | Brainwashing |
| .854 | Conformity |

## .9 Intelligence and aptitudes

Standard subdivisions are added for either or both topics in heading

Class here intellect, intelligence levels, multiple intelligences

Class emotional intelligence in 152.4; class factors in differential and developmental psychology that affect intelligence and aptitudes in 155

| [.902 87] | Testing and measurement |
|---|---|

Do not use for intelligence tests; class in 153.93. Do not use for aptitude tests; class in 153.94

| .93 | Intelligence tests |
|---|---|

Class here comprehensive works on testing and measurement of cognition, of conscious mental processes, of intelligence and personality

*For aptitude tests, see 153.94; for personality tests, see 155.28; for educational tests and measurements, see 371.26; for neuropsychological tests, see 616.80475*

| .94 | Aptitude tests |
|---|---|

Tests for special abilities

Class here vocational interest tests

Class use of aptitude and vocational interest tests for academic prognosis and placement in 371.264; class comprehensive works on vocational interests in 158.6

*See also 371.26 for achievement tests and measurements*

.940 001–.940 009     Standard subdivisions

.940 01–.949 99     Tests for aptitudes in specific fields

        Add to base number 153.94 notation 001–999, e.g., tests for musical ability 153.9478

.98     Superior intelligence

# 154    Subconscious and altered states and processes

### .2    The subconscious

Including works that emphasize the subconscious in treating relations among the id, ego, superego

Class works that emphasize the ego in 155.2

### .3    Daydreams, fantasies, reveries

Standard subdivisions are added for any or all topics in heading

*For daydreams, fantasies, reveries considered as aspects of imagination, see 153.3*

### .4    Altered states of consciousness

Including altered states due to use of drugs; hallucinations

### .6    Sleep phenomena

Class physiological aspects of sleep in 612.821

.63    Dreams

Class here dream interpretation, interdisciplinary works on dreams

*For parapsychological aspects of dreams, see 135.3; for physiological aspects of dreams, see 612.821*

.632    Nightmares

Use of this number for other types of dreams discontinued; class in 154.63

[.634]    Analysis of dreams

Number discontinued; class in 154.63

.64    Sleepwalking (Somnambulism)

### .7    Hypnotism

Class here interdisciplinary works on hypnotism

*For psychic aspects of hypnotism, see 133.89; for medical applications of hypnotism, see 615.8512*

.72    Animal magnetism

.76    Induction of hypnosis

.77    Hypnotic phenomena

.772            Phenomena during trance

.774            Posthypnotic phenomena

## 155    Differential and developmental psychology

Standard subdivisions are added for either or both topics in heading

Including role of play in development

Except for modifications shown under specific entries, add to each subdivision identified by * as follows:

2        Sensory perception, movement, emotions, physiological drives
             Add to 2 the numbers following 152 in 152.1–152.8, e.g., emotions 24, emotions of young people, of sixteen-year-olds 155.5124
                  Subdivisions are added for people of any specific age within an age group

3        Conscious mental processes and intelligence
             Standard subdivisions are added for conscious mental processes and intelligence together, for conscious mental processes alone
             Add to 3 the numbers following 153 in 153.1–153.9, e.g., creativity 335, intelligence tests 393, intelligence tests for young people, for sixteen-year-olds 155.51393; however, for aptitude tests, see 153.940008
                  Subdivisions are added for people of any specific age within an age group
             Class sensory perception, movement, emotions, physiological drives in 2

8        Individual, evolutionary, environmental psychology
             Including play

82       Individual psychology
             Add to 82 the numbers following 155.2 in 155.22–155.28, e.g., moral development 825, personality tests 828, personality tests for young people, for sixteen-year-olds 155.51828
                  Subdivisions are added for people of any specific age within an age group
             Class evolutionary psychology in 8; class environmental psychology in 89. Class application of individual psychology in general and application of broad, vaguely defined topics of individual psychology with the application in 9, e.g., personal improvement through self-actualization 91, improved interpersonal relations through self-esteem 92

89       Environmental psychology
8904          Special topics of environmental psychology
89042             Stress
                  Class here works on how to cope with stress
                  *For job stress, see 972*

891–896  Specific topics in environmental psychology
             Add to 89 the numbers following 155.9 in 155.91–155.96, e.g., influence of social environment 892, influence of social environment on young people, on sixteen-year-olds 155.51892; however, for influence of specific situations, see 155.93
                  Subdivisions are added for people of any specific age within an age group

                                                    (continued)

# 155 Differential and developmental psychology (continued)

9 Applied psychology

Class here application of individual psychology in general

Add to 9 the numbers following 158 in 158.1–158.9, e.g., personal improvement and analysis 91, interpersonal relations 92, job stress 972, personal improvement and analysis for young people, for sixteen-year-olds 155.5191

Subdivisions are added for people of any specific age within an age group

Class comprehensive works on stress in 89042. Class application of a specific branch of psychology (other than individual psychology in general 82) with the branch, e.g., how to control emotions 24, how to be creative 335, use of personality tests for self-knowledge and self-improvement 828

Unless other instructions are given, observe the following table of preference, e.g., reactions of African American school children to catastrophic fires 155.935 (*not* 155.424 or 155.8496073):

| | |
|---|---|
| Influence of specific situations | 155.93 |
| Psychology of specific ages | 155.4–155.6 |
| Ethnopsychology and national psychology | 155.8 |
| Evolutionary psychology | 155.7 |
| Environmental psychology (*except* 155.93) | 155.9 |
| Sex psychology; psychology of people by gender or sex, by sexual orientation | 155.3 |
| Individual psychology | 155.2 |

Class role of play in relation to a specific topic with the topic, e.g., role of play in child development 155.418

*See Manual at 155*

## SUMMARY

| | |
|---|---|
| **155.2** | **Individual psychology** |
| **.3** | **Sex psychology; psychology of people by gender or sex, by sexual orientation** |
| **.4** | **Child psychology** |
| **.5** | **Psychology of young people twelve to twenty** |
| **.6** | **Psychology of adults** |
| **.7** | **Evolutionary psychology** |
| **.8** | **Ethnopsychology and national psychology** |
| **.9** | **Environmental psychology** |

**.2** **Individual psychology**

Including defense mechanisms

Class here individual psychology of adults in general [*formerly* 155.6]; the self; character, identity, individuality, personality

Class individual psychology of adults by marital status and relationships in 155.64; class individual psychology of people in specific stages of adulthood in 155.65–155.67. Class defense mechanisms in relation to a specific topic with the topic, e.g., defense mechanisms and adaptability 155.24, defense mechanisms and reactions to death 155.937; class application of individual psychology in general and application of broad, vaguely defined topics of individual psychology with the application in 158, e.g., personal improvement through self-actualization 158.1, improved interpersonal relations through self-esteem 158.2

**[.202 87]** Testing and measurement

Do not use; class in 155.28

**.22** Individual differences

**.23** Traits and determinants of character and personality

**.232** Traits

Including altruism, bashfulness, dependence, extroversion, introversion, moral judgment, perfectionism, workaholism; comprehensive works on the psychology of aggression

Class interdisciplinary works on aggression, aggressive social interactions in 302.54. Class a specific aspect of a specific trait with the aspect, e.g., development of moral judgment 155.25

*For aggressive emotions, see 152.47; for aggressive drives, see 153.8*

**.234** Determinants

Class here environment versus heredity as determinants

Class comprehensive works on environment versus heredity in psychology in 155.7

*For environmental determinants, see 155.9*

**.24** Adaptability and adjustment

Standard subdivisions are added for either or both topics in heading

**.25** Development and modification of character and personality

Standard subdivisions are added for any or all topics in heading

Including maturity, development of self-control

*See also 153.85 for behavior modification and attitude change when reference is to bending the will or changing conscious intent*

**.26** Typology

Class a personality test based on a theory of personality types with the test in 155.28, e.g., Myers-Briggs Type Indicator® (personality inventory) 155.283

| | |
|---|---|
| .262 | Classical typology (Hippocrates' theory of temperaments) |
| .264 | Modern typology |

Including classification schemes of James, Kretschmer, Rorschach, Sheldon

| | |
|---|---|
| .264 4 | Typology of Jung |

Class here Myers-Briggs typology

| | |
|---|---|
| .28 | Appraisals and tests |

Standard subdivisions are added for either or both topics in heading

Class use of personality tests to determine vocational interests in 153.94; class use of personality tests to diagnose psychiatric disorders in 616.89075; class comprehensive works on appraisals and tests for intelligence and personality in 153.93

| | |
|---|---|
| .282 | Diagnostic graphology |

Class here interdisciplinary works on graphology

*For divinatory graphology, see 137; for handwriting analysis for the examination of evidence, see 363.2565; for handwriting analysis for screening of prospective employees, see 658.3112*

| | |
|---|---|
| .283 | Inventories and questionnaires |

Standard subdivisions are added for either or both topics in heading

| | |
|---|---|
| .284 | Projective techniques |
| .284 2 | Rorschach tests |
| .284 3 | Szondi tests |
| .284 4 | Thematic apperception tests |
| **.3** | **Sex psychology; psychology of people by gender or sex, by sexual orientation** |

Standard subdivisions are added for all the topics in the heading, for sex psychology alone

Class here sex psychology of adults in general [*formerly* 155.6], relations between the sexes, sex, sexual love

Class sex psychology of adults in specific age groups in 155.65–155.67; class interdisciplinary works on and social psychology of relations between the sexes, sex, sexual love in 306.7

| | |
|---|---|
| .31 | Erogeneity and libido |

Standard subdivisions are added for either or both topics in heading

| | |
|---|---|
| [.32] | Sex and personality |

Number discontinued; class in 155.3

.33 Psychology of people by gender or sex

Standard subdivisions are added for either or both topics in heading

Including display of behavior characteristics of both sexes or genders (androgynous behavior); intersex people; transgender people, transgenderists, transsexuals

Class here adults by gender or sex [*formerly* 155.63], gender identity, gender role, sex differences, sex role, the sexes; comprehensive works on psychology of men and women, of males and females

Class psychology of people by sexual orientation in 155.34; class sexual practices associated with specific sexes in 155.35; class female impersonation, male impersonation in 792.028

*For children by gender or sex, see 155.43; for young people twelve to twenty by gender or sex, see 155.53; for adults of either gender or sex by marital status and relationships, see 155.64; for people of either gender or sex in a specific stage of adulthood, see 155.65–155.67*

.332 †Men

Class here males; masculinity (presumed distinctive characteristics of males, whether overtly sexual or not)

.333 †Women

Class here females; femininity (presumed distinctive characteristics of females, whether overtly sexual or not)

[.334] Bisexuality

Use of this number for display of behavior characteristics of both sexes or genders (androgynous behavior) discontinued; class in 155.33

Bisexuality relocated to 155.343

.34 Psychology of people by sexual orientation

Including asexuals, heterosexuals

Class here adults in general by sexual orientation [*formerly* 155.60866]

Class sexual practices associated with specific orientations in 155.35; class adults in specific age groups by sexual orientation in 155.65–155.67; class interdisciplinary works on and social psychology of sexual orientation in 306.76

Use of this number for relations between the sexes discontinued; class in 155.3

.343 Bisexuals

Class here bisexuality [*formerly* 155.334]

.344 Gays

.344 1 General topics of psychology of gays

---

†Add as instructed under 155, except class evolutionary psychology in 155.7, ethnopsychology and national psychology in 155.8, environmental psychology in 155.9

| | |
|---|---|
| [.344 101–.344 109] | Standard subdivisions |
| | Do not use; class in 155.34401–155.34409 |
| .344 12–.344 19 | Sensory perception, movement, emotions, physiological drives; conscious mental processes and intelligence; individual and applied psychology |
| | Add to 155.3441 as instructed under 155, e.g., emotions of gays 155.344124; however, for evolutionary psychology, see 155.7; for ethnopsychology and national psychology, see 155.8; for environmental psychology, see 155.9 |
| .344 2 | †Gay men |
| .344 3 | †Lesbians |
| .35 | Sexual practices |

---

> ### 155.4–155.6 Psychology of specific ages

Class here developmental psychology

Class comprehensive works in 155

### .4 Child psychology

Through age eleven

Class interdisciplinary works on child development in 305.231

*See also 649.1 for child rearing*

| | |
|---|---|
| [.408 1] | People by gender or sex |
| | Do not use; class in 155.43 |
| [.408 2] | Women |
| | Do not use; class in 155.433 |
| [.408 3] | Young people |
| | Do not use for psychology of children in general; class in 155.4. Do not use for psychology of children in specific age groups; class in 155.42 |
| .408 5 | Relatives |
| [.408 55] | Siblings |
| | Do not use; class in 155.443 |
| .408 6 | People by miscellaneous social attributes |
| [.408 62] | People by social and economic levels |
| | Do not use; class in 155.456 |

†Add as instructed under 155, except class evolutionary psychology in 155.7, ethnopsychology and national psychology in 155.8, environmental psychology in 155.9

[.408 7]    People with disabilities and illnesses, gifted people

Do not use; class in 155.451–155.455

[.408 9]    Ethnic and national groups

Do not use; class in 155.457

.41    General topics of child psychology

Class national psychology of children in 155.4093–155.4099; class general topics applied to children by specific attributes in 155.42–155.45; class socialization in 303.32

[.410 1–.410 9]    Standard subdivisions

Do not use; class in 155.401–155.409

.412–.419    Sensory perception, movement, emotions, physiological drives; conscious mental processes and intelligence; individual, evolutionary, environmental, applied psychology

Add to 155.41 as instructed under 155, e.g., emotions of children 155.4124; however, interpersonal relationships relocated from 155.418 to 155.4192

> 155.42–155.45  Children by specific attributes

Unless other instructions are given, observe the following table of preference, e.g., boys aged three to five 155.423 (*not* 155.432):

| | |
|---|---|
| Exceptional children; children by social and economic levels, by ethnic or national group | 155.45 |
| Children by status and relationships | 155.44 |
| Children in specific age groups | 155.42 |
| Children by gender or sex | 155.43 |

Class comprehensive works in 155.4

.42    Children in specific age groups    —    *Use 155.4 for all age groups*

.422    Infants

From birth to age two

Class here comprehensive works on children from birth to age five

Add to 155.422 as instructed under 155, e.g., infants at play 155.4228; however, interpersonal relationships relocated from 155.4228 to 155.42292

*For children three to five, see 155.423*

.423      **Children three to five**

Class here preschool children, comprehensive works on children aged two to six or three to seven

Add to 155.423 as instructed under 155, e.g., conscious mental processes and intelligence of preschool children 155.4233; however, interpersonal relationships relocated from 155.4238 to 155.42392

*For children aged six and seven, see 155.424*

.424      **Children six to eleven**

Class here comprehensive works on school children to age fourteen

Add to 155.424 as instructed under 155, e.g., conscious mental processes and intelligence of school children 155.4243; however, interpersonal relationships relocated from 155.4248 to 155.42492

*For young people twelve to fourteen, see 155.5*

.43      **Children by gender or sex**

Class here sex psychology of children

*For children by sexual orientation, see 155.40866; for transgender and intersex children, see 155.40867*

.432      **Boys**

.433      **Girls**

.44      **Children by status and relationships**

Class here psychology of temporary or permanent separation from parents

.442      **The only child**

Class the adopted or foster only child in 155.445; class the institutionalized only child in 155.446

.443      **Siblings**

*For brothers and sisters of same birth, see 155.444; for adopted and foster children, see 155.445*

.444      **Brothers and sisters of same birth**

Standard subdivisions are added for either or both topics in heading

.445      **Adopted and foster children**

.446      **Institutionalized children**

Including children raised in communities that serve as collective parents, e.g., kibbutz children

.45      **Exceptional children; children by social and economic levels, by ethnic or national group**

Standard subdivisions are added for all topics in heading together, for exceptional children alone

| | |
|---|---|
| .451–.455 | Exceptional children |

Add to base number 155.45 the numbers following 371.9 in 371.91–371.95, e.g., psychology of gifted children 155.455

| | |
|---|---|
| .456 | Children by social and economic levels |
| .456 7 | Children with social disadvantages |

Including wild children (feral children)

Class here children with cultural disadvantages

Class psychoanalytic principles derived in part from study of wild children in 150.195

| | |
|---|---|
| .457 | Children by ethnic and national group |

Class here ethnopsychology

Class national psychology of children in 155.4093–155.4099

| | |
|---|---|
| .457 001–.457 009 | Standard subdivisions |
| .457 05–.457 09 | Children of mixed ancestry with ethnic origins from more than one continent, European children and children of European descent |

Add to base number 155.4570 the numbers following —0 in notation 05–09 from Table 5, e.g., children of European descent 155.4509, children of European descent in India 155.4509054

| | |
|---|---|
| .457 1–.457 9 | Specific ethnic and national groups |

Add to base number 155.457 notation 1–9 from Table 5, e.g., Japanese children 155.457956, Japanese-American children 155.457956073

| | |
|---|---|
| **.5** | **Psychology of young people twelve to twenty** |

Class vocational tests for young people twelve to twenty in 153.94000835; class youth twenty-one and over, comprehensive works on young adults in 155.65; class interdisciplinary works on development of young people twelve to twenty in 305.2355

| | |
|---|---|
| [.508 1] | People by gender or sex |

Do not use; class in 155.53

| | |
|---|---|
| [.508 2] | Women |

Do not use; class in 155.533

| | |
|---|---|
| .508 9 | Ethnic and national groups |

Class here ethnopsychology

| | |
|---|---|
| .51 | General topics of psychology of young people twelve to twenty |

Class ethnopsychology of young people twelve to twenty in 155.5089; class national psychology of young people twelve to twenty in 155.5093–155.5099; class general topics applied to young people twelve to twenty by gender or sex in 155.53; class socialization in 303.32

[.510 1–.510 9]    Standard subdivisions

Do not use; class in 155.501–155.509

.512–.519    Sensory perception, movement, emotions, physiological drives; conscious mental processes and intelligence; individual, evolutionary, environmental, applied psychology

Add to 155.51 as instructed under 155, e.g., emotions of young people twelve to twenty, emotions of sixteen-year-olds 155.5124; however, interpersonal relationships relocated from 155.518 to 155.5192

.53    Young people twelve to twenty by gender or sex

Class here sex psychology of young people twelve to twenty

*For young people twelve to twenty by sexual orientation, see 155.50866; for transgender and intersex young people twelve to twenty, see 155.50867*

[.530 85–.530 89]    Relatives; people by miscellaneous social attributes; people with disabilities and illnesses, gifted people; occupational and religious groups; ethnic and national groups

Do not use; class in 155.5085–155.5089

.532    Males twelve to twenty

[.532 085–.532 089]    Relatives; people by miscellaneous social attributes; people with disabilities and illnesses, gifted people; occupational and religious groups; ethnic and national groups

Do not use; class in 155.5085–155.5089

.533    Females twelve to twenty

[.533 085–.533 089]    Relatives; people by miscellaneous social attributes; people with disabilities and illnesses, gifted people; occupational and religious groups; ethnic and national groups

Do not use; class in 155.5085–155.5089

**.6    Psychology of adults**

Class sensory perception, movement, emotions, physiological drives, conscious mental processes and intelligence, individual psychology, sex psychology, evolutionary psychology, environmental psychology, applied psychology of adults by marital status relationships in 155.64; class sensory perception, movement, emotions, physiological drives, conscious mental processes and intelligence, individual psychology, sex psychology, evolutionary psychology, environmental psychology, applied psychology of people in specific stages of adulthood in 155.65–155.67

*See Manual at 155*

Sensory perception, movement, emotions, physiological drives of adults in general relocated to 152; conscious mental processes and intelligence of adults in general relocated to 153; individual psychology of adults in general relocated to 155.2; sex psychology of adults in general relocated to 155.3; evolutionary psychology of adults in general relocated to 155.7; environmental psychology of adults in general relocated to 155.9; applied psychology of adults in general relocated to 158

| [.608 1] | Adults by gender or sex |
| | Do not use; class in 155.33 |
| [.608 2] | Women |
| | Do not use; class in 155.333 |
| [.608 4] | Adults in specific stages of adulthood |
| | Do not use; class in 155.65–155.67 |
| [.608 5] | Relatives |
| | Do not use; class in 155.646 |
| .608 6 | Adults by miscellaneous social attributes |
| [.608 65] | Adults by marital status |
| | Do not use; class in 155.64 |
| [.608 66] | Adults in general by sexual orientation |
| | Relocated to 155.34 |
| [.608 9] | Ethnic and national groups |
| | Relocated to 155.82 |
| .609 | **History, geographic treatment, biography** |
| .609 3–.609 9 | Specific continents, countries, localities; extraterrestrial worlds |
| | National psychology of adults in general relocated to 155.89 |
| [.63] | **Adults by gender or sex** |
| | Relocated to 155.33 |
| .64 | **Adults by marital status and relationships** |
| | Class people in a specific stage of adulthood regardless of marital status and relationship in 155.65–155.67 |
| .642 | **Single status** |
| .642 2 | Men |
| .642 3 | Women |
| .643 | **Separated and divorced status** |
| | Standard subdivisions are added for either or both topics in heading |
| .643 2 | Men |
| .643 3 | Women |
| .644 | **Widowed status** |
| .644 2 | Men |
| .644 3 | Women |

| | |
|---|---|
| .645 | Married status |

Class married parents in 155.646

| | |
|---|---|
| .645 2 | Men |
| .645 3 | Women |
| .646 | Parents, grandparents, progeny, siblings |

Standard subdivisions are added for parents, grandparents, progeny, siblings together; for parents alone

Class unmarried parents in 155.642; class separated and divorced parents in 155.643; class widowed parents in 155.644

| | |
|---|---|
| .646 2 | Fathers |
| .646 3 | Mothers |

---

>         155.65–155.67 People in specific stages of adulthood

Class comprehensive works in 155.6

| | |
|---|---|
| .65 | *People in early adulthood |

Class here comprehensive works on young adults

*For young adults under twenty-one, see 155.5*

| | |
|---|---|
| .66 | *People in middle adulthood |
| .67 | People in late adulthood |
| .670 89 | Ethnic and national groups |

Class here ethnopsychology

| | |
|---|---|
| .671 | General topics of people in late adulthood |

Class ethnopsychology of people in late adulthood in 155.67089; class national psychology of people in late adulthood in 155.67093–155.67099

| | |
|---|---|
| [.671 01–.671 09] | Standard subdivisions |

Do not use; class in 155.6701–155.6709

| | |
|---|---|
| .671 2–.671 9 | Sensory perception, movement, emotions, physiological drives; conscious mental processes and intelligence; individual, evolutionary, environmental, applied psychology |

Add to 155.671 as instructed under 155, e.g., emotions of people in late adulthood 155.67124; however, interpersonal relationships relocated from 155.6718 to 155.67192; for adaptability of people in late adulthood, see 155.672

| | |
|---|---|
| .672 | Adaptability and adjustment |

Standard subdivisions are added for either or both topics in heading

Class here psychological aspects of retirement, change in status

---

*Add as instructed under 155

**.7** **Evolutionary psychology**

Evolution of basic human mental and psychological characteristics

Including behavior genetics

Class here evolutionary psychology of adults in general [*formerly* 155.6], comprehensive works on environment versus heredity in psychology

*For environment versus heredity in determining traits of character and personality, see 155.234; for environmental psychology, see 155.9*

*See also 304.5 for genetic bases of social behavior*

*See Manual at 302–307 vs. 150, T1—019*

**.8** **Ethnopsychology and national psychology**

Class here cross-cultural psychology

Class studies of cultural influence in 155.92

*See Manual at 155*

**.82** Ethnopsychology

Class here adults in general by ethnic and national group [*formerly* 155.6089], ethnic differences

*For psychology of specific ethnic groups, see 155.84*

**.84** Specific ethnic groups

Limited to ethnic groups in areas where they are not predominant

*See Manual at 155.89 vs. 155.84*

**.840 5–.840 9** Specific ethnic groups with ethnic origins from more than one continent, of European descent

Add to base number 155.840 the numbers following —0 in notation 05–09 from Table 5, e.g., ethnopsychology of people of mixed Asian and European ancestry 155.840595009, of people of mixed Asian and European ancestry in United States 155.840595009073

*See Manual at 155.89 vs. 155.84*

**.841–.849** Specific ethnic groups with other origins

Add to base number 155.84 notation 1–9 from Table 5, e.g., ethnopsychology of African Americans 155.8496073

**.89** National psychology

Class here national psychology of adults in general [*formerly* 155.6093–155.6099]

Add to base number 155.89 notation 3–9 from Table 2, e.g., Italian national psychology 155.8945

Class psychology of specific ethnic groups regardless of national origin in 155.84

*See Manual at 155.89 vs. 155.84*

.9      **Environmental psychology**

Class here environmental psychology of adults in general [*formerly* 155.6]; environmental influences, ways of coping with the influences

Unless other instructions are given, observe the following table of preference, e.g., the influence of family, friends, and work associates upon people coping with a loss through death 155.937 (*not* 155.92):

| | |
|---|---|
| Influence of specific situations | 155.93 |
| Influence of clothing | 155.95 |
| Influence of restrictive environments | 155.96 |
| Influence of injuries, diseases, physical disabilities, disfigurements | 155.916 |
| Influence of community and housing | 155.94 |
| Influence of social environment | 155.92 |
| Influence of physical environment and conditions (*except* 155.916) | 155.91 |

.904          Special topics of environmental psychology

.904 2             Stress

Class here works on how to cope with stress

*For job stress, see 158.72*

.91        Influence of physical environment and conditions

Standard subdivisions are added for either or both topics in heading

.911        Influence of sensory stimuli

Add to base number 155.911 the numbers following 152.1 in 152.14–152.18, e.g., psychology of color 155.91145

Class sensory influences associated with climate in 155.915; class sensory influences on people with injuries, diseases, physical disabilities, disfigurements in 155.916

.915        Influence of climate

Class influence of climate on people with injuries, diseases, physical disabilities, disfigurements in 155.916

.916        Influence of injuries, diseases, physical disabilities, disfigurements

.92        Influence of social environment

Including comprehensive works on forgiveness, on loneliness, on solitude

Add to base number 155.92 the numbers following 158.2 in 158.24–158.27, e.g., influence of family members, birth order 155.924

*For influence of community and housing, see 155.94; for forgiveness and loneliness in the context of improving interpersonal relations, see 158.2*

.93        Influence of specific situations

Including influence of divorce, loss of job

.935      Catastrophic disasters

> Including behavior patterns during bombings, earthquakes, fires, floods, hurricanes
>
> Class catastrophic accidents in 155.936; class death in catastrophic disasters in 155.937

.936      Accidents

> Class death in accidents in 155.937

.937      Death and dying

> Standard subdivisions are added for either or both topics in heading
>
> Class here reactions to death of others
>
> Class interdisciplinary works on death in 306.9

.937 08      Groups of people

> Use for people concerned about dying or affected by death of others, e.g., children grieving death of a loved one 155.937083, parents grieving the death of a child 155.937085, attitudes toward death and dying of people in late adulthood 155.9370846

.94      Influence of community and housing

> Standard subdivisions are added for influence of community and housing together, for influence of community alone

>      155.942–155.944   Specific types of communities

> Class housing in specific types of communities in 155.945; class comprehensive works in 155.94

.942      Urban communities

.943      Suburban communities

.944      Rural communities

.945      Housing

.95      Influence of clothing

.96      Influence of restrictive environments

.962      Prisons

.963      Submarine structures

.964      Subterranean structures

> Including behavior patterns in caves, mines, tunnels, underground shelters

.965      Aircraft

> Class here aviation psychology

.966 Spacecraft

Class here space psychology

## 156 Comparative psychology

Comparison of human psychology and the psychology of other organisms; study of other organisms to elucidate human behavior

Class behavior of nonhuman organisms in 591.5

*See Manual at 302–307 vs. 156*

---

> **156.2–156.5 Animals**

Class habits and behavior patterns of animals in 591.5; class comprehensive works in 156

.2 **Comparative psychology of sensory perception, movement, emotions, physiological drives of animals**

Add to base number 156.2 the numbers following 152 in 152.1–152.8, e.g., comparative reaction-time studies 156.283

.3 **Comparative conscious mental processes and intelligence of animals**

Standard subdivisions are added for comparative conscious mental processes and intelligence together, for comparative conscious mental processes alone

Add to base number 156.3 the numbers following 153 in 153.1–153.9, e.g., comparative learning curves 156.3158

.4 **Comparative subconscious and altered states and processes of animals**

.5 **Comparative differential and developmental psychology of animals**

.9 **Plants**

Class plant behavior in 575.9

## [157] [Unassigned]

Most recently used in Edition 19

# 158      Applied psychology

Class here applied psychology of adults in general [*formerly* 155.6], application of individual psychology in general; comprehensive works on how to better oneself and how to get along with other people; comprehensive works on psychological and parapsychological or occult techniques for achieving personal well-being, happiness, success

Class applied psychology of adults by marital status and relationships in 155.64; class applied psychology of people in specific stages of adulthood in 155.65–155.67; class aptitude tests (both general and applied to specific subjects) in 153.94; class interdisciplinary works on success in 650.1. Class a specific application of psychology with the application, e.g., Christian pastoral psychology 253.52; class application of a specific branch of psychology (other than individual psychology in general 155.2) with the branch, e.g., how to be creative 153.35, use of personality tests for self-knowledge and self-improvement 155.28

> *For parapsychological and occult techniques for achievement of well-being, happiness, success, see 131*

.1       **Personal improvement and analysis**

Standard subdivisions are added for either or both topics in heading

Including personality analysis and improvement

Class here works intended to make one a better person or to stave off failure, to solve problems or to adjust to a life that does not meet one's expectations; works on specific systems and schools of applied psychology written for people who wish to be improved or analyzed

Class works on how to get along with other people in 158.2; class works on specific systems and schools of applied psychology written for advisors and counselors to help them assist others in 158.9; class comprehensive works on how to better oneself and how to get along with other people in 158

> *See Manual at 616.86 vs. 158.1, 204.42, 248.8629, 292–299, 362.29*

.12      Personal improvement and analysis through meditation

Standard subdivisions are added for either or both topics in heading

.125     Transcendental meditation

.128     Meditations

Class here collections of thoughts for use in meditation

.2       **Interpersonal relations**

Relations between an individual and other people

Class here dominance, forgiveness, intimacy; overcoming loneliness; applications of assertiveness training, sensitivity training, transactional analysis

Class individual aspects of interpersonal communication in 153.6; class interpersonal relations in counseling and interviewing in 158.3; class interpersonal relations in leadership in 158.4; class interpersonal relations in negotiation in 158.5; class social psychology of communication in 302.2; class interactions within groups in 302.3; class comprehensive works on forgiveness, on loneliness in 155.92

| .24 | Interpersonal relations with family members |
|---|---|

Class guides to harmonious family relations in 646.78

| .25 | Interpersonal relations with friends and neighbors |
|---|---|

Standard subdivisions are added for either or both topics in heading

| .26 | Interpersonal relations with work associates |
|---|---|

*See also 158.7 for psychology of work*

| .27 | Interpersonal relationships with strangers |
|---|---|

| **.3** | **Counseling and interviewing** |
|---|---|

Standard subdivisions are added for counseling and interviewing together, for counseling alone

Class here helping behavior, personal coaching

Class helpfulness as a personality trait in 155.232; class interdisciplinary works on counseling in 361.06. Class counseling in a specific subject with the subject, e.g., personal coaching in the context of employee education and training under personnel management 658.3124, counseling services in the context of employee welfare under personnel management 658.385

| .35 | Group counseling |
|---|---|

| .39 | Interviewing |
|---|---|

Class interviewing in a specific discipline with the discipline, e.g., employee selection interviewing 658.31124

| **.4** | **Leadership** |
|---|---|

| **.5** | **Negotiation** |
|---|---|

| **.6** | **Vocational interests** |
|---|---|

Class aptitudes in 153.9; class interdisciplinary works on choice of vocation in 331.702

| [.602 87] | Testing and measurement |
|---|---|

Do not use; class in 153.94

| **.7** | **Industrial psychology** |
|---|---|

Works focusing on the psychology of the individual employee in relation to work or taking a broad view that encompasses the concerns of individual employees, union leaders, management

Class here psychology of work

Class workaholism as a personality trait in 155.232. Class industrial psychology applied to a specific subject outside psychology with the subject, plus notation 019 from Table 1, e.g., psychological principles of personnel management 658.30019

*See also 158.26 for psychology of interpersonal relations with work associates*

.72          Job stress

> Class comprehensive works on stress in 155.9042

.723        Job burnout

**.9**        **Systems and schools of applied psychology**

> Including transactional analysis

> Class here works about founders of systems and schools of applied psychology, works about systems and schools of applied psychology written for advisors and counselors to help them assist others with personal improvement or analysis

> Class works on systems and schools of applied psychology written for people who wish to be improved or analyzed in 158.1. Class application of systems and schools of applied psychology with the application, e.g., application of transactional analysis to interviewing 158.39

**[159]**      **[Unassigned]**

> Most recently used in Edition 19

# 160   Philosophical logic

> Science of reasoning

> Including logic operators, negation, truth tables

> Class here informal logic, syllogistic logic, term logic; formal logic, propositional calculus (sentential calculus), predicate calculus; first-order logic; critical thinking; axioms, modality, predication, propositions

> Class psychology of reasoning and problem solving in 153.43; class linguistic presupposition, implication, entailment in 401.45; class formal logic, propositional calculus (sentential calculus), predicate calculus, first-order logic, logic operators, truth tables from the perspective of symbolic (mathematical) logic; interdisciplinary works on logic in 511.3

   **.1**      **Philosophy and theory**

   .11      Systems

   .119     Specific systems of classical and nonclassical logic

> Including erotetic logic (logic of questions), free logic

   .119 8    Nonclassical logic

> Add to base number 160.1198 the numbers following 511.31 in 511.312–511.318, e.g., modal logic from the perspective of philosophical logic 160.11984, counterfactuals from the perspective of philosophical logic 160.11987

# 161   Induction

> *For hypotheses, see 167; for analogy, see 169*

# 162   Deduction

> *For syllogisms, see 166*

**[163]** **[Unassigned]**

Most recently used in Edition 16

**[164]** **[Unassigned]**

Most recently used in Edition 17

**165** **Fallacies and sources of error**

Standard subdivisions are added for either or both topics in heading

Including contradictions, fictions, paradoxes

**166** **Syllogisms**

**167** **Hypotheses**

**168** **Argument and persuasion**

Standard subdivisions are added for either or both topics in heading

**169** **Analogy**

# 170 Ethics (Moral philosophy)

Class here conscience, good and evil; ethics of specific subjects, interdisciplinary works on social ethics

*For religious ethics, see 205; for social ethics as a method of social control, see 303.372. For ethics of a specific religion, see the religion, e.g., Christian ethics 241*

### SUMMARY

| | |
|---|---|
| 170.1–.9 | **Standard subdivisions and special topics of ethics** |
| 171 | **Ethical systems** |
| 172 | **Political ethics** |
| 173 | **Ethics of family relationships** |
| 174 | **Occupational ethics** |
| 175 | **Ethics of recreation, leisure, public performances, communication** |
| 176 | **Ethics of sex and reproduction** |
| 177 | **Ethics of social relations** |
| 178 | **Ethics of consumption** |
| 179 | **Other ethical norms** |

.4 **Special topics of ethics**

.42 Metaethics

Class here comprehensive works on moral realism, moral anti-realism

Class bases for specific systems in 171

.44 Normative ethics

*For deontology, see 171.2; for virtue ethics, see 171.3; for consequentialism, utilitarianism, see 171.5*

[.440 8]    History and description with respect to groups of people

Do not use; class in 170.8

## .8 Groups of people

[.88]    Occupational and religious groups

Do not use for ethics of occupational groups; class in 174. Do not use for ethics of religious groups; class in 205

## .9 History, geographic treatment, biography

.92    Biography

*See Manual at 170.92 vs. 171*

# 171 Ethical systems

Regardless of time or place

Class comprehensive works on normative ethics in 170.44. Class a specific topic in ethics, regardless of the system within which it is treated, with the topic in 172–179, e.g., professional ethics 174

*See Manual at 170.92 vs. 171*

## .1 Systems based on authority

## .2 Systems based on intuition, moral sense, reason; on duty and rights

Including deontology (nonconsequentialism), empiricism, existentialism, humanism, natural law, naturalism, stoicism

Class comprehensive works on moral realism in 170.42

*For systems and doctrines based on conscience, see 171.6*

*See also 171.7 for systems based on biology, genetics, evolution; also 340.112 for natural law in legal theory*

## .3 Perfectionism

Systems based on self-realization, personal fulfillment, well-being

Class here virtue ethics

*See also 179.9 for individual virtues, virtue in general*

## .4 Hedonism

Systems based on achievement of individual pleasure or happiness

## .5 Consequentialism and utilitarianism

Standard subdivisions are added for either or both topics in heading

## .6 Systems based on conscience

Including casuistry

**.7**     **Systems based on biology, genetics, evolution, education, social factors**

Including communist ethics, relativism, situation ethics, sociobiological ethics

*See also 171.2 for systems based on natural law, naturalism*

**.8**     **Systems based on altruism**

*For utilitarianism, see 171.5*

**.9**     **Systems based on egoism**

*For hedonism, see 171.4*

---

>     **172–179 Applied ethics**

Class comprehensive works in 170

# 172     Political ethics

**.1**     **Relation of individuals to the state**

Including civic and political activity, military service, obedience to law, payment of taxes; civil war, resistance, revolution, terrorism

*See also 174.3 for jury ethics*

**.2**     **Duties of the state**

Duties of government toward citizens, e.g., education, freedom, personal security, welfare; duties of public officeholders and officials

Class here justice

**.4**     **International relations**

Including conduct of foreign affairs, disarmament, espionage

.42     War and peace

Standard subdivisions are added for either or both topics in heading

Including conscientious objection, just war theory, pacifism, ways and means of conducting warfare

Class occupational ethics of military personnel in 174.9355

*For civil war, see 172.1*

.422     Nuclear weapons and nuclear war

Standard subdivisions are added for either or both topics in heading

# 173     Ethics of family relationships

Including ethics of marriage, divorce, separation, parent-child relationships, sibling relationships

Class ethics of sex and reproduction in 176

# 174 Occupational ethics

Class here professional ethics; ethics of work

Occupational ethics for those involved in the recreation industry relocated to 175

## .1 Clergy

## .2 Medical and health professions

Class here comprehensive works on bioethics [*formerly* 174.957]

Class medical ethics related to human reproduction in 176

### .22 Hippocratic oath

### .26 Economic questions

Including advertising, fee splitting

### .28 Experimentation

Including embryo research

Class here experimentation on human subjects

Class embryo research relating to human reproduction in 176

*For experimentation on animals, see 179.4*

### .29 Specific topics and branches of medicine and health

Class here innovative procedures

Add to base number 174.29 the numbers following 61 in 610–618, e.g., nursing ethics 174.29073, pharmaceutical ethics 174.2951, psychiatric ethics 174.29689; however, for experimentation on human subjects and comprehensive works on medical experimentation, see 174.28; for human reproduction, see 176; for animal experimentation, see 179.4; for questions of life and death, see 179.7

## .3 Legal ethics

Class here professional conduct of judges, lawyers; jury ethics

*See also 172.1 for ethics of relation of individuals to the state other than service on juries*

## .4 Business ethics

Including industrial espionage

Class here economic ethics, ethics of finance, manufacturing, marketing, trade; corporate social responsibility

## .6 Gambling business

Including lottery management

*See also 175 for gambling*

**.9** **Other professions and occupations**

Not provided for elsewhere

Add to base number 174.9 notation 001–999, e.g., law enforcement ethics 174.936323; however, bioethics relocated from 174.957 to 174.2; for ethics of public administration, public officeholders and officials, see 172.2

## 175 Ethics of recreation, leisure, public performances, communication

Including occupational ethics for those involved in the recreation industry [*formerly* 174]; ethics of dancing, gambling, music, television; fair play, sportsmanship

*For ethics of hunting, see 179.3*

## 176 Ethics of sex and reproduction

*For abortion, see 179.76*

**.2** **Reproductive technology**

Including artificial insemination, embryo transfer, surrogate motherhood

*See also 174.28 for embryo research not for purpose of human reproduction*

**.22** Human cloning

Limited to use for human reproduction

**.3** **Birth control**

**.4** **Sexual relations**

Including celibacy, chastity, homosexuality, premarital and extramarital relations, promiscuity

*See also 177.65 for ethics of courtship; also 177.7 for ethics of love*

**.5** **Prostitution**

**.7** **Obscenity and pornography**

Standard subdivisions are added for either or both topics in heading

*For obscenity and pornography in literature, see 176.8; for obscenity in speech, see 179.5*

**.8** **Obscenity and pornography in literature**

Standard subdivisions are added for either or both topics in heading

## 177 Ethics of social relations

Limited to the topics provided for below

**.1** **Courtesy, hospitality, politeness**

Class etiquette in 395

.2 **Conversation**

> Including gossip

.3 **Truthfulness, lying, slander, flattery**

.4 **Personal appearance**

> Including exposure of person, ostentatious dress

.5 **Discriminatory practices and slavery**

> Standard subdivisions are added for either or both topics in heading

.6 **Friendship and courtship**

.62 Friendship

.65 Courtship

> Class sexual ethics in courtship in 176

.7 **Love**

> Including benevolence, caring, charity, kindness, liberality, philanthropy
>
> *See also 128.46 for love as human experience*

# 178 Ethics of consumption

> Including abstinence, gluttony, greed, overindulgence, temperance
>
> Class here use of natural resources, of wealth
>
> Class environmental and ecological ethics, respect for nature in 179.1; class consumption of meat in 179.3

.1 **Consumption of alcoholic beverages**

.7 **Consumption of tobacco**

.8 **Consumption of narcotics**

# 179 Other ethical norms

> Class here cruelty

[.01–.09] Standard subdivisions

> Do not use; class in 170

.1 **Respect for life and nature**

> Standard subdivisions are added for either or both topics in heading
>
> Class here environmental and ecological ethics
>
> *For ethics of consumption, see 178; for treatment of animals, see 179.3; for respect for human life, see 179.7*

.2 **Treatment of children**

> *For parent-child relationships, see 173*

**.3**     **Treatment of animals**

> Including ethics of hunting; vegetarianism
>
> *For experimentation on animals, see 179.4*

**.4**     **Experimentation on animals**

> Including vivisection

**.5**     **Blasphemy, profanity, obscenity in speech**

> Standard subdivisions are added for any or all topics in heading

**.6**     **Courage and cowardice**

**.7**     **Respect and disrespect for human life**

> Standard subdivisions are added for either or both topics in heading
>
> Including questions of life and death in medical ethics, capital punishment, dueling, euthanasia, genocide, homicide, suicide
>
> Class here comprehensive works on ethics of violence, of nonviolence
>
> Class ethics of contraception in 176; class comprehensive works on medical ethics in 174.2
>
> > *For ethics of violence, of nonviolence in political activity, see 172; for ethics of civil war, see 172.1; for ethics of war, see 172.42; for treatment of children, see 179.2*

**.76**     Abortion

**.8**     **Vices, faults, failings**

> Not otherwise provided for
>
> Including anger, cheating, covetousness, envy, hatred, jealousy, pride, procrastination, sloth

**.9**     **Virtues**

> Not otherwise provided for
>
> Including cheerfulness, gentleness, gratitude, honesty, humility, modesty, patience, prudence, respect, self-control, self-reliance, toleration
>
> Class here virtue
>
> > *See also 171.3 for virtue ethics as an ethical system*

---

> ## 180–190  History, geographic treatment, biography

Class here development, description, critical appraisal, collected writings, biography of individual philosophers regardless of viewpoint

Class comprehensive works on geographic treatment in 100; class comprehensive works on history in 109; class comprehensive works on collected biography in 109.2. Class critical appraisal of an individual philosopher's thought on a specific topic with the topic, plus notation 092 from Table 1, e.g., critical appraisal of Kant's theory of knowledge 121.092

*See Manual at 180–190*

## 180     Ancient, medieval, eastern philosophy

### SUMMARY

| | |
|---|---|
| 180.01–.09 | Standard subdivisions of ancient, medieval, eastern philosophy |
| .1–.9 | Standard subdivisions of ancient philosophy |
| 181 | Eastern philosophy |
| 182 | Pre-Socratic Greek philosophies |
| 183 | Sophistic, Socratic, related Greek philosophies |
| 184 | Platonic philosophy |
| 185 | Aristotelian philosophy |
| 186 | Skeptic and Neoplatonic philosophies |
| 187 | Epicurean philosophy |
| 188 | Stoic philosophy |
| 189 | Medieval western philosophy |

.01–.09     Standard subdivisions of ancient, medieval, eastern philosophy

**.1–.8     Standard subdivisions of ancient philosophy**

**.9     History and geographic treatment of ancient philosophy**

Do not use for ancient eastern philosophy; class in 181

Class specific schools of ancient western philosophy in 182–188

## 181     Eastern philosophy

Ancient, medieval, modern

.001–.007     Standard subdivisions

.008     Groups of people

.008 8     Occupational and religious groups

Do not use for religious groups; class in 181.04–181.09

[.008 9]     Ethnic and national groups

Do not use; class in 181.1–181.9

.009     History

Do not use for geographic treatment; class in 181.1–181.9

.04–.09　　Philosophies based on specific religions

> Add to base number 181.0 the numbers following 29 in 294–299, e.g.,
> Jewish philosophy 181.06, comprehensive works on Islamic philosophy
> 181.07; however, for Confucian philosophy, see 181.112; for Taoist
> philosophy, see 181.114; for Hindu-Brahmanical philosophy, see
> 181.41–181.48
>
> > *For Christian philosophy, see 190. For an individual Islamic philosopher*
> > *associated with a specific area, see the area, e.g., Arabia 181.92*
>
> > *See Manual at 200 vs. 100*

---

> **181.1–181.9  Philosophy of specific places**

> Class comprehensive works in 181. Class philosophical schools in a place with
> the place, e.g., Neo-Confucian philosophy in Korea 181.115 (*not* 181.112)
>
> (Option: To give local emphasis and a shorter number to philosophy of a
> specific country, use one of the following:
>
> (Option A: Place it first by use of a letter or other symbol, e.g., philosophy
> of Lebanon 181.L [preceding 181.1]
>
> (Option B: Class it in 181.1; in that case class comprehensive works on
> philosophy of Far East and South Asia in 181.9)

.1　　　　**\*Far East and South Asia**

> > *For philosophy of India, see 181.4*
>
> (Option: To give local emphasis and a shorter number to philosophy of a
> specific country, class it in this number; in that case class comprehensive works
> on philosophy of the Far East and South Asia in 181.9)

.11　　　　\*China and Korea

> Standard subdivisions are added for China and Korea together, for China
> alone

---

> 181.112–181.115  Schools of Chinese philosophy

> Class Buddhist philosophy in 181.043; class comprehensive works in 181.11

.112　　　　†Confucian philosophy

> Including Neo-Confucian philosophy
>
> Class here the Four Books of Confucius; interdisciplinary works on
> Confucianism
>
> Class the Five Confucian Classics in 299.51282
>
> > *For religious aspects of Confucianism, see 299.512*

.114　　　　†Taoist philosophy

---

\*Do not use notation 09 from Table 1
†Do not use notation 092 from Table 1

.115       †Mohist, Dialecticianist, Legalist philosophies

.119       *Korea

.12       *Japan

      Class Shinto philosophy in 181.09561

.15       *Pakistan and Bangladesh

.16       *Indonesia

.17       *Philippines

.19       *Southeast Asia

      Add to base number 181.19 the numbers for countries only following —59 in notation 591–597 from Table 2, e.g., philosophy of Thailand 181.193; however, do not add notation 09 from Table 1 for history, geographic treatment, biography

      *For Indonesia, see 181.16; for Philippines, see 181.17*

**.2**       **\*Egypt**

**.3**       **\*Palestine; Israel**

      Class Jewish philosophy in 181.06

**.4**       **\*India**

      Class here Hindu-Brahmanical philosophy

      Class Buddhist philosophy in 181.043; class Jainist philosophy in 181.044

      *See also 181.15 for philosophy of Pakistan and Bangladesh*

.41       †Sankhya

.42       †Mimamsa

.43       †Nyaya

.44       †Vaiśeṣika

.45       †Yoga

      Class here interdisciplinary works on the practice of yoga and yoga as a philosophical school

      *For yoga as a religious and spiritual discipline, see 204.36; for Hindu yoga as a religious and spiritual discipline, see 294.5436; for hatha yoga, physical yoga, see 613.7046*

.452       †Patañjali's philosophy

.46       †Lokāyata

      Class here Cārvāka school, Indian materialism

.48       †Vedanta

*Do not use notation 09 from Table 1
†Do not use notation 092 from Table 1

| .482 | †Śaṅkarācārya (Advaita) |
|---|---|
| .483 | †Rāmānujāchārya (Viśiṣṭādvaita) |
| .484 | †Dualistic school |
| .484 1 | †Madhvāchārya (Dvaita) |
| .484 2 | †Bhedabheda |
| .484 3 | †Nimbarka (Dvaitādvaita) |
| .484 4 | †Vallabhāchārya (Śuddhādvaita) |

**.5    *Iran (Persia)**

**.6    *Iraq**

> Class here Assyria, Babylonia, Chaldea, ancient Mesopotamia

**.8    *Syria and Lebanon**

> Including ancient Phoenicia

**.9    *Other eastern philosophy**

> Including philosophy of Central Asia, former Soviet Asia, Arabic-speaking North Africa other than Egypt

.92      *Arabia

> Class here individual Arabian Islamic philosophers

> Class Islamic philosophy not limited to one country in 181.07. Class an individual Islamic philosopher associated with another area with the area, e.g., Persia 181.5

---

> **182–188  Ancient western philosophy**

> Class comprehensive works in 180

# 182    †Pre-Socratic Greek philosophies

> Class comprehensive works on Sophistic philosophy in 183.1

**.1    †Ionic philosophy**

**.2    †Pythagorean philosophy**

**.3    †Eleatic philosophy**

**.4    †Heraclitean philosophy**

**.5    †Empedoclean philosophy**

**.7    †Democritean philosophy**

**.8    †Anaxagorean philosophy**

*Do not use notation 09 from Table 1
†Do not use notation 092 from Table 1

## 183    †Sophistic, Socratic, related Greek philosophies

.1      †Sophistic philosophy

> *For pre-Socratic Greek philosophies, see 182*

.2      †Socratic philosophy

.4      †Cynic philosophy

.5      †Cyrenaic philosophy

.6      †Megaric philosophy

.7      †Elian and Eretrian philosophies

## 184    †Platonic philosophy

Class here comprehensive works on ancient and modern Platonism

> *For modern Platonism, see 141.2*

## 185    †Aristotelian philosophy

Class here comprehensive works on Aristotelian and Neo-Aristotelian philosophy

> *For Neo-Aristotelianism, see 149.91*

## 186    †Skeptic and Neoplatonic philosophies

.1      †Pyrrhonic philosophy

.2      †New Academy

.3      †Eclectic philosophy

.4      †Neoplatonic philosophy

Class here Alexandrian philosophy, comprehensive works on ancient and modern Neoplatonism

> *For modern Neoplatonism, see 141.2*

## 187    †Epicurean philosophy

## 188    †Stoic philosophy

## 189    *Medieval western philosophy

Class here early Christian philosophy

.2      †Patristic philosophy

.4      †Scholastic philosophy

> *For neo-scholasticism, neo-Thomism, see 149.91*

*Do not use notation 09 from Table 1
†Do not use notation 092 from Table 1

.5     †**Mystic philosophy**

# 190    Modern western and other noneastern philosophy

Class here comprehensive works on Christian philosophy, on modern philosophy, on western philosophy, on modern western philosophy, on European philosophy

Modern philosophy of areas not provided for in 180 is classed here, even if not in the western tradition, e.g., North American native philosophy 191.08997, traditional African philosophy 199.6

*For ancient western and European philosophy, see 180; for early and medieval Christian philosophy, medieval western and European philosophy, see 189*

*See also 181 for eastern philosophy*

(Option: To give local emphasis and a shorter number to philosophy of a specific country, use one of the following:

(Option A: Place it first by use of a letter or other symbol, e.g., philosophy of Mexico 19M [preceding 191]

(Option B: Class it in 191; in that case class philosophy of United States and Canada in 199.7)

[.882 7]          Christian philosophy

Do not use; class in 190

[.89]     Philosophy of ethnic and national groups

Do not use; class in 191–199

[.94–.99]     Specific continents, countries, localities in modern world

Do not use; class in 191–199

---

> ## 191–199  Modern western and other noneastern philosophy by continent or country

Philosophy of an individual group is classed in the notation at the region or country level only, e.g., Arapaho philosophy 191.08997354, Sámi philosophy 198.0899457

Class comprehensive works on European philosophy; on modern western philosophy not limited by continent or country in 190

---

†Do not use notation 092 from Table 1

# 191 *Philosophy of United States and Canada

Standard subdivisions are added for either or both topics in heading

Class here North American philosophy

*For Middle American and Mexican philosophy, see 199.72*

(Option: To give local emphasis and a shorter number to philosophy of a specific country, class it in this number; in that case class philosophy of United States and Canada in 199.7)

# 192 *Philosophy of British Isles

Standard subdivisions are added for philosophy of British Isles together, for philosophy of England alone, for philosophy of Ireland alone, for philosophy of Northern Ireland alone, for philosophy of Scotland alone, for philosophy of United Kingdom alone, for philosophy of Wales alone

# 193 *Philosophy of Germany and Austria

Standard subdivisions are added for either or both topics in heading

# 194 *Philosophy of France

# 195 *Philosophy of Italy

# 196 *Philosophy of Spain and Portugal

.1    *Spain

.9    *Portugal

# 197 *Philosophy of Russia

Class here philosophy of former Soviet Union

*See also 181.9 for philosophy of former Soviet Asia*

Philosophy of Azerbaijan relocated to 199.4754; philosophy of Armenia relocated to 199.4756; philosophy of Georgia relocated to 199.4758; philosophy of Moldova relocated to 199.476; philosophy of Ukraine relocated to 199.477; philosophy of Belarus relocated to 199.478; philosophy of Lithuania relocated to 199.4793; philosophy of Latvia relocated to 199.4796; philosophy of Estonia relocated to 199.4798

# 198 *Philosophy of Scandinavia and Finland

Standard subdivisions are added for Scandinavia and Finland together, for Scandinavia alone

.1    *Norway

.5    *Sweden

.8    *Finland

*Do not use notation 09 from Table 1

.9          *Denmark

# 199          *Philosophy in other geographic areas

Add to base number 199 notation 4–9 from Table 2 for continent or country only, e.g., philosophy of Azerbaijan 199.4754 [*formerly* 197]; philosophy of Armenia 199.4756 [*formerly* 197]; philosophy of Georgia 199.4758 [*formerly* 197]; philosophy of Moldova 199.476 [*formerly* 197]; philosophy of Ukraine 199.477 [*formerly* 197]; philosophy of Belarus 199.478 [*formerly* 197]; philosophy of Lithuania 199.4793 [*formerly* 197]; philosophy of Latvia 199.4796 [*formerly* 197]; philosophy of Estonia 199.4798 [*formerly* 197]; Mexican philosophy 199.72; however, do not add notation 09 from Table 1 for history, geographic treatment, biography; for Asian philosophy, philosophy of Arabic-speaking North Africa, see 181; for European philosophy, see 190; for comprehensive works on North American philosophy, see 191

*Do not use notation 09 from Table 1

# 200 Religion

Beliefs, attitudes, practices of individuals and groups with respect to the ultimate nature of existences and relationships within the context of revelation, deity, worship

Including public relations for religion

Class here comparative religion; religions other than Christianity; works dealing with various religions, with religious topics not applied to specific religions; syncretistic religious writings of individuals expressing personal views and not claiming to establish a new religion or to represent an old one

Class a specific topic in comparative religion, religions other than Christianity in 201–209. Class public relations for a specific religion or aspect of a religion with the religion or aspect, e.g., public relations for a local Christian church 254.4

> *For government policy on religion, see 322.1*
>
> *See also 306.6 for sociology of religion*
>
> *See Manual at T1—0882 and 200; also at 130 vs. 200; also at 200 vs. 100; also at 201–209 and 292–299*

(Option: To give preferred treatment or shorter numbers to a specific religion other than Christianity, use one of the two options described at 290)

### SUMMARY

| | |
|---|---|
| 200.1–.9 | **Standard subdivisions** |
| 201 | **Religious mythology, general classes of religion, interreligious relations and attitudes, social theology** |
| 202 | **Doctrines** |
| 203 | **Public worship and other practices** |
| 204 | **Religious experience, life, practice** |
| 205 | **Religious ethics** |
| 206 | **Leaders and organization** |
| 207 | **Missions and religious education** |
| 208 | **Sources** |
| 209 | **Sects and reform movements** |
| | |
| 210 | **Philosophy and theory of religion** |
| .1 | **Theory of philosophy of religion** |
| 211 | **Concepts of God** |
| 212 | **Existence of God, ways of knowing God, attributes of God** |
| 213 | **Creation** |
| 214 | **Theodicy** |
| 215 | **Science and religion** |
| 218 | **Humankind** |

| | |
|---|---|
| 220 | Bible |
| .01–.09 | Standard subdivisions and special topics of Bible |
| .1–.9 | Generalities |
| 221 | Old Testament (Tanakh) |
| 222 | Historical books of Old Testament |
| 223 | Poetic books of Old Testament |
| 224 | Prophetic books of Old Testament |
| 225 | New Testament |
| 226 | Gospels and Acts |
| 227 | Epistles |
| 228 | Revelation (Apocalypse) |
| 229 | Apocrypha, pseudepigrapha, intertestamental works |
| | |
| 230 | Christianity |
| .002–.007 | Standard subdivisions of Christianity |
| .01–.09 | Standard subdivisions and specific types of Christian theology |
| .1–.9 | Doctrines of specific denominations and sects |
| 231 | God |
| 232 | Jesus Christ and his family |
| 233 | Humankind |
| 234 | Salvation and grace |
| 235 | Spiritual beings |
| 236 | Eschatology |
| 238 | Creeds, confessions of faith, covenants, catechisms |
| 239 | Apologetics and polemics |
| | |
| 240 | Christian moral and devotional theology |
| 241 | Christian ethics |
| 242 | Devotional literature |
| 243 | Evangelistic writings for individuals and families |
| 246 | Use of art in Christianity |
| 247 | Church furnishings and related articles |
| 248 | Christian experience, practice, life |
| 249 | Christian observances in family life |
| | |
| 250 | Local Christian church and Christian religious orders |
| .9 | History, geographic treatment, biography |
| 251 | Preaching (Homiletics) |
| 252 | Texts of sermons |
| 253 | Pastoral office and work (Pastoral theology) |
| 254 | Parish administration |
| 255 | Religious congregations and orders |
| 259 | Pastoral care of families, of specific groups of people |
| | |
| 260 | Christian social and ecclesiastical theology |
| .9 | History, geographic treatment, biography |
| 261 | Social theology and interreligious relations and attitudes |
| 262 | Ecclesiology |
| 263 | Days, times, places of religious observance |
| 264 | Public worship |
| 265 | Sacraments, other rites and acts |
| 266 | Missions |
| 267 | Associations for religious work |
| 268 | Religious education |
| 269 | Spiritual renewal |
| | |
| 270 | History, geographic treatment, biography of Christianity |
| .01–.09 | Standard subdivisions |
| .1–.8 | Historical periods |
| 271 | Religious congregations and orders in church history |
| 272 | Persecutions in general church history |
| 273 | Doctrinal controversies and heresies in general church history |
| 274–279 | Christianity by specific continents, countries, localities in modern world |

| | |
|---|---|
| 280 | **Denominations and sects of Christian church** |
| .01–.09 | **Standard subdivisions and special topics** |
| .2–.4 | **Branches** |
| 281 | **Early church and Eastern churches** |
| 282 | **Roman Catholic Church** |
| 283 | **Anglican churches** |
| 284 | **Protestant denominations of Continental origin and related bodies** |
| 285 | **Presbyterian churches, Reformed churches centered in America, Congregational churches, Puritanism** |
| 286 | **Baptist, Restoration movement, Adventist churches** |
| 287 | **Methodist churches; churches related to Methodism** |
| 289 | **Other denominations and sects** |
| | |
| 290 | **Other religions** |
| 292 | **Classical religion (Greek and Roman religion)** |
| 293 | **Germanic religion** |
| 294 | **Religions of Indic origin** |
| 295 | **Zoroastrianism (Mazdaism, Parseeism)** |
| 296 | **Judaism** |
| 297 | **Islam, Babism, Bahai Faith** |
| 299 | **Religions not provided for elsewhere** |

---

> **200.1–200.9 Standard subdivisions**

Limited to comparative religion, religion in general

.1 **Systems, scientific principles, psychology of religion**

Do not use for philosophy and theory; class in 210

.11 Systems

[.12] Classification

Do not use; class in 201.4

[.14] Communication

Do not use; class in 210.14

.15 Scientific principles

Class philosophic treatment of the relation of science and religion in 215

.19 Psychological principles

Class here psychology of religion

.2–.5 **Standard subdivisions**

[.6] **Organizations and management**

Do not use; class in 206

.7 **Education, research, related topics**

.71 Education

> Class here religion as an academic subject

> Class religious education to inculcate religious life and practice, comprehensive works on religious education in 207.5

> > *See also 379.28 for place of religion in public schools*

> > *See Manual at 207.5, 268 vs. 200.71, 230.071, 292–299*

**.8 Groups of people**

> Class here attitudes of religions to social groups; discrimination, equality, inequality, prejudice

**.9 History, geographic treatment, biography**

> *See Manual at 200.9 vs. 294, 299.5*

.901 2 To 4000 B.C.

> Do not use for prehistoric religions; class in 201.42

.92 Biography

> *See Manual at 200.92 and 201–209, 292–299*

---

> **201–209 Specific aspects of religion**

> Class treatment of religious topics with respect to philosophy of religion, natural theology in 210; class treatment with respect to Christianity in 230–280; class treatment with respect to a specific religion other than Christianity in 292–299; class comprehensive works on comparative religion in 200

> > *See Manual at 200.92 and 201–209, 292–299; also at 201–209 and 292–299*

**201 Religious mythology, general classes of religion, interreligious relations and attitudes, social theology**

### SUMMARY

| | |
|---|---|
| 201.3 | **Mythology and mythological foundations** |
| .4 | **General classes of religion** |
| .5 | **Interreligious relations** |
| .6 | **Religions and secular disciplines** |
| .7 | **Attitudes of religions toward social issues** |

[.012] Classification

> Do not use; class in 201.4

**.3 Mythology and mythological foundations**

> Stories of primeval history, beings, origins, and customs archetypally significant in the sacred life, doctrine, and ritual of religions

> Class myths on a specific subject with the subject, e.g., creation myths 202.4

> > *See Manual at 398.2 vs. 201.3, 230, 270, 292–299*

**.4**       **General classes of religion**

Including monotheistic, nontheistic, pantheistic, polytheistic religions

Class here classification of religions

Class concepts of God or the gods in world religions in 202.11; class philosophic treatment of concepts of God in 211

**.42**       Prehistoric religions

Use of this number for religions of nonliterate societies discontinued; class in 201.4

**.43**       Goddess religions

*See also 202.114 for female goddesses*

**.44**       Shamanism

Class shamanism in a specific religion with the religion, e.g., shamanism in religions of North American native origin 299.71144

**.5**       **Interreligious relations**

Including relations of religions with irreligion

**.6**       **Religions and secular disciplines**

Class guides to religious life and practice on specific topics in secular disciplines in 204.4

*For attitudes of religions toward social sciences, see 201.7*

**.600 01–.600 09**       Standard subdivisions

**.600 1–.619 9**       Computer science, information, philosophy, parapsychology and occultism, psychology

Add to base number 201.6 notation 001–199, e.g., religions and psychology 201.615

**.64–.69**       Language, natural sciences, mathematics, technology, arts, literature, rhetoric, geography, history

Add to base number 201.6 notation 400–900, e.g., religions and science 201.65; however, for ecology, see 201.77

**.7**       **Attitudes of religions toward social issues**

Attitudes of religions toward and influences on secular matters

Class here religion and culture, social theology

Class human ecology in 201.77; class guides to religious life and practice on specific topics in the social sciences in 204.4; class sociology of religion in 306.6

*For attitudes toward social groups, see 200.8; for attitudes toward various religions, see 201.5*

*See also 205 for religious ethics*

.72          Political affairs

Attitudes toward and influences on political activities and ideologies

Including civil war and revolution

Class secular view of religiously oriented political theories and ideologies in 320.55; class secular view of relation of state to religious organizations and groups in 322.1

*See Manual at 322.1 vs. 201.72, 261.7, 292–299*

.721         Theocracy

Supremacy of organized religion over civil government

.723         Civil rights

Including citizenship, religious freedom

.727         International affairs

.727 3            War and peace

Including conscientious objectors, disarmament, pacifism

*For nuclear weapons and nuclear war, see 201.7275*

.727 5            Nuclear weapons and nuclear war

.73          Economics

Class socioeconomic problems in 201.76

*For environment, natural resources, see 201.77*

.76          Social problems and services

Class here socioeconomic problems

*See also 361.75 for welfare work of religious organizations*

.762–.763    Specific social problems

Add to base number 201.76 the numbers following 36 in 362–363, e.g., poor people 201.7625, hunger 201.7638; however, for population problems, see 201.7; for environmental problems, see 201.77

.764         Crime and punishment

.77          Environment

Class here ecology, human ecology, environmental problems, natural resources, pollution

Class environmental ethics in 205.691

# 202          Doctrines

Class here beliefs, apologetics, polemics; comprehensive works on theology

*For social theologies, see 201.7; for religious ethics, see 205*

**.1          Objects of worship and veneration**

Class here animism, spiritism

| | |
|---|---|
| .11 | God, gods, goddesses, divinities and deities |

Class here supernatural beings

Class concepts of God in philosophy of religion in 211

| | |
|---|---|
| .112 | Attributes of God, of the gods |

*For attributes of male gods, see 202.113; for attributes of female goddesses, see 202.114*

| | |
|---|---|
| .113 | Male gods |
| .114 | Female goddesses |

*See also 201.43 for goddess religions*

| | |
|---|---|
| .117 | Relation to the world |

Including miracles, prophecy, providence, revelation, relation to and action in history

*For creation and cosmology, see 202.4*

| | |
|---|---|
| .118 | Theodicy |

Vindication of God's justice and goodness in permitting existence of evil and suffering

| | |
|---|---|
| .12 | Nature |

Including fire, sex, sun, trees, water

*See also 203.5 for sacred places*

| | |
|---|---|
| .13 | Persons |

Including ancestors, the dead, heroes, monarchs, saints

| | |
|---|---|
| .14 | Personified abstractions |
| .15 | Good spirits |

Class here angels

| | |
|---|---|
| .16 | Evil spirits |

Class here demons, devils

| | |
|---|---|
| .18 | Images |
| **.2** | **Humankind** |

Including atonement, creation of humankind, repentance, salvation, sin, soul

Class here comprehensive works on karma

Class creation of the world in 202.4

*For eschatology, see 202.3. For a specific aspect of karma, see the aspect, e.g., karma as a concept in Buddhist ethics 294.35*

| | |
|---|---|
| **.3** | **Eschatology** |

Including death, end of the world, heaven, hell, immortality, other worlds, punishments, purgatory, resurrection, rewards

.37          Reincarnation

**.4          Creation and cosmology**

*For creation of humankind, see 202.2*

# 203          Public worship and other practices

Practices predominantly public or collective in character

Unless other instructions are given, class a subject with aspects in two or more subdivisions of 203 in the number coming first, e.g., religious healing and ceremonies connected with it 203.1 (*not* 203.8)

Class leaders and organization in 206; class missions and religious education in 207; class comprehensive works on worship in 204.3

**.1          Religious healing**

*See Manual at 615.852 vs. 203.1, 234.131, 292–299*

**.2          Divination**

Including omens, oracles, prophecies

Class comprehensive works on divination in 133.3

**.3          Witchcraft**

Class religions based on modern revivals of witchcraft in 299.94; class comprehensive works on witchcraft in 133.43

**.4          Offerings, sacrifices, penances**

.42          Human sacrifice

**.5          Sacred places and pilgrimages**

Standard subdivisions are added for sacred places and pilgrimages together, for sacred places alone

Class here grottoes, holy buildings, pagodas, shrines, temples

Class monasteries in 206.57

.509 3–.509 9          Specific continents, countries, localities

Class here pilgrimages to specific sacred places

.51          Pilgrimages

[.510 93–.510 99]          Specific continents, countries, localities

Do not use; class in 203.5093–203.5099

**.6          Sacred times**

Including holy days, religious calendar, religious festivals

*See Manual at 203.6, 263.9, 292–299 vs. 394.265–394.267*

**.7**          **Symbolism, symbolic objects, sounds**

Including mandalas, mantras

Class here religious use, significance, purpose of the arts

*See also 201.67 for attitudes of religions toward the arts*

**.8**          **Rites and ceremonies**

Conduct and texts

Including liturgy, music, processions, public feasts and fasts, public prayer

Class interdisciplinary works on sacred music in 781.7; class interdisciplinary works on sacred vocal music in 782.22

.81          Birth rites

.82          Initiation rites

.85          Marriage rites

.88          Funeral and mourning rites

Standard subdivisions are added for either or both topics in heading

# 204          Religious experience, life, practice

Practices predominantly private or individual in character

Class here spirituality

Class religious ethics in 205

**.2**          **Religious experience**

Including conversion, enlightenment

.22          Mysticism

**.3**          **Worship, meditation, yoga**

Class here practical works on prayer, on contemplation; comprehensive works on worship

*For public worship, see 203*

.32          Devotional literature

Including meditations

.33          Prayer books

.35          Meditation

.36 Yoga

Religious and spiritual discipline

Including kundalini yoga

Class interdisciplinary works on yoga in 181.45

*For Hindu kundalini yoga, see 294.5436*

*See also 613.7046 for hatha yoga, physical yoga*

**.4** **Religious life and practice**

Class here guides to religious life and practice

*For worship, meditation, yoga, see 204.3*

[.408 5] Relatives

Do not use; class in 204.41

.408 6 People by miscellaneous social attributes

[.408 655] Married people

Do not use; class in 204.41

.408 7 Gifted people

Do not use for people with disabilities and illnesses; class in 204.42

.41 Marriage and family life

Including adoption, divorce, interreligious marriage, religious training of children in the home, single-parent family

Class here comprehensive works on marriage

*For abuse within the family, see 201.7628292; for marriage rites, see 203.85; for ethics of marriage, see 205.63*

.42 People experiencing illness, trouble, addiction, bereavement

*See Manual at 616.86 vs. 158.1, 204.42, 248.8629, 292–299, 362.29*

.46 Individual observances

Not provided for elsewhere

Including almsgiving, ceremonial and ritual observances, dietary limitations, observance of restrictions and limitations

.47 Asceticism

Including practice of celibacy, fasting and abstinence, poverty, solitude

**205** **Religious ethics**

Including conscience, sin

**.6** **Specific moral issues, sins, vices, virtues**

Add to base number 205.6 the numbers following 17 in 172–179, e.g., sexual relations 205.66, morality of discriminatory practices 205.675

## 206 Leaders and organization

Class here management

**.1 Leaders and their work**

Variant names: clergy, gurus, messiahs, priests, prophets, shamans

Role, function, duties

Including pastoral counseling and preaching

Class theologians in 202. Class a specific activity of a leader with the activity, e.g., religious healing by shamans 203.1

*For founders of religions, see 206.3*

*See Manual at 200.92 and 201–209, 292–299*

**[.109 2]** Biography

Do not use; class as instructed in Manual at 200.92 and 292–299

**.3 Founders of religions**

**[.309 2]** Biography

Do not use; class as instructed in Manual at 200.92 and 292–299

**.5 Organizations and organization**

Including associations, congregations, institutions, orders, parties; exercise of religious authority

Class laws and decisions in 208.4

**.57** Monasticism and monasteries

Class here religious orders

## 207 Missions and religious education

**.2 Missions**

**.5 Religious education**

Class here comprehensive works on religious education and religion as an academic subject

*For education in and teaching of comparative religion, religion as an academic subject, see 200.71; for religious training of children in the home, see 204.41*

*See Manual at 207.5, 268 vs. 200.71, 230.071, 292–299*

## 208 Sources

Class theology based on sacred sources in 202

**.2 Sacred books and scriptures**

*For sacred books and scriptures of sects and reform movements, see 208.5*

**.3**     **Oral traditions**

> *For oral traditions of sects and reform movements, see 208.5*

**.4**     **Laws and decisions**

Class civil law relating to religious matters in 340

> *For laws and decisions of sects and reform movements, see 208.5*

> *See also 364.188 for offenses against religion as defined and penalized by the state*

**.5**     **Sources of sects and reform movements**

**209**     **Sects and reform movements**

Class here new religious movements

Class specific aspects of sects and reform movements in 201–208

> *For specific sects and reform movements, see 280–290*

> *See Manual at 299.93*

# 210     Philosophy and theory of religion

Class here natural theology, philosophical theology; works that use observation and interpretation of evidence in nature, speculation, and reasoning, but not revelation or appeal to authoritative scriptures, to examine religious beliefs

Class a specific topic treated with respect to religions based on revelation or authority with the topic in 201–209, e.g., concepts of God in world religions 202.11; class a specific topic with respect to a specific religion with the religion, e.g., Christian concepts of God 231

(Option: To give local emphasis and a shorter number to a specific religion other than Christianity, class it in this number, and add to base number 21 the numbers following the base number for that religion in 292–299, e.g., Hinduism 210, Mahabharata 219.23; in that case class philosophy and theory of religion in 200, its subdivisions 211–218 in 200.1. Another option is described at 290)

**.1**     **Theory of philosophy of religion**

Including methodology of the philosophy of religion

**[.11]**     Systems

Do not use; class in 200.11

**[.12]**     Classification

Do not use; class in 201.4

**.14**     Communication

**[.15]**     Scientific principles

Do not use; class in 200.15

**[.19]**     Psychological principles

Do not use; class in 200.19

**211** **Concepts of God**

Including anthropomorphism

Class here comprehensive works on God, on The Holy

Class God, gods and goddesses in comparative religion in 202.11

*For existence of God, ways of knowing God, attributes of God, miracles, see 212*

**.2** **Pantheism**

**.3** **Theism**

*For pantheism, see 211.2*

.32 Polytheism

.33 Dualism

.34 Monotheism

**.4** **Rationalism (Free thought)**

**.5** **Deism**

**.6** **Humanism and secularism**

Standard subdivisions are added for either or both topics in heading

**.7** **Agnosticism and skepticism**

Standard subdivisions are added for either or both topics in heading

**.8** **Atheism**

**212** **Existence of God, ways of knowing God, attributes of God**

Including miracles

**.1** **Existence of God**

Including proofs

**.6** **Ways of knowing God**

Including role of faith, reason and revelation

Class proofs in 212.1

**.7** **Attributes of God**

Including love, omniscience

**213** **Creation**

Including creation of life and human life, evolution versus creation, evolution as method of creation

*See Manual at 231.7652 vs. 213, 500, 576.8*

**214**      **Theodicy**

> Vindication of God's justice and goodness in permitting existence of evil and suffering

> Class here good and evil

**.8**      **Providence**

**215**      **Science and religion**

> Including technology and religion

> Class religion and scientific theories of creation in 213

>> *See also 201.65 for various religions and science; also 261.55 for Christianity and science*

**.2**      **Astronomy**

> Including cosmology

**.3**      **Physics**

**.7**      **Life sciences**

> Including natural history, paleontology

> Class evolution versus creation, evolution as method of creation in 213; class anthropology and religion, ethnology and religion in 218

**[216]**      **[Unassigned]**

> Most recently used in Edition 21

**[217]**      **[Unassigned]**

> Most recently used in Edition 18

**218**      **Humankind**

> Including anthropology and religion, ethnology and religion, immortality

> *For creation of humankind, human evolution, see 213*

**[219]**      **[Unassigned]**

> Most recently used in Edition 19

**220**      **Bible**

> Holy Scriptures of Judaism and Christianity

> Class Christian Biblical theology in 230.041; class Biblical precepts in Christian codes of conduct in 241.52–241.54; class Jewish Biblical theology in 296.3; class Biblical precepts in Jewish codes of conduct in 296.36

> (If option A under 290 is chosen, class here sources of the specified religion; class Bible in 298)

## SUMMARY

.01–.02    Standard subdivisions

[.03]    Dictionaries, encyclopedias, concordances

> Do not use for dictionaries and encyclopedias; class in 220.3. Do not use for concordances; class in 220.4–220.5

.04    Special topics of Bible

.046    Apocalyptic passages

> Class apocalyptic passages in a book or group of books with the book or group of books, plus notation 0046 from add table under 221–229, e.g., apocalyptic passages in the prophets 224.0046, in Book of Daniel 224.50046

> *For Revelation (Apocalypse), see 228*

.05–.08    Standard subdivisions

.09    History, geographic treatment, biography

> Do not use for geography, history, chronology, persons of Bible lands in Bible times; class in 220.9

> Class the canon in 220.12

## SUMMARY

---

> ## 220.1–220.9 Generalities

> Class comprehensive works in 220. Class generalities applied to a specific part of the Bible with the part, plus notation 01–09 from add table under 221–229, e.g., a commentary on Job 223.107

.1    **Origins and authenticity**

| | | |
|---|---|---|
| .12 | | Canon |

Class here selection of the books accepted as Holy Scripture

.13 Inspiration

The Bible as revelation (word of God)

Including authority of Bible

.132 Inerrancy

.15 Biblical prophecy and prophecies

Class Christian messianic prophecies in 232.12; class Christian eschatological prophecies in 236; class Jewish messianic and eschatological prophecies in 296.33

*See also 224 for prophetic books of Old Testament*

**.3** **Encyclopedias and topical dictionaries**

*For dictionaries of specific texts, see 220.4–220.5*

---

> **220.4–220.5 Texts, versions, translations**

Class here critical appraisal of language and style; concordances, indexes, dictionaries of specific texts; complete texts; selections from more than one part; paraphrases

Class texts accompanied by commentaries in 220.77; class comprehensive works in 220.4. Class selections compiled for a specific purpose with the purpose, e.g., selections for daily meditations 242.2

**.4** **Original texts, early versions, early translations**

Class here original texts accompanied by modern translations, comprehensive works on texts and versions

*For modern versions and translations, see 220.5*

.404 Textual criticism and word studies

.404 6 Textual criticism (Lower criticism)

Use of scientific means to ascertain the actual original texts

.404 7 Theological studies of words or phrases

---

> 220.42–220.49 Texts in specific languages

Add to each subdivision identified by † the numbers following 220.404 in 220.4046–220.4047, regardless of specific version, e.g., textual criticism of Bible in Latin, of Vulgate 220.476, of Old Testament in Greek, of Septuagint 221.486

Class comprehensive works in 220.4

.42 †Aramaic versions

†Add as instructed under 220.42–220.49

| .43 | †Syriac versions |
| .44 | †Hebrew version |
| .45 | †Samaritan versions |
| .46 | Other Semitic language versions |

> Including Arabic, Ge'ez

| .47 | †Latin versions |
| .48 | †Greek versions |
| .49 | Other early versions |

> Including Armenian, Coptic

**.5** **Modern versions and translations**

.51 Polyglot

.52 Versions in English and Anglo-Saxon

> Standard subdivisions are added for versions in English and Anglo-Saxon, for English alone
>
> Class works containing translations in English and one other modern language with the other language, e.g., the Bible in English and German 220.531

.520 01–.520 09 Standard subdivisions

---

> 220.520 1–220.520 9 English

> Add to each subdivision identified by * as follows:
> 01–02 Standard subdivisions
> [03] Dictionaries, encyclopedias, concordances
> Do not use; class in 3
> 05–08 Standard subdivisions
> 09 Geographic treatment and biography
> Do not use for history of the translation; class in 8
> 2 Standard editions
> 3 Concordances, indexes, dictionaries
> 4 Special editions
> Including annotated editions, study editions, editions notable for illustrations
> 6 Selections
> 7 Paraphrases
> 8 History, criticism, explanation of the translation

> Class comprehensive works in 220.52

.520 1 English versions before 1582

> Including Coverdale, Tyndale, Wycliffe versions

---

†Add as instructed under 220.42–220.49

| | |
|---|---|
| .520 2 | *Douay version |

                 Class here Rheims-Douay, Rheims-Douay-Challoner versions

                     *See also 220.5205 for Confraternity-Douay-Challoner version*

| | |
|---|---|
| .520 3 | *Authorized version (King James version) |
| .520 4 | Revised version |

                 Including English Revised (1881–1885), American Revised (American Standard) (1901) versions

| | |
|---|---|
| .520 42 | *Revised Standard version (1946–1957) |
| .520 43 | *New Revised Standard version (1990) |
| .520 5 | *Confraternity Bible and New American Bible |

                 Class here Confraternity-Douay-Challoner version

                 Subdivisions are added for either or both topics in heading

                     *See also 220.5202 for Rheims-Douay, Rheims-Douay-Challoner versions*

| | |
|---|---|
| .520 6 | *New English Bible and Revised English Bible |

                 Subdivisions are added for either or both topics in heading

| | |
|---|---|
| .520 7 | *Jerusalem Bible and New Jerusalem Bible |

                 Subdivisions are added for either or both topics in heading

| | |
|---|---|
| .520 8 | Other English translations since 1582 |

                 Including New King James, New Century versions

                 *For translations by individuals, see 220.5209*

| | |
|---|---|
| .520 81 | *New International Version |
| .520 82 | *Today's English Bible (Good News Bible) |
| .520 83 | *Living Bible and New Living Translation |

                 Subdivisions are added for either or both topics in heading

| | |
|---|---|
| .520 9 | Translations by individuals |

                 Including Goodspeed, Knox, Moffatt, Phillips

| | |
|---|---|
| .529 | Anglo-Saxon |
| .53–.59 | Versions in other languages |

                 Add to base number 220.5 notation 3–9 from Table 6, e.g., the Bible in German 220.531

                 Works containing translations in two modern languages other than English are classed with the language coming later in Table 6; in more than two modern languages in 220.51

---

*Add as instructed under 220.5201–220.5209

**.6** **Interpretation and criticism (Exegesis)**

Class Christian meditations based on Biblical passages and intended for devotional use in 242.5; class material about the Bible intended for use in preparing Christian sermons in 251; class Christian sermons based on Biblical passages in 252; class material about the Bible for preparation of Jewish sermons and texts of Jewish sermons in 296.47; class Jewish meditations based on Biblical passages and intended for devotional use in 296.72

*For textual criticism, see 220.4046; for commentaries, see 220.7*

.601 Philosophy and theory

Class here hermeneutics

.61 General introductions to the Bible

Including isagogics (introductory studies prior to actual exegesis)

.64 Symbolism and typology

Standard subdivisions are added for either or both topics in heading

Class here interpretation of specific symbols

.65 Harmonies

.66 Literary criticism

Literary examination of the text in order to reach conclusions about its meaning, structure, authorship, date

Class here higher criticism, internal criticism, redaction criticism

Class language and style of specific texts in 220.4–220.5

*See also 809.93522 for the Bible as literature*

.663 Form criticism

Analysis of preliterary or oral forms and traditions in Biblical text

.67 Historical criticism

Interpretation of texts in light of the cultural, historical, religious, social milieu in which written

Class form criticism in 220.663

.68 Mythological, allegorical, numerical, astronomical interpretations

Including mythology in the Bible, demythologizing

**.7** **Commentaries**

Criticism and interpretation arranged in textual order

.77 Commentaries with text

**.8** **Nonreligious subjects treated in Bible**

Class a religious subject treated in Bible with the specific religion and topic, e.g., Christian theology 230, Jewish theology 296.3

.800 01–.800 09 Standard subdivisions

.800 1–.899 9      Specific nonreligious subjects

> Add to base number 220.8 notation 001–999, e.g., natural sciences in Bible 220.85; however, for geography, history, chronology, persons of Bible lands in Bible times, see 220.9

**.9**      **Geography, history, chronology, persons of Bible lands in Bible times**

> Class general history of Bible lands in ancient world in 930

.91      Geography

> Class here description and civilization
>
> Class civilization treated separately from geography in 220.95

.92      Collected biography

> Class an individual person with the part of the Bible in which the person is chiefly considered, e.g., Abraham 222.11092
>
> *See Manual at 220.92; also at 230–280*

.93      Archaeology (Material remains)

.95      History

> Including civilization treated separately from geography
>
> Class geographic description and civilization treated together in 220.91

.950 01–.950 09      Standard subdivisions

.950 5      Bible stories retold

> Including picture books

---

> ## 221–229 Specific parts of Bible, Apocrypha, pseudepigrapha, intertestamental works

> Add to each subdivision identified by * as follows (subdivisions from this table may be added for a part of any work that has its own number):
>
> 001–009     Standard subdivisions
>> Add to 0 the numbers following 220 in 220.01–220.09, e.g., apocalyptic passages in a book or group of books 0046
>
> 01–08     Generalities
>> Add to 0 the numbers following 220 in 220.1–220.8, e.g., interpretation of the work or of a part of the work 06
>
> 09     Geography, history, chronology, persons
>> Add to 09 the numbers following 221.9 in 221.91–221.95, e.g., biography 092
>
> Class comprehensive works in 220

# 221        Old Testament (Tanakh)

Holy Scriptures of Judaism, Old Testament of Christianity

Class Jewish Biblical theology in 296.3; class Biblical precepts in Jewish codes of conduct in 296.36

*For historical books, see 222; for Torah, see 222.1; for poetic books, Ketuvim, see 223; for prophetic books, Nevi'im, see 224*

*See Manual at 221*

[.03]        Dictionaries, encyclopedias, concordances

Do not use for dictionaries and encyclopedias; class in 221.3. Do not use for concordances; class in 221.4–221.5

.04        Special topics of Old Testament

.044            Megillot (Five scrolls)

*For a specific book of Megillot, see the book, e.g., Ruth 222.35*

.046            Apocalyptic passages

Class apocalyptic passages in a book or group of books with the book or group of books, plus notation 0046 from add table under 221–229, e.g., apocalyptic passages in the prophets 224.0046, in Book of Daniel 224.50046

.09        History, geographic treatment, biography

Do not use for geography, history, chronology, persons of Bible lands in Bible times; class in 221.9

Class the canon in 221.12

**.1–.8        Generalities**

Add to base number 221 the numbers following 220 in 220.1–220.8, e.g., Targums 221.42, commentaries 221.7

**.9        Geography, history, chronology, persons of Old Testament lands in Old Testament times**

Class general history of ancient areas in 930

.91        Geography

Class here description and civilization

Class civilization treated separately from geography in 221.95

.92        Persons

*See Manual at 220.92; also at 230–280*

.922            Collected treatment

.93        Archaeology (Material remains)

.95 History

Including civilization treated separately from geography

Class geographic description and civilization treated together in 221.91

.950 01–.950 09 Standard subdivisions

.950 5 Old Testament stories retold

Including picture books

---

> ## 222–224 Books of Old Testament

Class comprehensive works in 221

*See Manual at 221*

(Option: To arrange the books of the Old Testament (Tanakh) as found in Jewish Bibles, use one of the following:
(Option A: Use the optional arrangement of 222–224 given in the Manual at 221
(Option B: Class in 296.11

(A table giving the three numbers for each book is given in the Manual at 221)

## 222 *Historical books of Old Testament

.1 *Pentateuch (Torah)

Class here Hexateuch

*For Joshua, see 222.2*

.11 *Genesis

.12 *Exodus

*For Ten Commandments, see 222.16*

.13 *Leviticus

.14 *Numbers

.15 *Deuteronomy

*For Ten Commandments, see 222.16*

.16 *Ten Commandments (Decalogue)

Class Ten Commandments as code of conduct in Christianity in 241.52; class Ten Commandments as code of conduct in Judaism in 296.36

.2 *Joshua (Josue)

.3 *Judges and Ruth

.32 *Judges

.35 *Ruth

*Add as instructed under 221–229

| | |
|---|---|
| **.4** | **\*Samuel** |
| .43 | \*Samuel 1 |
| | Variant name: Kings 1 |
| .44 | \*Samuel 2 |
| | Variant name: Kings 2 |
| **.5** | **\*Kings** |
| .53 | \*Kings 1 |
| | Variant name: Kings 3 |
| .54 | \*Kings 2 |
| | Variant name: Kings 4 |
| **.6** | **\*Chronicles (Paralipomena)** |
| .63 | \*Chronicles 1 (Paralipomenon 1) |
| .64 | \*Chronicles 2 (Paralipomenon 2) |
| **.7** | **\*Ezra (Esdras 1)** |

> *See also 229.1 for Esdras 1 (also called Esdras 3) of the Apocrypha*

**.8**     **\*Nehemiah (Esdras 2, Nehemias)**

> *See also 229.1 for Esdras 2 (also called Esdras 4) of the Apocrypha*

(.86)     \*Tobit (Tobias)

> (Optional number; prefer 229.22)

(.88)     \*Judith

> (Optional number; prefer 229.24)

**.9**     **\*Esther**

> (Option: Class here deuterocanonical part of Esther; prefer 229.27)

# 223     **\*Poetic books of Old Testament**

> Class here Ketuvim (Hagiographa, Writings), wisdom literature

> *For Apocryphal wisdom literature, see 229.3. For a specific book of Ketuvim not provided for here, see the book, e.g., Ruth 222.35*

**.1**     **\*Job**

**.2**     **\*Psalms**

**.7**     **\*Proverbs**

**.8**     **\*Ecclesiastes (Qohelet)**

\*Add as instructed under 221–229

**.9**        **\*Song of Solomon (Canticle of Canticles, Song of Songs)**

(.96)        \*Wisdom of Solomon (Wisdom)

           (Optional number; prefer 229.3)

(.98)        \*Ecclesiasticus (Sirach)

           (Optional number; prefer 229.4)

# 224        *Prophetic books of Old Testament

Class here Major Prophets, Nevi'im

*For a specific book of Nevi'im not provided for here, see the book, e.g., Joshua 222.2*

**.1**        **\*Isaiah (Isaias)**

**.2**        **\*Jeremiah (Jeremias)**

**.3**        **\*Lamentations**

(.37)        \*Baruch

           (Optional number; prefer 229.5)

**.4**        **\*Ezekiel (Ezechiel)**

**.5**        **\*Daniel**

           (Option: Class here Song of the Three Children, Susanna, Bel and the Dragon; prefer 229.6)

**.6**        **\*Hosea (Osee)**

**.7**        **\*Joel**

**.8**        **\*Amos**

**.9**        **\*Minor Prophets**

           *For Hosea, see 224.6; for Joel, see 224.7; for Amos, see 224.8*

.91        \*Obadiah (Abdias)

.92        \*Jonah (Jonas)

.93        \*Micah (Micheas)

.94        \*Nahum

.95        \*Habakkuk (Habacuc)

.96        \*Zephaniah (Sophonias)

.97        \*Haggai (Aggeus)

.98        \*Zechariah (Zacharias)

.99        \*Malachi (Malachias)

\*Add as instructed under 221–229

(.997)  *Maccabees 1 and 2 (Machabees 1 and 2)

> (Optional number; prefer 229.73)

## 225 New Testament

> *For Gospels and Acts, see 226; for Epistles, see 227; for Revelation, see 228*

[.03]  Dictionaries, encyclopedias, concordances

> Do not use for dictionaries and encyclopedias; class in 225.3. Do not use for concordances; class in 225.4–225.5

.04  Special topics of New Testament

.046  Apocalyptic passages

> Class apocalyptic passages in a book or group of books with the book or group of books, plus notation 0046 from add table under 221–229, e.g., apocalyptic passages in Gospels 226.0046, in Gospel of Mark 226.30046

> *For Revelation (Apocalypse), see 228*

.09  History, geographic treatment, biography

> Do not use for geography, history, chronology, persons of Bible lands in Bible times; class in 225.9

> Class the canon in 225.12

**.1–.8  Generalities**

> Add to base number 225 the numbers following 220 in 220.1–220.8, e.g., Authorized Version 225.5203

**.9  Geography, history, chronology, persons of New Testament lands in New Testament times**

> Add to base number 225.9 the numbers following 221.9 in 221.91–221.95, e.g., individual persons 225.92; however, for Jesus Christ, Mary, Joseph, Joachim, Anne, John the Baptist, see 232

> *See Manual at 220.92; also at 230–280*

## 226 *Gospels and Acts

> Class here synoptic Gospels

> Subdivisions are added for Gospels and Acts together, for Gospels alone

> *See Manual at 230–280*

.095 05  Gospel stories retold

> Number built according to instructions under 221–229

> Class Jesus as a historical figure, biography and specific events in life of Jesus in 232.9

**.1  Harmonies of Gospels**

*Add as instructed under 221–229

> **226.2–226.5 Specific Gospels**

   Class comprehensive works in 226

   *For miracles, see 226.7; for parables, see 226.8*

.2  **\*Matthew**

   Class Golden Rule as code of conduct in 241.54

   *For Sermon on the Mount, see 226.9*

.3  **\*Mark**

.4  **\*Luke**

   Class Golden Rule as code of conduct in 241.54

   *For Sermon on the Mount, see 226.9*

.5  **\*John**

   Class here comprehensive works on Johannine literature

   *For Epistles of John, see 227.94; for Revelation (Apocalypse), see 228*

.6  **\*Acts of the Apostles**

.7  **\*Miracles**

   Class miracles in context of Jesus' life in 232.955

.8  **\*Parables**

   Class parables in context of Jesus' life in 232.954

.9  **\*Sermon on the Mount**

   Class Sermon on the Mount as code of conduct in 241.53

.93  **\*Beatitudes**

.96  **\*Lord's Prayer**

# 227  **\*Epistles**

   Class here Pauline epistles

.1  **\*Romans**

.2  **\*Corinthians 1**

   Class here comprehensive works on Epistles to Corinthians

   *For Corinthians 2, see 227.3*

.3  **\*Corinthians 2**

.4  **\*Galatians**

\*Add as instructed under 221–229

| .5  | **\*Ephesians** |
|-----|-----------------|
| .6  | **\*Philippians** |
| .7  | **\*Colossians** |
| .8  | **\*Other Pauline epistles** |
| .81 | \*Thessalonians 1 |

        Class here comprehensive works on Epistles to Thessalonians

        *For Thessalonians 2, see 227.82*

| .82 | \*Thessalonians 2 |
|-----|-------------------|
| .83 | \*Timothy 1 |

        Class here comprehensive works on Epistles to Timothy, on Pastoral Epistles

        *For Timothy 2, see 227.84; for Titus, see 227.85*

| .84 | \*Timothy 2 |
|-----|-------------|
| .85 | \*Titus |
| .86 | \*Philemon |
| .87 | \*Hebrews |
| **.9**  | **\*Catholic epistles** |
| .91 | \*James |
| .92 | \*Peter 1 |

        Class here comprehensive works on Epistles of Peter

        *For Peter 2, see 227.93*

| .93 | \*Peter 2 |
|-----|-----------|
| .94 | \*John 1 |

        Class here comprehensive works on Epistles of John

        *For John 2, see 227.95; for John 3, see 227.96*

| .95 | \*John 2 |
|-----|----------|
| .96 | \*John 3 |
| .97 | \*Jude |

# 228     **\*Revelation (Apocalypse)**

\*Add as instructed under 221–229

# 229     *Apocrypha, pseudepigrapha, intertestamental works

Apocrypha: works accepted as deuterocanonical in some Bibles

Pseudepigrapha, intertestamental works: works from intertestamental times connected with the Bible but not accepted as canonical

Subdivisions are added for Apocrypha, pseudepigrapha, intertestamental works together; for Apocrypha alone

---

> ### 229.1–229.7  Specific books and works of Apocrypha

Class comprehensive works in 229

### .1     *Esdras 1 and 2

Variant names: Esdras 3 and 4

*See also 222.7 for Ezra; also 222.8 for Nehemiah*

### .2     *Tobit, Judith, deuterocanonical part of Esther

.22         *Tobit (Tobias)

(Option: Class in 222.86)

.24         *Judith

(Option: Class in 222.88)

.27         *Deuterocanonical part of Esther

(Option: Class in 222.9)

### .3     *Wisdom of Solomon (Wisdom)

Class here Apocryphal wisdom literature

*For Ecclesiasticus, see 229.4*

(Option: Class in 223.96)

### .4     *Ecclesiasticus (Sirach)

(Option: Class in 223.98)

### .5     *Baruch and Epistle of Jeremiah

(Option: Class Baruch in 224.37)

### .6     *Song of the Three Children, Susanna, Bel and the Dragon, Prayer of Manasseh

(Option: Class Song of the Three Children, Susanna, Bel and the Dragon in 224.5)

### .7     *Maccabees (Machabees)

---

*Add as instructed under 221–229

.73      *Maccabees 1 and 2 (Machabees 1 and 2)

         (Option: Class in 224.997)

.75      *Maccabees 3 and 4 (Machabees 3 and 4)

---

>      **229.8–229.9   Pseudepigrapha, intertestamental works**

         Class comprehensive works in 229.9

         *For Maccabees 3 and 4, see 229.75*

**.8**      **\*Pseudo gospels**

         Including agrapha (Jesus' words not appearing in canonical Gospels), Gospel of Thomas

         Class comprehensive works on New Testament pseudepigrapha in 229.92

**.9**      **\*Pseudepigrapha**

         *For pseudo gospels, see 229.8*

.91      *Old Testament

         *For Maccabees 3 and 4, see 229.75*

.911      *Historical books

.912      *Poetic books

         Including Odes of Solomon

.913      *Prophetic books

         Including Apocalypse of Elijah, Ascension of Isaiah, Assumption of Moses, Books of Enoch, Jewish apocalypses

.914      *Testaments

         Including Testament of the Twelve Patriarchs

.92      *New Testament

         *For pseudo gospels, see 229.8; for Epistles, see 229.93; for Apocalypses, see 229.94*

.925      *Acts of the Apostles

.93      *Epistles

.94      *Apocalypses

*Add as instructed under 221–229

> ## 230–280 Christianity

Unless other instructions are given, observe the following table of preference for the history of Christianity and the Christian church (*except* for biography, explained in Manual at 230–280: Biography), e.g., Jesuit missions in India 266.254 (*not* 271.53054); persecution of Jesuits by Elizabeth I 272.7 (*not* 271.53042, 274.206, or 282.42):

| | |
|---|---|
| Specific topics | 220–260 |
| Persecutions in general church history | 272 |
| Doctrinal controversies and heresies in general church history | 273 |
| Religious congregations and orders in church history | 271 |
| Denominations and sects of Christian church | 280 |
| Christianity by continent, country, locality | 274–279 |
| History, geographic treatment, biography of Christianity (*except* 271–279) | 270 |

Class comprehensive works in 230

*For Bible, see 220*

*See Manual at 230–280*

(Option: To give local emphasis and shorter numbers to a specific religion other than Christianity, e.g., Buddhism, class it in these numbers, its sources in 220, comprehensive works in 230; in that case class the Bible and Christianity in 298. Another option is described at 290)

> ## 230–270 Specific elements of Christianity

Class here specific elements of specific denominations and sects
  (Option: Class specific elements of specific denominations and sects in 280)

Class comprehensive works in 230

## 230  Christianity

Including Christian mythology

Class here Christian theology, Christian doctrinal theology, contextual theology

Class doctrinal controversies in general church history in 273

*For Christian moral and devotional theology, see 240; for local Christian church and Christian religious orders, see 250; for Christian social and ecclesiastical theology, see 260; for history, geographic treatment, biography of Christianity, see 270; for denominations and sects of Christian church, see 280*

*See Manual at 398.2 vs. 201.3, 230, 270, 292–299*

## SUMMARY

| | |
|---|---|
| 230.002–.007 | **Standard subdivisions of Christianity** |
| .01–.09 | **Standard subdivisions and specific types of Christian theology** |
| .1–.9 | **Doctrines of specific denominations and sects** |
| 231 | **God** |
| 232 | **Jesus Christ and his family** |
| 233 | **Humankind** |
| 234 | **Salvation and grace** |
| 235 | **Spiritual beings** |
| 236 | **Eschatology** |
| 238 | **Creeds, confessions of faith, covenants, catechisms** |
| 239 | **Apologetics and polemics** |

[.001]      Philosophy and theory of Christianity

> Do not use; class in 230.01

.002–.003      Standard subdivisions of Christianity

.005      Serial publications of Christianity

[.006]      Organizations and management of Christianity

> Do not use; class in 260

.007      Education, research, related topics of Christianity

[.007 1]      Education

> Do not use; class in 230.071

[.008]      Groups of people in Christianity

> Do not use; class in 270.08

[.009]      History, geographic treatment, biography of Christianity

> Do not use; class in 270

.01      Philosophy and theory of Christianity, of Christian theology

.02–.03      Standard subdivisions of Christian theology

.04      Specific types of Christian theology

> Class theology of specific denominations and sects in 230.1–230.9
>
> *See Manual at 230–280*

[.040 1–.040 9]      Standard subdivisions

> Do not use; class in 230.01–230.09

.041      Biblical theology

> Class theology of a specific part of Old or New Testament with the part, e.g., theology of Pauline epistles 227.06; class biblical theology of a specific topic in doctrinal theology with the topic in 231–239, e.g., Old Testament minor prophets' view of repentance and forgiveness 234.509014; class biblical theology of a specific topic in moral and devotional theology, local Christian church and Christian religious orders, social and ecclesiastical theology with the topic in 240–260, e.g., New Testament writers' view of war and peace 261.87309015

| .041 1 | Christian theology of Old Testament |
|---|---|
| .041 5 | Christian theology of New Testament |

.042        Theology of Eastern and Roman Catholic churches

Class specific schools and systems of theology in 230.046

.044        Protestant theology

Class specific schools of Protestant theology in 230.046

.046        Specific schools and systems of theology

Including dominion, existentialist, liberal, neo-orthodox, process theologies

[.046 01–.046 09]        Standard subdivisions

Do not use; class in 230.01–230.09

| .046 2 | Evangelical and fundamentalist theology |
|---|---|
| .046 24 | Evangelical theology |
| .046 26 | Fundamentalist theology |
| .046 3 | Dispensationalist theology |
| .046 4 | Liberation theology |

.05–.06        Standard subdivisions of Christian theology

.07        Education, research, related topics of Christian theology

.071        Education in Christianity, in Christian theology

Class here Christianity as an academic subject

Class comprehensive works on Christian religious education, religious education to inculcate Christian faith and practice, catechetics in 268

*See Manual at 207.5, 268 vs. 200.71, 230.071, 292–299*

.071 1        Higher education in Christianity, in Christian theology

Class here Bible colleges, divinity schools, theological seminaries, graduate and undergraduate faculties of theology; education of ministers, pastors, priests, theologians

Class training for clergy in a specialized subject with the subject, plus notation 0711 from Table 1, e.g., education in pastoral counseling 253.50711

*For higher education for specific denominations and sects, see 230.073*

*See Manual at 207.5, 268 vs. 200.71, 230.071, 292–299*

.071 14–.071 19        Higher education in specific continents, countries, localities

Class here nondenominational and interdenominational schools and courses

| | |
|---|---|
| .073 | Higher education for specific denominations and sects |

> Add to base number 230.073 the numbers following 28 in 281–289, e.g., Roman Catholic seminaries 230.0732, a Roman Catholic seminary in Dublin 230.073241835

| | |
|---|---|
| .08–.09 | Standard subdivisions of Christian theology |

> *See Manual at 230–280*

**.1–.9    Doctrines of specific denominations and sects**

> Add to base number 230 the numbers following 28 in 281–289, e.g., Methodist doctrines 230.7

> *See Manual at 230–280; also at 270, 230.11–230.14 vs. 230.15–230.2, 281.5–281.9, 282*

> (Option: Class here specific doctrines of specific denominations and sects; prefer 231–236. If option is chosen, add as above, then add 0*and to the result add the numbers following 23 in 231–236, e.g., Methodist doctrines on salvation 230.704)

> ## 231–239  Christian doctrinal theology

> Class here antagonism between and reconciliation of a specific Christian doctrine and a secular discipline

> Class specific types of Christian doctrinal theology in 230.042–230.046; class comprehensive works on Christian doctrinal theology in 230; class comprehensive works on doctrines of specific denominations and sects in 230.1–230.9; class comprehensive works on antagonism between and reconciliation of Christian belief and a secular discipline in 261.5

> ## 231–236  Specific topics in Christian doctrinal theology

> Class here specific doctrines of specific denominations and sects
> (Option: Class specific doctrines of specific denominations and sects in 230.1–230.9)

> Class comprehensive works in 230

## 231      God

| | |
|---|---|
| .04 | Special topics of God |
| .042 | Ways of knowing God |

> Including faith, reason, tradition

> Class proofs of existence of God based on reason alone in 212.1; class revelation in 231.74

---

*Add 00 for standard subdivisions; see instructions at beginning of Table 1

.044        General concepts of God

Including non-Trinitarian concepts

Class here comprehensive works on Holy Trinity

---

>      **231.1–231.3 Holy Trinity**

Class comprehensive works in 231.044

**.1**      **God the Father**

**.2**      **God the Son**

*For Jesus Christ, see 232*

**.3**      **God the Holy Spirit**

*For gifts of and baptism in the Holy Spirit, see 234.13*

**.4**      **Attributes**

Including omnipotence, omnipresence, omniscience, transcendence

*For love and wisdom, see 231.6; for sovereignty, see 231.7; for justice and goodness, see 231.8*

**.5**      **Providence**

**.6**      **Love and wisdom**

**.7**      **Relation to the world**

Including relation to nature, sovereignty

Class here God's relation to individual believers

Class redemption in 234.3; class divine law in 241.2; class believers' experience of God in 248.2; class God's relation to the church in 262.7

*For Providence, see 231.5*

.72      Kingdom of God

Class Kingdom of God to come in 236

.73      Miracles

Class here miracles associated with saints, comprehensive works on miracles

*For miracles associated with Mary, see 232.917; for miracles of Jesus, see 232.955; for stigmata, see 248.29*

.74      Revelation

*For private visions, see 248.29*

.745      Prophecy

*For Biblical prophecy and prophecies, see 220.15; for messianic prophecies, see 232.12; for eschatological prophecies, see 236*

| | |
|---|---|
| .76 | Relation to and action in history |

Including covenant relationship, relationship to the Jewish people

| | |
|---|---|
| .765 | Creation |

*For creation of humankind, see 233.11*

| | |
|---|---|
| .765 2 | Relation of scientific and Christian viewpoints of origin of universe |

Class here creationism, creation science, evolution versus creation, reconciliation of evolution and creation

*See also 379.28 for teaching creationism in public schools*

*See Manual at 231.7652 vs. 213, 500, 576.8*

| | |
|---|---|
| **.8** | **Justice and goodness** |

Including good and evil

Class here theodicy (vindication of God's justice and goodness in permitting existence of evil and suffering)

*For providence, see 231.5; for Christian ethics, see 241*

## 232     Jesus Christ and his family

Class here Christology

---

| | |
|---|---|
| > | **232.1–232.8 Christology** |

Class life of Jesus in 232.9; class comprehensive works in 232

| | |
|---|---|
| **.1** | **Incarnation and messiahship of Christ** |

Including typology

| | |
|---|---|
| .12 | Messianic prophecies |
| **.2** | **Christ as Logos (Word of God)** |
| **.3** | **Christ as Redeemer** |

Including atonement

Class comprehensive works on the doctrine of redemption in 234.3

*For sacrifice of Christ, see 232.4*

| | |
|---|---|
| **.4** | **Sacrifice of Christ** |
| **.5** | **Resurrection of Christ** |

**.8    Divinity and humanity of Christ**

Including Person; offices as Prophet, Priest, King; intercession

Class here hypostatic union

Class non-Trinitarian concepts of Jesus in 232.9

> *For incarnation, see 232.1; for Christ as Logos, see 232.2; for Christ as Redeemer, see 232.3*

**.9    Family and life of Jesus**

Class here non-Trinitarian concepts of Jesus, rationalistic interpretations of Jesus

> *For Islamic doctrines about Jesus, see 297.2465*

> *See Manual at 230–280*

**.900 1–.900 9**    Standard subdivisions

**.901**    Life of Jesus

> *For birth, infancy, childhood of Jesus, see 232.92; for adulthood of Jesus, see 232.95–232.97*

**.903**    Character and personality of Jesus

**.904**    Jesus as teacher and exemplar

Including influence

Class teachings in 232.954

**.906**    Jewish interpretations of Jesus

**.908**    Historicity of Jesus

**.91**    Mary, mother of Jesus

Class here Mariology

Class Mary's husband and parents in 232.93

**.911**    Immaculate Conception

**.912**    Annunciation

**.913**    Virginity

**.914**    Assumption (Ascent to heaven)

**.917**    Miracles and apparitions

**.92**    Birth, infancy, childhood of Jesus

Including Holy Family, circumcision, massacre of innocents, flight into Egypt

Class here Christmas story

> *For Mary, see 232.91; for Joseph, see 232.932*

**.921**    Virgin birth

.922      Adoration of shepherds

.923      Wise men (Magi)

.927      Childhood of Jesus

> *For presentation in temple, see 232.928; for Jesus among doctors in temple, see 232.929*

.928      Presentation in temple

.929      Jesus among doctors in temple

.93      Mary's husband and parents

.932      Joseph

.933      Joachim and Anne

.94      John the Baptist

.95      Public life of Jesus

> Including baptism, temptation, calling of apostles

.954      Teachings

> Class texts and interpretations of New Testament passages narrating parables in 226.8

.955      Miracles

> Class texts and interpretations of New Testament passages narrating miracles in 226.7

.956      Transfiguration

.957      Last Supper

.958      Last words to disciples

.96      Passion and death of Jesus

.961      Betrayal by Judas

> Class comprehensive works on Judas Iscariot in 226.092

.962      Trial and condemnation

.963      Crucifixion and death

.963 5      Seven last words on cross

.964      Burial

.966      Relics of Passion

.967      Descent into hell

.97      Resurrection, appearances, ascension of Jesus

# 233      Humankind

> Class salvation in 234

**.1**      **Creation and fall**

.11          Creation

Including relation of human creation and human evolution

Class comprehensive works on creation in 231.765

.14          Original sin and fall

Class sins in 241.3

**.4          Accountability**

Including guilt

**.5          Nature**

Including body, soul, spirit, sexuality; humankind as image and likeness of God, as child of God

Class free will in 233.7

*For original sin, see 233.14; for death, see 236.1; for immortality, see 236.22*

**.7          Freedom of choice between good and evil**

Class predestination and free will in relation to salvation in 234.9

*For accountability, see 233.4*

**234        Salvation and grace**

Variant name for salvation: soteriology

Including election, innate virtues, merit, universal priesthood

**.1          Kinds and means of grace**

Including actual and sanctifying grace

.13          Spiritual gifts

Including interpretation of tongues, prophecy, working of miracles, helps, governments, apostleship, teaching, exhortation, speaking words of wisdom and knowledge

Class here gifts of and baptism in the Holy Spirit

*For faith, see 234.23*

.131        Healing

Spiritual, emotional, or physical

*For discussion of whether cures are miracles, see 231.73*

*See Manual at 615.852 vs. 203.1, 234.131, 292–299*

.132        Speaking in tongues (Glossolalia)

.16          Sacraments

Class liturgy and ritual of sacraments in 265

.161        Baptism

>          **235.3–235.4 Pure spirits**

Class comprehensive works in 235

*For God, see 231*

**.3**      **Angels**

Including archangels, celestial hierarchy, cherubim, seraphim

**.4**      **Devils (Demons)**

Class here spiritual warfare

.47      Satan (Lucifer)

# 236      Eschatology

Including Antichrist

Class here Kingdom of God to come

**.1**      **Death**

**.2**      **Future state (Life after death)**

Class resurrection of the dead in 236.8

*For intermediate state, see 236.4*

.21      Eternity

.22      Immortality

*For conditional immortality, see 236.23*

.23      Conditional immortality (Annihilationism)

.24      Heaven

.25      Hell

**.4**      **Intermediate state**

Probation after death

Including limbo of fathers (limbus patrum), limbo of infants (limbus infantium)

*For purgatory, see 236.5*

**.5**      **Purgatory**

**.8**      **Resurrection of the dead**

**.9**      **Last Judgment and related events**

Including Armageddon, Day of the Lord, end of the world, Judgment of Christ, millennium, rapture, Second Coming of Christ, tribulation

Class interdisciplinary works on end of the world in 001.9

**[237]** **[Unassigned]**

Most recently used in Edition 16

**238** **Creeds, confessions of faith, covenants, catechisms**

Class catechetics in 268. Class creeds and catechisms on a specific doctrine with the doctrine, e.g., attributes of God 231.4

**.1** **Early and Eastern creeds**

**.11–.19** Creeds of early church and Eastern churches

Add to base number 238.1 the numbers following 281 in 281.1–281.9, e.g., creeds of Eastern churches 238.15 [*formerly* 238.19]; creeds of Eastern Catholic churches (Eastern rite churches in communion with Rome) 238.152 [*formerly* 238.19]; creeds of Saint Thomas Christian churches 238.154 [*formerly* 238.19]; creeds of Oriental Orthodox churches 238.16 [*formerly* 238.19]; creeds of Assyrian Church of the East (Church of the East) 238.18 [*formerly* 238.19]; creeds of Orthodox Church 238.19

**.11** Creeds of Apostolic Church to the time of the great schism, 1054

Number built according to instructions under 238.11–238.19

Class here Apostles' Creed

*For creeds of Post-Nicene church, 325–1054, see 238.14*

**.14** Creeds of Post-Nicene church, 325–1054

Number built according to instructions under 238.11–238.19

**.142** Nicene Creed

Class here Niceno-Constantinopolitan Creed

**.144** Athanasian Creed

**.19** Creeds of Orthodox Church

Number built according to instructions under 238.11–238.19

Class Nicene Creed, Niceno-Constantinopolitan Creed in 238.142

**.2–.9** **Other denominations**

Add to base number 238 the numbers following 28 in 282–289, e.g., Lutheran catechisms 238.41

**239** **Apologetics and polemics**

Apologetics: systematic argumentation in defense of the divine origin and authority of Christianity

Standard subdivisions are added for either or both topics in heading

Class apologetics of specific denominations in 230.1–230.9. Class apologetics and polemics on a specific doctrine with the doctrine, e.g., on doctrine of Holy Trinity 231.044

*See also 273 for doctrinal controversies and heresies in general church history*

**.1**     **Apologetics and polemics in apostolic times**

> *For polemics against doctrines of specific groups in apostolic times, see 239.2–239.4*

---

> **239.2–239.4  Polemics against doctrines of specific groups in apostolic times**

Class comprehensive works in 239.1

**.2**     **Polemics against Jews in apostolic times**

**.3**     **Polemics against pagans and heathens in apostolic times**

**.4**     **Polemics against Neoplatonists in apostolic times**

**.7**     **Polemics against rationalists, agnostics, apostates, atheists in postapostolic times**

> Including polemics against deists, materialists, scientists, secular humanists

**.9**     **Polemics against other groups in postapostolic times**

> Class comprehensive postapostolic defenses of and attacks on doctrines of specific denominations or sects in 230.1–230.9. Class attacks on doctrines of a specific religion with the religion, e.g., doctrines of Judaism 296.3

**.93**     Polemics against new age groups and doctrines

# 240     Christian moral and devotional theology

### SUMMARY

| | |
|---|---|
| 241 | **Christian ethics** |
| 242 | **Devotional literature** |
| 243 | **Evangelistic writings for individuals and families** |
| 246 | **Use of art in Christianity** |
| 247 | **Church furnishings and related articles** |
| 248 | **Christian experience, practice, life** |
| 249 | **Christian observances in family life** |

# 241     Christian ethics

Variant name: Moral theology

> *See Manual at 241 vs. 261.8*

**.04**     Specific branches, denominations, sects

**.040 2**     Eastern and Roman Catholic churches

> *For ethics of Eastern churches, see 241.0415; for ethics of Roman Catholic Church, see 241.042*

**.040 4**     Protestant churches and Protestantism

> *For ethics of specific Protestant denominations and sects, see 241.043–241.049*

**.041–.049**     Specific denominations or sects

> Add to base number 241.04 the numbers following 28 in 281–289, e.g., Lutheran ethics 241.0441

**.1**     **Conscience**

**.2**     **Laws and bases of morality**

> Including divine law, natural law
>
> Class here relation of law and gospel
>
> *For codes of conduct, see 241.5*

**.3**     **Sin and vices**

> Standard subdivisions are added for either or both topics in heading
>
> Including specific vices
>
> Class original sin in 233.14
>
> *For specific moral issues, see 241.6*

**.31**     Mortal and venial sin

**.4**     **Virtues**

> Including specific virtues
>
> Class faith and hope as means of salvation in 234.2
>
> *For specific moral issues, see 241.6*

**.5**     **Codes of conduct**

> *For specific moral issues, see 241.6*

**.52**     Ten Commandments

**.53**     Sermon on the Mount

**.54**     Golden Rule

**.6**     **Specific moral issues**

> Add to base number 241.6 the numbers following 17 in 172–179, e.g., morality of warfare 241.6242, of abortion 241.6976; however, for specific vices, see 241.3; for specific virtues, see 241.4

**242**       **Devotional literature**

Class here texts of meditations, contemplations, prayers for individuals and families, religious poetry intended for devotional use

Unless other instructions are given, observe the following table of preference, e.g., prayers and meditations for daily use based on passages from the Bible 242.2 (*not* 242.5):

| | |
|---|---|
| Prayers and meditations for use in times of illness, trouble, bereavement | 242.4 |
| Prayers and meditations for specific groups of people | 242.6 |
| Prayers and meditations for daily use | 242.2 |
| Prayers and meditations for church year, other Christian feast and fast days | 242.3 |
| Prayers and meditations based on passages from the Bible | 242.5 |
| Specific prayers and groups of prayers | 242.7 |
| Collections of prayers | 242.8 |

Class devotional literature on a specific subject with the subject, e.g., meditations on passion and death of Jesus 232.96

*For evangelistic writings, see 243; for hymns, see 264.23*

.08       Groups of people

Do not use for devotional literature for specific groups of people; class in 242.6

Class here devotional literature by specific groups of people

.2       **Prayers and meditations for daily use**

Not limited to saints' days or specific parts of the church year

Including meditations and prayers for Sunday, Sabbath

Class prayers and meditations for daily use for specific groups of people in 242.6

.3       **Prayers and meditations for church year, other Christian feast and fast days**

Class prayers and meditations for church year, other Christian feast and fast days for specific groups of people in 242.6

---

>       242.33–242.36   Church year

Class comprehensive works in 242.3

*For Pentecost and time after Pentecost (Ordinary time), see 242.38*

.33       Advent and Christmas

.332       Advent

.335       Christmas season

Class here Christmas day

| | |
|---|---|
| .34 | Lent |

> *For Holy Week, see 242.35*

| | |
|---|---|
| .35 | Holy Week |
| .36 | Easter season |

> Including Ascension Day
>
> Class here Easter Sunday

| | |
|---|---|
| .37 | Other Christian feast and fast days |

> Including saints' days

| | |
|---|---|
| .38 | Pentecost and time after Pentecost (Ordinary time) |
| **.4** | **Prayers and meditations for use in times of illness, trouble, bereavement** |
| **.5** | **Prayers and meditations based on passages from the Bible** |

> Class interpretation and criticism of Bible passages for other than devotional use in 220.6; class Bible prayers in 242.722

| | |
|---|---|
| **.6** | **Prayers and meditations for specific groups of people** |

> Class here prayers and meditations for daily use, church year, other Christian feast and fast days for specific groups of people
>
> Add to base number 242.6 the numbers following 248.8 in 248.82–248.89, e.g., prayers and meditations for college students 242.634; however, for prayers and meditations for use in times of illness, trouble, bereavement, see 242.4
>
> Class collections of prayers for specific groups of people in 242.82–242.89

| | |
|---|---|
| **.7** | **Specific prayers and groups of prayers** |
| .72 | Specific types of prayers |

> Including doxologies
>
> Class here prayers to Father, Son, Holy Spirit

| | |
|---|---|
| .722 | Bible prayers |

---

| | |
|---|---|
| > | 242.74–242.76  Prayers addressed to spiritual beings other than God |

> Class comprehensive works in 242.7

| | |
|---|---|
| .74 | Prayers to Mary |

> Including Ave Maria (Hail Mary), Rosary

| | |
|---|---|
| .75 | Prayers to Joseph, Joachim, Anne |
| .76 | Prayers to saints and angels |

> *For Joseph, Joachim, Anne, see 242.75*

**.8** **Collections of prayers**

Class here prayer books

*For specific prayers and groups of prayers, see 242.7*

.800 1–.800 7 Standard subdivisions

.800 8 Groups of people

Do not use for collections of prayers for specific groups of people; class in 242.82–242.89

Class here collections of prayers by specific groups of people

.800 9 History, geographic treatment, biography

.801–.809 Collections of prayers by adherents of specific denominations and sects

Add to base number 242.80 the numbers following 28 in 281–289, e.g., collections of private prayers by Methodists 242.807

.82–.89 Collections of prayers for specific groups of people

Add to base number 242.8 the numbers following 248.8 in 248.82–248.89, e.g., collections of private prayers for college students 242.834

*For collections of prayers by adherents of specific denominations and sects, see 242.801–242.809*

**243** **Evangelistic writings for individuals and families**

Works designed to convert readers, promote repentance

Class evangelistic sermons in 252.3

**[244]** **[Unassigned]**

Most recently used in Edition 15

**[245]** **[Unassigned]**

Most recently used in Edition 21

**246** **Use of art in Christianity**

Religious meaning, significance, purpose

Class attitude of Christianity and Christian church toward secular art, the arts in 261.57; class creation, description, critical appraisal as art in 700

*For church furnishings and related articles, see 247*

———

> **246.1–246.4 Schools and styles**

Class specific elements by school and style in 246.5–246.9; class comprehensive works in 246. Class interdisciplinary works on schools and styles of Christian art with the school or style in 709, e.g., interdisciplinary works on early Christian art 709.0212

**.1** **Byzantine and Gothic art**

**.2**    **Early Christian and Romanesque art**

**.4**    **Renaissance and modern art**

>    Including Protestant art

---

> **246.5–246.9  Specific elements**

>    Class comprehensive works in 246

**.5**    **Icons, symbols, insignia**

**.53**    Icons

**.55**    Symbols

>    Including banners, emblems, incense, votive offerings

>    Class here Christian symbolism

>    *For colors and lights, see 246.6*

**.558**    Crosses and crucifixes

>    Standard subdivisions are added for either or both topics in heading

**.56**    Insignia

>    Including insignia of rank

**.6**    **Colors and lights**

**.7**    **Dramatic, musical, rhythmic arts**

>    Including dance, liturgical dance

**.72**    Dramatic arts

**.723**    Passion plays

**.725**    Puppetry

**.75**    Music

>    Class here comprehensive works on music in Christianity

>    Class attitude of Christianity and Christian church toward secular music in 261.578; class interdisciplinary works on Christian sacred music in 781.71

>    *For music in public worship, see 264.2*

**.9**    **Architecture**

>    Add to base number 246.9 the numbers following 726 in 726.4–726.9, e.g., cathedral church buildings 246.96; however, for church furnishings, see 247

**247**    **Church furnishings and related articles**

>    Including paintings, plastic arts, sculpture, structural decoration, textiles

**.1**    **Furniture**

## 248     Christian experience, practice, life

Class here spirituality

*See Manual at 230–280*

### SUMMARY

| | | |
|---|---|---|
| **248.06** | **Organizations and management** | |
| **.2** | **Religious experience** | |
| **.3** | **Worship** | |
| **.4** | **Christian life and practice** | |
| **.5** | **Witness bearing** | |
| **.6** | **Stewardship** | |
| **.8** | **Guides to Christian life for specific groups of people** | |

.06       Organizations and management

Class pious societies, sodalities, confraternities in 267

**.2**      **Religious experience**

.22       Mysticism

.24       Conversion

*For moral renewal and commitment, see 248.25*

————————

\>         248.242–248.246   Conversion from one system of belief to another

Class comprehensive works in 248.24

*For conversion of Christians to another religion, see the religion, e.g., conversion of Christians to Judaism 296.714*

.242      Conversion from Protestantism to Roman Catholicism

.244      Conversion from Roman Catholicism to Protestantism

.246      Conversion from non-Christianity to Christianity

.25       Moral renewal and commitment

.29       Other religious experiences

Including stigmata, private visions

Class spiritual gifts in 234.13; class speaking in tongues (glossolalia) in 234.132

**.3**      **Worship**

Class here comprehensive works on worship

Class texts of prayers and devotions in 242

*For observances in family life, see 249; for public worship, see 264*

.32       Prayer

.34       Meditation and contemplation

Standard subdivisions are added for either or both topics in heading

**.4**          **Christian life and practice**

>              Class here Christian marriage and family

>              *For Christian ethics, see 241; for worship, see 248.3; for witness bearing, see 248.5; for stewardship, see 248.6; for Christian observances in family life, see 249*

.408          Groups of people

>              Do not use for guides to Christian life for specific groups of people; class in 248.8

>              Class here guides to Christian life by specific groups of people

.46           Individual observances

>              Including ceremonial and ritual observances, observance of restrictions and limitations

>              *For asceticism, see 248.47; for pilgrimages, see 263.041*

.47           Asceticism

>              Attitudes and practices aside from and beyond normal moral duties adopted as aids to moral and spiritual development

>              Including practice of celibacy, fasting and abstinence, poverty, solitude, other physical austerities, e.g., flagellation

>              *For clerical celibacy, see 253.25; for practices of religious congregations and orders, see 255*

.48           Guides to Christian life by or for adherents of specific branches, denominations, sects

>              Class guides to Christian life for specific groups of people who are adherents of specific denominations and sects in 248.8

.480 2        Eastern and Roman Catholic churches

>              *For guides to Christian life by or for adherents of Eastern churches, see 248.4815; for guides to Christian life by or for adherents of Roman Catholic Church, see 248.482*

.480 4        Protestant churches and Protestantism

>              *For guides to Christian life by or for adherents of specific Protestant denominations and sects, see 248.483–248.489*

.481–.489     Specific denominations or sects

>              Add to base number 248.48 the numbers following 28 in 281–289, e.g., guides for Roman Catholics 248.482

**.5**          **Witness bearing**

**.6**          **Stewardship**

**.8** **Guides to Christian life for specific groups of people**

Limited to groups provided for below

Class here guides to Christian life for specific groups of people who are adherents of specific denominations and sects

Class guides to a specific aspect of Christian life with the aspect, e.g., prayer 248.32

| | |
|---|---|
| .808 | Groups of people |
| .808 1 | People by gender or sex |
| [.808 11] | Men |

Do not use; class in 248.842

| | |
|---|---|
| [.808 2] | Women |

Do not use; class in 248.843

| | |
|---|---|
| [.808 3] | Young people |

Do not use for children; class in 248.82. Do not use for young people twelve to twenty; class in 248.83

| | |
|---|---|
| [.808 4] | People in specific stages of adulthood |

Do not use; class in 248.84

| | |
|---|---|
| .808 5 | Relatives |

Do not use for parents; class in 248.845

| | |
|---|---|
| .808 6 | People by miscellaneous social attributes |
| .808 65 | People by marital status |

Do not use for men by marital status; class in 248.8422–248.8429. Do not use for women by marital status; class in 248.8432–248.8439

| | |
|---|---|
| [.808 653] | Separated and divorced people |

Do not use; class in 248.846

| | |
|---|---|
| [.808 655] | Married people |

Do not use; class in 248.844

| | |
|---|---|
| .808 7 | Gifted people |

Do not use for people with disabilities or illnesses; class in 248.86

| | |
|---|---|
| [.808 8] | Occupational and religious groups |

Do not use for adherents of specific denominations or sects; class in 248.48. Do not use for occupational groups; class in 248.88. Do not use for clergy or people in religious orders; class in 248.89

> 248.82–248.85  Guides to Christian life for specific age groups

> Class people of specific ages in specific occupational groups or experiencing illness, trouble, bereavement in 248.86–248.89; class comprehensive works in 248.8

.82        Children

> Through age eleven

.83        Young people twelve to twenty and college students

> Standard subdivisions are added for young people twelve to twenty and college students together, for young people twelve to twenty alone

.832       Males twelve to twenty

.833       Females twelve to twenty

.834       College students

> Male and female

.84      Adults

> *For people in late adulthood, see 248.85*

.842       Men

.842 1        Fathers

> Regardless of marital status

.842 2–.842 9    Men by marital status

> Add to base number 248.842 the numbers following —0865 in notation 08652–08659 from Table 1, e.g., guides for husbands 248.8425

> Class fathers in 248.8421

.843       Women

.843 1        Mothers

> Regardless of marital status

.843 2–.843 9    Women by marital status

> Add to base number 248.843 the numbers following —0865 in notation 08652–08659 from Table 1, e.g., guides for wives 248.8435

> Class mothers in 248.8431

.844       Married people

> Class husbands in 248.8425; class wives in 248.8435

.845       Parents

> Class here Christian child rearing, Christian religious training of children in the home

> *For fathers, see 248.8421; for mothers, see 248.8431*

.846 Separated and divorced people

*For separated and divorced men, see 248.8423; for separated and divorced women, see 248.8433*

.85 People in late adulthood

---

> 248.86–248.89 Guides to Christian life for occupational classes; people experiencing illness, trouble, bereavement

Class comprehensive works in 248.8

.86 People experiencing illness, trouble, bereavement

.861–.864 People experiencing specific illnesses and disabilities

Add to base number 248.86 the numbers following 362 in 362.1–362.4, e.g., people experiencing addiction 248.8629

*See Manual at 616.86 vs. 158.1, 204.42, 248.8629, 292–299, 362.29*

.866 People experiencing bereavement

.88 Occupational groups

*For religious groups, see 248.89*

.89 Religious groups

.892 Clergy

*For people in religious orders, see 248.894*

.894 People in religious orders

.894 2 Men

.894 22 Vocation

.894 25 Selection and novitiate

.894 3 Women

.894 32 Vocation

.894 35 Selection and novitiate

## 249 Christian observances in family life

Class here family prayer; family observance of religious restrictions, rites, ceremonies

---

> # 250–280 Christian church

Class comprehensive works in 260

# 250 Local Christian church and Christian religious orders

Standard subdivisions are added for local Christian church and Christian religious orders together, for local Christian church alone

Class public worship in 264; class missions in 266; class religious education in 268

### SUMMARY

[.68]    Management

> Do not use for management of local Christian church and Christian religious orders together; class in 250. Do not use for management of local Christian church; class in 254

.9    **History, geographic treatment, biography**

> Class general history of local church in specific continents, countries, localities in 274–279; class history, geographic treatment, biography of specific denominations in 280

---

>    ## 251–254 Local church

Class here basic Christian communities

Class the local church in overall church organization in 262.2; class comprehensive works in 250

*For pastoral care of families, of specific groups of people, see 259*

*See Manual at 260 vs. 251–254, 259*

# 251 Preaching (Homiletics)

Class texts of sermons in 252; class pastoral methods in 253.7

.001–.009    Standard subdivisions

.01    Preparation

.02    Sermon outlines

.03    Delivery

> Class here voice, expression, gesture

.07    Radio and television preaching

> Class specific aspects of radio and television preaching in 251.01–251.03

.08    Homiletic illustrations

**.1–.9        Material for preparation of sermons for specific occasions, for specific groups of people**

> Add to base number 251 the numbers following 252 in 252.1–252.9, e.g., material for preparation of sermons arranged for the church year 251.6

# 252        Texts of sermons

> Class sermons on a specific subject with the subject, e.g., God's Providence 231.5

**.001–.009        Standard subdivisions**

**.01–.09        Texts of sermons by specific denominations and sects**

> Add to base number 252.0 the numbers following 28 in 281–289, e.g., Anglican sermons 252.03

**.1        Texts of sermons for baptisms, confirmations, funerals, weddings**

> Class sermons for memorial occasions in 252.9

**.3        Texts of sermons for evangelistic meetings**

**.5        Texts of sermons for specific groups of people**

**.53        Children**

> Through age eleven

**.55        Young people twelve to twenty and college students**

> Including academic, chapel, convocation, commencement sermons

**.56        People in late adulthood, and people experiencing illness, trouble, bereavement**

**.58        Occupational groups**

> *For religious groups, see 252.59*

**.59        Religious groups**

**.592        Clergy**

> *For people in religious orders, see 252.594*

**.594        People in religious orders**

**.6        Texts of sermons for church year and public occasions**

> Standard subdivisions are added for texts of sermons for church year and public occasions together, for church year alone

> _____

> 252.61–252.64  Church year

> Class comprehensive works in 252.6

**.61        Advent and Christmas**

**.612        Advent**

| .615 | Christmas season |
|---|---|

.615  Christmas season

Class here Christmas day

.62  Lent

.625  Holy Week

.63  Easter season

Including Ascension Day

Class here Easter Sunday

.64  Pentecost and time after Pentecost (Ordinary time)

.67  Other feast and fast days

Including saints' days

.68  Secular occasions

Including elections, holidays, thanksgivings

**.7  Texts of sermons for consecrations, ordinations, installations**

**.9  Texts of sermons for memorial occasions**

# 253 Pastoral office and work (Pastoral theology)

Class here the work of priests, ministers, pastors, rectors, vicars, curates, chaplains, elders, deacons, assistants, laity in relation to the work of the church at the local level

Class local clergy and laity in relation to the government, organization and nature of the church as a whole in 262.1; class the ordination of women in 262.14; class the role of clergy in religious education in 268

.08  Groups of people

Do not use for pastoral care of specific groups of people; class in 259

Class here pastoral care performed by groups of people

.09  History, geographic treatment, biography

.092  Biography

Do not use for biography of clergy in the period prior to 1054; class in 270.1–270.3. Do not use for biography of clergy in the period subsequent to 1054; class in 280

*See Manual at 230–280*

**.2  Life and person**

Including professional and personal qualifications

Class education of clergy in 230.0711; class guides to Christian life for clergy in 248.892

.22  Families of clergy

.25        Clerical celibacy

> Add to base number 253.25 the numbers following 28 in 281–289, e.g., clerical celibacy in Orthodox church 253.2519, in Orthodox church in United States 253.251973

---

\>        **253.5–253.7 Pastoral duties and responsibilities**

> Class methods for services to families, to specific groups of people in 259; class comprehensive works in 253

> *For preaching, see 251; for parish administration, see 254*

.5        **Counseling and spiritual direction**

> Standard subdivisions are added for counseling and spiritual direction together, for counseling alone

> Class pastoral counseling, spiritual direction of specific groups of people in 259; class premarital, marriage, family counseling in 259.12–259.14

.52        Pastoral psychology

.53        Spiritual direction

.7        **Pastoral methods**

> Including group work, telephone work

.76        Pastoral methods in homes

.78        Use of radio and television

# 254    Parish administration

.001–.009        Standard subdivisions

.01–.09        Parish administration by specific denominations and sects

> Add to base number 254.0 the numbers following 28 in 281–289, e.g., administration of Roman Catholic parishes 254.02

.1        **Initiation of new churches**

.2        **Parish administration in specific kinds of communities**

> Class a specific activity in a specific kind of community with the activity, e.g., membership promotion 254.5

.22        Urban communities

.23        Suburban communities

.24        Rural communities

.3        **Use of communications media**

> Including use of audiovisual materials

.4        **Public relations and publicity**

> *For use of communications media, see 254.3*

**.5** **Membership**

Promotion and growth

**.6** **Programs**

Planning and execution

**.7** **Buildings, equipment, grounds**

**.8** **Finance**

Including budget, expenditures, income, methods of raising money

# 255 Religious congregations and orders

Class here monasticism, comprehensive works on Christian religious congregations and orders

When adding from 271 to indicate kinds of orders or specific orders, add only the notation for the kind or order. Do not use the footnote instruction to add as instructed under 271, but add notation from the table under 255.1–255.7 if it applies, or add notation 01–09 from Table 1. For example, the correct number for contemplative orders in the United Kingdom is 255.010941 (*not* 255.01041); for Benedictines in the United Kingdom 255.100941 (*not* 255.1041)

*For guides to Christian life for people in religious orders, see 248.894; for religious congregations and orders in church organization, see 262.24; for religious congregations and orders, monasticism in church history, see 271. For specific types of activity of religious congregations and orders, see the activity, e.g., pastoral counseling 253.5, missionary work 266*

.001–.009 Standard subdivisions

.01–.09 Specific kinds of congregations and orders

Add to base number 255.0 the numbers following 271.0 in 271.01–271.09 for the kind only, e.g., contemplative orders 255.01; then, for each kind having its own number, add notation 01–09 from Table 1 (*not* as instructed under 271), e.g., contemplative orders in the United Kingdom 255.010941

**.1–.7** **Roman Catholic orders of men**

Add to base number 255 the numbers following 271 in 271.1–271.7 for the order only, e.g., Benedictines 255.1; then, for each order having its own number, add further as follows (*not* as instructed at 271), e.g., Benedictines in the United Kingdom 255.100941, the rule of St. Benedict 255.106:

| | |
|---|---|
| 001–009 | Standard subdivisions |
| 02 | Constitutions |
| 04 | Statutes, ordinances, customs |
| 06 | Rule |

**.8** **Non-Roman Catholic orders of men**

.81 Monasticism of Eastern churches

Add to base number 255.81 the numbers following 281 in 281.5–281.9, e.g., Orthodox monasticism 255.819

.83 Anglican orders of men

**.9** **Congregations and orders of women**

| .900 1–.900 9 | Standard subdivisions |

.901–.909 Specific kinds of congregations and orders

> Add to base number 255.90 the numbers following 271.0 in 271.01–271.09 for the kind only, e.g., contemplative orders 255.901; then, for each kind having its own number, add notation 01–09 from Table 1 (*not* as instructed under 271), e.g., contemplative orders in the United Kingdom 255.9010941

.91–.97 Roman Catholic orders of women

> Add to base number 255.9 the numbers following 271.9 in 271.91–271.97 for the order only, e.g., Dominican sisters 255.972; then, for each order having its own number, add further as instructed under 255.1–255.7 (*not* as instructed at 271), e.g., Dominicans in the United Kingdom 255.97200941, the rule of the Dominicans 255.97206

.98 Non-Roman Catholic orders of women

.981 Monasticism of women of Eastern churches

> Add to base number 255.981 the numbers following 281 in 281.5–281.9, e.g., Orthodox monasticism of women 255.9819

.983 Anglican orders of women

## [256] [Unassigned]

Most recently used in Edition 14

## [257] [Unassigned]

Most recently used in Edition 14

## [258] [Unassigned]

Most recently used in Edition 17

## 259 Pastoral care of families, of specific groups of people

Performed by clergy or laity

Class here pastoral counseling of specific groups of people

Unless other instructions are given, observe the following table of preference, e.g., pastoral care of bereaved young people 259.6 (*not* 259.2):

| | |
|---|---|
| Pastoral care of the bereaved | 259.6 |
| Pastoral care of antisocial and asocial people | 259.5 |
| Pastoral care of people with disabilities, with physical or mental illnesses | 259.4 |
| Pastoral care of families | 259.1 |
| Pastoral care of young people | 259.2 |
| Pastoral care of people in late adulthood | 259.3 |

Class comprehensive works on pastoral care of more than one kind of person in 253

> See also 253.08 for pastoral care performed by groups of people; also 361.75 for works limited to social welfare work by religious organizations

> See Manual at 260 vs. 251–254, 259

| | |
|---|---|
| [.01–.07] | Standard subdivisions |
| | Do not use; class in 253.01–253.07 |
| .08 | Groups of people |
| | Do not use for bereaved people; class in 259.6 |
| [.083] | Young people |
| | Do not use; class in 259.2 |
| .084 | People in specific stages of adulthood |
| [.084 2] | People in early adulthood |
| | Do not use; class in 259.25 |
| [.084 6] | People in late adulthood |
| | Do not use; class in 259.3 |
| .086 | People by miscellaneous social attributes |
| [.086 92] | Antisocial and asocial people |
| | Do not use; class in 259.5 |
| .087 | Gifted people |
| | Do not use for people with disabilities and illnesses; class in 259.4 |
| .088 | Occupational and religious groups |
| [.088 378 198] | College students |
| | Do not use; class in 259.24 |
| [.09] | History, geographic treatment, biography |
| | Do not use; class in 253.09 |

**.1**      **Pastoral care of families**

.12      Family counseling

*For premarital counseling, see 259.13; for marriage counseling, see 259.14*

.13      Premarital counseling

.14      Marriage counseling

**.2**      **Pastoral care of young people**

.22      Pastoral care of children

Through age eleven

.23      Pastoral care of young people twelve to twenty

Class here comprehensive works on pastoral care of young adults

*For pastoral care of young adults over twenty-one, see 259.25*

.24          Pastoral care of college students

            Class here campus ministry

.25          Pastoral care of people in early adulthood

            Class here young adults over twenty-one

            *For pastoral care of college students, see 259.24*

**.3**         **Pastoral care of people in late adulthood**

**.4**         **Pastoral care of people with disabilities, with physical or mental illnesses**

            Class here programs for visiting the sick

            Add to base number 259.4 the numbers following 362 in 362.1–362.4, e.g., pastoral care of those who have attempted suicide 259.428

**.5**         **Pastoral care of antisocial and asocial people**

            Class here prison chaplaincy; pastoral care of juvenile delinquents and predelinquents, of offenders

**.6**         **Pastoral care of the bereaved**

# 260    Christian social and ecclesiastical theology

            Institutions, services, observances, disciplines, work of Christianity and Christian church

            Class here comprehensive works on Christian church

            *For local church and religious orders, see 250; for denominations and sects, see 280*

            *See Manual at 260 vs. 251–254, 259*

### SUMMARY

| | |
|---|---|
| 260.9 | **History, geographic treatment, biography** |
| 261 | **Social theology and interreligious relations and attitudes** |
| 262 | **Ecclesiology** |
| 263 | **Days, times, places of religious observance** |
| 264 | **Public worship** |
| 265 | **Sacraments, other rites and acts** |
| 266 | **Missions** |
| 267 | **Associations for religious work** |
| 268 | **Religious education** |
| 269 | **Spiritual renewal** |

**.9**         **History, geographic treatment, biography**

            Do not use for history, geographic treatment, biography of Christian church; class in 270

# 261    Social theology and interreligious relations and attitudes

Attitude of Christianity and Christian church toward and influence on secular matters, attitude toward other religions, interreligious relations

Class here Christianity and culture

Class sociology of religion in 306.6

**.1**      **Role of Christian church in society**

Class specific socioeconomic problems in 261.8

**.2**      **Christianity and other systems of belief**

.21      Christianity and irreligion

Including Christianity and communism, Christianity and the apostate and indifferent

.22–.29      Christianity and other religions

Add to base number 261.2 the numbers following 29 in 292–299, e.g., Christianity and Islam 261.27

**.5**      **Christianity and secular disciplines**

Class here antagonism between and reconciliation of Christian belief and a secular discipline

*For antagonism between and reconciliation of a specific Christian doctrine and a secular discipline, see the doctrine in 231–239, e.g., relation between Christian doctrine on the soul and modern biology 233.5*

*See Manual at 261.5*

.51      Philosophy, logic, related disciplines

.513      Parapsychology and occultism

.515      Psychology

.52      Communications media

Class here comprehensive works on attitude toward and use of communications media

*For a specific use of communications media by the church, see the use, e.g., use in parish administration 254.3*

.55      Science

Class the relation of scientific and Christian views on creation in 231.765; class ecology in 261.88

.56      Technology

.561      Medicine

.57      The arts

.578      Music

.58      Literature

| .7 | **Christianity and political affairs** |
|---|---|

Including civil war and revolution

Class here Christianity and civil rights

*For Christianity and international affairs, see 261.87*

*See Manual at 322.1 vs. 201.72, 261.7, 292–299*

| .72 | Religious freedom |
|---|---|
| .73 | Theocracy |

Supremacy of church over civil government

| .8 | **Christianity and socioeconomic problems** |
|---|---|

Class here comprehensive works on the Christian view of socioeconomic and political affairs

*For Christianity and political affairs, see 261.7*

*See also 361.75 for welfare services of religious organizations*

*See Manual at 241 vs. 261.8*

| .83 | Social problems and services |
|---|---|
| .832 | Social welfare problems and services |
| .832 1–.832 5 | Problems of and services to people with illnesses and disabilities, the poor |

Add to base number 261.832 the numbers following 362 in 362.1–362.5, e.g., Christian attitude toward alcoholism 261.832292, toward poor people 261.8325

| .832 6 | Hunger |
|---|---|
| .832 7 | Abuse within the family |
| .832 71 | Child abuse and neglect |

*For sexual abuse, see 261.83272*

| .832 72 | Sexual abuse |
|---|---|
| .832 73 | Adults who were victims of abuse as children |
| .832 8 | Refugees and victims of political oppression |
| .833 | Crime |

Add to base number 261.833 the numbers following 364 in 364.1–364.8, e.g., Christian attitude toward treason 261.833131, toward capital punishment 261.83366

| .835 | Sexual relations, marriage, family |
|---|---|

Add to base number 261.835 the numbers following 306 in 306.7–306.8, e.g., Christian attitude toward divorce 261.83589

Class abuse within the family in 261.8327

| | |
|---|---|
| .836 | Population |

Including abortion, family planning

Class ecology in 261.88

| | |
|---|---|
| .85 | Economics |

Including management of business enterprises

*For environment, natural resources, see 261.88*

| | |
|---|---|
| .87 | International affairs |
| .873 | War and peace |

*For civil war and revolution, see 261.7*

| | |
|---|---|
| .873 2 | Nuclear weapons and nuclear war |
| .88 | Environment |

Class here ecology, environmental problems, natural resources, pollution

Class environmental ethics in 241.691

# 262    Ecclesiology

Church government, organization, nature

*See Manual at 260 vs. 251–254, 259*

## SUMMARY

| | |
|---|---|
| **262.001–.009** | **Standard subdivisions, ecumenism, church renewal** |
| **.01–.09** | **Government and organization, ecclesiology of specific denominations and sects** |
| **.1** | **Governing leaders of churches** |
| **.2** | **Local church and religious congregations and orders in church organization** |
| **.3** | **Government and organization of systems governed by papacy and episcopacy** |
| **.4** | **Government and organization of systems governed by election** |
| **.5** | **General councils** |
| **.7** | **Nature of the church** |
| **.8** | **Church and ministerial authority and its denial** |
| **.9** | **Church law and discipline** |

| | |
|---|---|
| .001 | Philosophy and theory, ecumenism, church renewal |

Notation 01 from Table 1 as modified below

| | |
|---|---|
| .001 1 | Ecumenism |

Do not use for systems; class in 262.001

*See Manual at 280.042 vs. 262.0011*

| | |
|---|---|
| .001 109 | History, geographic treatment, biography |

Do not use for history of the ecumenical movement; class in 280.042

| | |
|---|---|
| .001 7 | Church renewal |

| .002–.005 | Standard subdivisions |
|---|---|
| .006 | Organizations |

.006 8      Particular aspects of administration

> Do not use for management without subdivision; class in 262

> Add notation 0681–0688 as appropriate for particular aspects of administration, e.g., financial administration of United Methodist Church 262.0760681

.007–.009      Standard subdivisions

.01–.09      Government and organization, ecclesiology of specific denominations and sects

> Add to base number 262.0 the numbers following 28 in 281–289, e.g., government and organization of the United Methodist Church 262.076

**.1**      **Governing leaders of churches**

> Authority, function, role

[.109 2]      Biography

> Do not use for biography of church leaders; class in 270. Do not use for biography of leaders of specific denominations; class in 280

> *See Manual at 230–280*

.11      Apostolic succession

---

> 262.12–262.15   Governing leaders by rank

> Class comprehensive works in 262.1

.12      Episcopacy

> Class here bishops, archbishops, national conferences of bishops

> Add to base number 262.12 the numbers following 28 in 281–289, e.g., episcopacy of Anglican churches 262.123, of Church of England 262.12342

> *For papacy and patriarchate, see 262.13*

.13      Papacy and patriarchate

> Standard subdivisions are added for papacy and patriarchate together, for Roman Catholic papacy alone

---

> 262.131–262.136   Specific aspects of Roman Catholic papacy

> Class comprehensive works in 262.13

.131      Papal infallibility

.132      Temporal power of the pope

.135      College of Cardinals

.136      Administration

Including congregations, offices of Curia Romana, Synod of Bishops, tribunals

*For national conferences of bishops, see 262.12; for College of Cardinals, see 262.135*

.14      Local clergy

Class here ordination of women

Add to base number 262.14 the numbers following 28 in 281–289, e.g., local Methodist clergy 262.147

Class works that treat the ordination of women only in relation to its effect on the local church in 253

.15      Laity

Body of church members

Add to base number 262.15 the numbers following 28 in 281–289, e.g., laity of Lutheran church 262.1541, in United States 262.154173

>      262.17–262.19   Governing leaders by system of government

Class leaders by rank in a specific system of government in 262.12–262.15; class comprehensive works in 262.1

.17      Governing leaders in papal and episcopal systems

.18      Governing leaders in presbyterian systems

.19      Governing leaders in congregational systems

.2      **Local church and religious congregations and orders in church organization**

*For administration of parishes, see 254; for government and administration of religious congregations and orders, see 255*

*See Manual at 260 vs. 251–254, 259*

.22      Parishes

.24      Religious congregations and orders

.26      Small groups

Including basic Christian communities

>      **262.3–262.4   Specific forms of church organization**

Class comprehensive works on government and organization of specific denominations and sects regardless of form of organization in 262.01–262.09; class comprehensive works in 262. Class a specific aspect of government and organization with the aspect, e.g., role of bishops in a system governed by episcopacy 262.12 (*not* 262.3)

**.3**      **Government and organization of systems governed by papacy and episcopacy**

> Including sees, dioceses, cathedral systems

**.4**      **Government and organization of systems governed by election**

> Including congregational systems, presbyteries, synods

**.5**      **General councils**

> Add to base number 262.5 the numbers following 28 in 281–289, e.g., ecumenical councils of Roman Catholic Church 262.52
>
> Class legal acts of general councils in 262.9. Class nonlegal decrees on a specific subject with the subject, e.g., statements on original sin 233.14

**.7**      **Nature of the church**

> Including God's relation to the church

.72      Attributes, marks, notes

> Including apostolicity, catholicity, credibility, holiness, infallibility, necessity, unity, visibility and invisibility

.73      Communion of saints

.77      Mystical body of Christ

**.8**      **Church and ministerial authority and its denial**

> Including heresy, schism

**.9**      **Church law and discipline**

> Class here canon (ecclesiastical) law
>
> Class civil law relating to church or religious matters in 340
>
> > *See also 364.188 for offenses against religion as defined and penalized by the state*

------

>      262.91–262.94   Roman Catholic law

> Class comprehensive works in 262.9

.91      Acts of the Holy See

> Including apostolic letters, briefs, encyclicals, papal bulls and decrees
>
> Class acts on a specific subject with the subject, e.g., on the nature of the church 262.7

.92      Early Roman Catholic codes

.922      Early codes to Gratian, ca. 1140

.923      Corpus iuris canonici

.924      Quinque compilationes antiquae

.93      Codex iuris canonici (1917)

| | |
|---|---|
| .931 | General principles (Canons 1–86) |
| .932 | Persons (Canons 87–725) |
| | Clergy, religious, laity |
| .933 | Things (Canons 726–1551) |
| | Including benefices, sacraments, sacred times and places, teaching office, temporal goods, worship |
| .934 | Procedure (Canons 1552–2194) |
| | Including trials, cases of beatification and canonization |
| .935 | Crimes and penalties (Canons 2195–2414) |
| .94 | Codex iuris canonici (1983) |
| | Unless other instructions are given, class a subject with aspects in two or more subdivisions of 262.94 in the number coming last, e.g., annulment of marriage 262.947 (*not* 262.944) |
| .941 | General norms (Canons 1–203) |
| .942 | The people of God (Canons 204–746) |
| | Including clergy, laity; hierarchical organization of the Church; religious congregations and orders |
| .943 | Teaching mission of the Church (Canons 747–833) |
| | Including Catholic education, catechetical instruction |
| .944 | Function of the Church (Canons 834–1253) |
| | Class here worship, sacred places and times; comprehensive works on canon law on sacraments |
| | *For a specific aspect of canon law on sacraments provided elsewhere, see the aspect, e.g., annulment of marriage 262.947* |
| .945 | Church temporal goods (Canons 1254–1310) |
| .946 | Sanctions (Canons 1311–1399) |
| | Class here crimes, penalties, delicts |
| .947 | Processes (Canons 1400–1752) |
| | Class here trials, judgments, procedures |
| .98 | Branches and other denominations and sects |
| .980 2 | Eastern and Roman Catholic churches |
| | *For church law of Eastern churches, see 262.9815; for church law of Roman Catholic Church, see 262.982* |
| .980 4 | Protestant churches and Protestantism |
| | *For church law of specific Protestant denominations and sects, see 262.983–262.989* |

.981–.989            Other specific denominations or sects

                     Add to base number 262.98 the numbers following 28 in 281–289, e.g.,
                     Anglican ecclesiastical law 262.983

# 263        Days, times, places of religious observance

.04          Special topics of days, times, places of religious observance

.041               Pilgrimages

[.041 093–.041 099]          Specific continents, countries, localities

                     Do not use; class in 263.0423–263.0429

.042               Holy places

                     Class here pilgrimages to holy places in specific continents, countries,
                     localities

                     *For works treating miracles and shrines associated with them, see
                     231.73; for miracles associated with Mary and shrines associated
                     with them, see 232.917; for miracles of Jesus and shrines associated
                     with them, see 232.955*

[.042 093–.042 099]          Specific continents, countries, localities

                     Do not use; class in 263.0423–263.0429

.042 3–.042 9          Specific continents, countries, localities

                     Add to base number 263.042 notation 3–9 from Table 2, e.g.,
                     Santiago de Compostela 263.0424611

---

>            **263.1–263.3  Sabbath and Sunday**

                     Class comprehensive works in 263.3

.1           **Biblical Sabbath**

.2           **Observance of the seventh day**

.3           **Sunday**

                     Class here Sunday observance, comprehensive works on Sabbath and Sunday

                     *For Biblical Sabbath, see 263.1; for observance of the seventh day, see
                     263.2*

.9           **Church year and other days and times**

                     Standard subdivisions are added for church year and other days and times
                     together, for church year alone

                     *See Manual at 203.6, 263.9, 292–299 vs. 394.265–394.267*

---

>            263.91–263.94  Church year

                     Class comprehensive works in 263.9

.91                Advent and Christmas

| .912 | Advent |
|---|---|

| .915 | Christmas season |
|---|---|

> Class here Christmas day

| .92 | Lent |
|---|---|

| .925 | Holy Week |
|---|---|

| .93 | Easter season |
|---|---|

> Including Ascension Day

> Class here Easter Sunday

| .94 | Pentecost and time after Pentecost (Ordinary time) |
|---|---|

| .97 | Other feast and fast days |
|---|---|

> *For saints' days, see 263.98*

| .98 | Saints' days |
|---|---|

> Standard subdivisions are added for individual saint's days

# 264 Public worship

Ceremonies, rites, services (liturgy and ritual)

Class works not limited by denomination or sect about sacraments, other rites and acts in 265; class Sunday school services in 268.7; class comprehensive works on worship in 248.3

## SUMMARY

| | | |
|---|---|---|
| **264.001–.009** | | **Standard subdivisions** |
| **.01–.09** | | **Public worship by denominations and sects** |
| **.1** | **Prayer** | |
| **.2** | **Music** | |
| **.3** | **Scripture readings and communion sacrament** | |
| **.4** | **Responsive readings** | |
| **.7** | **Prayer meetings, Holy Hours, novenas** | |
| **.9** | **Sacramentals** | |

| .001 | Philosophy and theory |
|---|---|

> Class here liturgical renewal

| .002–.009 | Standard subdivisions |
|---|---|

---

> 264.01 264.09  Public worship by denominations and sects

Class here works limited by denomination or sect about sacraments, other rites and acts

Class comprehensive works in 264; class comprehensive works on sacraments, other rites and acts in 265

.01 Early and Eastern churches

> Add to base number 264.01 the numbers following 281 in 281.1–281.9, e.g., liturgy and ritual of Orthodox churches 264.019; then add further as instructed under 264.04–264.09, e.g., Orthodox Divine Liturgy 264.019036

.02 Roman Catholic Church

.020 01–.020 09 Standard subdivisions

.020 1–.020 9 History, meaning, place of liturgy, ritual, prayers in public worship

> Add to base number 264.02 notation 01–09 from the table under 264.04–264.09, e.g., the Mass 264.02036; however, for texts, see 264.021–264.029

---

> 264.021–264.029 Texts of liturgy, ritual, prayers

Class comprehensive works in 264.02

.021 Texts of calendars and ordos

.022 Texts of ceremonials

> Ceremonials: canonization of saints, election and coronation of popes, creation of cardinals, other papal functions and services; instructions for bishops

.023 Texts of missals

> Class here sacramentaries
>
> *For lectionary, see 264.029*

.024 Texts of breviaries

> *For psalters, see 264.028*

.025 Texts of ritual

> Class here Pontificale Romanum, Rituale Romanum
>
> Add to base number 264.025 the numbers following 265 in 265.1–265.7, e.g., texts of baptism 264.0251

.027 Texts of special books

.027 2 Texts for special times of year

> Including Holy Week

.027 4 Texts for special liturgical services

> Including funeral services outside the Mass, litanies, novenas, stations of the cross

.028 Texts of psalters

.029 Texts of lectionary

| .03 | | Anglican churches |
|---|---|---|

Including rubrics

Class here Book of Common Prayer; Common Worship

| .030 01–.030 09 | Standard subdivisions |
|---|---|

| .030 1–.030 9 | History, meaning, place of liturgy, ritual, prayers in public worship |
|---|---|

Add to base number 264.03 notation 01–09 from the table under 264.04–264.09, e.g., prayer 264.0301; however, for texts, see 264.031–264.038

---

> **264.031–264.038 Texts of liturgy, ritual, prayers**

Class comprehensive works in 264.03

| .031 | Texts of calendars, festivals, fasts |
|---|---|
| .032 | Texts of lectionary |

Including texts of epistles, Gospels

| .033 | Texts of morning prayer and litany |
|---|---|
| .034 | Texts of evening prayer and vespers |
| .035 | Texts of sacraments, ordinances, services |

Add to base number 264.035 the numbers following 265 in 265.1–265.9, e.g., texts of baptism 264.0351

Class texts of morning prayer and litany in 264.033; class texts of evening prayer and vespers in 264.034

| .036 | Texts of collects |
|---|---|
| .038 | Texts of psalters |

.04–.09     Other specific denominations and sects

> Add to base number 264.0 the numbers following 28 in 284–289, e.g., United Methodist services 264.076; then add further as follows:
> 001–009     Standard subdivisions
> 01–07     Specific elements
> > History, meaning, place in public worship, texts
> > Add to 0 the numbers following 264 in 264.1–264.7, e.g., the Lord's Supper 036, the Lord's Supper in the United Methodist Church 264.076036
> 08     Sacraments
> > History, meaning, place in public worship, texts
> > Add to 08 the numbers following 265 in 265.1–265.7, e.g., the ceremony of baptism 081, the ceremony of baptism in the United Methodist Church 264.076081; however, for Holy Communion (Eucharist, Lord's Supper, Mass), see 036
> 09     Sacramentals, other rites and acts
> > History, meaning, place in public worship, texts
> 091     Sacramentals
> 098–099     Other rites and acts
> > Add to 09 the numbers following 265 in 265.8–265.9, e.g., funeral services 0985, United Methodist funerals 264.0760985

---

> ### 264.1–264.9 Specific elements

> History, meaning, place in public worship, texts

> Class specific elements in public worship of specific denominations and sects in 264.01–264.09; class use of the arts (*except* music), of color in public worship in 246; class liturgical year in 263.9; class comprehensive works in 264

> Specific elements as part of the Mass are classed in 264.36, e.g., Eucharistic prayers (*not* 264.1)

.1     **Prayer**

> Class prayers for a specific ceremony with the ceremony, e.g., prayers for funerals 265.85

.13     Texts of prayers

> Including litanies

> Class comprehensive collections of public and private prayers in 242.8

.15     Liturgy of the hours (Divine office)

> Including psalters

> Class here breviaries

.2     **Music**

> Class comprehensive works on music in Christianity in 246.75; class interdisciplinary works on Christian sacred music in 781.71; class interdisciplinary works on sacred vocal music in 782.22

.23          Hymns

> Class here texts of hymns for devotional use of individuals and families
>
> Class hymnals containing both text and music, interdisciplinary works on hymns in 782.27

**.3          Scripture readings and communion sacrament**

.34          Scripture readings

> Class here common lectionary

.36          Holy Communion (Eucharist, Lord's Supper, Mass)

> Including specific elements when part of the Mass
>
> *For viaticum, see 265.7*

**.4          Responsive readings**

**.7          Prayer meetings, Holy Hours, novenas**

**.9          Sacramentals**

> *For consecrations and dedications, see 265.92*

**265          Sacraments, other rites and acts**

> Standard subdivisions are added for sacraments and other rites and acts together, for sacraments alone
>
> Not limited by denomination or sect
>
> Class works limited by denomination or sect about sacraments, other rites and acts in 264.01–264.09

> ──────────────

>          **265.1–265.7  Sacraments**

> Class comprehensive works in 265
>
> *For Holy Communion (Eucharist, Lord's Supper, Mass), see 264.36*

**.1          Baptism**

.12          Infant baptism

.13          Adult baptism

> Class here Christian initiation (baptism and confirmation) of adults, catechumenate
>
> *For confirmation, see 265.2; for religious education for catechumens, see 268.434*

**.2          Confirmation (Chrismation)**

**.4          Holy Orders**

**.5          Matrimony**

**.6          Penance**

.61        Contrition

        Examination of conscience, prayers preparatory to confession

.62        Confession

.63        Satisfaction

        Penitential prayers and acts for the remission of sin

.64        Absolution

.66        Indulgences

**.7        Viaticum and anointing of the sick**

**.8        Rites in illness and death**

.82        Religious ceremonies for the afflicted

        *For viaticum and anointing of the sick, see 265.7*

.85        Religious ceremonies for the dead

        Class here funeral services

        *For requiem Mass, see 264.36*

**.9        Other acts**

        Including ceremonies of joining a church, foot washing, laying on of hands, love feasts (agapes)

.92        Consecrations and dedications

.94        Exorcism

**266        Missions**

        Class here missionary societies, religious aspects of medical missions

        Class medical services of medical missions in 362.1

        *For mission schools, see 371.071*

.001–.008        Standard subdivisions

.009        History, geographic treatment, biography

        Do not use for foreign missions originating in specific continents, countries, localities; class in 266.023. Do not use for history, geographic treatment, biography of missions of specific denominations and sects; class in 266.1–266.9

        Class here joint and interdenominational missions; foreign missions by continent, country, locality served

.02        Kinds of missions

.022        Home missions

.023        Foreign missions

| [.023 091–.023 099] | Geographic treatment and biography |
|---|---|

> Do not use for foreign missions characterized only by place served; class in 266.009. Do not use for foreign missions originating in specific areas; class in 266.0231–266.0239

| .023 1–.023 9 | Biography; foreign missions originating in specific areas |
|---|---|

> Add to base number 266.023 notation 1–9 from Table 2, e.g., missions originating in France 266.02344; then add 0* and again add notation 1–9 from Table 2 for place served, e.g., French missions to Africa 266.0234406

**.1–.9        Missions of specific denominations and sects**

> Add to base number 266 the numbers following 28 in 281–289, e.g., Anglican missions 266.3; Anglican missions serving Africa 266.36

# 267        Associations for religious work

Class here pious societies, sodalities, confraternities

*For religious congregations and orders, see 255; for missionary societies, see 266*

*See Manual at 230–280*

**.1        Associations for religious work for both men and women**

**.13        Interdenominational and nondenominational associations**

> *For Moral Rearmament, see 267.16*

**.16        Moral Rearmament**

**.18        Specific branches, denominations, sects**

**.180 2        Eastern and Roman Catholic churches**

> *For religious associations of Eastern churches, see 267.1815; for religious associations of Roman Catholic Church, see 267.182*

**.180 4        Protestant churches and Protestantism**

> *For religious associations of specific Protestant denominations and sects, see 267.183–267.189*

**.181–.189        Specific denominations or sects**

> Add to base number 267.18 the numbers following 28 in 281–289, e.g., Baptist Adult Union 267.186132

**.2        Men's associations**

**.23        Interdenominational and nondenominational associations**

> *For Young Men's Christian Associations, see 267.3*

**.24        Specific branches, denominations, sects**

---

*Add 00 for standard subdivisions; see instructions at beginning of Table 1

.240 2         Eastern and Roman Catholic churches

> *For men's religious associations of Eastern churches, see 267.2415; for men's religious associations of Roman Catholic Church, see 267.242*

.240 4         Protestant churches and Protestantism

> *For men's religious associations of specific Protestant denominations and sects, see 267.243–267.249*

.241–.249      Specific denominations or sects

> Add to base number 267.24 the numbers following 28 in 281–289, e.g., Baptist societies 267.246

**.3       Young Men's Christian Associations**

[.309]        History, geographic treatment, biography

> Do not use; class in 267.39

.39       History, geographic treatment, biography

.390 1–.390 5    Historical periods

> Add to base number 267.39 notation 01–05 from Table 2, e.g., Young Men's Christian Association in 21st century 267.3905

.391–.399      Geographic treatment, biography

> Add to base number 267.39 notation 1–9 from Table 2, e.g., Young Men's Christian Association in New York City 267.397471

**.4       Women's associations**

.43       Interdenominational and nondenominational associations

> *For Young Women's Christian Associations, see 267.5*

.44       Specific branches, denominations, sects

.440 2         Eastern and Roman Catholic churches

> *For women's religious associations of Eastern churches, see 267.4415; for women's religious associations of Roman Catholic Church, see 267.442*

.440 4         Protestant churches and Protestantism

> *For women's religious associations of specific Protestant denominations and sects, see 267.443–267.449*

.441–.449      Specific denominations or sects

> Add to base number 267.44 the numbers following 28 in 281–289, e.g., Baptist societies 267.446

**.5       Young Women's Christian Associations**

[.509]        History, geographic treatment, biography

> Do not use; class in 267.59

.59       History, geographic treatment, biography

.590 1–.590 5      Historical periods

> Add to base number 267.59 notation 01–05 from Table 2, e.g., Young Women's Christian Association in 21st century 267.5905

.591–.599      Geographic treatment, biography

> Add to base number 267.59 notation 1–9 from Table 2, e.g., Young Women's Christian Association in New York City 267.597471

## .6      Young adults' associations

.61      Interdenominational and nondenominational associations

> *For Young Men's Christian Associations, see 267.3; for Young Women's Christian Associations, see 267.5*

.62      Specific branches, denominations, sects

.620 2      Eastern and Roman Catholic churches

> *For young adults' religious associations of Eastern churches, see 267.6215; for young adults' religious associations of Roman Catholic Church, see 267.622*

.620 4      Protestant churches and Protestantism

> *For young adults' religious associations of specific Protestant denominations and sects, see 267.623–267.629*

.621–.629      Specific denominations or sects

> Add to base number 267.62 the numbers following 28 in 281–289, e.g., Baptist Young People's Union 267.626132

## .7      Boys' associations

> *For Young Men's Christian Associations, see 267.3*

## .8      Girls' associations

> *For Young Women's Christian Associations, see 267.5*

# 268      Religious education

> Class here catechetics (the science or art devoted to organizing the principles of religious teaching), curricula, comprehensive works on Christian religious education
>
> Class Christian religious schools providing general education in 371.071; class place of religion in public schools in 379.28. Class textbooks on a specific subject with the subject, e.g., textbooks on missions 266
>
> *For religious education at the university level, see 230.0711; for study of Christianity in secular secondary schools, see 230.0712*
>
> *See Manual at 207.5, 268 vs. 200.71, 230.071, 292–299*

[.068]      Management

> Do not use; class in 268.1

| | |
|---|---|
| .08 | Groups of people |

Do not use for education of specific groups of people; class in 268.4

Class here education, teaching performed by groups of people

[.088 2]    History and descriptions with respect to religious groups

Do not use; class in 268.8

**.1    Administration**

*For plant management, see 268.2; for personnel management, see 268.3*

**.2    Buildings and equipment**

**.3    Personnel**

Class here preparation, role, training, personnel management

*See Manual at 230–280*

**.4    Religious education of specific groups of people**

Class here curricula, records and rules, teaching methods, services for specific groups

[.408 3–.408 4]    Age groups

Do not use; class in 268.43

.43    Age groups

.432    Children

Through age eleven

*See also 372.84 for religion courses in secular primary schools*

(.432 04)    Special topics of children

(.432 045)    Textbooks

(Option: Class here religious education textbooks; prefer the specific subject, e.g., textbooks on Christianity 230, textbooks on missions 266)

.433    Young people twelve to twenty

(.433 04)    Special topics of young people twelve to twenty

(.433 045)    Textbooks

(Option: Class here religious education textbooks; prefer the specific subject, e.g., textbooks on Christianity 230, textbooks on missions 266)

.434    Adults

(.434 04)    Special topics of adults

| (.434 045) | Textbooks |
|---|---|

> (Option: Class here religious education textbooks; prefer the specific subject, e.g., textbooks on Christianity 230, textbooks on missions 266)

**.5          Records and rules**

> Including attendance, decorations, honor rolls, prizes, promotion

> Class records and rules for specific groups in 268.4

**.6          Methods of instruction and study**

> Class methods for a specific group with the group, e.g., methods for instruction of children 268.432071

.63          Lecture and audiovisual methods

.632            Lecture method

.635            Audiovisual methods

.67          Dramatic method

> Class use of dramatic arts for religious purposes not limited to religious education in 246.72

**.7          Services**

> Including anniversaries, festivals, music, rallies, special days

> Class services for specific groups in 268.4

**.8          Specific branches, denominations, sects**

.802            Eastern and Roman Catholic churches

> *For religious education of Eastern churches, see 268.815; for religious education of Roman Catholic Church, see 268.82*

.804            Protestant churches and Protestantism

> *For religious education of specific Protestant denominations and sects, see 268.83–268.89*

.81–.89          Specific denominations or sects

> Add to base number 268.8 the numbers following 28 in 281–289, e.g., Presbyterian religious education 268.85

> Class a specific element in religious education by specific denominations and sects with the element in 268.1–268.7, e.g., religious education of children in Baptist churches 268.432088286

**269          Spiritual renewal**

> Class history of the pentecostal movement in 270.82

**.2          Evangelism**

> *See also 243 for evangelistic writings for individuals and families; also 248.5 for witness bearing by individual lay Christians; also 252.3 for texts of evangelistic sermons; also 266 for missionary evangelization*

.24        Revival and camp meetings

.26        Evangelism by radio and television

**.6        Retreats**

Add to base number 269.6 the numbers following 248.8 in 248.82–248.89, e.g., retreats for men 269.642

---

>

# 270–280  History, geographic treatment, biography of Christianity; Church history; Christian denominations and sects

Unless other instructions are given, observe the following table of preference for the history of Christianity and the Christian church (*except* for biography, explained in Manual at 230–280), e.g., persecution of Jesuits by Elizabeth I 272.7 (*not* 271.53042, 274.206, or 282.42):

| | |
|---|---|
| Persecutions in general church history | 272 |
| Doctrinal controversies and heresies in general church history | 273 |
| Religious congregations and orders in church history | 271 |
| Denominations and sects of Christian church | 280 |
| Christianity and Christian church by continent, country, locality | 274–279 |
| General history, geographic treatment, biography of Christianity and Christian church (*except* 271–279) | 270 |

Class comprehensive works in 270

*See Manual at 230–280*

## 270  History, geographic treatment, biography of Christianity

Class here Church history, collected writings of apostolic and church fathers (patristics)

Observe table of preference under 230–280

*For history, geographic treatment, biography of specific denominations and sects, see 280*

*See Manual at 230–280; also at 270, 230.11–230.14 vs. 230.15–230.2, 281.5–281.9, 282; also at 398.2 vs. 201.3, 230, 270, 292–299*

### SUMMARY

| | |
|---|---|
| 270.01–.09 | **Standard subdivisions** |
| .1–.8 | **Historical periods** |
| 271 | **Religious congregations and orders in church history** |
| 272 | **Persecutions in general church history** |
| 273 | **Doctrinal controversies and heresies in general church history** |
| 274–279 | **Christianity by specific continents, countries, localities in modern world** |

| | |
|---|---|
| .01–.07 | Standard subdivisions |
| .08 | Groups of people |

Class here Christian attitudes toward social groups; discrimination, equality, inequality, prejudice

| | |
|---|---|
| .09 | Areas, regions, places in general; biography |
| [.093–.099] | Specific continents, countries, localities |

Do not use; class in 274–279

---

> **270.1–270.8 Historical periods**

Class historical periods in specific continents, countries, localities in 274–279; class comprehensive works in 270

| | |
|---|---|
| .1 | **Apostolic period to 325** |
| .2 | **Period of ecumenical councils, 325–787** |
| .3 | **787–1054** |

Class here comprehensive works on Middle Ages

*For a specific part of Middle Ages, see the part, e.g., late Middle Ages 270.5*

| | |
|---|---|
| .38 | Great schism, 1054 |
| .4 | **1054–1200** |
| .5 | **Late Middle Ages through Renaissance, 1200–1517** |
| .6 | **Period of Reformation and Counter-Reformation, 1517–1648** |

Including 17th century

*For 1648–1699, see 270.7*

| | |
|---|---|
| .7 | **Period from Peace of Westphalia to French Revolution, 1648–1789** |
| .8 | **Modern period, 1789–** |
| .81 | 1789–1900 |

.82       1900–1999

Class here comprehensive works on evangelicalism, fundamentalism, pentecostalism, charismatic movement

Add to base number 270.82 the numbers following —0904 in notation 09041–09049 from Table 1, e.g., 1960–1969 in church history 270.826

Class ecumenical movement in 280.042; class pentecostal churches that are independent denominations in 289.94; class evangelical churches, fundamentalist churches that are independent denominations in 289.95

*For evangelicalism, fundamentalism, pentecostalism, charismatic movement in the period 2000 to present, see 270.83. For evangelicalism, fundamentalism, pentecostalism, charismatic movement in a specific branch or denomination, see the branch or denomination, e.g., Protestant fundamentalism 280.4*

.83       2000–

---

>       **271–273 Special topics of church history**

Class comprehensive works in 270

# 271     Religious congregations and orders in church history

Class here history of monasticism, history of specific monasteries and convents even if not connected with a specific order

Add to each subdivision identified by * as follows:
    001–008     Standard subdivisions
    [009]       History
                 Do not use; class in base number without further addition
    [0091–0099]    Geographic treatment and biography
                  Do not use; class in 01–09
    01–09     Geographic treatment and biography
                  Add to 0 notation 1–9 from Table 2, e.g., collected biography 022, collected biography of Benedictines 271.1022, Benedictines in the United Kingdom 271.1041

Class persecutions involving religious congregations and orders in 272; class doctrinal controversies and heresies involving congregations and orders in 273

### SUMMARY

| | |
|---|---|
| 271.001–.009 | Standard subdivisions |
| .01–.09 | Specific kinds of congregations and orders |
| .1 | Benedictines |
| .2 | Dominicans (Friars Preachers, Black Friars) |
| .3 | Franciscans (Gray Friars) |
| .4 | Augustinians |
| .5 | Regular clerics |
| .6 | Passionists and Redemptorists |
| .7 | Roman Catholic orders of men not otherwise provided for |
| .8 | Non-Roman Catholic orders of men |
| .9 | Congregations and orders of women |

.001–.009     Standard subdivisions

> 271.01–271.09  Specific kinds of congregations and orders

Class comprehensive works in 271

.01     *Contemplative religious orders

.02     *Eremitical religious orders

.03     *Teaching orders

.04     *Preaching orders

.06     *Mendicant religious orders

.07     *Nursing orders

.08     *Canons regular

.09       Other specific kinds

.092        *Brothers

*See also 271.093 for lay brothers*

.093        *Lay brothers

.094        *Third orders

Secular and regular

.095        *Secular institutes

> **271.1–271.8  Specific orders of men**

Class comprehensive works in 271

> **271.1–271.7  Roman Catholic orders of men**

Class comprehensive works in 271

**.1      *Benedictines**

.11      *Confederated Benedictines

*For Olivetans, see 271.13*

.12      *Cistercians (Bernardines)

.125        *Trappists

.13      *Olivetans

.14      *Cluniacs

Including Camaldolese, Silvestrians, Monks of Saint Paul the Hermit

*For Carthusians, see 271.71*

.16      *Celestines

*Add as instructed under 271

| .17 | Mechitarists and Basilians |
|---|---|
| .18 | Antonines (Antonians), Maronites, Chaldeans, Syrians |
| .19 | *Canons |

> Including Crosier Fathers, Crosiers of the Red Star, Premonstratensians
>
> Class Augustinians in 271.4

**.2** **\*Dominicans (Friars Preachers, Black Friars)**

**.3** **\*Franciscans (Gray Friars)**

> Including Alcantarines, Observants, Recollects
>
> *See also 271.4 for Augustinian Recollects*

| .36 | *Capuchins |
|---|---|
| .37 | *Conventuals |
| .38 | *Third Order Regular |

**.4** **\*Augustinians**

> Including Augustinian Recollects

| .42 | *Trinitarians |
|---|---|
| .45 | *Mercedarians |
| .47 | *Servites |
| .49 | Other Augustinians |

> Including Brothers Hospitallers of St. John of God, Minims

**.5** **\*Regular clerics**

| .51 | *Theatines |
|---|---|
| .52 | *Barnabites |
| .53 | *Jesuits (Society of Jesus) |
| .54 | *Somaschi |
| .55 | *Camillians |
| .56 | *Minor Clerks Regular (Caracciolini) |
| .57 | *Clerks Regular of the Mother of God |
| .58 | *Piarists |

**.6** **\*Passionists and Redemptorists**

| .62 | *Passionists |
|---|---|
| .64 | *Redemptorists |

**.7** **Roman Catholic orders of men not otherwise provided for**

*Add as instructed under 271

| .71 | *Carthusians |
|---|---|

.73     *Carmelites (White Friars)

.75     *Sulpicians

.76     *Oblates

.77     *Lazarists (Vincentians)

.78     *Christian Brothers (Brothers of the Christian Schools)

.79          Other Roman Catholic orders of men

.791             *Orders of knighthood

Class here military orders

.791 2                *Knights of Malta (Knights Hospitalers of St. John of Jerusalem)

.791 3                *Knights Templars

.791 4                *Teutonic Knights

**.8     Non-Roman Catholic orders of men**

.81          Monasteries of Eastern churches

Add to base number 271.81 the numbers following 281 in 281.5–281.9, e.g., Orthodox monasteries 271.819, on Mount Athos 271.81949565

.83          Anglican orders of men

**.9     Congregations and orders of women**

.900 01–.900 08          Standard subdivisions

.900 09          History

[.900 091–.900 099]          Geographic treatment and biography

Do not use; class in 271.9001–271.9009

.900 1–.900 9          Geographic treatment and biography

Add to base number 271.900 notation 1–9 from Table 2, e.g., collected biography of women religious 271.90022, congregations and orders of women in France 271.90044

.901–.909          Specific kinds of congregations and orders

Add to base number 271.90 the numbers following 271.0 in 271.01–271.09, e.g., contemplative orders 271.901

---

> 271.91–271.98 Specific orders of women

Class comprehensive works in 271.9

*Add as instructed under 271

> 271.91–271.97 Roman Catholic orders of women

Class comprehensive works in 271.9

.91 *Sisters of Charity orders

.92 *Sisters of Mercy orders

.93 *Sacred Heart orders

.94 *Sisters of Bon Secours

.95 *Little Sisters of the Poor

.97 Other Roman Catholic orders of women

.971 *Carmelites

.972 *Dominicans

.973 *Franciscan orders

Class here Poor Clares

.974 *Ursulines

.975 *Visitation orders

.976 *Saint Joseph orders

.977 *Presentation orders

.98 Non-Roman Catholic orders of women

.981 Women's convents of Eastern churches

Add to base number 271.981 the numbers following 281 in 281.5–281.9, e.g., Orthodox convents of women 271.9819

.983 Anglican orders of women

## 272 Persecutions in general church history

Regardless of denomination

Class here martyrs

Class relation of state to church in 322.1

*See also 364.188 for offenses against religion as defined and penalized by the state*

**.1 Persecutions of Apostolic Church by imperial Rome**

**.2 Persecutions by Inquisition**

**.3 Persecutions of Waldenses and Albigenses**

**.4 Persecutions of Huguenots**

**.5 Persecutions of Molinists and Quietists**

*Add as instructed under 271

.6      **Persecutions of Anglican reformers by Mary I**

.7      **Persecutions of Roman Church by Elizabeth I and Anglicans**

.8      **Persecutions of Quakers, Baptists, witches by Puritans and others of Puritan times**

.9      **Modern persecutions and martyrs**

## 273      Doctrinal controversies and heresies in general church history

Class persecutions resulting from controversies and heresies in 272; class churches founded on specific doctrines in 280

*See also 239 for apologetics and polemics*

.1      **1st–2nd centuries**

Class here Christian gnosticism

Class comprehensive works and non-Christian Gnosticism in 299.932

*For gnosticism of 3rd century, see 273.2*

.2      **3rd century**

Including Christian Manicheism

Class comprehensive works and non-Christian Manicheism in 299.932

*For Sabellianism, see 273.3*

.3      **Sabellianism**

.4      **4th century**

Including Arianism, Donatism

.5      **5th century**

Including Pelagianism

.6      **6th–16th centuries**

Including Albigensianism, Catharism, Waldensianism

Class here antinomianism

*For later antinomianism, see 273.7–273.9; for Albigensian, Catharist, Waldensian churches, see 284.4*

.7      **17th century**

Including Molinism, Pietism; comprehensive works on Jansenism

*For Jansenist churches, see 284.84*

.8      **18th century**

.9      **19th century and later centuries**

Including modernism

**274–279 Christianity by specific continents, countries, localities in modern world**

> Class here Christian church history by continent, country, locality
>
> Add to base number 27 notation 4–9 from Table 2, e.g., Christianity, Christian church in Europe 274, in France 274.4; then add further as follows:
>
> | | |
> |---|---|
> | 001–008 | Standard subdivisions |
> | 009 | History, geographic treatment, biography |
> | | Do not use for historical periods; class in 01–08 |
> | 01–08 | Historical periods |
> | | Add the numbers following 27 in 270.1–270.8, e.g., Christian church in France during the Reformation 274.406 |
>
> Class geographic treatment of a specific subject with the subject, plus notation 09 from Table 1, e.g., persecutions in France 272.0944

**274      Christianity in Europe**

> Number built according to instructions under 274–279

**275      Christianity in Asia**

> Number built according to instructions under 274–279

**276      Christianity in Africa**

> Number built according to instructions under 274–279

**277      Christianity in North America**

> Number built according to instructions under 274–279

**278      Christianity in South America**

> Number built according to instructions under 274–279

**279      Christianity in Australasia, Pacific Ocean islands, Atlantic Ocean islands, Arctic islands, Antarctica**

> Number built according to instructions under 274–279

# 280    Denominations and sects of Christian church

Including nondenominational and interdenominational churches

Class here general history and geographic treatment of, comprehensive works on specific denominations and sects and their individual local churches

Class persecution of or by specific churches in 272

> *For a specific element of specific denominations and sects, see the element, e.g., doctrines 230*

> *See also 273 for doctrines of specific churches considered as heresies*

> *See Manual at 201–209 and 292–299; also at 230–280*

(Option: Class here specific elements of specific denominations and sects; prefer 230–270. If option is chosen, add to the number for each specific denomination, sect, group as follows:

| | |
|---|---|
| 001–008 | Standard subdivisions |
| [009] | History, geographic treatment, biography |
| | Do not use; class in 07 |
| 02 | Basic textual sources |
| | Class Bible in 220 |
| 03–06 | Doctrinal, moral, devotional, social, ecclesiastical theology |
| | Add to 0 the numbers following 2 in 230–260, e.g., the denomination and international affairs 06187 |
| 07 | History, geographic treatment, biography |
| 0701–0708 | Historical periods |
| | Add to 07 the numbers following 27 in 270.1–270.8, e.g., 20th century 07082 |
| 071–079 | Special topics of church history; Christianity by continent, country, locality |
| | Add to 07 the numbers following 27 in 271–279, e.g., Africa 076) |

### SUMMARY

.01–.03     Standard subdivisions

.04     Special topics of denominations and sects of Christian church

.042     Relations between denominations

Class here ecumenical movement

*See Manual at 280.042 vs. 262.0011*

.05–.09     Standard subdivisions

---

>        **280.2–280.4  Branches**

Class specific denominations and sects in 281–289; class comprehensive works in 280

.2       **Eastern and Roman Catholic churches**

Class comprehensive works on Roman Catholic Church and Eastern churches in communion with Rome in 282

*For Eastern churches, see 281.5; for Roman Catholic Church, see 282*

.4       **Protestant churches and Protestantism**

Standard subdivisions are added for either or both topics in heading

Class here dissenters, free churches, nonconformists (British context); works on Protestant evangelicalism, fundamentalism, pentecostalism, charismatic movement

Class comprehensive works on evangelicalism, fundamentalism, pentecostalism, charismatic movement in general church history in 270.82

*For specific Protestant denominations, see 283–289*

---

>        **281–289  Specific denomination or sect**

Class comprehensive works in 280

(Option: Class a specific denomination or sect requiring local emphasis in 289.2)

**281           Early church and Eastern churches**

---

>        **281.1–281.4  Early church**

Use these subdivisions only for building other numbers in 230–260, e.g., theology in the Ante-Nicene church 230.13; never use these subdivisions by themselves. When building numbers in 230–260 using these subdivisions, use 281.1 for comprehensive works

Class collected writings of apostolic and church fathers (patristics) in 270; class all works on early church in 270.1–270.3. Class a specific work of an apostolic or church father on a specific subject with the subject, e.g., philosophy 189.2

*See Manual at 270, 230.11–230.14 vs. 230.15–230.2, 281.5–281.9, 282*

.1       **Apostolic Church to the time of the great schism, 1054**

*For Apostolic Church to 100, see 281.2; for Ante-Nicene church, see 281.3; for Post-Nicene church, see 281.4*

.2       **Apostolic Church to 100**

.3       **Ante-Nicene church, 100–325**

**.4**      **Post-Nicene church, 325–1054**

**.5**      **Eastern churches**

> *For Oriental Orthodox churches, see 281.6; for Assyrian Church of the East (Church of the East), see 281.8; for Orthodox churches, see 281.9*
>
> *See Manual at 230–280; also at 270, 230.11–230.14 vs. 230.15–230.2, 281.5–281.9, 282*

**.52**      Eastern Catholic churches (Eastern rite churches in communion with Rome)

> Including Saint Thomas Christian churches in communion with Rome
>
> Class comprehensive works on Saint Thomas Christian churches in 281.54

**.54**      Saint Thomas Christian churches

> Including Mar Thoma Syrian Church, Malabar Independent Syrian Church, St. Thomas Evangelical Church of India
>
> > *For a specific church within the Saint Thomas Christian tradition not provided for here, see the church, e.g., Syriac Orthodox Church 281.63*

**.6**      **Oriental Orthodox churches**

> Former heading: Monophysite churches
>
> Including Eritrean Orthodox Church, Indian Orthodox Church
>
> Class here non-Chalcedonian churches
>
> > *For Coptic and Ethiopian churches, see 281.7*
>
> > *See Manual at 230–280; also at 270, 230.11–230.14 vs. 230.15–230.2, 281.5–281.9, 282*

**.62**      Armenian Church

**.63**      Syriac Church

> Former heading: Jacobite Church
>
> Class here Syriac Orthodox Church, Jacobite Patriarchate of Antioch
>
> > *See also 281.95691 for Orthodox Church in Syria*

**.7**      **Coptic and Ethiopian churches**

> *See Manual at 270, 230.11–230.14 vs. 230.15–230.2, 281.5–281.9, 282*

**.72**      Coptic Church (Coptic Orthodox Church)

**.75**      Ethiopian Church (Ethiopian Orthodox Tewahedo Church)

**.8**      **Assyrian Church of the East (Church of the East)**

> Former heading: Nestorian churches
>
> *See Manual at 270, 230.11–230.14 vs. 230.15–230.2, 281.5–281.9, 282*

**.9** **Orthodox churches**

> *See Manual at 230–280; also at 270, 230.11–230.14 vs. 230.15–230.2, 281.5–281.9, 282*

.909 History, geographic treatment, biography

[.909 3] Ancient world

> Do not use for early church; class in 270

[.909 4–.909 9] Specific continents, countries, localities in modern world

> Do not use for specific autocephalous, arbitrary autocephalous, autonomous, independent churches; class in 281.94–281.99

.94–.99 Specific autocephalous, arbitrary autocephalous, autonomous, independent churches

> Add to base number 281.9 notation 4–9 from Table 2 for the country of the seat of the church, e.g., Russian Orthodox Church, Russian Orthodox Church Outside Russia 281.947, Orthodox Church in America 281.973; then, for geographic treatment, add 0* and to the result add notation 4–9 from Table 2, e.g., Russian Orthodox Church Outside Russia in United States 281.947073

.947 Russia

> Number built according to instructions under 281.94–281.99

> Class here Moscow Patriarchate, Russian Orthodox Church

.947 7 Ukraine

> Number built according to instructions under 281.94–281.99

> Class here Ukrainian Autocephalous Orthodox Church, Ukrainian Orthodox Church (Kyivan Patriarchate), Ukrainian Orthodox Church (Moscow Patriarchate)

.949 5 Greece

> Number built according to instructions under 281.94–281.99

> Class here Orthodox Church of Greece

.949 6 Balkan Peninsula

> Number built according to instructions under 281.94–281.99

.949 61 Turkey in Eastern Europe

> Number built according to instructions under 281.94–281.99

> Class here Ecumenical Patriarchate of Constantinople (Church of Constantinople)

.949 71 Serbia

> Number built according to instructions under 281.94–281.99

> Class here Serbian Orthodox Church

---

*Add 00 for standard subdivisions; see instructions at beginning of Table 1

| | |
|---|---|
| .949 8 | Romania |

> Number built according to instructions under 281.94–281.99
>
> Class here Romanian Orthodox Church

| | |
|---|---|
| .973 | United States |

> Number built according to instructions under 281.94–281.99
>
> Class here Orthodox Church in America (OCA)
>
> Class specific Orthodox churches affiliated with a patriarchate or other national church with the patriarchate or church, e.g., Greek Orthodox Archdiocese of America (eparchy of the Ecumenical Patriarchate of Constantinople) 281.94961073

## 282 Roman Catholic Church

> Class here the Catholic traditionalist movement, comprehensive works on Roman Catholic Church and Eastern rite churches in communion with Rome
>
> Class modern schisms in Roman Catholic Church in 284.8
>
> *For Eastern rite churches in communion with Rome, see 281.52*
>
> *See Manual at 270, 230.11–230.14 vs. 230.15–230.2, 281.5–281.9, 282*

| | |
|---|---|
| .09 | History, geographic treatment, biography |

> *See Manual at 270, 230.11–230.14 vs. 230.15–230.2, 281.5–281.9, 282*

| | |
|---|---|
| [.093] | Ancient world |

> Do not use for early church; class in 270

| | |
|---|---|
| [.094–.099] | Specific continents, countries, localities in modern world |

> Do not use; class in 282.4–282.9

| | |
|---|---|
| **.4–.9** | **Specific continents, countries, localities in modern world** |

> Add to base number 282 notation 4–9 from Table 2, e.g., Roman Catholic Church in Latin America 282.8

---

## > 283–289 Protestant and other denominations

> Class comprehensive works on Protestant churches in 280.4; class comprehensive works on Protestant and other denominations in 280
>
> *See Manual at 283–289*

## 283 Anglican churches

| | |
|---|---|
| [.094–.099] | Specific continents, countries, localities in modern world |

> Do not use; class in 283.4–283.9

| | |
|---|---|
| **.3** | **Branches not in communion with the See of Canterbury** |

> Including Reformed Episcopal Church and its affiliates
>
> *See Manual at 230–280; also at 283–289*

.4–.9    **Specific continents, countries, localities in modern world**

> Class here national churches in communion with the See of Canterbury

> Add to base number 283 notation 4–9 from Table 2, e.g., Church of England 283.42, Episcopal Diocese of Long Island 283.74721

# 284    Protestant denominations of Continental origin and related bodies

> *For Protestant denominations of Continental origin not provided for here, see the denomination, e.g., Baptists 286*

.094 3            Germany and neighboring central European countries

> Class here Evangelische Kirche in Deutschland

## .1        Lutheran churches

[.109 4–.109 9]        Specific continents, countries, localities in modern world

> Do not use; class in 284.14–284.19

(.12)        (Permanently unassigned)

> (Optional number used to provide local emphasis or a shorter number for Lutheran church in a specific country other than the United States; prefer 284.14–284.19)

.13        Specific denominations, branches, synods centered in the United States

> *See Manual at 230–280; also at 283–289*

[.130 1–.130 9]        Standard subdivisions

> Do not use; class in 284.101–284.109

.131            *The American Lutheran Church

.131 2            *The Evangelical Lutheran Church

.131 3            *United Evangelical Lutheran Church

.131 4            *The Lutheran Free Church

.132            *The Evangelical Lutheran Synodical Conference of North America

> *For Wisconsin Evangelical Lutheran Synod, see 284.134*

.132 2            *The Lutheran Church—Missouri Synod

> *For Synod of Evangelical Lutheran Churches, see 284.1323*

.132 3            *Synod of Evangelical Lutheran Churches (Slovak)

.133        *The Lutheran Church in America

.133 2            *American Evangelical Lutheran Church

.133 3            *Augustana Evangelical Lutheran Church

.133 4            *Finnish Evangelical Lutheran Church

---

*Do not use notation 094–099 from Table 1; class in 284.14–284.19

| | |
|---|---|
| .133 5 | *The United Lutheran Church in America |
| .134 | *Wisconsin Evangelical Lutheran Synod |
| .135 | *Evangelical Lutheran Church in America |
| .14–.19 | Specific continents, countries, localities in modern world |

> Add to base number 284.1 notation 4–9 from Table 2, e.g., Lutheran Church of Sweden 284.1485, Memorial Evangelical Lutheran Church of Washington, D.C. 284.1753; however, Evangelische Kirche in Deutschland relocated from 284.143 to 284.0943
>
> (Option: Class Lutheran churches in a specific country other than the United States in 284.12)

**.2 Calvinistic and Reformed churches of European origin**

> Standard subdivisions are added for either or both topics in heading
>
> Class here comprehensive works on Calvinistic churches, on Reformed churches
>
> *For Huguenot churches, see 284.5; for Presbyterian churches, see 285; for Reformed churches centered in America, see 285.7*
>
> *See also 285.9 for Puritanism*

| | |
|---|---|
| [.209 4–.209 9] | Specific continents, countries, localities in modern world |

> Do not use; class in 284.24–284.29

| | |
|---|---|
| .24–.29 | Specific continents, countries, localities in modern world |

> Add to base number 284.2 notation 4–9 from Table 2, e.g., Reformed churches in Holland 284.2492, in South Africa 284.268

**.3 Hussite and Anabaptist churches**

> Including Lollards, Wycliffites
>
> *See also 289.7 for Mennonite churches*

**.4 Albigensian, Catharist, Waldensian churches**

**.5 Huguenot churches**

**.6 Moravian churches**

> *For Hussite churches, see 284.3*

| | |
|---|---|
| [.609 4–.609 9] | Specific continents, countries, localities in modern world |

> Do not use; class in 284.64–284.69

| | |
|---|---|
| .64–.69 | Specific continents, countries, localities in modern world |

> Add to base number 284.6 notation 4–9 from Table 2, e.g., Moravian churches in Germany 284.643

*Do not use notation 094–099 from Table 1; class in 284.14–284.19

**.8**       **Modern schisms in Roman Catholic Church**

Including Constitutional Church, Gallican schismatic churches, Liberal Catholic Church, Little Church of France, Old Catholic churches, Philippine Independent Church

.84       Jansenist churches

**.9**       **Arminian and Remonstrant churches**

# 285       Presbyterian churches, Reformed churches centered in America, Congregational churches, Puritanism

Standard subdivisions are added for Presbyterian churches, Reformed churches centered in America, Congregational churches together; for Presbyterian churches alone

---

>       **285.1–285.2  Presbyterian churches of United States, of British Commonwealth origin**

Class comprehensive works on Presbyterian churches, Presbyterian churches of other origin in 285

(If option under 280 is followed, use 285.001–285.008 for standard subdivisions, 285.02–285.07 for specific elements of Presbyterian churches)

**.1**       **Presbyterian churches of United States origin**

[.109 4–.109 9]       Specific continents, countries, localities in modern world

Do not use; class in 285.14–285.19

.13       Specific denominations

*See Manual at 230–280; also at 283–289*

[.130 1–.130 9]       Standard subdivisions

Do not use; class in 285.101–285.109

.131       *United Presbyterian Church in the U.S.A.

.132       *Presbyterian Church in the United States of America

.133       *Presbyterian Church in the United States

.134       *United Presbyterian Church of North America

.135       *Cumberland Presbyterian Church

.136       *Reformed Presbyterian churches

.137       *Presbyterian Church (U.S.A.)

.14–.19       Specific continents, countries, localities in modern world

Add to base number 285.1 notation 4–9 from Table 2, e.g., the Hudson River Presbytery 285.17473

---

*Do not use notation 094–099 from Table 1; class in 285.14–285.19

.2 **Presbyterian churches of British Commonwealth origin**

[.209 4–.209 9]    Specific continents, countries, localities in modern world

>    Do not use; class in 285.24–285.29

.23    Specific denominations

>    Including Countess of Huntingdon's Connexion

>    *See Manual at 230–280; also at 283–289*

[.230 1–.230 9]    Standard subdivisions

>    Do not use; class in 285.201–285.209

.232    †United Reformed Church in the United Kingdom

>    Class Congregational Church of England and Wales in 285.842

.233    †Church of Scotland

.234    †Free Church of Scotland

.235    †Presbyterian Church of Wales (Welsh Calvinistic Methodist Church)

.24–.29    Specific continents, countries, localities in modern world

>    Add to base number 285.2 notation 4–9 from Table 2, e.g., Presbyterianism in Ireland 285.2415, a Church of Scotland parish in Edinburgh 285.24134

>    Class United Church of Canada in 287.92; class Uniting Church in Australia in 287.93

.7    **Reformed churches centered in America**

[.709 4–.709 9]    Specific continents, countries, localities in modern world

>    Do not use; class in 285.74–285.79

.73    Specific denominations

>    *See Manual at 230–280; also at 283–289*

[.730 1–.730 9]    Standard subdivisions

>    Do not use; class in 285.701–285.709

.731    *Christian Reformed Church

.732    *Reformed Church in America (Dutch)

.733    *Reformed Church in the United States (German)

.734    *Evangelical and Reformed Church

.74–.79    Specific continents, countries, localities in modern world

>    Add to base number 285.7 notation 4–9 from Table 2, e.g., First Reformed Church of Schenectady, N.Y. 285.774744

.8    **Congregationalism**

*Do not use notation 094–099 from Table 1; class in 285.74–285.79
†Do not use notation 094–099 from Table 1; class in 285.24–285.29

| | |
|---|---|
| [.809 4–.809 9] | Specific continents, countries, localities in modern world |

> Do not use; class in 285.84–285.89

| | |
|---|---|
| (.82) | (Permanently unassigned) |

> (Optional number used to provide local emphasis or a shorter number for Congregational churches in a specific country other than the United States; prefer 285.84–285.89)

| | |
|---|---|
| .83 | Specific denominations centered in the United States |

> *See Manual at 230–280; also at 283–289*

| | |
|---|---|
| [.830 1–.830 9] | Standard subdivisions |

> Do not use; class in 285.801–285.809

| | |
|---|---|
| .832 | †Congregational Churches of the United States |
| .833 | †Congregational Christian Churches |
| .834 | †United Church of Christ |

> *For Evangelical and Reformed Church, see 285.734*

| | |
|---|---|
| .84–.89 | Specific continents, countries, localities in modern world |

> Class here specific denominations centered outside the United States

> Add to base number 285.8 notation 4–9 from Table 2, e.g., Congregational Church of England and Wales 285.842, Congregational churches in New England 285.874

> Class United Church of Canada in 287.92; class Uniting Church in Australia in 287.93

> (Option: Class Congregational churches in a specific country other than the United States in 285.82)

| | |
|---|---|
| .9 | **Puritanism** |

# 286 Baptist, Restoration movement, Adventist churches

> Standard subdivisions are added for Baptist, Restoration movement, Adventist churches together; for Baptist churches alone

---

> ## 286.1–286.5 Baptist churches

> Class comprehensive works in 286

> (If option under 280 is followed, use 286.001–286.008 for standard subdivisions, 286.02–286.07 for specific elements of Baptist churches)

| | |
|---|---|
| .1 | **Regular Baptists (Calvinistic Baptists)** |
| [.109 4–.109 9] | Specific continents, countries, localities in modern world |

> Do not use; class in 286.14–286.19

†Do not use notation 094–099 from Table 1; class in 285.84–285.89

(.12)      (Permanently unassigned)

> (Optional number used to provide local emphasis or a shorter number for Regular Baptist churches in a specific country other than the United States; prefer 286.14–286.19)

.13      Specific denominations centered in the United States

> *See Manual at 230–280; also at 283–289*

[.130 1–.130 9]      Standard subdivisions

> Do not use; class in 286.101–286.109

.131      *American Baptist Churches in the U.S.A.

> Former name: American (Northern) Baptist Convention

.132      *Southern Baptist Convention

.133      *National Baptist Convention of the United States of America

.134      *National Baptist Convention of America

.135      *Progressive National Baptist Convention

.136      *American Baptist Association

.14–.19      Specific continents, countries, localities in modern world

> Class here specific denominations centered outside the United States

> Add to base number 286.1 notation 4–9 from Table 2, e.g., Association of Regular Baptist Churches of Canada 286.171, a Southern Baptist association in Tennessee 286.1768

> (Option: Class Regular Baptist churches in a specific country other than the United States in 286.12)

**.2**      **Freewill Baptists**

**.3**      **Seventh-Day Baptists**

**.4**      **Old School Baptists**

> Including Antimission, Primitive Baptists

**.5**      **Other Baptist churches and denominations**

> Including Baptist General Conference, Church of the Brethren, Dunkers

**.6**      **Restoration movement**

> Former heading: Disciples of Christ (Campbellites)

[.609 4–.609 9]      Specific continents, countries, localities in modern world

> Do not use; class in 286.64–286.69

---

*Do not use notation 094–099 from Table 1; class in 286.14–286.19

.63      Specific denominations

Including Christian Church (Disciples of Christ), Christian Churches and Churches of Christ, Churches of Christ

Class a specific denomination in a specific geographic area with the area in 286.64–286.69

*See Manual at 230–280; also at 283–289*

[.630 1–.630 9]      Standard subdivisions

Do not use; class in 286.601–286.609

.64–.69      Specific continents, countries, localities in modern world

Class here specific denominations and specific churches in specific geographic areas

Add to base number 286.6 notation 4–9 from Table 2, e.g., the Christian Church (Disciples of Christ) in Florida 286.6759

## .7      Adventist churches

[.709 4–.709 9]      Specific continents, countries, localities in modern world

Do not use; class in 286.74–286.79

.73      Specific denominations

Including Advent Christian Church, Church of God General Conference

Class a specific denomination in a specific geographic area with the area in 286.74–286.79

*See Manual at 230–280; also at 283–289*

[.730 1–.730 9]      Standard subdivisions

Do not use; class in 286.701–286.709

.732      Seventh-Day Adventist Church

[.732 094–.732 099]      Specific continents, countries, localities in modern world

Do not use; class in 286.74–286.79

.74–.79      Specific continents, countries, localities in modern world

Class here specific denominations and specific churches in specific geographic areas

Add to base number 286.7 notation 4–9 from Table 2, e.g., Seventh-Day Adventists in South America 286.78

## 287      Methodist churches; churches related to Methodism

Standard subdivisions are added for Methodist churches and churches related to Methodism together; for Methodist churches alone

## .1      Wesleyan Methodist Church

[.109 4–.109 9]      Specific continents, countries, localities in modern world

Do not use; class in 287.14–287.19

.14–.19        Specific continents, countries, localities in modern world

> Add to base number 287.1 notation 4–9 from Table 2, e.g., Wesleyan Methodist Church in British Isles 287.141, Wesleyan Methodist Church in New South Wales 287.1944

**.2        Miscellaneous Methodist churches**

> Including Congregational Methodist Church, Free Methodist Church of North America

**.4        Primitive Methodist Church**

[.409 4–.409 9]        Specific continents, countries, localities in modern world

> Do not use; class in 287.44–287.49

.44–.49        Specific continents, countries, localities in modern world

> Add to base number 287.4 notation 4–9 from Table 2, e.g., Primitive Methodist Church in British Isles 287.441

**.5        Methodist churches in British Isles**

[.509 41–.509 42]        British Isles

> Do not use; class in 287.54

.53        Specific denominations

> Including Bible Christians, Methodist New Connexion, Protestant Methodists, United Methodist Church (Great Britain), United Methodist Free Churches, Wesleyan Conference, Wesleyan Reformers, Yearly Conference of People Called Methodists
>
> Class a specific denomination in a specific geographic area with the area in 287.54
>
> > *For Wesleyan Methodist Church in British Isles, see 287.141; for Primitive Methodist Church in British Isles, see 287.441*
> >
> > *See also 285.23 for Countess of Huntingdon's Connexion; also 285.235 for Welsh Calvinistic Methodist Church*
> >
> > *See Manual at 230–280; also at 283–289*

[.530 1–.530 9]        Standard subdivisions

> Do not use; class in 287.501–287.509

.532        *United Conference of Methodist Churches

.533        *Independent Methodists

.534        *Wesleyan Reform Union

.536        *Methodist Church of Great Britain

---

*Do not use notation 0941–0942 from Table 1; class in 287.54

.54 Country and locality

> Class here specific denominations and specific churches in specific geographic areas
>
> Add to base number 287.54 the numbers following —4 in notation 41–42 from Table 2, e.g., Methodist Church of Great Britain in Wales 287.5429

**.6 United Methodist Church**

> *See also 287.53 for United Methodist Church (Great Britain)*

[.609 4–.609 9] Specific continents, countries, localities in modern world

> Do not use; class in 287.64–287.69

.63 Specific antecedent denominations

> *For Methodist Protestant Church, see 287.7; for Evangelical United Brethren Church, see 289.9*
>
> *See Manual at 230–280; also at 283–289*

[.630 1–.630 9] Standard subdivisions

> Do not use; class in 287.601–287.609

.631 †The Methodist Church (1939–1968)

.632 †Methodist Episcopal Church

.633 †Methodist Episcopal Church, South

.64–.69 Specific continents, countries, localities in modern world

> Add to base number 287.6 notation 4–9 from Table 2, e.g., United Methodist churches in Ohio 287.6771

**.7 Methodist Protestant Church**

**.8 Black Methodist churches of United States origin**

[.809 4–.809 9] Specific continents, countries, localities in modern world

> Do not use; class in 287.84–287.89

.83 Specific denominations

> Including African Methodist Episcopal Church, African Methodist Episcopal Zion Church, Christian Methodist Episcopal Church
>
> Class a specific denomination in a specific geographic area with the area in 287.84–287.89
>
> *See Manual at 230–280; also at 283–289*

[.830 1–.830 9] Standard subdivisions

> Do not use; class in 287.801–287.809

---

†Do not use notation 094–099 from Table 1; class in 287.64–287.69

.84–.89     Specific continents, countries, localities in modern world

Class here specific denominations and specific churches in specific geographic areas

Add to base number 287.8 notation 4–9 from Table 2, e.g., Black Methodist churches in Georgia 287.8758, in Liberia 287.86662

## .9     Churches related to Methodism

Limited to those listed below

.92     United Church of Canada

.93     Uniting Church in Australia

.94     Church of South India

.95     Church of North India

.96     Salvation Army

.99     Church of the Nazarene

## [288]     [Unassigned]

Most recently used in Edition 19

## 289     Other denominations and sects

### SUMMARY

| | |
|---|---|
| 289.1 | Unitarian and Universalist churches |
| .3 | Latter-Day Saints (Mormons) |
| .4 | Church of the New Jerusalem (Swedenborgianism) |
| .5 | Church of Christ, Scientist (Christian Science) |
| .6 | Society of Friends (Quakers) |
| .7 | Mennonite churches |
| .8 | Shakers (United Society of Believers in Christ's Second Appearing) |
| .9 | Denominations and sects not provided for elsewhere |

## .1     Unitarian and Universalist churches

Class here Anti-Trinitarianism, Socinianism, Unitarianism

[.109 4–.109 9]     Specific continents, countries, localities in modern world

Do not use; class in 289.14–289.19

.13     Specific denominations

*See Manual at 230–280; also at 283–289*

[.130 1–.130 9]     Standard subdivisions

Do not use; class in 289.101–289.109

.132     *Unitarian Universalist Association

.133     *Unitarian churches

*Do not use notation 094–099 from Table 1; class in 289.14–289.19

.134          *Universalist churches

.14–.19          Specific continents, countries, localities in modern world

> Add to base number 289.1 notation 4–9 from Table 2, e.g., Unitarianism in Boston 289.174461

**(.2)          (Permanently unassigned)**

> (Optional number used to provide local emphasis or a shorter number for a specific denomination or sect; prefer the number for the specific denomination or sect in 281–289)

**.3          Latter-Day Saints (Mormons)**

[.309 4–.309 9]          Specific continents, countries, localities in modern world

> Do not use; class in 289.34–289.39

.32          Sources (Sacred books)

.322          Book of Mormon

.33          Specific branches

> *See Manual at 230–280; also at 283–289*

[.330 1–.330 9]          Standard subdivisions

> Do not use; class in 289.301–289.309

.332          Church of Jesus Christ of Latter-Day Saints

[.332 094–.332 099]          Specific continents, countries, localities in modern world

> Do not use; class in 289.34–289.39

.333          Community of Christ

> Former name: Reorganized Church of Jesus Christ of Latter-Day Saints

[.333 094–.333 099]          Specific continents, countries, localities in modern world

> Do not use; class in 289.34–289.39

.34–.39          Specific continents, countries, localities in modern world

> Add to base number 289.3 notation 4–9 from Table 2, e.g., Mormons in Utah 289.3792

**.4          Church of the New Jerusalem (Swedenborgianism)**

[.409 4–.409 9]          Specific continents, countries, localities in modern world

> Do not use; class in 289.44–289.49

.44–.49          Specific continents, countries, localities in modern world

> Add to base number 289.4 notation 4–9 from Table 2, e.g., Swedenborgianism in Europe 289.44

**.5          Church of Christ, Scientist (Christian Science)**

*Do not use notation 094–099 from Table 1; class in 289.14–289.19

[.509 4–.509 9]   Specific continents, countries, localities in modern world

> Do not use; class in 289.54–289.59

.52        Sources

> Writings by Mary Baker Eddy

.54–.59    Specific continents, countries, localities in modern world

> Add to base number 289.5 notation 4–9 from Table 2, e.g., First Church of Christ, Scientist, Boston 289.574461

.6         **Society of Friends (Quakers)**

[.609 4–.609 9]   Specific continents, countries, localities in modern world

> Do not use; class in 289.64–289.69

.63        Specific denominations

> *See Manual at 230–280; also at 283–289*

[.630 1–.630 9]   Standard subdivisions

> Do not use; class in 289.601–289.609

.64–.69    Specific continents, countries, localities in modern world

> Add to base number 289.6 notation 4–9 from Table 2, e.g., Quakers in England 289.642

.7         **Mennonite churches**

[.709 4–.709 9]   Specific continents, countries, localities in modern world

> Do not use; class in 289.74–289.79

.73        Specific branches

> Including Amish, Church of God in Christ, Defenseless Mennonites, General Conference Mennonites, Hutterian Brethren
>
> Class a specific denomination in a specific geographic area with the area in 289.74–289.79
>
> *See Manual at 230–280; also at 283–289*

[.730 1–.730 9]   Standard subdivisions

> Do not use; class in 289.701–289.709

.74–.79    Specific continents, countries, localities in modern world

> Class here specific denominations and specific churches in specific geographic areas
>
> Add to base number 289.7 notation 4–9 from Table 2, e.g., Amish churches in Lancaster County, Pennsylvania 289.774815

.8         **Shakers (United Society of Believers in Christ's Second Appearing)**

**.9**      **Denominations and sects not provided for elsewhere**

Including Christian and Missionary Alliance, Churches of God, Dukhobors, Evangelical Congregational Church, Evangelical United Brethren Church, Messianic Judaism (Jewish Christians), Plymouth Brethren, United Brethren in Christ

Class nondenominational and interdenominational churches in 280; class Protestant nondenominational and interdenominational churches in 280.4

*See Manual at 201–209 and 292–299*

(Option: Class a specific denomination or sect requiring local emphasis in 289.2)

**.92**      Jehovah's Witnesses

**.93**      African independent churches

Independent denominations originating in Africa and not connected to another denomination

Including Celestial Church of Christ, Cherubim and Seraphim Church, Eglise de Jésus-Christ sur la terre par le prophète Simon Kimbangu

**.94**      Pentecostal churches

Including Assemblies of God, United Pentecostal Church

Class comprehensive works on the pentecostal movement in general church history in 270.82

**.95**      Independent fundamentalist and evangelical churches

Including Evangelical Free Church of America, Independent Fundamental Churches of America

Class comprehensive works on fundamentalist, evangelical movements in general church history in 270.82

**.96**      Unification Church

**.97**      Unity School of Christianity

**.98**      New Thought

Class eclectic New Thought, comprehensive works in 299.93

# 290 Other religions

Limited to specific religions other than Christianity

Except for modifications shown under specific entries, add to each subdivision identified by † as follows:

01–05    Standard subdivisions

[06]      Organizations and management
          Do not use; class in 6

07        Education, research, related topics

071        Education
          Class here the religion as an academic subject
          Class comprehensive works on religious education, religious education to inculcate religious faith and practice in 75
          *See Manual at 207.5, 268 vs. 200.71, 230.071, 292–299*

08–09    Standard subdivisions

1–9    Specific elements
        Add the numbers following 20 in 201–209, e.g., organizations 65

Class religion in general, comprehensive works on religions other than Christianity in 200; class specific aspects of religion in 201–209

(Options: To give preferred treatment or shorter numbers to a specific religion, use one of the following:

(Option A: Class the sources of the religion in 220, other specific aspects of the religion in 230–280, comprehensive works on the religion in 230; in that case class the Bible and Christianity in 298

(Option B: Class in 210, and add to base number 21 the numbers following the base number for the religion in 292–299, e.g., Hinduism 210, Mahabharata 219.23; in that case class philosophy and theory of religion in 200, its subdivisions 211–218 in 200.1)

## SUMMARY

| | | |
|---|---|---|
| **292** | | **Classical religion (Greek and Roman religion)** |
| | **.001–.009** | **Standard subdivisions** |
| | **.07–.08** | **Classical religion by specific culture** |
| | **.1–.9** | **Specific elements** |
| **293** | | **Germanic religion** |
| **294** | | **Religions of Indic origin** |
| | **.3** | **Buddhism** |
| | **.4** | **Jainism** |
| | **.5** | **Hinduism** |
| | **.6** | **Sikhism** |
| **295** | | **Zoroastrianism (Mazdaism, Parseeism)** |
| **296** | | **Judaism** |
| | **.01–.09** | **Standard subdivisions** |
| | **.1** | **Sources** |
| | **.3** | **Theology, ethics, views of social issues** |
| | **.4** | **Traditions, rites, public services** |
| | **.6** | **Leaders, organization, religious education, outreach activity** |
| | **.7** | **Religious experience, life, practice** |
| | **.8** | **Denominations and movements** |

| | |
|---|---|
| 297 | **Islam, Babism, Bahai Faith** |
| .01–.09 | Standard subdivisions |
| .1 | **Sources of Islam** |
| .2 | **Islamic doctrinal theology ('Aqā'id and Kalām); Islam and secular disciplines; Islam and other systems of belief** |
| .3 | **Islamic worship** |
| .4 | **Sufism (Islamic mysticism)** |
| .5 | **Islamic ethics and religious experience, life, practice** |
| .6 | **Islamic leaders and organization** |
| .7 | **Protection and propagation of Islam** |
| .8 | **Islamic sects and reform movements** |
| .9 | **Babism and Bahai Faith** |
| | |
| 299 | **Religions not provided for elsewhere** |
| .1–.4 | **Religions of Indo-European, Semitic, Non-Semitic Afro-Asiatic, North and West Asian, Dravidian origin** |
| .5 | **Religions of East and Southeast Asian origin** |
| .6 | **Religions originating among Black Africans and people of Black African descent** |
| .7 | **Religions of North American native origin** |
| .8 | **Religions of South American native origin** |
| .9 | **Religions of other origin** |

## [291]    [Unassigned]

Most recently used in Edition 21

## 292    Classical religion (Greek and Roman religion)

> See also 299 for modern revivals of classical religions

> See Manual at 200.92 and 201–209, 292–299; also at 201–209 and 292–299; also at 203.6, 263.9, 292–299 vs. 394.265–394.267; also at 322.1 vs. 201.72, 261.7, 292–299; also at 398.2 vs. 201.3, 230, 270, 292–299; also at 615.852 vs. 203.1, 234.131, 292–299; also at 616.86 vs. 158.1, 204.42, 248.8629, 292–299, 362.29

.001–.005    Standard subdivisions

[.006]    Organizations and management

> Do not use; class in 292.6

.007    Education, research, related topics

.007 1    Education

> Class here classical religion as an academic subject

> Class comprehensive works on religious education, religious education to inculcate religious faith and practice in 292.75

> *See Manual at 207.5, 268 vs. 200.71, 230.071, 292–299*

.008–.009    Standard subdivisions

---

>    292.07–292.08  Classical religion by specific culture

> Class specific elements regardless of culture in 292.1–292.9; class comprehensive works in 292

.07    Roman religion

.08 Greek religion

**.1–.9 Specific elements**

> Add to base number 292 the numbers following 20 in 201–209, e.g., mythology 292.13, organizations 292.65

> Class classical religion as an academic subject in 292.0071

# 293 †Germanic religion

> Class here Scandinavian religion, Norse religion

> *See also 299 for modern revivals of Germanic religion*

> *See Manual at 200.92 and 201–209, 292–299; also at 201–209 and 292–299; also at 203.6, 263.9, 292–299 vs. 394.265–394.267; also at 207.5, 268 vs. 200.71, 230.071, 292–299; also at 322.1 vs. 201.72, 261.7, 292–299; also at 398.2 vs. 201.3, 230, 270, 292–299; also at 615.852 vs. 203.1, 234.131, 292–299; also at 616.86 vs. 158.1, 204.42, 248.8629, 292–299, 362.29*

# 294 Religions of Indic origin

> Including Divine Light Mission, Radha Soami Satsang

> *See Manual at 200.9 vs. 294, 299.5; also at 200.92 and 201–209, 292–299; also at 201–209 and 292–299; also at 203.6, 263.9, 292–299 vs. 394.265–394.267; also at 207.5, 268 vs. 200.71, 230.071, 292–299; also at 322.1 vs. 201.72, 261.7, 292–299; also at 398.2 vs. 201.3, 230, 270, 292–299; also at 615.852 vs. 203.1, 234.131, 292–299; also at 616.86 vs. 158.1, 204.42, 248.8629, 292–299, 362.29*

## SUMMARY

| | |
|---|---|
| 294.3 | **Buddhism** |
| .4 | **Jainism** |
| .5 | **Hinduism** |
| .6 | **Sikhism** |

**.3 Buddhism**

[.306] Organizations and management

> Do not use; class in 294.36

.307 Education, research, related topics

.307 1 Education

> Class here Buddhism as an academic subject

> Class comprehensive works on religious education, religious education to inculcate religious faith and practice in 294.375

> *See Manual at 207.5, 268 vs. 200.71, 230.071, 292–299*

†Add as instructed under 290

| | |
|---|---|
| .33 | Religious mythology, interreligious relations and attitudes, and social theology |

> Add to base number 294.33 the numbers following 201 in 201.3–201.7, e.g., social theology 294.337

| | |
|---|---|
| .34 | Doctrines and practices |
| .342 | Doctrines |

> *For social theology, see 294.337; for Buddhist ethics, see 294.35*

| | |
|---|---|
| .342 04 | Doctrines of specific branches, sects, reform movements |

> Add to base number 294.34204 the numbers following 294.39 in 294.391–294.392, e.g., Zen doctrines 294.3420427

| | |
|---|---|
| .342 1–.342 4 | Specific doctrines |

> Add to base number 294.342 the numbers following 202 in 202.1–202.4, e.g., reincarnation 294.34237

| | |
|---|---|
| .343–.344 | Public worship and other practices; religious experience, life, practice |

> Add to base number 294.34 the numbers following 20 in 203–204, e.g., religious experience 294.3442

| | |
|---|---|
| .35–.37 | Religious ethics, leaders and organization, missions, religious education |

> Add to base number 294.3 the numbers following 20 in 205–207, e.g., the Buddha 294.363, organizations 294.365

> *See Manual at 207.5, 268 vs. 200.71, 230.071, 292–299*

| | |
|---|---|
| .38 | Sources |
| .382 | Sacred books and scriptures (Tripiṭaka, Tipiṭaka) |

> Works sacred to both Theravadins and Mahayanists

> Class here comprehensive treatment of Theravadin and Mahayanist sacred texts

> *For works sacred only to Mahayanists, see 294.385*

| | |
|---|---|
| .382 2 | Vinayapiṭaka |
| .382 3 | Sūtrapiṭaka (Suttapiṭaka) |
| .382 32 | Khuddakanikāya |
| .382 322 | Dhammapada |
| .382 325 | Jatakas |
| .382 4 | Abhidharmapiṭaka (Abhidhammapiṭaka) |
| .383 | Oral traditions |
| .384 | Laws and decisions |
| .385 | Sources of branches, sects, reform movements |

> Including Buddhist Tantras, Mahayanist sacred works

.39            Branches, sects, reform movements

               Class specific aspects of branches, sects, reform movements in
               294.33–294.38

.391           Theravada Buddhism

               Variant names: Southern, Hinayana Buddhism

               Including Mahasanghika, Saravastivada, Sautrantika schools

.392           Mahayana Buddhism (Northern Buddhism)

               Including Madhyamika, Yogacara (Vijnana) schools

.392 3         Tibetan Buddhism (Lamaism)

               *See also 299.54 for Bon*

.392 5         Tantric Buddhism

.392 6         Pure Land sects

.392 7         Zen (Ch'an)

               Including Rinzai, Soto

.392 8         Nichiren Shoshu and Sōka Gakkai

**.4**         **†Jainism**

.49            Sects and reform movements

               Number built according to instructions under 290

               Class specific aspects of sects and reform movements in 294.41–294.48

.492           Svetambara

.493           Digambara

**.5**         **Hinduism**

               Class here Brahmanism

### SUMMARY

| | | |
|---|---|---|
| 294.501–.509 | **Standard subdivisions** | |
| .51–.53 | **Mythology, relations, doctrines, public worship and other practices** | |
| .54 | **Religious experience, life, practice, religious ethics** | |
| .55 | **Sects and reform movements** | |
| .56–.57 | **Leaders, organization, missions, religious education** | |
| .59 | **Sources** | |

[.506]         Organizations and management

               Do not use; class in 294.56

.507           Education, research, related topics

†Add as instructed under 290

| | | |
|---|---|---|
| .507 1 | | Education |

Class here Hinduism as an academic subject

Class comprehensive works on religious education, religious education to inculcate religious faith and practice in 294.575

*See Manual at 207.5, 268 vs. 200.71, 230.071, 292–299*

| | |
|---|---|
| .509 | History, geographic treatment, biography |
| .509 013 | 3999–1000 B.C. |

Class here religion of Vedic period

| | |
|---|---|
| .51–.53 | Mythology, relations, doctrines, public worship and other practices |

Add to base number 294.5 the numbers following 20 in 201–203, e.g., gods and goddesses 294.5211

| | |
|---|---|
| .54 | Religious experience, life, practice, religious ethics |

Practices predominantly private or individual in character

Class here spirituality

| | |
|---|---|
| .542 | Religious experience |

Including conversion, enlightenment

| | |
|---|---|
| .542 2 | Mysticism |
| .543 | Worship, meditation, yoga |

Class here description, interpretation, criticism, history, practical works on prayer, on contemplation; comprehensive works on worship

*For public worship, see 294.538*

| | |
|---|---|
| .543 2 | Devotional literature |

Including meditations

| | |
|---|---|
| .543 3 | Prayer books |
| .543 5 | Meditation |
| .543 6 | Yoga |

Religious and spiritual discipline

Including bhakti yoga, jnana yoga, karma yoga, kundalini yoga, raja yoga

Class yoga philosophy, raja yoga philosophy, interdisciplinary works on yoga in 181.45

*See also 613.7046 for hatha yoga, physical yoga*

| | |
|---|---|
| .544 | Religious life and practice |

Add to base number 294.544 the numbers following 204.4 in 204.41–204.47, e.g., asceticism 294.5447

| .548 | Religious ethics |
| | Including conscience, dharma, sin, vice |
| .548 6 | Specific moral issues, sins, vices, virtues |
| | Add to base number 294.5486 the numbers following 17 in 172–179, e.g., morality of family relationships 294.54863 |
| .55 | Sects and reform movements |
| | Class Buddhism in 294.3; class Jainism in 294.4; class Sikhism in 294.6. Class a specific aspect of a Hindu sect or reform movement with the subject, e.g., doctrines of Vishnuism 294.52 |
| .551 | Early Hindu sects |
| .551 2 | Vishnuism |
| | Including International Society for Krishna Consciousness |
| .551 3 | Shivaism |
| | Including Lingayats |
| .551 4 | Shaktaism |
| | Class here Tantric Hinduism |
| .551 5 | Ganapataism |
| .551 6 | Shanmukaism |
| .551 7 | Sauraism |
| .555 | Ramakrishna movement |
| .556 | Reformed Hinduism |
| .556 2 | Brahma Samaj |
| .556 3 | Arya-Samaj |
| .56–.57 | Leaders, organization, missions, religious education |
| | Add to base number 294.5 the numbers following 20 in 206–207, e.g., the role of the guru 294.561 |
| | Class Hinduism as an academic subject in 294.5071 |
| | *See Manual at 207.5, 268 vs. 200.71, 230.071, 292–299* |
| .59 | Sources |

.592 Sacred books and scriptures

> Add to each subdivision identified by * as follows:
>
> 04 Special topics
> 041 Sanskrit texts
> Including textual criticism
> Class Sanskrit texts accompanied by translations in 045; class Sanskrit texts accompanied by commentaries in 047
> 045 Translations
> Class here Sanskrit texts accompanied by translations
> Add to 045 notation 1–9 from Table 6, e.g., translations into English 04521
> Class texts accompanied by commentaries in 047
> 046 Interpretation and criticism
> *For textual criticism, see 041; for commentaries, see 047*
> 047 Commentaries
> Criticism and interpretation arranged in textual order
> Including texts accompanied by commentaries
> 048 Nonreligious subjects treated in sacred books and scriptures
> Class a religious subject treated in sacred books and scriptures with the subject, e.g., rites and ceremonies 294.538

.592 1 *Vedic literature

---

> 294.592 12–294.592 15 The Vedas
>
> Class here Samhitas, Brahmanas, Aranyakas
>
> Class Upanishads in 294.59218; class Vedic religion in 294.509013; class comprehensive works on the Vedas in 294.5921

.592 12 *Rigveda

.592 13 *Samaveda

.592 14 *Yajurveda

.592 15 *Atharvaveda

.592 18 Upanishads

.592 2 *Ramayana

.592 3 *Mahabharata

> *For Bhagavad Gita, see 294.5924*

.592 4 *Bhagavad Gita

.592 5 Puranas

.592 6 Dharmasastras

> Including Code of Manu

*Add as instructed under 294.592

| .593 | Oral traditions |
|------|------------------|
| .594 | Laws and decisions |
| .595 | Sources of sects and reform movements |

Including Hindu tantras

**.6          †Sikhism**

| .663 | Founders of Sikhism |
|------|---------------------|

Number built according to instructions under 290

Class here role and function of the ten Sikh gurus

## 295          †Zoroastrianism (Mazdaism, Parseeism)

Class Mithraism in 299.15

*See Manual at 200.92 and 201–209, 292–299; also at 201–209 and 292–299; also at 203.6, 263.9, 292–299 vs. 394.265–394.267; also at 207.5, 268 vs. 200.71, 230.071, 292–299; also at 322.1 vs. 201.72, 261.7, 292–299; also at 398.2 vs. 201.3, 230, 270, 292–299; also at 615.852 vs. 203.1, 234.131, 292–299; also at 616.86 vs. 158.1, 204.42, 248.8629, 292–299, 362.29*

## 296          Judaism

*See Manual at 200.92 and 201–209, 292–299; also at 201–209 and 292–299; also at 203.6, 263.9, 292–299 vs. 394.265–394.267; also at 322.1 vs. 201.72, 261.7, 292–299; also at 398.2 vs. 201.3, 230, 270, 292–299; also at 615.852 vs. 203.1, 234.131, 292–299; also at 616.86 vs. 158.1, 204.42, 248.8629, 292–299, 362.29*

### SUMMARY

| 296.01–.09 | Standard subdivisions |
|------------|------------------------|
| .1 | Sources |
| .3 | Theology, ethics, views of social issues |
| .4 | Traditions, rites, public services |
| .6 | Leaders, organization, religious education, outreach activity |
| .7 | Religious experience, life, practice |
| .8 | Denominations and movements |

| [.06] | Organizations and management |
|-------|------------------------------|

Do not use; class in 296.6

| .07 | Education, research, related topics |
|-----|-------------------------------------|
| .071 | Education |

Class here Judaism as an academic subject

Class comprehensive works on Jewish religious education, religious education to inculcate religious faith and practice in 296.68

*See Manual at 207.5, 268 vs. 200.71, 230.071, 292–299*

†Add as instructed under 290

.071 1             Higher education

> Class here Jewish theological faculties, rabbinical seminaries, yeshivot, education of rabbis

.08          Groups of people

> Class here Jewish attitudes toward social groups; discrimination, equality, inequality, prejudice

.09          History, geographic treatment, biography

> Class here history of specific synagogues

> *See also 320.54095694 for Zionism; also 909.04924 for world history of Jews*

---

\>        296.090 1–296.090 5   Historical periods

> Add to each subdivision identified by * as instructed under —0901–0905 in Table 1, e.g., museums of ancient Judaism 296.0901074

> Class comprehensive works in 296.09

.090 1         *To 499 A.D.

.090 13        *Earliest Judaism to 586 B.C.

.090 14        *Second Temple period, 586 B.C.–70 A.D.

.090 15        *Early rabbinic period, 70–499

.090 2–.090 5    6th–21st centuries

> Add to base number 296.090 the numbers following —090 in notation 0902–0905 from Table 1, e.g., Judaism in the Middle Ages 296.0902

.092          Biography

> Class here persons not associated with one activity or denomination

> Class a person associated with one activity or denomination with the activity or denomination with which the person is associated, e.g., a theologian 296.3092, a Reform rabbi 296.8341092

**.1**       **Sources**

> Class Jewish theology based on these sources in 296.3

> *For Torah and sacred scripture (Tanakh, Old Testament), see 221*

> *See Manual at 221*

---

*Add as instructed under 296.0901–296.0905

## SUMMARY

| | |
|---|---|
| **296.12** | **Talmudic literature** |
| **.14** | **Midrash** |
| **.15** | **Sources of specific sects and movements** |
| **.16** | **Cabalistic literature** |
| **.18** | **Halakhah (Legal literature)** |
| **.19** | **Aggadah (Nonlegal literature)** |

(.11)        Tanakh

> (Optional number; prefer 221)

> Arranged as found in Jewish Bibles

> *See Manual at 221: Optional numbers for books of Bible*

[.110 3]        Dictionaries, encyclopedias, concordances

> Do not use for dictionaries and encyclopedias; class in 296.1113. Do not use for concordances; class in 296.1114–296.1115

(.111)        Special topics; generalities; geography, history, chronology, persons of Bible lands in times of the Tanakh

> (Optional number; prefer 221)

(.111 04)        Special topics of Tanakh

(.111 044)        Megillot (Five scrolls)

> Relocated to 296.1164

(.111 046)        Apocalyptic passages

> Class apocalyptic passages in a book or group of books with the book or group of books, plus notation 0046 from add table under 221–229, e.g., apocalyptic passages in the prophets 296.1130046, in Book of Daniel 296.11650046

(.111 1–.111 8)        Generalities

> Add to base number 296.111 the numbers following 221 in 221.1–221.8, e.g., criticism and interpretation 296.1116

(.111 9)        Geography, history, chronology, persons of Bible lands in times of the Tanakh

> Add to base number 296.1119 the numbers following 221.9 in 221.91–221.95, e.g., archaeology 296.11193

(.112)        *‡Torah (Pentateuch)

(.112 1)        *‡Genesis

(.112 2)        *‡Exodus

> *For Ten Commandments, see 296.1126*

(.112 3)        *‡Leviticus

*Add as instructed under 221–229
‡(Optional number; prefer 222–224)

| | |
|---|---|
| (.112 4) | *‡Numbers |
| (.112 5) | *‡Deuteronomy |

> For Ten Commandments, see 296.1126

| | |
|---|---|
| (.112 6) | *‡Ten Commandments (Decalogue) |
| (.113) | *‡Prophetic books (Nevi'im) |
| (.113 1) | *Former Prophets (Nevi'im rishonim) |

(Optional number; prefer 222)

> For individual books of Former Prophets, see 296.1132–296.1135

| | |
|---|---|
| (.113 2) | *‡Joshua |
| (.113 3) | *‡Judges |
| (.113 4) | *‡Samuel |
| (.113 41) | *‡Samuel 1 |
| (.113 42) | *‡Samuel 2 |
| (.113 5) | *‡Kings |
| (.113 51) | *‡Kings 1 |
| (.113 52) | *‡Kings 2 |
| (.113 6) | *Later Prophets (Nevi'im aḥaronim) |

(Optional number; prefer 224)

> For Isaiah, see 296.1137; for Jeremiah, see 296.1138; for Ezekiel, see 296.1139; for Minor Prophets, see 296.114

| | |
|---|---|
| (.113 7) | *‡Isaiah |
| (.113 8) | *‡Jeremiah |
| (.113 9) | *‡Ezekiel |
| (.114) | *‡Minor Prophets |

> For Zephaniah, Haggai, Zechariah, Malachi, see 296.115

| | |
|---|---|
| (.114 1) | *‡Hosea |
| (.114 2) | *‡Joel |
| (.114 3) | *‡Amos |
| (.114 4) | *‡Obadiah |
| (.114 5) | *‡Jonah |
| (.114 6) | *‡Micah |
| (.114 7) | *‡Nahum |

*Add as instructed under 221–229
‡(Optional number; prefer 222–224)

| | |
|---|---|
| (.114 8) | *‡Habakkuk |
| (.115) | *‡Zephaniah, Haggai, Zechariah, Malachi |
| (.115 1) | *‡Zephaniah |
| (.115 2) | *‡Haggai |
| (.115 3) | *‡Zechariah |
| (.115 4) | *‡Malachi |
| (.116) | *‡Writings (Ketuvim) |
| (.116 1) | *‡Psalms |
| (.116 2) | *‡Proverbs |
| (.116 3) | *‡Job |
| (.116 4) | *Megillot (Five scrolls) [*formerly also* 296.111044] |
| | (Optional number; prefer 221.044) |
| (.116 41) | *‡Song of Solomon (Canticle of Canticles, Song of Songs) |
| (.116 42) | *‡Ruth |
| (.116 43) | *‡Lamentations |
| (.116 44) | *‡Ecclesiastes (Kohelet, Qohelet) |
| (.116 45) | *‡Esther |
| (.116 5) | *‡Daniel |
| (.116 6) | *‡Ezra |
| (.116 7) | *‡Nehemiah |
| (.116 8) | *‡Chronicles |
| (.116 81) | *‡Chronicles 1 |
| (.116 82) | *‡Chronicles 2 |
| (.118) | *Apocrypha |
| | (Optional number; prefer 229) |
| | *For pseudepigrapha, see 229.9* |
| (.118 1) | *Esdras 1 and 2 |
| | (Optional number; prefer 229.1) |
| | Variant names: Esdras 3 and 4 |
| | *See also 296.1166 for Ezra; also 296.1167 for Nehemiah* |
| (.118 2) | *Tobit, Judith, Additions to Esther |
| | (Optional number; prefer 229.2) |

*Add as instructed under 221–229
‡(Optional number; prefer 222–224)

| (.118 22) | *Tobit |
| | (Optional number; prefer 229.22) |
| (.118 24) | *Judith |
| | (Optional number; prefer 229.24) |
| (.118 27) | *Additions to Esther |
| | (Optional number; prefer 229.27) |
| (.118 3) | *Wisdom of Solomon (Wisdom) |
| | (Optional number; prefer 229.3) |
| | Class here Apocryphal wisdom literature |
| | *For Ecclesiasticus, see 296.1184* |
| (.118 4) | *Ecclesiasticus (Sirach) |
| | (Optional number; prefer 229.4) |
| (.118 5) | *Baruch and Epistle of Jeremiah |
| | (Optional number; prefer 229.5) |
| (.118 6) | *Song of the Three Children, Susanna, Bel and the Dragon |
| | (Optional number; prefer 229.6) |
| (.118 7) | *Maccabees (Machabees) |
| | (Optional number; prefer 229.7) |
| (.118 73) | *Maccabees 1 and 2 (Machabees 1 and 2) |
| | (Optional number; prefer 229.73) |
| (.118 75) | *Maccabees 3 and 4 (Machabees 3 and 4) |
| | (Optional number; prefer 229.75) |
| (.118 8) | *Prayer of Manasseh |
| | (Optional number; prefer 229.6) |

*Add as instructed under 221–229

>        296.12–296.14   Talmudic literature and Midrash

Add to each subdivision identified by ‡ as follows:

001–009     Standard subdivisions

04          Hebrew and Aramaic texts
           Including textual criticism
           Class texts accompanied by modern commentaries since 1500 in 07

05          Translations
           Add to 05 notation 1–9 from Table 6, e.g., literature in English 0521
           Class texts accompanied by modern commentaries since 1500 in 07

06          Interpretation and criticism (Exegesis)

0601       Philosophy and theory
           Class here hermeneutics

061–068     Subdivisions of interpretation and criticism (Exegesis)
           Add to 06 the numbers following 220.6 in 220.61–220.68, e.g., historical criticism 067
           *For textual criticism, see 04; for modern commentaries since 1500, see 07*

07          Modern commentaries since 1500
           Criticism and interpretation arranged in textual order
           Including texts accompanied by modern commentaries
           Commentaries written before 1500 are classed with the text without addition of 07

08          Nonreligious subjects treated in Talmudic literature and Midrash
           Add to 08 notation 001–999, e.g., natural sciences in Talmudic literature and Midrash 085
           Class a religious subject treated in Talmudic literature and Midrash with the subject, e.g., Jewish ethics 296.36

Class comprehensive works in 296.1

.12        ‡Talmudic literature

.120 092        Biography

           Number built according to instructions under 296.12–296.14

           Class here Soferim, Tannaim, Amoraim, Geonim

.123        ‡Mishnah

.123 1        ‡Order Zera'im

           Including tractates Berakhot, Bikkurim, Demai, Ḥallah, Kilayim, Ma'aser Sheni, Ma'aserot, Orlah, Pe'ah, Shevi'it, Terumot

.123 2        ‡Order Mo'ed

           Including tractates Beẓah, Eruvin, Ḥagigah, Megillah, Mo'ed Katan, Pesaḥim, Rosh Hashanah, Shabbat, Shekalim, Sukkah, Ta'anit, Yoma

‡Add as instructed under 296.12–296.14

| | |
|---|---|
| .123 3 | ‡Order Nashim |
| | Including tractates Gittin, Ketubbot, Kiddushin, Nazir, Nedarim, Sotah, Yevamot |
| .123 4 | ‡Order Nezikin |
| | Including tractates Avodah Zarah, Bava Batra, Bava Kamma, Bava Meẓia, Eduyyot, Horayot, Makkot, Sanhedrin, Shevuʻot |
| .123 47 | ‡Tractate Avot (Pirke Avot) |
| .123 5 | ‡Order Kodashim |
| | Including tractates Arakhin, Bekhorot, Ḥullin, Keritot, Kinnim, Meʻilah, Menaḥot, Middot, Tamid, Temurah, Zevaḥim |
| .123 6 | ‡Order Tohorot |
| | Including tractates Kelim, Makhshirin, Mikvaʼot, Negaʻim, Niddah, Oholot (Ahilot), Parah, Tevul Yom, Tohorot, Ukẓin, Yadayim, Zavim |
| .123 7 | Minor tractates |
| .124 | ‡Palestinian Talmud (Jerusalem Talmud, Talmud Yerushalmi) |
| .124 1–.124 7 | Individual orders and tractates |
| | Add to base number 296.124 the numbers following 296.123 in 296.1231–296.1237, e.g., Order Zeraʻim in Palestinian Talmud 296.1241 |
| .125 | ‡Babylonian Talmud |
| | Often called simply the Talmud |
| .125 1–.125 7 | Individual orders and tractates |
| | Add to base number 296.125 the numbers following 296.123 in 296.1231–296.1237, e.g., tractate Shabbat in Babylonian Talmud 296.1252 |
| .126 | Tosefta and Baraita |
| .126 2 | ‡Tosefta |
| .126 21–.126 27 | Individual orders and tractates |
| | Add to base number 296.1262 the numbers following 296.123 in 296.1231–296.1237, e.g., order Nezikin in Tosefta 296.12624 |
| .126 3 | ‡Baraita |
| .127 | Specific types of Talmudic literature |
| .127 4 | ‡Halakhah |
| .127 6 | ‡Aggadah |
| .14 | ‡Midrash |
| .141 | ‡Midrashic Halakhah |

‡Add as instructed under 296.12–296.14

| .142 | ‡Midrashic Aggadah |
|---|---|

.15 Sources of specific sects and movements

.155 Writings of Qumran community

Class here comprehensive works on Dead Sea Scrolls

*For Old Testament texts in Dead Sea Scrolls, see 221.44; for pseudepigrapha in Dead Sea Scrolls, see 229.91*

*See also 296.815 for comprehensive works on Qumran community*

.16 Cabalistic literature

Class here interdisciplinary works on cabala

The texts of religious cabalistic works are classed here even if the editor introduces and annotates them from an occult or Christian point of view

Class Jewish mystical experience in 296.712; class Jewish mystical movements in 296.8

*For cabalistic traditions in occultism, see 135.47*

.162 Zohar

.18 Halakhah (Legal literature)

Including early rabbinical legal writings, comprehensive works on rabbinical writings to 1400

Class here commandments (mitzvot) treated as laws, the 613 commandments, comprehensive works on Jewish law

Class commandments (mitzvot) treated as ethical values in 296.36; class Jewish law relating to secular matters in 340.58

*For Torah, see 222.1; for Talmudic Halakhah, see 296.1274; for Midrashic Halakhah, see 296.141. For early rabbinical writings to 1400 on a specific subject, see the subject, e.g., creation 296.34; for laws on a specific religious topic, see the topic, e.g., laws concerning marriage rites 296.444*

.180 92 Biography

Class here Rishonim, Aharonim

.181 Legal writings of Maimonides

Class here comprehensive works on writings of Maimonides

*For philosophical writings of Maimonides, see 181.06. For writings on a specific religious topic, see the topic, e.g., the Thirteen Articles of Faith 296.3*

.181 2 Mishneh Torah

.182 Work of Joseph Caro

Class here Shulḥan ʻarukh

‡Add as instructed under 296.12–296.14

**.185**          Responsa

> Class responsa on a specific religious topic with the topic, e.g., responsa concerning marriage rites 296.444

**.185 4**          Responsa of reform movements

> Add to base number 296.1854 the numbers following 296.834 in 296.8341–296.8344, e.g., Reform responsa 296.18541

**.188**          Nonreligious subjects treated in halakhah

**.188 000 1–.188 000 9**          Standard subdivisions

**.188 001–.188 999**          Specific nonreligious subjects treated in halakhah

> Add to base number 296.188 notation 001–999, e.g., agriculture in halakhah 296.18863

**.19**          Aggadah (Nonlegal literature)

> Stories, legends, parables, proverbs, anecdotes, ancient or modern, told for religious edification

> Class here comprehensive works on Aggadah

> Class Jewish folklore in 398.2089924

> *For Talmudic Aggadah, see 296.1276; for Midrashic Aggadah, see 296.142*

> *See also 296.45371 for Passover Haggadah*

**.3**          **Theology, ethics, views of social issues**

> Standard subdivisions are added for theology, ethics, social issues together; for theology alone

> Class here Biblical theology, the Thirteen Articles of Faith

> *See also 181.06 for Jewish philosophy*

> *See Manual at 200 vs. 100*

**.31**          God and spiritual beings

**.311**          God

**.311 2**          Attributes and names of God

**.311 4**          Relation to the world

> *For revelation, see 296.3115; for miracles, see 296.3116; for relation to and action in history, see 296.3117; for creation, see 296.34*

**.311 5**          Revelation

**.311 55**          Prophecy

> Class Biblical prophecy and prophecies in 221.15; class the prophetic books of the Bible in 224; class messianic prophecies in 296.336

**.311 6**          Miracles

.37 Judaism and secular disciplines

> Class here attitudes of Judaism toward and influence on secular issues, religious views and teachings about secular disciplines, works treating relation between Jewish belief and a secular discipline

> Class Jewish philosophy of a secular discipline and Jewish theories within a secular discipline with the discipline, e.g., Jewish philosophy 181.06

>> *For Judaism and social issues, see 296.38*

>> *See also 296.12–296.14 for nonreligious subjects treated in Talmudic literature and Midrash; also 296.188 for nonreligious subjects treated in halakhah*

.371 Judaism and philosophy, parapsychology and occultism, psychology

.375 Judaism and natural sciences, mathematics

.376 Judaism and technology

> Including Judaism and medicine

.377 Judaism and the arts

.38 Judaism and social sciences

> Attitudes of Judaism toward and influence on social issues

> Including Judaism and environment

> Class here Judaism and socioeconomic problems, Jewish social theology

> Class Judaism ad ecology in 296.38; class Jewish view of marriage and family in 296.74

.382 Judaism and politics

> Attitude toward and influence on political activities and ideologies

> Class here Judaism and civil rights

>> *See Manual at 322.1 vs. 201.72, 261.7, 292–299*

.382 7 International affairs, war and peace

> Including attitude of Judaism toward civil and revolutionary wars, conscientious objectors, pacifism

.383 Judaism and economics

> Class Judaism and environment in 296.38

.39 Judaism and other systems of belief

> Including Judaism and atheism, Judaism and irreligion

.396 Judaism and Christianity

.397 Judaism and Islam

**.4 Traditions, rites, public services**

> Class individual observances not provided for here in 296.7

## SUMMARY

.41      Sabbath

> Class liturgy and prayers for Sabbath in 296.45

.412      Prohibited activity

---

>    296.43–296.44 Festivals, holy days, fasts; rites and customs for occasions that occur generally once in a lifetime

> Class here personal ritual observances to be performed at specific times or in conjunction with specific rites

> Class comprehensive works in 296.43

> *For specific rites of ancient Judaism to 70 A.D. not provided for elsewhere, see 296.49*

.43      Festivals, holy days, fasts

> *For liturgy and prayers for festivals, holy days, fasts, see 296.453; for Sabbath, see 296.41*

> *See Manual at 203.6, 263.9, 292–299 vs. 394.265–394.267*

.431      High Holy Days

> *For Yom Kippur (Day of Atonement), see 296.432*

.431 5      Rosh Hashanah (New Year)

.432      Yom Kippur (Day of Atonement)

.433      Sukkot (Feast of Tabernacles)

.433 9      Simḥat Torah

.435      Hanukkah (Feast of the Dedication)

.436      Purim (Feast of Lots)

.437      Pesach (Passover)

.438      Shavuot (Feast of Weeks, Pentecost)

.439      Other festivals, holy days, fasts

> Including Lag b'Omer, Tishah b'Av

.439 1      Festivals, holy days, fasts associated with the land of Israel

> Including Sabbatical Year (shemittah)

| | |
|---|---|
| .44 | Rites and customs for occasions that occur generally once in a lifetime |

> *See also 296.7 for rites and customs which continue throughout life*
>
> *For liturgy and prayers for occasions that occur generally once in a lifetime, see 296.454*

| | |
|---|---|
| .442 | Special rites for male Jews |
| .442 2 | Berit milah (Circumcision) |
| .442 3 | Pidyon haben (Redemption of first-born male) |
| .442 4 | Bar mitzvah |
| .443 | Special rites for female Jews |

Including naming ceremonies

> *For observance of laws of family purity, see 296.742*

| | |
|---|---|
| .443 4 | Bat mitzvah |
| .444 | Marriage and divorce rites and traditions |

Standard subdivisions are added for marriage and divorce rites and traditions together, for marriage rites alone, for marriage traditions alone

Including issues concerning who may be married, descent of Jewish identity

> *For guides to marriage and family life, see 296.74*

| | |
|---|---|
| .444 3 | Interreligious marriage |
| .444 4 | Divorce rites and traditions |

Standard subdivisions are added for either or both topics in heading

| | |
|---|---|
| .445 | Burial and mourning rites and traditions |

Standard subdivisions are added for any or all topics in heading

Including memorial services

| | |
|---|---|
| .446 | Synagogue dedication |
| .45 | Liturgy and prayers |

Description, interpretation, conduct, texts of rites and public services; private and public prayers, blessings, benedictions

Including prayer at meals

Class here Ashkenazic liturgy; worship; liturgy and prayers for Sabbath; prayer books, e.g., siddurim

Class devotional reading for the individual in 296.72

| | |
|---|---|
| .450 4 | Liturgy of specific groups |

Including Ari liturgy

Class Ashkenazic liturgy or liturgy of unspecified group in 296.45

| | |
|---|---|
| [.450 401–.450 409] | Standard subdivisions |
| | Do not use; class in 296.4501–296.4509 |
| .450 42 | Sephardic liturgy |
| .450 44 | Hasidic liturgy |
| .450 46 | Reform liturgy |
| .450 47 | Conservative liturgy |
| .450 48 | Reconstructionist liturgy |
| .452 | Piyyutim |

---

>      296.453–296.454 Liturgy and prayers for festivals, holy days, fasts; for occasions that occur generally once in a lifetime

Add to each subdivision identified by * the numbers following 296.45 in 296.45042–296.45048, e.g., Passover Haggadah of the Sephardic rite 296.45371042

Class comprehensive works in 296.45

| | |
|---|---|
| .453 | *Liturgy and prayers for festivals, holy days, fasts |

Class here Mahzorim

| | |
|---|---|
| .453 1–.453 6 | Liturgy and prayers for High Holy Days, Sukkot, Hanukkah, Purim |

Add to base number 296.453 the numbers following 296.43 in 296.431–296.436, e.g., liturgy and prayers for High Holy Days 296.4531; then add further as instructed under 296.453–296.454, e.g., Reform prayer books for High Holy Days 296.4531046

| | |
|---|---|
| .453 7 | *Liturgy and prayers for Pesach (Passover) |
| .453 71 | *Passover Haggadah (Seder service) |
| .453 8–.453 9 | Liturgy and prayers for Shavuot, other festivals, holy days, fasts |

Add to base number 296.453 the numbers following 296.43 in 296.438–296.439, e.g., prayers for Shavuot 296.4538; then add further as instructed under 296.453–296.454, e.g., prayers for Shavuot of the Sephardic rite 296.4538042

| | |
|---|---|
| .454 | Liturgy and prayers for occasions that occur generally once in a lifetime |

Add to base number 296.454 the numbers following 296.44 in 296.442–296.446, e.g., liturgy and prayers for weddings 296.4544; then add further as instructed under 296.453–296.454, e.g., Reform prayer books for weddings 296.4544046

| | |
|---|---|
| .46 | Use of the arts and symbolism |

Including synagogue buildings

---

*Add as instructed under 296.453–296.454

.461            Liturgical articles

> Including mezuzot, prayer shawls

.461 2          Phylacteries (Tefillin)

.461 5          Torah scrolls

> Class here scribes (soferim)

.462            Music

> Class here cantors

> Class works containing both text and music, interdisciplinary works on Jewish liturgical music in 782.36

.47             Sermons and preaching (Homiletics)

> Add to base number 296.47 the numbers following 296.4 in 296.41–296.44, e.g., High Holy Day sermons 296.4731

> Class sermons on a specific subject with the subject, e.g., sermons on social issues 296.38

.48             Pilgrimages and sacred places

[.480 93–.480 99]        Specific continents, countries, localities

> Do not use; class in 296.482–296.489

.481            Pilgrimages

> Class pilgrimages to specific sacred places in 296.482–296.489

.482            Jerusalem

.483–.489       Sacred places in specific continents, countries, localities

> Add to base number 296.48 notation 3–9 from Table 2, e.g., sacred places in Iraq 296.48567; however, for Jerusalem, see 296.482

> Class the Land of Israel as a theme in Jewish theology in 296.31173

.49             Traditions, rites, public services of ancient Judaism to 70 A.D.

> Not provided for elsewhere

.491            The Temple

.492            Sacrifices and offerings

.493            Ark of the Covenant

.495            Ancient priesthood

**.6            Leaders, organization, religious education, outreach activity**

.61            Leaders and their work

Role, function, duties

Class here ordination, work of rabbis; activities of leaders and other congregational workers designed to promote religious and social welfare of social groups in community, pastoral care; chaplaincy

*For ancient priesthood, see 296.495*

*See also 296.4615 for scribes; also 296.462 for cantors*

[.610 92]            Biography

Do not use for biography of religious leaders primarily associated with a specific religious activity; class in 296.1–296.7 e.g., a theologian 296.3092. Do not use for biography of religious leaders primarily associated with a specific denomination or movement; class in 296.8 e.g., a Reform rabbi 296.8341092. Do not use for biography of other religious leaders; class in 296.092

.65            Synagogues and congregations

Role and function

*See also 296.46 for synagogue buildings*

.650 9            History, geographic treatment, biography

Class history of specific synagogues in 296.09

.67            Organizations and organization

Theory and history of organizations other than synagogues and congregations

Including religious authority, excommunication, schism; sanhedrin

Class laws and decisions in 296.18. Class organizations sponsored by one denomination with the denomination in 296.8, e.g., Union of Orthodox Congregations of America 296.83206073

*For synagogues and congregations, see 296.65*

*See also 369.3924 for Jewish service and fraternal associations, e.g., B'nai B'rith*

.68            Religious education

Class Judaism as an academic subject in 296.071

*For religious education at the level of higher education, see 296.0711*

*See Manual at 207.5, 268 vs. 200.71, 230.071, 292–299*

.680 83            Young people

Class here afternoon weekday schools, Hebrew schools, Jewish religious schools, Sunday schools; religious education in Jewish day schools

Class comprehensive works on Jewish day schools in 371.076

.69            Outreach activity for the benefit of converts and nonobservant Jews

.7    **Religious experience, life, practice**

Standard subdivisions are added for religious experience, life, practice together; for religious life and practice together

Practices which continue throughout life

Including asceticism

Class here guides to religious life, spirituality

*For ethics, see 296.36; for traditions, rites, public services, see 296.4*

[.708 5]    Relatives

Do not use; class in 296.74

.708 6    People by miscellaneous social attributes

[.708 655]    Married people

Do not use; class in 296.74

.71    Religious experience

.712    Mysticism

Class cabalistic literature in 296.16; class Jewish mystical movements in 296.8

.714    Conversion

Class here conversion of non-Jews to Judaism

Class outreach activity for the benefit of converts and nonobservant Jews in 296.69. Class conversion of Jews to another religion with the religion, e.g., conversion of Jews to Christianity 248.246

.715    Return of Jews from non-observance to religious observance

.72    Devotional reading for the individual

Including meditation and meditations

Class devotional literature in the form of Aggadah in 296.19

.73    Kosher observance (Kashrut observance)

Observance of dietary laws

Including ritual slaughter (shehitah)

.74    Marriage and family life

Including Jewish child rearing

Class here social theology of marriage and family, comprehensive works on marriage

*For ethics of marriage, see 296.363; for marriage and divorce rites and traditions, see 296.444*

.742    Observance of laws of family purity

*For ritual bath (mikveh), see 296.75*

| | |
|---|---|
| .75 | Ritual bath (Mikveh) |
| .76 | People experiencing illness, trouble, bereavement |
| **.8** | **Denominations and movements** |

Class specific aspects of denominations and movements in 296.1–296.7

| | |
|---|---|
| .81 | Denominations and movements of ancient origin |

Including Hellenistic movement, Karaites, Zealots

| | |
|---|---|
| .812 | Pharisees |
| .813 | Sadducees |
| .814 | Essenes |

*For Qumran community, see 296.815*

| | |
|---|---|
| .815 | Qumran community |

*See also 296.155 for writings of Qumran community*

| | |
|---|---|
| .817 | Samaritans |
| .82 | Medieval and early modern denominations and movements to ca. 1750 |

Including Sabbatianism

| | |
|---|---|
| .83 | Modern denominations and movements after ca. 1750 |
| .832 | Orthodox Judaism |
| .833 | Mystical Judaism |
| .833 2 | Hasidism |
| .833 22 | Habad Lubavitch Hasidism |
| .834 | Reform movements |

Including Humanistic Judaism

| | |
|---|---|
| .834 1 | Reform Judaism |
| .834 2 | Conservative Judaism |
| .834 4 | Reconstructionist Judaism |

## 297  Islam, Babism, Bahai Faith

Standard subdivisions are added for Islam, Babism, Bahai Faith together; for Islam alone

*See Manual at 200.92 and 201–209, 292–299; also at 201–209 and 292–299; also at 203.6, 263.9, 292–299 vs. 394.265–394.267; also at 322.1 vs. 201.72, 261.7, 292–299; also at 398.2 vs. 201.3, 230, 270, 292–299; also at 615.852 vs. 203.1, 234.131, 292–299; also at 616.86 vs. 158.1, 204.42, 248.8629, 292–299, 362.29*

## SUMMARY

[.06]      Organizations and management

        Do not use; class in 297.6

.07      Education, research, related topics

.071      Education

        Class here Islamic religion as an academic subject

        Class comprehensive works on Islamic religious education, religious education to inculcate religious faith and practice in 297.77

        *See Manual at 207.5, 268 vs. 200.71, 230.071, 292–299*

.09      History, geographic treatment, biography

        Notation 09 from Table 1 as modified below

        Class here religious aspects of Islamic fundamentalism

        Class prophets prior to Muḥammad in 297.246; class political science aspects of Islam, of Islamic fundamentalism in 320

        *For religious aspects of Islamic fundamentalism in a specific sect or reform movement, see 297.8*

        *See also 909.09767 for Islamic civilization*

        *See Manual at 320.557 vs. 297.09, 297.272, 322.1*

.090 2      610–1499

.090 21      610–1204

        Use of this notation for 500–609 discontinued because without meaning in context 201104

.090 211      Period of Revelation, 610–632

        From first revelation to Muḥammad the Prophet until his death

        Class biography of and comprehensive works on Muḥammad the Prophet in 297.63; class biography of and comprehensive works on his family and Companions in 297.64; class Hijrah (emigration from Mecca to Medina, 622) in relation to Muḥammad the Prophet and his family and Companions in 297.634; class Hijrah in general history in 953.802

| | |
|---|---|
| .090 212 | Period of Four Rightly-Guided Caliphs, 632–661 |

Class here 7th century, Rashidun Caliphate

Class religious biography and theological discussion of the first four caliphs in 297.648. Class interdisciplinary biographies of the first four caliphs with the subject in 950, e.g., Abu Bakr 953.02092

*For 661–699, see 297.090213*

| | |
|---|---|
| .090 213 | Period of Naissance, 661–718 |
| .090 214 | Period of Recording and Emergence of Islamic Schools of Thought, 718–912 |
| .090 215 | Period of Comprehensive Works, 912–1204 |
| .090 22 | 1204–1499 |

Including 14th century, 1300–1399 [*formerly* 297.09023]; 15th century, 1400–1499 [*formerly* 297.09024]

Class here period of Explanations and Briefs, 1204–1495

| | |
|---|---|
| [.090 23] | 14th century, 1300–1399 |

Relocated to 297.09022

| | |
|---|---|
| [.090 24] | 15th century, 1400–1499 |

Relocated to 297.09022

| | |
|---|---|
| .090 3–.090 5 | 16th–21st centuries |

Add to base number 297.090 the numbers following —090 in notation 0903–0905 from Table 1, e.g., Islam in 20th century 297.0904

| | |
|---|---|
| .092 | Biography |

Class interdisciplinary works on caliphs as civil and religious heads of state with the subject in 940–990, e.g., Abu Bakr 953.02092

*For Muslims primarily associated with a specific religious activity, see 297.1–297.7; for founders of Sufi orders, see 297.48; for Muhammad the Prophet, see 297.63; for Muhammad's family and companions (including religious biography of the first four caliphs), see 297.64; for Muslims primarily associated with a specific sect or reform movement, see 297.8*

*See Manual at 297.092*

---

> **297.1–297.8 Islam**

Class comprehensive works in 297

---

> **297.1–297.3 Sources of Islam; Islamic doctrinal theology ('Aqā'id and Kalām); Islam and secular disciplines; Islam and other systems of belief; Islamic worship**

Class comprehensive works in 297

**.1**          **Sources of Islam**

### SUMMARY

**.12**          Koran and Hadith

>          Class theology based on Koran and Hadith in 297.2

**.122**          Koran

**.122 03**          Topical dictionaries and encyclopedias

>          Do not use for concordances or non-topical dictionaries; class in 297.1224–297.1225

**.122 09**          History, geographic treatment, biography

>          Class here geography, history, chronology of the Middle East in Koran times in relation to the Koran

>          Class origin of Koran, commentary about historical occasions on which passages of Koran were revealed in 297.1221; class compilation and recording of Koran in 297.1224042; class comprehensive works on geography, history, chronology of the Middle East in Koran times in 939.4

**.122 092**          Biography

>          *For Muḥammad, see 297.63; for Muḥammad's family and companions, see 297.64; for prophets prior to Muḥammad, see 297.246*

**.122 1**          Origin and authenticity

>          Including inspiration, revelation, commentary about historic occasions on which passages were revealed; Koranic prophecy and prophecies

>          Class compilation and recording of Koran in 297.1224042

**.122 2**          Koran stories retold

>          Including picture books

------

>          297.122 4–297.122 5  Texts

>          Class comprehensive works in 297.122

>          *For texts accompanied by commentaries, see 297.1227*

**.122 4**          Arabic texts

>          Class here textual criticism

>          Class Arabic texts accompanied by translations in 297.1225

**.122 404**          Special topics of Arabic texts

**.122 404 2**          Compilation and recording of Koran

| | |
|---|---|
| .122 404 5 | Recitation and readings |

Standard subdivisions are added for either or both topics in heading

Class here art of melodic reading, tajwīd (adornment of recitation); qirā'āt (science of the readings, which treats various renditions of the text according to different oral traditions)

| | |
|---|---|
| .122 5 | Translations |

Class here Arabic texts accompanied by translations

Add to base number 297.1225 notation 1–9 from Table 6, e.g., the Koran in English 297.122521

| | |
|---|---|
| .122 6 | Interpretation and criticism (Exegesis) |

Class art of recitation in 297.1224045

*For textual criticism, see 297.1224; for commentaries, see 297.1227*

| | |
|---|---|
| .122 601 | Philosophy and theory |

Class here hermeneutics, principles and methods of Koranic exegesis

| | |
|---|---|
| .122 61 | General introductions to the Koran |

Including general introductions to the sciences necessary to study the Koran

| | |
|---|---|
| .122 67 | Historical criticism |
| .122 68 | Allegorical and numerical interpretations |
| .122 7 | Commentaries |

Criticism and interpretation arranged in textual order

Class here texts accompanied by commentaries

| | |
|---|---|
| .122 8 | Nonreligious subjects treated in the Koran |

Class a religious subject treated in the Koran with the subject, e.g., Islamic ethics 297.5

| | |
|---|---|
| .122 800 01–.122 800 09 | Standard subdivisions |
| .122 800 1–.122 899 9 | Specific nonreligious subjects treated in the Koran |

Add to base number 297.1228 notation 001–999, e.g., natural sciences in the Koran 297.12285

| | |
|---|---|
| .122 9 | Individual suras and groups of suras |

Origins, authenticity; geography, history, chronology of Koran lands in Koran times; texts; criticism, interpretation; commentaries; nonreligious subjects treated in the suras

| | |
|---|---|
| [.124] | Hadith (Traditions) |

Relocated to 297.125

| | |
|---|---|
| .125 | Hadith (Traditions) [*formerly* 297.124] |
| .125 012 | Classification |
| | Do not use for muṣṭalaḥ al-Ḥadīth; class in 297.1252 |
| .125 09 | History, geographic treatment, biography |
| | Notation 09 from Table 1 as modified under 297.09 |
| .125 1 | General topics of Hadith |
| | Class texts of Hadith, works about specific Hadith and compilations of Hadith in 297.1254–297.1259 |
| [.125 101–.125 109] | Standard subdivisions |
| | Do not use; class in 297.12501–297.12509 |
| .125 12 | Hadith stories retold |
| | Including picture books |
| .125 16 | Interpretation |
| | Class here riwayah (study of text of Hadith) |
| .125 160 1 | Philosophy and theory |
| | Class here hermeneutics, principles and methods of interpretation of Hadith |
| .125 161 | General introductions to Hadith |
| | Class here sciences of Hadith |
| | *For dirāyah (science of authenticity of Hadith), see 297.1252* |
| .125 162 | Asbāb wurūd al-Ḥadīth (Causes and circumstances of Hadith) |
| .125 163 | Al-Nāsikh wa-al-mansūkh (Abrogation of Hadith) |
| .125 18 | Nonreligious subjects treated in Hadith |
| | Class a religious subject treated in Hadith with the subject, e.g., Islamic ethics 297.5 |
| .125 180 001–.125 180 009 | Standard subdivisions |
| .125 180 01–.125 189 99 | Specific nonreligious subjects treated in Hadith |
| | Add to base number 297.12518 the notation 001–999, e.g., natural sciences in Hadith 297.125185 |

.125 2　　　　　　　Dirāyah (Science of authenticity of Hadith)

　　　　　　　　　　Class here muṣṭalaḥ al-Ḥadīth (classification of Hadith)

　　　　　　　　　　Unless other instructions are given, class a subject with aspects in two
　　　　　　　　　　or more subdivisions of 297.1252 in the number coming last, e.g.,
　　　　　　　　　　Hadith that are ṣaḥīḥ (authentic) and mutawātir (have a large number
　　　　　　　　　　of transmitters) 297.12523 (*not* 297.12521)

　　　　　　　　　　Class texts of Hadith in 297.1254–297.1259. Class authenticity of
　　　　　　　　　　specific Hadith with the Hadith in 297.1254–297.1259, plus notation
　　　　　　　　　　01 from add table under 297.1254–297.1259, e.g., weak Hadith of Ibn
　　　　　　　　　　Mājah, Muḥammad ibn Yazīd 297.1255201

.125 21　　　　　　Al-ṣaḥīḥ (Authentic Hadith) and al-hasan (Good Hadith)

　　　　　　　　　　Standard subdivisions are added for either or both topics in
　　　　　　　　　　heading

　　　　　　　　　　Including al-marfūʿ (narration attributed to the Prophet
　　　　　　　　　　specifically), al-mawqūf (narration attributed to a Companion
　　　　　　　　　　of the Prophet), al-maqṭūʿ (narration attributed to the tabiʿī, the
　　　　　　　　　　Successors of the Companions)

　　　　　　　　　　Class here al-muttaṣil (Hadith with uninterrupted chain of
　　　　　　　　　　transmission back to Prophet)

.125 22　　　　　　Al-daʿīf (Weak Hadith)

　　　　　　　　　　Including al-muʿallaq (discontinuity in the beginning of
　　　　　　　　　　transmission chain), al-muʿḍal (two or more consecutive
　　　　　　　　　　transmitters are dropped), al-munqatiʿ (chain of transmission is
　　　　　　　　　　disconnected at any point), and al-shadh (reported by trustworthy
　　　　　　　　　　transmitter but contradicts report of more trustworthy transmitter)

.125 222　　　　　　Al-mursal (Hadith in which transmitter between Successor and
　　　　　　　　　　Prophet is omitted from a given chain of transmission)

.125 225　　　　　　Al-mawḍuʿ (Fabricated Hadith)

.125 23　　　　　　Al-mutawātir (Hadith with large number of transmitters at all stages
　　　　　　　　　　of transmission)

.125 24　　　　　　Al-āḥād (Hadith with one or a few transmitters)

　　　　　　　　　　Including al-mashhūr (Hadith with more than two transmitters),
　　　　　　　　　　al-ʿazīz (Hadith with only two transmitters), al-gharīb (Hadith with
　　　　　　　　　　only one transmitter)

.125 26　　　　　　Al-jarḥ wa al-taʿdīl (Principles of disparagement and crediting of
　　　　　　　　　　transmitters of Hadith)

.125 261　　　　　　Ṭabaqāt al-ruwāh (Rankings of transmitters)

.125 262　　　　　　Al-thiqāt (Trustworthy transmitters)

.125 263　　　　　　Al-ḍuʿafāʾ (Untrustworthy transmitters)

.125 264　　　　　　Asmāʾ al-ruwāh (Names of transmitters)

　　　　　　　　　　Including al-muttafiq wa-al-muftariq (same name, different
　　　　　　　　　　identity)

.125 264 2 Al-Mu'talif wa-al-mukhtalif (Different names, written similarly but pronounced differently)

---

> 297.125 4–297.125 9 Texts of Hadith

Class here texts of specific Hadith and compilations of Hadith, works about specific Hadith and compilations of Hadith

Add to each subdivision identified by * as follows:
001–009 Standard subdivisions
01–08 Generalities
Add to 0 the numbers following 297.122 in 297.1221–297.1228, e.g., authenticity 01, interpretation 06

Class comprehensive works in 297.125

---

> 297.125 4–297.125 8 Texts of Hadith of Sunnites

Class comprehensive works in 297.125

.125 4 *Jawāmiʻ (Comprehensive compilations), ṣiḥāḥ (Authentic compilations), mustadrākāt

Subdivisions are added for jawāmiʻ, ṣiḥāḥ, mustadrākāt together, for jawāmiʻ alone, for ṣiḥāḥ alone

.125 41 *Al-Bukhārī, Muḥammad ibn Ismāʻīl

.125 42 *Muslim ibn al-Ḥajjāj al-Qushayrī

.125 43 *Al-Tirmidhī, Muḥammad ibn ʻĪsá

.125 45 Mustadrākāt (Compilations of Hadith meeting the conditions of other compilers but not found in their books)

.125 5 *Sunan (Compilations according to Islamic law hierarchy), musannafat, muwaṭṭaʻāt

Subdivisions are added for sunan, musannafat, muwaṭṭaʻāt together, for sunan alone

.125 51 *Abū Dāʻūd Sulaymān ibn al-Ashʻath al-Sijistānī

.125 52 *Ibn Mājah, Muḥammad ibn Yazīd

.125 53 *Al-Nasāʻī, Aḥmad ibn Shuʻayb

.125 54 *Al-Dārimī, ʻAbd Allāh ibn ʻAbd al-Raḥmān

.125 56 *Musannafat (Compilations according to topics)

Including muṣannaf of Ibn Abī Shaybah, ʻAbd Allāh ibn Muḥammad and muṣannaf of ʻAbd al-Razzāq ibn Hammām al-Ḥimyari

.125 58 *Muwaṭṭaʻāt (The well-trodden path of Hadith)

Class here Muwaṭṭaʻ of Mālik ibn Anas

---

*Add as instructed under 297.1254–297.1259

| | |
|---|---|
| .125 6 | Masānīd, aṭrāf, maʻājim, zawāʼid |
| .125 61 | *Masānīd (Compilations arranged by first transmitter in the chain of transmission) |
| .125 612 | *Ibn Ḥanbal, Aḥmad ibn Muḥammad |
| .125 613 | *Al-Mawṣilī, Abū Yaʻlá Aḥmad ibn ʻAlī |
| .125 62 | *Aṭrāf (Compilations of the beginnings, or the most well known words of a specific Hadith) |
| | Class here Mizzī, Yūsuf ibn al-Zakī ʻAbd al-Raḥmān |
| .125 63 | *Maʻājim (Compilations arranged alphabetically according to names of the compilers' sheikhs) |
| | Class here al-Ṭabarānī, Sulaymān ibn Aḥmad |
| .125 64 | *Zawāʼid (Compilations of Hadith found in one compilation but not another) |
| | Class here Haythamī, Nūr al-Dīn ʻAlī ibn Abī Bakr |
| .125 7 | *Mustakhrajat (Compilations containing Hadith of other compilers with different chains of transmission) and takhrījāt (Compilations that define the degree of verification of another compilation) |
| | Subdivisions are added for either or both topics in heading |
| | Class mustakhrajat and takhrījāt of a specific work with the work, e.g., takhrījāt of maʻājim of al-Ṭabarānī, Sulaymān ibn Aḥmad 297.12563 |
| .125 8 | *Al-Aḥādīth al-Qudusīyah (Sacred Hadith) |
| | Sayings of the Prophet Muḥammad divinely communicated to him |
| .125 9 | Texts of Hadith of sects other than Sunnites |
| .125 92 | Hadith of Shiites |
| .125 921 | *Twelvers (Ithna Asharites) |
| .125 921 1 | *Kulaynī, Muḥammad ibn Yaʻqūb |
| .125 921 2 | *Ibn Bābawayh al-Qummī, Muḥammad ibn ʻAlī |
| .125 921 3 | *Ṭūsī, Muḥammad ibn al-Ḥasan (Abū Jaʻfar) |
| .125 922 | *Seveners (Ismailites) |
| .125 924 | *Zaydites |
| .125 93 | Hadith of other sects |
| .125 933 | *Ibadites |

*Add as instructed under 297.1254–297.1259

.14 Religious and ceremonial laws and decisions

> Class here fiqh in relation to religious and ceremonial laws and decisions, sharia in relation to religious and ceremonial laws and decisions

> Class Islamic law relating to secular matters, interdisciplinary works on Islamic law in 340.59. Class religious law on a specific topic with the topic, e.g., religious law concerning ḥajj 297.352

.18 Stories, legends, parables, proverbs, anecdotes told for religious edification

> Class here comprehensive works on Islamic legends

> Class Islamic folklore in 398.2088297

> *For Islamic legends on a specific topic, see the topic, e.g., Islamic legends about pre-Islamic prophets 297.246*

**.2 Islamic doctrinal theology ('Aqā'id and Kalām); Islam and secular disciplines; Islam and other systems of belief**

> Standard subdivisions are added for Islamic doctrinal theology, Islam and secular disciplines, Islam and other systems of belief together; for Islamic doctrinal theology alone

> Class Islamic ethics in 297.5; class doctrines concerning Muḥammad the Prophet in 297.63

### SUMMARY

| | |
|---|---|
| 297.204 | **Doctrines of specific sects** |
| .21 | **God and spiritual beings** |
| .22 | **Humankind** |
| .23 | **Eschatology** |
| .24 | **Other doctrines** |
| .26 | **Islam and secular disciplines** |
| .27 | **Islam and social sciences** |
| .28 | **Islam and other systems of belief** |
| .29 | **Apologetics and polemics** |

.204 Doctrines of specific sects

> Add to base number 297.204 the numbers following 297.8 in 297.81–297.87, e.g., doctrines of Shiites 297.2042

---

> 297.21–297.24 Specific topics in Islamic doctrinal theology ('Aqā'id and Kalām)

> Class comprehensive works in 297.2

> *For doctrines of specific sects, see 297.204; for apologetics and polemics, see 297.29; for shahāda (profession of faith), see 297.34*

.21 God and spiritual beings

.211 God

.211 2        Attributes and names of God

Class vindication of God's justice and goodness in permitting existence of evil and suffering in 297.2118

*For tawhid (unity of God), see 297.2113*

.211 3        Tawhid (Unity of God)

.211 4        Relation to the world

Including relation to and action in history

*For revelation, see 297.2115; for creation, see 297.242*

.211 5        Revelation

Including prophecy

Class Koranic prophecy in 297.1221; class prophets and prophethood in 297.246

.211 8        Theodicy

Vindication of God's justice and goodness in permitting existence of evil and suffering

.215          Angels

.216          Devils

.217          Jinn

.22           Humankind

Including faith, repentance

*For eschatology, see 297.23*

.221          Creation

Class comprehensive works on creation in 297.242

.225          Nature

Including soul

Class free will and predestination in 297.227

.227          Free will and predestination

Class here freedom of choice between good and evil

.23           Eschatology

Including day of judgment, death, eternity, future life, heaven, hell, punishment, resurrection, rewards

Class doctrines of Hidden Imam, of Mahdi in 297.24

.24           Other doctrines

Including doctrines of Hidden Imam, of Mahdi

| .242 | Creation |
|---|---|

    Including origin of life

    Class here Islamic cosmology

      *For creation of humankind, see 297.221*

| .246 | Prophets prior to Muḥammad |
|---|---|

    Including Adam, Moses

    Class here comprehensive works on prophets and prophethood in Islam

      *For Muḥammad the Prophet, see 297.63*

| .246 3 | Abraham |
|---|---|
| .246 5 | Jesus, son of Mary |
| .26 | Islam and secular disciplines |

    Class here attitudes of Islam toward and influence on secular issues, Islamic views and teachings about secular disciplines

    Class relation of a specific Islamic doctrine and a secular discipline with the doctrine in 297.2, e.g., relation of Islamic doctrine about creation and scientific theories about creation 297.242; class work influenced by Islam and Islamic theories within a secular discipline with the discipline, e.g., Islamic philosophy 181.07, architecture in the Islamic world 720.91767

      *For Islam and social sciences, see 297.27*

      *See also 297.1228 for nonreligious subjects treated in Koran; also 297.12518 for nonreligious subjects treated in Hadith*

      *See Manual at 297.26–297.27*

| .261 | Islam and philosophy, parapsychology and occultism, psychology |
|---|---|
| .265 | Islam and natural sciences, mathematics |
| .266 | Islam and technology |
| .267 | Islam and the arts |
| .27 | Islam and social sciences |

    Attitudes of Islam toward and influence on social issues

    Including environment, war and peace

    Class here Islam and socioeconomic problems, Islamic social theology

    Class Islamic view of marriage and family in 297.577

      *See Manual at 297.26–297.27*

| .272 | Islam and politics |
|---|---|

Including civil rights, international affairs, nationalism

Class political science view of religiously oriented political theories and ideologies in 320.55; class political science view of relation of state to religious organizations and groups in 322.1; class political science view of religious political parties in 324.2182

*See Manual at 320.557 vs. 297.09, 297.272, 322.1*

| .273 | Islam and economics |
|---|---|

Including Islam and communism

*See also 297.289 for Islam and atheism*

| .28 | Islam and other systems of belief |
|---|---|

Attitudes toward and relations with other systems of belief

Class apologetics and polemics in 297.29

| .282 | Islam and Judaism |
|---|---|

Class Biblical figures as prophets prior to Muḥammad in 297.246

| .283 | Islam and Christianity |
|---|---|

Class Biblical figures as prophets prior to Muḥammad in 297.246

| .284 | Islam and religions of Indic origin |
|---|---|

Add to base number 297.284 the numbers following 294 in 294.3–294.6, e.g., Islam and Hinduism 297.2845

| .289 | Islam and irreligion |
|---|---|

Including Islam and atheism

| .29 | Apologetics and polemics |
|---|---|
| .292 | Polemics against Judaism |
| .293 | Polemics against Christianity |
| .294 | Polemics against religions of Indic origin |
| .298 | Polemics against scientists and materialists |
| **.3** | **Islamic worship** |

Including use of arts and symbolism in worship

Class here comprehensive works on Islamic worship, on non-Sufi worship, on Islamic private worship, on non-Sufi private worship, public worship

Class Pillars of Islam (Pillars of the Faith) in 297.31. Class applications of the arts and symbolism in worship of specific sects with the sect in 297.301–297.307, e.g., use of arts and symbolism in Sunni worship 297.301; class applications of the arts and symbolism in specific aspects of worship with the aspect in 297.31–297.38, e.g., use of arts and symbolism in mosques 297.351

*For Sufi worship, see 297.43*

| | | |
|---|---|---|
| .300 1–.300 9 | | Standard subdivisions |
| .301–.307 | | Specific sects |

Add to base number 297.30 the numbers following 297.8 in 297.81–297.87, e.g., Shiite rites 297.302

.31      Pillars of Islam (Pillars of the Faith)

Comprehensive works only

*For shahāda (profession of faith), see 297.34; for ḥajj (pilgrimage to Mecca), see 297.352; for ṣawm Ramaḍān (annual fast of Ramadan), see 297.362; for ṣalāt (prayer five times daily), see 297.3822; for zakat, see 297.54*

*See also 297.72 for jihad*

.34      Shahāda (Profession of faith)

.35      Sacred places and pilgrimages

Standard subdivisions are added for sacred places and pilgrimages together, for sacred places alone

Including non-Sufi pilgrimages, comprehensive works on Islamic pilgrimages

Class here rites and ceremonies associated with sacred places and pilgrimages

Class pilgrimages to specific places in 297.352–297.359

*For Sufi pilgrimages, see 297.435*

[.350 93–.350 99]      Specific continents, countries, localities

Do not use; class in 297.353–297.359

.351      Mosques

Class here interdisciplinary works

*For organizational role and function of mosques, see 297.65; for architecture of mosques, see 726.2*

[.351 093–.351 099]      Specific continents, countries, localities

Do not use; class in 297.352–297.359

.352      Mecca

Class here ḥajj (pilgrimage to Mecca)

.353–.359      Specific continents, countries, localities

Add to base number 297.35 notation 3–9 from Table 2, e.g., Medina 297.35538, Jerusalem 297.35569442; however, for Mecca, see 297.352

.36          Special days and seasons

Including Jum'ah (Friday prayer); 'Āshūrā' (Tenth of Muḥarram); Mawlid al-Nabī (Prophet's birthday); 'Īd al-Aḍḥā, 'Īd al-Fiṭr

Class here rites and ceremonies associated with special days and seasons, Islamic religious calendar

*See also 297.37 for sermons for special days and seasons*

.362         Ṣawm Ramaḍān (Annual fast of Ramadan)

Including Laylat al-Qadr

Class comprehensive works on fasting in 297.53

.37          Sermons and preaching

Class sermons on a specific subject with the subject, e.g., sermons on day of judgment 297.23

.38          Rites, ceremonies, prayer, meditation

Conduct and texts

Including ablutions

Class ablutions associated with prayer and meditations in 297.382; class ablutions associated with burial and mourning in 297.385; class rites and ceremonies associated with sacred places and pilgrimages in 297.35; class rites and ceremonies associated with special days and seasons in 297.36

*See also 297.37 for sermons and preaching*

.382        Prayer and meditation

Standard subdivisions are added for prayer and meditation together, for prayer alone

Including dhikr (remembrance), qiblah (direction of prayer)

Class here practical works on prayer and meditation

Class prayer and meditation associated with sacred places and pilgrimages in 297.35; class prayer and meditation associated with special days and seasons in 297.36. Class prayer and meditation associated with specific rites and ceremonies with the rites and ceremonies, e.g., funerals in 297.385; class prayers and meditations on a specific subject with the subject, e.g., unity of God 297.2113

.382 2      Ṣalāt (Prayer five times daily)

*For texts of prayers, see 297.3824*

.382 4      Texts of prayers and meditations

Class here prayer books

.385        Burial and mourning rites

.39 Popular practices

> Including controversial practices, e.g., divination and occultism

> Class occult practices not regarded as Islamic practices in 130; class Islamic views of occultism regarded as a secular topic in 297.261; class sociological studies of Islamic popular practices in 306.69739. Class popular practices associated with a topic provided elsewhere with the topic, e.g., popular practices associated with burial and mourning 297.385

**.4 Sufism (Islamic mysticism)**

.41 Sufi doctrinal theology; Sufism and secular disciplines; Sufism and non-Islamic systems of belief

> Standard subdivisions are added for Sufi doctrinal theology, Sufism and secular disciplines, Sufism and non-Islamic systems of belief together; for Sufi doctrinal theology alone

> Add to base number 297.41 the numbers following 297.2 in 297.21–297.29, e.g., Sufi concept of God 297.4111

> Class Sufi doctrines concerning Muḥammad the Prophet in 297.4; class Sufi ethics in 297.45

.43 Sufi worship

.430 01–.430 09 Standard subdivisions

.430 1–.430 7 Specific sects

> Add to base number 297.43 the numbers following 297.3 in 297.301–297.307, e.g., Sunni Sufi orders 297.4301

.431–.438 Subdivisions of Sufi worship

> Add to base number 297.43 the numbers following 297.3 in 297.31–297.38, e.g., Sufi pilgrimages 297.435, Sufi observance of ṣawm Ramaḍān 297.4362, Sufi prayer and meditation 297.4382

> Comprehensive works on Islamic worship, on non-Sufi worship, on Islamic private worship, on non-Sufi private worship relocated to 297.3

.44 Sufi religious life and practice

> Class here guides to Sufi religious life

> Class Sufi ethics in 297.45

> *For Sufi worship, see 297.43*

.446 Sufi individual observances

> Including Sufi ascetic practices, dietary laws and observance

> *For Sufi fasting, see 297.45*

.45 Sufi ethics

> Including Sufi almsgiving, fasting, ṣadaqah, zakat

> *For Sufi observance of ṣawm Ramaḍān, see 297.4362*

.48 Sufi orders

Including Bektashi, Naqshabandiyah, Qādirīyah, Tijānīyah

*See also 297.835 for Kadarites (Islamic sect)*

.482 Mevleviyeh

**.5** **Islamic ethics and religious experience, life, practice**

Standard subdivisions are added for ethics and religious experience, life, practice together; for ethics alone

Including conscience; general works on duty, sin, vice, virtue

Class a specific duty, sin, vice, virtue in 297.56

*For Pillars of Islam (Pillars of the Faith), see 297.31; for jihad, see 297.72*

.53 Ṣawm (Fast)

Class here comprehensive works on fasting

*For ṣawm Ramaḍān (Annual Fast of Ramadan), see 297.362*

.54 Zakat

Class here almsgiving, ṣadaqah

.56 Specific vices, virtues, moral issues

Add to base number 297.56 the numbers following 17 in 172–179, e.g., Islamic sexual ethics 297.566; however, for almsgiving, see 297.54

Class comprehensive works on vices, on virtues in 297.5

.57 Religious experience, life, practice

Standard subdivisions are added for any or all topics in heading

Class here non-Sufi and comprehensive works on Islamic religious experience, life, practice; non-Sufi and comprehensive guides to religious life

Class Islamic ethics in 297.5

*For worship, see 297.3; for mysticism and Sufi religious experience, see 297.4; for Sufi life and practice, see 297.44*

[.570 85] Relatives

Do not use; class in 297.577

.570 86 People by miscellaneous social attributes

[.570 865 5] Married people

Do not use; class in 297.577

.574 Conversion

Class here conversion of non-Muslims to Islam

Class da'wah in 297.74. Class conversion of Muslims to another religion with the religion, e.g., conversion of Muslims to Christianity 248.246

.576          Individual observances

    Including ascetic practices, dietary laws and observance, ritual slaughter of animals to conform with dietary laws

    *For pilgrimages, see 297.35; for fasting, see 297.53; for almsgiving, see 297.54*

.577          Marriage and family life

    Including Muslim child rearing

    Class here comprehensive works on marriage, on family life

    *For ethics of marriage and family, see 297.563*

**.6          Islamic leaders and organization**

.61          Leaders and their work

    Role, function, duties

    Class here ayatollahs, caliphate, caliphs, imamate, imams, ulama

    *For doctrine of Hidden Imam, see 297.24; for Muḥammad the Prophet, see 297.63; for Muḥammad's family and companions (including first four caliphs), see 297.64*

[.610 92]          Biography

    Do not use for biography of religious leaders primarily associated with a specific religious activity; class in 297.1–297.7 e.g., founders of Sufi orders 297.48. Do not use for biography of Muḥammad; class in 297.63. Do not use for biography of Muḥammad's family and companions (including first four caliphs); class in 297.64. Do not use for biography of Islamic leaders primarily associated with a specific sect or reform movement; class in 297.8. Do not use for biography of other religious leaders; class in 297.092

.63          Muḥammad the Prophet

    Class here comprehensive works on Muḥammad and his family and companions

    Class Hadith in 297.125

    *For Muḥammad's family and companions, see 297.64*

.630 92          Biography

    Do not use for Muḥammad the Prophet; class in 297.63

    Class here scholars who specialize in the life and works of Muḥammad the Prophet

.632          Period prior to call to prophethood

    Including birth, childhood

    *See also 297.36 for Mawlid al-Nabī (holiday of Prophet's birthday)*

.633 Period at Mecca

Including Isrā' (Night Journey to Jerusalem) and Mi'rāj (Ascent to Heaven)

Class comprehensive works on prophetic career in 297.635

*For period prior to call to prophethood, see 297.632*

.634 Hijrah (Emigration from Mecca)

.635 Period at Medina

*For emigration from Mecca to Medina, see 297.634*

.64 Muḥammad's family and companions

Standard subdivisions are added for family and companions together, for family alone

Including descendants of Muḥammad

.642 Wives

.644 Children

.648 Ṣaḥābah (Companions)

Including religious biography and theological discussion of the first four caliphs

Class interdisciplinary biographies of the first four caliphs with the subject in 950, e.g., Abu Bakr 953.02092

.65 Organizations and organization

Role and function

Including associations, congregations, mosques

Class Islamic organizations in relation to political affairs in 297.272; class a specific organization limited to a specific sect or reform movement in 297.8; class political science view of relation of state to religious organizations and groups in 322.1; class political science view of religious political parties in 324.2182; class interdisciplinary works on mosques in 297.351

**.7 Protection and propagation of Islam**

.72 Jihad

.74 Da'wah

Class here call to Islam, missionary work

.77 Islamic religious education

Class Islam as an academic subject in 297.071; class comprehensive works on madrasah education, treating both religious education and other subjects, in 371.077

*For religious education at the level of higher education, see 297.0711*

*See Manual at 207.5, 268 vs. 200.71, 230.071, 292–299*

.770 83            Young people

> Class here Islamic religious schools, religious education in Islamic schools that teach all subjects

> Class comprehensive works on Islamic schools that teach all subjects in 371.077

## .8     Islamic sects and reform movements

> Class specific aspects of sects and reform movements in 297.1–297.7; class secular view of relation of state to religious organizations and groups in 322.1; class secular view of religious political parties in 324.2182

> *For Sufism, see 297.4*

.804            Special topics of Islamic sects and reform movements

.804 2            Relations among sects and reform movements

> Class here relations between Sunni and Shia Islam

.81            Sunnites

> Class relations between Sunnites and Shiites in 297.8042

.811            Hanafites

.812            Shafiites

.813            Malikites

.814            Hanbalites and Wahhābīyah

.82            Shiites

> Class relations between Shiites and Sunnites in 297.8042

.821            Twelvers (Ithna Asharites)

.822            Seveners (Ismailites)

> Including Mustalians, Nizaris

.824            Zaydites

.83            Other sects and reform movements

> Including Kharijites

.833            Ibadites

.834            Motazilites

.835            Kadarites

> *See also 297.48 for Qādirīyah (Sufi order)*

.837            Murjiites

.85            Druzes

.86            Ahmadiyya movement

| | |
|---|---|
| .87 | Black Muslim movement |

Including American Muslim Mission, Nation of Islam, World Community of al-Islam in the West

| | |
|---|---|
| **.9** | **Babism and Bahai Faith** |
| .92 | Babism |
| .93 | Bahai Faith |
| .931–.937 | Specific aspects |

Add to base number 297.93 the numbers following 20 in 201–207, e.g., Bahai ethics 297.935

| | |
|---|---|
| .938 | Sources |
| .938 2 | Sacred books |

*For works by the Bab, see 297.92*

| | |
|---|---|
| .938 22 | Works by Bahá'u'lláh |
| .938 24 | Works by 'Abdu'l-Bahá |
| .938 6 | Authoritative interpretation |

Class here works by Shoghi Effendi

| | |
|---|---|
| .938 7 | Elucidation and legislation |

Class here works of the Universal House of Justice

## (298)    (Permanently unassigned)

(Optional number used for Christianity if option A under 290 is chosen. Another option is described at 290)

## 299    Religions not provided for elsewhere

Including Urantia, modern revivals of long dormant religions

Class syncretistic religious writings of individuals expressing personal views and not claiming to establish a new religion or to represent an old one in 200

If a religion not named in the schedule claims to be Christian, class it in 289.9 even if it is unorthodox or syncretistic

*See Manual at 200.92 and 201–209, 292–299; also at 201–209 and 292–299; also at 203.6, 263.9, 292–299 vs. 394.265–394.267; also at 207.5, 268 vs. 200.71, 230.071, 292–299; also at 322.1 vs. 201.72, 261.7, 292–299; also at 398.2 vs. 201.3, 230, 270, 292–299; also at 615.852 vs. 203.1, 234.131, 292–299; also at 616.86 vs. 158.1, 204.42, 248.8629, 292–299, 362.29*

(Options for giving local emphasis and shorter numbers for a specific religion are described at 290)

## SUMMARY

### .1–.4  Religions of Indo-European, Semitic, Non-Semitic Afro-Asiatic, North and West Asian, Dravidian origin

Not otherwise provided for

Add to base number 299 the numbers following —9 in notation 91–94 from Table 5, e.g., Mithraism 299.15

Class modern revivals of long dormant religions in 299

### .1  Religions of Indo-European origin

Number built according to instructions under 299.1–299.4

### .16  Celtic religion

Number built according to instructions under 299.1–299.4

### .161  Specific aspects of Celtic religion

Add to base number 299.161 the numbers following 20 in 201–209, e.g., Celtic mythology 299.16113

### .3  Religions of Non-Semitic Afro-Asiatic origin

Number built according to instructions under 299.1–299.4

### .31  †Ancient Egyptian religion

Number built according to instructions under 299.1–299.4

### .5  Religions of East and Southeast Asian origin

*See Manual at 200.9 vs. 294, 299.5*

### .51  Religions of Chinese origin

### .511  Specific aspects of Chinese religions

Add to base number 299.511 the numbers following 20 in 201–209, e.g., Chinese gods and goddesses 299.511211

### .512  †Confucianism

Class the Four books of Confucius, interdisciplinary works on Confucianism in 181.112

### .514  †Taoism

†Add as instructed under 290

.54          Religions of Tibetan origin

Class here Bon

.56          Religions of Japanese and Ryukyuan origin

.561            †Shinto

.57–.59      Other religions of East and Southeast Asian origin

Add to base number 299.5 the numbers following —95 in notation 957–959 from Table 5, e.g., Caodaism 299.592

**.6          Religions originating among Black Africans and people of Black African descent**

*For Black Muslims, see 297.87; for religions originating among peoples who speak, or whose ancestors spoke, Ethiopian languages, see 299.28; for religions originating among Cushitic and Omotic peoples, see 299.35; for religions originating among the Hausa, see 299.37; for religions originating among the Malagasy, see 299.923*

[.609 61–.609 69]        Religions in specific areas in Africa

Do not use; class in 299.691–299.699

.61          Specific aspects

Add to base number 299.61 the numbers following 20 in 201–208, e.g., mythology and mythological foundations 299.6113

Class specific aspects of specific religions and movements, of religions of specific groups and peoples in 299.67–299.68

.67          Specific religions and movements

Class here doctrines; practices, rites, ceremonies; mythology and mythological foundations; and other specific aspects of specific religions and movements

.672            †Umbanda

.673            †Candomblé

.674            †Santeria

.675            †Voodoo

Including zombiism

Class voodoo as an occult practice without regard to its religious significance in 133.4

.676            †Ras Tafari movement

†Add as instructed under 290

.68    Religions of specific groups and peoples

> Class here doctrines; practices, rites, ceremonies; mythology and mythological foundations; and other specific aspects of specific religions and movements
>
> Class specific religions and movements of specific groups and peoples in 299.67

.681    Religions of Khoikhoi and San

.683–.685    Religions of peoples who speak, or whose ancestors spoke, Niger-Congo, Nilo-Saharan languages

> Add to base number 299.68 the numbers following —96 in notation 963–965 from Table 6, e.g., religion of the Yoruba 299.68333; then add further as follows:
> 001–009    Standard subdivisions
> 01–08    Specific aspects
>    Add to 0 the numbers following 20 in 201–208, e.g., mythology 013, Yoruba mythology 299.68333013

.686–.688    Religions of national groups in Africa

> Add to base number 299.68 the numbers following —6 in notation 66–68 from Table 2, e.g., religion of Ugandans 299.68761
>
> Class national groups that predominate in specific areas in Africa in 299.69

.689    Religions of other national groups of largely African descent

> Add to base number 299.689 notation 4–9 from Table 2, e.g., African religion of Haitians 299.6897294
>
> Class religions of such national groups in areas where they predominate in 299.609, e.g., African religion of Haitians in Haiti 299.6097294

.69    Religions of specific areas in Africa

> Add to base number 299.69 the numbers following —6 in notation 61–69 from Table 2, e.g., religions of West Africa 299.696
>
> Class specific aspects of religions of specific areas in 299.61; class specific religions and movements in specific areas in 299.67; class religions of specific groups and peoples in specific areas in 299.68

**.7    Religions of North American native origin**

[.709 71–.709 79]    Religions in specific areas in North America

> Do not use; class in 299.791–299.799

.71    Specific aspects

> Add to base number 299.71 the numbers following 20 in 201–208, e.g., mythology and mythological foundations 299.7113
>
> Class specific aspects of religions of specific groups and peoples in 299.78

.78        Religions of specific groups and peoples

Add to base number 299.78 the numbers following —97 in notation 971–979 from Table 5, e.g., religion of Aztecs 299.78452; then add further as follows (*not* as instructed at Table 5):
   001–009    Standard subdivisions
   01–08    Specific aspects
        Add to 0 the numbers following 20 in 201–208, e.g., mythology and mythological foundations 013, Aztec mythology 299.78452013

.79        Religions of specific areas in North America

Add to base number 299.79 the numbers following —7 in notation 71–79 from Table 2, e.g., religions of Indians of Mexico 299.792

Class religions of specific groups and peoples in specific areas in 299.78

**.8          Religions of South American native origin**

[.809 81–.809 89]        Religions of specific areas in South America

Do not use; class in 299.891–299.899

.81        Specific aspects

Add to base number 299.81 the numbers following 20 in 201–208, e.g., mythology and mythological foundations 299.8113

Class specific aspects of religions of specific groups and peoples in 299.88

.88        Religions of specific groups and peoples

Add to base number 299.88 the numbers following —98 in notation 982–989 from Table 5, e.g., religion of Incas 299.88323; then add further as follows (*not* as instructed at Table 5):
   001–009    Standard subdivisions
   01–08    Specific aspects
        Add to 0 the numbers following 20 in 201–208, e.g., mythology and mythological foundations 013, Inca mythology 299.88323013

.89        Religions of specific areas in South America

Add to base number 299.89 the numbers following —8 in notation 81–89 from Table 2, e.g., religions of Indians of the Amazon 299.8911

Class religions of specific groups and peoples in specific areas in 299.88

**.9          Religions of other origin**

.92        Religions of other ethnic origin

Add to base number 299.92 the numbers following —99 in notation 991–999 from Table 5, e.g., religion of Polynesians 299.924; then add further as follows (*not* as instructed at Table 5):
   001–009    Standard subdivisions
   01–08    Specific aspects
        Add to 0 the numbers following 20 in 201–208, e.g., mythology and mythological foundations 013

.93            Religions of eclectic and syncretistic origin

Religions and applied religious philosophies of eclectic, syncretistic, universal nature

Including Eckankar, a Course in Miracles, Great White Brotherhood, New Thought, systems of Bhagwan Shree Rajneesh and Meher Baba, United Church of Religious Science

Class here New Age religions

Class syncretistic religious writings of individuals expressing personal views and not claiming to establish a new religion or to represent an old one in 200

*See also 289.98 for Christian New Thought*

*See Manual at 299.93; also at 201–209 and 292–299*

.932         Gnosticism

Including Manicheism

Class Christian gnosticism in 273.1; class Christian Manicheism in 273.2

.933         Subud

.934         Theosophy

.935         Anthroposophy

.936         Scientology

Including dianetics

.94            Modern paganism, neopaganism, wicca

Standard subdivisions are added for any or all topics in heading

Class here religions based on modern revivals of witchcraft

# 300

<hr>

## 300    Social sciences

Class here behavioral sciences, social studies

Class a specific behavioral science with the science, e.g., psychology 150; class military, diplomatic, political, economic, social, welfare aspects of a war with the history of the war, e.g., Vietnamese War 959.7043

*For language, see 400; for history, see 900*

*See Manual at 300 vs. 600; also at 300–330, 355–390 vs. 342–347, 352–354; also at 300, 320.6 vs. 352–354*

### SUMMARY

| | |
|---|---|
| 300.1–.9 | **Standard subdivisions** |
| 301 | **Sociology and anthropology** |
| 302 | **Social interaction** |
| 303 | **Social processes** |
| 304 | **Factors affecting social behavior** |
| 305 | **Groups of people** |
| 306 | **Culture and institutions** |
| 307 | **Communities** |
| | |
| 310 | **Collections of general statistics** |
| 314–319 | **General statistics of specific continents, countries, localities in modern world** |
| | |
| 320 | **Political science (Politics and government)** |
| .01–.09 | **Standard subdivisions** |
| .1–.9 | **[Structure and functions of government, ideologies, political situation and conditions, related topics]** |
| 321 | **Systems of governments and states** |
| 322 | **Relation of the state to organized groups and their members** |
| 323 | **Civil and political rights** |
| 324 | **The political process** |
| 325 | **International migration and colonization** |
| 326 | **Slavery and emancipation** |
| 327 | **International relations** |
| 328 | **The legislative process** |
| | |
| 330 | **Economics** |
| .01–.09 | **Standard subdivisions** |
| .1–.9 | **[Systems, schools, theories, economic situation and conditions]** |
| 331 | **Labor economics** |
| 332 | **Financial economics** |
| 333 | **Economics of land and energy** |
| 334 | **Cooperatives** |
| 335 | **Socialism and related systems** |
| 336 | **Public finance** |
| 337 | **International economics** |
| 338 | **Production** |
| 339 | **Macroeconomics and related topics** |

| 340 | Law |
| .02–.09 | Standard subdivisions |
| .1–.9 | [Philosophy and theory of law, comparative law, law reform, legal systems, conflict of laws] |
| 341 | Law of nations |
| 342 | Constitutional and administrative law |
| 343 | Military, defense, public property, public finance, tax, commerce (trade), industrial law |
| 344 | Labor, social service, education, cultural law |
| 345 | Criminal law |
| 346 | Private law |
| 347 | Procedure and courts |
| 348 | Laws, regulations, cases |
| 349 | Law of specific jurisdictions, areas, socioeconomic regions, regional intergovernmental organizations |

| 350 | Public administration and military science |
| 351 | Public administration |
| 352 | General considerations of public administration |
| 353 | Specific fields of public administration |
| 354 | Public administration of economy and environment |
| 355 | Military science |
| 356 | Foot forces and warfare |
| 357 | Mounted forces and warfare |
| 358 | Air and other specialized forces and warfare; engineering and related services |
| 359 | Sea forces and warfare |

| 360 | Social problems and services; associations |
| 361 | Social problems and services |
| 362 | Social problems of and services to groups of people |
| 363 | Other social problems and services |
| 364 | Criminology |
| 365 | Penal and related institutions |
| 366 | Secret associations and societies |
| 367 | General clubs |
| 368 | Insurance |
| 369 | Associations |

| 370 | Education |
| .1–.9 | Standard subdivisions, education for specific objectives, educational psychology |
| 371 | Schools and their activities; special education |
| 372 | Primary education (Elementary education) |
| 373 | Secondary education |
| 374 | Adult education |
| 375 | Curricula |
| 378 | Higher education (Tertiary education) |
| 379 | Public policy issues in education |

| 380 | Commerce, communications, transportation |
| .1–.9 | Standard subdivisions |
| 381 | Commerce (Trade) |
| 382 | International commerce (Foreign trade) |
| 383 | Postal communication |
| 384 | Communications |
| 385 | Railroad transportation |
| 386 | Inland waterway and ferry transportation |
| 387 | Water, air, space transportation |
| 388 | Transportation |
| 389 | Metrology and standardization |

| 390 | Customs, etiquette, folklore |
|---|---|
| .01–.09 | Standard subdivisions of customs |
| .1–.4 | Customs of specific economic, social, occupational classes |
| 391 | Costume and personal appearance |
| 392 | Customs of life cycle and domestic life |
| 393 | Death customs |
| 394 | General customs |
| 395 | Etiquette (Manners) |
| 398 | Folklore |
| 399 | Customs of war and diplomacy |

**.1**      **Philosophy and theory**

**.2**      **Miscellany**

.21        Tabulated and related materials

         Do not use for statistics; class in 310

**.3–.9**    **Standard subdivisions**

# 301     Sociology and anthropology

Standard subdivisions are added for either or both topics in heading

Class here interdisciplinary works on society, humans

Class social problems and social welfare in 361–365

> *For specific topics in sociology and anthropology, see 302–307; for criminal anthropology, see 364.2; for customs, etiquette, folklore, see 390; for physical anthropology, see 599.9. For a specific aspect of society not provided for in 302–307, see the aspect, e.g., general history 900*
>
> *See Manual at 301–307 vs. 361–365*

[.019]      Psychological principles

         Do not use; class in 302

**.7**      **Nonliterate societies**

---

> ## 302–307 Specific topics in sociology and anthropology

Unless other instructions are given, observe the following table of preference, e.g., friendship among women 302.34082 (*not* 305.4):

| | |
|---|---|
| Factors affecting social behavior | 304 |
| Social processes | 303 |
| Social interaction | 302 |
| Culture and institutions | 306 |
| Groups of people | 305 |
| Communities | 307 |

Class comprehensive works in 301. Class effect of one factor on another with the factor affected, e.g., effect of climate on social change 303.4

> *See Manual at 301–307 vs. 361–365; also at 302–307 vs. 150, T1—019; also at 302–307 vs. 156; also at 302–307 vs. 320; also at 363 vs. 302–307, 333.7, 570–590, 600*

## 302     Social interaction

Class here psychological principles of sociology, interpersonal relations, social psychology

Class social psychology of a specific situation with the situation, e.g., social psychology of ethnic groups 305.8

*See also 155.92 for effect of social environment upon individuals; also 158.2 for individual aspects of interpersonal relations*

### SUMMARY

| | | |
|---|---|---|
| 302.01–.09 | | **Standard subdivisions** |
| | .1 | **General topics of social interaction** |
| | .2 | **Communication** |
| | .3 | **Social interaction within groups** |
| | .4 | **Social interaction between groups** |
| | .5 | **Relation of individual to society** |

.015 195        Statistical mathematics

Class here sociometry

*See Manual at 519.5, T1—015195 vs. 001.422, T1—0727*

[.019]     Psychological principles

Do not use; class in 302

.072     Research

[.072 7]     Statistical methods

Do not use; class in 302.015195

### .1     General topics of social interaction

.12     Social understanding

Including attribution, risk perception

*For social learning, see 303.32; for perception of norms, see 303.37*

.13     Social choice

Including attraction, influence

.14     Social participation

Including communalism, competition, cooperation, encounter groups, sensitivity training, voluntarism

Class here social acceptance, social adjustment, social skills, success

*See also 302.4 for intergroup aspects of participation*

.15     Social role (Role theory)

Including role conflict

Class social role of a specific group of people or institution with the group or institution in 305–306, e.g., social role of women 305.42

.17 Social dysfunction

Dysfunction affecting a substantial portion of society, e.g., mass hysteria, crazes

Including apathy, fear, panic

Class here social psychoanalysis

Class dysfunctional responses of individuals to society in 302.542

**.2** **Communication**

Including failures and disruptions of communication

Class here interdisciplinary works on communication, content analysis, semiotics

*For information theory, see 003.54; for censorship, see 303.376. For the semiotics of a specific subject, see the subject, plus notation 014 from Table 1, e.g., semiotics of biology 570.14*

.22 Kinds of communication

.222 Nonverbal communication

Including drumbeats, smoke signals; body language, gestures; flower language

Class here means of nonverbal communication, interdisciplinary works on nonlinguistic communication (nonstructured communication)

Class comprehensive works on means of verbal and nonverbal communication in 302.23; class sign languages for deaf people in 419

*For iconography, see 704.9; for insignia, see 929.9*

.222 3 Symbols

Class here interdisciplinary works on symbols, on symbolism

*For religious symbolism, see 203.7; for Christian religious symbols, see 246.55. For symbols in a specific subject other than religion, see the subject, plus notation 0148 from Table 1, e.g., symbols in electrical engineering 621.30148*

.224 Verbal communication

Class media in 302.23

*For language, see 400*

.224 2 Oral communication

Including listening

*For conversation, see 302.346*

.224 4 Written communication

Class here literacy, illiteracy

*See also 301.7 for nonliterate societies*

.23 Media (Means of communication)

Including signboards, signs

Class here electronic media, mass media, sociology of journalism

Class the effect of mass media on a specific subject other than social groups with the subject, e.g., effect on social change 303.4833, on a company's advertising policy 659.111; class interdisciplinary works on a specific medium with the medium, e.g., newspapers 070, television 384.55

.230 8 Groups of people

Class here effect of mass media on specific groups, on social stratification

Portrayal of a specific group in mass media relocated to the group in 305–306, e.g., minorities in mass media 305, scientists in mass media 306.45, gays in mass media 306.766

.231 Digital media

Including electronic publications, Internet, World Wide Web

.232 Print media

Class interdisciplinary works on the book in 002

.232 2 Newspapers

.232 4 Periodicals and journals

Standard subdivisions are added for either or both topics in heading

.234 Motion pictures, radio, television

.234 3 Motion pictures

.234 4 Radio

.234 5 Television

.235 Telephony and telegraphy

Standard subdivisions are added for telephony and telegraphy together, for telephony alone

.24 Content

Including gossip, rumor

*See also 070.1 for journalistic aspect of content*

**.3 Social interaction within groups**

Including teasing

Class here group decision-making processes, group dynamics, negotiation, social networks

.302 85 Computer applications

Class here online social networks

*For computer science aspects of online social networks, see 006.754*

.33 Social interaction in abstract and temporary groups

> Including audiences, crowds, mobs

> Class media audiences in 302.23

.34 Social interaction in primary groups

> Groups small enough for all members to engage in face-to-face relationships at one time

> Including committees, gangs

> Class here friendship

> Class family in 306.85

>> *See also 362.74 for predelinquent gangs; also 364.1066 for gangs engaging in crime*

.343 Bullying

> Class bullying in a specific institution with the institution, e.g., bullying in school 371.58

.346 Conversation

> Including conversational rhythm

.35 Social interaction in complex groups

> Class here bureaucracies, hierarchically organized groups, organizational behavior, sociology of management

> Class general works that emphasize how to manage in 658. Class works that emphasize how to manage in a specific field of activity with the field, plus notation 068 from Table 1, e.g., management of commercial banks 332.12068

**.4** **Social interaction between groups**

> Including ingroups and outgroups

> Class social interaction between a specific group of people and other groups of people in 305

**.5** **Relation of individual to society**

> *See also 155.92 for psychological effects of social environment upon the individual*

.54 Response of individuals

> Including ambition

> Class here aggression, dysfunctional responses, individualism

>> *For conformity, see 303.32*

>> *See also 302.17 for mass manifestations of social dysfunction*

.542 Deviation

> Class here madness considered as a form of interaction of individuals with society

.544            Alienation

.545            Isolation

# 303      Social processes

*For social interaction, see 302; for factors affecting social behavior, see 304*

### SUMMARY

| | |
|---|---|
| 303.3 | Coordination and control |
| .4 | Social change |
| .6 | Conflict and conflict resolution |

.3        **Coordination and control**

Standard subdivisions are added for coordination and control together, for coordination alone

Class here policy formulation, power

Class coordination and control in and through specific institutions in 306

### SUMMARY

| | |
|---|---|
| 303.32 | Socialization |
| .33 | Social control |
| .34 | Leadership |
| .35 | Utilitarian control |
| .36 | Coercion |
| .37 | Social norms |
| .38 | Public opinion |

.32        Socialization

Including social learning

Class here conformity

Class interdisciplinary works on child development in 305.231

*For education, see 370*

.323        Socialization by family

.324        Socialization by school

.325        Socialization by religious organizations

.327        Socialization by peer group

Class here peer pressure

.33        Social control

*For socialization, see 303.32; for social control through specific means, see 303.34–303.38*

---

> 303.34–303.38  Social control through specific means

Class socialization through specific means of control in 303.32; class comprehensive works in 303.33

| .34 | Leadership |
|---|---|

.342    Persuasion

By individuals

Class here interdisciplinary works on persuasion

*For a specific aspect of persuasion, see the aspect, e.g., individual psychology of persuasion 153.852, persuasion by media 302.23, persuasion by propaganda 303.375*

.35    Utilitarian control

Use of rewards and incentives

.36    Coercion

Including authority, punishment, restraint, threat

*See also 364.6 for treatment and punishment of offenders*

.37    Social norms

Including perception of norms

*For public opinion, see 303.38*

.372    Belief systems and customs

Standard subdivisions are added for either or both topics in heading

Class here social ethics as a method of social control; justice, values

Class rightness or wrongness of conduct as it affects individuals or society, interdisciplinary works on social ethics in 170

*See also 361.61 for values in social policy toward welfare problems*

.375    Propaganda

.376    Censorship

*See Manual at 363.31 vs. 303.376, 791.4*

.38    Public opinion

Class here attitudes, attitude formation and change

Class propaganda in 303.375. Class public opinion on a specific subject with the subject, e.g., public opinion on racial stereotypes 305.8, on the political process 324

*See also 302.12 for social understanding*

.385    Prejudice

Class here social stereotypes and stereotyping

Class prejudices held by groups of people with specific attributes in 303.386; class prejudices held by ethnic and national groups in 303.387; class prejudices held by occupational groups in 303.388; class prejudices regarding a specific group in 305

.386        Opinions held by groups of people with specific attributes

> Add to base number 303.386 the numbers following —08 in notation 081–088 from Table 1, e.g., opinions of young people 303.3863, opinions of Catholics 303.3868282
>
> *For opinions held by ethnic and national groups, see 303.387; for opinions held by occupational groups, see 303.388*

.387        Opinions held by ethnic and national groups

> Add to base number 303.387 notation 1–9 from Table 5, e.g., opinions of Canadians 303.38711

.388        Opinions held by occupational groups

> Add to base number 303.388 notation 001–999, e.g., opinions of dentists 303.3886176

**.4**        **Social change**

> Including evolutionary and revolutionary change
>
> Class social change in a specific aspect of society with the aspect in 302–307, e.g., changes in religious institutions 306.6

[.401 12]        Forecasting and forecasts

> Do not use; class in 303.49

.44        Growth and development

> Standard subdivisions are added for either or both topics in heading
>
> Class here progress, specialization

.45        Deterioration and decay

> Standard subdivisions are added for either or both topics in heading

.48        Causes of change

.482        Contact between cultures

> Class here acculturation, assimilation; social effects of international assistance, of commerce
>
> Class multicultural education in 370.117

.482 09        History and biography

> Do not use for geographic treatment; class in 303.4821–303.4829

| .482 1–.482 9 | Contact between specific areas |
|---|---|

Add to base number 303.482 notation 1–9 from Table 2, e.g., cultural exchanges with China 303.48251; then add 0* and again add notation 1–9 from Table 2, e.g., cultural exchange between China and Japan 303.48251052

Give priority in notation to the nation most affected. If this cannot be determined, give priority to the one coming first in Table 2
(Option: Give priority to the area requiring local emphasis, e.g., in United States class cultural exchange between United States and France in 303.48273044)

| .483 | Development of science and technology |
|---|---|

Class government policy on science in 338.926

*See Manual at 303.483 vs. 306.45, 306.46*

| .483 2 | Transportation |
|---|---|
| .483 3 | Communication |

Class here information technology

Class government policy on information in 338.926

| .483 4 | Computers |
|---|---|

Class here automation, microelectronics, robots

| .484 | Purposefully induced change |
|---|---|

Including dissent, radicalism

Class here social innovation, social reform, social reform movements

Class political aspects of reform movements in 322.44; class role of reform movements in addressing social problems in 361–365. Class innovation and reform directed to a specific end with the end, e.g., reform of banking 332.1

| .485 | Disasters |
|---|---|

Including earthquakes, pandemics, wars

| .49 | Social forecasts |
|---|---|

Class here futurology, social forecasting

Class interdisciplinary works on forecasting in 003.2. Class forecasting in and forecasts of a specific subject with the subject, plus notation 0112 from Table 1, e.g., future of U.S. Democratic Party 324.27360112

| .490 9 | History and biography |
|---|---|

Do not use for geographic treatment; class in 303.491–303.499

| .491–.499 | Forecasts for specific areas |
|---|---|

Add to base number 303.49 notation 1–9 from Table 2, e.g., Eastern Europe in the year 2010 303.4947

*Add 00 for standard subdivisions; see instructions at beginning of Table 1

**.6**          **Conflict and conflict resolution**

Class a specific form of conflict provided elsewhere in 302–306 with the form, e.g., bullying 302.343, racial conflict 305.8, spouse abuse 306.872; class a specific conflict considered an historical event with the event in 900, e.g., disturbances of May-June 1968 in France 944.0836

.61          Civil disobedience

Including hunger strikes, passive resistance, sit-ins

Class here nonviolence

.62          Civil disorder

*For civil war and revolution, see 303.64*

.623          Riots

.625          Terrorism

Class interdisciplinary works on terrorism in 363.325

.64          Civil war and revolution

Standard subdivisions are added for either or both topics in heading

Class terrorism in 303.625

.66          War and peace

Including pacifism, sociology of war

Class war as a cause of social change in 303.485; class prevention of war in 327.172; class causes of war in 355.027; class the art and science of warfare in 355–359. Class military, diplomatic, political, economic, social, welfare aspects of a specific war with the history of the war, e.g., of World War II 940.53

*For civil war, see 303.64*

.69          Conflict resolution

Including mediation

Class here conflict management

Class resolution of a specific kind of conflict with the kind of conflict, e.g., resolution of war 303.66

# 304          Factors affecting social behavior

**.2**          **Human ecology**

Class here ecological anthropology, human geography

*See Manual at 578 vs. 304.2, 508, 910*

.208 2          Women

Class here ecofeminism [*formerly* 305.42]

.23 Geographic, space, time factors

Including territoriality

.237 Time factors

Class aspects of time in relation to a specific subject with the subject in 302–307, e.g., time and conversation 302.346, leisure activities 306.4812

*See also 650.11 for time management*

.25 Climatic and weather factors

.27 Biological factors

Other than human

*For genetic factors, see 304.5*

.28 Environmental abuse

Including greenhouse effect

Class here social consequences of pollution, of misuse of resources

Class interdisciplinary works on resources in 333.7; class interdisciplinary works on pollution in 363.73

*See Manual at 333.72 vs. 304.28, 320.58, 363.7*

**.5** **Genetic factors**

Class here sociobiology (biosociology), study of genetic bases of human social behavior

Class a specific aspect of sociobiology with the aspect in 302–307, e.g., sociobiology of conflict 303.6

*For sociobiology of plants and animals, see 577.8*

*See also 304.27 for biological factors*

**.6** **Population**

Class here demographic anthropology, demography; population composition, geography, size; comprehensive works on population

*For movement of people, see 304.8*

.61 Population characteristics

Including density

.62 Growth and decline

*See also 304.63 for births; also 304.64 for deaths; also 304.8 for movement of people*

| | | |
|---|---|---|
| .63 | | Births |

Including birth intervals, family size

Class here comprehensive works on births and deaths

*For deaths, see 304.64*

*See also 304.62 for growth and decline of population*

.632    Fertility

.64    Deaths (Mortality)

.645    Life expectancy

.645 09    History and biography

Do not use for geographic treatment; class in 304.6451–304.6459

.645 1–.645 9    Geographic treatment

Add to base number 304.645 notation 1–9 from Table 2, e.g., life expectancy in Canada 304.64571

.66    Demographic effects of population control efforts

Class population policy, comprehensive works on population control in 363.9

.663    Genocide

Class here ethnic cleansing

.666    Family planning

Class here birth control

*See also 363.96 for family planning programs; also 613.94 for birth control techniques*

.667    Abortion

.668    Infanticide

**.8    Movement of people**

*For movement to, from, within communities, see 307.2*

.809    History, geographic treatment, biography

Class here internal movement, emigration from specific areas

*For emigration to specific areas, see 304.83–304.89*

.81    Causes

.82    International movement

Class international emigration in 304.809; class international immigration in 304.83–304.89

*See also 325 for political aspects of international movement*

.83–.89    Migration

Add to base number 304.8 notation 3–9 from Table 2, e.g., migration to Australia 304.894; then add 0* and to the result add notation 1–9 from Table 2 for the place of origin, e.g., migration from United States to Australia 304.894073

# 305    **Groups of people**

Class here portrayal of a specific group in mass media [*formerly* 302.2308]; minorities; culture and institutions of specific groups; subcultures of specific groups; consciousness-raising groups; problems, role, social status of specific groups; group identity, social identity; discrimination; social stratification, equality, inequality; interactions between a specific group and other groups

Unless other instructions are given, observe the following table of preference, e.g., African American male youths 305.235108996073 (*not* 305.3889607300835 or 305.896073008351):

| | |
|---|---|
| People with disabilities and illnesses, gifted people | 305.908 |
| Age groups | 305.2 |
| People by gender or sex | 305.3–305.4 |
| People by social and economic levels | 305.5 |
| Religious groups | 305.6 |
| Ethnic and national groups | 305.8 |
| Language groups | 305.7 |
| People by occupation and miscellaneous social statuses (*except* 305.908) | 305.9 |

Class effect of mass media on specific groups, on social stratification in 302.2308; class opinions of specific groups in 303.38; class interactions, problems, role, social status of specific groups, discrimination against and conflict involving specific groups in 305.2–305.9; class specific problems of, welfare services to groups of people in 362. Class role of a specific group in a specific institution with the institution, e.g., father-child relationship 306.8742, women in education 370.82; class people by sexual orientation with the sexual orientation in 306.76, e.g., middle-aged gay men 306.76620844; class people by kinship or marital status with the kinship or marital status in 306.8, e.g., African American mothers 306.874308996073; class a specific aspect of discrimination with the aspect, plus notation 08 from Table 1, e.g., sex discrimination against women in sports 796.082

*See also 920.008 for general collections of biography of members of a specific group*

*See Manual at 306 vs. 305, 909, 930–990; also at 920.008 vs. 305–306, 362*

### SUMMARY

| | | |
|---|---|---|
| **305.2** | **Age groups** | |
| **.3** | **People by gender or sex** | |
| **.4** | **Women** | |
| **.5** | **People by social and economic levels** | |
| **.6** | **Religious groups** | |
| **.7** | **Language groups** | |
| **.8** | **Ethnic and national groups** | |
| **.9** | **People by occupation and miscellaneous social statuses; people with disabilities and illnesses, gifted people** | |

*Add 00 for standard subdivisions; see instructions at beginning of Table 1

[.08]          Specific groups of people

Do not use; class in 305.2–305.9

[.085]          Relatives

Do not use; class in 306.87

## .2          Age groups

Class here comprehensive works on generation gap

*For generation gap within families, see 306.874*

### SUMMARY

| | |
|---|---|
| 305.23 | **Young people** |
| .24 | **Adults** |
| .26 | **People in late adulthood** |

[.208 1–.208 4]          People by gender or sex; specific age groups

Do not use; class in 305.23–305.26

.23          Young people

Through age twenty

Class here interdisciplinary works on children

*For a specific aspect of children, see the aspect, e.g., social welfare of children 362.7*

.230 811          Boys

.230 82          Girls

[.230 83–.230 84]          Age groups

Do not use for young people in general; class in 305.23. Do not use for specific age groups; class in 305.232–305.235

.230 86          Children by miscellaneous social attributes

.230 869 23          Predelinquent children

Do not use for juvenile delinquents; class in 364.36

Class here runaway children

.231          Child development

Class here interdisciplinary works on child development

Class socialization in 303.32

*For psychological development of children, see 155.4; for physical development of children, see 612.65*

.232          Infants

Children from birth through age two

| .233 | Children three to five |
| | Class here preschool children |

| .234 | Children six to eleven |
| | Class here preteens, school children |

*For school children over eleven, see 305.235*

| .235 | Young people twelve to twenty |

Variant names: adolescents, teenagers, young adults, youth

Class young people twenty-one and over in 305.242

| [.235 081 1] | Men |

Do not use; class in 305.2351

| [.235 082] | Women |

Do not use; class in 305.2352

| [.235 083–.235 084] | Age groups |

Do not use; class in 305.235

| .235 1 | Males |

| .235 2 | Females |

| .235 5 | Development |

Class here interdisciplinary works on development of young people twelve to twenty

*For psychological development, see 155.5; for physical development, see 612.661*

| .24 | Adults |

Class here adulthood

Class adult men in 305.31; class adult women in 305.4

*For late adulthood, see 305.26*

| .242 | People in early adulthood |

Class here comprehensive works on young adults

*For young adults under twenty-one, see 305.235*

| [.242 081 1] | Men |

Do not use; class in 305.2421

| [.242 082] | Women |

Do not use; class in 305.2422

| [.242 083–.242 084] | Age groups |

Do not use; class in 305.242

| .242 1 | Young men |

| .242 2 | Young women |
| --- | --- |
| .244 | People in middle adulthood |

Class here middle age

| [.244 081 1] | Men |
| --- | --- |

Do not use; class in 305.2441

| [.244 082] | Women |
| --- | --- |

Do not use; class in 305.2442

| [.244 083–.244 084] | Age groups |
| --- | --- |

Do not use; class in 305.244

| .244 1 | Middle-aged men |
| --- | --- |
| .244 2 | Middle-aged women |
| .26 | People in late adulthood |

Class sociology of retirement in 306.38

*See also 646.79 for guides to retirement*

| [.260 811] | Men |
| --- | --- |

Do not use; class in 305.261

| [.260 82] | Women |
| --- | --- |

Do not use; class in 305.262

| [.260 83–.260 84] | Age groups |
| --- | --- |

Do not use; class in 305.26

| .261 | Older men |
| --- | --- |
| .262 | Older women |

**.3 People by gender or sex**

Standard subdivisions are added for either or both topics in heading

Class here interdisciplinary works on men and women, gender identity, gender role, sex role, the sexes

Class sex psychology, psychology of people by gender or sex, by sexual orientation in 155.3; class sexual division of labor in 306.3615; class the relations between the sexes and within the sexes in 306.7–306.8. Class the relation of a specific gender or sex to a specific subject with the subject, plus notation 081–082 from Table 1, e.g., women in U.S. history 973.082

*For young and middle-aged men and women, see 305.24; for men and women in late adulthood, see 305.26; for women, see 305.4; for transgender and intersex people, see 306.768. For a specific aspect of gender identity, gender role, or sex role, see the aspect, e.g., psychology of gender identity 155.33*

.31 Men

Class here interdisciplinary works on men, on males

*For specific aspects of sociology of men, see 305.32–305.38. For a specific aspect of men not provided for in 305.3, see the aspect, e.g., legal status of men 346.013*

[.310 8] Groups of people

Do not use; class in 305.33–305.38

.310 9 History, geographic treatment, biography

.310 92 Biography

*See also 920.71 for general biography of men*

*See Manual at 920.008 vs. 305–306, 362*

.32–.38 Specific aspects of sociology of men

Add to base number 305.3 the numbers following 305.4 in 305.42–305.48, e.g., African American men 305.38896073; however, for engaged men, see 306.7340811; for men by sexual orientation, see 306.76; for gay men, see 306.7662; for single men, see 306.8152; for men by kinship characteristics, see 306.87; for married men, see 306.8722; for widowers, see 306.882; for separated and divorced men, see 306.892

Class comprehensive works in 305.31

**.4** **Women**

Class here interdisciplinary works on women, on females

*For a specific aspect of women not provided for here, see the aspect, e.g., women's suffrage 324.623, legal status of women 346.0134*

[.408] Groups of people

Do not use; class in 305.43–305.48

.409 History, geographic treatment, biography

.409 2 Biography

*See also 920.72 for general biography of women*

*See Manual at 920.008 vs. 305–306, 362*

.42 Social role and status of women

Standard subdivisions are added for either or both topics in heading

Class here discrimination against women, feminism, women's movements

Class social role and status of specific groups of women with the group in 305.43–305.48, e.g., role of housewives 305.4364 (*not* 305.4208864)

Ecofeminism relocated to 304.2082

.43        Women by occupation

Add to base number 305.43 notation 001–999, e.g., women physicians 305.43610695

*See also 331.4 for economic aspects of women by occupation*

.48        Specific groups of women

Class women by occupation in 305.43; class women with disabilities and illnesses, gifted women in 305.908

*For engaged women, see 306.734082; for women by sexual orientation, see 306.76; for lesbians, see 306.7663; for single women, see 306.8153; for women by kinship characteristics, see 306.87; for married women, see 306.8723; for unmarried mothers, see 306.87432; for widows, see 306.883; for separated and divorced women, see 306.893*

[.480 1–.480 9]        Standard subdivisions

Do not use; class in 305.401–305.409

.482        Women by social and economic levels [*formerly* 305.48962]

Class here women by level of cultural development [*formerly* 305.48963]

Add to base number 305.482 the numbers following —0862 in notation 08621–08625 from Table 1, e.g., working class women 305.48923

.484        Women by miscellaneous social statuses [*formerly* 305.48969]

Add to base number 305.484 the numbers following —0869 in notation 08691–08697 from Table 1, e.g., homeless women 305.48442; however, for women offenders, see 364.374; for women inmates of penal institutions, see 365.6082

.486–.488        Women by specific religious, language, ethnic, national groups

Add to base number 305.48 the numbers following 305 in 305.6–305.8, e.g., Muslim women 305.48697

[.489]        Miscellaneous groups

Number discontinued; class in 305.48

[.489 6]        Women by social and economic levels; by miscellaneous social statuses

Number discontinued; class in 305.48

[.489 62]        Women by social and economic levels

Relocated to 305.482

[.489 63]        Women by level of cultural development

Relocated to 305.482

[.489 69]        Women by miscellaneous social statuses

Relocated to 305.484

**.5**        **People by social and economic levels**

Class here class struggle, people by level of cultural development, social classes

*For theory of class struggle in Marxism, see 335.411*

*See Manual at 305.9 vs. 305.5*

.51        General principles of social classes

.512        Principles of stratification

.512 2        Caste systems

.513        Social mobility

.52        Upper class

Class here aristocracy, elites

Class intellectual elites in 305.552

.522        Upper class by birth

Class here nobility, royalty

.523        Upper class by economic status

.523 2        Landowners with large estates and landed gentry

.523 4        Rich people

*For landowners with large estates, see 305.5232*

.524        Upper class by political status

Including cabinet ministers, commissars, judges, legislative representatives

.55        Middle class (Bourgeoisie)

Class here moderately well-to-do, white collar workers

Class working class in 305.562

.552        Intelligentsia

Class here intellectual elites

.553        Professional classes

.554        Managerial and entrepreneurial classes

Standard subdivisions are added for either or both topics in heading

[.556]        White collar classes

Use of this number for white collar workers discontinued; class in 305.55

Office workers relocated to 305.96513; clerks relocated to 305.965137

.56       Lower, alienated, excluded classes

Class here people with cultural and social disadvantages, interdisciplinary works on nondominant groups

*For a specific nondominant group, see the group, e.g., nondominant ethnic groups 305.8*

Use of this number for comprehensive works on minorities discontinued; class in 305

.562      Working class

Variant names: laboring class, proletariat

Including migrant workers

Class here blue collar workers

Class agricultural laborers in 305.563; class slaves in 306.362

.563      Agricultural lower classes

Including agricultural laborers, migrant agricultural workers

*For agricultural workers, see 305.963; for serfs, sharecroppers, see 306.365*

.563 3      Peasants

[.565]      People with cultural disadvantages

Number discontinued; class in 305.56

.568      Alienated and excluded classes

Tramps relocated to 305.569

.568 8      Dalits

Variant names: scheduled castes, untouchables

.569      Poor people

Including tramps [*formerly* 305.568]

.569 2      Homeless people

**.6      Religious groups**

Add to base number 305.6 the numbers following 2 in 230–299, e.g., Christians 305.67, Christians in Indonesia 305.67598, Christian Scientists 305.6895, Christian Scientists in France 305.689544, Orthodox Jews 305.696832

*See Manual at 305.6 vs. 305.92, 306.6*

.696      Jews as a religious group

Number built according to instructions under 305.6

Class comprehensive works on Jews in 305.8924

**.7**        **Language groups**

Add to base number 305.7 notation 1–9 from Table 6, e.g., English-speaking people 305.721; then add 0* and to the result add notation 1–9 from Table 2, e.g., English-speaking people of South Africa 305.721068

**.8**        **Ethnic and national groups**

Class here indigenous ethnic and national groups; ethnic and national groups associated with a specific language; ethnology, cultural ethnology, ethnography; race relations; racial groups, racism; treatment of biculturalism and multiculturalism in which difference in language is not a central element

Class physical ethnology in 599.97; class biculturalism and multiculturalism among residents in an area of divergent cultural traditions centered upon different languages in 306.446

*See also 909.04 for the comprehensive history of specific ethnic and national groups; also 920.0092 for general collections of biography of members of a specific ethnic or national group*

*See Manual at 920.008 vs. 305–306, 362*

**.800 1–.800 9**        Standard subdivisions

**.805–.809**        Ethnic and national groups with ethnic origins from more than one continent, of European descent

Add to base number 305.80 the numbers following 0 in notation 05–09 from Table 5, e.g., ethnic national groups of European descent 305.809

**.81–.89**        Specific ethnic and national groups

Add to base number 305.8 notation 1–9 from Table 5, e.g., comprehensive works on Jews 305.8924, Chinese 305.8951, Chinese Australians 305.8951094, Inuit 305.89712

*For Jews as a religious group, see 305.696*

**.9**        **People by occupation and miscellaneous social statuses; people with disabilities and illnesses, gifted people**

Standard subdivisions are added for all topics in heading together, for people by occupation alone

Unless other instructions are given, class a subject with aspects in two or more subdivisions of 305.9 in the number coming last, e.g., unemployed librarians 305.9092 (*not* 305.90694)

Class here occupational mobility

Class men by occupation in 305.33; class women by occupation in 305.43; class comprehensive works on nonagricultural occupations in 306.368

*See Manual at 305.9 vs. 305.5*

**.900 1–.900 9**        Standard subdivisions

**.906**        People by miscellaneous social statuses

*For victims of crime, see 362.88*

*Add 00 for standard subdivisions; see instructions at beginning of Table 1

| | |
|---|---|
| .906 9 | People with status defined by changes in residence; antisocial, asocial, unemployed people; victims of war; veterans |
| .906 91 | People with status defined by changes in residence |

Class here aliens, expatriates, foreigners

Class runaway children in 305.23086923; class migrant workers in 305.562; class tramps in 305.569; class people of a specific ethnic or national group in 305.8

| | |
|---|---|
| .906 912 | Immigrants |

Class displaced persons, refugees in 305.906914

| | |
|---|---|
| .906 914 | Displaced persons |

Class here exiles, refugees, stateless persons

> *For a specific aspect of displaced persons or refugees, see the aspect, e.g., political aspects of refugees 325.21*

| | |
|---|---|
| .906 918 | Nomads |
| .906 92 | Antisocial and asocial people |

> *For offenders, see 364.3; for inmates of penal institutions, see 365.6*

| | |
|---|---|
| .906 94 | Unemployed people |
| .906 95 | Victims of war |
| .906 97 | Veterans of military service |
| .908 | People with disabilities and illnesses, gifted people |

Add to base number 305.908 the numbers following —087 in notation 0871–0879 from Table 1, e.g., blind people 305.9081, deaf people 305.9082, gifted people 305.9089

Class here people with physical disabilities

| | |
|---|---|
| .909 | Generalists |

Add to base number 305.909 the numbers following 0 in 001–099, e.g., computer programmers 305.909051, librarians 305.9092

| | |
|---|---|
| .91–.99 | People by occupation other than generalists |

Add to base number 305.9 notation 100–999, e.g., office workers 305.96513 [*formerly* 305.556], clerks 305.965137 [*formerly* 305.556], religious occupations 305.92, postal workers 305.9383, farmers 305.963

*See Manual at 305.6 vs. 305.92, 306.6*

# 306 Culture and institutions

Culture: the aggregate of a society's beliefs, folkways, mores, science, technology, values, arts

Institutions: patterns of behavior in social relationships

Including the roles, functions, and patterns within which the groups and members of a society conduct their lives

Class here mass culture (popular culture), cultural and social anthropology

Class cultural exchange in 303.482; class physical anthropology in 599.9; class history of a specific ethnic group in 900

> *For customs and folklore, see 390. For government policy on a specific aspect of culture, see the aspect, e.g., government policy on the arts 700*

> *See Manual at 306 vs. 305, 909, 930–990; also at 920.008 vs. 305–306, 362*

### SUMMARY

| | |
|---|---|
| 306.1 | **Subcultures** |
| .2 | **Political institutions** |
| .3 | **Economic institutions** |
| .4 | **Specific aspects of culture** |
| .6 | **Religious institutions** |
| .7 | **Sexual relations** |
| .8 | **Marriage and family** |
| .9 | **Institutions pertaining to death** |

[.08]    Groups of people

Do not use for culture and institutions of a specific group not provided for here; class in 305

[.085]    Relatives

Do not use; class in 306.87

## .1    Subcultures

Including counterculture, drug culture

Class subcultures of specific groups in 305; class drug usage considered as a social problem in 362.29

---

> ## 306.2–306.6  Cultural institutions

Except for modifications shown under specific entries, add to each subdivision identified by * as follows:
     01–07    Standard subdivisions
     [08]    Groups of people
          Do not use; class in the specific subject plus notation 08 from Table 1, e.g., women in education 370.82, women in sports 796.082
     09    History, geographic treatment, biography

Class comprehensive works in 306

*See Manual at T1—08 and 306.2–306.6*

**.2          *Political institutions**

Institutions maintaining internal and external peace

Class here political sociology; comprehensive works on patronage, on client relationships

Class political science in 320; class law in 340; class public administration and military science in 350

*For patronage and client relationships in a specific institution, see the institution, e.g., in systems of production 306.34, in art 306.47*

*See Manual at 320 vs. 306.2*

---

>          306.23–306.25  Governmental institutions

Class comprehensive works in 306.2

.23          *Legislative institutions

.24          *Executive institutions

Class military institutions in 306.27; class police in 306.28

.25          *Judicial institutions

.26          *Political parties

.27          *Military institutions

Class here military sociology

*See also 355 for military science*

.28          *Police institutions

*See also 363.2 for police services*

**.3          *Economic institutions**

Social arrangements for production, distribution

Class here economic anthropology; economic sociology; sociology of economic development, of consumption

Class specific occupational groups in 305.909–305.99

*For economic institutions relating to housing, see 307.336*

*See also 305.5 for social classes; also 330 for economics*

.32          *Property systems

Including kinds of land tenure

*For agricultural land tenure systems, see 306.349*

*Add as instructed under 306.2–306.6

.34     *Systems of production and exchange

        Standard subdivisions are added for either or both topics in heading

        Including cooperation, syndicalism

        Class here sociology of industrial conflict and relations

           *See also 302.35 for organizational behavior; also 303.482 for commerce (trade) as agent of social change*

.342     *Capitalism (Free enterprise)

           *See also 330.122 for economic aspects*

.345     *Socialism

        Class interdisciplinary works on socialism in 335

           *See Manual at 335 vs. 306.345, 320.53*

.349     *Agricultural systems

        Including plantation as a system of production

        Class here agricultural sociology, land tenure systems

           *For agricultural production systems not involving ownership of land, see 306.364*

.36     *Systems of labor

        Including free labor systems

        Class here industrial sociology, sociology of work

        Class sociology of industrial conflict and relations in 306.34; class economic aspects of work in 331

.361     *General aspects of systems of labor

        Including absenteeism, quality of work life, unemployment

.361 3     Work ethic

           *See also 174 for philosophical aspects of ethics of work*

.361 5     Sexual division of labor

.362     Slavery

        Class here slaves, interdisciplinary works on slave trade

           *For a specific aspect of the slave trade, see the aspect, e.g., economic aspects of slave trade 381.44*

.363     *Contract and indentured labor

        Standard subdivisions are added for either or both topics in heading

*Add as instructed under 306.2–306.6

.364        *Agricultural systems of labor

Class here systems of agricultural production not involving ownership of land, e.g., fishing, hunting, gathering systems

Class agricultural slavery in 306.362; class contract and indentured labor in agriculture in 306.363

*For agricultural occupations in general, see 305.963; for agricultural shared return systems, see 306.365*

.365        Agricultural shared return systems

Class here serfdom, serfs; sharecropping, sharecroppers

.368        *Nonagricultural occupations

Class here division of labor

Class social groups defined by occupation in 305.9

*For sexual division of labor, see 306.3615*

.38         Retirement

Class here retired people

*See also 646.79 for guides to retirement*

**.4         Specific aspects of culture**

Not provided for elsewhere

Including magic and witchcraft, symbols

.42         *Sociology of knowledge

Class here sociology of intellectual life, of information

Class specific instances of sociology of knowledge in 306.43–306.48

.43         *Education

Class here educational anthropology

*See also 370.115 for education for social responsibility*

.432        School and society

Including interdisciplinary works on relations of teachers and society, on relations of colleges and universities with society

*For community-school relations in education, see 371.19; for community-school relations in higher education, see 378.103*

*Add as instructed under 306.2–306.6

.44 Language

Including pragmatics

Class here anthropological linguistics, ethnolinguistics, sociolinguistics

*See Manual at 401.43 vs. 306.44, 401.45, 401.9, 412, 415*

Interdisciplinary works on pragmatics relocated to 401.45

.446 Bilingualism and multilingualism

Standard subdivisions are added for either or both topics in heading

Class here biculturalism and multiculturalism among residents in an area of divergent cultural traditions centered upon different languages

Class treatment of biculturalism and multiculturalism in which difference in language is not a central element in 305.8; class treatment of bilingualism and multilingualism in context of language planning and policy formulation in 306.449

*See also 404.2 for linguistic aspects of bilingualism*

.449 Language planning and policy

Standard subdivisions are added for either or both topics in the headings

Class here development of policies on language to solve communication problems of a community that uses more than one language

[.449 094–.449 099] Specific continents, countries, localities in modern world

Do not use; class in 306.4494–306.4499

.449 4–.449 9 Specific continents, countries, localities in modern world

Add to base number 306.449 notation 4–9 from Table 2, e.g., language policy of India 306.44954
Subdivisions are added for language planning, language policy, or both

.45 *Science

Class here works contrasting scientific and humanistic cultures

*See Manual at 303.483 vs. 306.45, 306.46*

.46 *Technology

Class here material culture

*See Manual at 303.483 vs. 306.45, 306.46*

.461 *Medicine and health

Standard subdivisions are added for either or both topics in heading

Class here sociology of illness

Class social aspects of medical welfare problems and services in 362.1042

*Add as instructed under 306.2–306.6

.461 3　　　　　　　*Personal health

　　　　　　　　　　　Including body image, body shape, eating, physical fitness

.47　　　　　*Art

　　　　　　　　Including arts and crafts

.48　　　　　*Recreation and performing arts

　　　　　　　Standard subdivisions are added for recreation and performing arts together, for recreation alone

　　　　　　　*For motion pictures, radio, television, see 302.234*

.481　　　　　　*General topics of recreation

　　　　　　　　Including play, pleasure, wit and humor

.481 2　　　　　　　*Leisure

　　　　　　　　　Class here free time

.481 25　　　　　　　*Vacations (Holidays)

.481 9　　　　　　　*Travel and tourism

　　　　　　　　　Standard subdivisions are added for either or both topics in heading

.482　　　　　*Gambling

.483　　　　　*Sports

　　　　　　　Class gambling on athletic events in 306.482

.484　　　　　*Music, dance, theater

　　　　　　　Class here performing arts

　　　　　　　*For motion pictures, radio, television, see 302.234*

.484 2　　　　　　Music

[.484 208]　　　　　　　Groups of people

　　　　　　　　　Do not use; class in 780.8

.484 22–.484 29　　　Traditions of music

　　　　　　　Add to base number 306.4842 the numbers following 781.6 in 781.62–781.69, e.g., jazz 306.48425; however, do not add notation 08 from Table 1 for groups of people; class in 781.62–781.69, plus notation 08 from Table 1, e.g., women and jazz 781.65082

.484 6　　　　　　*Dance

.484 8　　　　　　*Theater

.487　　　　　*Games and hobbies

　　　　　　　Class gambling on games in 306.482; class sports in 306.483

.488　　　　　*Reading

*Add as instructed under 306.2–306.6

**.6** **Religious institutions**

Religious institutions considered from a secular, nonreligious viewpoint

Class here sociology of religion

*See also 201.7 for social theology; also 261 for Christian social theology*

*See Manual at 305.6 vs. 305.92, 306.6*

**[.608]** Groups of people

Do not use; class in 200.8

**.63–.69** Institutions of specific religions

Add to base number 306.6 the numbers following 2 in 230–290, e.g., comprehensive works on Christian institutions 306.63, Sunday school as a social institution 306.668, synagogue as a social institution 306.69665; however, do not add notation 08 from Table 1 for groups of people; class in 230–290, plus notation 08 from Table 1, e.g., women and Christianity 270.082

**.7** **Sexual relations**

Class here interdisciplinary works on relations between the sexes, sex, sexual love

*For sexual ethics, see 176; for problems and controversies concerning various sexual relations, see 363.4; for sex offenses, see 364.153; for customs pertaining to relations between the sexes, see 392.6; for sexual hygiene, see 613.95; for sexual techniques, see 613.96*

**.73** General institutions

Class here dating behavior

*For marriage, see 306.81*

*See also 646.77 for practical guidance on dating behavior*

**.732** Celibacy

**.733** Premarital sexual relations

**.734** Courtship and engagement

Class here engaged people

*See also 392.4 for customs of courtship*

**.736** Extramarital relations

Including lovers, mistresses, paramours

**.74** Prostitution

Class here prostitutes

*See also 331.76130674 for prostitution as an occupation; also 363.44 for prostitution as a social problem; also 364.1534 for prostitution as a crime*

| | | |
|---|---|---|
| .740 811 | Men | |

> Do not use for prostitution by males; class in 306.743

| | |
|---|---|
| .740 82 | Women |

> Do not use for prostitution by females; class in 306.742

| | |
|---|---|
| .740 83 | Young people |

> Do not use for prostitution by children; class in 306.745

| | |
|---|---|
| .742 | Prostitution by females |

> Class child prostitution in 306.745

| | |
|---|---|
| .743 | Prostitution by males |

> Class child prostitution in 306.745

| | |
|---|---|
| .745 | Prostitution by children |
| .76 | Sexual orientation, transgenderism, intersexuality |

> Standard subdivisions are added for sexual orientation, transgenderism, intersexuality together; for sexual orientation and transgenderism together; for sexual orientation alone

> Including asexuality, asexuals

> Class here people by sexual orientation

> Class practices associated with specific orientations in 306.77

| | |
|---|---|
| [.762] | Asexuality |

> Number discontinued; class in 306.76

| | |
|---|---|
| .764 | Heterosexuality |

> Class here heterosexuals

| | |
|---|---|
| .765 | Bisexuality |

> Class here bisexuals

| | |
|---|---|
| .766 | Homosexuality |

> Class here gay liberation movement, gays, homophobia

| | |
|---|---|
| .766 2 | Male homosexuality |

> Class here gay men

| | |
|---|---|
| .766 3 | Lesbianism |

> Class here lesbians

.768 Transgenderism and intersexuality

> Standard subdivisions are added for transgenderism and intersexuality together, for transgenderism alone

> Including female-to-male transgender people, male-to-female transgender people

> Class here transsexuality; transgender people, transgenderists, transsexuals

> Class practices associated with transgenderism and intersexuality in 306.77

.768 5 Intersexuality

> Class here intersex people

.77 Sexual and related practices

> Standard subdivisions are added for sexual and related practices together, for sexual practices alone

> Including fetishism, group sex, pornography, sodomy

> Class transvestic fetishism in 306.778

>> *For sexual practices viewed as medical disorders, see 616.8583*

>> *See also 363.47 for pornography as a social problem; also 364.174 for pornography as an offense against public morals; also 364.153 for sex crimes*

.772 Masturbation

.774 Oral sex

.775 Sadism

> Class here sadomasochism

>> *For masochism, see 306.776*

.776 Masochism

.778 Transvestism

> Class here cross dressing

> Class female impersonation, male impersonation in 792.028

**.8** **Marriage and family**

> *See also 362.8286 for premarital and marriage counseling*

| .81 | Marriage and marital status |
|---|---|

Standard subdivisions are added for either or both topics in heading

Class here people by marital status; interdisciplinary works on marriage, on marital status

Class patterns of mate selection in 306.82; class married people in 306.872; class alteration of marriage arrangements in 306.88

> *For types of marriage, see 306.84. For other aspects of marriage, see the aspect, e.g., sexual techniques 613.96*

| .815 | Single marital status |
|---|---|

Class here single people; comprehensive works on single, divorced and widowed marital status; people who have never been married

Class single parents in 306.856

> *For widowed people, see 306.88; for separation and divorce, see 306.89*

| [.815 081 1] | Men |
|---|---|

Do not use; class in 306.8152

| [.815 082] | Women |
|---|---|

Do not use; class in 306.8153

| .815 2 | Single men |
|---|---|

Class single fathers in 306.87422

| .815 3 | Single women |
|---|---|

Class single mothers in 306.87432

| .82 | Patterns in mate selection |
|---|---|

Including endogamy, exogamy

Class courtship in 306.734

> *See also 392.4 for the customs of mate selection; also 646.77 for practical guidance on choosing a mate and dating behavior*

| .83 | Types of kinship systems |
|---|---|

Including matrilineal, patrilineal, totemic systems

| .84 | Types of marriage and relationships |
|---|---|

Including remarriage

Class married people in 306.872

| .841 | Partnerships and unions |
|---|---|

Class here civil unions, common-law marriage, de facto relationships, domestic partnerships, registered partnerships; unmarried couples living together (cohabitation)

| .842 | Marriage by number of spouses |
|---|---|

| .842 2 | Monogamy |
|--------|----------|

.842 3          Polygamy

             Including ménage à trois

             Class here polyandry, polygyny; polygamists

.843         Interreligious marriage

             Marriage in which the spouses belong to different religions or different branches of same religion

.845         Intercultural marriage

             Class here marriage between citizens of different countries

.846         Interracial marriage

.848         Same-sex marriage

.85         Family

             Class here interdisciplinary works on family

             *For kinship systems, see 306.83; for intrafamily relationships, see 306.87; for stepfamilies, see 306.8747; for alteration of family arrangements, see 306.88. For a specific aspect of family, see the aspect, e.g., achieving harmonious family relations 646.78*

             *See also 155.924 for psychological influence of family on individual members*

.852         Rural family

             *See also 307.72 for rural sociology*

.854         Urban family

             *See also 307.76 for urban sociology*

.855         Nuclear family

             Class the single-parent family in 306.856

.856         Single-parent family

             Class here divorced families with single-parent custody, unmarried parents, unmarried parenthood

             *For single fatherhood, see 306.87422; for single motherhood, see 306.87432*

.857         Extended family

             Class kinship systems in extended family in 306.83

.858         Patriarchal family

.859         Matriarchal family

| .87 | Intrafamily relationships |
|---|---|

Including abuse within family; birth order; childlessness; collateral relationships between aunts/uncles and nieces/nephews; collateral relationships between cousins; dysfunctional relationships; in-law relationships

Class incest in 306.877. Class abuse in a specific family relationship with the relationship, e.g., spouse abuse 306.872

*For alteration of family arrangements, see 306.88*

*See also 362.82 for social services to families; also 646.78 for practical guides to harmonious family relationships*

| .872 | Spousal relationship |
|---|---|

Including dual-career families

Class here husband-wife relationship, married people

Class sexual practices in 306.77

*For polygamists, see 306.8423*

*See also 613.96 for sexual techniques*

| .872 081 1 | Men |
|---|---|

Do not use for husbands; class in 306.8722

| .872 082 | Women |
|---|---|

Do not use for wives; class in 306.8723

| .872 2 | Husbands |
|---|---|
| .872 3 | Wives |
| .874 | Parent-child relationship |

Including adopted children, children of unmarried parents, only child

Class here generation gap within families

Class comprehensive works on generation gap in 305.2

*See also 649.1 for child rearing (parenting)*

| .874 2 | Father-child relationship |
|---|---|

Including teenage fatherhood

Class here sociology of fatherhood

Class single teenage fatherhood in 306.87422

| .874 22 | Single fatherhood |
|---|---|

Class here single fathers, unmarried fathers, unmarried fatherhood

| .874 3 | Mother-child relationship |

Including surrogate motherhood, teenage motherhood

Class here sociology of motherhood

Class single teenage motherhood in 306.87432

| .874 32 | Single motherhood |

Class here single mothers, unmarried mothers, unmarried motherhood

| .874 5 | Grandparent-child relationship |

| .874 7 | Stepparent-stepchild relationship |

Class here blended families; stepchildren, stepfamiles, stepparents

| .875 | Sibling relationships |

| .875 2 | Brother-brother relationship |

| .875 3 | Brother-sister relationship |

| .875 4 | Sister-sister relationship |

| .877 | Incest |

| .88 | Alteration of family arrangements |

Including desertion

Class here widowed people

*For separation and divorce, see 306.89*

| .880 811 | Men |

Do not use for widowers; class in 306.882

| .880 82 | Women |

Do not use for widows; class in 306.883

| .882 | Widowers |

| .883 | Widows |

| .89 | Separation and divorce |

Standard subdivisions are added for either or both topics in heading

Including binuclear family, shared custody

Class here separated and divorced people

Class divorced families with single-parent custody in 306.856; class parent-child relationship in divorced families in 306.874

| [.890 811] | Men |

Do not use; class in 306.892

| [.890 82] | Women |

Do not use; class in 306.893

.892 Separated and divorced men

> Standard subdivisions are added for either or both topics in heading

.893 Separated and divorced women

> Standard subdivisions are added for either or both topics in heading

**.9 Institutions pertaining to death**

Class here interdisciplinary works on death

*For a specific aspect of death, see the aspect, e.g., psychology of death 155.937, funeral rites and ceremonies 393.9*

# 307 Communities

*See Manual at 307*

---

> **307.1–307.3 Specific aspects of communities**

Add to each subdivision identified by * as follows:
1     Specific kinds of communities
        Add to 1 the numbers following 307.7 in 307.72–307.77, e.g., cities 16

Class comprehensive works in 307

**.1 \*Planning and development**

.12 \*Planning

> *See also 711 for the physical aspect of area planning*

.14 \*Development

Class here human settlement

Class resettlement in 307.2; class redevelopment in 307.34

**.2 \*Movement of people to, from, within communities**

Including resettlement

Class comprehensive works on population in 304.6

.24 \*Movement from rural to urban communities

Class here rural exodus

.26 \*Movement from urban to rural communities

Class here urban exodus

**.3 \*Structure**

Class movement within communities in 307.2

.32 \*Physical setting

.33 \*Patterns of use

---

\*Add as instructed under 307.1–307.3

| | |
|---|---|
| .332 | *Industrial use |
| .333 | *Commercial use |
| | Class here business districts |
| .334 | *Recreational use |
| .336 | *Residential use |
| | Including housing succession |
| | Class here housing patterns, sociology of housing |
| | *See also 363.58 for housing programs* |
| | *See Manual at 363.5 vs. 307.336, 307.34* |
| .336 2 | *Neighborhoods |
| | Class ghettos in 307.3366 |
| .336 4 | *Slums |
| .336 6 | *Ghettos |
| .34 | *Redevelopment |
| | Class community planning in 307.12 |
| | *See Manual at 363.5 vs. 307.336, 307.34* |
| .342 | *City core |
| | Class here inner cities |
| .344 | *Slum clearance |
| .346 | *Parks and recreational facilities |
| **.7** | **Specific kinds of communities** |
| | Class a specific aspect of specific kinds of communities in 307.1–307.3 |
| .72 | Rural communities |
| | Including plantations considered as communities |
| | Class here rural sociology, rural villages |
| | Class agricultural sociology, the plantation considered as a system of production in 306.349 |
| .74 | Suburban communities |
| .740 9 | History and biography |
| | Do not use for geographic treatment; class in 307.7609 |

*Add as instructed under 307.1–307.3

| | |
|---|---|
| .76 | Urban communities |

Class here urban policy (government policy on cities), urban sociology, interdisciplinary works on cities

*For suburban communities, see 307.74. For a specific aspect of cities, see the aspect, e.g., public administration of cities 352.16*

| | |
|---|---|
| .760 9 | History, geographic treatment, biography |

Class here specific suburban communities, specific urban communities regardless of size or kind

---

> 307.762–307.764 Urban communities by size

Class specific urban communities regardless of size in 307.7609; class comprehensive works in 307.76

| | |
|---|---|
| .762 | Small urban communities |

Class here comprehensive works on villages

*For rural villages, see 307.72*

| | |
|---|---|
| .763 | Medium-sized urban communities |
| .764 | Large urban communities |

Class here metropolitan areas as communities

*For medium-sized communities, see 307.763*

---

> 307.766–307.768 Urban communities by kind

Class specific urban communities regardless of kind in 307.7609; class comprehensive works in 307.76

| | |
|---|---|
| .766 | Mining and industrial towns |

Class company towns in 307.767

| | |
|---|---|
| .767 | Company towns |
| .768 | New towns |
| .77 | Self-contained communities |

Class here voluntary socialist and anarchist communities

| | |
|---|---|
| .772 | Tribal communities |

Class tribal communities considered in context of culture and institutions of indigenous ethnic and national groups in 305.8

| | |
|---|---|
| .774 | Communes |

Class kibbutzim in 307.776

| | |
|---|---|
| .776 | Kibbutzim and moshavim |

Standard subdivisions are added for either or both topics in heading

**[308]** **[Unassigned]**

> Most recently used in Edition 16

**[309]** **[Unassigned]**

> Most recently used in Edition 18

# 310 Collections of general statistics

> Class works on collecting statistical data in 001.433. Class statistics of a specific subject, other than general statistics of a place, with the subject, plus notation 021 from Table 1, e.g., statistics on deaths by crimes of violence 364.15021
>
> *See also 001.422 for analysis of statistical data; also 001.4226 for methods of presenting statistical data*

[.94–.99] Specific continents, countries, localities in modern world

> Do not use; class in 314–319

**[311]** **[Unassigned]**

> Most recently used in Edition 17

**[312]** **[Unassigned]**

> Most recently used in Edition 19

**[313]** **[Unassigned]**

> Most recently used in Edition 14

# 314–319 General statistics of specific continents, countries, localities in modern world

> Add to base number 31 notation 4–9 from Table 2, e.g., statistics of France 314.4

## 314 General statistics of Europe

> Number built according to instructions under 314–319

## 315 General statistics of Asia

> Number built according to instructions under 314–319

## 316 General statistics of Africa

> Number built according to instructions under 314–319

## 317 General statistics of North America

> Number built according to instructions under 314–319

## 318 General statistics of South America

> Number built according to instructions under 314–319

## 319 General statistics of Australasia, Pacific Ocean islands, Atlantic Ocean islands, Arctic islands, Antarctica

> Number built according to instructions under 314–319

# 320    Political science (Politics and government)

Class sociology of political institutions and processes in 306.2

*For law, see 340; for public administration and military science, see 350*

*See Manual at 302–307 vs. 320; also at 320 vs. 306.2; also at 324 vs. 320; also at 909, 930–990 vs. 320*

## SUMMARY

| | |
|---|---|
| 320.01–.09 | Standard subdivisions |
| .1 | The state |
| .3 | Comparative government |
| .4 | Structure and functions of government |
| .5 | Political ideologies |
| .6 | Policy making |
| .8 | Local government |
| .9 | Political situation and conditions |
| | |
| 321 | Systems of governments and states |
| .001–.009 | Standard subdivisions |
| .01–.09 | [Systems of relating parts of a state to the whole, kinds of states, change in system of government] |
| .1 | Family-based government |
| .3 | Feudalism |
| .5 | Elitist systems |
| .6 | Absolute monarchy |
| .8 | Democratic government |
| .9 | Authoritarian government |
| | |
| 322 | Relation of the state to organized groups and their members |
| .1 | Religious organizations and groups |
| .2 | Labor movements and groups |
| .3 | Business and industry |
| .4 | Political action groups |
| .5 | Armed services |
| | |
| 323 | Civil and political rights |
| .01–.09 | Standard subdivisions; citizen participation; resistance, repression, persecution |
| .1 | Civil and political rights of nondominant groups |
| .3 | Civil and political rights of other social groups |
| .4 | Specific civil rights; limitation and suspension of civil rights |
| .5 | Political rights |
| .6 | Citizenship and related topics |
| | |
| 324 | The political process |
| .09 | History, geographic treatment, biography |
| .1 | International party organizations, auxiliaries, activities |
| .2 | Political parties |
| .3 | Auxiliary party organizations |
| .4 | Interest and pressure groups |
| .5 | Nominating candidates |
| .6 | Election systems and procedures; suffrage |
| .7 | Conduct of election campaigns |
| .9 | History and geographic treatment of elections |

| | | |
|---|---|---|
| **325** | | **International migration and colonization** |
| | **.1** | **Immigration** |
| | **.2** | **Emigration** |
| | **.3** | **Colonization** |
| | **.4–.9** | **International migration to and colonization in specific continents, countries, localities in modern world** |

| | | |
|---|---|---|
| **326** | | **Slavery and emancipation** |
| | **.8** | **Emancipation** |

| | | |
|---|---|---|
| **327** | | **International relations** |
| | **.02–.09** | **Standard subdivisions** |
| | **.1** | **Foreign policy and specific topics in international relations** |
| | **.2** | **Diplomacy** |
| | **.3–.9** | **Foreign relations of specific continents, countries, localities** |

| | | |
|---|---|---|
| **328** | | **The legislative process** |
| | **.06** | **Organizations and management** |
| | **.1** | **Rules and procedures of legislative bodies** |
| | **.2** | **Initiative and referendum** |
| | **.3** | **Specific topics of legislative bodies** |
| | **.4–.9** | **The legislative process in specific continents, countries, localities in modern world** |

**.01**       Philosophy and theory

Class general theory in 320.011

**.011**       General theory; systems

Including theory of liberty

Class here nature, legitimacy, role of government; political change, political justice

Class systems in 320.0113; class biography of general theory in 320.092; class specific theories in the sense of ideologies in 320.5; class personal liberty in 323.44. Class theories on a specific aspect of political science with the aspect, e.g., social contract as a theory of origin of the state 320.11

**.011 3**       Systems

The word "systems" here refers only to concepts derived from 003, e.g., systems theory, models

Add to base number 320.0113 the numbers following 003 in 003.1–003.8, e.g., forecasting and forecasts 320.01132, computer modeling and simulation 320.01133; however, for forecasting and forecasts for a specific period or area, see 320.9

Class systems of governments and states in 321

**.014**       Communication

Class here political persuasion and political propaganda

Class interdisciplinary works on persuasion in 303.342; class interdisciplinary works on propaganda in 303.375

**.019**       Psychological principles

Class political persuasion and propaganda in 320.014

**.02–.08**       Standard subdivisions

| | | |
|---|---|---|
| .09 | | History, geographic treatment, biography |

Do not use for political situation and conditions, for forecasting and forecasts in a specific period or area; class in 320.9

.092        Biography

Do not use for biography of political thinkers identified with specific ideologies; class in 320.5

Class here political philosophers and political scientists

## .1     The state

Class systems by which states are organized in 321

.101        Philosophy and theory

Do not use for theories of origin of the state; class in 320.11

.101 1        Systems

The word "systems" here refers only to concepts derived from 003, e.g., systems theory, models

Class systems of governments and states in 321

.11        Theories of origin

Class here social contract

.12        Territory

Including boundaries

Class here geopolitics

Class acquisition of territory in 325.32; class territory in law of nations in 341.42; class history of territorial changes in 911

*For geopolitics in international relations, see 327.101*

.15        Sovereignty

Class here national self-determination

Class states with restricted sovereignty in 321.08

## .3     Comparative government

Class comparison of a specific aspect of government with the aspect, e.g., comparison of committee systems in different legislatures 328.365

## .4     Structure and functions of government

Class here civics

Class analysis of systems by which government is structured in 321

*For comparative government, see 320.3*

*See Manual at 320.9, 320.4 vs. 351; also at 909, 930–990 vs. 320.4, 321, 321.09*

| | |
|---|---|
| .404 | Separation of powers |

Class here interdisciplinary works on branches of government

Class systems of selecting chief executives in 324; class legislative control and oversight of executive branch in 328.3456

*For legislative branch, see 328; for judicial branch, see 347; for executive branch, see 351*

| | |
|---|---|
| .404 09 | History and biography |

Do not use for geographic treatment; class in 320.41–320.49

| | |
|---|---|
| .404 9 | Vertical separation of powers |

Class here relation of central governments with regional and local jurisdictions

*For relation of local government to higher levels of government, see 320.8; for relation of federal to state, regional, provincial governments, see 321.023*

| | |
|---|---|
| .409 | History and biography |

Do not use for geographic treatment; class in 320.41–320.49

| | |
|---|---|
| .41–.49 | Geographic treatment |

Class here systems of state and government in specific countries

Add to base number 320.4 notation 1–9 from Table 2, e.g., structure of government in Cuba 320.47291; then to the result add standard subdivisions as modified under 320.4, e.g., separation of powers in Cuba 320.4729104

| | |
|---|---|
| **.5** | **Political ideologies** |

Except as provided under 320.53209, use notation 09 from Table 1 for variants of basic ideologies formulated and practiced in specific nations, e.g., Titoism 320.532309497, apartheid 320.560968

Class ideologies with respect to a specific aspect of political science with the aspect, e.g., ideologies with respect to revolution 321.094

*See Manual at 324 vs. 320.5, 320.9, 909, 930–990*

| | |
|---|---|
| .508 | Groups of people |

Ideologies based on groups of people relocated to 320.56

| | |
|---|---|
| .51 | Liberalism |
| .512 | Traditional liberalism |

Ideologies and theories stressing rationalism, individualism, limited government

Including libertarianism

*See also 320.52 for conservatism*

| | |
|---|---|
| .513 | Modern liberalism |

Ideologies and theories stressing responsibility of the state for welfare of its citizens

.52        Conservatism

Ideologies and theories stressing limits of human reason and virtue, value of tradition, caution in effecting social change

*See also 320.512 for traditional liberalism*

.53        Collectivism and fascism

Standard subdivisions are added for collectivism and fascism together, for collectivism alone

Class here new left, radicalism, totalitarianism, comprehensive works on authoritarianism

*For religiously oriented authoritarianism, see 320.55*

*See Manual at 335 vs. 306.345, 320.53*

---

>        320.531–320.532   Specific collectivist ideologies

Class comprehensive works in 320.53

.531        Socialism

Nonauthoritarian systems

Class authoritarian systems of socialism in 320.532; class interdisciplinary works on socialism in 335

.531 2        Non-Marxian and quasi-Marxian socialism

Including Christian socialism, Fabian socialism

.531 5        Marxian socialism (Democratic socialism, Social democracy)

Class comprehensive political works on Marxian systems of collectivism in 320.532

.532        Communism

Class here authoritarian systems of socialism, comprehensive political works on Marxian systems of collectivism

Class interdisciplinary works on Marxism in 335.4

*For nonauthoritarian Marxian socialism, see 320.5315*

.532 093–.532 099        Specific continents, countries, localities

Class communism as formulated and practiced in former Soviet Union in 320.5322; class systems of communism as formulated and practiced in specific nations outside of former Soviet Union in 320.5323093–320.5323099, e.g., Maoism 320.53230951

.532 2        Marxism-Leninism

Class here communism as formulated and practiced in former Soviet Union

*For variant forms of Marxism-Leninism, see 320.5323*

.532 3          Variant forms of communism

Systems of communism, of Marxism-Leninism, other than ones accepted in former Soviet Union

Including Trotskyism

.533          Fascism

Class here falangism, national socialism, neo-Nazism

Class interdisciplinary works on fascism in 335.6

*See also 320.569924 for anti-Semitism*

.54          Nationalism, regionalism, internationalism

Standard subdivisions are added for nationalism, regionalism, internationalism together; for nationalism and regionalism together; for nationalism alone; for regionalism alone

Class here regional nationalism, ethnic nationalism, pan-nationalism

.540 1–.540 7          Standard subdivisions

Standard subdivisions of nationalism and regionalism by areas, regions, places in general relocated to 320.54091, plus notation 01–07 from table under 320.54091; standard subdivisions of nationalism and regionalism by specific continents, countries, localities relocated to 320.54093–320.54099, plus notation 01–07 from table under 320.54093–320.54099

.540 8          Groups of people

Nationalism and regionalism with respect to groups of people by areas, regions, places in general relocated to 320.54091, plus notation 08 from table under 320.54091; nationalism and regionalism with respect to groups of people by specific continents, countries, localities relocated to 320.54093–320.54099, plus notation 08 from table under 320.54093–320.54099

.540 899 6          Africans and people of African descent

Do not use for Black nationalism; class in 320.546

.540 9          History, geographic treatment, biography

.540 91          Areas, regions, places in general

Add to base number 320.54091 the numbers following
—1 in notation 11–19 from Table 2, e.g., Arab nationalism
320.5409174927; then add further as follows:

| | |
|---|---|
| 01–07 | Standard subdivisions [*formerly* 320.5401–320.5407] |
| 08 | Groups of people [*formerly* 320.5408] |
| 08996 | Africans and people of African descent |
| |      Do not use for Black nationalism; class in 320.546 |
| 09 | History, geographic treatment, biography |
| 092 | Biography [*formerly* 320.54092] |

| | |
|---|---|
| .540 92 | Biography |

> Biography of nationalism and regionalism with respect to groups of people by areas, regions, places in general relocated to 320.54091, plus notation 092 from table under 320.54091; biography of nationalism and regionalism with respect to groups of people by specific continents, countries, localities relocated to 320.54093–320.54099, plus notation 092 from table under 320.54093–320.54099

| | |
|---|---|
| .540 93–.540 99 | Specific continents, countries, localities |

> Add to base number 320.5409 notation 3–9 from Table 2, e.g., Swedish nationalism 320.5409485; then add further as follows:
> 01–07    Standard subdivisions [*formerly* 320.5401–320.5407]
> 08    Groups of people [*formerly* 320.5408]
> 08996        Africans and people of African descent
>             Do not use for Black nationalism; class in 320.546
> 09    History, geographic treatment, biography
> 092        Biography [*formerly* 320.54092]

| | |
|---|---|
| .540 956 94 | Palestine; Israel |

> Number built according to instructions under 320.54093–320.54099

> Class here Zionism

| | |
|---|---|
| .540 96 | Africa |

> Number built according to instructions under 320.54093–320.54099

> Class here Pan-Africanism

| | |
|---|---|
| .546 | Black nationalism |

> *See also 320.54096 for Pan-Africanism*

| | |
|---|---|
| .548 | Internationalism |

> Ideology based on political activity that focuses on the universal human condition rather than the narrow interests of a particular nation

| | |
|---|---|
| [.549] | Regional nationalism |

> Number discontinued; class in 320.54

| | |
|---|---|
| .55 | Religiously oriented ideologies |

> Including theocracy

> Class Zionism in 320.54095694

> *For Christian socialism, see 320.5312*

| | |
|---|---|
| .557 | Islamic ideologies |

> Class here Islamic fundamentalism, Islamism

> *For ideologies of Black Muslim movement, see 320.558*

> *See Manual at 320.557 vs. 297.09, 297.272, 322.1*

.558          Black Muslim movement

   Class interdisciplinary works on the Black Muslim movement in 297.87

.56          Ideologies based on groups of people [*formerly* 320.508]

   Unless other instructions are given, class a subject with aspects in two or
   more subdivisions of 320.56 in the number coming last, e.g., multicultural
   feminism 320.5622 (*not* 320.561)

.561          Multiculturalism

   Ideologies based on preserving the various cultural identities within a
   society

.562          Ideologies by gender or sex

.562 2          Feminism

   Ideologies based on equality of the sexes

.566          Ideologies by miscellaneous social statuses

.566 2          Populism

   Ideologies based on defending the interests of the common people

.569          Ideologies by ethnic and national groups

   Class here racism (ideologies based on assumptions of racial superiority)

   Class Nazism in 320.533

   *For multiculturalism, see 320.561*

.569 001–.569 009          Standard subdivisions

.569 05–.569 09          People of mixed ancestry with ethnic origins from more than one
   continent; Europeans and people of European descent

   Add to base number 320.569 notation 05–09 from Table 5, e.g.,
   white supremacy as a political ideology 320.56909

.569 1–.569 9          Specific ethnic and national groups

   Add to base number 320.569 notation 1–9 from Table 5, e.g.,
   anti-Semitism as a political ideology 320.569924

.57          Anarchism

   Class interdisciplinary works on anarchism in 335.83

.58          Environmentalist political ideologies

   Class here ecologism, environmentalism, green politics

   *See Manual at 333.72 vs. 304.28, 320.58, 363.7*

**.6** **Policy making**

Class here decision making, planning, formulation of programs and proposals, policy studies, public policy

Class a specific aspect of policy making with the aspect, e.g., policy making on religion 322.1, legislative lobbying 328.38

*For policy making in a specific subject, see the subject, e.g., policy making for economic development 338.9*

*See Manual at 300, 320.6 vs. 352–354: Public policy*

**.8** **Local government**

Including boundaries and forms of local government

Class here relation of local government to higher levels of government

Class boundaries and forms of specific kinds of local governments in 320.83–320.85; class comprehensive works on relation of parts of a state to the whole in 321.01

*For local administration, see 352.14*

**.83** Intermediate levels

Government levels between national, state, or large provincial government and local municipalities

Class here arrondissements, counties, districts, Landkreise, provinces as intermediate level units

*For provinces as state-level units, see 321.023*

*See Manual at 352.13 vs. 352.15*

**.84** Rural government

**.85** City government

Including incorporation

Class here urban government

*See also 321.06 for city-states*

**.854** Forms of city government

Including city manager, commission, mayor-council government

**.859** Annexation

**.9** **Political situation and conditions**

Class general political history in 900

*See Manual at 320.9, 320.4 vs. 351; also at 324 vs. 320.5, 320.9, 909, 930–990; also at 909, 930–990 vs. 320*

**.900 1–.900 8** Standard subdivisions

[.900 9]      History, geographic treatment, biography

> Do not use for history; class in 320.901–320.905. Do not use for geographic treatment and biography; class in 320.91–320.99

.901–.905      History

> Add to base number 320.9 notation 01–05 from Table 2, e.g., political conditions in 19th century 320.9034

.91–.99      Geographic treatment and biography

> Add to base number 320.9 notation 1–9 from Table 2, e.g., political conditions in Egypt 320.962

# 321      Systems of governments and states

Class here kinds of states

Class selecting chief executives in 324; class comprehensive works on heads of state and administration in 352.23. Class a kind of head of state or administration characteristic of a specific system of government with the system, e.g., prime ministers responsible to legislatures 321.8043, constitutional monarchs 321.87

*See Manual at 909, 930–990 vs. 320.4, 321, 321.09*

## SUMMARY

| | |
|---|---|
| 321.001–.009 | **Standard subdivisions** |
| .01–.09 | **[Systems of relating parts of a state to the whole, kinds of states, change in system of government]** |
| .1 | **Family-based government** |
| .3 | **Feudalism** |
| .5 | **Elitist systems** |
| .6 | **Absolute monarchy** |
| .8 | **Democratic government** |
| .9 | **Authoritarian government** |

.001–.009      Standard subdivisions

.01      *Systems of relating parts of a state to the whole

> Class here unitary states (states in which full control is vested in central governments)
>
> Class systems of relating parts of a state to the whole in specific kinds of states in 321.02–321.08

---

>      321.02–321.08   Kinds of states

Class kinds of states in specific jurisdictions in 320.43–320.49; class comprehensive works in 321

*For comprehensive works on unitary states, see 321.01; for kinds of states defined by source or exercise of governmental authority, see 321.3–321.9*

---

*Do not use notation 093–099 from Table 1 for systems of governments and states in a specific jurisdiction; class in 320.43–320.49

| | |
|---|---|
| .02 | *Federations |

    Class here confederations

    *For proposed regional and world federations, see 321.04*

| | |
|---|---|
| .023 | *Relation of federal to state, regional, provincial governments |

    Standard subdivisions are added for any or all topics in heading

    Class here states and provinces in federal systems

| | |
|---|---|
| .03 | Empires |

    Systems in which a group of states are governed by a single sovereign power

    *See also 325.32 for imperialism*

| | |
|---|---|
| .04 | Proposed regional and world unions |

    Unitary or federal

    Class here supranational states

| | |
|---|---|
| .040 94 | Europe |

    Class European Union in 341.2422

| | |
|---|---|
| .05 | *Nation-states |

    States considered as political embodiments of ethnic groups

    Class a national state or nation in the sense of a sovereign state in 320.1

| | |
|---|---|
| .06 | *Small states |

    Including city-states, ministates

    *See also 320.85 for cities as local governments; also 327.101 for international role of small states*

| | |
|---|---|
| .07 | Ideal states (Utopias) |

    Including anarchy as an ideal system

    Class proposed regional and world unions in 321.04

| | |
|---|---|
| .08 | *States with restricted sovereignty and non-self-governing territories |

    Including colonies, mandates, protectorates

| | |
|---|---|
| .09 | Change in system of government |

    Including coups d'état

    *See Manual at 909, 930–990 vs. 320.4, 321, 321.09*

| | |
|---|---|
| .094 | Revolution |

    Class interdisciplinary works on revolution in 303.64

---

*Do not use notation 093–099 from Table 1 for systems of governments and states in a specific jurisdiction; class in 320.43–320.49

**.1**      **Family-based government**

Ancient and modern

Class here government in nonliterate societies, tribal government

---

>      **321.3–321.9 Systems of government defined by source or exercise of authority**

Class here kinds of states defined by source or exercise of governmental authority

Class comprehensive works in 321

**.3**      *Feudalism

**.5**      *Elitist systems

Including aristocracy, oligarchy, plutocracy, theocracy

**.6**      *Absolute monarchy

Including divine right of kings

Class here autocracy

**.8**      *Democratic government

.804      Systems defined by method of selecting chief executives

.804 2      *Presidential government

Government by a chief executive selected independently of a legislature

.804 3      *Cabinet government

Government by a cabinet of ministers (including a chief executive) responsible to a legislature

.86      *Republics

Class republics defined by method of selecting chief executives in 321.804

.87      *Limited monarchy (Constitutional monarchy)

Class cabinet government in limited monarchies in 321.8043

**.9**      *Authoritarian government

Class here despotism, dictatorship, totalitarian government

*For elitist systems, see 321.5; for absolute monarchy, see 321.6*

---

*Do not use notation 093–099 from Table 1 for systems of governments and states in a specific jurisdiction; class in 320.43–320.49

.92 \*Communist government

> Class here proletarian dictatorship
>
> Class communism as a political ideology in 320.532; class interdisciplinary works on communism in 335.4

.94 \*Fascist government

> Including corporate state
>
> Class here Nazi system
>
> Class fascism as a political ideology in 320.533; class interdisciplinary works on fascism in 335.6

# 322 Relation of the state to organized groups and their members

> Relation of the state to groups other than regular political parties
>
> *For groups organized for a specific purpose not provided for here, see the purpose, e.g., groups organized to promote political rights 323.5*

## .1 Religious organizations and groups

> Class here church and state, religion and state; government policy on religion
>
> Class freedom of religion in 323.442
>
> *See Manual at 320.557 vs. 297.09, 297.272, 322.1; also at 322.1 vs. 201.72, 261.7, 292–299*

## .2 Labor movements and groups

> Including general strikes
>
> *For general strikes directed primarily toward employers or focused upon limited economic objectives, see 331.8925*
>
> *See also 323.3223 for relation of the state to the working class*

## .3 Business and industry

## .4 Political action groups

> Class here protest groups; nonelectoral tactics used by political action groups, e.g., civil disobedience; specific kinds of conflicts between political action groups and constituted authorities, e.g., riots
>
> Class political action committees (United States fund-raising groups) in 324.4; class interdisciplinary works on conflicts and their resolution in 303.6

---

\*Do not use notation 093–099 from Table 1 for systems of governments and states in a specific jurisdiction; class in 320.43–320.49

**.42**          Revolutionary and subversive groups

>   Standard subdivisions are added for either or both topics in heading

>   Class here revolutionary and subversive activities and branches of political parties

>   Class comprehensive works on parties and international party organizations engaged in both nonviolent political activity and revolutionary activity in 324.2

**.420 93–.420 99**          Specific continents, countries, localities

>>   Class here specific revolutionary and subversive groups irrespective of political persuasion or stated goals, e.g., Ku Klux Klan 322.420973

>>   Class impact of specific revolutionary and subversive groups on general history in 930–990

**.43**          Pressure groups

>   Groups striving for immediate and relatively limited goals

>   Class a pressure group working for a specific goal with the goal, e.g., a group working for better law enforcement 363.23

**.44**          Reform movements

>   Groups seeking to change a substantial social function

>   Class interdisciplinary works on social reform in 303.484. Class a movement seeking to reform a specific social function with the function, e.g., women's suffrage movement 324.623, welfare reform 361.68

**.5**          **Armed services**

# 323          Civil and political rights

>   Standard subdivisions are added for civil and political rights together, for civil rights alone

>   Class here civil liberties, human rights, individual freedom, rights of humanity; relations of the state to its residents

>   Class welfare aspects of human rights in 361.614

>   *For relation of the state to organized groups other than political parties and related organizations, see 322; for relation of the state to political parties and related organizations, see 324; for human rights law, see 341.48; for civil rights law, see 342.085*

### SUMMARY

| | |
|---|---|
| 323.01–.09 | Standard subdivisions; citizen participation; resistance, repression, persecution |
| .1 | Civil and political rights of nondominant groups |
| .3 | Civil and political rights of other social groups |
| .4 | Specific civil rights; limitation and suspension of civil rights |
| .5 | Political rights |
| .6 | Citizenship and related topics |

.01      Philosophy and theory

> Class here natural rights

.04      Citizen participation; resistance, repression, persecution

.042      Citizen participation

> Class here participation of citizens in governmental processes, participatory democracy

> Class citizen participation in a specific issue with the issue, e.g., participation in public school evaluation 379.158

.044      Resistance, repression, persecution

> Class limitation and suspension of civil rights in 323.49

.08      Groups of people

> Class here groups of people enforcing civil and political rights, groups of people participating in the abuse of civil and political rights, groups of people working for civil and political rights in general

> Do not use for civil and political rights of nondominant groups; class in 323.1. Do not use for civil and political rights of other social groups; class in 323.3

**.1**      **Civil and political rights of nondominant groups**

> Standard subdivisions are added for either civil or political rights or both

> Class specific civil rights of nondominant groups in 323.4; class specific political rights of nondominant groups in 323.5; class interdisciplinary works on nondominant groups in 305.5

> *For civil and political rights of specific nondominant groups other than members of ethnic and national groups, see 323.3*

[.109 3–.109 9]      Specific continents, countries, localities

> Do not use; class in 323.13–323.19

.11      Ethnic and national groups

> Standard subdivisions are added for either civil or political rights or both

> Class interdisciplinary works on ethnic and national groups in 305.8

[.110 93–.110 99]      Specific continents, countries, localities

> Do not use; class in 323.13–323.19

.111–.119      Specific ethnic and national groups

> Add to base number 323.11 notation 1–9 from Table 5, e.g., civil rights of Jews 323.11924, of African Americans 323.1196073
> Subdivisions are added for either civil or political rights or both
> (Option: Class civil and political rights of North American native peoples in 970.5; prefer 323.1197
> (Option: Class civil and political rights of South American native peoples in 980.5; prefer 323.1198)

> Class members of specific ethnic and national groups who are also members of other social groups in 323.3

.13–.19     Nondominant groups, ethnic and national groups in specific continents, countries, localities

> Add to base number 323.1 notation 3–9 from Table 2, e.g., civil rights of national minorities in China 323.151
>> Subdivisions are added for either civil or political rights or both
>
> Class specific ethnic and national groups in specific continents, countries, localities in 323.111–323.119; class other specific nondominant groups in specific continents, countries, localities in 323.3

**.3          Civil and political rights of other social groups**

> Groups other than ethnic and national groups
>
> Class a specific civil right of social groups in 323.4; class a specific political right of social groups in 323.5

[.301–.309]     Standard subdivisions

> Do not use; class in 323.01–323.09

.32          Groups identified by miscellaneous social attributes

> Add to base number 323.32 the numbers following —086 in notation 0862–0869 from Table 1, e.g., working class 323.3223, intellectuals 323.3231
>> Subdivisions are added for either civil or political rights or both

.34          Women

> Standard subdivisions are added for either civil or political rights or both
>
> Class women identified by miscellaneous social characteristics in 323.32

.35          Age groups

> Standard subdivisions are added for either civil or political rights or both
>
> Class age groups identified by miscellaneous social characteristics in 323.32; class women regardless of age group in 323.34

.352          Young people

> Standard subdivisions are added for either civil or political rights or both
>
> Class here children

.353          Young and middle-aged adults

> Standard subdivisions are added for either civil or political rights or both
>
> Class comprehensive works on adults in 323

.354          People in late adulthood

> Standard subdivisions are added for either civil or political rights or both

**.4          Specific civil rights; limitation and suspension of civil rights**

[.401–.409]     Standard subdivisions

> Do not use; class in 323.01–323.09

.42          Equal protection of law

| | |
|---|---|
| .43 | Personal security |

Including right to bear arms, right to life

Class right to privacy in 323.448; class legal aspects of right to life in 342.085

| | |
|---|---|
| .44 | Freedom of action (Liberty) |

Class here freedom of expression, intellectual freedom

*For rights of assembly and association, see 323.47; for right of petition, see 323.48*

| | |
|---|---|
| .442 | Freedom of conscience and religion |
| .443 | Freedom of speech |
| .445 | Freedom of publication |

Class here freedom of information, freedom of the press

| | |
|---|---|
| .448 | Right to privacy |
| .448 2 | Freedom from government surveillance |

Surveillance by interception of mail, electronic monitoring, other means

Class governmental databases in 323.4483

| | |
|---|---|
| .448 3 | Freedom from misuse of information in databases and government records |
| .46 | Property rights |

Including freedom of contract

Class interdisciplinary works on economic rights in 330

| | |
|---|---|
| .47 | Rights of assembly and association |
| .48 | Right of petition |

Class here comprehensive works on rights of petition and assembly

*For right of assembly, see 323.47*

| | |
|---|---|
| .49 | Limitation and suspension of civil rights |

Including harassment through abuse of power, e.g., detention of dissidents for alleged mental health problems

Class limitation and suspension of specific rights in 323.42–323.48

| | |
|---|---|
| [.490 8] | Groups of people |

Do not use for limitation and suspension of rights of nondominant groups; class in 323.1. Do not use for limitation and suspension of rights of other social groups; class in 323.3

**.5** **Political rights**

Including right to hold office, right to representation

Class right of assembly in 323.47; class right of petition in 323.48; class exercise of political rights in 324

*For citizenship and related rights, see 323.6; for voting rights, see 324.62*

**[.508]** Groups of people

Do not use for political rights of nondominant groups; class in 323.1. Do not use for political rights of other social groups; class in 323.3

**.6** **Citizenship and related topics**

Standard subdivisions are added for citizenship and related topics together, for citizenship alone

**.62** Acquisition of citizenship

Including acquisition of citizenship by marriage

**.623** Naturalization

**.63** Relation of the state to aliens and people with citizenship problems

Including dual nationality, stateless persons

**.631** Aliens

Including asylum

Class naturalization of aliens in 323.623

**.64** Expatriation and repatriation

Class comprehensive works on refugees in 325.21

**.65** Duties and obligations of citizens

Standard subdivisions are added for either or both topics in heading

Including loyalty, loyalty oaths

**.67** Passports and visas

**324** **The political process**

Class here elections

*See Manual at 324 vs. 320; also at 324 vs. 320.5, 320.9, 909, 930–990; also at 909, 930–990 vs. 320*

**SUMMARY**

[.023]           Politics as a profession, occupation, hobby

Do not use; class in 324.22

.09           History, geographic treatment, biography

Do not use for history and geographic treatment of elections; class in 324.9

## .1     International party organizations, auxiliaries, activities

Not directly controlled by specific national parties

Class revolutionary and subversive activities and branches of party organizations in 322.42

---

>     324.13–324.17 International organizations, auxiliaries, activities of parties identified primarily by position on right-to-left spectrum

Class organizations, auxiliaries, activities of parties not primarily identified by position on right-to-left spectrum in 324.18; class comprehensive works in 324.1

.13           International organizations of rightist parties

Including international anticommunist leagues and their activities, monarchist parties

.14           International organizations of conservative parties

.15           International organizations of centrist parties

.16           International organizations of liberal parties

*For international organizations of social democratic parties, see 324.172*

.17           International organizations of leftist and labor-oriented parties

Including First International

.172          International organizations of social democratic parties

.174          International organizations of nonauthoritarian socialist parties

Including Second and Socialist Internationals

*For international organizations of social democratic parties, see 324.172*

.175        International organizations of communist parties

> Including Third (Communist) and Fourth (Trotskyist) Internationals, Cominform

.18        International organizations of other parties

> Not primarily identified by position on right-to-left spectrum

> Including libertarian parties

> Add to base number 324.18 the numbers following 08 in notation 082–087 from table under 324.24–324.29, e.g., international organizations of religious parties 324.182

## .2     Political parties

> *For revolutionary and subversive activities and branches of parties, see 322.42; for international party organizations and activities, see 324.1; for auxiliary organizations, see 324.3*

### SUMMARY

[.202 3]        Party politics as a profession, occupation, hobby

> Do not use; class in 324.22

.204        Relation of political parties to state and government

> Including political patronage

.209        History, geographic treatment, biography

.209 4–.209 9        Specific continents, countries, localities in modern world

> Do not use for parties in specific countries and localities; class in 324.24–324.29

> *See Manual at 324.2094–324.2099 and 324.24–324.29*

.21        Kinds of parties

> Class here party finance, membership, organization; political machines

.210 94–.210 99        Specific continents, countries, localities in modern world

> Do not use for kinds of parties in specific countries and localities; class in 324.24–324.29. Do not use for party finance, membership, organizations of parties in specific countries and localities; class in 324.24–324.29 plus notation 011 from table under 324.24–324.29

.212–.218      Specific kinds of parties

> Add to base number 324.21 the numbers following 0 in notation 02–08 from table under 324.24–324.29, e.g., centrist parties 324.215
>
> *For leadership of specific kinds of parties, see 324.22; for programs and ideologies of specific kinds of parties, see 324.23; for specific parties and kinds of parties in a specific country or part of a country in modern world, see 324.24–324.29; for campaign finance of specific kinds of parties, see 324.78*

.218 2      Religious parties

> Number built according to instructions under 324.212–324.218
>
> Class here comprehensive works on Christian democratic parties
>
> *For nominally religious parties identified primarily by position on right-to-left spectrum or other ideology, see the position or ideology, e.g., conservative, secular Christian democratic parties 324.214*

.22      Leadership

> Including selection of leaders
>
> Class here politics as a profession, occupation, hobby; politicians as a type of person
>
> *For nominating candidates, see 324.5*

.220 94–.220 99      Specific continents, countries, localities in modern world

> Do not use for party leadership in specific countries and localities; class in 324.24–324.29 plus notation 012 from table under 324.24–324.29

.23      Programs and ideologies

> Standard subdivisions are added for either or both topics in heading
>
> Class here platforms, campaign literature
>
> *For campaign literature on a specific subject, see the subject, e.g., campaign literature on United States participation in Vietnamese War 959.7043373*

.230 94–.230 99      Geographic areas in modern world other than specific countries and states

> Do not use for party programs and ideologies in specific countries and localities; class in 324.24–324.29 plus notation 013 from table under 324.24–324.29

.232–.238      Programs and ideologies of specific kinds of parties

> Add to base number 324.23 the numbers following 0 in notation 02–08 from table under 324.24–324.29, e.g., programs of centrist parties 324.235
>
> *For programs and ideologies of specific parties and kinds of parties in a specific country or part of a country in modern world, see 324.24–324.29*

.24–.29    Parties in specific countries and localities in modern world

The following add table is limited to countries and localities other than the United Kingdom, Germany, Austria, Italy, Switzerland, Canada, United States, Australia; special developments for those countries follow the add table

Except where specifically instructed to the contrary below, for a country or for localities within a country add to base number 324.2 notation 4–9 from Table 2 for the specific country, e.g., parties of France 324.244; then add to the number according to the table below, e.g., parties in Paris 324.24400944361, French Communist Party 324.244075, French Communist Party in Paris 324.2440750944361:

| | |
|---|---|
| 001–009 | Standard subdivisions |
| 01 | General topics |
| | Class general topics of specific parties in 02–08 |
| 011 | Organization, membership, finance |
| | Class here political machines |
| | Class leadership in 012; class comprehensive works on party organization, membership, finance in 324.21 |
| 012 | Leadership |
| | Including selection of leaders |
| | Class nominating candidates in 015; class comprehensive works on party leadership in 324.22 |
| 013 | Programs and ideologies |
| | Standard subdivisions are added for either or both topics in heading |
| | Class here platforms, campaign literature |
| | Class comprehensive works on party programs and ideologies in 324.23 |
| | *For campaign literature on a specific subject, see the subject, e.g., campaign literature on United States participation in Vietnamese War 959.7043373* |
| 014 | Auxiliary party organizations |
| | Class comprehensive works on auxiliary party organizations in 324.3 |
| 015 | Nominating party candidates |
| | Class here nomination campaigns; results of campaigns, e.g., delegate counts |
| | Class comprehensive works on nominating candidates in 324.5; class comprehensive works on nomination and election campaigns in 324.9 |
| 0152 | Nominating by caucuses and co-optation |
| 0154 | Nominating by primaries |
| 0156 | Nominating by conventions |
| | *For selecting delegates to nominating conventions by caucuses and co-optation, see 0152; for selecting delegates to nominating conventions by primaries, see 0154* |
| 02 | Parties existing only prior to 1945 |
| | Parties existing prior to 1945 and ceasing existence after 1945 relocated to 03–08 |
| | Class comprehensive works on parties existing only prior to 1945 in 324.212 |

(continued)

.24–.29     Parties in specific countries and localities in modern world (continued)

      >03–08    Parties founded or in existence after 1945
             Class here parties existing prior to 1945 and ceasing existence after 1945 [*formerly* 02]
             Class comprehensive works on specific kinds of parties founded or in existence after 1945 in 324.21; class comprehensive works on parties founded or in existence after 1945 in specific countries in base number for the country in 324.24–324.29

      >03–07    Parties founded or in existence after 1945 identified primarily by position on right-to-left spectrum
             Class parties that are identified by position on right-to-left spectrum and another ideology in 08; class comprehensive works in base number for the country in 324.24–324.29

        03        Rightist parties
             Including monarchist parties

        038       Neofascist and neo-Nazi parties
             Standard subdivisions are added for either or both topics in heading
                *See also 02 for fascist and Nazi parties founded before 1945*

        04        Conservative parties
        05        Centrist parties
        06        Liberal parties
        07        Leftist and worker parties
        072       Social democratic parties
        074       Socialist parties
             *For social democratic parties, see 072*
        075       Communist parties

        08        Parties founded or in existence after 1945 not identified primarily by position on right-to-left spectrum
             Including libertarian, farmers' parties

        082       Religious parties
             Class nominally religious parties identified primarily by position on right-to-left spectrum or other ideology with the position or ideology, e.g., centrist, secular Christian democratic parties 05

        083       Nationalist parties
        084       Regionalist parties
             Class here separatist, sovereigntist parties

        087       Environmentalist parties (Green parties)

      (Option: Arrange specific parties of a specific country alphabetically, e.g., Labour Party of United Kingdom 324.241)

      Class comprehensive works on parties in 324.2; class comprehensive works on specific kinds of parties in 324.21

      *See Manual at 324.2094–324.2099 and 324.24–324.29*

      **Special developments follow for selected specific countries whose party systems deviate from the above pattern**

## SUMMARY

| | |
|---|---|
| .241 | Parties of United Kingdom |

.241 001–.241 009    Standard subdivisions

.241 01    General topics of parties of United Kingdom

Add to base number 324.24101 the numbers following 01 in notation 011–015 from table under 324.24–324.29, e.g., campaign literature of parties of United Kingdom 324.241013

Class general topics of specific parties of United Kingdom in 324.24102–324.24109

.241 02    Parties existing only prior to 1945

Class here parties of Great Britain before union with Ireland, of England and Wales before union with Scotland

Parties existing prior to 1945 and ceasing existence after 1945 relocated to 324.24104–324.24109

---

>     324.241 04–324.241 09  Parties founded or in existence after 1945

Class here parties existing prior to 1945 and ceasing existence after 1945 [*formerly* 324.24102]

.241 04    Conservative Party

.241 06    Liberal Party and its successors

Standard subdivisions are added for any or all liberal parties

Class here Liberal Democrats

.241 07    Labour Party

.241 09    Other parties

Add to base number 324.24109 the numbers following 0 in notation 03–08 from table under 324.24–324.29, e.g., Communist Party 324.2410975

| | |
|---|---|
| .243 | Parties of Germany |

.243 001–.243 009    Standard subdivisions

.243 01            General topics

> Add to base number 324.24301 the numbers following 01 in notation 011–015 from table under 324.24–324.29, e.g., campaign literature of parties of Germany 324.243013

> Class general topics of specific parties of Germany in 324.24302–324.24308

.243 02            Parties existing only prior to 1945

> Parties existing prior to 1945 and ceasing existence after 1945 relocated to 324.24303–324.24308

.243 023           Rightist parties

> Including monarchist parties

> Class here rightist nationalist parties

.243 023 8          National Socialist German Labor Party (Nazi Party)

.243 024           Conservative parties

.243 025           Centrist parties

> Class here German Center Party

.243 026           Liberal parties

.243 027           Leftist and worker parties

---

>      324.243 03–324.243 08   Parties founded or in existence after 1945

> Class here parties existing prior to 1945 and ceasing existence after 1945 [*formerly* 324.24302]

> Class comprehensive works in 324.243

---

>      324.243 03–324.243 07   Parties founded or in existence after 1945 identified primarily by position on right-to-left spectrum

> Class parties that are identified by position on right-to-left spectrum and another ideology in 324.24308; class comprehensive works in 324.243

.243 03           Rightist parties

> Including monarchist parties

> Class here rightist nationalist parties, German People's Union, National Democratic Party of Germany; Republican Party of Germany

.243 038          Neofascist and neo-Nazi parties

> Standard subdivisions are added for either or both topics in heading

> > See also 324.2430238 for National Socialist German Labor Party (Nazi Party)

| | |
|---|---|
| .243 04 | Conservative parties |

Class here conservative religious parties, Christian Democratic Union of Germany (CDU), Christian Social Union (CSU)

| | |
|---|---|
| .243 05 | Centrist parties |
| .243 06 | Liberal parties |

Class here Free Democratic Party

| | |
|---|---|
| .243 07 | Leftist and worker parties |
| .243 072 | Social democratic parties |

Class here Social Democratic Party of Germany (SPD)

| | |
|---|---|
| .243 074 | Socialist parties |

Class here Party of Democratic Socialism, The Left

*For social democratic parties, see 324.243072*

| | |
|---|---|
| .243 075 | Communist parties |

Class here German Communist Party, Communist Party of Germany, Socialist Unity Party of Germany (SED)

| | |
|---|---|
| .243 08 | Parties founded or in existence after 1945 not identified primarily by position on right-to-left spectrum |

Including libertarian, farmers' parties

| | |
|---|---|
| .243 082 | Religious parties |

Class conservative religious parties, Christian Democratic Union of Germany, Christian Social Union in 324.24304

| | |
|---|---|
| .243 083 | Nationalist parties |

Class rightist nationalist parties, National Democratic Party of Germany in 324.24303

| | |
|---|---|
| .243 084 | Regionalist parties |

Class here separatist, sovereigntist parties

| | |
|---|---|
| .243 087 | Environmentalist parties (Green parties) |

Class here Greens

| | |
|---|---|
| .243 6 | Parties of Austria |
| .243 600 1–.243 600 9 | Standard subdivisions |
| .243 601 | General topics |

Add to base number 324.243601 the numbers following 01 in notation 011–015 from table under 324.24–324.29, e.g., campaign literature of parties in Austria 324.2436013

Class general topics of specific parties of Austria in 324.243602–324.243608

| | |
|---|---|
| .243 602 | Parties existing only prior to 1945 |

Parties existing prior to 1945 and ceasing existence after 1945 relocated to 324.243603–324.243608

| | |
|---|---|
| .243 602 3 | Rightist parties |

Class here rightist Pan-German national parties, Pan-German People's Party (GDVP), Rural Federation (LB)

| | |
|---|---|
| .243 602 38 | National socialist parties |

Class here German National Socialist Labor Party (DNSAP), National Socialist German Labor Party (NSDAP), National Socialist Labor Party (NSAP)

| | |
|---|---|
| .243 602 4 | Conservative parties |

Class here Christian Social Party (CSP), Homeland Bloc

| | |
|---|---|
| .243 602 43 | Fatherland Front |
| .243 602 6 | Liberal parties |
| .243 602 7 | Leftist and worker parties |

Class here Social Democratic Worker Party (SDAP)

---

>     324.243 603–324.243 608  Parties founded or in existence after 1945

Class here parties existing prior to 1945 and ceasing existence after 1945 [*formerly* 324.243602]

Class comprehensive works in 324.2436

---

>     324.243 603–324.243 607  Parties founded or in existence after 1945 identified primarily by position on right-to-left spectrum

Class parties that are identified by position on right-to-left spectrum and another ideology in 324.243608; class comprehensive works in 324.2436

| | |
|---|---|
| .243 603 | Rightist parties |

Class here rightist populist parties, Freedom Party of Austria (FPÖ), Alliance for the Future of Austria (BZÖ) [*all formerly* 324.243608]; rightist Pan-German nationalist parties, Federation of Independents (VdU) [*both formerly* 324.2436083]

| | |
|---|---|
| .243 603 8 | Neofascist and neo-Nazi parties |

Standard subdivisions are added for either or both topics in heading

Class here National Democratic Party (NDP)

*See also 324.24360238 for national socialist parties*

| | |
|---|---|
| .243 604 | Conservative parties |

Class here Austrian People's Party (ÖVP)

| [.243 605] | Centrist parties |
| | Number discontinued; class in 324.2436 |
| .243 606 | Liberal parties |
| | Class here Liberal Forum (LiF) |
| .243 607 | Leftist and worker parties |
| .243 607 2 | Social democratic parties |
| | Class here Social Democratic Party of Austria (SPÖ) |
| .243 607 5 | Communist parties |
| | Class here Communist Party of Austria (KPÖ) |
| .243 608 | Parties founded or in existence after 1945 not identified primarily by position on right-to-left spectrum |
| | Rightist populist parties, Freedom Party of Austria (FPÖ), Alliance for the Future of Austria (BZÖ) relocated to 324.243603 |
| [.243 608 2] | Religious parties |
| | Number discontinued; class in 324.243608 |
| .243 608 3 | Nationalist parties |
| | Rightist Pan-German nationalist parties, Federation of Independents (VdU) relocated to 324.243603 |
| .243 608 7 | Environmental parties (Green parties) |
| | Class here Greens (Austrian Green Party) |
| .245 | Parties of Italy |
| .245 001–.245 009 | Standard subdivisions |
| .245 01 | General topics |
| | Add to base number 324.24501 the numbers following 01 in notation 011–015 from table under 324.24–324.29, e.g., campaign literature of parties in Italy 324.245013 |
| | Class general topics of specific parties of Italy in 324.24502–324.24508 |
| .245 02 | Parties existing only prior to 1945 |

> 324.245 023 -324.245 027  Parties existing only prior to 1945 identified primarily by position on right-to-left spectrum

Class parties that are identified by position on right-to-left spectrum and another ideology in 324.245028; class comprehensive works in 324.24502

| .245 023 | Rightist parties |

| | |
|---|---|
| .245 023 8 | Fascist parties |
| | Including Fascist Republican Party |
| | Class here National Fascist Party |
| .245 024 | Conservative parties |
| .245 025 | Centrist parties |
| .245 026 | Liberal parties |
| | Including Action Party (1853–1867) |
| | *See also 324.24506 for Action Party (1942–1947)* |
| .245 027 | Leftist parties |
| | Including Party of Italian Workers, Socialist Party of Italian Workers (1893–1895), Socialist Party of Italian Workers (1925–1927), United Socialist Party (1922–1930) |
| | *See also 324.2450722 for Socialist Party of Italian Workers (1947–1951), United Socialist Party (1969–1971)* |
| .245 028 | Parties existing only prior to 1945 not identified primarily by position on right-to-left spectrum |
| .245 028 2 | Religious parties |
| | Class here Italian Popular Party (1919–1926) |
| | Class comprehensive works on Italian Popular Party (1919–1926) and Christian Democracy in 324.2450822 |
| | *See also 324.245082 for Italian Popular Party (1994–2002)* |

---

>      324.245 03–324.245 08   Parties founded or in existence after 1945

Class comprehensive works in 324.245

---

>      324.245 03–324.245 07   Parties founded or in existence after 1945 identified primarily by position on right-to-left spectrum

Class parties that are identified by position on right-to-left spectrum and another ideology in 324.24508; class comprehensive works in 324.245

| | |
|---|---|
| .245 03 | Rightist parties |
| | Including monarchist parties |
| .245 038 | Neofascist parties |
| | Including Italian Social Movement, Italian Social Movement-Right National |
| | Class National Alliance in 324.24504 |

| | |
|---|---|
| .245 04 | Conservative parties |

Including Forward Italy, Italian Liberal Party (1943–1994), Italian Liberal Party (2004–), National Alliance

| | |
|---|---|
| .245 05 | Centrist parties |

Including Democracy is Freedom-Daisy (Daisy), Italian Republican Party

Class Democratic Party in 324.24506

| | |
|---|---|
| .245 06 | Liberal parties |

Including Action Party (1942–1947), Democratic Party, Radical Party, Transnational Radical Party

*See also 324.245026 for Action Party (1853–1867); also 324.24504 for Italian Liberal Party (1943–1994), Italian Liberal Party (2004–)*

| | |
|---|---|
| .245 07 | Leftist and worker parties |

Including Democratic Party of the Left, Democrats of the Left

Class Democratic Party in 324.24506

| | |
|---|---|
| .245 072 | Social democratic parties |

Including Italian Democratic Socialist Party (2004–)

*See also 324.2450722 for Italian Democratic Socialist Party (1954–1995)*

| | |
|---|---|
| .245 072 2 | Italian Democratic Socialist Party (1952–1995) |

Class here Socialist Party of Italian Workers (1947–1951), United Socialist Party (1969–1971)

*See also 324.245027 for Socialist Party of Italian Workers (1893–1895), Socialist Party of Italian Workers (1925–1927), United Socialist Party (1922–1930); also 324.245072 for Italian Democratic Socialist Party (2004–)*

| | |
|---|---|
| .245 074 | Socialist parties |

Including Socialist Party of Proletarian Unity (1947–1951)

*For social democratic parties, see 324.245072*

*See also 324.2450742 for Socialist Party of Proletarian Unity (1943–1947)*

| | |
|---|---|
| .245 074 2 | Italian Socialist Party |

Class here Socialist Party of Proletarian Unity (1943–1947)

*See also 324.245074 for Socialist Party of Proletarian Unity (1947–1951)*

| | |
|---|---|
| .245 075 | Communist parties |
| | Including Communist Refoundation Party, Party of Italian Communists |
| | Class Democratic Party of the Left, Democrats of the Left in 324.24507 |
| .245 075 2 | Italian Communist Party |
| .245 08 | Parties founded or in existence after 1945 not identified primarily by position on right-to-left spectrum |
| .245 082 | Religious parties |
| | Including Christian Democratic Center, Italian Popular Party (1994–2002), Union of Christian and Center Democrats, United Christian Democrats |
| | *See also 324.2450282 for Italian Popular Party (1919–1926)* |
| .245 082 2 | Christian Democracy |
| | Class here comprehensive works on Italian Popular Party (1919–1926) and Christian Democracy together; on Italian Popular Party (1919–1926), Christian Democracy, Italian Popular Party (1994–2002) together |
| | Class Italian Popular Party (1994–2002) in 324.245082 |
| | *For Italian Popular Party (1919–1926), see 324.2450282* |
| .245 083 | Nationalist parties |
| .245 084 | Regionalist parties |
| | Including Northern League, South Tyrolean People's Party, Valdotanian Union |
| | Class here separatist, sovereigntist parties |
| .245 087 | Environmentalist parties (Green parties) |
| | Class here Federation of the Greens |
| .245 1–.245 9 | Parties of regions and provinces of Italy |
| | Add to base number 324.245 the numbers following —45 in notation 451–459 from Table 2 for region or province, e.g., parties in Veneto region 324.2453; then add 0* and to the result add the numbers following 324.2450 in 324.24501–324.24508, e.g., Venetian League 324.2453084 |
| .249 4 | Parties of Switzerland |
| .249 400 1–.249 400 9 | Standard subdivisions |

*Add 00 for standard subdivisions; see instructions at beginning of Table 1

.249 401                    General topics

> Add to base number 324.249401 the numbers following 01 in notation 011–015 from table under 324.24–324.29, e.g., campaign literature of parties in Switzerland 324.2494013
>
> Class general topics of specific parties of Switzerland in 324.249402–324.249408

.249 402                    Parties existing only prior to 1945

> Parties existing prior to 1945 and ceasing existence after 1945 relocated to 324.249403–324.249408

---

> 324.249 403–324.249 408  Parties founded or in existence after 1945
>
> Class here parties existing prior to 1945 and ceasing existence after 1945 [*formerly* 324.249402]
>
> Class comprehensive works in 324.2494

---

> 324.249 403–324.249 407  Parties founded or in existence after 1945 identified primarily by position on right-to-left spectrum
>
> Class parties that are identified by position on right-to-left spectrum and another ideology in 324.249408; class comprehensive works in 324.2494

.249 403                    Rightist parties

> Class here rightist national parties, National Action for People and Homeland (NA), Swiss Democrats (SD) [*all formerly* 324.2494083]; Swiss Peoples Party (SVP), Freedom Party of Switzerland (FPS)

.249 404                    Conservative parties

> Class here conservative religious parties, Christian Democratic People's Party of Switzerland (CVP) [*both formerly* 324.2494082]

.249 405                    Centrist parties

.249 406                    Liberal parties

> Class here FDP.The Liberals, Radical Democratic Party (FDP, Free Democratic Party, Freethinking Democratic Party, Liberal Democratic Party, Radical Free Democratic Party), Swiss Liberal Party (LPS)

.249 407                    Leftist and worker parties

> Class here leftist religious parties, Christian Social Party (CSP) [*both formerly* 324.2494082]

.249 407 2                  Social democratic parties

> Class here Social Democratic Party of Switzerland (SPS)

.249 407 4        Socialist parties

Class here Swiss Labour Party (PdA)

*For social democratic parties, see 324.2494072*

.249 407 5        Communist parties

Class here Revolutionary Marxist League (RML), Socialist Worker Party (SAP)

.249 408        Parties founded or in existence after 1945 not identified primarily by position on right-to-left spectrum

Including libertarian parties, farmers' parties

Class here National Alliance of Independents (LdU)

.249 408 2        Religious parties

Class here Protestant People's Party of Switzerland (EVP), Confederal Democratic Union (EDU)

Conservative religious parties, Christian Democratic People's Party of Switzerland (CVP) relocated to 324.249404; leftist religious parties, Christian Social Party (CSP) relocated to 324.249407

.249 408 3        Nationalist parties

Rightist national parties, National Action for People and Homeland (NA), Swiss Democrats (SD) relocated to 324.249403

.249 408 4        Regionalist parties

Class here separatist, sovereigntist parties; Ticino League

.249 408 7        Environmental parties (Green parties)

Class here Green Party of Switzerland (GPS), Green Alliance (GB)

.271        Parties of Canada

.271 001–.271 009        Standard subdivisions

.271 01        General topics of parties of Canada

Add to base number 324.27101 the numbers following 01 in notation 011–015 from table under 324.24–324.29, e.g., campaign literature of parties of Canada 324.271013

Class general topics of specific parties of Canada in 324.27102–324.27109

.271 02        Parties existing only prior to 1945

Parties existing prior to 1945 and ceasing existence after 1945 relocated to 324.27104–324.27109

>         324.271 04–324.271 09  Parties founded or in existence after 1945

        Class here parties existing prior to 1945 and ceasing existence after 1945 [*formerly* 324.27102]

.271 04         Conservative Party of Canada (2003–) and its predecessors

        Including Reform Party of Canada, Canadian Reform Conservative Alliance

        Class here Conservative Party of Canada (1938–1942) and the party under former names, e.g., Liberal-Conservative Party; Progressive Conservative Party

.271 05         Social Credit Party of Canada

.271 06         Liberal Party of Canada

.271 07         New Democratic Party of Canada

.271 09         Other parties

        Add to base number 324.27109 the numbers following 0 in notation 03–08 from table under 324.24–324.29, e.g., nationalist parties 324.2710983

.271 098 4         Regionalist parties

        Number built according to instructions under 324.27109

        Class here separatist, sovereigntist parties; Bloc québécois

        *See also 324.27140984 for Parti québécois*

.271 1–.271 9         Parties of provinces and territories of Canada

        Add to base number 324.271 the numbers following —71 in notation 711–719 from Table 2 for province or territory, e.g., parties in the Yukon Territory 324.27191; then add 0* and to the result add the numbers following 324.2710 in 324.27101–324.27109, e.g., Yukon Party 324.2719104

.271 409 84         Regionalist parties of Quebec

        Number built according to instructions under 324.2711–324.2719

        Class here separatist, sovereigntist parties; Parti québécois

        *See also 324.2710984 for Bloc québécois*

.273         Parties of United States

        *For parties in specific states and District of Columbia, see 324.274–324.279*

.273 01–.273 09         Standard subdivisions

*Add 00 for standard subdivisions; see instructions at beginning of Table 1

.273 1        General topics of parties of United States

> Add to base number 324.2731 the numbers following 01 in notation 011–015 from table under 324.24–324.29, e.g., campaign literature of parties of United States 324.27313

> Class general topics of specific parties of United States in 324.2732–324.2738

.273 2        Parties existing only prior to 1945

> Including American ("Know-Nothing") Party, Free Soil Party

> Parties existing prior to 1945 and ceasing existence after 1945 relocated to 324.2733–324.2738

.273 22        Federalist Party

> Variant name: Federal Party

.273 23        Whig Party

> Including National Republican Party

.273 26        Jeffersonian Republican Party

> Variant name: Anti-federalist Party

.273 27        Populist and progressive parties

> Including Progressive ("Bull Moose") Party

> *See also 324.2737 for Progressive Party (1948)*

---

>        324.273 3–324.273 8   Parties founded or in existence after 1945

> Class here parties existing prior to 1945 and ceasing existence after 1945 [*formerly* 324.2732]

.273 3        Nationalist parties of the right

> Including American Independent Party; sectionalist parties, e.g., States' Rights Party (Dixiecrats)

.273 38        National Socialist White People's Party

> Former name: American Nazi Party

.273 4        Republican Party

.273 6        Democratic Party

> Including Democratic-Republican Party

.273 7        Leftist and worker parties

> Including Progressive Party (1948), Socialist Labor Party, Socialist Party, Socialist Workers Party

> *See also 324.27327 for Progressive ("Bull Moose") Party*

.273 75        Communist Party

| .273 8 | Other parties founded or in existence after 1945 |
|---|---|

Including environmentalist, libertarian, prohibitionist, religious, separatist parties

*See also 324.2733 for sectionalist parties*

| .274–.279 | Parties of states of United States and District of Columbia |
|---|---|

Add to base number 324.27 the numbers following —7 in notation 74–79 from Table 2 for state or District of Columbia, e.g., parties in New York State 324.2747; then add 0*, and to the result add the numbers following 324.273 in 324.2731–324.2738, e.g., Republican Party in New York State 324.274704

Class comprehensive works in 324.273

*For parties in Hawaii, see 324.2969*

**A development for New York follows**

| .274 7 | Parties in New York |
|---|---|
| .274 700 1–.274 700 9 | Standard subdivisions |
| .274 701–.274 702 | General topics and parties existing only prior to 1945 |

Add to base number 324.27470 the numbers following 324.273 in 324.2731–324.2732, e.g., Whig Party 324.2747023

| .274 703 | Nationalist parties of the right |
|---|---|
| .274 704 | Republican Party |
| .274 706 | Democratic Party |
| .274 707 | Leftist and worker parties |
| .274 707 5 | Communist Party |
| .274 708 | Other parties founded or in existence after 1945 |

Including Conservative Party, Liberal Party

| .294 | Parties of Australia |
|---|---|
| .294 001–.294 009 | Standard subdivisions |
| .294 01 | General topics of parties of Australia |

Add to base number 324.29401 the numbers following 01 in notation 011–015 from table under 324.24–324.29, e.g., campaign literature of parties of Australia 324.294013

Class general topics of specific parties of Australia in 324.29402–324.29409

| .294 02 | Parties existing only prior to 1945 |
|---|---|

Parties existing prior to 1945 and ceasing existence after 1945 relocated to 324.29404–324.29409

*Add 00 for standard subdivisions; see instructions at beginning of Table 1

> 324.294 04–324.294 09  Parties founded or in existence after 1945

Class here parties existing prior to 1945 and ceasing existence after 1945 [*formerly* 324.29402]

| | |
|---|---|
| .294 04 | The Nationals |

Former names: Australian Country Party, National Country Party, National Party of Australia

| | |
|---|---|
| .294 05 | Liberal Party of Australia |
| .294 06 | Democratic Labor Party |
| .294 07 | Australian Labor Party |
| .294 09 | Other parties |

Add to base number 324.29409 the numbers following 0 in notation 03–08 from table under 324.24–324.29, e.g., Australian Democrats 324.294095

.294 1–.294 8    Parties in states and territories of Australia

Add to base number 324.294 the numbers following —94 in notation 941–948 from Table 2 for state or territory, e.g., parties in New South Wales 324.2944; then add 0* and to the result add the numbers following 324.2940 in 324.29401–324.29409, e.g., Australian Labor Party in New South Wales 324.294407

.296 9    Parties in Hawaii

.296 900 1–.296 900 9    Standard subdivisions

.296 901–.296 908    Parties in Hawaii

Add to base number 324.29690 the numbers following 324.273 in 324.2731–324.2738, e.g., Democratic Party in Hawaii 324.296906

**.3    Auxiliary party organizations**

Organizations attached to political parties, e.g., political clubs, women's organizations, youth groups

Class revolutionary and subversive branches of political parties in 322.42

*For auxiliary organizations of international party organizations, see 324.1*

.309 4–.309 9    Geographic areas in modern world other than specific countries and states

Do not use for auxiliary party organizations in a specific country or state; class in 324.24–324.29 plus notation 014 from table under 324.24–324.29

*Add 00 for standard subdivisions; see instructions at beginning of Table 1

**.4          Interest and pressure groups**

Class here influence and activities of groups in extragovernmental processes; political action committees (PACs, United States fund-raising groups); comprehensive works on lobbying

Class comprehensive works on interest groups, political action groups in 322.4; class comprehensive works on pressure groups in 322.43

> *For legislative lobbying, see 328.38. For lobbying for a specific goal, see the goal, e.g., lobbying for penal reform 364.6*

**.5          Nominating candidates**

Class here campaigns for nomination; results of campaigns, e.g., delegate counts

Class comprehensive works on nomination and election campaigns in 324.9

**.509 4–.509 9**          Geographic areas in modern world other than specific countries and states

Do not use for nominating party candidates in a specific country or state; class in 324.24–324.29 plus notation 015 from table under 324.24–324.29

**.52          Nominating by caucuses and co-optation**

**.520 94–.520 99**          Geographic areas in modern world other than specific countries and states

Do not use for nominating party candidates by caucuses and co-optation in a specific country or state; class in 324.24–324.29 plus notation 0152 from table under 324.24–324.29

**.54          Nominating by primaries**

**.540 94–.540 99**          Geographic areas in modern world other than specific countries and states

Do not use for nominating party candidates by primaries in a specific country or state; class in 324.24–324.29 plus notation 0154 from table under 324.24–324.29

**.56          Nominating by conventions**

> *For selecting delegates to nominating conventions by caucuses and co-optation, see 324.52; for selecting delegates to nominating conventions by primaries, see 324.54*

> *See also 324.21 for convention finance*

**.560 94–.560 99**          Geographic areas in modern world other than specific countries and states

Do not use for nominating party candidates by conventions in a specific country or state; class in 324.24–324.29 plus notation 0156 from table under 324.24–324.29

**.6**     **Election systems and procedures; suffrage**

Standard subdivisions are added for election systems and procedures, suffrage together; for election systems alone; for election procedures alone

Class here comprehensive works on systems and procedures for nominations and elections

Class conduct of election campaigns in 324.7

*For nominating candidates, see 324.5; for manuals outlining election procedures that discuss laws or administrative regulations, see 342.07*

**.62**     Suffrage

Class here qualifications for voting, voting rights

Class comprehensive works on political rights in 323.5

**[.620 82]**     Women's suffrage

Do not use; class in 324.623

**.623**     Women's suffrage

**.63**     Electoral systems

Including direct and indirect elections, electoral colleges

*For electoral basis of representation in legislative bodies, see 328.3347*

**.64**     Registration of voters

**.65**     Voting procedures

Including absentee voting, ballots and ballot systems, counting and certification of votes, election monitoring, election officials, procedures for contested elections, voting machines

**.66**     Election fraud

Class irregularities in campaign finance in 324.78; class election fraud as a crime in 364.1324

**.68**     Recall

Removal of an official from office by popular vote

**.7**     **Conduct of election campaigns**

Variant name: practical politics

Class here public relations for conduct of political election campaigns

*See also 324.5 for conduct of campaigns for nomination*

**.72**     Strategy

Including citizen participation

*For use and effect of media, see 324.73*

**.73**     Use and effect of media

Class here advertising for political election campaigns

.78          Campaign finance

Class party finance in 324.21

**.9          History and geographic treatment of elections**

Class here election returns and results, studies of voting behavior; comprehensive works on campaigns

Class platforms, campaign literature in 324.23

*For campaigns for nomination, see 324.5; for conduct of election campaigns, see 324.7*

.900 1–.900 8          Standard subdivisions

[.900 9]          History, geographic treatment, biography

Do not use for comprehensive works on history; class in 324.9. Do not use for geographic treatment; class in 324.91–324.99

[.900 901–.900 905]          Historical periods

Do not use; class in 324.901–324.905

[.900 92]          Biography

Do not use; class in 324.092

.901–.905          Historical periods

Add to base number 324.90 the numbers following —090 in notation 0901–0905 from Table 1, e.g., election campaigns in 19th century 324.9034

.91–.99          Geographic treatment

Add to base number 324.9 notation 1–9 from Table 2, e.g., political campaigns in the United Kingdom 324.941; then to the result add historical period numbers from appropriate subdivisions of 930–990, e.g., election campaign of 1997 in the United Kingdom 324.9410859. In all cases use one 0* except 00† for North America and South America, e.g., the election of 1992 in United States 324.9730928, elections in South America between World Wars 324.980033

**325          International migration and colonization**

Standard subdivisions are added for international migration and colonization together, for international migration alone

Including population transfers

Class interdisciplinary works on international movement of people in 304.82. Class movement of people associated with a specific event in world history with the event in 909, e.g., Jewish Diaspora 909.04924; class movement of people associated with a specific event in the history of a country or region with the event in 930–990, e.g., emigration of Jews as a consequence of the Holocaust 940.5318142

*Add 00 for standard subdivisions; see instructions at beginning of Table 1
†Add 000 for standard subdivisions; see instructions at beginning of Table 1

[.094–.099]    Specific continents, countries, localities in modern world

>Do not use; class in 325.4–325.9

## .1    Immigration

*For illegal immigration, see 364.137*

[.109 4–.109 9]    Specific continents, countries, localities in modern world

>Do not use; class in 325.4–325.9

## .2    Emigration

[.209 3–.209 9]    Specific continents, countries, localities

>Do not use; class in 325.23–325.29

### .21    Refugees

>Class here displaced persons, exiles, political refugees

>Class interdisciplinary works on displaced persons, refugees in 305.906914

.210 93–.210 99    Specific continents, countries, localities

>>Refugees from one country in another country are classed in country of origin, e.g., Polish political refugees in Canada 325.21094380971

### .23–.29    Emigration from specific continents, countries, localities

>Add to base number 325.2 notation 3–9 from Table 2, e.g., emigration from Japan 325.252, emigration from Japan to United States 325.2520973

## .3    Colonization

>Class here exercise of political dominion over distant territories, decolonization

.309 3    Ancient world

>Do not use for colonization by specific countries in ancient world; class in 325.33

.309 4–.309 9    Specific continents, countries, localities in modern world

>Do not use for colonization by specific countries in modern world; class in 325.34–325.39. Do not use for colonization in specific places in modern world; class in 325.4–325.9

### .32    Imperialism

>The policy, practice, or advocacy of acquiring political dominion over territories outside the natural boundaries of a country

>Class comprehensive works on foreign policy in 327.1

### .33–.39    Colonization by specific countries

>Add to base number 325.3 notation 3–9 from Table 2, e.g., colonization by United Kingdom 325.341, colonization by United Kingdom in West Africa 325.3410966

>Class imperialism of specific countries in 325.32093–325.32099

**.4–.9     International migration to and colonization in specific continents, countries, localities in modern world**

> Add to base number 325 notation 4–9 from Table 2, e.g., migration to Israel 325.5694
>> Subdivisions are added for either or both topics in heading
>
> Class emigration from specific continents, countries, localities in modern world to specific continents, countries, localities in 325.24–325.29; class colonization by specific countries in modern world in specific continents, countries, localities in 325.34–325.39; class comprehensive works on colonization by and in specific continents, countries, localities in modern world in 325.3094–325.3099

# 326     Slavery and emancipation

> Standard subdivisions are added for slavery and emancipation together, for slavery alone
>
> Class interdisciplinary works on slavery in 306.362

**.8     Emancipation**

> Class here abolitionism, antislavery movements

# 327     International relations

> Class military science in 355; class interdisciplinary works on relations among countries in 303.482
>
> *For international relations with respect to a specific subject, see the subject, e.g., commerce between United Kingdom and communist bloc 382.094101717*
>
> *See Manual at 341 vs. 327*

### SUMMARY

| | |
|---|---|
| 327.02–.09 | **Standard subdivisions** |
| .1 | **Foreign policy and specific topics in international relations** |
| .2 | **Diplomacy** |
| .3–.9 | **Foreign relations of specific continents, countries, localities** |

**[.01]     Philosophy and theory**

> Do not use; class in 327.101

**.06     Organizations**

> *For intergovernmental organizations, see 341.2*

**[.068]     Management**

> Do not use; class in 353.13

**.09     History, geographic treatment, biography**

> Class here diplomatic history, international relations of or in areas, regions, places in general, not limited by continent, country, locality, e.g., foreign relations of former Communist bloc 327.091717

**.092     Biography**

> Do not use for diplomats; class in 327.2092

[.093–.099]      Foreign relations of specific continents, countries, localities

> Do not use; class in 327.3–327.9

**.1        Foreign policy and specific topics in international relations**

> Standard subdivisions are added for foreign policy
>
> Class here imperialism in international relations, international politics, power politics
>
> Class comprehensive works on imperialism, imperialism as national policy in 325.32
>
> *For diplomacy, see 327.2*

.101        Philosophy and theory of international relations, of foreign policy

> Including role and position of small states, economic bases of international relations
>
> Class here geopolitics in international relations, nature of power in international relations
>
> Class comprehensive works on geopolitics in 320.12

.102–.108      Standard subdivisions of foreign policy

.109        History, geographic treatment, biography of foreign policy

.109 2      Biography

> Do not use for diplomats; class in 327.2092

[.109 3–.109 9]      Foreign relations of specific continents, countries, localities

> Do not use; class in 327.3–327.9

.11        Specific means of attaining foreign policy goals

> Including government information services
>
> *For espionage and subversion, see 327.12; for propaganda and war of nerves, see 327.14*

.111        Economic activities

> Including foreign aid
>
> Class boycotts and sanctions in 327.117

.112        Balance of power

.114        Spheres of influence

.116        Alliances

> Class here collective security

.117        Use of force and threats of force

> Including boycotts, sanctions, terrorism
>
> Class war of nerves in 327.14; class war in 355.02

.12       Espionage and subversion

Standard subdivisions are added for either or both topics in heading

Class here interdisciplinary works on espionage, subversion, intelligence gathering

*For military espionage, see 355.3432; for military subversion, see 355.3437*

.120 93–.120 99       Specific continents, countries, localities

Do not use for espionage and subversion by specific nations; class in 327.123–327.129

.123–.129       Espionage and subversion by specific nations

Add to base number 327.12 notation 3–9 from Table 2, e.g., espionage by France 327.1244; then for espionage and subversion by that country in another area add 0* and to the result add notation 1–9 from Table 2, e.g., espionage by France in developing countries 327.124401724
Subdivisions are added for either or both topics in heading

.14       Propaganda and war of nerves

Including disinformation activities

Class comprehensive works on political propaganda in 320.014; class comprehensive works on use of force and threats of force in 327.117; class interdisciplinary works on propaganda in 303.375

.16       International conflict

Class war in 355.02; class conflict involving specific means of attaining foreign policy goals in 327.117

*See also 327.17 for peaceful resolution of international conflict*

.17       International cooperation

Class here internationalism, conflict resolution

Class international governmental organizations in 341.2; class interdisciplinary works on conflict resolution in 303.69

*For law of international cooperation, see 341.7*

.172       Promotion of peace and international order

.174       Disarmament and arms control

.174 3       Conventional weapons limitation

.174 5       Chemical and biological disarmament

Standard subdivisions are added for either or both topics in heading

Class here disarmament of weapons of mass destruction, of specific chemical and biological weapons

*For nuclear disarmament, see 327.1747*

*Add 00 for standard subdivisions; see instructions at beginning of Table 1

.174 7                          Nuclear disarmament

                                Class here strategic arms limitation, limitation of specific nuclear
                                weapons

**.2          Diplomacy**

                    Including protocol

                    Use 327.2 for methods and style of diplomacy; 327 for substance and content of
                    diplomatic relations

                    *For law of diplomacy, see 341.33*

.209 2                          Biography

                                Do not use for biography of diplomats of specific nations; class in
                                327.3–327.9

**.3–.9      Foreign relations of specific continents, countries, localities**

                    Class here foreign policy

                    Add to base number 327 notation 3–9 from Table 2, e.g., foreign relations of
                    Brazil 327.81, of eastern European countries 327.47, in Middle East 327.56;
                    then, for relations between that nation or region and another nation or region,
                    add 0* and to the result add notation 1–9 from Table 2, e.g., relations between
                    Brazil and France 327.81044, between Brazil and Arab world 327.810174927

                    Give priority in notation to the nation or region emphasized. If emphasis is
                    equal, give priority to the nation or region coming first in Table 2
                        (Option: Give priority in notation to the nation or region requiring local
                        emphasis, e.g., libraries in the United States class foreign relations between
                        the United States and France in 327.73044)

                    Class specific topics in international relations of specific nations or regions in
                    327.11–327.17

                    *See Manual at T1—092: Comprehensive biography: Public figures; also at
                    920.009, 920.03–920.09 vs. 909.09, 909.1–909.8, 930–990*

**328          The legislative process**

                    Class here legislative branch, legislative bodies

                    *See Manual at 909, 930–990 vs. 320*

### SUMMARY

| | |
|---|---|
| 328.06 | **Organizations and management** |
| .1 | **Rules and procedures of legislative bodies** |
| .2 | **Initiative and referendum** |
| .3 | **Specific topics of legislative bodies** |
| .4–.9 | **The legislative process in specific continents, countries, localities in modern world** |

.060 1                          International organizations

                                Class here interparliamentary unions

*Add 00 for standard subdivisions; see instructions at beginning of Table 1

.068          Management

> Class here public administration of legislative branch

> Do not use for management of members' offices; class in 328.331068. Do not use for public administration of legislative branch of specific jurisdiction; class in 328.4–328.9 plus notation 0068 from table under 328.4–328.9

[.094–.099]      The legislative process in specific continents, countries, localities in modern world

> Do not use; class in 328.4–328.9

**.1      Rules and procedures of legislative bodies**

> Including rules and procedures for reporting legislative sessions, e.g., television coverage

> Class comprehensive rules of order in 060.42

> *For rules of committees of legislative bodies, see 328.3653*

.109 4–.109 9     Specific continents and localities in modern world

> Do not use for rules and procedures of specific legislative bodies in modern world; class in 328.4–328.9 plus notation 05 from table under 328.4–328.9

**.2      Initiative and referendum**

.209 4–.209 9     Specific continents and localities in modern world

> Do not use for treatment in specific jurisdictions in modern world; class in 328.24–328.29

.22          Initiative

.220 94–.220 99    Specific continents and localities in modern world

> Do not use for initiative in specific jurisdictions in modern world; class in 328.24–328.29

.23          Referendum

.230 94–.230 99    Specific continents and localities in modern world

> Do not use for referendum in specific jurisdictions in modern world; class in 328.24–328.29

.24–.29      Initiative and referendum in specific jurisdictions in modern world

> Add to base number 328.2 notation 4–9 from Table 2, e.g., initiative in California 328.2794
> Subdivisions are added for either or both topics in heading

**.3      Specific topics of legislative bodies**

> Class specific topics of legislative bodies of specific jurisdictions in modern world in 328.4–328.9, plus notation 07 from table under 328.4–328.9

> *For rules and procedures of legislative bodies, see 328.1*

## SUMMARY

[.301–.303]   Standard subdivisions

> Do not use; class in 328.01–328.03

.304   Legislative reform

> *For reform of basis of representation, see 328.334; for reform of internal organization, see 328.36*

[.305–.309]   Standard subdivisions

> Do not use; class in 328.05–328.09

.31   Upper houses

> Class comprehensive works on upper and lower houses in 328.39. Class a specific aspect of upper houses with the aspect, e.g., treaty making power of upper houses 328.346

.32   Lower houses

> Class a specific aspect of lower houses with the aspect, e.g., basis of representation of lower houses 328.334

.33   Members and membership

> Including qualifications, term of office, term limitation

> Class comprehensive biography of members in 328.092; class biography of members of specific legislative bodies in modern world in 328.4–328.9, plus notation 092 from table under 328.4–328.9

> > *For personal privileges, see 328.347; for officers and leaders, see 328.362; for discipline of members, see 328.366*

.331   Work and activity of individual members

> Class here constituency services, work of members' offices

.334   Basis of representation

.334 5   Election districts

> Class here apportionment and reapportionment, redistricting

> > *For districts used in proportional representation, see 328.3347*

.334 55   Gerrymandering

.334 7   Proportional representation

.34       Powers, privileges, restrictions

Class here legislative duties

Class enactment of legislation in 328.37

.341       General powers

*For treaty and war powers, see 328.346*

.341 2       Financial power

Power over appropriation, borrowing and lending, currency, taxation

.341 3       General economic and public welfare powers

.345       Extralegislative powers

Including control and oversight of judicial branch

Class here hearings

*For hearings on a specific subject, see the subject, e.g., hearings on laws 348.01*

.345 2       Investigative power

Including ombudsman role

Class interdisciplinary works on ombudsmen in 352.88

.345 3       Judicial power

Including power to impeach

.345 4       Electoral power

.345 5       Power over appointments

.345 6       Control and oversight of executive branch

Class here general relations with executive branch

Class cabinet system of executives in 321.8043; class control of foreign relations in 328.346

*For ombudsman role, see 328.3452*

.346       Treaty and war powers

Class here control of international relations

.347       Personal privileges of legislators

*For legislative immunity, see 328.348*

.348       Legislative immunity

.349       Restrictions on legislative power

Including constitutional restrictions, checks exercised by other branches and by the electorate

.35       Sessions

Class a specific aspect of legislative sessions with the aspect, e.g., internal organization of a session 328.36

| .36 | Internal organization and discipline |
|---|---|

Including caucuses

Class legislative reference bureaus in 027.65; class party caucuses in 328.369; class comprehensive works on rules and procedures in 328.1

| .362 | Officers and leaders |
|---|---|

Class party organization in legislative bodies in 328.369

| .365 | Committees |
|---|---|

Class committee hearings and reports on a specific subject that emphasize proposed legislation with the subject in 340, e.g., hearing on bills governing armed services 343.013; class committee hearings and reports on a specific subject that do not emphasize proposed legislation with the subject in 001–999, e.g., general reports on military affairs 355

| .365 3 | Rules |
|---|---|

Including rules of specific committees, of specific types of committees

| .365 7 | Specific types of committees |
|---|---|

Including conference, joint, select committees

Class rules of specific types of committees in 328.3653; class specific types of committees with specific subject jurisdiction in 328.3658

| .365 8 | Committees of specific subject jurisdiction |
|---|---|

Including rules committees

Class rules of committees of specific subject jurisdiction in 328.3653

| .366 | Discipline of members |
|---|---|
| .369 | Party organization in legislative bodies |

Including opposition, opposition parties, party caucuses

| .37 | Enactment of legislation |
|---|---|

Including repeal of legislation

*See also 328.365 for committee procedures*

| .372 | Origin of legislation |
|---|---|

Submission by members, by executive, by outside interests

| .373 | Drafting legislation |
|---|---|
| .375 | Passage of legislation |

Including votes and voting procedures

| .377 | Enactment of resolutions |
|---|---|

| | |
|---|---|
| .378 | Enactment of special types of legislation |

Including private bills, procedures for legislative enactment of budgets

> *For enactment of resolutions, see 328.377; for enactment of budgets,*
> *see 352.48*

| | |
|---|---|
| .38 | Lobbying |
| .39 | Forms of legislative bodies |

Unicameral, bicameral

Do not use for description of various legislatures that happen to be of one form or another

> *For upper houses, see 328.31; for lower houses, see 328.32*

| | |
|---|---|
| **.4–.9** | **The legislative process in specific continents, countries, localities in modern world** |

Add to base number 328 notation 4–9 from Table 2, e.g., the legislative process in the Canadian Parliament or in the provincial legislatures of Canada 328.71, in eastern Europe 328.47; then add further as follows:

| | |
|---|---|
| 001–008 | Standard subdivisions |
| [009] | History and biography |
| | Do not use; class in 09 |
| 01 | Journals and calendars |
| 02 | Debates |
| | Including collections of speeches by individual members |
| 03 | Abstracts |
| 04 | Other documents |
| | Class here series of miscellaneous parliamentary papers and documents |
| 05 | Rules and procedures |
| | Including legislative manuals |
| | Class committee rules in 07653 |
| 07 | Specific topics of legislative bodies |
| | *For rules and procedures, see 05* |
| [0701–0703] | Standard subdivisions |
| | Do not use; class in 001–003 |
| 0704 | Legislative reform |
| [0705–0708] | Standard subdivisions |
| | Do not use; class in 005–008 |
| [0709] | History and biography |
| | Do not use; class in 09 |
| 071–079 | Other topics of legislative bodies |
| | Add to 07 the numbers following 328.3 in 328.31–328.39, e.g., specific committees 07658 |
| 09 | History and biography |
| 092 | Biography |
| | *See Manual at T1—092: Comprehensive biography: Public figures; also at 920.009, 920.03–920.09 vs. 909.09, 909.1–909.8, 930–990* |

> *For initiative and referendum in specific jurisdictions in modern world, see*
> *328.24–328.29*

**[329]**     **[Unassigned]**

Most recently used in Edition 18

# 330     Economics

Including interdisciplinary works on economic rights

Class here comprehensive works on economics and management

Unless other instructions are given, observe the following table of preference, e.g., finance as an economic factor in international economics 332.042 (*not* 337):

| | |
|---|---|
| Cooperatives | 334 |
| Public finance | 336 |
| Economics of labor, finance, land, energy | 331–333 |
| Production, Commerce (381–382), Communications (383–384), Transportation (385–388) | 338 |
| Macroeconomics and related topics | 339 |
| International economics | 337 |
| Socialism and related systems | 335 |

Class economic rights in the sense of welfare rights in 361.614

> *For management, see 658. For a specific kind or aspect of economic rights, see the kind or aspect, e.g., political aspects of property rights 323.46*
>
> *See Manual at 330 vs. 650, 658*

## SUMMARY

| | |
|---|---|
| 330.01–.09 | **Standard subdivisions** |
| .1 | **Systems, schools, theories** |
| .9 | **Economic situation and conditions** |
| | |
| 331 | **Labor economics** |
| .01–.09 | **Standard subdivisions and industrial relations by industry and occupation** |
| .1 | **Labor force and market** |
| .2 | **Conditions of employment** |
| .3 | **Workers by age group** |
| .4 | **Women workers** |
| .5 | **Workers by personal attributes other than age** |
| .6 | **Workers by ethnic and national origin** |
| .7 | **Labor by industry and occupation** |
| .8 | **Labor unions, labor-management bargaining and disputes** |
| | |
| 332 | **Financial economics** |
| .01–.09 | **Standard subdivisions, personal finance, special topics of financial economics** |
| .1 | **Banks** |
| .2 | **Specialized banking institutions** |
| .3 | **Credit and loan institutions** |
| .4 | **Money** |
| .5 | **Barter, commercial paper, social credit money** |
| .6 | **Investment** |
| .7 | **Credit** |
| .8 | **Interest** |
| .9 | **Counterfeiting, forgery, alteration** |

| 333 | | Economics of land and energy |
|---|---|---|
| | .001–.009 | Standard subdivisions |
| | .01–.08 | [Theories and land surveys] |
| | .1 | Public ownership of land |
| | .2 | Ownership of land by nongovernmental groups |
| | .3 | Private ownership of land |
| | .4 | Absentee ownership |
| | .5 | Renting and leasing land |
| | .7 | Land, recreational and wilderness areas, energy |
| | .8 | Subsurface resources |
| | .9 | Other natural resources |
| | | |
| 334 | | Cooperatives |
| | .1 | Housing cooperatives |
| | .2 | Banking and credit cooperatives |
| | .5 | Consumer cooperatives |
| | .6 | Producers' cooperatives |
| | .7 | Benefit societies |
| | | |
| 335 | | Socialism and related systems |
| | .001–.009 | Standard subdivisions |
| | .02 | Utopian systems and schools |
| | .1 | Systems of English origin |
| | .2 | Systems of French origin |
| | .3 | Systems of American origin |
| | .4 | Marxian systems |
| | .5 | Democratic socialism |
| | .6 | Fascism |
| | .7 | Christian socialism |
| | .8 | Other systems |
| | | |
| 336 | | Public finance |
| | .001–.008 | Standard subdivisions |
| | .01–.09 | [Public finance by governmental level; revenue; history, geographic treatment, biography; associations of sovereign states] |
| | .1 | Nontax revenues |
| | .2 | Taxes |
| | .3 | Public debt and expenditures |
| | .4–.9 | Public finance of specific continents, countries, localities in modern world |
| | | |
| 337 | | International economics |
| | .1 | Multilateral economic cooperation |
| | .3–.9 | Foreign economic policies and relations of specific jurisdictions and groups of jurisdictions |
| | | |
| 338 | | Production |
| | .001–.008 | Standard subdivisions |
| | .01–.09 | [General topics] |
| | .1 | Agriculture |
| | .2 | Extraction of minerals |
| | .3 | Other extractive industries |
| | .4 | Secondary industries and services |
| | .5 | General production economics |
| | .6 | Organization of production |
| | .7 | Business enterprises |
| | .8 | Combinations |
| | .9 | Economic development and growth |
| | | |
| 339 | | Macroeconomics and related topics |
| | .2 | Distribution of income and wealth |
| | .3 | Product and income accounts |
| | .4 | Factors affecting income and wealth |
| | .5 | Macroeconomic policy |

| | |
|---|---|
| .01 | Philosophy and theory |

Do not use for theories; class in 330.1

| | |
|---|---|
| .015 1 | Mathematical principles |

*See also 330.1543 for mathematical economics as a school of economics*

| | |
|---|---|
| .015 195 | Statistical mathematics |

Class here econometrics

*See Manual at 519.5, T1—015195 vs. 001.422, T1—0727*

| | |
|---|---|
| .02–.08 | Standard subdivisions |
| .09 | History, geographic treatment, biography of economics as a discipline |

Do not use for economic situation and conditions; class in 330.9

| | |
|---|---|
| **.1** | **Systems, schools, theories** |

*For economic rent, see 333.012; for law of supply and demand, see 338.521*

| | |
|---|---|
| .12 | Systems |
| .122 | Free enterprise economy |

Including open economy (the economy of an area in which trade with other areas is unrestricted)

Class here capitalism

Class laissez-faire economic theory in 330.153

*See also 382.7 for trade barriers and restrictions*

| | |
|---|---|
| .124 | Planned economies |

Class here command economies

Class schools of thought featuring planned economies in 335

*See also 338.9 for economic planning*

| | |
|---|---|
| .126 | Mixed economies |

Including interventionism, social market economy, welfare state systems

*See also 330.1556 for welfare economics as a school of economic thought*

| | |
|---|---|
| .15 | Schools of economic thought |

*For socialist and related schools, see 335*

| | |
|---|---|
| .151 | Pre-classical schools |

*For physiocracy, see 330.152*

| | |
|---|---|
| .151 2 | Ancient and medieval theories |
| .151 3 | Mercantilism |

| .152 | Physiocracy |
|---|---|

Class here school of Quesnay

| .153 | Classical economics |
|---|---|

Class here schools of Smith, Ricardo, Malthus, Mill, Say; laissez-faire economic theory

*See also 330.157 for neoclassical school*

| .154 | Historical and mathematical schools |
|---|---|
| .154 2 | Historical school |

Class here the schools of Roscher, Knies, Hildebrand, Schmoller, Bücher, Knapp

| .154 3 | Mathematical school |
|---|---|

Class here schools of Cournot, Dupuit, Pareto

Class mathematical economics in 330.0151

*See also 330.157 for marginal utility school*

| .155 | Miscellaneous schools |
|---|---|

Only those named below

Including school of Henry George (single-tax school)

| .155 2 | Institutional economics |
|---|---|

Class economics of institutions in 330

| .155 3 | Chicago school of economics (Monetarism) |
|---|---|

Class monetary theory in 332.401

| .155 4 | Supply-side economics |
|---|---|
| .155 6 | Welfare economics school |
| .156 | Keynesian economics |

Class here post-Keynesian economics

| .157 | Marginal utility school |
|---|---|

Variant names: Austrian school, neoclassical school

Class here schools of Jevons, Menger, Walras, Wieser, Böhm-Bawerk, Von Mises; utility theory

*See also 330.1543 for schools of Cournot, Dupuit, Pareto*

| (.159) | Socialist and related schools |
|---|---|

(Optional number; prefer 335)

Add to base number 330.159 the numbers following 335 in 335.1–335.8, e.g., Marxian systems 330.1594

| .16 | Theories of wealth |
|---|---|

Class macroeconomic aspects of wealth in 339

| | |
|---|---|
| .17 | Theories of property |
| **.9** | **Economic situation and conditions** |

> Standard subdivisions are added for either or both topics in heading
>
> Class here economic geography, economic history; works describing situation and conditions at both macroeconomic and microeconomic levels
>
> Class policies to promote economic growth and development in 338.9; class macroeconomic policies in 339.5

| | |
|---|---|
| .900 1–.900 8 | Standard subdivisions |
| [.900 9] | History, geographic treatment, biography |

> Do not use for comprehensive works on history, on geographic treatment; class in 330.9

| | |
|---|---|
| [.900 901–.900 905] | Historical periods |

> Do not use; class in 330.901–330.905

| | |
|---|---|
| [.900 91] | Areas, regions, places in general |

> Do not use; class in 330.91

| | |
|---|---|
| [.900 92] | Biography |

> Do not use; class in 330.092

| | |
|---|---|
| [.900 93–.900 99] | Specific continents, countries, localities |

> Do not use; class in 330.93–330.99

| | |
|---|---|
| .901–.905 | Historical periods |

> Add to base number 330.90 the numbers following —090 in notation 0901–0905 from Table 1, e.g., economic situation in 1960–1969 330.9046

| | |
|---|---|
| .91 | Areas, regions, places in general |

> Add to base number 330.91 the numbers following —1 in notation 11–19 from Table 2, e.g., economic situation and conditions in developing countries 330.91724; then add 0* and to the result add the numbers following 909 in 909.1–909.8, e.g., economic situation and conditions in developing countries in 1980–1989 330.917240828
>> Use 0 plus notation 0112 from Table 1 for forecasting and forecasts, e.g., forecasting and forecasts of economic situation and conditions in developing countries 330.9172400112. Do not use historical periods for forecasting and forecasts
>
> (Option: Class in 910.13301)

*Add 00 for standard subdivisions; see instructions at beginning of Table 1

.93–.99     Specific continents, countries, localities

Add to base number 330.9 notation 3–9 from Table 2, e.g., economic
situation and conditions in France 330.944; then to the result add historical
period numbers from appropriate subdivisions of 930–990, e.g., economic
situation and conditions in France under Louis XIV 330.944033. In all cases
use one 0* except 00† for North and South America, e.g., economic situation
in the United States during Reconstruction period 330.97308, in South
America in 20th century 330.980033

Use 0 or 00 plus notation 0112 from Table 1 for forecasting and
forecasts, e.g., forecasting and forecasts of economic situation and
conditions in France 330.94400112. Do not use historical periods for
forecasting and forecasts

(Option: Class in 910.13303–910.13309)

---

> ## 331–333 Economics of labor, finance, land, energy

Class comprehensive works on economics of labor, finance, land, energy in
330; class comprehensive works on labor, capital, land considered as factors of
production in 338.01

## 331     Labor economics

Class here industrial relations, interdisciplinary works on labor

Unless other instructions are given, observe the following table of preference,
e.g., compensation of women in banking 331.42813321 (*not* 331.2813321 or
331.7613321):

| | |
|---|---|
| Choice of vocation | 331.702 |
| Labor force by personal attributes | 331.3–331.6 |
| Labor force and market | 331.1 |
| Conditions of employment | 331.2 |
| Labor unions, labor-management bargaining and disputes | 331.8 |
| Labor by industry and occupation (*except* 331.702) | 331.7 |

Class economic conditions of working class in 330.9; class relations between
management and labor unions in 331.8; class full employment policy in 339.5

*For a specific noneconomic aspect of labor, see the aspect, e.g., relation of
labor movements to the state 322.2, managerial aspects of labor 658.3*

*See also 305.562 for sociology of working class; also 306.36 for sociology of
labor*

---

*Add 00 for standard subdivisions; see instructions at beginning of Table 1
†Add 000 for standard subdivisions; see instructions at beginning of Table 1

## SUMMARY

| | |
|---|---|
| 331.01–.09 | **Standard subdivisions and industrial relations by industry and occupation** |
| .1 | **Labor force and market** |
| .2 | **Conditions of employment** |
| .3 | **Workers by age group** |
| .4 | **Women workers** |
| .5 | **Workers by personal attributes other than age** |
| .6 | **Workers by ethnic and national origin** |
| .7 | **Labor by industry and occupation** |
| .8 | **Labor unions, labor-management bargaining and disputes** |

.01        Philosophy and theory

Notation 01 from Table 1 as modified below

Do not use for value of labor; class in 331.013

.011        Rights and position of labor

Do not use for systems analysis applied to labor economics; class in 331.01. Do not use for systems of labor; class in 331.117

Standard subdivisions are added for either or both topics in heading

Class here employment rights

*For open shop, right to work, see 331.8892*

.011 2        Industrial democracy

Class producer cooperatives in 334.6; class guild socialism in 335.15; class syndicalism in 335.82; class worker control of industry in 338.6; class employee representation in management discussed from the managerial viewpoint in 658.3152

*For role of labor unions in industrial democracy, see 331.88*

.012        Satisfactions and dissatisfactions of labor

Do not use for classification of occupations; class in 331.70012

Standard subdivisions are added for either or both topics in heading

.013        Freedom, dignity, value of labor

.04        Industrial relations by industry and occupation

Standard subdivisions are added for either or both topics in heading

.041        Industrial relations in industries and occupations other than extractive, manufacturing, construction

Standard subdivisions are added for industries, occupations, or both

Class here industrial relations in service industries and occupations

.041 000 1–.041 000 9        Standard subdivisions

.041 001–.041 999      Subdivisions for industrial relations in industries and occupations other than extractive, manufacturing, construction

> Add to base number 331.041 notation 001–999, e.g., industrial relations in clerical occupations 331.04165137
>> Subdivisions are added for industries, occupations, or both

.042–.049      Industrial relations in extractive, manufacturing, construction industries and occupations

> Add to base number 331.04 the numbers following 6 in 620–690, e.g., industrial relations in chemical industries 331.046
>> Subdivisions are added for industries, occupations, or both

.08      Groups of people

> Do not use for discrimination; class in 331.133

> Class here labor force by personal attributes [*formerly* 331.1143], comprehensive works on minorities in the labor force

[.081]      People by gender or sex

> Do not use; class in 331.56

[.082]      Women

> Do not use; class in 331.4

[.083–.084]      Age groups

> Do not use; class in 331.3

[.086]      People by miscellaneous social attributes

> Do not use; class in 331.5

[.087]      People with disabilities and illnesses, gifted people

> Do not use; class in 331.5

[.088]      Occupational and religious groups

> Do not use for religious groups; class in 331.58. Do not use for occupational groups; class in 331.7

[.089]      Ethnic and national groups

> Do not use; class in 331.6

.1      **Labor force and market**

> Class here comprehensive works on employment and unemployment

> Class employment in 331.125; class unemployment in 331.137

### SUMMARY

| | |
|---|---|
| **331.11** | **Labor force** |
| **.12** | **Labor market** |
| **.13** | **Discrimination in employment, labor shortages, unemployment** |

| .11 | Labor force |
|---|---|

Class here human resources, labor supply, size of labor force, work force

Class labor force in relation to demand for labor in 331.12

*See also 331.8732 for union membership*

| .114 | Qualifications |
|---|---|

| .114 2 | Qualifications by level of skills |
|---|---|

Including semiskilled, unskilled employees

Use of this number for comprehensive works on qualifications discontinued; class in 331.114

| .114 22 | Skilled workers |
|---|---|

Use of this number for qualifications by level of skills discontinued; class in 331.1142

| [.114 224] | Skilled workers |
|---|---|

Number discontinued; class in 331.11422

| [.114 23] | Qualifications by level of education |
|---|---|

Relocated to 331.1144

| [.114 3] | Labor force by personal attributes |
|---|---|

Comprehensive works on labor force by personal attributes relocated to 331.08; programs for workplace diversity relocated to 331.133

| .114 4 | Qualifications by level of education [*formerly* 331.11423] |
|---|---|

| .114 43 | High school graduates |
|---|---|

| .114 45 | College graduates |
|---|---|

Regardless of degree obtained

| .117 | Systems of labor |
|---|---|

*See also 306.36 for social aspects of systems of labor*

| .117 2 | Free labor |
|---|---|

| .117 3 | Compulsory labor |
|---|---|

| .117 32 | State labor (Drafted workers) |
|---|---|

| .117 34 | Slave labor |
|---|---|

| .118 | Labor productivity |
|---|---|

Class industrial productivity in 338.06

.119 Labor force by industry and occupation

Standard subdivisions are added for either or both topics in heading

Class qualifications of labor force by industry and occupation in 331.114; class systems of labor by industry and occupation in 331.117; class labor productivity by industry and occupation in 331.118; class comprehensive works on labor by industry and occupation in 331.7

.119 04 Special topics of labor force by industry and occupation

.119 042 Labor force in general categories of occupations

Including blue collar, civilian, governmental (public service), service, white collar occupations

.119 1 Labor force in industries and occupations other than extractive, manufacturing, construction

Standard subdivisions are added for industries, occupations, or both

Class here labor force in service industries and occupations

.119 100 01–.119 100 09 Standard subdivisions

.119 100 1–.119 199 9 Subdivisions for labor force in industries and occupations other than extractive, manufacturing, construction

Add to base number 331.1191 notation 001–999, e.g., labor force in stenography 331.11916513741; however, for labor force in general categories of occupations, e.g., governmental (public service) occupations, see 331.119042
Subdivisions are added for industries, occupations, or both

.119 2–.119 9 Labor force in extractive, manufacturing, construction industries and occupations

Add to base number 331.119 the numbers following 6 in 620–690, e.g., labor force in automotive manufacturing 331.119292
Subdivisions are added for industries, occupations, or both

.12 Labor market

Class here supply of labor in relation to demand

Class job creation in 331.120424

*For discrimination in employment, labor shortages, unemployment, underemployment, see 331.13*

### SUMMARY

| | | |
|---|---|---|
| 331.120 4 | **Special topics of labor market** | |
| .123 | **Demand for labor** | |
| .124 | **Job vacancies (Job openings)** | |
| .125 | **Labor actively employed** | |
| .126 | **Labor turnover** | |
| .127 | **Labor mobility** | |
| .128 | **Placement** | |
| .129 | **Labor market by industry and occupation** | |

.120 4 Special topics of labor market

.120 42            Government policy on labor market

> *For policy with respect to a specific aspect of labor force and market, see the aspect, e.g., assistance in finding jobs 331.128*
>
> *See also 362.85 for social programs for working class; also 370 for education*

.120 424          Full employment policies

Class here job creation

Class policies designed to secure full employment through fiscal and monetary policy in 339.5

> *See Manual at 331.120424 vs. 331.1377*

.123          Demand for labor

Class here labor requirements

> *For job vacancies, see 331.124; for shortages, see 331.136; for surpluses, see 331.137*

.123 1          Demand for labor in industries and occupations other than extractive, manufacturing, construction

Standard subdivisions are added for industries, occupations, or both

Class here demand for labor in service industries and occupations

.123 100 01–.123 100 09          Standard subdivisions

.123 100 1–.123 199 9          Subdivisions for demand for labor in industries and occupations other than extractive, manufacturing, construction

Add to base number 331.1231 notation 001–999, e.g., demand for teachers 331.12313711
     Subdivisions are added for industries, occupations, or both

.123 2–.123 9          Demand for labor in extractive, manufacturing, construction industries and occupations

Add to base number 331.123 the numbers following 6 in 620–690, e.g., demand for carpenters 331.12394
     Subdivisions are added for industries, occupations, or both

.124          Job vacancies (Job openings)

.124 1          Job vacancies in industries and occupations other than extractive, manufacturing, construction

Standard subdivisions are added for industries, occupations, or both

Class here job vacancies in service industries and occupations

.124 100 01–.124 100 09          Standard subdivisions

.124 100 1–.124 199 9          Subdivisions for job vacancies in industries and occupations other than extractive, manufacturing, construction

> Add to base number 331.1241 notation 001–999, e.g., opportunities in librarianship 331.124102
>> Subdivisions are added for industries, occupations, or both

.124 2–.124 9          Job vacancies in extractive, manufacturing, construction industries and occupations

> Add to base number 331.124 the numbers following 6 in 620–690, e.g., openings in paper manufacture 331.12476
>> Subdivisions are added for industries, occupations, or both

.125          Labor actively employed

> Class here employment, utilization of human resources, comprehensive works on employment and compensation

> Class comprehensive works on employment and unemployment in 331.1

> *For compensation, see 331.21*

> *See also 331.126 for turnover; also 331.137 for unemployment*

.125 1          Labor actively employed in industries and occupations other than extractive, manufacturing, construction

> Standard subdivisions are added for industries, occupations, or both

> Class here labor actively employed in service industries and occupations

.125 100 01–.125 100 09          Standard subdivisions

.125 100 1–.125 199 9          Subdivisions for labor actively employed in industries and occupations other than extractive, manufacturing, construction

> Add to base number 331.1251 notation 001–999, e.g., labor actively employed in education 331.125137
>> Subdivisions are added for industries, occupations, or both

.125 2–.125 9          Labor actively employed in extractive, manufacturing, construction industries and occupations

> Add to base number 331.125 the numbers following 6 in 620–690, e.g., labor actively employed in the plumbing industry 331.125961
>> Subdivisions are added for industries, occupations, or both

.126          Labor turnover

.126 1          Labor turnover in industries and occupations other than extractive, manufacturing, construction

> Standard subdivisions are added for industries, occupations, or both

> Class here turnover in service industries and occupations

.126 100 01–.126 100 09          Standard subdivisions

.126 100 1–.126 199 9          Subdivisions for turnover in industries and occupations other than extractive, manufacturing, construction

> Add to base number 331.1261 notation 001–999, e.g., turnover of nurses 331.126161073
>> Subdivisions are added for industries, occupations, or both

.126 2–.126 9          Labor turnover in extractive, manufacturing, construction industries and occupations

> Add to base number 331.126 the numbers following 6 in 620–690, e.g., turnover of miners 331.12622
>> Subdivisions are added for industries, occupations, or both

.127          Labor mobility

.127 09          History and biography

> Do not use for geographic treatment; class in 331.1279

.127 2          Occupational mobility

.127 9          Geographic mobility

.127 91          International mobility

> Including brain drain

.127 93–.127 99          Geographic mobility within specific countries and smaller areas

> Add to base number 331.1279 notation 3–9 from Table 2, e.g., mobility of labor within Canada 331.127971

> Class mobility between countries and continents in 331.12791

.128          Placement

> Class here employment agencies, job banks, labor exchanges, sources of job information

> Class job vacancies in 331.124

> *See also 362.0425 for employment services viewed as a solution to social welfare problems; also 650.14 for success in, techniques of job hunting*

.129          Labor market by industry and occupation

> Standard subdivisions are added for either or both topics in heading

> *For specific aspects of labor market by industry and occupation, see 331.123–331.128*

.129 04          Special topics of labor market by industry and occupation

.129 042          Labor market by general categories of occupations

> Including blue collar, civilian, governmental (public service), service, white collar occupations

.129 1          Labor market by industries and occupations other than extractive, manufacturing, construction

> Standard subdivisions are added for industries, occupations, or both

> Class here labor market in service industries and occupations

.129 100 01–.129 100 09        Standard subdivisions

.129 100 1–.129 199 9        Subdivisions for labor market by industries and occupations other than extractive, manufacturing, construction

> Add to base number 331.1291 notation 001–999, e.g., labor market in stenography 331.12916513741; however, for labor market in general categories of occupations, e.g., governmental (public service) occupations, see 331.129042
> Subdivisions are added for industries, occupations, or both

.129 2–.129 9        Labor market by extractive, manufacturing, construction industries and occupations

> Add to base number 331.129 the numbers following 6 in 620–690, e.g., labor market in automotive manufacturing 331.129292
> Subdivisions are added for industries, occupations, or both

.13        Discrimination in employment, labor shortages, unemployment

> Including underemployment

> Class here maladjustments in labor market, programs to prevent or provide relief from maladjustments

.133        Discrimination in employment

> Class here programs for workplace diversity [*formerly* 331.1143], affirmative action in employment, equal employment opportunity programs, hostile work environments

> Class discrimination against workers with specific personal attributes in 331.3–331.6; class personnel aspects of discrimination in government employment in 352.608; class comprehensive works on work environment in 331.256; class comprehensive works about personnel policies on discrimination in 658.3008

> > *For discrimination in relation to a specific aspect of industrial relations, see the aspect, e.g., discrimination as a factor affecting compensation 331.2153, discrimination by unions 331.8732*

.136        Labor shortages

.137        Unemployment

> Class here labor surpluses, unemployed people

.137 04        Kinds of unemployment

.137 041        Structural unemployment

> *For technological unemployment, see 331.137042*

.137 042        Technological unemployment

.137 044        Seasonal unemployment

| .137 045 | Frictional unemployment |
|---|---|
| .137 047 | Cyclical unemployment |
| [.137 09] | History, geographic treatment, biography |

Do not use; class in 331.1379

| .137 2 | Causes of unemployment |
|---|---|

*For macroeconomic causes, see 339. For a cause of unemployment that defines a specific kind of unemployment, see the kind in 331.13704, e.g., structural unemployment 331.137041*

| .137 3 | Effects of unemployment |
|---|---|
| .137 7 | Prevention and relief of unemployment |

Standard subdivisions are added for either or both topics in heading

*For a specific measure of prevention or relief, see the measure, e.g., work sharing 331.2572, economic stabilization 339.5, welfare 362.85*

*See Manual at 331.120424 vs. 331.1377*

| .137 8 | Unemployment among general groups of labor, unemployment by industry and occupation |
|---|---|

Class specific elements regardless of group, industry, occupation in 331.1372–331.1377

| .137 804 | General groups of unemployed people |
|---|---|

Groups defined by level of education, skill, experience

Class unemployed people having specific personal attributes in 331.3–331.6

| .137 81 | Unemployment in industries and occupations other than extractive, manufacturing, construction |
|---|---|

Standard subdivisions are added for industries, occupations, or both

Class here unemployment in service industries and occupations

| .137 810 001–.137 810 009 | Standard subdivisions |
|---|---|
| .137 810 01–.137 819 99 | Subdivisions for unemployment in industries and occupations other than extractive, manufacturing, construction |

Add to base number 331.13781 notation 001–999, e.g., unemployment in clerical occupations 331.1378165137
Subdivisions are added for industries, occupations, or both

.137 82–.137 89         Unemployment in extractive, manufacturing, construction industries and occupations

> Add to base number 331.1378 the numbers following 6 in 620–690, e.g., unemployment in the automotive industry 331.1378292
> > Subdivisions are added for industries, occupations, or both

.137 9                 History, geographic treatment, biography

> Class history of specific elements of unemployment in 331.1372–331.1377; class history of unemployment among general groups of labor and by industry and occupation in 331.1378

.137 900 1–.137 900 8       Standard subdivisions

[.137 900 9]               History

> Do not use; class in 331.1379

.137 901–.137 905          Historical periods

> Add to base number 331.13790 the numbers following —090 in notation 0901–0905 from Table 1, e.g., unemployment in 20th century 331.137904

.137 91–.137 99          Geographic treatment and biography

> Add to base number 331.1379 notation 1–9 from Table 2, e.g., unemployment in the United States 331.137973

> Class geographic treatment of specific elements of unemployment in 331.1372–331.1377; class geographic treatment and biography of unemployment among general groups of labor and by industry and occupation in 331.1378

.2            **Conditions of employment**

> Class here comprehensive works on collective bargaining to determine conditions of employment and the resulting conditions of employment

> Class conditions of employment discussed from the managerial viewpoint in 658.312

> *For collective bargaining to determine conditions of employment, see 331.89*

### SUMMARY

|  |  |
|---|---|
| 331.204 | **Conditions of employment by industry and occupation** |
| .21 | **Compensation** |
| .22 | **Compensation differentials** |
| .23 | **Guaranteed-wage plans** |
| .25 | **Other conditions of employment** |
| .28 | **Compensation by industry and occupation** |
| .29 | **History, geographic treatment, biography of compensation** |

.204            Conditions of employment by industry and occupation

> Standard subdivisions are added for either or both topics in heading

| | |
|---|---|
| .204 1 | Conditions of employment in industries and occupations other than extractive, manufacturing, construction |

> Standard subdivisions are added for industries, occupations, or both

> Class here conditions of employment in service industries and occupations

| | |
|---|---|
| .204 100 01–.204 100 09 | Standard subdivisions |
| .204 100 1–.204 199 9 | Subdivisions for conditions of employment in industries and occupations other than extractive, manufacturing, construction |

> Add to base number 331.2041 notation 001–999, e.g., conditions of employment in clerical occupations 331.204165137
> > Subdivisions are added for industries, occupations, or both

| | |
|---|---|
| .204 2–.204 9 | Conditions of employment in extractive, manufacturing, construction industries and occupations |

> Add to base number 331.204 the numbers following 6 in 620–690, e.g., conditions of employment in chemical industries 331.2046
> Subdivisions are added for industries, occupations, or both

| | |
|---|---|
| .21 | Compensation |

> Class here wages, wage policy

> Class incomes policy (wage-price policy) in 339.5

> *For compensation differentials, see 331.22; for employee benefits (fringe benefits), see 331.255; for compensation by industry and occupation, see 331.28*

| | |
|---|---|
| .210 1 | Philosophy and theory |

> Including bargain theory, marginal productivity theory, national income theory, subsistence theory ("iron law"), wages fund theory

| | |
|---|---|
| [.210 9] | History, geographic treatment, biography |

> Do not use; class in 331.29

| | |
|---|---|
| .215 | Factors affecting compensation |

> Including methods of determination, e.g., intraindustry and interindustry comparison; criteria used in determination, e.g., cost of living as a compensation determinant

> *For minimum-wage policies, see 331.23*

> *See also 332.415 for wage-price controls to combat inflation; also 339.5 for wage control as a factor in economic stabilization*

| | |
|---|---|
| .215 08 | Groups of people |

> Do not use for discrimination in compensation; class in 331.2153

.215 3     Discrimination and anti-discrimination policies

> Standard subdivisions are added for either or both topics in heading
>
> Class here equal pay for equal work, pay equity
>
> Class discrimination because of a specific personal characteristic in 331.3–331.6

.216     Methods of compensation

> Class here wage payment systems
>
> Class employee benefits (fringe benefits) in 331.255

.216 2     Time payments

> Including hourly, weekly, monthly, annual periods; overtime pay
>
> Class guaranteed-wage plans in 331.23

.216 4     Incentive compensation

> Including bonuses, merit pay, performance awards; piecework, combined timework and piecework
>
> Class tips in 331.2166

.216 47     Profit sharing

> Class here gain sharing

.216 49     Employee stock ownership plans

> Class here employee stock options, employee stock purchase plans
>
> Class stock options as a form of speculation in 332.632283; class comprehensive works on employee ownership in 338.69

.216 6     Other methods of compensation

> Including longevity pay, locality pay (weighting), professional and subcontracting fees, severance pay, tips
>
> Class paid leave in 331.2576

.22     Compensation differentials

> Including differences among, firms, industries, occupations, regions
>
> Class differentials as a factor affecting compensation in 331.215

.220 9     History, geographic treatment, biography

> Class geographic treatment of compensation not emphasizing differentials in 331.29

.23     Guaranteed-wage plans

> Class here minimum wage
>
> Class guaranteed minimum income in 362.582

.236     Guaranteed annual wage

.25     Other conditions of employment

## SUMMARY

| | |
|---|---|
| 331.252 | Pensions |
| .255 | Employee benefits (Fringe benefits) |
| .256 | Work environment |
| .257 | Hours |
| .259 | Training, worker security, regulation of worker conduct |

.252         Pensions

Including retirement age

Class here retirement benefits, superannuation, interdisciplinary works on pensions

Class pensions for government (public service) employees in 331.25291351

*For pensions provided by unions, see 331.8735; for retirement planning, see 332.024014; for public administration of pensions for government workers, see 353.549; for pensions (annuities) provided through insurance, see 368.37; for government pension plans for the population at large, see 368.43; for comprehensive works on administration of pensions, see 658.3253*

.252 2         Pension reform

Class here preservation, transfer of vested rights in pensions

.252 4         Pension funds

Class investment by pension funds in 332.67254

.252 9         Pensions by industry and occupation

Standard subdivisions are added for either or both topics in heading

.252 91         Pensions in industries and occupations other than extractive, manufacturing, construction

Standard subdivisions are added for industries, occupations, or both

Class here pensions in service industries and occupations

.252 910 001–.252 910 009         Standard subdivisions

.252 910 01–.252 919 99         Subdivisions for pensions in industries and occupations other than extractive, manufacturing, construction

Add to base number 331.25291 notation 001–999, e.g., military pensions 331.25291355
Subdivisions are added for industries, occupations, or both

.252 92–.252 99         Pensions in extractive, manufacturing, construction industries and occupations

Add to base number 331.2529 the numbers following 6 in 620–690, e.g., pensions in construction trades 331.252924
Subdivisions are added for industries, occupations, or both

.255        **Employee benefits (Fringe benefits)**

Class here employee assistance programs, insurance, interdisciplinary works on employee benefits

*For stock ownership and purchase plans, see 331.21649; for pensions, see 331.252; for benefits provided by unions, see 331.8735; for benefits for veterans of military service and their survivors, see 362.86; for benefits provided through insurance, see 368.3; for benefits provided through government-sponsored social insurance, see 368.4; for comprehensive works on administration of employee benefits, see 658.325*

.255 2        Unemployment compensation

Class interdisciplinary works on unemployment insurance in 368.44

.255 4        Health services

Class interdisciplinary works on health insurance in 368.382

.256        **Work environment**

Class here physical working conditions, quality of work life, working facilities, workplace relationships; work stress

*For hostile work environment caused by hostile and discriminatory behavior, see 331.133*

.256 7        Home labor

Producing goods at home for an outside employer

Class here cottage industries, comprehensive works on work at home

*For telecommuting, see 331.2568*

.256 8        Telecommuting

.257        **Hours**

Including reduced workweek

Class here workweek

.257 2        Alternative work schedules; workday

Including overtime, work sharing

.257 22        Compressed workweek

Including four-day forty-hour week

.257 23        Workday

Class a specific alternative workday schedule with the alternative work schedule elsewhere in 331.2572, e.g., part-time schedule 331.25727

*For rest periods, see 331.2576*

.257 24        Flexible hours

*See also 331.2567 for home labor; also 331.2568 for telecommuting; also 331.25722 for compressed workweek*

| .257 25 | Shift work |
|---|---|

*See also 331.2574 for night work*

| .257 27 | Part-time work |
|---|---|
| .257 277 | Job sharing |

*See also 331.2572 for work sharing*

| .257 29 | Temporary employment |
|---|---|

Class here temporary employees

Class services to provide temporary help in 331.128

| .257 4 | Night, holy day, Sunday, holiday work |
|---|---|

*See also 331.2572 for shift work*

| .257 6 | Leave and rest periods (breaks) |
|---|---|

Standard subdivisions are added for leave and rest periods together, for leave alone

Class here annual leave, holidays, paid vacations

| .257 62 | Sick leave |
|---|---|
| .257 63 | Special-purpose leave |

Including educational, paternity, sabbatical leave

*For maternity leave, see 331.44*

| .259 | Training, worker security, regulation of worker conduct |
|---|---|
| .259 2 | Training |

Not related to a specific industry

Class here interdisciplinary works on on-the-job vocational training, on vocational training provided by industry

Class interdisciplinary works on vocational education conducted by an educational institution in 370.113

*For managerial aspects of training by the employer, see 658.3124. For on-the-job training in a specific occupation, see the occupation, plus notation 07155 from Table 1, e.g., on-the-job apprenticeship of plumbers 696.107155*

| .259 22 | Apprenticeship |
|---|---|

*For apprentices as a special class of workers, see 331.55; for work experience as part of education, see 371.227*

| .259 24 | Retraining |
|---|---|
| .259 6 | Worker security |

Including dismissal of employees; employment security, job tenure; right to organize, rights of transfer and promotion, seniority

.259 8            Regulation of worker conduct

                    Class here discipline

.259 88           Absenteeism

.28          Compensation by industry and occupation

                    Standard subdivisions are added for either or both topics in heading

                    Class specific elements of compensation by industry and occupation in 331.21–331.23

.281        Compensation in industries and occupations other than extractive, manufacturing, construction

                    Standard subdivisions are added for industries, occupations, or both

                    Class here compensation in service industries and occupations

.281 000 1–.281 000 9       Standard subdivisions

.281 001–.281 999       Subdivisions for compensation in industries and occupations other than extractive, manufacturing, construction

                          Add to base number 331.281 notation 001–999, e.g., compensation of legislators 331.28132833
                              Subdivisions are added for industries, occupations, or both

.282–.289      Compensation in extractive, manufacturing, construction industries and occupations

                      Add to base number 331.28 the numbers following 6 in 620–690, e.g., compensation in the mining industry 331.2822, average factory compensation 331.287
                      Subdivisions are added for industries, occupations, or both

.29         History, geographic treatment, biography of compensation

                    Class history of factors affecting compensation and history of methods of compensation in 331.215–331.216; class history of compensation differentials and history of guaranteed-wage plans in 331.22–331.23; class history of compensation by industries and occupations in 331.28; class wage-price policies in relation to stabilizing the economy in 339.5

.290 01–.290 08      Standard subdivisions

[.290 09]          History

                    Do not use; class in 331.29

.290 1–.290 5       Historical periods

                    Add to base number 331.290 the numbers following —090 in notation 0901–0905 from Table 1, e.g., compensation in 20th century 331.2904

.291–.299      Geographic treatment and biography

> Add to base number 331.29 notation 1–9 from Table 2, e.g., compensation in Australia 331.2994
>
> Class geographic treatment and biography of specific elements of compensation in 331.215–331.23; class geographic treatment and biography of compensation by industries and occupations in 331.28

---

> **331.3–331.6 Labor force by personal attributes**
>
> Class here labor force and market, conditions of employment, industries and occupations, labor unions, labor-management bargaining with respect to special groups of workers
>
> Unless other instructions are given, class a subject with aspects in two or more subdivisions of 331.3–331.6 in the number coming first, e.g., young North American native women 331.34408997 (*not* 331.408997 or 331.6997)
>
> Class choice of vocation for people with specific personal attributes in 331.702; class comprehensive works on groups of people in 331.08. Class employment services as a form of social service to a specific group of people with the group in 362.6–362.8, e.g., sheltered employment for people in late adulthood 362.64

.3       **Workers by age group**

.31      Children

> Through age thirteen
>
> *See also 364.15554 for criminal aspects of child labor*

.318     Children through age thirteen by industry and occupation

> Standard subdivisions are added for either or both topics in heading

.34      Young workers

> Through age thirty-five
>
> *For children through age thirteen, see 331.31; for young workers by industry and occupation, see 331.38*

.341–.342    Specific aspects of employment of young workers

> Add to base number 331.34 the numbers following 331 in 331.1–331.2, e.g., training of young workers 331.342592
>
> Class specific aspects of employment of specific kinds of young workers in 331.344–331.346

.344–.346    Employment of specific kinds of young workers

> Add to base number 331.34 the numbers following 331 in 331.4–331.6, e.g., African American youth 331.346396073; however, for apprentices, see 331.55

.347              Workers aged 14 through 20

                 Class employment of specific groups of workers aged 14 through 20 in
                 331.344–331.346

                 *For specific aspects of employment of workers aged 14 through 20,*
                 *see 331.341–331.342*

.38          Young workers by industry and occupation

                 Standard subdivisions are added for either or both topics in heading

                 Through age thirty-five

                 Class employment of specific kinds of young workers by industry and
                 occupation in 331.344–331.346

                 *For children through age thirteen by industries and occupations, see*
                 *331.318; for specific aspects of employment of young workers by industry*
                 *and occupation, see 331.341–331.342*

.381             Young workers in industries and occupations other than extractive,
                 manufacturing, construction

                 Standard subdivisions are added for industries, occupations, or both

                 Class here young workers in service industries and occupations

.381 000 1–.381 000 9        Standard subdivisions

.381 001–.381 999            Subdivisions for young workers in industries and occupations
                             other than extractive, manufacturing, construction

                             Add to base number 331.381 notation 001–999, e.g., young
                             workers in clerical occupations 331.38165137
                             Subdivisions are added for industries, occupations, or both

.382–.389            Young workers in extractive, manufacturing, construction industries
                     and occupations

                     Add to base number 331.38 the numbers following 6 in 620–690, e.g.,
                     young textile workers 331.3877
                     Subdivisions are added for industries, occupations, or both

.39          Other age groups

.394             Middle-aged workers

.398             Older workers

.398 1–.398 2        Specific aspects on employment of older workers

                     Add to base number 331.398 the numbers following 331 in
                     331.1–331.2, e.g., discrimination against older workers 331.398133

.398 8           Older workers by industry and occupation

                 Standard subdivisions are added for either or both topics in heading

.398 81 — Older workers in industries and occupations other than extractive, manufacturing, construction

Standard subdivisions are added for industries, occupations, or both

Class here older workers in service industries and occupations

.398 810 001–.398 810 009 — Standard subdivisions

.398 810 01–.398 819 99 — Subdivisions for older workers in industries and occupations other than extractive, manufacturing, construction

Add to base number 331.39881 notation 001–999, e.g., older workers in clerical occupations 331.3988165137
Subdivisions are added for industries, occupations, or both

.398 82–.398 89 — Older workers in extractive, manufacturing, construction industries and occupations

Add to base number 331.3988 the numbers following 6 in 620–690, e.g., older agricultural workers in 331.39883
Subdivisions are added for industries, occupations, or both

## .4 Women workers

Unless other instructions are given, observe the following table of preference, e.g., women clothing workers in labor unions 331.478187 (*not* 331.4887):

| | |
|---|---|
| Working mothers | 331.44 |
| Married women | 331.43 |
| Labor unions and labor-management bargaining and disputes | 331.47 |
| Specific aspects of employment of women | 331.41–331.42 |
| Women workers by industry and occupation | 331.48 |

*See also 305.43 for sociology of women's occupations*

.41–.42 Specific aspects of employment of women

Add to base number 331.4 the numbers following 331 in 331.1–331.2, e.g., discrimination against women 331.4133

.43 Married women

.44 Working mothers

Including expectant mothers, maternity leave

.47 Labor unions and labor-management bargaining and disputes

Add to base number 331.47 the numbers following 331.8 in 331.87–331.89, e.g., women in labor unions 331.478

.48 Women workers by industry and occupation

Standard subdivisions are added for either or both topics in heading

.481      Women workers in industries and occupations other than extractive, manufacturing, construction

> Standard subdivisions are added for industries, occupations, or both

> Class here women in service industries and occupations

.481 000 1–.481 000 9      Standard subdivisions

.481 001–.481 999      Subdivisions for women workers in industries and occupations other than extractive, manufacturing, construction

> Add to base number 331.481 notation 001–999, e.g., women in advertising 331.4816591
> Subdivisions are added for industries, occupations, or both

.482–.489      Women workers in extractive, manufacturing, construction industries and occupations

> Add to base number 331.48 the numbers following 6 in 620–690, e.g., women clothing workers 331.4887
> Subdivisions are added for industries, occupations, or both

## .5      Workers by personal attributes other than age

> Including transgender and intersex people, retired people

> *For immigrants and aliens, see 331.62; for native-born workers by ethnic group, see 331.63*

.51      Prisoners and ex-convicts

> Standard subdivisions are added for either or both topics in heading

> Including political and war prisoners

.52      Veterans

> *See also 331.25291355 for pensions received because of military service; also 331.761355 for military labor*

.53      Gays

> Class here gay men

.54      Workers in special economic situations

> Class here economically disadvantaged workers not provided for elsewhere

> Class unemployed workers in 331.137

.542      Contract workers

.544      Migrant and casual workers

> Standard subdivisions are added for migrant and casual workers together, for migrant workers alone

> Class here migrant agricultural laborers

> *See also 331.62 for immigrant and alien workers*

.55      Apprentices

> Class training of apprentices in 331.25922

.56 Workers by gender or sex

Class transgender and intersex people in 331.5

*For women, see 331.4*

.561 Men

.58 Workers by religious group

Add to base number 331.58 the numbers following 2 in 230–299, e.g., Catholics 331.5882, Muslims 331.5897

.59 Workers with disabilities and illnesses

Class here workers with physical disabilities

Add to base number 331.59 the numbers following —087 in notation 0871–0877 from Table 1, e.g., workers with impaired vision 331.591

**.6 Workers by ethnic and national origin**

.62 Immigrants and aliens

Standard subdivisions are added for either or both topics in heading

*See also 331.544 for migrant workers*

.620 9 History, geographic treatment, biography

Class here immigrant and alien workers in specific areas, e.g., immigrant workers in Canada 331.620971

*For immigrant and alien workers from specific jurisdictions, see 331.621–331.629*

---

> 331.621–331.629 Immigrants and aliens by place of origin

Class comprehensive works in 331.62

*See also 331.6209 for immigrant and alien workers in specific areas*

.621 Immigrants and aliens from areas, regions, places in general

Add to base number 331.621 the numbers following —1 in notation 11–19 from Table 2, e.g., immigrant workers from developing regions 331.621724; then add 0* and to the result add notation 1–9 from Table 2, e.g., immigrant workers from developing regions in California 331.6217240794
Subdivisions are added for either or both topics in heading

.623–.629 Immigrants and aliens from specific continents, countries, localities

Add to base number 331.62 notation 3–9 from Table 2 for place of origin, e.g., immigrant workers from China 331.6251; then, for area located, add 0* and to the result add notation 1–9 from Table 2, e.g., immigrant workers from China in California 331.62510794
Subdivisions are added for either or both topics in heading

---

*Add 00 for standard subdivisions; see instructions at beginning of Table 1

.63          Native-born workers by ethnic group

Class here indigenous ethnic groups [*formerly* 331.69], native-born nonindigenous ethnic groups

.630 01–.630 07          Standard subdivisions

.630 08          Groups of people

[.630 089]          Ethnic and national groups

Do not use for comprehensive works on native-born ethnic groups; class in 331.63. Do not use for specific native-born ethnic groups; class in 331.6305–331.6399

.630 09          History, geographic treatment, biography

.630 5–.630 9          Native-born workers of mixed ancestry with ethnic origins from more than one continent, native-born European workers and native-born workers of European descent

Add to base number 331.63 notation 05–09 from Table 5, e.g., native-born workers of European descent 331.6309, native-born workers of European descent in Australia 331.6309094

.631–.639          Native-born workers of other ethnic groups

Add to base number 331.63 notation 1–9 from Table 5, e.g., African Americans 331.6396073, African American workers in Alabama 331.63960730761, Aboriginal Australians 331.639915, Aboriginal Australian workers in Queensland 331.6399150943

[.69]          Indigenous ethnic groups

Relocated to 331.63

.7          **Labor by industry and occupation**

Standard subdivisions are added for either or both topics in heading

Class comprehensive works on industrial occupations in 331.794

*For professional relationships in a specific industry or occupation, see the industry or occupation, plus notation 023 from Table 1, e.g., professional relationships in accounting 657.023*

.700 1–.700 9          Standard subdivisions

.702          Choice of vocation

Class here choice of vocation for people with specific personal attributes, e.g., veterans; interdisciplinary works describing vocations and occupational specialties; interdisciplinary works on career opportunities and vocational counseling

Class studies of vocational interest in 158.6; class job hunting in 650.14

*For vocational counseling in schools, see 371.425. For descriptions of, career opportunities in, choice of vocation with regard to specific vocations and occupational specialties, see the vocation or specialty, plus notation 023 from Table 1, e.g., career opportunities in accounting 657.023*

.702 3          Choice of vocation for people at specific educational levels

[.702 301–.702 309]          Standard subdivisions

Do not use; class in 331.70201–331.70209

.702 33          Choice of vocation for high school graduates

.702 35          Choice of vocation for college graduates

Regardless of degree obtained

.71          Professional occupations

*For specific professional occupations, see 331.761*

.76          Specific industries and occupations

Class specific groups of occupations in 331.79

[.760 1–.760 9]          Standard subdivisions

Do not use; class in 331.7001–331.7009

.761          Industries and occupations other than extractive, manufacturing, construction

Standard subdivisions are added for industries, occupations, or both

Class comprehensive works on service industries and occupations in 331.793

.761 000 1–.761 000 9          Standard subdivisions

.761 001–.761 999          Subdivisions for industries and occupations other than extractive, manufacturing, construction

Add to base number 331.761 notation 001–999, e.g., managerial occupations 331.761658; however, for governmental (public service) occupations, see 331.795
Subdivisions are added for industries, occupations, or both

.762–.769          Extractive, manufacturing, construction industries and occupations

Add to base number 331.76 the numbers following 6 in 620–690, e.g., food processing 331.7664
Subdivisions are added for industries, occupations, or both

Class comprehensive works on industrial occupations in 331.794

.79          General occupation groups and government occupations

Occupational groups not defined by industry or discipline

Unless other instructions are given, class a subject with aspects in two or more subdivisions of 331.79 in the number coming last, e.g., white collar governmental (public service) occupations 331.795 (*not* 331.792)

*For professional occupations, see 331.71*

[.790 1–.790 9]          Standard subdivisions

Do not use; class in 331.7001–331.7009

.792          White collar occupations

.793      Service occupations

> Class here labor in service industries

.794      Industrial occupations

> Including the work of artisans and supervisors; skilled, semiskilled work
>
> *For unskilled work, see 331.798*

.795      Governmental occupations (Public service occupations)

> Including elected civil servants

.798      Unskilled work

## .8      Labor unions, labor-management bargaining and disputes

> Class here interdisciplinary works on labor movements
>
> Class comprehensive works on labor relations (all relations between management and individual employees or employee groups) in 331; class comprehensive works on industrial democracy in 331.0112
>
> *For a specific aspect of labor movements, see the aspect, e.g., political activities of labor movements 322.2*

### SUMMARY

| | |
|---|---|
| 331.87 | **Labor union organization** |
| .88 | **Labor unions (Trade unions)** |
| .89 | **Labor-management bargaining and disputes** |

.87      Labor union organization

> Class comprehensive works on labor unions in 331.88

.871      Constitutions, bylaws, rules

.872      Levels of organization

> Including locals, national unions, union federations
>
> Class international unions in 331.88091; class descriptions of individual unions and federations, comprehensive works on unions in specific areas in 331.8809

.873      Specific aspects of union organization

> Including discipline of members

[.873 01–.873 09]      Standard subdivisions

> Do not use; class in 331.8701–331.8709

.873 2      Membership

> Class here membership policies
>
> Class discrimination by unions against workers with specific personal attributes with the characteristic in 331.3–331.6, e.g., discrimination against women 331.47732

| | |
|---|---|
| .873 3 | Officers |

        Including shop stewards

        Class here union leaders

        Class biography of union leaders in 331.88092

| | |
|---|---|
| .873 5 | Benefits, funds, property |
| .874 | Union elections and conventions |

        Standard subdivisions are added for union elections and conventions together, for union elections alone

| | |
|---|---|
| .88 | Labor unions (Trade unions) |

        Class here unions organized along religious lines, e.g., Christian trade unions

        Class right of workers to organize in 331.2596

        *For labor union organization, see 331.87; for managerial viewpoint on labor unions, see 658.3153*

        *See also 322.2 for political activities of labor unions*

| | |
|---|---|
| .880 1 | Philosophy and theory |

        Including countermonopoly theory; theories of unions as instruments of class struggle, as instruments of industrial democracy, as instruments for worker control of industry

        *See also 331.0112 for industrial democracy; also 338.69 for worker control of industry*

| | |
|---|---|
| .880 9 | History, geographic treatment, biography |
| .880 91 | Areas, regions, places in general |

        Class here international unions

        Class international unions with members from only two countries in 331.88094–331.88099, using the comprehensive notation from Table 2 for the two countries, e.g., unions with United States and Canadian workers 331.880973

| | |
|---|---|
| .881 | Labor unions by industry and occupation |

        Standard subdivisions are added for either or both topics in heading

| | |
|---|---|
| .881 1 | Labor unions in industries and occupations other than extractive, manufacturing, construction |

        Standard subdivisions are added for industries, occupations, or both

        Class here labor unions in service industries and occupations

| | |
|---|---|
| .881 100 01–.881 100 09 | Standard subdivisions |

.881 100 1–.881 199 9     Subdivisions for labor unions (trade unions) in industries and occupations other than extractive, manufacturing, construction

> Add to base number 331.8811 notation 001–999, e.g., teachers' unions 331.88113711
>> Subdivisions are added for industries, occupations, or both

.881 2–.881 9     Labor unions in extractive, manufacturing, construction industries and occupations

> Add to base number 331.881 the numbers following 6 in 620–690, e.g., garment workers' unions 331.88187
>> Subdivisions are added for industries, occupations, or both

.883     Kinds of unions

> Class blue-collar unions in 331.88; class specific kinds of unions by industry and occupation in 331.881

> *For revolutionary unions, see 331.886*

.883 2     Craft unions

> Class semi-industrial unions in 331.8833

.883 3     Industrial unions

> Class here semi-industrial unions

.883 4     Company unions

.883 6     White collar unions

.886     Revolutionary unions

> Class Industrial Workers of the World (IWW) in 331.8860973

.889     Union security issues

.889 2     Open and closed shop

> Standard subdivisions are added for either or both topics in heading

> Class here right to work, agency shop, union shop; general arrangements for union security

> Class specific issues of union security in 331.8896; class comprehensive works on rights of labor in 331.011

.889 6     Other union security issues

> Including control of hiring, layoffs, apprenticeships; preferential hiring, sole bargaining rights; dues checkoff, featherbedding

> Class general arrangements for union security in 331.8892

[.889 601–.889 609]     Standard subdivisions

> Do not use; class in 331.88901–331.88909

.889 66     Grievance procedures

.89              Labor-management bargaining and disputes

Standard subdivisions are added for either or both topics in heading

Variant name for labor-management bargaining: collective bargaining

Class conditions of work determined by collective bargaining in 331.2; class
grievance procedures to resolve disputes in 331.88966; class works treating
collective bargaining from the managerial viewpoint in 658.3154

### SUMMARY

| | |
|---|---|
| 331.890 4 | **Labor-management bargaining and disputes by industry and occupation** |
| .891 | **Contracts and related topics** |
| .892 | **Strikes** |
| .893 | **Other labor measures** |
| .894 | **Management measures** |
| .898 | **Government measures** |

.890 4           Labor-management bargaining and disputes by industry and occupation

Standard subdivisions are added for any or all topics in heading

.890 41          Labor-management bargaining and disputes in industries and
occupations other than extractive, manufacturing, construction

Standard subdivisions are added for any or all topics in heading

Class here labor-management bargaining and disputes in service
industries and occupations

.890 410 001–.890 410 009           Standard subdivisions

.890 410 01–.890 419 99           Subdivisions for labor-management bargaining and
disputes in industries and occupations other than extractive,
manufacturing, construction

Add to base number 331.89041 notation 001–999,
e.g., labor-management bargaining in hospitals
331.8904136211
Subdivisions are added for any or all topics in
heading

.890 42–.890 49          Labor-management bargaining and disputes in extractive,
manufacturing, construction industries and occupations

Add to base number 331.8904 the numbers following 6 in
620–690, e.g., labor-management bargaining and disputes in the
garment industry 331.890487
Subdivisions are added for any or all topics in heading

.891             Contracts and related topics

Standard subdivisions are added for contracts and related topics, for
contracts alone

.891 2           Organizing and contract negotiation

Including negotiation during life of contract, recognition of unions

Class conciliation measures in 331.8914

| .891 4 | Conciliation measures |
|---|---|
| .891 42 | Mediation |
| .891 43 | Arbitration |
| .892 | Strikes |

> *For management measures with respect to strikes, see 331.894; for government measures with respect to strikes, see 331.898*

> *See also 331.8914 for conciliation measures*

| .892 01 | Philosophy and theory |
|---|---|

Including right to strike, general theories about effects of strikes

Class effects of strikes on a specific thing with the thing, e.g., effect of strikes on profitability of mining industries 338.23

| [.892 09] | History, geographic treatment, biography |
|---|---|

Do not use; class in 331.8929

| .892 5 | General strikes |
|---|---|

Class interdisciplinary works on general strikes in 322.2

| .892 7 | Picketing |
|---|---|
| .892 8 | Strikes by industry and occupation |

Standard subdivisions are added for either or both topics in heading

| .892 81 | Strikes in industries and occupations other than extractive, manufacturing, construction |
|---|---|

Standard subdivisions are added for industries, occupations, or both

Class here strikes in service industries and occupations

| .892 810 001–.892 810 009 | Standard subdivisions |
|---|---|
| .892 810 01–.892 819 99 | Subdivisions for strikes in industries and occupations other than extractive, manufacturing, construction |

Add to base number 331.89281 notation 001–999, e.g., teachers' strikes 331.892813711
Subdivisions are added for industries, occupations, or both

| .892 82–.892 89 | Strikes in extractive, manufacturing, construction industries and occupations |
|---|---|

Add to base number 331.8928 the numbers following 6 in 620–690, e.g., strikes of rubber workers 331.8928782
Subdivisions are added for industries, occupations, or both

| .892 9 | History, geographic treatment, biography |
|---|---|
| .892 900 1–.892 900 8 | Standard subdivisions |

| [.892 900 9] | History |
| | Do not use; class in 331.8929 |

| .892 901–.892 905 | Historical periods |

Add to base number 331.89290 the numbers following —090 in notation 0901–0905 from Table 1, e.g., strikes in 20th century 331.892904

Class general strikes in specific periods in 331.8925; class strikes by industry and occupations in specific periods in 331.8928

| .892 91–.892 99 | Geographic treatment and biography |

Add to base number 331.8929 notation 1–9 from Table 2, e.g., strikes in Great Britain 331.892941

Class general strikes in specific places in 331.8925; class strikes by industry and occupations in specific places in 331.8928

| .893 | Other labor measures |

Including boycotts, injunctions, sabotage

Class here comprehensive works on labor violence

*For violence in strikes, see 331.892*

| .894 | Management measures |

Including blacklisting, injunctions, labor espionage, lockouts, strikebreaking, yellow-dog contracts

Class comprehensive works on strikes in 331.892

| .898 | Government measures |

*For conciliation measures, see 331.8914*

*See also 331.8892 for right to work*

| .898 4 | Use of troops |

# 332    Financial economics

*For public finance, see 336*

*See Manual at 332, 336 vs. 339; also at 332 vs. 338, 658.15*

## SUMMARY

| 332.01–.09 | Standard subdivisions, personal finance, special topics of financial economics |
| --- | --- |
| .1 | Banks |
| .2 | Specialized banking institutions |
| .3 | Credit and loan institutions |
| .4 | Money |
| .5 | Barter, commercial paper, social credit money |
| .6 | Investment |
| .7 | Credit |
| .8 | Interest |
| .9 | Counterfeiting, forgery, alteration |

.02      Miscellany and personal finance

     Notation 02 from Table 1 as modified below

.024      Personal finance

     Do not use for works on financial economics for people in specific occupations; class in 332.02

     Including prevention of identity theft

     Class here management of household finances

     *For a specific aspect of personal finance not provided for here, see the aspect, e.g., investing in stocks 332.6322, consumer information 381.33*

.024 001–.024 009      Standard subdivisions

.024 01      Increasing income, net worth, financial security

     Standard subdivisions are added for any or all topics in heading

     Class here financial independence

.024 014      Retirement planning

.024 014 5      Retirement investment plans

     Class here individual retirement accounts (IRAs), 401(k) plans, Keogh plans, other investment plans regardless of name; annuities

.024 016      Estate planning

.024 02      Personal debt management

.04      Special topics of financial economics

.041      Capital

     *For international aspects of capital, see 332.042*

.041 2      Working capital

     Including cash, inventories

.041 4      Fixed capital

     *For land, see 333*

.041 5      Capital formation and saving

     Standard subdivisions are added for either or both topics in heading

     Class here capital markets, interdisciplinary works on raising money for investment in capital assets

     *For capital formation discussed in relation to production in specific kinds of industries, see 338.1–338.4; for financing of firms, see 338.6041; for savings and investment as a factor affecting national income, see 339.43*

[.041 506 8]      Management

     Do not use; class in 658.1522

.041 52       Self-financing

Class here retained profits

Class managerial aspects of self-financing in 658.15226

.041 54       Venture capital

.042       International finance

Class international monetary system in 332.45; class comprehensive works on international economics in 337

*For international banking, see 332.15; for international investment, see 332.673*

.042 4       Capital movements

Class here currency movements

*For exchange of currencies, see 332.45; for international exchange of securities, see 332.65; for balance of payments, see 382.17*

.042 46       Emigrant remittances

*For a specific aspect of emigrant remittances, see the aspect, e.g., impact of emigrant remittances on economic development in Latin America 338.98*

.06       Organizations

Do not use for financial institutions and their management; class in 332.1

**.1**       **Banks**

Including bank failures

Class here banking; comprehensive works on money and banking, on financial institutions and their functions

Class government guaranty of deposits in 368.854

*For specialized banking institutions, see 332.2; for credit and loan institutions, see 332.3; for money, see 332.4; for credit, see 332.7; for credit unions, see 334.22. For a specific nonbanking activity of a bank, see the activity, e.g., banks selling real estate 333.33*

### SUMMARY

| | | |
|---|---|---|
| **332.11** | **Central banks** | |
| **.12** | **Commercial banks** | |
| **.15** | **International banks** | |
| **.16** | **Banks with multiple outlets** | |
| **.17** | **Banking services** | |

.11       Central banks

Specific central banks are classed here, e.g., United States Board of Governors of the Federal Reserve System 332.110973

| .112 | Relation to monetary policy |
|---|---|

Including issuance of bank notes

Class role of central bank in carrying out macroeconomic policy in 339.53; class comprehensive works on bank notes in 332.4044

*For interest rates, reserve requirements, see 332.113; for open-market operations, see 332.114*

| .113 | Relation to commercial banks |
|---|---|

Including clearance, interest rates (discount rates), loans, reserve requirements

| .114 | Open-market operations |
|---|---|

Including purchase of government securities

| .12 | Commercial banks |
|---|---|

Class here clearing banks, clearing houses

Class relation to central banks in 332.113; class commercial banks with multiple outlets in 332.16

*For international operations of commercial banks, see 332.15; for other banking services of commercial banks, see 332.17*

| .122 | Incorporated banks |
|---|---|

Class here chartered banks

| .122 3 | National banks |
|---|---|

*See also 332.11 for central banks*

| .122 4 | State and provincial banks |
|---|---|

Class state and provincial chartered private banks in 332.123

| .123 | Private banks |
|---|---|

| .15 | International banks |
|---|---|

Class here international operations of commercial and other banks, role of banks in international borrowing and debt

Class comprehensive works on international borrowing and debt in 336.3435

| .152 | International banks for monetary stabilization and balance of payments |
|---|---|

Standard subdivisions are added for either or both topics in heading

Class here International Monetary Fund

Class comprehensive works on balance of payments in 382.17

.153 **International banks for development of resources and production**

Standard subdivisions are added for either or both topics in heading

Including International Development Association, International Finance Corporation

Class here comprehensive works on development banks

Class banks for development of resources and production in a specific region in 332.15309

*For development banks serving one country, see 332.28*

.153 094 Europe

*For European Investment Bank, see 332.1534*

.153 097 North America

*For Inter-American Development Bank, see 332.1538*

.153 2 International Bank for Reconstruction and Development (World Bank)

.153 4 European Investment Bank

.153 8 Inter-American Development Bank

.154 **International banks for promotion and facilitation of trade**

Standard subdivisions are added for either or both topics in heading

.155 **International banks for international settlements**

Class here Bank for International Settlements

.16 **Banks with multiple outlets**

Class here branch banks, chain banks, interstate banking; bank holding companies, mergers, syndicates

.17 **Banking services**

*For international operations, see 332.15; for services of specialized banking institutions, see 332.2*

*See also 332.7 for credit functions not limited to a specific type of financial institution*

.175 **General banking services**

.175 2 Deposits

Including time deposits, e.g., certificates of deposit, savings accounts; savings departments

.175 22 Checking accounts

Including NOW (negotiable order of withdrawal) accounts

Class here demand deposits

.175 3 Loans

.175 4        Investments

> See also 332.66 for investment banks

.178        Special banking services

Including clearing services, debit and smart cards, electronic funds transfers, internet banking, safe-deposit services, trust services

.178 8        Credit cards

Class comprehensive works on credit cards in 332.765

**.2**        **Specialized banking institutions**

> For international banks, see 332.15; for agricultural institutions, see 332.31; for investment banks, see 332.66; for banking cooperatives, see 334.2

.21        Savings banks

Including government savings banks

Class here mutual savings banks

Class comprehensive works on thrift institutions in 332.32

> For postal savings banks, see 332.22

.22        Postal savings banks

.26        Trust companies

.28        Development banks serving one country

Variant name: industrial development banks

Class banks for development of agriculture in 332.31; class comprehensive works on development banks in 332.153

**.3**        **Credit and loan institutions**

Standard subdivisions are added for either or both topics in heading

Including credit and loan functions of enterprises whose primary function is not credit and loan, e.g., credit function of retail stores, travel agencies

Class credit and loan functions of insurance companies in 332.38

.31        Agricultural institutions

Including land banks

.32        Savings and loan associations

Variant names: building and loan associations, building societies, home loan associations, mortgage institutions

Class here comprehensive works on thrift institutions

> For savings banks, see 332.21; for credit unions, see 334.22

.34        Pawnshops

Class here pawnbrokers, pawnbroking

| .35 | Consumer and sales finance institutions |
|---|---|

Standard subdivisions are added for either or both topics in heading

| .37 | Labor and employee banks |
|---|---|

Standard subdivisions are added for either or both topics in heading

*For credit unions, see 334.22*

*See also 332.35 for banks specializing in consumer loans*

| .38 | Credit and loan functions of insurance companies |
|---|---|

Standard subdivisions are added for either or both topics in heading

Class interdisciplinary works on insurance companies in 368.0065

**.4        Money**

Class here mediums of exchange

Class monetary policy in 332.46; class comprehensive works on money and banking in 332.1

*For barter, commercial paper, social credit money, see 332.5*

### SUMMARY

| 332.401–.408 | **Standard subdivisions and forms and units of money** |
|---|---|
| **.41** | **Value of money** |
| **.42** | **Monetary standards** |
| **.45** | **Foreign exchange** |
| **.46** | **Monetary policy** |
| **.49** | **History, geographic treatment, biography of money and monetary policy** |

| .401 | Philosophy and theory |
|---|---|

Including circulation and velocity theory, equation of exchange theory, income and cash balance theories, quantity theory, supply and demand theory

| .404 | Forms and units of money |
|---|---|

| .404 2 | Gold and silver coins |
|---|---|

Class here interdisciplinary works on coins

*For token coins, coins of nonprecious metals, see 332.4043. For a specific aspect of coins not provided for here, see the aspect, e.g., coins as an investment 332.63, artistic aspect of coins 737.4*

| .404 3 | Token coins |
|---|---|

Coins with an intrinsic value less than their nominal value

Class here coins of nonprecious metals

| .404 4 | Paper money |
|---|---|

Class here bank notes

| [.409] | History, geographic treatment, biography |
|---|---|

Do not use; class in 332.49

| .41 | Value of money |
|---|---|

Class here inflation, stagflation, deflation; purchasing power

Class the personal financial problem of coping with changing value of money in 332.024; class comprehensive works on purchasing power in 339.42

*See also 331.1372 for effects of inflation on unemployment*

| .414 | Factors affecting fluctuations in value |
|---|---|

Including variations in money supply

*For stabilization measures, see 332.415*

| .414 2 | Devaluation |
|---|---|
| .415 | Stabilization measures |

Including wage-price policy to combat inflation

Class monetary policy in 332.46; class fiscal policy in 336.3; class comprehensive works on economic stabilization policies, on wage-price policy in 339.5

| .42 | Monetary standards |
|---|---|

Class here credit, fiat, paper money; bank notes; legal tender; paper standard

*For paper money as a form of currency, see 332.4044*

| .422 | Monometallic standards |
|---|---|
| .422 2 | Gold standard |
| .422 3 | Silver standard |

Class silver question in 332.4230973

| .423 | Bimetallism |
|---|---|

Class here bimetallism based on gold and silver

| .45 | Foreign exchange |
|---|---|

Class here forward exchange (foreign exchange futures), international monetary systems, special drawing rights

Class Eurocurrency and Eurodollar market in 332.456094; class Euro in 332.494; class comprehensive works on international finance in 332.042; class comprehensive works on financial futures in 332.632; class comprehensive works on speculation in 332.645; class comprehensive works on balance of payments in 382.17

*See also 332.152 for International Monetary Fund*

| .452 | Foreign exchange with a gold standard |
|---|---|
| .456 | Exchange rates |

Class here currency convertibility

| .456 01–.456 08 | Standard subdivisions |
|---|---|

Class standard subdivisions of specific currencies and groups of currencies in 332.45609

.456 09            History, geographic treatment, biography

.456 091           Exchange rates of specific currencies and groups of currencies in areas, regions, places in general

Add to base number 332.456091 the numbers following —1 in notation 11–19 from Table 2, e.g., exchange rates of currencies of developing countries 332.456091724; then add 0* and to the result add notation 1–9 from Table 2, e.g., exchange rate between currencies of developing countries and Europe 332.45609172404
Do not follow add instructions under —091 in Table 1

Give priority in notation to the currency of a jurisdiction or group of jurisdictions coming first in Table 2
(Option: Give priority in notation to the currency of the jurisdiction requiring local emphasis, e.g., libraries in Europe class exchange rate between currencies of Europe and developing countries in 332.45609401724)

.456 093–.456 099   Exchange rates of specific currencies and groups of currencies in specific continents, countries, localities

Add to base number 332.45609 notation 3–9 from Table 2, e.g., exchange rates of currency of United Kingdom 332.4560941; then add 0* and to the result add notation 1–9 from Table 2, e.g., exchange rate between currencies of United Kingdom and United States 332.4560941073
Do not use add table under —093–099 in Table 1

Give priority in notation to the currency of a jurisdiction or group of jurisdictions coming first in Table 2
(Option: Give priority in notation to the currency of the jurisdiction requiring local emphasis, e.g., libraries in United States class exchange rate between currencies of United States and United Kingdom in 332.4560973041)

.456 2             Floating exchange rates (Fluctuating exchange rates)

Class managed floating rates in 332.4564

.456 4             Fixed and flexible exchange rates

*For determination by international agreement, see 332.4566*

.456 6             Determination by international agreement

Class here international monetary policy, international monetary reform

Class Internation Monetary Fund in 332.152; class comprehensive works on monetary policy in 332.46

*Add 00 for standard subdivisions; see instructions at beginning of Table 1

| .46 | Monetary policy |
|---|---|

Including minting policies and practices

Class here currency question, managed currency

*For relation of central banks to monetary policy, see 332.112; for international monetary policy, see 332.4566; for use of monetary policy for economic stabilization, see 339.53*

| [.460 9] | History, geographic treatment, biography |
|---|---|

Do not use; class in 332.49

| .49 | History, geographic treatment, biography of money and monetary policy |
|---|---|

Standard subdivisions are added for money, monetary policy, or both

| .490 01–.490 08 | Standard subdivisions |
|---|---|

| [.490 09] | History |
|---|---|

Do not use; class in 332.49

| .490 1–.490 5 | Historical periods |
|---|---|

Add to base number 332.490 the numbers following —090 in notation 0901–0905 from Table 1, e.g., money and monetary policy in 20th century 332.4904
Subdivisions are added for money, monetary policy, or both

| .491–.499 | Geographic treatment and biography |
|---|---|

Add to base number 332.49 notation 1–9 from Table 2, e.g., money and monetary policy in India 332.4954
Subdivisions are added for money, monetary policy, or both

| **.5** | **Barter, commercial paper, social credit money** |
|---|---|
| .54 | Barter |
| .55 | Commercial paper as medium of exchange |

Class comprehensive works on commercial paper in 332.77

| .56 | Social credit money |
|---|---|
| **.6** | **Investment** |

Class here investments, domestic investment, individual investment, private investment; investment prospectuses, portfolio analysis and management

Class investment guides in 332.678; class description and analysis of business enterprises issuing securities in 338.7

**SUMMARY**

| | |
|---|---|
| **332.604** | **Special topics of investment** |
| **.62** | **Securities brokers** |
| **.63** | **Specific forms of investment** |
| **.64** | **Exchange of securities and commodities; speculation** |
| **.65** | **International exchange of securities** |
| **.66** | **Investment banks** |
| **.67** | **Investments in specific industries, in specific kinds of enterprise, by specific kinds of investors; international investment; investment guides** |

[.601 12]       Forecasting

Do not use; class in 332.678

.604       Special topics of investment

.604 2       Investment for specific purposes

Including socially responsible investment

Class retirement investment plans in 332.0240145

[.604 201–.604 209]       Standard subdivisions

Do not use; class in 332.601–332.609

.604 22       Tax shelters

.62       Securities brokers

Including discount brokers

Class here investment brokers, investment counselors

Class real estate brokerage in 333.33

.63       Specific forms of investment

Including art, coins, stamps

Class here speculation in specific forms of investment

Class speculation in multiple forms of investment, comprehensive works on speculation in 332.645; class investment in specific kinds of enterprises regardless of form in 332.6722

[.630 1–.630 9]       Standard subdivisions

Do not use; class in 332.601–332.609

.632 Securities, real estate, commodities

Standard subdivisions are added for securities, real estate, commodities together; for securities alone

Class here valuation (value); speculation in securities; comprehensive works on financial futures

Class evaluation techniques in 332.632042; class buying and selling procedures for securities and commodities in 332.64; class buying and selling procedures for real estate in 333.33; class comprehensive works on speculation, on futures in 332.645

*For forward exchange (foreign exchange futures), see 332.45*

.632 04 Special topics of securities, real estate, commodities

.632 042 Evaluation techniques for securities, real estate, commodities

Including analyzing corporate balance sheets, reading financial pages and ticker tapes

Class the valuation given to securities, real estate and commodities in 332.632

.632 044 General types of securities

Including fixed rate, variable rate securities; gilt-edged securities

Class stocks in 332.6322; class bonds in 332.6323

*See Manual at 332.632044 vs. 332.6323*

.632 2 Stocks (Shares)

Including rights and warrants

Class here common stock

*See Manual at 332.6322 vs. 332.6323*

.632 21 Valuation

Including dividends paid, price-earnings ratio

*For prices, see 332.63222*

.632 22 Prices

.632 220 21 Tabulated and related materials

Do not use for statistics; class in 332.63222

.632 25 Preferred stock

Class valuation in 332.63221; class prices in 332.63222; class speculation in 332.63228

.632 28 Stock speculation

Including buying on margin, day trading, stock index futures

Class comprehensive works on speculation in 332.645

| .632 283 | Options |
|---|---|

Class here puts and calls

*See also 331.21649 for employee stock options*

| .632 3 | Bonds |
|---|---|

Including mortgage bonds and certificates

Class here interest rate futures and options

*See Manual at 332.632044 vs. 332.6323; also at 332.6322 vs. 332.6323*

| .632 32 | Government securities |
|---|---|

Class here government or treasury bonds, bills, certificates, notes

*For municipal bonds, see 332.63233*

| .632 33 | Municipal bonds |
|---|---|
| .632 34 | Corporate bonds |
| .632 4 | Real estate |

Class real estate finance in 332.72; class comprehensive works on fixed capital in 332.0414; class comprehensive works on real estate business in 333.33

| .632 42 | Land |
|---|---|
| .632 43 | Buildings and other fixtures |

Standard subdivisions are added for buildings and other fixtures, for buildings alone

*See also 647.92–647.94 for management of multiple dwellings*

| .632 44 | Mortgages |
|---|---|

*See also 332.6323 for mortgage bonds*

| .632 47 | Real estate investment trusts |
|---|---|

Including real estate syndication

| .632 7 | Investment company securities |
|---|---|

Including closed-end mutual funds, money market funds

Class here mutual funds, open-end mutual funds, investment companies, investment trusts, unit trusts

*For real estate investment trusts, see 332.63247*

| .632 8 | Commodities |
|---|---|

Class here commodity futures and options, speculation in commodities

.64 Exchange of securities and commodities; speculation

Class here security and commodity exchanges

*See also 332.632 for advice on investing in specific forms of securities and commodities; also 332.678 for general investment guides*

.642 Exchange of securities

Including initial public offerings, tender offers

Class here securities exchanges, stock exchanges, stock market

Class brokerage firms in 332.62; class speculation in securities in 332.632

*For over-the-counter markets, see 332.643; for international exchange of securities, see 332.65*

[.642 094–.642 099] Specific continents, countries, localities in modern world

Do not use; class in 332.6424–332.6429

.642 4–.642 9 Exchange of securities in specific continents, countries, localities in modern world

Add to base number 332.642 notation 4–9 from Table 2, e.g., exchange of securities in the Netherlands 332.642492
When adding from Table 2 for a specific exchange, use the number for the primary area served by the exchange, e.g., New York Stock Exchange 332.64273, Pacific Stock Exchange 332.64279

.643 Over-the-counter markets

.644 Exchange of commodities

Class here commodity exchanges, commodity futures and options markets

Class speculation in 332.645

.644 1 Products of agriculture

Add to base number 332.6441 the numbers following 63 in 633–638, e.g., soybeans 332.6441334

.644 2 Products of mineral industries

Add to base number 332.6442 the numbers following 553 in 553.2–553.9, e.g., copper 332.644243

.645 Speculation

Including arbitrage, buying on margin

Class here speculation in multiple forms of investment

Class speculation in specific forms of investment in 332.63; class guides to speculation in 332.678

*See also 332.45 for speculation in foreign exchange*

.645 2 Futures

| .645 24 | Hedging |
|---------|---------|
| .645 3  | Options |

Class here puts and calls

| .645 7 | Derivatives |
|--------|-------------|
| .65 | International exchange of securities |

Class comprehensive works on international investment in 332.673

| .66 | Investment banks |
|-----|------------------|

Class here investment banking, issuing houses

*For international investment banks, see 332.15*

*See also 332.1754 for investment services of commercial banks*

| .67 | Investments in specific industries, in specific kinds of enterprise, by specific kinds of investors; international investment; investment guides |
|-----|---------|

Class investment in a specific form of securities with the form in 332.63, e.g., investment in railroad stocks 332.6322 (*not* 332.6722); class a specific aspect of investment with the aspect in 332.64–332.66, e.g., speculation by pension funds 332.645 (*not* 332.67254)

### SUMMARY

|  |  |
|--|--|
| 332.672 | **Investment in specific industries, in specific kinds of enterprises, by specific kinds of investors** |
| .673 | **International investment** |
| .678 | **Investment guides** |

| [.670 1–.670 9] | Standard subdivisions |
|-----------------|-----------------------|

Do not use; class in 332.601–332.609

| .672 | Investment in specific industries, in specific kinds of enterprises, by specific kinds of investors |
|------|---------|

Class foreign investment in specific industries, in specific kinds of enterprises, by specific kinds of investors in 332.673

| [.672 01–.672 09] | Standard subdivisions |
|-------------------|-----------------------|

Do not use; class in 332.601–332.609

| .672 2 | Investment in specific industries and kinds of enterprises |
|--------|---------|

Including insurance companies, railroads

Class here domestic investment in specific industries and specific kinds of enterprises

Class investment in specific industries and kinds of enterprises by specific kinds of investors in 332.6725

*See Manual at 332 vs. 338, 658.15*

| [.672 201–.672 209] | Standard subdivisions |
|---------------------|-----------------------|

Do not use; class in 332.67201–332.67209

| | |
|---|---|
| .672 22 | Small business |
| .672 5 | Investment by specific kinds of investors |

Other than investment by private investors in general or by individual investors

Class here domestic investment by specific kind of investors

| | |
|---|---|
| [.672 501–.672 509] | Standard subdivisions |

Do not use; class in 332.67201–332.67209

| | |
|---|---|
| .672 52 | Investment by governments and their agencies |

Standard subdivisions are added for either or both topics in heading

| | |
|---|---|
| .672 53 | Investment by institutional investors |

Class here domestic investment by specific kinds of institutions other than pension funds

Class investments by banks in 332.1754

*For investment by pension funds, see 332.67254*

| | |
|---|---|
| .672 532 | Insurance companies |
| .672 54 | Investment by pension funds |
| .673 | International investment |

Class here foreign investment

Class international investment banking in 332.15; class specific forms of foreign investment in 332.63; class history and description of multinational business ventures and subsidiaries in 338.88; class initiation of international business enterprises (including subsidiaries) in 658.1149

*For international exchange of securities, see 332.65*

| | |
|---|---|
| .673 09 | History, geographic treatment, biography |

Class here the advantages and disadvantages of establishing businesses in specific areas, investment in specific areas not originating in other specific areas

Class the advantages and disadvantages of establishing businesses in specific areas resulting from government policy in 332.6732

*See also 338.09 for works describing where in fact industry is located*

*See Manual at 338.091–338.099 vs. 332.67309, 338.6042*

| | |
|---|---|
| .673 093–.673 099 | Specific continents, countries, localities |

*For investment originating in specific continents and countries, see 332.6733–332.6739*

| | |
|---|---|
| .673 1 | International investment by specific kinds of investors |
| | Other than investment by private investors in general |
| | Including individual investors |
| [.673 101–.673 109] | Standard subdivisions |
| | Do not use; class in 332.67301–332.67309 |
| .673 12 | International investment by governments |
| .673 14 | International investment by institutional investors |
| .673 2 | Government policy |
| | Including international control |
| .673 209 3–.673 209 9 | Specific continents, countries, localities |

Class incentives and obstacles in country of investment in 332.67322; class incentives and obstacles in country of investor in 332.67324

.673 22          Incentives and obstacles in country of investment

Class here incentives and obstacles in specific continent and region of investment

Add to base number 332.67322 notation 3–9 from Table 2, e.g., incentives and obstacles in Brazil 332.6732281
Subdivisions are added for either or both topics in heading

.673 24          Incentives and obstacles in country of investor

Class here incentives and obstacles in specific continent and region of investor

Add to base number 332.67324 notation 3–9 from Table 2, e.g., incentives and obstacles to overseas investment by British citizens 332.6732441
Subdivisions are added for either or both topics in heading

.673 3–.673 9        Investment originating in specific continents and countries

Add to base number 332.673 notation 3–9 from Table 2 for origin of investment, e.g., British foreign investments 332.67341; then add 0* and to the result add notation 1–9 from Table 2, e.g., British foreign investments in Brazil 332.67341081

Class policies of specific governments in 332.6732

*Add 00 for standard subdivisions; see instructions at beginning of Table 1

.678            Investment guides

Including forecasting, formula plans, speculation

Class here guides to domestic investment in general, guides to investment by private investors in general, by individual investors in general

Class guides to specific forms of investment in 332.63; class guides to investment in specific industry, by kind of enterprise, by kind of investor (other than private investors in general and individual investors) in 332.672; class guides to foreign investment in 332.673

**.7**      **Credit**

Class here loans

Class credit functions of banks in 332.1; class credit functions of specialized banking institutions in 332.2; class credit functions of credit and loan institutions in 332.3

*For interest, see 332.8*

.71            Agricultural credit

.72            Real estate finance and mortgages

Standard subdivisions are added for either or both topics in heading

Class here discrimination in mortgage loans; mortgage delinquencies and defaults

Class finance on farm real estate in 332.71

*See also 332.32 for mortgage institutions; also 332.6323 for mortgage bonds and certificates; also 332.63244 for mortgages as an investment*

.722           Home finance (Residential finance)

.74            Other forms of credit

Class credit instruments facilitating a specific form of credit in 332.76

.742           Commercial, mercantile, industrial credit

Including export credit, small business loans

.743           Personal loans

Including consumer credit

.75            Insolvency and credit restrictions

Standard subdivisions are added for insolvency and credit restrictions together, for insolvency alone

Class here bankruptcy

.76            Credit instruments

> Including checks, debit cards, money orders, smart cards

> Class certificates of deposit in 332.1752

>> *For commercial paper, see 332.77. For credit instruments issued by a specific type of financial institution, see the type in 332.1, e.g., commercial banks 332.178*

.765           Credit cards

> Class here comprehensive works on credit cards

.77            Commercial paper

> Including acceptances, drafts, letters of credit, promissory notes

> Class here comprehensive works on commercial paper

>> *For commercial paper as medium of exchange, see 332.55*

**.8            Interest**

> *See also 332.6323 for interest rate futures*

.83            Usury

.84            Discount

> Including rediscount

**.9            Counterfeiting, forgery, alteration**

> Class comprehensive works on counterfeiting in 364.1334; class comprehensive works on forgery in 364.1635

>> *See also 737.4 for counterfeit coins; also 769.55 for counterfeit paper money; also 769.562 for counterfeit stamps*

**333            Economics of land and energy**

> Land: all natural and man-made resources over which possession of the earth gives control

> Standard subdivisions are added for land and energy together, for land alone

> Class here land as a factor of production

>> *See Manual at 333.73–333.78 vs. 333, 333.1–333.5*

### SUMMARY

| | |
|---|---|
| 333.001–.009 | **Standard subdivisions** |
| .01–.08 | **[Theories and land surveys]** |
| .1 | **Public ownership of land** |
| .2 | **Ownership of land by nongovernmental groups** |
| .3 | **Private ownership of land** |
| .4 | **Absentee ownership** |
| .5 | **Renting and leasing land** |
| .7 | **Land, recreational and wilderness areas, energy** |
| .8 | **Subsurface resources** |
| .9 | **Other natural resources** |

| | |
|---|---|
| .001 | Philosophy and theory |

> Do not use for theories; class in 333.01

| | |
|---|---|
| .001 2 | Classification |

> *For land classification, see 333.73012*

| | |
|---|---|
| .002–.009 | Standard subdivisions |
| .01 | Theories |
| .012 | Rent theories |

> Including Ricardo's theory of earning power of land in terms of its marginal productivity
>
> Class here economic rent
>
> Class comprehensive works on rent in 333.5

| | |
|---|---|
| .08 | Land surveys |

> Class here work of chartered surveyors (United Kingdom)
>
> *For land surveying techniques, see 526.9. For a specific kind of land survey, see the kind, e.g., public land surveys 333.18, land use surveys 333.7313*
>
> *See also 631.47 for surveys that focus on agricultural use of soils*

---

>         **333.1–333.5 Ownership of land**

> Ownership: right to possession and use; right to transfer of possession and use
>
> Land: all natural and man-made resources over which possession of the earth gives control
>
> Class here the kind of control that stems from ownership; ownership of natural resources
>
> Class comprehensive economic works on ownership of land in 333.3; class interdisciplinary works on economic and legal aspects of ownership and transfer of land in 346.043
>
> *See also 333.7–333.9 for usage of natural resources, for control of such usage not stemming from ownership*
>
> *See Manual at 333.73–333.78 vs. 333, 333.1–333.5*

| | |
|---|---|
| **.1** | **Public ownership of land** |

> Class public control of privately owned lands in 333.717; class comprehensive works on land policy in 333.73
>
> *See also 333.2 for ownership and control of land by peoples subordinate to another jurisdiction; also 343.02 for law of public property*

| | |
|---|---|
| .11 | Acquisition and disposal of specific kinds of lands |

> Including forests, roads, recreational lands

[.110 1–.110 9]       Standard subdivisions

           Do not use; class in 333.1

.13            Acquisition

           Including eminent domain, expropriation, purchase

           Class here evaluation of lands for government acquisition

           Class acquisition of specific kinds of land in 333.11

           *For nationalization, see 333.14*

.14            Nationalization

.16            Disposal

           Including grants, leases, sale

           Class disposal of specific kinds of land in 333.11

.18            Public land surveys

           Class surveys of public land use in 333.7313; class interdisciplinary works on land surveys in 333.08

           *See also 526.9 for surveying techniques*

**.2**            **Ownership of land by nongovernmental groups**

           Including common lands; enclosure of common lands; open-field system; ownership and control of land by peoples subordinate to another jurisdiction, e.g., lands of American native peoples in United States

           *For corporate ownership, see 333.324*

**.3**            **Private ownership of land**

           Including subdivision of private land

           Class here comprehensive works on land ownership (land tenure)

           *For public ownership, see 333.1; for ownership by nongovernmental groups, see 333.2; for absentee ownership, see 333.4*

### SUMMARY

| | | |
|---|---|---|
| **333.31** | **Land reform** | |
| **.32** | **Types of tenure** | |
| **.33** | **Transfer of possession and of right to use** | |

.31            Land reform

           Class here land redistribution, settlement and resettlement of people on the land

           *See also 333.2 for enclosure of common lands*

[.310 94–.310 99]       Specific continents, countries, localities in modern world

           Do not use; class in 333.314–333.319

| | |
|---|---|
| .314–.319 | Land reform in specific continents, countries, localities in modern world |

Add to base number 333.31 notation 4–9 from Table 2, e.g., land reform in Latin America 333.318

| | |
|---|---|
| .32 | Types of tenure |
| .322 | Feudal tenure |
| .323 | Individual tenure |

*For corporate ownership, see 333.324*

| | |
|---|---|
| .323 2 | Ownership in fee simple |
| .323 4 | Qualified ownership |

Including easements, entails, life estates, time-sharing

| | |
|---|---|
| .324 | Corporate ownership |
| .33 | Transfer of possession and of right to use |

Standard subdivisions are added for either or both topics in heading

Including consolidation of holdings

Class here comprehensive works on real estate business

Class land reform in 333.31

*For government acquisition and disposal, see 333.1; for renting and leasing, see 333.5; for real estate development, see 333.7315*

*See also 332.6324 for real estate investment; also 332.72 for real estate finance*

| | |
|---|---|
| .332 | Value and price of land |

Standard subdivisions are added for value and price together, for value alone

Class here valuation (appraisal)

Class valuation for government acquisition and disposal in 333.11–333.16; class value and price of specific kinds of land in 333.335–333.339; class valuation for tax purposes in 352.44

| | |
|---|---|
| .332 2 | Real estate market |

Class here economic and social factors affecting exchange of real estate

Class price in 333.3323

| | |
|---|---|
| .332 3 | Price |
| .332 302 1 | Tabulated and related materials |

Do not use for statistics; class in 333.3323

.333            Sale and gift

Standard subdivisions are added for sale and gift together, for sale alone

Class sale and gift of specific kinds of land in 333.335–333.339

---

> 333.335–333.339 Transfer of possession and use of specific kinds of land

Except for modifications shown under specific entries, add to each subdivision identified by * as follows:
2       Value and price
        Standard subdivisions are added for value and price together, for value alone
        Class here valuation (appraisal)
22      Real estate market
            Class here economic and social factors affecting exchange of real estate
            Class price in 23
23      Price
3       Sale and gift
        Standard subdivisions are added for sale and gift together, for sale alone
5       Renting and leasing
        Standard subdivisions are added for renting and leasing together, for renting alone
        Add to 5 the numbers following 333.5 in 333.53–333.56, e.g., share renting 563

Class comprehensive works in 333.33

.335            *Rural lands

Class here agricultural lands

.335 7              *Forest lands

.336            *Industrial lands

Including transportation space, e.g., right of way

Class works that emphasize buildings in 333.338

.337            *Urban lands

Residential and commercial lands

Class works that emphasize buildings in 333.338

*For industrial lands, see 333.336*

.338            *Buildings and other fixtures

Including apartment houses, condominiums, mobile homes

Class here residential buildings

*See also 643.12 for the homemakers approach to buying and selling housing*

---

*Add as instructed under 333.335–333.339

.338 7                    *Commercial and industrial buildings

                              Subdivisions are added for either or both topics in heading

.339                      Other natural resources

                              Appraisal, gift, leasing, renting, sale, market

                              Including rights to use of minerals, water, air space

**.4          Absentee ownership**

**.5          Renting and leasing land**

                  Class renting and leasing specific kinds of land in 333.335–333.339

                  *For renting and leasing public land, see 333.16; for renting and leasing
                  land owned by nongovernmental groups other than private corporations and
                  partnerships, see 333.2; for absentee ownership, see 333.4*

.53           Tenancy

                  Including tenancy for years (for a specified time period), tenancy from year
                  to year, tenancy at will

                  *For landlord-tenant relations, see 333.54*

.54           Landlord-tenant relations

.56           Types of renting

.562              Cash renting

.563              Share renting

                  Class here percentage renting

                  *For sharecropping, see 333.335563*

*Add as instructed under 333.335–333.339

>      **333.7–333.9 Natural resources and energy**

Aspects other than ownership

Class here raw materials

Except for modifications shown under specific entries, add to each subdivision identified by * as follows:

     01–09     Standard subdivisions
     1        General topics
             Class comprehensive works on specific topics in 333.71
   [101–109]    Standard subdivisions
             Do not use; class in 01–09
     11       Reserves
             Variant names: stock, supply
             Including shortages
     12      Requirements
             Variant names: need, demand
     13      Consumption (Utilization)
             Class consumption control in 17
             Do not add for specific uses (e.g., water for irrigation); class with the subject in 333.7–333.9 without further subdivision
             Class interdisciplinary works on consumption in 339.47
     137     Abuse and wastage
             Standard subdivisions are added for either or both topics in heading
             Class here description of abused resources, consequences of abuse and wastage
             Class reclamation, rehabilitation, restoration of abused resources in 153; class prevention of abuse and wastage in 16; class pollution in 363.73
     14      Environmental impact studies
             Class studies emphasizing abuse and wastage in 137. Class impact on a specific environment or resource with the impact, e.g., economic impact on Rome of a major new waste treatment facility 330.945632, impact of the same treatment plant on the waters of the Tiber River 333.916214094562; class projected impacts with the program or development that is being studied, e.g., projected impact of proposed standards for water pollution 363.739462
   >15–17    Management and control
             Class here citizen participation, planning, policy
             Class comprehensive works in 333.7–333.9 without adding from this table
     15      Development
     152     Improvement
     153     Reclamation, rehabilitation, restoration
             Standard subdivisions are added for any or all topics in heading
             Class reclamation that is not restoration to a previous state in 152
     158     Subsidies

(continued)

> **333.7–333.9 Natural resources and energy (continued)**

16      Conservation and protection
         Standard subdivisions are added for either or both topics in
         heading
         Class control of usage in 17; class comprehensive works on
         conservation and protection in 333.72

17      Control of usage
         Including allocation, price control, rationing, ways and means of
         efficient use
         Do not add for specific uses (e.g., water for irrigation); class
         with the subject in 333.7–333.9 without further subdivision

Class ownership of land and other natural resources in 333.1–333.5; class
economic geology in 553; class comprehensive works on natural resources and
energy in 333.7

*See Manual at 333.7–333.9 vs. 363.1, 363.73, 577; also at 333.7–333.9 vs.
363.6; also at 333.7–333.9 vs. 508, 913–919, 930–990*

.7      **Land, recreational and wilderness areas, energy**

Class here interdisciplinary works on the environment, on natural resources

Class environmentalism in 333.72

*For ownership aspects of natural resources, see 333.1–333.5; for subsurface
resources, see 333.8; for natural resources other than land, recreational and
wilderness areas, energy, subsurface resources, see 333.9. For noneconomic
aspects of the environment, of natural resources, see the aspect, e.g.,
environmental protection 363.7, conservation technology 639.9*

*See Manual at 363 vs. 302–307, 333.7, 570–590, 600*

### SUMMARY

| | |
|---|---|
| 333.71 | **General topics of land, recreational and wilderness areas, energy** |
| .72 | **Conservation and protection** |
| .73 | **Land** |
| .74 | **Grasslands** |
| .75 | **Forest lands** |
| .76 | **Rural lands** |
| .77 | **Urban lands** |
| .78 | **Recreational and wilderness areas** |
| .79 | **Energy** |

.71      General topics of land, recreational and wilderness areas, energy

Add to base number 333.71 the numbers following 1 in notation 11–17
from table under 333.7–333.9, e.g., development 333.715; however, for
conservation and protection, see 333.72

.72        Conservation and protection

       Standard subdivisions are added for either or both topics in heading

       Class here environmentalism, comprehensive works on conservation and protection of natural resources

       *For conservation and protection with respect to energy or a specific type of natural resource, see the resource in 333.73–333.95, plus notation 16 from table under 333.7–333.9, e.g., conservation of wilderness areas 333.78216*

       *See Manual at 333.72 vs. 304.28, 320.58, 363.7*

.73        Land

       Aspects other than ownership

       Including kinds of land by physical condition, e.g., mountainous land, sand dunes

       Class here government policy on land; river basins

       Class ownership aspects of land in 333.1–333.5; class arid and semiarid lands in 333.736

       *For kinds of land by use, see 333.74–333.78; for shorelands and related areas, see 333.917; for wetlands and submerged lands, see 333.918*

       *See Manual at 333.73–333.78 vs. 333, 333.1–333.5*

.731        General topics of land

       Add to base number 333.731 the numbers following 1 in notation 11–17 from table under 333.7–333.9, e.g., real estate development 333.7315, comprehensive works on soil and water conservation 333.7316

       Class soil and water conservation in rural lands in 333.7616; class real estate development in urban lands in 333.7715; class zoning of urban lands in 333.7717; class water conservation in 333.9116; class pollution control in 363.73966; class comprehensive works on real estate business in 333.33

       *For a specific type of natural areas established for conservation, see the type, e.g., wilderness areas 333.782*

.736        *Arid lands

       Class here semiarid lands, desertification

---

>        333.74–333.78 Kinds of land by use

       Class comprehensive works in 333.73

       *See Manual at 333.73–333.78 vs. 333, 333.1–333.5*

.74        *Grasslands

       Class here grazing lands, pasture lands

---

*Add as instructed under 333.7–333.9

.75          *Forest lands

Class here national forests; jungles, rain forests, woodlands; old-growth forests

Class parks, recreational, wilderness areas in 333.78

*See also 333.95397 for wood as a fuel*

.751 1        Reserves

Number built according to instructions under 333.7–333.9

Class here forest reserves, timber reserves

Class supply of cut timber, comprehensive works on timber in 338.17498

.751 2        Requirements

Number built according to instructions under 333.7–333.9

Class here requirements for timber discussed in terms of effect on forest land and supply of uncut timber

Class requirements for timber discussed in terms of how much timber will need to be cut to meet demand in 338.17498

.751 3        Consumption (Utilization)

Number built according to instructions under 333.7–333.9

Class here consumption of forest products in terms of effect on future forest resources

Class utilization of forests to provide products for sale in 338.17498

.751 5        Development

Number built according to instructions under 333.7–333.9

Class here measures to promote growth of forests as long-term resources

Class development of ways to exploit forest products in 338.17498

.76          *Rural lands

Class here agricultural lands

Class rural lands of a specific physical condition not devoted to a specific use in 333.73; class rural recreational lands in 333.78

*For grasslands, see 333.74; for forest lands, see 333.75*

.765         *Mined lands

Class here surface-mined lands

---

*Add as instructed under 333.7–333.9

| | |
|---|---|
| .77 | *Urban lands |

Including commercial, industrial, residential lands; streets

Class urban mined lands in 333.765; class urban recreational lands in 333.78

| | |
|---|---|
| .78 | *Recreational and wilderness areas |

Subdivisions are added for recreational and wilderness areas together, for recreational areas alone

Class wildlife in 333.954; class wildlife refuges in 333.95416

*See also 363.68 for park and recreation services*

| | |
|---|---|
| .782 | *Wilderness areas |

*For specific kinds of wilderness areas, see 333.784*

| | |
|---|---|
| .783 | *Parks |
| .784 | Specific kinds of recreational and wilderness areas |

Including forests, mountains

| | |
|---|---|
| [.784 01–.784 09] | Standard subdivisions |

Do not use; class in 333.7801–333.7809

---

| | |
|---|---|
| > | 333.784 4–333.784 5   Recreational use of water |

Class here recreational use of land adjoining water, e.g., beaches, shores

Class comprehensive works on recreational use of water in 333.7844; class comprehensive works on uses of water and land adjoining it in 333.91

| | |
|---|---|
| .784 4 | *Recreational use of lakes |

Class here comprehensive works on recreational use of water

*For recreational use of rivers and streams, see 333.7845; for recreational use of reservoirs, see 333.7846*

| | |
|---|---|
| .784 5 | *Recreational use of rivers and streams |

Standard subdivisions are added for either or both topics in heading

| | |
|---|---|
| .784 6 | *Recreational use of reservoirs |

Class comprehensive works on lakes and reservoirs in 333.7844

*Add as instructed under 333.7–333.9

.79            ‡Energy

Class here power resources, production of energy, interdisciplinary works on energy

Class electric power in 333.7932; class extraction of energy resources and comprehensive works on the economics of mineral fuels in 338.2; class comprehensive works on production economics of processing and manufacturing fuels in 338.476626; class interdisciplinary works on mineral fuels in 553

> *For a specific form of energy not provided for here, see the form, e.g., wind energy 333.92; for a specific energy resource not provided for here, see the resource, e.g., fossil fuels 333.82; for a noneconomic aspect of energy, see the aspect, e.g., technology of photovoltaic power generation 621.31244*

### SUMMARY

| | |
|---|---|
| 333.791 37 | **Abuse and wastage** |
| .792 | **Primary forms of energy** |
| .793 | **Secondary forms of energy** |
| .794 | **Renewable energy resources** |
| .796 | **Energy for specific uses** |

.791 37        Abuse and wastage

Number built according to instructions under 333.7–333.9

Class utilization of waste heat in 333.793

.792            †Primary forms of energy

Resources used directly to perform work, to produce other forms of energy

.792 3          †Solar energy

Including electricity derived from solar energy, e.g., with photovoltaic cells

Class distribution of electricity derived from solar energy in 333.7932

.792 33         Financial aspects

Including prices

.792 4          †Nuclear energy

Class here electricity derived from nuclear energy

Class distribution of electricity derived from nuclear energy in 333.7932; class nuclear fuels in 333.85

.792 43         Financial aspects

Including prices

†Add as instructed under 333.7–333.9, except use 15 for both development and generation of energy
‡Add as instructed under 333.7–333.9, except class utilization of waste heat in 333.793

.793                †Secondary forms of energy

Energy produced through use of other resources

Including cogeneration of electric power and heat, district heating, waste heat

Class economics of synthetic fuel production in 338.4766266

*For secondary forms of energy derived from a specific resource, see the resource, e.g., electricity derived from nuclear energy 333.7924*

.793 2              †Electrical energy

Including distribution of electrical energy regardless of resource from which the electricity was derived, rural electrification

Class here electricity derived from fossil fuels, electrical utilities, comprehensive works on electrical energy

*For electricity derived from a specific resource other than fossil fuels, see the resource, e.g., electricity derived from water 333.914*

.793 23             Financial aspects

.793 231            Prices

.793 8              †Energy from waste materials

Class distribution of electricity derived from waste materials in 333.7932; class production economics of making fuel from waste materials in 338.4766287; class chemical technology of energy from waste materials in 662.87

*For energy from biological wastes, see 333.9539*

.794                †Renewable energy resources

Class here alternative energy resources

Class distribution of electricity derived from renewable energy resources in 333.7932

*For a specific renewable or alternative energy resource, see the resource, e.g., solar energy 333.7923*   nuclear 333.7924

*[handwritten margin note: Use for wind power, biomass, water power]*

.796                Energy for specific uses

Including energy for military use

Unless other instructions are given, class a subject with aspects in two or more subdivisions of 333.796 in the number coming last, e.g., energy use in school buildings 333.7964 (*not* 333.7962)

Class a specific kind of energy for specific uses with the kind of energy, e.g., energy from petroleum for transportation use 333.8232 (*not* 333.7968)

[.796 01–.796 09]   Standard subdivisions

Do not use; class in 333.7901–333.7909

---

†Add as instructed under 333.7–333.9, except use 15 for both development and generation of energy

| .796 2 | *Energy for use in buildings |
| | Including use in construction |

*See also 624 for technical aspects of energy use in construction*

| .796 3 | *Energy for residential use |
| .796 4 | *Energy for social service institutions |

Including churches, hospitals, prisons, schools

| .796 5 | *Energy for industrial use |

Class here manufacturing use

Class energy use in construction of buildings in 333.7962

*For food processing use, see 333.7966*

| .796 6 | *Energy for use in agriculture and food processing |
| .796 8 | *Energy for use in transportation and commerce |

Subdivisions are added for transportation and commerce together, for transportation alone

| .796 89 | *Energy for commercial use |

**.8 Subsurface resources**

Class here strategic materials

Class mined lands, including surface-mined lands, in 333.765; class extraction of subsurface resources and comprehensive works on the economics of subsurface resources in 338.2; class interdisciplinary works on subsurface resources in 553

*For ownership aspects of subsurface resources, see 333.1–333.5; for groundwater, see 333.9104*

| .81 | General topics of subsurface resources |

Add to base number 333.81 the numbers following 1 in notation 11–17 from table under 333.7–333.9, e.g., reserves in storage of subsurface resources 333.811; however, for development, see 338.2

| .82 | Fossil fuels |

Class here nonrenewable fuels

Class electricity derived from fossil fuels in 333.7932

*For nuclear fuels, see 333.85493*

| .821 | General topics of fossil fuels |

Add to base number 333.821 the numbers following 1 in notation 11–17 from table under 333.7–333.9, e.g., reserves in storage of fossil fuels 333.8211; however, for development, see 338.272; for reserves in nature, see 553.2

| .822 | Coal |

*Add as instructed under 333.7–333.9

.822 1            General topics of coal

> Add to base number 333.8221 the numbers following 1 in notation 11–17 from table under 333.7–333.9, e.g., reserves in storage of coal 333.82211; however, for development, see 338.2724; for reserves in nature, see 553.24

.823         Oil and natural gas

.823 1            General topics of oil and natural gas

> Add to base number 333.8231 the numbers following 1 in notation 11–17 from table under 333.7–333.9, e.g., reserves in storage of oil and natural gas 333.82311; however, for development, see 338.2728; for reserves in nature, see 553.28

.823 2            Oil

> Petroleum limited to oil

> Class petroleum covering oil and natural gas in 333.823

.823 21            General topics of oil

> Add to base number 333.82321 the numbers following 1 in notation 11–17 from table under 333.7–333.9, e.g., reserves in storage of oil 333.823211; however, for development, see 338.27282; for reserves in nature, see 553.282

.823 3            Natural gas

> *See also 363.63 for gas distribution services of public utilities*

.823 31            General topics of natural gas

> Add to base number 333.82331 the numbers following 1 in notation 11–17 from table under 333.7–333.9, e.g., reserves in storage of natural gas 333.823311; however, for development, see 338.27285; for reserves in nature, see 553.285

.85         Minerals

> Class comprehensive works on the economics of minerals in 338.2; class interdisciplinary works on nonmetallic minerals in 553; class interdisciplinary works on metals in 669

.851         General topics of minerals

> Add to base number 333.851 the numbers following 1 in notation 11–17 from table under 333.7–333.9, e.g., reserves in storage of minerals 333.8511; however, for development, see 338.2; for reserves in nature, see 553

.852–.859         Specific minerals

> Add to base number 333.85 the numbers following 553 in 553.2–553.9, e.g., tin 333.85453, uranium 333.854932; however, for fossil fuels, see 333.82; for groundwater, see 333.9104

> Class nuclear energy in 333.7924

.88          *Geothermal energy

>    Class here electricity derived from geothermal energy, thermal waters
>
>    Class distribution of electricity derived from geothermal energy in 333.7932

### .9          **Other natural resources**

> *For ownership aspects of other natural resources, see 333.1–333.5*

### SUMMARY

| | |
|---|---|
| 333.91 | **Water and lands adjoining bodies of water** |
| .92 | **Air** |
| .94 | **Space** |
| .95 | **Biological resources** |

.91          Water and lands adjoining bodies of water

>    Standard subdivisions are added for water and lands adjoining bodies of water together, for water alone
>
>    Class here aquatic resources, comprehensive works on the economics of aquatic resources
>
>    Class interdisciplinary works on water in 553.7
>
> > *For a specific aquatic resource, see the resource, e.g., minerals 333.85, fishes 333.956; for a specific aspect of water not provided for here, see the aspect, e.g., recreational use of water and lands adjoining bodies of water 333.7844–333.7845, regulation and control of distribution of water to consumers 363.61*
> >
> > *See Manual at 363.61*

.910 01–.910 09          Standard subdivisions

.910 4          †Groundwater (Subsurface water)

> > *For subsurface thermal waters, see 333.88*

.911          General topics of water

>    Class water for specific uses in 333.912–333.915; class comprehensive works on soil and water conservation in 333.7316. Class general topics of a specific kind of water with the kind, e.g., general topics of rivers and streams 333.9162

[.911 01–.911 09]          Standard subdivisions

>    Do not use; class in 333.91001–333.91009

.911 1–.911 7          Subdivisions for topics of water

>    Add to base number 333.911 the numbers following 1 in notation 11–17 from table under 333.7–333.9, e.g., reserves in storage, as in reservoirs and storage tanks 333.9111; however, for water pollution, see 363.7394; for reserves in nature, see 553.7

---

*Add as instructed under 333.7–333.9

†Add as instructed under 333.7–333.9, except use 11 only for reserves in storage; class reserves in nature in 553.7

>        333.912–333.915   Water for specific uses

             Class comprehensive works in 333.91

             *For recreational use, see 333.7844*

.912          †Water for domestic and industrial uses

.912 2        †Water for domestic use

             Including drinking and washing

.912 3        †Water for industrial use

             Class water for generation of energy in 333.914; class water for transportation in 333.915

.913          †Water for irrigation

.914          *Water for generation of energy

             Including thermal ocean power conversion

             Class here hydroelectricity

.914 11       Reserves

             Number built according to instructions under 333.7–333.9

             Class here energy-producing potential of water

.914 15       Development

             Number built according to instructions under 333.7–333.9

             Class here development and generation of energy

.915          †Water for transportation

>        333.916–333.918   Specific bodies of water, shorelands, wetlands and related areas

             Class specific uses of water, shorelands, wetlands, and related areas in 333.912–333.915; class comprehensive works in 333.91

.916          Specific bodies of water

             Class specific uses of specific bodies of water in 333.912–333.915; class lands adjoining specific bodies of water in 333.917; class wetlands and submerged lands related to specific bodies of water in 333.918

.916 2        †Rivers and streams

             Subdivisions are added for either or both topics in heading

             Class river basins in 333.73

---

*Add as instructed under 333.7–333.9

†Add as instructed under 333.7–333.9, except use 11 only for reserves in storage; class reserves in nature in 553.7

.916 3   †Lakes and ponds

   Subdivisions are added for either or both topics in heading

   *For saltwater lakes, see 333.9164*

.916 4   ‡Oceans and seas

   Including bays, estuaries, gulfs, salt lakes

   Subdivisions are added for either or both topics in heading

.917   *Lands adjoining bodies of water

   Including beaches, floodplains, tidelands (lands that are overflowed by the tide but exposed by low water)

   Class here coasts, seashores, shorelands

   Class river basins in 333.73; class comprehensive works on tidelands in 333.918

   *For wetlands and submerged lands, see 333.918*

.918   *Wetlands and submerged lands

   Including continental shelves, tidelands (lands underlying the ocean beyond the low tidemark but within a nation's territorial waters), comprehensive works on tidelands

   Subdivisions are added for wetlands and submerged lands together, for wetlands alone

   Class recreational use in 333.784

   *For tidelands (lands that are overflowed by the tide but exposed by low water), see 333.917*

   *See also 333.916 for works focusing on bodies of water rather than the land they submerge*

.92   *Air

   Class here wind energy, use of wind for generation of electricity

   Class distribution of wind-generated electricity in 333.7932

.94   Space

   Class industrialization of space in 338.0919

.95   *Biological resources

   Class here biodiversity, biosphere

   Unless other instructions are given, class a subject with aspects in two or more subdivisions of 333.95 in the number coming last, e.g., game birds 333.95829 (*not* 333.9549)

---

*Add as instructed under 333.7–333.9

†Add as instructed under 333.7–333.9, except use 11 only for reserves in storage; class reserves in nature in 553.7

‡Add as instructed under 333.7–333.9, except class reserves in 551.46

## SUMMARY

|  |  |
|---|---|
| **333.952** | **Specific kinds of biological resources** |
| **.953** | **Plants and microorganisms** |
| **.954** | **Animals** |
| **.955** | **Invertebrates** |
| **.956** | **Fishes** |
| **.957** | **Reptiles and amphibians** |
| **.958** | **Birds** |
| **.959** | **Specific kinds of mammals** |

.952        Specific kinds of biological resources

Not limited by kind of organisms

> *For genetic and germ plasm resources, see 333.9534; for biomass energy, see 333.9539*

[.952 01–.952 09]    Standard subdivisions

Do not use; class in 333.9501–333.9509

.952 2      *Rare and endangered species

Class here extinction, threatened species, vanishing species

Subdivisions are added for either or both topics in heading

.952 3      *Nonnative species

Class here alien, exotic, introduced, invasive, naturalized species

.952 8      *Aquatic biological resources

Class here freshwater biological resources

> *For marine biological resources, see 333.956*

.952 88      *Wetland biological resources

.953      *Plants and microorganisms

Subdivisions are added for plants and microorganisms together, for plants alone

> *For forests, comprehensive works on timber resources, see 333.75*

> *See also 333.82 for peat*

.953 2      *Rare and endangered plants

Class here threatened, vanishing plants

Subdivisions are added for either or both topics in heading

*Add as instructed under 333.7–333.9

.953 3         *Nonnative and native plants

> Standard subdivisions are added for nonnative and native plants together, for nonnative plants alone

> Class here alien, exotic, introduced, invasive, naturalized plants

> Class rare and endangered nonnative and native plants in 333.9532

.953 4         *Germ plasm resources

> Class here plant varieties; interdisciplinary works on genetic resources, on germ plasm

>> *For animal genetic resources, germ plasm, see 333.954; for germ plasm, plant varieties in agriculture, see 631.523*

.953 8         *Seaweeds

> Class here algae, kelp

.953 9         †Plants as sources of energy

> Class here interdisciplinary works on biomass energy

>> *For animal biomass as an energy resource, see 333.954; for production economics of making biomass fuel, see 338.4766288; for biomass fuel engineering, see 662.88*

.953 97         *Fuelwood

.954         *Animals

> Including biomass energy, genetic resources, germ plasm

> Class here wildlife; comprehensive works on mammals, on vertebrates

>> *For invertebrates, see 333.955; for fishes, see 333.956; for reptiles and amphibians, see 333.957; for birds, see 333.958; for specific kinds of mammals, see 333.959*

.954 11         Reserves

> Number built according to instructions under 333.7–333.9

> Class here supply of uncaught animals in nature, statistics of catches used in estimating population of animals in nature

> Class catches from fishing, whaling, hunting, trapping industries in 338.372

.954 15         Development

> Number built according to instructions under 333.7–333.9

> Class here measures to increase supply of animals in nature

.954 2         *Rare and endangered animals

> Class here threatened, vanishing animals

> Subdivisions are added for either or both topics in heading

*Add as instructed under 333.7–333.9
†Add as instructed under 333.7–333.9, except use 15 for both development and generation of energy

| | | |
|---|---|---|
| .954 3 | | *Nonnative animals |

Class here alien, exotic, introduced, invasive, naturalized animals

.954 8             *Aquatic animals

*For marine animals, see 333.956*

.954 88           *Wetland animals

.954 9             *Game animals

Class economics of hunting in 338.3729

*For big game animals, see 333.9596*

---

>      **333.955–333.959 Specific taxonomic groups of animals**

Class comprehensive works in 333.954

*See Manual at 333.955–333.959 vs. 639.97*

.955          *Invertebrates

Class here marine invertebrates, shellfish

---

>      **333.955 3–333.955 5 Marine invertebrates**

Class comprehensive works in 333.955

.955 3           *Coral reefs

---

>      **333.955 4–333.955 5 Shellfish**

Class comprehensive works in 333.955

.955 4           *Mollusks

Class here Bivalvia

Class comprehensive works on shellfish in 333.955

.955 41–.955 48      Specific kinds of mollusks

Add to base number 333.9554 the numbers following 639.4 in 639.41–639.48, e.g., scallops 333.95546; then add further as instructed under 333.7–333.9 (*not* as instructed under 592–599), e.g., supply of scallops 333.9554611

.955 5           *Crustaceans

Class here Decapoda

.955 54–.955 58      Specific kinds of crustaceans

Add to base number 333.9555 the numbers following 595.38 in 595.384–595.388, e.g., lobsters 333.95554; then add further as instructed under 333.7–333.9 (*not* as instructed under 592–599), e.g., consumption of lobsters 333.9555413

*Add as instructed under 333.7–333.9

.955 7    *Insects

.956     *Fishes

> Class here marine biological resources, comprehensive works on finfish and shellfish

> *For shellfish, see 333.955. For a specific kind of marine biological resource not provided for below, see the kind, e.g., marine algae 333.9538, marine mammals 333.9595*

.956 2–.956 7  Specific kinds of fishes

> Add to base number 333.956 the numbers following 597 in 597.2–597.7, e.g., salmon 333.95656; then add further as instructed under 333.7–333.9 (*not* as instructed under 592–599), e.g., restoration of salmon fisheries 333.95656153

.956 8    *Rare and endangered fishes

> Subdivisions are added for either or both topics in heading

> Class specific kinds of rare and endangered fishes in 333.9562–333.9567

.956 9    *Game fishes

> Class specific kinds of game fishes in 333.9562–333.9567; class game fishes (salmonids) in 333.95655; class economics of fishing in 338.3727

.957     *Reptiles and amphibians

> Subdivisions are added for reptiles and amphibians together, for reptiles alone

.957 2    *Rare and endangered reptiles and amphibians

> Subdivisions are added for all topics in heading together, for rare reptiles alone, for endangered reptiles alone

.957 8–.957 9  Amphibians, specific reptiles

> Add to base number 333.957 the numbers following 597 in 597.8–597.9, e.g., sea turtles 333.957928; then add further as instructed under 333.7–333.9 (*not* as instructed under 592–599), e.g., protection of sea turtles 333.95792816; however, for comprehensive works on reptiles, on reptiles and amphibians, see 333.957

.958     *Birds

.958 2    Specific nontaxonomic kinds of birds

[.958 201–.958 209]  Standard subdivisions

> Do not use; class in 333.9501–333.9509

.958 22    *Rare and endangered birds

> Class here threatened, vanishing birds

> Subdivisions are added for either or both topics in heading

---

*Add as instructed under 333.7–333.9

| | |
|---|---|
| .958 28 | *Aquatic birds |

Class here water birds

Class waterfowl in 333.95841

| | |
|---|---|
| .958 287 | *Sea birds |
| .958 29 | *Game birds |

Class lowland game birds in 333.95841; class upland game birds in 333.9586

| | |
|---|---|
| .958 3–.958 9 | Specific kinds of birds |

Add to base number 333.958 the numbers following 598 in 598.3–598.9, e.g., wild turkeys 333.958645; then add further as instructed under 333.7–333.9 (*not* as instructed under 592–599), e.g., demand for wild turkeys 333.95864513

| | |
|---|---|
| .959 | Specific kinds of mammals |

Class comprehensive works in 333.954

| | |
|---|---|
| [.959 01–.959 09] | Standard subdivisions |

Do not use; class in 333.95401–333.95409

| | |
|---|---|
| .959 2–.959 8 | Subdivisions for specific kinds of mammals |

Add to base number 333.959 the numbers following 599 in 599.2–599.8, e.g., marine mammals, whales 333.9595, big game animals, ungulates 333.9596, carnivores, fur-bearing animals 333.9597; then add further as instructed under 333.7–333.9 (*not* as instructed under 592–599), e.g., supply of big game 333.959611

# 334 Cooperatives

## .1 Housing cooperatives

Class here building cooperatives

Class cooperative building associations that are also cooperative savings and loan associations in 334.2

## .2 Banking and credit cooperatives

Standard subdivisions are added for either or both topics in heading

| | |
|---|---|
| .22 | Credit unions |

Class comprehensive works on thrift institutions in 332.32

## .5 Consumer cooperatives

Class consumer housing cooperatives in 334.1; class comprehensive works on cooperative marketing in 334.6

| | |
|---|---|
| [.506 88] | Management of distribution (Marketing) |

Do not use; class in 658.87

*Add as instructed under 333.7–333.9

**.6** **Producers' cooperatives**

Class here marketing, production cooperatives

*For consumer cooperatives, see 334.5*

.68 Producers' cooperatives by industry

.681 Producers' cooperatives in industries other than extractive, manufacturing, construction

Class here service industries

.681 000 1–.681 000 9 Standard subdivisions

.681 001–.681 999 Subdivisions for producer's cooperatives in industries other than extractive, manufacturing, construction

Add to base number 334.681 notation 001–999 (but not 381–382), e.g., cooperative legal services 334.68134; however, for banking and credit cooperatives, see 334.2

.682–.688 Producers' cooperatives in extractive, manufacturing, construction industries

Class here cooperative marketing by producers in extractive, manufacturing, construction industries

Add to base number 334.68 the numbers following 6 in 620–680, e.g., agricultural cooperatives 334.683; however, for kibbutzim and moshavim, see 307.776; for Communist collective farms, see 338.763

*For building cooperatives, see 334.1*

**.7** **Benefit societies**

Class here benevolent, friendly, fraternal benefit, mutual aid, provident societies

Class a specific function of a benefit society with the function, e.g., insurance 368.3

# 335 Socialism and related systems

Standard subdivisions are added for socialism and related systems together, for socialism alone

Class here schools of thought featuring planned economies, state socialism, interdisciplinary works on socialism and related systems

Class socialism (communism) in 335.43; class comparisons of Communism (Marxism-Leninism) with other systems in 335.437; class socialism (democratic socialism) in 335.5

*For socialism as a political ideology, see 320.53; for socialist and communist political parties, see 324.217. For a specific topic of economics treated from a socialist or communist point of view, see the topic in economics, e.g., interest 332.8*

*See Manual at 335 vs. 306.345, 320.53*

(Option: Class in 330.159)

## SUMMARY

.001–.009     Standard subdivisions

.02       Utopian systems and schools

> Standard subdivisions are added for either or both topics in heading
>
> *For specific utopian systems, see 335.1–335.3*
>
> *See also 301 for ideal societies; also 321.07 for ideal states*

---

> **335.1–335.3 Non-Marxian and quasi-Marxian socialism**

Class comprehensive works in 335

> *For national socialism, see 335.6; for Christian socialism, see 335.7*
>
> *See also 307.77 for voluntary socialist communities*

**.1**      **Systems of English origin**

.12       Utopian socialism

> Including Owenism

.14       Fabian socialism

.15       Guild socialism

**.2**      **Systems of French origin**

> Including Babouvism, Icarianism

.22       Saint-Simonism

.23       Fourierism (Phalansterianism)

**.3**      **Systems of American origin**

**.4**      **Marxian systems**

> Class here Marxism
>
> *For democratic Marxian systems, see 335.5*

.401      Philosophy

> Do not use for philosophic foundations; class in 335.411. Do not use for comprehensive works on theory of Marxian systems; class in 335.4

| | |
|---|---|
| [.409 034] | 19th century, 1800–1899 |
| | Do not use; class in 335.42 |
| .409 04 | 20th century, 1900–1999 |
| .409 041 | 1917–1919 |
| | Do not use for 1900–1917; class in 335.423 |
| .41 | Philosophic foundations, economic concepts, aims |
| | Including social ownership of means of production |
| .411 | Philosophic foundations |
| | Including theory of class struggle |
| | *For the philosophic foundations of Marxian economics, see 335.412* |
| .411 2 | Dialectical materialism |
| | Class comprehensive works on dialectical materialism in 146.32 |
| .411 9 | Historical materialism |
| .412 | Economic concepts |
| | Including labor theory of value |
| .42 | Marxian systems, 1848–1917 |
| .422 | Early Communism, 1848–1875 |
| | Period of Communist manifesto |
| .423 | Scientific socialism, 1875–1917 |
| | Class scientific socialism of Lenin (Marxism-Leninism) in 335.43 |
| | *For democratic socialism, see 335.5* |
| .43 | Communism (Marxism-Leninism) |
| | Class here former Soviet communism, democratic centralism |
| | *For communism as a political ideology, see 320.532* |
| .430 9 | History, geographic treatment, biography |
| | Do not use for national variants as schools of thought; class in 335.434 |
| .433 | Trotskyist doctrines |
| .434 | National variants as schools of thought |
| | Use 335.4309 for communism in specific nations viewed as actual economic systems rather than schools of thought, e.g., Cuban communism as an existing system 335.43097291 (*not* 335.4347) |
| | Soviet communism as a school of thought is classed in 335.43, as the economic system of the former Soviet Union in 335.430947 |
| [.434 094–.434 099] | Specific continents, countries, localities in modern world |
| | Do not use; class in 335.434 |

| | |
|---|---|
| .434 4 | Communism of Yugoslavia (1918–1991) |
| | Class here Titoism |
| .434 5 | Chinese communism |
| | Class here Maoism |
| | Class comprehensive works on Asian national variants of communism in 335.4346 |
| .434 6 | Asian national variants |
| | Including North Korean, Vietnamese communism |
| | *For Chinese communism, see 335.4345* |
| .434 7 | Cuban communism (Castroism) |
| | Including ideas of Che Guevara |
| .437 | Comparative studies |
| | Comparison of communism with capitalism, cooperation, democratic socialism, other forms of collectivism |

## .5      Democratic socialism

Marxian and non-Marxian socialism

*For Fabian socialism, see 335.14; for Christian socialism, see 335.7*

*See also 307.77 for voluntary socialist communities*

## .6      Fascism

Class here falangism, national socialism, Neo-Nazism

*For fascism as a political ideology, see 320.533*

## .7      Christian socialism

*For Christian socialism as a political ideology, see 320.5312*

## .8      Other systems

| | |
|---|---|
| .82 | Syndicalism |
| | Class here anarcho-syndicalism |
| .83 | Anarchism |
| | *For anarchism as a political ideology, see 320.57; for anarcho-syndicalism, see 335.82* |
| | *See also 307.77 for voluntary anarchist communities* |

# 336      Public finance

Class here intergovernmental fiscal relations, comprehensive works on public finance and financial administration of governments

*For public financial administration and budgets, see 352.4*

*See Manual at 332, 336 vs. 339*

## SUMMARY

.001–.005    Standard subdivisions

.006    Organizations

.006 01        International organizations

> Class associations of sovereign states in 336.0916

[.006 8]        Management

> Do not use; class in 352.4

.007–.008    Standard subdivisions

[.009]        History, geographic treatment, biography

> Do not use for treatment by governmental level; class in 336.01. Do not use for history and biography for treatment by areas, regions, places in general, for ancient world; class in 336.09

[.009 4–.009 9]    Specific continents, countries, localities in modern world

> Do not use; class in 336.4–336.9

.01    Public finance by governmental level

> Class here public finance in three or more jurisdictions at a specific level

> Class public finance at a specific level in one or two specific jurisdictions in ancient world in 336.093; class public finance at a specific level in one or two specific jurisdictions in modern world in 336.4–336.9

.012    Public finance at national level

[.012 091]        Areas, regions, places in general

> Do not use; class in 336.0121

[.012 093–.012 099]    Specific continents, countries

> Do not use for specific continents; class in 336.0123–336.0129. Do not use for specific countries in ancient world; class in 336.093. Do not use for specific countries in modern world; class in 336.4–336.9

.012 1        Public finance at national level in areas, regions, places in general

> Add to base number 336.0121 the numbers following —1 in notation 11–19 from Table 2, e.g., national public finance in developing countries 336.0121724

.012 3–.012 9       Public finance at national level in specific continents

Add to base number 336.012 notation 3–9 from Table 2, e.g., national public finance in Europe 336.0124

Class public finance at national level in specific nations in ancient world in 336.093; class public finance at national level in specific nations in modern world in 336.4–336.9

.013           Public finance at state and provincial level

[.013 091]         Areas, regions, places in general

Do not use; class in 336.0131

[.013 093–.013 099]     Specific continents, countries, localities

Do not use for specific continents, countries; class in 336.0133–336.0139. Do not use for specific states and provinces in ancient world; class in 336.093. Do not use for specific states and provinces in modern world; class in 336.4–336.9

.013 1          Public finance at state and provincial level in areas, regions, places in general

Add to base number 336.0131 the numbers following —1 in notation 11–19 from Table 2, e.g., state and provincial public finance in developing countries 336.0131724

.013 3–.013 9      Public finance at state and provincial level in specific continents, countries

Add to base number 336.013 notation 3–9 from Table 2, e.g., provincial public finance in Canada 336.01371

Class public finance at state and provincial level in specific states and provinces in ancient world in 336.093; class public finance at state and provincial level in specific states and provinces in modern world in 336.4–336.9

.014           Public finance at local level

[.014 091]         Areas, regions, places in general

Do not use; class in 336.0141

[.014 093–.014 099]     Specific continents, countries, localities

Do not use for specific continents, countries, states and provinces; class in 336.0143–336.0149. Do not use for specific localities in ancient world; class in 336.093. Do not use for specific localities in modern world; class in 336.4–336.9

.014 1          Public finance at local level in areas, regions, places in general

Add to base number 336.0141 the numbers following —1 in notation 11–19 from Table 2, e.g., local public finance in developing countries 336.0141724

.014 3–.014 9     Public finance at local level in specific continents, countries, states and provinces

> Add to base number 336.014 notation 3–9 from Table 2, e.g., local public finance in Pennsylvania 336.014748

> Class public finance at local level in specific localities in ancient world in 336.093; class public finance at local level in specific localities in modern world in 336.4–336.9

.02     Revenue

> *For specific forms of revenue, see 336.1–336.2*

[.020 91]     Areas, regions, places in general

> Do not use; class in 336.021

[.020 93–.020 99]     Specific continents, countries, localities

> Do not use; class in 336.023–336.029

.021     Revenue in areas, regions, places in general

> Add to base number 336.021 the numbers following —1 in notation 11–19 from Table 2, e.g., revenue in developing countries 336.021724

.023–.029     Revenue in specific continents, countries, localities

> Add to base number 336.02 notation 3–9 from Table 2, e.g., revenue in France 336.0244

.09     History, geographic treatment, biography; associations of sovereign states

.090 1–.090 5     Historical periods

> Add to base number 336.090 the numbers following —090 in notation 0901–0905 from Table 1, e.g., public finance in the 19th century 336.09034

.091     Areas, regions, places in general; associations of sovereign states

.091 6     Associations of sovereign states

.091 62     League of Nations

.091 63     United Nations

.091 68     Regional associations

> Including League of Arab States

> Class regional associations limited to specific continents in 336.4–336.9

.091 7     Socioeconomic regions

> Add to base number 336.0917 the numbers following —17 in notation 171–177 from Table 2, e.g., public finance in developing countries 336.091724; however, for public finance in socioeconomic regions by governmental level, see 336.01

> Class regional associations of sovereign states in 336.09168

.092       Biography

> Add to base number 336.092 the numbers following —092 in notation 0922–0929 from Table 1, e.g., collected biography 336.0922

.093       Ancient world

> Add to base number 336.093 the numbers following —3 in notation 31–39 from Table 2, e.g., public finance in Roman Empire 336.0937; however, for public finance in ancient world by governmental level, see 336.01

[.094–.099]       Specific continents, countries, localities in modern world

> Do not use; class in 336.4–336.9

---

> ## 336.1–336.2 Specific forms of revenue

Class comprehensive works in 336.02

.1       **Nontax revenues**

> *For public borrowing, see 336.34*

---

> ### 336.12–336.15 Commercial revenues

Class revenue from franchises in 333.16; class comprehensive works in 336.1

*For revenues from public industries and services, see 336.19*

.12       Commercial revenues from public lands

> Including revenue from rent, mineral rights

.15       Commercial revenues from deposits, investments, loans

.16       Administrative revenues

> Including revenue from franchises, fines, gifts, profits on coinage, user and license fees

.17       Revenues from lotteries

.18       Intergovernmental and intragovernmental revenues

> Standard subdivisions are added for intergovernmental and intragovernmental revenues together, for intergovernmental revenues alone

.182       Revenues from reparations and interest on war loans

.185       Revenues from one government unit to another

> Including grants from higher units, payment in lieu of taxes, technical assistance funds

.188       Revenues from international grants

.19       Revenue from public industries and services

> Standard subdivisions are added for either or both topics in heading

**.2**      **Taxes**

Class here taxation, internal (inland) revenue, interdisciplinary works on taxes

*For tax law, see 343.04; for tax administration, see 352.44*

*See Manual at 343.04–343.06 vs. 336.2, 352.44*

### SUMMARY

| | |
|---|---|
| 336.200 1–.200 9 | **Standard subdivisions** |
| .201–.207 | **General topics of taxes** |
| .22 | **Real property taxes** |
| .23 | **Personal property taxes** |
| .24 | **Income taxes** |
| .25 | **Poll taxes** |
| .26 | **Customs (Tariff)** |
| .27 | **Other taxes** |
| .29 | **Principles of taxation** |

.200 1–.200 8      Standard subdivisions

.200 9      History, geographic treatment, biography

Do not use for general works on taxes by governmental level; class in 336.201

---

> 336.201–336.207  General topics of taxes

Unless other instructions are given, class a subject with aspects in two or more subdivisions of 336.201–336.207 in the number coming last, e.g., local business taxes 336.207 (*not* 336.2014)

Class comprehensive works in 336.2

.201      Taxes by governmental level

Class here taxes in three or more jurisdictions at the same level

Class taxes in one or two specific jurisdictions at a specific level in 336.20093–336.20099

.201 2      National taxes

[.201 209 1]      Areas, regions, places in general

Do not use; class in 336.20121

[.201 209 3–.201 209 9]      Specific continents, countries

Do not use for specific countries; class in 336.20093–336.20099. Do not use for specific continents; class in 336.20123–336.20129

.201 21      National taxes in areas, regions, places in general

Add to base number 336.20121 the numbers following —1 in notation 11–19 from Table 2, e.g., national taxes in developing countries 336.20121724

| .201 23–.201 29 | National taxes in specific continents |
|---|---|

Add to base number 336.2012 notation 3–9 from Table 2, e.g., national taxes in Europe 336.20124

Class national taxes in specific nations in 336.20093–336.20099

| .201 3 | State and provincial taxes |
|---|---|

| [.201 309 1] | Areas, regions, places in general |
|---|---|

Do not use; class in 336.20131

| [.201 309 3–.201 309 9] | Specific continents, countries |
|---|---|

Do not use for specific states or provinces; class in 336.20093–336.20099. Do not use for specific continents, countries; class in 336.20133–336.20139

| .201 31 | State and provincial taxes in areas, regions, places in general |
|---|---|

Add to base number 336.20131 the numbers following —1 in notation 11–19 from Table 2, e.g., provincial taxes in developing countries 336.20131724

| .201 33–.201 39 | State and provincial taxes in specific continents, countries |
|---|---|

Add to base number 336.2013 notation 3–9 from Table 2, e.g., provincial taxes in Canada 336.201371

Class state and provincial taxes in specific states or provinces in 336.20093–336.20099

| .201 4 | Local taxes |
|---|---|

| [.201 409 1] | Areas, regions, places in general |
|---|---|

Do not use; class in 336.20141

| [.201 409 3–.201 409 9] | Specific continents, countries, localities |
|---|---|

Do not use for local taxes in specific local jurisdictions; class in 336.20093–336.20099. Do not use for local taxes in specific continents, countries, states or provinces; class in 336.20143–336.20149

| .201 41 | Local taxes in areas, regions, places in general |
|---|---|

Add to base number 336.20141 the numbers following —1 in notation 11–19 from Table 2, e.g., local taxes in developing countries 336.20141724

| .201 43–.201 49 | Local taxes in specific continents, countries, states and provinces |
|---|---|

Add to base number 336.2014 notation 3–9 from Table 2, e.g., local taxes in Pennsylvania 336.2014748

Class local taxes in specific local jurisdictions in 336.20093–336.20099

| .205 | Tax reform |
|---|---|

Class here proposals and innovations

Class reform of taxes at a specific governmental level in 336.201

.206 Provisions that allow tax avoidance

> Including tax credits, deductions, incentives, rebates

> Class here loopholes, tax expenditure (reductions in government revenue through preferential tax treatment)

.207 Business taxes

> Including taxes on manufacturing, small business, international business

.22 Real property taxes

> Variant name: rates (United Kingdom)

> Class here comprehensive works on property taxes

> Class comprehensive works on taxes on personal wealth in 336.24

> *For personal property taxes, see 336.23*

.222 Rates and assessment

> Class rates and assessment of specific kinds of real property in 336.225

.225 Specific kinds of real property

> Including commercial, farm, residential property; land value taxation

[.225 01–.225 09] Standard subdivisions

> Do not use; class in 336.2201–336.2209

.23 Personal property taxes

> On tangible and intangible property

> Including mobile homes

> Class comprehensive works on property taxes in 336.22

.24 Income taxes

> Class here comprehensive works on taxes on personal wealth

> *For property taxes, see 336.22; for estate, inheritance, gift taxes, see 336.276*

.241 General topics of income taxes

> Class general topics applied to personal income tax in 336.242; class general topics applied to corporate income tax in 336.243

[.241 01–.241 09] Standard subdivisions

> Do not use; class in 336.2401–336.2409

.241 5 Reform

> Class reform of taxes on business income in 336.2417

.241 6 Provisions that allow tax avoidance

> Class provisions allowing avoidance of taxes on business income in 336.2417

.241 7 Taxes on business income

| | |
|---|---|
| .242 | Personal income taxes (Individual income taxes) |

*See also 362.582 for negative income tax*

| | |
|---|---|
| .242 1 | General topics of personal income taxes |

Class general topics applied to taxes on specific kinds of personal income in 336.2422–336.2428

| | |
|---|---|
| [.242 101–.242 109] | Standard subdivisions |

Do not use; class in 336.24201–336.24209

| | |
|---|---|
| .242 15 | Reform |
| .242 16 | Provisions that allow tax avoidance |
| .242 2 | Income from wages |

Including withholding tax

| | |
|---|---|
| .242 3 | Self-employment income |

Including income from individual proprietorships, from partnerships

Class here small business income

*For small corporation income, see 336.243*

| | |
|---|---|
| .242 4 | Capital gains |

Including capital loss deduction

Class here comprehensive works on taxation of individual and corporate capital gains and losses

*For taxation of corporate capital gains, see 336.243*

| | |
|---|---|
| .242 6 | Interest income |

Class here comprehensive works on taxation of individual and corporate interest income

*For taxation of corporate interest income, see 336.243*

| | |
|---|---|
| .242 8 | Retirement income |
| .243 | Corporate income taxes |

Including capital gains taxes, interest income

Class comprehensive works on business taxes in 336.207; class comprehensive works on business income tax in 336.2417

| | |
|---|---|
| .243 1 | General topics of corporate income taxes |

Class general topics applied to profits taxes in 336.2432

| | |
|---|---|
| [.243 101–.243 109] | Standard subdivisions |

Do not use; class in 336.24301–336.24309

| | |
|---|---|
| .243 15 | Reform |
| .243 16 | Provisions that allow tax avoidance |

Including oil depletion allowance

.243 2                    Excess and undistributed profits taxes

> Standard subdivisions are added for excess and undistributed profits taxes together, for excess profits tax alone

.249                      Social security taxes

> Class actuarial and administrative aspects of finance for social security in 368.401; class actuarial and administrative aspects of rates and rate making for social security in 368.4011

.25         Poll taxes

.26         Customs (Tariff)

> Class interdisciplinary works on customs (tariff) in 382.7

.263        Export and transit taxes

> Standard subdivisions are added for export and transit taxes together, for export taxes alone

.264        Import taxes

> *For import tax schedules, see 336.265; for import taxes on specific products, see 336.266*

.265        Import tax schedules

> *For import tax schedules on specific products, see 336.266*

.266        Import taxes and tax schedules on specific products

[.266 000 1–.266 000 9]          Standard subdivisions

> Do not use for import taxes; class in 336.26401–336.26409. Do not use for import tax schedules; class in 336.26501–336.26509

.266 001–.266 999          Subdivisions of import taxes and tax schedules on specific products

> Add to base number 336.266 notation 001–999, e.g., import taxes on paintings 336.26675
> Subdivisions are added for either or both topics in heading

.27         Other taxes

.271        Excise, sales, value-added, related taxes

> Including luxury, use taxes

.271 3      Sales tax

.271 4      Value-added tax

.271 6      Severance tax

.272        Stamp tax and revenue stamps

> Standard subdivisions are added for either or both topics in heading

.276          Estate, inheritance, gift taxes

Standard subdivisions are added for any or all topics in heading

Class here death duties, death tax

Class estate planning in 332.024016; class comprehensive works on taxes on personal wealth in 336.24

.278          Taxes on products, services, industries

Standard subdivisions are added for any or all topics in heading

Class a specific kind of tax on a product, service, industry with the kind of tax, e.g., import taxes on coal 336.26655324, severance taxes on coal 336.2716

.278 000 1–.278 000 9          Standard subdivisions

.278 001–.278 999          Taxes on specific products, services, industries

Add to base number 336.278 notation 001–999, e.g., coal industry taxes 336.2783382724
Subdivisions are added for any or all topics in heading

.29          Principles of taxation

Class principles of specific kinds of taxes in 336.22–336.27

.291          General principles of taxation

Including adequacy (yield), certainty, diversity, economy and convenience of collection, justice

.293          Kinds of rate

Including progressive, proportional, regressive rates

.294          Incidence

The final burden of tax payment and the people on whom it falls

Including direct, indirect, double taxation

**.3          Public debt and expenditures**

Class here fiscal policy, comprehensive works on monetary and fiscal policy

*For monetary policy, see 332.46; for use of fiscal and monetary policy in economic stabilization, see 339.5*

**SUMMARY**

| | |
|---|---|
| 336.31 | **Government securities** |
| .34 | **Public debt** |
| .36 | **Debt management** |
| .39 | **Public expenditures** |

.31          Government securities

Including short-term securities, Eurobonds

Class comprehensive works on government securities in 332.63232

.34 Public debt

Class here public borrowing

*For public securities, see 336.31; for debt management, see 336.36*

.340 9 History, geographic treatment, biography

Do not use for general works on domestic public debt by governmental level; class in 336.343

.343 Public debt by governmental level

Class here public debt in three or more jurisdictions at a specific level

Class public debt in one or two jurisdictions at the same level in 336.34093–336.34099; class international public debt regardless of jurisdiction or level in 336.3435; class flotation of loans regardless of level in 336.344; class debt limits regardless of level in 336.346

.343 1 Local level

[.343 109 1] Areas, regions, places in general

Do not use; class in 336.34311

[.343 109 3–.343 109 9] Specific continents, countries, localities

Do not use for specific continents, countries, states and provinces; class in 336.3409. Do not use for specific localities; class in 336.34313–336.34319

.343 11 Local public debt in areas, regions, places in general

Add to base number 336.34311 the numbers following —1 in notation 11–19 from Table 2, e.g., local public debt in developing countries 336.34311724

.343 13–.343 19 Local public debt in specific continents, countries, states and provinces

Add to base number 336.3431 notation 3–9 from Table 2, e.g., local public debt in Pennsylvania 336.3431748

Class local public debt in specific localities in 336.34093–336.34099

.343 2 State and provincial level

[.343 209 1] Areas, regions, places in general

Do not use; class in 336.34321

[.343 209 3–.343 209 9] Specific continents, countries, localities

Do not use for specific states and provinces; class in 336.34093–336.34099. Do not use for specific continents, countries; class in 336.34323–336.34329

.343 21 State and provincial public debt in areas, regions, places in general

Add to base number 336.34321 the numbers following —1 in notation 11–19 from Table 2, e.g., state and provincial public debt in developing countries 336.34321724

.343 23–.343 29      State and provincial public debt in specific continents, countries

Add to base number 336.3432 notation 3–9 from Table 2, e.g., provincial public debt in Canada 336.343271

Class state and provincial public debt in specific states and provinces in 336.34093–336.34099

.343 3      National level

*For borrowing by one nation from another nation, see 336.3435*

[.343 309 1]      Areas, regions, places in general

Do not use; class in 336.34331

[.343 309 3–.343 309 9]      Specific continents, countries, localities

Do not use for specific countries; class in 336.34093–336.34099. Do not use for specific continents; class in 336.34333–336.34339

.343 31      National public debt in areas, regions, places in general

Add to base number 336.34331 the numbers following —1 in notation 11–19 from Table 2, e.g., national public debt in developing countries 336.34331724

.343 33–.343 39      National public debt in specific continents

Add to base number 336.3433 notation 3–9 from Table 2, e.g., national public debt in Europe 336.34334

Class national public debt in specific countries in 336.34093–336.34099

.343 5      International public debt

Borrowing by one nation from another, public debts owed by one nation to another

Class here comprehensive works on international borrowing and debts

*For role of banks in international borrowing and debts, see 332.15*

.344      Flotation of government securities

Including forced loans

Class government securities in 336.31

.346      Debt limits

.36      Debt management

Class debt limits in 336.346

*See also 339.523 for deficit financing in macroeconomic policy*

.363      Repayment and redemption

Standard subdivisions are added for either or both topics in heading

Including sinking funds

.368            Repudiation

> Class here public insolvency

.39             Public expenditures

> Class tax expenditure in 336.206

> *For expenditure in macroeconomic policy, see 339.522. For expenditures by a specific agency or on a specific activity, see the agency or activity in 352–354, plus notation 249 from table under 352–354, e.g., expenditures on transportation 354.76249*

**.4–.9     Public finance of specific continents, countries, localities in modern world**

> Add to base number 336 notation 4–9 from Table 2, e.g., public finance of Australia 336.94; however, for general works on public finance by governmental level, see 336.01

# 337     International economics

> Class here international economic planning; comprehensive works on international economic relations, on international economic cooperation

> *For a specific aspect of international economics not provided for here, see the aspect, e.g., multinational business enterprises 338.88, international commerce 382*

[.093–.099]     Specific continents, countries, localities

> Do not use; class in 337.3–337.9

**.1     Multilateral economic cooperation**

> Class here economic integration, multilateral agreements and multistate organizations for economic cooperation

> Class bilateral economic cooperation in 337.3–337.9; class interdisciplinary works on intergovernmental organizations in 341.2

> *For trade agreements, see 382.9*

> *See Manual at 337.3–337.9 vs. 337.1*

.109            History and biography

> Do not use for geographic treatment; class in 337.11–337.19

.11             Multilateral economic cooperation in areas, regions, places in general

> Add to base number 337.11 the numbers following —1 in notation 17–18 from Table 2, e.g., multilateral economic cooperation in developing regions 337.11724

.14             European multilateral cooperation

.142            European Union

> Class here European Common Market, European Community, European Economic Community

.143            European Free Trade Association (EFTA)

.147 Council for Mutual Economic Assistance (COMECON)

.15–.19 Multilateral cooperation in continents other than Europe

> Add to base number 337.1 notation 5–9 from Table 2, e.g., Andean Group 337.18

.3–.9 **Foreign economic policies and relations of specific jurisdictions and groups of jurisdictions**

> Class here bilateral economic cooperation

> Add to base number 337 notation 3–9 from Table 2, e.g., economic policy of United Kingdom 337.41; then, for foreign economic relations between two jurisdictions or groups of jurisdictions, add 0* and to the result add notation 1–9 from Table 2, e.g., economic relations between United Kingdom and France 337.41044

> Give priority in notation to the jurisdiction or group of jurisdictions emphasized. If the emphasis is equal, give priority to the one coming first in Table 2
> > (Option: Give priority in notation to the jurisdiction or group of jurisdictions requiring local emphasis, e.g., libraries in the United States class foreign economic relations between the United States and France in 337.73044)

> Class multilateral economic cooperation in 337.1

> *See Manual at 337.3–337.9 vs. 337.1*

**338 Production**

> Class here interdisciplinary works on industry, on production

> *For specific factors of production, see 331–333; for production economics of financial industries, see 332; for production economics of real estate business, see 333.33; for production economics of energy production, see 333.79; for economics of cooperative production, see 334; for production economics of insurance industry, see 368; for commerce, communications, transportation, see 380. For a specific noneconomic aspect of industry and production, see the aspect, e.g., law of industry 343.07, production technology 620–690*

> *See Manual at T1—025 vs. T1—029; also at 332 vs. 338, 658.15; also at 363.5, 363.6, 363.8 vs. 338*

### SUMMARY

| | |
|---|---|
| 338.001–.008 | Standard subdivisions |
| .01–.09 | [General topics] |
| .1 | Agriculture |
| .2 | Extraction of minerals |
| .3 | Other extractive industries |
| .4 | Secondary industries and services |
| .5 | General production economics |
| .6 | Organization of production |
| .7 | Business enterprises |
| .8 | Combinations |
| .9 | Economic development and growth |

*Add 00 for standard subdivisions; see instructions at beginning of Table 1

| .001 | Philosophy and theory |
|---|---|

*For a specific theory, see the theory, e.g., law of diminishing marginal utility 338.5212*

| .001 12 | Forecasting |
|---|---|

Do not use for forecasting of products and services; class in 338.020112. Do not use for general production forecasting; class in 338.544

| .002–.008 | Standard subdivisions |
|---|---|
| [.009] | History, geographic treatment, biography |

Do not use; class in 338.09

| .01 | Factors of production |
|---|---|

Class here comprehensive and theoretical works on factors of production

Class factors of production as part of industrial conditions and situation in 338.09; class factors of production as costs of production in 338.512

*For labor, see 331; for capital, see 332; for land, see 333*

| .02 | Products and services |
|---|---|

Standard subdivisions are added for products and services together, for products alone

Class general production economics in 338.5; class consumption in 339.47; class shipments and sales in 381

*For specific products, see 338.1–338.4; for services alone, see 338.47*

*See Manual at T1—025 vs. T1—029*

| .020 12 | Classification |
|---|---|

Class here standard industrial classifications

Add to base number 338.02012 notation 4–9 from Table 2, e.g., standard industrial classifications of Canada 338.0201271

| .04 | Entrepreneurship |
|---|---|
| .06 | Production efficiency |

Including cost-output ratio

Class here industrial productivity

Class conservation of energy in 333.7916

*For labor productivity, see 331.118*

.064       Effect of technological innovations

> Class here effect of automation, comprehensive works on effect of technological innovations on the economy
>
> *For effect of technological innovations on a specific aspect of the economy, see the aspect, e.g., effect on working conditions 331.25, effect on banking 332.1*
>
> *See also 303.483 for effect of technological innovation on society*

.09       History, geographic treatment, biography

> Class here history, geographic treatment, biography of general principles and theories; existing and potential resources for production, industrial conditions and situation, industrial surveys, location of industry
>
> Class a specific resource with the resource, e.g., water for power 333.914

.090 01–.090 08       Standard subdivisions

[.090 09]       History

> Do not use; class in 338.09

.090 1–.090 5       Historical periods

> Add to base number 338.090 the numbers following —090 in notation 0901–0905 from Table 1, e.g., industrial surveys in 20th century 338.0904

.091–.099       Geographic treatment and biography

> Add to base number 338.09 notation 1–9 from Table 2, e.g., industrial surveys of Canada 338.0971
>
> *See also 338.6042 for rationale for and process of locating business enterprises*
>
> *See Manual at 338.091–338.099 vs. 332.67309, 338.6042*

.092       Biography

> Number built according to instructions under 338.091–338.099
>
> *See Manual at 338.092*

> ### 338.1–338.4 Specific kinds of industries

Class here finance, general production economics of specific kinds of industries

Class results of market surveys; supply and demand in relation to trade, to marketing opportunities in 381; class comprehensive works in 338; class interdisciplinary works on capital formation in 332.0415

> *For financial industries, see 332; for credit for specific kinds of industries, see 332.7; for real estate business, see 333.33; for energy production, see 333.79; for cooperatives in specific kinds of industries, see 334; for organization of production in specific kinds of industries, see 338.6; for business enterprises other than cooperatives in specific kinds of industries, see 338.7; for commerce, communications, transportation, see 380. For biographies of entrepreneurs in a specific kind of industry, see the kind of industry in 338.6–338.8, e.g., biographies of small-business owners 338.642092, biographies of entrepreneurs in textile manufacturing 338.76770092; for biographies of people known for their contributions in a specific type of technology, see the type of technology in 600, e.g., biographies of mining engineers 622.092*

> ### 338.1–338.3 Primary industries (Extractive industries)

Class comprehensive works in 338

.1      **Agriculture**

Class agricultural cooperatives in 334.683; class government farm policies in 338.18

> *See Manual at 338.1 vs. 631.558*

.13      Financial aspects

Class here capital formation and other investment in agriculture, costs, prices received by farmers, farm income

Add to base number 338.13 the numbers following 63 in 633–638, e.g., prices of rice 338.13318

Class government policies that affect financial aspects in 338.18; class food prices in 338.19

> *For agricultural credit, see 332.71*

> *See also 338.16 for production efficiency*

> *See Manual at 332 vs. 338, 658.15*

.14      Factors affecting production

Including drought, plant and animal diseases, shortages of materials and equipment used in farming

> *For financial factors, see 338.13; for production efficiency, see 338.16; for surpluses and shortages of farm products, see 338.17; for government policies, see 338.18*

.16       Production efficiency

Including cost-output ratio, size of farm, use of labor

Class here agricultural productivity; science, technological innovation in agriculture

Class energy conservation in agriculture in 333.7966; class comprehensive works on factors affecting production in 338.14

*For labor productivity, see 331.118*

.161       Mechanization

Class here automation

Class mechanization of harvesting methods in 338.163

.162       Agricultural methods

Including crop rotation; use of fertilizers, of insecticides

*For harvesting methods, see 338.163*

.163       Harvesting methods

.17       Products

Including seed industry as a whole

Class here surpluses and shortages of farm products, forecasts and projections of supply and demand

Add to base number 338.17 the numbers following 63 in 633–638, e.g., rice or seed rice 338.17318, forestry 338.1749, forest products 338.17498; however, for supply of timber in nature, see 333.7511; for demand for timber, see 333.7512

Class specific elements of production applied to specific products and groups of products in 338.13–338.16; class government farm policies applied to specific products and groups of products in 338.18; class supply, surpluses, shortages of food in 338.19; class specific producers in 338.763. Class a specific kind of seed with the kind, e.g., corn (maize) seed 338.17315

.174 98       Forest products

Number built according to instructions under 338.17

Class here supply of cut timber, comprehensive works on timber

*For uncut timber, timber reserves, see 333.7511*

.18       Government farm policies

Class here acreage allotments, agricultural credit, drought relief, price supports, subsidies

Class government policies with respect to food supply in 338.19

[.180 93–.180 99]       Specific continents, countries, localities

Do not use; class in 338.183–338.189

.181            International policies

Policies and programs of international bodies

.183–.189       Specific continents, countries, localities

Add to base number 338.18 notation 3–9 from Table 2, e.g., government farm policies of India 338.1854; however, for international policies, see 338.181

.19             Food supply

Class here economic causes and effects of, economic remedies for maladjustments in food supply; measures for attaining and maintaining adequate amounts of food; food requirements (demand); reserves (stocks, supply) of food; prices of food to the consumer; comprehensive works on the economics of production, storage, distribution of food

Class interdisciplinary works on food supply in 363.8

*For production of food, see 338.13–338.18; for supply of specific food commodities, see 338.17; for food processing, see 338.47664; for distribution of food, see 381.41*

*See Manual at 363.5, 363.6, 363.8 vs. 338*

[.190 91]       Areas, regions, places in general

Do not use; class in 338.191

[.190 93–.190 99]  Specific continents, countries, localities

Do not use; class in 338.193–338.199

.191            Food supply in areas, regions, places in general

Add to base number 338.191 the numbers following —1 in notation 11–19 from Table 2, e.g., food supply in developing countries 338.191724

.193–.199       Food supply in specific continents, countries, localities

Add to base number 338.19 notation 3–9 from Table 2, e.g., food supply in Africa 338.196

.2      **Extraction of minerals**

Class here extraction of energy resources, comprehensive works on economics of extraction and processing of minerals and energy resources

Class conservation of mineral and energy resources in 333.7–333.9; class mined lands in 333.765

*For processing of minerals and raw materials of energy, see 338.47*

.23      Financial aspects

> Class here capital formation and other investment in industries engaged in extraction of minerals; costs, income, prices
>
> Add to base number 338.23 the numbers following 553 in 553.2–553.9, e.g., prices of tin 338.23453
>
> Class production efficiency in 338.26
>
> > *For industrial credit, see 332.742*
> >
> > *See Manual at 332 vs. 338, 658.15*

.26      Production efficiency

> Including automation, cost-output ratio, effect of technological innovation, factors of production
>
> Class here industrial productivity
>
> Class energy conservation in mineral extraction industries in 333.7965
>
> > *For labor productivity, see 331.118*

.27      Products

> Add to base number 338.27 the numbers following 553 in 553.2–553.9, e.g., coal 338.2724
>
> Class supply in storage, shortages, surpluses, demand, and projections of these in 333.8; class specific elements of production applied to specific products in 338.23–338.26; class specific producers doing extraction only in 338.7622; class specific producers doing both extraction and processing in 338.766; class supply in nature in 553.2–553.9

**.3**      **Other extractive industries**

> Including financial aspects, production efficiency
>
> Class energy conservation in extractive industries in 333.7965
>
> > *For industrial credit, see 332.742*
> >
> > *See Manual at 332 vs. 338, 658.15*

.37      Products

> Class specific producers in 338.763

.371      Products of culture of invertebrates and cold-blooded vertebrates; aquaculture

> Add to base number 338.371 the numbers following 639 in 639.3–639.8, e.g., culture of oysters 338.37141, aquaculture 338.3718; however, for insect culture, see 338.178
>
> Class comprehensive works on fishing and the culture of fishes and other water animals in 338.3727

.372             **Products of fishing, whaling, hunting, trapping**

Class here catches from fishing, whaling, hunting, trapping industries

Add to base number 338.372 the numbers following 59 in 592–599, e.g., fishing for mollusks, comprehensive works on shellfishing 338.3724; fishing for crustaceans 338.3753; finfishing, comprehensive works on fishing 338.3727; then add further as follows:
01–08     Standard subdivisions
09        History, geographic treatment, biography
            Use number for the area in which industry is based, not the place where fishes or other animals are caught, e.g., fishing fleet based at Los Angeles 338.37270979494, not 338.372709722 or 338.3727091641

Class supply of uncaught animals in nature in 333.95411; class measures to increase supply of animals in nature in 333.95415; class culture of invertebrates and cold-blooded vertebrates in 338.371. Class supply of a specific non-taxonomic kind of uncaught animals in nature, statistics of catches of a specific non-taxonomic kind of animal used in estimating its population in nature, with the kind of animal in 333.9542–333.9549, plus notation 11 from table under 333.7–333.9, e.g., supply of uncaught aquatic animals 333.9594811, statistics of game animal catches used in estimating population of game animals 333.954911; class supply of a specific taxonomic kind of uncaught animals in nature, statistics of catches of a specific taxonomic kind of animal used in estimating its population in nature, with the kind of animal in 333.955–333.959, plus notation 11 from table under 333.7–333.9, e.g., supply of uncaught deer 333.9596511, statistics of game bird catches used in estimating population of game birds 333.9582911; class measures to increase supply of a specific non-taxonomic kind of animals in nature with the kind in 333.9542–333.9549, plus notation 15 from table under 333.7–333.9, e.g., development of game animals in nature 333.954915; class measures to increase supply of a specific taxonomic kind of animals in nature with the kind in 333.955–333.959, plus notation 15 from table under 333.7–333.9, e.g., development of fishes in nature 333.95615

.4       **Secondary industries and services**

Standard subdivisions are added for secondary industries and services together, for secondary industries alone

Class here products of secondary industries

Class government policies in 338.48; class comprehensive works on products in 338.02; class comprehensive works on service industries, on services in 338.47

*See Manual at T1—025 vs. T1—029*

.43       Financial aspects

Class here capital formation and other investments, costs, income, prices

Class production efficiency in 338.45

*For industrial credit, see 332.742*

*See Manual at 332 vs. 338, 658.15*

.430 001–.430 009        Standard subdivisions

| | |
|---|---|
| .430 01–.439 99 | Specific industries and services |

Add to base number 338.43 notation 001–999, e.g., automobile prices 338.43629222; however, for financial aspects of financial industries, see 332; for financial aspects of real estate, see 333.33; for financial aspects of energy production, see 333.79; for financial aspects of cooperative production, see 334; for financial aspects of insurance industry, see 368.01; for financial aspects of commerce, communications, transportation, see 380

Subdivisions are added for either or both topics in heading

**.45      Production efficiency**

Including cost-output ratio, factors of production (land, labor, capital), production capacity

Class here industrial productivity

Class energy conservation in secondary industries in 333.796516

*For labor productivity, see 331.118*

**.454      Automation**

*For automation in specific industries, see 338.456*

**.456      Production efficiency in specific industries and groups of industries**

Class here automation in specific industries

[.456 01–.456 09]      Standard subdivisions

Do not use; class in 338.4501–338.4509

.456 1      Production efficiency in industries other than extractive, manufacturing, construction

Class here service industries

.456 100 01–.456 100 09      Standard subdivisions

.456 100 1–.456 199 9      Subdivisions for production efficiency in industries other than extractive, manufacturing, construction

Add to base number 338.4561 notation 001–999, e.g., production efficiency in hospital services 338.456136211; however, for production efficiency in financial industries, see 332; for production efficiency in real estate business, see 333.33; for production efficiency in cooperative enterprises, see 334; for production efficiency in the insurance industry, see 368; for production efficiency in commerce, communications, transportation, see 380

.456 2–.456 9      Production efficiency in manufacturing and construction industries

Add to base number 338.456 the numbers following 6 in 620–690, e.g., power equipment in textile manufacture 338.456770285; however, for production efficiency in energy production, see 333.79; for production efficiency in cooperative enterprises, see 334

**.46      Professional services**

Class specific elements of production applied to professional services in 338.43–338.45; class specific professional services in 338.47

.47 Services and specific products

Class here quantities produced, shortages, surpluses, stockpiles, forecasts and projections of supply and demand; comprehensive works on service industries, on economics of services

Class specific elements of production applied to services and specific products in 338.43–338.45; class specific producers in 338.76; class comprehensive works on products of secondary industries in 338.4

*For comprehensive works on professional services, see 338.46*

.470 001–.470 009 Standard subdivisions of services

.470 01–.479 99 Subdivisions for products and services

Add to base number 338.47 notation 001–999, e.g., pharmaceutical industry 338.476151, tourist industry 338.4791; however, for production economics of financial industries, see 332; for production economics of real estate business, see 333.33; for production economics of energy production, see 333.79; for production economics of cooperative enterprises, see 334; for production economics of commerce, communications, transportation, see 380

Subdivisions are added for either or both topics in heading

.476 626 Fuel industry

Number built according to instructions under 338.47001–338.47999

Class here comprehensive works on processing and manufacturing fuels

*For processing or manufacturing a specific fuel, see the fuel, e.g., biomass fuel 338.4766288, gasoline 338.4766553827*

.48 Government policies

Class government policies with respect to a specific aspect of secondary industries and services in 338.43–338.47

**.5 General production economics**

Including risk

Class here microeconomics (economics of the firm)

Class production economics of specific kinds of industries in 338.1–338.4

*For organization of production, see 338.6*

[.501 12] Forecasting

Do not use; class in 338.544

.51 Costs

.512 Factors of production as costs of production

Including law of diminishing marginal returns, of factor proportions

Class comprehensive works on factors of production in 338.01

| .514 | Elements in cost calculation |
| --- | --- |
| .514 2 | Kinds of cost |

Including average, fixed, marginal, variable costs

| .514 4 | Size of enterprise |
| --- | --- |

Including economies and diseconomies of scale

| .516 | Profits |
| --- | --- |

Including relation of marginal cost to marginal revenue

| .52 | Prices |
| --- | --- |

Class here price determination, effects of changes, comprehensive works on prices

Class effect of money on prices in 332.41; class effect of costs on prices in 338.516

*For a specific aspect of prices not provided for here, see the aspect, e.g., effects of prices on the whole economy 339.42*

| .520 1 | Philosophy and theory |
| --- | --- |

Do not use for theories; class in 338.521

| .520 2 | Miscellany |
| --- | --- |
| .520 21 | Tabulated and related materials |

Do not use for statistics; class in 338.528

| .521 | Price theories |
| --- | --- |

Class here law of supply and demand, theories of value

*For Marxian labor theory of value, see 335.412*

*See also 333.7 for supply and demand for natural resources and energy; also 338.1–338.4 for supply and demand for specific products*

| .521 2 | Theory of demand |
| --- | --- |

Including law of diminishing marginal utility, price-demand relationship

| .521 3 | Theory of supply |
| --- | --- |

Including price-supply relationship

---

>     338.522–338.526 Price determination

Class comprehensive works in 338.52

| .522 | Price determination in free markets |
| --- | --- |

Including interproduct competition, e.g., butter versus margarine

| .523 | Price determination by monopolies, oligopolies |
| --- | --- |

Including price fixing, price leadership

| .526 | Price determination by government regulation (Price control) |
|---|---|
| .528 | Price levels |

Class here indexes, statistics

*See also 339.42 for cost of living*

.528 021              Tabulated and related materials

Do not use for statistics; class in 338.528

.54          Economic fluctuations

Including seasonal variations, secular trends

[.540 112]              Forecasting

Do not use; class in 338.544

.542          Business cycles

Including prosperity, recession, depression, recovery; panics

Class remedial and preventive measures in 338.543. Class comprehensive economic works on a specific period of prosperity or depression with the economic conditions of the specific time or place in 330.9, e.g., worldwide depression in 1930s 330.9043, economic prosperity in Germany, 1949–1962 330.9430875

.543          Remedial and preventive action

Standard subdivisions are added for either or both topics in heading

Class comprehensive works on economic stabilization in 339.5

.544          General production forecasting and forecasts

*See also 658.40355 for forecasting as a technique of managerial decision-making*

.544 2              Methods of forecasting

Class comprehensive works on economic forecasting in 330.0112

.544 3              Forecasts

Class forecasts of economic situation in 330.900112

**.6          Organization of production**

Class here organization of production in specific kinds of industries

*For business enterprises and their structure, see 338.7*

*See Manual at 338.092*

.604          Special topics of organization of production

.604 1              Finance

Class finance of specific kinds of industries in 338.1–338.4; class interdisciplinary works on capital formation in 332.0415

| | |
|---|---|
| .604 2 | Location |

Class here proximity to sources of power, raw materials, labor supply, transportation, markets

*See Manual at 338.091–338.099 vs. 332.67309, 338.6042*

| | |
|---|---|
| .604 6 | Specialization and comparative advantage |

Standard subdivisions are added for either or both topics in heading

Class works on specialization and comparative advantage that emphasize international commerce in 382.1042

| | |
|---|---|
| .604 8 | Competition and restraint |

Standard subdivisions are added for either or both topics in heading

Class monopoly and monopolies in 338.82

| | |
|---|---|
| .61 | Private enterprise |

Class specific systems of private enterprise in 338.63; class specific sizes of private enterprise in 338.64

| | |
|---|---|
| .62 | Public enterprise |
| .63 | Systems of production |

*For factory system, see 338.65*

| | |
|---|---|
| .632 | Guild system |
| .634 | Domestic system |

Class here cottage industry

| | |
|---|---|
| .64 | Size of enterprises |

Including downsizing

Class relation of size of enterprise to cost of production in 338.5144; class specific types of enterprises of specific sizes in 338.7–338.8

| | |
|---|---|
| .642 | Small business |

Including custom production

Class here small industry

Class cottage industry in 338.634

| | |
|---|---|
| .642 089 | Ethnic and national groups |

Class minority enterprises in 338.6422

| | |
|---|---|
| .642 2 | Minority enterprises |

Class handicraft industries operated by minorities in 338.6425

| | |
|---|---|
| .642 5 | Handicraft industries |
| .644 | Big business |

Class here large industry

Class monopoly and monopolies in 338.82

.65 Factory system

.69 Worker control of industry

Class here employee ownership, worker self-management

Class role of unions in achieving worker control of industry in 331.8801; class guild socialism in 335.15; class syndicalism in 335.82; class employee participation in management in 658.3152

*For employee stock ownership plans, see 331.21649*

**.7** **Business enterprises**

Not limited to private or capitalist enterprises

Class here structure of business enterprises; interdisciplinary works on business enterprises, on organizations for production

*For cooperatives, see 334; for combinations, see 338.8*

*See Manual at T1—025 vs. T1—029; also at 338.092*

.71 Initiation and dissolution of business enterprises

---

> 338.72–338.74 Specific kinds of business enterprises

Class specific kinds of business enterprises in specific industries and groups of industries in 338.76; class comprehensive works in 338.7

.72 Individual proprietorships

.73 Partnerships

.74 Corporations

Open and closed

*See Manual at T1—025 vs. T1—029*

.749 Government corporations

Class here interdisciplinary works on government corporations

*For a specific aspect of government corporations, see the aspect, e.g., law 346.067, public administration of government corporations 352.266*

[.749 068] Management

Do not use; class in 352.266

.76 Business enterprises by industry

Class here specific individual business enterprises, biographies of entrepreneurs in specific fields

*For biographies of people known for their contribution to technology, see the kind of contribution in 600, plus notation 092 from Table 1, e.g., biographies of mining engineers 622.092*

*See Manual at T1—025 vs. T1—029*

.761            Business enterprises in industries other than extractive, manufacturing, construction

                Class here service industries

.761 000 1–.761 000 9       Standard subdivisions

.761 001–.761 999         Subdivisions for business enterprises in industries other than extractive, manufacturing, construction

                     Add to base number 338.761 notation 001–999, e.g., law firms 338.76134; however, for financial institutions, see 332.1–332.6; for real estate business enterprises, see 333.33; for cooperative enterprises, see 334; for insurance companies, see 368.0065; for enterprises engaged in commerce, communications, transportation, see 380

.762–.769         Business enterprises in extractive, manufacturing, construction industries

                     Add to base number 338.76 the numbers following 6 in 620–690, e.g., agriculture 338.763; however, for enterprises engaged in production of energy, see 333.79; for cooperative enterprises, see 334.682–334.688

.8       **Combinations**

                Organization and structure for massive production and control of production

                Class here antitrust policies, economic concentration

                To be classed here, works about specific individual enterprises must stress that they are combinations; otherwise, the works are classed in 338.76

                *See Manual at 338.092*

### SUMMARY

| | | |
|---|---|---|
| 338.804 | **Special topics of combinations** | |
| .82 | **Restrictive practices** | |
| .83 | **Mergers** | |
| .85 | **Trusts** | |
| .86 | **Holding companies** | |
| .87 | **Informal arrangements** | |
| .88 | **Multinational business enterprises** | |

.804          Special topics of combinations

.804 2        Kinds of combinations

                Including horizontal, vertical, conglomerate

.82        Restrictive practices

                Class here monopoly and monopolies, oligopoly and oligopolies

                Class price determination in 338.523; class restrictive practices of multinational business enterprises in 338.884

.826        Restrictive practices in specific industries, groups of industries, fields of enterprise

[.826 01–.826 09]        Standard subdivisions

> Do not use; class in 338.8201–338.8209

.826 1        Restrictive practices in industries and fields of enterprise other than extractive, manufacturing, construction

> Class here service industries

.826 100 01–.826 100 09        Standard subdivisions

.826 100 1–.826 199 9        Subdivisions for restrictive practices in industries and fields of enterprise other than extractive, manufacturing, construction

> Add to base number 338.8261 notation 001–999, e.g., restrictive practices in publishing 338.82610705; however, for restrictive practices by combinations in the financial industries, see 332.1–332.6; for restrictive practices by combinations in real estate business, see 333.33; for restrictive practices by combinations in cooperative enterprise, see 334; for restrictive practices by combinations in the insurance industry, see 368; for restrictive practices by combinations in commerce, communications, transportation, see 380

.826 2–.826 9        Restrictive practices in extractive, manufacturing, construction industries and fields of enterprise

> Add to base number 338.826 the numbers following 6 in 620–690, e.g., restrictive practices by combinations engaged in computer engineering 338.8262139; however, for restrictive practices by combinations engaged in energy production, see 333.79; for restrictive practices by cooperatives, see 334

---

>        338.83–338.87 Specific forms of combinations and their practices

> Class international combinations regardless of form in 338.88; class comprehensive works in 338.8

.83        Mergers

> Class here acquisitions, amalgamations

.836        Mergers in specific industries, groups of industries, fields of enterprise

[.836 01–.836 09]        Standard subdivisions

> Do not use; class in 338.8301–338.8309

.836 1        Mergers in industries and fields of enterprise other than extractive, manufacturing, construction

> Class here service industries

.836 100 01–.836 100 09        Standard subdivisions

.836 100 1–.836 199 9      Subdivisions for mergers in industries and fields of enterprise other than extractive, manufacturing, construction

> Add to base number 338.8361 notation 001–999, e.g., mergers of publishers 338.83610705; however, for mergers of financial institutions, see 332.1–332.6; for mergers of real estate business enterprises, see 333.33; for mergers of cooperatives, see 334; for mergers of enterprises in the insurance industry, see 368.0065; for mergers of enterprises engaged in commerce, communications, transportation, see 380

.836 2–.836 9      Mergers in extractive, manufacturing, construction industries and fields of enterprise

> Add to base number 338.836 the numbers following 6 in 620–690, e.g., mergers of automotive companies 338.836292; however, for mergers of enterprises engaged in energy production, see 333.79; for mergers of cooperatives, see 334

.85      Trusts

.86      Holding companies

.87      Informal arrangements

> Including cartels, interlocking directorates, pools

.88      Multinational business enterprises

> Class here foreign-owned and mostly foreign-owned enterprises, enterprises with mostly international operations

## SUMMARY

| | |
|---|---|
| 338.880 9 | **History and biography** |
| .881 | **Growth, expansion, power** |
| .883 | **Role in international economic development** |
| .884 | **Restrictive practices and their control** |
| .887 | **Multinational business enterprises in specific industries, groups of industries, fields** |
| .888 | **Multinational business enterprises by location of operations** |
| .889 | **Multinational business enterprises by location of owners** |

.880 9      History and biography

> Do not use for geographic treatment; class in 338.888–338.889

.881      Growth, expansion, power

> Standard subdivisions are added for any or all topics in heading

> Class growth, expansion, power of multinational enterprises engaged in specific fields in 338.887

> *See also 322.3 for political influence of multinational enterprises*

.881 09      History and biography

> Do not use for geographic treatment; class in 338.888–338.889

.883            Role in international economic development

Class role in international economic development of multinational enterprises engaged in specific fields in 338.887

.883 09              History and biography

Do not use for geographic treatment; class in 338.888–338.889

.884            Restrictive practices and their control

Standard subdivisions are added for either or both topics in heading

Class here international monopoly, oligopoly

Class restrictive practices of multinational enterprises engaged in specific fields in 338.887

.884 09              History and biography

Do not use for geographic treatment; class in 338.888–338.889

.887            Multinational business enterprises in specific industries, groups of industries, fields

[.887 01–.887 08]       Standard subdivisions

Do not use; class in 338.8801–338.8808

[.887 09]          History

Do not use for history; class in 338.8809. Do not use for geographic treatment; class in 338.888–338.889

[.887 092]          Biography

Do not use; class in 338.88092

.887 1          Multinational business enterprises in industries and fields of enterprise other than extractive, manufacturing, construction

Class here service industries

.887 100 01–.887 100 09       Standard subdivisions

.887 100 1–.887 199 9        Subdivisions for multinational business enterprises in industries and fields of enterprise other than extractive, manufacturing, construction

Add to base number 338.8871 notation 001–999, e.g., multinational enterprises engaged in advertising 338.88716591; however, for multinational enterprises in financial industries, see 332.1–332.6; for multinational enterprises in real estate business, see 333.33; for multinational cooperatives, see 334; for multinational enterprises in the insurance industry, see 368.0065; for multinational enterprises in commerce, communications, transportation, see 380

.887 2–.887 9      Multinational business enterprises in extractive, manufacturing, construction industries and fields of enterprise

> Add to base number 338.887 the numbers following 6 in 620–690, e.g., multinational enterprises engaged in mining petroleum and natural gas 338.88722338; however, for multinational enterprises engaged in energy production, see 333.79; for multinational cooperatives, see 334

.888      Multinational business enterprises by location of operations

> Class multinational enterprises in specific industries and groups of industries in 338.887; class multinational enterprises by location of owners in 338.889

[.888 01–.888 08]      Standard subdivisions

> Do not use; class in 338.8801–338.8808

[.888 09]      History

> Do not use; class in 338.8809

[.888 091]      Areas, regions, places in general

> Do not use; class in 338.8881

[.888 092]      Biography

> Do not use; class in 338.88092

[.888 093–.888 099]      Specific continents, countries, localities

> Do not use; class in 338.8883–338.8889

.888 1      Multinational business enterprises in areas, regions, places in general

> Add to base number 333.8881 the numbers following —1 in notation 11–19 from Table 2, e.g., multinational enterprises in developing countries 338.8881724

.888 3–.888 9      Multinational enterprises in specific continents, countries, localities

> Add to base number 338.888 notation 3–9 from Table 2, e.g., multinational enterprises in Europe 338.8884

.889      Multinational business enterprises by location of owners

> Class multinational enterprises in specific industries or groups of industries in 338.887; class multinational enterprises in a specific area without regard to location of owners in 338.888

[.889 01–.889 08]      Standard subdivisions

> Do not use; class in 338.8801–338.8808

[.889 09]      History

> Do not use; class in 338.8809

[.889 091]      Areas, regions, places in general

> Do not use; class in 338.8891

| [.889 092] | Biography |
| | Do not use; class in 338.88092 |
| [.889 093–.889 099] | Specific continents, countries, localities |
| | Do not use; class in 338.8893–338.8899 |

.889 1        Multinational business enterprises by owners residing in areas, regions, places in general

> Add to base number 338.8891 the numbers following —1 in notation 11–19 from Table 2, e.g., multinational enterprises owned by citizens of developing countries 338.8891724; then, for area in which enterprise is located, add 0* and to the result add notation 1–9 from Table 2, e.g., multinational enterprises owned by citizens of developing countries and located in Africa 338.889172406

.889 3–.889 9    Multinational business enterprises by owners residing in specific continents, countries, localities

> Add to base number 338.889 notation 3–9 from Table 2, e.g., multinational enterprises owned by United States nationals 338.88973; then, for area in which enterprise is located, add 0* and to the result add notation 1–9 from Table 2, e.g., multinational enterprises owned by United States nationals in Canada 338.88973071

## .9 Economic development and growth

Standard subdivisions are added for either or both topics in heading

Including autarky and interdependence

Class here economic planning, government policies and programs

> *For economic development and growth with respect to specific kinds of industries, see 338.1–338.4. For economic development and growth with respect to a specific subject not provided for here, see the subject, e.g., international development banks 332.153*
>
> *See also 330.124 for planned economies*

.900 1–.900 8    Standard subdivisions

.900 9        History, geographic treatment, biography

[.900 93–.900 99]    Specific continents, countries, localities

        Do not use; class in 338.93–338.99

.91        International development and growth

Standard subdivisions are added for either or both topics in heading

Class here assistance by international organizations, foreign aid, technical assistance

Class foreign economic policies and relations of specific jurisdictions and groups of jurisdictions in 337.3–337.9

---

*Add 00 for standard subdivisions; see instructions at beginning of Table 1

.910 91                 Areas, regions, places in general

> Do not use for assistance given by specific groups of jurisdictions in areas, regions, places in general to other jurisdictions; class in 338.911
>
> Class here assistance given to specific groups of jurisdictions in areas, regions, places in general

.910 93–.910 99     Specific continents, countries, localities

> Do not use for assistance given by specific jurisdictions and groups of jurisdictions to other jurisdictions; class in 338.913–338.919
>
> Class here assistance given to specific jurisdictions and groups of jurisdictions

.911                   International assistance by specific groups of jurisdictions in areas, regions, places in general

> Add to base number 338.911 the numbers following —1 in notation 11–19 from Table 2, e.g., assistance by countries where Arabs predominate 338.91174927; then, for assistance by a specific group of jurisdictions to another group of jurisdictions or to a specific jurisdiction, add 0* and to the result add notation 1–9 from Table 2, e.g., assistance by Arab countries to Africa 338.9117492706

.913–.919         International assistance by specific jurisdictions and groups of jurisdictions in specific continents, countries, localities

> Add to base number 338.91 notation 3–9 from Table 2, e.g., assistance by United Kingdom 338.9141; then, for assistance by a specific jurisdiction or group of jurisdictions to another jurisdiction or group of jurisdictions, add 0* and again add notation 1–9 from Table 2, e.g., assistance by United Kingdom to Nigeria 338.91410669

.92           Specific policies

[.920 1–.920 8]      Standard subdivisions

> Do not use; class in 338.9001–338.9008

[.920 9]             History, geographic treatment, biography

> Do not use; class in 338.9009

[.920 93–.920 99]      Specific continents, countries, localities

> Do not use; class in 338.93–338.99

.922                   †Subsidies and grants

> Standard subdivisions are added for either or both topics in heading
>
> Including government loans

---

*Add 00 for standard subdivisions; see instructions at beginning of Table 1
†Do not use notation 093–099 from Table 1 for specific policies in specific areas; class in 338.93–338.99

.924 †Nationalization

> Class here expropriation

.925 †Privatization

> Class here denationalization

.926 †Information policy

> Class here science policy, technology transfer

> *See Manual at 338.926 vs. 352.745, 500*

.927 †Appropriate technology

> Class here alternative technology, environmental economics, sustainable development

.93–.99 Economic development and growth in specific continents, countries, localities

> Add to base number 338.9 notation 3–9 from Table 2, e.g., economic policies of United Kingdom 338.941; then add 0* and to the result add the numbers following 338.92 in 338.922–338.927, e.g., subsidies in United Kingdom 338.94102
> Subdivisions are added for either or both topics in heading

## 339 Macroeconomics and related topics

> Standard subdivisions are added for macroeconomics and related topics together, for macroeconomics alone

> *For economic fluctuations, see 338.54*

> *See Manual at 332, 336 vs. 339*

### SUMMARY

| | |
|---|---|
| 339.2 | **Distribution of income and wealth** |
| .3 | **Product and income accounts** |
| .4 | **Factors affecting income and wealth** |
| .5 | **Macroeconomic policy** |

.2 **Distribution of income and wealth**

> Standard subdivisions are added for either or both topics in heading

> Class product and income accounts in 339.3; class factors affecting income and wealth in 339.4; class income redistribution in 339.52; class transfer payments in 339.522

.21 Distribution of income and wealth among factors of production

> Factors of production: land, labor, capital, entrepreneurship, corporate profits

> Standard subdivisions are added for either or both topics in heading

---

*Add 00 for standard subdivisions; see instructions at beginning of Table 1
†Do not use notation 093–099 from Table 1 for specific policies in specific areas; class in 338.93–338.99

.22            Distribution of aggregate personal income and wealth

      Standard subdivisions are added for either or both topics in heading

      Class here consumer income, household income

      Class income in relation to consumption, household budget, in 339.41; class poverty in 339.46

.23            Input-output analysis (Interindustry analysis)

      Including data on specific industries

.26            Flow-of-funds accounts

**.3            Product and income accounts**

      *For distribution of income and wealth, see 339.2; for factors affecting income and wealth, see 339.4*

[.309 3–.309 9]            Specific continents, countries, localities

      Do not use for specific countries and localities; class in 339.33–339.39

.31            Product accounts

      Class here gross domestic product (GDP), gross national product (GNP)

      *For net national product (NNP), see 339.32*

[.310 93–.310 99]            Specific continents, countries, localities

      Do not use for specific countries and localities; class in 339.33–339.39

.32            Income accounts

      Class here net national product (NNP), national income (NI), personal income (PI), disposable personal income (DPI)

      *For distribution of aggregate personal income, see 339.22*

[.320 93–.320 99]            Specific continents, countries, localities

      Do not use for specific countries and localities; class in 339.33–339.39

.33–.39            Product and income accounts of specific continents, countries, localities

      Class here product accounts of specific continents, income accounts of specific continents

      Add to base number 339.3 notation 3–9 from Table 2, e.g., gross national product of United States 339.373
        Subdivisions are added for product accounts, income accounts, or both

**.4            Factors affecting income and wealth**

      Standard subdivisions are added for either or both topics in heading

      *For economic stabilization, see 339.5*

.41      Income in relation to consumption

Including acceleration principle, consumer responses to decreases and increases in income, household budgets as a measure of relation of income to consumption

Class purchasing power, effect of prices on consumption in 339.42; class multiplier, relation of consumption and savings, in 339.43

*See also 658.834 for consumer research in marketing management*

.42      Cost of living

Including effect of rising costs of specific commodities on consumers

Class here purchasing power, effect of prices on consumers

Class price statistics and indexes in 338.528

*For purchasing power of money, see 332.41*

.43      Savings and investment

Standard subdivisions are added for either or both topics in heading

Including multiplier, relation of consumption and savings

Class here capital formation

Class interdisciplinary works on capital formation and saving in 332.0415

.46      Poverty

Class here economic causes of poverty

Class comprehensive works on poverty in 362.5

.47      Consumption (Spending)

Class here standard of living, interdisciplinary works on consumption

Class consumption in relation to income in 339.41; class consumption in relation to cost of living in 339.42; class consumption in relation to savings and investment in 339.43; class consumption in relation to poverty in 339.46; class government spending in 339.522; class consumption as a measure of marketing opportunities or volume and value of trade in 381

*For sociology of consumption, see 306.3; for consumption as utilization of natural resources and energy, see 333.713; for consumption of specific products and services, of specific groups of products and services, see 339.48*

*See also 658.834 for consumer research in marketing management*

.48      Consumption of specific products and services, of specific groups of products and services

[.480 001–.480 009]      Standard subdivisions

Do not use; class in 339.4701–339.4709

| .480 01–.489 99 | Subdivisions for consumption of specific products and services, of specific groups of products and services |

> Add to base number 339.48 notation 001–999, e.g., consumption of agricultural products 339.4863; however, for consumption in the sense of utilization of specific natural resources, see 333.7–333.9

**.49**      Conservation of economic resources

> Economic resources: the sum total of economic resources of a nation or other area, e.g., natural resources, human resources, resources that result from human activities

> *For conservation of natural resources, see 333.72*

**[.490 91]**      Areas, regions, places in general

> Do not use; class in 339.491

**[.490 93–.490 99]**      Specific continents, countries, localities

> Do not use; class in 339.493–339.499

**.491**      Conservation of economic resources in areas, regions, places in general

> Add to base number 339.491 the numbers following —1 in notation 11–19 from Table 2, e.g., conservation of economic resources of developing countries 339.491724

**.493–.499**      Conservation of economic resources in specific continents, countries, localities

> Add to base number 339.49 notation 3–9 from Table 2, e.g., conservation of economic resources of India 339.4954

**.5**      **Macroeconomic policy**

> Class here incomes policy (wage-price policy), economic stabilization and growth, equilibrium, full employment policy

> Class wage-price policies of specific jurisdictions in 331.29

> *For wage policy, see 331.21; for measures to combat inflation, see 332.415; for price policy, see 338.52; for measures to control economic fluctuations, see 338.543; for measures to promote growth and development, see 338.9*

**.52**      Use of fiscal policy

> Class here income redistribution

**.522**      Government spending

> Including transfer payments

**.523**      Budget surpluses and deficits

**.525**      Taxes

.53      Use of monetary policy

> Including discount rates, reserve requirements, open-market operations, regulation of bank credit

> Class comprehensive works on relation of central banks to monetary policy in 332.112; class comprehensive works on monetary policy in 332.46

# 340     Law

> Class here jurisprudence

> Instructions for building classification numbers for works on law of a jurisdiction or area are found at 342–349

> *See Manual at 340 vs. 808.06634; also at 340, 342–347 vs. 340.56; also at 340, 342–347 vs. 340.57; also at 342–349*

## SUMMARY

| | |
|---|---|
| 343 | Military, defense, public property, public finance, tax, commerce (trade), industrial law |
| .001–.009 | Standard subdivisions; laws, regulations, cases, procedure, courts |
| .01 | Military and defense law, veterans' law |
| .02 | Law of public property |
| .03 | Law of public finance |
| .04 | Tax law |
| .05 | Kinds of taxes by base |
| .06 | Kinds of taxes by incidence |
| .07 | Regulation of economic activity |
| .08 | Regulation of commerce (trade) |
| .09 | Control of public utilities |
| .1 | Socioeconomic regions |
| .2 | Regional intergovernmental organizations |
| .3–.9 | Specific jurisdictions and areas |
| | |
| 344 | Labor, social service, education, cultural law |
| .001–.009 | Standard subdivisions; laws, regulations, cases, procedure, courts |
| .01 | Labor |
| .02 | Government-sponsored insurance |
| .03 | Social service |
| .04 | Miscellaneous social problems and services |
| .05 | Police services, other aspects of public safety, matters concerning public morals and customs |
| .06 | Public works |
| .07 | Education |
| .08 | Educational and cultural exchanges |
| .09 | Culture and religion |
| .1 | Socioeconomic regions |
| .2 | Regional intergovernmental organizations |
| .3–.9 | Specific jurisdictions and areas |
| | |
| 345 | Criminal law |
| .001–.009 | Standard subdivisions; laws, regulations, cases, procedure, courts |
| .01 | Criminal courts |
| .02 | Criminal offenses |
| .03 | Offenders |
| .04 | Liability, responsibility, guilt |
| .05 | Criminal procedure |
| .06 | Evidence |
| .07 | Trials |
| .08 | Juvenile procedure and courts |
| .1 | Socioeconomic regions |
| .2 | Regional intergovernmental organizations |
| .3–.9 | Specific jurisdictions and areas |

| | | |
|---|---|---|
| **346** | | **Private law** |
| | .001–.009 | **Standard subdivisions; laws, regulations, cases, procedure, courts; equity** |
| | .01 | **Persons and domestic relations** |
| | .02 | **Juristic acts, contracts, agency** |
| | .03 | **Torts (Delicts)** |
| | .04 | **Property** |
| | .05 | **Inheritance, succession, fiduciary trusts, trustees** |
| | .06 | **Organizations (Associations)** |
| | .07 | **Commercial law** |
| | .08 | **Banks and insurance** |
| | .09 | **Investment and negotiable instruments** |
| | .1 | **Socioeconomic regions** |
| | .2 | **Regional intergovernmental organizations** |
| | .3–.9 | **Specific jurisdictions and areas** |
| | | |
| **347** | | **Procedure and courts** |
| | .001–.009 | **Standard subdivisions; laws, regulations, cases, procedure, courts** |
| | .01 | **Courts** |
| | .02 | **Courts with general original jurisdiction** |
| | .03 | **Appellate courts** |
| | .04 | **Courts with specialized jurisdiction** |
| | .05 | **Procedure** |
| | .06 | **Evidence** |
| | .07 | **Trials** |
| | .08 | **Appellate procedure** |
| | .09 | **Dispute resolution** |
| | .1 | **Socioeconomic regions** |
| | .2 | **Regional intergovernmental organizations** |
| | .3–.9 | **Specific jurisdictions and areas** |
| | | |
| **348** | | **Laws, regulations, cases** |
| | .001–.009 | **Standard subdivisions and codification** |
| | .01 | **Preliminary materials** |
| | .02 | **Laws and regulations** |
| | .04 | **Cases** |
| | .05 | **Advisory opinions of attorneys-general (ministers of justice)** |
| | .1 | **Socioeconomic regions** |
| | .2 | **Regional intergovernmental organizations** |
| | .3–.9 | **Specific jurisdictions and areas** |
| | | |
| **349** | | **Law of specific jurisdictions, areas, socioeconomic regions, regional intergovernmental organizations** |
| | .1 | **Law of specific socioeconomic regions** |
| | .2 | **Law of regional intergovernmental organizations** |
| | .4–.9 | **Law of specific jurisdictions and areas of modern world** |

[.01]    Philosophy and theory

Do not use; class in 340.1

---

>    340.02–340.09 Standard subdivisions

Class comprehensive works in 340

*See Manual at 340.02–340.09 vs. 349*

.02    Miscellany

| | |
|---|---|
| .023 | Law as a profession, occupation, hobby |

Class here legal personnel, nature of duties, characteristics of profession

Class professional ethics of legal personnel in 174.3. Class works that emphasize procedures of work performed by legal personnel with the subject without adding notation 023 from Table 1, e.g., works that emphasize procedures of conducting a lawsuit 347.0504

| | |
|---|---|
| .03–.08 | Standard subdivisions |
| .09 | History, geographic treatment, biography of law |

Do not use for history and geographic treatment of law of traditional societies; class in 340.52. Do not use for comprehensive works on law of specific jurisdictions and areas in modern world; class in 349

| | |
|---|---|
| [.091 7] | Socioeconomic regions |

Do not use; class in 349.1

| | |
|---|---|
| .092 | Biography |

Do not use for theorists; class in 340.1092

| | |
|---|---|
| [.093] | Ancient world |

Do not use; class in 340.53

| | |
|---|---|
| **.1** | **Philosophy and theory of law** |

Class here methodology, schools of thought

*For theory of specific legal systems, see 340.5*

| | |
|---|---|
| .11 | Special topics of philosophy and theory of law |

Including origin, sources, nature, limits of law; rule of law; legal reasoning; equal protection of the law

Class interdisciplinary works on equal protection of the law in 323.42

| | |
|---|---|
| .112 | Law and ethics |

Class here civil rights, law and morality, legal positivism, natural law

Class social justice in 340.115

| | |
|---|---|
| .114 | Justice |

*For distributive justice, social justice, see 340.115*

| | |
|---|---|
| .115 | Law and society |

Including distributive justice, social justice

Class here sociological jurisprudence

| | |
|---|---|
| .12–.19 | Specific aspects of philosophy and theory |

Add to base number 340.1 the numbers following —01 in notation 012–019 from Table 1, e.g., classification of law 340.12

**.2**      **Comparative law**

> Limited to methodological works
>
> Class comparison of specific branches of law in 342–347
>
> > (If option A under 342–349 is chosen, class comparative law in 349
> >
> > (If option B under 342–349 is chosen, class comparative law in 342)

**.3**      **Law reform**

**.5**      **Legal systems**

> History and theory
>
> Class here customary law
>
> Class conflict of laws on a specific subject in specific systems of law with the subject in 340.9, e.g., conflict of divorce laws in ancient Roman law 340.91660937, conflict of divorce laws in civil law 340.9166; class a specific subject in specific systems of law with the subject in 341–347, e.g., juristic persons in Islamic law 346.167013, in ancient Roman law 346.37013, in Byzantine law 346.495013, in civil law 346.013; class religious and ceremonial laws of a specific religious body with the body, e.g., Christian canon law 262.9

**.52**      Law of traditional societies

> Class here ethnological jurisprudence
>
> *See Manual at 340.52*

**[.520 93]**      Law of traditional societies in ancient world

> Do not use; class in 340.53

**[.520 94–.520 99]**      Law of traditional societies in specific continents, countries, localities in modern world

> Do not use; class in 340.524–340.529

**.524–.529**      Law of traditional societies in specific continents, countries, localities in modern world

> Add to base number 340.52 notation 4–9 from Table 2, e.g., traditional law of the Sahara 340.5266

**.53**      Ancient law

> Add to base number 340.53 the numbers following —3 in notation 31–39 from Table 2, e.g., law of ancient Greece 340.538; however, for Roman law, see 340.54
>
> Class ancient Oriental law in 340.5
>
> (If option B under 342–349 is chosen, class here branches of the law in jurisdictions of the ancient world by adding to the number for the jurisdiction facet indicator 0*, notation for the branch of law, and notation for the subordinate subject in branch of law, e.g., criminal law of ancient Greece 340.53805, law of criminal trials of ancient Greece 340.538057)

---

*Add 00 for standard subdivisions; see instructions at beginning of Table 1

.54      **Roman law**

Including Byzantine law

Class comprehensive works on Roman-derived law in specific jurisdictions and areas in modern world in 349

*For medieval Roman law, see 340.55*

(If option B under 342–349 is chosen, class here branches of the law in Roman Empire by adding to base number 340.54 facet indicator 0\*, notation for the branch of law, and notation for the subordinate subject in branch of law, e.g., criminal law of Roman Empire 340.5405, law of criminal trials of Roman Empire 340.54057)

---

>      340.55–340.59 **Medieval, modern, religious systems of law**

Class comprehensive works in 340.5; class comprehensive works on law of specific jurisdictions and areas in modern world in 349

.55      **Medieval European law**

Including feudal law, medieval Roman law

Class medieval civil law in 340.56; class medieval common law in 340.57

.56      **Civil law systems**

Systems of law derived from Roman law

Including Roman-Dutch law

*See Manual at 340, 342–347 vs. 340.56*

.57      **Common law systems**

*See Manual at 340, 342–347 vs. 340.57*

.58      **Jewish law**

*For religious and ceremonial law of Judaism, see 296.18*

.59      **Islamic law**

Class here fiqh, sharia

*For religious and ceremonial law of Islam, fiqh and sharia in relation to religious and ceremonial laws and decisions, see 297.14*

\*Add 00 for standard subdivisions; see instructions at beginning of Table 1

**.9**      **Conflict of laws**

Body of rules governing choice of jurisdiction in cases in private law that fall under laws of two or more such jurisdictions

Class here private international law

Add to base number 340.9 the numbers following 346.0 in 346.01–346.09, e.g., conflict of divorce laws 340.9166

*For comparative law, see 340.2; for domestic conflict of laws, see 342.042. For a specific aspect of conflict of laws and of private international law not provided for here, see the aspect in 342–345, e.g., citizenship 342.083, air transportation 343.097*

*See also 341 for international law*

*See Manual at 340.9*

**341**      **Law of nations**

Class here international law, public international law

Class comprehensive works on public law in 342

*See also 340.9 for private international law*

*See Manual at 341 vs. 327*

(Option: Class law of nations of a specific subject with the subject, plus notation 026 from Table 1, e.g., international disarmament law 327.174026, not 341.733)

### SUMMARY

| | |
|---|---|
| 341.01–.09 | **Standard subdivisions; treaties, codes, cases; relation of law of nations and domestic law** |
| .1 | **Sources of law of nations** |
| .2 | **The world community** |
| .3 | **Relations between states** |
| .4 | **Jurisdiction over physical space; human rights** |
| .5 | **Disputes and conflicts between states** |
| .6 | **Law of war** |
| .7 | **International cooperation** |

**.02**      Miscellany; treaties, codes, cases

Notation 02 from Table 1 as modified below

**.026**      Treaties, codes, cases

Texts of treaties, codes, cases; guides, e.g., checklists, citators, digests, indexes

Class here conventions, protocols

Class treaties as a source of law of nations in 341.1; class comprehensive works on treaties in 341.37. Class treaties on a specific subject in law of nations with the subject in 341.2–341.7, plus notation 026 from add table under 341.2–341.7, e.g., collections of disarmament treaties 341.733026; class text of treaties on a specific subject in domestic law with the subject in 342–347, plus notation 0261 from add table under 342–347, e.g., text of commercial treaties 346.070261

>        341.026 1–341.026 6   Texts of treaties

          Class comprehensive works in 341.026

>        341.026 1–341.026 3   Series of treaties compiled by intergovernmental organizations

          Class specific kinds of treaties regardless of the organization compiling them in 341.0265–341.0266; class comprehensive works in 341.026

.026 1        League of Nations series of treaties

          Class a League of Nations series relating to a specific area in 341.0264

.026 2        United Nations series of treaties

          Class a United Nations series relating to a specific area in 341.0264

.026 3        Series of treaties compiled by regional organizations

          Add to base number 341.0263 the numbers following 341.24 in 341.242–341.249, e.g., a series compiled by Organization of American States 341.02635

.026 4        Collections of treaties by area

          Add to base number 341.0264 notation 1–9 from Table 2, e.g., treaties on Philippines 341.0264599

          Class collections of treaties relating to a specific area compiled by regional organizations in 341.0263; class collections of specific kinds of treaties by area in 341.0265–341.0266

>        341.026 5–341.026 6   Kinds of treaties

          Collections and individual treaties

          Class comprehensive works in 341.026

.026 5        Multilateral treaties

          Class an agreement between an intergovernmental organization and a specific country in 341.026

.026 6        Bilateral treaties

          Add to base number 341.0266 notation 3–9 from Table 2, e.g., treaties of the United Kingdom 341.026641; then add 0* and again add notation 3–9 from Table 2, e.g., treaties between United Kingdom and France 341.026641044

          Give priority in notation to the country coming first in Table 2 (Option: Give priority in notation to the country requiring local emphasis, e.g., libraries in United States class treaties between United Kingdom and the United States in 341.026673041)

*Add 00 for standard subdivisions; see instructions at beginning of Table 1

.026 7          Codes

> Class codes of a specific subject in law of nations with the subject in 341.2–341.7, plus notation 0267 from add table under 341.2–341.7, e.g., disarmament codes 341.7330267; class codes of a specific subject in domestic law with the subject in 342–347, plus notation 02632 from add table under 342–347, e.g., commercial codes 346.0702632

.026 8          Cases

> Decisions and reports

> Class here general collections of cases on international matters tried in any court system

> Add to base number 341.0268 notation 3–9 from Table 2, e.g., cases brought by United Kingdom 341.026841; then, for cases brought by that nation against another nation, add 0* and again add notation 3–9 from Table 2, e.g., cases brought by United Kingdom against United States 341.026841073
>> (Option: Give priority in notation to the nation requiring local emphasis, e.g., libraries in United States class all cases involving United States and United Kingdom in 341.026873041)

> Class cases about a specific subject in law of nations with the subject in 341.2–341.7, plus notation 0268 from add table under 341.2–341.7, e.g., disarmament cases 341.7330268; class cases about a specific subject in domestic law with the subject in 342–347, plus notation 0264 from add table under 342–347, e.g., commercial cases 346.070264

.04          Relation of law of nations and domestic law

> Class here works on whether domestic law or law of nations prevails in a certain situation

> Class the law of a nation or lesser jurisdiction that carries out the provisions of an international agreement in 342–347

.09          History, geographic treatment, biography

.092          Biography

> Do not use for critical works on individual publicists; class in 341.1

**.1          Sources of law of nations**

> Treaties, judicial decisions, custom, general principles of law, works of publicists (theorists)

> Class here critical works on individual publicists (theorists)

> Class texts of treaties and reports of judicial decisions in 341.026; class comprehensive works on treaties in 341.37. Class writings of publicists on a specific subject with the subject in 341–347, e.g., international rivers 341.442, international commerce 343.087

---

*Add 00 for standard subdivisions; see instructions at beginning of Table 1

>      **341.2–341.7 Specific topics**

Add to each subdivision identified by † as follows:

| | | |
|---|---|---|
| 01 | | Philosophy and theory |
| | | Notation 01 from Table 1 as modified below |
| 011 | | Special topics of philosophy and theory of law |
| | | Including origin, sources, nature, limits of law; rule of law; legal reasoning; equal protection of the law; law and ethics; justice; law and society |
| | | Use of this number for systems discontinued; class in 01 |
| 02 | | Miscellany |
| | | Notation 02 from Table 1 as modified below |
| 023 | | Law as a profession, occupation, hobby |
| | | Class here legal personnel, nature of duties, characteristics of profession |
| | | Class professional ethics of legal personnel in 174.3; class comprehensive works on legal personnel in 340.023. Class works that emphasize procedures of work performed by legal personnel with the subject without adding notation 023 from Table 1, e.g., works that emphasize procedures of adjudicating matters of public international law 341.55 |
| 026 | | Treaties, codes, cases |
| | | Texts of treaties, codes, cases; guides, e.g., checklists, citators, digests, indexes |
| | | Do not use for discussions, commentaries, or popular works; class with the subject in 341.2–341.7 without further subdivision |
| | | Class here conventions, protocols |
| | | Class texts of treaties on a specific subject in domestic law with the subject in 342–347, plus notation 0261 from add table under 342–347, e.g., text of commercial treaties 346.070261 |
| 0261–0266 | | Text of treaties |
| | | Add to 026 the numbers following 341.026 in 341.0261–341.0266, e.g., multilateral treaties 0265 |
| 0267 | | Codes |
| | | Class codes of a specific subject in domestic law with the subject in 342–347, plus notation 02632 from add table under 342–347, e.g., commercial codes 346.0702632 |

(continued)

> **341.2–341.7  Specific topics (continued)**

> 0268 Cases
> Decisions and reports
> Class here general collections of cases on international matters tried in any court system
> Add to base number 0268 notation 3–9 from Table 2, e.g., cases brought by United Kingdom 026841; then, for cases brought by that nation against another nation, add 0* and again add notation 3–9 from Table 2, e.g., cases brought by United Kingdom against United States 026841073
>> (Option: Give priority in notation to the nation requiring local emphasis, e.g., libraries in United States class all cases involving United States and United Kingdom in 026873041)
> Class cases about a specific subject in domestic law with the subject in 342–347, plus notation 0264 from add table under 342–347, e.g., commercial cases 346.070264

> 03–08 Standard subdivisions
> 09 History, geographic treatment, biography
> *See Manual at 342–349*

Class comprehensive works in 341

**.2** **The world community**

Class here international legal personality

**.21** World government

Proposals and schemes

> 341.22–341.24  Intergovernmental organizations

Class here legal responsibilities of officials; privileges and immunities; interdisciplinary works on intergovernmental organizations

Class comprehensive works on intergovernmental organizations in 341.2; class interdisciplinary works on international organizations in 060. Class comprehensive works on the laws of a specific intergovernmental organization with the organization in 349, e.g., laws of European Union 349.24

> *For administration of intergovernmental organizations, see 352.11. For a specialized intergovernmental organization, see the subject with which it deals, plus notation 0601 from Table 1, e.g., Interpol 363.20601; for legal aspects of a specialized intergovernmental organization, see the subject with which it deals in 341–347, e.g., Interpol 345.052; for treaties, codes, cases on a specific subject in domestic law of a non-specialized intergovernmental organization, see the specific subject in 342–347, e.g., economic law of European Union 343.2407; for a nonlegal aspect of an intergovernmental organization, see the aspect, e.g., economic aspects of European Union 337.142*

**.22** League of Nations

---

*Add 00 for standard subdivisions; see instructions at beginning of Table 1

| [.220 13] | Value |
|---|---|
| | Number discontinued; class in 341.2201 |
| [.220 68] | Management |
| | Do not use; class in 352.112 |

.221–.229      Functions, activities, organization, general relations with specific nations

> Add to base number 341.22 the numbers following 341.23 in 341.231–341.239, e.g., Covenant of the League 341.222

.23      United Nations

.230 1      Philosophy and theory

> Notation 01 from Table 1 as modified below
>
> Do not use for value; class in 341.23013

.230 13      Value

> Evaluation of and opinions about the effectiveness and worth of the United Nations

[.230 68]      Management

> Do not use; class in 352.113

.231      †Functions and activities

> Class functions and activities of specific branches of the United Nations in 341.232. Class a specific function or activity with the function or activity in 341–347, e.g., role in the peaceful settlement of disputes 341.523, role of UNICEF in child welfare 344.0327

.232      †Organization

> Including charter
>
> Class here rules of procedure
>
> *For legal responsibility of officials, see 341.233; for Secretariat, see 352.113*

.232 2      †General Assembly

.232 3      †Security Council

.232 5      †Economic and Social Council

.233      †Admission and membership

> *For organization, see 341.232*

†Add as instructed under 341.2–341.7

| .234–.239 | General relations with specific nations |
|---|---|

Add to base number 341.23 notation 4–9 from Table 2, e.g., relations with United States 341.2373

Class relations dealing with a specific subject with the subject in 341–347, e.g., United Nations peacekeeping operations in Serbia 341.584094971, United Nations human rights activities in the United States 342.73085

| .24 | Regional organizations |
|---|---|

*For comprehensive works on the laws of regional intergovernemental organizations, see 349.2*

| .242 | European regional organizations |
|---|---|

| .242 1 | †Council of Europe |
|---|---|

Class laws promulgated by Council of Europe with the subject in 341–347, e.g., protection of rights of individuals 342.24085

| .242 2 | †European Union |
|---|---|

Class here European Common Market, European Community, European Economic Community

Class political integration of European Union member states in 320.94; class economic integration of European Union member states in 337.142. Class laws promulgated by European Union with the subject in 341–347, e.g., copyright laws 346.240482

| .242 202 65 | Multilateral treaties |
|---|---|

Number built according to instructions under 341.2–341.7

Class here texts of founding treaties, e.g., Treaty Establishing the European Community, Maastricht Treaty on European Union; texts of treaties amending founding treaties, e.g., Treaty of Nice; Treaty Establishing a Constitution for Europe (2004)

Class texts of accession treaties in 341.242230265

| [.242 206 8] | Management |
|---|---|

Do not use; class in 352.114

| .242 209 | History, geographic treatment, biography |
|---|---|

Notation 09 from Table 1 as modified below

| .242 209 4–.242 209 9 | Specific continents, countries, localities; extraterrestrial worlds |
|---|---|

Class here general relations with specific nations

Class relations dealing with a specific subject with the subject in 341–347, e.g., admission to European Union 341.24223, relations concerning antitrust law and competition law 343.240721, effect of European Union law on national law of Germany 349.43

†Add as instructed under 341.2–341.7

| | |
|---|---|
| .242 22 | †Organization |

    Class here rules of procedure

    Class legislative process in European Union in 328.4

    *For legal responsibility of officials, see 341.24223*

| | |
|---|---|
| .242 222 | †Council of the European Union |
| .242 224 | †European Parliament [*formerly* 341.2424] |
| .242 226 | †European Commission |
| .242 228 | †Courts of the European Union |

    *For European Court of Human Rights, see 342.240850269*

| | |
|---|---|
| .242 228 2 | †Court of First Instance of the European Communities |
| .242 228 4 | †Court of Justice of the European Communities |
| .242 23 | †Admission and membership |

    Subdivisions are added for either or both topics in heading

    *For organization, see 341.24222*

| | |
|---|---|
| .242 230 265 | Multilateral treaties |

    Number built according to instructions under 341.2–341.7

    Class here texts of accession treaties

| | |
|---|---|
| .242 24 | †Relationship between European Union law and national law of European Union countries |

    Class here effect of European Union law on national law of European Union countries, harmonization of national law of European Union countries

    *For relationship of European Union law on a specific branch or subject of law with national law of a specific member state, see the branch or subject of national law in 342–347, e.g., Italian labor law regulated by European Union law 344.4501; for comprehensive works on relationship of European Union law on a specific branch or subject and national law of member countries, see the branch or subject in 342–347 plus the notation for European regional intergovernmental organizations, e.g., effect of European Union law on labor law of member states 344.2401; for comprehensive works on relationship of European Union law and national law of a specific member state, see the national law in 349, e.g., effect of European Union law on national law of Italy 349.45*

| | |
|---|---|
| [.242 4] | European Parliament |

    Relocated to 341.242224

| | |
|---|---|
| .242 7 | †Council for Mutual Economic Assistance |

†Add as instructed under 341.2–341.7

| | |
|---|---|
| .243 | Atlantic regional organizations |
| .245 | Western Hemisphere regional organizations |

Including Organization of American States

| | |
|---|---|
| .246 | Pacific regional organizations |
| .247 | Asian regional organizations |
| .247 3 | Far East regional organizations |

Including ASEAN (Association of East Asian Nations)

| | |
|---|---|
| .247 7 | Western Asia regional organizations |

Including League of Arab States

Class here Middle East organizations

| | |
|---|---|
| .249 | African regional organizations |

*For League of Arab States, see 341.2477*

| | |
|---|---|
| .26 | †States |

Including recognition of states and governments; mergers, self-determination, liability, sovereignty, succession of states; liability of states to aliens

Class liability of states with respect to a specific subject in law of nations with the subject in 341.2–341.7, e.g., liability for damages caused by testing nuclear weapons 341.734; class liability of states with respect to a specific subject in other branches of law with the subject in 342–347, e.g., liability for breach of contract 346.022

*For semisovereign states, see 341.27; for relations between states, see 341.3; for jurisdiction over physical space, see 341.4*

| | |
|---|---|
| .27 | †Semisovereign states |

Including mandates, protectorates, trusteeships

| | |
|---|---|
| .28 | †Non-self-governing territories |

Class here colonies

| | |
|---|---|
| .29 | †Areas having special status in international law |

Including partitioned areas, e.g., Antarctica, Cyprus

| | |
|---|---|
| **.3** | **†Relations between states** |

*For jurisdictional relations, see 341.4; for disputes and conflicts, see 341.5; for international cooperation, see 341.7*

†Add as instructed under 341.2–341.7

.302 6        Treaties, codes, cases

Number built according to instructions under 341.2–341.7

Class here texts of treaties limited to general relations between states

Class works about treaties in 341.37. Class text of treaties on a specific subject in law of nations with the subject in 341.2–341.7, plus notation 026 from add table under 341.2–341.7, e.g., text of disarmament treaties 341.733026, text of a disarmament treaty between Russia and the United States 341.733026647073; class text of treaties on a specific subject in domestic law with the subject in 342–347, plus notation 0261 from add table under 342–347, e.g., text of copyright treaties 346.04820261

.33        †Diplomatic law

Including legal aspects of functions, immunities, privileges, status of diplomatic personnel and agencies; delegations to international organizations and their staffs

Class officials and employees of intergovernmental organizations in 341.22–341.24; class interdisciplinary works on diplomacy in 327.2

*For consular law, see 341.35*

.35        †Consular law

.37        Treaties

Including negotiation and ratification, validity and binding force, termination, interpretation

Class treaties on a specific subject in law of nations with the subject in 341.2–341.7, e.g., disarmament treaties 341.733; class treaties on a specific subject in domestic law with the subject in 342–347, e.g., copyright treaties 346.0482

*For general collections of texts of treaties, see 341.026; for treaties as sources of law of nations, see 341.1*

**.4        †Jurisdiction over physical space; human rights**

Class here conservation and development of extraterritorial natural resources; extraterritoriality; jurisdiction over physical space; servitudes and easements; right of innocent passage

Subdivisions are added for jurisdiction over physical space and human rights together, for jurisdiction over physical space alone

*See also 346.044 for conservation and development of territorial natural resources*

---

>        341.42–341.47   Jurisdiction over physical space

Class comprehensive works in 341.4

†Add as instructed under 341.2–341.7

.42          †Territory

Including acquisition, boundaries, border disputes

Class mergers of states in 341.26; class boundary rivers in 341.442

.44          †Bodies of water

*For high seas, see 341.45*

.442          †Rivers

National, semi-national, boundary, internationalized rivers

Including combined river, lake, canal systems, e.g., Saint Lawrence
Seaway

Class canalized rivers in 341.446

.444          †Lakes and inland seas

Subdivisions are added for either or both topics in heading

Class combined river, lake, canal systems in 341.442

.446          †Canals and straits

Class combined river, lake, canal systems in 341.442

.448          †Territorial waters

Including bays, continental shelves

Class access to the sea, comprehensive works on ocean and sea waters in
341.45

.45          †High seas

Class here comprehensive works on international law of ocean and sea
waters

Class ocean transportation in 343.0962; class oceanographic research in
344.0955

*For territorial waters, see 341.448*

*See Manual at 341.45 vs. 343.0962*

.455          †Seabed (Ocean bottom)]
.46          †Airspace

Class air transportation in 343.097; class meteorological research in
344.0955

.47          †Extraterrestrial space

Including the moon, planets

Class space transportation in 343.0979; class space research in 344.0952

---

†Add as instructed under 341.2–341.7

| .48 | Human rights |
|---|---|

Class jurisdiction over persons in 342.08; class civil rights in 342.085; class personal property in 346.047; class interdisciplinary works on human rights in 323

*See Manual at 342.085 vs. 341.48*

| .480 2 | Miscellany |
|---|---|

Notation 02 from Table 1 as modified below

| .480 26 | Treaties, codes, cases |
|---|---|

Add to base number 341.48026 the numbers following 341.026 in 341.0261–341.0268, e.g., text of multilateral treaties 341.480265

| [.480 8] | Groups of people |
|---|---|

Do not use; class in 341.485

| .483 | Specific human rights |
|---|---|

Class specific rights of specific social groups in 341.485

| [.483 01–.483 09] | Standard subdivisions |
|---|---|

Do not use; class in 341.4801–341.4809

| .483 2–.483 8 | Subdivisions for specific human rights |
|---|---|

Add to base number 341.483 the numbers following 342.085 in 342.0852–342.0858, e.g., freedom of religion 341.4832

| .485 | Rights of specific social groups |
|---|---|

| [.485 01–.485 09] | Standard subdivisions |
|---|---|

Do not use; class in 341.4801–341.4809

| .485 2–.485 8 | Subdivisions for rights of specific social groups |
|---|---|

Add to base number 341.485 the numbers following 342.087 in 342.0872–342.0878, e.g., rights of women 341.4858; however, for rights of stateless persons and refugees, see 341.486

| .486 | †Rights of stateless persons and refugees |
|---|---|

Class jurisdiction over stateless persons and refugees in 342.083

| **.5** | **†Disputes and conflicts between states** |
|---|---|

Class disputes on a specific subject with the subject in 341–347, e.g., jurisdictional disputes 341.4

*For law of war, see 341.6*

| .52 | †Peaceful settlement |
|---|---|

Including mediation

*For adjudication, see 341.55*

---

†Add as instructed under 341.2–341.7

| .522 | †Arbitration |
| .522 2 | †Permanent Court of Arbitration |
| .523 | †Role of intergovernmental organizations |

Class peace conferences in 341.73

| .55 | †Adjudication |

Courts and court procedure

Including role of domestic courts in adjudicating matters of public international law, interpretation of general law of nations in courts

Class interpretation of a specific subject with the subject in 341–347, e.g., interpretation of war crimes 341.69, interpretation of civil rights 342.085

| .552 | †International Court of Justice |
| .58 | †Coercive methods of settlement short of war |

Including ultimatums

| .582 | †Sanctions |

Including boycotts, embargoes, reprisals

| .584 | †Intervention |

Including blockades, deploying peacekeeping forces, humanitarian intervention

| **.6** | **†Law of war** |
| .62 | †Initiation of war |

Including aggression

| .63 | †Conduct of war |

Including prize law

| .64 | †Neutrality and neutral states |

Class status of nationals of neutral nations in 341.67

| .65 | †Treatment of prisoners |

Including granting of quarter

Class humanitarian law in 341.67

| .66 | Termination of war |

Including indemnification, reparations, restitution; laws of occupation

Class here military government of occupied countries

*For war claims by private individuals of one country against another country, see 340.9*

†Add as instructed under 341.2–341.7

.660 2          Miscellany

              Notation 02 from Table 1 as modified below

.660 26         Treaties and cases

              Class here text of treaties limited to termination of war

              Add to base number 341.66026 the numbers following 341.026 in 341.0261–341.0268, e.g., text of multilateral treaties 341.660265

              Class texts of treaties that are signed at termination of a war but cover topics other than termination of the war in 341.026

.67         †Humanitarian law

              Including status of enemy aliens and their property, nationals of neutral nations, combatants, noncombatants, war victims

              *For treatment of prisoners, see 341.65*

.68         †Law of nations and civil war

              Including responsibility of the state for acts of unsuccessful insurgent governments

.69         †War crimes

.690 268        Cases

              Number built according to instructions under 341.2–341.7

              Class here trials of war criminals, e.g., Tokyo war crime trials

**.7**        **†International cooperation**

.72         †Mutual security

              Including international security forces

              Class here legal aspects of international mutual security pacts, e.g., NATO (North Atlantic Treaty Organization)

              Class military and defense law in 343.01; class civil defense in 344.0535; class interdisciplinary works on international mutual security pacts in 355.031

.722        †Peaceful occupation (Friendly occupation)

.73         †Peace and disarmament

              Class here peace conferences, general efforts to gain acceptance of renunciation of war as an instrument of national policy

              Subdivisions are added for peace and disarmament together, for peace alone

              Class peaceful settlement of disputes in 341.52

†Add as instructed under 341.2–341.7

| .733 | †Disarmament |
|---|---|

Including suspension of weapons testing

Class the abolition and control of specific kinds of weapons in 341.734–341.738

| .734 | †Control of nuclear weapons |
|---|---|

| .735 | †Control of chemical and biological weapons |
|---|---|

Class here control of weapons of mass destruction

*For control of nuclear weapons, see 341.734*

| .738 | †Control of strategic weapons during time of peace |
|---|---|

Class control of nuclear strategic weapons in 341.734; class control of chemical and biological strategic weapons in 341.735

---

> ## 342–349  Branches of law; laws, regulations, cases; law of specific jurisdictions, areas, socioeconomic regions

Classification numbers for law of specific jurisdictions and areas are built from five elements, which can be arranged in different ways to produce standard or optional numbers, according to instructions following this table:

(1)    34, the base number, indicating law
(2)    A digit indicating specific branch of law, original materials, or comprehensive works as follows:

2    Constitutional and administrative law
3    Military, defense, public property, public finance, tax, trade (commerce), industrial law
4    Labor, social service, education, cultural law
5    Criminal law
6    Private law
7    Procedure and courts
8    Laws, regulations, cases not limited to a specific branch
9    Comprehensive works

(3)    The facet indicator 0*
(4)    One or more digits indicating a subject subordinate to specific branch of law or type of original material
        Example: 1 Courts (from 345.01 under 345 Criminal law)
(5)    Notation from Table 2 indicating the jurisdiction or area
        Example: —94 Australia

To show comprehensive works on a specific jurisdiction or area in modern world, arrange the elements as follows, using law of Australia as an example:
    Base number: 34
    Digit indicating comprehensive works: 9
    Jurisdiction or area: Australia, —94
    The complete number is 349.94

(continued)

---

*Add 00 for standard subdivisions; see instructions at beginning of Table 1
†Add as instructed under 341.2–341.7

> ## 342–349 Branches of law; laws, regulations, cases; law of specific jurisdictions, areas, socioeconomic regions (continued)

To show a specific branch, a specific subject, or a kind of original material, arrange the elements as follows, using criminal courts of Australia as an example:
> Base number: 34
> Branch of law: Criminal law, 5
> Jurisdiction or area: Australia, —94
> Facet indicator: 0*
> Subordinate subject in branch of law: Courts, 1
> The complete number is 345.9401

Class comprehensive works in 340; class comprehensive works on law of specific ancient jurisdictions, areas, socioeconomic regions in 340.53; class comprehensive works on law of specific jurisdictions, areas, socioeconomic regions in 349

*See Manual at 342–349*

(Option: To give preferred treatment to the law of a specific jurisdiction, to jurisdictions in general, to branch of law and its subordinate subjects, or to subject, use one of the following options or the option at 342–347:

(Option A: To give local emphasis and a shorter notation to law of a specific jurisdiction or area, e.g., Australia, arrange the elements as follows, using criminal courts of Australia as an example:
> Base number: 34
> Branch of law: Criminal law, 5
> Facet indicator: 0*
> Subordinate subject in the branch of law: Courts, 1
> The complete number is 345.01

(For law of a jurisdiction subordinate to the emphasized jurisdiction or area, insert between the branch of law and facet indicator the notation indicating the subordinate jurisdiction

> (To show subordinate jurisdictions of an area with regular notation from Table 2, derive the notation by dropping from the area number for subordinate jurisdiction all digits that apply to preferred jurisdiction. For example, drop area number for Australia —94 from area number for Tasmania —946 to obtain notation 6, which is used for Tasmania. Thus, the number for criminal procedure of Tasmania is 345.605

> (To show subordinate jurisdictions of an area with irregular notation from Table 2, i.e., with numbers for subdivisions that are coordinate with the number for the entire area, derive notation by dropping the digits from area number that all subdivisions have in common. For example, Sudan's area number is —624, while the numbers for its regions and provinces are —625–629. Drop —62 from full area number for Darfur region —627 to obtain the notation 7, which is used for Darfur region. Thus, the number for criminal procedure of the Darfur region is 345.705

(continued)

---

*Add 00 for standard subdivisions; see instructions at beginning of Table 1

> ## 342–349 Branches of law; laws, regulations, cases; law of specific jurisdictions, areas, socioeconomic regions (continued)

(Class comprehensive works on law of the preferred jurisdiction or area in 342; class comparative law and law of other jurisdictions and areas in 349

(Option B: To give preferred treatment to jurisdictions in general, arrange the elements as follows, using criminal courts of Australia as an example:
Base number: 34
Jurisdiction or area: Australia, —94
Facet indicator: 0*
Branch of law: Criminal law, 5
Subordinate subject in branch of law: Courts, 1
The complete number is 349.4051. Other examples: criminal courts of Tasmania 349.46051, texts of welfare laws of Hobart 349.4610430263

(Class law of jurisdictions in the ancient world in 340.53–340.54; class comparative law in 342; class law of socioeconomic regions in 343.1; class law of regional intergovernmental organizations in 343.2

(Option C: To give preferred treatment to branch of law and its subordinate subjects, arrange the elements as follows, using criminal courts of Australia as an example:
Base number: 34
Branch of law: Criminal law, 5
Subordinate subject in branch of law: Courts, 1
Facet indicator: 0*
Jurisdiction or area: Australia, —94
The complete number is 345.1094)

*Add 00 for standard subdivisions; see instructions at beginning of Table 1

> ## 342–347 Branches of law

Class here comprehensive works on specific subjects of law

Except for modifications shown under specific entries, add to each subdivision identified by * as follows:

| 01 | Philosophy and theory |
| | Notation 01 from Table 1 as modified below |
| 011 | Special topics of philosophy and theory of law |
| | Including origin, sources, nature, limits of law; rule of law; legal reasoning; equal protection of the law; law and ethics; justice; law and society |
| | Use of this number for systems discontinued; class in 01 |
| 02 | Miscellany |
| | Notation 02 from Table 1 as modified below |
| 023 | Law as a profession, occupation, hobby |
| | Class here legal personnel, nature of duties, characteristics of profession |
| | Class professional ethics of legal personnel in 174.3; class comprehensive works on legal personnel in 340.023. Class works that emphasize procedures of work performed by legal personnel with the subject without adding notation 023 from Table 1, e.g., works that emphasize procedures of conducting a lawsuit 347.0504 |
| 026 | Laws, regulations, cases, procedure, courts |
| | Standard subdivisions may be added to 026 and its subdivisions |
| | (Option: Class laws, regulations, cases on specific subjects in law in 348) |
| 0261 | Treaties |
| | Including negotiation and ratification, validity and binding force, termination, interpretation |
| | Class here bilateral and multilateral treaties |
| | Do not use for commentaries and criticism; class with the subject in 342–347 without further subdivision |
| | Add to 0261 notation 3–9 from Table 2, e.g., bilateral treaties with Great Britain 026141 |
| 0262 | Preliminary materials |
| | Including bills, hearings, reports, executive messages, statements of witnesses, legislative histories, slip laws |
| | Do not use for commentaries and critical works; class with the subject in 342–347 without further subdivision |
| | *See Manual at 300–330, 355–390 vs. 342–347, 352–354* |
| 0263 | Laws and regulations |
| | Do not use for commentaries and criticism; class with the subject in 342–347 without further subdivision |
| 02632 | Individual and collected laws |
| | Including codes |
| 02636 | Administrative regulations |
| | Collections and individual regulations |
| 02638 | Guides to laws and regulations |
| | Digests, citators, checklists, tables, indexes |

(continued)

> ## 342–347  Branches of law (continued)

| | |
|---|---|
| 0264 | Cases |
| | Do not use for casebooks, for popular works; class with the subject in 342–347 without further subdivision |
| 02642 | Reports |
| 02643 | Court decisions |
| | Class here official court decisions |
| | Do not use for treatises on court decisions and popular treatment of cases; class with the subject in 342–347 without further subdivision |
| 02646 | Decisions (Rulings) of regulatory agencies |
| 02648 | Guides to cases |
| | Including digests, citators, checklists, tables, indexes, loose-leaf services |
| | Class here guides to laws, regulations, cases |
| | *For guides to laws and regulations, see 02638* |
| 0265 | Advisory opinions of attorneys-general (ministers of justice) |
| 0269 | Courts and procedure |
| | Including administrative courts, regulatory agencies; practice, rules, form books, legal costs and fees |
| | (Option: Class courts and procedure in specific fields in 347) |
| 03–05 | Standard subdivisions |
| 06 | Organizations and management |
| | Notation 06 from Table 1 as modified below |
| | Class regulation of associations engaged in a specific type of enterprise with the enterprise in 343.076–343.078, e.g., regulation of law partnerships 343.07834; class organization of associations engaged in specific types of enterprises with the kind of association in 346.06, e.g., laws for forming a law partnership 346.0682 |
| 0601 | International organizations |
| | Law limited to a specific regional intergovernmental organization is classed under the area of the organization before indicating the subject of a branch of law, e.g., economic law of European Union 343.2407. Further instructions are given under 342–349 |
| 07–08 | Standard subdivisions |
| 09 | History, geographic treatment, biography |
| [0917] | Socioeconomic regions |
| | Law limited to a specific socioeconomic region is classed under the region before indicating the subject of a branch of law, e.g., railroad law in developing countries 343.124095 (*not* 343.095091724) |

(continued)

> ## 342–347 Branches of law (continued)

093–099     Specific localities

Limited to application of law of a specific jurisdiction to a limited area within that jurisdiction

Law limited to a specific jurisdiction or area is classed under the jurisdiction before indicating the subject of a branch of law, e.g., railroad law of Germany 343.43095 (*not* 343.0950943). Once the jurisdiction has been specified, notation 093–099 may be added for application of law of that jurisdiction to a limited area within the jurisdiction, e.g., application of German railroad law in Bavaria 343.4309509433

*See Manual at 342–349*

Class general laws, regulations, cases in 348; class comprehensive works in 340

*For a specific subject in law of nations, see the subject in 341, e.g., disarmament law 341.73*

*See Manual at 340, 342–347 vs. 340.56; also at 340, 342–347 vs. 340.57*

(Option: Class the law of a specific subject with the subject, plus notation 026 from Table 1, e.g., law of education 370.26, not 344.07)

## 342   Constitutional and administrative law

Standard subdivisions are added for constitutional and administrative law together, for constitutional law alone

Class here comprehensive works on public law

*For law of nations, see 341. For constitutional law on a specific subject not provided for here, see the subject in 343–347, e.g., criminal law 345*

(If option A under 342–349 is chosen, class here comprehensive works on the law of preferred jurisdiction, e.g., [assuming Australia to be preferred jurisdiction] comprehensive works on law of Australia 342, on law of Tasmania 342.6. Class specific branches of the law of preferred jurisdiction in 342–348

(If option B under 342–349 is chosen, class here comparative law and law without jurisdiction by adding to base number 342 the numbers following 34 in 342–348, but omitting the first 0 after decimal point, e.g., comparative criminal procedure 342.55 [*not* 342.505])

### SUMMARY

| | |
|---|---|
| 342.001–.009 | **Standard subdivisions; laws, regulations, cases, procedure, courts** |
| .02 | **Basic instruments of government** |
| .03 | **Revision and amendment of basic instruments of government** |
| .04 | **Structure, powers, functions of government** |
| .05 | **Legislative branch of government** |
| .06 | **Executive branch of government** |
| .07 | **Election law** |
| .08 | **Jurisdiction over persons** |
| .09 | **Local government** |
| .1 | **Socioeconomic regions** |
| .2 | **Regional intergovernmental organizations** |
| .3–.9 | **Specific jurisdictions and areas** |

| | |
|---|---|
| .001–.008 | Standard subdivisions |

Notation from Table 1 as modified under 342–347, e.g., cases 342.00264

| | |
|---|---|
| .009 | History, geographic treatment, biography |
| [.009 17] | Socioeconomic regions |

Do not use; class in 342.1

| | |
|---|---|
| [.009 3–.009 9] | Specific continents, countries, localities |

Do not use; class in 342.3–342.9

| | |
|---|---|
| .02 | *Basic instruments of government |

Class here constitutions, municipal charters

*For revision and amendment, see 342.03. For constitutional provisions dealing with a specific subject, see the subject in 342–347, e.g., individual rights 342.085*

| | |
|---|---|
| [.020 9] | History, geographic treatment, biography |

Do not use; class in 342.029

| | |
|---|---|
| .023 | Texts of constitutions |

Including texts of proposed constitutions

| | |
|---|---|
| .024 | Sources |

Class commentary on source documents without text in 342.0292

| | |
|---|---|
| .024 2 | Convention proceedings |

Including debates, journals, minutes

| | |
|---|---|
| .024 3 | Other convention documents |

Including enabling acts, memoranda, proposals, rules

| | |
|---|---|
| .029 | Constitutional history |

*For sources, see 342.024*

| | |
|---|---|
| .029 2 | History of conventions |

Class proceedings and documents of conventions in 342.024; class constitutional conventions dealing with revision and amendment of constitutions in 342.03

| | |
|---|---|
| .03 | Revision and amendment of basic instruments of government |

Class here constitutional reform

Class proposals for and formation of new constitutions in 342.02

*For amendments dealing with a specific subject, see the subject in 342–347, e.g., an amendment establishing an income tax 343.052*

| | |
|---|---|
| [.030 9] | History, geographic treatment, biography |

Do not use; class in 342.039

*Add as instructed under 342–347

| .032 | *Amendment procedure |
|---|---|
| .035 | Proposed and pending amendments |

        Class here collected texts of constitutional amendments

        Class texts of proposed constitutions in 342.023

| .039 | History of amendments |
|---|---|

        Including defeated amendments not limited to a specific subject

| .04 | *Structure, powers, functions of government |
|---|---|

        Class government corporations in 346.067

| .041 | *Powers and functions of government |
|---|---|

        *For jurisdiction over persons, see 342.08*

| .041 2 | *Conduct of relations with foreign governments |
|---|---|

        Including military assistance and missions; power to regulate foreign diplomatic and consular personnel, to wage war; comprehensive works on power to acquire territory from or cede it to other jurisdictions

        Class military and defense law in 343.012–343.019

        *For municipal annexation, see 342.0413*

        *See also 342.0418 for police powers; also 342.062 for war and emergency powers of executives*

| .041 3 | *Jurisdiction over territory, dependencies, colonies |
|---|---|

        Including municipal annexation

        Class comprehensive works on the power to acquire territory from or cede it to other jurisdictions in 342.0412

| .041 8 | *Police powers |
|---|---|

        Powers to exercise control in interests of general security, health, safety, morals, welfare

        Class individual rights in 342.085. Class the exercise of a specific police power with the power in 342–347, e.g., exclusion of undesirable aliens 342.082, regulation of public health 344.04

        *See also 342.062 for war and emergency powers of executives*

| .042 | *Levels of government |
|---|---|

        Including federal structure; relations between levels, relations among subordinate units of same level; domestic conflict of laws; home rule; interstate compacts

        Class levels of government with respect to a specific subject with the subject in 342–347, e.g., interstate compacts on seaports and their facilities 343.0967

        *See also 342.09 for local governments*

*Add as instructed under 342–347

| .044 | *Branches of government |
|---|---|

Including distribution and separation of powers, relations between branches

Class relations of a specific branch of government with government institutions at a different level in 342.042

> *For legislative branch, see 342.05; for executive branch, see 342.06; for judicial branch, see 347*

| .05 | *Legislative branch of government |
|---|---|

Class here lobbying

Class relations of legislative branch with government institutions at a different level in 342.042

| .052 | *Duties, functions, powers |
|---|---|

| .053 | *Basis of representation |
|---|---|

Including apportionment, districting

| .055 | *Membership |
|---|---|

Including qualifications, terms of office

| .057 | *Organization and procedure |
|---|---|

> *For preliminary materials, see 348.01*

| .06 | *Executive branch of government |
|---|---|

Class here administrative law

Class relations of executive branch with governmental institutions at a different level in 342.042. Class standards set by an agency in connection with a specific subject with the subject outside of law, e.g., standards for safety in health care facilities 363.1562

> *For administrative law on a specific subject, see the subject in 342–347, e.g., air traffic control 343.0976*

| .062 | *Chief and deputy chief executives |
|---|---|

Including impeachment; war and emergency powers

Subdivisions are added for either or both topics in heading

| .062 8 | *Martial law |
|---|---|

| .064 | *Executive departments (Ministries) and agencies |
|---|---|

Class departments and agencies dealing with a specific subject with the subject in 342–347, e.g., revenue agencies 343.036

| .066 | *Administrative procedure |
|---|---|

Class maintenance of privacy in 342.0858

> *See also 344.0531 for information control laws*

*Add as instructed under 342–347

.066 2       *Public records

> Class here privacy of government records, right to information, sunshine laws

.066 4       *Administrative courts and regulatory agencies

> Including hearing examiners, provisional courts

> Class executive function of administering and enforcing the law in 351–354. Class administrative courts, regulatory agencies dealing with a specific subject with the subject in 342–347, plus notation 0269 from table under 342–347, e.g., agencies regulating civil aeronautics 343.0970269

.066 7       *Ombudsmen

.068       *Officials and employees

> Including impeachment

> Class here civil service

> Class labor-management bargaining in government service in 344.018904135

> *For chief and deputy chief executives, see 342.062; for official and employees involved with administrative procedure, see 342.066*

.068 4       *Employee rights and discipline

> Including conflict of interest, loyalty oaths, political activity of employees, security measures

.068 6       *Conditions of employment

> Including compensation, fringe benefits, leave, retirement benefits, tenure, training

.07       *Election law

> Class here manuals of election procedures that discuss laws or administrative regulations

> Class manuals of election procedures limited to political aspects in 324.6; class apportionment, districting in 342.053

> *For electing legislators, see 342.055; for electing executives, see 342.068*

.072       *Voting rights and qualifications for voting

> Subdivisions are added for either or both topics in heading

.075       *Voting procedures

> Including absentee voting, voter registration

.078       *Campaign practices

> Including finance

*Add as instructed under 342–347

.08        *Jurisdiction over persons

Including census law

.082       *Entrance to and exit from national domain

Including immigration, passports, visas, emigration

Class entry and exit of diplomatic and consular personnel in 342.0412

.083       *Citizenship and nationality

Including right of asylum, status of aliens, jurisdiction over stateless persons and refugees

Subdivisions are added for either or both topics in heading

Class liability of states to aliens in 341.26; class status of enemy aliens in 341.67; class status of diplomatic and consular personnel in 342.0412

.084       *Abortion

Class here comprehensive works

*For rights of fetuses, see 342.085; for rights of women, see 342.0878; for medical aspects, see 344.04192; for abortion for population control, see 344.048; for abortion control, see 344.0546; for criminal abortion, see 345.0285*

.085       *Rights and activities of individuals

Including individual rights of military personnel, rights of fetuses

Class here civil rights; comprehensive works on individual rights

Class constitutional rights of aliens in 342.083; class constitutional rights of specific social groups in 342.087; class comprehensive works on abortion in 342.084; class interdisciplinary works on civil rights, on individual rights in 323

*For a specific right not provided for here, see the right, e.g., right to vote 342.072, right to education 344.079*

*See Manual at 342.085 vs. 341.48*

.085 2     *Religious activities

.085 3     *Freedom of information and opinion

Including freedom of speech, freedom of the press

Subdivisions are added for either or both topics in heading

Class fairness doctrine in 343.09945; class censorship and information control laws in 344.0531; class relation of freedom of the press to the judicial process in 347.05

*For freedom of political opinion, see 342.0854; for academic freedom, see 344.078*

*See also 342.0662 for access to public records; also 344.0547 for obscenity and pornography laws*

*Add as instructed under 342–347

.085 4      *Political activity

       Including civil disobedience and dissent, rights of assembly and petition

       Class election law in 342.07

         *For political activity of government employees, see 342.0684*

.085 8      *Maintenance of privacy

       Class privacy of government records in 342.0662

.087      *Groups of people

       Including slaves

       Class here affirmative action, legal status

         *For aliens, displaced persons, refugees, see 342.083*

         *See also 342.085 for rights and activities of individuals*

[.087 08]      Groups of people

       Do not use; class in 342.087

.087 2      *Indigenous and aboriginal peoples

       Subdivisions are added for either or both topics in heading

       Class women in 342.0878

.087 3      *Ethnic and national groups

       Class indigenous and aboriginal peoples of specific ethnic and national groups in 342.0872; class women of specific ethnic and national groups in 342.0878

.087 7      *Age groups

       Class women regardless of age group in 342.0878

.087 72      *Young people

       Class here children

.087 74      *People in late adulthood

.087 8      *Women

       Including abortion rights

       Class comprehensive works on abortion in 342.084

.088      *Government liability

       Including liability for abuse of power, corruption, denial of civil rights

       Class liability in a specific field with the field in 342–347, e.g., liability of military units 343.013, liability of schools, of school officials, of school districts 344.075

*Add as instructed under 342–347

.09      *Local government

Including municipal corporations, municipal government

Class home rule in 342.042; class specific local governments in 342.3–342.9. Class a specific aspect of local government with the aspect in 342–347, e.g., local real estate taxation 343.054

.1      **Socioeconomic regions**

Add to base number 342.1 the numbers following —17 in notation 171–177 from Table 2, e.g., constitutional and administrative law of developing countries 342.124; then to the result add as follows:
001–009     Standard subdivisions
           Notation from Table 1 as modified under 342–347
02–09     Topics of constitutional and administrative law
           Add the numbers following 342 in 342.02–342.09,
           e.g., election law of developing countries 342.12407,
           administrative regulations for elections in developing countries
           342.1240702636

Class socioeconomic regions of a specific regional intergovernmental organization in 342.2; class socioeconomic regions of a specific jurisdiction or area in 342.3–342.9

.2      **Regional intergovernmental organizations**

Class here relationship between the organization's law and national law of member countries

Add to base number 342.2 notation 3–9 from Table 2, e.g., harmonization of national constitutional and administrative law of European Union countries 342.24; then to the result add as follows:
001–009     Standard subdivisions
           Notation from Table 1 as modified under 342–347
02–09     Topics of constitutional and administrative law
           Add the numbers following 342 in 342.02–342.09, e.g.,
           harmonization of national citizenship law of European
           Union countries 342.24083, harmonization of administrative
           regulations of citizenship law of European Union countries
           342.2408302636

Class relationship of organization's law and national law of a specific member country with the national law in 342.3–342.9, e.g., effect of European Union laws on national constitutional and administrative law of Germany 342.43

*See Manual at 342–349*

.24      Regional intergovernmental organizations of Europe

Number built according to instructions under 342.2

*Add as instructed under 342–347

.240 2      Basic instruments of government

Class founding treaties, basic legal instruments of European Union in 341.2422

Class here effect of European Union law on and harmonization of national constitutions of European Union countries

Number built according to instructions under 342.2

.240 8      Jurisdiction over persons

Number built according to instructions under 342.2

Class here European Union law itself, effect of European Union law on and harmonization of national laws of European Union countries

.240 85      Rights and activities of individuals

Number built according to instructions under 342.2

.240 850 261      Treaties

Number built according to instructions under 342.2

Class here Charter of Fundamental Rights of the European Union, European Convention on Human Rights

.240 850 269      Courts and procedure

Number built according to instructions under 342.2

Class here European Court of Human Rights

**.3–.9    Specific jurisdictions and areas**

Add to base number 342 notation 3–9 from Table 2, e.g., constitutional and administrative law of Australia 342.94, of New South Wales 342.944, of African states 342.6; then to the result add as follows:
001–009      Standard subdivisions
        Notation from Table 1 as modified under 342–347
02–09      Topics of constitutional and administrative law
        Add the numbers following 342 in 342.02–342.09, e.g., election law of Australia 342.9407, of New South Wales 342.94407, of African states 342.607, administrative regulations for elections in Australia 342.940702636

*For regional intergovernmental organizations, relationship between the organization's laws and national laws of all member states, see 342.2*

*See Manual at 342–349*

**343     Military, defense, public property, public finance, tax, commerce (trade), industrial law**

(If option B under 342–349 is chosen, class here law of socioeconomic regions and of regional intergovernmental organizations; however, for law of jurisdictions in the ancient world, see 340.53)

# SUMMARY

.001–.008     Standard subdivisions

Notation from Table 1 as modified under 342–347, e.g., cases 343.00264

.009     History, geographic treatment, biography

Notation 09 from Table 1 as modified below

[.009 17]     Socioeconomic regions

Do not use; class in 343.1

[.009 3–.009 9]     Specific continents, countries, localities

Do not use; class in 343.3–343.9

.01     *Military and defense law, veterans' law

Class here national security, war and emergency legislation

Subdivisions are added for two or more topics in heading, for military law alone, for defense law alone

*For war claims, see 341.66; for martial law, see 342.0628*

.011     *Veterans' law

Class here veterans' welfare law

Class veterans' insurance claims in 346.086364

.011 2     *Veterans' pensions

Including benefits to survivors of veterans

.011 3     *Education and training for veterans

Subdivisions are added for either or both topics in heading

.011 4     *Employment for veterans

*Add as instructed under 342–347

.011 5          *Health care and rehabilitation for veterans

Subdivisions are added for either or both topics in heading

Class disability compensation in 343.0116

.011 6          *Disability compensation for veterans

---

> 343.012–343.019 Military and defense law

Class comprehensive works in 343.01. Class a specific aspect of military or defense law not provided for here with the aspect in 342–347, e.g., regulation of industry 343.07

.012          *Manpower procurement

Including voluntary enlistment

Class reserve officers' training corps and military academies in 344.0769

*For manpower procurement of a specific service other than the army in general, see the service in 343.015–343.019, e.g., manpower procurement of mercenary troops 343.015354, naval manpower procurement 343.01922*

.012 2          *Draft and selective service

Including draft resistance

Subdivisions are added for either or both topics in heading

Class individual rights of military personnel in 342.085; class treatment of conscientious objectors in 343.0126

.012 6          *Conscientious objectors

.013          *Military life, customs, resources

Including rank, pay, promotion, demotion, leave, allowances, living conditions

Class individual rights of military personnel in 342.085

*For civilian employees of military services, see 342.068; for manpower procurement, see 343.012; for discipline and conduct, see 343.014. For military life, customs, resources of a specific service other than the army in general, see the service in 343.015–343.019, e.g., military resources of mercenary troops 343.015354, naval military resources 343.0192*

.014          *Discipline and conduct

Including desertion

Subdivisions are added for either or both topics in heading

*For discipline and conduct of a specific service other than the army in general, see the service in 343.015–343.019, e.g., discipline and conduct of mercenary troops 343.015354, naval discipline and conduct 343.01913*

---

*Add as instructed under 342–347

| [.014 026 9] | Courts and procedure |
|---|---|

Do not use; class in 343.0143

.014 3      *Military courts and procedure

Including procedural rights of military personnel in military courts

Subdivisions are added for either or both topics in heading

Class international war crime trials in 341.69; class procedural rights in nonmilitary courts in 347.05

*See also 342.085 for general rights of military personnel*

.014 6      *Military penology

*For military prisons, see 344.03548*

.015–.019      Specific aspects of military and defense law

Add to base number 343.01 the numbers following 35 in 355–359, e.g., organization 343.0153, training 343.0155, military installations and bases 343.0157, naval law 343.019; then add further as instructed under 342–347, e.g., cases involving naval law 343.0190264; however, for military assistance to foreign nations, see 342.0412; for manpower procurement, see 343.012; for military life, customs, resources, see 343.013; for discipline and conduct, see 343.014

.02      *Law of public property

.023      *Personal property

.025      *Real property

.025 2      *Acquisition

Including nationalization of alien property, condemnation, eminent domain (expropriation); comprehensive works on nationalization

*For acquisition of territory from other jurisdictions, see 342.0412*

.025 3      *Disposal

*See also 342.0412 for cession of territory to other jurisdictions*

.025 6      *Control and use

Including construction and maintenance of government buildings

Subdivisions are added for either or both topics in heading

Class regulation of construction of government buildings in 343.07869051; class comprehensive works on control and use of public and private real property, control of natural resources in 346.044

.03      *Law of public finance

Class here international financial law

*For banks, see 346.082; for government securities, see 346.0922*

*Add as instructed under 342–347

.032      *Monetary law

Including coinage

Class here currency

Class comprehensive works on commemorative medals in 344.091; class comprehensive works on central banks in 346.0821

.032 1–.032 6      Specific aspects of monetary law

Add to base number 343.032 the numbers following 332.4 in 332.41–332.46, e.g., foreign exchange 343.0325, monetary policy 343.0326; then add further as instructed under 342–347, e.g., cases involving foreign exchange 343.03250264

.034      *Budgeting and expenditure

Including fiscal policy, accounting and auditing, economic stabilization, grants-in-aid, intergovernmental financial relations, revenue sharing

Subdivisions are added for either or both topics in heading

Class revenue law, revenue sharing as revenue in 343.036; class budgets and their preparation in 352.48. Class bills for authorization of expenditure for a specific purpose with the purpose in 342–347, e.g., price supports 343.0742

*See also 343.083 for regulation of prices; also 346.063 for public accounting*

.036      *Revenue law

*For public borrowing and debt, see 343.037; for tax law, see 343.04*

.037      *Public borrowing and debt

Including government bankruptcy and insolvency

.04      *Tax law

Class here internal revenue law; tax auditing, avoidance, planning

Class fiscal policy in 343.034; class tax planning applied to a specific kind of tax in 343.05–343.06; class tax evasion in 345.0233; class interdisciplinary works on taxes in 336.2

*For specific kinds of taxes, see 343.05–343.06*

*See Manual at 343.04–343.06 vs. 336.2, 352.44*

.042      *Tax assessment and collection

Including tax accounting, tax appeals

Class assessment and collection of taxes at specific levels in 343.043; class assessment and collection of specific kinds of taxes in 343.05–343.06

---

*Add as instructed under 342–347

.043 Taxes by level

National, state and provincial, local

Class here only comprehensive works and comparisons, e.g., national taxes in North America 343.7043, state taxes in the United States 343.73043, local taxes of the jurisdictions of Pennsylvania 343.748043

Class a specific kind of tax regardless of level with the kind in 343.05–343.06, e.g., income tax law of Michigan 343.774052

Taxes of a specific jurisdiction are classed in 343.3–343.9, plus notation 04 from 343.04, e.g., United States taxes 343.7304

---

> 343.05–343.06 Specific kinds of taxes

Class comprehensive works in 343.04

*See Manual at 343.04–343.06 vs. 336.2, 352.44*

.05 Kinds of taxes by base

### SUMMARY

| | |
|---|---|
| 343.052 | **Income tax** |
| .053 | **Estate, inheritance, gift taxes** |
| .054 | **Property taxes** |
| .055 | **Excise and turnover taxes** |
| .056 | **Customs taxes (Tariff)** |
| .057 | **Stamp taxes** |

.052 *Income tax

Class internal revenue law in 343.04

.052 04 Special topics of income tax

.052 042 *Assessment of income taxes

.052 044 *Preparation of returns

.052 3 *Provisions that allow tax avoidance

.052 304 *Tax incentives

.052 32 *Charitable deductions

.052 33 *Individual retirement accounts

Including Keogh plans

.052 34 *Depreciation and depletion allowances

Subdivisions are added for either or both topics in heading

.052 36 *Business losses

Including bad debts

.052 37 *Tax credits

*Add as instructed under 342–347

| | |
|---|---|
| .052 38 | *Tax shelters |
| .052 4 | Taxes on specific types of income |

Including proceeds from insurance, retirement income

Class reductions in taxes on specific types of income in 343.0523

| | |
|---|---|
| .052 42 | *Wages |

Including payroll taxes, social security taxes

| | |
|---|---|
| .052 424 | *Withholding tax |
| .052 44 | *Profits |
| .052 45 | *Capital gains |
| .052 46 | *Investment income |

Including income from bonds, deposits, stocks

*For taxes on capital gains, see 343.05245; for taxes on real estate transactions, see 343.0546*

| | |
|---|---|
| .052 48 | *Foreign income |

Class taxes on specific types of foreign income in 343.05242–343.05246

| | |
|---|---|
| .052 6 | Income taxes by incidence |

Including taxes on citizens resident in foreign countries, on self-employed persons

Class here double taxation

Add to base number 343.0526 the numbers following 343.06 in 343.062–343.068, e.g., corporation income taxes 343.05267; then add further as instructed under 342–347, e.g., cases involving corporation income taxes 343.052670264; however, for reduction in taxation regardless of incidence, see 343.0523; for taxes on specific types of income regardless of incidence, see 343.0524

| | |
|---|---|
| .053 | *Estate, inheritance, gift taxes |

Standard subdivisions are added for estate, inheritance, gift taxes together; for estate taxes alone; for inheritance taxes alone

Class here death duties, death tax, estate planning

Subdivisions are added for estate, inheritance, gift taxes together; for estate taxes alone; for inheritance taxes alone

*For taxes on fiduciary trusts, see 343.05264*

| | |
|---|---|
| .053 5 | *Gift taxes |
| .054 | *Property taxes |

Real and personal property

| | |
|---|---|
| .054 2 | *Assessment |

*Add as instructed under 342–347

.054 3                    *Exemptions

.054 6                    *Taxes on real estate transactions

                Including real estate sales tax

                Class a specific aspect of real estate tax not provided for here with the aspect in 342–347, e.g., tax assessment 343.0542

.055                      *Excise and turnover taxes

                Including luxury, severance, transfer, use, value-added taxes; user fees

                *For taxes on real estate transactions, see 343.0546*

.055 2                    *Sales taxes

                Class sales taxes on specific commodities and services in 343.0558

.055 3                    *Excise taxes

                Class excise taxes on specific commodities and services in 343.0558

.055 8                    Taxes on specific commodities and services

                Class comprehensive works on sales taxes in 343.0552; class comprehensive works on excise taxes in 343.0553

[.055 801–.055 809]        Standard subdivisions

                Do not use; class in 343.05501–343.05509

.055 81–.055 85           Subdivisions for taxes on specific commodities and services

                Add to base number 343.0558 the numbers following 381.4 in 381.41–381.45, e.g., taxes on products of secondary industries 343.05585, on cigarettes 343.0558567973; then add further as instructed under 342–347, e.g., cases involving taxes on cigarettes 343.0558679730264

.056                      *Customs taxes (Tariff)

                Including custom taxes (tariff) on specific commodities

.057                      *Stamp taxes

.06                       Kinds of taxes by incidence

                Class taxes on specific bases regardless of incidence in 343.05

.062                      *Taxes on individuals

                Class here poll tax

.064                      *Taxes on fiduciary trusts

                Including pension trusts

.066                      *Taxes on organizations

                Class here tax-exempt organizations

                *For taxes on corporations, see 343.067*

*Add as instructed under 342–347

.066 2             *Partnerships

.066 8             *Charitable foundations and trusts

> Subdivisions are added for either or both topics in heading

.067        *Taxes on corporations

.068        *Taxes on business enterprises

> Including small business taxes

> Class taxes on individuals engaged in business in 343.062; class taxes on specific types of business organizations in 343.066

.07         *Regulation of economic activity

> Including daylight saving time, nationalization of industry, rationing

> Class here international economic law, international economic organizations; comprehensive works on regulation of small business, licensing, industry and commerce

> Class regulation of the practice of specific occupations in 344.01; class public health in 344.04; class safety measures in 344.047; class regulation of organizations in 346.06

> *For regulation of commerce, see 343.08*

> *See also 346 for impact of economic activity upon private persons and corporate bodies*

### SUMMARY

|         |                                |
|---------|--------------------------------|
| 343.071 | Consumer protection            |
| .072    | Unfair practices               |
| .074    | Economic assistance            |
| .075    | Production controls            |
| .076    | Agricultural industries        |
| .077    | Mineral industries             |
| .078    | Secondary industries and services |

.071        *Consumer protection

> Class a specific aspect of consumer protection with the aspect in 342–347, e.g., protection against misleading advertising 343.082

---

>          343.072–343.075  Specific aspects of regulation

> Class regulation of specific industries and services regardless of aspect in 343.076–343.078; class regulation of public utilities regardless of aspect in 343.09; class comprehensive works in 343.07. Class a specific aspect of industrial regulation not provided for here with the aspect in 342–347, e.g., wages 344.0121

.072          *Unfair practices

> Including monopoly, industrial espionage

*Add as instructed under 342–347

| | |
|---|---|
| .072 1 | *Antitrust law |

Class here competition law

*For restraint of trade, see 343.0723; for price fixing and discrimination, see 343.0725*

| | |
|---|---|
| .072 3 | *Restraint of trade |
| .072 5 | *Price fixing and discrimination |

Subdivisions are added for either or both topics in heading

| | |
|---|---|
| .074 | *Economic assistance |

Class here technology transfer

Class assistance to specific industries and services in 343.076–343.078

---

> 343.074 2–343.074 6  Domestic economic assistance

Class comprehensive works in 343.074

| | |
|---|---|
| .074 2 | Specific kinds of assistance |

Including loans, mortgage insurance, price supports, subsidies

| | |
|---|---|
| .074 5 | *Rural development |

Class specific kinds of assistance to rural areas in 343.0742; class assistance to agriculture in 343.076

| | |
|---|---|
| .074 6 | *Regional development |

Class specific kinds of assistance in 343.0742; class development of rural regions in 343.0745

| | |
|---|---|
| .074 8 | *Foreign economic assistance (Foreign aid) |
| .075 | *Production controls |

Including standardization, weights and measures, packaging (containers)

*See also 344.042 for product control*

---

> 343.076–343.078  Regulation of specific industries and services

Class here regulating the production of and commerce in specific goods and services

Class comprehensive works in 343.07

*For commerce in specific goods and services, see 343.085; for public utilities, see 343.09; for regulation of labor of specific occupations, see 344.0176*

*See also 346.07 for commercial law*

*Add as instructed under 342–347

.076      *Agricultural industries

     Including agricultural assistance

     Class here comprehensive works on primary industries

     *For mineral industries, see 343.077*

     *See also 344.049 for veterinary public health*

.076 1      Specific production controls

     Including acreage allotments, price supports, production quotas

     Class controls of specific commodities in 343.0763–343.0769

.076 3–.076 9      Specific commodities

     Add to base number 343.076 the numbers following 63 in 633–639, e.g., products of fishing 343.07692, products of whaling 343.076928, products of sealing 343.076929, products of fishery of invertebrates 343.07694, forest products 343.076498; then add further as instructed under 342–347, e.g., cases involving forest products 343.0764980264

.077      *Mineral industries

     *See also 346.043 for mineral rights; also 346.04685 for conservation of minerals*

.077 2      *Oil, oil shales, tar sands, natural gas

.077 5      *Mining of coal and nonfuel minerals

.077 52      *Coal

.077 55      *Nonfuel minerals

.078      Secondary industries and services

     *See Manual at 343.078 vs. 343.08*

.078 000 1–.078 000 9      Standard subdivisions

     Notation from Table 1 as modified under 342–347, e.g., cases 343.078000264

.078 001–.078 999      Specific secondary industries and services

     Add to base number 343.078 notation 001–999, e.g., regulation of tourist industry 343.07891, regulation of shipbuilding industry 343.07862382; then add further as instructed under 342–347, e.g., cases involving shipbuilding industry 343.078623820264; however, for regulation of advertising industry, see 343.082; for regulation of marketing, see 343.08; for regulation of closely regulated industries, such as transportation and communication, see 343.09; for regulation of health services, see 344.0321

*Add as instructed under 342–347

| | |
|---|---|
| .08 | *Regulation of commerce (trade) |

Including guarantees, warranties

Class here commodity exchanges, marketing, domestic trade, exchange transactions

Unless other instructions are given, observe the following table of preference, e.g., retail trade of agricultural commodities 343.0851 (*not* 343.0811):

| | |
|---|---|
| International commerce (Foreign trade) | 343.087 |
| Specific commodities | 343.085 |
| Retail and wholesale trade, interstate commerce | 343.081 |
| Prices | 343.083 |
| Advertising and labeling | 343.082 |

Class regulation of real estate business in 346.0437; class law of sale in 346.072; class regulation of banks in 346.082; class regulation of insurance companies and agencies in 346.086; class regulation of organizations engaged in marketing securities in 346.0926; class comprehensive works on regulation of industry and trade in 343.07

*See Manual at 343.078 vs. 343.08*

| | |
|---|---|
| .081 | Retail and wholesale trade, interstate commerce |
| [.081 01–.081 09] | Standard subdivisions |

Do not use; class in 343.0801–343.0809

| | |
|---|---|
| .081 1 | *Retail trade |

Including auctions

Class here wholesale trade through specific marketing channels [*formerly* 343.0812], marketing channels

| | |
|---|---|
| .081 14 | Retail channels by merchandising pattern |
| [.081 140 1–.081 140 9] | Standard subdivisions |

Do not use; class in 343.081101–343.081109

| | |
|---|---|
| .081 142 | *Electronic commerce; mail-order, telephone-order, television shopping |

Class here online shopping, teleshopping

Subdivisions are added for electronic commerce, mail-order, telephone-order, television shopping together; for electronic commerce alone

Class online auctions in 343.0811

| | |
|---|---|
| [.081 142 028 5] | Computer applications |

Do not use; class in 343.081142

*Add as instructed under 342–347

.081 142 8            *Mail-order, telephone-order, television shopping

                     Class here catalog shopping

                     Subdivisions are added for any or all topics in heading

.081 2          *Wholesale trade

                     Wholesale trade through specific marketing channels relocated to 343.0811

.081 5          *Interstate commerce

                     Class interstate retail commerce in 343.0811; class interstate wholesale commerce in 343.0812

.082          *Advertising and labeling

                     Class restrictions on posting advertisements in 346.045

.083          *Prices

                     Class price supports in 343.0742; class price supports for a specific industry or service in 343.076–343.078

[.084]          Marketing

                     Number discontinued; class in 343.08

.085          Specific commodities

                     Class international commerce of a specific commodity in 343.0871–343.0875

[.085 01–.085 09]          Standard subdivisions

                     Do not use; class in 343.0801–343.0809

.085 1–.085 5          Subdivisions for specific commodities

                     Class here domestic trade of specific commodities

                     Add to base number 343.085 the numbers following 381.4 in 381.41–381.45, e.g., agricultural commodities 343.0851, rice 343.0851318; then add further as instructed under 342–347, e.g., cases involving rice 343.08513180264

.087          *International commerce (Foreign trade)

                     Class here combined treatment of trade, tariffs, and general shipping

                     *For tariffs, see 343.056; for shipping, see 343.096*

.087 1–.087 5          Specific commodities

                     Add to base number 343.087 the numbers following 381.4 in 381.41–381.45, e.g., agricultural commodities 343.0871, rice 343.0871318; then add further as instructed under 342–347, e.g., cases involving rice 343.08713180264

.087 7          *Imports

                     Class imports of specific commodities in 343.0871–343.0875

*Add as instructed under 342–347

.087 8       *Exports

> Class exports of specific commodities in 343.0871–343.0875

.09       *Control of public utilities

### SUMMARY

.091       *General considerations of control of public utilities

> Including rates, operations, facilities, services

> Class general considerations applied to specific utilities in 343.092–343.099

.092       *Water and power supply

> Subdivisions are added for water and power supply together, for power supply alone

.092 4       *Water

.092 5       *Nuclear energy

.092 6       *Oil and gas

> Class extraction in 343.0772; class processing in 343.0786655–343.0786657

.092 7       *Coal

> Class extraction in 343.07752; class processing in 343.07866262

.092 8       *Solar energy

.092 9       *Electric power

> Including cogeneration of heat and electricity

> Class a specific source of electric power with the source in 342–347, e.g., nuclear power 343.0925

.093       *Transportation

> Class here comprehensive works on ground transportation, on the law of carriers

> Class transportation insurance in 346.0862

> *For specific kinds of transportation and ground transportation, see 343.094–343.098*

*Add as instructed under 342–347

| .093 2 | *Freight services |
|---|---|
| | Including transportation of specific goods |
| .093 22 | *Hazardous materials |
| .093 3 | *Passenger services |
| | Class here mass transportation |
| .093 8 | *Transportation safety |
| | Class private law of transportation accidents in 346.0322 |
| .093 9 | *Pipeline transportation |
| .093 95 | *Oil (Petroleum) |
| .093 96 | *Natural gas |
| .093 97 | *Coal |
| | Class here coal slurry |

---

> 343.094–343.098 Specific kinds of transportation and ground transportation

Class comprehensive works in 343.093

*For pipeline transportation, see 343.0939*

.094      *Road transportation

Class here highway transportation

Class comprehensive works on ground transportation in 343.093

*For street traffic, see 343.0982*

.094 2      *Roads

Class here highways

.094 4      *Vehicles

Including licensing, registration

Class vehicle operation in 343.0946; class commercial vehicular services in 343.0948; class vehicle product liability in 346.038; class property laws relating to vehicles in 346.047

*See also 346.043 for mobile homes*

.094 6      *Vehicle operation and traffic control

Including drivers' licenses, speed limits, traffic signals

Subdivisions are added for either or both topics in heading

Class police traffic services in 344.052332; class traffic offenses in 345.0247

---

*Add as instructed under 342–347

| | |
|---|---|
| .094 8 | *Commercial services |

Class commercial vehicles in 343.0944; class operation of commercial vehicles in 343.0946

| | |
|---|---|
| .094 82 | *Bus |
| .094 83 | *Truck |
| .095 | *Railroad transportation |
| .095 2 | *Stationary facilities |

Including signals, terminals, tracks, yards

| | |
|---|---|
| .095 5 | *Rolling stock |

Including cars, locomotives

| | |
|---|---|
| .095 8 | *Services |

Passenger, freight

| | |
|---|---|
| .096 | *Water transportation |

Including prize law

Class here maritime, admiralty law

Class a specific subject of maritime or admiralty law not provided for here with the subject in 342–347, e.g., maritime contracts 346.022

---

> 343.096 2–343.096 4  Specific kinds of water transportation

Class facilities, operations, services of specific kinds of transportation in 343.0965–343.0968; class comprehensive works in 343.096

| | |
|---|---|
| .096 2 | *Ocean transportation |

Class interoceanic waterways in 343.0964

*See Manual at 341.45 vs. 343.0962*

| | |
|---|---|
| .096 4 | *Inland waterway transportation |

Including interoceanic canals

---

> 343.096 5–343.096 8  Facilities, operations, services

Class comprehensive works in 343.096

| | |
|---|---|
| .096 5 | *Ships |

Including pilot's license

| | |
|---|---|
| .096 6 | *Navigation |

Class here rule of the road at sea

*Add as instructed under 342–347

| | |
|---|---|
| .096 7 | *Ports |
| | Including piloting, tug services |
| .096 8 | *Services |
| | Including freight, passenger services; salvage operations |
| | Class services of ports in 343.0967 |
| .097 | *Air transportation and space transportation |
| | Subdivisions are added for air and space transportation together, for air transportation alone |

>         343.097 5–343.097 8  Air transportation

Class comprehensive works in 343.097

| | |
|---|---|
| .097 5 | *Aircraft |
| | Including pilot's license |
| .097 6 | *Air navigation and traffic control |
| | Subdivisions are added for either or both topics in heading |
| .097 7 | *Airports |
| | Class here landing fields |
| | *For traffic control, see 343.0976* |
| .097 8 | *Air transportation services |
| | Including freight, passenger services |
| | Class services of airports and landing fields in 343.0977 |
| .097 9 | *Space transportation |
| .098 | *Local transportation |
| | Class police traffic services in 344.052332; class traffic offenses in 345.0247 |
| | *For local water transportation, see 343.096; for local air transportation, see 343.097* |
| .098 1 | *Pedestrian traffic |
| .098 2 | *Vehicular traffic |
| | Including parking facilities |
| | Class traffic control in 343.0946 |
| .098 3 | *Rail transit systems |
| | Surface, subsurface, elevated |

*Add as instructed under 342–347

.099          **\*Communications**

             Class here mass media law

             Class censorship in 344.0531; class criminal libel in 345.0256; class libel as a tort in 346.034

.099 2       **\*Postal service**

             Class postal offenses in 345.0236

.099 23      **\*Postal rates**

.099 25      **\*Postal organization**

             Including routes

.099 4       **\*Telecommunication**

             Including telegraph

.099 43      **\*Telephone**

             Class radiotelephony in 343.09945

.099 44      **\*Computer communications**

             Class comprehensive works on computer law in 343.0999

.099 45      **\*Radio**

             Including radiotelephony, comprehensive works on fairness doctrine

             Class here wireless communication

               *For fairness doctrine related to television, see 343.09946*

.099 46      **\*Television**

             Including cable television

.099 8       **\*Press law**

             Class here publishing law

             Class freedom of the press in 342.0853

.099 9       **\*Information storage and retrieval**

             Class here comprehensive works on computer law

               *For a specific aspect of computer law, see the aspect in 342–347, e.g., invasion of privacy 342.0858*

\*Add as instructed under 342–347

**.1**      **Socioeconomic regions**

Add to base number 343.1 the numbers following —17 in notation 171–177 from Table 2, e.g., miscellaneous public law of developing countries 343.124; then to the result add as follows:

001–009     Standard subdivisions
               Notation from Table 1 as modified under 342–347
01–09     Topics of military, defense, public property, public finance, tax, commerce (trade), industrial law
               Add the numbers following 343 in 343.01–343.09, e.g., tax law of developing countries 343.12404, administrative regulations on taxes of developing countries 343.1240402636

Class socioeconomic regions of a specific regional intergovernmental organization in 343.2; class socioeconomic regions of a specific jurisdiction or area in 343.3–343.9

(If option B under 342–349 is chosen, class here law of socioeconomic regions by adding to base number 343.1 the numbers following —17 in notation 171–177 from Table 2, e.g., law of developing countries 343.124, then adding facet indicator 0*, notation for the branch of law, and notation for the subordinate subject in branch of law, e.g., private law of developing countries 343.12406, banking law of developing countries 343.1240682)

**.2**      **Regional intergovernmental organizations**

Class here relationship between the organization's law and national law of member countries

Add to base number 343.2 notation 3–9 from Table 2, e.g., miscellaneous public law of European Union 343.24; then to the result add as follows:

001–009     Standard subdivisions
               Notation from Table 1 as modified under 342–347
01–09     Topics of military, defense, public property, public finance, tax, commerce (trade), industrial law
               Add the numbers following 343 in 343.01–343.09, e.g., economic law of European Union 343.2407, administrative regulations of economic law of European Union 343.240702636

Class relationship of organization's law and national law of a specific member country with the national law in 343.3–343.9, e.g., effect of European Union laws on national economic law of Germany 343.43

*See Manual at 342–349*

(If option B under 342–349 is chosen, class here law of regional intergovernmental organizations by adding to base number 343.2 notation 4–9 from Table 2, e.g., law of the European Union 343.24, then adding facet indicator 0*, notation for the branch of law, and notation for the subordinate subject in branch of law, e.g., private law of the European Union 343.2406, banking law of the European Union 343.240682)

---

*Add 00 for standard subdivisions; see instructions at beginning of Table 1

.240 7            Regulation of economic activity

Number built according to instructions under 343.2

Class here comprehensive works on Four Freedoms of European Union

*For a specific aspect of the Four Freedoms, see the aspect, e.g., prohibition of customs duties on goods moving from one country to another within European Union 343.24056*

### .3–.9     Specific jurisdictions and areas

Add to base number 343 notation 3–9 from Table 2, e.g., miscellaneous public law of Australia 343.94, of New South Wales 343.944, of African states 343.6; then to the result add as follows:
001–009     Standard subdivisions
01–09     Topics of military, defense, public property, public finance, tax, commerce (trade), industrial law
         Add the numbers following 343 in 343.01–343.09, e.g., tax law of Australia 343.9404, of New South Wales 343.94404, of African states 343.604, administrative regulations on taxes of Australia 343.940402636

*For regional intergovernmental organizations, relationship between the organization's laws and national laws of all member states, see 343.2*

*See Manual at 342–349*

## 344     Labor, social service, education, cultural law

### SUMMARY

| | |
|---|---|
| 344.001–.009 | **Standard subdivisions; laws, regulations, cases, procedure, courts** |
| .01 | **Labor** |
| .02 | **Government-sponsored insurance** |
| .03 | **Social service** |
| .04 | **Miscellaneous social problems and services** |
| .05 | **Police services, other aspects of public safety, matters concerning public morals and customs** |
| .06 | **Public works** |
| .07 | **Education** |
| .08 | **Educational and cultural exchanges** |
| .09 | **Culture and religion** |
| .1 | **Socioeconomic regions** |
| .2 | **Regional intergovernmental organizations** |
| .3–.9 | **Specific jurisdictions and areas** |

.001–.008     Standard subdivisions

Notation from Table 1 as modified under 342–347, e.g., cases 344.00264

.009     History, geographic treatment, biography

[.009 17]     Socioeconomic regions

Do not use; class in 344.1

[.009 3–.009 9]     Specific continents, countries, localities

Do not use; class in 344.3–344.9

.01          *Labor

             Class here social law, social legislation

             *For social insurance, see 344.02; for public welfare, see 344.0316*

.010 1            Philosophy and theory

                  Including job and labor rights

.011–.018    Specific aspects of labor

             Add to base number 344.01 the numbers following 331 in 331.1–331.8,
             e.g., child labor law 344.0131; then add further as instructed under
             342–347, e.g., cases involving child labor law 344.01310264; however,
             for government officials and employees, see 342.068; for military
             personnel, see 343.013–343.019; for medical personnel, see 344.041; for
             certification and licensing of teachers, see 344.078

.02          *Government-sponsored insurance

             Class here social insurance

             Class comprehensive works on insurance in 346.086

             *For a type of government-sponsored insurance not provided for here, see
             the type in 346.0861–346.0868, e.g., crop insurance 346.086121, bank
             deposit insurance 346.086854*

             *See also 344.03 for social service law; also 343.05242 for social security
             taxes*

             *See Manual at 363 vs. 344.02–344.05, 353–354*

.021         *Workers' compensation insurance (Workmen's compensation
             insurance)

             Class disability compensation for veterans in 343.0116

.021 7            Occupations and industries

                  Class disabilities and injuries in specific occupations and industries in
                  344.0218

.021 8            Disabilities and injuries

.022         *Health and accident insurance

             Subdivisions are added for health and accident insurance together, for
             health insurance alone

             Class health benefits for veterans in 343.0115

             *For workers' compensation insurance, see 344.021*

[.022 084 6]            Insurance for people in late adulthood

                       Do not use; class in 344.0226

.022 4            *Maternity insurance

.022 6            *Accident and health insurance for people in late adulthood

*Add as instructed under 342–347

| .023 | *Old age and survivors' insurance |
|---|---|

Class accident and health insurance for people in late adulthood in 344.0226

| .024 | *Unemployment insurance |
|---|---|
| .028 | *Insurance against crimes of violence |
| .03 | *Social service |

*For social insurance, see 344.02; for miscellaneous social problems and services, see 344.04; for police services, other aspects of public safety, matters concerning public morals and customs, see 344.05; for public works, see 344.06; for insurance, see 346.086*

*See Manual at 363 vs. 344.02–344.05, 353–354*

| .031 | Specific topics of social service in general |
|---|---|

Class specific topics of a specific social problem or service in 344.032–344.035

| [.031 001–.031 009] | Standard subdivisions |
|---|---|

Do not use; class in 344.0301–344.0309

| .031 02–.031 06 | Subdivisions for specific kinds of assistance in social service in general |
|---|---|

Add to base number 344.031 the numbers following 361 in 361.02–361.06, e.g., laws governing counseling 344.03106; then add further as instructed under 342–347, e.g., cases involving counseling 344.031060264

| .031 1–.031 8 | Social problems and social action |
|---|---|

Add to base number 344.031 the numbers following 361 in 361.1–361.8, e.g., laws governing charitable trusts 344.0317632; then add further as instructed under 342–347, e.g., cases involving charitable trusts 344.03176320264

| .032 | Social welfare problems and services |
|---|---|
| .032 01 | Philosophy and theory |

Notation 01 from Table 1 as modified under 342–347, e.g., sources of law 344.032011

| .032 02 | Miscellany |
|---|---|

Notation 02 from Table 1 as modified under 342–347, e.g., cases 344.0320264

| .032 03 | Dictionaries, encyclopedias, concordances |
|---|---|
| .032 04 | Special topics of social problems of and services to groups of people |

Add to base number 344.03204 the numbers following 362.04, e.g., social action law 344.0320425; then add further as instructed under 342–347, e.g., cases involving social action law 344.03204250264

*Add as instructed under 342–347

| | |
|---|---|
| .032 05–.032 07 | Standard subdivisions |

Notation from Table 1 as modified under 342–347

| | |
|---|---|
| [.032 08] | Groups of people |

Do not use; class in 344.0321–344.0328

| | |
|---|---|
| .032 09 | History, geographic treatment, biography |

Notation 09 from Table 1 as modified under 342–347

| | |
|---|---|
| .032 1–.032 8 | Specific social welfare problems and services |

Add to base number 344.032 the numbers following 362 in 362.1–362.8, e.g., child welfare law 344.0327; then add further as instructed under 342–347, e.g., cases involving child welfare 344.03270264; however, for veterans' welfare, see 343.011; for comprehensive works on public health, see 344.04; for medical personnel and their activities, see 344.041; for mental and emotional illnesses and disturbances, see 344.044; for adoption, see 346.0178

| | |
|---|---|
| .033 | *Food supply |
| .035 | *Penal institutions |
| .035 3–.035 7 | Specific aspects of penal institutions |

Add to base number 344.035 the numbers following 365 in 365.3–365.7, e.g., law governing convict labor 344.03565; then add further as instructed under 342–347, e.g., cases involving convict labor 344.035650264

| | |
|---|---|
| .04 | Miscellaneous social problems and services |

Only those named below

Class here comprehensive works on public health

*For an aspect of public health not provided for here, see the aspect, e.g., emergency medical services 344.03218*

*See Manual at 363 vs. 344.02–344.05, 353–354*

## SUMMARY

| | |
|---|---|
| 344.041 | **Medical personnel and their activities** |
| .042 | **Product control** |
| .043 | **Control of disease** |
| .044 | **Mental health services and services to substance abusers** |
| .045 | **Disposal of dead** |
| .046 | **Environmental protection** |
| .047 | **Safety** |
| .048 | **Population control** |
| .049 | **Veterinary public health** |

*Add as instructed under 342–347

| | |
|---|---|
| .041 | *Medical personnel and their activities |

        Subdivisions are added for either or both topics in heading

        Class military medicine in 343.013; class medical institutions and their services in 344.03211–344.03216

        *For control of disease, see 344.043*

| | |
|---|---|
| .041 1 | *Medical malpractice |

        Class medical malpractice by a specific kind of medical personnel in 344.0412–344.0416; class medical malpractice related to a specific medical problem in 344.0419

        *See also 344.03211 for malpractice by hospitals and other medical institutions*

---

>         344.041 2–344.041 6  Specific medical personnel and their activities

        Class a specific type of medical personnel involved with specific problems in 344.0419; class comprehensive works in 344.041

| | |
|---|---|
| .041 2 | *Physicians and their activities |

        Including informed consent

        Subdivisions are added for either or both topics in heading

| | |
|---|---|
| .041 21 | *Malpractice |

        Works specifically emphasizing physicians

| | |
|---|---|
| .041 3 | *Dentists and dentistry |

        Including dental assistants, dental technicians

        Subdivisions are added for either or both topics in heading

| | |
|---|---|
| .041 4 | *Nurses and nursing |

        Subdivisions are added for either or both topics in heading

| | |
|---|---|
| .041 5 | *Midwives and midwifery |

        Subdivisions are added for either or both topics in heading

| | |
|---|---|
| .041 6 | *Pharmacists and pharmacy |

        Subdivisions are added for either or both topics in heading

| | |
|---|---|
| .041 9 | Problems in medical practice |
| .041 92 | *Abortion |

        Class comprehensive works in 342.084

| | |
|---|---|
| .041 94 | *Oversight of the human body and its parts |

        Including blood transfusion, organ donation, transplants

        Class rights regarding frozen embryos in 346.0171

*Add as instructed under 342–347

| .041 96 | *Human experimentation |
| | Including medical genetics |
| .041 97 | *Terminal care |
| | Class here euthanasia, right to die |
| .042 | *Product control |
| | Including recall of unsafe products |
| | *For motor vehicle recall, see 343.0944* |
| .042 3 | *Food, drugs, cosmetics, clothing, toys |
| .042 32 | *Food |
| | Including food additives |
| .042 33 | *Drugs |
| .042 35 | *Clothing and toys |
| .042 4 | *Chemicals |
| | Class food additives, drugs, cosmetics in 344.0423 |
| .043 | *Control of disease |
| | Including control of carriers, quarantine, immunization measures |
| | Class control of carriers, quarantine, immunization measures of a specific disease in 344.0436–344.0438 |
| .043 6–.043 8 | Control of specific diseases |
| | Add to base number 344.043 the numbers following 61 in 616–618, e.g., control of AIDS 344.04369792; then add further as instructed under 342–347, e.g., cases involving control of AIDS 344.043697920264; however, for control of mental diseases, see 344.044 |
| .044 | *Mental health services and services to substance abusers |
| | Subdivisions are added for mental health services and services to substance abusers together, for mental health services alone |
| | Class capacity and status of persons with mental illness and disabilities in 346.0138 |
| .044 6 | *Services to substance abusers |
| | Class here addiction |
| .044 61 | *Alcoholics |
| | Class control of trade in alcoholic beverages in 344.0541 |

*Add as instructed under 342–347

| | |
|---|---|
| .044 63–.044 69 | Other kinds of substance abusers |

Add to base number 344.0446 the numbers following 362.29 in 362.293–362.299 for the substance only, e.g., heroin abusers 344.04463; then add further as instructed under 342–347, e.g., cases involving heroin abusers 344.044630264

Class control of drug traffic in 344.0545

| | |
|---|---|
| .045 | *Disposal of dead |
| .046 | *Environmental protection |

Class here liability for environmental damages, comprehensive works on environmental law

Class conservation of natural resources in 346.044

*For an aspect of environmental law not provided for here, see the aspect, e.g., government control and regulation of natural resources 346.044*

| | |
|---|---|
| .046 2 | *Wastes |

Including recycling

Class here waste disposal, management

| | |
|---|---|
| .046 22 | Kinds of waste |

Including sewage; animal, chemical, solid wastes

Class disposal of specific kinds of wastes into specific environments in 344.04626

| | |
|---|---|
| .046 26 | Disposal into specific environments |

Including dumping into oceans

| | |
|---|---|
| .046 3 | *Pollution and noise |
| .046 32 | *Pollution |

Class waste disposal in 344.0462

*For pollutants, see 344.04633; for pollution of specific environments, see 344.04634*

| | |
|---|---|
| .046 33 | *Pollutants |
| .046 332 | *Oil |
| .046 334 | *Pesticides |
| .046 335 | *Asbestos |
| .046 336 | *Acid rain |

*Add as instructed under 342–347

| .046 34 | Pollution of specific environments |
|---|---|

Including soil pollution

Class pollution of specific environments by specific pollutants in 344.04633

| .046 342 | *Air pollution |
|---|---|
| .046 343 | *Water pollution |
| .046 38 | *Noise |
| .046 4 | *Sanitation in places of public assembly |

Including hotels

*For industrial sanitation, see 344.0465*

| .046 5 | *Industrial sanitation and safety |
|---|---|
| .047 | *Safety |

*For transportation safety, see 343.0938; for product safety, see 344.042; for industrial safety, see 344.0465; for other aspects of public safety, see 344.053*

| .047 2 | *Safety in use of hazardous materials and devices |
|---|---|

Class safety in use of hazardous materials in industry in 344.0465

| .047 6 | *Safety in recreation |
|---|---|
| .048 | *Population control |

Class here birth control

| .049 | *Veterinary public health |
|---|---|

Including animal welfare, humane law

| .05 | Police services, other aspects of public safety, matters concerning public morals and customs |
|---|---|

Add to base number 344.05 the numbers following 363 in 363.2–363.4, e.g., disasters 344.0534, civil defense 344.0535, fire protection 344.0537, smoking laws 344.054; then add further as instructed under 342–347, e.g., cases involving fire protection 344.05370264; however, for criminal investigation and law enforcement, see 345.052

Class comprehensive works on public safety in 344.047

*See Manual at 363 vs. 344.02–344.05, 353–354*

| .06 | Public works |
|---|---|

Public programs not provided for elsewhere

| .060 001–.060 009 | Standard subdivisions |
|---|---|

Notation from Table 1 as modified under 342–347, e.g., cases 344.06000264

---

*Add as instructed under 342–347

.060 01–.069 99       Specific kinds of public works

> Add to base number 344.06 notation 001–999, e.g., public housing 344.063635; then add further as instructed under 342–347, e.g., cases involving public housing 344.0636350264

.07       *Education

Class here schools

Unless other instructions are given, class a subject with aspects in two or more subdivisions of 344.07 in the number coming last, e.g., finance of primary public schools by local governments 344.07682 (*not* 344.074, 344.073, or 344.071)

*For educational exchanges, see 344.08*

---

>       344.071–344.074   Kinds of education

Class comprehensive works in 344.07

.071       *Public education

.072       *Private education

.073       Education by level of government

National, state, local

.074       Education by level of education

Primary, secondary, higher, adult

.075       *Liability of schools, of school officials, of school districts

.076       *Finance

Public and private education

Class financial aid to students in 344.0795

.076 2       *Financial resources

Including investments, natural resources, tax receipts

*For aid to education, see 344.0763*

.076 3       *Aid to education by higher levels of government

.076 5       *Expenditure

.076 7       Kinds of schools

Including trade, vocational schools

.076 8       Levels of education and schools

.076 82       *Preschool and primary education

Subdivisions are added for preschool and primary education together, for primary education alone

---

*Add as instructed under 342–347

| .076 83 | *Secondary education |
|---------|---------------------|
| .076 84 | *Higher education |
| .076 85 | *Adult education |
| .076 9 | Educational programs |

Including medical and public health education; schools devoted to specific educational programs, e.g., military, merchant marine academies

| .077 | *Curricula and educational materials |
|------|--------------------------------------|
| .078 | *Teachers and teaching |

Including academic freedom

Subdivisions are added for either or both topics in heading

Class employment rights in 344.0101

| .079 | *Students |
|------|-----------|

Including authority of the law over students, compulsory education, right to education

| .079 1 | *Education of specific groups of students |
|--------|-------------------------------------------|

Class here special education

Class finance in 344.0769

| .079 11–.079 15 | Specific groups of students |
|-----------------|------------------------------|

Add to base number 344.0791 the numbers following 371.9 in 371.91–371.95, e.g., education of students with visual impairments 344.079111; then add further as instructed under 342–347, e.g., cases involving education of students with visual impairments 344.0791110264

| .079 2 | *Attendance |
|--------|-------------|

Including school year and day, truancy

| .079 3 | *Discipline and student rights |
|--------|--------------------------------|

*See also 342.085 for general rights of students*

| .079 4 | *Student services |
|--------|-------------------|

Including counseling

| .079 42 | *School lunch programs |
|---------|------------------------|
| .079 5 | *Financial aid to students |

Including loans, scholarships

| .079 6 | *Religion and the student |
|--------|---------------------------|

Including prayer in public schools

*Add as instructed under 342–347

| | |
|---|---|
| .079 8 | *Segregation and discrimination |
| .08 | *Educational and cultural exchanges |
| .09 | *Culture and religion |

Including information exchange, flag code, language code (the official language or languages of a specific jurisdiction)

Subdivisions are added for culture and religion together, for culture alone

*For education, see 344.07; for educational and cultural exchanges, see 344.08*

| | |
|---|---|
| .091 | *Historic commemoration and patriotic events |

Subdivisions are added for either or both topics in heading

Class commemorative medals and coins that are legal tender in 343.032

| | |
|---|---|
| .092 | *Libraries and archives |

Subdivisions are added for either or both topics in heading

| | |
|---|---|
| .093 | *Museums and galleries |

Subdivisions are added for either or both topics in heading

| | |
|---|---|
| .094 | *Historic preservation |

Including archaeology, antiquities

Class here historical buildings, monuments

Class historic commemoration and patriotic events in 344.091

| | |
|---|---|
| .095 | *Science and technology |

Subdivisions are added for either or both topics in heading

| | |
|---|---|
| .095 2 | *Astronomy and space research |

Subdivisions are added for either or both topics in heading

| | |
|---|---|
| .095 3 | *Physics and applied physics |

Subdivisions are added for either or both topics in heading

| | |
|---|---|
| .095 4 | *Chemistry and chemical technology |

Subdivisions are added for either or both topics in heading

| | |
|---|---|
| .095 5 | *Geology |

Including weather control, meteorology, oceanography

| | |
|---|---|
| .095 7 | *Agriculture and biology |

Subdivisions are added for either or both topics in heading

| | |
|---|---|
| .096 | *Religion |

*Add as instructed under 342–347

.097       \*Arts and humanities

> *For museums and galleries, see 344.093*

.099       \*Amusements

> Including sports law; comprehensive works on gambling
>
> Class here recreation law
>
> Class arts and humanities in 344.097
>
> *For gambling as a social problem, see 344.0542*

## .1     Socioeconomic regions

> Add to base number 344.1 the numbers following —17 in notation 171–177 from Table 2, e.g., social law of developing countries 344.124; then to the result add as follows:
> | | |
> |---|---|
> | 001–009 | Standard subdivisions |
> | | Notation from Table 1 as modified under 342–347 |
> | 01–09 | Topics of labor, social service, education, cultural law |
> | | Add the numbers following 344 in 344.01–344.09, e.g., labor law of developing countries 344.12401, administrative regulations on labor in developing countries 344.1240102636 |
>
> Class socioeconomic regions of a specific regional intergovernmental organization in 344.2; class socioeconomic regions of a specific jurisdiction or area in 344.3–344.9

## .2     Regional intergovernmental organizations

> Class here relationship between the organization's law and national law of member countries
>
> Add to base number 344.2 notation 3–9 from Table 2, e.g., social law of European Union 344.24; then to the result add as follows:
> | | |
> |---|---|
> | 001–009 | Standard subdivisions |
> | | Notation from Table 1 as modified under 342–347 |
> | 01–09 | Topics of labor, social service, education, cultural law |
> | | Add the numbers following 344 in 344.01–344.09, e.g., labor law of European Union 344.2401, administrative regulations of labor law of European Union 344.240102636 |
>
> Class relationship of organization's law and national law of a specific member country with the national law in 344.3–344.9, e.g., effect of European Union laws on national social law of France 344.44
>
> *See Manual at 342–349*

\*Add as instructed under 342–347

**.3–.9     Specific jurisdictions and areas**

> Add to base number 344 notation 3–9 from Table 2, e.g., social law of Australia 344.94, of New South Wales 344.944, of African states 344.6; then to the result add as follows:
>
> 001–009     Standard subdivisions
> > Notation from Table 1 as modified under 342–347
>
> 01–09     Topics of labor, social service, education, cultural law
> > Add the numbers following 344 in 344.01–344.09, e.g., labor law of Australia 344.9401, of New South Wales 344.94401, of African states 344.601, administrative regulations on labor in Australia 344.940102636
>
> *For regional intergovernmental organizations, relationship between the organization's laws and national laws of all member states, see 344.2*
>
> *See Manual at 342–349*

# 345     Criminal law

> Class here international criminal law
>
> Class comprehensive works on civil and criminal procedure and courts in 347; class interdisciplinary works on criminal justice in 364. Class civil actions linked to crimes with the subject in 342–344 or 346–347, e.g., employers' civil tort liability 346.031

### SUMMARY

| | |
|---|---|
| 345.001–.009 | **Standard subdivisions; laws, regulations, cases, procedure, courts** |
| .01 | **Criminal courts** |
| .02 | **Criminal offenses** |
| .03 | **Offenders** |
| .04 | **Liability, responsibility, guilt** |
| .05 | **Criminal procedure** |
| .06 | **Evidence** |
| .07 | **Trials** |
| .08 | **Juvenile procedure and courts** |
| .1 | **Socioeconomic regions** |
| .2 | **Regional intergovernmental organizations** |
| .3–.9 | **Specific jurisdictions and areas** |

**.001–.008     Standard subdivisions**

> Notation from Table 1 as modified under 342–347, e.g., cases 345.00264

**.009     History, geographic treatment, biography**

**[.009 17]     Socioeconomic regions**

> Do not use; class in 345.1

**[.009 3–.009 9]     Specific continents, countries, localities**

> Do not use; class in 345.3–345.9

| | |
|---|---|
| .01 | *Criminal courts |

Courts specializing in criminal cases, general and other specialized courts considered with respect to their functions in criminal cases

Class appellate courts hearing both civil and criminal cases in 347.03

*For juvenile courts, see 345.081*

| | |
|---|---|
| .012 | General considerations, administration and personnel, legal aid |
| .012 2 | *General considerations of criminal courts |

Including criminal jurisdiction, judicial cooperation in criminal cases, judicial discretion, judicial error, judicial review, letters rogatory

| | |
|---|---|
| .012 3 | *Judicial administration of criminal courts |

*For judges, see 345.0124; for court officials other than judges, see 345.0126*

| | |
|---|---|
| .012 4 | *Criminal court judges |

Class judges associated with a specific criminal court with the court, e.g., judges of a juvenile court 345.081

| | |
|---|---|
| .012 6 | Other criminal court officials |

Including coroners

| | |
|---|---|
| .012 62 | *Public prosecutors |

Class here district attorneys

| | |
|---|---|
| .012 63 | *Public defenders |
| .012 7 | *Legal aid in criminal cases |

Class legal aid as a welfare service, interdisciplinary works on legal aid in 362.58

*Add as instructed under 342–347

.014 Criminal courts with specific kinds of jurisdiction

> Add to each subdivision identified by † as follows:
> 01–09 Standard subdivisions
> Notation from Table 1 as modified under 342–347, e.g., cases 0264
> 2 General considerations
> Including functions, jurisdiction, organization, powers
> 3 Judicial administration
> 34 Judges
> 36 Other criminal court officials
> Including coroners
> 362 Public prosecutors
> Class here district attorneys
> 363 Public defenders
> 5 Procedure
> *For evidence, see 345.06; for trials, see 345.07; for juvenile procedure, see 345.08*
> 504 Special topics of criminal procedure
> Add to 504 the numbers following 345.0504 in 345.05042–345.05044, e.g., prosecution 5042
> 52–56 Criminal investigation and law enforcement, rights of suspects
> Add to 5 the numbers following 345.05 in 345.052–345.056, e.g., rights of suspects 56

.014 2 †Courts with original jurisdiction

Class here courts of first instance, local courts, trial courts

.014 4 †Appellate courts

Class here comprehensive works on appellate procedure in criminal cases [*formerly* 347.08]

*For appellate courts with specialized jurisdiction, see 345.0148*

.014 42 †Intermediate appellate courts

Class here courts of second instance, courts of first appeal

.014 44 †Courts of last resort (Supreme courts)

Class here courts of third instance, courts of second appeal, courts of final appeal

.014 8 †Courts with specialized jurisdiction

Class courts dealing with a specific subject with the subject in 342–347, plus notation 0269 from table under 342–347 if needed, e.g., military courts 343.0143

---

> 345.02–345.04 General considerations

Class comprehensive works in 345

---

†Add as instructed under 345.014

.02      *Criminal offenses

> Class here contraventions, crimes, crimes without victims
>
> *See Manual at 345.02 vs. 346.03*

.023–.028      Specific crimes and classes of crime

> Class here specific trials of specific crimes and classes of crime, e.g., trials of offenses against the person 345.025, a specific trial for murder 345.02523
>
> Add to base number 345.02 the numbers following 364.1 in 364.13–364.18, e.g., terrorism 345.02317, genocide 345.0251, hijacking 345.02552, piracy 345.0264, drug traffic 345.0277, white collar crime 345.0268; then add further as instructed under 342–347, e.g., court decisions on white collar crime 345.026802643
>
> Class defenses for a specific crime in 345.04

.03      *Offenders

> Including juvenile delinquents
>
> Class here criminals

.04      *Liability, responsibility, guilt

> Including criminal capacity; criminal intent; double jeopardy; defenses, e.g., duress; defenses for a specific crime, e.g., self-defense
>
> Subdivisions are added for any or all topics in heading
>
> *See also 345.05044 for defense*

.05      *Criminal procedure

> Including legal costs and fees
>
> Class here administration of criminal justice, court rules, participants in criminal proceedings
>
> Class procedure in specific courts devoted exclusively to criminal cases in 345.01; class procedure in specific courts hearing both civil and criminal cases in 347.02–347.04. Class participants in criminal proceedings provided for elsewhere with the subject, e.g., criminal court judges 345.0124, witnesses 345.066
>
> > *For evidence, see 345.06; for trials and trial procedures, see 345.07; for juvenile procedure, see 345.08*

.050 4      Special topics of criminal procedure

.050 42      *Prosecution

> Including prosecutorial discretion
>
> Class district attorneys, public prosecutors in 345.01262

---

*Add as instructed under 342–347

| .050 44 | *Defense |
|---|---|

Class public defenders in 345.01263; class defenses in 345.04; class right to counsel in 345.056

| .050 46 | *Victims of crime |
|---|---|

Class a specific role of victims in criminal procedure with the role, e.g., witness 345.066; class a specific use of victim impact statements with the use, e.g., use of victim impact statements at sentencing 345.0772. Class social services for victims of crime in 362.88

| .052 | *Criminal investigation and law enforcement |
|---|---|

Including extradition, judicial assistance

Class here Interpol, manuals on what police may legally do in course of carrying out their duties

Class rights of suspects in 345.056; class admissibility of evidence in 345.062

| .052 2 | *Search and seizure |
|---|---|

Subdivisions are added for either or both topics in heading

| .052 7 | *Arrest |
|---|---|

Including preventive detention

*See also 346.0334 for false arrest*

| .056 | *Rights of suspects |
|---|---|

Including habeas corpus, jury trial, protection from self-incrimination, right to counsel

Class legal aid in 345.0127

| .06 | *Evidence |
|---|---|

Including confessions

| .062–.067 | Specific aspects of evidence |
|---|---|

Add to base number 345.06 the numbers following 347.06 in 347.062–347.067, e.g., admissibility of evidence 345.062; then add further as instructed under 342–347, e.g., cases involving admissibility of evidence 345.0620264

| .07 | *Trials |
|---|---|

Class trials of specific offenses in 345.02; class hearings and trials in juvenile cases in 345.087; class comprehensive works on criminal procedure in 345.05; class comprehensive works on appellate procedure in criminal cases in 345.0144

*Add as instructed under 342–347

| .072 | *Pretrial procedure |
|---|---|

Including arraignment, discovery, grand jury proceedings, indictment, plea bargaining, pleading, preliminary hearings, pretrial release, summons

| .075 | *Trial procedure (Courtroom procedure) |
|---|---|

Including juries and jury selection, examination of witnesses, instructions to juries, verdicts

*For final disposition of cases, see 345.077*

| .077 | *Final disposition of cases |
|---|---|

Including pardon, parole, probation, rehabilitation

| .077 2 | *Sentencing |
|---|---|

*For penalties, see 345.0773*

| .077 3 | *Penalties |
|---|---|

Including death penalty

| .08 | *Juvenile procedure and courts |
|---|---|

Subdivisions are added for procedure and courts together, for procedure alone

Class juvenile offenders in 345.03; class liability, responsibility, guilt of juveniles in 345.04

| .081 | *Juvenile courts |
|---|---|
| .087 | *Hearings, trials, disposition of cases |

## .1      Socioeconomic regions

Add to base number 345.1 the numbers following —17 in notation 171–177 from Table 2, e.g., criminal law of developing countries 345.124; then to the result add as follows:
     001–009     Standard subdivisions
                  Notation from Table 1 as modified under 342–347
     01–08     Topics of criminal law
                  Add the numbers following 345 in 345.01–345.08, e.g., the law of evidence in developing countries 345.12406, decisions on evidence in developing countries 345.1240602643

Class socioeconomic regions of a specific regional intergovernmental organization in 345.2; class socioeconomic regions of a specific jurisdiction or area in 345.3–345.9

*Add as instructed under 342–347

## .2     Regional intergovernmental organizations

Class here relationship between the organization's law and national law of member countries

Add to base number 345.2 notation 3–9 from Table 2, e.g., criminal law of European Union 345.24; then to the result add as follows:
    001–009     Standard subdivisions
                    Notation from Table 1 as modified under 342–347
    01–08    Topics of criminal law
                  Add the numbers following 345 in 345.01–345.08, e.g., law of evidence of European Union 345.2406, administrative regulations of law of evidence of European Union 345.240602636

Class relationship of organization's law and national law of a specific member country with the national law in 345.3–345.9, e.g., effect of European Union laws on national criminal law of Spain 345.46

*See Manual at 342–349*

## .3–.9    Specific jurisdictions and areas

Add to base number 345 notation 3–9 from Table 2, e.g., criminal law of Australia 345.94, of New South Wales 345.944, of African states 345.6; then to the result add as follows:
    001–009     Standard subdivisions
                    Notation from Table 1 as modified under 342–347
    01–08    Topics of criminal law
                  Add the numbers following 345 in 345.01–345.08, e.g., the law of evidence in Australia 345.9406, in New South Wales 345.94406, in African states 345.606, decisions on evidence in Australia 345.940602643

*For regional intergovernmental organizations, relationship between the organization's laws and national laws of all member states, see 345.2*

*See Manual at 342–349*

### Special developments for Scotland and England follow

.411                 Criminal law of Scotland

.411 001–.411 009         Standard subdivisions

.411 01               *Criminal courts

Including Crown Counsel, Lord Advocate, Solicitor-General; procurators fiscal

Class here appellate courts devoted exclusively to criminal cases

Class appellate courts hearing both civil and criminal cases in 347.41103

*For Children's Hearings (juvenile courts), see 345.41108*

.411 012          *District Court

.411 014          *Sheriff Court

*Add as instructed under 342–347

| | |
|---|---|
| .411 016 | *High Court of Justiciary |
| .411 016 2 | *Court of First Instance |
| .411 016 3 | *Court of Appeal |
| .411 02–.411 07 | General considerations and procedure |

> Add to base number 345.4110 the numbers following 345.0 in 345.02–345.07, e.g., general criminal procedure 345.41105

| | |
|---|---|
| .411 08 | *Juvenile procedure |

> Including Children's Hearings (juvenile courts)

> Class juvenile offenders in 345.41103; class liability, responsibility, guilt of juveniles in 345.41104

| | |
|---|---|
| .42 | Criminal law of England |
| .420 01–.420 09 | Standard subdivisions |
| .420 1 | *Criminal courts |

> Including Attorney-General, Director of Public Prosecutions

> Class here appellate courts devoted exclusively to criminal cases

> Class appellate courts hearing both civil and criminal cases in 347.4203

> *For juvenile courts, see 345.42081*

| | |
|---|---|
| .420 12 | *Magistrates Court |

> *For civil jurisdiction of Magistrates Court, see 347.42023*

| | |
|---|---|
| .420 14 | *Crown Court |
| .420 16 | *Divisional Court of Queen's Bench Division of High Court of Justice |
| .420 18 | *Criminal Division of Court of Appeal |
| .420 2–.420 8 | General considerations, procedure, juvenile courts and procedure |

> Add to base number 345.420 the numbers following 345.0 in 345.02–345.08, e.g., juvenile courts 345.42081

# 346 Private law

> *See also 340.9 for private international law*

---

*Add as instructed under 342–347

## SUMMARY

.001        Philosophy and theory

> Notation 01 from Table 1 as modified under 342–347, e.g., sources of law 346.0011

.002        Miscellany

> Notation 02 from Table 1 as modified below and under 342–347, e.g., cases 346.00264

.002 3        Private law as a profession, occupation, hobby

> Class here nature of duties, characteristics of profession of civil-law notaries, of other notaries required to have legal education

> Class lay notaries in 347.016. Class works that emphasize procedures of work performed by notaries with the subject without adding notation 023 from Table 1, e.g., private international law 340.9, transfer of real property 346.0436

.003        Dictionaries, encyclopedias, concordances

.004        *Equity

.005–.008        Standard subdivisions

.009        History, geographic treatment, biography

[.009 17]        Socioeconomic regions

> Do not use; class in 346.1

[.009 3–.009 9]        Specific continents, countries, localities

> Do not use; class in 346,3–346.9

.01        *Persons and domestic relations

.012        *Persons

> Including names of persons

> *For capacity and status of persons, see 346.013*

> *See also 346.048 for business names*

*Add as instructed under 342–347

.013            *Capacity and status of persons

           Capacity: the attribute of persons (personal or corporate) which enables them to perform civil or juristic acts

           Including capacity and status of aliens; of people in late adulthood; of people with disabilities; of ethnic, national, economic groups; of slaves

           Subdivisions are added for either or both topics in heading

           Class liability of states to aliens in 341.26; class individual rights in 342.085; class the rehabilitation of a criminal's personal rights lost by judicial sentence in 345.077

           *For criminal capacity, see 345.04*

[.013 08]        Groups of people

           Do not use; class in 346.013

.013 4          *Women

.013 5          *Minors

           Including age of majority

.013 8          *People with mental illness and disabilities

.015            *Domestic relations (Family law)

           Class here comprehensive works on domestic relations and inheritance and succession

           *For marriage, partnerships, unions, see 346.016; for parent and child, see 346.017; for inheritance and succession, see 346.052*

.016            *Marriage, partnerships, unions

           Including civil unions, common-law marriage, de facto relationships, domestic partnerships, registered partnerships; unmarried couples living together (cohabitation)

           Subdivisions are added for marriage, partnerships, unions together; for marriage alone

           Class same-sex marriage in 346.0168

.016 3          *Spouses

           Rights and duties

           Including legal status of homemakers

           Class here husband and wife, married people

           Class legal status of married women in 346.0134; class rights and duties in relation to divorce, annulment, separation in 346.0166

.016 6          *Divorce, annulment, separation

           Subdivisions are added for divorce, annulment, separation together; for divorce alone

---

*Add as instructed under 342–347

>       346.016 62–346.016 64   Specific aspects of divorce, annulment, separation

      Class comprehensive works in 346.0166

> *For specific aspects of annulment, see 346.01665; for specific aspects of separation, see 346.01668*

.016 62       *Prenuptial contracts (Antenuptial contracts)

> *For support aspects of the contract, see 346.01663; for marital property aspects of the contract, see 346.01664*

.016 63       *Support

      Class here alimony

> *For separate maintenance, see 346.01668; for child support, see 346.0172*

.016 64       *Marital property in divorce, annulment, separation

      Including community and separate property in divorce, annulment, separation

      Comprehensive works on marital, community, separate property relocated to 346.042

.016 65       *Annulment

.016 68       *Separation

      Including separate maintenance

.016 8       *Same-sex marriage

      Class rights and duties of spouses in 346.0163; class divorce, annulment, separation in 346.0166

.017       *Parent and child

      Including surrogate motherhood

      Class here parental rights and duties regardless of marital status of parents

.017 1       *Unborn children

> *For a specific aspect of unborn children, see the aspect, e.g., rights of fetuses 342.085*

.017 2       *Child support

.017 3       *Custody of children

      Class here joint custody, visitation rights

.017 5       *Paternity

.017 8       *Adoption

.018       *Guardian and ward

*Add as instructed under 342–347

.02      *Juristic acts, contracts, agency

> Subdivisions are added for juristic acts, contracts, and agency together; for juristic acts alone

> Class juristic acts dealing with a specific legal aspect not provided for here with the aspect in 342–347, e.g., personal property 346.047

.021      General considerations of juristic acts

> Including cause, form, object, declaration of will

.022      *Contracts

> Including breach of contract, parties to contract, rescission, subcontracting

> Class here comprehensive works on liability

> Class sale in 346.072; class loan in 346.073. Class contractual aspects of specific subjects in law with the subject in 342–347, e.g., partnership contracts 346.0682; class nonlegal aspects of contracts concerning a specific nonlegal subject with the subject, e.g., materials management aspects of roofing contracts 695.0687

>> *For government liability, see 342.088; for liability of schools, of school officials, of school districts, see 344.075; for criminal liability, see 345.04; for specific kinds of contracts, see 346.023–346.025; for extracontractual liability, see 346.03*

.023      *Public contracts (Government contracts)

> Including defense, research and development contracts

> Class governmental contracts themselves in 352.53

.024      *Contracts of service

> Including master-servant relationships, mechanics' liens

> Class labor contracts in 344.01891; class public contracts of service in 346.023; class contracts of service involving bailments in 346.025; class agency in 346.029

>> *See also 346.074 for liens in secured transactions*

.025      *Contracts involving bailments

> Including bills of lading, pawnbroking

> Class public contracts involving bailments in 346.023

.029      *Agency and quasi contract

> Including power of attorney, unjust enrichment

> Subdivisions are added for either or both topics in heading

---

*Add as instructed under 342–347

| .03 | *Torts (Delicts) |

.03    *Torts (Delicts)

Class here liability for the torts of others, e.g., employees

Class remedies in 347.077

*See Manual at 345.02 vs. 346.03*

.031    Liability of specific classes of persons

Including liability of employers, directors of corporations, hospitals

Class liability of specific classes of persons in specific situations in 346.032–346.038

*For personal liability of government officials, see 342.068*

.032    *Negligence

Including contributory negligence

Class environmental liability and negligence in 344.046; class malpractice in 346.033

.032 2    *Accidents

Class accidents resulting in personal injury and wrongful death in 346.0323

.032 3    *Personal injury and wrongful death

.033    *Torts against the person

Including assault and battery, invasion of privacy, malpractice (professional liability)

*For accidents, see 346.0322; for injury through negligence, see 346.0323; for libel and slander, see 346.034. For malpractice pertaining to a specific profession, see the profession in 342–347, e.g., malpractice of lay notaries 347.016, malpractice of lawyers 347.05041*

.033 4    *Malicious prosecution

Class here false arrest and imprisonment

.034    *Libel and slander (Defamation)

Class libel and slander as crimes in 345.0256

.036    *Torts involving property

Including nuisance, trespass, trover and conversion, wrongful entry

Class wrongful entry as invasion of privacy in 346.033

.038    *Product liability

Class here strict liability

.04    *Property

*For property of enemy aliens, see 341.67; for public property, see 343.02*

*Add as instructed under 342–347

## SUMMARY

.040 869 1      Property of people with status defined by changes in residence

Class here alien property

*For nationalization of alien property, see 343.0252*

.042      Kinds of interest in property

Including comprehensive works on marital, community, separate property [*all formerly* 346.01664]; joint tenancy, future interests

*For marital, community, separate property in divorce, annulment, separation, see 346.01664*

.043      *Real property

Land, permanent fixtures, natural resources

Including mobile homes

Class here interdisciplinary works on economic and legal aspects of ownership and transfer of land

*For economic aspects of ownership and transfer of land, see 333.1–333.5; for government control and regulation of real property, see 346.044*

*See also 343.0944 for motorized homes*

.043 2      *Ownership (Land tenure)

Including incidents of ownership, e.g., riparian rights, water rights; recovery, squatter's right; types of estate, e.g., fee simple

*For joint tenancy, see 346.042*

.043 3      *Horizontal property and cooperative ownership

Variant name for horizontal property: condominium

Including time-sharing

.043 4      *Tenancy

Including eviction

Class here landlord and tenant

Class ejectment in 346.0432

*Add as instructed under 342–347

| | | |
|---|---|---|
| .043 44 | | *Rent |
| | | Including rent control |
| .043 46 | | *Leases |
| .043 462 | | *Commercial leases |
| .043 48 | | *Farm tenancy |
| | | Class rent in 346.04344; class leases in 346.04346 |
| .043 5 | | *Easements and servitudes |
| | | Including right of way |
| .043 6 | | *Transfer |
| | | Including consolidation of land holdings, restrictions on alienation |
| | | Class inheritance and succession in 346.052 |
| | | *For conveyancing, see 346.0438* |
| .043 62 | | *Acquisition and purchase |
| .043 63 | | *Sale |
| | | Class real estate business in 346.0437 |
| .043 64 | | *Mortgages |
| | | Class here foreclosure |
| .043 7 | | *Real estate business |
| | | Including valuation of real property |
| | | Class regulation of a specific general administrative function of real estate business with the function in 342–347, e.g., wages 344.0128133333, organization 346.065 |
| .043 71 | | *Malpractice |
| | | Class malpractice pertaining to closing and settlements in 346.04373; class malpractice pertaining to subdivision in 346.04377 |
| .043 73 | | *Closing and settlements |
| | | Including escrows |
| .043 77 | | *Subdivision |
| .043 8 | | *Conveyancing |
| | | Including deeds, registration and description of land, title examinations, titles |

---

*Add as instructed under 342–347

.044      *Government control and regulation of real property

> Class here conservation of natural resources; land reform; comprehensive works on government control and regulation of public and private real property

> Subdivisions are added for either or both topics in heading

> Class government as landlord or tenant in 346.0434; class comprehensive works on environmental law in 344.046

> > *For control and use of public real property, see 343.0256; for rent control, see 346.04344; for regional and local community planning, see 346.045; for control of specific kinds of land and natural resources, see 346.046*

> > *See also 341.4 for conservation of extraterritorial natural resources*

.045      *Regional and local community planning

> Variant name for local community planning: city planning

> Including building codes that relate to regional or local community planning or land use; land use; restrictions on posting advertisements; zoning

> Class regulations governing construction of buildings in 343.07869

.046      Government control and regulation of specific kinds of land and natural resources

> Class here protection of specific resources

> Add to base number 346.046 the numbers following 333 in 333.7–333.9, e.g., control of power and power resources 346.04679, control of recreational lands 346.04678; then add further as instructed under 342–347, e.g., cases involving control of recreational lands 346.046780264

> Class comprehensive works in 346.044

.047      *Personal property

> Movable property

> Including leasing of personal property, e.g., a truck

> Class mobile homes in 346.043

> > *For intangible property, see 346.048; for sale, see 346.072*

.048      *Intangible property

> Including public lending rights

> Class here intellectual property, industrial property (intangible property of an industrial nature, e.g., business names, franchises)

> > *For negotiable instruments, see 346.096*

.048 2      *Copyright

*Add as instructed under 342–347

| .048 4 | *Design protection |
| .048 6 | *Patents |
| .048 8 | *Trademarks |
| .05 | *Inheritance, succession, fiduciary trusts, trustees |
| .052 | *Inheritance and succession |

Class here estate planning, probate practice

Subdivisions are added for either or both topics in heading

Class comprehensive works on domestic relations and inheritance and succession in 346.015

*For estate planning to avoid taxes, see 343.053; for wills, see 346.054; for administration of estates, see 346.056*

| .054 | *Wills |
| .056 | *Administration of estates |

Including execution of wills

*For unclaimed estates, see 346.057*

| .057 | *Unclaimed estates |
| .059 | *Fiduciary trusts |
| .06 | *Organizations (Associations) |

Class here organization of associations engaged in specific types of enterprises, e.g., an organization of railroad companies

Class organization of labor unions in 344.0187. Class operation of organizations engaged in a specific type of enterprise with the type of enterprise, e.g., operation of railroad companies 343.095

| .063 | *Accounting |

Class accounting for specific kinds of organizations in 346.064–346.068

*See also 343.034 for government accounting*

| .063 1 | *Malpractice |
| .064 | *Nonprofit organizations |

Including charitable trusts and foundations, trade associations, unincorporated societies

*Add as instructed under 342–347

.065       *Business enterprises

Including combinations, record requirements, sale, valuation

Class record requirements for a specific kind of organization with the kind in 342–347, e.g., record requirements for a government corporation 346.067; class record requirements for a specific subject with the subject in 342–347, e.g., workers' compensation insurance records 344.021

*For corporations, see 346.066; for unincorporated business enterprises, see 346.068*

.065 2       *Small business

Class small corporations in 346.066

.066       *Corporations (Companies)

Class comprehensive works on corporate and commercial law in 346.07

*For government corporations, see 346.067*

*See also 342.09 for municipal corporations*

.066 2       *Organization

Including investment banking, liquidation

.066 22       *Incorporation

.066 26       *Reorganization

Including acquisitions and mergers

.066 4       *Management

Including records

.066 42       *Officers

.066 45       *Meetings

Class shareholders' meetings in 346.0666

.066 48       *Accounting

.066 6       *Securities and security holders

Including shareholders' voting and meetings

Standard subdivisions are added for either or both topics in heading

Class tender offers for corporate stock in 346.0662; class securities marketing in 346.092

---

*Add as instructed under 342–347

.066 8    Kinds of corporations (Kinds of companies)

Including close corporations; cooperatives; credit unions; holding, limited, public limited companies

Class specific aspects of corporate law applied to specific kinds of corporations in 346.0662–346.0666

*For nonprofit corporations, see 346.064; for government corporations, see 346.067*

.067    *Government corporations

Including quangos

Class municipal corporations in 342.09

.068    *Unincorporated business enterprises

Including land trusts, sole traders

.068 2    *Partnerships

Class here joint ventures

.07    *Commercial law

Class here commercial contracts, conduct of business; laws of a specific jurisdiction governing business investment by foreign nationals, e.g., laws of China governing the conduct of business in China by foreign nationals 346.5107; comprehensive works on business law

*For a specific subject of commercial law, of business law not provided for here, see the subject in 342–347, e.g., tax law 343.04, insurance law 346.086*

.072    *Sale

Class sale of real property in 346.04363; class sale of business enterprises in 346.065; class conditional and secured sales transactions in 346.074

.073    *Loan

Including agricultural and consumer credit, interest, truth in lending, usury

Class here credit

Class secured loan transactions in 346.074

.074    *Secured transactions

Including chattel mortgages; conditional, installment sales; guaranty, liens, suretyship

Class comprehensive works on mortgages in 346.04364

*See also 346.024 for mechanics' liens*

.077      *Debtor and creditor

         Including collection of debts

         *For bankruptcy, see 346.078*

.078      *Bankruptcy

         Including receivership

         Class here insolvency

.08      *Banks and insurance

.082      *Banks

         Class here banking

         Class investment banking in 346.0662. Class regulation of a specific general administrative function with the function in 342–347, e.g., wages 344.012813321, corporate organization 346.0662

         *For loan, see 346.073*

.082 1–.082 3      Specific topics of banks

         Add to base number 346.082 the numbers following 332 in 332.1–332.3, e.g., international banks 346.08215, specialized banking institutions 346.0822, credit and loan institutions 346.0823, commercial banks 346.08212; then add further as instructed under 342–347, e.g., cases involving commercial banks 346.082120264

.086      Insurance

         Class regulation of a specific general administrative function with the function in 342–347, e.g., wages 344.01281368, corporate organization 346.0662

.086 000 1–.086 000 9      Standard subdivisions

         Notation from Table 1 as modified under 342–347, e.g., cases 346.086000264

.086 01      General principles

         Add to base number 346.08601 the numbers following 368.01 in 368.011–368.019, e.g., underwriting 346.086012; then add further as instructed under 342–347, e.g., cases involving underwriting 346.0860120264

.086 02      *Malpractice

.086 06–.086 09      Risks and sales groupings

         Add to base number 346.0860 the numbers following 368.0 in 368.06–368.09, e.g., automobile insurance 346.086092; then add further as instructed under 342–347, e.g., cases involving automobile insurance 346.0860920264

---

*Add as instructed under 342–347

.086 1–.086 8     Specific topics of insurance

Add to base number 346.086 the numbers following 368 in 368.1–368.8, e.g., fire insurance 346.08611; then add further as instructed under 342–347, e.g., cases involving fire insurance 346.086110264; however, for government-sponsored insurance, social insurance, see 344.02

.09          *Investment and negotiable instruments

.092          *Investment

Class here investments

.092 2          Specific types of investments

Including bonds, government securities, mutual funds, stocks; commodities, real estate

Class here securities

Class initial promotion of securities in 346.0662; class what a corporation must do to make certain a security is valid in 346.0666; class organizations marketing specific types of securities in 346.0926

*See also 346.074 for secured transactions*

[.092 201–.092 209]     Standard subdivisions

Do not use; class in 346.09201–346.09209

.092 6          *Marketing agents and arrangements

Including securities brokers; exchange of securities, stock exchanges

Class investment banking in 346.0662. Class regulation of a specific general administrative function of organizations engaged in marketing securities with the function in 342–347, e.g., wages 344.01281332642, organization 346.065

*For commodity exchanges, see 343.08*

.096          *Negotiable instruments

Including bills of exchange, checks (cheques), promissory notes, trade acceptances, warehouse receipts

*For securities, see 346.092*

*Add as instructed under 342–347

**.1          Socioeconomic regions**

Add to base number 346.1 the numbers following —17 in notation 171–177 from Table 2, e.g., private law of developing countries 346.124; then to the result add as follows:
001–009     Standard subdivisions
                    Notation from Table 1 as modified under 342–347
01–09      Topics of private law
                    Add the numbers following 346 in 346.01–346.09, e.g., property law of developing countries 346.12404, cases involving property law in developing countries 346.124040264

Class socioeconomic regions of a specific regional intergovernmental organization in 346.2; class socioeconomic regions of a specific jurisdiction or area in 346.3–346.9

**.2          Regional intergovernmental organizations**

Class here relationship between the organization's law and national law of member countries

Add to base number 346.2 notation 3–9 from Table 2, e.g., private law of European Union 346.24; then to the result add as follows:
001–009     Standard subdivisions
                    Notation from Table 1 as modified under 342–347
01–09      Topics of private law
                    Add the numbers following 346 in 346.01–346.09, e.g., property law of European Union 346.2404, administrative regulations of property law of European Union 346.240402636

*See Manual at 342–349*

Class relationship of organization's law and national law of a specific member country with the national law in 346.3–346.9, e.g., effect of European Union laws on national private law of Italy 346.45

**.3–.9       Specific jurisdictions and areas**

Add to base number 346 notation 3–9 from Table 2, e.g., private law of Australia 346.94, of New South Wales 346.944, of African states 346.6; then to the result add as follows:
001–009     Standard subdivisions
                    Notation from Table 1 as modified under 342–347
01–09      Topics of private law
                    Add the numbers following 346 in 346.01–346.09, e.g., family law of Australia 346.94015, of New South Wales 346.944014, of African states 346.6015, cases involving family law of Australia 346.940150264

*For regional intergovernmental organizations, relationship between the organization's laws and national laws of all member states, see 346.2*

*See Manual at 342–349*

# 347          Procedure and courts

Class here civil procedure and courts; comprehensive works on civil and criminal procedure and courts, judicial branch of government, administration of justice, legal services

*For administrative procedure, see 342.066; for criminal procedure and courts, see 345*

*See Manual at 347*

(Option: Class here courts and procedure in a specific field of law; prefer specific field in 342–347, plus notation 0269 from table under 342–347)

## SUMMARY

| | |
|---|---|
| 347.001–.009 | **Standard subdivisions; laws, regulations, cases, procedure, courts** |
| .01 | **Courts** |
| .02 | **Courts with general original jurisdiction** |
| .03 | **Appellate courts** |
| .04 | **Courts with specialized jurisdiction** |
| .05 | **Procedure** |
| .06 | **Evidence** |
| .07 | **Trials** |
| .08 | **Appellate procedure** |
| .09 | **Dispute resolution** |
| .1 | **Socioeconomic regions** |
| .2 | **Regional intergovernmental organizations** |
| .3–.9 | **Specific jurisdictions and areas** |

.001–.005          Standard subdivisions

Notation from Table 1 as modified under 342–347, e.g., cases 347.00264

.006          Organizations

[.006 8]          Management

Do not use; class in 347.013

.007–.008          Standard subdivisions

.009          History, geographic treatment, biography

[.009 17]          Socioeconomic regions

Do not use; class in 347.1

[.009 3–.009 9]          Specific continents, countries, localities

Do not use; class in 347.3–347.9

.01          *Courts

Class provisional courts in 342.0664

*For juvenile courts, see 345.081; for courts with specific kinds of jurisdiction, see 347.02–347.04*

*Add as instructed under 342–347

.012          *General considerations of courts

                Including judicial cooperation, letters rogatory; judicial discretion, judicial error, judicial review, jurisdiction of courts

                Class criminal contempt of court in 345.0234; class general considerations of specific aspects of courts in 347.013–347.017

                *See Manual at 347*

.013          *Judicial administration (Court management)

                Including court calendars, records

                *For judges, see 347.014; for court officials other than judges, see 347.016*

.014          *Judges

                Class judges associated with a specific court with the court, e.g., judges of a juvenile court 345.081, judges of the High Court of Justice in England 347.4202534

.016          Other officials

                Including clerks, coroners, court reporters, justices of the peace, marshals, lay notaries, sheriffs

                Class nature of duties, characteristics of profession of civil-law notaries, of other notaries required to have legal education in 346.0023. Class the work of court officials with respect to a specific subject with the subject, e.g., justices of the peace and domestic relations 346.015

.017          *Legal aid

                Class legal aid in criminal cases in 345.0127; class legal aid as a welfare service, interdisciplinary works on legal aid in 362.58

---

*Add as instructed under 342–347

>         **347.02–347.04 Courts with specific kinds of jurisdiction**

Add to each subdivision identified by † as follows:
01–09    Standard subdivisions
         Notation from Table 1 as modified under 342–347, e.g., cases
         0264
2       General considerations
         Including functions, jurisdiction, organization, powers
3       Judicial administration
34      Judges
36      Other officials
5       Procedure
         *For evidence, see 347.06; for trials, see 347.07; for appellate*
         *procedure, see 347.08*
504     Practice
         Form, manner, order of instituting and conducting a suit,
         court case, or other judicial proceeding through its successive
         stages to its end in accordance with rules and principles laid
         down by law or by regulations and precedents of the courts
5041    Malpractice
51–57    Specific topics of procedure
         Add to 5 the numbers following 347.05 in 347.051–347.057,
         e.g., formbooks 55
         Class practice in 504

Class comprehensive works in 347.01

>         **347.02–347.03 Courts with general jurisdiction**

Class procedure in specific levels of courts in 347.05–347.08; class
comprehensive works in 347.01

.02       †Courts with general original jurisdiction

Class here comprehensive works on courts of first instance, local courts,
trial courts, on courts that have names such as Circuit, District, County,
Municipal, Superior Court

.03       †Appellate courts

*For appellate courts devoted exclusively to criminal cases, see 345.0144;*
*for appellate courts with specialized jurisdiction, see 347.04*

.033      †Intermediate appellate courts

Class here courts of second instance, courts of first appeal

.035      †Courts of last resort (Supreme courts)

Class here courts of third instance, courts of second appeal, courts of
final appeal

†Add as instructed under 347.02–347.04

.04 †Courts with specialized jurisdiction

Including admiralty courts, small-claims courts

Class courts dealing with a specific subject with the subject in 342–347, plus notation 0269 from table under 342–347, e.g., tax courts 343.040269

.05 *Procedure

Class here procedure in specific levels of courts, relation of a fair trial to freedom of the press, comprehensive works on procedure

Class procedure in a specific court with the court in 347.02–347.04, plus notation 5 from add table under 347.02–347.04, e.g., practice in supreme courts 347.035504; class procedure with respect to a specific subject with the subject in 342–347, plus notation 0269 from table under 342–347, e.g., court procedure in tax matters 343.040269

*For evidence, see 347.06; for trials, see 347.07; for appellate procedure, see 347.08*

.050 4 *Practice

Form, manner, order of instituting and conducting a suit, court case, or other judicial proceeding through its successive stages to its end in accordance with rules and principles laid down by law or by regulations and precedents of the courts

*See also 340.023 for practice of law as a profession*

.050 41 *Malpractice

.051 *Court rules

Class rules about legal costs and fees in 347.057; class rules of specific courts, of courts having specific kinds of jurisdiction in 347.02–347.04

.052 Motions, limitation of actions, parties to trial, jury trial

Class here advocacy

.053 Kinds of actions

Including class actions, lawsuits

.055 Forms and form books

Standard subdivisions are added for either or both topics in heading

.057 Legal costs and fees

Standard subdivisions are added for either or both topics in heading

Rules and guidelines

Class ethical aspects of legal costs and fees in 174.3; class financial management of law firms in 340.0681; class economics of salaries of legal personnel in 331.28134; class economics of law firms in 338.7–338.8; class interdisciplinary works on legal costs and fees in 338.4334

*Add as instructed under 342–347
†Add as instructed under 347.02–347.04

.057 2        Fees for legal professional services

       Class here lawyers' fees, contingent or conditional fees

.06        *Evidence

.062        *Admissibility

.064        Kinds of evidence

       *For witnesses, see 347.066*

.066        *Witnesses

       Class examination of witnesses in 347.075

       *For expert testimony, see 347.067*

.067        *Expert testimony

       Class forensic science in 363.25; class medical jurisprudence, forensic medicine, forensic psychiatry in 614.1

.07        *Trials

       Class a trial dealing with a specific subject with the subject in 342–347, e.g., a product liability trial 346.038; class procedures of trials dealing with a specific subject with the subject in 342–347, plus notation 0269 from table under 342–347, e.g., procedures of product liability trials 346.0380269

.072        *Pretrial procedure

       Including discovery, pleading, service of process, summons

.075        *Trial procedure (Courtroom procedure)

       Including examination of witnesses, summations, verdicts

.075 2        *Juries

       Class here jury selection

       Class instructions to juries in 347.0758

.075 8        *Instructions to juries

.077        *Judgments

       Including attachment and garnishment, legal costs and fees awarded as part of judgments, executions of judgment, remedies

.08        *Appellate procedure

       Class here comprehensive works on appellate procedure in civil and criminal cases

       *For procedure in specific appellate courts hearing both civil and criminal cases, specific appellate courts devoted exclusively to civil cases, see 347.03–347.04; for procedure in appellate courts devoted exclusively to criminal cases, see 345.0144*

       Comprehensive works on appellate procedure in criminal cases relocated to 345.0144

---

*Add as instructed under 342–347

.09     *Dispute resolution

Class here arbitration, conciliation, mediation

**.1**     **Socioeconomic regions**

Add to base number 347.1 the numbers following —17 in notation 171–177 from Table 2, e.g., civil procedure and courts of developing countries 347.124; then to the result add as follows:
001–009     Standard subdivisions
          Notation from Table 1 as modified under 342–347
01–09     Topics of procedure and courts
          Add the numbers following 347 in 347.01–347.09, e.g., the law of evidence in developing countries 347.12406, court decisions on evidence in developing countries 347.1240602643

Class socioeconomic regions of a specific regional intergovernmental organization in 347.2; class socioeconomic regions of a specific jurisdiction or area in 347.3–347.9

**.2**     **Regional intergovernmental organizations**

Class here effect of organization's law on and harmonization of national laws of member countries

Add to base number 347.2 notation 3–9 from Table 2, e.g., harmonization of national laws on procedure and courts of European Union countries 347.24; then to the result add as follows:
001–009     Standard subdivisions
          Notation from Table 1 as modified under 342–347
01–09     Topics of procedure and courts
          Add the numbers following 347 in 347.01–347.09, e.g., harmonization of national law of evidence of European Union 347.2406, harmonization of individual and collected laws of evidence of European Union countries 347.240602632
          Class effect of organization's laws on national laws of a specific member country with the national laws, e.g., effect of European Union laws on national laws on procedures and courts of France 347.44

Class relationship of organization's law and national law of a specific member country with the national law in 347.3–347.9, e.g., effect of European Union laws on national German laws on procedure and courts 347.43

*See Manual at 342–349*

.24     Regional intergovernmental organizations of Europe

Number built according to instructions under 347.2

Class here effect of European Union law on and harmonization of national laws on procedure and courts of European Union countries

Class effect of European Union law on national laws of a specific member country with the national law, e.g., effect of European Union laws on national French laws on procedures and courts 347.44

---

*Add as instructed under 342–347

**.3–.9     Specific jurisdictions and areas**

Add to base number 347 notation 3–9 from Table 2, e.g., civil procedure and courts of Australia 347.94, of New South Wales 347.944, of African states 347.6; then to the result add as follows:

    001–009     Standard subdivisions

                   Notation from Table 1 as modified under 342–347

    01–09    Topics of procedure and courts

                   Add the numbers following 347 in 347.01–347.09, e.g., the law of evidence in Australia 347.9406, in New South Wales 347.94406, in African states 347.606; Australian court decisions on evidence in 347.940602643

*For regional intergovernmental organizations, relationship between the organization's laws and national laws of all member states, see 347.2*

*See Manual at 342–349*

**Special developments for Scotland, England, the United States follow**

.411              Civil procedure and courts of Scotland

.411 001–.411 009       Standard subdivisions

.411 01           *Courts

                   *For courts with specific kinds of jurisdiction, see 347.41102–347.41104*

.411 012–.411 017       Specific aspects of courts

                   Add to base number 347.41101 the numbers following 347.01 in 347.012–347.017, e.g., general considerations 347.411012

---

>       347.411 02–347.411 04   Courts with specific kinds of jurisdiction

                   Add to each subdivision identified by † as instructed under 347.02–347.04, e.g., jurisdiction of the Sheriff Court 347.4110212

                   Class comprehensive works in 347.41101

---

>       347.411 02–347.411 03   Courts with general jurisdiction

                   Class procedure in specific levels of courts in 347.41105–347.41108; class comprehensive works in 347.41101

.411 02           †Courts with original jurisdiction

.411 021          †Sheriff Court

                   *For criminal jurisdiction of Sheriff Court, see 345.411014; for appellate jurisdiction of Sheriff-Principal, see 347.411032*

---

*Add as instructed under 342–347
†Add as instructed under 347.02–347.04

| | |
|---|---|
| .411 023 | †Court of Session |

> *For Outer House, see 347.411024; for Inner House, see 347.411035*

| | |
|---|---|
| .411 024 | †Outer House of Court of Session |
| .411 03 | †Courts with appellate jurisdiction |

Class here comprehensive works on appellate courts

> *For appellate courts devoted exclusively to criminal cases, see 345.41101; for appellate courts with specialized jurisdiction, see 347.41104*

| | |
|---|---|
| .411 032 | †Sheriff-Principal |
| .411 035 | †Inner House of Court of Session |
| .411 039 | †House of Lords (Court of last resort) |
| .411 04 | †Courts with specialized jurisdiction |

Including Court of the Lord Lyon, Licensing Appeals Courts, Licensing Courts

Class courts dealing with a single specific subject with the subject in 342–347, plus notation 0269 from table under 342–347, e.g., Court of Exchequer 343.411040269

| | |
|---|---|
| .411 05–.411 09 | Procedure and arbitration |

Add to base number 347.4110 the numbers following 347.0 in 347.05–347.09, e.g., evidence 347.41106

| | |
|---|---|
| .42 | Civil procedure and courts of England |
| .420 01–.420 09 | Standard subdivisions |
| .420 1 | *Courts |

> *For courts with specific kinds of jurisdiction, see 347.4202–347.4204*

| | |
|---|---|
| .420 12–.420 17 | Specific aspects of courts |

Add to base number 347.4201 the numbers following 347.01 in 347.012–347.017, e.g., general considerations 347.42012

---

> 347.420 2–347.420 4  Courts with specific kinds of jurisdiction

Add to each subdivision identified by † as instructed under 347.02–347.04, e.g., jurisdiction of County Court 347.420212

Class comprehensive works in 347.4201

---

*Add as instructed under 342–347
†Add as instructed under 347.02–347.04

>      347.420 2–347.420 3   Courts with general jurisdiction

Class procedure in specific levels of courts in 347.4205–347.4208; class comprehensive works in 347.4201

.420 2        †Courts with original jurisdiction

.420 21       †County Court

.420 23       †Domestic Court of Magistrates Court

Class comprehensive works on Magistrates Court in 345.42012

.420 25       †High Court of Justice

*For Family Division, see 346.420150269; for Chancery Division, see 347.42026; for Queen's Bench Division, see 347.42027*

.420 26       †Chancery Division of the High Court of Justice

.420 27       †Queen's Bench Division of High Court of Justice

*For Divisional Court of Queen's Bench Division, see 345.42016*

.420 29       †Supreme Court of Judicature

*For Crown Court, see 345.42014; for High Court of Justice, see 347.42025; for Court of Appeal, see 347.42032*

.420 3        †Courts with appellate jurisdiction

Class here comprehensive works on appellate courts

*For appellate courts devoted exclusively to criminal cases, see 345.4201; for appellate courts with specialized jurisdiction, see 347.4204*

.420 32       †Court of Appeal

*For Criminal Division, see 345.42018; for Civil Division, see 347.42035*

.420 35       †Civil Division of Court of Appeal

.420 39       †House of Lords (Court of last resort)

Criminal and civil jurisdiction

.420 4        †Courts with specialized jurisdiction

Including Judicial Committee of the Privy Council

Class courts dealing with a specific subject with the subject in 342–347, plus notation 0269 from table under 342–347, e.g., Lands Tribunal 346.420430269

†Add as instructed under 347.02–347.04

| | | |
|---|---|---|
| .420 5–.420 9 | | Procedure and arbitration |

> Add to base number 347.420 the numbers following 347.0 in 347.05–347.09, e.g., evidence 347.4206

.73        Civil procedure and courts of the United States

> Federal procedure and courts; national and regional treatment of state and local procedure and courts
>
> *For civil procedure and courts of specific states and localities, see 347.74–347.79*

.730 01–.730 09        Standard subdivisions

.731        *Courts

> *For specific court systems, see 347.732–347.734*

.731 2–.731 7        Specific aspects of courts

> Add to base number 347.731 the numbers following 347.01 in 347.012–347.017, e.g., judges 347.7314

---

>        347.732–347.734  Specific court systems

Class comprehensive works in 347.731

.732        Federal courts

> Add 0 to base number 347.732; then add further as instructed under 347.02–347.04, e.g., periodicals about federal courts 347.732005, federal judges 347.732034

---

>        347.732 2–347.732 8  Federal courts with specific kinds of jurisdiction

Class here procedure in specific courts

Add to each subdivision identified by † as instructed under 347.02–347.04, e.g., Supreme Court rules 347.732651

Class comprehensive works in 347.732

---

>        347.732 2–347.732 6  Federal courts with general jurisdiction

Class procedure in specific levels of courts in 347.735–347.738; class comprehensive works in 347.732

.732 2                †District courts

> Courts of original jurisdiction

.732 4                †Courts of appeal

> *For Supreme Court, see 347.7326*

.732 6                †Supreme Court

*Add as instructed under 342–347
†Add as instructed under 347.02–347.04

| | |
|---|---|
| .732 8 | †Courts of specialized jurisdiction |

Including United States Court of Customs and Patent Appeals

Class courts dealing with a specific subject with the subject in United States law, plus notation 0269 from table under 342–347, e.g., tax courts 343.73040269

| | |
|---|---|
| .733 | *State courts |

Class courts of specific states in 347.74–347.79

| | |
|---|---|
| .733 2–.733 8 | Specific aspects of state courts |

Add to base number 347.733 the numbers following 347.732 in 347.7322–347.7328, e.g., state supreme courts 347.7336

| | |
|---|---|
| .734 | *Local courts |

Class courts of specific localities in 347.74–347.79

| | |
|---|---|
| .735–.738 | Procedure |

Class here procedure in specific levels of federal courts

Add to base number 347.73 the numbers following 347.0 in 347.05–347.08, e.g., rules of evidence 347.736

Class procedure in specific courts in 347.732–347.734

| | |
|---|---|
| .739 | *Arbitration, mediation, conciliation |

Subdivisions are added for any or all topics in heading

| | |
|---|---|
| .74–.79 | Civil procedure and courts of specific states and localities of the United States |

Add to base number 347 notation 74–79 from Table 2, e.g., civil procedure and courts of Pennsylvania 347.748, of Philadelphia 347.74811; then to the result add as follows:
001–009     Standard subdivisions
                Notation from Table 1 as modified under 342–347
01–09     Topics of procedure and courts
                Add the numbers following 347 in 347.01–347.09, e.g.,
                the Supreme Court of Pennsylvania 347.748035, courts of
                Philadelphia 347.7481101

Class regional treatment of state and local procedure and courts in 347.73; class civil procedure and courts of Hawaii in 347.969

*Add as instructed under 342–347
†Add as instructed under 347.02–347.04

# 348 Laws, regulations, cases

Original materials and their guides listed here are comprehensive in nature, covering the whole of the law of a specific jurisdiction or a major portion thereof

Class treatises on the whole law of a specific jurisdiction in 349. Class original materials and their guides limited to a specific branch or subject with the branch or subject in 342–347, plus notation 026 from table under 342–347, e.g., a digest of tax laws 343.0402638

(Option: Class here laws, regulations, cases covering specific subjects in law; prefer specific subject in 342–347, plus notation 026 from table under 342–347)

## SUMMARY

| | |
|---|---|
| 348.001–.009 | Standard subdivisions and codification |
| .01 | Preliminary materials |
| .02 | Laws and regulations |
| .04 | Cases |
| .05 | Advisory opinions of attorneys-general (ministers of justice) |
| .1 | Socioeconomic regions |
| .2 | Regional intergovernmental organizations |
| .3–.9 | Specific jurisdictions and areas |

.001–.003     Standard subdivisions

.004     Codification

> Class proposed codes in 348.023

.005     Serial publications

.006     Organizations and management

> Notation 06 from Table 1 as modified below

.006 01     International organizations

> Laws, regulations, cases limited to a specific regional intergovernmental organization are classed under the area of the organization before indicating the subject of a branch of law, e.g., regulations of European Union 348.24025. Further instructions are given under 342–349

.007–.008     Standard subdivisions

.009     History, geographic treatment, biography

[.009 17]     Socioeconomic regions

> Do not use; class in 348.1

[.009 3–.009 9]     Specific continents, countries, localities

> Do not use; class in 348.3–348.9

.01            *Preliminary materials

               Including bills; legislative hearings, histories; slip laws; statistical reports of
               bills passed or vetoed, reports on the status of bills

.02            *Laws and regulations

               Standard subdivisions are added for laws and regulations together, for laws
               alone

               Class here statutes

               Including laws arranged in alphabetical order

               (If option under 348 is chosen, class here individual laws)

.020 1–.020 8        Standard subdivisions

---

\>        348.022–348.024 Laws

               Class guides to laws in 348.026–348.028; class comprehensive works in 348.02

.022           *Laws arranged in chronological order

               Including session laws

.023           *Codes

               Compilations of laws in classified order

               Including compiled and consolidated statutes

.024           *Selected laws

.025           *Regulations

               Class guides to regulationss in 348.026–348.028

.025 01–.025 08      Standard subdivisions

---

\>        348.026–348.028 Guides to laws and regulations

               Class comprehensive works and guides in 348.026. Class guides to a specific
               collection of laws with the collection, e.g., a citator to the U.S. Code 348.7323

.026           *Digests of laws and regulations

               Standard subdivisions are added for either or both topics in heading

               Including summaries of changes

               Class here comprehensive guides to laws and regulations

               *For citators to laws and regulations, see 348.027; for checklists,
               tables, indexes of laws and regulations, see 348.028*

---

*Do not use notation 0601 from Table 1 for a specific regional intergovernmental organization;
class in 348.2. Do not use notation 0917 from Table 1 for socioeconomic regions; class in 348.1.
Do not use notation 093–099 from Table 1 for specific continents, countries, localities; class in
348.3–348.9

| .027 | *Citators to laws and regulations |
|------|------------------------------------|

Standard subdivisions are added for either or both topics in heading

| .028 | *Checklists, tables, indexes of laws and regulations |
|------|------------------------------------------------------|

Standard subdivisions are added for any or all topics in heading

Class union lists of legal material in 016.34

| .04 | *Cases |
|------|--------|

Do not use for casebooks; class with the subject in 342–347 without further subdivision

Class cases in a specific subject in law with the subject in 343–347, plus notation 0264 from table under 342–347, e.g., cases involving tax law 344.040264

---

> ### 348.041–348.043 Reports

Reports of cases contain a relatively full treatment of each case as well as the ultimate decision

Class comprehensive works in 348.04

| .041 | *National reports |
|------|-------------------|
| .042 | *Regional reports |
| .043 | *State and provincial reports |

Standard subdivisions are added for either or both topics in heading

| .044 | *Court decisions |
|------|------------------|

Texts of decisions with or without accompanying information

| .045 | *Decisions (Rulings) of regulatory agencies |
|------|---------------------------------------------|

---

> ### 348.046–348.048 Guides to cases

Class here combined guides to laws, regulations, cases

Class comprehensive works and guides in 348.046. Class guides to a specific set of court reports with the reports, e.g., a citator to U.S. Supreme Court reports 348.73413

*For guides to laws and regulations, see 348.026–348.028*

| .046 | *Digests of cases |
|------|-------------------|

Class here comprehensive guides to cases

*For citators to cases, see 348.047; for checklists, tables, indexes of cases, see 348.048*

---

*Do not use notation 0601 from Table 1 for a specific regional intergovernmental organization; class in 348.2. Do not use notation 0917 from Table 1 for socioeconomic regions; class in 348.1. Do not use notation 093–099 from Table 1 for specific continents, countries, localities; class in 348.3–348.9

.047        *Citators to cases

.048        *Checklists, tables, indexes of cases

> Standard subdivisions are added for any or all topics in heading

.05         *Advisory opinions of attorneys-general (ministers of justice)

**.1        Socioeconomic regions**

> Add to base number 348 the numbers following —17 in notation 171–177 from Table 2, e.g., laws, regulations, cases of developing countries 348.124; then to the result add as follows:
> 001–009    Standard subdivisions
> > Notation from Table 1 as modified under 348.001–348.009
> 01–05    Topics of laws, regulations, cases
> > Add the numbers following 348 in 348.01–348.05, e.g., selected laws of developing countries 348.124024

> Class socioeconomic regions of a specific regional intergovernmental organization in 348.2; class socioeconomic regions of a specific jurisdiction or area in 348.3–348.9

**.2        Regional intergovernmental organizations**

> Add to base number 348.2 notation 3–9 from Table 2, e.g., laws, regulations, cases of European Union 348.24; then to the result add as follows:
> 001–009    Standard subdivisions
> > Notation from Table 1 as modified under 348.001–348.009
> 01–05    Topics of laws, regulations, cases
> > Add the numbers following 348 in 348.01–348.05, e.g., selected laws of European Union 348.24024

> *See Manual at 342–349*

---

*Do not use notation 0601 from Table 1 for a specific regional intergovernmental organization; class in 348.2. Do not use notation 0917 from Table 1 for socioeconomic regions; class in 348.1. Do not use notation 093–099 from Table 1 for specific continents, countries, localities; class in 348.3–348.9

**.3–.9**      **Specific jurisdictions and areas**

Class here general collections of repealed laws

Add to base number 348 notation 3–9 from Table 2, e.g., laws, regulations, cases of Australia 348.94, of New South Wales 348.944, of African states 348.6; then to the result add as follows:

      001–009     Standard subdivisions

                     Notation from Table 1 as modified under 348.001–348.009

      01–05    Topics of laws, regulations, cases

                   Add the numbers following 348 in 348.01–348.05, e.g., selected laws of Australia 348.94024, of New South Wales 348.944024, of African states 348.6024

Class the legislative procedure involved in enacting or repealing a law in 328.37. Class repealed laws on a specific subject with the subject in 342–347, e.g., repeal of a prohibition on the sale and consumption of alcohol 344.0541

*For regional intergovernmental organizations, relationship between the organization's laws and national laws of all member states, see 348.2*

*See Manual at 342–349*

**A special development for the United States follows**

**.73**      Federal laws, regulations, cases of the United States

Including national and regional treatment of state and local laws, regulations, cases

*For laws, regulations, cases of specific states and localities, see 348.74–348.79*

**.730 4**      Codification

      Class proposed codes in 348.7323

**.731**      Preliminary materials

      Including bills; legislative hearings, histories; slip laws

**.732**      Federal laws and regulations

Standard subdivisions are added for federal laws and regulations together, for federal laws alone

Class here federal statutes

(If option under 348 is chosen, class here individual laws)

---

&gt;       348.732 2–348.732 4  Federal laws

Class guides to federal laws in 348.7326–348.7328; class comprehensive works in 348.732

**.732 2**      Federal laws in chronological order

**.732 3**      United States Code

**.732 4**      Selected Federal laws

| .732 5 | Federal regulations |
|---|---|

Class guides to federal regulations in 348.7326–348.7328

---

> 348.732 6–348.732 8 Guides to federal laws and regulations

Class comprehensive works and guides in 348.7326

| .732 6 | Digests of federal laws and regulations |
|---|---|

Standard subdivisions are added for either or both topics in heading

Including summaries of changes

Class here comprehensive guides to federal laws and regulations

*For citators to federal laws and regulations, see 348.7327; for checklists, tables, indexes of federal laws and regulations, see 348.7328*

| .732 7 | Citators to federal laws and regulations |
|---|---|

Standard subdivisions are added for either or both topics in heading

| .732 8 | Checklists, tables, indexes of federal laws and regulations |
|---|---|

Standard subdivisions are added for any or all topics in heading

| .734 | Federal cases |
|---|---|

Do not use for casebooks; class with the subject in 342–347 without further subdivision

---

> 348.734 1–348.734 2 Reports of federal cases

Class comprehensive works and reports in 348.734

| .734 1 | Federal court reports |
|---|---|
| .734 13 | Supreme Court |
| .734 15 | Lower Federal courts |
| .734 2 | National reporter system |
| .734 22 | Atlantic federal reporter system |
| .734 23 | Northeastern federal reporter system |
| .734 24 | Northwestern federal reporter system |
| .734 25 | Southeastern federal reporter system |
| .734 26 | Southwestern federal reporter system |
| .734 27 | Southern federal reporter system |
| .734 28 | Pacific federal reporter system |
| .734 4 | Court decisions |
| .734 5 | Decisions of regulatory agencies (Rulings of regulatory agencies) |

>        348.734 6–348.734 8   Guides to federal cases

       Class here combined guides to federal laws, regulations, cases

       Class comprehensive works and guides to federal cases in 348.7346

       *For guides to federal laws and regulations, see 348.7326–348.7328*

.734 6        Digests of federal cases

       Class here comprehensive guides to federal cases

       *For citators to federal cases, see 348.7347; for checklists, tables,*
       *indexes of federal cases, see 348.7348*

.734 7        Citators to federal cases

.734 8        Checklists, tables, indexes of federal cases

       Standard subdivisions are added for any or all topics in heading

.735        Advisory opinions of Attorney-General

.74–.79        Laws, regulations, cases of specific states and localities of the United States

       Add to base number 348 notation 74–79 from Table 2, e.g., laws, regulations, cases of Pennsylvania 348.748, of Philadelphia 348.74811; then to the result add the numbers following 348 in 348.001–348.05, e.g., Pennsylvania statutes 348.748022, Philadelphia code of ordinances 348.74811023

       Class national and regional treatment of state and local laws, regulations, cases in 348.73; class laws, regulations, cases of Hawaii in 348.969

## 349   Law of specific jurisdictions, areas, socioeconomic regions, regional intergovernmental organizations

       *For law of specific ancient jurisdictions, areas, socioeconomic regions, see 340.53; for specific branches of law of a specific jurisdiction, area, socioeconomic region, regional intergovernmental organization, see 342–347; for original materials on law of a specific jurisdiction, area, socioeconomic region, regional intergovernmental organization, see 348*

       *See Manual at 340.02–340.09 vs. 349; also at 342–349*

       (If option A under 342–349 is chosen, class here comparative law and law of jurisdictions other than the preferred jurisdiction by adding to base number 349 the numbers following 34 in 342–348, e.g., comparative criminal procedure 349.505, criminal procedure of New Zealand 349.59305. Assuming Australia to be the preferred jurisdiction, criminal procedure of Australia 345.05. Class comprehensive works on law of jurisdictions other than the preferred jurisdiction in 349.9)

**.1     Law of specific socioeconomic regions**

Add to base number 349.1 the numbers following —17 in notation 171–177 from Table 2, e.g., works on ordinances from developing countries 349.124; however, for Islamic law, see 340.59

Class socioeconomic regions of a specific regional intergovernmental organization in 349.2; class law of specific socioeconomic regions of a specific jurisdiction or area in 349.4–349.9

**.2     Law of regional intergovernmental organizations**

Add to base number 349.2 notation 3–9 from Table 2, e.g., works on the ordinances of European Union 349.24

Class comprehensive works on regional intergovernmental organizations themselves in 341.2

**.24     Regional intergovernmental organizations of Europe**

Number built according to instructions under 349.2

Class comprehensive works on effect of European Union laws on national laws of member states in 341.24224. Class effect of European Union laws on national laws of a specific member state with the laws of the member state, e.g., effect on laws of Italy 349.45

**.4–.9     Law of specific jurisdictions and areas in modern world**

Add to base number 349 notation 4–9 from Table 2, e.g., works on the ordinances of the City of Los Angeles 349.79494

*For regional intergovernmental organizations, see 349.2*

**.9     Law of other parts of world**

Number built according to instructions under 349.4–349.9

(If option A under 342–349 is chosen, class here law of specific jurisdictions, areas, socioeconomic regions, regional intergovernmental organizations

*(For law of specific ancient jurisdictions, areas, socioeconomic regions, see 340.53)*

**(.91)     Law of specific socioeconomic regions**

(Optional number; prefer 349.1)

(If option A under 342–349 is chosen, add to base number 349.91 the numbers following —17 in notation 171–177 from Table 2, e.g., works on ordinances from developing countries 349.9124; however, for Islamic law, see 340.59

(Class socioeconomic regions of a specific regional intergovernmental organization in 349.92; class law of specific socioeconomic regions of a specific jurisdiction or area in 349.94–349.99)

| | |
|---|---|
| (.92) | Law of regional intergovernmental organizations |

(Optional number; prefer 349.2)

(If option A under 342–349 is chosen, add to base number 349.92 notation 3–9 from Table 2, e.g., works on the ordinances of European Union 349.924)

| | |
|---|---|
| .93–.99 | Law of Australasia, Pacific Ocean islands, Atlantic Ocean islands, Arctic islands, Antarctica |

Number built according to instructions under 349.4–349.9

(If option A under 342–349 is chosen, class here law of specific jurisdictions and areas of modern world other than the preferred jurisdiction, adding to base number 349.9 notation 4–9 from Table 2, e.g., works on the ordinances of the City of Los Angeles 349.979494. Assuming Australia to be the preferred jurisdiction, works on the ordinances of Australia 342

*(For law of regional intergovernmental organizations, see 349.92)*

# 350    Public administration and military science

## SUMMARY

| | |
|---|---|
| **351** | **Public administration** |
| **.01–.09** | **Standard subdivisions** |
| **.1** | **Administration in areas, regions, places in general** |
| **.3–.9** | **Administration in specific continents, countries, localities** |
| | |
| **352** | **General considerations of public administration** |
| **.1** | **Jurisdictional levels of administration** |
| **.2** | **Organization of administration** |
| **.3** | **Executive management** |
| **.4** | **Financial administration and budgets** |
| **.5** | **Property administration and related topics** |
| **.6** | **Personnel management (Human resource management)** |
| **.7** | **Public administration of general forms of assistance** |
| **.8** | **Public administration of general forms of control** |
| | |
| **353** | **Specific fields of public administration** |
| **.1** | **Public administration of external and national security affairs** |
| **.3** | **Public administration of services related to domestic order** |
| **.4** | **Public administration of justice** |
| **.5** | **Public administration of social welfare** |
| **.6** | **Public administration of health services** |
| **.7** | **Public administration of culture and related activities** |
| **.8** | **Public administration of agencies supporting and controlling education** |
| **.9** | **Public administration of safety, sanitation, waste control** |
| | |
| **354** | **Public administration of economy and environment** |
| **.08** | **Groups of people** |
| **.2** | **General considerations of public administration** |
| **.3** | **Public administration of environment and natural resources** |
| **.4** | **Public administration of energy and energy-related industries** |
| **.5** | **Public administration of agriculture** |
| **.6** | **Public administration of construction, manufacturing, service industries** |
| **.7** | **Public administration of commerce, communications, transportation** |
| **.8** | **Public administration of financial institutions, money, credit** |
| **.9** | **Public administration of labor and professions** |

# 351     Public administration

Class here executive branch of government, programs administered by executive branch, civil service in the sense of all units of public administration outside armed services

Class relation of executive branch to other branches, works that deal comprehensively with more than one branch of government in 320.404; class civil service in the sense of merit system in 352.63; class interdisciplinary works on management in 658. Class management of government-owned enterprises operating a service with the service, plus notation 068 from Table 1, e.g., management of public hospitals 362.11068, of nationalized railroads 385.068

> *For administration of legislative branch, see 328.068; for administration of judicial branch, see 347.013; for specific topics of public administration, see 352–354*

> *See Manual at T1—068 vs. 353–354; also at 320.9, 320.4 vs. 351; also at 351 vs. 352.29*

### SUMMARY

.025       Directories of persons and organizations

> Class directories of elected public officials in 324.025

.05       Serial publications

> Class here official gazettes, serial administrative reports of governmental organizations

.06       Nongovernmental organizations

> Do not use for governmental organizations; class in 351. Do not use for serial administrative reports of governmental organizations; class in 351.05
>
> *See Manual at T1—0601–T1—0609*

[.068]       Management

> Do not use; class in 351

.07       Education, research, related topics

.076       Review and exercise

> Class here interdisciplinary works on civil service examinations
>
> *For civil service examinations in a specific subject, see the subject, plus notation 076 from Table 1, e.g., examinations in accounting 657.076*
>
> (Option: Class here civil service examinations in specific subjects; prefer the subject in 001–999, plus notation 076 from Table 1. If option is chosen, add to base number 351.076 notation 001–999, e.g., civil service examinations in accounting 351.076657)

.08       Groups of people

> Do not use for programs directed to groups of people; class in 353.53

.09       History and biography

[.091]       Areas, regions, places in general

> Do not use; class in 351.1

[.093–.099]       Specific continents, countries, localities

> Do not use; class in 351.3–351.9

**.1       Administration in areas, regions, places in general**

> Not limited by continent, country, locality
>
> Add to base number 351.1 the numbers following 1 in notation 11–19 from Table 2, e.g., administration in developing regions 351.1724; however, for urban administration, see 352.16; for rural administration, see 352.17

**.3–.9**     **Administration in specific continents, countries, localities**

Class here administration of specific jurisdictions, practical works on administration of specific subordinate jurisdictions, e.g., specific provinces

Add to base number 351 notation 3–9 from Table 2, e.g., public administration in Germany 351.43

Class theoretical works on specific kinds of subordinate jurisdictions in 352.13–352.19

*See Manual at 351.3–351.9 vs. 352.13–352.19*

(Option A: Class here treatment of specific topics of public administration in specific continents, countries, localities; prefer 352–354, plus notation 09 from table under 352–354. If option is chosen, add to each geographic subdivision as follows:

| | |
|---|---|
| 001–007 | Standard subdivisions |
| | Notation from Table 1 as modified under 351, e.g., serial administrative reports 005 |
| 008 | Groups of people |
| | Class programs directed to groups of people in 0353 |
| 009 | History, geographic treatment, biography |
| | Use for geographic treatment only when area of interest is narrower than area of jurisdiction, e.g., United States federal administration in Gulf Coast states 351.7300976 |
| 02–04 | Specific topics of public administration |
| | Add to 0 the numbers following 35 in 352–354, e.g., social welfare administration 035, programs directed to groups of people 0353 |

(Option B: Class here treatment of specific topics of public administration in specific continents, countries, localities not requiring local emphasis; prefer 352–354, plus notation 09 from table under 352–354. If option B is chosen, add to each geographic subdivision as instructed under option A)

> ## 352–354 Specific topics of public administration

Class here public administration of specific departments and agencies

Except for modifications shown under specific entries, add to each subdivision identified by * as follows:

01–07    Standard subdivisions
        Notation from Table 1 as modified under 351, e.g., serial administrative reports 05

08      Groups of people
        Class here programs directed to groups of people; equal opportunity programs

09      History, geographic treatment, biography

093–099    Specific continents, countries, localities
        (Option A: Class treatment of specific topics of public administration by specific continents, countries, localities in 351.3–351.9)
        (Option B: In order to provide local emphasis and shorter notation, class specific topics of public administration treated in jurisdictions requiring local emphasis in 352–354 without adding notation 09 from this table, and class specific topics of public administration in specific continents, countries, localities not requiring local emphasis in 351.3–351.9)

2       General considerations of public administration

21      Jurisdictional levels

2101–2109    Standard subdivisions
        Add to 210 the numbers following 352.10 in 352.101–352.109, e.g., nongovernmental organizations 2106

211–219    Specific jurisdictional levels
        Add to 21 the numbers following 352.1 in 352.11–352.19, e.g., international administration 211
        Class administration at national level, combined treatment of national and other levels (*except* works that emphasize differences between administration at different levels) in base number without use of notation 21

22–26    Specific topics in management
        Add to 2 the numbers following 352 in 352.2–352.6, e.g., governing boards and commissions 225, contracts and procurement 253; however; planning and policy making of a specific subject relocated from 234 to the subject outside 354, e.g., government policy on arts 700

27–28    Public administration of supporting and controlling functions of government
        Do not use when redundant
        Add to 2 the numbers following 352 in 352.7–352.8, e.g., promoting and disseminating knowledge 274, regulation 28

Unless other instructions are given, class a subject with aspects in two or more subdivisions of 352–354 in the number coming last, e.g., chief executive of a department of agriculture 354.52293 (*not* 352.293)

Class misconduct in office regardless of topic in 353.46; class comprehensive works in 351

*See Manual at 352–354; also at 300–330, 355–390 vs. 342–347, 352–354; also at 300, 320.6 vs. 352–354*

# 352     General considerations of public administration

Class here general considerations of public administration applying to two or more branches of government, e.g., financial administration of the legislative and judicial branches 352.4

Class general considerations of public administration applied to a specific field with the field in public administration, plus notation 2 from table under 352–354, e.g., local safety administration 353.9214

*See Manual at 352–354*

## SUMMARY

| | |
|---|---|
| 352.1 | Jurisdictional levels of administration |
| .2 | Organization of administration |
| .3 | Executive management |
| .4 | Financial administration and budgets |
| .5 | Property administration and related topics |
| .6 | Personnel management (Human resource management) |
| .7 | Public administration of general forms of assistance |
| .8 | Public administration of general forms of control |

[.01–.09]     Standard subdivisions

Do not use; class in 351.01–351.09

## .1     Jurisdictional levels of administration

Class programs directed to specific groups of people at specific levels of administration in 353.5321. Class a specific topic in administrative management, support, control at a specific jurisdictional level of administration with the topic in 352.2–352.8, plus notation 21 from table under 352–354, e.g., financial administration and budgets of international agencies 352.4211, regulation by local government 352.8214

Use 351 for combined treatment of national and other levels of administration except for works that emphasize differences between administration at different levels

*For administration at national level, see 351*

### SUMMARY

| | |
|---|---|
| 352.101–.109 | Standard subdivisions |
| .11 | International administration |
| .13 | State and provincial administration |
| .14 | Local administration |
| .15 | Intermediate units of local administration |
| .16 | Urban administration |
| .17 | Rural administration |
| .19 | Administration of special service districts |

### .105     Serial publications

Class here official gazettes, serial administrative reports of governmental organizations

| .106 | Nongovernmental organizations |
|---|---|

Do not use for governmental organizations; class in 352.1. Do not use for serial administrative reports of governmental organizations; class in 352.105

| [.106 8] | Management |
|---|---|

Do not use; class in 352.1

| .108 | Groups of people |
|---|---|

Do not use for programs at specific levels of administration directed toward groups of people; class in 353.5321

| .11 | International administration |
|---|---|

Class here administration of intergovernmental organizations

Class interdisciplinary works on intergovernmental organizations in 341.2

| .110 5 | Serial publications |
|---|---|

Class here official gazettes, serial administrative reports of government organizations

| .110 6 | Nongovernmental organizations |
|---|---|

Do not use for governmental organizations; class in 352.11. Do not use for serial administrative reports of governmental organizations; class in 352.1105

| [.110 68] | Management |
|---|---|

Do not use; class in 352.11

| .110 8 | Groups of people |
|---|---|

Do not use for international programs directed to groups of people; class in 353.53211

| .110 9 | History, geographic treatment, biography |
|---|---|

| [.110 94–.110 99] | Specific continents, countries, localities in modern world |
|---|---|

Do not use; class in 352.114–352.119

| .112 | League of Nations |
|---|---|
| .113 | United Nations |

Class here secretariat

Class interdisciplinary works on United Nations in 341.23

| .114–.119 | International administration in specific continents and parts of continents |
|---|---|

Class here administration of international organizations serving continents and parts of continents

Add to base number 352.11 notation 4–9 from Table 2, e.g., international administration in southeast Asia 352.1159, Organization of American States 352.117

> 352.13–352.19 Administration of subordinate jurisdictions

Except for modifications shown under specific entries, add to each subdivision
identified by † as follows:
01–07    Standard subdivisions
         Notation from Table 1 as modified under 351, e.g., serial
         administrative reports 05
08       Groups of people
         Do not use for programs directed to groups of people; class in
         353.53213
09       History, geographic treatment, biography
093–099  Specific continents, countries, localities
         Limited to comprehensive, theoretical, comparative
         treatment, e.g. administration of Länder in Germany
         352.130943
         Class administration of or in a specific subordinate
         jurisdiction with the jurisdiction in 351.3–351.9 (*not*
         093–099), e.g., administration of Bavaria 351.433
              *See Manual at 351.3–351.9 vs. 352.13–352.19*
3        Administrative cooperation among subordinate jurisdictions
         Class here administrative relations among subordinate jurisdictions
         that do not involve support and control by a higher jurisdiction,
         e.g., relations among coordinate city and county governments
         Class comprehensive works on administrative cooperation among
         subordinate jurisdictions in 352.143
              *See also 353.33 for support and control of subordinate*
              *jurisdictions by higher jurisdictions*
301–308  Standard subdivisions
         Notation from Table 1 as modified under 351, e.g., serial
         administrative reports 305
309      History, geographic treatment, biography

Class comprehensive works on administration of subordinate jurisdictions in
352.14. Class administration of or in a specific subordinate jurisdiction with the
jurisdiction in 351.3–351.9, e.g., administration of Bavaria 351.433

*See Manual at 351.3 351.9 vs. 352.13–352.19*

.13      †State and provincial administration

States and provinces: regularly constituted territorial subdivisions of
large countries, with responsibilities cutting across several fields of
administration, and usually encompassing many local units

Subdivisions are added for either or both topics in heading

*See Manual at 352.13 vs. 352.15*

†Add as instructed under 352.13–352.19

.14          †Local administration

Limited to comprehensive and comparative treatment, e.g., local administration in Germany 352.140943

Class here comprehensive works on administration of subordinate jurisdictions

Class local government, combined treatment of local government and local administration in 320.8; class regional divisions of administrative agencies in 352.288. Class administration in or of a specific subordinate jurisdiction with the jurisdiction in 351.3–351.9, e.g., administration of Nuremberg 351.43324

*For state and provincial administration, see 352.13; for administration of specific kinds of local jurisdictions, see 352.15–352.19; for support and control of subordinate jurisdictions by higher jurisdictions, see 353.33*

*See Manual at 351.3–351.9 vs. 352.13–352.19*

---

>            352.15–352.19  Administration of specific kinds of local jurisdictions

Class comprehensive works in 352.14

.15          †Intermediate units of local administration

Intermediate units: regularly constituted relatively local territorial subdivisions, with responsibilities cutting across several fields of administration, and usually containing few component units

Class here arrondissements, counties, shires, territorial departments; provinces of small countries

*See Manual at 352.13 vs. 352.15*

.16          †Urban administration

Class here city administration

*See also 354.2793 for public administration of urban development*

.167         †Administration of metropolitan regions

.169         †Suburban administration

.17          †Rural administration

*See also 354.2794 for public administration of rural development*

.19          †Administration of special service districts

Local districts or authorities established to provide one or a few services

Class regional divisions of state and national agencies in 352.288. Class administration of specific kinds of special service districts with the service they administer, e.g., metropolitan districts to coordinate administration of health services 353.6219, local rail transit authorities that operate trains 388.42065

†Add as instructed under 352.13–352.19

.193        Administrative cooperation among jurisdictions served by special
            service districts

            Number built according to instructions under 352.13–352.19

            Class here control of special service districts by higher jurisdictions and
            by other local authorities

> **352.2–352.6  Specific topics of management in public administration**

Except for modifications shown under specific entries, add to each subdivision
identified by ‡ as follows:

01–09    Standard subdivisions
              Add to 0 the numbers following 0 in notation 01–09 from table
              under 352–354, e.g., programs directed to groups of people 08
2        General considerations of public administration
21           Jurisdictional levels
2101–2109    Standard subdivisions
              Add to 210 the numbers following 352.10 in
              352.101–352.109, e.g., nongovernmental organizations
              2106
211–219    Specific jurisdictional levels
              Add to 21 the numbers following 352.1 in 352.11–352.19,
              e.g., international administration 211
              Class administration at national level, combined treatment
              of national and other levels (*except* works that emphasize
              differences between administration at different levels) in base
              number without use of notation 21
22–26    Specific topics in management
              Add to 2 the numbers following 352 in 352.2–352.6, e.g.,
              governing boards and commissions 225, planning and policy
              making 234, contracts and procurement 253

Class comprehensive works on administrative aspects in 351; class
interdisciplinary works on management, on specific topics of management in
658

.2    **‡Organization of administration**

Class comprehensive works on executive management in public administration
in 352.3; class interdisciplinary works on organization in management in 658.1

### SUMMARY

| | |
|---|---|
| 352.23 | **Chief executives** |
| .24 | **Cabinets and cabinet-level committees** |
| .25 | **Governing boards and commissions** |
| .26 | **Special kinds of agencies** |
| .28 | **Internal organization** |
| .29 | **Organization and structure of departments and agencies** |

‡Add as instructed under 352.2–352.6

.23 ‡Chief executives

Class here presidents, prime ministers, monarchs; comprehensive works on heads of state

Class governing boards and commissions in 352.25

*For heads of departments and agencies, see 352.293. For a specific aspect of heads of state, see the aspect, e.g., presidential government 321.8042*

.230 92 Biography

Do not use for collected biographies of chief executives; class in 930–990 plus notation 0099 from table under 930–990, e.g., collected biography of kings and queens of Great Britain 941.0099. Do not use for individual biographies of chief executive; class in 930–990 plus notation 01–09 for the period of the person's administration from table under 930–990, plus notation 092 from Table 1, e.g., biography of Queen Elizabeth of England 942.055092

Class here biography of chief executives as administrators

*See Manual at T1—092: Comprehensive biography: Public figures; also at 920.009, 920.03–920.09 vs. 909.09, 909.1–909.8, 930–990*

.233 ‡Heads of state lacking administrative powers

Presidents in countries where prime ministers are head of administration; constitutional monarchs and their representatives, e.g., governors-general in Commonwealth of Nations countries

.233 092 Biography

Do not use for collected biographies of heads of states lacking administrative powers; class in 930–990 plus notation 0099 from table under 930–990, e.g., collected biography of constitutional monarchs of Great Britain 941.0099. Do not use for individual biographies of heads of states lacking administrative powers; class in 930–990 plus notation 01–09 for the period of the person's administration from table under 930–990, plus notation 092 from Table 1, e.g., biography of Queen Elizabeth of Great Britain 941.085092

*See Manual at T1—092: Comprehensive biography: Public figures; also at 920.009, 920.03–920.09 vs. 909.09, 909.1–909.8, 930–990*

.235 ‡Powers and privileges of chief executives

Class abuse of power in 353.46

.236 ‡Leadership role of chief executives

.237 ‡Office of chief executive

‡Add as instructed under 352.2–352.6

| .237 229 3 | Heads and deputy heads of office of chief executive |
|---|---|

Number built according to instructions under 352–354

Class here chief of staff to chief executive

.238          ‡Executive messages, speeches, writings

Collections, history, description, criticism

*For messages, speeches, writings on a specific subject, see
the subject, e.g., budget messages of specific jurisdictions
352.493–352.499, messages on German budget 352.4943013,
executive messages on economics 330, executive messages on
economy of Germany 330.943*

.238 4          ‡Addresses to legislatures

.238 6          ‡Inaugural addresses

.239          ‡Deputy chief executives

.239 092          Biography

Do not use for collected biographies of deputy chief
executives; class in 930–990 plus notation 0099 from table
under 930–990, e.g., collected biography of deputy prime
ministers of Australia 994.0099. Do not use for individual
biographies of deputy chief executives; class in 930–990 plus
notation 01–09 for the period of the person's administration
from table under 930–990, plus notation 092 from Table 1, e.g.,
biography of Deputy Prime Minister Tim Fischer of Australia
994.066092

Class here biographies of deputy chief executives as
administrators

*See Manual at T1—092: Comprehensive biography:
Public figures; also at 920.009, 920.03–920.09 vs. 909.09,
909.1–909.8, 930–990*

.24          ‡Cabinets and cabinet-level committees

Class here councils of ministers, executive councils

Subdivisions are added for either or both topics in heading

*For a cabinet-level committee charged with a specific activity, see the
activity, plus notation 224 from table under 352–354, e.g., cabinet
councils on the economy 354.224*

.243          ‡Cabinet secretariats

.243 229 3          Heads and deputy heads of cabinet secretariats

Number built according to instructions under 352–354

Class here cabinet secretaries, ministers with a portfolio of
cabinet affairs

.246          ‡Domestic councils

‡Add as instructed under 352.2–352.6

.25            ‡Governing boards and commissions

> Multimember bodies (other than cabinets and cabinet-level committees) selecting executives and or participating in executive decisions

> Subdivisions are added for either or both topics in heading

> Class a specific board or commission with the topic it administers, plus notation 09 (*not* 225) from table under 352–354, e.g., United States National Labor Relations Board 354.970973 (*not* 354.972250973)

>> *For regulatory boards and commissions, see 352.8*

>> *See also 352.743 for advisory bodies*

.26            ‡Special kinds of agencies

>> *For a special kind of agency not provided for here, see the kind, e.g., cabinets 352.24*

.264           ‡Independent agencies

> Agencies that are not parts of larger (cabinet-level) departments

> Avoid using notation 2264 from table under 352–354 for specific independent agencies, e.g., independent regulatory agencies 352.8 (*not* 352.82264)

> Class autonomous authorities of local scope in 352.19

.266           ‡Government corporations (Public enterprises)

> Class interdisciplinary works on government corporations in 338.749

.28            ‡Internal organization

> Class here levels of management

>> *For supervision, see 352.66*

.283           ‡Distribution and delegation of authority

> Including centralization, decentralization

> Class here line and staff organization

> Subdivisions are added for either or both topics in heading

>> *For regional divisions of administrative departments, see 352.288*

.284           ‡Middle management

.285           ‡Top management

.288           ‡Regional divisions of administrative agencies

> Class here field offices, regional offices

‡Add as instructed under 352.2–352.6

.29 ‡Organization and structure of departments and agencies

Limited to generalities of organization and structure

Subdivisions are added for either or both topics in heading

Class description and purposes of departments and agencies in general in 351. Class organization and structure of a specific kind of department or agency with the kind, plus notation 22 (*not* 229) from table under 352–354, e.g., structure of governing boards 352.2522, structure of governing boards in Germany 352.25220943

*See Manual at 351 vs. 352.29; also at 352–354*

.293 ‡Heads and deputy heads of departments and agencies

Class here cabinet officers, ministers of state, secretaries of state

Class cabinet secretaries, ministers with a portfolio of cabinet affairs in 352.2432293; class secretaries of state of specific states of United States in 352.3870974–352.3870979; class secretaries of state for foreign affairs in 353.132293; class prime ministers, comprehensive works on chief executives in 352.23

*See also 352.39 for executive development*

*See Manual at 352–354*

.3 ‡**Executive management**

Class here interdisciplinary works on public administrators

Class interdisciplinary works on executive management in 658.4

*For internal organization, see 352.28. For a specific aspect of public administrators, see the aspect, e.g., biography 351.092, law 342.068*

.33 ‡Decision making

Class specific means of obtaining guidance for decision making in 352.37

.34 ‡Planning and policy making

Subdivisions are added for either or both topics in heading

Class specific means of obtaining guidance for planning and policy making in 352.37

*See Manual at 300, 320.6 vs. 352–354*

.35 ‡Internal control

Including internal inspection, agency ombudsmen

Class here accountability in public administration, administrative responsibility, oversight

Class legislative oversight in 328.3456; class administration of control of society by government in 352.8

*For oversight by outside agencies, see 352.88*

‡Add as instructed under 352.2–352.6

| .357 | ‡Quality control |
|---|---|

Class quality control by managerial accounting in 352.43

| .36 | ‡Objectives of administration |
|---|---|

Class here management by objective (MBO)

Class means of obtaining objectives in 352.37

| .365 | ‡Project management |
|---|---|
| .367 | ‡Managing change |

Class here modernization

| .37 | ‡Means of obtaining objectives |
|---|---|

Class here specific means of obtaining guidance for policy and decision making

Class comprehensive works on decision making in 352.33; class comprehensive works on policy in 352.34; class management by objectives in 352.36

*For use of information, see 352.38; for fact-finding and advisory bodies, see 352.743*

| .373 | ‡Use of consultants |
|---|---|
| .375 | ‡Promotion of efficiency |
| .379 | ‡Intelligence and security |

Including computer and office security, security classification

Class military security classification in 355.3433

*See also 353.1 for administration of external and national security*

| .38 | ‡Information management |
|---|---|

Class fact-finding and advisory bodies in 352.743

| .384 | ‡Communication in management |
|---|---|
| .387 | ‡Records management |

Class here maintaining official records

Class archival treatment of public records in 025.1714; class secretaries of state in specific states of United States in 352.3870974–352.3870979; class programs supporting archives in 352.744

*See Manual at 352–354*

| .39 | ‡Managing executive personnel |
|---|---|

Class here executive development, leadership, management environment

*For leadership role of chief executive, see 352.236; for specific aspects of managing of executive personnel, see 352.6*

‡Add as instructed under 352.2–352.6

**.4**      ‡**Financial administration and budgets**

Class here management of public finance; treasury departments and ministries; works covering both government financial administration and administration of financial institutions, money, credit

Subdivisions are added for financial administration and budgets together, for financial administration alone

Class interdisciplinary works on public finance in 336; class interdisciplinary works on financial management in 658.15

> *For administration of financial institutions, money, credit, see 354.8*

> *See also 332.46 for monetary policy; also 336.3 for fiscal policy*

.43      ‡Financial control

Class here managerial accounting (financial and nonfinancial); agencies that perform management, performance, program auditing, e.g., general accounting offices

Class ordinary accounting of government agencies in 657.835

.439      ‡Management, performance, program audits

Internal or external audits or comparable reviews to evaluate efficiency, conformance to policies and standards, and effectiveness of expenditures of funds or other administrative activities

Class here reports of general accounting offices

Subdivisions are added for any or all topics in heading

Class financial auditing of government agencies in 657.835045

.44      ‡Revenue administration

Class here tax administration, tax collection

> *See also 353.43 for tax litigation*

> *See Manual at 343.04–343.06 vs. 336.2, 352.44*

.448      ‡Customs administration

.45      ‡Debt management

.46      ‡Public expenditures

> *For payroll administration, see 352.47; for contracts, see 352.53; for financial assistance, see 352.73*

.47      ‡Payroll administration

> *See also 352.67 for wage and salary scales of government workers; also 354.98 for wages and salaries of labor and professions*

‡Add as instructed under 352.2–352.6

.48      ‡Budgeting

Including adoption of budgets, budget messages; specific kinds of budgets, e.g., capital, estimated, legislative budgets

Class here comprehensive works on budgets

*For procedures for legislative enactment of budgets, see 328.378; for budgets of specific international organizations and specific jurisdictions, see 352.49*

.49      Budgets for specific international organizations and specific jurisdictions

Class comprehensive works on budgets in 352.48

[.490 1–.490 9]      Standard subdivisions

Do not use; class in 352.4801–352.4809

.491      Budgets for specific international organizations

Add to base number 352.491 the numbers following 352.11 in 352.112–352.119, e.g., budgets for United Nations 352.4913; then add further as instructed under 352.493–352.499, e.g., proposed budgets for United Nations 352.491301

‡Add as instructed under 352.2–352.6

.493–.499     Budgets for specific jurisdictions

> Add to base number 352.49 notation 3–9 from Table 2, e.g., a budget of Germany 352.4943; then add further as follows:

     001–007    Standard subdivisions

> > Notation from Table 1 as modified under 351, e.g., official serial reports on budgets 005

     008–009    Standard subdivisions

     >01–03    Comprehensive budgets in specific stages of adoption

> > Class here operating budgets
> >
> > Class partial budgets in specific stages of adoption in 04–08; class comprehensive works in 352.493–352.499 without use of notation from this table

     01    Proposed budgets

> > Class here estimated budgets, executive budgets, budget requests from recipient agencies
> >
> > *For budgets in legislative process, see 02*

     013    Executive budget messages and supporting documents

     02    Budgets in legislative process

> > Class here legislative budgets, legislative authorizations

     023    Legislative hearings and reports on budgets

> > Hearings that concentrate on the objectives that a budget is to achieve are usually classed with the subject outside public administration, e.g., a hearing on the prospect that a budget will help achieve economic stabilization and growth 339.522
> >
> > *See Manual at 300–330, 355–390 vs. 342–347, 352–354*

     03    Adopted budgets

     >04–08    Partial budgets

> > Class comprehensive works in 352.493–352.499 without use of notation from this table. Class budgets for a specific jurisdiction limited to a specific subject with the subject, plus notation 249 from table under 352–354, e.g., agricultural budgets in specific jurisdictions 354.5249, agricultural budgets for Germany 354.524943
> >
> > *For operating budgets, see 01–03*

     04    Revenue budgets

     05    Capital budgets

     08    Supplemental budgets

> Class works on budgeting, on budgets in general in 352.48

.5     ‡**Property administration and related topics**

> Class here general services agencies

> Subdivisions are added for property administration and related topics together, for property administration alone

> Class records management in 352.387

‡Add as instructed under 352.2–352.6

.53 ‡Contracts and procurement

> Class here procurement of property, comprehensive works on public contracts

> Subdivisions are added for either or both topics in heading

>> *For procurement of specific forms of property, see 352.55–352.57. For public contracts not related to property, see the subject, plus notation 253 from table under 352–354, e.g., personnel contracts 352.65253*

.538 ‡Contracting for services

> Class here contracting out

> Class use of consultants in 352.373

.54 ‡Maintenance, utilization, disposal of property

> Including inventory

>> *For maintenance, utilization, disposal of specific forms of property, see 352.55–352.57*

.55 *Equipment and supplies

> Subdivisions are added for either or both topics in heading

> Class interdisciplinary works on supply management in 658.7

.553 *Contracts and procurement

> Subdivisions are added for either or both topics in heading

.554 *Maintenance, utilization, disposal

.56 *Buildings and their utilities

> Class here plant management

> Subdivisions are added for buildings and their utilities, for buildings alone

> Class interdisciplinary works on plant management in 658.2

>> *For public land management, see 352.57*

.563 *Contracts and procurement

> Subdivisions are added for either or both topics in heading

.564 *Maintenance, utilization, disposal

.57 *Public lands

> Class comprehensive works on land resources in 354.34

.573 *Contracts and procurement

> Subdivisions are added for either or both topics in heading

.574 *Maintenance, utilization, disposal

*Add as instructed under 352–354
‡Add as instructed under 352.2–352.6

.6 ‡**Personnel management (Human resource management)**

> Use subdivisions of 352.6 for specific aspects of management of executive personnel
>
> Class contracting out in 352.538; class interdisciplinary works on personnel management in 658.3
>
> *For general management of executive personnel, see 352.39*

.602 5 Directories of people and organizations in personnel management

> Class directories of public officials and employees in 351.025

.608 Groups of people

> Class here equal employment opportunity programs for government employees
>
> Class comprehensive works on equal employment opportunity programs in 354.908

.63 ‡Civil service system

> Government service in which appointments are determined by merit and examination rather than by political patronage
>
> Including management of office workers
>
> Class here government service, merit system, interdisciplinary works on government workers
>
> Class civil service in the sense of all units of public administration other than armed services in 351; class civil service examinations in 351.076
>
> *For a specific aspect of government service and government workers, see the aspect, e.g., labor economics 331.795, wage and salary scales 352.67*

.64 ‡Job description

> Including job analysis and classification

.65 ‡Recruiting and selection

.650 8 Groups of people

> Class here preferential hiring

.66 ‡Utilization and training

> Including discipline, evaluation, motivation, placement, supervision; absenteeism, turnover
>
> Subdivisions are added for utilization and training, for utilization alone

.669 ‡Training

‡Add as instructed under 352.2–352.6

.67      ‡Conditions of employment

Including fringe benefits, e.g., counseling, health services; hours of work, work environment

Class here compensation

Class payroll administration in 352.47; class public administration of pensions for government workers in 353.549; class comprehensive works on conditions of employment for all workers in 354.98

*For training, see 352.669*

.68      ‡Employer-employee relationships

Including labor unions and collective bargaining, other employee organizations, employee participation in management, grievances

Class comprehensive works on grievances against government in 352.885; class comprehensive works on labor unions and collective bargaining for all workers in 354.97

.69      ‡Separation from service

Including dismissal, layoffs, reduction in force, retirement

Class public administration of pensions for government workers in 353.549

---

>      **352.7–352.8 Public administration of supporting and controlling functions of government**

Class comprehensive works in 351. Class public administration of support and control of a specific topic of management with the topic, plus notation 27–28 from add table under 352–354, e.g., support for commerce and trade 354.7327, advisory bodies in commerce and trade 354.732743

.7      *****Public administration of general forms of assistance**

Class here the promotional and supporting role of administration when considered apart from its restraining and limiting role; administration of research and development in noneconomic fields

Class comprehensive works on public administration of research and development in 354.27

*See also 352.8 for the restraining and limiting role of administration*

### SUMMARY

| | |
|---|---|
| 352.73 | **Financial assistance** |
| .74 | **Promoting and disseminating knowledge** |
| .75 | **Census and surveys** |
| .76 | **Promoting museums and exhibitions** |
| .77 | **Public works** |
| .78 | **Sponsorship of volunteers and public service activities** |
| .79 | **Assistance to urban, suburban, rural areas** |

---

*Add as instructed under 352–354
‡Add as instructed under 352.2–352.6

.73         *Financial assistance

Financial assistance to subordinate jurisdictions or to private parties

Class here grants, grants-in-aid, revenue sharing

Class comprehensive works on support and control of subordinate jurisdictions in 353.33

*For price supports, see 352.85*

.734         Financial support for specific kinds of subordinate jurisdictions

Add to base number 352.734 the numbers following 352.1 in 352.13–352.19, e.g., grants to states and provinces 352.7343, grants to local governments from either national governments or states and provinces 352.7344

.736         *Loans and loan guarantees

Subdivisions are added for either or both topics in heading

.74         *Promoting and disseminating knowledge

Class here promoting research

Subdivisions are added for either or both topics in heading

Class governmental publishers in 070.595

*For census and surveys, see 352.75; for promoting museums and exhibitions, see 352.76; for public administration of agencies supporting and controlling education, see 353.8*

.743         *Fact-finding and advisory bodies

Bodies advising the government or the public

Temporary and permanent

Class here counseling bodies, royal commissions

Subdivisions are added for either or both topics in heading

*See also 352.25 for governing boards and commissions*

.744         *Promoting libraries and historical research

Class here programs supporting archives

Subdivisions are added for either or both topics in heading

Class library administration in 025.1; class archives administration in 025 1714; class records management in 352.387

*For public administration of agencies supporting public libraries, see 353.73*

*Add as instructed under 352–354

.745        *Promoting general fields of knowledge

Including natural sciences, social and behavioral sciences, technology; specific field of knowledge not provided for elsewhere, e.g., physics, space

Class here promoting experimental research

Class promoting museums and exhibitions in 352.76. Class promoting a specific field of knowledge provided for elsewhere with the field in public administration, plus notation 274 (*not* 2745) from table under 352–354 if not redundant, e.g., promoting environmental knowledge by an environmental protection agency 354.328274, but promoting public libraries 353.73 (*not* 353.73274)

*For promoting arts and humanities, see 353.77*

*See also 338.926–338.927 for science policy, policies to promote economic development through use of science and technology; also 355.07 for military research and development*

*See Manual at 338.926 vs. 352.745, 500*

.746        *Consumer information programs

Class here consumer protection

Class interdisciplinary works on consumer information in 381.33; class interdisciplinary works on consumer protection in 381.34

*For a specific aspect of consumer protection, see the aspect, e.g., price and cost controls 352.85*

.748        *Publicity activities

Publicity for government's own activities

Class here public relations

Class interdisciplinary works on public relations in 659.2

.749        *Protecting intellectual property

Regardless of subject or field

Including copyright, patents, trademarks

.75         *Census and surveys

Class here public administration of descriptive research

Subdivisions are added for either or both topics in heading

*Add as instructed under 352–354

.76      *Promoting museums and exhibitions

> Class here government participation in fairs and expositions
>
> Subdivisions are added for either or both topics in heading
>
> Class comprehensive works on public administration of culture and related activities in 353.7
>
> *See also 069 for government policy on museums*

.77      *Public works

> *For a specific program of public works, see the program, e.g., transportation public works 354.76277*

.78      *Sponsorship of volunteers and public service activities

> Subdivisions are added for either or both topics in heading

.79      *Assistance to urban, suburban, rural areas

> Class specific form of assistance to urban and rural areas in 352.73–352.78; class comprehensive works on public administration of urban and rural development in 354.279
>
> *See also 352.7091724 for assistance to underdeveloped areas*

.793      *Urban and suburban areas

> Including community planning
>
> Subdivisions are added for either or both topics in heading
>
> Class community planning for rural areas in 352.794; class community action programs in 353.52793; class comprehensive works on public administration of community development in 354.2793
>
> > *See also 353.5333 for programs directed to residents of disadvantaged urban areas*

.794      *Rural areas

> *See also 353.5334 for programs directed to residents of rural areas*

## .8      *Public administration of general forms of control

> Class here the restraining and limiting role of administration when considered apart from its promotional and supporting role; regulation, regulatory agencies, quasi-judicial agencies
>
> Class internal control of administrative activities in 352.35; class watchdog agencies in 352.88
>
> *See also 352.7 for promotional and supporting role of administration*

.83      *Setting standards

> Class here inspection, establishing weights and measures
>
> Class inspection as a form of internal control in 352.35

*Add as instructed under 352–354

.84        \*Licensing, accreditation, certification, chartering, registration; incorporation

> Class here interdisciplinary works on licensing, accreditation, certification, chartering, registration

> Subdivisions are added for any or all topics in heading

> Class interdisciplinary works on incorporation in 346.06622

>> *For licensing, accreditation, certification, chartering by nongovernmental organizations, see 060*

.85        \*Price and cost controls

> Class here price supports

> Subdivisions are added for either or both topics in heading

.86        \*Rationing

> Class here allocation

.88        \*Use of watchdog and oversight agencies

> Including ethics agencies

> Class here promotion of procedural rights, agencies providing checks and balances to administrative operations, interdisciplinary works on ombudsmen

> Subdivisions are added for either or both topics in heading

> Class oversight in executive management, ombudsmen within agencies in 352.35; class quasi-judicial agencies in 352.8; class misconduct in office in 353.46

>> *For ombudsman role in legislative bodies, see 328.3452*

>> *See also 342.06 for administrative law*

.885       \*Processing claims against government

> Class here government liability, grievances against government

>> *For government-employee grievances, see 352.68; for international claims, see 353.44*

# 353    Specific fields of public administration

> *For public administration of economy and environment, see 354*

> *See Manual at T1—068 vs. 353–354; also at 352–354; also at 363 vs. 344.02–344.05, 353–354*

---

\*Add as instructed under 352–354

## SUMMARY

[.01–.09]  Standard subdivisions

    Do not use; class in 351.01–351.09

**.1**   ***Public administration of external and national security affairs**

    Subdivisions are added for external and national security affairs together, for national security affairs alone

    Class interdisciplinary works on national security in 355.03

    *For military and defense administration, see 355.6*

    *See also 352.379 for intelligence and security in executive management*

.122 4    Cabinet-level national security councils

     Number built according to instructions under 352–354

.13    *Foreign and diplomatic relations

     Class here departments and ministries of foreign affairs

     Subdivisions are added for either or both topics in heading

     Class interdisciplinary works on foreign relations in 327

.132 63    Foreign service

     Number built according to instructions under 352–354

     Class here consular and diplomatic services

.132 73    Financial assistance

     Number built according to instructions under 352–354

     Class here foreign aid

     Class use of foreign aid to attain foreign policy objectives in 327.111; class interdisciplinary works on foreign aid in 338 91

.132 74    Promotion and dissemination of knowledge

     Number built according to instructions under 352–354

     Class here government information services

     Class interdisciplinary works on government information services in 327.11

*Add as instructed under 352–354

.15    *Administration of non-self-governing territories

   Class here administration of colonies, of semisovereign states

   Class military government of occupied territories in 355.49

.150 93–.150 99    Specific continents, countries, localities

   Do not use for administration of specific non-self-governing territories; class in 351.3–351.9 e.g., British colonial administration in Kenya 351.67620904

   Limited to administration of more than one jurisdiction, e.g., British colonial administration 353.150941, British colonial administration in Africa 353.150941096

.159    Administration of territories under international control

.17    *Intelligence and counterintelligence

   Limited to administration of operations primarily focused on foreign threats

   Class here espionage, subversion

   Subdivisions are added for either or both topics in heading

   Class activities of domestic police services relating to intelligence and subversion in 363.23; class interdisciplinary works on espionage, subversion, intelligence in 327.12

**(.2)    Military and defense administration**

   (Optional number; prefer 355.6)

   Class here army administration

   *For specific topics in military and defense administration, see 355.6*

(.25)    Naval administration

   (Optional number; prefer 359.6)

   *For specific topics in naval administration, see 359.6*

(.27)    Air forces administration

   (Optional number; prefer 358.416)

   *For specific topics in air forces administration, see 358.416*

(.29)    Administration of other military forces

   (Optional number; prefer numbers for specific forces in 356–359)

   *For specific topics in administration of other specific forces, see the specific force, plus notation 6 from table under 356–359, e.g., executive management of marine forces 359.966*

*Add as instructed under 352–354

> **353.3–353.9 Public administration in domestic fields not related to economy and environment**

Many works classed here will concern activities of national or state and provincial governments to regulate, control, or support services provided by local government agencies. These activities are in contrast to those of local governments which provide the actual services. Works on managing local agencies that directly serve the ultimate recipients are usually classed with the service outside public administration, e.g., management of city police departments 363.2068 (*not* 353.36216), of parole boards 364.62068 (*not* 353.39), of local school systems 371.2 (*not* 353.8214)

Class comprehensive works in 351

*See Manual at T1—068 vs. 353–354*

.3 **\*Public administration of services related to domestic order**

Class here home departments and ministries, European style interior ministries

*For public administration of justice, see 353.4*

*See also 354.30973 for United States Department of the Interior*

.33 \*Support and control of subordinate jurisdictions by higher jurisdictions

Subdivisions are added for either or both topics in heading

Class comprehensive works on administration of subordinate jurisdictions in 352.14

*For financial support of subordinate jurisdictions, see 352.73*

.332 13–.332 19 Administration by subordinate jurisdictions

Numbers built according to instructions under 352–354

Class support and control of specific kinds of subordinate jurisdictions in 353.333–353.339

.333–.339 Support and control of specific kinds of subordinate jurisdictions

Unless it is redundant, add to base number 353.33 the numbers following 352.1 in 352.13–352.19, e.g., support and control of counties 353.335, but comprehensive works on support and control of local administration by states and provinces or by unitary national administration 353.33 (*not* 353.334); however,

for control of special service districts, see 352.193; for support of urban, suburban, rural areas, see 352.79

.36 \*Police services

Including control of crowds, explosives, guns; crime prevention

Class operational management of police services in 363.2068; class operational management of bureaus of investigation in 363.25068

*For regulating personal conduct, see 353.37*

\*Add as instructed under 352–354

.37    *Regulating personal conduct

Including public administration of censorship; control of alcohol, drugs, gambling, pornography, prostitution, sexual mores and morals

Class personal liberty in 323.44; class police control of personal conduct in 363.23; class censorship in 363.31; class interdisciplinary works on controversies relating to public morals and customs in 363.4

.39    *Corrections

Including parole and probation services

Class here prisons

Class interdisciplinary works on administration of correctional activities in 364.6068; class interdisciplinary works on parole administration in 364.62068; class interdisciplinary works on probation administration in 364.63068; class interdisciplinary works on prison administration in 365.068

.4    **Public administration of justice**

Class here public administration of criminal justice, departments of justice

*For judicial administration, see 347.013; for police services, see 353.36; for correctional activities, see 353.39*

.43    *Criminal matters

Including antitrust and tax litigation

Class here criminal prosecution

Class marshals service in 347.016; class criminal litigation to promote civil rights in 353.48; class administration of police services in 363.25068; class interdisciplinary works on criminal procedure in 345.05

.44    *Civil matters

Including international-claims litigation

Class administrative processing of claims against government in 352.885; class civil litigation to promote citizenship and rights in 353.48; class interdisciplinary works on civil procedure in 347.05

.46    *Misconduct in office

Regardless of topic or field

Class here abuse of power, civil rights violations, conflict of interest, corruption, whistle blowing

Class problems resolvable by routine administrative procedures in 352.88; class interdisciplinary works on misconduct in office in 364.132

*Add as instructed under 352–354

.463      \*Public investigations and inquiries

> Other than normal administrative and legislative oversight

> Subdivisions are added for either or both topics in heading

> Class legislative oversight hearings on administrative matters with the subject in public administration, e.g., on public administration of social welfare 353.5

> > *See also 328.3452 for legislative investigative power; also 352.88 for normal administrative oversight and watchdog agencies*

.465      Misconduct in specific areas of public administration

> Add to base number 353.465 the numbers following 35 in 352–354, e.g., misconduct in treasury departments 353.46524

.48      \*Exercise of citizenship and rights

> Including litigation

> Class here promotion of civil rights

> Class election procedures in 324.6

> > *For administration of public defenders, see 345.01; for promotion of procedural rights, see 352.88*

.484      \*Immigration and naturalization services

> Subdivisions are added for either or both topics in heading

> Class comprehensive works on activities relating to population and settlement in 353.59

**.5      \*Public administration of social welfare**

> Class here human services, social security in the sense of social welfare

> Class social security in the sense of retirement income in 353.54

> *For public administration of health services, see 353.6*

> *See Manual at 361–365 vs. 353.5*

### SUMMARY

| | |
|---|---|
| 353.508 | **Groups of people** |
| .53 | **Programs directed to groups of people** |
| .54 | **Income maintenance** |
| .55 | **Housing** |
| .56 | **Nutrition and food** |
| .59 | **Activities relating to population and settlement** |

.508      Groups of people

> Do not use for programs directed to groups of people; class in 353.53

\*Add as instructed under 352–354

.53              *Programs directed to groups of people

Class here equal opportunity programs; programs for minorities, for socially disadvantaged groups; comprehensive works on programs in public administration directed to groups of people

Class programs directed to victims of crime and political oppression regardless of other group characteristic in 353.5337–353.5338; class programs directed to ethnic minorities in 353.5339. Class a program directing a specific kind of service to groups of people with the kind of service, plus notation 08 from Table 1, e.g., personnel programs directed to minorities 352.608, administrative support for children's recreation 353.78083

*For programs directed to labor and professional groups, see 354.9*

.533             Specific miscellaneous groups

Only those named below

[.533 01–.533 09]        Standard subdivisions

Do not use; class in 353.5301–353.5309

.533 1           *Families

Class here unmarried mothers

*See also 353.536 for children*

.533 2           *Poor people

Class poor residents of disadvantaged urban and suburban areas in 353.5333; class poor residents of disadvantaged rural and sparsely populated areas in 353.5334

.533 3           *Residents of disadvantaged urban and suburban areas

Class here residents of inner cities, of slums

Subdivisions are added for either or both topics in heading

Class comprehensive works on assistance to urban and suburban areas in 352.793

*See also 354.2793 for urban and suburban development*

.533 4           *Residents of rural and sparsely populated areas

Subdivisions are added for either or both topics in heading

Class comprehensive works on assistance to rural areas in 352.794

*See also 354.2794 for rural development*

.533 7           *Victims of crime

Regardless of other group characteristics or kind of crime

Class people who are victims of both crime and political oppression in 353.5338

*Add as instructed under 352–354

| .533 8 | *Victims of oppression |
|---|---|

Regardless of other group characteristics or of reason for oppression

Class here refugees, victims of religious persecution

| .533 9 | *Ethnic and national groups in general |
|---|---|

Class here programs directed to ethnic minorities

*For specific ethnic and national groups, see 353.534*

| .534 | Specific ethnic and national groups |
|---|---|

| [.534 001–.534 009] | Standard subdivisions |
|---|---|

Do not use; class in 353.533901–353.533909

| .534 05–.534 09 | Specific ethnic and national groups with ethnic origins from more than one continent, of European descent |
|---|---|

Add to base number 353.534 notation 05–09 from Table 5, e.g., programs directed to ethnic groups of European descent 353.53409

| .534 1–.534 9 | Specific ethnic groups with other origins |
|---|---|

Add to base number 704.03 notation 1–9 from Table 5, e.g., programs for Spanish Americans 353.53468

| .535 | *Women |
|---|---|
| .536 | *Young people to age twenty |

Class here children

| .536 5 | Young people twelve to twenty |
|---|---|

Variant names: adolescents, teenagers, young adults, youth

| .537 | *People in late adulthood |
|---|---|
| .538 | *Veterans |
| .539 | *People with disabilities and illnesses |

Programs not predominantly health related, e.g., access for people with disabilities

Subdivisions are added for either or both topics in heading

Class health programs for people with disabilities and illnesses in 353.6

---

*Add as instructed under 352–354

.54      *Income maintenance

Including guaranteed minimum income, unemployment insurance

Class here pensions, social security in the sense of retirement income, comprehensive works on public administration of government sponsored insurance

Class social security in the sense of social welfare in 353.5; class comprehensive works on insurance in 354.85

*For government-sponsored health insurance, see 353.69*

.548      Public administration of pensions limited to specific occupations and groups of occupations

Add to base number 353.548 the numbers following 354.9 in 354.93–354.95, e.g., public administration of railroad pensions 353.5485385

*For pensions of government workers, see 353.549*

*See also 331.252 for pension benefits*

.549      *Public administration of pensions for government workers

*See also 352.69 for retirement of government workers*

.55      *Housing

Including public housing, assistance to home owners

.56      *Nutrition and food

*For food purity, designation of nutritional content, see 353.997*

.59      *Activities relating to population and settlement

Including birth and death certificates, birth control, population movement

*For immigration and naturalization services, see 353.484*

**.6      *Public administration of health services**

Including disposal of the dead

Class here rehabilitation services, services for physical illness

Class comprehensive works on public administration of social welfare in 353.5

.627 4      Promoting and disseminating knowledge

Number built according to instructions under 352–354

Class here health promotion, physical fitness programs

.628      General forms of control

Number built according to instructions under 352–354

Class here disease control, medical screening

*Add as instructed under 352–354

.63     Specific kinds of physical diseases

Including cancer, communicable diseases

.64     *Mental health services

Including services for substance abuse

*For services for people with mental retardation, see 353.65*

.65     *Services for people with mental retardation

.66     *Services for people with physical disabilities

.68     *Health care facilities

.69     *Health insurance

Including workers' compensation insurance

Class here hospital insurance; specific health insurance programs, e.g., United States Medicaid and Medicare 353.690973

## .7     *Public administration of culture and related activities

Including programs to support and control religion, language programs

Subdivisions are added for culture and related activities together, for culture alone

Class public administration of communications in 354.75

*For promoting museums and exhibitions, see 352.76; for public administration of education, see 353.8*

*See also 306 for government policy on culture; also 322.1 for government policy on religion; also 353.48 for promotion of religious freedom*

.73     *Public libraries

Public administration of agencies supporting and controlling public libraries and library systems

Class administration of public libraries and library systems in 025.1974; class public administration of support for libraries in general in 352.744

[.732 25]     Governing boards and commissions

Do not use; class in 021.82

.77     *Arts and humanities

Including crafts, performing arts, celebrations, historical preservation

*For recreation, see 353.78*

*See also 001.3 for government policy on humanities; also 306.449 for government policy on language; also 700 for government policy on arts*

*Add as instructed under 352–354

.78     *Recreation

    Including parks, recreational use of environment, sports hunting and fishing

    Class here sports

    Class comprehensive works on hunting in 354.349; class comprehensive works on fishing in 354.57

    *For crafts and performing arts, see 353.77*

.8     **\*Public administration of agencies supporting and controlling education**

    Class here agencies supporting and controlling primary education, supporting and controlling secondary education

    Class school administration and management in 371.2; class public policy issues in education in 379; class comprehensive works on promotion and dissemination of knowledge in 352.74

    *See Manual at 371 vs. 353.8, 371.2, 379*

.822 5     Governing boards and commissions

    Number built according to instructions under 352–354

    *For local school boards, see 379.1531*

.824     Financial administration of public education

    Number built according to instructions under 352–354

    Class here financial administration of agencies supporting and controlling public education

    Class financial management of schools and school systems in 371.206

.84     *Adult education

.88     *Higher education

.89     *Special education

.9     **\*Public administration of safety, sanitation, waste control**

    Subdivisions are added for public administration of safety, sanitation, waste control together, for public administration of safety alone

.93     *Sanitation and waste control

    Including cleanup of pollution, recycling

    Subdivisions are added for either or both topics in heading

    Class operational management of waste control and disposal services in 363.728068; class comprehensive works on public administration of pollution in 354.335

    *For sanitation in public facilities, see 353.94; for hazardous wastes, see 353.994*

*Add as instructed under 352–354

.94   *Sanitation in public facilities

   Including sanitation in common carriers, eating and drinking places, health facilities, streets, workplaces

   Class operational management of sanitary services in 363.72068

---

>   353.95–353.99   Public administration of safety

   Class here accidents, public administration of safety in economy and environment

   Class comprehensive works in 353.9

   *For police services, see 353.36; for contagious diseases, see 353.63*

.95   *Preparation for disasters

   Class here civil defense, emergency planning

   Class management of disaster relief in 363.348068

.96   *Industrial and occupational safety

   Standard subdivisions are added for either or both topics in heading

   Class here workplace safety

   Class workplace sanitation in 353.93

.966   Safety in specific extractive, manufacturing, construction occupations

   Add to base number 353.966 the numbers following 6 in 620–690, e.g., mine safety 353.96622

.97   *Safety in miscellaneous areas

   Including domestic, outdoor, sports safety

   Class here safety in public facilities

   *For workplace safety, see 353.96; for transportation safety, see 353.98*

.979   *Fire safety

   Class management of fire departments in 363.37068

.98   *Transportation safety

   Including space transportation safety

   Class here ground-transportation safety

   Class comprehensive works on transportation in 354.76

.987   *Water-transportation safety

   Class here water safety

   *For water-sports safety, see 353.97*

*Add as instructed under 352–354

.988          *Air-transportation safety

.99          *Hazardous products and materials

> Including medical instruments and supplies

> Class here hazardous machinery

> Subdivisions are added for hazardous products and materials together, for hazardous products alone

.993          *Hazardous materials

> Class hazardous wastes in 353.994

> *For radioactive materials, see 353.999*

.994          *Hazardous wastes

> *For radioactive wastes, see 353.999*

.997          *Food safety

> Class here food purity, designation of nutritional content

> Class comprehensive works on nutrition and food services in 353.56

.998          *Drugs and medicines

> Class here drug safety

> Subdivisions are added for either or both topics in heading

.999          *Radioactive products

> Including radioactive wastes

> Class here radiation safety, radioactive materials

## 354    *Public administration of economy and environment

> Subdivisions are added for public administration of economy and environment together, for public administration of economy alone

> Class public administration of safety in economy and environment in 353.95–353.99

> *See Manual at T1—068 vs. 353–354; also at 352–354; also at 363 vs. 344.02–344.05, 353–354*

### SUMMARY

| | |
|---|---|
| 354.08 | **Groups of people** |
| .2 | **General considerations of public administration** |
| .3 | **Public administration of environment and natural resources** |
| .4 | **Public administration of energy and energy-related industries** |
| .5 | **Public administration of agriculture** |
| .6 | **Public administration of construction, manufacturing, service industries** |
| .7 | **Public administration of commerce, communications, transportation** |
| .8 | **Public administration of financial institutions, money, credit** |
| .9 | **Public administration of labor and professions** |

*Add as instructed under 352–354

.08    Groups of people

      Class here equal economic opportunity programs

.27    General forms of assistance

      Number built according to instructions under 352–354

      Class here comprehensive works on public administration of development, on public administration of research and development

      Class urban and community development in 354.2793; class rural development in 354.2794; class comprehensive works on public administration of research and development in noneconomic fields in 352.7; class interdisciplinary works on research and development in 338.9. Class public administration of research and development of a specific economic activity with the activity in 354, plus notation 27 from table under 352–354, e.g., development of agriculture 354.527

.274    Promotion and dissemination of knowledge

      Number built according to instructions under 352–354

      Class protection of intellectual property in 352.749

.279    Assistance to urban, suburban, rural areas; to small business

      Number built according to instructions under 352–354

.279 9    *Assistance to small business

      *For a specific form of assistance to small business, see the form, e.g., assistance in securing government contracts 352.5327, small business loans 354.2736*

---

> ### 354.3–354.8 Public administration of specific fields of economic and environmental activity

      Class here public administration of industries associated with specific fields of economic and environmental activity

      Class public administration of labor and professions in specific fields of economic and environmental activity in 354.9; class comprehensive works in 354

.3    **\*Public administration of environment and natural resources**

      Class here departments of natural resources, public administration of primary industries

      Subdivisions are added for either or both topics in heading

      *For public administration of recreational use of environment, see 353.78; for public administration of sanitation and waste control, see 353.93; for public administration of energy and energy-related resources, see 354.4; for public administration of agriculture, see 354.5*

---

\*Add as instructed under 352–354

## SUMMARY

|  |  |
|---|---|
| 354.327–.328 | [General forms of assistance and control] |
| .33 | Special forms of environmental protection and control |
| .34 | Land and biological resources |
| .35 | Urban land |
| .36 | Water |
| .37 | Air and atmospheric phenomena |
| .39 | Mineral resources |

.327       General forms of assistance

Number built according to instructions under 352–354

Class here natural resources development

Class interdisciplinary works on natural resources development in 333.715

.328       General forms of control

Number built according to instructions under 352–354

Class here environmental protection

Class interdisciplinary works on environmental protection in 363.7

*For special forms of environmental protection and control, see 354.33*

.33       Special forms of environmental protection and control

Not provided for in subdivisions of 354.328

Class comprehensive works on public administration of environmental protection and control in 354.328. Class public administration of a special form of protection and control relating to a specific environment with the form of protection and control in 354.34–354.37, plus notation 3 from table under 354.34–354.37, e.g., water conservation 354.3634

.333       *Resource use planning

Class here zoning

Class urban zoning in 354.353; class interdisciplinary works on zoning in 333.7317

.334       *Conservation

Class interdisciplinary works on conservation in 333.72

.335       *Prevention and control of pollution

Class here comprehensive works on public administration of pollution

Class public administration of cleanup of pollution in 353.93; class interdisciplinary works on pollution in 363.73

.338       *Noise control

Regardless of environment

*Add as instructed under 352–354

.339      *Pest control

Regardless of environment

---

>      354.34–354.37   Specific environments

Except for modifications shown under specific entries, add to each subdivision identified by † as follows:
01–09    Standard subdivisions
       Add as instructed under 352–354, e.g., equal opportunity programs 08
2         General considerations of administration
       Add as instructed under 352–354, e.g., state and provincial administration of the topic 213
3         Special forms of protection and control
       Add to 3 the numbers following 354.33 in 354.333–354.335, e.g., conservation 34

Class noise control in specific environments in 354.338; class pest control in specific environments in 354.339; class mineral resources derived from a specific environment in 354.39; class comprehensive works on administration of environment in 354.3

.34      †Land and biological resources

Including wetlands

Class here real estate, real property

Subdivisions are added for land and biological resources together, for land alone

Class parks in 353.78

*For public lands, see 352.57; for urban land, see 354.35*

.349      †Biological resources

Including hunting

Class here animal resources

*For sports hunting, see 353.78; for forestry, see 354.55; for aquatic biological resources, fishing and fisheries, see 354.57*

.35      *Urban land

.353      *Land use planning

Class here city planning, urban zoning

Class comprehensive works on public administration of zoning in 354.333; class interdisciplinary works on city planning in 307.1216; class interdisciplinary works on urban zoning in 333.7717

---

*Add as instructed under 352–354
†Add as instructed under 354.34–354.37

| .36 | †Water |
|---|---|

Including groundwater, estuaries

*For aquatic biological resources, fishing and fisheries, see 354.57*

| .362 7 | General forms of assistance |
|---|---|

Number built according to instructions under 354.34–354.37

Class here development of water resources, of electricity from water resources; flood control

Class distribution of electricity derived from water power in 354.49

| .366 | †Water supply |
|---|---|

*For irrigation projects, see 354.367*

| .367 | †Irrigation projects |
|---|---|
| .369 | †Oceans |
| .37 | †Air and atmospheric phenomena |

Class here weather bureaus

| .39 | *Mineral resources |
|---|---|

Class here geological surveys, mining bureaus, subsurface resources

*For mineral energy resources, see 354.4*

| .393 | *Conservation of mineral resources |
|---|---|

| **.4** | **\*Public administration of energy and energy-related industries** |
|---|---|

Class here departments of energy; public administration of energy resources, public administration of mineral energy resources

Subdivisions are added for either or both topics in heading

*For development of water power, see 354.3627*

| .428 | General forms of control |
|---|---|

Number built according to instructions under 352–354

Class here control of public utilities supplying energy

Class energy conservation in 354.43; class comprehensive works on control of public utilities in 354.728. Class control of a specific energy utility with the form of energy, plus notation 28 from table under 352–354, e.g., a gas utility 354.4628

| .43 | *Energy conservation |
|---|---|

Class energy conservation for a specific form of energy with the form, plus notation 3 from the table under 354.44–354.49, e.g., petroleum conservation 354.453

---

\*Add as instructed under 352–354
†Add as instructed under 354.34–354.37

>      354.44–354.49   Specific energy resources and electricity

Except for modifications shown under specific entries, add to each subdivision identified by ‡ as follows:

01–09      Standard subdivisions
          Add as instructed under 352–354, e.g., equal opportunity programs 08
2        General considerations of administration
          Add as instructed under 352–354, e.g., international administration of the topic 211
3        Conservation
301–309      Standard subdivisions
          Add as instructed under 352–354, e.g., equal opportunity programs 308
32       General considerations of administration
          Add as instructed under 352–354, e.g., international administration of the topic 3211

Class comprehensive works in 354.4

>      354.44–354.48   Specific energy resources

Class distribution of electricity derived from specific energy resources in 354.49; class comprehensive works on energy resources in 354.4

.44      ‡Fossil fuels

Including coal

*For oil and gas, see 354.45*

.45      ‡Oil

Class here comprehensive works on petroleum

*For gas, see 354.46*

.46      ‡Gas

Natural and manufactured

.47      ‡Nuclear fuels

Class radiation safety, radioactive wastes in 353.999

.472 7        General forms of assistance

Number built according to instructions under 354.44–354.49

Class here development of electricity from nuclear fuels

Class distribution of electricity derived from nuclear fuels in 354.49

.48      ‡Other energy resources

Including geothermal and solar energy

.49      ‡Electricity

‡Add as instructed under 354.44–354.49

.492 7       General forms of assistance

Number built according to instructions under 354.44–354.49

Class here comprehensive works on development of electricity

Class development of electricity from a specific resource with the resource, plus notation 27 from table under 354.44–354.49, e.g., from water power 354.3627, from nuclear fuels 354.4727

.492 8       General forms of control

Number built according to instructions under 354.44–354.49

Class here control of electric utilities, of distribution of electricity regardless of resource from which it is derived

Class development of electricity in 354.4927

### .5       *Public administration of agriculture

Class nutrition and food programs in 353.56; class rural development in 354.2794; class soil conservation in 354.3434; class irrigation projects in 354.367; class agricultural price supports in 354.5285; class agricultural credit in 354.86

*For hunting, see 354.349*

.54       *Plant crops

*For forestry, see 354.55*

.55       *Forestry

.56       *Animal husbandry

.57       *Fishing and fisheries

Class here aquatic biological resources, marine biological resources

Subdivisions are added for either or both topics in heading

Class comprehensive works on resources derived from water in 354.36

*For sports fishing, see 353.78*

.59       *Commodity programs

Including marketing services

Class here farm produce

Class programs that combine inspection and marketing in 354.59283

*For agricultural price supports, see 354.5285*

*See also 354.88 for commodity exchanges*

### .6       *Public administration of construction, manufacturing, service industries

Class here administration of secondary industries

---

*Add as instructed under 352–354

.64       \*Construction

           Class public works in 352.77

.66       \*Manufacturing

.68       \*Service industries

           *For commerce, communications, transportation, see 354.7; for financial services, see 354.8*

.7       **\*Public administration of commerce, communications, transportation**

### SUMMARY

| | |
|---|---|
| 354.728 | **General forms of control** |
| .73 | **Commerce** |
| .74 | **Foreign commerce** |
| .75 | **Communications** |
| .76 | **Transportation** |
| .77 | **Road transportation** |
| .78 | **Water transportation** |
| .79 | **Air and space transportation** |

.728       General forms of control

           Number built according to instructions under 352–354

           Class here comprehensive works on control of public utilities

           *For control of a specific public utility, see the utility, plus notation 28 from table under 352–354, e.g., control of electric utilities 354.4928*

.73       \*Commerce

           Including tourist trade regardless of origin

           Class here domestic commerce

           *For consumer protection, see 352.746; for foreign commerce, see 354.74*

           *See also 354.76280973 for United States Interstate Commerce Commission*

.74       \*Foreign commerce

           Class foreign tourism in 354.73

.75       \*Communications

           Class here telecommunications

           Class management, business organizations, and description of facilities, activities, services of a publicly owned communications system with the system in 384, e.g., business organization of a publicly owned telephone system 384.6065

           *See Manual at T1—068 vs. 353–354; also at 380: Add table: 09 vs. 065*

---

\*Add as instructed under 352–354

.759          *Postal service

> Class operational management of postal service in 383.068; class postal organization in 383.4

.76          *Transportation

> Class here ground transportation
>
> Class transportation safety in 353.98
>
>> *For road transportation, see 354.77; for water transportation, see 354.78; for air and space transportation, see 354.79*

.763          *Passenger services

> Class passenger service in a specific form of transportation with the form in 354.765–354.79, e.g., rail passenger service 354.7673

.764          *Freight services

> Including pipeline transportation
>
> Class freight service in a specific form of transportation with the form in 354.765–354.79, e.g., rail freight service 354.7674

.765          *Automotive transportation

> Including parking facilities
>
>> *For road transportation, see 354.77*

.765 284          Licensing, accreditation, certification, chartering, registration; incorporation

> Number built according to instructions under 352–354
>
> Class here licensing to drive, registration of passenger automobiles for general use
>
>> *For licensing to drive and registration of passenger automobiles for hire, see 354.7653284*

.765 3          *Passenger service

.765 328 4          Licensing, accreditation, certification, chartering, registration; incorporation

> Number built according to instructions under 352–354
>
> Class here licensing to drive, registration of passenger vehicles for hire
>
>> *For licensing to drive, registration of passenger automobiles for general use, see 354.765284*

.765 4          *Freight service

.767          *Railroad transportation

> Class urban rail transportation in 354.769

.767 3          *Passenger service

*Add as instructed under 352–354

| .767 4 | *Freight service |
|---|---|

.769            *Urban mass transportation

> Class here local bus transportation, local rail transportation, comprehensive works on local transportation
>
> *For a specific form of local transportation not provided for here, see the form, e.g., taxi service 354.7653, helicopter service 354.79*

.769 3           *Passenger service

.769 4           *Freight service

.77            *Road transportation

.772 8            General forms of control

> Number built according to instructions under 352–354
>
> Class here traffic control, traffic engineering

.773           *Passenger service

.774           *Freight service

.78           *Water transportation

> Class here inland water transportation, ocean transportation

.783           *Passenger service

.784           *Freight service

.79           *Air and space transportation

> Subdivisions are added for air and space transportation together, for air transportation alone

.793           *Passenger service

.794           *Freight service

**.8            *Public administration of financial institutions, money, credit**

> Subdivisions are added for financial institutions, money, credit together; for financial institutions alone
>
> Class works covering public administration of both financial system and government finances in 352.4
>
> *See also 332.46 for monetary policy*

.84           *Money

> Class credit institutions in 354.86

.85           *Insurance

> *For government-sponsored insurance, see 353.54; for government-sponsored health insurance, see 353.69*

---

*Add as instructed under 352–354

| | |
|---|---|
| .86 | *Credit institutions |

      Class here banks, savings and loan institutions

      Class government loans and loan guarantees in 352.736

| | |
|---|---|
| .88 | *Securities and investments |
| **.9** | ***Public administration of labor and professions** |

      Class here departments of labor

      Subdivisions are added for labor and professions together, for labor alone

      Class occupational safety in 353.96

| | |
|---|---|
| .908 | Groups of people |

      Class here affirmative action programs, equal employment opportunity programs

      Class affirmative action programs for a government's own employees in 352.608

| | |
|---|---|
| .927 | General forms of assistance |

      Number built according to instructions under 352–354

      Class here job creation

| | |
|---|---|
| .93 | Labor in specific groups of occupations |

      Including blue collar, industrial, professional occupations

      Class labor in specific extractive, manufacturing, construction occupations in 354.94; class labor in specific occupations other than extraction, manufacturing, construction in 354.95

      *For government workers, see 352.63*

| | |
|---|---|
| .94 | Labor in specific extractive, manufacturing, construction occupations |

      Add to base number 354.94 the numbers following 6 in 620–690, e.g., miners 354.9422

| | |
|---|---|
| .95 | Labor in other specific occupations |

      Add to base number 354.95 notation 001–999, e.g., railroad workers 354.95385

*Add as instructed under 352–354

> 354.96–354.98 Specific programs for labor and professions

Not provided for in subdivisions of 354.927 derived from 352.7

Except for modifications shown under specific entries, add to each subdivision identified by † as follows:
01–09 Standard subdivisions
Add as instructed under 352–354, e.g., programs directed to groups of people 08
2 General considerations of administration
Add as instructed under 352–354, e.g., state and provincial administration of the topic 213
3 Specific groups of occupations
Class specific extractive, manufacturing, construction occupations in 4; class other specific occupations in 5
*For government workers, see 352.63*
4 Specific extractive, manufacturing, construction occupations
Add to 4 the numbers following 6 in 620–690, e.g., miners 422
5 Other specific occupations
Add to 5 notation 001–999, e.g., railroad workers 5385

Class comprehensive works in 354.9

.96 †Employment and related services

Subdivisions are added for employment and related services together, for employment services alone

.968 †Promoting training

Class here promoting apprenticeship

*See also 352.669 for training of government's own workers*

.97 †Labor unions and collective bargaining

Class here employer-employee relationships

Subdivisions are added for either or both topics in heading

.98 †Conditions of employment

Class here compensation

Class pensions, unemployment insurance in 353.54; class workers' compensation insurance in 353.69

# 355 Military science

Class here armed forces and services, ground forces and services

Class sociology of military institutions in 306.27

*For specific kinds of military forces and warfare, see 356–359*

*See also 322.5 for relation of the state to military organizations; also 327.174 for disarmament; also 343.01 for military and defense law*

*See Manual at 355–359 vs. 623; also at 930–990 vs. 355.009, 355–359*

†Add as instructed under 354.96–354.98

### SUMMARY

| | |
|---|---|
| 355.001–.009 | **Standard subdivisions** |
| .02–.07 | **Basic considerations of military science** |
| .1 | **Military life and customs** |
| .2 | **Military resources** |
| .3 | **Organization and personnel of military forces** |
| .4 | **Military operations** |
| .5 | **Military training** |
| .6 | **Military administration** |
| .7 | **Military installations** |
| .8 | **Military equipment and supplies (Matériel)** |

.001          Philosophy and theory

.002          Miscellany

[.002 8]          Auxiliary techniques and procedures; apparatus, equipment, materials

> Do not use; class in 355.8

.003–.005          Standard subdivisions

.006          Organizations

[.006 8]          Management

> Do not use; class in 355.6

.007          Education and related topics

.007 1          Education

> Do not use for reserve training; class in 355.2232

.007 11          Higher education

> Class here military colleges and universities

> > *For mid-career training of officers at academically accredited armed forces schools, see 355.55*

> > *See Manual at 378.4–378.9 vs. 355.00711*

.007 113–.007 119          Specific continents, countries, localities

> Official service academies are classed in notation at the country level only, e.g., Royal Military Academy (Sandhurst, England) 355.0071141

[.007 155]          On-the-job training

> Do not use; class in 355.5

[.007 2]          Research

> Do not use; class in 355.07

.008          Groups of people

.009            History, geographic treatment, biography

Class historical and geographic treatment of military situation and policy in 355.033

*See Manual at 930–990 vs. 355.009, 355–359*

.009 3–.009 9       Specific continents, countries, localities

Class organization of specific national armies in 355.3093–355.3099

*For military history of a specific war, see the war in 930–990, e.g., military history of Vietnamese War 959.70434*

---

>         355.02–355.07   Basic considerations of military science

Class comprehensive works in 355

.02            War and warfare

Class here conventional warfare, total war; comprehensive works on military strategy

Class defense in 355.03

*For strategy in military operations, see 355.4*

*See also 341.6 for law of war*

.020 11          Systems

Do not use for models; class in 355.48

.021            General topics of war and warfare

[.021 01–.021 09]     Standard subdivisions

Do not use; class in 355.0201–355.0209

.021 3          Militarism

Class here antimilitarism, interdisciplinary works on military-industrial complex

Class relation of military organizations to the state in 322.5; class promotion of peace in 327.172

*For economic aspects of military-industrial complex, see 338.47355*

.021 5          Limited war

.021 7          Nuclear warfare

         Including issues of deterrence

         Class here comprehensive works on nuclear forces

         Class comprehensive works on warfare with weapons of mass destruction in 358.3

         *For a specific nuclear force and its warfare, see the force, e.g., nuclear missile forces and warfare 358.17*

         *See also 327.1747 for nuclear disarmament*

.021 8          Insurgent, resistance, revolutionary warfare

         Standard subdivisions are added for any or all topics in heading

         Class here civil war, guerrilla warfare

         Class guerrilla tactics in 355.425

.027          Causes of war

         *For causes of specific wars, see 930–990*

.027 2          Political and diplomatic causes

.027 3          Economic causes

.027 4          Social causes

         *See also 303.66 for sociology of war*

.027 5          Psychological causes

.028          Aftermath of war

         Including military occupation

         Class here dislocation, reconstruction

         Class government of occupied territories in 355.49

         *For aftermath of specific wars, see 930–990*

.03          Military situation and policy

         Class here defense

         Class defense operations in 355.4

[.030 9]          History and geographic treatment

         Do not use; class in 355.033

[.030 92]          Biography

         Do not use; class in 355.0092

.031          Military relations

         Class here military alliances, mutual security pacts

         *For military assistance, see 355.032*

.031 09                     History, geographic treatment, biography

> Class here military relations between two regions or countries, e.g., military relations of China 355.0310951, then for relations between that nation and another nation or region add as instructed under —093–099 in Table 1, e.g., military relations between China and Myanmar 355.031095109591

.032               Military assistance

> Class here military attachés, military missions

.032 093–.032 099           Specific continents, countries, localities

> Do not use for military assistance to specific continents, countries, localities; class in 355.0323–355.0329

.032 3–.032 9       Military assistance to specific continents, countries, localities

> Add to base number 355.032 notation 3–9 from Table 2, e.g., military assistance to Vietnam 355.032597

.033               General history and description

> Class general history and description of military relations in 355.031

.033 000 1–.033 000 8       Standard subdivisions

[.033 000 9]                History, geographic treatment, biography

> Do not use for biography; class in 355.0092. Do not use for history without subdivision; class in 355.033. Do not use for historical periods; class in 355.033001–355.033005. Do not use for areas, regions, places in general; class in 355.03301. Do not use for specific continents, countries, localities; class in 355.03303–355.03309

.033 001–.033 005           Historical periods

> Add to base number 355.03300 the numbers following —090 in notation 0901–0905 from Table 1, e.g., military situation and policy in 1930s 355.0330043

.033 01                     Areas, regions, places in general

> Add to base number 355.03301 the numbers following —1 in notation 11–19 from Table 2, e.g., military situation and policy in developing countries 355.03301724

.033 03–.033 09             Specific continents, countries, localities

> Add to base number 355.0330 notation 3–9 from Table 2, e.g., military situation of Brazil 355.033081

.033 2             Military capability

> Class here combat readiness

> Class combat readiness of specific units in 355.3

.033 209 1–.033 209 9]      Geographic treatment and biography

> Do not use; class in 355.03321–355.03329

.033 21–.033 29       Geographic treatment and biography of military capability

> Add to base number 355.0332 notation 1–9 from Table 2, e.g., military capability of Sweden 355.0332485

.033 5       Military policy

[.033 509 1–.033 509 9]       Geographic treatment and biography

> Do not use; class in 355.03351–355.03359

.033 51–.033 59       Geographic treatment and biography of military policy

> Add to base number 355.0335 notation 1–9 from Table 2, e.g., military policy of Italy 355.033545

.07       Military research and development

> Limited to military aspects

> Class here relation of military science to science and technology; comprehensive works on military aspects of research and development of equipment, supplies, weapons

> Class interdisciplinary works on military research and development in 338.4735507

> *For procurement and contracting aspects of research and development of equipment and supplies, see 355.6212; for military aspects of research and development (other than procurement and contracting) of specific kinds of equipment and supplies, see 355.8*

## .1       Military life and customs

> Class here conditions of military employment

> *For social and welfare services provided to soldiers and dependents, see 355.34*

### SUMMARY

| | | |
|---|---|---|
| **355.11** | **Service periods, promotion and demotion, termination** | |
| **.12** | **Living conditions** | |
| **.13** | **Conduct and rewards** | |
| **.14** | **Uniforms** | |
| **.15** | **Colors and standards** | |
| **.16** | **Celebrations, commemorations, memorials** | |
| **.17** | **Ceremonies** | |

.11       Service periods, promotion and demotion, termination

.111       Length of service

.112       Promotion and demotion

.113       Inactive periods

> Including furloughs, leaves, missing in action, reserve status, status during captivity or internment

> Class reserve training in 355.2232

.114 Termination of service

Including resignation, retirement; reinstatement

.12 Living conditions

Class here living conditions of dependents, comprehensive works on military housing

*For quarters for personnel at military installations, see 355.71*

.123 Morale and motivation

.129 Living conditions in specific situations

Class morale in specific situations in 355.123

*For life in military prisons and prison camps (other than prisoner-of-war camps), see 365.48*

.129 2 Living conditions in regular quarters

Including quarters during basic training

.129 3 Living conditions during maneuvers, aboard ship, in transit

.129 4 Living conditions in combat zones

.129 6 Living conditions in prisoner-of-war camps

.13 Conduct and rewards

Class here discipline, soldierly qualities

*See also 343.014 for law of discipline and conduct*

.133 Regulation of conduct

Class rewards in 355.134

.133 2 Enforcement and punishment

Class offenses in 355.1334

.133 23 Enforcement

Including criminal investigation, military police

.133 25 Punishment

Class military prisons in 365.48

.133 4 Offenses against military discipline

Including desertion, mutiny

Class interdisciplinary works on mutinies in 364.131

*See also 364.138 for war crimes*

.133 6 Etiquette

Class dress regulations, etiquette of uniforms in 355.14

.134              Rewards

        Including special privileges

        Class here awards, citations

.134 092              Biography

        Class a military awardee who is associated with another subject with the subject, e.g., biography of an awardee who is also a movie star 791.43028092

.134 2              Honorary insignia

        Including badges, decorations, medals

        Class here comprehensive works on insignia

        Class comprehensive works on insignia and uniforms in 355.14

        *For insignia of rank, see 355.14*

.134 9              Gifts and gun salutes

.14              Uniforms

        Including accessories, insignia of rank and service

        Class here etiquette of uniforms, comprehensive works on insignia and uniforms

        Class issue and use of uniforms in 355.81

        *For honorary insignia, comprehensive works on insignia, see 355.1342*

.140 9              History, geographic treatment, biography

        *See Manual at 355.1409*

.15              Colors and standards

        Standard subdivisions are added for either or both topics in heading

        Class here flag presentations

.16              Celebrations, commemorations, memorials

        Standard subdivisions are added for any or all topics in heading

.17              Ceremonies

        Class ceremonies for a specific occasion with the occasion, e.g., gun salutes 355.1349, military celebrations 355.16

**.2**              **Military resources**

.21              Preparation, evaluation, preservation

        Class preparation, evaluation, preservation of specific resources in 355.22–355.27

---

>              355.22–355.27 Specific resources

        Class comprehensive works in 355.2

.22 Human resources

*For civilian personnel, see 355.23*

[.220 68] Management

Do not use for management of human resources other than recruiting; class in 355.61. Do not use for recruiting; class in 355.223

.223 Recruiting and reserve training

Standard subdivisions are added for recruiting and reserve training together, for recruiting alone

Class here enlistment

.223 2 Reserve training

.223 207 11 Higher education

Class here reserve training in academic settings, e.g., United States Reserve Officers' Training Corps 355.2232071173

.223 4 Qualifications for service

.223 6 Specific methods and procedures of recruiting

Including registration, commissioning

[.223 601–.223 609] Standard subdivisions

Do not use; class in 355.22301–355.22309

.223 62 Voluntary enlistment

Class here all-volunteer army

.223 63 Draft (Conscription)

*For universal military service, see 355.225*

.224 Conscientious objectors

Class here draft resistance

Class ethics of conscientious objection in 172.1; class techniques for evading draft in 355.22363

.225 Universal military training

Class here universal military service

.23 Civilian workers

[.230 68] Management

Do not use; class in 355.619

.24 Raw materials

Class here strategic materials, comprehensive works on nonhuman resources

*For industrial resources, see 355.26; for transportation and communication facilities, see 355.27*

| | | |
|---|---|---|
| .242 | | Metals |
| .243 | | Nonmetallic minerals |
| .245 | | Agricultural products |
| .26 | | Industrial resources |

> Military appraisal and utilization
>
> Class here manufacturing war matériel

| | |
|---|---|
| .27 | Transportation and communications facilities |
| .28 | Mobilization |

> Including commandeering, requisition
>
> Class mobilization of specific resources in 355.22–355.27

| | |
|---|---|
| .29 | Demobilization |

> Class demobilization of specific resources in 355.22–355.27

**.3      Organization and personnel of military forces**

> Standard subdivisions are added for organization and personnel together, for organization alone
>
> Class here organization of national armies, combat readiness of specific units
>
> Class comprehensive works on combat readiness in 355.0332

### SUMMARY

| | |
|---|---|
| 355.31 | **Kinds of military units** |
| .33 | **Personnel and their hierarchy** |
| .34 | **Noncombat services** |
| .35 | **Combat units according to field of service** |
| .37 | **Reserves** |

| | |
|---|---|
| .31 | Kinds of military units |

> Including armies, regiments, squads; districts
>
> Class here combat units
>
> Class organization of national armies in 355.3
>
>> *For a specific kind of unit limited to a specific service, see the service, e.g., reserve units 355.37, armored units 358.183*

| | |
|---|---|
| .33 | Personnel and their hierarchy |

> Including labor relations and military employee organizations
>
> Class biography of soldiers in 355.0092; class promotion and demotion in 355.112

| | |
|---|---|
| .330 4 | Line and staff organization |

| | |
|---|---|
| .330 41 | Line organization |

Including evaluation, leadership, supervision

Class here command and control systems, command functions

*For motivation, see 355.123*

| | |
|---|---|
| .330 42 | Staff organization |

Class here general staffs, joint chiefs of staff

*For line functions of chiefs of staff, see 355.33041*

| | |
|---|---|
| .331 | General and flag officers |

Officers above rank of colonel (naval rank of captain)

| | |
|---|---|
| .332 | Commissioned and warrant officers |

Standard subdivisions are added for commissioned and warrant officers together, for commissioned officers alone

Class officers' manuals in 355

*For general and flag officers, see 355.331*

| | |
|---|---|
| .338 | Enlisted personnel |

Including noncommissioned officers

Class noncommissioned officers' manuals in 355

*See also 331.8811355 for military unions*

| | |
|---|---|
| .34 | Noncombat services |

Including propaganda, social services for dependents, interdisciplinary works on civic action of armed forces

Class here operations of noncombat services, social services for soldiers

*For a specific noncombat service not provided for here, see the service, e.g., housing 355.12, personnel management 355.61; for a specific civic action of armed forces, see the action, e.g., civil works program of U.S. Army Corps of Engineers 363.0973*

| | |
|---|---|
| .341 | Supply issuing and related services |

Including canteens, mess services, post exchanges

Class officers' and noncommissioned officers' clubs in 355.346; class comprehensive works on supply services in 355.621

| | |
|---|---|
| .342 | Public relations |
| .343 | Unconventional warfare services |
| .343 2 | Intelligence |

Including cryptanalysis, mapping, weather forecasting

Class here military espionage

Class counterintelligence in 355.3433; class interdisciplinary works on espionage in 327.12

| | |
|---|---|
| .343 3 | Counterintelligence |
| | Including security classification |
| .343 4 | Psychological warfare |
| .343 7 | Subversion and sabotage |
| | Class interdisciplinary works on subversion in 327.12 |
| .345 | Health services |
| | Including ambulance, sanitation, veterinary services |
| | Class here medical services |
| | Class technology of medical services in 610; class technology of health services in 613.6; class sanitation engineering in 623.75; class veterinary sciences in 636.089 |
| .346 | Recreational services |
| | Including library services, officers' and noncommissioned officers' (NCO) clubs |
| | Class library and informational sciences in 020; class recreational arts in 790 |
| .347 | Religious services |
| | Standard subdivisions are added for specific religions, e.g., history of Jewish services 355.34709 |
| | Class care of military personnel by religious leaders in general in 206.1; class Christian pastoral care of military personnel in 259.088355 |
| .348 | Women's units |
| | Class women in armed forces in 355.0082; class women as a military resource in 355.22082. Class a specific service performed by women with the service, plus notation 082 from Table 1, e.g., women in intelligence services 355.3432082, women in combat 355.4082 |
| .35 | Combat units according to field of service |
| | Class comprehensive works on combat units in 355.31 |
| .351 | Units serving wholly within national or local frontiers |
| | Class here frontier troops, active units called home guards |
| | Class reserve units called home guards in 355.37 |
| .352 | Expeditionary forces |
| | Class here expeditionary forces of colonies, forces of mother countries dedicated to service in colonies |
| .354 | Mercenary troops |
| | Class here soldiers of fortune |

.356          Allied and coalition forces

> Standard subdivisions are added for either or both topics in heading

> Class here multinational forces

> Class joint operations of allied and coalition forces in 355.46

>> *For multinational forces commanded by international bodies, see 355.357*

.357          International forces

> Troops serving under command of international bodies

> Including peacekeeping forces

> Class interdisciplinary works on peaceful resolution of conflict in 327.17

>> *See also 341.58 for legal aspects of international forces*

.359          Foreign legions

> Units of national armies consisting primarily of foreign recruits

> Class here auxiliaries (troops of foreign countries serving with a state's armies)

.37          Reserves

> Class here home guards, home reserves, militia, national guards; military departments devoted to reserve or national guard affairs

> Class training of reserves in 355.2232; class active units called home guards in 355.351. Class reserve units of a specific kind of military force with the force, e.g., army engineer reserves 358.223

**.4**          **Military operations**

> Including mine clearing operations, peacekeeping operations

> Class here attack and defense operations, combat; strategy in military operations

>> *For mine clearing operations by civilians, see 363.34988; for engineering of mine clearing, see 623.26*

[.409 1]          Areas, regions, places in general

> Do not use; class in 355.471

[.409 3–.409 9]          Specific continents, countries, localities

> Do not use; class in 355.473–355.479

.41          Support operations

> Including camouflage, deception, handling prisoners of war

> Class support operations in a specific situation with the situation, e.g., logistics of siege warfare 355.44

.411          Logistics

> Including troop movements

>> *For troop support, see 355.415*

.412            Encampment

.413            Reconnaissance

> Class here patrolling

.415            Troop support

> Operations for providing immediate necessities for maintenance of troops
>
> Class comprehensive works on operations for provisioning troops in 355.411
>
>> *For a specific aspect of troop support, see the aspect, e.g., medical service 355.345*

.42             Tactics

>> *For nuclear tactics, see 355.43; for tactics of siege warfare, see 355.44; for tactics of defense of home territory, see 355.45*

.422            Specific tactics

> Including antiaircraft defenses, attacks and counterattacks, debarkation and landing, prevention of friendly fire casualties, retreats, skirmishing; mobile (blitz), commando (hit-and-run), infiltration tactics
>
> Class specific tactics in specific conditions in 355.423–355.426

[.422 01–.422 09]       Standard subdivisions

> Do not use; class in 355.4201–355.4209

---

>          355.423–355.426  Tactics in specific conditions

> Class comprehensive works in 355.42

.423            Tactics in various kinds of terrain, climate, weather; night tactics

.424            Use of animals

.425            Guerrilla tactics

> Class here tribal fighting
>
> Class guerrilla warfare in 355.0218

.426            Tactics in cities

> Class here house-to-house fighting, street fighting, urban warfare
>
> Class siege warfare in 355.44

.43             Nuclear operations

> Class nuclear warfare in 355.0217

.44             Siege and trench warfare, blockades

> Class urban warfare in 355.426; class naval blockades in 359.44

.45             Defense of home territory

> Class defensive forts and installations in 355.7

.46       Combined operations

Joint operations of two or more kinds of military forces

Including operations of forces of more than one nation

Class here amphibious operations

Class amphibious operations in which marines are main land component in 359.9646

.47       Military geography

[.470 91–.470 99]       Geographic treatment and biography

Do not use; class in 355.471–355.479

.471–.479       Geographic treatment and biography of military geography

Class here geographic treatment of military operations

Add to base number 355.47 notation 1–9 from Table 2, e.g., military geography of Russia 355.4747

.48       Technical analyses of military events

Including real and imaginary wars, campaigns, battles

Class here war games

*See also 793.92 for recreational war games*

.49       Occupation of conquered territory

Including military government

Class occupation as an aftermath of war in 355.028

**.5       Military training**

Training of individuals and units

*For reserve training, see 355.2232; for universal military training, see 355.225. For military training in a specific subject, see the subject, plus notation 0715 from Table 1, e.g., military training in computer engineering 621.390715*

.507 1       Education in military training

Class military training in a specific country with the country in 355.5093–355.5099, e.g., military training in Switzerland 355.509494 (*not* 355.50710494)

.52       Maneuvers

.54       Basic training

Including drill, survival training, tactical exercises

.544       Encampment and field training

Including setting up and dismantling camps, constructing temporary fortifications, running obstacle courses

.547        Small arms and bayonet practice

> Class here manual of arms
>
> If emphasis is on use by infantry, class in 356.115

.548        Self-defense

> Unarmed combat and combat with knife
>
> If emphasis is on use by infantry, class in 356.115

.55        Training of officers

> Class here mid-career training at academically accredited armed forces schools
>
> Class training through war games in 355.48; class comprehensive works on university-level service academies in 355.00711

.56        Technical training

**.6**        **Military administration**

> Class here defense administration, departments of defense
>
> Class administration of a function not provided for here with the function, plus notation 068 from Table 1, e.g., administration of installations 355.7068
>
> *For organization of military forces, see 355.3*
>
> (Option: Class comprehensive works in 353.2. If option is chosen, change heading to "Specific topics in military administration," and do not add standard subdivisions)

[.606 8]        Management

> Do not use; class in 355.6

.609 1        Areas, regions, places in general

> Class here international military and defense administration
>
> Class administration of international peacekeeping troops in 355.357068
>
> (If option under 355.6 is chosen, class international military and defense administration in 353.2211)

.61        Personnel management (Human resource management)

> *For service periods, promotion and demotion, termination, see 355.11; for motivation, see 355.123; for personnel and their hierarchy, see 355.33; for wage and salary administration, see 355.64*

.614        Job description for military personnel

> Including job analysis and classification

.619        Civilian workers

> Add to base number 355.619 the numbers following 352.6 in 352.63–352.69, e.g., recruiting civilian personnel 355.6195
>
> Class civilian workers as a military resource in 355.23

.62       Supply and financial administration and related topics

.621       Supply administration and related topics

> Class here administration of specific kinds of equipment and supplies

>> *For product development, see 355.07; for supply issuing and related services, see 355.341; for supply depots and installations, see 355.75*

.621 2       Contracts and procurement

> Standard subdivisions are added for either or both topics in heading

> Class here comprehensive works on military contracts

>> *For contracts for a specific nonsupply item, see the item, plus notation 068 from Table 1, e.g., contracts for real property 355.70681*

.621 3       Internal control and disposal of supplies

> Including warehouse management

.621 32       Inventory control

.621 37       Surplus supplies and their disposal

> Standard subdivisions are added for either or both topics in heading

.622       Financial administration

> Add to base number 355.622 the numbers following 352.4 in 352.43–352.49, e.g., defense budget 355.6229, defense budget of United States 355.622973

> *For payroll administration, see 355.64*

.64       Salary administration

> Class here wage and payroll administration

.68       Executive management

> Add to base number 355.68 the numbers following 352.3 in 352.33–352.38, e.g., inspection 355.685; however, for intelligence, see 355.3432; for counterintelligence, see 355.3433

> Class command and control systems in 355.33041

> *For managing executive personnel, see 355.33*

.69       Military mail; graves registration and burial services

.693       Military mail

.699       Graves registration and burial services

.7       **Military installations**

> Class here military bases, forts, permanent camps, posts, reservations

.709 3–.709 9      Specific continents, countries, localities

> Class here specific forts or systems of fortifications, installations having two or more functions

> Use notation for area of installation, not country maintaining it, e.g., United States bases in Panama Canal Area 355.70972875

.71      Quarters for personnel

> Housing at military installations

> Including barracks, prisoner-of-war camps

> Class comprehensive works on military housing in 355.12

.72      Medical installations

> Class medical supply depots in 355.75; class veterans' hospitals in 362.11; class comprehensive works on medical services in 355.345

.73      Artillery installations

> Class army artillery installations in 358.127

.74      Engineering installations

> Class army engineering installations in 358.227

.75      Supply depots and installations

> Class comprehensive works on supply services in 355.621

.79      Land

**.8      Military equipment and supplies (Matériel)**

> Limited to equipment and supplies common to two or more land forces, or to at least two of the three major defense forces, e.g., missiles and tanks, supplies of land and sea forces

> Including auxiliary techniques and procedures

> Class here weapons (ordnance); apparatus, equipment, materials; military aspects of research and development (other than procurement and contracting) of specific kinds of equipment and supplies

> Class mobilization of military industrial resources in 355.28; class comprehensive works on military aspects of research and development of equipment and supplies, of weapons in 355.07; class weapons limited to a specific land force in 356–357. Class interdisciplinary works on research and development of a specific kind of supplies and equipment with the kind in 338.47, e.g., small arms 338.4762344

> *For administration of specific kinds of equipment and supplies, see 355.621*

[.806 8]      Management

> Do not use; class in 355.621

[.807 2]      Research

> Do not use; class in 355.07

.81      Clothing, food, camp equipment, office supplies

.82      Specific kinds of weapons (ordnance)

Class specific kinds of weapons limited to a specific land force in 356–357

*For combat vehicles, see 355.83*

*See also 327.174 for problems of arms limitation and of verifying arms-control treaty provisions for specific kinds of weapons*

*See Manual at 355–359 vs. 623*

[.820 1–.820 9]      Standard subdivisions

Do not use; class in 355.801–355.809

.821      Artillery

Class army artillery in 358.1282

*For specific pieces of artillery, see 355.822; for artillery projectiles, see 355.82513*

.822      Specific pieces of artillery

Class specific pieces of army artillery in 358.1282

.823–.826      Other specific kinds of weapons

Add to base number 355.82 the numbers following 623.4 in 623.43–623.46, e.g., nuclear weapons 355.825119, artillery projectiles 355.82513; however, for comprehensive works on missiles, see 358.17182; for comprehensive works on chemical, biological, radiological weapons, on weapons of mass destruction, see 358.3; for ordnance of a force or service dedicated to a specific kind of weapon, see the force or service in 356–359, plus notation 82 or 83 from table at 356–359, e.g., tank ammunition 358.1882

.825 1      Charge-containing devices

Number built according to instructions under 355.823–355.826

Class here interdisciplinary works on bombs

*For military engineering of bombs, see 623.451*

.83      Transportation equipment and supplies

Including fuel; aircraft used outside air forces, ships used outside naval forces, support vehicles, trains

Class here combat vehicles

Class comprehensive works on aircraft in 358.4183; class comprehensive works on ships in 359.83

.85      Communication equipment

Class army communication equipment in 358.248

.88      Medical supplies

Class ambulances in 355.83

> ## 356–359   Specific kinds of military forces and warfare

Class here history of specific military forces not limited to any one war, services and units dedicated to specific forces, countermeasures against specific forces

All notes under 355 are applicable here

Except for modifications shown under specific entries, add to each subdivision identified by * as follows:

| | | |
|---|---|---|
| 01–09 | | Standard subdivisions |
| | | Notation from Table 1 as modified under 355.001–355.009, e.g., management 6 (*not* 068), management of artillery forces 358.126 (*not* 358.12068); however, class research, statistical methods in 072 |
| 1 | | Military life and customs |
| 14 | | Uniforms |
| 3 | | Organization and personnel |
| | | Class here units |
| | | *For personnel management, see 6* |
| 309 | | History, geographic treatment, biography |
| | | Class here units of specific countries regardless of size of unit |
| 4 | | Operations |
| | | Class here tactics |
| 5 | | Training |
| 6 | | Administration |
| | | Including administration of equipment and supplies, executive management, financial administration, personnel management |
| | | *For administration of a specific topic not provided for here, see the topic, plus notation 068 from Table 1, e.g., administration of installations 7068* |
| | | (Option: Class comprehensive works on administration in 353.29. If option is chosen, change heading to "Specific topics in administration," and do not add standard subdivisions) |
| 7 | | Installations |
| 8 | | Equipment and supplies (Matériel) |
| | | Class here weapons |
| [8068] | | Management |
| | | Do not use; class in 6 |
| 82 | | Weapons other than combat vehicles |
| 83 | | Combat vehicles |

Class comprehensive works in 355. Class a specific countermeasure with the force wielding it, e.g., coast artillery 358.16 (*not* 359)

*See Manual at 355–359 vs. 623; also at 930–990 vs. 355.009, 355–359*

> ## 356–357   Land forces and warfare

Class comprehensive works in 355

*For artillery, missile, armored forces, see 358.1; for chemical, biological, radiological warfare, see 358.3*

## 356     Foot forces and warfare

Standard subdivisions are added for either or both topics in heading

**.1**    **Infantry**

.11    General topics of infantry

    Class general topics of irregular troops in 356.15; class general topics of troops having special combat functions in 356.16

[.110 1–.110 9]  Standard subdivisions

    Do not use; class in 356.101–356.109

.111–.118  Specific topics of infantry

    Add to base number 356.11 notation 1–8 from table under 356–359, e.g., infantry training 356.115

.15    *Irregular troops

    Including guerrillas, partisans

.16    Troops having special combat functions

    Including motorized infantry

.162    Troops specializing in specific weapons

    Including bazookamen, grenadiers, machine gunners, sharpshooters (snipers)

.164    *Mountain and ski troops

    Subdivisions are added for either or both topics in heading

.166    *Paratroops

.167    *Commandos and rangers

    Subdivisions are added for either or both topics in heading

# 357  Mounted forces and warfare

    Standard subdivisions are added for either or both topics in heading

.04    General topics of mounted forces and warfare

[.040 1–.040 9]  Standard subdivisions

    Do not use; class in 357.01–357.09

.041    Military life and customs

.041 4    Uniforms

.043    Organization and personnel

    Class here comprehensive works on units that served as horse cavalry and mechanized or armored cavalry, e.g., U.S. Third Cavalry Division 357.0430973

    Class a specific period of service of a unit which changed kinds of mounts with the kind of mount, e.g., U.S. Third Cavalry Division as a horse unit 357.1830973

*Add as instructed under 356–359

.044–.048     Operations, training, administration, installations, equipment and supplies

> Add to base number 357.04 notation 4–8 from table under 356–359, e.g., training mounted forces 357.045

### .1      Horse cavalry

Class here dragoons, lancers

*For remount services, see 357.2*

*See also 358.12 for horse artillery*

.18      General topics of horse cavalry

[.180 1–.180 9]     Standard subdivisions

> Do not use; class in 357.101–357.109

.181–.188     Special topics of horse cavalry

> Add to base number 357.18 notation 1–8 from table under 356–359, e.g., uniforms of horse cavalry 357.1814

### .2      Remount services

### .5      Mechanized cavalry

*For armored cavalry, see 358.18*

.52      *Bicycle troops

.53      *Motorcycle troops

.54      Large motor-vehicle cavalry

Including jeep and truck cavalry

## 358     Air and other specialized forces and warfare; engineering and related services

### SUMMARY

| | | |
|---|---|---|
| 358.1 | Missile forces; army artillery and armored forces | |
| .2 | Army engineering and related services | |
| .3 | Chemical, biological, radiological warfare | |
| .4 | Air forces and warfare | |
| .8 | Space forces | |

### .1      Missile forces; army artillery and armored forces

.12      *Army artillery forces

Including antitank artillery forces

Class here field artillery forces

> *For antiaircraft artillery forces, see 358.13; for coast artillery forces, see 358.16*

*Add as instructed under 356–359

| | |
|---|---|
| .13 | *Antiaircraft artillery forces |
| .16 | *Coast artillery forces |
| .17 | Guided missile forces |

Class here strategic missile forces, nuclear missile forces

Class strategic land missile forces in 358.1754

*For air guided missile forces, see 358.42; for naval guided missile forces, see 359.9817*

| | |
|---|---|
| .171 | General topics of guided missile forces |

Class general topics of specific missile forces in 358.174–358.176

| | |
|---|---|
| [.171 01–.171 09] | Standard subdivisions |

Do not use; class in 358.1701–358.1709

| | |
|---|---|
| .171 1–.171 8 | Specific topics of guided missile forces |

Add to base number 358.171 notation 1–8 from table under 356–359, e.g., training of missile forces 358.1715

| | |
|---|---|
| .171 82 | Weapons other than combat vehicles |

Number built according to instructions under 358.1711–358.1718

Class here comprehensive works on missiles

*For military engineering of missiles, see 623.451*

| | |
|---|---|
| .174 | *Antimissile defense forces |

Class here Strategic Defense Initiative (SDI, star wars), surface-to-air missile forces

Class a specific defense other than surface-to-air missiles with the defense, e.g., beam weapon forces 358.39, air-to-air missile forces 358.43

| | |
|---|---|
| .175 | Specific surface-to-surface missile forces |
| [.175 01–.175 09] | Standard subdivisions |

Do not use; class in 358.1701–358.1709

| | |
|---|---|
| .175 2 | *Short-range missile forces |

Class here tactical missile forces

| | |
|---|---|
| .175 3 | *Intermediate-range missile forces |
| .175 4 | *Long-range missile forces |

Class here strategic land missile forces

| | |
|---|---|
| .176 | *Surface-to-underwater missile forces |
| .18 | *Armored forces |

Class here tank forces, armored cavalry

*Add as instructed under 356–359

.2          **Army engineering and related services**

.22          *Engineering services

>   Including property maintenance
>
>   Class here construction engineer services
>
>   Class communications services in 358.24; class transportation services in 358.25; class civil activities of army engineering services in 363

.23          *Demolition services

>   Including bomb disposal units

.24          *Communications forces (Signal forces)

>   Including military cryptography services

.25          *Transportation services

.3          **Chemical, biological, radiological warfare**

>   Regardless of service or force to which assigned
>
>   Class here warfare with weapons of mass destruction; interdisciplinary works on chemical, biological, radiological warfare; interdisciplinary works on weapons of mass destruction
>
>   *For nuclear warfare, see 355.0217. For a specific aspect of weapons of mass destruction, see the aspect, e.g., disarmament of weapons of mass destruction 327.1745*

.34          *Chemical warfare

.38          *Biological warfare

.39          *Radiation and beam warfare

>   Class here passive defense against nuclear radiation

.4          **Air forces and warfare**

>   Standard subdivisions are added for either or both topics in heading
>
>   *For naval air forces, see 359.94*

.400 1–.400 9          Standard subdivisions

>   Notation from Table 1 as modified under 355.001–355.009, e.g., air forces administration 358.416 (*not* 358.40068)

.403          Situation and policy

>   Standard subdivisions are added for either or both topics in heading
>
>   Class air defense operations in 358.414

*Add as instructed under 356–359

.407       Air force research and development

Limited to air force aspects

Class here relation of air force and warfare to science and technology, comprehensive works on air force aspects of research and development of equipment and supplies

Class interdisciplinary works on air force research and development in 338.47358407

*For procurement and contracting aspects of research and development of air force supplies and equipment, see 358.416212; for air force aspects of research and development (other than procurement and contracting) of specific kinds of equipment and supplies, see 358.418*

.41       General topics of air forces and warfare

Class general topics of specific forces in 358.42–358.47

[.410 1–.410 9]       Standard subdivisions

Do not use; class in 358.4001–358.4009

.411–.418       Specific topics of air forces and warfare

Add to base number 358.41 the numbers following 355 in 355.1–355.8, e.g., uniforms 358.4114, comprehensive works on military aircraft 358.4183; however, for aircraft of specific forces, see 358.42–358.47

---

>       358.42–358.47 Specific forces

Class chemical, biological, radiological warfare in 358.3; class comprehensive works in 358.4

.42       *Bombing forces

Including air-to-underwater guided missile forces

Class here strategic missions of air forces; air-to-surface guided missile forces; comprehensive works on air guided missile forces, on air nuclear forces

*For air-to-air guided missile forces, air-to-air nuclear forces, see 358.43*

.43       *Pursuit and fighter forces

Standard subdivisions are added for either or both topics in heading

Including air-to-air guided missile forces, air-to-air nuclear forces, air artillery

Class here tactical missions of air forces

.44       *Transportation services

.45       *Reconnaissance forces and operations

Including antisubmarine reconnaissance

*Add as instructed under 356–359

.46          *Communications services

> Class here signal services

.47          *Engineering services

**.8      *Space forces**

> *See also 358.17 for missile forces when either launch or target is from or to the earth or its atmosphere*

# 359      Sea forces and warfare

> Standard subdivisions are added for either or both topics in heading

> Class here naval forces and warfare

## SUMMARY

| | | |
|---|---|---|
| 359.001–.009 | | **Standard subdivisions** |
| .03–.07 | | **[Situation and policy, naval research and development]** |
| .1–.2 | | **Naval life and resources** |
| .3 | | **Organization and personnel of naval forces** |
| .4–.7 | | **Naval operations, training, administration, installations** |
| .8 | | **Naval equipment and supplies (Naval matériel)** |
| .9 | | **Specialized combat forces; engineering and related services** |

.001–.009      Standard subdivisions

> Notation from Table 1 as modified under 355.001–355.006, e.g., naval administration 359.6 (*not* 359.0068)

.03          Situation and policy

> Standard subdivisions are added for either or both topics in heading

> Class here naval defense

> Class naval defense operations in 359.4

.07          Naval research and development

> Limited to naval aspects

> Class here relation of naval science to science and technology; comprehensive works on naval aspects of research and development of equipment, supplies, weapons

> Class interdisciplinary works on naval research and development in 338.4735907

> *For procurement and contracting aspects of research and development of naval equipment and supplies, see 359.6212; for naval aspects of research and development (other than procurement and contracting) of specific kinds of equipment and supplies, see 359.81–359.88*

**.1–.2      Naval life and resources**

> Add to base number 359 the numbers following 355 in 355.1–355.2, e.g., uniforms 359.14

---

*Add as instructed under 356–359

**.3**      **Organization and personnel of naval forces**

.31      Naval units

> Including fleets, squadrons, flotillas, divisions
>
> Class noncombat services in 359.34; class reserves in 359.37
>
> *For ships as naval units, see 359.32*

.32      Ships as naval units

> Class here crews of ships
>
> Class comprehensive works on ships in the navy in 359.83
>
> *See Manual at 359.32 vs. 359.83*

.322      Sailing ships as naval units

> Class here sailing ships of war

.325–.326      Specific kinds of powered ships as naval units

> Add to base number 359.32 the numbers following 623.82 in 623.825–623.826, e.g., cruisers 359.3253; however, for submarines, see 359.933; for aircraft carriers, see 359.9435; for military supply and transport ships, see 359.9853

.33–.37      Personnel, noncombat services, fields of combat service, reserves

> Add to base number 359.3 the numbers following 355.3 in 355.33–355.37, e.g., noncombat services 359.34

**.4–.7**      **Naval operations, training, administration, installations**

> Add to base number 359 the numbers following 355 in 355.4–355.7, e.g., naval blockades 359.44

**.8**      **Naval equipment and supplies (Naval matériel)**

> Including auxiliary techniques and procedures
>
> Class here weapons (ordnance); apparatus, equipment, materials; naval aspects of research and development (other than procurement and contracting) of specific kinds of supplies and equipment
>
> Class mobilization of naval industrial resources in 359.28. Class interdisciplinary works on research and development of a specific kind of naval supplies and equipment with the kind in 338.47, e.g., warships 338.47623825

[.806 8]      Management

> Do not use; class in 359.621

[.807 2]      Research

> Do not use; class in 359.07

.81–.88      Specific kinds of naval equipment and supplies

> Add to base number 359.8 the numbers following 355.8 in 355.81–355.88, e.g., clothing 359.81; however, for ordnance on specific kinds of ships, see 359.83; for artillery, see 359.981282; for guided missiles, see 359.981782

.83  Transportation equipment and supplies

> Number built according to instructions under 359.8

> Including fuel, support vehicles

> Class here comprehensive works on ships in armed forces

>> *For ships as naval units, see 359.32. For ships used outside the naval forces, see the force using them, e.g., coast guard ships 359.9783*

>> *See Manual at 359.32 vs. 359.83*

.832  Sailing ships as equipment

> Class here sailing ships of war

.835–.836  Specific kinds of power-driven warships as equipment

> Add to base number 359.83 the numbers following 623.82 in 623.825–623.826, e.g., cruisers 359.8353; however, for submarines, see 359.9383; for aircraft carriers, see 359.94835; for military supply and transport ships, see 359.98583

## .9  Specialized combat forces; engineering and related services

> Class chemical, biological, radiological warfare in 358.3

.93  *Submarine forces

.933  Organization and personnel

> Number built according to instructions under 356–359

> Class here units, submarines as units

>> *See Manual at 359.32 vs. 359.83*

.938  Equipment and supplies (Matériel)

> Number built according to instructions under 356–359

.938 3  Ships as equipment

> Number built according to instructions under 356–359

> Class here submarines as equipment

>> *See Manual at 359.32 vs. 359.83*

.938 32  Conventionally powered submarines

.938 34  Nuclear powered submarines

.94  *Naval air forces

.943  Organization and personnel

> Number built according to instructions under 356–359

> Class here units

*Add as instructed under 356–359

| .943 4 | Aircraft units |
|---|---|

Including flights, groups, squadrons, wings

| .943 5 | Aircraft carriers as units |
|---|---|

*See Manual at 359.32 vs. 359.83*

| .948 | Equipment and supplies (Matériel) |
|---|---|

Number built according to instructions under 356–359

| .948 3 | Combat vehicles |
|---|---|

Number built according to instructions under 356–359

Class combat vehicles as units in 359.943

| .948 34 | Aircraft |
|---|---|
| .948 35 | Aircraft carriers as equipment |

*See Manual at 359.32 vs. 359.83*

| .96 | Marine forces |
|---|---|

Add to base number 359.96 the numbers following 355 in 355.1–355.8, e.g., training 355.965

| .97 | *Coast guard |
|---|---|

As a military service

Class coast guard as a police service, interdisciplinary works on coast guard in 363.286

| .98 | Artillery and guided missile forces; engineering and related services |
|---|---|
| .981 | Artillery and guided missile forces |
| .981 2 | *Artillery services |

Class artillery units aboard specific kinds of ships in 359.32; class artillery ordnance aboard specific kinds of ships in 359.83

| .981 7 | *Guided missile forces |
|---|---|

Class guided missile units aboard specific kinds of ships in 359.32; class guided missile ordnance aboard specific kinds of ships in 359.83

| .982 | *Engineering services |
|---|---|
| .983 | *Communications services (Signal services) |
| .984 | Special warfare services |

Including frogmen, underwater demolition units, underwater reconnaissance operations; sea, air, land teams

| .985 | *Transportation services |
|---|---|

Class here military sealift commands

*Add as instructed under 356–359

| .985 3 | Organization and personnel |
|---|---|
| | Number built according to instructions under 356–359 |
| | Including troopships as units |
| | Class here units, military supply ships as units |
| | *See Manual at 359.32 vs. 359.83* |
| .985 8 | Supplies and equipment (Matériel) |
| | Number built according to instructions under 356–359 |
| .985 83 | Military supply ships as equipment |
| | Number built according to instructions under 356–359 |
| | Including troopships |
| | *See Manual at 359.32 vs. 359.83* |

# 360          Social problems and services; associations

## SUMMARY

| 361 | Social problems and services |
|---|---|
| .001–.008 | Standard subdivisions |
| .02–.06 | Specific kinds of assistance |
| .1 | Social problems |
| .2 | Social action |
| .3 | Social work |
| .4 | Group work |
| .6 | Governmental action |
| .7 | Private action |
| .8 | Community action |
| .9 | History, geographic treatment, biography |
| | |
| 362 | Social problems of and services to groups of people |
| .04 | Special topics of social problems of and services to groups of people |
| .1 | People with physical illnesses |
| .2 | People with mental illness and disabilities |
| .3 | People with mental retardation |
| .4 | People with physical disabilities |
| .5 | Poor people |
| .6 | People in late adulthood |
| .7 | Young people |
| .8 | Other groups of people |
| .9 | History, geographic treatment, biography |
| | |
| 363 | Other social problems and services |
| .1 | Public safety programs |
| .2 | Police services |
| .3 | Other aspects of public safety |
| .4 | Controversies related to public morals and customs |
| .5 | Housing |
| .6 | Public utilities and related services |
| .7 | Environmental problems |
| .8 | Food supply |
| .9 | Population problems |

| | | |
|---|---|---|
| **364** | | **Criminology** |
| | .01–.09 | Standard subdivisions and special topics of criminology |
| | .1 | Criminal offenses |
| | .2 | Causes of crime and delinquency |
| | .3 | Offenders |
| | .4 | Prevention of crime and delinquency |
| | .6 | Penology |
| | .8 | Discharged offenders |
| | .9 | History, geographic treatment, biography of crime and its alleviation |
| | | |
| **365** | | **Penal and related institutions** |
| | .3 | Kinds of penal institutions |
| | .4 | Institutions for specific classes of inmates |
| | .5 | Prison plant |
| | .6 | Inmates |
| | .7 | Reform of penal institutions |
| | .9 | History, geographic treatment, biography |
| | | |
| **366** | | **Secret associations and societies** |
| | .01–.09 | Standard subdivisions |
| | .1 | Freemasonry |
| | .2 | Knights of Pythias |
| | .3 | Independent Order of Odd Fellows |
| | .5 | Benevolent and Protective Order of Elks |
| | | |
| **367** | | **General clubs** |
| | .9 | History, geographic treatment, biography |
| | | |
| **368** | | **Insurance** |
| | .001–.009 | Standard subdivisions and insurance companies |
| | .01–.09 | [General principles, specific forms of risk, sales groupings] |
| | .1 | Insurance against damage to and loss of property |
| | .2 | Insurance against damage to and loss of property in transit |
| | .3 | Old-age insurance and insurance against death, illness, injury |
| | .4 | Government-sponsored insurance |
| | .5 | Liability insurance |
| | .6 | Glass insurance |
| | .7 | Insurance against industrial casualties (accidents) |
| | .8 | Other casualty insurance |
| | .9 | Insurance by specific continents, countries, localities in modern world |
| | | |
| **369** | | **Associations** |
| | .01–.09 | Standard subdivisions |
| | .1 | Hereditary, military, patriotic societies of United States |
| | .2 | Hereditary, military, patriotic societies |
| | .3 | Ethnic clubs |
| | .4 | Young people's societies |
| | .5 | Service clubs |

## 361 Social problems and services

Class here social welfare; work and policy of government agencies that enforce the law in matters of social problems and services; interdisciplinary works on socioeconomic planning and development, on programs and services covering several branches of social sciences, on social problems and services

Class law of social services, including draft laws, enforcement of the law by courts, in 344.02–344.05; class the internal administration of governmental agencies dealing with social services, including their administrative annual reports, in 353.5; class insurance in 368; class personal health and safety in 613; class description of present or past social conditions in 930–990

> *For social problems considered purely as social phenomena, see 301–307; for community planning and development, see 307.1; for economic planning and development, see 338.9; for social services in armed forces, see 355–359; for specific problems and services, see 362–365; for school social services, see 371.7; for social services in specific wars, see 900*

> *See Manual at 361–365; also at 301–307 vs. 361–365; also at 361–365 vs. 353.5; also at 361 vs. 362–363*

### SUMMARY

| | |
|---|---|
| 361.001–.008 | Standard subdivisions |
| .02–.06 | Specific kinds of assistance |
| .1 | Social problems |
| .2 | Social action |
| .3 | Social work |
| .4 | Group work |
| .6 | Governmental action |
| .7 | Private action |
| .8 | Community action |
| .9 | History, geographic treatment, biography |

.001–.007    Standard subdivisions

.008    Groups of people

Do not use for social problems of and services to groups of people; class in 362

[.009]    History, geographic treatment, biography

Do not use; class in 361.9

---

>    361.02–361.06  Specific kinds of assistance

Class here general discussions covering various problems and client groups, and both governmental and private assistance

Class comprehensive works in 361. Class assistance with respect to a specific problem with the problem, e.g., free assistance to people in late adulthood 362.6

> *For governmental assistance, see 361.6; for private assistance, see 361.7*

.02    Free assistance

Class specific kinds of free assistance in 361.05–361.06

.04 **Paid assistance**

Assistance for which the recipient pays all or part of cost

Class specific kinds of paid assistance in 361.05–361.06

.05 **Material assistance**

Including direct provision of food, clothing, shelter (temporary housing); financial aid; institutional care; recreational activities and facilities; relief

.06 **Counseling, guidance, related services**

Standard subdivisions are added for counseling, guidance, related services together; for counseling alone; for guidance alone

Services directed toward enabling individuals and groups to assist themselves

Including citizens advice bureaus; telephone counseling, e.g., hot lines

Class social work in 361.3

**.1 Social problems**

History, description, appraisal of areas and kinds of social breakdown, of problems endemic to human society

Including risk assessment

*For specific problems, see 362–363*

**.2 Social action**

Class change as a social phenomenon in 303.4

*For a specific aspect of social action not provided for here, see the aspect in 361.3–361.8, e.g., social work 361.3*

.23 **Dissent and protest**

Standard subdivisions are added for either or both topics in heading

.24 **Reform movements**

.25 **Action within established social framework**

Class here planning, policy, programs, proposals; citizen participation; comprehensive works on governmental and private action

*For international action, see 361.26; for social work, see 361.3; for governmental action, see 361.6; for private action, see 361.7; for combined governmental and private community action, see 361.8*

.26 **International action**

Class governmental international action in 361.6; class private international action in 361.77

**.3 Social work**

.32        Practice of social work

         Class here casework

         *For counseling, see 361.06; for group work, see 361.4*

.322       Interviewing

.37        Volunteer social work

         *For a specific aspect of volunteer social work, see the aspect, e.g.,*
         *interviewing 361.322*

**.4**        **Group work**

         Class counseling in group work in 361.06

.43        Self-help groups

         Class here mutual aid, support groups

**.6**        **Governmental action**

         Class here intergovernmental assistance and planning, governmental
         international action, interdisciplinary works on government-sponsored
         socioeconomic planning and development

         Class combined governmental and private action in 361.25; class governmental
         social work in 361.3; class combined governmental and private community
         action in 361.8

         *For management of governmental agencies regulating social welfare*
         *services, see 353.5*

.61        Social policy

         Class welfare reform in 361.68

.612       Goals, values, priorities

.613       Relation of politics and social action

         Class effect of social action on political structures and values in 320

.614       Relation of welfare and human rights

         Including use of compulsory remedial action

         Class interdisciplinary works on human rights in 323

.615       Relation of government and private sectors

         Class welfare state in 361.65

.65        Welfare state

         Class economics of welfare state in 330.126

.68        Welfare reform

**.7**        **Private action**

         Class combined governmental and private action in 361.25; class private social
         work in 361.3; class relation of government and private sectors in 361.615; class
         combined governmental and private community action in 361.8

| | |
|---|---|
| .706 | Organizations and management |

Do not use for a specific kind of organization; class in 361.75–361.77 with the kind e.g., nonprofit organizations 361.763

| | |
|---|---|
| .706 81 | Organization and financial management |

Class here fund raising

Class charity, thrift shops in 381.19

| | |
|---|---|
| .708 | Groups of people |

Do not use for private action to a group of people; class in 362

| | |
|---|---|
| .74 | Individual philanthropy |

Class an organization that controls the use of the money donated by a philanthropist with the organization, e.g., Rockefeller Foundation 361.7632

| | |
|---|---|
| .75 | Religious organizations |
| .76 | Private organizations |

Class religious organizations in 361.75; class private international organizations in 361.77

| | |
|---|---|
| .763 | Nonprofit organizations |

Including CARE

| | |
|---|---|
| .763 2 | Charitable foundations and trusts |
| .763 4 | National Red Cross and Red Crescent societies |

Standard subdivisions are added for either or both topics in heading

Class here affiliated national societies, e.g., Red Crystal

Class comprehensive works on International Committee of the Red Cross, International Federation of Red Cross and Red Crescent Societies in 361.772

| | |
|---|---|
| .765 | Business organizations |

Class ways that management can deal with charitable donations in 658.153; class programs of employers for employees in 658.38

| | |
|---|---|
| .766 | Labor unions |
| .77 | Private international organizations |

*See also 361.76 for local organizations providing services worldwide*

| | |
|---|---|
| .772 | International Committee of the Red Cross; International Federation of Red Cross and Red Crescent Societies |

Standard subdivisions are added for either or both topics in heading

*For Red Cross, Red Crescent, affiliated societies of a specific nation, see 361.7634*

**.8**      **Community action**

Including community chests, united charities

Class community development in 307.14; class governmental community action in 361.6; class private community action in 361.7

**.9**      **History, geographic treatment, biography**

Class history, geographic treatment, biography of specific kinds of social action in 361.2–361.8

.901–.905      Historical periods

Add to base number 361.90 the numbers following —090 in notation 0901–0905 from Table 1, e.g., welfare work in 20th century 361.904

.91–.99      Geographic treatment, biography

Add to base number 361.9 notation 1–9 from Table 2, e.g., welfare work in Arizona 361.9791

---

>      **362–363   Specific social problems and services**

Except for modifications shown under specific entries, add to each subdivision identified by * as follows:

| | |
|---|---|
| 01 | Philosophy and theory |
| 02 | Miscellany |
| [0218] | Standards |
| | Do not use; class in 62 |
| [0289] | Safety measures |
| | Do not use; class in 363.1 |
| 03–05 | Standard subdivisions |
| 06 | Organizations and management |
| 0681 | Organization and financial management |
| | Including managerial cost control |
| | Class social measures to hold down costs in 5 |
| 07 | Education, research, related topics |
| 08 | Groups of people |

Do not use for discrimination as social cause; class in 1. Do not use for actions against discrimination; class in 5

*See also 3 for people close to those with a problem*

| | |
|---|---|
| 09 | History, geographic treatment, biography |
| >1–4 | Characteristics of problem |

Class comprehensive works in 362–363 without adding from this table

| | |
|---|---|
| 1 | Social causes |

Including discrimination

Class here sources

| | |
|---|---|
| 2 | Incidence, extent, severity |

Standard subdivisions are added for any or all topics in heading

Including risk assessment

(continued)

> **362–363 Specific social problems and services (continued)**

3     Effects on people close to those with a problem
> Including effects on co-workers, on neighbors
> Class here families
> Class aftereffects on people close to those with a problem in 4; class family problems in 362.82

4     Aftereffects of people with a problem
> Either effects on the individual with the problem that occur after the problem has ceased, or effects on other people that occur after the problem has ceased or the other people are no longer close to the individual with the problem
> Class here adult children of people with a problem
> Class a specific aftereffect with the aftereffect, e.g., social aspects of alcoholism in victims of child abuse 362.292, medical aspects of depression in adult victims of child abuse 616.8527

5     Social action
> Class here social action to relieve discrimination, social measures to hold down costs
> Add to 5 the numbers following 361 in 361.2–361.8, e.g., international action 526, social work 53, rationing 56
> Class governmental administration of rationing programs in 352.86; class comprehensive works on social action in 361.2
> *For specific forms of action, see 6–8*

>6–8     Specific forms of action
> Class comprehensive works in 5
> Works containing topics from any two of these subdivisions are classed in 5

6     Control
> Elimination and reduction of hazards, of sources and causes of difficulty
> Class measures to protect against and to limit effects of problems in 7

62     Standards

63     Monitoring, surveillance, reporting
> Standard subdivisions are added for any or all topics in heading

64     Inspection and testing
> Standard subdivisions are added for either or both topics in heading

65     Investigation of specific incidents
> Class criminal investigation of specific incidents in 364.1

66     Certification

7     Measures to prevent, protect against, limit effects of problems
> Class here preparedness
> Class measures that both control and prevent problems in 6
> *For safety measures, see 363.1*

72     Protective measures
> Including design of environments, warning and guidance systems

(continued)

> ## 362–363 Specific social problems and services (continued)

| | |
|---|---|
| 8 | Remedial measures, services, forms of assistance |
| | Measures applicable primarily to individuals, even if in large groups |
| | Class here material assistance |
| | Class remedial measures directed toward altering a social function, e.g., cost control, in 5; class social work in 53; class comprehensive works on material assistance in 361.05 |
| 809 | History, geographic treatment, biography |
| | Class here the area receiving assistance, e.g., relief to Italy provided by the United States 809450973 |
| | Class the area providing assistance in 8 without adding from Table 1, e.g., relief provided by the United States to many countries 8, not 80973 |
| 81 | Rescue operations |
| 82 | Financial assistance |
| | Class social insurance in 368.4 |
| 83 | Provision of food, shelter (temporary housing), household assistance, clothing, other related necessities; recreation |
| | Class long-term housing in 363.59 |
| 84 | Employment services |
| | Including vocational rehabilitation |
| 85 | Residential care |
| | Care within institutions existing for the purpose |
| 86 | Counseling and guidance |
| | Standard subdivisions are added for either or both topics in heading |
| | Including legal aid |
| | Class comprehensive works on counseling and guidance in 361.06 |

Class discrimination in 305; class comprehensive works in 361

*For criminology, see 364*

*See Manual at 361 vs. 362–363; also at 362–363 vs. 364.1*

## 362    Social problems of and services to groups of people

Class here social security

Unless other instructions are given, observe the following table of preference, e.g., mentally ill veterans 362.208697 (*not* 362.860874):

| | |
|---|---|
| People with physical illnesses | 362.1 |
| People with mental illness and disabilities | 362.2 |
| People with mental retardation | 362.3 |
| People with physical disabilities | 362.4 |
| Displaced persons | 362.87 |
| Victims of crimes and war | 362.88 |
| Veterans of military service | 362.86 |
| People in late adulthood | 362.6 |
| Young people | 362.7 |
| Working class | 362.85 |
| Women | 362.83 |
| Transgender and intersex people | 362.897 |
| People by sexual orientation | 362.896 |
| People with status defined by changes in residence | 362.8991 |
| Retired people | 362.8996 |
| Poor people | 362.5 |
| Unemployed people | 362.8994 |
| People by miscellaneous social attributes (without subdivisions) | 362.899 |
| People by social and economic levels | 362.892 |
| Miscellaneous groups of people (without subdivisions) | 362.89 |
| Families | 362.82 |
| Ethnic and national groups | 362.84 |
| Other groups of people (without subdivisions) | 362.8 |
| History, geographic treatment, biography | 362.9 |

Use notation 08 from Table 1 to indicate the specific group of people to whom the service is rendered, e.g., young adults addicted to narcotics 362.293084, poor veterans of military service 362.86086942. Do not use notation 08 from Table 1 to indicate services rendered by groups of people, e.g., services rendered by young adults to people addicted to narcotics 362.293, not 362.2930842

> For social problems of and services to military personnel, see 355.34; for social problems of and services to prisoners, see 365.66; for social security as a form of social insurance, see 368.4; for social problems of and services to students, see 371.7

> See also 920.008 for general collections of biography of members of a specific group that share a social problem

> See Manual at 920.008 vs. 305–306, 362

## SUMMARY

|  |  |
|---|---|
| **362.04** | **Special topics of social problems of and services to groups of people** |
| **.1** | **People with physical illnesses** |
| **.2** | **People with mental illness and disabilities** |
| **.3** | **People with mental retardation** |
| **.4** | **People with physical disabilities** |
| **.5** | **Poor people** |
| **.6** | **People in late adulthood** |
| **.7** | **Young people** |
| **.8** | **Other groups of people** |
| **.9** | **History, geographic treatment, biography** |

.04        Special topics of social problems of and services to groups of people

.042        Social problems

.042 2        Incidence, extent, severity

> Including social effects

.042 3        Social causes

.042 4        Prevention

.042 5        Social action

> Including remedial measures
>
> Class prevention in 362.0424

[.08]        Groups of people

> Do not use; class in 362.1–362.8

[.09]        History, geographic treatment, biography

> Do not use; class in 362.9

---

> ### 362.1–362.4 People with illnesses and disabilities

Class incidence of and public measures to prevent physical diseases in 614.4–614.5; class comprehensive works in 362.1

*See Manual at 362.1–362.4 vs. 610; also at 362.1–362.4 and 614.4–614.5*

### .1        People with physical illnesses

Class here interdisciplinary works on illness and disability, on medical care and treatment, on medical missions, on public health

*For religious aspects of medical missions, see 266; for sociology of medicine, of health, of illness, see 306.461; for mental illness, see 362.2; for mental retardation, see 362.3; for problems of and services to people with a specific physical disability regardless of cause, see 362.4; for technology of medicine, see 610*

# SUMMARY

.102 3    Services to people with physical illnesses as a profession, occupation, hobby

Class here interdisciplinary works on health occupations peripheral to the medical and paramedical professions

Class works covering both the medical and peripheral occupations in 610

*For a specific peripheral profession, see the profession, e.g., medical social workers 362.10425, hospital secretaries 651.3741*

.104    Special topics of people with physical illnesses

.104 2    Social aspects

Class preventive measures in 614.44–614.48

.104 22    Social effects

Class incidence in 614.42

.104 25    Forms of assistance

Including medical social work

Class here comprehensive works on health assistance and health and accident insurance

*For health and accident insurance, see 368.382; for government sponsored health and accident insurance, see 368.42*

.104 252    Financial assistance

.104 256    Counseling and guidance

Standard subdivisions are added for either or both topics in heading

.104 257    Rural health services

.104 258    Managed care plans

.104 258 4    Health maintenance organizations (HMOs)

.106 8    Management

Class here peer reviews

Class the result of a peer reviews with the result, e.g., the result of the evaluation of New York City hospitals 362.11097471

| | | |
|---|---|---|
| .108 | | Groups of people |

> Do not use for services rendered by groups of people; class in 362.1
>
> Class physical illness among groups of people in 616.008

.108 3          Young people

> Do not use for infants and children up to puberty; class in 362.19892

.108 4          People in specific stages of adulthood

[.108 46]          People in late adulthood

> Do not use; class in 362.19897

.109          History, geographic treatment, biography

[.109 173 4]          Rural regions

> Do not use; class in 362.104257

---

> 362.11–362.19  Medical services

Free and paid

Class medical treatment in 616; class comprehensive works in 362.1

---

> 362.11–362.16  Services of specific kinds of institutions

Class services of health maintenance organizations in 362.1042584; class specific kinds of services provided by a specific institution in 362.17; class services by a specific institution to patients with specific conditions in 362.19; class comprehensive works in 362.1

.11          Hospitals and related institutions

Standard subdivisions are added for hospitals and related institutions together, for hospitals alone

*For clinics and related institutions, see 362.12; for extended medical care facilities, see 362.16*

.12          Clinics and related institutions

Standard subdivisions are added for clinics and related institutions together, for clinics alone

Including dispensaries, health centers, outpatient departments of general hospitals

Class here ambulatory care, community health services

.14          Professional home care

Including visiting nurses' services, services of health visitors

*See also 649.8 for home care by family members*

**.16**      Extended medical care facilities

Including convalescent homes, sanatoriums for people suffering from chronic diseases

Class here extended medical care facilities for people in late adulthood, institutions providing complete medical care, nursing homes providing complete medical care

Class comprehensive works on life care communities in 362.61

**[.160 846]**      People in late adulthood

Do not use; class in 362.16

**.17**      Specific services

Class here social provision of specific kinds of medical services, interdisciplinary works covering both social provision and technology of specific kinds of medical services

Unless other instructions are given, class a subject with aspects in two or more subdivisions of 362.17 in the number coming last, e.g., diagnostic services by doctors 362.177 (*not* 362.172)

Class forms of assistance in 362.10425; class specific kinds of services to patients with specific conditions in 362.19; class group practice in 610.65

> *For emergency services, see 362.18; for technology of medical services, see 610; for preventive services, see 614.44*

**.172**      Services of physicians

Including referral and consulting services

**.173**      Services of nurses

Class visiting nurses' services in 362.14

**.173 068**      Management of services of nurses

Class here nonmedical aspects of ward management

**.174**      Intensive care

**.175**      Terminal care

**.175 6**      Hospices

**.176**      Nutritional services

Class here feeding of sick, comprehensive works on the provision of special diets for various classes of people with illnesses

Class nutritional programs for the population at large in 363.8

> *For nutritional services applied to nutrition disorders, see 362.19639*

**.177**      Diagnostic and screening services

Including radiology services

**.178**      Therapeutic services

| | |
|---|---|
| .178 2 | Pharmaceutical services |

Class nutritional services in 362.176

| | |
|---|---|
| .178 3 | Organ and tissue banks |

Standard subdivisions are added for either or both topics in heading

Including eye banks

*For blood and blood plasma banks, see 362.1784*

| | |
|---|---|
| .178 4 | Blood and blood plasma banks |

Standard subdivisions are added for either or both topics in heading

| | |
|---|---|
| .178 6 | Rehabilitation services |
| .18 | Emergency services |

Including trauma centers

| | |
|---|---|
| .188 | Ambulance services |
| .19 | Services to patients with specific conditions |

Class here living with a physical disease

Class incidence of and public measures to prevent specific diseases in 614.5

*See also 362.10425 for indigent patients; also 362.175 for terminal patients*

| | |
|---|---|
| [.190 1–.190 9] | Standard subdivisions |

Do not use; class in 362.101–362.109

| | |
|---|---|
| .196–.198 | Specific conditions |

Add to base number 362.19 the numbers following 61 in 616–618 for the condition only, e.g., services to patients with diabetes 362.196462, dental care 362.1976, maternity services 362.1982; then add further as follows (*not* as instructed under 616.1–616.9, 617, or 618.1–618.8); however, for 362.19892 pediatric care, add 0 before adding further, e.g., periodicals on pediatric care 362.198920005:

> 001–009    Standard subdivisions
> > Notation from Table 1 as modified under 616.1–616.9, e.g., biography of an individual with diabetes 362.1964620092, periodicals on dental care 362.1976005
>
> 02–08    Specific services
> > Add to base number 0 the numbers following 362.17 in 362.172–362.178, e.g., intensive care 04

*For services to people with mental illness, see 362.2*

| | |
|---|---|
| [.198 18] | Birth control services |

Do not use; class in 363.96

.198 88 Abortion services

Number built according to instructions under 362.196–362.198

Class here interdisciplinary works [*formerly* 363.46]

> *For a specific aspect of abortion, see the aspect, e.g., abortion as a controversy 363.46, abortion as a crime 364.185, medical aspects of abortion 618.88*

## .2 †People with mental illness and disabilities

Standard subdivisions are added for either or both topics in heading

Class here mental disabilities that consist of mental retardation combined with mental illness

Class life with a psychiatric disorder in 616.890092

> *For mental retardation, see 362.3*

### SUMMARY

| | |
|---|---|
| 362.204 | **Special topics of people with mental illness and disabilities** |
| .21 | **Mental health facilities** |
| .22 | **Community mental health services** |
| .23 | **Extended care facilities** |
| .24 | **Professional home care** |
| .25 | **Neuroses** |
| .26 | **Psychoses** |
| .27 | **Disorders of personality, intellect, impulse control** |
| .28 | **Suicide** |
| .29 | **Substance abuse** |

.204 Special topics of people with mental illness and disabilities

.204 2 Social aspects

.204 22 Incidence, extent, severity

Including social effects

.204 25 Prevention and forms of assistance

Class here psychiatric social work

.204 251 Emergency and rescue operations

Standard subdivisions are added for either or both topics in heading

Class here hot lines

.204 252 Financial assistance

.204 256 Counseling and guidance

Standard subdivisions are added for either or both topics in heading

---

†Do not use notation 08 from Table 1 to indicate services rendered by groups of people; class in base number

> **362.21–362.24 Medical services**

Class care for specific problems in 362.25–362.29; class medical treatment in 616.8; class comprehensive works in 362.2

.21 Mental health facilities

Class here psychiatric hospitals

*For psychiatric clinics, see 362.22; for nursing homes and sanatoriums, see 362.23*

.22 Community mental health services

Class here psychiatric clinics

.223 Group homes

.23 Extended care facilities

Class here nursing homes, sanatoriums

.24 Professional home care

> **362.25–362.29 Specific problems**

Class comprehensive works in 362.2

.25 †Neuroses

Including anorexia nervosa, compulsive gambling, depression

.26 †Psychoses

Including schizophrenia

.27 †Disorders of personality, intellect, impulse control

Including food addiction, kleptomania

*For suicide, see 362.28; for substance abuse, see 362.29*

.28 *†Suicide

Class here suicidal behavior

.288 1 Rescue operations

Number built according to instructions under 362–363

Class here emergency services, hot lines

*Add as instructed under 362–363
†Do not use notation 08 from Table 1 to indicate services rendered by groups of people; class in base number

.29          †Substance abuse

Class here drug abuse; interdisciplinary works on substance abuse, addiction, habituation, intoxication

Class works on drug abuse limited to narcotic abuse in 362.293

*For subculture of substance abusers, see 306.1; for drug traffic, see 363.45; for illegal sale, possession, use of drugs, see 364.177; for drug use as a custom, see 394.1; for medical aspects of substance abuse, see 616.86*

*See also 362.27 for food addiction*

*See Manual at 616.86 vs. 158.1, 204.42, 248.8629, 292–299, 362.29*

.291          Aspects of substance abuse

Class aspects of a specific substance in 362.292–362.299

[.291 01–.291 09]          Standard subdivisions

Do not use; class in 362.2901–362.2909

.291 1–.291 8          Specific aspects of substance abuse

Add to base number 362.291 notation 1–8 from table under 362–363, e.g., prevention of substance abuse 362.2917; however, for control of drug traffic, see 363.45

Notation 1–8 from table under 362–363 is added for both specific aspects of two or more of the substances provided for in 362.292–362.298 and for a combination of substances provided for in 362.292–362.298 and in 362.299, e.g., counseling for alcohol and cocaine abuse, for narcotics and stimulant abuse 362.29186

.292          *†Alcohol

Class here interdisciplinary works on alcoholism

*For a specific aspect of alcoholism, see the aspect, e.g., medical aspects 616.861*

[.292 6]          Control of sale of alcoholic beverages

Do not use; class in 363.41

.292 8          Remedial measures, services, forms of assistance

Number built according to instructions under 362–363

.292 86          Counseling and guidance

Number built according to instructions under 362–363

Class here services of Alcoholics Anonymous

---

*Add as instructed under 362–363

†Do not use notation 08 from Table 1 to indicate services rendered by groups of people; class in base number

| .293 | *†Narcotics |
|------|-------------|

Opium and its derivatives and synthetic equivalents

Class here specific narcotics, e.g., heroin, morphine

| .294 | *†Hallucinogens and psychedelics |
|------|----------------------------------|

Class here specific hallucinogens and psychedelics, e.g., LSD, mescaline, PCP

Subdivisions are added for either or both topics in heading

Class cannabis in 362.295

| .295 | *†Cannabis |
|------|------------|

Class here specific kinds of cannabis, e.g., hashish, marijuana

| .296 | *†Tobacco |
|------|-----------|

| .298 | *†Cocaine |
|------|-----------|

Class here specific forms of cocaine, e.g., crack

| .299 | †Other substances |
|------|-------------------|

Including analgesics, depressants, inhalants, sedatives, stimulants

Class here designer drugs (synthetic drugs of abuse), prescription drugs

Class alcohol in 362.292; class cocaine in 362.298

*For designer hallucinogens, see 362.294*

| [.299 1] | Aspects of more than one substance |
|----------|-------------------------------------|

Number discontinued; class in 362.299

| .299 3 | *†Inhalants |
|--------|-------------|

Class here gases and solvents used as inhalants; individual gases or solvents, e.g., amyl nitrate, glue

| .299 5 | *†Stimulants |
|--------|--------------|

Class here specific kinds of stimulants, e.g., amphetamine, ephedrine, methamphetamine

Class cocaine in 362.298

| .3 | *†**People with mental retardation** |
|----|--------------------------------------|

Class comprehensive works on problems of and services to people with developmental disabilities (those who have neurological diseases combined with mental retardation and whose problems exhibit themselves before age 18) in 362.1968; class comprehensive works on treatment of mental retardation and mental illness in 362.2

*Add as instructed under 362–363

†Do not use notation 08 from Table 1 to indicate services rendered by groups of people; class in base number

**.4          †People with physical disabilities**

> Regardless of cause
>
> Class here comprehensive works on people with disabilities, people with physical and mental disabilities
>
> Class comprehensive medical works in 617
>
> *For people with mental disabilities, see 362.3*

.404          Special topics of people with physical disabilities, people with physical and mental disabilities

> Add to base number 362.404 notation 1–8 from table under 362–363, e.g., social work with people with physical disabilities 362.40453 Subdivisions are added for either or both topics in heading

.404 84          Employment services

> Number built according to instructions under 362–363

.404 848          Sheltered employment

.41          *†People with blindness and visual impairments

> Class here people who are blind-deaf
>
> Subdivisions are added for either or both topics in heading
>
> *For people who are deaf, see 362.42*

.42          *†People with hearing impairments

> Class here people who are deaf
>
> Class comprehensive works on people with linguistic and communication disabilities in 362.196855; class people who are blind-deaf in 362.41
>
> *See also 371.912 for teaching people who are deaf*

.43          *†People with mobility impairments

> Subdivisions are added for services to people with specific mobility impairments, e.g., residential care for paraplegics 362.4385

**.5          *†Poor people**

> Class economic causes and effects of poverty in 339.46

.508          Groups of people

> Do not use for services rendered by groups of people; class in 362.5

[.508 3]          Young people

> Do not use for poor young people through age seventeen; class in 362.77569

---

*Add as instructed under 362–363
†Do not use notation 08 from Table 1 to indicate services rendered by groups of people; class in base number

| [.508 35] | Young people eighteen to twenty |
| | Relocated to 362.77569 |
| .508 6 | People by miscellaneous social attributes |
| [.508 694 1] | Unemployed people |
| | Relocated to 362.594 |
| [.508 694 2] | Homeless people |
| | Do not use; class in 362.592 |
| .508 9 | Ethnic and national groups [*formerly* 362.84] |

.57      Measures to prevent, protect against, limit effects of poverty

Number built according to instructions under 362–363

Class economic measures to prevent poverty in 339

.58      Remedial measures, services, forms of assistance

Number built according to instructions under 362–363

Class birth control as a remedy for poverty in 363.96; class assistance to poor people under social security in 368.4

*For food stamp programs, see 363.882*

.582      Financial assistance

Number built according to instructions under 362–363

Including guaranteed minimum income, negative income tax

Class here supplementary social security for low income people

Class aid to families with dependent children (AFDC) in 362.713

.583      Provision of shelter (temporary houusing) [*formerly* 363.58]; provision of clothing, other related necessities; recreation

Number built according to instructions under 362–363

Do not use for food programs; class in 363.8

Class long-term housing in 363.5

.586      Counseling and guidance

Number built according to instructions under 362–363

Including interdisciplinary works on legal aid

*For law of legal aid, see 347.017*

.59      Homeless and unemployed people

.592      *†Homeless people

---

*Add as instructed under 362–363

†Do not use notation 08 from Table 1 to indicate services rendered by groups of people; class in base number

.594       \*†Unemployed people [*formerly* 362.5086941]

**.6**       **People in late adulthood**

         Class here social gerontology

[.608]       Groups of people

         Relocated to 362.69

---

>       362.61–362.66 Remedial measures, services, forms of assistance

         Class comprehensive works in 362.63

         *For specific problems, see 362.68; for services to groups of people in late adulthood, see 362.69*

.61       Residential care

         Class here assisted living; facilities providing minimal medical care, e.g., medication maintenance; services of life care communities (continuing care retirement communities), old age homes, rest homes

         Class institutions providing complete medical care in 362.16; class housing in 363.5946

.63       Remedial measures, services, forms of assistance

         Measures applicable primarily to individuals, even if in large groups

         Class here material assistance

         Including provision of financial aid, food, shelter (temporary housing), household assistance, clothing, recreation

         Class remedial measures directed toward altering a social function, e.g., cost control, in 362.675; class social work in 362.6753

         *For residential care, see 362.61; for employment services, see 362.64; for counseling and guidance, see 362.66; for specific problems, see 362.68; for services to groups of people, see 362.69*

.64       Employment services

         Including vocational rehabilitation

.66       Counseling and guidance

         Standard subdivisions are added for either or both topics in heading

.67       Characteristics of problems, social action

         Add to base number 362.67 notation 1–7 from table under 362–363, e.g., effects on families 362.673

         *For remedial measures, services, forms of assistance, see 362.63; for specific problems, see 362.68; for problems of groups of people in late adulthood, see 362.69*

\*Add as instructed under 362–363

†Do not use notation 08 from Table 1 to indicate services rendered by groups of people; class in base number

.68       Specific problems

> *For problems of groups of people, see 362.69*

.682       †Elder abuse

> Class parent abuse in 362.8292; class elder abuse as a crime in 364.1555. Class elder abuse in a specific situation with the situation, e.g., elder abuse in nursing homes 362.16

.69       Groups of people [*formerly* 362.608]

.691–.698       Miscellaneous specific groups of people

> Add to base number 362.69 the numbers following —08 in notation 081–088 from Table 1, e.g., women in late adulthood 362.692; then add further as follows:
>
> 001–007    Standard subdivisions
> 008         Groups of people
>            Do not use for services rendered by groups of people; class in base number
> 009         History, geographic treatment, biography
> 01–08    Characteristics of problems, social action
>            Add to 0 notation 1–8 from table under 362–363, e.g., effects on families of women in late adulthood 362.6923

.699       People in late adulthood by ethnic or national group

> Class treatment with respect to miscellaneous specific groups of people in late adulthood of a specific ethnic and national group with the kind of people in 362.691–362.698, e.g., Chinese women in late adulthood 362.692

.699 001–.699 007       Standard subdivisions

.699 008       Groups of people

> Do not use for services rendered by groups of people; class in 362.699

.699 009       History, geographic treatment, biography

.699 05–.699 09       †People in late adulthood of mixed ancestry with ethnic origins from more than one continent, Europeans in late adulthood and people in late adulthood of European descent

> Add to base number 362.6990 the numbers following 0 in notation 05–09 from Table 5, e.g., people in late adulthood of European descent 362.69909, people in late adulthood of European descent in Australia 362.69909094

.699 1–.699 9       †People in late adulthood by specific ethnic or national groups

> Add to base number 362.699 notation 1–9 from Table 5, e.g., people in late adulthood of Italian descent 362.69951, people in late adulthood of Italian descent in United States 362.69951073

---

†Do not use notation 08 from Table 1 to indicate services rendered by groups of people; class in base number

.7      **Young people**

Through age twenty

Class here children

## SUMMARY

| | |
|---|---|
| **362.708** | **Groups of people** |
| **.71** | **Remedial measures, services, forms of assistance** |
| **.72** | **Characteristics of problems, social action** |
| **.73** | **Institutional and related services** |
| **.74** | **Troubled young people** |
| **.76** | **Abused and neglected young people** |
| **.77** | **Specific groups of young people** |
| **.78** | **Transgender and intersex young people, young people by sexual orientation, young people in intrafamily relationships** |

.708        Groups of people

Do not use for services rendered by groups of people; class in 362.7

.708 3      Young people twelve to twenty

Do not use for children; class in 362.7

· Including young women eighteen to twenty [*formerly* 362.830835]

Class here young men and women twelve to twenty

Class remedial measures, services, forms of assistance in 362.71; class characteristics of problems, social action in 362.72; class specific groups of young people twelve to twenty, other than young men and women, in 362.77; class young people twenty-one and over, comprehensive works on young men and women in 362

[.708 35]      Young people twelve to twenty

Do not use; class in 362.7083

.708 5      Relatives

Young people as parents relocated to 362.7874

[.708 6]      Young people by miscellaneous social attributes

Relocated to 362.77

[.708 66]      Young people by sexual orientation

Relocated to 362.786

[.708 67]      Transgender and intersex young people

Do not use; class in 362.785

[.708 9]      Ethnic and national groups

Relocated to 362.778

>      362.71–362.73   Specific kinds of services to young people

Class services to maladjusted young people in 362.74; class services to abused and neglected children in 362.76; class comprehensive works in 362.7

.71      Remedial measures, services, forms of assistance

Measures applicable primarily to individuals, even if in large groups

Including recreational services

Class here material assistance

Class remedial measures directed toward altering a social function, e.g., cost control, in 362.725; class social work in 362.7253

*For institutional and related services, see 362.73; for services to groups of young people, see 362.77*

.712      Day care services

.713      Aid to families with dependent children (AFDC)

.716      Counseling and guidance

Standard subdivisions are added for either or both topics in heading

Including legal aid

.72      Characteristics of problems, social action

Add to base number 362.72 notation 1–7 from table under 362–363, e.g., effects on families 362.723

*For remedial measures, services, forms of assistance, see 362.71; for problems of groups of young people, see 362.77*

.723      Effects on people close to those with a problem

Number built according to instructions under 362.72

Class here a family problem when focused on the child

Class a family problem when focused on the parent with the problem in 362.82, e.g., families with missing children 362.8297

.73      Institutional and related services

Class here abandoned children, orphans

.732      Institutional care

Including children's homes, orphanages; houseparents

.733      Foster home care

Class here comprehensive works on foster home care and adoption

*For adoption, see 362.734*

.734        Adoption

Including confidentiality of adoption records

Class comprehensive works on the activities of adopted people seeking their natural parents in 362.8298

---

>      362.74–362.78   Groups of young people

Unless other instructions are given, observe the following table of preference, e.g., poor gay abused young people 362.76 (*not* 362.77569 or 362.7866):

| | |
|---|---|
| Troubled young people | 362.74 |
| Abused and neglected young people | 362.76 |
| Young people by intrafamily relationships | 362.787 |
| Young people by sexual orientation | 362.786 |
| Transgender and intersex young people | 362.785 |
| Transgender and intersex young people, young people by sexual orientation, young people by intrafamily relationships (without subdivision) | 362.78 |
| Young people by social and economic levels | 362.775 |
| Young people by religious groups | 362.776 |
| Young people by ethnic and national group | 362.778 |
| Young people by language groups | 362.77 |
| Unemployed young people | 362.7794 |
| Young people with status defined by changes in residence | 362.7791 |
| Young people with status defined by changes in residence, unemployed young people (without subdivision) | 362.779 |
| Specific groups of young people (without subdivision) | 362.77 |

Class comprehensive works in 362.7

---

>      362.74–362.76   Specific kinds of young people

Class comprehensive works in 362.7

*For abandoned children, orphans, see 362.73*

.74      *†Troubled young people

> Former heading: Maladjusted young people

> Including predelinquents, runaways

> Class here halfway houses for young people who have not committed any crimes

> Class young people with mental illness in 362.2083; class families with missing children in 362.8297; class halfway houses for the transition from reform school to society in 365.42

> *For juvenile delinquents, see 364.36*

.76      *†Abused and neglected young people

> Subdivisions are added for either or both topics in heading

> Class child abuse as a crime in 364.15554

.77      Specific groups of young people

> Class here young people by miscellaneous social attributes [*formerly* 362.7086]

> *For transgender and intersex young people, see 362.785; for young people by sexual orientation, see 362.786; for young people in intrafamily relationships, see 362.787*

[.770 1–.770 9]      Standard subdivisions

> Do not use; class in 362.701–362.709

.775–.777      Young people by social and economic levels, religious groups, language groups

> Add to base number 362.77 the numbers following 305 in 305.5–305.7, e.g., young workers eighteen to twenty 362.77562 [*formerly* 362.850835], poor young people 362.77569; then add further as follows:
> 001–007    Standard subdivisions
> 008         Groups of people
>              Do not use for services rendered by groups of people; class in base number
> 009         History, geographic treatment, biography
> 01–08    Characteristics of problems, social action
>              Add to 0 notation 1–8 from table under 362–363, e.g., effects on families of poor young people 362.7756903

> *For abandoned children, orphans, see 362.73; for abused children, see 372.76*

---

*Add as instructed under 362–363

†Do not use notation 08 from Table 1 to indicate services rendered by groups of people; class in base number

| | |
|---|---|
| .775 69 | *†Poor young people |

> Number built according to instructions under 362.775–362.777
>
> Class here poor young people eighteen to twenty [*formerly* 362.50835]
>
> Class aid to families with dependent children in 362.713

| | |
|---|---|
| .778 | †Young people by ethnic or national group [*formerly* 362.7089] |

> Class here young people eighteen to twenty by ethnic or national group [*formerly* 362.84]

| | |
|---|---|
| .778 001–.778 007 | Standard subdivisions |
| .778 008 | Groups of people |

> Do not use for services rendered by groups of people; class in 362.778

| | |
|---|---|
| .778 009 | History, geographic treatment, biography |
| .778 05–.778 09 | †Young people of mixed ancestry with ethnic origins from more than one continent, European young people and young people of European descent |

> Add to base number 362.7780 the numbers following 0 in notation 05–09 from Table 5, e.g., young people of European descent 362.77809, young people of European descent 362.77809094

| | |
|---|---|
| .778 1–.778 9 | †Specific ethnic and national groups |

> Add to base number 362.778 notation 1–9 from Table 5, e.g., young people of Italian descent 362.77851, young people of Italian descent in United States 362.77851073

| | |
|---|---|
| .779 | Young people with status defined by changes in residence, unemployed youth |
| .779 1 | Young people with status defined by changes in residence |

> Class here aliens, expatriates, foreigners

| | |
|---|---|
| .779 100 1–.779 100 7 | Standard subdivisions |
| .779 100 8 | Groups of people |

> Do not use for services rendered by groups of people; class in 362.7791

| | |
|---|---|
| .779 100 9 | History, geographic treatment, biography |
| .779 101–.779 108 | Characteristics of problems, social action |

> Add to base number 362.77910 notation 1–8 from table under 362–363, e.g., effects on families of young aliens 362.779103

---

*Add as instructed under 362–363

†Do not use notation 08 from Table 1 to indicate services rendered by groups of people; class in base number

| | |
|---|---|
| .779 12 | *†Immigrant young people |

Class immigrant young people of a specific ethnic or national group in 362.778

| | |
|---|---|
| .779 14 | *†Displaced young people |

Class here exiles, refugees, stateless young people

| | |
|---|---|
| .779 18 | *†Nomadic young people |
| .779 4 | *†Unemployed young people |

Class poverty-stricken and destitute unemployed young people in 362.77569

.78      Transgender and intersex young people, young people by sexual orientation, young people in intrafamily relationships

.785      *†Transgender and intersex young people

Including female-to-male transgender young people, male-to-female transgender young people

Class here transgenderists, transsexuals

Subdivisions are added for transgender and intersex young people together, for transgender young people alone

.786      †Young people by sexual orientation [*formerly* 362.70866]

Including asexual young people

.786 2–.786 6      Young people by specific sexual orientation

Add to base number 362.786 the numbers following 306.76 in 306.762–306.766, e.g., gay young people 362.77866; then add further as follows:

| | |
|---|---|
| 001–007 | Standard subdivisions |
| 008 | Groups of people |
| | Do not use for services rendered by groups of people; class in base number |
| 009 | History, geographic treatment, biography |
| 01–08 | Characteristics of problems, social action |
| | Add to 0 notation 1–8 from table under 362–363, e.g., effects on families of gay young people 362.7786603 |

.787      †Young people by intrafamily relationships

Class here young people eighteen to twenty [*formerly* 362.820835]

Unless other instructions are given, class a subject with aspects in two or more subdivisions of 362.787 in the number coming last, e.g., 362.78792 (*not* 362.78742)

---

*Add as instructed under 362–363

†Do not use notation 08 from Table 1 to indicate services rendered by groups of people; class in base number

.787 2–.787 5          Young people in husband-wife, parent-child, sibling relationships

> Add to base number 362.787 the numbers following 306.87 in 306.872–306.874, e.g., single young mothers 362.787432; then add further as follows:
> 001–007    Standard subdivisions
> 008         Groups of people
>             Do not use for services rendered by groups of people; class in base number
> 009         History, geographic treatment, biography
> 01–08   Characteristics of problems, social action
>             Add to 0 notation 1–8 from table under 362–363, e.g., financial assistance to single young women 362.787432082

.787 4          *†Parent-child relationship

> Number built according to instructions under 362.7872–362.7875

> Class here young people as parents [*formerly* 362.7085]

.787 43          *†Mother-child relationship

> Number built according to instructions under 362.7872–362.7875

> Class here teenage pregnancy

.787 432          *†Single motherhood

> Number built according to instructions under 362.7872–362.7875

> Class here unmarried mothers eighteen to twenty [*formerly* 362.8392], single young mothers

> Class comprehensive works on single motherhood in 362.839532

.787 8–.787 9          Young people in altered family arrangements

> Add to base number 362.787 the numbers following 306.8 in 306.88–306.89, e.g., divorce young mothers 362.78793; then add further as follows:
> 001–007    Standard subdivisions
> 008         Groups of people
>             Do not use for services rendered by groups of people; class in base number
> 009         History, geographic treatment, biography
> 01–08   Characteristics of problems, social action
>             Add to 0 notation 1–8 from table under 362–363, e.g., financial assistance to divorces young women 362.78793082

**.8          Other groups of people**

---

*Add as instructed under 362–363

†Do not use notation 08 from Table 1 to indicate services rendered by groups of people; class in base number

## SUMMARY

| | | |
|---|---|---|
| 362.82 | | **Families** |
| | .83 | **Women** |
| | .84 | **Ethnic and national groups** |
| | .85 | **Working class** |
| | .86 | **Veterans of military service** |
| | .87 | **Displaced persons** |
| | .88 | **Victims of crimes and war** |
| | .89 | **Miscellaneous groups of people** |

.82     *Families

> Class here parents, family problems focused on the parent

> Class family welfare when synonymous with general welfare in 362; class family welfare when synonymous with general welfare of a specific ethnic or national group in 362.84. Class a family problem when focused on the child with the problem in 362.7, e.g., abused children 362.76

.820 8          Groups of people

> Do not use for services rendered by groups of people; class in 362.82

[.820 83]          Young people by intrafamily relationships

> Do not use for young people through age seventeen; class in 362.787

[.820 835]          Young people eighteen to twenty

> Relocated to 362.787

.820 86          People by miscellaneous social attributes

[.820 865 3]          Separated parents, divorced parents

> Relocated to 362.8294

[.820 865 4]          Widowed people

> Relocated to 362.8293

.820 865 5          Married people

> Do not use for married women; class in 362.83952

.820 89          Ethnic and national groups [*formerly* 362.84]

.828          Remedial measures, services, forms of assistance

> Number built according to instructions under 362–363

> Class services and forms of assistance for specific problems in 362.829; class family planning programs in 363.96

.828 2          Financial assistance

> Number built according to instructions under 362–363

> Class aid to families with dependent children (AFDC) in 362.713

*Add as instructed under 362–363

.828 3      Provision of food, shelter (temporary housing), household assistance, clothing, other related necessities; recreation

> Number built according to instructions under 362–363

> Including visiting housekeepers

> Class day care in 362.712

.828 6      Counseling and guidance

> Number built according to instructions under 362–363

> Including premarital and marriage counseling

.829      Specific problems

> Class a problem not provided for here with the problem, plus notation 3 from the table under 362–363, e.g., alcoholism within the family setting 362.2923

.829 2      *†Abuse within the family

> Class here parent, spouse abuse; domestic violence

> Class elder abuse in 362.682; class abused children in 362.76; class abuse as a crime in 364.1555

.829 3      *†Widowed people [*formerly also* 362.8208654, 362.8294]

> Class here widowers

> Class widowers in late adulthood in 362.6954

> *For widows, see 362.83958*

.829 4      *†Single-parent family

> Class here separated parents, divorced parents [*both formerly also* 362.8208653]

> Class separated and divorced parents in late adulthood in 362.69653

> *For unmarried mothers, see 362.839532; for separated women, divorced women, see 362.83959*

> Widowed people relocated to 363.8293

.829 5      *†Parents in prison

.829 7      *†Missing children

> Class here parental kidnapping

> Class runaway children in 362.74

.829 8      *†Relationship between adoptees and their biological parents

> Class adoption in 362.734. Class a specific aspect of children seeking their biological parents with the aspect, e.g., confidentiality of adoption records 362.734, genealogical searching 929.1

---

*Add as instructed under 362–363
†Do not use notation 08 from Table 1 to indicate services rendered by groups of people; class in base number

.83        *Women

Class wife abuse, battered women, sexually abused women in 362.8292; class rape in 362.883; class transgender and intersex people in 362.896

[.830 8]        Groups of people

Relocated to 362.839

[.830 83]        Young women

Do not use for young women through age seventeen; class in 362.7083

[.830 835]        Young women eighteen to twenty

Relocated to 362.7083

.839        †Groups of people [*formerly also* 362.8308]

### SUMMARY

| | |
|---|---|
| 362.839 5 | **Women by intrafamily relationships** |
| .839 6 | **Women by sexual orientation** |
| .839 8 | **Women with status defined by changes in residence, retired women, poor women** |
| .839 9 | **Women by ethnic or national group** |

[.839 2]        Unmarried mothers

Unmarried mothers eighteen to twenty relocated to 362.787432; unmarried mothers twenty-one and over relocated to 362.839532

.839 5        †Women by intrafamily relationships

Unless other instructions are given, class a subject with aspects in two or more subdivisions of 362.8395 in the number coming last, e.g., divorced mothers 362.83959 (*not* 306.83953)

Class women by intrafamily relationships and by sexual orientation in 362.8396; class women by intrafamily relationships and with special social status in 362.8398

.839 52        *†Spouses

.839 53        *†Mother-child relationship

.839 532        *†Single motherhood

Class here unmarried mothers twenty-one and over [*formerly* 362.8392], single mothers, comprehensive works on single motherhood

Class comprehensive works on single-parent family in 362.8294

*For single motherhood through age twenty, see 362.787432*

.839 55        *†Grandmother-child relationship

---

*Add as instructed under 362–363

†Do not use notation 08 from Table 1 to indicate services rendered by groups of people; class in base number

| | |
|---|---|
| .839 57 | *†Stepmother-child relationship |
| .839 58 | *†Widows |

> Class widows in late adulthood in 362.6954; class comprehensive works on widowed parents in 362.8293

| | |
|---|---|
| .839 59 | *†Separated and divorced women |

> Subdivisions are added for either or both topics in heading

> Class comprehensive works on single-parent family in 362.8294

| | |
|---|---|
| .839 6 | †Women by sexual orientation |

> Including asexual women

| | |
|---|---|
| .839 62–.839 68 | Women by specific sexual orientation |

> Add to base number 362.8396 the numbers following 306.76 in 306.762–306.768, e.g., lesbians 362.83966; then add further as follows:

| | |
|---|---|
| 001–007 | Standard subdivisions |
| 008 | Groups of people |
| | Do not use for services rendered by groups of people; class in base number |
| 009 | History, geographic treatment, biography |
| 01–08 | Characteristics of problems, social action |
| | Add to 0 notation 1–8 from table under 362–363, e.g., effects on families of lesbians 362.8396603 |

> Class women by specific sexual orientation and with status defined by changes in residence in 362.83981; class retired women by sexual orientation in 362.83984; class poor women by sexual orientation in 362.83985

| | |
|---|---|
| .839 8 | †Women with status defined by changes in residence, retired women, poor women |
| .839 81 | Women with status defined by changes in residence |

> Class here aliens, expatriates, foreigners

| | |
|---|---|
| .839 810 01–.839 810 07 | Standard subdivisions |
| .839 810 08 | Groups of people |

> Do not use for services rendered by groups of people; class in 362.83981

| | |
|---|---|
| .839 810 09 | History, geographic treatment, biography |
| .839 810 1–.839 810 8 | Characteristics of problems, social action |

> Add to base number 362.839810 notation 1–8 from table under 362–363, e.g., effects on families of women expatriates 362.8398103

---

*Add as instructed under 362–363
†Do not use notation 08 from Table 1 to indicate services rendered by groups of people; class in base number

| | |
|---|---|
| .839 812 | *†Immigrant women |
| | Class immigrant women of a specific ethnic or national group in 362.8399 |
| .839 814 | *†Displaced women |
| | Class here exiles, refugees, stateless women |
| .839 818 | *†Nomadic women |
| .839 84 | *†Retired women |
| .839 85 | *†Poor women |
| | Including homeless women |
| .839 9 | Women by ethnic or national group |
| | Class women of a specific ethnic or national group in intrafamily relationships in 362.8395; class women of a specific ethnic or national group by sexual orientation in 362.8396; class women of a specific ethnic or national group with a specific social status in 362.8398 |
| .839 900 1–.839 900 7 | Standard subdivisions |
| .839 900 8 | Groups of people |
| | Do not use for services rendered by groups of people; class in 362.8399 |
| .839 900 9 | History, geographic treatment, biography |
| .839 905–.839 909 | †Women of mixed ancestry with ethnic origins from more than one continent, European women and women of European descent |
| | Add to base number 362.83990 the numbers following 0 in notation 05–09 from Table 5, e.g., women of European descent 362.839909, women of European descent in Australia 362.839909094 |
| .839 91–.839 99 | †Specific ethnic and national groups |
| | Add to base number 362.8399 notation 1–9 from Table 5, e.g., women of Italian descent 362.839951, women of Italian descent in United States 362.839951073 |
| .84 | Ethnic and national groups |
| | Poor people by ethnic or national group relocated to 362.5089; young people eighteen to twenty by ethnic or national group relocated to 362.778; families by ethnic or national group relocated to 362.82089 |
| .840 01–.840 07 | Standard subdivisions |
| .840 08 | Groups of people |
| | Do not use for services rendered by groups of people; class in 362.84 |

*Add as instructed under 362–363
†Do not use notation 08 from Table 1 to indicate services rendered by groups of people; class in base number

| | |
|---|---|
| .840 09 | History, geographic treatment, biography |
| .840 5–.840 9 | †People of mixed ancestry with ethnic origins from more than one continent, Europeans and people of European descent |

> Add to base number 362.840 the numbers following 0 in notation 05–09 from Table 5, e.g., people of European descent 362.8409, people of European descent in Australia 362.8409094

| | |
|---|---|
| .841–.849 | †Specific ethnic and national groups |

> Add to base number 362.84 notation 1–9 from Table 5, e.g., Italians in United States 362.8451073

> Class a social problem of a specific ethnic or national group in a place where the group predominates with the problem, plus notation 093–099 from Table 1, e.g., poor Italians in Rome 362.50945632; class comprehensive works on the social problems of a specific ethnic or national group in a place where the group predominates with the place in 362.9, e.g., social problems of Italians in Italy 362.945

| | |
|---|---|
| .85 | *Working class |

> Including migrant workers

| | |
|---|---|
| .850 8 | Groups of people |

> Do not use for services rendered by groups of people; class in 362.85

| | |
|---|---|
| [.850 83] | Young people |

> Do not use for young workers through age seventeen from lower class; class in 362.77562

| | |
|---|---|
| [.850 835] | Young people eighteen to twenty |

> Relocated to 362.77562

| | |
|---|---|
| .86 | *†Veterans of military service |

> Class here veterans' rights and benefits

| | |
|---|---|
| .868 2 | Financial assistance |

> Number built according to instructions under 362–363

> Class veterans' pensions in 331.25291355

> *For veterans' education benefits, see 371.223; for veterans' higher education benefits, see 378.32*

| | |
|---|---|
| .87 | *†Displaced persons |

> Former heading: Victims of oppression

> Class here exiles, refugees, stateless persons

> Victims of war relocated to 362.88

---

*Add as instructed under 362–363
†Do not use notation 08 from Table 1 to indicate services rendered by groups of people; class in base number

| | |
|---|---|
| .88 | **Victims of crimes and war** |

Standard subdivisions are added for victims of crimes and war together, for victims of crimes alone

Including inmates of concentration or internment camps

Class here victimology

Class services to abused family members, victims of domestic violence in 362.8292; class crime prevention for society as a whole in 364.4; class prevention by individuals in 613.6; class comprehensive works on crimes in 364.1

*For works on why people become victims of specific crimes, see 364.1*

| | |
|---|---|
| .880 8 | Groups of people |

Do not use for services rendered by groups of people; class in 362.88

| | |
|---|---|
| .880 83 | †Young people |

Class neglected children in 362.76

| | |
|---|---|
| .881 | **Characteristics of problems, social action** |

Add to base number 362.881 notation 1–8 from table under 362–363, e.g., effects on families of victims of crime 362.88103

| | |
|---|---|
| .883 | †Rape |

Class rape prevention by individuals in 613.663

| | |
|---|---|
| .885 | †Assault and battery |

Standard subdivisions are added for either or both topics in heading

Class here victims of abuse

| | |
|---|---|
| .885 083 | †Young people |

Class abused children in 362.76

| | |
|---|---|
| .885 084 | †People in specific ages of adulthood |
| .885 084 6 | †People in late adulthood |

Class elder abuse in 362.682

| | |
|---|---|
| .89 | **Miscellaneous groups of people** |

Limited to the groups provided for below

| | |
|---|---|
| .892 | *†People by social and economic levels |

Class here social classes

*For working class, see 362.85*

---

*Add as instructed under 362–363

†Do not use notation 08 from Table 1 to indicate services rendered by groups of people; class in base number

| | | |
|---|---|---|
| .896 | *†People by sexual orientation | |

Including asexuals

| | | |
|---|---|---|
| .896 2 | *†Heterosexuals | |
| .896 3 | *†Bisexuals | |
| .896 4 | *†Gays | |
| .897 | *†Transgender and intersex people | |

Including female-to-male transgender people, male-to-female transgender people

Class here transgenderists, transsexuals

Subdivisions are added for transgender and intersex people together, for transgender people alone

.899       People by miscellaneous social attributes

*For poor people, see 362.5; for unmarried mothers, see 362.839532; for victims of crime and war, see 362.88; for offenders, see 364.3*

.899 1       People with status defined by changes in residence

Class here aliens, expatriates, foreigners

Class retired people with status defined by changes in residence in 362.8994

*For displaced persons, see 362.87*

.899 100 1–.899 100 7       Standard subdivisions

.899 100 8       Groups of people

Do not use for services rendered by groups of people; class in 362.8991

.899 100 9       History, geographic treatment, biography

.899 101–.899 108       Characteristics of problems, social action

Add to base number 362.89910 notation 1–8 from table under 362–363, e.g., effects on families of expatriates 362.899103

.899 12       *†Immigrants

Class here comprehensive works on immigration

*For immigrants of a specific ethnic or national group, see 362.84; for population problems, see 363.9; for illegal immigration, see 364.137*

.899 4       *†Unemployed people

.899 6       *†Retired people

---

*Add as instructed under 362–363

†Do not use notation 08 from Table 1 to indicate services rendered by groups of p̲ number

**.9      History, geographic treatment, biography**

Class here comprehensive works on the social problems of a specific ethnic or national group in a place where the group predominates, e.g., social problems of Italians in Italy 362.945

Class history, geographic treatment, biography of specific social problems in 362.1–362.8

> *For a social problem of a specific ethnic or national group in a place where the group predominates, see the problem, plus notation 093–099 from Table 1, e.g., poor Italians in Rome 362.50945632*

**.901–.905      Historical periods**

> Add to base number 362.90 the numbers following —090 in notation 0901–0905 from Table 1, e.g., social welfare in 20th century 362.904

**.91–.99      Geographic treatment, biography**

> Add to base number 362.9 notation 1–9 from Table 2, e.g., social welfare in France 362.944

# 363    Other social problems and services

Standard subdivisions are added for comprehensive treatment of environmental and safety problems of society, e.g., assuring a safe and secure environment for Japan 363.0952

Class here public works

> *For communication facilities, see 384; for transportation facilities, see 388*

> *See Manual at 363 vs. 302–307, 333.7, 570–590, 600; also at 363 vs. 344.02–344.05, 353–354*

## SUMMARY

| | |
|---|---|
| 363.1 | Public safety programs |
| .2 | Police services |
| .3 | Other aspects of public safety |
| .4 | Controversies related to public morals and customs |
| .5 | Housing |
| .6 | Public utilities and related services |
| .7 | Environmental problems |
| .8 | Food supply |
| .9 | Population problems |

## .1 Public safety programs

Class here safety measures, interdisciplinary works on safety

Unless other instructions are given, observe the following table of preference, e.g., use of hazardous materials in health care facilities 363.17 (*not* 363.15):

| | |
|---|---|
| Hazardous materials | 363.17 |
| Hazards in sports and recreation | 363.14 |
| Transportation hazards | 363.12 |
| Hazardous machinery | 363.18 |
| Product hazards | 363.19 |
| Domestic hazards | 363.13 |
| Hazards in health care facilities | 363.15 |
| Occupational and industrial hazards | 363.11 |

Class terrorism and responses to terrorism associated with a particular aspect of public safety in 363.325; class managerial response to safety requirements, comprehensive works on safety management in 658.408. Class safety management in a specific industry with the industry, plus notation 0684 from Table 1, e.g., safety management in petroleum industry 665.50684

> For police services, see 363.2; for aspects of public safety not provided for here, see 363.3; for personal safety, see 613.6; for survival after accidents, see 613.69. For a specific kind of remedial measure other than rescue operations, see the measure, e.g., medical care for the injured 362.1; for safety technology of a specific subject, see the subject, plus notation 0289 from Table 1, e.g., safety technology in hydraulic engineering 627.0289

> See Manual at 363.1; also at 333.7–333.9 vs. 363.1, 363.73, 577; also at 363.1 vs. 600

### SUMMARY

| | | |
|---|---|---|
| 363.100 | 1–.100 9 | **Standard subdivisions** |
| | .101–.108 | **[General topics of public safety programs]** |
| | .11 | **Occupational and industrial hazards** |
| | .12 | **Transportation hazards** |
| | .13 | **Domestic hazards** |
| | .14 | **Hazards in sports and recreation** |
| | .15 | **Hazards in health care facilities** |
| | .17 | **Hazardous materials** |
| | .18 | **Hazardous machinery** |
| | .19 | **Product hazards** |

.100 1–.100 9      Standard subdivisions

As modified under 362–363

.101–.105      General topics of public safety programs

Add to base number 363.10 notation 1–5 from table under 362–363, e.g., public action to promote safety 363.1056

.106      Public control of safety

.106 2      Standards

.106 3      Monitoring, surveillance, reporting

Standard subdivisions are added for any or all topics in heading

| | |
|---|---|
| .106 4 | Inspection and testing |

> Standard subdivisions are added for either or both topics in heading

| | |
|---|---|
| .106 5 | Investigation of specific incidents |

> Class here interdisciplinary works on safety investigation

> *For a technical or engineering aspect of the investigation, see the aspect in 600, e.g., safety engineering 620.86, wreckage studies of automobile accidents 629.2826; for accounts of a specific incident that affected general social life and history, see the incident in 900, e.g., San Francisco earthquake of 1906 979.461051*

| | |
|---|---|
| .106 6 | Certification |
| .107–.108 | Measures to prevent, protect against, limit effects of problems; remedial measures, services, forms of assistance |

> Add to base number 363.10 notation 7–8 from table under 362–363, e.g., alarm and warning systems 363.1072, counseling 363.1086

| | |
|---|---|
| .11 | *Occupational and industrial hazards |

> Subdivisions are added for either or both topics in heading

| | |
|---|---|
| .119 | Occupational and industrial hazards in specific industries and occupations |
| [.119 000 1–.119 000 9] | Standard subdivisions |

> Do not use; class in 363.1101–363.1109

| | |
|---|---|
| .119 001–.119 999 | Subdivisions for specific industries and occupations |

> Add to base number 363.119 notation 001–999, e.g., school safety programs 363.119371, hazards in coal mining 363.119622334; however, for hazards to transportation workers, see 363.12; for hazards to domestic workers, see 363.13; for hazards to professional athletes, see 363.14; for hazards to workers in health care facilities, see 363.15

| | |
|---|---|
| .12 | Transportation hazards |

> Class here accidents, fires resulting from accidents

> Class comprehensive works on fires in transportation facilities in 363.379

> *See Manual at 900: Historic events vs. nonhistoric events*

| | |
|---|---|
| .120 01–.120 09 | Standard subdivisions |

> As modified under 362–363

| | |
|---|---|
| .120 1–.120 8 | Characteristics of transportation hazards, social action |

> Add to base number 363.120 notation 1–8 from table under 362–363, e.g., accident prevention 363.1207

| | |
|---|---|
| .122 | *Rail transportation |

*Add as instructed under 362–363

| .123 | *Water transportation |
|------|----------------------|

Class here water safety

Class safety in water sports in 363.14

| .124 | *Air and space transportation |
|------|-------------------------------|

Subdivisions are added for either or both topics in heading

| .124 1 | Causes of air and space accidents |
|--------|-----------------------------------|

Number built according to instructions under 362–363

| .124 12 | Natural factors |
|---------|-----------------|

Including birds, clear-air turbulence (CAT)

| .124 14 | Operator failures |
|---------|-------------------|

| .124 16 | Vehicle failures |
|---------|------------------|

| .124 18 | Failures of traffic control |
|---------|-----------------------------|

Class comprehensive works on air traffic control in 387.740426

| .124 6 | Control of air and space transportation |
|--------|-----------------------------------------|

Number built according to instructions under 362–363

| .124 65 | Investigation of specific air and space accidents |
|---------|---------------------------------------------------|

Number built according to instructions under 362–363

Class here general investigations of aircraft accidents

Class wreckage studies in 629.13255

| .124 9 | Specific types of accidents and accidents in specific types of services |
|--------|-------------------------------------------------------------------------|

| .124 92 | Specific types of accidents |
|---------|-----------------------------|

Including midair collisions, takeoff accidents

| .124 93 | Accidents in specific types of services |
|---------|-----------------------------------------|

Including air-taxi services, helicopter services

Class specific types of accidents in specific types of services in 363.12492

| .125 | *Highway and urban vehicular transportation |
|------|---------------------------------------------|

Subdivisions are added for either or both topics in heading

| .125 1 | Causes of accidents |
|--------|---------------------|

Number built according to instructions under 362–363

Including road rage

*See also 364.147 for traffic offenses as causes of accidents*

*Add as instructed under 362–363

| | |
|---|---|
| .125 14 | Use of drugs |
| | Class here drunk driving |
| .125 6 | Control of highway and urban vehicular transportation |
| | Number built according to instructions under 362–363 |
| | Class traffic control by the police in 363.2332 |
| .125 65 | Investigation of specific vehicular and highway accidents |
| | Number built according to instructions under 362–363 |
| | Class here general investigations of automobile accidents |
| | Class wreckage studies in 629.2826 |
| .125 9 | Hazards in use of specific types of vehicles other than automobiles |
| | Including bicycles, motorcycles, trucks |
| .13 | *Domestic hazards |
| .14 | *Hazards in sports and recreation |
| | Subdivisions are added for either or both topics in heading |
| .15 | *Hazards in health care facilities |
| .17 | *Hazardous materials |
| | Manufacture, transportation, use |

Class here interdisciplinary works on hazardous materials, works on the control of such materials in their ordinary commercial setting (manufacture, sale, commercial and industrial use, disposal)

*For hazardous materials as components of articles that become hazardous products, see 363.19; for hazardous materials as impurities in the water supply, see 363.61; for hazardous wastes, see 363.728; for hazardous materials as environmental pollutants, see 363.738; for hazardous materials as a cause of disease or injury in an organism, see 571.95; for hazardous materials as an environmental factor affecting the natural ecology, see 577.275; for hazardous materials technology, see 604.7; for chemicals as a cause of injury to people, see 615.9; for radiation hazards as a cause of injury to people, see 616.9897*

| | |
|---|---|
| .176 3 | Monitoring, surveillance, reporting |
| | Number built according to instructions under 362–363 |

Class here studies on the applicability of both social and technical findings of environmental chemistry and additive toxicology to the monitoring of hazardous materials

| | |
|---|---|
| .179 | Specific types of hazardous materials |
| | Including corrosive materials |

*Add as instructed under 362–363

| .179 1 | Toxic chemicals |
|---|---|

Including asbestos, lead

Class toxic agricultural chemicals in 363.1792

| .179 2 | *Agricultural chemicals |
|---|---|

Class here pesticides

| .179 8 | Explosives [*formerly also* 363.33], fuels, related products |
|---|---|

Class here explosions [*formerly* 363.3497], safety considerations with respect to especially flammable materials

> *See also 363.19 for products e.g., sweaters, mattresses) that might constitute unsuspected fire hazards; also 363.377 for measures to control accumulation of ordinary combustible materials*

| .179 9 | *Radioactive materials |
|---|---|

Class here nuclear accidents

| .18 | *Hazardous machinery |
|---|---|
| .189 | Specific kinds of hazardous machinery |

Including electrical and x-ray equipment

| .19 | Product hazards |
|---|---|

Adulteration, contamination, safety, adequacy, effectiveness of products offered for human consumption and use

Including household appliances, medical instruments and supplies, textiles, toys

Class here hazards due to containers and applicators that accompany products

| .192 | *Foods |
|---|---|
| .192 9 | Specific foods |

Including beverages, canned goods, dairy products, meats

| .194 | *Drugs and medicines |
|---|---|

Subdivisions are added for either or both topics in heading

| .196 | *Cosmetics |
|---|---|
| **.2** | **Police services** |

Class police services in control of factors affecting public morals in 363.4. Class a social service function of police with the function in 362, e.g., counseling of rape victims 362.883; class police committing a crime with the crime in 364.1, e.g., police violation of civil rights 364.1322

| [.206 83] | Personnel management (Human resource management) |
|---|---|

Do not use; class in 363.22

---

*Add as instructed under 362–363

.22       **Personnel**

Duties, functions, activities

Class here personnel management (human resource management)

Class specific duties, functions, activities in 363.23–363.25

---

>               **363.23–363.25 Specific aspects of police services**

Class specific aspects of services of special kinds of security and law enforcement agencies in 363.28; class comprehensive works in 363.2

.23       **Police functions**

Class here law enforcement, prevention of crime by police

*For detection of crime, see 363.25. For police functions in relation to a type of social conflict, see the type, e.g., control of terrorism 363.32516*

*See Manual at 363 vs. 344.02–344.05, 353–354: Law enforcement*

.232       **Patrol and surveillance**

Including pursuit and apprehension of lawbreakers, use of deadly force, undercover work

*For highway patrol, see 363.2332*

.233       **Enforcement of civil laws**

Including enforcement of building codes, licensing laws and ordinances, sanitation laws

.233 2       Traffic control

Including highway patrol

Class general investigations of traffic accidents in 363.12565; class investigation of traffic offenses in 363.25; class wreckage studies in 629.2826; class comprehensive works on traffic control in 363.1256

.233 6       Location of missing persons

.24       **Auxiliary services**

Including communications services, evidence preservation, fingerprint and photograph files, police records

.25       **Detection of crime (Criminal investigation)**

Class here forensic science (criminalistics); evidence, circumstantial evidence

Class general investigations of transportation accidents in 363.12065

*For evidence preservation, see 363.24; for forensic medicine, see 614.1*

*See also 364.1 for criminal offenses*

>      363.252–363.258   Specific techniques and kinds of evidence

Class comprehensive works in 363.25; class comprehensive works on detection of a specific kind of crime in 363.259. Class detection of a specific crime with the crime in 364.1, e.g., detection of a murder in New York City 364.1523097471

>      363.252–363.256   Procurement and analysis of evidence

Class evidence used in identification of criminals not listed here in 363.258; class comprehensive works in 363.25

.252       Procurement of evidence

Including electronic surveillance, search and seizure, use of informers and secret agents

*For interrogation of witnesses, see 363.254*

.254       Interrogation of witnesses

Including use of polygraph (lie detector)

.256       Analysis of evidence

Class here laboratories

Class files resulting from criminal investigations in 363.24

.256 2      Physical evidence

Including analysis of blood and hair, use of ballistics

.256 5      Documentary evidence

Including analysis of handwriting and typewriting

.258       Identification of criminals

Including artists' sketches, fingerprints, lineups, photographs, voice prints

Class files resulting from criminal investigations in 363.24

.259       Detection of specific types of offenses

Add to base number 363.259 the numbers following 364.1 in 364.13–364.18, e.g., investigation of murder 363.259523

Class specific techniques of investigation of specific types of offenses in 363.252–363.258. Class detection of a specific crime with the crime in 364.1, e.g., detection of a murder in New York City 364.1523097471

.28       Services of special kinds of security and law enforcement agencies

Including park police

Class agencies to carry out specific police functions in 363.23; class agencies to investigate specific kinds of crime in 363.259

*For narcotics agents, see 363.45; for postal inspectors, see 383.46*

.282        Marshals and sheriffs

   Standard subdivisions are added for either or both topics in heading

.283        Secret police

.285        Border patrols

.286        Coast guards and harbor patrols

   Standard subdivisions are added for coast guards and harbor patrols together, for coast guards alone

   Class here interdisciplinary works on coast guards

   *For coast guards as a military service, see 359.97; for inland waterway security services, see 363.2872*

.287        Transportation security services

   *For automobile traffic control, see 363.2332; for harbor patrols, see 363.286*

   *See also 363.379 for transportation fire hazards*

.287 2      Inland waterway security services

   Class here river security services

.287 4      Railway security services

.287 6      Air transportation security services

   Including airport police, sky marshals

.289        Private detective and police services

   Standard subdivisions are added for either or both topics in heading

   Including bodyguards, campus police, store detectives

**.3        Other aspects of public safety**

   *See Manual at 363.1*

.31         Censorship

   Class here control of information, press control; censorship as routine governmental function; interdisciplinary works on censorship

   *For a specific aspect of censorship not provided for here, see the aspect, e.g., censorship as social control 303.376, legal aspects of censorship 344.0531*

   *See Manual at 363.31 vs. 303.376, 791.4*

.32         Social conflict

   Class here civil disorder [*formerly* 363.3497], civil disobedience; violence

   Class interdisciplinary works on conflict in 303.6; class interdisciplinary works on civil disorder and disobedience in 303.62

.321      Aspects of social conflict

> Class aspects of a specific kind of civil disorder or disobedience in 363.323–363.325

[.321 01–.321 09]      Standard subdivisions

> Do not use; class in 363.3201–363.3209

.321 1–.321 8      Specific aspects of social conflict

> Add to base number 363.321 notation 1–8 from table under 362–363, e.g., social causes of violence 363.3211

.321 5      Social action

> Number built according to instructions under 362–363

> Class here conflict resolution

> Class interdisciplinary works on conflict resolution in 303.69

.323      *Crowds

> Class here riots [*formerly* 363.3497]; demonstrations; crowd control, riot control

[.323 6]      Control

> Do not use; class in 363.323

.325      Terrorism

> Including cyberterrorism

> Class here bombing; terrorism and responses to terrorism associated with a particular aspect of public safety; interdisciplinary works on terrorism

> Class comprehensive works on data security and cyberterrorism in 005.8; class comprehensive works on aspects of public safety and terrorism and responses to terrorism associated with the aspect in 363.1

> > *For sociology of terrorism, see 303.625; for terrorism as a crime, see 364.1317; for cyberterrorism as a crime, see 364.168*

.325 1      Aspects of terrorism

> Class aspects of bioterrorism and chemical terrorism in 363.3253; class aspects of nuclear terrorism in 363.3255; class aspects of a specific target of terrorism in 363.3259

[.325 101–.325 109]      Standard subdivisions

> Do not use; class in 363.32501–363.32509

.325 11–.325 18      Specific aspects of terrorism

> Add to base number 363.3251 notation 1–8 from table under 362–363, e.g., social causes of terrorism 363.32511

---

*Add as instructed under 362–363

.325 3         *Bioterrorism and chemical terrorism

> Standard subdivisions are added for either or both topics in heading
>
> Class bioterrorism and chemical terrorism against a specific target in 363.3259

.325 5         *Nuclear terrorism

> Class nuclear terrorism against a specific target in 363.3259

.325 9         Specific targets of terrorism

> Add to base number 363.3259 notation 001–999, e.g., terrorist attacks on food supply 363.32593638, terrorist attacks on nuclear power plants 363.3259621483

.33       Control of firearms

> Class here interdisciplinary works on gun control
>
> *For gun control as a civil rights issue, see 323.43*
>
> Explosives relocated to 363.1798

.34       *Disasters

> Class survival after disasters in 613.69
>
> *For disasters caused by terrorism, see 363.325*
>
> *See Manual at 900: Historic events vs. nonhistoric events*

.348       Remedial measures, services, forms of assistance

> Number built according to instructions under 362–363
>
> Class here disaster relief
>
> Class raising funds for mounting and carrying out disaster relief in 363.34570681. Class disaster relief for a specific type of disasters with the type, plus notation 8 from table under 362–363, e.g., disaster relief for flood victims 363.34938
>
> > *For a specific kind of remedial measure other than those applied immediately at the time and site of the disaster, see the measure, e.g., medical care for the injured 362.1; for a specific form of disaster relief not provided for here, see the form of relief, e.g., long-range planning to replace housing lost due to a volcanic eruption 363.58*

.348 1       Rescue operations

> Number built according to instructions under 362–363
>
> Forms of assistance applied immediately at time and site of disaster
>
> Class here salvage operations; comprehensive works on rescue and salvage operations for disasters in general
>
> Class rescue and salvage operations for a specific type of disaster with the type, plus notation 81 from table under 362–363, e.g., rescue operations for flood victims 363.349381

*Add as instructed under 362–363

.349      Specific kinds of disasters

> *For epidemics and pandemics, see 362.1; for fires, see 363.37. For a disaster resulting from one of the hazards listed in 363.1, see the hazard, e.g., shipwrecks 363.123, nuclear accidents 363.1799*

.349 2      Disasters caused by weather conditions

Class here storms

> *For floods, see 363.3493*

.349 21      Aspects of disasters caused by weather conditions

Class an aspect of disasters caused by a specific weather condition in 363.34922–363.34929

[.349 210 1–.349 210 9]      Standard subdivisions

Do not use; class in 363.349201–363.349209

.349 211–.349 218      Specific aspects of disasters caused by weather conditions

Add to base number 363.34921 notation 1–8 from table under 362–363, e.g., rescue operations during storms 363.3492181

.349 22–.349 26      Specific kinds of storms

Add to base number 363.3492 the numbers following 551.55 in 551.552–551.556, e.g., ice storms 363.34926; then add further as instructed under 362–363, e.g., rescue operations during ice storms 363.3492681

> *For dust storms, see 363.34929*

.349 29      *Droughts

Including dust storms

.349 3      *Floods

> *See also 363.3494 for tsunamis*

.349 36      Control

Number built according to instructions under 362–363

Class technology of flood control in 627.4

.349 4      *Tsunamis

> *See also 363.3493 for floods*

.349 5      *Earthquakes and volcanoes

Subdivisions are added for earthquakes and volcanoes together, for earthquakes alone

> *See also 363.3494 for tsunamis*

*Add as instructed under 362–363

| [.349 7] | Disasters induced by human activity |
|---|---|

Number discontinued; class in 363.34

Explosions relocated to 363.1798; civil disorder relocated to 363.32; riots relocated to 363.323

| .349 8 | *War |
|---|---|

*For civil defense, see 363.35*

*See also 303.66 for sociology of war*

| [.349 87] | Measures to prevent, protect against, limit effects of war |
|---|---|

Do not use; class in 327.17

| .349 88 | Remedial measures, services, forms of assistance |
|---|---|

Number built according to instructions under 362–363

Including mine clearing operations by civilians

Class here war relief

Class problems of war refugees when not treated directly in the context of war relief in 362.87; class interdisciplinary works on mine clearing operations in 355.4. Class war relief during a specific war with the war, e.g., relief work of Switzerland during World War II 940.54778494

| .35 | Civil defense |
|---|---|

Measures to defend civilian populations against war

Class comprehensive works on civil defense and emergency preparedness in 363.347

| .37 | *Fire hazards |
|---|---|

Class fire fighting and fire safety technology in 628.92

| .377 | Measures to prevent, protect against, limit effects of problems |
|---|---|

Number built according to instructions under 362–363

Class here fire prevention, measures to control accumulation of ordinary combustible materials

Class safety considerations with respect to especially flammable materials in 363.1798; class safety of products (e.g., sweaters, mattresses) that might constitute unsuspected fire hazards in 363.19

| .378 | Remedial measures, services, forms of assistance |
|---|---|

Number built according to instructions under 362–363

Class here fire fighting

*Add as instructed under 362–363

.379      Fire hazards in specific situations

> Including fire hazards in high-rise buildings, schools, transportation; forest fires

> *For fires resulting from transportation accidents, see 363.12*

**.4**      **Controversies related to public morals and customs**

> Treated as social problems

> Class censorship and control of information in 363.31. Class a controversy treated other than as a social issue with the aspect of the controversy, e.g., ethics of gambling 175 (*not* 363.42)

.41      Sale of alcoholic beverages

> Class problems of and services to alcoholics in 362.292; class comprehensive works on criminal offenses associated with alcoholic beverages in 364.173

> *For sale of alcoholic beverages as an offense against revenue, comprehensive works on criminal offenses associated with alcoholic beverages, see 364.1332*

.42      Gambling

> Class compulsive gambling in 362.25; class gambling as a crime in 364.172

.44      Prostitution

> Class prostitution as a crime in 364.1534

.45      Drug traffic

> Class here narcotics agents

> Class problems of and services to drug addicts in 362.29

> *For criminal offenses associated with drugs, see 364.177*

> *See also 363.41 for sale of alcoholic beverages*

.46      Abortion

> Class abortion as a crime in 364.185

> Interdisciplinary works on abortion relocated to 362.19888

.47      Obscenity and pornography

> Class obscenity and pornography as crimes in 364.174

.48      Premarital and extramarital relations

> Class premarital and extramarital relations as crimes in 364.153

> *For prostitution, see 363.44*

.49      Homosexuality

> Class interdisciplinary works in 306.766

**.5**      **\*Housing**

Class here housing as a social problem, comprehensive works on housing for poor people, interdisciplinary works on housing

*For a specific aspect of housing, see the aspect, e.g., sociological aspects 307.336, economic aspects 333.338, provision of shelter 361.05*

*See Manual at 363.5, 363.6, 363.8 vs. 338; also at 363.5 vs. 307.336, 307.34; also at 363.5 vs. 643.1*

[.508]      Housing for groups of people

Do not use; class in 363.59

.51      Social causes

Number built according to instructions under 362–363

Class here housing conditions

[.52]      Incidence, extent, severity of housing problems

Do not use; class in 363.51

.58      Programs and services

Do not use subdivisions of 8 from the table under 362–363

Provision of shelter (temporary houusing) relocated to 362.583

.582      Financial assistance

Class here housing allowances, rental subsidies, subsidized housing

.583      Programs and services for specific objectives

Including home ownership, payment of energy bills, rehabilitation, resettlement, urban homesteading, weatherization

.585      Public operated housing

Class here council housing

.59      Housing for groups of people

Add to base number 363.59 the numbers following —08 in notation 081–089 from Table 1, e.g., housing for people in late adulthood 363.5946; however, for extended medical care for older adults, see 362.16; for comprehensive works on homelessness, see 362.5; for residential care for healthy older adults, see 362.61; for comprehensive works on housing for poor people, see 363.5

Class specific aspects of housing for poor people, of low-income housing in 363.51–363.58

*For provision of shelter for a specific group of people, see the group in 362.1–362.8, plus notation 83 from table under 362–363, e.g., shelter for women 362.8383*

---

\*Add as instructed under 362–363

**.6**      **Public utilities and related services**

> Standard subdivisions are added for public utilities and related services together, for public utilities alone
>
> Class here problems of allocation among end users, measures to assure abundance of immediately available supplies and services
>
> > *For electrical utilities, see 333.7932; for communication, see 384; for transportation, see 388*
> >
> > *See Manual at 333.7–333.9 vs. 363.6; also at 363.5, 363.6, 363.8 vs. 338*

**.61**      Water supply

> Class here comprehensive works on water supply, on water-related public works, e.g., a study covering waterworks, treatment plants, canals, flood control, hydroelectric generation
>
> > *For a specific topic of water supply, see the topic, e.g., flood control 363.34936*
> >
> > *See Manual at 363.61*

**.63**      Gas

**.68**      Park and recreation services

> Class here services maintained or proposed after land has been designated for parks, establishment and operation of recreational centers primarily serving the general public
>
> Class park policy and park development in 333.783; class recreational centers in 790.068. Class a specific cultural institution maintained by park and recreation services with the institution, e.g., museums 069, theaters 792

**.69**      Historic preservation

> Including identification and designation of historic buildings and areas
>
> Class here public policies to protect and restore historic buildings and areas and to promote appreciation of them
>
> Class technology of building restoration and preservation in 720.288
>
> > *See Manual at 913–919: Historic sites and buildings; also at 930–990: Historic preservation*

**.7**      **Environmental problems**

> Class here environmental protection; impact of wastes, of pollution, of actions to control waste and pollution
>
> Class interdisciplinary works on the environment in 333.7
>
> > *See Manual at 333.72 vs. 304.28, 320.58, 363.7*

## SUMMARY

| | |
|---|---|
| **363.700 1–.700 9** | **Standard subdivisions** |
| **.701–.708** | **Characteristics of environmental problems, social action** |
| **.72** | **Sanitation** |
| **.73** | **Pollution** |
| **.74** | **Noise** |
| **.75** | **Disposal of the dead** |
| **.78** | **Pest control** |

.700 1–.700 9      Standard subdivisions

> Notation from Table 1 as modified under 362–363, e.g., managerial cost control 363.700681

.701–.708      Characteristics of environmental problems, social action

> Add to base number 363.70 notation 1–8 from table under 362–363, e.g., international action to protect the environment 363.70526

.72      *Sanitation

.728      Wastes

> Do not use for other remedial measures, services, forms of assistance; class in 363.72

> Class here industrial, municipal wastes; waste disposal, management

> Unless other instructions are given, class a subject with aspects in two or more subdivisions of 363.728 in the number coming last, e.g., recycling scrap metal 363.7288 (*not* 363.7282)

> Class dangerous wastes still in hands of processors or users in 363.17; class pollution by waste disposal in 363.73; class dangerous wastes which have escaped both safety and sanitary controls in 363.738

.728 2      Recycling

.728 4      *Liquid wastes

> Including urban water runoff; dredging spoil, water reuse planning

> Class here wastewater management

> *See Manual at 363.61*

.728 49      Specific kinds of liquid wastes

[.728 490 1–.728 490 9]      Standard subdivisions

> Do not use; class in 363.728401–363.728409

.728 493      *Sewage

> Class here biosolids, sewage sludge, wastes from combined sewers

.728 5      *Solid wastes

.728 7      *Hazardous wastes

*Add as instructed under 362–363

| .728 8 | Specific kinds of wastes |

Including agricultural, domestic, medical wastes; beverage containers, garbage, scrap metal

*For radioactive wastes, see 363.7289*

| .728 9 | *Radioactive wastes |
| .729 | Sanitation in specific environments |
| .729 1 | Streets |
| .729 2 | Recreational areas |

Including swimming pools

| .729 3 | Common carriers |
| .729 4 | Public toilets |
| .729 5 | Workplaces |
| .729 6 | Food service establishments |
| .729 7 | Health facilities |

Including ambulances

| .729 8 | Residential buildings |

Other than private family dwellings

| .729 9 | Barbershops, beauty shops, laundries |
| .73 | *Pollution |

Class works that discuss waste and sanitation problems as well as pollution in 363.7; class sanitation in 363.72; class noise in 363.74; class management responsibilities and measures with respect to protection and preservation of the environment in 658.408

*See Manual at 333.7–333.9 vs. 363.1, 363.73, 577; also at 363.73 vs. 571.95, 577.27*

| .731 | Social causes |

Number built according to instructions under 362–363

Including industrial pollution

Class specific pollutants from specific sources in 363.738

| .732 | Incidence, extent, severity |

Number built according to instructions under 362–363

Class incidence, extent, severity of pollution from specific sources in 363.731

*Add as instructed under 362–363

| | |
|---|---|
| .735 | Social action |
| | Number built according to instructions under 362–363 |
| | Class here remedial measures |
| .737 | Measures to prevent, protect against, limit effects of pollution |
| | Number built according to instructions under 362–363 |
| | Class waste disposal as a method of pollution prevention in 363.728; class technology of pollution prevention in 628.5 |
| .738 | Pollutants |
| | Do not use for remedial measures; class in 363.735 |
| | Class here chemical pollutants |
| .738 2 | *Oil |
| .738 4 | *Toxic chemicals |
| .738 49 | Specific types of toxic chemicals |
| .738 492 | *Lead |
| .738 494 | *Asbestos |
| .738 498 | *Pesticides |
| | Class here agricultural pollution, agricultural runoff |
| | Class pollution by animal wastes, feedlot runoff, fertilizers in 363.738 |
| .738 6 | *Acid rain |
| .738 7 | Fumes, gases, smoke |
| | Class lead emissions in 363.7384 |
| .738 74 | *Greenhouse gases |
| | Gases contributing to greenhouse effect (global warming) |
| | Class here interdisciplinary works on greenhouse effect (global warming) |
| | *For a specific aspect of greenhouse effect (global warming) not provided for here, see the aspect, e.g., changes in earth's temperature 551.5253, effect on ecology 577.276* |
| .738 75 | *Gases contributing to ozone layer depletion |
| | Class here interdisciplinary works on ozone layer depletion |
| | *For a specific aspect of ozone layer depletion not provided for here, see the aspect, e.g., chemical changes in earth's ozone layer 551.5142, effect on ecology 577.276* |

*Add as instructed under 362–363

| | | |
|---|---|---|
| .739 | | Pollution of specific environments |

Class specific pollutants in specific environments in 363.738

.739 2      *Air pollution

.739 4      *Water pollution

Class here comprehensive works on water pollution

*For assurance of clean water supply, see 363.61*

*See Manual at 363.61*

.739 6      *Soil pollution

.74      *Noise

.741      Sources of noise

Number built according to instructions under 362–363

Including forms of transportation, e.g., aircraft, automobile traffic; construction equipment, industry

Class effects of specific sources of noise in 363.742

.742      Incidence, extent, severity

Number built according to instructions under 362–363

Class incidence, extent, severity of noise from specific sources in 363.741

.75      Disposal of the dead

Class here interdisciplinary works on social aspects and services, customs, technology

Class interdisciplinary works on death in 306.9

*For death customs, see 393; for technology of disposal of the dead, see 614.6*

.78      Pest control

Including dog pounds, rat and mosquito abatement programs, removal of animal carcasses

Class here interdisciplinary works on pest control

*For control of disease-carrying pests, see 614.43; for comprehensive works on the technology of pest control, see 628.96; for control of agricultural pests, see 632.9; for control of household pests, see 648.7*

*Add as instructed under 362–363

**.8**      **\*Food supply**

> Class here famine, hunger; interdisciplinary works on food supply, on nutrition
>
> Class food stamp programs in 363.882; class food relief in 363.883
>
>> *For economics of food supply, see 338.19; for problems of malnutrition, see 362.19639; for prevention of malnutrition, see 614.5939*
>>
>> *See Manual at 363.5, 363.6, 363.8 vs. 338; also at 363.8 vs. 613.2, 641.3*

**.808**      Groups of people

> Do not use for food supply problems of and services to groups of people, other than poor people; class in 362.1–362.8, plus notation 83 from table under 362–363

**.82**      Incidence, extent, severity of food supply problems

> Number built according to instructions under 362–363
>
> Class here nutrition surveys

**.85**      Social action

> Number built according to instructions under 362–363

**.856**      Governmental action

> Number built according to instructions under 362–363
>
> Class here food rationing

**.9**      **Population problems**

> Class here interdisciplinary works on population problems
>
> Class immigration in 362.89912; class interdisciplinary works on population in 304.6
>
>> *For a specific manifestation of a population problem, see the manifestation, e.g., population growth as a cause of poverty 362.51, pressure on food supply leading to famine 363.8*
>>
>> *See Manual at 301–307 vs. 361–365*

**.91**      Population quantity

> Overpopulation and underpopulation
>
> Class remedial measures for overpopulation in 363.96

**.92**      Population quality

> Class here interdisciplinary works on eugenics
>
>> *For eugenic measures to reduce crime, see 364.4. For a specific aspect of eugenics, see the aspect, e.g., civil rights 323, involuntary sterilization 363.97*
>>
>> *See also 613.94 for family planning techniques*

\*Add as instructed under 362–363

.96     **Birth control**

Class here remedial measures for overpopulation; interdisciplinary works on birth control, on family planning programs

Class abortion in 362.19888

*For sterilization, see 363.97; for personal health aspects of birth control, see 613.94; for comprehensive medical works on birth control, see 618.18*

.97     **Sterilization**

Including involuntary sterilization

Class here voluntary sterilization

# 364     Criminology

Crime and its alleviation

Class here comprehensive works on criminology and criminal law, on criminal justice that includes criminology, police services, and criminal law

Unless other instructions are given, observe the following table of preference, e.g., punishment of specific types of offenders 364.6 (*not* 364.3):

| | |
|---|---|
| Penology | 364.6 |
| Discharged offenders | 364.8 |
| Offenders | 364.3 |
| Prevention of crime and delinquency | 364.4 |
| Causes of crime and delinquency | 364.2 |
| Criminal offenses | 364.1 |
| History, geographic treatment, biography of crime and its alleviation | 364.9 |

Class social services to victims of crimes and crime prevention for the individual in 362.88

*For criminal law, see 345; for police services, see 363.2*

### SUMMARY

| | |
|---|---|
| 364.01–.09 | **Standard subdivisions and special topics of criminology** |
| .1 | **Criminal offenses** |
| .2 | **Causes of crime and delinquency** |
| .3 | **Offenders** |
| .4 | **Prevention of crime and delinquency** |
| .6 | **Penology** |
| .8 | **Discharged offenders** |
| .9 | **History, geographic treatment, biography of crime and its alleviation** |

.019     **Psychological principles**

*For criminal psychology of specific offenses, see 364.1; for criminal psychology of offenders in general, see 364.3*

.04     **Special topics of criminology**

.042 Extent and incidence of crime

Criminal offenses and offenders

Class criminal offenses in 364.1; class offenders in 364.3

.08 Groups of people

Class works on why people become victims of specific crimes in 364.1

[.086 923] Juvenile delinquents and predelinquents

Do not use for predelinquents; class in 362.74. Do not use for juvenile delinquents; class in 364.36

[.086 927] Offenders

Do not use for offenders; class in 364.3. Do not use for convicts; class in 365.6

.086 949 Victims of war

Do not use for victims of crimes; class in 362.88

.09 History, geographic treatment, biography of criminology as a discipline

Do not use for history, geographic treatment, biography of crime and its alleviation; class in 364.9

**.1 Criminal offenses**

Class here conspiracy to and incitement to commit an offense, individuals identified with a specific offense or type of offense, investigation of specific crimes, crimes without victims

Class social services to victims of crimes in 362.88; class investigation of specific types of offenses in 363.259; class crime as an event in history in 900

*See Manual at 362–363 vs. 364.1; also at 900: Historic events vs. nonhistoric events*

### SUMMARY

| | |
|---|---|
| 364.101–.109 | **Standard subdivisions and organized crime** |
| .13 | **Political and related offenses** |
| .14 | **Offenses against public health, safety, order, environment** |
| .15 | **Offenses against the person** |
| .16 | **Offenses against property** |
| .17 | **Offenses against public morals** |
| .18 | **Other offenses** |

.106 Organized crime

Do not use for organizations dealing with criminal offenses; class in 364.06

Class here Mafia

[.106 092] Biography

Do not use for organized crime figures not associated with a specific offense; class in 364.1092. Do not use for organized crime figures associated with a specific offense; class in 364.13–364.18 with the offense e.g., a hired killer 364.1523092

| | |
|---|---|
| .106 6 | Gangsterism |

Engagement of organized groups in piracy, robbery, theft, hijacking

| | |
|---|---|
| .106 7 | Racketeering |

Engagement of organized groups in extortion from legitimate or illegitimate enterprises through intimidation and force

Including union racketeering

| | |
|---|---|
| .106 8 | Syndicated crime |

Engagement of organized groups in furnishing illegal goods or services

| | |
|---|---|
| .109 2 | Biography |

Criminals are classed with the crime for which they are most noted unless they are discussed with relationship to a specific crime, e.g., a general biography of Jesse James, a bank robber, is classed in 364.1552092, but a study of Jesse James' killings is classed in 364.1523092

Class comprehensive works on offenders in 364.3

| | |
|---|---|
| .13 | Political and related offenses |
| .131 | Political offenses |

Including espionage, rebellion, seditious libel, subversion, treason

Class genocide in 364.151; class assassination of heads of state and government in 364.1524; class sabotage in 364.164

*For war crimes, see 364.138*

| | |
|---|---|
| .131 7 | Terrorism |

Class interdisciplinary works on terrorism in 363.325

*For terrorism as a war crime, see 364.138. For a specific type of terrorism, see the type, e.g., cyberterrorism 364.168*

| | |
|---|---|
| .132 | Offenses against proper government |

*For offenses against administration of justice, see 364.134*

| | |
|---|---|
| .132 2 | Denial and violation of civil rights |

Standard subdivisions are added for either or both topics in heading

| | |
|---|---|
| .132 3 | Corruption |

Including bribery of officials, graft

| | |
|---|---|
| .132 4 | Election offenses |

Including bribery of voters, fraudulent reporting of votes, illegal voting, violations of campaign finance laws

| | |
|---|---|
| .133 | Offenses against revenue |

| .133 2 | Bootlegging |
|---|---|

Class here production, sale, transportation of alcoholic beverages; illicit distilling; comprehensive works on criminal offenses associated with alcoholic beverages

*For smuggling of alcoholic beverages, see 364.13361; for possession and use of alcoholic beverages, see 364.173*

*See also 363.41 for sale of alcoholic beverages; also 364.1662 for bootlegging of copyrighted property, e.g., software piracy*

| .133 4 | Counterfeiting of mediums of exchange |
|---|---|

Class here counterfeiting money, comprehensive works on counterfeiting

*For counterfeiting of merchandise, see 364.1668*

| .133 6 | Smuggling |
|---|---|

Including smuggling of tobacco products, e.g., cigarettes

Class here comprehensive works on importing or exporting items on which duties have not been paid or illegal items

*For human smuggling, see 364.137. For a smuggled item not provided for here, see the item, e.g., medicine 364.142*

| .133 61 | Alcoholic beverages |
|---|---|

Class bootlegging in 364.1332

| .133 65 | Drugs |
|---|---|

Class here narcotics

Class drug traffic in 363.45; class comprehensive works on criminal offenses associated with drugs in 364.177

| .133 67 | Animals |
|---|---|

Class here wildlife smuggling

*For violation of animal or plant quarantine, see 364.142*

| .133 8 | Tax evasion |
|---|---|
| .134 | Offenses against administration of justice |

Including collusion, contempt of court, lynching, perjury, subornation of perjury

| .135 | International offenses |
|---|---|

*For a specific international offense, see the offense, e.g., piracy 364.164*

| .136 | Offenses against postal laws |
|---|---|
| .137 | Illegal immigration |

Class here human smuggling

| | |
|---|---|
| .138 | War crimes |

Class here terrorism as a war crime

Class comprehensive works on terrorism in 364.1317

*For a specific war crime, see the crime, e.g., genocide 364.151*

*See also 341.69 for law of war crimes*

| | |
|---|---|
| .14 | Offenses against public health, safety, order, environment |
| .142 | Offenses against public health and safety |

Including adulteration of food and drugs, violations of product and building safety laws

| | |
|---|---|
| .143 | Offenses against public order |

Including carrying concealed weapons, disorderly conduct, rioting, unlawful assembly

| | |
|---|---|
| .145 | Offenses against the environment |

Class here violation of pollution laws

| | |
|---|---|
| .147 | Traffic offenses and misuse of communications facilities |

Class offenses against postal laws in 364.136

| | |
|---|---|
| .148 | Vagrancy |
| .15 | Offenses against the person |

Class here hate crimes

Class prevention of crimes by individuals in 613.6

| | |
|---|---|
| .151 | Genocide |
| .152 | Homicide |

*For lynching, see 364.134; for genocide, see 364.151*

| | |
|---|---|
| .152 2 | Suicide |

Class assisted suicide in 364.1523

| | |
|---|---|
| .152 3 | Murder |

Including assisted suicide

*For assassination, see 364.1524*

| | |
|---|---|
| .152 32 | Serial murder |
| .152 34 | Mass murder |
| .152 4 | Assassination |
| .152 5 | Manslaughter |
| .153 | Sex offenses |

Including adultery, indecent exposure, seduction, statutory rape

Class rape in 364.1532; class bigamy in 364.183

.153 2                    Rape

> Class social services aspects of rape in 362.883
>
> *See also 364.153 for statutory rape*

.153 4                    Prostitution

> *See also 363.44 for prostitution as a public morals issue*

.153 6                    Sexual deviations

> Including incest, sodomy

.154                 Abduction, kidnapping, taking and holding of hostages

> Class parental kidnapping in 362.8297

.155                 Other violent offenses against the person

.155 2                    Robbery

> Thefts including threat of violence or bodily harm, or actual occurrence of violence
>
> Class here comprehensive works on hijacking
>
> > *For a specific type of hijacking, see the type, e.g., taking hostages 364.154*

.155 5                    Assault and battery

> Standard subdivisions are added for either or both topics in heading
>
> Including elder abuse
>
> Class elder abuse as a social problem in 362.6

.155 53                  Spouse abuse

> Class social services to battered wives, spouse abuse as a social problem in 362.8292

.155 54                  Child abuse

> Class here child neglect
>
> Class child abuse as a social problem in 362.76
>
> > *See also 364.1536 for incest; also 364.174 for pornography*

.156                 Offenses against reputation and honor

> Including defamation, invasion of privacy, libel, slander
>
> Class seditious libel in 364.131

.158                 Stalking

.16               Offenses against property

> Class here looting, pillage, plundering
>
> Class prevention of crimes by individuals in 613.6

.162       Theft

> Class here larceny
>
> Class robbery in 364.1552; class fraud in 364.163; class identity theft in 364.1633

.162 2       Theft from residential and related buildings

> Standard subdivisions are added for theft from residential and related buildings together, for theft from residential buildings alone
>
> Including theft from garages
>
> Class here burglary
>
> Class theft of a specific item from residential or related buildings in 364.1628
>
> *For theft from nonresidential buildings, see 364.1623*

.162 3       Theft from nonresidential buildings

> Class here theft from commercial buildings, employee theft
>
> Class theft of a specific item from nonresidential buildings in 364.1628

.162 32       Shoplifting

.162 4       Embezzlement

> Class comprehensive works on business offenses, white collar crime in 364.168

.162 7       Fencing

> Class fencing of a specific item in 364.1628

.162 8       Theft of specific items

> *See also 364.1662 for theft of intellectual property*

[.162 800 01–.162 800 09]       Standard subdivisions

> Do not use; class in 364.16201–364.16209

.162 800 1–.162 809 9       Theft of computers, books, related objects

> Add to base number 364.1628 notation 001–099, e.g., computer theft 364.1628004

.162 81–.162 89       Theft of other specific items

> Add to base number 364.1628 notation 100–900, e.g., art thefts 364.16287

.162 859 1       Theft of wildlife

> Number built according to instructions under 364.16281–364.16289
>
> Class here poaching, comprehensive works on wildlife crimes
>
> *For wildlife smuggling, see 364.13367*

| | | |
|---|---|---|
| .162 862 904 | | Transportation vehicle thefts |

           Number built according to instructions under 364.16281–364.16289

           Class here theft of the vehicles, theft from the vehicles

           *For theft of a specific item, other than the vehicle, see the item, e.g., theft of computers from motor vehicles 364.1628004*

.163        Fraud

        Including welfare fraud, e.g., Medicare fraud

        Class mail fraud in 364.136

.163 2      Phishing

        Class use of information obtained by phishing for identity theft in 364.1633

.163 3      Identity theft

        Class here impersonation (false personation)

.163 5      Forgery

        Class product conterfeiting in 364.1668

.164        Violent offenses against property

        Including piracy, sabotage

        Class robbery, comprehensive works on hijacking in 364.1552; class prevention by individuals of violent offenses against property in 613.66

        *See also 364.1662 for copyright piracy*

.164 2      Arson

.164 4      Vandalism

.165        Extortion

        Including blackmail

.166        Intellectual property infringement

.166 2      Copyright infringement

        Including bootlegging (making, distribution, or trafficking in copyrighted material); copyright piracy, e.g., software piracy, pirated editions (bootlegged editions)

        *For counterfeiting of copyrighted products, see 364.1668*

        *See also 364.1332 for bootlegging as an offense against revenue*

.166 3      Trademark infringement

        *For counterfeiting of trademarked products, see 364.1668*

.166 8         Product counterfeiting

> Class here counterfeiting of copyrighted products, counterfeiting of trademarked products, passing off

> Class comprehensive works on counterfeiting in 364.1334

.168         Business, financial, professional offenses

> Including criminal usury, cyberterrorism, unfair trade practices; violation of antitrust laws, of laws with respect to securities and their exchange

> Class here computer, white collar crime

> *For embezzlement, see 364.1624; for fraud, see 364.163. For a specific type of computer crime not provided for here, see the type, e.g., tax evasion 364.1338*

> *See also 364.1628004 for theft of computers*

.17     Offenses against public morals

> *For sex offenses, see 364.153*

.172     Gambling

> *See also 363.42 for gambling as a public morals question*

.173     Possession and use of alcoholic beverages

> Standard subdivisions are added for either or both topics in heading

> Including public drunkenness

> Class drunk driving in 364.147; class comprehensive works on criminal offenses associated with alcoholic beverages in 364.1332

> *See also 363.41 for sale of alcoholic beverages*

.174     Obscenity and pornography

> *See also 363.47 for obscenity and pornography as a public morals question*

.177     Drugs

> Class here production, sale, possession, use

> Class drug traffic in 363.45

> *For smuggling of drugs, see 364.13365*

> *See also 364.173 for alcoholic beverages*

.18     Other offenses

> Including illegal adoption

.183     Bigamy

.185     Criminal abortion

> Class abortion as a public morals question in 363.46; class interdisciplinary works on abortion in 362.19888

.187     Cruelty to animals

.188               **Offenses against religion**

                    Offenses defined and penalized by the state

                    Including blasphemy, heresy, sacrilege

                    Class offenses against church law in 262.9

.2               **Causes of crime and delinquency**

                    Class here criminal anthropology

                    Class victimology in 362.88

.22               Influence of physical environment

                    Including climate, seasons, weather

.24               Influence of personal factors

                    Including biological factors, e.g., effects of heredity, genetic defects, physical typology; psychological factors

.25               Influence of social factors

                    Including leisure and recreation

.253              Influence of family and peer group

.254              Influence of mass media

                    Including books, motion pictures, radio, television

.256              Influence of social conflict

                    Including class, ethnic group, religion, socioeconomic conditions

.3               **Offenders**

                    Including recidivists

                    Class here criminal psychology

                    Class a specific aspect of the justice system for specific types of offenders with the aspect, e.g., determination of sentences for juvenile offenders 364.650835, offenders as prisoners in 365.6

                    *For individuals chiefly identified with a specific offense or type of offense, see 364.1*

[.308 11]         Men

                    Do not use; class in 364.373

[.308 2]          Women

                    Do not use; class in 364.374

[.308 3]          Young people

                    Do not use; class in 364.36

.308 6           People by miscellaneous social characteristics

| [.308 692 3] | Juvenile delinquents and predelinquents |
| --- | --- |
| | Do not use; class in 364.36 |
| [.308 692 7] | Offenders |
| | Do not use; class in 364.3 |
| [.308 74] | People with mental illnesses and disabilities |
| | Do not use; class in 364.38 |
| [.308 9] | Ethnic and national groups |
| | Do not use; class in 364.34 |

.34    Offenders of ethnic and national groups

Class juvenile delinquents of specific ethnic and national groups in 364.36; class women in 364.374; class offenders with mental illnesses and disabilities in 364.38

.340 5–.340 9    Offenders of mixed ancestry with ethnic origins from more than one continent, European offenders and offenders of European descent

Add to base number 364.34 notation 05–09 from Table 5, e.g., offenders of European descent 364.3409

.341–.349    Specific ethnic and national groups

Add to base number 364.34 notation 1–9 from Table 5, e.g., Germans as offenders

.36    Juvenile delinquents

Including status offenders (juveniles who have broken laws pertaining only to their age group, e.g., curfew laws, drinking below legal age)

Class here comprehensive works on juvenile delinquency, juvenile delinquents, juvenile justice system together

Class comprehensive works on maladjusted young people in 362.74

*For legal aspects, see 345*

.37    Men and women

Class adult offenders with mental illnesses and disabilities in 364.38. Class men and women with attributes of a specific group with the grouop, e.g., 364.30846

.373    Men

Works specifically emphasizing male sex

.374    Women

.38    Offenders with mental illnesses and disabilities

Class here offenders with mental retardation

Class juvenile offenders with mental illnesses and disabilities in 364.36

**.4**          **Prevention of crime and delinquency**

Including curfew, eugenic measures

Class here what society does to prevent crime

Class penalties as a deterrent in 364.601

> *For law enforcement, see 363.23. For a specific aspect of prevention by a potential victim, see the aspect, e.g., prevention of identity theft 332.024, prevention by individuals of crimes 613.6, household security 643.16, business intelligence and security 658.47*

.404          Special topics of prevention of crime and delinquency

.404 5              Social action

> Add to base number 364.4045 the numbers following 361 in 361.2–361.8, e.g., social policy 364.404561

.41          Identification of potential offenders

Including genetic screening

.43          Citizen participation

Class individual action in 362.88

.44          Welfare services

Including financial assistance; foster home care; recreational services, e.g., camps, playgrounds

Class preventive police work in 363.23

> *For counseling and guidance, see 364.48*

.48          Counseling and guidance

Standard subdivisions are added for either or both topics in heading

.49          Environmental design

**.6**          **Penology**

Class here welfare services to offenders, reform of penal system

Class welfare services to prisoners in 365.66; class reform of penal institutions in 365.7

> *For discharged offenders, see 364.8; for institutions for correction of offenders, see 365*

.601          Philosophy and theory

> Class here punishment as retribution, deterrent, protection to society, reformation of offenders

.62          Parole and indeterminate sentence

Standard subdivisions are added for parole and indeterminate sentence together, for parole alone

Class services to prisoners to prepare them for parole in 365.66

.63      Probation and suspended sentence

Standard subdivisions are added for probation and suspended sentence together, for probation alone

Including reprieve

Class here comprehensive works on probation and parole

*For parole, see 364.62*

.65      Determination of sentence

Including amnesty, commutation of sentence, pardon

Class a specific punishment with the punishment, e.g., probation 364.63, imprisonment 365

.66      Capital punishment

.67      Corporal punishment

.68      Noninstitutional penalties

Including community service, deportation, fines, loss of citizenship, loss of vote

*For capital punishment, see 364.66; for corporal punishment, see 364.67*

**.8**      **Discharged offenders**

**.9**      **History, geographic treatment, biography of crime and its alleviation**

*For extent and incidence of crime, see 364.042*

.901–.905      Historical periods

Add to base number 364.90 the numbers following —090 in notation 0901–0905 from Table 1, e.g., crime and its alleviation in 20th century 364.904

.91–.99      Geographic treatment, biography

Add to base number 364.9 notation 1–9 from Table 2, e.g., people associated with crime and its alleviation 364.92; however, for victims, see 362.88; for police, see 363.2; for criminologists, see 364.092; for offenders associated with specific kinds of crime, see 364.1; for comprehensive works on offenders, see 364.3; for penologists, see 364.6092

# 365     Penal and related institutions

Institutions for correction of offenders and for incarceration of other groups considered socially undesirable

Standard subdivisions are added for penal and related institutions together, for penal institutions alone

Class here imprisonment and detention

Unless other instructions are given, class a subject with aspects in two or more subdivisions of 365 in the number coming last, e.g., maximum security prisons for women 365.43 (*not* 365.33)

Class parole and indeterminate sentence in 364.62; class probation and suspended sentence in 364.63

[.068 2]         Plant management

            Do not use; class in 365.5

[.09]       History, geographic treatment, biography

            Do not use; class in 365.9

**.3**     **Kinds of penal institutions**

        Class specific institutions in 365.93–365.99

.32       Institutions by level of government

        National, state or provincial, local

.33       Institutions by degree of security

.34       Institutions by purpose or type of program

        Including jails, penal colonies, penitentiaries, prerelease guidance centers, prison farms, reformatories, work camps

        Class penal colonies as a part of history of a place with the place in 930–990, e.g., penal colony of Botany Bay as founding settlement of New South Wales 994.402

**.4**     **Institutions for specific classes of inmates**

        Including debtors' prisons

        Class here personal narratives of specific classes of inmates

        Class specific institutions in 365.93–365.99; class comprehensive works on inmates in 365.6

.42       Institutions for juveniles

        Including borstals, reformatories; industrial, reform, training schools; halfway houses for the transition from reform school to society

.43       Institutions for adult women

.44       Institutions for adult men

        Works specifically emphasizing inmates of the male sex

        Class institutions in general, specific kinds of institutions for men in 365.3

.45      Institutions for political prisoners and related groups of people

> Standard subdivisions are added for either or both topics in heading

> Class here concentration camps

>> *For concentration camps associated with a specific war, see the war, e.g., World War II concentration camps 940.5317*

.46      Institutions for the criminally insane

.48      Military prisons and prison camps

> Institutions whose inmates are military personnel

> Class institutions for prisoners of war in 355.1296; class military institutions for the insane in 365.46

## .5      Prison plant

> Buildings, equipment, grounds

> Class prison architecture in 725.6

## .6      Inmates

> Including reception and classification

> Class here offenders as inmates; community-based corrections; social aspects of prison life, e.g., conjugal rights, drug abuse

> Class institutions for specific classes of inmates, personal narratives of inmates in 365.4

.602 1      Tabulated and related materials

> Class statistics of inmates when used to indicate general statistics of offenders in 364.3021

.609 2      Biography

> Class a personal narrative of a specific class of inmate with the class of inmate in 365.4, plus notation 092 from Table 1, e.g., a personal narrative of a political prisoner 365.45092

.64      Security, discipline, daily routine, release and discharge

> Class here treatment of inmates

.641      Security

> Including escapes, riots

.643      Discipline

> Rules, rights, privileges

> Including furloughs

> Class work furloughs in 365.65

>> *For punishments, see 365.644*

.644      Punishments for infractions of prison discipline

.646          Daily routine

> *For labor, see 365.65; for services to prisoners, see 365.66*

.647          Release and discharge

> Class work release in 365.65; class services to prepare prisoners for release in 365.66

.65          Labor

> Including chain gangs, contract system, lease system, work furloughs, work release

.66          Services to prisoners

---

> 365.661–365.663 **Counseling, rehabilitation, prerelease programs**

> Class here how to provide the service, how to perform the service

> Class comprehensive works in 365.66

.661          Counseling and rehabilitation

> Standard subdivisions are added for either or both topics in heading

> Class a specific service providing counseling or rehabilitation with the service, e.g., religious counseling 365.665

.663          Prerelease programs

> Class prerelease institutions in 365.34

---

> 365.665–365.668 **Religious, educational, medical, recreational services**

> How to provide the service is classed here. How to perform the service is classed with the activity in 000–999

> Class comprehensive works in 365.66

.665          Religious services

> Class care of prisoners by religious leaders in general in 206.1; class Christian pastoral care of prisoners in 259.5

.666          Educational services

> Class education of delinquent students in 371.93; class adult education of prisoners in 374.1826927

.667          Health services

> Class here medical services

> Class technology of medical serives in 610; class technology of health serives in 613

.667 2          Mental health services

.667 29          Substance abuse treatment

| | |
|---|---|
| .668 | Recreational services |

Class recreational arts in 790

**.7    Reform of penal institutions**

Class reform of penal system, reform to eliminate prisons as form of punishment for certain types of crimes in 364.6

**.9    History, geographic treatment, biography**

Class specific aspects of penal institutions in specific times and places, of specific kinds of institutions in 365.3–365.7

| | |
|---|---|
| .901–.905 | Historical periods |

Add to base number 365.90 the numbers following —090 in notation 0901–0905 from Table 1, e.g., penal institutions in 20th century 365.904

| | |
|---|---|
| .91–.99 | Geographic treatment, biography |

Add to base number 365.9 notation 1–9 from Table 2, e.g., prison administrators 365.92; however, for inmates, see 365.6092

# 366    Secret associations and societies

Standard subdivisions are added for either or both topics in heading

Class here semisecret associations and societies

*For Rosicrucianism, see 135.43; for orders of knighthood, see 929.71. For secret associations and societies not provided for here, see the associations and societies, e.g., student secret associations 371.83*

Comprehensive works on associations relocated to 369

| | |
|---|---|
| [.001–.008] | Standard subdivisions of associations |

Relocated to 369.01–369.08

| | |
|---|---|
| [.009] | History, geographic treatment, biography of associations |

Relocated to 369.09

| | |
|---|---|
| .01–.08 | Standard subdivisions |
| .09 | History, geographic treatment, biography |
| .093–.099 | Specific continents, countries, localities |

Do not use for specific associations or societies not provided for in 366.1–366.5; class in 366

**.1    Freemasonry**

| | |
|---|---|
| .108 2 | Women in Freemasonry |

*For Order of the Eastern Star, see 366.18*

| | |
|---|---|
| .12 | Rituals |
| .16 | Nobles of the Mystic Shrine (Shriners) |
| .18 | Order of the Eastern Star |

.2      **Knights of Pythias**

.3      **Independent Order of Odd Fellows**

.308 2        Women

> *For International Association of Rebekah Assemblies, see 366.38*

.38        International Association of Rebekah Assemblies

.5      **Benevolent and Protective Order of Elks**

# 367    General clubs

Including social clubs, study clubs

Class here social clubs for specific types of people, e.g., social clubs for actors

Class clubs dealing with a specific subject with the subject, plus notation 06 from Table 1, e.g., pinochle clubs 795.41606

[.09]        History, geographic treatment, biography

         Do not use; class in 367.9

.9      **History, geographic treatment, biography**

.901–.905     Historical periods

         Add to base number 367.90 the numbers following —090 in notation 0901–0905 from Table 1, e.g., general clubs in 20th century 367.904

.91–.99     Geographic treatment, biography

         Add to base number 367.9 notation 1–9 from Table 2, e.g., The Lamb (social club in New York City composed chiefly of actors, musicians, and playwrights) 367.97471

# 368    Insurance

Class here risk, insurance industry

Class risk management as part of management in 658.155

*See also 658.153 for managerial decisions on choosing insurance*

### SUMMARY

| | |
|---|---|
| 368.001–.009 | Standard subdivisions and insurance companies |
| .01–.09 | [General principles, specific forms of risk, sales groupings] |
| .1 | Insurance against damage to and loss of property |
| .2 | Insurance against damage to and loss of property in transit |
| .3 | Old-age insurance and insurance against death, illness, injury |
| .4 | Government-sponsored insurance |
| .5 | Liability insurance |
| .6 | Glass insurance |
| .7 | Insurance against industrial casualties (accidents) |
| .8 | Other casualty insurance |
| .9 | Insurance by specific continents, countries, localities in modern world |

.001        Philosophy and theory

| | |
|---|---|
| [.001 51] | Mathematical principles |
| | Do not use; class in 368.01 |
| .002–.005 | Standard subdivisions |
| .006 | Organizations and management; insurance companies |
| | Notation 06 from Table 1 as modified below |
| .006 5 | Insurance companies |
| | For-profit and nonprofit organizations |
| | Class here interdisciplinary works on insurance companies |
| | Add to base number 368.0065 notation 4–9 from Table 2, e.g., insurance companies of Texas 368.0065764 |
| | Class government agencies that provide insurance in 353.54 |
| | *For credit and loan functions of insurance companies, see 332.38* |
| .007–.008 | Standard subdivisions |
| .009 | History, geographic treatment, biography |
| [.009 4–.009 9] | Specific continents, countries, localities in modern world |
| | Do not use; class in 368.9 |
| .01 | General principles |
| | Class here actuarial science, finance, mathematical principles |
| | Class investments by insurance companies in 332.672532 |
| .011 | Rates |
| | Class here rate making |
| .012 | Underwriting |
| | Risk selection and estimation |
| .012 2 | Reinsurance |
| .014 | Claims |
| | Including adjustment of claims, fraudulent claims, settlement of losses |
| | Class fraudulent claims, insurance fraud as crimes in 364.163 |
| .016 | Lapse, persistence, termination |
| | Standard subdivisions are added for any or all topics in heading |
| .019 | Government policies with respect to insurance, insurance industry |

---

>     368.06–368.08   Specific forms of risk

Class comprehensive works in 368

.06          Property risks

> Risk of loss from impairment or destruction of property
>
> Class risk of consequential loss in 368.08

.062          Risks to tangible property

.063          Risks to intangible property

.07          Personal risks

> Risk of loss of income or augmented expenditure due to hazards to the person

.08          Other risks

> Including liability risks, risk of consequential loss, risks due to the failure of others, statutory liability risks

.09          Conventional comprehensive sales groupings

> Combinations of different lines of insurance, e.g., property-casualty, property-casualty-life and health
>
> Class here all-risk, multiple-line coverage
>
> Class a single line of insurance with the line, e.g., homeowner's liability insurance 368.56

.092          Motor vehicle insurance

> Class here automobile insurance
>
> *For motor vehicle transportation insurance as a branch of inland marine insurance, see 368.232; for motor vehicle liability insurance, see 368.572*

.093          Aviation insurance

> *For air transportation insurance as a branch of inland marine insurance, see 368.24; for aviation liability insurance, see 368.576*

.094          Business insurance

> Broad property and liability coverage
>
> Class here businessowners insurance, comprehensive business policies; commercial insurance, commercial multi-peril insurance; special multi-peril insurance (SMP)
>
> *For a single line of insurance, see the line, e.g., business liability insurance 368.81*

.096          Multi-peril real property insurance

> Coverage of perils associated with land and whatever is growing on or affixed to it
>
> Class here homeowner's insurance

> **368.1–368.8 Specific kinds of insurance**

Add to each subdivision identified by * as follows:
001–005   Standard subdivisions
006         Organizations and management; insurance companies
               Notation 06 from Table 1 as modified below
0065       Insurance companies
               For-profit and nonprofit organizations
               Add to 0065 notation 4–9 from Table 2, e.g., insurance
               companies in Great Britain 006541
007–009   Standard subdivisions
01          General principles
               Add to 01 the numbers following 368.01 in 368.011–368.019,
               e.g., underwriting 012

Class comprehensive works in 368

**.1**     ***Insurance against damage to and loss of property**

Subdivisions are added for either or both topics in heading

Class multi-peril real property insurance in 368.096. Class property damage (liability) insurance as part of a specific type of liability insurance with the type, e.g., property damage insurance as part of public liability 368.56

*For insurance against damage to and loss of property in transit, see 368.2; for casualty insurance, see 368.5–368.8*

**.11**     ***Fire insurance**

*For extended coverage endorsement, see 368.129*

*See also 368.12 for allied fire insurance lines*

**.12**     ***Allied fire insurance lines and extended coverage endorsement**

Perils and losses traditionally associated with fire insurance

Including explosion, smoke damage, vandalism and malicious mischief (VMM) insurance

Class here commercial property insurance

Subdivisions are added for allied fire insurance lines and extended coverage endorsement together, for allied fire insurance lines alone

Class business interruption insurance in 368.815

*See also 368.56 for livestock liability insurance*

**.121**     ***Crop insurance**

Class here government-sponsored crop insurance

*Add as instructed under 368.1–368.8

.122      *Disaster insurance

> Including insurance against damage and loss from storms

> > *For insurance for damage to crops from storms and other disasters, see 368.121*

.122 2      *Flood insurance

.122 6      *Earthquake insurance

.125      *Civil commotion and riot insurance

> Subdivisions are added for either or both topics in heading

.129      *Extended coverage endorsement

.14      *War risk insurance

> Class ocean marine war risk insurance in 368.22; class war risk life insurance in 368.364

**.2      *Insurance against damage to and loss of property in transit**

> Variant names: Marine insurance, Transportation insurance

> Including postal and satellite insurance

> Class here insurance against damage to and loss of instrumentalities of transportation

> Class a combination of transportation property insurance and transportation liability insurance in 368.09

.22      *Ocean marine insurance

> Over-the-sea transportation insurance

> Including ocean marine war risk insurance

.23      *Inland marine insurance

> Land or over-the-land (including over inland waterways) transportation insurance

> > *For air transportation insurance, see 368.24*

.232      *Motor vehicle insurance

> Class here automobile insurance

> Class comprehensive works on all types of motor vehicle insurance in 368.092

.233      *Railroad insurance

.24      *Air transportation insurance

> Class comprehensive works on all types of air transportation and aviation insurance in 368.093

---

*Add as instructed under 368.1–368.8

**.3**      **\*Old-age insurance and insurance against death, illness, injury**

Class here comprehensive works on private and government-sponsored old-age insurance and insurance against death, illness, injury; comprehensive works on group insurance, on industrial insurance, on old-age and survivors' insurance, on survivors' insurance

Class personnel management of insurance as a fringe benefit in 658.3254; class comprehensive works on insurance as a fringe benefit in 331.255

> *For government-sponsored insurance, see 368.4. For a specific type of group insurance, of industrial insurance, of old-age and survivors' insurance, of survivors' insurance not provided for here, see the type, e.g., group credit insurance 368.87*

**.32**      \*Life insurance

> *For special fields of life insurance, see 368.36*

**.322**      \*Endowment insurance

**.323**      \*Term life insurance

**.324**      \*Universal life insurance

**.325**      \*Variable life insurance

**.326**      \*Whole life insurance

**.36**      Special fields of life insurance

**.362**      \*Industrial life insurance

**.363**      \*Fraternal insurance

**.364**      \*Life insurance for members of armed services

> Including National Service Life Insurance, veterans' life insurance, war risk life insurance

**.366**      \*Burial insurance

**.37**      \*Annuities

> Class pensions as an element of personnel management in 658.3253; class comprehensive works on pensions in 331.252

**.375**      \*Variable annuities

**.38**      \*Health insurance, accident insurance, disability income insurance

\*Add as instructed under 368.1–368.8

.382      *Health insurance

> Including disability insurance; health maintenance organizations, preferred provider plans; long-term care insurance, Medigap (Medicare supplement insurance); reimbursement health insurance (insurance in which the insured first pays the bills)
>
> Class here insurance aspects of managed care, prepaid health insurance (insurance in which the insurer first pays the bills), specific health insurance organizations or plans without regard to type, comprehensive works on health and accident insurance
>
> Class interdisciplinary works on delivery of health care in 362.1
>
> *For accident insurance, see 368.384*
>
> *See also 368.386 for disability income insurance*

---

>     368.382 2–368.382 7   Basic health insurance coverage for specific kinds of services

> Class here policies limited to coverage for specific kinds of services, works that focus on specific types of benefits of broader policies
>
> Class catastrophic health insurance in 368.3828; class comprehensive works in 368.382

.382 2      *Medical and surgical insurance

> Subdivisions are added for medical and surgical insurance together, for medical insurance alone
>
> Class major medical insurance in 368.3828

.382 3      *Dental insurance

.382 4      *Pharmaceutical services insurance

.382 5      *Mental health insurance

> Including coverage for treatment of substance abuse

.382 7      *Hospital insurance

> Class coverage for psychiatric hospitalization in 368.3825; class major medical insurance in 368.3828

.382 8      *Catastrophic health insurance (Major medical insurance)

> Insurance providing protection for potentially large health care expenses after basic health care insurance benefits have been exhausted

.384      *Accident insurance

.386      *Disability income insurance

> *See also 368.382 for disability insurance*

*Add as instructed under 368.1–368.8

**.4**      **\*Government-sponsored insurance**

Class here social insurance, social security as a form of social insurance

Class comprehensive works on social security taxes in 336.249

*For a type of government-sponsored insurance not provided for here, see the type, e.g., crop insurance 368.121, bank deposit insurance 368.854*

.400 68             Management

Class personnel management of insurance for government employees in 352.67

.400 9              History, geographic treatment, biography

.400 973                United States

Do not use for social security in United States; class in 368.4300973

**.41**      **\*Workers' compensation insurance (Workmen's compensation insurance)**

Protection against losses incurred through disablements caused on the job

Class here comprehensive works on workers' compensation insurance and employers' liability insurance

*For employers' liability insurance (insurance of an employer's liability for compensation to his employees in case of accident), see 368.56*

**.42**      \*Health and accident insurance

Subdivisions are added for health and accident insurance together, for health insurance alone

Class comprehensive works on health and accident insurance in 368.382

*For workers' compensation insurance, see 368.41*

*See also 362.1042520973 for United States' Medicaid financial benefits; also 362.10973 for United States' Medicaid health services*

[.420 084 6]            Accident and health insurance for people in late adulthood

Do not use; class in 368.426

.420 085 2             Accident and health insurance for mothers

Do not use for maternity insurance; class in 368.424

**.424**      \*Maternity insurance

**.426**      \*Accident and health insurance for people in late adulthood

Class comprehensive works on accident and health insurance for people in late adulthood in 368.38200846

\*Add as instructed under 368.1–368.8

.43        *Old-age and survivors' insurance

> Class here comprehensive works on government-sponsored old-age and survivors' insurance and government-sponsored accident and health insurance for people in late adulthood
>
> Class supplementary social security for low-income people in 362.582; class comprehensive works on old-age and survivors' insurance in 368.3
>
> *For government-sponsored accident and health insurance for people in late adulthood, see 368.426*

.430 097 3             United States

> Class here social security in United States

.44        *Unemployment insurance

.48        *Insurance against crimes of violence

> Class comprehensive works on crime insurance in 368.82

---

>        **368.5–368.8 Casualty insurance**

> Class comprehensive works in 368.5

.5        **\*Liability insurance**

> Including no-fault insurance, umbrella or excess liability insurance
>
> Class here comprehensive works on casualty insurance
>
> Class no-fault insurance, umbrella or excess liability insurance of a specific type with the type, e.g., umbrella personal insurance 368.56, no-fault motor vehicle insurance 368.5728
>
> *For glass insurance, see 368.6; for insurance against industrial casualties, see 368.7; for other casualty insurance, see 368.8*

.56        Miscellaneous lines of liability insurance

> Only those lines named below
>
> Including commercial general, contractual, elevator, employers', homeowners', landlords', owners', tenants' liability insurance; livestock liability insurance; personal liability insurance
>
> Class here public liability insurance
>
> *See also 368.121 for crop insurance*

.562        *Product liability insurance

.563        *Environmental impairment liability insurance

> Class here pollution liability insurance

.564        *Professional liability insurance

> Class here errors and omissions insurance, malpractice insurance

*Add as instructed under 368.1–368.8

.564 2               *Medical malpractice insurance

Class here physicians' liability insurance

.57          *Instrumentalities of transportation

.572             *Motor vehicle liability insurance

Class here automobile liability insurance

Class comprehensive works on all types of motor vehicle insurance in 368.092

.572 8             *No-fault motor vehicle insurance

.576             *Aviation liability insurance

Class comprehensive works on all types of aviation insurance in 368.093

**.6        *Glass insurance**

Including coverage on plate glass, windows

**.7        *Insurance against industrial casualties (accidents)**

Including boiler and machinery, nuclear (nuclear energy, nuclear hazards), power interruption, power plant insurance

**.8        Other casualty insurance**

.81          *Business liability insurance

Casualty aspects only

Class comprehensive works on business insurance in 368.094

.815             *Business interruption insurance

Including strike insurance

.82          *Burglary, robbery, theft insurance

Including extortion, kidnap and ransom insurance

Class here comprehensive works on crime insurance

Subdivisions are added for any or all topics in heading

*For a specific type of crime insurance not provided for here, see the type, e.g., government-sponsored insurance against crimes of violence 368.48*

.83          *Fidelity bonds

Guarantee against loss to employers because of dishonesty of employees

Class here comprehensive works on fidelity and surety bonds

*For surety bonds, see 368.84*

.84          *Surety bonds

Guarantee against loss due to failure to perform an obligation or fulfill a contract

*Add as instructed under 368.1–368.8

.85 Guarantees

> *For a specific guarantee not provided for here, see the guarantee, e.g., surety bonds 368.84*

.852 *Mortgage insurance

.853 *Investment guarantees

.854 *Bank deposit insurance

> Class here government guaranty of deposits

.87 *Credit insurance

> Insurance of creditor against loss due to debtor's insolvency

.88 *Title insurance

**.9 Insurance by specific continents, countries, localities in modern world**

> Add to base number 368.9 notation 4–9 from Table 2, e.g., insurance in South America 368.98

> *For a specific type of insurance in a specific place, see the type, e.g., transportation insurance in South America 368.20098*

**369 Associations [*formerly* 366]**

Organizations formed for fraternizing or for mutual assistance

Class interdisciplinary works on organizations in 060; class general rules of order in 060.42

> *For secret associations and societies, see 366; for general clubs, see 367; for orders of knighthood, see 929.71*

> *See also 200 for religious associations; also 368.363 for fraternal insurance*

.01–.08 Standard subdivisions [*formerly* 366.001–366.008]

.09 History, geographic treatment, biography [*formerly* 366.009]

.093–.099 Specific continents, countries, localities

> Do not use for specific associations not provided for in 369.1–369.5; class in 369

**.1 Hereditary, military, patriotic societies of United States**

Standard subdivisions are added for any or all topics in heading

Including state and local societies

(Option: To give local emphasis and a shorter number to hereditary, military, patriotic societies of a specific country, class them in this number; in that case, class hereditary, military, patriotic societies of United States in 369.273)

.11 General societies

> Including military and naval orders, Medal of Honor Legion, Military Order of Foreign Wars of the United States, Veterans of Foreign Wars

*Add as instructed under 368.1–368.8

| | |
|---|---|
| .12 | Colonial America societies |

Including General Society of Colonial Wars, General Society of Mayflower Descendants, National Society of the Colonial Dames of America

| | |
|---|---|
| .13 | Revolutionary War societies |

Including Society of the Cincinnati, Sons of the American Revolution

| | |
|---|---|
| .135 | Daughters of the American Revolution |
| .14 | Societies commemorating events of 1789–1861 |
| .15 | Union Civil War societies |

Including Grand Army of the Republic

Class here comprehensive works on societies of Civil War

*For Confederate Civil War societies, see 369.17*

| | |
|---|---|
| .17 | Confederate Civil War societies |

Including United Confederate Veterans, United Daughters of the Confederacy

| | |
|---|---|
| .18 | Societies commemorating wars from 1898 to present |
| .181 | Spanish-American War, 1898 |
| .186 | World Wars I and II and later wars |
| .186 1 | American Legion |
| .186 2 | American Veterans of World War II, Korea, and Vietnam (AMVETS) |
| .186 3 | Disabled American Veterans |
| **.2** | **Hereditary, military, patriotic societies** |

Standard subdivisions are added for any or all topics in heading

Class here nationality clubs

(Option: To give local emphasis and a shorter number to hereditary, military, patriotic societies of a specific country, use one of the following:

(Option A: Place them first by use of a letter or other symbol, e.g., hereditary, military, patriotic societies of France 369.F [preceding 369.1]

(Option B: Class them in 369.1; in that case, class hereditary, military, patriotic societies of United States in 369.273)

| | |
|---|---|
| [.209 3–.209 9] | Specific continents, countries, localities |

Do not use; class in 369.23–369.29

| | |
|---|---|
| .21 | International societies |

**.23–.29** Specific continents, countries, localities

> Add to base number 369.2 notation 3–9 from Table 2, e.g., patriotic societies of Italy 369.245; however, for hereditary, military, patriotic societies of United States, see 369.1
>> Notation 09 from Table 1 is added to indicate nationality clubs not located with the nation of interest, e.g., Order Sons of Italy in America 369.2450973
>
> Class clubs of ethnic groups not defined by specific country or locality in 369.3

**.3** **Ethnic clubs**

> Class clubs of ethnic groups defined by specific country or locality in 369.23–369.29

**.305–.309** Ethnic clubs for people of mixed ancestry with ethnic origins from more than one continent, ethnic clubs for Europeans and for people of European descent

> Add to base number 369.3 notation 05–09 from Table 5, e.g., ethnic clubs for people of European descent 369.309

**.31–.39** Specific ethnic and national groups

> Add to base number 369.3 notation 1–9 from Table 5, e.g., B'nai B'rith 369.3924

**.4** **Young people's societies**

> Class a specific aspect of young people's societies with the aspect, e.g., Boy Scout camps 796.5422

**.42** Boys' societies

> *For Boy Scouts, see 369.43*

**.43** Boy Scouts

> Including Cub Scouts, Explorers

**.46** Girls' societies

> *For Explorers, see 369.43; for Camp Fire, see 369.47*

**.463** Girl Scouts and Girl Guides

**.47** Camp Fire

**.5** **Service clubs**

> Including Lions International

**.52** Rotary International

# 370 Education

Class here basic education, public education

Unless other instructions are given, observe the following table of preference, e.g., special education at primary level 371.90472 (*not* 372):

| | |
|---|---|
| Public policy issues in education | 379 |
| Special education | 371.9 |
| Specific levels of education | 372–374 |
| Higher education | 378 |
| Schools and their activities (*except* 371.9) | 371 |
| Education for specific objectives | 370.11 |
| Curricula | 375 |
| Standard subdivisions, educational psychology (*except* 370.11) | 370.1–370.9 |

Class sociology of education in 306.43; class special education in a specific subject in 371.9; class primary education in a specific subject in 372.3–372.8. Class comprehensive works on education in a specific subject and on secondary, higher, and adult education in a specific subject with the subject, plus notation 071 from Table 1, e.g., education in science 507.1

## SUMMARY

| | |
|---|---|
| 370.1–.9 | **Standard subdivisions, education for specific objectives, educational psychology** |
| **371** | **Schools and their activities; special education** |
| .001–.009 | **Standard subdivisions** |
| .01–.07 | **Specific kinds of schools** |
| .1 | **Teachers and teaching, and related activities** |
| .2 | **School administration; administration of student academic activities** |
| .3 | **Methods of instruction and study** |
| .4 | **Student guidance and counseling** |
| .5 | **School discipline and related activities** |
| .6 | **Physical plant; materials management** |
| .7 | **Student welfare** |
| .8 | **Students** |
| .9 | **Special education** |
| **372** | **Primary education (Elementary education)** |
| .01–.08 | **Standard subdivisions, primary education for specific objectives** |
| .1 | **Organization and activities in primary education** |
| .2 | **Specific levels of primary education** |
| .3 | **Knowledge, computer science, library and information sciences, science, technology** |
| .4 | **Reading** |
| .5 | **The arts** |
| .6 | **Language arts (Communication skills)** |
| .7 | **Mathematics** |
| .8 | **Other studies** |
| .9 | **History, geographic treatment, biography of primary education** |

| | | |
|---|---|---|
| 373 | | Secondary education |
| | .01–.09 | Standard subdivisions, secondary education for specific objectives |
| | .1 | Organization and activities in secondary education |
| | .2 | Secondary schools and programs of specific kinds, levels, curricula, focus |
| | .3–.9 | Secondary education in specific continents, countries, localities |

| | | |
|---|---|---|
| 374 | | Adult education |
| | .001–.008 | Standard subdivisions |
| | .01 | Adult education for specific objectives |
| | .1 | Organization and activities in adult education |
| | .2 | Groups, media, computers in adult education |
| | .4 | Distance education |
| | .8 | Specific kinds of institutions and agencies in adult education |
| | .9 | History, geographic treatment, biography |

| | | |
|---|---|---|
| 375 | | Curricula |
| | .000 1–.000 9 | Standard subdivisions |
| | .001–.006 | [Curriculum development, required and elective courses] |

| | | |
|---|---|---|
| 378 | | Higher education (Tertiary education) |
| | .001–.009 | Standard subdivisions |
| | .01–.07 | [Higher education for specific objectives, specific kinds of colleges and universities] |
| | .1 | Organization and activities in higher education |
| | .2 | Academic degrees and related topics |
| | .3 | Student aid and related topics |
| | .4–.9 | Higher education in specific continents, countries, localities in modern world |

| | | |
|---|---|---|
| 379 | | Public policy issues in education |
| | .1 | Specific elements of support and control of public education |
| | .2 | Specific policy issues in public education |
| | .3 | Public policy issues in private education |
| | .4–.9 | Public policy issues in specific continents, countries, localities in modern world |

**.1 Philosophy and theory, education for specific objectives, educational psychology**

Notation 01 from Table 1 as modified below

Do not use for philosophical foundations; class in 370.12. Do not use for value; class in 370.13

**.11 Education for specific objectives**

Do not use for systems; class in 370.1

Class here curricula directed toward specific educational objectives

*See also 371 for school systems*

**.111 Fundamental education**

Preparation of educationally disadvantaged students for participation in community life

Class here compensatory education

Class fundamental education of adults in 374.012

**.112 Humanistic education (Liberal education)**

.113 Vocational education

>Class here career education, occupational training, vocational schools

>Class on-the-job training, vocational training provided by industry in 331.2592

>>*For vocational education at secondary level, see 373.246; for adult vocational education, see 374.013*

>>*See also 331.702 for choice of vocation; also 371.425 for vocational guidance in schools*

.114 Moral, ethical, character education

>Standard subdivisions are added for any or all topics in heading

>Class education for social responsibility in 370.115; class moral and character training of children at home in 649.7

.115 Education for social responsibility

>Including critical pedagogy, education for democracy, popular education (education for socioeconomic transformation); social education

>Class education for international understanding in 370.116

>>*See also 306.43 for sociology of education*

.116 Education for international understanding

>Class here educational exchanges, foreign study

.116 2 Exchange of students

>Class grants for student exchanges in 371.223

.116 3 Exchange of teachers

.117 Multicultural and bilingual education

>Multicultural education: programs to promote mutual understanding among cultures

>Standard subdivisions are added for multicultural and bilingual education together, for multicultural education alone

.117 5 Bilingual education

.118 Education for creativity

.119 Education for effective use of leisure

>Class here education for individual fulfillment

.12 Classification and philosophical foundations

>Including idealism, pragmatism, realism

.13 Value of education

.14 Communication

| | |
|---|---|
| .15 | Educational psychology |

Do not use for scientific principles; class in 370.1

Class here psychology of teaching

Class interdisciplinary works on psychology in 150. Class psychology of a specific topic in education with the topic, plus notation 019 from Table 1, e.g., psychology of special education 371.9019

*See also 153.15 for studies that use students as subjects for research into fundamental processes of learning*

| | |
|---|---|
| .151 | Differential psychology |

Class a specific aspect of psychology of specific groups of people in 370.152–370.158

| | |
|---|---|
| .152 | Conscious mental processes and intelligence |

Subdivisions are added for conscious mental processes and intelligence together, for conscious mental processes alone

Including critical thinking

Class here cognition

*For emotions, see 370.1534; for perception, see 370.155; for creativity and imagination, see 370.157*

| | |
|---|---|
| .152 2 | Memory |
| .152 3 | Learning |

*For motivation to learn, see 370.154*

| | |
|---|---|
| .152 4 | Reasoning |

Class here problem solving

| | |
|---|---|
| .152 8 | Behavior modification |

Class behavior modification methods of instruction in 371.393

| | |
|---|---|
| .152 9 | Intelligence |

Class here multiple intelligences

*For emotional intelligence, see 370.1534*

| | |
|---|---|
| .153 | Personality and emotions |

Class behavior modification in 370.1528

| | |
|---|---|
| .153 2 | Personality |
| .153 4 | Emotions |

Class here feelings

| | |
|---|---|
| .154 | Motivation to learn |

Class comprehensive works on learning in 370.1523

| .155 | Perception, movement, psychological drives |
| | Including motor skills, sensory perception |
| | Class emotions in 370.1534 |
| .157 | Creativity and imagination |
| | Standard subdivisions are added for either or both topics in heading |
| | *See also 370.118 for education to promote creativity* |
| .158 | Psychological adjustment to education |
| | Class here effect of school education and environment on students |
| [.19] | Psychological principles |
| | Do not use; class in 370.15 |
| **.2** | **Miscellany** |
| .28 | Auxiliary techniques and procedures |
| [.284] | Apparatus, equipment, materials |
| | Do not use; class in 371.67 |
| [.287] | Testing and measurement |
| | Do not use; class in 371.26 |
| [.288] | Maintenance and repair |
| | Do not use; class in 371.68 |
| **.6** | **Organizations** |
| [.68] | Management |
| | Do not use; class in 371.2 |
| **.7** | **Education, research, related topics** |
| | Class here education, research, related topics in teaching |
| | Class education, research, related topics at a specific level with the level, e.g., education for teachers at primary level 372.071 |
| .71 | Education |
| | Class here practice teaching |
| **.8** | **Groups of people** |
| | Do not use for students; class in 371.8. Do not use for education of specific groups of students; class in 371.82, e.g., education of ethnic minorities 371.829 |
| | Class here discrimination in education [*formerly* 379.26] |
| .82 | Women in education |
| | Do not use for education of women; class in 371.822 |

**.9** **History, geographic treatment, biography**

Class here comparative education

## 371 Schools and their activities; special education

Standard subdivisions are added for schools and their activities, special education together; for schools and their activities together; for schools alone

Class here school systems, school policy; comprehensive works on schools, school activities, public policy issues in education together

Class schools and their activities in primary, secondary, and adult education in 372–374; class schools and their activities in higher education in 378

*For curricula, see 375; for public policy issues in education, see 379*

*See Manual at 371 vs. 353.8, 371.2, 379*

### SUMMARY

| | |
|---|---|
| 371.001–.009 | **Standard subdivisions** |
| .01–.07 | **Specific kinds of schools** |
| .1 | **Teachers and teaching, and related activities** |
| .2 | **School administration; administration of student academic activities** |
| .3 | **Methods of instruction and study** |
| .4 | **Student guidance and counseling** |
| .5 | **School discipline and related activities** |
| .6 | **Physical plant; materials management** |
| .7 | **Student welfare** |
| .8 | **Students** |
| .9 | **Special education** |

**.001** Philosophy and theory

**.001 1** Systems

The word "systems" as used here refers only to concepts derived from 003, e.g., systems theory, analysis, and design applied to schools and school systems

*See also 371.01–371.07 for specific kinds of school systems*

**.002** Miscellany

**[.002 8]** Auxiliary techniques and procedures

Do not use; class in 370.28

**[.002 84]** Apparatus, equipment, materials

Do not use; class in 371.67

**[.002 87]** Testing and measurement

Do not use; class in 371.26

**[.002 88]** Maintenance and repair

Do not use; class in 371.68

**.003–.005** Standard subdivisions

**.006** Organizations

| [.006 8] | Management |
|---|---|

Do not use; class in 371.2

| .007 | Education, research, related topics |
|---|---|

| .008 | Groups of people |
|---|---|

Do not use for schools for specific groups of people; class in 371.82

| .009 | History, geographic treatment, biography |
|---|---|

| .009 4–.009 9 | Specific continents, countries, localities in modern world |
|---|---|

Class here specific all-age schools and school systems

---

>       371.01–371.07 Specific kinds of schools

Class here specific kinds of school systems; types of education characteristic of specific kinds of schools other than public and community schools

Class comprehensive works in 371. Class a specific topic with respect to a specific kind of school with the topic in 371.1–371.8, e.g., teaching in private schools 371.102; class a specific kind of school defined by a method of instruction or study with the method, e.g., Montessori schools 371.392; class a specific kind of school for a specific group of students with the group in 371.82, e.g., schools for ethnic minorities 371.829, schools for African Americans 371.82996073

*See Manual at 371.01–371.8 vs. 372–374, 378*

| .01 | Public schools |
|---|---|

Class public education in 370; class public community schools in 371.03; class public alternative schools in 371.04; class publicly supported religious schools in 371.07; class public policy issues concerning public schools in 379

Public schools distinguished by source of funding, locus of control, and mandate relocated to 371.05

| .02 | Private schools |
|---|---|

Class here publicly supported private schools, schools not under government control

Class private community schools in 371.03; class private alternative schools in 371.04; class public policy issues in private education in 379.3

*For religious schools, see 371.07*

| .03 | Community schools |
|---|---|

| .04 | Alternative schools |
|---|---|

Class here experimental schools, free schools

| .042 | Home schools |
|---|---|

Class here home schooling

*See also 371.39 for home instruction by visiting teachers*

.05        Public schools distinguished by source of funding, locus of control, and mandate [*formerly* 371.01]

       Class here academy schools, charter schools

.07        Religious schools

       Class religious education to encourage belief and to promote religious life and practice in 207

.071        Christian religious schools

       Add to base number 371.071 the numbers following 28 in 281–289, e.g., Catholic schools 371.0712, Catholic schools in Quebec 371.0712714

       Class Christian education to encourage belief and to promote religious life and practice in 268

.072–.079        Other religious schools

       Add to base number 371.07 the numbers following 29 in 292–299, e.g., Islamic schools 371.077

---

>        **371.1–371.8 Schools and their activities**

       Class schools and their activities in special education in 371.9; class public policy issues relating to schools and their activities taken as a whole in 379; class comprehensive works in 371

       *For comprehensive works on specific kinds of schools, see 371.01–371.07*

       *See Manual at 371.01–371.8 vs. 372–374, 378*

.1        **Teachers and teaching, and related activities**

       Standard subdivisions are added for a combination of two or more topics in heading, for teachers alone

.100 1–.100 6        Standard subdivisions

.100 7        Research and related topics

[.100 71]        Education

       Do not use; class in 370.71

.100 8–.100 9        Standard subdivisions

.102        Teaching

       Class here mentoring

       Class substitute teaching in 371.14122; class evaluation of teachers in 371.144; class team teaching in 371.148

       *For practice teaching, see 370.71; for methods of instruction, see 371.3*

[.102 019]        Psychology of teaching

       Do not use; class in 370.15

| | |
|---|---|
| [.102 07] | Education, research, related topics |
| | Do not use; class in 370.7 |
| .102 2 | Communication in teaching |
| .102 3 | Teacher-student relations |
| .102 4 | Classroom management |
| | Class here classroom discipline |
| | Class classroom techniques of instruction in 371.3; class comprehensive works on school discipline in 371.5 |
| .103 | Teacher-parent conferences |
| | One-on-one teacher-parent relations |
| | Class comprehensive works on teacher-parent relations in 371.192 |
| .104 | Academic status |
| | Privileges, prerogatives, immunities, responsibilities |
| | Including academic freedom, sabbatical leave, tenure |
| | *For teacher-community relations, see 371.19* |
| | *See also 331.2596 for economic aspects of tenure* |
| .106 | Relation of teachers to school administration and nonteaching staff |
| | Including teacher participation in administration |
| | Class labor unions in 331.88113711; class collective bargaining in 331.890413711 |
| [.11] | Personal characteristics of teachers |
| | Number discontinued; class in 371.1 |
| .12 | Professional qualifications of teachers |
| | Class here teacher certification |
| .14 | Organization of teaching force |
| | Including teacher turnover |
| | Class performance contracting in 371.15 |
| .141 | Staffing and nonteaching activities |
| .141 2 | Staffing |
| | Including teacher workload |
| | *For team teaching, see 371.148* |
| .141 22 | Substitute teaching |
| .141 23 | Differentiated staffing |
| | Class use of teacher aides in 371.14124 |

| | |
|---|---|
| .141 24 | Use of teacher aides (teachers' assistants) |
| | Paid or volunteer |
| .141 4 | Nonteaching activities |

*For teacher participation in management, see 371.106*

| | |
|---|---|
| .144 | Evaluation of teachers |

Class here accountability, probation

*See also 371.15 for performance contracting; also 379.158 for overall educational accountability*

| | |
|---|---|
| .148 | Team teaching |

Two or more people teaching a class

| | |
|---|---|
| .15 | Performance contracting |

*See also 371.144 for teacher accountability*

| | |
|---|---|
| .19 | Community-school relations |

Including teacher-community relations

Class here community involvement in schools, community-school partnerships, school involvement in the community

Class interdisciplinary works on relations of schools and society, teachers and society in 306.432

| | |
|---|---|
| .192 | Parent-school relations |

Class here parent participation in schools; comprehensive works on teacher-parent relations

*For teacher-parent conferences, see 371.103*

| | |
|---|---|
| .192 06 | Organizations and management |

Class here home and school associations, parent-teacher associations

| | |
|---|---|
| .195 | Industry-school relations |

Class here industry involvement in schools, industry-school partnerships

*See also 370.113 for vocational education; also 371.227 for student employment in connection with ongoing academic work*

| | |
|---|---|
| **.2** | **School administration; administration of student academic activities** |

Standard subdivisions are added for either or both topics in heading

*See Manual at 371 vs. 353.8, 371.2, 379*

## SUMMARY

.200 1          Philosophy and theory

.200 2          Miscellany

[.200 28]          Auxiliary techniques and procedures

Do not use; class in 370.28

[.200 284]          Apparatus, equipment, materials

Do not use; class in 371.67

[.200 288]          Maintenance and repair

Do not use; class in 371.68

.200 3–.200 5     Standard subdivisions

.200 6          Organizations

[.200 68]          Management

Do not use; class in 371.2

.200 7–.200 8     Standard subdivisions

.200 9          History, geographic treatment, biography

.200 92          Biography

Class here collected biography of school administrators and biography of specific administrators not associated with a specific level of education or school

Class biography of school administrators best known as leaders in education in 370.92; class biography of administrators best known as leaders in primary education in 372.92; class biography of administrators best known as leaders in adult education in 374.92. Class biography of administrators best known as leaders at a specific level of education other than primary and adult limited to a specific area or school with the geographic area under the specific level, plus notation 092 from Table 1, e.g., a biography of a president of University of California at Berkeley 378.79467092

> 371.201–371.207 School administration

Class comprehensive works in 371.2. Class management of a specific function with the function in 371, plus notation 068 from Table 1, e.g., management of student welfare 371.7068

*For plant management, see 371.6; for materials management, see 371.67*

.201                     Personnel management

Class here staff

*For teachers, see 371.1; for support staff, see 371.202*

.201 1                   School administrators

Role and function

Including school superintendents

Class here leadership, top and middle management

Class education of school administrators in 371.20071; class biography of school administrators in 371.20092

*For principals, see 371.2012*

.201 2                   Principals

.202                     Personnel management of support staff

Other than administrators and teachers

Class personnel management of staff providing a specific function with the function, plus notation 0683 from Table 1, e.g., personnel management of school nurses 371.7120683

.202 3                   Management of administrative support personnel

.203                     School supervision (Instructional supervision)

*See also 375.001 for curriculum development*

.206                     Financial management

Including tuition

Class here financial administration of public schools and school systems

Class financial administration of agencies supporting public education in 353.824; class student aid in 371.22

.207                     Executive management

Including internal organization

Class here planning, school improvement programs

Class government policies in 379

*For leadership, school administrators, top and middle management, see 371.2011; for school boards, see 379.1531*

> 371.21–371.29 Administration of student academic activities

Class methods of instruction in 371.3; class student participation in administration in 371.59; class comprehensive works in 371.2

*For educational and vocational guidance, see 371.42*

.21 Admissions and related topics

Standard subdivisions are added for admissions and related topics, for admissions alone

Class here articulation, matriculation

.216 Admission procedures

.217 Entrance requirements

Class entrance examinations in 371.262; class academic prognosis and placement in 371.264

.218 Credits

Class use of credits in placement in 371.264; class use of credits to determine promotion and failure in 371.28

.219 School enrollment

.219 09 History and biography

Do not use for geographic treatment; class in 371.2191–371.2199

.219 1–.219 9 Geographic treatment of school enrollment

Add to base number 371.219 notation 1–9 from Table 2, e.g., school enrollment in Russia 371.21947

.22 Student aid and cooperative education

Standard subdivisions are added for student aid and cooperative education together, for student aid alone

*See also 371.206 for tuition*

.223 Scholarships and fellowships

Standard subdivisions are added for either or both topics in heading

Including veterans' education benefits

Class here grants

.224 Student loans

.225 Student employment

Including employment for service to the community

Class here employment of students by their own school, work-study programs

*For employment by industry and nonschool agencies in connection with ongoing academic work, see 371.227*

.227      Cooperative education

> Student employment by industry and nonschool agencies in connection with ongoing academic work
>
> Class here apprenticeship programs, work-study plan
>
> Class apprenticeship programs without school sponsorship, interdisciplinary works on apprenticeship in 331.25922

.23      School year

> Class here school calendar

.232      Summer school

.236      Year-round school

> Class here extended school year

.24      Schedules and school day

> *See also 371.294 for school attendance*

.242      Schedules

> Including flexible scheduling
>
> Class here scheduling, school week

.244      School day

> Class here length of school day
>
> Class scheduling within school day in 371.242

.25      Grouping students for instruction

> Including multigraded classes (mixed-level classrooms, combination of grades)
>
> Class here school classes
>
> Class one-room schools in 372.125

.251      Class size

.252      Mixed ability grouping (Heterogeneous grouping)

> Class here mainstreaming outside context of special education
>
> Class comprehensive works on mainstreaming in 371.9046

.254      Ability grouping (Homogeneous grouping)

> Class here streaming
>
> Class mainstreaming for ordinary students in 371.252; class nongraded grouping in 371.255

.255      Nongraded grouping

.256      **Open classroom grouping**

         Class here open plan schools

         Class open classroom methods of instruction in 371.3941

.26      **Examinations and tests; academic prognosis and placement**

         Standard subdivisions are added for examinations and tests, academic prognosis and placement together; for examinations alone; for tests alone

         Including test-taking skills

         Class use of examinations and tests in guidance in 371.42

         *For classroom and school examinations and tests, see 371.271*

.260 1      **Philosophy and theory, validity and reliability of tests**

         Notation 01 from Table 1 as modified below

.260 13      **Validity and reliability of tests**

         Including test bias

         Class here comprehensive works on validity and reliability of standardized tests

         *For validity and reliability of specific kinds of standardized tests, see 371.262*

.261      **Test construction**

         Class evaluation of tests in 371.26013

.262      **Standardized tests**

         Class here organizations producing standardized tests, comprehensive works on specific kinds of educational tests and their validity and reliability

         Class comprehensive works on validity and reliability of standardized tests in 371.26013; class interdisciplinary works on intelligence tests in 153.93; class interdisciplinary works on aptitude tests in 153.94. Class standardized tests for a specific subject in primary school with the subject in 372.3–372.8, plus notation 076 from Table 1, e.g., mathematics tests for primary school 372.7076; class standardized tests for a specific subject at secondary or higher level with the subject in 001–999, plus notation 076 from Table 1, e.g., mathematics tests for secondary school 510.76

         *For construction of standardized tests, see 371.261; for specific kinds of educational tests devised by individual teachers, see 371.271*

         *See Manual at 371.262 vs. 371.264*

.264      **Academic prognosis and placement**

         Including accreditation of prior learning (APL), advanced placement

         Class standardized tests, use of specific tests of academic achievement and general education, comprehensive works on specific kinds of educational tests in 371.262

         *See Manual at 371.262 vs. 371.264*

| | |
|---|---|
| .27 | Classroom and school examinations and tests; marking systems |
| .271 | Classroom and school examinations and tests |

> Tests devised by individual teacher or school

> Standard subdivisions are added for any or all topics in heading

| | |
|---|---|
| .272 | Marking systems |

> Methods used for recording and reporting students achievement

| | |
|---|---|
| .28 | Promotion and failure |

> Including educational acceleration, underachievement

| | |
|---|---|
| .283 | Promotion |
| .285 | Failure |

> Including grade repetition

| | |
|---|---|
| .29 | Student mobility and school attendance |
| .291 | Student mobility |
| .291 2 | School completion |

> Class here graduation; diplomas, other certificates of completion

| | |
|---|---|
| .291 3 | Dropouts (Early school leavers) |

> Class student failure in 371.285

| | |
|---|---|
| .291 4 | Transfers |
| .294 | School attendance |

> Class compulsory education in 379.23

> *For truancy, school attendance officers, see 371.295*

| | |
|---|---|
| .295 | Truancy |

> Class here school attendance officers, truant officers

> Class dropouts in 371.2913

**.3**      **Methods of instruction and study**

Class here classroom techniques, creative activities, seatwork

Class classroom management in 371.1024; class comprehensive works on teaching in 371.102. Class methods of instruction in a specific subject at primary level with the subject in 372.3–372.8, plus notation 044 from table under 372.3–372.8, e.g., methods of teaching mathematics in primary school 372.7044; class methods of instruction in a specific subject at secondary and higher levels with the subject in 001–999, plus notation 071 from Table 1, e.g., methods of teaching mathematics in secondary school 510.712

## SUMMARY

.302 8    Auxiliary techniques and procedures, techniques of study, lesson plans

Notation 028 from Table 1 as modified below

.302 81    Techniques of study

Including book reports, homework, note-taking, reading for content, report writing

Class here techniques for parents, study skills

[.302 84]    Apparatus, equipment, materials

Do not use; class in 371.33

[.302 85]    Computer applications

Do not use; class in 371.334

[.307 8]    Use of apparatus, equipment, materials in study and teaching

Do not use; class in 371.33

.32    Use of textbooks

Including textbook bias

Class public control of textbooks in 379.156. Class textbooks on a specific subject with the subject in 001–999, e.g., textbooks on mathematics 510

.33    Teaching aids, equipment, materials

Class here educational media, educational technology; use of teaching aids, equipment, materials in study and teaching

Class public control of teaching materials in 379.156. Class teaching aids, equipment, materials used in a specific method of instruction with the method, e.g., materials used in Montessori method 371.392

*For textbooks, see 371.32*

*See also 027.7 for instructional materials centers*

.333    Audio materials and equipment

Standard subdivisions are added for either or both topics in heading

*See also 371.335 for audiovisual materials*

.333 1    Radio

| | |
|---|---|
| .333 2 | Sound recordings and their players |

Standard subdivisions are added for either or both topics in heading

| | |
|---|---|
| .334 | Computer science |

Class here data processing, computer-assisted instruction (CAI), electronic programmed instruction

Unless it is redundant, add to base number 371.334 the numbers following 00 in 004–006, e.g., instructional use of software 371.33453, use of computer graphics in teaching 371.33466

*For computer modeling and simulation, see 371.397*

| | |
|---|---|
| .335 | Audiovisual and visual materials and equipment |

Standard subdivisions are added for audiovisual and visual materials or equipment together, for audiovisual materials or equipment alone

Class audio materials and equipment in 371.333

*See also 371.32 for textbooks*

| | |
|---|---|
| .335 2 | Slides and filmstrips, motion pictures and video, pictures |
| .335 22 | Slides and filmstrips |

Standard subdivisions are added for either or both topics in heading

| | |
|---|---|
| .335 23 | Motion pictures and video recordings |

Standard subdivisions are added for either or both topics in heading

| | |
|---|---|
| .335 6 | Bulletin boards |
| .335 8 | Television |

Including videoconferencing

Class video recordings in 371.33523

| | |
|---|---|
| .337 | Educational games and toys |

Standard subdivisions are added for either or both topics in heading

*See also 371.397 for simulation*

| | |
|---|---|
| .35 | Distance education |

Class here extension services, open and distance learning (ODL)

| | |
|---|---|
| .356 | Correspondence courses |
| .358 | Electronic distance education |

Including teleconferencing

Class here instructional use of mass media

*For distance education by radio, see 371.3331; for distance education by computer, see 371.334; for distance education by television, see 371.3358*

.36    Project methods (Cooperative learning)

> Methods that emphasize student direction of group projects

> Class here group work, unit method

> Class group teaching (in which class is divided into groups, but activity is still directed by teacher) in 371.395

.37    Recitation and discussion

> Including seminars

.38    Methods employed outside classroom

> *See also 371.39 for home instruction by visiting teachers*

.382    Laboratory method

> Class laboratory method with electronic and visual materials and equipment in 371.33

.384    Outdoor education

> Class here field trips to indoor locations, open air schools

.39    Other methods of instruction

> Including home instruction by educational personnel, monitorial system of education, Morrison plan, rote learning

> *See also 371.042 for home schooling*

.391    Waldorf method

.392    Montessori method

> Montessori method is usually limited to primary level in 372.1392. Discussion of advancing it to higher grades is classed with higher level

.393    Behavior modification methods

> Including student performance contracting

> Class use of behavior modification in classroom discipline in 371.1024

.394    Individualized instruction

> Class here tutoring

.394 1    Open classroom instruction

> Class grouping students for open classroom instruction in 371.256

.394 2    Honors work

> Class here honors programs, honors courses

> *See also 371.264 for advanced placement*

.394 3    Independent study

> Class independent honors work in 371.3942

> *For programmed instruction, see 371.3944*

| | |
|---|---|
| .394 4 | Programmed instruction |

> *For electronic programmed instruction, see 371.334*

| | |
|---|---|
| .395 | Group teaching |

Teaching in which class is divided into groups, but activity is still directed by teacher

Class group work that emphasizes student direction of group projects in 371.36

> *See also 371.148 for team teaching*

| | |
|---|---|
| .396 | Lecture method |
| .397 | Simulation |

Class here computer modeling and simulation

Class comprehensive works on instructional use of computers in 371.334

| | |
|---|---|
| .399 | Use of drama |

Class here use of theater

| | |
|---|---|
| **.4** | **Student guidance and counseling** |

Standard subdivisions are added for either or both topics in heading

Class here student personnel services, services of deans of students

> *For a specific student personnel service not provided for here, see the service, e.g., student employment 371.225*

| | |
|---|---|
| .404 | Teachers and students in guidance and counseling |
| .404 6 | Role of teachers in guidance and counseling |
| .404 7 | Peer counseling |

Counseling by other students

| | |
|---|---|
| .42 | Educational and vocational guidance |
| .422 | Educational guidance |

Other than vocational

| | |
|---|---|
| .425 | Vocational guidance |

Class interdisciplinary works on vocational guidance in 331.702. Class vocational guidance in a specific occupation with the occupation, plus notation 023 from Table 1, e.g., guidance in science 502.3

| | |
|---|---|
| .46 | Personal counseling |

Counseling of students with emotional, personal, social problems by staff other than psychologists and medical personnel

Including school social workers

Class personal counseling by other students in 371.4047; class student welfare programs in 371.7

**.5**      **School discipline and related activities**

> Standard subdivisions are added for school discipline and related activities together, for school discipline alone

> *For classroom discipline, see 371.1024*

**.51**      General regulations for student conduct

> Including honor system

**.53**      Rewards

> Class rewards to discourage specific disciplinary problems in 371.58

**.54**      Punishment

> Class punishment for specific discipline problems in 371.58

**.542**      Corporal punishment

**.543**      Probation, suspension, expulsion

**.58**      Specific discipline problems

> Class comprehensive works on crime, delinquency, sexual abuse, substance abuse, vandalism, violence in schools in 371.78

> *For truancy, see 371.295*

**.59**      Student participation in administration

> Including monitors, student participation in maintenance of discipline

> Class here student government

> *See also 371.39 for monitorial system of education*

**.6**      **Physical plant; materials management**

> Standard subdivisions are added for physical plant and materials management together; for physical plant alone

> Class here plant management, educational buildings, school facilities

> *See also 727 for architecture of educational buildings*

**[.602 84]**      Apparatus, equipment, materials

> Do not use; class in 371.67

**[.602 88]**      Maintenance and repair

> Do not use; class in 371.68

**.61**      School grounds, sites, location

**.62**      Specific kinds of buildings and rooms

> Class here furnishings, apparatus, equipment, supplies for specific kinds of buildings and rooms

> Class teaching aids, equipment, materials regardless of kind of building or room in 371.33

.621      Instructional spaces

> Including study facilities

> Class here classrooms

> *For laboratories, see 371.623*

.623      Laboratories

.625      Noninstructional facilities

> Class facilities for a specific noninstructional objective with the objective, e.g., cafeterias 371.716

.63      School furnishings

> Class furnishings for specific kinds of buildings and rooms in 371.62

.67      Apparatus, equipment, materials

> Class here materials management

> Class apparatus, equipment, supplies for specific kinds of buildings and rooms in 371.62

> *For teaching aids, equipment, materials, see 371.33; for school furnishings, see 371.63*

.68      Custodial and maintenance services, renovation

> Standard subdivisions are added for a combination of two or more topics in heading, for custodial services alone, for maintenance services alone

> Including repair services

> *For technical maintenance and repair of a specific facility or piece of equipment, see the facility or piece of equipment, plus notation 0288 from Table 1, e.g., repair of educational computers 371.3340288; for custodial and maintenance services, renovation of a specific noninstructional facility, see the facility, plus notation 0682 from Table 1, e.g., maintenance services for school cafeterias 371.7160682*

**.7**      **Student welfare**

> Class here school social services

> *For a specific provision for student welfare not provided for here, see the provision, e.g., personal counseling 371.46, student housing 371.871*

.71      Student health and related topics

> Standard subdivisions are added for student health and related topics together, for student health alone

.712      School nursing programs

> Class use of school nurses in mental welfare programs in 371.713; class use of school nurses in birth control, pregnancy, sex hygiene programs in 371.714

.713        Mental health services

          Class here school psychologists

          *For substance abuse programs, see 371.784*

.714        Sex hygiene, birth control, pregnancy programs

          Standard subdivisions are added for sex hygiene, birth control, pregnancy programs together; for sex hygiene programs alone

.716        Food services

          Including milk programs, nutrition programs

          Class here school cafeterias, school lunch programs

.78        School programs related to crime, substance abuse, sexual abuse

          Class here crime, substance abuse, sexual abuse problems in schools; assistance to victims of crime and abuse

          Class crime, substance abuse, sexual abuse as school discipline problems in 371.58

.782        Crime prevention and alleviation

          Standard subdivisions are added for either or both topics in heading

          Class here delinquency in schools, school violence

          Class campus police in 363.289; class prevention and alleviation of crime relating to substance abuse in 371.784; class prevention and alleviation of crime related to sexual abuse in 371.786; class interdisciplinary works on victims of crime in 362.88; class interdisciplinary works on crime prevention in 364.4

.784        Substance abuse programs

.786        Sexual abuse programs

**.8**        **Students**

          Including class reunions

          Class here extracurricular activities, student life

          *For a specific aspect of students not provided for here, see the aspect, e.g., student discipline 371.5*

.801 9       Student psychology

          Class educational psychology in 370.15

.805        Serial publications

          Limited to serials about students, student life, extracurricular activities

          *See also 371.897 for student journalism*

.806        Organizations and management

          Do not use for student organizations; class in 371.83

| [.808] | Groups of people |
|---|---|

> Do not use; class in 371.82

.81  Student movements

> Student efforts to achieve reform on campus and social change

> Including student strikes

> Class here student activism, protest, unrest

> Class a student movement to achieve a specific objective with the objective, e.g., a movement to achieve electoral reform 324.63

.82  Specific groups of students; schools for specific groups of students

> Class here discrimination, group identity, minorities; education of young people; comprehensive works on education of specific groups of students

> *For a specific aspect of education of specific groups of students, see the aspect, e.g., counseling for women students 371.4082*

[.820 1–.820 9]  Standard subdivisions

> Do not use; class in 371.801–371.809

.821–.829  Subdivisions for specific groups of students; for schools for specific groups of students

> Add to base number 371.82 the numbers following —08 in notation 081–089 from Table 1, e.g., education of females 371.822, education of students of specific ethnic or national origin 371.829; however, education of young people discontinued from 371.823 to 371.82; education of boys relocated from 371.823 to 371.8211; education of girls relocated from 371.823 to 371.822; for students who are the focus of special education, delinquent and problem students, students with disabilities and illnesses, gifted students, see 371.9

.83  Student organizations

> Class here student clubs

> Class student movements in 371.81. Class a student organization in a specific field with the field, plus notation 06 from Table 1, e.g., student literary societies 806

> *For Greek-letter societies, see 371.85*

.85  Greek-letter societies

> Class here alumni units

> Class a Greek-letter society in a specific field with the field, plus notation 06 from Table 1, e.g., a Greek-letter medical society 610.6

.852  Honor societies

.855  Men's Greek-letter social societies

> Class here fraternities

.856  Women's Greek-letter social societies

> Class here sororities

.87      Housing and transportation of students

.871      Housing

.872      Transportation

Class busing for school integration in 379.263

*See also 363.1259 for school bus safety*

.89      Miscellaneous student activities

Only those named here or below

Including competitions

*For a specific student competition, see the competition, plus notation 079 from Table 1, e.g., a photographic competition 770.79*

.895      School assemblies

.897      Student journalism

Class interdisciplinary student journals in 050. Class a student journal on a specific subject with the subject, plus notation 05 from Table 1, e.g., a journal on student life and extracurricular activities 371.805, a student literary journal 805

.897 4      Producing newspapers

.897 5      Producing magazines

.897 6      Producing yearbooks

Class a yearbook of a specific school with the school, e.g., a yearbook of a preparatory school in New York city 373.7471

**.9**      **Special education**

Class here exceptional students, learning disabilities, underachievers in special education; schools and school activities pertaining to special education

Except for modifications shown under specific entries, add to each subdivision identified by * as follows:

| | |
|---|---|
| [0284] | Apparatus, equipment, materials |
| | Do not use; class in 5 |
| [0288] | Maintenance and repair |
| | Do not use; class in 5 |
| [0682] | Plant management |
| | Do not use; class in 5 |
| 3–7 | General topics |

Add to base number the numbers following 371.904 in 371.9043–371.9047, e.g., equipment 5, equipment for students with reading disorders 371.91445

Unless other instructions are given, observe the following table of preference, e.g., emotionally disturbed gifted students 371.95 (*not* 371.94):

| | |
|---|---|
| Gifted students | 371.95 |
| Students with mental disabilities | 371.92 |
| Students with emotional disturbances | 371.94 |
| Students with physical disabilities | 371.91 |
| Delinquent and problem students | 371.93 |

Class comprehensive works on underachievers in 371.28

## SUMMARY

| | |
|---|---|
| 371.901–.909 | **Standard subdivisions and general topics of special education** |
| .91 | **Students with physical disabilities** |
| .92 | **Students with mental disabilities** |
| .93 | **Delinquent and problem students** |
| .94 | **Students with emotional disturbances** |
| .95 | **Gifted students** |

[.902 84]      Apparatus, equipment, materials

Do not use; class in 371.9045

[.902 88]      Maintenance and repair

Do not use; class in 371.9045

.904      General topics of special education

.904 3      Teaching methods

Including academic prognosis and placement

.904 302 8      Auxiliary techniques and procedures, techniques of study, lesson plans

Notation 028 from Table 1 as modified below

| | | |
|---|---|---|
| .904 302 81 | | Techniques of study |

Including book reports, homework, note-taking, reading for content, report writing

Class here techniques for parents, study skills

[.904 302 84]      Apparatus, equipment, materials

Do not use; class in 371.90433

[.904 302 85]      Computer applications

Do not use; class in 371.904334

[.904 307 8]      Use of apparatus, equipment, materials in study and teaching

Do not use; class in 371.90433

.904 32–.904 39      Specific teaching methods

Add to base number 371.9043 the numbers following 371.3 in 371.32–371.39, e.g., project methods 371.90436

.904 4      Programs in specific subjects

Class here curricula

Add to base number 371.9044 the numbers following 372 in 372.3–372.8, e.g., mathematics 371.90447

.904 5      Buildings, rooms, furnishings, apparatus, equipment, supplies

Including maintenance and repair

Class here plant management

.904 6      Mainstreaming

Educating exceptional students in regular school programs

Including identifying students for special education

Class here inclusive education

*See also 371.252 for mainstreaming outside the context of special education*

.904 7      Special education by level

Class a specific topic in special education at a specific level with the topic, e.g., teaching at primary level 371.9043

.904 72      Special education at primary level

.904 73      Special education at secondary level

.904 74      Special education at higher level

.904 75      Adult special education

Other than in colleges and universities

[.906 82]      Plant management

Do not use; class in 371.9045

.908            Groups of people

Do not use for groups of students requiring special education; class in 371.9

.91            Students with physical disabilities

Including general works on students with brain damage

Unless other instructions are given, observe the following table of preference, e.g., students with blindness and mobility impairments 371.916 (*not* 371.911):

Students with linguistic disorders            371.914
Students with mobility impairments            371.916
Students with blindness and visual impairments   371.911
Students with hearing impairments            371.912

Class students with a specific disorder caused by brain damage with the disorder in 371.911–371.94, e.g., emotional disorders caused by brain damage 371.94

.911            *Students with blindness and visual impairments

Subdivisions are added for either or both topics in heading

.912            Students with hearing impairments

Class here deaf students

[.912 028 4]            Apparatus, equipment, materials

Do not use; class in 371.9125

[.912 028 8]            Maintenance and repair

Do not use; class in 371.9125

[.912 068 2]            Plant management

Do not use; class in 371.9125

.912 3–.912 6            Teaching methods, specific subjects, facilities, mainstreaming

Add to base number 371.912 the numbers following 371.904 in 371.9043–371.9046, e.g., instruction in lipreading 371.91246, teaching methods 371.9123

.912 8            Education by level

Add to base number 371.9128 the numbers following 371.9047 in 371.90472–371.90475, e.g., university education for deaf people 371.91284

.914            Students with linguistic disorders

.914 2            *Students with speaking disorders

Including aphasia, stuttering

*Add as instructed under 371.9

| | |
|---|---|
| .914 4 | *Students with reading disorders |

     Class here dyslexia

     *See also 372.43 for remedial reading in primary education*

| | |
|---|---|
| .916 | *Students with mobility impairments |
| .92 | Students with mental disabilities |

     Class here students with developmental disabilities

     Class students with mental illness in 371.94

| | |
|---|---|
| .926 | *Students with moderate mental disabilities |
| .928 | Students with severe mental disabilities |
| .928 001 | Philosophy and theory |
| .928 002 | Miscellany |
| [.928 002 84] | Apparatus, equipment, materials |

      Do not use; class in 371.92805

| | |
|---|---|
| [.928 002 88] | Maintenance and repair |

      Do not use; class in 371.92805

| | |
|---|---|
| .928 003–.928 005 | Standard subdivisions |
| .928 006 | Organizations and management |
| [.928 006 82] | Plant management |

      Do not use; class in 371.92805

| | |
|---|---|
| .928 007–.928 009 | Standard subdivisions |
| .928 03–.928 07 | General topics of students with mental retardation |

     Add to base number 371.9280 the numbers following 371.904 in 371.9043–371.9047, e.g., teaching methods 371.92803

| | |
|---|---|
| .93 | *Delinquent and problem students |

    Not suffering emotional disturbances

    Including maladjusted students

    Subdivisions are added for either or both topics in heading

    Class delinquent and problem students suffering emotional disturbances in 371.94

*Add as instructed under 371.9

.94     \*Students with emotional disturbances

> Including attention-deficit-disordered students, autistic students, hyperactive students

> Class here students with mental illness

>> *For delinquent and problem students not suffering severe emotional disturbances, see 371.93*

.95     Gifted students

[.950 284]     Apparatus, equipment, materials

> Do not use; class in 371.955

[.950 288]     Maintenance and repair

> Do not use; class in 371.955

[.950 682]     Plant management

> Do not use; class in 371.955

.952     Mainstreaming

> Educating gifted students in regular school programs

> Including identification

.953     Programs in specific subjects

> Class here curricula

> Add to base number 371.953 the numbers following 372 in 372.3–372.8, e.g., programs in mathematics 371.9537

.955     Buildings, rooms, furnishings, apparatus, equipment, supplies

> Including maintenance and repair

> Class here plant management

.956     Teaching methods

> Including motivating gifted underachievers

.956 028     Auxiliary techniques and procedures, techniques of study, lesson plans

> Notation 028 from Table 1 as modified below

.956 028 1     Techniques of study

> Including book reports, homework, note-taking, reading for content, report writing

> Class here techniques for parents, study skills

[.956 028 4]     Apparatus, equipment, materials

> Do not use; class in 371.9563

\*Add as instructed under 371.9

| [.956 028 5] | Computer applications |
|---|---|

Do not use; class in 371.95634

| [.956 078] | Use of apparatus, equipment, materials in study and teaching |
|---|---|

Do not use; class in 371.9563

| .956 2–.956 9 | Specific teaching methods |
|---|---|

Add to base number 371.956 the numbers following 371.3 in 371.32–371.39, e.g., use of computers 371.95634

| .957 | Education by level |
|---|---|

Add to base number 371.957 the numbers following 371.9047 in 371.90472–371.90475, e.g., educating gifted students at primary level 371.9572

---

> ## 372–374 Specific levels of education

Unless other instructions are given, class works treating two sublevels of education that are not subdivisions of the same number with the higher level, e.g., kindergarten and first grade 372.241 (*not* 372.218)

Class special education at any level in 371.9; class public policy issues relating to a specific level of education taken as a whole in 379; class comprehensive works on education and works dealing comprehensively with primary and secondary education, with secondary and higher education in 370; class comprehensive works on schools in 371

*For higher education, see 378*

*See Manual at 371.01–371.8 vs. 372–374, 378*

## 372  Primary education (Elementary education)

Class here elementary schools, primary schools; lower sections of all-age schools

*For adult primary education, see 374.012*

### SUMMARY

| 372.01–.08 | **Standard subdivisions, primary education for specific objectives** |
|---|---|
| .1 | **Organization and activities in primary education** |
| .2 | **Specific levels of primary education** |
| .3 | **Knowledge, computer science, library and information sciences, science, technology** |
| .4 | **Reading** |
| .5 | **The arts** |
| .6 | **Language arts (Communication skills)** |
| .7 | **Mathematics** |
| .8 | **Other studies** |
| .9 | **History, geographic treatment, biography of primary education** |

| .01 | Philosophy and theory; primary education for specific objectives |
|---|---|

Notation 01 from Table 1 as modified below

.011            Primary education for specific objectives

                Do not use for systems; class in 372.01

                Class here curricula directed toward specific educational objectives

                Add to base number 372.011 the numbers following 370.11 in
                370.111–370.119, e.g., character education 372.0114

                Class a specific topic with respect to primary education for a specific
                objective with the topic in 372.11–372.18, e.g., administration of primary
                schools 372.12

                *See also 372.1042 for specific kinds of primary school systems*

[.028 4]        Apparatus, equipment, materials

                Do not use; class in 372.167

[.028 7]        Testing and measurement

                Do not use; class in 372.126

[.028 8]        Maintenance and repair

                Do not use; class in 372.168

[.068]          Management

                Do not use; class in 372.12

.08             Groups of people

                Do not use for students; class in 372.18. Do not use for education of specific
                groups of students; class in 372.182, e.g., education of ethnic minorities
                372.1829

[.09]           History, geographic treatment, biography

                Do not use; class in 372.9

**.1            Organization and activities in primary education**

                *For comprehensive works on primary education for specific objectives, see
                372.011; for comprehensive works on specific levels of primary education,
                see 372.2*

[.101–.103]     Standard subdivisions

                Do not use; class in 372.01–372.03

.104            Special topics of primary schools

.104 2            Specific kinds of primary schools

> Class here specific kinds of school systems, kinds of primary education (other than public primary education) defined by specific kinds of schools

> Add to base number 372.1042 the numbers following 371.0 in 371.01–371.07, e.g., primary church schools 372.104271, Catholic primary schools 372.1042712

> Class a specific kind of primary schools at a specific level in 372.2; class specific schools regardless of kind in 372.9. Class a specific topic with respect to a specific kind of primary school with the topic in 372.11–372.19, e.g., administration of primary private schools 372.12

[.105–.108]     Standard subdivisions

> Do not use; class in 372.05–372.08

[.109]           History, geographic treatment, biography

> Do not use; class in 372.9

.11–.18      School organization and activities in primary education

> Add to base number 372.1 the numbers following 371 in 371.1–371.8, e.g., administration 372.12; however, for use of drama as a method of instruction, see 372.66

.19              Primary education in subject areas

> Class here curricula

> Class curricula directed toward a specific primary education objective in 372.011

> *For primary education in a specific subject, see 372.3–372.8*

**.2         Specific levels of primary education**

> Class specific schools at a specific level in 372.9. Class a specific topic with respect to primary education at a specific level with the topic in 372.11–372.19, e.g., administration of kindergarten 372.12

[.201–.208]     Standard subdivisions

> Do not use; class in 372.01–372.08

[.209]           History, geographic treatment, biography

> Do not use; class in 372.9

.21             Preschool education

> School-based or center-based pre-primary education

> Class here early childhood education

> Class preschool education by parents in the home as part of child-rearing in 649.68

[.216]           Nursery schools

> Number discontinued; class in 372.21

| | |
|---|---|
| .218 | Kindergarten |
| .24 | Specific levels of primary education |

Class primary education covering grades 1–4 in 372

*See Manual at 372.24 and 373.23*

| | |
|---|---|
| [.240 1–.240 8] | Standard subdivisions |

Do not use; class in 372.01–372.08

| | |
|---|---|
| [.240 9] | History, geographic treatment, biography |

Do not use; class in 372.9

| | |
|---|---|
| .241 | Lower level |

Class here grades 1–3

| | |
|---|---|
| .242 | Intermediate level |

Former heading: Upper level

Class here grades 4–6

Class lower secondary schools, middle schools (grades 5–8), junior high schools (grades 7–9) in 373.236

(Option: Class lower secondary level, grades 7–10 of compulsory primary education in 372.243)

| | |
|---|---|
| (.243) | Upper level |

(Optional number; prefer 373.236)

Class here lower secondary level, grades 7–10 of compulsory primary education

---

> ### 372.3–372.8 Primary education in specific subjects

Add to each subdivision identified by * as follows:

| | |
|---|---|
| 04 | General topics |
| 042 | Place of subject in education |
| 043 | Curricula |
| 044 | Teaching |
| | Class here methods of instruction, teaching materials |
| | Class textbooks with the subject in 001–999, e.g., primary textbooks on arithmetic 513 |
| (045) | Textbooks |
| | (Optional number; prefer the subject in 001–999, e.g., primary textbooks on arithmetic 513) |
| | Including readers (if option at 372.4122 is used) |
| 049 | Instruction at specific levels |
| | Including kindergarten |
| | Class a specific aspect of instruction at a given level with the aspect, e.g., curricula for kindergarten 043 |

Class comprehensive works in 372.19

**.3**     **Knowledge, computer science, library and information sciences, science, technology**

> Including discussion of ideas from many fields, interdisciplinary approach to knowledge
>
> Class interdisciplinary approach to knowledge with a focus on a specific subject with the subject in 372.3–372.8, e.g., environmental studies with components of civics and geography 372.357, writing across the curriculum 372.623

**.34**     *Computer science; library and information sciences

> Class here digital literacy, information literacy
>
> Subdivisions are added for any or all topics in heading
>
> Class use of computers as a method of instruction in 372.1334. Class use of computers as a method of instruction in a specific subject with the subject in 372.3–372.8, plus notation 044 from table under 372.3–372.8, e.g., computer-assisted instruction in arithmetic 372.72044

**.35**     *Science and technology

> Subdivisions are added for science and technology together, for science alone
>
> *For mathematics, see 372.7*

**.357**     *Nature study

> Class here environmental studies

**.358**     *Technology (Applied sciences)

> Including robots
>
> Class here industrial arts
>
> > *For personal health and safety, home and family management, see 372.37; for physical education, see 372.86*
> >
> > *See also 372.5 for manual arts*

**.37**     *Personal health and safety; social skills

> Including comprehensive works on home and family management [*formerly* 372.82]
>
> Class here life skills
>
> Subdivisions are added for personal health and safety, social skills together; for personal health and safety together; for personal health alone
>
> Class food in 372.373; class social skills in 372.374
>
> *For sewing, see 372.54; for physical education, see 372.86*

**.372**     *Sex education

> Including human reproductive physiology

---

*Add as instructed under 372.3–372.8

| | | |
|---|---|---|
| .373 | | *Nutrition and food |
| | | Including cooking |
| | | Subdivisions are added for either or both topics in heading |
| .374 | | *Social skills |
| | | Class here family life, interpersonal relations |
| .378 | | *Substance abuse |

**.4**      **Reading**

Class here reading instruction in home schools

Unless other instructions are given, class a subject with aspects in two or more subdivisions of 372.4 in the number coming last, e.g., vocabulary building by phonetic methods 372.465 (*not* 372.44)

| | | |
|---|---|---|
| .402 84 | | Apparatus and equipment |
| | | Do not use for materials; class in 372.412 |
| [.402 87] | | Testing and measurement |
| | | Do not use; class in 372.48 |
| .41 | | Instructional materials, reading readiness, methods of instruction and study |
| .412 | | Instructional materials |
| (.412 2) | | Readers |

(Optional number; prefer specific language in 420–490, plus notation 86 from Table 4, e.g., English-language readers 428.6

(If option under this number is chosen, class readers on a specific subject with the subject in 372.3–372.8, plus notation 045 from table under 372.3–372.8, e.g., science readers 372.35045)

| | | |
|---|---|---|
| .414 | | Reading readiness |
| .416 | | Methods of instruction and study |

*For a method of instruction or study not provided for here, see the method elsewhere in 372.4, e.g., individualized reading instruction 372.417, word-attack strategies 372.46*

| | | |
|---|---|---|
| .416 2 | | Small-group reading instruction |
| .416 4 | | Whole-class reading instruction |
| .417 | | Individualized reading instruction (Personalized reading instruction) |

*See also 372.454 for independent reading*

| | | |
|---|---|---|
| .42 | | Reading motivation |
| .423 | | Use of national and commercial programs |

*Add as instructed under 372.3–372.8

| | |
|---|---|
| .425 | Community-school programs |

Class here parent participation in reading

| | |
|---|---|
| .427 | School-based programs |

Classroom and library programs

| | |
|---|---|
| .43 | Remedial reading |

Including reading failure

Class reading difficulties treated in special education in 371.9144

| | |
|---|---|
| .44 | Vocabulary development |
| .45 | Reading-skill strategies |

*For word-attack strategies, see 372.46; for reading comprehension strategies, see 372.47*

| | |
|---|---|
| .452 | Oral reading |
| .454 | Independent reading |
| [.455] | Speed reading |

Provision discontinued because without meaning in context

| | |
|---|---|
| .46 | Word-attack strategies (Decoding strategies) |
| .462 | Whole-word method (Sight method) |

Class here word-recognition method

| | |
|---|---|
| .465 | Part-word method (Phonetic method) |

Including teaching alphabets

Class here phonetics in elementary education

Class pronunciation in a specific communication skill with the skill, e.g., pronunciation in speech 372.622

| | |
|---|---|
| .47 | Reading comprehension strategies |
| .472 | Strategies using standardized materials |

Including cloze procedure

Class a strategy using standardized materials in a specific subject with the subject in 372.3–372.8, plus notation 044 from table under 372.3–372.8, e.g., cloze procedure in science instruction 372.35044

Use of this number for SQ3R technique discontinued; class in 372.47

| | |
|---|---|
| .474 | Cognitive strategies |

Including critical thinking

| | |
|---|---|
| .475 | Whole-language approach |

Class here language experience approach

| | |
|---|---|
| .476 | Reading in content areas |

| .48 | Evaluation of reading skills |
|---|---|

Class here testing and measurement

Class evaluation of reading readiness in 372.414

| .482 | Standardized testing |
|---|---|
| .484 | Classroom and school testing |

Standard subdivisions are added for either or both topics in heading

| .486 | Diagnostic testing |
|---|---|
| **.5** | ***The arts** |

*For literature, see 372.64; for drama, see 372.66; for dance, see 372.868; for music, see 372.87*

| .52 | *Drawing, painting, design |
|---|---|
| .53 | *Modeling and sculpture |

Subdivisions are added for either or both topics in heading

| .54 | *Sewing |
|---|---|

Including weaving

Class here needlework

| .55 | *Handicrafts |
|---|---|

Including paper work

*For needlework, see 372.54*

| **.6** | ***Language arts (Communication skills)** |
|---|---|

Including fingerspelling, lipreading, sign languages

Class here literacy education

*For reading, see 372.4*

(Option: Class here language arts (communication skills) in a language other than English; in that case, class language arts (communication skills) in English in 372.6521)

| .61 | Grammar |
|---|---|

Including language usage, word study

| .62 | Written and spoken expression |
|---|---|

Class here language experience approach, whole-language approach

*For whole-language approach in reading, see 372.475. For a specific aspect of language experience in language arts, see the aspect, e.g., listening 372.69*

*Add as instructed under 372.3–372.8

| .622 | Speech |
|------|--------|

Including pronunciation

Class oral presentations other than public speaking in 372.66

> *See also 372.465 for phonetic methods of reading instruction; also 372.66 for drama*

| .623 | *Composition |
|------|--------------|

Class here comprehensive works on written expression

*For spelling and handwriting, see 372.63*

| .63 | Spelling and handwriting |
|-----|--------------------------|
| .632 | *Spelling (Orthography) |

Class fingerspelling in 372.6

| .634 | *Handwriting (Penmanship) |
|------|---------------------------|
| .64 | *Literature appreciation |

Class plays taught as theater in 372.66

| .65 | *Foreign, official, second languages; bilingual instruction |
|-----|-------------------------------------------------------------|

Languages other than the language given preference in 372.6

Subdivisions are added for all topics in heading together, for foreign languages alone, for official languages alone, for second languages alone

| .651 | *Bilingual instruction |
|------|------------------------|

Class comprehensive works on bilingual education in 370.1175

---

*Add as instructed under 372.3–372.8

.652–.659       Specific foreign, official, second languages

Subdivisions are added for any or all topics in heading

Add to base number 372.65 notation 2–9 from Table 6, e.g., Spanish 372.6561, English as a second language 372.6521; then add further as follows:

| | |
|---|---|
| 04 | General topics |
| 041 | Language arts in foreign, official, second languages |
| | Add to 041 the numbers following 372.6 in 372.61–372.64, e.g., Spanish composition 372.656104123 |
| 042 | Place of subject in education |
| 043 | Curricula |
| 044 | Teaching |
| | Class here methods of instruction, teaching materials |
| | Class textbooks with the subject in 001–999, e.g., primary textbooks on arithmetic 513 |
| (045) | Textbooks |
| | (Optional number; prefer the subject in 001–999, e.g., primary textbooks on arithmetic 513) |
| | Including readers (if option at 372.4122 is used) |
| 049 | Instruction at specific levels |
| | Including kindergarten |
| | Class a specific aspect of instruction at a given level with the aspect, e.g., curricula for kindergarten 043 |

.66       *Drama (Theater)

Class here school plays, comprehensive works on oral presentations

Class plays taught as literature in 372.64

*For public speaking, see 372.622; for other oral presentations, see 372.67. For use of drama as a method of instruction in a specific subject in elementary education, see the subject in 372.3–372.8, plus notation 044 from table under 372.3–372.8, e.g., use of drama in teaching history 372.89044*

.67       Other oral presentations

Other than drama and public speaking

Class here activities related to oral presentations

.672       *Media production and presentation

Subdivisions are added for either or both topics in heading

Class media production of a specific dramatic art with the art, e.g., storytelling for media 372.677

.674       *Puppetry

Limited to instructional use in elementary education

Class here puppet theater

Class interdisciplinary works on puppetry in 791.53

*Add as instructed under 372.3–372.8

| | |
|---|---|
| .676 | *Choral speaking |

Class here readers' theater

| | |
|---|---|
| .677 | *Storytelling |
| .69 | *Listening |
| **.7** | **\*Mathematics** |

Including measurement

| | |
|---|---|
| .71 | *Algebra |
| .72 | *Arithmetic |

Class here numeracy

| | |
|---|---|
| .76 | *Geometry |
| .79 | *Probabilities and statistical mathematics |

Subdivisions are added for either or both topics in heading

| | |
|---|---|
| **.8** | **Other studies** |
| [.801–.809] | Standard subdivisions |

Do not use; class in 372.1901–372.1909

| | |
|---|---|
| [.82] | Home and family management |

Relocated to 372.37

| | |
|---|---|
| .83 | *Civics (Citizenship) |

Comprehensive works on social studies relocated to 372.89

| | |
|---|---|
| [.832] | Civics (Citizenship) |

Number discontinued; class in 372.83

| | |
|---|---|
| .84 | *Religion |

Class religious education of children under auspices of religious bodies to inculcate religious faith and practice in 207.5; class religious education of children under church auspices to inculcate Christian faith and practice in 268.432

| | |
|---|---|
| .86 | *Physical education and dance |

Subdivisions are added for physical education and dance together, for physical education alone

| | |
|---|---|
| .868 | *Dance |

Class here movement education

| | |
|---|---|
| .87 | *Music |

*See also 372.868 for dance*

| | |
|---|---|
| .872 | Appreciation |

*Add as instructed under 372.3–372.8

| | |
|---|---|
| .873 | Performance |

Including reading music

| | |
|---|---|
| .874 | Composition |
| .89 | History and geography |

Standard subdivisions are added for history and geography together, for history alone

Class here comprehensive works on social studies [*formerly* 372.83]; civilization

> *For environmental studies, see 372.357; for social skills, see 372.374; for civics, see 372.83*

| | |
|---|---|
| .890 4 | General topics of history and geography |
| .890 42–.890 44 | Place of history and geography in education; curricula, teaching |

Add to base number 372.8904 the numbers following 04 in notation 042–044 from table under 372.3–372.8, e.g., teaching history 372.89044

| | |
|---|---|
| (.890 45) | Textbooks |

(Optional number; prefer 909)

> *For textbooks on history and civilization of ancient world, of specific continents, countries, localities, see 372.893–372.899*

| | |
|---|---|
| .890 49 | Instruction at specific levels |

Class a specific aspect of instruction at a given level with the aspect, e.g., history curricula for primary grades 372.89043

| | |
|---|---|
| .891 | Geography |
| .891 04 | General topics of geography |
| .891 042–.891 044 | Place of geography in education; curricula, teaching |

Add to base number 372.89104 the numbers following 04 in notation 042–044 from the table under 372.3–372.8, e.g., using maps in geography 372.891044

| | |
|---|---|
| (.891 045) | Textbooks |

(Optional number; prefer 910)

> *For textbooks on geography of specific places, see 372.8911–372.8919*

| | |
|---|---|
| .891 049 | Instruction at specific levels |

Class a specific aspect of instruction at a given level with the aspect, e.g., geography curricula for primary grades 372.891043

(.891 1–.891 9)     Textbooks on geography of specific places

> (Optional numbers; prefer 910.91 for geography in general, 913–919 for geography of specific continents, countries, localities)

> Add to base number 372.891 notation 1–9 from Table 2, e.g., geography textbooks on Asia 372.8915

(.893–.899)     Textbooks on history and civilization of ancient world, of specific continents, countries, localities

> (Optional numbers; prefer 930–990)

> Add to base number 372.89 notation 3–9 from Table 2, e.g., textbooks on ancient Egypt 372.8932

> *For textbooks on geography of specific places, see 372.8911–372.8919*

**.9     History, geographic treatment, biography of primary education**

> Class here specific schools and school systems

.901–.905     Historical periods

> Add to base number 372.9 notation 01–05 from Table 2, e.g., primary education in the 21st century 372.905

.91–.99     Geographic treatment, biography

> Add to base number 372.9 notation 1–9 from Table 2, e.g., primary education in Brazil 372.981

# 373     Secondary education

> Class here upper sections of all-age schools

> *For secondary education in a specific subject, see the subject, plus notation 0712 from Table 1, e.g., secondary education in agriculture 630.712*

### SUMMARY

| | | |
|---|---|---|
| 373.01–.09 | | Standard subdivisions, secondary education for specific objectives |
| .1 | | Organization and activities in secondary education |
| .2 | | Secondary schools and programs of specific kinds, levels, curricula, focus |
| .3–.9 | | Secondary education in specific continents, countries, localities |

.01     Philosophy and theory, secondary education for specific objectives

> Notation 01 from Table 1 as modified below

.011      Secondary education for specific objectives

Do not use for systems; class in 373.01

Class here curricula directed toward specific educational objectives

Add to base number 373.011 the numbers following 370.11 in 370.111–370.119, e.g., education for social responsibility in high school 373.0115; however, for vocational education, see 373.246

Class a specific topic with respect to secondary education for a specific objective with the topic in 373.11–373.18, e.g., professional qualifications for teaching social responsibility in high school 373.112

*See also 373.21–373.22 for specific kinds of secondary school systems*

.02      Miscellany

[.028 4]      Apparatus, equipment, materials

Do not use; class in 373.167

[.028 7]      Testing and measurement

Do not use; class in 373.126

[.028 8]      Maintenance and repair

Do not use; class in 373.168

.06      Organizations

[.068]      Management

Do not use; class in 373.12

.08      Groups of people

Do not use for students; class in 373.18. Do not use for schools and education for specific groups of students; class in 373.182 e.g., secondary schools for ethnic minorities 373.1829

.082      Women in secondary education

Do not use for secondary education of young women; class in 373.182352

.09      History, geographic treatment, biography

[.093–.099]      Specific continents, countries, localities

Do not use; class in 373.3–373.9

**.1      Organization and activities in secondary education**

*For comprehensive works on secondary education for specific objectives, see 373.011; for comprehensive works on schools and programs of specific kinds, levels, curricula, focus, see 373.2*

[.101–.109]      Standard subdivisions

Do not use; class in 373.01–373.09

.11–.18        School organization and activities in secondary education

> Add to base number 373.1 the numbers following 371 in 371.1–371.8, e.g., professional qualifications of teachers 373.112, secondary education of young women 373.182352; however, for cooperative education, see 373.28

.19            Curricula

> Class curricula directed toward specific secondary educational objectives in 373.011; class education in secondary schools identified by specific types of curricula in 373.24–373.26

.2             **Secondary schools and programs of specific kinds, levels, curricula, focus**

> Class here types of education (other than public education in general) provided by schools and programs of specific kinds, levels, curricula, focus

> Unless other instructions are given, class a subject with aspects in two or more subdivisions of 373.2 in the number coming last, e.g., public senior vocational schools 373.246 (*not* 373.224 or 373.238)

> Class a specific topic relating to schools and programs of a specific kind, level, curriculum, focus in 373.11–373.18; class a specific school regardless of kind, level, curriculum, focus in 373.3–373.9; class continuation schools in 374.8; class folk high schools in 374.83

### SUMMARY

| | |
|---|---|
| 373.21 | **Community, alternative, religious secondary schools; public secondary schools distinguished by source of funding, locus of control, and mandate** |
| .22 | **Private and public secondary schools** |
| .23 | **Specific levels of secondary education** |
| .24 | **Academic, military, vocational schools** |
| .25 | **Comprehensive secondary schools** |
| .26 | **General secondary schools** |
| .27 | **Apprenticeship programs in secondary education** |
| .28 | **Cooperative education** |

[.201–.209]    Standard subdivisions

> Do not use; class in 373.01–373.09

---

> 373.21–373.22   Specific kinds of schools

> Class comprehensive works in 373

.21            Community, alternative, religious secondary schools; public secondary schools distinguished by source of funding, locus of control, and mandate

> Add to base number 373.21 the numbers following 371.0 in 371.03–371.07, e.g., public secondary schools distinguished by source of funding, locus of control, and mandate 373.215 [*formerly* 373.224]

.22            Private and public secondary schools

> Class private and public community, alternative, religious secondary schools in 373.21

.222       **Private secondary schools (Preparatory schools)**

Class here public schools (private secondary schools), comprehensive works on boarding schools

Class private schools (other than academic schools) identified by type of curriculum in 373.24–373.26

*For a specific kind of boarding school (other than private secondary schools), see the kind, e.g., private primary boarding schools 372.10422, military boarding schools 373.243*

.224       **Public secondary schools**

Class comprehensive works on public secondary education in 373

*For specific levels of public secondary schools, see 373.23; for public secondary schools identified by a specific type of curriculum, see 373.24–373.26*

Public secondary schools distinguished by source of funding, locus of control, and mandate relocated to 373.215

.23       **Specific levels of secondary education**

Class private schools regardless of level in 373.222; class schools identified by a specific type of curriculum regardless of level in 373.24–373.26; class comprehensive works on levels of secondary schools, four-year high schools not of a specific type in 373

*See Manual at 372.24 and 373.23*

[.230 1–.230 9]       Standard subdivisions

Do not use; class in 373.01–373.09

.236       **Lower level**

Including grades above 6 in primary schools

Class here middle schools (grades 5–8), junior high schools (grades 7–9); grades 7–10 of compulsory primary education

*For lower grades of middle schools, see 372.242*

(Option: Class lower secondary level, grades 7–10 of compulsory primary education in 372.243)

.238       **Upper level**

Including high school equivalency programs

Class here senior high schools (grades 10–12); high school postgraduate programs

---

&gt;       **373.24–373.26 Secondary schools identified by type of curriculum**

Class here private schools (other than academic schools) identified by type of curriculum

Class comprehensive works in 373

.24       **Academic, military, vocational schools**

| .241 | Academic schools |
|---|---|

Schools preparing for higher education

Class here classical schools [*formerly* 373.242]; comprehensive works on magnet schools (specialist schools)

Class private academic schools in 373.222; class preparing for higher education in military schools in 373.243; class preparing for higher education in comprehensive secondary schools in 373.25; class comprehensive works on secondary schools preparing for higher education in 373

> *For a specific type of magnet school, see the type, e.g., magnet public primary schools 372.10421, magnet vocational schools 373.246, magnet secondary schools for science 507.12, magnet secondary schools for arts 700.712*

| [.242] | Classical schools |
|---|---|

Relocated to 373.241

| .243 | Military schools |
|---|---|

Secondary schools offering professional military education but remaining basically academic in nature

Class here naval schools

Class schools concentrating on professional military education in 355.0071

| .246 | Vocational schools |
|---|---|

Class here technical secondary schools, vocational education

Class vocational education in comprehensive secondary schools in 373.24; class comprehensive works on vocational education in 370.113

| .25 | Comprehensive secondary schools |
|---|---|

Schools offering academic, vocational, general programs when considered distinct from undifferentiated secondary schools

| .26 | General secondary schools |
|---|---|

Schools offering nonvocational, general terminal education when considered distinct from undifferentiated secondary schools

| .27 | Apprenticeship programs in secondary education |
|---|---|

Class apprenticeship programs offered by industry in 331.25922; class work-study plan in 373.28; class apprenticeship training as part of personnel management in 658.3124

| .28 | Cooperative education |
|---|---|

Class here work-study plan

**.3–.9**    **Secondary education in specific continents, countries, localities**

Class here specific schools and school systems

Add to base number 373 notation 3–9 from Table 2, e.g., secondary schools of Australia 373.94

*For a specific school devoted primarily to a specific discipline, see the discipline, plus notation 0712 from Table 1, e.g., a science high school 507.12*

# 374    Adult education

Class here continuing, further, lifelong, permanent, recurrent education

Class on-the-job training in 331.2592; class adult high school equivalency programs in 373.238

*For adult education in a specific subject, see the subject, plus notation 0715 from Table 1, e.g., sculpture courses for adults 730.715*

.001          Philosophy and theory

.002          Miscellany

[.002 84]          Apparatus, equipment, materials

                       Do not use; class in 374.167

[.002 87]          Testing and measurement

                       Do not use; class in 374.126

[.002 88]          Maintenance and repair

                       Do not use; class in 374.168

.003–.005          Standard subdivisions

.006          Organizations

[.006 8]          Management

                       Do not use; class in 374.12

.007          Education, research, related topics

.008          Groups of people

                       Do not use for students; class in 374.18. Do not use for education of specific groups of students; class in 374.182, e.g., adult education of ethnic minority students 374.1829

[.009]          History, geographic treatment, biography

                       Do not use; class in 374.9

.01       Adult education for specific objectives

> Class here curricula directed toward specific adult educational objectives, kinds of agencies promoting specific objectives
>
> Class specific agencies for adult education regardless of objective in 374.94–374.99. Class a specific topic with respect to a specific adult educational objective with the topic in 374.11–374.18, e.g., testing in adult basic education 374.126

.012       Adult basic education

> Class here adult primary, fundamental, remedial education

.012 4       Literacy programs

> Limited to general discussion of programs to promote ability of adults to read and write up to a sixth-grade level
>
> Class comprehensive works on literacy programs in 379.24; class adult education in effective composition (writing) in 808.00715. Class adult education in standard usage of a specific language with the language, plus notation 800715 from Table 4, e.g., a course in basic English for adults 428.00715

.013–.019       Vocational, moral, ethical, character education; education for social responsibility, for international understanding; multicultural and bilingual education; education for creativity, for effective use of leisure

> Add to base number 374.01 the numbers following 370.11 in 370.113–370.119, e.g., adult education for effective use of leisure 374.019

.1       **Organization and activities in adult education**

> *For groups, media, computers in adult education, see 374.2; for comprehensive works on adult education for specific objectives, see 374.01; for comprehensive works on distance education, see 374.4; for comprehensive works on specific kinds of institutions and agencies, see 374.8*

[.101–.108]       Standard subdivisions

> Do not use; class in 374.001–374.008

[.109]       History, geographic treatment, biography

> Do not use; class in 374.9

.11–.18       School organization and activities in adult education

> Add to base number 374.1 the numbers following 371 in 371.1–371.8, e.g., testing 374.126; however, for use of media and computers, electronic distance education, see 374.26; for distance education, correspondence schools and courses, see 374.4

.2       **Groups, media, computers in adult education**

.22        Groups in adult education

Class here discussion, reading, special-interest, study groups

Class self-help groups in 361.4

*See also 374.182 for specific groups of people as students*

.26        Use of mass media and computers

Standard subdivisions are added for either or both topics in heading

Class here electronic distance education

**.4**        **Distance education**

Class here correspondence schools and courses, open and distance learning (ODL), open learning

*For electronic distance education, see 374.26*

**.8**        **Specific kinds of institutions and agencies in adult education**

Including community centers for adult education; continuation, evening, vacation schools

Class here specific kinds of schools

Class adult education role of libraries in 021.24; class specific institutions and agencies regardless of kind in 374.94–374.99. Class a specific topic with respect to a specific kind of institution or agency in adult education with the topic in 374.11–374.18, e.g., vacation school students 374.18

*For kinds of agencies promoting adult education for specific objectives, see 374.01; for correspondence schools, see 374.4; for alternative colleges and universities as agencies for adult education, see 378.03; for university extension services as agencies for adult education, see 378.175*

[.801–.808]        Standard subdivisions

Do not use; class in 374.001–374.008

[.809]        History, geographic treatment, biography

Do not use; class in 374.9

.83        Folk high schools

.830 9        History, geographic treatment, biography

Class specific folk high schools in 374.9

**.9**        **History, geographic treatment, biography**

.901–.905        Historical periods

Add to base number 374.9 notation 01–05 from Table 2, e.g., adult education in the 21st century 374.905

.91–.99        Geographic treatment, biography

Add to base number 374.9 notation 1–9 from Table 2, e.g., adult education in Sweden 374.9485

# 375 Curricula

*For curricula of a specific subject at the primary level, see 372.3–372.8. For curricula of a specific subject for a specific level other than primary level and for more than one level, see the subject, plus notation 071 from Table 1, e.g., curricula for health 613.071; for curricula for a specific level, see the level, e.g., secondary-school curricula 373.19*

.000 1–.000 9      Standard subdivisions

.001      Curriculum development

Class here curriculum planning

Class comprehensive works on curriculum development and instructional supervision in 371.203

*For curriculum evaluation and change, see 375.006*

.002      Required courses

Class here core curriculum

.004      Elective courses

.006      Evaluation and change

(.01–.03)      Curricula and courses in bibliography, library and information sciences, encyclopedias

(Optional numbers; prefer 010–030, plus notation 071 from Table 1)

Add to base number 375 notation 010–030, e.g., curricula in cataloging and classification 375.0253

(.04)      Curricula and courses in knowledge, systems study, computer science

(Optional number; prefer 001–006, plus notation 071 from Table 1)

Add to base number 375.04 the numbers following 00 in 001–006, e.g., curricula in computer science 375.044

(.05–.09)      Curricula and courses of study in general serial publications; general organizations and museology; documentary media, educational media, news media; journalism; publishing; general collections; manuscripts, rare books, other rare printed materials

(Optional numbers; prefer 050–090, plus notation 071 from Table 1)

Add to base number 375 notation 050–090, e.g., journalism curricula 375.0704

**(.1–.9)**      **Curricula and courses of study in other specific subjects**

(Optional numbers; prefer 100–900, plus notation 071 from Table 1)

Add to base number 375 notation 100–900, e.g., history curricula 375.9

# [376]      [Unassigned]

Most recently used in Edition 20

**[377]**     **[Unassigned]**

Most recently used in Edition 20

**378**     **Higher education (Tertiary education)**

Class here college education, university education; universities

Class four-year colleges in 378.1542

*For higher education in a specific subject, see the subject, plus notation 0711 from Table 1, e.g., medical schools 610.711*

*See Manual at 371.01–371.8 vs. 372–374, 378*

**SUMMARY**

| | |
|---|---|
| 378.001–.009 | **Standard subdivisions** |
| .01–.07 | **[Higher education for specific objectives, specific kinds of colleges and universities]** |
| .1 | **Organization and activities in higher education** |
| .2 | **Academic degrees and related topics** |
| .3 | **Student aid and related topics** |
| .4–.9 | **Higher education in specific continents, countries, localities in modern world** |

.001          Philosophy and theory

.001 1          Systems

The word "systems" as used here refers only to concepts derived from 003, e.g., systems theory, analysis, and design applied to schools and school systems

*See also 378.03–378.07 for specific kinds of college and university systems*

.002          Miscellany

[.002 84]          Apparatus, equipment, materials

Do not use; class in 378.1967

[.002 87]          Testing and measurement

Do not use; class in 378.166

[.002 88]          Maintenance and repair

Do not use; class in 378.1968

.003–.005     Standard subdivisions

.006          Organizations

[.006 8]          Management

Do not use; class in 378.101

.007          Education, research, related topics

.008          Groups of people

> Do not use for students; class in 378.198. Do not use for higher education of specific groups of student; class in 378.1982 e.g., higher education of ethnic minorities 378.19829

.008 2          Women in higher education

> Do not use for higher education of women; class in 378.19822. Do not use for higher education of young women; class in 378.1982422

.009          History, geographic treatment, biography

.009 2          Biography

> Class here administrators

> Class persons associated with specific colleges and universities in 378.4–378.9

[.009 4–.009 9]          Specific continents, countries, localities in modern world

> Do not use; class in 378.4–378.9

.01          Higher education for specific objectives

> Class here curricula directed toward specific higher educational objectives

> Add to base number 378.01 the numbers following 370.11 in 370.111–370.119, e.g., professional education 378.013

> Class professional schools in 378.155. Class a specific topic with respect to a specific higher educational objective with the topic in 378.101–378.198, e.g., seminars in professional education 378.177

---

> 378.03–378.07    Specific kinds of colleges and universities

> Class here specific kinds of higher education (other than public higher education) characteristic of specific kinds of colleges and universities, specific kinds of college and university systems

> Class a specific kind of college and university at a specific level in 378.15; class schools for specific groups of students in 378.1982; class specific institutions in 378.4–378.9; class comprehensive works in 378. Class a specific topic with respect to a specific kind of college or university with the topic in 378.1, e.g., graduate school fraternities 378.19855

.03          Alternative colleges and universities

> Standard subdivisions are added for either or both topics in heading

> Class here experimental schools of higher education, free universities, open universities, universities without walls

> *See also 378.175 for extension services*

---

> 378.04–378.05    Private and public colleges and universities

> Class public and private alternative colleges and universities in 378.03; class public and private colleges and universities related to religious bodies in 378.07; class comprehensive works in 378

| .04 | Private colleges and universities |
|---|---|

Standard subdivisions are added for either or both topics in heading

| .05 | Public colleges and universities |
|---|---|

Standard subdivisions are added for either or both topics in heading

Class two-year public colleges in 378.1543; class comprehensive works on public higher education in 378

| .052 | Municipal colleges and universities |
|---|---|

Standard subdivisions are added for either or both topics in heading

Class here county, regional colleges and universities

| .053 | State and provincial colleges and universities |
|---|---|

Standard subdivisions are added for either state or provincial colleges and universities

*For municipal colleges supported by state and provincial governments, see 378.052*

| [.054–.055] | Land-grant colleges and universities, national colleges and universities |
|---|---|

Numbers discontinued; class in 378.05

| .07 | Colleges and universities related to religious bodies |
|---|---|

Add to base number 378.07 the numbers following 371.07 in 371.071–371.079, e.g., church-related universities 378.071, Jewish universities 378.076
Subdivisions are added for either or both topics in heading

| **.1** | **Organization and activities in higher education** |
|---|---|

Including university autonomy

*For academic degrees and related topics, see 378.2; for student aid and related topics, see 378.3; for comprehensive works on higher education for specific objectives, see 378.01; for comprehensive works on specific kinds of colleges and universities, see 378.03–378.07*

### SUMMARY

| | |
|---|---|
| 378.101–.107 | **[Administration, community relations, cooperation]** |
| .11 | **Personnel management** |
| .12 | **Faculty and teaching** |
| .15 | **Specific levels of higher education** |
| .16 | **Administration of student academic activities** |
| .17 | **Methods of instruction and study** |
| .19 | **Guidance, discipline, physical plant, welfare, students, curricula** |

| [.100 1–.100 9] | Standard subdivisions |
|---|---|

Do not use; class in 378.001–378.009

| | |
|---|---|
| .101 | College and university administration |

Standard subdivisions are added for either or both topics in heading

Class administrators in 378.111

*For financial management, see 378.106; for executive management, see 378.107; for personnel management, see 378.11; for plant and materials management, see 378.196*

| | |
|---|---|
| .101 1 | Governing bodies |
| .101 2 | Policies and regulations |
| .103 | Community relations |

Including volunteer student service (for credit or not for credit)

Class interdisciplinary works on relations of colleges and universities with society in 306.432

| | |
|---|---|
| .103 5 | Industry relations |

Class here industry involvement in higher education, industry-school partnerships

Class technology transfer in 338.926

*See also 378.37 for cooperative education*

| | |
|---|---|
| .104 | Cooperation in higher education |

Class here consortia in higher education

Class a specific instance of cooperation with the instance, e.g., cooperation in computer networking 004.6

| | |
|---|---|
| .106 | Financial management |

Including tuition

*For student aid and related topics, see 378.3*

| | |
|---|---|
| .107 | Executive management |

Class here planning

*For governing bodies, see 378.1011; for administrators, leadership, top and middle management, see 378.111*

| | |
|---|---|
| .11 | Personnel management |

Class here staff

*For faculty, see 378.12*

| | |
|---|---|
| .111 | Administrators |

Including leadership, top and middle management

*For biography of administrators, see 378.0092. For administrators of a specific function, see the function, e.g., directors of admissions 378.161*

.112          Staff personnel

> Other than administrators and faculty

> *For a specific kind of staff personnel, see the kind, e.g., counselors 378.194*

.12       Faculty and teaching

> Standard subdivisions are added for faculty and teaching together, for faculty alone

[.120 71]          Education of faculty

> Do not use; class in 378.0071

.121          Academic status

> Privileges, prerogatives, immunities, responsibilities

> Including sabbatical leave

.121 3          Academic freedom

.121 4          Tenure

.122          Organization of teaching force

> Including hierarchy

> Add to base number 378.122 the numbers following 371.14 in 371.141–371.148, e.g., faculty workload 378.12212, evaluation of faculty 378.1224

.124          Professional qualifications

> Use of this number for personal qualifications discontinued; class in 378.12

.125          Teaching

> *For methods of instruction and study, see 378.17*

[.125 07]          Education, research, related topics in teaching

> Do not use; class in 378.007

.15       Specific levels of higher education

> Class specific institutions in 378.4–378.9. Class a specific topic of higher education with respect to a specific level of higher education with the topic in 378.1, e.g., teaching at the graduate level 378.125

[.150 1–.150 9]          Standard subdivisions

> Do not use; class in 378.001–378.009

.154          Undergraduate level

> Institutions conferring degrees or their equivalent at the undergraduate level within the national qualification structure for higher education

| .154 2 | Programs leading to a bachelor's degree |
|---|---|

Class here four-year colleges, three-year institutions conferring the equivalent of a bachelor's degree, undergraduate departments and schools of universities

| .154 3 | Programs leading to degrees below the bachelor's degree |
|---|---|

Class here institutions conferring degrees below the bachelor's level, two-year colleges

| .155 | Graduate level |
|---|---|

Including postdoctoral programs

Class here independent institutions conferring advanced degrees, graduate departments and schools of universities, comprehensive works on professional schools

Class comprehensive works on professional education in 378.013

*For professional schools at undergraduate level, see 378.154*

| [.158] | Evening school in higher education |
|---|---|

Number discontinued; class in 378.1

| .16 | Administration of student academic activities |
|---|---|

Add to base number 378.16 the numbers following 371.2 in 371.21–371.29, e.g., admissions and related topics 378.161, standardized tests at college level 378.1662; however, for academic degrees and related topics, see 378.2; for student aid and related topics, see 378.3

Class methods of instruction in 378.17; class student participation in management in 378.1959

| .17 | Methods of instruction and study |
|---|---|
| .170 28 | Auxiliary techniques and procedures, techniques of study, lesson plans |

Notation 028 from Table 1 as modified below

| .170 281 | Techniques of study |
|---|---|

Including book reports, homework, note-taking, reading for content, report writing

Class here techniques for parents, study skills

| [.170 284] | Apparatus, equipment, materials |
|---|---|

Do not use; class in 378.173

| [.170 285] | Computer applications |
|---|---|

Do not use; class in 378.1734

| [.170 78] | Use of apparatus, equipment, materials in study and teaching |
|---|---|

Do not use; class in 378.173

.172–.179     Specific methods of instruction and study

> Add to base number 378.17 the numbers following 371.3 in 371.32–371.39, e.g., extension services 378.175, seminars 378.177

.19     Guidance, discipline, physical plant, welfare, students, curricula

.194–.198     Guidance, discipline, physical plant, welfare, students

> Add to base number 378.19 the numbers following 371 in 371.4–371.8, e.g., school discipline 378.195, higher education of specific kinds of students 378.1982

.199     Curricula

> Class curricula directed toward specific educational objectives in 378.01

**.2     Academic degrees and related topics**

> Standard subdivisions are added for academic degrees and related topics together, for academic degrees alone

.24     Requirements for earned degrees

.241     Course, residence, subject requirements

> Class here college majors

.242     Thesis and dissertation requirements

> Class preparation of theses and dissertations in 808.066378

.25     Honorary degrees

.28     Academic costume

**.3     Student aid and related topics**

> Standard subdivisions are added for student aid and related topics together, for student aid alone
>
> *For student aid in a specific field, see the field, plus notation 079 from Table 1, e.g., student aid in medical education 610.79*

.32     Veterans' higher education benefits

.33     Fellowships and grants

> Class comprehensive works on student exchanges in higher education in 378.0162

.34     Scholarships

.36     Loans and employment

.362     Student loans

.365            Student employment

Including employment for service to the community

Class here employment of students by their own schools, work-study programs

> *For volunteer student service to community, see 378.103; for employment in connection with fellowships, see 378.33; for employment by industry and nonschool agencies in connection with ongoing academic work, see 378.37*

.37             Cooperative education

Student employment by industry and nonschool agencies in connection with ongoing academic work

Class here work-study plan

Class general work-study programs for student employment in 378.365

.38             Costs and expenditures

Standard subdivisions are added for either or both topics in heading

**.4–.9         Higher education in specific continents, countries, localities in modern world**

Class here specific schools

Add to base number 378 notation 4–9 from Table 2, e.g., higher education in Mexico 378.72
(Option: If it is desired to give local emphasis and a shorter number to a specific college or university, place it first by use of a letter or other symbol, e.g., University of South Africa 378.S [preceding 378.4])

> *For a school or department of a college or university devoted to a specific subject, see the subject, plus notation 0711 from Table 1, e.g., Harvard Law School 340.07117444*

> *See Manual at 378.4–378.9 vs. 355.00711*

**379        Public policy issues in education**

Public policy issues at any level of education

Class public administration of education in 353.8; class school administration in 371.2

> *For public policy issues on a topic not provided for here, see the topic, e.g., policy on school admissions 371.21, on medical schools 610.711*

> *See Manual at 371 vs. 353.8, 371.2, 379*

### SUMMARY

[.094–.099]       Specific continents, countries, localities in modern world

> Do not use; class in 379.4–379.9

**.1**       **Specific elements of support and control of public education**

> Class support and control of activities involved in specific policy issues in public education in 379.2

### SUMMARY

| | |
|---|---|
| 379.11 | **Support of public education** |
| .12 | **Support by specific level of government, international support** |
| .13 | **Revenue sources** |
| .15 | **Control of public education** |

[.101–.109]       Standard subdivisions

> Do not use; class in 379.01–379.09

.11       Support of public education

> Class here financial support; comprehensive works on financial support of education

> *For support by specific levels of government, international support, see 379.12; for revenue sources, see 379.13; for financial support of private education, see 379.32*

> *See also 353.824 for financial administration of agencies supporting public education*

.111       Educational vouchers

> Regardless of level of government

> Class here school choice

> Class educational vouchers for a specific level of education in 379.112–379.118; class educational vouchers for special education in 379.119

> *For use of educational vouchers in private education, see 379.32*

.112       Support of public primary education

.112 2       Support of public preschool education

.113       Support of public secondary education

.114       Public support of adult education

.118       Support of public higher education

.119       Public support of special education

.12       Support by specific level of government, international support

> Class educational vouchers regardless of level of government providing them in 379.111; class revenue sources of specific levels of government in 379.13

| [.120 1–.120 9] | Standard subdivisions |
| | Do not use; class in 379.01–379.09 |

.121 **Support by national governments**

.121 2 National support of primary education

.121 22 National support of preschool education

.121 3 National support of secondary education

.121 4 National support of higher education

.121 5 National support of adult education

.121 6 National support of special education

.122 **Support by state, provincial, regional governments**

Add to base number 379.122 the numbers following 379.121 in 379.1212–379.1216, e.g., state support of adult education 379.1225

.123 **Local support**

.128 **Support by regional intergovernmental organizations**

.128 2–.128 9 Support by specific regional intergovernmental organizations

Add to base number 379.128 the numbers following 341.24 in 341.242–341.249, e.g., support by European Union 379.12822

.129 **International support**

Class here international multicultural educational aid

.129 09 History, geographic treatment, biography

Do not use for geographic treatment by recipient area; class in 379.1291–379.1299

.129 1–.129 9 Geographic treatment by recipient area

Add to base number 379.129 notation 1–9 from Table 2, e.g., educational aid to Asia 379.1295; then, for area providing support, add 0*, and again add notation 1–9 from Table 2, e.g., French educational aid to Asia 379.1295044

.13 **Revenue sources**

Class here school taxes

Class financial assistance from higher levels of government in 379.12

.15 **Control of public education**

Class here autonomy

---

> 379.151–379.154 Control by specific governmental level

Class control of specific aspects of education regardless of level in 379.155–379.158; class comprehensive works in 379.15

---

*Add 00 for standard subdivisions; see instructions at beginning of Table 1

| .151 | Control by national governments |
|------|--------------------------------|
| .152 | Control by state, provincial, regional governments |
| .153 | Control by local governments |
| .153 1 | School boards |
| .153 5 | School districts |

        Including centralization and consolidation of schools, changing school attendance boundaries

| .154 | Control by regional intergovernmental organizations |
|------|--------------------------------|
| .154 2–.154 9 | Control by specific regional intergovernmental organizations |

        Add to base number 379.154 the numbers following 341.24 in 341.242–341.249, e.g., control by European Commission 379.1542226

---

> 379.155–379.158 **Control of specific aspects of education**

Class comprehensive works in 379.15

*For control of a specific aspect of education not provided for here, see the aspect, e.g., control of school discipline 371.5*

| .155 | Control of curriculum |
|------|------------------------|

*See also 379.28 for place of religion in public education*

| .156 | Control of teaching materials |
|------|-------------------------------|

Class here control of textbooks

| .157 | Control of teachers and administrators |
|------|----------------------------------------|

Class control of specific aspects of teachers and teaching in 371.1; class control of specific aspects of school administrators in 371.2011

| .158 | School standards and accreditation |
|------|------------------------------------|

Standard subdivisions are added for either or both topics in heading

Class here educational evaluation, school accountability

*See also 353.8284 for government commissions on standards and accreditation; also 371.26 for examinations and tests*

| **.2** | **Specific policy issues in public education** |
|--------|------------------------------------------------|

Not otherwise provided for

| [.201–.209] | Standard subdivisions |
|-------------|------------------------|

Do not use; class in 379.01–379.09

| .23 | Compulsory education |
|-----|----------------------|

Including school-leaving age

| .24 | Literacy policies |
|---|---|

Class here right to read

| .26 | Educational equalization (Equal educational opportunity) |
|---|---|

Class here affirmative action, right to education

Discrimination in education relocated to 370.8

| .263 | School desegregation |
|---|---|
| .28 | Place of religion in public schools |

Regardless of faith or denomination

Including teaching creationism in public schools

| **.3** | **Public policy issues in private education** |
|---|---|
| .32 | Public support of private education |

Class here educational vouchers, financial support

Class comprehensive works on financial support of education in 379.11

| .322 | Public support of private primary education |
|---|---|
| .322 2 | Public support of private preschool education |
| .323 | Public support of private secondary education |
| .324 | Public support of private higher education |
| .326 | Public support of private adult education |
| .328 | Public support of private special education |
| .34 | Public control of private education |

Add to base number 379.34 the numbers following 379.32 in 379.322–379.328, e.g., public control of private primary education 379.342

| **.4–.9** | **Public policy issues in specific continents, countries, localities in modern world** |
|---|---|

Add to base number 379 notation 4–9 from Table 2, e.g., public educational policies in United States 379.73

# 380    Commerce, communications, transportation

Except for modifications shown under specific entries, add to each subdivision identified by * as follows:

025       Directories of persons and organizations

06       Organizations and management; business enterprises
           Notation 06 from Table 1 as modified below

065      Business enterprises
          Including individual proprietorships, partnerships, companies, public and private corporations, combinations
          Add to 065 notation 3–9 from Table 2, e.g., business enterprises of France 06544
          Class directories of business enterprises, membership lists with directory information in 025; class organizations whose members are business enterprises, e.g., trade associations and chambers of commerce, in 06
              *See Manual at T1—025 vs. T1—0601–0609; also at 380: Add table: 09 vs. 065*

068      Management
          Public and private

09       History, geographic treatment, biography
          Class specific business enterprises in 065
             *See Manual at 380: Add table: 09 vs. 065*

Class public regulation and control in 354.7

*See Manual at 380*

## SUMMARY

| | | |
|---|---|---|
| 380.1–.9 | Standard subdivisions | |
| 381 | Commerce (Trade) | |
| 382 | International commerce (Foreign trade) | |
| 383 | Postal communication | |
| 384 | Communications | |
| 385 | Railroad transportation | |
| 386 | Inland waterway and ferry transportation | |
| 387 | Water, air, space transportation | |
| 388 | Transportation | |
| 389 | Metrology and standardization | |

[.01]      Philosophy and theory

        Relocated to 380.1

[.02–.09]    Standard subdivisions

        Relocated to 380.2–380.9

**.1**      **Philosophy and theory [*formerly* 380.01]**

**.2–.9**      **Standard subdivisions [*formerly* 380.02–380.09]**

# 381    *Commerce (Trade)

Class here internal commerce (domestic trade), warehousing, interdisciplinary works on marketing

Unless other instructions are given, observe the following table of preference, e.g., retail trade in rice 381.41318 (*not* 381.1):

| | |
|---|---|
| Specific products and services | 381.4 |
| Marketing channels | 381.1 |
| Wholesale trade | 381.2 |
| Interregional and interstate commerce | 381.5 |
| Commercial policy | 381.3 |

Class supply and demand in 338.1–338.5; class restrictive practices in business organizations engaged in commerce in 338.82; class comprehensive works on warehousing in 388.044; class interdisciplinary works on consumption in 339.47. Class cooperative, labor, finance, land, energy economics in relation to commerce with the branch of economics in 330, e.g., cooperative marketing 334.6

*For international commerce, see 382; for management of marketing, see 658.8*

*See Manual at T1—025 vs. T1—029*

### SUMMARY

| | | |
|---|---|---|
| **381.029** | | **Commercial miscellany** |
| | **.1** | **Marketing channels** |
| | **.2** | **Wholesale trade** |
| | **.3** | **Commercial policy** |
| | **.4** | **Specific products and services** |
| | **.5** | **Interregional and interstate commerce** |

**.029**     Commercial miscellany

Do not use for evaluation and purchasing manuals; class in 381.33

Notation 029 from Table 1 is seldom used with the subdivisions of 381

Class here interdisciplinary works on commercial miscellany

*For commercial miscellany with respect to a specific product or service, see the noncommercial number for the product or service, plus notation 029 from Table 1, e.g., buyers' guides for passenger automobiles 629.222029*

*See Manual at T1—025 vs. T1—029*

*Add as instructed under 380

.1      **\*Marketing channels**

Including exhibitions, trade fairs (trade shows)

Class here retail trade; markets, shops, stores

Class street fairs in 381.186; class consumer problems and their alleviation in 381.3; class interdisciplinary works on exhibitions, on fairs in 907.4. Class marketing channels and marketing enterprises limited to or predominantly for a specific product or service with the product or service in 381.4, e.g., food supermarkets, comprehensive works on food and grocery trade 381.456413

Management of marketing channels limited to or predominantly for a specific product or service is classed with the product or service in 381.4, e.g., management of chain bookstores 381.45002068, management of food supermarkets 381.4564130068. Management of marketing channels not limited to or predominantly for a specific product or service is classed in 658.87, e.g., management of all kinds of chain stores 658.8702, management of supermarkets that are not predominantly food stores 658.879

> *For consumer cooperatives, see 334.5; for producer cooperatives, see 334.6*

.101–.105      Standard subdivisions

.106      Organizations, business enterprises

Notation 06 from Table 1 as modified under 380

[.106 8]      Management

Do not use; class in 658.87

.107–.109      Standard subdivisions

.11      †Shopping centers

.12      †Chain stores

Class chain stores with a specific merchandising pattern in 381.14

.13      †Franchise businesses

Class franchise businesses with a specific merchandising pattern in 381.14

.14      Retail channels by merchandising pattern

> *For factory outlets, see 381.15; for outdoor and street markets, see 381.18*

[.140 1–.140 9]      Standard subdivisions

Do not use; class in 381.101–381.109

.141      †Department stores

Class department stores that are discount stores in 381.149

---

*Add as instructed under 380
†Add as instructed under 380, except observe special instructions for management at 381.1

.142            †Teleshopping

                Class here catalog shopping, mail-order shopping, online shopping, telephone and television shopping; comprehensive works on electronic commerce

                *For online auctions, see 381.177*

[.142 028 5]            Computer applications

                Do not use; class in 381.142

.147            †Convenience stores

                Including forecourt sales

                Class convenience stores that are mainly grocery stores in 381.456413

.149            †Discount stores

                Including customer clubs, warehouse clubs, wholesale clubs

                Class here supermarkets that are not predominantly food stores, hypermarkets, superstores

                Class food retailing in supermarkets in 381.456413

.15            †Outlet stores

                Class here discount stores that are outlet stores, factory outlets, manufacturers' outlets, wholesale outlet stores

.17            †Auctions

[.170 285]            Computer applications

                Do not use; class in 381.177

.177            †Online auctions

.18            †Outdoor and street markets

                Class here street vending

                Subdivisions are added for either or both topics in heading

                *For outdoor and street markets for secondhand goods, see 381.19*

.186            †Street fairs

                *See also 381.457451 for antique fairs; also 381.45790132 for collectors' fairs*

.19            †Outlets for secondhand goods

                Including estate sales; charity, thrift shops

                Class outdoor and street markets selling both new and secondhand goods in 381.18. Class a specific kind of estate sale with the kind, e.g., estate yard sales 381.195

                *For auctions of second hand goods, see 381.17*

†Add as instructed under 380, except observe special instructions for management at 381.1

| | |
|---|---|
| .192 | †Flea markets |
| .195 | †Garage, rummage, and related sales |

> Sales held over a short time period of goods owned or contributed by individuals who no longer need them
>
> Standard subdivisions are added for any or all topics in heading
>
> Class here car boot, jumble, tag, white elephant, yard sales

**.2      Wholesale trade**

> Class wholesale trade through specific marketing channels in 381.1

.206         Organizations, business enterprises

> Notation 06 from Table 1 as modified below

.206 5        Business enterprises

> Including individual proprietorships, partnerships, companies, public and private corporations, combinations
>
> Add to 381.2065 notation 3–9 from Table 2, e.g., wholesale trade business enterprises of France 381.206544
>
> Class organizations whose members are business enterprises, e.g., trade associations, in 381.206
>
> *See Manual at 380: Add table: 09 vs. 065*

[.206 8]       Management

> Do not use for comprehensive works on management of wholesale trade; class in 658.86. Do not use for management of wholesale trade limited to or predominantly in a specific product or service; class with the product or service in 381.4 e.g., management of wholesale trade in food 381.4564130068

.209        History, geographic treatment, biography

> Class specific business enterprises in 381.2065
>
> *See Manual at 380: Add table: 09 vs. 065*

**.3      Commercial policy**

> Class here consumer problems and their alleviation, consumerism

.32        Consumer movements

> Class specific activities of consumer movements in 381.33–381.34

---

†Add as instructed under 380, except observe special instructions for management at 381.1

.33 Consumer information

Including consumer information aspects of product labeling; research, testing of products

Class here consumer education, comprehensive works on evaluation of products and services to be purchased, interdisciplinary evaluation and purchasing manuals

> *For evaluation and purchasing guides and consumer education for household and personal products and services, see 640.73. For evaluation and purchasing manuals for a specific product or service, see the product or service, plus notation 029 from Table 1, e.g., manual on evaluating passenger automobiles 629.222029*

.34 Consumer protection

Class product hazards in 363.19; class fraud in 364.163

.347 Better business bureaus

**.4 Specific products and services**

Class here works discussing consumption as a measure of the volume, value, or kind of trade in specific products; management of enterprises selling specific products and services

Class interdisciplinary works on consumption of specific products and services in 339.48

[.401–.409] Standard subdivisions

Do not use; class in 381.01–381.09

.41 *Products of agriculture

Class here farmers' markets, produce trade

[.410 29] Commercial miscellany

Do not use; class in 630.209

.413–.418 Specific products

Add to base number 381.41 the numbers following 63 in 633–638, e.g., rice 381.41318

.42 *Products of mineral industries

[.420 29] Commercial miscellany

Do not use; class in 553.029

.422–.429 Specific products

Add to base number 381.42 the numbers following 553 in 553.2–553.9, e.g., oil 381.42282

.43 *Products of other extractive industries

*Add as instructed under 380

| | | |
|---|---|---|
| [.430 29] | | Commercial miscellany |

Do not use; class in 639.029

.431       *Products of culture of invertebrates and cold-blooded vertebrates

Class products of insect culture in 381.418

[.431 029]       Commercial miscellany

Do not use; class in 639.029

.431 3–.431 7       Specific products

Add to base number 381.431 the numbers following 639 in 639.3–639.7, e.g., oysters 381.43141

.432–.439       Products of fishing, whaling, hunting, trapping

Add to base number 381.43 the numbers following 59 in 592–599, e.g., fur 381.4397, comprehensive works on products of both finfishing and shellfishing industries 381.437

.44       *Slave trade

Limited to works that emphasize economic aspects of slave trade

Class interdisciplinary works on slave trade in 306.362

.45       Products of secondary industries and services

Standard subdivisions are added for either or both topics in heading

.450 001–.450 009       Standard subdivisions

Notation from Table 1 as modified under 380, e.g., companies 381.4500065

.450 01–.459 99       Specific products and services

Add to base number 381.45 notation 001–999, e.g., clothing 381.45687; then add further as instructed under 380, e.g., clothing stores 381.45687065
Subdivisions are added for either or both topics in heading

*See Manual at 709.2 vs. 381.457092*

.456 413       *Food trade

Number built according to instructions under 381.45001–381.45999

Class here food retailing in supermarkets; grocery stores

Class supermarkets that are not predominantly food stores in 381.149

*For produce trade, see 381.41; for trade in commercially processed foods, see 381.45664. For trade in a specific food, see the food in 381.41–381.45, e.g., oysters 381.43141*

---

*Add as instructed under 380

**.5**      **\*Interregional and interstate commerce**

Commerce between parts of a single jurisdiction

Standard subdivisions are added for either or both topics in heading

# 382    \*International commerce (Foreign trade)

Class here trade between nations and their colonies, protectorates, trusts

Unless other instructions are given, observe the following table of preference, e.g., import trade in rice 382.41318 (*not* 382.5):

| | |
|---|---|
| Specific products and services | 382.4 |
| Tariff policy | 382.7 |
| Import and export trade | 382.5–382.6 |
| General topics of international commerce | 382.1 |
| Trade agreements | 382.9 |
| Commercial policy | 382.3 |

Class interdisciplinary works on international finance in 332.042; class interdisciplinary works on international economics in 337

### SUMMARY

| | |
|---|---|
| 382.01–.09 | **Standard subdivisions and business enterprises** |
| .1 | **General topics of international commerce** |
| .3 | **Commercial policy** |
| .4 | **Specific products and services** |
| .5 | **Import trade** |
| .6 | **Export trade** |
| .7 | **Tariff policy** |
| .9 | **Trade agreements** |

**.01**      Philosophy and theory

Do not use for theories of international commerce; class in 382.104

**.06**      Organizations and management; business enterprises

Notation 06 from Table 1 as modified under 380

Do not use for organizations associated with trade agreements; class in 382.9 e.g., World Trade Organization 382.92

**.09**      History, geographic treatment, biography

\*Add as instructed under 380

.091 International commerce of areas, regions, places in general

> Add to base number 382.091 the numbers following —1 in notation 11–19 from Table 2, e.g., international commerce of developing countries 382.091724; then, for commerce between an area, region, or place and another area, region, place or a continent, country, locality, add 0† and add notation 1–9 from Table 2, e.g., commerce between developing countries and United Kingdom 382.091724041
> > Do not follow add instructions under —091 in Table 1

> Give priority in notation to the region, area, place emphasized. If emphasis is equal, give priority to the one coming first in Table 2
> > (Option: Give priority in notation to the region, area, place requiring local emphasis, e.g., libraries in United States class trade between developing nations and United States in d382.097301724)

.093–.099 International commerce in specific continents, countries, localities

> Add to base number 382.09 notation 3–9 from Table 2, e.g., international commerce of United Kingdom 382.0941; then, for commerce between two continents, countries, localities or between a continent, country, locality and a region, area, place, add 0† and add notation 1–9 from Table 2, e.g., commerce between United Kingdom and communist bloc 382.094101717
> > Do not use add table under —093–099 in Table 1

> Give priority in notation to the continent, country, locality emphasized. If emphasis is equal, give priority to the one coming first in Table 2
> > (Option: Give priority in notation to the continent, country, locality requiring local emphasis, e.g., libraries in United States class trade between United Kingdom and United States in 382.0973041)

## .1 General topics of international commerce

.104 Theories

.104 2 Specialization and comparative advantage

> Standard subdivisions are added for either or both topics in heading

> Class comprehensive works on specialization and comparative advantage in 338.6046

.17 Balance of payments

> Class here balance of trade

## .3 Commercial policy

> Class economic imperialism in 337

## .4 Specific products and services

> Class here works discussing consumption as a measure of the volume, value, or kind of trade in specific products

> Class interdisciplinary works on consumption of specific products and services in 339.48

---

†Add 00 for standard subdivisions; see instructions at beginning of Table 1

[.401–.409]        Standard subdivisions

> Do not use; class in 382.01–382.09

.41–.45        Specific products and services

> Add to base number 382.4 the numbers following 381.4 in 381.41–381.45, e.g., foreign trade in products of agriculture 382.41, of rice 382.41318
> Subdivisions are added for either or both topics in heading

**.5        \*Import trade**

> Class here nontariff trade barriers

> Class the combined import and export trade of a country, the trade between two countries in 382.09; class agreements on nontariff trade barriers in 382.9

.52        Import quotas

.53        Embargoes on imports

.54        Licensing of imports

**.6        \*Export trade**

> Class the combined import and export trade of a country, the trade between two countries in 382.09

.609            History, geographic treatment, biography

> Do not use for the area to which goods are being exported; class in 382.6109

.61            Export trade by export market area

.610 9            History, geographic treatment, biography

> Class here the area to which goods are being exported

> Class the area doing the exporting in 382.609

.63            Export policy

> Including subsidies, export trade promotion

> *For export controls and restrictions, see 382.64*

.64            Export controls and restrictions

> Standard subdivisions are added for either or both topics in heading

> Including inspection, licensing

**.7        Tariff policy**

> Including drawbacks

> Class here interdisciplinary works on customs duties

> Class international agreements on tariffs in 382.9

> *For a specific aspect of customs duties, see the aspect, e.g., law 343.056*

\*Add as instructed under 380

| | |
|---|---|
| .71 | Free trade |

Class international free trade agreements in 382.9

| | |
|---|---|
| .72 | Revenue tariffs |
| .73 | Protectionism |

Class here protective and prohibitive tariffs, comprehensive works on trade barriers and restrictions

*For nontariff trade barriers, see 382.5; for single and multiple column tariffs, see 382.75*

| | |
|---|---|
| .75 | Single and multiple column tariffs |
| .752 | Single column tariffs |

Single rates for each product

| | |
|---|---|
| .753 | Multiple column tariffs |

Varying rates on the same product designed to favor certain countries of origin

Including generalized system of preference (GSP)

| | |
|---|---|
| .78 | Tariff exemptions (Duty-free importation) |

Including educational, scientific, tourist exemptions

## .9 Trade agreements

Class here agreements on nontariff trade barriers, on tariffs

Class general economic cooperation and international arrangements for this purpose in 337; class texts of treaties on tariffs in 343.0560261; class texts of treaties on international commerce in 343.0870261

| | |
|---|---|
| .906 | Organizations and management |

Do not use for organizations associated with multilateral agreements; class in 382.91–382.92. Do not use for organizations associated with bilateral agreements; class in 382.93–382.99

| | |
|---|---|
| .909 | History, geographic treatment, biography |

Do not use for multilateral agreements; class in 382.91. Do not use for bilateral agreements; class in 382.93–382.99

| | |
|---|---|
| .91 | Multilateral agreements |

Class here customs unions

Class bilateral agreements in 382.93–382.99; class interdisciplinary works on intergovernmental organizations in 341.2

*For World Trade Organization, see 382.92*

| | |
|---|---|
| [.910 91] | Area, regions, places in general |

Do not use; class in 382.911

| | |
|---|---|
| .910 93 | Multilateral agreements in ancient world [*formerly* 382.913] |

[.910 94–.910 99]          Specific continents, countries, localities in modern world

> Do not use; class in 382.914–382.919

.911          Multilateral agreements in areas, regions, places in general

> Add to base number 382.911 the numbers following —1 in notation 11–19 from Table 2, e.g., western bloc nations 382.911713

[.913]          Multilateral agreements in ancient world

> Relocated to 382.91093

---

> 382.914–382.919 Multilateral agreements in specific continents, countries, localities in modern world

> Class comprehensive works in 382.91

.914          Multilateral agreements in Europe

.914 2          European Union

> Class here European Common Market, European Community, European Economic Community

.914 3          European Free Trade Association (EFTA)

.914 7          Multilateral agreements in Eastern Europe

> Former heading: Council for Mutual Economic Assistance (COMECON)

.915–.919          Multilateral agreements in other continents and regions

> Add to base number 382.91 notation 5–9 from Table 2, e.g., southeast Asia 382.9159

.92          World Trade Organization (WTO)

> Class here General Agreement on Tariffs and Trade (GATT)

.93–.99          Trade agreements by specific countries

> Add to base number 382.9 notation 3–9 from Table 2, e.g., trade agreements of United Kingdom 382.941; then, for bilateral agreements, add 0† and again add notation 3–9 from Table 2, e.g., agreements between United Kingdom and France 382.941044
> Do not use add table under —093–099 in Table 1

> Give priority in notation to the country emphasized. If emphasis is equal, give priority to the one coming first in Table 2
> (Option: Give priority in notation to the country requiring local emphasis, e.g., libraries in United States class agreements between United Kingdom and United States in 382.973041)

---

†Add 00 for standard subdivisions; see instructions at beginning of Table 1

> ## 383–388 Communications and transportation

Class comprehensive works on communications in 384; class comprehensive works on communications and transportation together, on transportation alone in 388

Comprehensive works on the activities, services, and facilities of a system are classed in the number for the system, e.g., radio broadcasting activities, services, and facilities 384.54, not 384.544

## 383     Postal communication

Class comprehensive works on communications in 384

*See also 769.56 for philately*

| | |
|---|---|
| .06 | Organizations and management |

Do not use for postal organizations; class in 383.4

| | |
|---|---|
| [.09] | History, geographic treatment, biography |

Do not use; class in 383.49

**.1**     **Mail handling**

.12     Classes of mail

Class a specific mode of transportation for a specific class of mail in 383.141–383.144. Class a specific service for a specific class of mail with the service, e.g., special delivery of letters 383.183

.120 01–.120 09     Standard subdivisions

---

> 383.120 2–383.120 5   Special classes

Class comprehensive works in 383.12

.120 2     Free mail

Including franking privileges

.120 5     Nonmailable matter

Including obscene and subversive material

.122     Letters, postcards, sealed material

Class here first-class mail

.123     Newspapers and periodicals

Class here second-class mail

.124     Printed material

Not provided for elsewhere

Including books, catalogs, circulars; bulk mailings

Class here third-class mail

.125      Parcels

         Class here fourth-class mail

         Class printed matter in 383.124

.14      Transportation systems, collection, delivery

         Standard subdivisions are added for transportation systems, collection, delivery together; for transportation systems alone

>       383.141–383.144   Transportation systems

         Class comprehensive works in 383.14

.141      Facsimile transmission

.142      Sea mail

.143      Overland mail

         Including inland waterway, railroad mail; star routes

.144      Air mail

         Including mail carried through space

.145      Collection and delivery

         Including postal zones

         Class collection and delivery of mail within the military services in 355.69; class star routes in 383.143; class special delivery in 383.183

.145 5      Postal codes

         Class here zip code

.18      Other services

         Including express mail

.182      Insured and registered mail

         Standard subdivisions are added for either or both topics in heading

.183      Special delivery and special handling

         Standard subdivisions are added for either or both topics in heading

.184      Cash on delivery (Collect on delivery, COD)

.186      Dead letter services

**.2**      **Economic aspects of production**

         Class economic aspects of mail handling in 383.1

         *See also 330 for other economic aspects, e.g., postal workers' unions 331.8811383*

.23      Rates and costs

         Including use of postage stamps

| .24 | Efficiency of operation |
|---|---|

Including use of mechanization and automation

**.4          Postal organization**

[.409]          History, geographic treatment, biography

Do not use; class in 383.49

| .41 | International systems and conventions |
|---|---|
| .42 | Post offices |
| .46 | Internal services |

Including postal inspection

.49          History, geographic treatment, biography of postal communication, of postal organizations and systems

Add to base number 383.49 notation 1–9 from Table 2, e.g., postal communication in Europe 383.494

# 384      *Communications

Including recordings, visual signaling

Class here interdisciplinary works on telecommunication

Class sociology of communication in 302.2; class services designed to facilitate communication by people with disabilities in 362.40483; class services designed to facilitate communication by people in late adulthood in 362.63; class comprehensive works on communications and transportation in 388

*For postal communication, see 383. For a specific aspect of telecommunication, see the aspect, e.g., telecommunication engineering 621.382*

### SUMMARY

| 384.04 | Special topics of communications |
|---|---|
| .1 | Telegraphy |
| .3 | Computer communication |
| .5 | Wireless communication |
| .6 | Telephony |
| .8 | Motion pictures |

| .04 | Special topics of communications |
|---|---|
| .041 | Economic aspects of production |

Class economic aspects of facilities in 384.042; class economic aspects of activities and services in 384.043

*See also 330 for other economic aspects, e.g., telecommunication workers' unions 331.8811384*

*Add as instructed under 380

.042        Facilities

> Including stations
>
> Class use of facilities in specific activities and services in 384.043

.043        Activities and services

> Standard subdivisions are added for either or both topics in heading

---

>        **384.1–384.6 Telecommunication**
>
> Class comprehensive works in 384

.1        **\*Telegraphy**

> Class here submarine cable telegraphy
>
> *For radiotelegraphy, see 384.52*

.102 84        Materials

> Do not use for apparatus and equipment; class in 384.15

.13        Economic aspects of production

> Class economic aspects of activities and services in 384.14; class economic aspects of facilities in 384.15
>
> *See also 330 for other economic aspects, e.g., telegraphy workers' unions 331.88113841*

.14        **\*Activities and services**

> Including Morse and other code telegraphy, printing telegraphy; stock tickers, teletype, telex; comprehensive works on facsimile transmission
>
> Subdivisions are added for either or both topics in heading
>
> Class comprehensive works on electronic mail in 384.34
>
> *For postal facsimile transmission, see 383.141*

.15        Facilities

> Class use of facilities in specific activities and services in 384.14

.3        **\*Computer communication**

> Transfer of computer-based information by any of various media ( e.g., coaxial cable or radio waves) from one computer to another or between computers and terminals
>
> Class here computer communications networks, links between computers via telephone lines
>
> Class Internet telephony in 384.6; class interdisciplinary works on computer communications in 004.6
>
> *See Manual at 004.6 vs. 384.3*

---

\*Add as instructed under 380

.302 85       Computer applications

> Class here computer science applied to economic and related aspects of providing computer communication to the public

.31       Economic aspects of production

> Class economic aspects of production of computer communication hardware and software and comprehensive works on production and sale in 338.470046; class sale of computer communication hardware and software in 381.450046; class economic aspects of facilities in 384.32; class economic aspects of activities and services in 384.33

>> *See also 330 for other economic aspects, e.g., computer communication workers' unions 331.88113843*

.32       Facilities

> Class use of facilities in specific activities and services in 384.33

.33       Activities and services

> Standard subdivisions are added for either or both topics in heading

> Including services of value-added networks

>> *For electronic mail, see 384.34; for videotex, see 384.35*

>> *See Manual at 004.678 vs. 006.7, 025.042, 384.33*

.34       *Electronic mail

> Class here comprehensive works on electronic mail

> Class interdisciplinary works on electronic mail in 004.692

>> *For a specific kind of electronic mail, see the kind, e.g., postal facsimile transmission 383.141*

.35       *Videotex

**.5       *Wireless communication**

### SUMMARY

| | |
|---|---|
| 384.51 | Satellite communication |
| .52 | Radiotelegraphy |
| .53 | Radiotelephony |
| .54 | Radiobroadcasting |
| .55 | Television |

.51       *Satellite communication

>> *For a specific form of satellite communication, see the form, e.g., television transmission by satellite 384.552*

.52       *Radiotelegraphy

---

*Add as instructed under 380

.523–.525     Economic aspects, activities and services, facilities

> Add to base number 384.52 the numbers following 384.1 in 384.13–384.15, e.g., apparatus 384.525

.53     *Radiotelephony

> Including ship-to-shore communication, citizens band radio

> Class here portable telephones

.533–.535     Economic aspects, activities and services, facilities

> Add to base number 384.53 the numbers following 384.6 in 384.63–384.65, e.g., transmitting and receiving equipment 384.535

.54     *Radiobroadcasting

> Class here public broadcasting (noncommercial broadcasting), public aspects of amateur radio, interdisciplinary works on radiobroadcasting and television broadcasting

> *For television broadcasting, see 384.55*

> *See Manual at 384.54, 384.55, 384.8 vs. 791.4*

.540 65     Business enterprises

> Number built according to instructions under 380

> Including network affiliates, public (noncommercial) networks and stations

> Class here stations and networks

> *See Manual at 384.54, 384.55, 384.8 vs. 791.4*

.543     Economic aspects of production

> Class economic aspects of activities and services in 384.544; class economic aspects of facilities in 384.545

> *See also 330 for other economic aspects, e.g., radiobroadcasting workers' unions 331.881138454*

.544     *Activities and services

> Subdivisions are added for either or both topics in heading

.544 2     Scheduling

> Including sale of time

.544 3     Programs

> Class techniques of producing programs in 791.44. Class a specific type of program with the type, e.g., news broadcasts 070.43

.545     Facilities

> Class use of facilities in specific activities and services in 384.544

---

*Add as instructed under 380

| | |
|---|---|
| .545 2 | Broadcasting channels |

Class listings of stations by channel (assigned frequency) in 384.5453025

| | |
|---|---|
| .545 24 | Frequency allocation |
| .545 3 | Stations |

Including AM, FM stations

Class stations as business enterprises in 384.54065

| | |
|---|---|
| .545 5 | Networks |

Class networks as business enterprises in 384.54065

| | |
|---|---|
| .545 6 | Satellites |
| .55 | Television |

Including low power television (LPTV) stations (stations that rebroadcast the programs of full-service stations, originate programming that often includes pay television, and are usually limited in power to 10–1000 watts and a 10–mile to 15–mile broadcasting radius)

Unless other instructions are given, class a subject with aspects in two or more subdivisions of 384.55 in the number coming last, e.g., economic aspects of cable television and controlled transmission television 384.5561 (*not* 384.5551)

*See Manual at 384.54, 384.55, 384.8 vs. 791.4*

| | |
|---|---|
| .550 65 | Business enterprises |

Number built according to instructions under 380

Enterprises engaged in two or more aspects of television, e.g., pay television enterprises that produce video products

Including network affiliates; nonaffiliated commercial, private television

Class here stations and networks

*See Manual at 384.54, 384.55, 384.8 vs. 791.4*

| | |
|---|---|
| .551 | Economic aspects of production of television in general |

*See also 330 for other economic aspects, e.g., television workers' unions 331.881138455*

| | |
|---|---|
| .552 | Facilities and channels of television in general |

Class here direct broadcast satellite (DBS) systems, satellites, satellite dishes

| | |
|---|---|
| .552 1 | Broadcasting channels |

Including frequency allocation

| | |
|---|---|
| .552 2 | Stations |

Class stations as business enterprises in 384.55065

| | | |
|---|---|---|
| .552 3 | | Networks |
| | | Class networks as business enterprises in 384.55065 |
| .553 | | *Activities and services of television in general |
| | | Subdivisions are added for either or both topics in heading |
| .553 1 | | Scheduling |
| | | Including sale of time |
| .553 2 | | Programs |
| | | Class technique of producing programs in 791.45. Class a specific type of program with the type, e.g., news broadcasts 070.43 |
| .554 | | *General broadcasting (Free television) |
| | | Transmitting signals over the air for use by the general public |
| | | Including translator stations (low-power stations for transmitting the signals of television broadcast stations to areas where reception is unsatisfactory) |
| | | Class here public television (noncommercial television) |
| | | Class works combining both general broadcasting and cable television in 384.55 |
| .554 3 | | Economic aspects of production |
| | | *See also 330 for other economic aspects, e.g., public television workers' unions 331.8811384554* |
| .554 4 | | *Activities and services |
| | | Subdivisions are added for either or both topics in heading |
| .554 42 | | Scheduling |
| | | Including sale of time |
| .554 43 | | Programs |
| | | Including local programming |
| | | Class techniques of producing programs in 791.45. Class a specific type of program with the type, e.g., news broadcasts 070.43 |
| .554 5 | | Facilities and channels |
| | | Class here direct broadcast satellite (DBS) systems, satellites, satellite dishes |
| | | Class use of facilities and channels in specific activities and services in 384.5544 |
| .554 52 | | Broadcasting channels |
| .554 53 | | Stations |
| | | Class stations as business enterprises in 384.554065 |

*Add as instructed under 380

| | |
|---|---|
| .554 55 | Networks |

> Class networks as business enterprises in 384.554065

| | |
|---|---|
| .554 6 | *Community antenna television systems (CATV systems) |

> Systems that provide television reception to remote communities, using a tall antenna, usually limited to no more than 12 channels

| | |
|---|---|
| .554 61–.554 63 | Economic aspects, activities and services, facilities |

> Add to base number 384.5546 the numbers following 384.55 in 384.551–384.553, e.g., networks 384.554623

| | |
|---|---|
| .555 | *Pay television |

> Systems that receive and distribute signals to customers who pay for the service

> Class here cable television

> Class works combining general broadcasting and cable television in 384.55; class pay television in Canada in 384.5554; class use of cable television in closed-circuit television in 384.556

| | |
|---|---|
| .555 1–.555 3 | Economic aspects, facilities and channels, activities and services |

> Add to base number 384.555 the numbers following 384.55 in 384.551–384.553, e.g., networks 384.55523

| | |
|---|---|
| .555 4 | *Premium television (Subscription television) |

> Systems that scramble signals that are decoded for a fee

> Class here pay-cable, pay television in Canada

> *See also 384.55 for low power television (LPTV) stations*

| | |
|---|---|
| .555 41–.555 43 | Economic aspects, activities and services, facilities |

> Add to base number 384.5554 the numbers following 384.55 in 384.551–384.553, e.g., facilities 384.55542

| | |
|---|---|
| .556 | *Controlled transmission television (Closed-circuit television) |

> Systems where the signals are carried to a specific audience

> Including theater television

> Class here industrial uses, e.g., surveillance, monitoring of hazardous industrial processes

| | |
|---|---|
| .556 1–.556 3 | Economic aspects, activities and services, facilities |

> Add to base number 384.556 the numbers following 384.55 in 384.551–384.553, e.g., rates 384.5561

*Add as instructed under 380

| | |
|---|---|
| .558 | *Video production |

Including camcorders, video recorders, laser optical discs

Class video production associated with a specific aspect of television communication with the aspect, e.g., video production in cable television 384.555

### .6          *Telephony

Class here Internet telephony; comprehensive works on wire and cable communication

*For telegraphy, see 384.1; for radiotelephony, portable telephones, see 384.53; for cable television, see 384.555*

.602 5          Directories of persons and organizations

*See also 914–919, plus notation 0025 from table under 913–919, for telephone directories, e.g., New York City telephone directory 917.4710025*

.63          Economic aspects of production

Class economic aspects of activities and services in 384.64; class economic aspects of facilities in 384.65

*See also 330 for other economic aspects, e.g., telephone unions workers' 331.88113846*

.64          *Activities and services

Including caller ID telephone service; conference calls; emergency services; local, long-distance, overseas service

Subdivisions are added for either or both topics in heading

.646          *Audiotex

Including dial-a-message telephone calls

.65          Facilities

Including stations, lines, switchboards, dialing systems, transmitting and receiving equipment

Class use of facilities in specific activities and services in 384.64

### .8          *Motion pictures

*See Manual at 384.54, 384.55, 384.8 vs. 791.4*

.83–.85          Economic aspects, activities and services, facilities

Add to base number 384.8 the numbers following 384.1 in 384.13–384.15, e.g., activities 384.84

*Add as instructed under 380

## 385    *Railroad transportation

Class here standard-gage and broad-gage railways

Class comprehensive works on transportation, on ground transportation in 388

> *For local rail transit systems, see 388.42*

> *See Manual at 629.046 vs. 388*

.065        Business enterprises

Number built according to instructions under 380

Class here railroad companies

> *See also 385.5065 for narrow-gage and special-duty railroad companies; also 385.6065 for inclined and mountain railroad companies*

---

> **385.1–385.3 Specific aspects**

Class specific aspects of narrow-gage and special-duty railroads in 385.5; class specific aspects of inclined and mountain railroads in 385.6; class comprehensive works in 385

**.1**        **Economic aspects of production**

Class economic aspects of activities and services in 385.2; class economic aspects of facilities in 385.3

> *See also 330 for other economic aspects, e.g., railroad workers' unions 331.8811385*

**.2**        **Activities and services**

Standard subdivisions are added for either or both topics in heading

.204        Special topics of activities and services

.204 2        Basic activities

Including dispatching, routing, scheduling, traffic control

> *For operation of rolling stock, see 385.2044*

.204 4        Operation of rolling stock

---

> **385.22–385.24 Transportation activities and services**

Class comprehensive works in 385.2

.22        *Passenger services

Including baggage, meal, sleeper services

.23        *Express transportation of goods

---

*Add as instructed under 380

.24       *Freight services

         Class unitized cargo services in 385.72

          *For express transportation of goods, see 385.23*

.26       Activities and services of terminals and stations

         Standard subdivisions are added for either or both topics in heading

         Including fueling

.262      *Passenger services

         Including passenger amenities, reservation systems

.264      *Freight services

         Including freight handling, warehousing, storage

          *For railroad mail, see 383.143*

## .3       Facilities and vehicles

         Class use of facilities and vehicles in specific activities and services in 385.2

.31       Stationary facilities

.312      The way

         Including bridges, grade crossings, tracks, tunnels

         Class comprenensive works on tunnels in 388.13; class comprehensive works on bridges in 388.132

.314      Terminals and stations

         Including yards, roundhouses, train sheds, shop buildings

.316      Communications facilities

         Including signals

.32–.34    Cars

         Add to base number 385.3 the numbers following 625.2 in 625.22–625.24, e.g., dining cars 385.33

         Class comprehensive works in 385.37

.36       Locomotives

         Add to base number 385.36 the numbers following 625.26 in 625.261–625.266, e.g., steam locomotives 385.361

.37       Rolling stock

          *For cars, see 385.32–385.34; for locomotives, see 385.36; for rolling stock of local rail transit systems, see 388.42*

*Add as instructed under 380

**.5**      **\*Narrow-gage and special-purpose railroads**

> *For inclined and mountain railroads, see 385.6; for special-purpose railroads located entirely within a metropolitan region, see 388.42–388.46*

> Monorail systems relocated to 388.44; interurban railroads (streetcar lines running between urban areas or from urban to rural areas) relocated to 388.46

**.52**      **\*Narrow-gage railroads**

> Class narrow-gage industrial railroads in 385.54

**.54**      **\*Industrial railroads**

> Subdivisions are added for any purpose of the railroad, e.g., lumber railroads in Georgia 385.5409758, mine railroads in Colorado 385.5409788

**.6**      **\*Inclined and mountain railroad systems**

> Including cable, funicular, rack railroads

**.7**      **Railroad combined with other transportation systems**

**.72**      **\*Unitized cargo services**

> Including piggyback transportation (trucks, trailers, buses, private automobiles on flatcars)

> *For container-ship operations, see 387.5442*

**.77**      **\*Ship railroads**

> Rail transportation of vessels overland between bodies of water

# 386      **\*Inland waterway and ferry transportation**

> Subdivisions are added for inland waterway and ferry transportation together, for inland waterway transportation alone

> Class comprehensive works on water transportation in 387; class comprehensive works on transportation in 388

> *See Manual at 629.046 vs. 388*

**.1**      **Economic aspects of production**

> Class economic aspects of facilities in 386.2; class economic aspects of activities and services in 386.24; class economic aspects of specific kinds of inland water and ferry transportation in 386.3–386.6

> *See also 330 for other economic aspects, e.g., inland-waterway transportation workers' unions 331.8811386*

**.2**      **Activities, services, facilities, ships**

> Class activities and facilities (*except* for ships and ports) of specific types of inland water systems in 386.3–386.6; class activities, services, facilities of ports in 386.8

---

\*Add as instructed under 380

| | |
|---|---|
| .22 | Ships |

Including air-cushion vehicles

Add to base number 386.22 the numbers following 623.82 in 623.821–623.829, e.g., tugboats 386.2232

Class use of ships in specific activities and services in 386.24

| | |
|---|---|
| .24 | Activities and services |

Standard subdivisions are added for either or both topics in heading

| | |
|---|---|
| .240 4 | Special topics of activities and services |
| .240 42 | Basic activities |

Including dispatching, routing, scheduling, traffic control

*For operation of ships, see 386.24044*

| | |
|---|---|
| .240 44 | Operation of ships |
| .242 | *Passenger services |

Including baggage, meal, sleeper services

| | |
|---|---|
| .244 | *Freight services |

*For inland waterway mail, see 383.143*

---

> ### 386.3–386.6   Specific kinds of inland water and ferry transportation

Class here activities, services, facilities

Class ships for specific kinds of inland water transportation in 386.22; class ports for specific kinds of inland water transportation in 386.8; class comprehensive works in 386

---

> ### 386.3–386.5   Specific kinds of waters

Class ferry transportation on specific kinds of waters in 386.6; class comprehensive works in 386

| | |
|---|---|
| .3 | *River transportation |

Class here transportation by canalized rivers

Class combined river, lake, canal systems in 386.5

| | |
|---|---|
| .32 | The way |
| .35 | Activities and services |

Standard subdivisions are added for either or both topics in heading

| | |
|---|---|
| .350 4 | Special topics of activities and services |

*Add as instructed under 380

| | | |
|---|---|---|
| .350 42 | | Basic activities |

> Including dispatching, routing, scheduling, traffic control
>
> *For operation of ships, see 386.35044*

| | | |
|---|---|---|
| .350 44 | | Operation of ships |
| .352 | | *Passenger services |

> Including baggage, meal, sleeper services

| | | |
|---|---|---|
| .354 | | *Freight services |

> *For inland waterway mail, see 383.143*

**.4          *Canal transportation**

> Class canalized rivers in 386.3; class combined river, lake, canal systems in 386.5

| | |
|---|---|
| .404 | Special topics of canal transportation |
| .404 2 | Activities and services |

> Standard subdivisions are added for either or both topics in heading

| | |
|---|---|
| .404 204 | Special topics of activities and services |
| .404 204 2 | Basic activities |

> Including dispatching, routing, scheduling, traffic control
>
> *For operation of ships, see 386.4042044*

| | |
|---|---|
| .404 204 4 | Operation of ships |
| .404 22 | *Passenger services |

> Including baggage, meal, sleeper services

| | |
|---|---|
| .404 24 | *Freight services |

> *For inland waterway mail, see 383.143*

---

> 386.42–386.48  Specific canals and kinds of canals
>
> Existing and proposed
>
> Class comprehensive works in 386.4

| | |
|---|---|
| .42 | Interoceanic canals |

> *For canals connecting specific oceans, see 386.43–386.45*

---

> 386.43–386.45  Canals connecting specific oceans
>
> Class comprehensive works in 386.42

*Add as instructed under 380

.43      Canals connecting Indian and Atlantic Oceans

       Class here Suez Canal

.44      Canals connecting Atlantic and Pacific Oceans

       Class here Panama Canal

.445      Proposed Nicaragua Canal

.447      Proposed Tehuantepec Canal

.45      Canals connecting Pacific and Indian Oceans

.46      Noninteroceanic canals

       Including canals connecting parts of one ocean

       *For kinds of noninteroceanic canals, see 386.47–386.48*

---

>      386.47–386.48   Kinds of noninteroceanic canals

       Class here specific canals

       Class comprehensive works in 386.46

.47      *Ship canals

.48      *Small craft and barge canals

       Subdivisions are added for either or both topics in heading

**.5**      **\*Lake transportation**

       Class here transportation on combined river, lake, canal systems, e.g., Saint Lawrence Seaway 386.509714

.52      The way

.54      Activities and services

       Standard subdivisions are added for either or both topics in heading

.540 4      Special topics of activities and services

.540 42      Basic activities

       Including dispatching, routing, scheduling, traffic control

       *For operation of ships, see 386.54044*

.540 44      Operation of ships

.542      *Passenger services

       Including baggage, meal, sleeper services

.544      *Freight services

       *For inland waterway mail, see 383.143*

---

*Add as instructed under 380

.6 **\*Ferry transportation**

>    Oceanic and inland

.8 **\*Ports**

>    Class here ports on nontidal waters

.82–.86 Physiographic location, facilities, activities, services; free ports

>    Add to base number 386.8 the numbers following 387.1 in 387.12–387.16, e.g., freight terminals 386.853

# 387 Water, air, space transportation

> Class here comprehensive works on water transportation
>
> Class comprehensive works on transportation in 388
>
> *For inland waterway and ferry transportation, see 386*

## SUMMARY

| | |
|---|---|
| 387.01–.09 | **Standard subdivisions of water transportation** |
| .1 | **Ports** |
| .2 | **Ships** |
| .5 | **Ocean transportation (Marine transportation)** |
| .7 | **Air transportation** |
| .8 | **Space transportation** |

[.001–.009] Standard subdivisions of water transportation

>    Relocated to 387.01–387.09

.01–.09 Standard subdivisions of water transportation [*formerly* 387.001–387.009]

>    Notation from Table 1 as modified under 380, e.g., water transportation business enterprises 387.065; however, do not use for water, air, space transportation together; class in 388.01–388.09

.1 **Ports**

>    Class here ports on tidal waters
>
>    *For inland ports, see 386.8*

.12 Physiographic location of ports

>    Including ports on tidal rivers, roadsteads
>
>    Class facilities of specific types of ports in 387.15; class activities and services of specific types of ports in 387.16

.120 9 History, geographic treatment, biography

>    Class a specific port in 387.109

---

\*Add as instructed under 380

| .13 | Free ports |
| | Class facilities of free ports in 387.15; class activities and services of free ports in 387.16 |
| .130 9 | History, geographic treatment, biography |
| | Class a specific free port in 387.109 |
| .15 | Port facilities |
| | Including docks, marinas, piers, quays |
| | Class use of port facilities in specific activities and services in 387.16 |
| .152 | Passenger terminals |
| .153 | Freight terminals |
| .155 | Navigational aids |
| | Class here lighthouses |
| | Class piloting in 387.166 |
| .16 | Activities and services |
| | Standard subdivisions are added for either or both topics in heading |
| | Including port maintenance |
| .162 | *Passenger services |
| | Including booking services |
| .164 | *Freight services |
| | Including freight handling, warehousing, storage, connection with land transportation |
| .166 | Operational services |
| | Including piloting, ship-to-shore communication, towing, tug services |
| .168 | Auxiliary services |
| | Including fueling |

**.2** **Ships**

Including air-cushion vehicles

Class use of ships in inland waterway transportation in 386.22; class use of ships in specific activities and services in 387.54

*See Manual at 629.046 vs. 388*

.204      General types

Add to base number 387.204 the numbers following 623.820 in 623.8202–623.8205, e.g., sailing craft 387.2043

---

*Add as instructed under 380

| .21–.29 | Specific types |
|---|---|

> Add to base number 387.2 the numbers following 623.82 in 623.821–623.829, e.g., cargo ships 387.245

**.5** **\*Ocean transportation (Marine transportation)**

> *For seaports, see 387.1; for ships, see 387.2*
>
> *See Manual at 629.046 vs. 388*

| .51 | Economic aspects of production |
|---|---|

> Class economic aspects of ships in 387.2; class economic aspects of routes and kinds of routes in 387.52; class economic aspects of activities and services in 387.54; class economic aspects of facilities in 387.58
>
> *See also 330 for other economic aspects, e.g., ocean transportation workers' unions 331.88113875*

| .52 | Routes and kinds of routes |
|---|---|

> Class here specific routes
>
> Class activities and services on routes and kinds of routes in 387.54; class use of facilities on routes and kinds of routes in 387.58

| .522 | Intercoastal routes |
|---|---|
| .523 | Auxiliary, irregular, tramp routes |
| .524 | Coastwise routes |
| .54 | Activities and services |

> Standard subdivisions are added for either or both topics in heading
>
> Class activities and services of ports in 387.16

| .540 4 | Special topics of activities and services |
|---|---|
| .540 42 | Basic activities |

> Including dispatching, routing, scheduling, traffic control
>
> *For operation of ships, see 387.54044*

| .540 44 | Operation of ships |
|---|---|

> Including life and activities of marine personnel at sea

| .542 | \*Passenger services |
|---|---|

> Including baggage, meal, sleeper services

| .544 | \*Freight services |
|---|---|
| .544 2 | \*Container-ship operations |

> Class unitized cargo in 385.72; class carriage of specific kinds of cargo in container-ship operations in 387.5448

\*Add as instructed under 380

.544 8        Carriage of specific kinds of cargo

> Including dry cargo, fertilizer, petroleum
>
> *For sea mail, see 383.142*

.55        *Salvage

.58        Facilities

> Class facilities of ports in 387.15; class ships in 387.2; class use of facilities in specific activities and services in 387.54
>
> *For lighthouses, see 387.155*

## .7        *Air transportation

> *See Manual at 629.046 vs. 388*

.71        Economic aspects of production

> Class economic aspects of routes in 387.72; class economic aspects of facilities in 387.73; class economic aspects of activities and services in 387.74
>
> *See also 330 for other economic aspects, e.g., air transportation workers' unions 331.88113877*

.712        Rates and fares

.72        Routes

> Including helicopter routes to and from airports
>
> Class use of facilities on routes and kinds of routes in 387.73; class activities and services on routes in 387.74

.73        Aircraft and facilities

> Standard subdivisions are added for aircraft and facilities together, for aircraft alone

.732–.733        Specific types of aircraft

> Add to base number 387.73 the numbers following 629.133 in 629.1332–629.1333, e.g., helicopters 387.73352
>
> Class use of aircraft in specific activities and services in 387.74

.736        Airports

> Class here landing fields

.736 2        Facilities

> Including hangars, runways, terminal buildings; access to airports
>
> Class use of facilities in specific activities and services in 387.7364

*Add as instructed under 380

| | |
|---|---|
| .736 4 | Activities and services |

> Standard subdivisions are added for either or both topics in heading
>
> Including booking, fueling, passenger services

| | |
|---|---|
| .74 | Activities and services |

> Standard subdivisions are added for either or both topics in heading
>
> Class activities and services of airports and landing fields in 387.7364

| | |
|---|---|
| .740 4 | Special topics of activities and services |
| .740 42 | Basic activities |

> Including dispatching, routing, scheduling; airport noise and its alleviation
>
> *For operation of aircraft, see 387.74044*

| | |
|---|---|
| .740 426 | Air traffic control |

> *See Manual at 629.1366 vs. 387.740426*

| | |
|---|---|
| .740 44 | Operation of aircraft |

> Class here operating personnel, flight crews
>
> Class maintenance and maintenance personnel in 387.73

| | |
|---|---|
| .742 | *Passenger services |

> Including baggage, meal, sleeper services

| | |
|---|---|
| .742 2 | *Reservation systems |
| .742 8 | *Charter services |
| .744 | *Freight services |

> Including all-cargo plane services
>
> *For air mail, see 383.144*

| | |
|---|---|
| **.8** | ***Space transportation** |

> *See Manual at 629.046 vs. 388*

---

*Add as instructed under 380

# 388    *Transportation

Class here ground transportation, comprehensive works on communications and transportation, interdisciplinary works on transportation

Comprehensive works on the activities, services, and facilities of a system are classed in the number for the system, e.g., seaport activities, services, and facilities 387.1, not 387.15 nor 387.16

Class services designed to facilitate the use of transportation by people with disabilities in 362.40483; class services designed to facilitate the use of transportation by people in late adulthood in 362.63; class transportation of students in 371.872

*For transportation safety and safety measures, see 363.12; for transportation security, see 363.287; for postal transportation, see 383.14; for communications, see 384; for railroad transportation, see 385; for water, air, space transportation, see 387; for transportation technology, see 629.04*

*See also 385.7 for railroad combined with other transportation systems*

*See Manual at 629.046 vs. 388*

## SUMMARY

|  |  |
|---|---|
| 388.04 | **Special topics of transportation** |
| .1 | **Roads** |
| .3 | **Vehicular transportation** |
| .4 | **Local transportation** |
| .5 | **Pipeline transportation** |

.04      Special topics of transportation

Including facilities, vehicles

.041      Activities and services

Standard subdivisions are added for either or both topics in heading

Including routing, scheduling, dispatching, traffic control

Class specific kinds of services in 388.042–388.044

.042      *Passenger services

Including baggage, reservation, meal, sleeper services

Class here mass transportation

.044      *Freight services

Including handling, storage; comprehensive works on warehousing

Class unitized cargo services in 385.72

*For commerce aspects of warehousing, see 381*

.047      Comparative studies of kinds of transportation

Class a comparative study of a specific kind of transportation with the kind, e.g., comparative study of local transportation 388.4

*Add as instructed under 380

.049                    Economic aspects of transportation

Class economic aspects of activities and services in 388.041; class
economic aspects of passenger services in 388.042; class economic
aspects of freight services in 388.044

*See also 330 for other economic aspects, e.g., transportation workers'
unions 331.8811388*

**.1        *Roads**

Class here highways

*For highway services and use, see 388.31; for urban roads, see 388.411*

[.102 23]                   Maps, plans, diagrams

Do not use; class in 912

.11                     Economic aspects of production

Class economic aspects of kinds of roads in 388.12; class economic aspects
of special road features in 388.13. Class economic effects of roads on a
specific aspect of an economic activity with the activity, e.g., effect on
business location 338.6042

*See also 330 for other economic aspects, e.g., road transportation
workers' unions 331.88113881*

.112                    Costs

.114                    Finance

Including user charges, tolls

.12                     Kinds of roads

Including primary and secondary roads, bicycle paths, pedestrian paths

Class special features of kinds of roads in 388.13

*For access roads, see 388.13*

.122                    Expressways

Variant names: beltways, freeways, motorways, parkways, throughways,
tollways, turnpikes

.13                     Special road features

Including access roads, grade separations, intersections, interdisciplinary
works on tunnels

Class signs and signals for traffic control in 388.3122

*For railroad tunnels, see 385.312. For a specific aspect of tunnels, see
the aspect, e.g., tunnel engineering 624.193*

*Add as instructed under 380

| .132 | Bridges |
|---|---|

Class here interdisciplinary works on bridges

*For railroad bridges, see 385.312. For a specific aspect of bridges, see the aspect, e.g., bridge engineering 624.2*

| **.3** | ***Vehicular transportation** |
|---|---|

Class urban vehicular transportation in 388.41

| .31 | Traffic flow and maintenance |
|---|---|

| .312 | Highway services |
|---|---|

Including lighting, roadside park facilities, snow removal

*For traffic control by police, see 363.2332; for speed limits, see 388.3144*

| .312 2 | Traffic control through signs and signals |
|---|---|

Standard subdivisions are added for either or both topics in heading

| .312 4 | Driver information |
|---|---|

Information supplied en route

Including information on traffic patterns via commercial radio

| .314 | Highway use |
|---|---|

| .314 2 | Traffic volume |
|---|---|

Class peak hours in 388.3143

| .314 3 | Traffic patterns |
|---|---|

Including patterns by origin, by destination; peak hours; use by specific kinds of vehicles

| .314 4 | Speed limits |
|---|---|

| .32 | *Vehicular activities and services |
|---|---|

Subdivisions are added for either or both topics in heading

*See also 388.34 for vehicles*

*See Manual at 629.046 vs. 388*

| .321 | *Services of private passenger automobiles |
|---|---|

Including limousine services

| .322 | *Bus services |
|---|---|

Class here passenger services

Class services of terminals, stations, stops in 388.33

| .322 04 | Special topics of bus services |
|---|---|

---

*Add as instructed under 380

| | |
|---|---|
| .322 042 | Basic activities |

Including dispatching, routing, scheduling, traffic control

*For operation of vehicles, see 388.322044*

| | |
|---|---|
| .322 044 | Operation of vehicles |
| .322 1 | Routes |

Intercity and trunk

Class services offered on specific routes and kinds of routes in 388.3222

| | |
|---|---|
| .322 2 | Types of services |

Including charter, baggage, meal, small package and express services; tourism

| | |
|---|---|
| .322 8 | *Stagecoach services |

Class stagecoach routes in 388.3221

*For types of stagecoach services, see 388.3222*

| | |
|---|---|
| .324 | *Trucking services |

Class services of terminals in 388.33

| | |
|---|---|
| .324 04 | Special topics of trucking services |
| .324 042 | Basic activities |

Including dispatching, routing, scheduling, traffic control

*For operation of vehicles, see 388.324044*

| | |
|---|---|
| .324 044 | Operation of vehicles |
| .324 2 | Routes |

Including long-haul, line-haul, intercity routes

| | |
|---|---|
| .324 3 | Kinds of carriers |

Including common (for-hire), contract, private carriers

| | |
|---|---|
| .33 | Terminals, stations, stops |

Including activities, services, facilities (e.g., vehicle sheds, docks, booking facilities)

*Add as instructed under 380

.34             Vehicles

Including electric-powered vehicles, natural gas vehicles, snowmobiles, trolleybuses

Class here interdisciplinary works on land vehicles

Class use of vehicles in specific services, vehicle operation in 388.32

> *For railroad rolling stock, see 385.37; for air-cushion vehicles, see 388.35; for rolling stock of local rail transit systems, see 388.42. For a specific aspect of vehicles, see the aspect, e.g., engineering of motor land vehicles 629.2*

> *See Manual at 629.046 vs. 388*

.341            Carts, wagons, carriages, stagecoaches

Including rickshaws, animal-drawn omnibuses

Class here nonmotor land vehicles

Class cycles in 388.347

.342–.348       Gasoline-powered, oil-powered, human-powered vehicles

Add to base number 388.34 the numbers following 629.22 in 629.222–629.228, e.g., buses 388.34233, bicycles 388.3472

> *For rickshaws, see 388.341*

.35             Air-cushion vehicles

Class here comprehensive works on air-cushion vehicles

> *For air-cushion ships for inland waterways, see 386.22; for air-cushion ships for ocean transportation, see 387.2*

**.4          *Local transportation**

Class here urban and suburban transportation, rapid transit, mass transit, commuter services

.404            Special topics of local transportation

.404 2             Economic aspects of production

> *See also 330 for other economic aspects, e.g., local transportation workers' unions 331.88113884*

---

> 388.41–388.46  Specific kinds of local transportation

Class terminals and parking facilities for specific kinds of transportation in 388.47; class comprehensive works in 388.4

> *See Manual at 629.046 vs. 388*

*Add as instructed under 380

.41        Vehicular and pedestrian traffic

> Including moving sidewalks
>
> Class vehicles in 388.34–388.35

.411        Urban roads

> Including parkways, expressways, arterial and side streets, sidewalks, bicycle paths (bikeways); intersections, traffic circles (roundabouts)
>
> Class here streets
>
> Class operation, services, use of urban roads in 388.4131

.413        Activities and services

> Standard subdivisions are added for either or both topics in heading

.413 1        Traffic flow and maintenance

> Add to base number 388.4131 the numbers following 388.31 in 388.312–388.314, e.g., peak hours 388.413143

.413 2        Vehicular services

.413 21        *Services by private passenger automobiles

.413 212        *Car and van pools

> Class here ridesharing
>
> Subdivisions are added for either or both topics in heading

.413 214        *Taxicabs and limousines

.413 22        *Bus services

> Including animal-drawn omnibuses
>
> *For guided-way systems, see 388.42*

.413 223        *Trolleybus services

.413 24        *Trucking services

.42        *Local rail transit systems

> Including monorail systems [*formerly* 385.5], guided-way systems
>
> Class here elevated rail transit systems [*formerly* 388.44], local surface rail systems using conventional (heavy) rail technology [*formerly* 388.46]; rolling stock; underground systems; comprehensive works on local rail transit systems with multiple transit modes
>
> Class rail terminals and stations in 388.472
>
> *For light rail transit systems, see 388.46*
>
> *See also 388.34 for trolleybuses; also 388.413223 for trolleybus services*

*Add as instructed under 380

| [.428] | Underground systems (Subway systems) |
|---|---|

Number discontinued; class in 388.42

| .44 | *Elevated rail transit systems |
|---|---|

Relocated to 388.42

| .46 | *Light rail transit systems |
|---|---|

Class here interurban railroads (streetcar lines running between urban areas or from urban to rural areas) [*formerly* 385.5]; streetcar systems, tramways, trolley-car systems

Local surface rail systems using conventional (heavy) rail technology relocated to 388.42

| .47 | Terminals, stations, parking facilities |
|---|---|
| .472 | Rail terminals and stations |
| .473 | Truck and bus stations and terminals |

Including bus stops

| .474 | Parking facilities |
|---|---|

Including on-street and off-street parking facilities, facilities located above and below street level

Class here interdisciplinary works on parking

> For a specific aspect of parking, see the aspect, e.g., city planning 711.73

| **.5** | **\*Pipeline transportation** |
|---|---|
| .55 | *Oil (Petroleum) |
| .56 | *Natural gas |
| .57 | *Coal |

Class here coal slurry

# 389        Metrology and standardization

| **.1** | **Metrology** |
|---|---|

Class interdisciplinary works on measurement in 530.8

| .15 | Systems of measurement |
|---|---|

Including metric system (système international, SI), imperial (British) system

Class adoption of metric system in 389.16; class mathematical tables of conversion from one system to another in 530.81

*Add as instructed under 380

.16          Adoption of metric system (système international, SI)

> *See also 658.4062 for management measures for coping with conversion to metric system*

.17          Time systems and standards

> Including conversion tables; daylight saving, standard, universal time; time zones

> Class interdisciplinary works on chronology in 529

**.6          Standardization**

> Class here interdisciplinary collections of standards [*formerly* 602.18], interdisciplinary works on standards

> *For law of standardization and standards, see 343.076; for public administration aspects of standardization and standards, see 352.83; for production management aspects of standardization and standards, see 658.562. For standardization and standards of a specific topic, see the topic, plus notation 0218 from Table 1, e.g., technical standards 602.18*

.62          Standardization of quantity and size

> Class here standardization for interchangeability

.63          Standardization of quality

> Class here performance standards

# 390          Customs, etiquette, folklore

> Standard subdivisions are added for customs, etiquette, folklore together; for customs alone

> Class here folkways; interdisciplinary works on ceremonies, on rites

> *For customs of military life, see 355.1. For a type of ceremony or rite not provided for here, see the type, e.g., religious rites 203.8, military ceremonies 355.17*

### SUMMARY

|  |  |
|---|---|
| 390.01–.09 | **Standard subdivisions of customs, etiquette, folklore together; standard subdivisions of customs** |
| .1–.4 | **Customs of specific economic, social, occupational classes** |
| 391 | **Costume and personal appearance** |
| 392 | **Customs of life cycle and domestic life** |
| 393 | **Death customs** |
| 394 | **General customs** |
| 395 | **Etiquette (Manners)** |
| 398 | **Folklore** |
| 399 | **Customs of war and diplomacy** |

.01–.07          Standard subdivisions

.08          Groups of people

.086          People by miscellaneous social attributes

[.086 2]   People by social and economic levels

> Do not use for people by economic status; class in 390.1. Do not use for people by social class; class in 390.2

.088   Religious groups

> Do not use for occupational groups; class in 390.4

.09   History, geographic treatment, biography

---

> **390.1–390.4 Customs of specific economic, social, occupational classes**

> Class comprehensive works in 390

.1   **Customs of people by economic status**

> Class customs of slaves and serfs in 390.25

.2   **Customs of people by social class**

.22   Customs of royalty

.23   Customs of nobility

.24   Customs of common people

> Class customs of common people of specific economic statuses in 390.1; class customs of specific occupations in 390.4

.25   Customs of slaves and serfs

.4   **Customs of people by occupation**

> Add to base number 390.4 notation 001–999, e.g., customs of lawyers 390.434; however, for customs of military personnel, see 355.1; for customs of diplomats, see 399

---

> **391–394 Customs**

> Class comprehensive works in 390

> *For customs of specific economic, social, occupational classes, see 390.1–390.4; for customs of war and diplomacy, see 399*

# 391   Costume and personal appearance

Standard subdivisions are added for costume and personal appearance together, for costume alone

Class here interdisciplinary works on costume, clothing (apparel, garments), fashion; casual wear (sportswear)

Class costume and clothing associated with a specific occasion with the occasion in 392–394, e.g., wedding clothes 392.54

*For fashion design, see 746.92. For a specific aspect of costume and clothing, see the aspect, e.g., stage costuming 792.026, clothing construction 646.4*

*See Manual at 391 vs. 646.3, 746.92*

| | |
|---|---|
| .001–.007 | Standard subdivisions |
| .008 | Groups of people |
| .008 1 | People by gender or sex |
| [.008 11] | Men |

> Do not use; class in 391.1

| | |
|---|---|
| [.008 2] | Women |

> Do not use; class in 391.2

| | |
|---|---|
| .008 3 | Young people |

> Do not use for children under twelve; class in 391.3

| | |
|---|---|
| .008 4 | People in specific stages of adulthood |

> Do not use for clothing for men in specific stages of adulthood; class in 391.1. Do not use for clothing for women in specific stages of adulthood; class in 391.2

| | |
|---|---|
| .008 6 | People by miscellaneous social attributes |
| [.008 62] | People by social and economic levels |

> Do not use for people by economic status; class in 391.01. Do not use for people by social class; class in 391.02

| | |
|---|---|
| .008 8 | Religious groups |

> Do not use for occupational groups; class in 391.04

| | |
|---|---|
| .009 | History, geographic treatment, biography |
| .01–.04 | Costume of economic, social, occupational groups |

> Add to base number 391.0 the numbers following 390 in 390.1–390.4, e.g., costume of royalty 391.022; however, for military costume, see 355.14; for costume of diplomats, see 399

---

> ### 391.1–391.3 Costume of men, women, children

> Class costume for men, women, children by specific economic, social, occupational groups in 391.01–391.04; class kinds of garments for men, women, children in 391.4; class accessories for men, women, children in 391.44; class comprehensive works in 391

> Outerwear for men, women, children relocated to 391.46; specific kinds of garments for men, women, children relocated to 391.47; garments for special purposes for men, women, children relocated to 391.48

| | |
|---|---|
| **.1** | **Costume of men** |
| **.2** | **Costume of women** |
| **.3** | **Costume of children** |
| **.4** | **Kinds of garments; accessories; buttons** |

> Class comprehensive works on garments in 391

| | |
|---|---|
| [.401–.409] | Standard subdivisions |

> Do not use; class in 391.001–391.009

| | |
|---|---|
| .41 | Gloves, mittens, footwear, neckwear |

> Including scarves, ties

> Muffs relocated to 391.44

| | |
|---|---|
| .412 | Gloves and mittens |

> Standard subdivisions are added for either or both topics in heading

| | |
|---|---|
| .413 | Footwear |

> Class here shoes and boots

> Hosiery relocated to 391.423

| | |
|---|---|
| .42 | Undergarments, hosiery, sleepwear, loungewear |
| .423 | Hosiery [*formerly* 391.413] and undergarments |

> Standard subdivisions are added for undergarments and hosiery together, for undergarments alone

> > *See also 391.473 for vests (waistcoats); also 391.476 for pants (trousers)*

| | |
|---|---|
| .426 | Sleepwear and loungewear |

> Variant name for sleepwear: nightclothes

> Standard subdivisions are added for either or both topics in heading

| | |
|---|---|
| .43 | Headwear |

> Including headscarves, helmets, protective headwear

> Class here bonnets, caps, hats

| | |
|---|---|
| .434 | Masks |
| .44 | Accessories |

> Including muffs [*formerly* 391.41], canes, combs, eyeglasses, fans, flowers, handbags, parasols

> > *For gloves, mittens, footwear, neckwear, see 391.41; for headwear, see 391.43; for jewelry, see 391.7*

| | |
|---|---|
| .45 | Buttons |
| .46 | Outerwear |

> Including capes, cloaks, stoles, sweaters

> Class here outerwear for men, women, children [*all formerly* 391.1–391.3]; overcoats, topcoats, raincoats; comprehensive works on coats and jackets

> Class garments for specific purposes in 391.48

> > *For suit jackets, sport coats, see 391.473*

| .47 | Specific kinds of garments |
|---|---|

Not provided for elsewhere

Class here specific kinds of garments for men, women, children [*all formerly* 391.1–391.3]

Class garments for specific purposes in 391.48

| .472 | Dresses |
|---|---|

| .473 | Suits |
|---|---|

Class here jackets, sport coats, vests (waistcoats)

Class skirts in 391.477; class outerwear, comprehensive works on coats and jackets in 391.46

*For pants (trousers), see 391.476*

*See also 391.423 for vests (undergarments)*

| .475 | Shirts, blouses, tops |
|---|---|

Standard subdivisions are added for any or all topics in heading

| .476 | Pants (Trousers) |
|---|---|

*See also 391.423 for pants (undergarments)*

| .477 | Skirts |
|---|---|

| .48 | Garments for special purposes |
|---|---|

Including activewear (clothing for athletic and outdoor sports), costumes, maternity garments

Class here garments for special purposes for men, women, children [*all formerly* 391.1–391.3]

Class headwear for special purposes in 391.43; class accessories for special purposes in 391.44

*For sleepwear and loungewear, see 391.426; for wedding clothes, see 392.54*

*See also 391 for casual wear (sportswear)*

| .486 | Evening and formal dress |
|---|---|

Standard subdivisions are added for either or both topics in heading

| **.5** | **Hairstyles** |
|---|---|

Including beards, wigs

| **.6** | **Personal appearance** |
|---|---|

*For hairstyles, see 391.5*

| .62 | Body contours |
|---|---|

| .63 | Use of cosmetics and perfume |
|---|---|

| .64 | Personal cleanliness and hygiene |
|---|---|

Including bathing

| .65 | Tattooing and scarification |
|---|---|

Standard subdivisions are added for tattooing and scarification together, for tattooing alone

*See also 391.7 for body piercing*

**.7** **Jewelry**

Including body piercing

Class here interdisciplinary works on jewelry

*For jewelry making, see 739.27*

| .72 | Finger rings |
|---|---|

**392** **Customs of life cycle and domestic life**

*For death customs, see 393*

**.1** **Customs of birth, puberty, majority**

| .12 | Birth customs |
|---|---|

Including baptism, couvade, infanticide, name giving

| .13 | Child-rearing customs |
|---|---|
| .14 | Customs relating to attainment of puberty |

Including initiation rites

| .15 | Customs relating to attainment of majority |
|---|---|

Including debuts

**.3** **Customs relating to dwelling places and domestic arts**

| .36 | Dwelling places |
|---|---|

Class here furnishings, heating, lighting, sanitation

| .37 | Cooking |
|---|---|

Class comprehensive works on food and meals in 394.12

**.4** **Courtship and engagement customs**

Standard subdivisions are added for courtship and engagement customs together, for courtship customs alone

Including bride purchase, bundling, infant betrothal, matchmaking

**.5** **Wedding and marriage customs**

Standard subdivisions are added for either or both topics in heading

*See also 395.22 for etiquette of weddings*

| .54 | Wedding clothes |
|---|---|

**.6**          **Customs of sexual relations**

Including chaperonage

*For courtship and engagement customs, see 392.4; for wedding and marriage customs, see 392.5*

**393          Death customs**

Customs relating to disposal of the dead and to mourning

**.1**          **Burial**

Including entombment

**.2**          **Cremation**

**.3**          **Embalming**

**.4**          **Exposure**

**.9**          **Mourning**

Including wakes

.93          Funerals

.930 954                    India and neighboring south Asian countries

Including sati

**394          General customs**

Including kissing, swearing

Class etiquette in 395

**SUMMARY**

| | |
|---|---|
| 394.1 | **Eating, drinking; using drugs** |
| .2 | **Special occasions** |
| .3 | **Recreational customs** |
| .4 | **Official ceremonies and observances** |
| .5 | **Pageants, processions, parades** |
| .6 | **Fairs** |
| .7 | **Customs of chivalry** |
| .8 | **Dueling and suicide** |
| .9 | **Cannibalism** |

**.1**          **Eating, drinking; using drugs**

Situations and methods of use, prohibited uses

.12          Eating and drinking

Class here food

Class table manners in 395.54

*For cooking, see 392.37; for drinking of alcoholic beverages, see 394.13; for customs of tea, see 394.15; for food taboos, see 394.16*

.125          Meals

| .125 2 | First meal of the day [*formerly* 394.15] |
|---|---|

Class here breakfasts, brunches

| .125 3 | Light meals [*formerly* 394.15] |
|---|---|

Class here snacks; dinners, lunches, suppers, teas as light meals

Class breakfasts, brunches in 394.1252; class dinners, lunches, suppers, teas as main meals in 394.1254

*See also 394.15 for Japanese tea ceremony*

| .125 4 | Main meal of the day [*formerly* 394.15] |
|---|---|

Class here dinners; lunches, suppers, teas as main meals

Class breakfasts, brunches in 394.1252; class dinners, lunches, suppers, teas as light meals in 394.1253

| .13 | Drinking of alcoholic beverages |
|---|---|
| .14 | Use of drugs |

Including marijuana, narcotics, tobacco

*For alcoholic beverages, see 394.13*

| .15 | Customs of tea |
|---|---|

Class here tea ceremonies

*See also 394.1253 for teas as a light meal*

First meal of the day relocated to 394.1252; light meals relocated to 394.1253; main meal of the day relocated to 394.1254

| .16 | Food taboos |
|---|---|
| **.2** | **Special occasions** |

Including anniversaries, birthdays, celebrations, fast days

Class official ceremonies in 394.4; class pageants, processions, parades in 394.5

| .25 | Carnival |
|---|---|

Pre-Lenten festival

Class here Mardi Gras; festivals of pre-Lenten origin

*See also 394.26 for carnivals other than pre-Lenten festivals*

| .26 | Holidays |
|---|---|

Class here carnivals other than pre-Lenten festivals, festivals; independence days; patriotic, seasonal, secular holidays

Class a season associated with a holiday with the holiday, e.g., the Christmas season 394.2663; class a technology or craft associated with holidays with the technology or craft, e.g., making fireworks 662.1, decorating Easter eggs 745.5944

*For Carnival, Mardi Gras, see 394.25*

[.260 9]        History, geographic treatment, biography

Do not use; class in 394.269

---

>       394.261–394.264  Secular holidays

Class here patriotic holidays, seasonal holidays

Class religious holidays of a specific season in 394.265; class comprehensive works in 394.26

.261        Holidays of December, January, February

Class here wintertime holidays of the northern hemisphere, summertime holidays of the southern hemisphere

.261 2        Kwanzaa

.261 4        New Year

.261 8        Valentine's Day

.262        Holidays of March, April, May

Class here springtime holidays of the northern hemisphere, autumn holidays of the southern hemisphere

.262 7        May Day

Class here May Day as a springtime festival, as a labor holiday'

.262 8        Mother's Day

Class here Mothering Sunday

.263        Holidays of June, July, August

Class here summertime holidays of the northern hemisphere, wintertime holidays of the southern hemisphere

.263 4        Fourth of July

.263 5        Bastille Day

.264        Holidays of September, October, November

Class here autumn holidays of the northern hemisphere, springtime holidays of the southern hemisphere

.264 4        Oktoberfest

.264 6        Halloween

.264 9        Thanksgiving

.265          Religious holidays

              Add to base number 394.265 the numbers following 29 in 292–299 for
              the religion only, e.g., Hindu holidays 394.26545; however, for Jewish
              holidays, see 394.267

              Class secular holidays with a religious or quasi-religious origin in
              394.261–394.264

              *For Christian holidays, see 394.266*

              *See Manual at 203.6, 263.9, 292–299 vs. 394.265–394.267*

.266          Christian holidays

              Holidays of the church year

              *For pre-Lenten festivals, see 394.25*

.266 3        Christmas

.266 7        Easter

.267          Jewish holidays

.269          History, geographic treatment, biography

              Class history, geographic treatment, biography of specific holidays and
              of specific kinds of holidays in 394.261–394.267

.269 01–.269 05    Historical periods

              Add to base number 394.2690 the numbers following —090 in
              notation 0901–0905 from Table 1, e.g., holidays in 20th century
              394.26904

.269 1–.269 9     Geographical treatment, biography

              Add to base number 394.269 notation 1–9 from Table 2, e.g., holidays
              of Mexico 394.26972

**.3**        **Recreational customs**

              Including dances, gambling, games, toys

**.4**        **Official ceremonies and observances**

              Including coronations, inaugurations, jubilees, state visits, triumphs

              *For military ceremonies, see 355.17*

**.5**        **Pageants, processions, parades**

              Class planning, promoting, staging of pageants, processions, parades in 791.6.
              Class pageants, processions, parades associated with a specific activity with the
              activity, e.g., Thanksgiving Day parades 394.2649

**.6**        **Fairs**

**.7**        **Customs of chivalry**

| | |
|---|---|
| **.8** | **Dueling and suicide** |

> Standard subdivisions are added for dueling and suicide together, for dueling alone

| | |
|---|---|
| .88 | Suicide |
| **.9** | **Cannibalism** |

# 395 Etiquette (Manners)

Prescriptive and practical works on social behavior

Unless other instructions are given, class a subject with aspects in two or more subdivisions of 395 in the number coming last, e.g., table manners for children 395.54 (*not* 395.122)

Class customs in 391–394

> *For protocol of diplomacy, see 327.2*

| | |
|---|---|
| [.081–.084] | People by gender or sex; age groups |

> Do not use; class in 395.1

| | |
|---|---|
| **.1** | **Etiquette for people by gender or sex; for age groups** |
| .12 | Etiquette for age groups |
| .122 | Children |

> From birth through age eleven

| | |
|---|---|
| .123 | Young people twelve to twenty |

> Variant names: adolescents, teenagers, young adults, youth
>
> People in early adulthood, comprehensive works on young adults relocated to 395.124

| | |
|---|---|
| .123 2 | Males twelve to twenty |
| .123 3 | Females twelve to twenty |
| .124 | People in early adulthood [*formerly* 395.123] |

> Class here comprehensive works on young adults [*formerly* 395.123]
>
> *For young adults under twenty-one, see 395.123*

| | |
|---|---|
| .124 1 | Young men |
| .124 2 | Young women |
| .126 | Adults aged sixty-five and over |
| .14 | Etiquette for people by gender or sex |

> Class etiquette for age groups regardless of gender or sex in 395.12

| | |
|---|---|
| .142 | Male |
| .144 | Female |
| **.2** | **Etiquette for stages in life cycle** |

.22       Engagements and weddings

.23       Funerals

.24       Occasions associated with birth, puberty, majority

> Including christening, confirmation, bar mitzvah, debut

**.3       Etiquette for social occasions**

> Including dances
>
> Class here hospitality and entertainment
>
> Class etiquette for stages in life cycle in 395.2; class invitations in 395.4

**.4       Social correspondence**

> Including invitations and announcements
>
> Class here written and spoken styles and forms of address and greeting

**.5       Etiquette by situations**

> Including online, school, sports etiquette

.52       Business and office etiquette

.53       Public behavior

> Including etiquette in church, at theater, in stores and shops

.54       Table manners

.59       Conversation

> Class here telephone etiquette

## [396]       [Unassigned]

> Most recently used in Edition 16

## [397]       [Unassigned]

> Most recently used in Edition 16

## 398       Folklore

> *See also 201.3 for religious mythology; also 800 for belles-lettres by identifiable authors, anonymous literary classics*

### SUMMARY

| | |
|---|---|
| 398.09 | **History, geographic treatment, biography of folklore** |
| .2 | **Folk literature** |
| .3 | **Real phenomena as subjects of folklore** |
| .4 | **Paranatural and legendary phenomena as subjects of folklore** |
| .6 | **Riddles** |
| .7 | **Jokes and jests** |
| .8 | **Rhymes and rhyming games** |
| .9 | **Proverbs** |

.09       History, geographic treatment, biography of folklore

> *For history, geographic treatment, biography of folk literature, see 398.209*

**.2**       **Folk literature**

Folklore as literature

Standard subdivisions may be added to subdivisions of this number for any topic even if the subject of the work does not approximate the whole, e.g., 18th century folktales about elves 398.2109033

Class here fairy tales, literary appraisal and criticism of folk literature; interdisciplinary works on mythology

Class an anonymous classic or a work by a known author with the classic or work in 800, e.g., Icelandic sagas 839.63, fairy tales by Hans Christian Andersen 839.8136

> *For religious mythology, see 201.3; for riddles, see 398.6; for rhymes and rhyming games, see 398.8; for proverbs, see 398.9; for folk poetry other than rhymes and rhyming games, see 808.81; for folk drama, see 808.82*

> *See Manual at 398.2; also at 398.2 vs. 201.3, 230, 270, 292–299; also at 398.2 vs. 398.3–398.4; also at 800 vs. 398.2*

Jokes and jests relocated to 398.7

.204       Folk literature by language

> Add to base number 398.204 notation 1–9 from Table 6, e.g., folk tales from French-speaking areas of the world 398.20441; however, for tales of a specific language from an area where that language predominates, see the area in 398.209, e.g., French folk tales from France 398.20944, from Quebec 398.209714

.208       Groups of people

.208 9       Ethnic and national groups

> Class here individual tales, collections of tales, lore on a specific topic

> Class collections of tales or lore by ethnic and national groups from a specific continent, country, locality where they predominate with the continent, country, locality in 398.2093–398.2099, e.g., French tales and lore from France 398.20944, from Quebec 398.209714; class individual tales, collections of tales, lore on a specific topic by ethnic and national groups from a specific continent, country, locality where they predominate with the continent, country, locality in 398.2093–398.2099, plus the notation for the topic from table under 398.2093–398.2099, e.g., French tales and lore from France about witches 398.2094401, from Quebec about witches 398.20971401

.209       History, geographic treatment, biography

.209 3–.209 9       Specific continents, countries, localities

Class here individual tales, collections of tales, lore on a specific topic from a specific continent, country, locality; collections of tales and lore from a specific continent, country, locality; works consisting equally of the tales and lore and criticism of them

Unless other instructions are given in the add table below, observe the following table of preference, e.g., periodicals of statistics 0021 (*not* 005):

| | |
|---|---|
| Tales and lore on a specific topic | 01–08 |
| Forecasting and forecasts | 001 |
| Museums, collections, exhibits | 0074 |
| Collecting folk literature | 0075 |
| Illustrations | 0022 |
| Statistics | 0021 |
| Serial publications | 005 |

Add to base number 398.209 notation 3–9 from Table 2, e.g., folk literature of France 398.20944; then add further as follows (*not* as instructed under notation 093–099 from Table 1):

| | |
|---|---|
| 001 | Forecasting and forecasts |
| 002 | Statistics and illustrations |
| 0021 |     Statistics |
| 0022 |     Illustrations |
| |         Including cartoons, drawings, pictures, pictorial charts and designs, sketches; graphs; maps, plans, diagrams |
| |         Class statistical drafts in 0021; class humorous cartoons in 398.2093–398.2099 without adding from this table |
| 005 | Serial publications |
| |     Regardless of form (print or electronic) or frequency |
| |     Class here house organs, magazines, newspapers, yearbooks |
| 007 | Museums, collections, exhibits; collecting objects |
| 0074 |     Museums, collections, exhibits |
| |     Class here exhibitions, fairs, festivals; catalogs, lists regardless of whether or not articles are offered for sale; guidebooks, history and description |
| |     Add to base number 0074 notation 4–9 from Table 2, e.g., museums in Germany 007443 |
| 0075 |     Collecting folk literature |
| |     Class here collectibles, memorabilia, price trends for collectors |

(continued)

| | | |
|---|---|---|
| .209 3–.209 9 | | Specific continents, countries, localities (continued) |

> **01–08**    Tales and lore on a specific topic
> Class here literary criticism
> Add to base number the numbers following 398.2 in 398.21–398.28, e.g., animal tales 045
> Class comprehensive works in the base number for the specific continent, country, locality in 398.2093–398.2099. Class comprehensive works on history and criticism of a specific topic with the topic in 398.3–398.4, e.g., history and criticism of tales and lore about witches 398.45
> *See Manual at 398.2 vs. 398.3–398.4*

> **09**    History and geographic treatment
> Class here literary criticism

> **09005**    Serial publications

> **0901–0905**    Historical periods
> Class here literary criticism
> Add to base number 090 the numbers following —090 in notation 0901–0905 from Table 1, e.g., folk literature of Middle Ages 0902

> **091**    Areas, regions, places in general
> Add to base number 091 the numbers following —1 in notation 11–19 from Table 2, e.g., folk literature of urban regions 091732

> **093–099**    Specific continents, countries, localities
> Add to base number 09 notation 3–9 from Table 2, e.g., folk literature of United States 0973
> Use to add notation for a specific continent, country, locality when first area notation is used to specify area of origin of the tales and lore, while second one identifies area in which the tales and lore are discussed or modified, e.g., French tales 398.20944, Haitian version of French tales 398.20944097294

(Option: Class individual tales, collections of tales, lore on a specific topic from a specific continent, country, locality in 398.21–398.28)

> 398.21–398.28  Tales and lore on a specific topic

Add to each subdivision identified by * as follows:
- 01–07  Standard subdivisions
- 08  Groups of people
- [089]  Individual tales, collections of tales, lore on a specific topic by ethnic and national groups
  - Do not use; class in 398.2089
  - (Option: Continue to use 089; prefer 398.2089)
- 09  History, geographic treatment, biography
  - Class here literary criticism
  - Class comprehensive works on history and criticism of a specific topic with the topic in 398.3–398.4, e.g., history and criticism of tales and lore about witches 398.45
  - *See Manual at 398.2 vs. 398.3–398.4*
- [093–099]  Individual tales, collections of tales, lore on a specific topic from a specific continent, country, locality
  - Do not use; class in 398.2093–398.2099
  - (Option: Continue to use 093–099; prefer 398.2093–398.2099)

Class comprehensive works in 398.2

.21        *Tales and lore of paranatural beings of human and semihuman form

> *For werewolves, see 398.2454; for ghosts, see 398.25*

> *See also 398.2 for comprehensive works on fairy tales (tales of paranatural beings)*

.22        *Tales and lore of persons without paranormal powers

Class here legendary or mythological persons

.23        *Tales and lore of places and times

Class historical and quasi-historical events in 398.27

.232        *Real places

Class tales of real places at special times in 398.236

> *See also 398.209 for tales originating in specific places*

.232 1–.232 9    Specific places

Add to base number 398.232 notation 1–9 from Table 2, e.g., tales about India 398.23254; then add further as instructed under 398.21–398.28, e.g., 18th century tales about India 398.2325409033

.234        *Legendary places

.236        *Times

Class here holidays, seasons

*Add as instructed under 398.21–398.28

.24      *Tales and lore of plants and animals

         Class here agriculture

         Class comprehensive works on tales and lore involving science in 398.26

.242      *Plants

         Real and legendary

.245      *Animals

         *See Manual at 800, T3C—362 vs. 398.245, 590, 636*

.245 2      *Real animals

.245 22–.245 29      Specific animals

         Add to base number 398.2452 the numbers following 59 in 592–599, e.g., cats 398.24529752; then add further as instructed under 398.21–398.28, e.g., 18th century tales about cats 398.2452975209033

.245 4      *Legendary animals

.25      *Ghost stories

.26      *Tales and lore involving physical and natural phenomena

         Real and legendary

         Class here comprehensive works on tales and lore involving scientific and technical themes

         *For tales and lore of plants and animals, see 398.24; for tales and lore involving technical themes, see 398.27*

.27      *Tales and lore of humanity and human existence

         *For tales and lore of persons without paranormal powers, see 398.22; for tales and lore of agriculture, see 398.24*

         Tales and lore of other topics relocated to 398.28

.273–.278      Specific human, social, technical, artistic, recreational, literary, historical, political, military themes

         Add to base number 398.27 the numbers following —35 in notation 353–358 from Table 3C, e.g., tales of everyday life 398.275, of historical events 398.278; then add further as instructed under 398.21–398.28, e.g., 18th century tales about everyday life 398.27509033

.28      *Tales and lore of other topics [*formerly* 398.27]

         Tales and lore not provided for elsewhere

*Add as instructed under 398.21–398.28

> **398.3–398.4 History and criticism of specific subjects of folklore**

Standard subdivisions may be added to subdivisions of 398.3–398.4 for any topic even if the subject of the work does not approximate the whole, e.g., history and criticism of folktales from France about elves 398.450944

Limited to works without extended text of folk tales

Class here origin, role, function of themes and subjects of folklore as cultural and social phenomena

Class comprehensive works in 398.09. Class literary criticism of individual tales, collections of tales, lore on a specific topic by a specific ethnic or national group with the group in 398.2089, e.g., literary criticism of Navajo tales and lore about witches 398.20899726; class literary criticism of individual tales, collections of tales, lore on a specific topic from a specific continent, country, locality with the continent, country, locality in 398.2093–398.2099, plus the notation for the topic from table under 398.2093–398.2099, plus notation 09 from table under 398.21–398.28, e.g., literary criticism of French tales and lore about witches 398.209440109; class comprehensive treatment of literary criticism of tales or lore on a specific topic with the topic in 398.2, plus notation 09 from table under 398.21–398.28, e.g., literary criticism of tales and lore about witches 398.2109

*See Manual at 398.2 vs. 398.3–398.4*

| | |
|---|---|
| **.3** | **Real phenomena as subjects of folklore** |
| .32 | Places |
| .322 | Physiographic regions |
| .329 | Specific places |

Class historical and political themes, historical events in specific places in 398.358

| | |
|---|---|
| [.329 01–.329 09] | Standard subdivisions |

Do not use; class in 398.3201–398.3209

| | |
|---|---|
| .329 3–.329 9 | Specific continents, countries, localities |

Add to base number 398.329 notation 3–9 from Table 2, e.g., London as a subject for folklore 398.329421

| | |
|---|---|
| .33 | Times |

Class here holidays, seasons

| | |
|---|---|
| .35 | Humanity and human existence |
| .352 | Persons without paranormal powers |

.353–.358　Specific human, social, technical, artistic, recreational, literary, historical, political, military themes

> Add to base number 398.35 the numbers following —35 in notation 353–358 from Table 3C, e.g., tales of historical events 398.358; however, medical folklore relocated from 398.353 to 398.3561; food relocated from 398.355 to 398.3564; recreation relocated from 398.55 to 398.3579

> Class specific human, social, technical, artistic, recreational, literary, historical, political, military themes related to a specific kind of person without paranomal powers in 398.352; class pecific human, social, technical, artistic, recreational, literary, historical, political, military themes related to paranatural beings of human and semihuman form in 398.45; class agriculture, comprehensive works on scientific and technical themes in 398.36

.36　Scientific themes

> Class here agriculture, nature, physical phenomena, comprehensive works on scientific and technical themes

> *For technical themes, see 398.356*

.362　Heavenly bodies

.363　Weather

.364　Fire and water

.365　Minerals

.368　Plants

> Add to base number 398.368 the numbers following 58 in 582–588, e.g., flowers 398.368213

.369　Animals

> Add to base number 398.369 the numbers following 59 in 592–599, e.g., rabbits 398.369932

**.4　Paranatural and legendary phenomena as subjects of folklore**

> Class here magic

> *See also 133.43 for magic in occultism*

.41　Folk beliefs

> Class here superstitions

.42　Legendary places

.45　Paranormal beings of human and semihuman form

> *For ghosts, see 398.47*

.46　Legendary minerals, plants, animals

.465　Minerals

> Class here philosopher's stone

.468　Plants

.469          Animals

.47          Ghosts

> Class here haunted places

**[.5]**        **Chapbooks**

> Interdisciplinary works on chapbooks relocated to 002; chapbooks with content limited to a specific subject relocated to the subject, e.g., murder 364.1523, 18th-century English fiction 823.5

**.6**         **Riddles**

> Class riddles as a type of puzzle similar to logic puzzles in 793.735; class riddle as jokes by known authors in 808.882

> *See Manual at T3A—8 + 02, T3B—802, T3B—8 + 02 vs. 398.6, 793.735*

> Interdisciplinary works on riddles relocated to 808.882

**.7**         **Jokes and jests [*both formerly* 398.2]**

> Standard subdivisions are added for either or both topics in heading

> Class here jokebooks, jestbooks

> Class jokes and jests by known authors, interdisciplinary works on jokes and jests in 808.882

> *See Manual at 800 vs. 398.2*

**.8**         **Rhymes and rhyming games**

> Standard subdivisions are added for either or both topics in heading

> Including jump rope rhymes, lullabies, tongue twisters

> Class here anonymous children's rhymes from the oral tradition, nursery rhymes

> Class forms of folk poetry not provided for here with the form in 800, e.g., medieval metrical romances 808.8133

> *See Manual at 800 vs. 398.2*

> Interdisciplinary works on tongue twisters relocated to 808.882

**[.808 3]**        Young people

> Do not use; class in 398.8

.84          Counting-out rhymes (Counting rhymes)

.87          Street cries and songs

**.9**         **Proverbs**

> Class here folk aphorisms

> Add to base number 398.9 notation 1–9 from Table 6, e.g., French proverbs 398.941

> *See Manual at 800 vs. 398.2*

## 399     Customs of war and diplomacy

Including dances, peace pipe

Class protocol of diplomacy in 327.2; class customs of military life in 355.1; class cannibalism in 394.9

# 400 Language

Class here interdisciplinary works on language and literature

*For government policy on language, see 306.449; for literature, see 800; for rhetoric, see 808. For the language of a specific subject, see the subject, plus notation 014 from Table 1, e.g., language of science 501.4*

(Option A: To give local emphasis or a shorter number to a specific language, class in 410, where full instructions appear

(Option B: To give local emphasis or a shorter number to a specific language, place before 420 through use of a letter or other symbol. Full instructions appear under 420–490)

### SUMMARY

| | |
|---|---|
| 401–409 | **Standard subdivisions, international languages, special topics of languages** |
| 410 | **Linguistics** |
| 420 | **English and Old English (Anglo-Saxon)** |
| 430 | **German and related languages** |
| 440 | **French and related Romance languages** |
| 450 | **Italian, Dalmatian, Romanian, Rhaetian, Sardinian, Corsican** |
| 460 | **Spanish, Portuguese, Galician** |
| 470 | **Latin and related Italic languages** |
| 480 | **Classical Greek and related Hellenic languages** |
| 490 | **Other languages** |

## 401 Philosophy and theory; international languages

Notation 01 from Table 1 as modified below

Class interdisciplinary works on philosophy of language in 121.68

### .3 International languages

Class here universal languages; general discussions of international languages, e.g., diplomatic languages, lingua francas

Class artificial languages in 499.99. Class a specific international sign language with the language in 419, e.g., American Sign Language as a universal language 419.7; class a other specific international languages with the language in 420–490, e.g., Latin as a diplomatic language 470, Swahili as a lingua franca 496.392

**.4**         **Communication; semantics, pragmatics, languages for special purposes**

Notation 014 from Table 1 as modified below

Class here lexicology, interdisciplinary works on terminology

Class interdisciplinary works on communication, content analysis, semiotics in 302.2. Class the semiotics of a specific subject with the subject, plus notation 014 from Table 1, e.g., semiotics of biology 570.14

> *For dictionaries of linguistics, see 410.3; for general polyglot dictionaries, see 413; for lexicography, see 413.028; for applied linguistics treatment of terminology, see 418. For terminology (including pronunciation and spelling) of a specific subject, see the subject, plus notation 014 from Table 1, e.g., terminology of linguistics 410.14, terminology of engineering 620.0014*

> *See also 121.68 for semiotics as a topic in philosophy*

**.41**         Discourse analysis

Including pragmatics in discourse analysis

Class discourse analysis of languages for special purposes in 401.47; class interdisciplinary works on pragmatics in 401.45. Class discourse analysis of a specific subject with the subject, plus notation 014 from Table 1, e.g., discourse analysis of political science 320.014

Use of this number for content analysis, semiotics discontinued; class in 401.4

**[.42]**         Etymology

Do not use; class in 412

**.43**         Semantics

> *For history of word meanings, see 412*

> *See also 121.68 for semantics as a topic in philosophy; also 149.94 for general semantics as a philosophical school*

> *See Manual at 401.43 vs. 306.44, 401.45, 401.9, 412, 415*

**.430 285**         Computer applications

**.430 285 635**         Natural language processing

Class here word sense disambiguation

**.45**         Pragmatics

Class here interdisciplinary works on pragmatics [*formerly* 306.44]

> *For pragmatics in sociolinguistics, see 306.44; for pragmatics in discourse analysis, see 401.41; for pragmatics in psycholinguistics, see 401.9*

**.452**         Speech acts

Class here illocutionary acts

.454 Presupposition

Class here implication, entailment

Class presupposition, implication, entailment in logic in 160

.456 Reference

Class here anaphora, deixis; comprehensive works on reference

Class reference in philosophy of language in 121.68

.47 Languages for special purposes

Class here sublanguages, discourse analysis of languages for special purposes

Class teaching of languages for special purposes as second languages in 418.0071; class translation of languages for special purposes in 418.03. Class dictionaries of languages for special purposes with the purpose, plus notation 03 from Table 1, e.g., medical dictionaries 610.3

[.48] Abbreviations, acronyms, symbols

Do not use for abbreviations, acronyms, symbols as part of writing systems; class in 411. Do not use for dictionaries of abbreviations, acronyms, symbols; class in 413.15

**.5** **Scientific principles**

.51 Mathematical principles

Class mathematical linguistics in 410.151

**.9** **Psychological principles, language acquisition, speech perception**

Notation 019 from Table 1 as modified below

Including speech errors

Class here psycholinguistics

Class speech errors in language acquisition in 401.93; class psychology of bilingualism in 404.2019

*See also 306.44 for sociolinguistics*

*See Manual at 401.43 vs. 306.44, 401.45, 401.9, 412, 415*

.93 Language acquisition

*See also 418.0071 for study and teaching of language; also 418.4019 for psychology of reading*

*See Manual at 407.1, T1—071 vs. 401.93, T4—019, 410.71, 418.0071, T4—80071*

.95 Speech perception

*See also 152.15 for auditory perception*

**402** **Miscellany**

.85              Computer applications

Class computational linguistics in 006.35

# 403    Dictionaries, encyclopedias, concordances

*For dictionaries, encyclopedias, concordances of linguistics, see 410.3; for general polyglot dictionaries, see 413; for dictionaries, encyclopedias, concordances of literature, see 803*

# 404    Special topics of language

### .2    Bilingualism

Class here multilingualism

Specific instances of bilingualism are classed with the language dominant in the country in which the linguistic interaction occurs, e.g., a discussion of Spanish-English bilingualism in Los Angeles 420.42610979494. If neither language is dominant, class with the one coming later in 420–490 (if both languages are sign languages, class with the one coming later in 419)

*See also 306.446 for sociology of bilingualism and multilingualism*

# 405    Serial publications

# 406    Organizations and management

# 407    Education, research, related topics

*See Manual at 407.1, T1—071 vs. 401.93, T4—019, 410.71, 418.0071, T4—80071*

### .2    Research

.21              Research methods

Class corpus-based research methods in 410.188

# 408    Groups of people

*See also 306.44 for sociology of language*

### .9    Treatment of language with respect to ethnic and national groups

Class ethnolinguistics in 306.44

# 409    Geographic treatment and biography

Do not use for language history not limited by area; class in 417.7

Class specific sign languages and groups of sign languages in 419; class other specific languages and groups of languages in 420–490

*See also 410.9 for geographic treatment and biography of linguistics*

# 410    Linguistics

Class here descriptive, synchronic linguistics; comprehensive works on Eurasiatic languages, on Indo-European languages, on Indo-Germanic languages, on Indo-Hittite languages

Class linguistics of specific sign languages in 419; class linguistics of other specific languages in 420–490

> *For sociolinguistics, see 306.44; for lexicology, semiotics, see 401.4; for semantics, see 401.43; for specific Indo-European languages other than east Indo-European languages and Celtic languages, see 420–480; for east Indo-European and Celtic languages, see 491*

> *See Manual at 410*

(Option A: To give local emphasis and a shorter number to a specific language, e.g., Russian, class it here and add to base number 41 as instructed under 420–490; in that case class linguistics in 400, its subdivisions in 401–409, standard subdivisions of language and of linguistics in 400.1–400.9. Option B is described under 420–490)

### SUMMARY

| | |
|---|---|
| 410.1–.9 | Standard subdivisions |
| 411 | Writing systems of standard forms of languages |
| 412 | Etymology of standard forms of languages |
| 413 | Dictionaries of standard forms of languages |
| 414 | Phonology and phonetics of standard forms of languages |
| 415 | Grammar of standard forms of languages |
| 417 | Dialectology and historical linguistics |
| 418 | Standard usage (Prescriptive linguistics) |
| 419 | Sign languages |

.1    **Philosophy and theory**

Notation 01 from Table 1 as modified below

Do not use for philosophy and theory of language and languages; class in 401. Do not use for schools and theories of linguistics; class in 410.18

.151    Mathematical principles

Class here mathematical linguistics

.18    Schools, theories, methodologies of linguistics

Including functionalism, structural linguistics

> *For works on schools, theories, methodologies of linguistics that stress syntax, or syntax and phonology, see 415.018*

| | |
|---|---|
| .188 | **Corpus linguistics** |

Including language data samples collected as corpora to support corpus-based analysis, corpus linguistics applied to texts in a specific subject

Class corpus linguistics applied to a specific topic in linguistics with the topic, e.g., corpus-based analysis of noun phrases 415.5; class corpus linguistics applied to a specific work or the works of a specific author with the work or author, e.g., versions of the Bible 220.4, Shakespeare's works 822.33

| | |
|---|---|
| .19 | **Psychological principles** |

Class psycholinguistics in 401.9

| | |
|---|---|
| **.2** | **Miscellany** |

Do not use for miscellany of language and languages; class in 402

| | |
|---|---|
| .285 | **Computer applications** |

Class computer applications in corpus linguistics in 410.188. Class a computational linguistics application of a linguistic process with the process, plus notation 0285635 from Table 1, e.g., part-of-speech tagging 415.0285635

*See Manual at 006.35 vs. 410.285*

Computational linguistics relocated to 006.35

| | |
|---|---|
| **.3–.9** | **Standard subdivisions** |

Do not use for standard subdivisions of language and languages; class in 403–409

*See Manual at 407.1, T1—071 vs. 401.93, T4—019, 410.71, 418.0071, T4—80071*

# 411     Writing systems of standard forms of languages

Including alphabets, ideographs, syllabaries; braille; abbreviations, acronyms, capitalization, punctuation, spelling, transliteration

Class dictionaries of abbreviations and acronyms in 413.15; class writing systems of geographic variations, of modern nongeographic variations of languages in 417.2; class manual alphabets, fingerspelling in 418

*See also 652 for practical works on how to write by hand or machine, e.g., penmanship 652.1*

| | |
|---|---|
| **.7** | **Paleography and epigraphy** |

Study of ancient and medieval handwriting and inscriptions

Standard subdivisions are added for either or both topics in heading

*See also 417.7 for paleography covering all aspects of early writings*

**412       Etymology of standard forms of languages**

> Class etymology of geographic variations, of modern nongeographic variations of languages in 417.2; class comprehensive works on historical linguistics in 417.7; class interdisciplinary works on onomastics in 929.97. Class a specific aspect of etymology with the aspect, e.g., phonetic development of words 414
>
> *See Manual at 401.43 vs. 306.44, 401.45, 401.9, 412, 415*

.03       Dictionaries, encyclopedias, concordances

> Including dictionaries of eponyms [*formerly* 413.1]

**413       Dictionaries of standard forms of languages**

> Class here polyglot dictionaries
>
> Class dictionaries of geographic variations, of modern nongeographic variations of languages in 417.2
>
> *For bilingual dictionaries, see the language, plus notation 32–39 from Table 4, e.g., French-English dictionary 443.21*

.028      Auxiliary techniques and procedures; apparatus, equipment, materials

> Class here basic techniques and procedures; lexicography

**.1       Specialized dictionaries**

> Including synonym dictionaries
>
> Class etymological dictionaries in 412.03. Class subject dictionaries with the subject, plus notation 03 from Table 1, e.g., dictionary of medicine 610.3
>
> *For crossword-puzzle dictionaries, see 793.73203*
>
> Dictionaries of eponyms relocated to 412.03

.15       Dictionaries of abbreviations, acronyms, symbols

> Standard subdivisions are added for any or all topics in heading
>
> Class subject dictionaries of abbreviations, acronyms, symbols with the subject, plus notation 0148 from Table 1, e.g., dictionary of scientific abbreviations and acronyms 501.48

.17       Picture dictionaries

> Limited to dictionaries with pictures of what words represent
>
> *See also 419.03 for dictionaries with pictures of sign-language signs*

**.2–.9    Polyglot dictionaries with entry words or definitions in only one language**

> Add to base number 413 notation 2–9 from Table 6, e.g., a dictionary with terms in English, French, and German, but with definitions only in English 413.21

## 414 Phonology and phonetics of standard forms of languages

Standard subdivisions are added for phonology and phonetics together, for phonology alone

Class here consonants, vowels; morphophonology, morphophonemics, phonemics

Class phonology and phonetics of geographic variations, of modern nongeographic variations of languages in 417.2; class comprehensive works on phonology, morphology, syntax; on phonology and morphology; on phonology and syntax in 415

### .6 Suprasegmental features

Phonology and phonetics of vocal effects extending over more than one sound element

Including juncture (pauses), pitch, stress

Class here intonation

### .8 Phonetics

*For phonetic aspects of suprasegmental features, see 414.6*

## 415 Grammar of standard forms of languages

Class here grammatical categories, sentences, syntax, topic and comment; word order; comprehensive works on phonology, morphology, syntax; on phonology and morphology; on phonology and syntax

Class grammar of geographic variations, of modern nongeographic variations of languages in 417.2

Unless other instructions are given, class a subject with aspects in two or more subdivisions of 415 in the number coming last, e.g., number expressed by verbs 415.6 (*not* 415.5)

*For phonology, see 414; for prescriptive grammar, see 418*

*See Manual at 401.43 vs. 306.44, 401.45, 401.9, 412, 415*

.01        Philosophy and theory

Notation 01 from Table 1 as modified below

Do not use for schools and theories of grammar; class in 415.018

.018        Schools, theories, methodologies

Including case, categorial, relational grammar

.018 2        Generative grammar

.018 4        Dependency grammar

.02        Miscellany

.028 5        Computer applications

.028 563 5        Natural language processing

Class here part-of-speech tagging, parsing

> **415.5–415.7 Word classes**

Class here parts of speech

Class comprehensive works in 415

**.5 Nouns, pronouns, adjectives, articles**

Including case, number, person

Class here noun phrases

**.54 Nouns**

**.55 Pronouns**

**.6 Verbs**

Including modality, mood, voice; comprehensive works on words derived from verbs, on infinitives, on participles

Class here verb phrases

Class works that treat a specific function (other than the verb function) of words derived from verbs with the function, e.g., gerunds as nouns 415.54

**.62 Tense**

**.63 Aspect**

**.7 Miscellaneous word classes**

Including conjunctions, interjections, particles, prepositions, prepositional phrases

Class clitics in 415.92

**.76 Adverbs**

Including adverbials

**.9 Morphology**

Class morphophonology, morphophonemics in 414

*For morphology of specific word classes, see 415.5–415.7*

**.92 Word formation**

Including affixes (infixes, prefixes, suffixes), clitics; formation of compound words

Class here derivational morphology

Class etymology in 412

**.95 Inflection**

*For inflectional schemata designed for use as aids in learning a language, see 418*

## [416]     [Unassigned]

Most recently used in Edition 18

## 417     Dialectology and historical linguistics

### .2     Dialectology

Including argot, cant, jargon, slang

Class here dialects, patois, provincialisms

Works on writing systems, etymology, dictionaries, phonology, phonetics, grammar, applied linguistics are classed here when applied to geographic variations, to modern nongeographic variations, e.g., morphology of geographic variations

### .22     Pidgins, creoles, mixed languages

Standard subdivisions are added for any or all topics in heading

*See Manual at T4—7*

### .7     Historical linguistics (Diachronic linguistics)

Study of development of language over time

Class here language history not limited by area, language change, paleography covering all aspects of early writings

*For change in and history of a specific element of language, see the element, e.g., paleography limited to study of ancient and medieval handwriting 411.7, grammar 415*

*See also 409 for geographic treatment of language history; also 410.9 for history of linguistics*

*See Manual at 410*

## 418     Standard usage (Prescriptive linguistics)

General, formal, informal usage

Including comprehensive works on instruction in lipreading with respect to multiple languages, comprehensive works on use of signs and fingerspelling for manual coding of multiple standard spoken languages

Class here applied linguistics

Class purely descriptive linguistics in 411–415; class prescriptive and applied linguistics applied to geographic variations, to modern nongeographic variations of languages in 417.2; class dictionaries in 413; class lexicography in 413.028

*For rhetoric, see 808.04. For use of signs and fingerspelling for manual coding of a specific spoken language, see the language plus notation 891 from Table 4, e.g., use of signs and fingerspelling to represent standard English 428.91, use of British Sign Language signs to represent standard English 428.9141; for lipreading a specific language, see the language, plus notation 8954 from Table 4, e.g., lipreading English 428.954*

### .001–.006     Standard subdivisions

### .007     Education, research, related topics

| | |
|---|---|
| .007 1 | Education |

Class here second language teaching

*See Manual at 407.1, T1—071 vs. 401.93, T4—019, 410.71, 418.0071, T4—80071*

| | |
|---|---|
| .008–.009 | Standard subdivisions |
| .02 | Translating |

Class here interpreting

Translating materials on specific subjects relocated to 418.03; translating literature (belles-lettres) and rhetoric relocated to 418.04

| | |
|---|---|
| .020 285 | Computer applications |
| .020 285 635 | Natural language processing |

Class here machine translation

| | |
|---|---|
| .03 | Translating materials on specific subjects [*formerly* 418.02] |

Class here interpreting materials on specific subjects

Add to base number 418.03 three-digit numbers 001–999 (but stop before any zero that follows a non-zero number), e.g., translating natural history materials 418.035 (*not* 418.03508), translating medical materials 418.0361

Class translating a specific work or the works of a specific author with the work, translations of the work, or author, e.g., translating the Bible 220, translating the Bible into English 220.52, translating the works of Aristotle 185

*For translating literature (belles-lettres) and rhetoric, see 418.04*

| | |
|---|---|
| .04 | Translating literature (belles-lettres) and rhetoric [*formerly* 418.02] |

Class here interpreting literature and rhetoric, translating works about literature, rhetoric

Class translating a specific work or works of a specific author with the work or author, e.g., translating the Aeneid 873.01, translating the works of Shakespeare 822.33

| | |
|---|---|
| .041–.048 | Translating specific forms of literature |

Add to base number 418.04 one-digit notation 1–8 from Table 3B, e.g., translating poetry 418.041, translating tragedy 418.042 (*not* 418.0420512)

| | |
|---|---|
| .07 | Multilingual phrase books |
| **.4** | **Reading** |

# 419 Sign languages

Class here comprehensive works on fingerspelling, use of fingerspelling as part of sign languages

Class nonlinguistic (nonstructured) communication (e.g., use of gestures) in 302.222

*For comprehensive works on use of signs and fingerspelling for manual coding of multiple standard spoken languages, see 418; for use of signs and fingerspelling for manual coding of specific standard spoken languages, see notation 891 from Table 4*

.03 Dictionaries, encyclopedias, concordances

Class a dictionary of a specific sign language with the language, e.g., dictionary of American Sign Language 419.703

.09 History, geographic treatment, biography

[.094–.099] Specific continents, countries, localities in modern world

Do not use for sign languages used primarily for purposes other than communication among deaf people or between hearing and deaf people; class in 419.1. Do not use for sign languages used primarily for communication among deaf people or between hearing and deaf people; class in 419.4–419.9. Do not use for comprehensive works on all types of sign languages; class in 419

.1 **Sign languages used primarily for purposes other than communication of deaf people**

Including monastic sign languages, sign languages used as lingua francas among hearing people

(Option: To give local emphasis and a shorter number to a specific sign language used primarily for purposes other than communication of deaf people, class it in 419.3. Prefer 419.1)

(.3) **Specific sign language**

(Optional number; prefer 419.1 or 419.4–419.9)

.4–.9 **Sign languages used primarily for communication among deaf people or between hearing and deaf people**

Class here indigenous sign languages of deaf communities, comprehensive works on methods of communication of deaf-blind people

Add to base number 419 notation 4–9 from Table 2, e.g., British Sign Language 419.41, Spanish Sign Language 419.46, Catalonian Sign Language 419.467, American Sign Language 419.7; then for a specific sign language add 0 and to the result add further as instructed at beginning of Table 4, e.g., grammar of British Sign Language 419.4105, grammar of Spanish Sign Language 419.4605, grammar of Catalonian Sign Language 419.46705, grammar of American Sign Language 419.705

Class sign languages used primarily for purposes other than communication of deaf people in 419.1

*For braille, see 411*

(Option: To give local emphasis and a shorter number to a specific sign language used primarily for communication among deaf people or between hearing and deaf people, class it in 419.3. Prefer 419.4–419.9)

> # 420–490 Specific languages

Class here comprehensive works on specific languages and their literatures

Except for modifications shown under specific entries, add to base number for each language identified by * as instructed at beginning of Table 4, e.g., grammar of Japanese 495.65. The base number is the number given for the language unless the schedule specifies a different number
  (Option: For any group of languages, add notation 04 to the base number and then add as instructed at beginning of Table 4, e.g., grammar of Celtic languages 491.6045)

The numbers used in this schedule for individual languages do not necessarily correspond exactly with those in 810–890 or with notation in Table 6. Use notation from Table 6 only when so instructed, e.g., at 494

Class polyglot dictionaries in 413; class comprehensive works in 410

*For specific sign languages, see 419; for literatures of specific languages, see 810–890*

*See Manual at 420–490*

(Option B: To give local emphasis and a shorter number to a specific language, place it first by use of a letter or other symbol, e.g., Arabic language 4A0 [preceding 420], for which the base number is 4A. Option A is described under 410)

> # 420–480 Specific Indo-European languages other than east Indo-European languages and Celtic languages

Class comprehensive works on Indo-European languages in 410

# 420 English and Old English (Anglo-Saxon)

.1–.9 **Standard subdivisions of English**

Notation from Table 1 as modified under —01–09 in Table 4, e.g., semantics of Italian 420.143

## 421–428 Subdivisions of English

Class here comprehensive works on English and Old English (Anglo-Saxon)

Except for modifications shown under specific entries, add to base number 42 notation 1–8 from Table 4, e.g., phonology of English 421.5

*For Old English (Anglo-Saxon), see 429*

## 421 Writing system, phonology, phonetics of standard English

Number built according to instructions under 421–428

.52 Spelling (Orthography) and pronunciation

Number built according to instructions under 421–428

Including standard Canadian spelling and pronunciation

*For standard American (U.S.) spelling and pronunciation, see 421.54; for standard British spelling and pronunciation, see 421.55*

.54 Standard American (U.S.) spelling and pronunciation

.55 Standard British spelling and pronunciation

## 422 Etymology of standard English

Number built according to instructions under 421–428

## 423 Dictionaries of standard English

Number built according to instructions under 421–428

## [424] [Unassigned]

Most recently used in Edition 16

## 425 Grammar of standard English

Number built according to instructions under 421–428

## [426] [Unassigned]

Most recently used in Edition 18

## 427 Historical and geographic variations, modern nongeographic variations of English

Number built according to instructions under 421–428

*For Old English (Anglo-Saxon), see 429*

.001–.008 Standard subdivisions

.009 History, geographic treatment, biography

| [.009 02] | 6th–15th centuries, 500–1499 |
|---|---|

> Do not use for Middle English; class in 427.02

| [.009 4–.009 9] | Specific continents, countries, localities in modern world |
|---|---|

> Do not use; class in 427.9

| .02 | Middle English, 1100–1500 |
|---|---|

> *See also 429 for Old English (Anglo-Saxon)*

| [.09] | Modern nongeographic variations |
|---|---|

> Number discontinued; class in 427

**[.1–.8]    Geographic variations in parts of England**

> Relocated to 427.9421–427.9428

**.9    Geographic variations**

| [.901–.909] | Standard subdivisions |
|---|---|

> Do not use; class in 427.001–427.009

| .91 | Geographic variations in areas, regions, places in general |
|---|---|

> Add to base number 427.91 the numbers following —1 in notation 11–19 from Table 2, e.g., dialects of the British empire 427.9171241

| .94–.99 | Geographic variations in specific continents, countries, localities in modern world |
|---|---|

> Add to base number 427.9 notation 4–9 from Table 2, e.g., geographic variations in parts of England 427.9421–427.9428 [*formerly* 427.1–427.8], slang of British Isles 427.941, geographic variations in England 427.942, dialects of Canada 427.971, Tok Pisin 427.9953

> *For geographic variations of Middle English, see 427.02094–427.02099*

**428    Standard English usage (Prescriptive linguistics)**

> Number built according to instructions under 421–428

> Class here Basic English

**429    *Old English (Anglo-Saxon)**

> *See also 427.02 for Middle English*

# 430    German and related languages

> Class here Germanic languages

> *For English and Old English (Anglo-Saxon), see 420*

| .01–.03 | Standard subdivisions of Germanic languages |
|---|---|

> Notation from Table 1 as modified under —01–03 in Table 4, e.g., semantics of Germanic languages 430.0143

*Add to base number as instructed under 420–490

.04 Special topics of Germanic languages

> Add to base number 430.04 notation 1–8 from Table 4, e.g., grammar of Germanic languages 430.045

.05–.09 Standard subdivisions of Germanic languages

**.1–.9 Standard subdivisions of German**

> Notation from Table 1 as modified under —01–09 in Table 4, e.g., semantics of German 430.143

# 431–438 Subdivisions of German

> Except for modifications shown under specific entries, add to base number 43 notation 1–8 from Table 4, e.g., phonology of German 431.5

## 431 Writing systems, phonology, phonetics of standard German

> Number built according to instructions under 431–438

## 432 Etymology of standard German

> Number built according to instructions under 431–438

## 433 Dictionaries of standard German

> Number built according to instructions under 431–438

## [434] [Unassigned]

> Most recently used in Edition 16

## 435 Grammar of standard German

> Number built according to instructions under 431–438

## [436] [Unassigned]

> Most recently used in Edition 18

## 437 Historical and geographic variations, modern nongeographic variations of German

> Number built according to instructions under 431–438

> Class Low German in 439.4

.001–.008 Standard subdivisions

.009 History, geographic treatment, biography

[.009 02] 6th–15th centuries, 500–1499

> Do not use for Old High German; class in 437.01. Do not use for Middle High German and Early New High German; class in 437.02

[.009 4–.009 9] Specific continents, countries, localities in modern world

> Do not use; class in 437.9

| .01 | Old High German to 1100 |
|---|---|
| .02 | Middle High German and Early New High German, 1100–1500 |

Standard subdivisions are added for either or both topics in heading

| [.09] | Modern nongeographic variations |
|---|---|

Number discontinued; class in 437

**[.1–.5]** **Geographic variations in parts of Germany**

Relocated to 437.9431–437.9435

**[.6]** **Geographic variations in Austria**

Relocated to 437.9436

**.9** **Geographic variations**

*See also 439.1 for Yiddish*

**[.901–.909]** Standard subdivisions

Do not use; class in 437.001–437.009

**.91** Geographic variations in areas, regions, places in general

Add to base number 437.91 the numbers following —1 in notation 11–19 from Table 2, e.g., dialects of rural regions 437.91734

**.94–.99** Geographic variations in specific continents, countries, localities in modern world

Add to base number 437.9 notation 4–9 from Table 2, e.g., geographic variations in parts of Germany 437.9431–437.9435 [*formerly* 437.1–437.5], geographic variations in Austria 437.9436 [*formerly* 437.6], geographic variations in Germany 437.943, German dialects of Alsace 437.94439

*For geographic variations of Old High German, see 437.01094–437.01099; for geographic variations of Middle High German and Early New High, see 437.02094–437.02099*

**438** **Standard German usage (Prescriptive linguistics)**

Number built according to instructions under 431–438

**439** **Other Germanic languages**

**.1** **\*Yiddish**

---

**>** **439.2–439.4 Low Germanic languages**

Class here West Germanic languages

Class comprehensive works in 439

---

\*Add to base number as instructed under 420–490

**.2**    **\*Frisian**

> Including Old Frisian

**.3**    **Netherlandish languages**

**.31**    \*Dutch

> Including Old Low Franconian
>
> Class here Flemish

**.36**    \*Afrikaans

**.4**    **\*Low German (Plattdeutsch)**

> Including Old Low German, Old Saxon

**.5**    **North Germanic languages (Nordic languages)**

> Including proto-Nordic language
>
> Class here comprehensive works on east Scandinavian languages, comprehensive works on west Scandinavian languages, comprehensive works on modern west Scandinavian languages; comprehensive works on languages in the Nordic countries
>
> *For specific North Germanic languages, see 439.6–439.8; for Finnish, see 494.541; for Sámi, see 494.57*

---

\>    **439.6–439.8  Specific North Germanic languages**

> Class comprehensive works in 439.5

**.6**    **Old Norse (Old Icelandic), Icelandic, Faroese**

> Class comprehensive works on west Scandinavian languages in 439.5

[.600 1–.600 9]    Standard subdivisions of comprehensive works on Old Norse (Old Icelandic), Icelandic, Faroese

> Relocated to 439.601–439.609

.601–.609    Standard subdivisions of comprehensive works on Old Norse (Old Icelandic), Icelandic, Faroese [*formerly* 439.6001–439.6009]; Old Norse (Old Icelandic)

> Notation from Table 1 as modified under —01–09 in Table 4, e.g., semantics of Old Norse 439.60143

.61–.68    Subdivisions of Old Norse (Old Icelandic)

> Add to base number 439.6 notation 1–8 from Table 4, e.g., grammar of Old Norse 439.65

---

\*Add to base number as instructed under 420–490

| .69 | Icelandic and Faroese |
|---|---|

Icelandic ca. 1500–

Class comprehensive works on modern west Scandinavian languages in 439.5

| [.690 01–.690 09] | Standard subdivisions of comprehensive works on Icelandic and Faroese |
|---|---|

Relocated to 439.6901–439.6909

| .690 1–.690 9 | Standard subdivisions of comprehensive works on Icelandic and Faroese [*formerly* 439.69001–439.69009]; Icelandic |
|---|---|

Notation from Table 1 as modified under —01–09 in Table 4, e.g., semantics of Icelandic 439.690143

| .691–.698 | Subdivisions of Icelandic |
|---|---|

Add to base number 439.69 notation 1–8 from Table 4, e.g., grammar of Icelandic 439.695

| .699 | *Faroese |
|---|---|

| **.7** | **\*Swedish** |
|---|---|

| .77 | Historical and geographic variations, modern nongeographic variations |
|---|---|

Number built according to instructions under 420–490

| .770 01–.770 09 | Standard subdivisions |
|---|---|

| [.770 090 1] | To 499 A.D. |
|---|---|

Do not use; class in 439.5

| [.770 090 2] | 6th–15th centuries, 500–1499 |
|---|---|

Do not use for proto-Nordic language; class in 439.5. Do not use for Old Swedish; class in 439.7701

| [.770 094–.770 099] | Specific continents, countries, localities in modern world |
|---|---|

Do not use; class in 439.779

| .770 1 | Old Swedish to 1526 |
|---|---|

| [.776–.778] | Geographic variations in parts of Sweden |
|---|---|

Relocated to 439.779486–439.779488

| .779 | Geographic variations |
|---|---|

| [.779 01–.779 09] | Standard subdivisions |
|---|---|

Do not use; class in 439.77001–439.77009

| .779 1 | Geographic variations in areas, regions, places in general |
|---|---|

Add to base number 439.7791 the numbers following —1 in notation 11–19 from Table 2, e.g., dialects of rural regions 439.7791734

*Add to base number as instructed under 420–490

.779 4–.779 9     Geographic variations in specific continents, countries, localities in modern world

> Add to base number 439.779 notation 4–9 from Table 2, e.g., geographic variations in parts of Sweden 439.779486–439.779488 [*formerly* 439.776–439.778], geographic variations in Sweden 439.779485, dialects of Finland 439.7794897

## .8     Danish and Norwegian

.81     *Danish

> Class Dano-Norwegian in 439.82

.817     Historical and geographic variations, modern nongeographic variations

> Number built according to instructions under 420–490

.817 001–.817 009     Standard subdivisions

[.817 009 01]     To 499 A.D.

> Do not use; class in 439.5

[.817 009 02]     6th–15th centuries, 500–1499

> Do not use for proto-Nordic language; class in 439.5. Do not use for Old Danish; class in 439.81701

[.817 009 4–.817 009 9]     Specific continents, countries, localities in modern world

> Do not use; class in 439.8179

.817 01     Old Danish to 1500

[.817 1–.817 5]     Geographic variations in parts of Denmark

> Relocated to 439.81794891–439.81794895

.817 9     Geographic variations

[.817 901–.817 909]     Standard subdivisions

> Do not use; class in 439.817001–439.817009

.817 91     Geographic variations in areas, regions, places in general

> Add to base number 439.81791 the numbers following —1 in notation 11–19 from Table 2, e.g., dialects of rural regions 439.81791734

.817 94–.817 99     Geographic variations in specific continents, countries, localities in modern world

> Add to base number 439.8179 notation 4–9 from Table 2, e.g., geographic variations in parts of Denmark 439.81794891–439.81794895 [*formerly* 439.8171–439.8175], geographic variations in Denmark 439.8179489, dialects of Germany 439.817943

*Add to base number as instructed under 420–490

.82        *Norwegian

> Class here Bokmål, Dano-Norwegian, Riksmål; New Norse, Landsmål

.827       Historical and geographic variations, modern nongeographic variations

> Number built according to instructions under 420–490

.827 001–.827 009        Standard subdivisions

[.827 009 01]        To 499 A.D.

> Do not use; class in 439.5

[.827 009 02]        6th–15th centuries, 500–1499

> Do not use for proto-Nordic language; class in 439.5. Do not use for Old Norse; class in 439.6. Do not use for Middle Norwegian; class in 439.82702

.827 009 03        Modern period, 1500–

> Do not use for Middle Norwegian; class in 439.82702

[.827 009 4–.827 009 9]        Specific continents, countries, localities in modern world

> Do not use; class in 439.8279

.827 02        Middle Norwegian, 1350–1525

[.827 2–.827 4]        Geographic variations in parts of Norway

> Relocated to 439.8279482–439.8279484

.827 9        Geographic variations

[.827 901–.827 909]        Standard subdivisions

> Do not use; class in 439.827001–439.827009

.827 91        Geographic variations in areas, regions, places in general

> Add to base number 439.82791 the numbers following —1 in notation 11–19 from Table 2, e.g., dialects of rural regions 439.82791734

.827 94–.827 99        Geographic variations in specific continents, countries, localities in modern world

> Add to base number 439.8279 notation 4–9 from Table 2, e.g., geographic variations in parts of Norway 439.8279482–439.8279484 [*formerly* 439.8272–439.8274], geographic variations in Norway 439.8279481, dialects of United States 439.827973

**.9        East Germanic languages**

> Including Burgundian, Gothic, Vandalic

---

*Add to base number as instructed under 420–490

# 440 French and related Romance languages

Class here Romance languages

Class comprehensive works on Italic languages in 470

*For Italian, Dalmatian, Romanian, Rhaetian, Sardinian, Corsican, see 450; for Spanish, Portuguese, Galician, see 460*

.01–.03     Standard subdivisions of Romance languages

Notation from Table 1 as modified under —01–03 in Table 4, e.g., semantics of Romance languages 440.0143

.04     Special topics of Romance languages

Add to base number 440.04 notation 1–8 from Table 4, e.g., grammar of Romance languages 440.045

.05–.09     Standard subdivisions of Romance languages

**.1–.9     Standard subdivisions of French**

Notation from Table 1 as modified under —01–09 in Table 4, e.g., semantics of French 440.143

## 441–448 Subdivisions of French

Except for modifications shown under specific entries, add to base number 44 notation 1–8 from Table 4, e.g., phonology of French 441.5

## 441 Writing systems, phonology, phonetics of standard French

Number built according to instructions under 441–448

## 442 Etymology of standard French

Number built according to instructions under 441–448

## 443 Dictionaries of standard French

Number built according to instructions under 441–448

## [444] [Unassigned]

Most recently used in Edition 16

## 445 Grammar of standard French

Number built according to instructions under 441–448

## [446] [Unassigned]

Most recently used in Edition 18

## 447 Historical and geographic variations, modern nongeographic variations of French

Number built according to instructions under 441–448

*See also 449 for Occitan, Franco-Provençal*

.001–.008     Standard subdivisions

| | |
|---|---|
| .009 | History, geographic treatment, biography |
| [.009 02] | 6th–15th centuries, 500–1499 |

> Do not use for Old French; class in 447.01. Do not use for Middle French; class in 447.02

| | |
|---|---|
| [.009 031] | 16th century, 1500–1599 |

> Do not use; class in 447.02

| | |
|---|---|
| [.009 4–.009 9] | Specific continents, countries, localities in modern world |

> Do not use; class in 447.9

| | |
|---|---|
| .01 | Old French to 1400 |
| .02 | Middle French, 1400–1600 |
| [.09] | Modern nongeographic variations |

> Number discontinued; class in 447

**[.1–.8]**     **Geographic variations in parts of France**

> Relocated to 447.9441–447.9448

**.9**       **Geographic variations**

| | |
|---|---|
| [.901–.909] | Standard subdivisions |

> Do not use; class in 447.001–447.009

| | |
|---|---|
| .91 | Geographic variations in areas, regions, places in general |

> Add to base number 447.91 the numbers following —1 in notation 11–19 from Table 2, e.g., dialects of the overseas regions of the French Republic 447.9171244

| | |
|---|---|
| .94–.99 | Geographic variations in specific continents, countries, localities in modern world |

> Add to base number 447.9 notation 4–9 from Table 2, e.g., geographic variations in parts of France 447.9441–447.9448 [*formerly* 447.1–447.8], geographic variations in France 447.944, dialects of Quebec 447.9714, Haitian Creole 447.97294

> *For geographic variations of Old French, see 447.01094–447.01099; for geographic variations of Middle French, see 447.02094–447.02099*

> *See also 449.709449 for Provençal dialect of Occitan; also 459.984 for Corsican*

**448**     **Standard French usage (Prescriptive linguistics)**

> Number built according to instructions under 441–448

**449**     **Occitan, Catalan, Franco-Provençal**

> Class here Langue d'oc; Provençal (Occitan)

> Class Provençal (dialect of Occitan) in 449.709449

.01–.09 Standard subdivisions of Occitan, Langue d'oc

> Notation from Table 1 as modified under —01–09 in Table 4, e.g., semantics of Occitan 449.0143
>
> Subdivisions are added for either or both topics in heading

**.1–.8 Subdivisions of Occitan, Langue d'oc**

> Add to base number 449 notation 1–8 from Table 4, e.g., grammar of Occitan 449.5
>
> Subdivisions are added for either or both topics in heading

.709 449 Provençal dialect

> Number built according to instructions under 449.1–449.8
>
> Class Provençal (Occitan) in 449
>
> *See also 449 for Franco-Provençal*

**.9 *Catalan**

# 450 Italian, Dalmatian, Romanian, Rhaetian, Sardinian, Corsican

> Class Dalmatian in 457.94972; class comprehensive works on Romance languages in 440; class comprehensive works on Italic languages in 470

**.1–.9 Standard subdivisions of Italian**

> Notation from Table 1 as modified under —01–09 in Table 4, e.g., semantics of Italian 450.143

## 451–458 Subdivisions of Italian

> Except for modifications shown under specific entries, add to base number 45 notation 1–8 from Table 4, e.g., phonology of Italian 451.5

## 451 Writing systems, phonology, phonetics of standard Italian

> Number built according to instructions under 451–458

## 452 Etymology of standard Italian

> Number built according to instructions under 451–458

## 453 Dictionaries of standard Italian

> Number built according to instructions under 451–458

## [454] [Unassigned]

> Most recently used in Edition 16

## 455 Grammar of standard Italian

> Number built according to instructions under 451–458

*Add to base number as instructed under 420–490

**[456]     [Unassigned]**

> Most recently used in Edition 18

**457     Historical and geographic variations, modern nongeographic variations of Italian**

> Number built according to instructions under 451–458

.001–.008     Standard subdivisions

.009     History, geographic treatment, biography

[.009 02]          6th–15th centuries, 500–1499

> Do not use for Old Italian; class in 457.01. Do not use for Middle Italian; class in 457.02

[.009 031]          16th century, 1500–1599

> Do not use; class in 457.02

[.009 4–.009 9]     Specific continents, countries, localities in modern world

> Do not use; class in 457.1–457.9

.01     Old Italian to 1300

.02     Middle Italian, 1300–1600

[.09]     Modern nongeographic variations

> Number discontinued; class in 457

**[.1–.7]     Geographic variations in parts of Italian Peninsula**

> Relocated to 457.9451–457.9457

**[.8]     Geographic variations in Sicily**

> Relocated to 457.9458

**.9     Geographic variations**

> *For geographic variations of Old Italian, see 457.01094–457.01099; for geographic variations of Middle Italian, see 457.02094–457.02099*

> Sardinian relocated to 459.982

[.901–.909]     Standard subdivisions

> Do not use; class in 457.001–457.009

.91     Geographic variations in areas, regions, places in general

> Add to base number 457.91 the numbers following —1 in notation 11–19 from Table 2, e.g., dialects of rural regions 457.91734

> Geographic variations in Cagliari province of Sardinia relocated to 459.98271

[.92]     Geographic variations in Nuoro province of Sardinia

> Relocated to 459.98272

| [.93] | Geographic variations in Sassari province of Sardinia |
|---|---|

Relocated to 459.98273

.94    Geographic variations in Europe

Add to base number 457.94 the numbers following —4 in notation 41–49 from Table 2, e.g., geographic variations in parts of Italian Peninsula 457.9451–457.9457 [*formerly* 457.1–457.7], geographic variations in Sicily 457.9458 [*formerly* 457.8], Dalmatian language 457.94972 [*formerly* 457.994972], geographic variations in Italian Peninsula 457.945

Geographic variations in Oristano province of Sardinia relocated to 459.98274

.949 72        Dalmatian language

.95    Geographic variations in Asia

Add to base number 457.95 the numbers following —5 in notation 51–59 from Table 2, e.g., geographic variations in Philippines 457.9599

Corsican relocated to 459.984

.96–.98    Geographic variations in Africa, North America, South America

Add to base number 457.9 notation 6–8 from Table 2, e.g., geographic variations in Libya 457.9612

.99    Geographic variations in other parts of world

Add to base number 457.99 the numbers following —9 in notation 91–98 from Table 2, e.g., geographic variations in Australia 457.994

[.994 972]        Dalmatian language

Relocated to 457.94972

# 458    Standard Italian usage (Prescriptive linguistics)

Number built according to instructions under 451–458

# 459    Romanian, Rhaetian, Sardinian, Corsican

.01–.09    Standard subdivisions of Romanian

Notation from Table 1 as modified under —01–09 in Table 4, e.g., semantics of Romanian 459.0143

## .1–.8    Subdivisions of Romanian

Add to base number 459 notation 1–8 from Table 4, e.g., grammar of Romanian 459.5

## .9    Rhaetian languages; Sardinian, Corsican

.92    *Friulian language

.94    *Ladin language

*See also 467.9496 for Judeo-Spanish (Ladino)*

*Add to base number as instructed under 420–490

.96          *Romansch language

.98          Sardinian and Corsican

.982            *Sardinian [*formerly* 457.9]

.982 7              Historical and geographic variations, modern nongeographic variations

Number built according to instructions under 420–490

[.982 709 459 1–.982 709 459 4]        Treatment by localities in Sardinia

Do not use; class in 459.98271–459.98274

---

\>          459.982 71–459.982 74  Geographic variations in Sardinia [*formerly* 457.91–457.94]

Class comprehensive works in 459.9827

.982 71              Geographic variations in Cagliari province of Sardinia [*formerly* 457.91]

.982 72              Geographic variations in Nuoro province of Sardinia [*formerly* 457.92]

.982 73              Geographic variations in Sassari province of Sardinia [*formerly* 457.93]

.982 74              Geographic variations in Oristano province of Sardinia [*formerly* 457.94]

.984            *Corsican [*formerly* 457.95]

# 460    Spanish, Portuguese, Galician

Class comprehensive works on Romance languages in 440

.01–.09      Standard subdivisions of comprehensive works on Spanish, Portuguese, Galician

### .1–.9    Standard subdivisions of Spanish

Notation from Table 1 as modified under —01–09 in Table 4, e.g., semantics of Spanish 460.143

### 461–468 Subdivisions of Spanish

Except for modifications shown under specific entries, add to base number 46 notation 1–8 from Table 4, e.g., phonology of Spanish 461.5

# 461    Writing systems, phonology, phonetics of standard Spanish

Number built according to instructions under 461–468

# 462    Etymology of standard Spanish

Number built according to instructions under 461–468

*Add to base number as instructed under 420–490

**463**        **Dictionaries of standard Spanish**

> Number built according to instructions under 461–468

**[464]**      **[Unassigned]**

> Most recently used in Edition 16

**465**        **Grammar of standard Spanish**

> Number built according to instructions under 461–468

**[466]**      **[Unassigned]**

> Most recently used in Edition 18

**467**        **Historical and geographic variations, modern nongeographic variations of Spanish**

> Number built according to instructions under 461–468

.001–.008      Standard subdivisions

.009           History, geographic treatment, biography

[.009 02]              6th–15th centuries, 500–1499

> Do not use for Old Spanish; class in 467.01. Do not use for Middle Spanish; class in 467.02

[.009 031]             16th century, 1500–1599

> Do not use; class in 467.02

[.009 4–.009 9]     Specific continents, countries, localities in modern world

> Do not use; class in 467.9

.01            Old Spanish to 1100

.02            Middle Spanish, 1100–1600

[.09]          Modern nongeographic variations

> Number discontinued; class in 467

**[.1–.8]**     **Geographic variations in parts of Spain**

> Relocated to 467.9461–467.9468

**.9**          **Geographic variations**

[.901–.909]       Standard subdivisions

> Do not use; class in 467.001–467.009

.91            Geographic variations in areas, regions, places in general

> Add to base number 467.91 the numbers following —1 in notation 11–19 from Table 2, e.g., dialects of rural regions 467.91734

.94–.99      Geographic variations in specific continents, countries, localities in modern world

Add to base number 467.9 notation 4–9 from Table 2, e.g., geographic variations in parts of Spain 467.9461–467.9468 [*formerly* 467.1–467.8], geographic variations in Spain 467.946, Judeo-Spanish (Ladino) 467.9496, Papiamento 467.972986, Latin American dialects 467.98

*For geographic variations of Old Spanish, see 467.01094–467.01099; for geographic variations of Middle Spanish, see 467.02094–467.02099*

# 468      Standard Spanish usage (Prescriptive linguistics)

Number built according to instructions under 461–468

# 469      *Portuguese

.01–.09      Standard subdivisions of Portuguese

Notation from Table 1 as modified under —01–09 in Table 4, e.g., semantics of Portuguese 469.0143

### .1–.5      Subdivisions of Portuguese

Except for modifications shown under specific entries, add to base number 469 notation 1–5 from Table 4, e.g., phonology of Portuguese 469.15

### .7      Historical and geographic variations, modern nongeographic variations

Number built according to instructions under 420–490

.700 1–.700 8      Standard subdivisions

.700 9      History, geographic treatment, biography

[.700 902]      6th–15th centuries, 500–1499

Do not use for Old Portuguese; class in 469.701. Do not use for Middle Portuguese; class in 469.702

[.700 903 1]      16th century, 1500–1599

Do not use; class in 469.702

[.700 94–.700 99]      Specific continents, countries, localities in modern world

Do not use; class in 469.79

.701      Old Portuguese to 1100

.702      Middle Portuguese, 1100–1600

[.709]      Modern nongeographic variations

Number discontinued; class in 469.7

*Add to base number as instructed under 420–490

[.71–.76]     Geographic variations in Portuguese parts of Iberian Peninsula

> Geographic variations of Portuguese in Portuguese parts of Iberian Peninsula relocated to 469.794691–469.794696; geographic variations of Galician in Portuguese parts of Iberian Peninsula relocated from 469.71–469.72 to 469.9

[.78]     Geographic variations in Madeira

> Relocated to 469.794698

.79     Geographic variations

> Class here pidgins, creoles

[.790 1–.790 9]     Standard subdivisions

> Do not use; class in 469.7001–469.7009

.791     Geographic variations in areas, regions, places in general

> Add to base number 469.791 the numbers following —1 in notation 11–19 from Table 2, e.g., dialects of the Portuguese Empire 469.791712469
>
> Geographic variations in Azores relocated to 469.794699

.794     Geographic variations in Europe

> Add to base number 469.794 the numbers following —4 in notation 41–49 from Table 2, e.g., geographic variations in Portuguese parts of Iberian Peninsula 469.794691–469.794696 [*formerly* 469.71–469.76], geographic variations in Madeira 469.794698 [*formerly* 469.78], geographic variations in Azores 469.794699 [*formerly* 469.791], geographic variations in Spain 469.7946, geographic variations in Portugal 469.79469
>
> > *For geographic variations of Old Portuguese, see 469.701094–469.701099; for geographic variations of Middle Portuguese, see 469.702094–469.702099*
>
> Geographic variations of Galician in Spain relocated to 469.9

.795–.797     Geographic variations in Asia, Africa, North America

> Add to base number 469.79 notation 5–7 from Table 2, e.g., Crioulo of Guinea-Bissau 469.796657 [*formerly* 469.7996657], Crioulo of Cape Verde Islands and comprehensive works on Crioulo 469.796658 [*formerly* 469.7996658]
>
> > *See also 467.972986 for Papiamento*

.798     Geographic variations in South America

> Add to base number 469.798 the numbers following —8 in notation 81–89 from Table 2, e.g., geographic variations in Brazil 469.7981, dialects of São Paulo 469.798161
> > Notation 81–87 from Table 2 replaces notation 811–817 from Table 2 with the result that many numbers have been reused with new meanings

.799     Geographic variations in other parts of world

> Add to base number 469.799 the numbers following —9 in notation 93–98 from Table 2, e.g., geographic variations of Australia 469.7994

[.799 01–.799 09]      Standard subdivisions

> Do not use; class in 469.79001–469.79009

.799 1      Geographic variations in areas, regions, places in general

> Add to base number 469.7991 the numbers following —1 in notation 11–19 from Table 2, e.g., dialects of rural regions 469.7991734

[.799 665 7]      Crioulo of Guinea-Bissau

> Relocated to 469.796657

[.799 665 8]      Crioulo of Cape Verde Islands; comprehensive works on Crioulo

> Relocated to 469.796658

**.8**      **Standard Portuguese usage (Prescriptive linguistics)**

> Add to base number 469.8 the numbers following —8 in notation 8001–8955 from Table 4, e.g., reading Portuguese 469.84

**.9**      **\*Galician [*formerly* 469.71–469.72, 469.794]**

> Class here Gallegan

# 470    Latin and related Italic languages

> Class here Italic languages
>
> Class comprehensive works on Latin and Greek in 480
>
> *For Romance languages, see 440*

.01–.09      Standard subdivisions of Italic languages

**.1–.9**      **Standard subdivisions of Latin**

> Notation from Table 1 as modified under —01–09 in Table 4, e.g., semantics of Latin 470.143

## 471–478 Subdivisions of Latin

> Except for modifications shown under specific entries, add to base number 47 notation 1–8 from Table 4, e.g., phonology of Latin 471.5
>
> *See Manual at 471–475, 478 vs. 477*

## 471    Writing systems, phonology, phonetics of classical Latin

> Number built according to instructions under 471–478

## 472    Etymology of classical Latin

> Number built according to instructions under 471–478

## 473    Dictionaries of classical Latin

> Number built according to instructions under 471–478

---

\*Add to base number as instructed under 420–490

**[474]**      **[Unassigned]**

> Most recently used in Edition 16

**475**      **Grammar of classical Latin**

> Number built according to instructions under 471–478

**[476]**      **[Unassigned]**

> Most recently used in Edition 18

**477**      **Old, postclassical, Vulgar Latin**

> Standard subdivisions are added for any or all topics in heading
>
> Variant name for Old Latin: preclassical Latin
>
> Number built according to instructions under 471–478

**478**      **Classical Latin usage (Prescriptive linguistics)**

> Number built according to instructions under 471–478
>
> Class here classical-revival Latin usage during medieval or modern times

**479**      **Other Italic languages**

> **.4–.9**      **Specific languages**
>
> > Add to base number 479 the numbers following —79 in notation 794–799 from Table 6, e.g., Umbrian 479.9

**480**      **Classical Greek and related Hellenic languages**

> Classical Greek: the Greek that flourished between 750 and 350 B.C.
>
> Class here Hellenic languages, comprehensive works on classical (Greek and Latin) languages
>
> > *For Latin, see 470*

> **.01–.09**      Standard subdivisions of classical (Greek and Latin) languages
>
> **.1–.9**      **Standard subdivisions of Hellenic languages, of classical Greek**

**481–488**      **Subdivisions of classical, preclassical, postclassical Greek**

> Except for modifications shown under specific entries, add to base number 48 notation 1–8 from Table 4, e.g., phonology of classical Greek 481.5
>
> Dialects of classical Greek are classed in the numbers for classical Greek (480.1–480.9, 481–485, 488)
>
> > *For standard subdivisions of classical Greek, see 480.1–480.9*

**481**      **Writing systems, phonology, phonetics of classical Greek**

> Number built according to instructions under 481–488

**482 Etymology of classical Greek**

> Number built according to instructions under 481–488

**483 Dictionaries of classical Greek**

> Number built according to instructions under 481–488

**[484] [Unassigned]**

> Most recently used in Edition 16

**485 Grammar of classical Greek**

> Number built according to instructions under 481–488

**[486] [Unassigned]**

> Most recently used in Edition 18

**487 Preclassical and postclassical Greek**

> Number built according to instructions under 481–488

**.1 Preclassical Greek**

> Including Mycenaean Greek, Linear B
>
> *See also 492.6 for Linear A*

**.3 Postclassical Greek**

> Including Byzantine Greek
>
> *For Koine, see 487.4*

**.4 Koine (Hellenistic Greek)**

> Class here Biblical Greek

**488 Classical Greek usage (Prescriptive linguistics)**

> Number built according to instructions under 481–488

**489 Other Hellenic languages**

**.3 *Modern Greek**

> Including Demotic, Katharevusa

# 490 Other languages

*Add to base number as instructed under 420–490

## SUMMARY

| | |
|---|---|
| 491 | East Indo-European and Celtic languages |
| 492 | Afro-Asiatic languages |
| 493 | Non-Semitic Afro-Asiatic languages |
| 494 | Altaic, Uralic, Hyperborean, Dravidian languages, miscellaneous languages of south Asia |
| 495 | Languages of east and southeast Asia |
| 496 | African languages |
| 497 | North American native languages |
| 498 | South American native languages |
| 499 | Non-Austronesian languages of Oceania, Austronesian languages, miscellaneous languages |

## 491    East Indo-European and Celtic languages

Class comprehensive works on Indo-European languages in 410

## SUMMARY

| | |
|---|---|
| 491.1 | Indo-Iranian languages |
| .2 | Sanskrit |
| .3 | Middle Indo-Aryan languages |
| .4 | Modern Indo-Aryan languages |
| .5 | Iranian languages |
| .6 | Celtic languages |
| .7 | Russian and related East Slavic languages |
| .8 | Slavic (Slavonic) languages |
| .9 | Baltic and other Indo-European languages |

### .1    Indo-Iranian languages

Class here comprehensive works on languages of south Asia

> *For Indo-Aryan languages, see 491.2–491.4; for Iranian languages, see 491.5; for Dravidian languages and miscellaneous languages of south Asia, see 494.8; for languages of south Asia closely related to languages of east and southeast Asia, see 495; for Andamanese languages, see 495.9*

---

> ### 491.2–491.4   Indo-Aryan languages

Class comprehensive works in 491.1

### .2    *Sanskrit

.29       Vedic (Old Indo-Aryan)

### .3    Middle Indo-Aryan languages

Former heading: Middle Indic languages

Class here comprehensive works on Prakrit languages

> *For modern Prakrit languages, see 491.4*

.37       *Pali

---

*Add to base number as instructed under 420–490

.4 **Modern Indo-Aryan languages**

> Former heading: Modern Indic languages

> Class here modern Prakrit languages

> Class comprehensive works on Prakrit languages in 491.3

.41 Sindhi and Lahnda

.410 1–.410 9 Standard subdivisions of Sindhi

> Notation from Table 1 as modified under —01–09 in Table 4, e.g., semantics of Sindhi 491.40143

.411–.418 Subdivisions of Sindhi

> Add to base number 491.41 notation 1–8 from Table 4, e.g., grammar of Sindhi 491.415

.419 *Lahnda

.42 *Panjabi

.43 Western Hindi languages

> Class here comprehensive works on Hindi languages

> *For languages of east central zone of Indo-Aryan languages (Eastern Hindi languages), see 491.492*

[.430 01–.430 09] Standard subdivisions of Western Hindi languages

> Relocated to 491.4301–491.4309

.430 1–.430 9 Standard subdivisions of Western Hindi languages [*formerly* 491.43001–491.43009], Hindi

> Notation from Table 1 as modified under —01–09 in Table 4, e.g., semantics of Hindi 491.430143

.431–.438 Subdivisions of Hindi

> Add to base number 491.43 notation 1–8 from Table 4, e.g., grammar of Hindi 491.435

.439 *Urdu

.44 *Bengali

> Class here comprehensive works on Bengali and Assamese

> *For Assamese, see 491.451*

.45 Assamese, Bihari, Oriya

.451 *Assamese

.454 *Bihari

---

*Add to base number as instructed under 420–490

| | |
|---|---|
| .454 7 | Historical and geographic variations, modern nongeographic variations |
| | Number built according to instructions under 420–490 |
| | Including Bhojpuri, Magahi, Maithili |
| .456 | *Oriya |
| .46 | Marathi and Konkani |
| .460 1–.460 9 | Standard subdivisions of Marathi |
| | Notation from Table 1 as modified under —01–09 in Table 4, e.g., semantics of Marathi 491.460143 |
| .461–.468 | Subdivisions of Marathi |
| | Add to base number 491.46 notation 1–8 from Table 4, e.g., grammar of Marathi 491.465 |
| .467 | Historical and geographic variations, modern nongeographic variations of Marathi |
| | Number built according to instructions under 491.4601–491.468 |
| | *For Konkani, see 491.469* |
| .469 | *Konkani |
| .47 | Gujarati, Bhili, Rajasthani |
| .470 1–.470 9 | Standard subdivisions of Gujarati |
| | Notation from Table 1 as modified under —01–09 in Table 4, e.g., semantics of Gujarati 491.470143 |
| .471–.478 | Subdivisions of Gujarati |
| | Add to base number 491.47 notation 1–8 from Table 4, e.g., grammar of Gujarati 491.475 |
| .479 | *Rajasthani |
| .479 7 | Historical and geographic variations, modern nongeographic variations |
| | Number built according to instructions under 420–490 |
| | Including Jaipuri, Marwari |
| .48 | Sinhalese-Maldivian languages |
| | Class here Sinhalese (Sinhala) |
| .480 1–.480 9 | Standard subdivisions of Sinhalese (Sinhala) |
| | Notation from Table 1 as modified under —01–09 in Table 4, e.g., semantics of Sinhalese 491.480143 |
| .481–.488 | Subdivisions of Sinhalese (Sinhala) |
| | Add to base number 491.48 notation 1–8 from Table 4, e.g., grammar of Sinhalese 491.485 |

*Add to base number as instructed under 420–490

| .489 | *Divehi (Maldivian) |
|---|---|

.49      Other Indo-Aryan languages

        Including Nuristani (Kafiri)

        *See also 494.8 for Dravidian languages; also 495.4 for Tibeto-Burman languages; also 495.95 for Munda languages*

.492      Languages of east central zone of Indo-Aryan languages (Eastern Hindi languages)

        Including Awadhi, Bagheli, Chattisgarhi, Fijian Hindustani (Fiji Hindi)

        Class comprehensive works on Hindi languages in 491.43

.495      *Nepali language

.496      Pahari languages

        Including Garhwali

        Class here languages of northern zone of Indo-Aryan languages

        *For Nepali, see 491.495*

.497      *Romani

.499      Dardic (Pisacha) languages

        Including Kashmiri, Khowar, Kohistani, Shina

**.5**      **Iranian languages**

.51      *Old Persian

        Class here ancient west Iranian languages

        *See also 491.52 for Avestan language*

.52      *Avestan

        Class here ancient east Iranian languages

.53      Middle Iranian languages

        Including Khotanese (Saka), Pahlavi (Middle Persian), Sogdian

.55      *Modern Persian (Farsi)

        Class Tajik in 491.57

.56      *Dari

.57      *Tajik

.59      Other modern Iranian languages

        Including Pamir languages; Osetin (Ossetic)

.593      *Pashto (Afghan)

---

*Add to base number as instructed under 420–490

| | |
|---|---|
| .597 | Kurdish languages |

Including central and southern Kurdish

Class here Kurdish (Kurmanji, northern Kurdish)

| | |
|---|---|
| .597 01–.597 09 | Standard subdivisions of Kurdish (Kurmanji) |

Notation from Table 1 as modified under —01–09 in Table 4, e.g., semantics of Kurdish 491.5970143

| | |
|---|---|
| .597 1–.597 8 | Subdivisions of Kurdish (Kurmanji) |

Add to base number 491.597 notation 1–8 from Table 4, e.g., grammar of Kurdish 491.5975

| | |
|---|---|
| .598 | *Baluchi |
| **.6** | **Celtic languages** |

Including Gaulish

| | |
|---|---|
| .62 | *Irish Gaelic |
| .63 | *Scottish Gaelic |
| .64 | *Manx |
| .66 | *Welsh (Cymric) |
| .67 | *Cornish |
| .68 | *Breton |
| **.7** | **Russian and related East Slavic languages** |

Class here East Slavic languages

Class comprehensive works on Slavic (Slavonic) languages in 491.8

| | |
|---|---|
| .700 1–.700 9 | Standard subdivisions of East Slavic languages |
| .701–.709 | Standard subdivisions of Russian |

Notation from Table 1 as modified under —01–09 in Table 4, e.g., semantics of Russian 491.70143

| | |
|---|---|
| .71–.75 | Writing systems, phonology, phonetics, etymology, dictionaries, grammar of Russian |

Add to base number 491.7 notation 1–5 from Table 4, e.g., grammar of Russian 491.75

| | |
|---|---|
| .77 | Historical and geographic variations, modern nongeographic variations of Russian |
| .770 01–.770 08 | Standard subdivisions |
| .770 09 | History, geographic treatment, biography |
| [.770 090 2] | 6th–15th centuries, 500–1499 |

Do not use; class in 491.7701

*Add to base number as instructed under 420–490

| | |
|---|---|
| [.770 090 31] | 16th century, 1500–1599 |
| | Do not use for Old Russian; class in 491.7701. Do not use for Middle Russian; class in 491.7702 |
| [.770 090 32] | 17th century, 1600–1699 |
| | Do not use; class in 491.7702 |
| .770 090 33 | 18th century, 1700–1799 |
| | Do not use for Middle Russian; class in 491.7702 |
| [.770 094–.770 099] | Specific continents, countries, localities in modern world |
| | Do not use; class in 491.774–491.779 |
| .770 1 | Old Russian to 1550 |
| .770 2 | Middle Russian, 1550–1750 |
| [.770 9] | Modern nongeographic variations |
| | Number discontinued; class in 491.77 |
| .774–.779 | Geographic variations |

> Add to base number 491.77 notation 4–9 from Table 2, e.g., dialects of Far Eastern Siberia 491.77577
>
> *For geographic variations of Old Russian, see 491.7701094–491.7701099; for geographic variations in Middle Russian, see 491.7702094–491.7702099*

| | |
|---|---|
| .78 | Standard Russian usage (Prescriptive linguistics) |
| .780 01–.780 09 | Standard subdivisions |
| .780 2–.780 4 | Translating |

> Add to base number 491.78 the numbers following —8 in notation 802–804 from Table 4, e.g., translating Russian literature (belles-lettres) and rhetoric 491.7804

| | |
|---|---|
| .781–.786 | Words, approaches to expression, reading, readers |

> Add to base number 491.78 the numbers following —8 in notation 81–86 from Table 4, e.g., reading Russian 491.784

| | |
|---|---|
| .79 | Ukrainian and Belarusian |
| .790 1–.790 9 | Standard subdivisions of Ukrainian |

> Notation from Table 1 as modified under 01–09 in Table 4, e.g., semantics of Ukrainian 491.790143

| | |
|---|---|
| .791–.798 | Subdivisions of Ukrainian |

> Add to base number 491.79 notation 1–8 from Table 4, e.g., grammar of Ukrainian 491.795

| | |
|---|---|
| .799 | *Belarusian |

*Add to base number as instructed under 420–490

**.8**       **Slavic (Slavonic) languages**

Including Common Slavic

Class here comprehensive works on Balto-Slavic languages

*For East Slavic languages, see 491.7; for Baltic languages, see 491.9*

**.801–.803**       Standard subdivisions

Notation from Table 1 as modified under —01–03 in Table 4, e.g., semantics of Slavic languages 491.80143

**.804**       Special topics of Slavic languages

Add to base number 491.804 notation 1–8 from Table 4, e.g., grammar of Slavic languages 491.8045

**.805–.809**       Standard subdivisions

**.81**       Bulgarian and related South Slavic languages

Class here South Slavic languages

*For Serbian, see 491.82; for Croatian and Bosnian, see 491.83; for Slovenian, see 491.84*

**[.810 01–.810 09]**       Standard subdivisions of South Slavic languages

Relocated to 491.8101–491.8109

**.810 1–.810 9**       Standard subdivisions of South Slavic languages [*formerly* 491.81001–491.81009], Bulgarian

Notation from Table 1 as modified under —01–09 in Table 4, e.g., semantics of Bulgarian 491.810143

**.811–.815**       Writing systems, phonology, phonetics, etymology, dictionaries, grammar of Bulgarian

Except for modifications shown under specific entries, add to base number 491.81 notation 1–5 from Table 4, e.g., phonology of Bulgarian 491.8115

Class comprehensive works in 491.81

**.817**       Historical and geographic variations, modern nongeographic variations of Bulgarian

Number built according to instructions under 420–490

**.817 001–.817 008**       Standard subdivisions

**.817 009**       History, geographic treatment, biography

Do not use for Old Bulgarian; class in 491.81701

**.817 01**       *Old Bulgarian (Church Slavic)

**.818**       Standard Bulgarian usage (Prescriptive linguistics)

**.818 001–.818 009**       Standard subdivisions

---

*Add to base number as instructed under 420–490

| | |
|---|---|
| .818 02–.818 04 | Translating |

Add to base number 491.818 the numbers following —8 in notation 802–804 from Table 4, e.g., translating Bulgarian literature (belles-lettres) and rhetoric 491.81804

| | |
|---|---|
| .818 1–.818 6 | Words, approaches to expression, reading, readers |

Add to base number 491.818 the numbers following —8 in notation 81–86 from Table 4, e.g., reading Bulgarian 491.8184

| | |
|---|---|
| .819 | *Macedonian |
| .82 | *Serbian |

Class here Serbo-Croatian (languages of Serbs, Croats, and Bosnians treated together as a single language)

Croatian relocated to 491.83; Bosnian relocated to 491.839

| | |
|---|---|
| .83 | *Croatian [*formerly* 491.82] and Bosnian |

Subdivisions are added for Croatian and Bosnian together, for Croatian alone

| | |
|---|---|
| .839 | *Bosnian [*formerly* 491.82] |
| .84 | *Slovenian |
| .85 | Polish and related West Slavic languages |

Including Kashubian

Class here West Slavic languages

*For Czech, see 491.86; for Slovak, see 491.87; for Wendish, see 491.88; for Polabian, see 491.89*

| | |
|---|---|
| [.850 01–.850 09] | Standard subdivisions of West Slavic languages |

Relocated to 491.8501–491.8509

| | |
|---|---|
| .850 1–.850 9 | Standard subdivisions of West Slavic languages [*formerly* 491.85001–491.85009], Polish |

Notation from Table 1 as modified under —01–09 in Table 4, e.g., semantics of Polish 491.850143

| | |
|---|---|
| .851–.858 | Subdivisions of Polish |

Add to base number 491.85 notation 1–8 from Table 4, e.g., grammar of Polish 491.855

| | |
|---|---|
| .86 | *Czech |
| .867 | Historical and geographic variations, modern nongeographic variations |

Number built according to instructions under 420–490

Including Moravian dialects

| | |
|---|---|
| .87 | *Slovak |

*Add to base number as instructed under 420–490

| | |
|---|---|
| .88 | *Wendish (Lusatian, Sorbian) |
| .89 | *Polabian |

**.9      Baltic and other Indo-European languages**

---

>         491.91–491.93 Baltic languages

        Class comprehensive works in 491.9

| | |
|---|---|
| .91 | Old Prussian |
| .92 | *Lithuanian |
| .93 | *Latvian (Lettish) |
| .99 | Other Indo-European languages |

        Add to base number 491.99 the numbers following —9199 in notation 91991–91998 from Table 6, e.g., Albanian 491.991, Phrygian 491.993; then to the number given for each language listed below add further as instructed at beginning of Table 4, e.g., grammar of Albanian 491.9915

        491.991 Albanian

        491.992 Armenian

        491.994 Tocharian

        491.998 Hittite

# 492     Afro-Asiatic languages

        Class here Semitic languages

        *For non-Semitic Afro-Asiatic languages, see 493*

| | |
|---|---|
| .01–.03 | Standard subdivisions |

        Notation from Table 1 as modified under —01–03 in Table 4, e.g., semantics of Semitic languages 492.0143

| | |
|---|---|
| .04 | Special topics of Afro-Asiatic and Semitic languages |

        Add to base number 492.04 notation 1–8 from Table 4, e.g., grammar of Semitic languages 492.045

| | |
|---|---|
| .05–.09 | Standard subdivisions |

**.1      East Semitic languages**

        Including Assyrian, Babylonian

        Class here Akkadian (Assyro-Babylonian)

        *For Eblaite, see 492.6*

        *See also 499.95 for Sumerian*

*Add to base number as instructed under 420–490

.101–.109      Standard subdivisions of Akkadian (Assyro-Babylonian)

> Notation from Table 1 as modified under —01–09 in Table 4, e.g., semantics of Akkadian 492.10143

.11–.18      Subdivisions of Akkadian (Assyro-Babylonian)

> Add to base number 492.1 notation 1–8 from Table 4, e.g., grammar of Akkadian 492.15; dialects of Assyrian, Babylonian 492.17

---

> **492.2–492.9 West Semitic languages**

> Class comprehensive works in 492

.2      **Aramaic languages**

> *For Eastern Aramaic languages, see 492.3*

.29      Western Aramaic languages

> Including Biblical Aramaic (Chaldee) and Samaritan

.3      **Eastern Aramaic languages**

> Class here Syriac

.301–.309      Standard subdivisions of Syriac

> Notation from Table 1 as modified under —01–09 in Table 4, e.g., semantics of Syriac 492.30143

.31–.38      Subdivisions of Syriac

> Add to base number 492.3 notation 1–8 from Table 4, e.g., grammar of Syriac 492.35

.4      **\*Hebrew**

.6      **Canaanite languages**

> Including Ammonite, Eblaite, Moabite, Phoenician; Linear A and its language

> Class here comprehensive works on Canaanitic languages

> *For Hebrew, see 492.4*

> *See also 487.1 for Linear B*

> *See Manual at T6—926*

.67      \*Ugaritic

.7      **Arabic and Maltese**

> Class here Classical Arabic, modern standard Arabic

> *See also 492.9 for South Arabian languages*

---

\*Add to base number as instructed under 420–490

.701–.709    Standard subdivisions of Arabic

> Notation from Table 1 as modified under —01–09 in Table 4, e.g., semantics of Arabic 492.70143

.71–.78    Subdivisions of Arabic

> Add to base number 492.7 notation 1–8 from Table 4, e.g., grammar of Arabic 492.75

> Class Maltese in 492.79

.79    *Maltese

**.8    Ethiopian languages**

> Including Gurage, Harari

> Class here comprehensive works on South Semitic languages

> *For South Arabian languages, see 492.9*

.81    *Ge'ez language

.82    *Tigré

.83    *Tigrinya

.87    *Amharic

.877    Historical and geographic variations, modern nongeographic variations

> Number built according to instructions under 420–490

**.9    South Arabian languages**

> Including Mahri, Sokotri

> Class comprehensive works on South Semitic languages in 492.8

> *See also 492.7 for Arabic*

---

*Add to base number as instructed under 420–490

## 493     Non-Semitic Afro-Asiatic languages

Add to base number 493 the numbers following —93 in notation 931–937 from Table 6, e.g., Afar 493.5, Oromo 493.55; then to the number for each language listed below add further as instructed at beginning of Table 4, e.g., grammar of Oromo 493.555

493.1 Egyptian

493.2 Coptic

493.33 Tamazight

493.34 Kabyle

493.38 Tamashek

493.54 Somali

493.55 Oromo

493.72 Hausa

## 494     Altaic, Uralic, Hyperborean, Dravidian languages, miscellaneous languages of south Asia

Add to base number 494 the numbers following —94 in notation 941–948 from Table 6, e.g., Mongolian 494.23, Altai 494.33; then to the number for each language listed below add further as instructed at beginning of Table 4, e.g., grammar of Mongolian 494.235

494.23 Mongolian proper, Halh Mongolian (Khalkha Mongolian)

494.315 Chuvash

494.323 Uighur

494.325 Uzbek

494.332 Yakut

494.345 Kazakh

494.347 Kyrgyz

494.35 Turkish, Osmanli, Ottoman Turkish

494.361 Azerbaijani

494.364 Turkmen

494.387 Tatar

494.388 Crimean Tatar

494.511 Hungarian (Magyar)

(continued)

**494        Altaic, Uralic, Hyperborean, Dravidian languages, miscellaneous languages of south Asia (continued)**

> 494.541 Finnish (Suomi)
>
> 494.542 Tornedalen Finnish, Meänkieli
>
> 494.545 Estonian
>
> 494.5722 South Sámi
>
> 494.5743 Lule Sámi
>
> 494.5745 North Sámi
>
> 494.811 Tamil
>
> 494.812 Malayalam
>
> 494.814 Kannada (Kanarese)
>
> 494.823 Gondi
>
> 494.824 Kui (Khond, Kandh)
>
> 494.827 Telugu
>
> 494.83 Brahui
>
> 494.892 Burushaski
>
> *For Japanese, see 495.6; for Korean, see 495.7*
>
> *See also 497.1 for Inuit, Yupik, Aleut languages*

**495        Languages of east and southeast Asia**

> Including Karen
>
> Here are classed languages of south Asia closely related to the languages of east and southeast Asia
>
> Class here Sino-Tibetan languages
>
> *For Austronesian languages of east and southeast Asia, see 499.2*

**.1        *Chinese**

> Class here Beijing dialect; Mandarin (Putonghua) (standard written Chinese)

**.17        Historical and geographic variations, modern nongeographic variations of Chinese**

> Number built according to instructions under 420–490
>
> Class Mandarin Chinese in 495.1

*Add to base number as instructed under 420–490

[.170 94–.170 99]     Specific continents, countries, localities in modern world

Do not use; class in 495.179

[.171–.178]     Geographic variations in parts of China

Relocated to 495.179511–495.179518

.179     Geographic variations

[.179 01–.179 09]     Standard subdivisions

Do not use; class in 495.17001–495.17009

.179 1     Geographic variations in areas, regions, places in general

Add to base number 467.91 the numbers following —1 in notation 11–19 from Table 2, e.g., dialects of rural regions 495.1791734

.179 4–.179 9     Geographic variations in specific continents, countries, localities in modern world

Add to base number 495.179 notation 4–9 from Table 2, e.g., geographic variations in parts of China 495.179511–495.179518 [*formerly* 495.171–495.178]; dialects of Guangdong Sheng, comprehensive works on Yue (Cantonese) dialects 495.1795127 [*formerly* 495.1727]; works that focus narrowly on the Cantonese dialect as spoken in the municipality of Canton 495.17951275 [*formerly* 495.17275]; geographic variations in China 495.17951, Chinese dialects in Malaysia 495.179595, Yue (Cantonese) dialects as spoken in North America 495.1797

**.4     Tibetan and related Tibeto-Burman languages**

Including Baric, Bodish, Loloish languages

Class here Tibeto-Burman languages

Class Karen in 495

*For Burmese, see 495.8*

[.400 1–.400 9]     Standard subdivisions of Tibeto-Burman languages

Relocated to 495.401–495.409

.401–.409     Standard subdivisions of Tibeto-Burman languages [*formerly* 495.4001–495.4009], Tibetan

Notation from Table 1 as modified under —01–09 in Table 4, e.g., semantics of Tibetan 495.40143

.41–.48     Subdivisions of Tibetan

Add to base number 495.4 notation 1–8 from Table 4, e.g., grammar of Tibetan 495.45

.49     Eastern Himalayan languages

Including Chepang, Limbu, Magari, Sunwar; Newari

Class here Kiranti languages, Mahakiranti languages

*See also 491.495 for Nepali*

**.6**     **\*Japanese**

**.7**     **\*Korean**

**.8**     **\*Burmese**

**.9**     **Miscellaneous languages of southeast Asia; Munda languages**

> Only those languages provided for below
>
> Including Kadai languages, Kam-Sui languages
>
> Class here Daic languages
>
> Class Austroasiatic languages in 495.93
>
> *For Austronesian languages, see 499.2*

.91     Thai (Siamese) and related Tai languages

> Class here Tai languages

[.910 01–.910 09]     Standard subdivisions of Tai languages

> Relocated to 495.9101–495.9109

.910 1–.910 9     Standard subdivisions of Tai languages [*formerly* 495.91001–495.91009], Thai (Siamese)

> Notation from Table 1 as modified under —01–09 in Table 4, e.g., semantics of Thai 495.910143

.911–.918     Subdivisions of Thai (Siamese)

> Add to base number 495.91 notation 1–8 from Table 4, e.g., grammar of Thai 495.915

.919     Other Tai languages

> Including Shan
>
> *For Viet-Muong languages, see 495.92*

.919 1          \*Lao

.92–.97     Viet-Muong, Austroasiatic, Munda, Hmong-Mien (Miao-Yao) languages

> Add to base number 495.9 the numbers following —959 in notation 9592–9597 from Table 6, e.g., Vietnamese 495.922, Khasi 495.93; then to the number for each language listed below add further as instructed at beginning of Table 4, e.g., grammar of Vietnamese 495.9225
>
> 495.922 Vietnamese
>
> 495.932 Khmer (Cambodian)
>
> 495.972 Hmong (Miao)
>
> 495.978 Yao

\*Add to base number as instructed under 420–490

## 496     African languages

Class Afrikaans in 439.36; class Malagasy in 499.3. Class an African creole having a non-African primary source language with the source language, plus notation 7 from Table 4, e.g., Krio 427.9664

*For Ethiopian languages, see 492.8; for non-Semitic Afro-Asiatic languages, see 493*

**.1**     **Khoisan languages**

Including Khoikhoi, San

**.3**     **Niger-Congo languages**

Including Ijoid, Kordofanian languages; Dogon

.32     West Atlantic languages

.321     Senegambian languages

Former heading: Senegal group

Including Serer (Serer-Sine)

*For Fula, see 496.322*

.321 4     *Wolof

.322     *Fula (Fulani)

.33     Igboid, Defoid, Edoid, Idomoid, Nupoid, Akpes, Oko, Ukaan languages; Kwa languages; Kru languages

Igboid, Defoid, Edoid, Idomoid, Nupoid, Akpes, Oko, Ukaan languages, formerly considered Kwa languages, are now considered Benue-Congo languages

Add to base number 496.33 the numbers following —9633 in notation 96332–96338 from Table 6, e.g., Yoruba 496.333, Baoulé 496.338; then to the number for each language listed below add further as instructed at beginning of Table 4, e.g., grammar of Yoruba 496.3335

496.332 Ibo (Igbo)

496.333 Yoruba

496.3374 Ewe

496.3378 Gã

496.3385 Akan, Fante, Twi

Class comprehensive works on Benue-Congo languages in 496.36

.34     Mande languages

.345     Manding-Mokole languages

Class here Mandekan languages

*Add to base number as instructed under 420–490

.345 2          *Bambara

.348          Mende-Bandi languages

        Including Bandi (Gbandi)

        Class here Mende

.348 01–.348 09          Standard subdivisions of Mende

        Notation from Table 1 as modified under —01–09 in Table 4, e.g., semantics of Mende 496.3480143

.348 1–.348 8          Subdivisions of Mende

        Add to base number 496.348 notation 1–8 from Table 4, e.g., grammar of Mende 496.3485

.35          Gur (Voltaic) languages

        Including Dagomba, Moré, Senufo

        Class Dogon in 496.3

.36          Benue-Congo and Adamawa-Ubangi languages

        Standard subdivisions are added for Benue-Congo and Adamawa-Ubangi languages together, for Benue-Congo languages alone

        Including Bamileke

        Class here Bantoid languages

        Class Mbam languages (from zone A) in 496.396

        *For Igboid, Defoid, Edoid, Idomoid, Nupoid, Akpes, Oko, Ukaan languages, see 496.33; for Bantu languages, see 496.39*

.361          Adamawa-Ubangi languages

        Including Gbaya, Zande

.361 6          *Sango

.364          Cross River languages

        Including Ibibio

.364 2          *Efik

.39          Bantu languages

        Bantu proper (Narrow Bantu)

        *See also 496.36 for Bantoid languages other than Bantu proper*

        *See Manual at T6—9639*

.390 1–.390 3          Standard subdivisions

        Notation from Table 1 as modified under —01–03 in Table 4, e.g., semantics of Bantu languages 496.390143

---

*Add to base number as instructed under 420–490

| .390 4 | Special topics of Bantu languages |
|---|---|

Add to base number 496.3904 notation 1–8 from Table 4, e.g., grammar of Bantu languages 496.39045

| .390 5–.390 9 | Standard subdivisions |
|---|---|
| .391–.399 | Specific Bantu languages and language families |

Add to base number 496.39 the numbers following —9639 in notation 96391–96399 from Table 6, e.g., Ewondo 496.396, Zulu 496.3986; then to the number for each language listed below add further as instructed at beginning of Table 4, e.g., grammar of Zulu 496.39865

496.3915 Bemba

496.3918 Nyanja, Chichewa (Chewa)

496.392 Swahili

496.3931 Kongo (Koongo)

496.3932 Mbundu (Kimbundu)

496.39461 Rwanda (Kinyarwanda)

496.39465 Rundi

496.3954 Kikuyu

496.3957 Ganda (Luganda)

496.3962 Duala

496.39686 Lingala

496.3975 Shona

496.3976 Venda (Tshivenda)

496.39771 Northern Sotho

496.39772 Southern Sotho

496.39775 Tswana

496.3978 Tsonga

496.3985 Xhosa

496.3986 Zulu

496.3987 Swazi (siSwati)

496.3989 Ndebele (South Africa)

**.5**     **Nilo-Saharan languages**

> Including Nilotic, Nubian languages; Luo, Songhai
>
> Class here Chari-Nile (Macrosudanic) languages

# 497    North American native languages

> Class here comprehensive works on North and South American native languages
>
> *For South American native languages, see 498*

**.1–.2**     **Inuit, Yupik, Aleut, Na-Dene languages**

> Add to base number 497 the numbers following —97 in notation 971–972 from Table 6, e.g., Na-Dene languages 497.2, Navajo 497.26; then to the number for each language listed below add further as instructed at beginning of Table 4, e.g., grammar of Navajo 497.265
>
> > 497.124 Eastern Canadian Inuktitut
> >
> > 497.19 Aleut
> >
> > 497.256 Mescalero-Chiricahua Apache (Chiricahua, Mescalero)
> >
> > 497.26 Navajo (Diné)
> >
> > 497.27 Tlingit
> >
> > 497.28 Haida

**.3**     **Algic and Muskogean languages**

> Standard subdivisions are added for Algic and Muskogean languages together, for Algic languages alone
>
> Including Lumbee, Yurok
>
> Class here Algonquian languages

.31–.38        Specific Algic and Muskogean languages and language families

Add to base number 497.3 the numbers following —973 in notation
9731–9738 from Table 6, e.g., Cree 497.323, Muskogean languages 497.38;
then to the number for each language listed below add further as instructed
at beginning of Table 4, e.g., grammar of Cree 497.3235

497.312 Kickapoo

497.313 Menomini

497.314 Mesquakie, Fox

497.315 Miami

497.316 Potawatomi

497.317 Shawnee

497.323 Cree

497.333 Ojibwa, Chippewa

497.336 Ottawa

497.343 Micmac

497.344 Mohegan, Narragansett

497.345 Unami (Delaware, Lenni Lenape)

497.347 Powhatan

497.348 Wampanoag

497.352 Blackfoot, Siksika

497.353 Cheyenne

497.354 Arapaho

497.385 Muskogee (Creek)

497.3859 Seminole

497.386 Chickasaw

497.387 Choctaw

.4        **Penutian, Mayan, Mixe-Zoque, Uto-Aztecan, Kiowa Tanoan languages**

.41–.49 Specific Penutian, Mayan, Mixe-Zoque, Uto-Aztecan, Kiowa Tanoan languages and language families

> Add to base number 497.4 the numbers following —974 in notation 9741–9749 from Table 6, e.g., Uto-Aztecan languages 497.45, Nahuatl 497.452; then to the number for each language listed below add further as instructed at beginning of Table 4, e.g., grammar of Nahuatl 497.4525

> 497.4122 Klamath, Modoc

> 497.4124 Nez Percé

> 497.4127 Yakama

> 497.4128 Tsimshian

> 497.4133 Miwok

> 497.422 Cakchikel

> 497.423 Quiché

> 497.427 Maya, Yucatec Maya

> 497.4287 Tzotzil

> 497.452 Nahuatl (Aztec)

> 497.4542 Yaqui

> 497.4544 Huichol

> 497.4546 Tarahumara

> 497.4552 Tohono O'odham

> 497.45529 Akimel O'odham

.5 **Siouan, Iroquoian, Hokan, Chumash, Yuki languages**

> Class Keresan languages in 497.9; class Caddoan languages in 497.93

> *See also 497.9 for Yuchi*

.52–.58     Specific Siouan, Iroquoian, Hokan, Chumash, Yuki languages and language families

Add to base number 497.5 the numbers following —975 in notation 9752–9758 from Table 6, e.g., Iroquoian languages 497.55, Cherokee 497.557; then to the number for each language listed below add further as instructed at beginning of Table 4, e.g., grammar of Cherokee 497.5575

497.522 Mandan

497.5243 Dakota

497.5244 Lakota

497.5253 Omaha

497.52539 Ponca

497.5254 Osage

497.526 Winnebago

497.5272 Crow

497.5274 Hidatsa

497.5542 Mohawk

497.5543 Oneida

497.5546 Seneca

497.555 Wyandot, Huron

497.557 Cherokee

497.5722 Mohave

497.5724 Havasupai, Walapai, Yavapai

497.576 Washo

**.6–.9**   **Oto-Manguean, Chibchan languages of North America, Misumalpan, other North American languages**

Add to base number 497 the numbers following —97 in notation 976–979 from Table 6, e.g., Oto-Manguean languages 497.6, Zapotec 497.68; then to the number for each language listed below add further as instructed at beginning of Table 4, e.g., grammar of Zapotec 497.685

497.63 Mixtec

497.68 Zapotec

497.83 San Blas Kuna (San Blas Cuna)

497.882 Miskito

497.922 Taino

497.932 Arikara

497.933 Pawnee

497.9435 Kalispel, Pend d'Oreille

497.953 Kwakiutl

497.955 Nootka

497.96 Purépecha (Tarasco)

497.992 Kutenai

497.994 Zuni

**498**   **South American native languages**

Add to base number 498 the numbers following —98 in notation 982–989 from Table 6, e.g., Quechua 498.323, Tucanoan languages 498.35; then to the number for each language listed below add further as instructed at beginning of Table 4, e.g., grammar of Quechua 498.3235

498.323 Quechua (Kechua)

498.324 Aymara

498.372 Shuar

498.3822 Paraguayan Guaraní

498.3832 Tupí (Nhengatu)

498.422 Carib (Galibi)

498.72 Mapudungun (Mapuche)

498.92 Yanomamo

# 499 Non-Austronesian languages of Oceania, Austronesian languages, miscellaneous languages

Add to base number 499 the numbers following —99 in notation 991–999 from Table 6, e.g., Polynesian languages 499.4, Maori 499.442; then to the number for each language listed below add further as instructed at beginning of Table 4, e.g., grammar of Maori 499.4425; however, for sign languages, see 419

499.211 Tagalog (Filipino)

499.221 Indonesian (Bahasa Indonesia)

499.222 Javanese

499.2232 Sunda (Sundanese)

499.2234 Madura (Madurese)

499.2238 Bali (Balinese)

499.2242 Aceh (Achinese)

499.2244 Minangkabau

499.22462 Batak Toba

499.22466 Batak Dairi

499.2248 Lampung

499.2256 Banjar (Banjarese)

499.2262 Bugis (Buginese)

499.2264 Makasar

499.28 Malay (Bahasa Malaysia, Standard Malay)

499.3 Malagasy

499.42 Hawaiian

499.442 Maori

499.444 Tahitian

499.462 Samoan

499.482 Tongan (Tonga)

499.484 Niue (Niuean)

(continued)

**499**      **Non-Austronesian languages of Oceania, Austronesian languages, miscellaneous languages (continued)**

499.59 Fijian

499.92 Basque

499.95 Sumerian

499.9623 Abkhaz

499.9625 Adyghe

499.969 Georgian

499.992 Esperanto

499.993 Interlingua

# 500

---

## 500    Natural sciences and mathematics

Natural sciences: sciences that deal with matter and energy, or with objects and processes observable in nature

Class here interdisciplinary works on natural and applied sciences

Class natural history in 508. Class scientific principles of a subject with the subject, plus notation 015 from Table 1, e.g., scientific principles of photography 770.15

> *For government policy on science, see 338.926; for applied sciences, see 600*
>
> *See Manual at 231.7652 vs. 213, 500, 576.8; also at 338.926 vs. 352.745, 500; also at 500 vs. 001*

### SUMMARY

| | |
|---|---|
| **530** | **Physics** |
| .01–.09 | Standard subdivisions |
| .1–.8 | [Theories, mathematical physics, states of matter, instrumentation, measurement] |
| **531** | Classical mechanics |
| **532** | Fluid mechanics |
| **533** | Pneumatics (Gas mechanics) |
| **534** | Sound and related vibrations |
| **535** | Light and related radiation |
| **536** | Heat |
| **537** | Electricity and electronics |
| **538** | Magnetism |
| **539** | Modern physics |
| | |
| **540** | **Chemistry and allied sciences** |
| .1–.9 | Standard subdivisions |
| **541** | Physical chemistry |
| **542** | Techniques, procedures, apparatus, equipment, materials |
| **543** | Analytical chemistry |
| **546** | Inorganic chemistry |
| **547** | Organic chemistry |
| **548** | Crystallography |
| **549** | Mineralogy |
| | |
| **550** | **Earth sciences** |
| **551** | Geology, hydrology, meteorology |
| **552** | Petrology |
| **553** | Economic geology |
| **554–559** | Earth sciences by specific continents, countries, localities in modern world; extraterrestrial worlds |
| | |
| **560** | **Paleontology** |
| .1–.9 | Standard subdivisions; stratigraphic paleontology; special topics of paleontology and paleozoology |
| **561** | Paleobotany; fossil microorganisms |
| **562** | Fossil invertebrates |
| **563** | Miscellaneous fossil marine and seashore invertebrates |
| **564** | Fossil Mollusca and Molluscoidea |
| **565** | Fossil Arthropoda |
| **566** | Fossil Chordata |
| **567** | Fossil cold-blooded vertebrates |
| **568** | Fossil Aves (birds) |
| **569** | Fossil Mammalia |
| | |
| **570** | **Biology** |
| .1–.9 | Standard subdivisions |
| **571** | Physiology and related subjects |
| **572** | Biochemistry |
| **573** | Specific physiological systems in animals, regional histology and physiology in animals |
| **575** | Specific parts of and physiological systems in plants |
| **576** | Genetics and evolution |
| **577** | Ecology |
| **578** | Natural history of organisms and related subjects |
| **579** | Natural history of microorganisms, fungi, algae |

| | | |
|---|---|---|
| 580 | | **Plants** |
| | .1–.9 | **Standard subdivisions** |
| 581 | | **Specific topics in natural history of plants** |
| 582 | | **Plants noted for specific vegetative characteristics and flowers** |
| 583 | | **Magnoliopsida (Dicotyledons)** |
| 584 | | **Liliopsida (Monocotyledons)** |
| 585 | | **Pinophyta (Gymnosperms)** |
| 586 | | **Cryptogamia (Seedless plants)** |
| 587 | | **Pteridophyta** |
| 588 | | **Bryophyta** |
| | | |
| 590 | | **Animals** |
| | .1–.9 | **Standard subdivisions** |
| 591 | | **Specific topics in natural history of animals** |
| 592 | | **Invertebrates** |
| 593 | | **Miscellaneous marine and seashore invertebrates** |
| 594 | | **Mollusca and Molluscoidea** |
| 595 | | **Arthropoda** |
| 596 | | **Chordata** |
| 597 | | **Cold-blooded vertebrates** |
| 598 | | **Aves (Birds)** |
| 599 | | **Mammalia (Mammals)** |

### .2 Physical sciences

> *For astronomy and allied sciences, see 520; for physics, see 530; for chemistry and allied sciences, see 540; for earth sciences, see 550*

### .5 Space sciences

> *For astronomy, see 520; for earth sciences in other worlds, see 550. For space sciences aspects of a specific subject, see the subject, plus notation 0919 from Table 1, e.g., chemical reactions in space 541.390919*
>
> *See Manual at 520 vs. 500.5, 523.1, 530.1, 919.9*

### .8 Groups of people

> Add to base number 500.8 the numbers following —08 in notation 081–089 from Table 1, e.g., women in science 500.82

# 501 Philosophy and theory

> Class scientific method as a general research technique in 001.42; class scientific method applied in the natural sciences in 507.21

# 502 Miscellany

### .8 Auxiliary techniques and procedures; apparatus, equipment, materials

> Notation 028 from Table 1 as modified below

.82 Microscopy

  Including photomicrography, stereology

  Class here microscopes; interdisciplinary works on microscopy

  Class interdisciplinary works on photomicrography in 778.31

  *For manufacture of microscopes, see 681.413. For microscopy in a specific subject, see the subject, plus notation 028 from Table 1, e.g., microscopy in archaeology 930.1028*

.823 Compound microscopy

  Class stereology with compound microscopes in 502.82

.825 Electron microscopy

  Class stereology with electron microscopes in 502.82

.84 Apparatus, equipment, materials

  Do not use for microscopes; class in 502.82

## 503 Dictionaries, encyclopedias, concordances

## [504] [Unassigned]

  Most recently used in Edition 16

## 505 Serial publications

## 506 Organizations and management

## 507 Education, research, related topics

### .2 Research

  Class research covering the sciences in the broad sense of all knowledge in 001.4

  *See Manual at 500 vs. 001*

.21 Research methods

  Class scientific method as a general research technique in 001.42

### .8 Use of apparatus and equipment in study and teaching

  Class here science fair projects, science projects in schools

## 508 Natural history

  Do not use for groups of people; class in 500.8

  Class here description and surveys of phenomena in nature

  Class natural history of organisms in 578

  *See Manual at 333.7–333.9 vs. 508, 913–919, 930–990; also at 578 vs. 304.2, 508, 910*

.09       History and biography

> Do not use for geographic treatment; class in 508.3–508.9

**.2**     **Seasons**

> Class here interdisciplinary works on seasons

> *For a specific aspect of seasons, see the aspect, e.g., effect of seasons on organisms 577.23*

**.3**     **Areas, regions, places in general; specific continents, countries, localities in ancient world**

.31       Areas, regions, places in general

> Add to base number 508.31 the numbers following —1 in notation 11–19 from Table 2, e.g., natural history of the sea 508.3162

.33       Specific continents, countries, localities in ancient world

> Add to base number 508.33 the numbers following —3 in notation 31–39 from Table 2, e.g., natural history of ancient Greece 508.338

**.4–.9**     **Specific continents, countries, localities in modern world**

> Add to base number 508 notation 4–9 from Table 2, e.g., natural history of Brazil 508.81

## 509     History, geographic treatment, biography

> Class history, geographic treatment, biography of natural phenomena in 508

## 510     Mathematics

> Class here pure mathematics

> *See Manual at 510; also at 510, T1—0151 vs. 003, T1—011; also at 510, T1—0151 vs. 004–006, T1—0285*

### SUMMARY

| | |
|---|---|
| 510.1 | Philosophy and theory |
| 511 | General principles of mathematics |
| 512 | Algebra |
| 513 | Arithmetic |
| 514 | Topology |
| 515 | Analysis |
| 516 | Geometry |
| 518 | Numerical analysis |
| 519 | Probabilities and applied mathematics |

**.1**     **Philosophy and theory**

> Including metamathematics

> Class mathematical logic in 511.3

## 511     General principles of mathematics

> Class general principles applied to a specific branch of mathematics with the branch, e.g., finite geometry 516.11

### SUMMARY

## .1     Finite mathematics

Class here discrete mathematics

*For a specific aspect of finite mathematics, see the aspect, e.g., finite groups 512.23*

*See Manual at 004.0151 vs. 511.1, 511.35*

## .3     Mathematical logic (Symbolic logic)

Including logic operators, truth tables; axiom of choice, completeness theorem, decidability, formal languages, Gödel's theorem, type theory; combinatory logic, intermediate logic

Class here formal logic, propositional calculus (sentential calculus), predicate calculus; first-order logic, higher-order logic; axioms, hypotheses; interdisciplinary works on logic

Class formal logic, propositional calculus (sentential calculus), predicate calculus, first-order logic, logic operators, truth tables from the perspective of philosophical logic in 160

*For philosophical logic, see 160; for category theory, see 512.62*

### .31     Nonclassical logic

Including abduction; default, defeasible, nonmonotonic logic; linear, paraconsistent, relevance, substructural logic

Unless other instructions are given, class a subject with aspects in two or more subdivisions of 511.31 in the number coming last, e.g., conditional probability 511.318 (*not* 511.317)

*For intuitionistic logic, see 511.36*

### .312     Many-valued logic (Multiple-valued logic)

### .313     Fuzzy logic

Class here fuzzy mathematics, fuzzy systems

Class fuzzy sets in 511.3223

### .314     Modal logic

Including alethic, deontic, dynamic, epistemic, provability, temporal logic; possible worlds

### .317     Conditional logic

Including counterfactuals

| .318 | Probabilistic logic |
|---|---|

> *See also 161 for induction; also 519.2 for applied mathematical probabilities*

| .32 | Sets |
|---|---|

> *For point sets, see 511.33; for partially ordered sets, see 511.332*

| .322 | Set theory |
|---|---|

Including axiomatic set theory, cardinal numbers, combinatorial set theory, continuum hypothesis, transfinite numbers

> *For natural numbers, see 512.72*

| .322 3 | Fuzzy sets |
|---|---|

| .324 | Set algebra |
|---|---|

Class here Boolean algebra

| .326 | Functions and relations |
|---|---|

Including automorphisms, equations, isomorphisms, variables

Class here mappings, transformations

| .33 | Order, lattices, ordered algebraic structures |
|---|---|

Standard subdivisions are added for any or all topics in heading

Including point sets

> *See also 511.326 for functions and relations*

| .332 | Partially ordered sets |
|---|---|

| .34 | Model theory |
|---|---|

> *See also 511.8 for mathematical models*

| .35 | Recursion theory |
|---|---|

Including cellular automata, lambda calculus, Petri nets, recursive functions

Class here automata theory, machine theory, sequential machines, Turing machines

Class computer mathematics in 004.0151

> *See Manual at 004.0151 vs. 511.1, 511.35*

| .352 | Recursive functions |
|---|---|

Including NP-complete problems

Class here computability, computable functions, computational complexity

| .36 | Proof theory and constructive mathematics |
|---|---|

Standard subdivisions are added for either or both topics in heading

Including intuitionistic logic, intuitionistic mathematics

**.4** **Approximations and expansions**

Class numerical approximation in 518.5; class stochastic approximation in 519.623

.42 Methods

Including curve fitting, least squares

.422 Interpolation

.422 3 Splines

.43 Error analysis

**.5** **Graph theory**

Including network theory

Class interdisciplinary works on network theory in 003.72; class matching theory in 511.66

*See also 518.23 for nomography*

.52 Trees

.54 Directed graphs (Digraphs)

Including tournaments

.56 Coloring of graphs

Class here map coloring

**.6** **Combinatorics (Combinatorial analysis)**

Including algebraic combinatorics; combinatorial configurations and designs; matroids

Class graph theory in 511.5; class design of experiments in 519.57

.62 Enumeration

.64 Permutations and combinations

Including Latin and magic squares

.65 Choice

*See also 511.3 for axiom of choice; also 519.3 for decision making in game theory*

.66 Extremal combinatorics

Including matching theory

Class here maxima, minima

**.8** **Mathematical models (Mathematical simulation)**

*See also 511.34 for model theory*

Algorithms relocated to 518.1

# 512        Algebra

Class here universal algebra, modern algebra (abstract algebra combined with number theory)

Class foundations of algebra in 512.9

*For numerical algebra, see 518.42*

### SUMMARY

| | |
|---|---|
| **512.001–.009** | **Standard subdivisions** |
| **.02** | **Abstract algebra** |
| **.1** | **Algebra combined with other branches of mathematics** |
| **.2** | **Groups and group theory** |
| **.3** | **Fields** |
| **.4** | **Rings** |
| **.5** | **Linear algebra** |
| **.6** | **Category theory, homological algebra, K-theory** |
| **.7** | **Number theory** |
| **.9** | **Foundations of algebra** |

.001–.009        Standard subdivisions

.02        Abstract algebra

*For subdivisions of abstract algebra, see 512.2–512.5*

## .1        Algebra combined with other branches of mathematics

*For arithmetic and algebra, see 513.12*

*See Manual at 510: Combination of topics*

.12        Algebra and Euclidean geometry

.13        Algebra and trigonometry

.14        Algebra and analytic geometry

.15        Algebra and calculus

---

> ## 512.2–512.5  Subdivisions of abstract algebra

Class comprehensive works in 512.02

## .2        Groups and group theory

Standard subdivisions are added for either or both topics in heading

Class here cosets, subgroups

*For Brauer groups, see 512.46; for topological and related algebras and groups, see 512.55; for groups, semigroups, groupoids viewed as categories, see 512.62; for algebraic topology, see 514.2*

.21        Permutation groups

.22        Representations of groups

| .23 | Finite groups |
|---|---|

*For finite Abelian groups, see 512.25*

| .25 | Abelian groups (Commutative groups) |
|---|---|

Including cyclic groups

Class here finite Abelian groups

| .27 | Semigroups |
|---|---|
| .28 | Groupoids |

**.3**     **Fields**

Class here field theory

Class linear algebra in 512.5; class differential algebras in 512.56; class number theory in 512.7

| .32 | Galois theory |
|---|---|

**.4**     **Rings**

Including algebras based on group properties, flexible algebras, free algebras, subrings; extension theory

Class here integral domains, radical theory

Class algebras defined by dimension of space in 512.5; class topological algebras in 512.55

*For fields, see 512.3*

| .42 | Modules and ideals |
|---|---|
| .44 | Commutative rings |

Class here commutative algebras

| .46 | Associative rings |
|---|---|

Including Brauer groups

Class here associative algebras, noncommutative algebras, noncommutative rings

| .48 | Nonassociative rings |
|---|---|

Including Jordan algebras

Class here nonassociative algebras

| .482 | Lie algebras and groups |
|---|---|

**.5**     **Linear algebra**

Including Cayley algebra, multidimensional algebra, multilinear algebra, quaternions

Class here linear algebra combined with analytic geometry; vector algebra

Class foundations of algebra in 512.9; class analysis combined with linear algebra in 515.14; class numerical linear algebra in 518.43

.52      Vector spaces

       Class bilinear forms in 512.944; class topological vector spaces in 515.73

.55      Topological and related algebras and groups

       Standard subdivisions are added for topological and related algebras and groups together, for topological algebras alone, for topological groups alone

       Including Fréchet, Hopf, reductive, Stein, uniform algebras and their groups

       *For Lie algebras and groups, see 512.482; for differential algebras, see 512.56; for factor algebras, see 512.57; for homological algebra, see 512.64*

       *See also 512.62 for category theory; also 512.64 for algebraic K-theory; also 514.2 for algebraic topology*

.554     Banach algebras

.556     Self-adjoint operator algebras

       Including C*-algebras, Von Neumann algebras, W*-algebras

       Class here operator algebras

.56      Differential algebras

       Class here difference algebras

.57      Factor algebras

       Including Clifford, exterior, spinor, tensor algebras

**.6**      **Category theory, homological algebra, K-theory**

.62      Category theory

       Including Abelian categories; functors, morphisms, toposes

.64      Homological algebra

.66      K-theory

       Including algebraic K-theory

       *For topological K-theory, see 514.23*

**.7**      **Number theory**

       Class numerical methods in 518.47

       *For theory of equations, see 512.94*

.72      Elementary number theory

       Including congruences, continued fractions, Diophantine equations, divisibility, factorization, Fibonacci numbers, integers, natural numbers, operations, power residues, quadratic residues, residues, roots, sequences of integers

.723     Prime numbers

.73      Analytic number theory

> Including Diophantine approximations, distribution theory of prime numbers, functions, L-functions, modular forms, multiplicative properties, number theoretic functions, partitions, Riemann hypothesis, sieves, transcendental numbers, Zeta function

.74      Algebraic number theory

> Including algebraic function theory, class groups, class numbers, discriminants, Fermat's last theorem, field extensions, fields, ideals, p-adic numbers, quadratic forms, reciprocity, rings, unit theory

> *For factorization, see 512.72*

.75      Geometry of numbers

.76      Probabilistic number theory

.78      Specific fields of numbers

.782      Rational numbers

> Including specific rational numbers which are not integers

> Class rational functions in 512.96

.784      Algebraic numbers

> Including specific algebraic numbers which are not rational numbers

.786      Real numbers

> Class transcendental numbers in 512.73; class real functions in 515.8

.788      Complex numbers

> Class here imaginary numbers

> Class complex functions in 515.9

**.9**      **Foundations of algebra**

> Class algebra combined with other branches of mathematics in 512.1

[.900 1–.900 9]      Standard subdivisions

> Relocated to 512.901–512.909

.901–.909      Standard subdivisions [*formerly* 512.9001–512.9009]

.92      Algebraic operations

> Class here addition, subtraction, multiplication, division

.922      Exponents and logarithms

.923      Root extraction

> Including factorization

.924      Approximation, ratio, proportion

.94      Theory of equations

.942      Specific types and systems of equations

| .942 2 | Polynomial equations |
|---|---|

Including binomial, cubic, quartic equations

| .942 22 | Quadratic equations |
|---|---|
| .942 6 | Simultaneous equations |
| .943 | Determinants and matrices |
| .943 2 | Determinants |
| .943 4 | Matrices |

Class determinants of matrices in 512.9432

*For eigenvalues and eigenvectors, see 512.9436*

| .943 6 | Eigenvalues and eigenvectors |
|---|---|

Standard subdivisions are added for either or both topics in heading

| .944 | Theory of forms and algebraic invariant theory |
|---|---|

Standard subdivisions are added for either or both topics in heading

| .96 | Algebra of non-equation functions |
|---|---|

Including rational functions

*For inequalities, see 512.97*

| .97 | Inequalities |
|---|---|

# 513 Arithmetic

Including numeracy

Class numerical methods in 518.45

| **.1** | **Arithmetic combined with other branches of mathematics** |
|---|---|

*See Manual at 510: Combination of topics*

| .12 | Arithmetic and algebra |
|---|---|
| .13 | Arithmetic and geometry |
| .14 | Arithmetic, algebra, geometry |
| **.2** | **Arithmetic operations** |

*For approximations, see 511.4*

| .21 | Basic operations |
|---|---|
| .211 | Addition |

Including counting

| .212 | Subtraction |
|---|---|
| .213 | Multiplication |
| .214 | Division |

| | |
|---|---|
| .22 | Exponents and logarithms |
| .23 | Root extraction |

Including factorization; square root, cube root

| | |
|---|---|
| .24 | Ratio and proportion |
| .245 | Percentage |
| .26 | Fractions |

*For ratio, see 513.24; for percentage, see 513.245*

*See also 512.782 for rational numbers*

| | |
|---|---|
| .265 | Decimal fractions |
| **.5** | **Numeration systems** |

Including base 3, 5, 20 systems

| | |
|---|---|
| .52 | Binary system (Base 2 system) |
| .55 | Decimal system (Base 10 system) |

Class decimal fractions in 513.265

| | |
|---|---|
| **.6** | **Modular arithmetic** |
| **.9** | **Rapid calculations** |

Class here mental arithmetic, ready reckoners, shortcuts

## 514    Topology

Class here analysis situs, homeomorphisms, homogeneous spaces, mappings

Class topology combined with analysis in 515.13; class topology combined with geometry in 516

*For topological vector spaces, see 515.73*

| | |
|---|---|
| **.2** | **Algebraic topology** |

*See also 512.55 for topological algebras*

| | |
|---|---|
| .22 | Combinatorial topology |
| .223 | Combinatorial elements |

Including simplexes, complexes, nets

| | |
|---|---|
| .224 | Structures and spaces |

Standard subdivisions are added for either or both topics in heading

Including braids, fiber bundles, fiber spaces, links, path spaces, sheaves, vector bundles

| | |
|---|---|
| .224 2 | Knots |

.23      Homology and cohomology theories

> Standard subdivisions are added for either or both topics in heading
>
> Including topological K-theory
>
> Class homological algebra in 512.64; class K-theory in 512.66
>
> *See also 512.55 for topological groups*

.24      Homotopy theory

> Including retracts, shape theory

**.3**      **Topology of spaces**

> Class here metric topology

.32      Systems and spaces

> Standard subdivisions are added for either or both topics in heading

.322      Point set topology (General topology)

.323      Proximity spaces

.325      Metric spaces

.34      Topological manifolds

> Class here manifold topology
>
> *For differentiable manifolds, see 516.36*

**.7**      **Analytic topology**

.72      Differential topology

> Including cobordism theory, differentiable mappings, foliations

.74      Global analysis

> Including Hodge theory, index theorems
>
> *For differentiable manifolds, see 516.36*
>
> *See also 515.39 for dynamical systems*

.742      Fractals

.744      Catastrophes

.746      Singularity theory

> Class here comprehensive works on singularities
>
> *For singularities in a specific subject, see the subject, e.g., singularities in functions of several complex variable 515.94*

# 515        Analysis

> Class here calculus; comprehensive works on the theory of functions

> Class probabilities in 519.2

> *For numerical analysis, see 518. For theory of a specific function or group of functions, see the function or group of functions, e.g., analysis of continued fractions 512.72*

## SUMMARY

**.1        Analysis and calculus combined with other branches of mathematics**

> *For algebra and calculus, see 512.15*

> *See Manual at 510: Combination of topics*

**.13        Analysis and topology**

**.14        Analysis and linear algebra**

**.15        Calculus and analytic geometry**

**.16        Calculus and trigonometry**

**.2        General aspects of analysis**

> Class a specific application with the application, e.g., operations on functions of real variables 515.823

**.22        Properties of functions**

**.222        Continuity, dimension, limit**

> Class here continuous functions

**.23        Operations on functions**

> *For differentiation, see 515.33; for integration, see 515.43*

**.24        Sequences and series**

> Standard subdivisions are added for sequences and series together, for sequences alone

> Including algebraic progressions, arithmetic progressions, geometric progressions

> Class here infinite processes

| | |
|---|---|
| .243 | Series |

    Including summability

    Class here infinite series

    Class number theory of continued fractions in 512.72

| | |
|---|---|
| .243 2 | Power series |
| .243 3 | Fourier and harmonic analysis |

    Standard subdivisions are added for either or both topics in heading

    Including wavelets

    Class here Fourier series

    Class Fourier transforms in 515.723

    *For abstract harmonic analysis, see 515.785*

| | |
|---|---|
| .25 | Equations and functions |

    Standard subdivisions are added for either or both topics in heading

| | |
|---|---|
| .252 | Equations and functions by degree |

    Including linear, nonlinear, quadratic equations

| | |
|---|---|
| .253 | Equations and functions by property |

    Including homogeneous, indeterminate, reciprocal equations

| | |
|---|---|
| .26 | Inequalities |
| **.3** | **Differential calculus and equations** |

    Class differential topology in 514.72; class differential operators in 515.7242; class differential geometry in 516.36; class comprehensive works on differential and integral calculus and equations in 515

| | |
|---|---|
| .33 | Differential calculus |

    Including ordinary, partial, total differentiations; total and directional derivatives, mean value theorems

    Class vector differentiation in 515.63; class numerical differentiation in 518.53; class probability calculus in 519.2

| | |
|---|---|
| .35 | Differential equations |

    Class here Cauchy problem; orders, degrees; comprehensive works on boundary-value problems

    Class mixed equations in 515.38; class numerical solutions in 518.63

    *For dynamical systems, see 515.39 For boundary-value problems of finite differences, see 515.62*

| | |
|---|---|
| .352 | Ordinary differential equations |
| .353 | Partial differential equations |
| .353 3 | Elliptic equations |

| | |
|---|---|
| .353 4 | Parabolic equations |
| .353 5 | Hyperbolic equations |
| .354 | Linear differential equations |

Class linear ordinary differential equations in 515.352; class linear partial differential equations in 515.353

| | |
|---|---|
| .355 | Nonlinear differential equations |

Class nonlinear ordinary differential equations in 515.352; class nonlinear partial differential equations in 515.353

| | |
|---|---|
| .357 | Inverse problems |

Class inverse problems of specific kinds of equations in 515.352–515.355

| | |
|---|---|
| .36 | Differential inequalities |
| .37 | Differential forms |
| .38 | Mixed equations |

Including differential-difference and integro-differential equations

| | |
|---|---|
| .39 | Dynamical systems |

Including chaos theory, Hamiltonian systems

| | |
|---|---|
| .392 | Stability theory |

Including bifurcation theory, perturbation theory

| | |
|---|---|
| **.4** | **Integral calculus and equations** |

Class special functions in 515.5; class integral transforms in 515.723; class integral geometry in 516.362

| | |
|---|---|
| .42 | Theory of measure and integration |

Standard subdivisions are added for either or both topics in heading

Class here abstract measure theory

*For functionals, see 515.7*

Ergodic theory relocated to 515.48

| | |
|---|---|
| .43 | Integral calculus |

Including integration, summation, arc length, convolutions, cubature, quadrature; Cauchy, definite, Denjoy, Green, Haar, improper, Lebesgue, line, Poisson, Poisson-Stieltjes, proper, Riemann, Stokes', surface integrals

Class vector integration in 515.63; class numerical integration in 518.54; class probability integration in 519.2

| | |
|---|---|
| .45 | Integral equations |

Class mixed equations in 515.38; class numerical solutions in 518.66

| | |
|---|---|
| .46 | Integral inequalities |
| .48 | Ergodic theory |

**.5** **Special functions**

.52 Eulerian integrals

Including beta and gamma functions

.53 Harmonic functions

Including Bessel, Hankel, Laplace, Legendre, Neumann functions

.54 Mathieu functions

.55 Orthogonal polynomials

Including Chebyshev, Hermite, hypergeometric, Jacobi, Lagrange, Laguerre, Legendre polynomials

.56 Zeta function

Class application of Riemann zeta function with respect to prime number theory in 512.73

**.6** **Other analytic methods**

*For functional analysis, see 515.7*

.62 Calculus of finite differences

Class here boundary-value problems when either limit has a numerical value

.625 Difference equations

Class difference-differential equations in 515.38

.63 Vector, tensor, spinor analysis

Standard subdivisions are added for vector, tensor, spinor analysis together; for vector analysis alone; for tensor analysis alone

Including vector and tensor calculus

Class algebraic vector analysis in 512.52; class geometric vector analysis in 516.182

.64 Calculus of variations

.642 Control theory

Class here optimal control

Class optimization in 519.6

*See also 003.5 for interdisciplinary works on control theory; also 629.8312 for control theory in engineering*

**.7** **Functional analysis**

Class here comprehensive works on real-valued, complex-valued, vector-valued functions

Class theory of measure and integration in 515.42; class potential theory in 515.9

*For topological algebras, see 512.55; for functions of real variables, see 515.8; for functions of complex variables, see 515.9*

.72        **Operational calculus**

> Class a specific application with the application, e.g., differential operators in topological vector spaces 515.73

.722        **Spectral and representation theories**

.722 2        Spectral theory

> Class spectral theory of a specific kind of operator with the kind of operator, e.g., spectral theory of differential operators 515.7242

.722 3        Representation theory

> Class abstract harmonic analysis in 515.42

.723        **Transforms (Integral operators, integral transforms)**

> Including Fourier, Hilbert, Laplace, Legendre, Radon, Z transforms

.724        **Operator theory**

> *For integral operators, see 515.723*

.724 2        Differential operators

> Including elliptic operators

.724 6        Linear operators

> Class linear integral operators in 515.723; class linear differential operators in 515.7242

.724 8        Nonlinear operators

> Class here nonlinear functional analysis

> Class nonlinear integral operators in 515.723; class nonlinear differential operators in 515.7242

.73        **Topological vector spaces**

> Including spaces of analytic functions; spaces of continuous functions; spaces of measurable functions, e.g., $L^p$ spaces, Orlicz spaces; Hermitian (unitary) and Riesz spaces

> Class here linear topological spaces

> *For functionals, see 515.7*

.732        **Banach spaces**

> Class here normed linear spaces

> *For Hilbert spaces, see 515.733*

.733        Hilbert spaces

> Class here inner product spaces

.75        **Functional equations**

> Class difference equations in 515.625

.78        **Special topics of functional analysis**

.782      Distribution theory

        Including duality, Sobolev spaces

        Class here generalized functions

.785      Abstract harmonic analysis

        Including Fourier analysis on groups

**.8**      **Functions of real variables**

        Class here real analysis

        Class combined treatment of functions of real and complex variables in 515.9

        *See also 512.786 for real numbers*

.82      General aspects of functions of real variables

        Add to base number 515.82 the numbers following 515.2 in 515.22–515.26, e.g., expansion of functions 515.823

        Class a specific application with the application, e.g., expansion of functions of several real variables 515.84

.83      Functions of one real variable

        Including fractional calculus

.84      Functions of several real variables

.88      Specific types of real variable functions

        Including real variable analytic functions

.882      Convex functions

        Class here convex analysis

**.9**      **Functions of complex variables**

        Class here automorphic functions, complex analysis, conformal mapping

        *See also 512.788 for complex numbers*

.92      General aspects of functions of complex variables

        Add to base number 515.92 the numbers following 515.2 in 515.22–515.26, e.g., expansion of functions 515.923

        Class a specific application with the application, e.g., expansion of functions of several complex variables 515.94

.93      Functions of one complex variable

        Including Riemann surfaces

.94      Functions of several complex variables

        Including singularities in functions of several complex variables, Teichmüller spaces

        Class comprehensive works in singularities in 514.746

| | |
|---|---|
| .942 | Analytic spaces |

Generalization of Riemann surfaces to n-dimensional spaces

| | |
|---|---|
| .946 | Complex manifolds |
| .96 | Potential theory |

*For a specific application of potential theory, see the application, e.g., harmonic analysis and potential theory 515.2433*

| | |
|---|---|
| .98 | Specific types of complex variable functions |

Including entire, holomorphic, pseudoanalytic functions

| | |
|---|---|
| .982 | Meromorphic functions |
| .983 | Elliptic functions |

Class special elliptic functions in 515.5

| | |
|---|---|
| .984 | Theta function |

# 516      Geometry

Class here geometry combined with topology

Class algebra combined with geometry in 512.1; class arithmetic combined with geometry in 513.13; class analysis combined with geometry in 515.1; class geometric probability in 519.2

*For topology, see 514*

## SUMMARY

| | |
|---|---|
| 516.001–.009 | **Standard subdivisions** |
| .02–.08 | **[Classical and modern geometry; manifolds, convex sets]** |
| .1 | **General aspects of geometry** |
| .2 | **Euclidean geometry** |
| .3 | **Analytic geometries** |
| .4 | **Affine geometry** |
| .5 | **Projective geometry** |
| .6 | **Abstract descriptive geometry** |
| .9 | **Non-Euclidean geometries** |

| | |
|---|---|
| .001–.009 | Standard subdivisions |
| .02 | Classical geometry |
| .04 | Modern geometry |
| .07 | Manifolds |

*For topological manifolds, see 514.34*

| | |
|---|---|
| .08 | Convex sets |

Class here convex geometry

**.1**         **General aspects of geometry**

Including symmetry

Class here automorphisms, metric geometry, transformations

Class general aspects applied to a specific geometry with the geometry, e.g., conic sections in Euclidean geometry 516.2152

.11         Finite geometry

Class here discrete geometry

.12         Incidence geometry

.13         Combinatorial geometry

.132         Tilings

Class here tessellations

.15         Geometric configurations

Including mensuration, patterns, sizes, space

Class here measures, shapes

Class geometric configurations in a specific subject with the subject, e.g., measuring the sphere in solid geometry 516.23

.152         One-dimensional configurations

Including angles, circles, conic sections, lines, spirals

Class here curves

.154         Two-dimensional configurations

Including cones, cylinders, disks, polygons, spheres, squares, triangles

Class here planes, surfaces

*See also 516.22 for plane geometry*

.156         Three-dimensional configurations

Including balls, cubes, polyhedra, prisms, pyramids

Class here solids

*See also 516.23 for solid geometry*

.158         Four-dimensional and higher-dimensional configurations

Including hypercubes, polytopes

.16         Coordinate systems

Including Cartesian, curvilinear, homogeneous systems

.18         Nonpoint base geometries

.182         Vector geometry

Class vector algebra in 512.5

.183         Line geometry

**.2**        **Euclidean geometry**

Class here congruences, similarity, metric geometry

Class a specific type of Euclidean geometry with the type, e.g., Euclidean analytic geometry 516.3

**.200 1–.200 9**        Standard subdivisions

**.204**        Famous problems

Including trisecting an angle, squaring the circle, doubling the cube

**.21**        General aspects of Euclidean geometry

Add to base number 516.21 the numbers following 516.1 in 516.12–516.18, e.g., conic sections 516.2152

Class a specific application with the application, e.g., conic sections in plane geometry 516.22

**.22**        Plane geometry

Including Pythagorean theorem

**.23**        Solid geometry

**.24**        Trigonometry

**.242**        Plane trigonometry

**.244**        Spherical trigonometry

**.246**        Trigonometric functions

Class analytic trigonometry in 516.34

**.3**        **Analytic geometries**

Class linear algebra combined with analytic geometry in 512.5; class analytic affine geometry in 516.4; class analytic projective geometry in 516.5

**.32**        Plane analytic geometry

**.33**        Solid analytic geometry

**.34**        Analytic trigonometry

Plane and spherical

**.35**        Algebraic geometry

Geometries based on linear algebra

Including enumerative geometry, lattice point geometry, singularities

Class here birational and conformal transformations, connections, dual geometries, intersections; bilinear and sesquilinear forms; complex multiplication

Class comprehensive works in singularities in 514.746

.352 Curves and surfaces on projective and affine planes

> Standard subdivisions are added for either or both topics in heading

> Including Mordell conjecture

> Class here theory of curves

.353 Algebraic varieties of higher dimensions

> Including Abelian varieties

.36 Differential and integral geometry

> Standard subdivisions are added for differential and integral geometry together, for differential geometry alone

> Including symplectic manifolds

> Class here curves, differentiable manifolds, surfaces, torsion

> *For metric differential geometries, see 516.37*

.362 Integral geometry (Global differential geometry)

> Including arc length, curvature, evolutes, geodesics, involutes, tangent space at a point; analytic, convex, developable, minimal, ruled surfaces; analytic, asymptotic, minimal curves; Riemannian manifolds, symmetric spaces

> Class here modern differential geometry

> *For fiber bundles, fiber spaces, see 514.224*

.37 Metric differential geometries

.373 Riemannian geometry

> Including Sasakian geometry

.374 Minkowski geometry

> Including Einstein geometry

.375 Finsler geometry

.376 Cartan geometry

**.4 Affine geometry**

> Class affine differential geometry in 516.36

**.5 Projective geometry**

> Class projective differential geometry in 516.36

**.6 Abstract descriptive geometry**

> *See also 604.2015166 for descriptive geometry in technical drawing*

**.9**        **Non-Euclidean geometries**

Including Bolyai, elliptic, Gauss, hyperbolic, inversive, Lobachevski geometries; imbeddings of non-Euclidean spaces in other geometries

Class a specific type of non-Euclidean geometry with the type, e.g., non-Euclidean analytic geometries 516.3

## [517]        [Unassigned]

Most recently used in Edition 17

## 518        Numerical analysis

Class here applied numerical analysis, numerical calculations, numerical mathematics

Class approximations and expansions in 511.4

*For numerical statistical mathematics, see 519.5*

**.1**        **Algorithms**

**.2**        **Specific numerical methods**

Class specific numerical methods applied to a particular field in 518.4–518.6

.23        Graphic methods

Including nomography

.25        Finite element analysis

Class here finite strip method, finite volume method

.26        Iterative methods

.28        Probabilistic methods

Class here statistical methods, stochastic methods

.282        Monte Carlo method

**.4**        **Numerical methods in algebra, arithmetic, number theory**

.42        Numerical methods in algebra

Class here numerical algebra

*For numerical linear algebra, see 518.43*

.43        Numerical linear algebra

.45        Numerical methods in arithmetic

.47        Numerical methods in number theory

**.5**        **Numerical approximation**

.53        Numerical differentiation

.54        Numerical integration

**.6** **Numerical methods in analysis**

> Class here numerical methods in calculus

> Class numerical approximation in 518.5

**.63** Numerical solutions of ordinary differential equations

> Including Galerkin method, relaxation methods, Runge-Kutta method

**.64** Numerical solutions of partial differential equations

**.66** Numerical solutions of integral equations

# 519 Probabilities and applied mathematics

> Standard subdivisions are added for probabilities and applied mathematics together; for applied mathematics alone

> Class a specific application with the application, e.g., statistics in physics 530.1595, game theory in gambling 795.01

### SUMMARY

| | |
|---|---|
| 519.2 | **Probabilities** |
| .3 | **Game theory** |
| .5 | **Statistical mathematics** |
| .6 | **Mathematical optimization** |
| .7 | **Programming** |
| .8 | **Special topics of applied mathematics** |

**.2** **Probabilities**

> Class here conditional probabilities, geometric probability, probability calculus

> Class probabilistic methods of numerical analysis in 518.28; class probabilities applied to statistical mathematics in 519.5

**.22** Stochastic analysis

**.23** Random processes (Stochastic processes)

> *For queuing processes, see 519.82*

**.232** Stationary processes

> Including time series

**.233** Markov processes

> Including Markov chains

**.234** Branching processes

**.236** Martingales

**.24** Probability distribution

> Including binomial distribution, Poisson distribution

.27          Games of chance (Stochastic games)

> Class here gambling

>> *See Manual at 795.015192 vs. 519.27*

.28          Special topics of probabilities

.282          Random walks

.287          Expectation and prediction

> Standard subdivisions are added for either or both topics in heading

> Including estimation, reliability, renewal theories; Markov risk

**.3**          **Game theory**

> Class games of chance in 519.27

.32          Differential games

**.5**          **Statistical mathematics**

> Class here parametric and nonparametric methods

>> *See Manual at 519.5, T1—015195 vs. 001.422, T1—0727*

.52          Theory of sampling

.53          Descriptive statistics, multivariate analysis, analysis of variance and covariance

> Including cluster analysis

.532          Frequency distributions

.533          Measures of central tendency

> Including median, mean, mode

> Class here averaging

.534          Measures of deviation

> Including standard deviation

.535          Multivariate analysis

> Including latent structure analysis

>> *For regression analysis, see 519.536; for correlation analysis, see 519.537*

.535 4          Factor analysis

> Including principal components analysis

.536          Regression analysis

> Including autoregression

.537          Correlation analysis (Association analysis)

> Including autocorrelation

.538 Analysis of variance and covariance

> Standard subdivisions are added for either or both topics in heading

.54 Statistical inference

> Including bootstrap methods, confidence regions, expectation, nonparametric inference, parametric inference, prediction, resampling methods, sequential analysis

.542 Decision theory

> Including Bayesian statistical decision theory

.544 Estimation theory

.546 Survival analysis

> Class here censored observations

.55 Time-series analysis

.56 Hypothesis testing

> Including chi-square test, goodness-of-fit tests

.57 Design of experiments

> Including factorial experiment designs

**.6 Mathematical optimization**

> Class control theory in 515.642

> *For a specific mathematical optimization technique, see the technique, e.g., mathematical programming 519.7*

> *See also 511.65 for choice and decision making in combinatorial analysis*

.62 Stochastic optimization

.623 Stochastic approximation

.625 Genetic algorithms

.64 Combinatorial optimization

**.7 Programming**

.700 1–.700 9 Standard subdivisions

.702 Single-stage programming

.703 Multistage programming

> Including dynamic programming

.72 Linear programming

.76 Nonlinear programming

> Including convex and quadratic programming

> Class integer programming in 519.77

.77 Integer programming

**.8**        **Special topics of applied mathematics**

.82        Queuing

>    Including congestion

>    Class here queuing processes

.83        Inventory and storage

.84        Success runs

.85        Epidemics and fluctuations

.86        Quality control

# 520        Astronomy and allied sciences

*See Manual at 520 vs. 500.5, 523.1, 530.1, 919.9; also at 520 vs. 523.1, 523.112, 523.8*

### SUMMARY

| | |
|---|---|
| 521 | **Celestial mechanics** |
| 522 | **Techniques, procedures, apparatus, equipment, materials** |
| 523 | **Specific celestial bodies and phenomena** |
| 525 | **Earth (Astronomical geography)** |
| 526 | **Mathematical geography** |
| 527 | **Celestial navigation** |
| 528 | **Ephemerides** |
| 529 | **Chronology** |

[.153]        Physical principles

>    Do not use; class in 523.01

[.154]        Chemical principles

>    Do not use; class in 523.02

[.28]        Auxiliary techniques and procedures; apparatus, equipment, materials

>    Do not use; class in 522

---

>        **521–525  Astronomy**

>    Class comprehensive works in 520

>    *For geodetic astronomy, see 526.6*

# 521        Celestial mechanics

>    Including equilibrium, problems of three and n bodies

>    Class here motion

>    Class applications to specific celestial bodies and phenomena in 523

**.1**        **Gravitation**

**.3** **Orbits**

> Class here Kepler's laws

**.4** **Perturbations**

**.9** **Precession**

> Including nutation
>
> Class corrections of precession in 522.9

# 522 Techniques, procedures, apparatus, equipment, materials

> Class here astrometry, positional and practical astronomy
>
> Class positional astronomy as an aspect of mathematical geography in 526.6

**[.028]** Auxiliary techniques and procedures; apparatus, equipment, materials

> Do not use for general works; class in 522. Do not use for specific auxiliary techniques and procedures; class in 522.8

---

> **522.1–522.6 Practical astronomy**
>
> Class comprehensive works in 522
>
> *For corrections, see 522.9; for practical astronomy of specific celestial bodies and phenomena, see 523*

**.1** **Observatories**

> Optical and nonoptical

**.109** History and biography

> Do not use for geographic treatment; class in 522.19

**.19** Geographic treatment

> Add to base number 522.19 notation 1–9 from Table 2, e.g., space observatories 522.1919, observatories in China 522.1951

**.2** **Astronomical instruments**

> Including meridional instruments [*formerly* 522.3], extrameridional instruments [*formerly* 522.4]
>
> Class here movable nonspace telescopes; comprehensive works on telescopes
>
> *For auxiliary instruments, see 522.5; for astronomical instruments used in nonoptical astronomy, see 522.68; for sextants, see 527.0284*

**.29** Fixed-location and space telescopes

**.290 9** History and biography

> Do not use for geographic treatment; class in 522.291–522.299

.291–.299   Geographic treatment

> Add to base number 522.29 notation 1–9 from Table 2, e.g., fixed location telescopes in Chile 522.2983

**[.3]   Meridional instruments**

> Relocated to 522.2

**[.4]   Extrameridional instruments**

> Extrameridional instruments relocated to 522.2; sextants relocated to 527.0284

**.5   Auxiliary instruments**

> Including chronographs, chronometers
>
> *For auxiliary instruments in special methods of observation, see 522.6*

**.6   Special methods of observation**

.62   Photometry

.622   Photographic photometry

.623   Photoelectric photometry

.63   Photography

> *For photographic photometry, see 522.622*

.65   Polarimetry

.67   Spectroscopy

> Class spectroscopy of a specific celestial body with the body, plus notation 0287 from Table 1, e.g., spectroscopy of planets 523.40287

.68   Nonoptical astronomy

> Class here nonoptical telescopes
>
> *For nonoptical observatories, see 522.1*

.682   Radio astronomy

.683   Infrared astronomy

.686   Particle methods of observation

.686 2   Gamma-ray astronomy

.686 3   X-ray astronomy

**.7   Spherical astronomy**

> Including celestial reference systems
>
> Class comprehensive works on geodetic coordinates in 526.6

.8 **Specific auxiliary techniques and procedures**

Add to base number 522.8 the numbers following —028 in notation 0285–0289 from Table 1, e.g., testing and measurement 522.87

Class spectroscopy in 522.67

.9 **Corrections**

Corrections of aberration, astronomical refraction, parallax, precession; of instrumental errors

# 523 Specific celestial bodies and phenomena

Including zodiac

Class phenomena of celestial bodies directly comparable to terrestrial phenomena with the terrestrial phenomena in 550, e.g., volcanic activity on Mars 551.21099923

*See Manual at 523 vs. 550*

## SUMMARY

| | |
|---|---|
| 523.01–.02 | **[Astrophysics and cosmochemistry]** |
| .1 | **The universe, galaxies, quasars** |
| .2 | **Planetary systems** |
| .3 | **Moon** |
| .4 | **Planets, asteroids, trans-Neptunian objects of solar system** |
| .5 | **Meteors, solar wind, zodiacal light** |
| .6 | **Comets** |
| .7 | **Sun** |
| .8 | **Stars** |
| .9 | **Satellites and rings; eclipses, transits, occultations** |

[.001–.009]   Standard subdivisions

Do not use; class in 520.1–520.9

.01   Astrophysics

*For celestial mechanics, see 521*

.013   Heat

Add to base number 523.013 the numbers following 536 in 536.1–536.7, e.g., heat transfer 523.0132

.015   Light and related radiation

Standard subdivisions are added for light and related radiation together, for light alone

.015 01   Infrared and ultraviolet radiation; philosophy and theory of light and related radiation

Class here radiation of nonvisible spectral regions

Add to base number 523.01501 the numbers following 535.01 in 535.012–535.019, e.g., infrared radiation 523.015012

Class a specific element of infrared and ultraviolet radiation in 523.0152–523.0156

| .015 1–.015 8 | Specific aspects of light and related radiation |
|---|---|

Add to base number 523.015 the numbers following 535 in 535.1–535.8, e.g., polarization 523.01552

| .018 | Electricity and magnetism |
|---|---|

Add to base number 523.018 the numbers following 53 in 537–538, e.g., magnetism 523.0188

| .019 | Molecular, atomic, nuclear physics |
|---|---|

Add to base number 523.019 the numbers following 539 in 539.1–539.7, e.g., cosmic rays 523.0197223

| .02 | Cosmochemistry |
|---|---|

### .1        The universe, galaxies, quasars

Standard subdivisions are added for the universe, galaxies, quasars together; for the universe alone

Class here cosmology

*See also 523.8875 for black holes*

*See Manual at 520 vs. 500.5, 523.1, 530.1, 919.9; also at 520 vs. 523.1, 523.112, 523.8*

| .11 | Galaxies and quasars |
|---|---|
| .112 | Galaxies |

*For Milky Way, see 523.113*

*See Manual at 520 vs. 523.1, 523.112, 523.8: Stars and galaxies*

| .112 5 | Interstellar and intergalactic matter |
|---|---|

Standard subdivisions are added for interstellar and intergalactic matter together, for interstellar matter alone

Class here cosmic dust

*See also 523.1126 for dark matter*

| .112 6 | Dark matter |
|---|---|
| .113 | Milky Way |
| .113 5 | Interstellar matter |

Including diffuse and planetary nebulas

*For dark matter, see 523.1126*

| .115 | Quasars |
|---|---|
| .12 | Cosmogony |

*For expanding universe theories, see 523.18*

| .18 | Expanding universe theories |
|---|---|

Class here big bang theory

.19    End of universe theories

**.2    Planetary systems**

    Class here solar system

      *For specific parts of solar system, see 523.3–523.7*

.24    Extrasolar systems

    Class here extrasolar planets

———————

\>     **523.3–523.7  Specific parts of solar system**

    Class comprehensive works in 523.2

**.3    Moon**

.31    Constants and dimensions

    Including gravity, size, mass

.32    Optical, electromagnetic, radioactive, thermal phenomena

    Including phases

.33    Orbit and motions

    Including librations, sidereal month

.38    Eclipses

**.4    Planets, asteroids, trans-Neptunian objects of solar system**

    Standard subdivisions are added for planets, asteroids, trans-Neptunian objects of solar system together, for planets of solar system alone

    Class here comprehensive works on planets, satellites, rings of solar system

    Add to notation for each number identified by * the numbers following 523.3 in 523.31–523.33, e.g., orbit of Jupiter 523.453

      *For meteors, see 523.51; for satellites and rings, see 523.98; for transits, occultations, see 523.99; for earth, see 525*

      *See also 523.24 for extrasolar planets*

.41    *Mercury

.42    *Venus

.43    *Mars

.44    Asteroids (Planetoids)

    Including Ceres

    Class comprehensive works on meteors and asteroids in 523.5

.45    *Jupiter

*Add as instructed under 523.4

.46        *Saturn

.47        *Uranus

.48        *Neptune

> Former heading: Trans-Uranian planets
>
> Trans-Neptunian objects relocated to 523.49

.481        Constants and dimensions

> Number built according to instructions under 523.4
>
> Use of this number for Neptune discontinued; class in 523.48

.482        Optical, electromagnetic, radioactive, thermal phenomena

> Number built according to instructions under 523.4
>
> Pluto relocated to 523.4922

.49        Trans-Neptunian objects [*formerly* 523.48]

.492        Kuiper belt objects

.492 2        *Pluto [*formerly* 523.482]

.494        Scattered disk objects

.497        Oort cloud objects

**.5        Meteors, solar wind, zodiacal light**

> Class here interplanetary matter, comprehensive works on meteors and asteroids
>
> *For asteroids, see 523.44*

.51        Meteors

> Class here meteoroids, meteorites
>
> *For meteor showers, see 523.53*

.53        Meteor showers

> Including radiant points

.58        Solar wind

.59        Zodiacal light

> Including counterglow (gegenschein)

**.6        Comets**

.63        Motion and orbits

> Class motion and orbits of specific comets in 523.64

.64        Specific comets

*Add as instructed under 523.4

| [.640 1–.640 9] | Standard subdivisions |
|---|---|
| | Do not use; class in 523.601–523.609 |
| .642 | Halley's comet |
| .66 | Physical phenomena and constitution |
| | Class physical phenomena and constitution of specific comets in 523.64 |

**.7          Sun**

| .702 1 | Tabulated and related materials |
|---|---|
| | Class sun tables indicating orbits and motions of earth in 525.38 |
| .71 | Constants and dimensions |
| | Including gravity, size, mass |
| .72 | Optical, electromagnetic, radioactive, thermal phenomena |
| | Class here solar energy, solar radiation |

*For phenomena of photosphere, see 523.74; for phenomena of chromosphere and corona, see 523.75*

*See also 523.59 for zodiacal light*

| .73 | Motions |
|---|---|
| | Including apparent motion, rotation |
| .74 | Photosphere |
| | Including faculae, solar granulation, sunspots |
| .75 | Chromosphere and corona |
| | Including solar flares and prominences |

*See also 523.58 for solar wind*

| .76 | Solar interior |
|---|---|
| .78 | Eclipses |

**.8          Stars**

Class here comprehensive works on stars and galaxies

*For galaxies, see 523.112; for sun, see 523.7*

*See also 523.115 for quasars; also 523.24 for extrasolar systems*

*See Manual at 520 vs. 523.1, 523.112, 523.8: Stars and galaxies*

| [.802 87] | Testing and measurement |
|---|---|
| | Do not use; class in 523.87 |

>            523.81–523.83   Properties and phenomena

Class comprehensive works in 523.8

*For physical constitution, see 523.86. For properties and phenomena of a specific kind of star or aggregation of stars, see the kind or aggregation, e.g., properties of supernovas 523.84465, properties of spectral types 523.87*

.81         Constants and dimensions

Including gravity, size, mass, parallax

.82         Optical, electromagnetic, radioactive, thermal phenomena

Class here stellar radiation

.822        Magnitudes

.83         Motion

Including velocity

.84         Aggregations and variable stars

Standard subdivisions are added for aggregations and variable stars together, for aggregations alone

Class here comprehensive works on binary stars and clusters

*For clusters, see 523.85*

*See also 523.112 for galaxies*

.841        Binary and multiple stars

Standard subdivisions are added for binary and multiple stars together, for binary stars alone

Including optical and visual binaries

Class here astrometric binaries

*For spectroscopic binaries, see 523.842; for eclipsing binaries, see 523.8444*

.842        Spectroscopic binaries

.844        Variable stars

.844 2       Intrinsic variables

*For eruptive variables, see 523.8446*

.844 25      Pulsating variables

Class here Cepheids

*For long-period and semiregular variables, see 523.84426; for pulsars, see 523.8874*

.844 26      Long-period and semiregular variables

.844 4       Eclipsing binaries (Extrinsic variables)

| | |
|---|---|
| .844 6 | Eruptive variables |
| | Including flare stars, novas |
| .844 65 | Supernovas |
| .85 | Clusters |
| .852 | Open clusters |
| .855 | Globular clusters |
| .86 | Physical constitution |

Class physical constitution of a specific kind or aggregation of star with the kind or aggregation, e.g., constitution of neutron stars 523.8874

| | |
|---|---|
| .87 | Spectral types |

Class here spectroscopy, testing and measurement

Class spectral types representative of specific stages in the evolution of stars in 523.88. Class spectroscopy of a specific kind or aggregation of star with the kind or aggregation, plus notation 0287 from Table 1, e.g., spectroscopy of neutron stars 523.88740287

| | |
|---|---|
| .88 | Kinds of stars characteristic of stages of stellar evolution |

Including giant (R, N, or S spectral type), main sequence, red dwarf, Wolf-Rayet stars; star formation

Class here stellar evolution

*For intrinsic variables, see 523.8442*

| | |
|---|---|
| .887 | Terminal stages |
| | Including white dwarfs |
| .887 4 | Neutron stars |
| | Class here pulsars |
| .887 5 | Black holes |
| **.9** | **Satellites and rings; eclipses, transits, occultations** |
| .91 | Transits of Mercury |
| .92 | Transits of Venus |
| .98 | Satellites and rings |

Variant name for satellites: moons

Add to base number 523.98 the numbers following 523.4 in 523.43–523.48, e.g., satellites of Jupiter 523.985, orbits of Jovian satellites 523.9853

Subdivisions are added for either or both topics in heading

*For earth's moon, see 523.3*

| | |
|---|---|
| .99 | Eclipses, transits, occultations |

> *For transits of Mercury, see 523.91; for transits of Venus, see 523.92. For eclipses of a specific celestial body, see the body, e.g., eclipses of the moon 523.38*

## [524]    [Unassigned]

Most recently used in Edition 14

## 525    Earth (Astronomical geography)

> *For magnetic properties, see 538.7*

| | |
|---|---|
| .1 | **Constants and dimensions** |

Including size, shape

Class determination of size and shape in 526.1

> *For gravity, see 531.14*

| | |
|---|---|
| .2 | **Optical, radioactive, thermal properties** |
| .3 | **Orbit and motions** |
| .35 | Rotation |
| .36 | Foucault's pendulum |
| .38 | Sun tables |

Class here sunrise and sunset tables

| | |
|---|---|
| .5 | **Seasons and zones of latitude** |

Standard subdivisions are added for seasons and zones of latitude together, for seasons alone

Limited to astronomical causes of seasons and zones of latitude

Class climatology in 551.6; class interdisciplinary works on seasons in 508.2

| | |
|---|---|
| .7 | **Twilight** |

Class here dawn

## 526    Mathematical geography

Class here cartography, map drawing, map making

Class map making for a specific purpose with the purpose, e.g., military map making 623.71

> *For astronomical geography, see 525*

> *See also 912.014 for map reading*

| | |
|---|---|
| .1 | **Geodesy** |

> *For geodetic surveying, see 526.3; for geodetic astronomy and geographic positions, see 526.6; for gravity determinations, see 526.7*

**.3**        **Geodetic surveying**

> Surveying in which curvature of earth is considered

.31        Reconnaissance surveys

.32        Bench marks

.320 9        History and biography

> Do not use for geographic treatment; class in 526.321–526.329

.321–.329        Geographic treatment

> Add to base number 526.32 notation 1–9 from Table 2, e.g., bench marks in California 526.32794

.33        Triangulation, trilateration, traversing

> Standard subdivisions are added for triangulation, trilateration, traversing together; for triangulation alone

> Including base lines, nets

.36        Leveling

> Class here spirit leveling

> *For bench marks, see 526.32; for barometric leveling, see 526.37; for trigonometric leveling, see 526.38*

.37        Barometric leveling

.38        Trigonometric leveling

**.6**        **Geodetic astronomy and geographic positions**

> Standard subdivisions are added for geodetic astronomy and geographic positions together, for geodetic astronomy alone

> Class here geodetic aspects of positional astronomy; comprehensive works on geodetic coordinates

> Class comprehensive works on positional astronomy in 522

> *For coordinates in spherical astronomy, see 522.7*

.61        Latitude

> *For latitude in celestial navigation, see 527.1*

.62        Longitude

> *For longitude in celestial navigation, see 527.2*

.63        Azimuth

.64        Geographic positions

> Including effect of irregularities of earth's surface on determining geographic positions

**.7**        **Gravity determinations**

**.8**          **Map projections**

Class map reading in 912.014

.82          Conformal projections (Orthomorphic projections)

.85          Equal-area projections (Equivalent projections)

**.9**          **Surveying**

Class here plane surveying (surveying in which curvature of earth is disregarded), land surveying

Class work of chartered surveyors (United Kingdom), interdisciplinary works on land surveys in 333.08; class engineering surveys in 622–629

*For geodetic surveying, see 526.3*

.98          Topographic surveying

.981          Contour surveying

.982          Photogrammetry

Class here aerial and space surveying

.982 5          Ground photogrammetry (Terrestrial photogrammetry)

.99          Hydrographic surveying

**527**          **Celestial navigation**

*For celestial navigation of specific craft, see the craft, e.g., navigation of nautical craft 623.89*

.028 4          Apparatus, equipment, materials

Including sextants [*formerly* 522.4]

**.1**          **Latitude**

**.2**          **Longitude**

**.3**          **Position determination**

Including Sumner's method

*For determination of latitude, see 527.1; for determination of longitude, see 527.2*

**528**          **Ephemerides**

Variant names: astronomical, nautical almanacs

Class tables of specific celestial bodies in 523

.093–.099          Treatment in ancient world, treatment by specific continent

Do not use for treatment by specific country or locality; class in 528.1–528.8

**.1–.8          Ephemerides of specific countries and localities**

Add to base number 528 the numbers following 06 in 061–068, e.g., ephemerides of England 528.2

**.9          Ephemeris making**

# 529          Chronology

**.1          Days**

Including apparent and mean days, equation of time, sidereal and solar days

**.2          Intervals of time**

Including years, months, weeks

*For sidereal month, see 523.33; for days, see 529.1*

*See also 525.5 for seasons*

**.3          Calendars**

*For western calendars, see 529.4; for calendar reform, see 529.5*

.32          Calendars of specific religions and traditions

Add to base number 529.32 the numbers following 29 in 292–299, e.g., Jewish calendar 529.326; however, for Julian calendar, see 529.42

*For Christian calendars, see 529.4*

**.4          Western calendars**

Class here Christian calendars

.42          Julian calendar

.43          Gregorian calendar

.44          Christian church calendar

Including determination of movable feasts and fast days

**.5          Calendar reform**

**.7          Horology**

Finding and measuring time

Class time systems and standards in 389.17

*For manufacture of instruments for measuring time, see 681.11*

# 530    Physics

Class here energy, matter, antimatter, classical physics; comprehensive works on classical and quantum mechanics

Class quantum mechanics, energy in quantum mechanics in 530.12; class classical mechanics in 531; class energy in classical mechanics in 531.6; class physical chemistry in 541

*For astrophysics, see 523.01*

## SUMMARY

| | |
|---|---|
| 530.01–.09 | Standard subdivisions |
| .1 | Theories and mathematical physics |
| .4 | States of matter |
| .7 | Instrumentation |
| .8 | Measurement |
| | |
| 531 | Classical mechanics |
| .015 195 | Statistical mathematics |
| .1 | Dynamics, statics, mass and gravity, particle mechanics |
| .2 | Solid statics |
| .3 | Solid dynamics |
| .4 | Friction and viscosity of solids |
| .5 | Mass and gravity of solids; projectiles |
| .6 | Energy |
| | |
| 532 | Fluid mechanics |
| .001–.009 | Standard subdivisions |
| .02–.05 | Fluid statics and dynamics |
| .2 | Hydrostatics |
| .4 | Mass, density, specific gravity of liquids |
| .5 | Hydrodynamics |
| | |
| 533 | Pneumatics (Gas mechanics) |
| .1 | Statics; mass, density, specific gravity |
| .2 | Dynamics |
| .5 | Vacuums |
| .6 | Aeromechanics |
| .7 | Kinetic theory of gases |
| | |
| 534 | Sound and related vibrations |
| .1 | Generation of sound |
| .2 | Transmission of sound |
| .3 | Characteristics of sound |
| .5 | Vibrations related to sound |
| | |
| 535 | Light and related radiation |
| .01–.09 | Infrared and ultraviolet radiation; standard subdivisions |
| .1 | Theories |
| .2 | Physical optics |
| .3 | Transmission, absorption, emission of light |
| .4 | Dispersion of light |
| .5 | Beams |
| .6 | Color |
| .8 | Special developments of light and related radiation |

| 536 | Heat |
|---|---|
| .01 | Philosophy and theory |
| .1 | Theories |
| .2 | Heat transfer |
| .3 | Radiation |
| .4 | Effects of heat on matter |
| .5 | Temperature |
| .6 | Specific heat |
| .7 | Thermodynamics |
| | |
| 537 | Electricity and electronics |
| .01 | Philosophy and theory |
| .1 | Theories |
| .2 | Electrostatics |
| .5 | Electronics |
| .6 | Electrodynamics (Electric currents) and thermoelectricity |
| | |
| 538 | Magnetism |
| .3 | Magnetic properties and phenomena |
| .4 | Magnetic substances and their characteristic phenomena |
| .6 | Magnetohydrodynamics |
| .7 | Geomagnetism and related phenomena |
| | |
| 539 | Modern physics |
| .01 | Philosophy and theory |
| .1 | Structure of matter |
| .2 | Radiation (Radiant energy) |
| .6 | Molecular physics |
| .7 | Atomic and nuclear physics |

.01      Philosophy and theory

> Do not use for theories; class in 530.1

[.015 1]      Mathematical physics

> Do not use; class in 530.15

.02      Miscellany

.028 4      Materials

> Do not use for apparatus and equipment; class in 530.7

[.028 7]      Testing and measurement

> Do not use; class in 530.8

.03–.09      Standard subdivisions

## .1      Theories and mathematical physics

> Standard subdivisions are added for theories and mathematical physics together, for theories alone
>
> Including space
>
> Class applications to specific states of matter in 530.4
>
> *See Manual at 520 vs. 500.5, 523.1, 530.1, 919.9*

.11 Relativity theory

Including fourth dimension

Class here conservation of mass-energy, equivalence of mass-energy ($E=mc^2$), space-time

Class specific relativistic theories in 530.12–530.14

.12 Quantum mechanics (Quantum theory)

Class here relativistic, nonrelativistic quantum mechanics

*For quantum statistics, see 530.133; for quantum kinetic theories, see 530.136; for quantum field theory, see 530.143; for quantum electronics, see 537.5*

*See Manual at 530.475 vs. 530.12, 531.16*

.122 Matrix mechanics (Heisenberg representation)

.124 Wave mechanics

Waves considered as a fundamental property of matter

Class here Schrödinger wave mechanics

*See also 530.141 for waves in electromagnetic theory; also 531.1133 for waves in classical physics*

.13 Statistical mechanics

Class here relativistic, nonrelativistic statistical mechanics

Including percolation theory

.132 Classical statistical mechanics (Boltzmann statistics)

.133 Quantum statistics (Quantum statistical mechanics)

.136 Kinetic theories

Class here quantum, combined quantum-classical kinetic theories

*For classical kinetic theory, see 531.113*

.138 Transport theory

.14 Field and wave theories

Classical, quantum, relativistic, nonrelativistic theories accounting for fundamental particles and interactions

Standard subdivisions are added for field and wave theories together, for field theories alone

Including problem of few bodies, theory of continuum physics

*For wave mechanics, see 530.124; for string and superstring theories, see 539.7258*

.141 Electromagnetic theory

> Electromagnetic fields and waves considered in terms of fundamental structure of matter

> Including Maxwell's equations

> Class electromagnetic spectrum and waves in 539.2

>> *See also 537.1 for theories of electricity; also 538.01 for theories of magnetism*

.142 Unified field theory

> Class here grand unified theory

.142 3 Supergravity

> Class here comprehensive works on supergravity and supersymmetry

>> *For supersymmetry, see 539.725*

.143 Quantum field theory

.143 3 Quantum electrodynamics

.143 5 Gauge fields

.144 Problem of many bodies

.15 Mathematical physics

> Add to base number 530.15 the numbers following 51 in 511–519, e.g., statistics 530.1595

> Class mathematical description of physical phenomena according to a specific theory with the theory in 530.1, e.g., statistical mechanics 530.13

**.4 States of matter**

> Class here quantum mechanics of specific states of matter; sound, light, heat, electricity, magnetism as properties of a specific state of matter

> Unless other instructions are given, class a subject with aspects in two or more subdivisions of 530.4 in the number coming last, e.g., tunneling in thin films 530.4175 (*not* 530.416)

> *For superconductivity and superconductors, see 537.623*

.41 Solid-state physics

> Class here physics of condensed matter

>> *For liquid-state physics, see 530.42; for crystallography, see 548*

>> *See Manual at 548 vs. 530.41*

.411 Structure

> Including electron arrangement, lattice dynamics

.412 Properties

> Including elastic, electrical, magnetic, optical, thermal properties

| | |
|---|---|
| .413 | Kinds |

Including amorphous, crystalline and noncrystalline, metallic and nonmetallic, ordered and disordered, organic, porous solids; polymers; solid particles

> *For dielectric matter, see 537.24; for semiconductors, see 537.622; for crystals, see 548*

| | |
|---|---|
| .414 | Phase transformations |

Transformations between different phases of condensed matter, between solid and gas phases

| | |
|---|---|
| .415 | Diffusion and mass transfer |

Standard subdivisions are added for either or both topics in heading

Class transport theory in 530.138

| | |
|---|---|
| .416 | Responsive behavior and energy phenomena |

Including bombardment, collisions, emission, excitation, excited states, excitons, field effects, internal friction, ion implantation, Jahn-Teller effect, Josephson effect, oscillation, phonons, radiation effect, relaxation, scattering, sputtering, tunneling, vibration

Class responsive behavior and energy phenomena in semiconductors in 537.622

> *See Manual at 530.416 vs. 539.75*

| | |
|---|---|
| .417 | Surface physics |

Class here interface with other states of matter

Class surface physics of semiconductors in 537.622

| | |
|---|---|
| .417 5 | Thin films |

Class comprehensive works on thin films in 530.4275

| | |
|---|---|
| .42 | Liquid-state physics |

Including superfluidity

Class here fluid-state physics

> *For gaseous-state physics, see 530.43*

| | |
|---|---|
| .424 | Phase transformations |

Transformations between different fluid phases

Including critical points

Class phase transformations between fluids and solids in 530.414

| | |
|---|---|
| .425 | Diffusion and mass transfer |

Standard subdivisions are added for either or both topics in heading

Including Brownian motion in liquids, osmosis

> *See Manual at 530.475 vs. 530.12, 531.16*

.427 Surface physics

Including capillarity, drops, surface tension

Class here interface with gases

Class interface with solids in 530.417; class surface tension of thin films in 530.4275

.427 5 Thin films

Class here bubbles

.429 Liquid crystals

Including liquid polymers

.43 Gaseous-state physics

Class interface with solids in 530.417; class interface with liquids in 530.427; class ionization of gases in 530.444

*For plasma physics, see 530.44*

.435 Diffusion and mass transfer

Standard subdivisions are added for either or both topics in heading

.44 Plasma physics

Physics of ionized gases

Add to base number 530.44 the numbers following 530.41 in 530.412–530.416, e.g., optical properties of plasmas 530.442, ionization of gases 530.444

*See also 537.532 for ionization of gases in electronics*

.47 Generalities of states of matter

*For generalities of specific states of matter, see 530.41–530.44*

.474 Phase transformations

Variant names: phase changes, phase transitions

Including critical phenomena, e.g., critical points; phase diagrams, equilibria, stability; triple points

Class here analysis of phase transformations to matter at the molecular and submolecular level; changes of state

Class phase transformations between different phases of condensed matter, between solids and gases in 530.414; class phase transformations between fluid phases in 530.424; class phase transformations between plasmas and other states of matter in 530.444

.475 Diffusion and mass transfer

Standard subdivisions are added for either or both topics in heading

Variant name for mass transfer: mass transport

Class here Brownian motion

*For heat transfer, see 536.2*

*See Manual at 530.475 vs. 530.12, 531.16*

**.7 Instrumentation**

Instrumentation for measurement, control, recording

**.8 Measurement**

Including dimensional analysis, testing

Class here interdisciplinary works on measurement, on mensuration

Class instrumentation for measurement in 530.7

*For horology, see 529.7. For measurement, mensuration in a specific subject, see the subject, plus notation 0287 from Table 1, e.g., psychological measurement 150.287*

*See also 516.15 for geometric mensuration*

.801 Philosophy and theory

Class here measurement theory

.802 Miscellany

[.802 1] Tabulated and related material

Do not use; class in 530.81

.81 Physical units and constants

Standard subdivisions are added for physical units and constants together, for physical units alone

Including dimensions, interdisciplinary works on size

Class here conversion tables between systems, systems of measurement, tabulated and related materials, weights and measures

Class units of dimension and size in metric system in 530.812; class units of dimension and size in British system in 530.813

*For social aspects of systems of measurement, see 389.1. For a specific aspect of size, see the aspect, e.g., size of business enterprise 338.64*

[.810 21] Tabulated and related material

Do not use; class in 530.81

.812 Metric system (Système international, SI)

.813              British system

                  Variant names: English, Imperial system

                  Class here United States customary units

# 531     Classical mechanics

                  Variant names: mechanics, continuum mechanics, Newtonian mechanics

                  Class here solid mechanics

                  *For fluid mechanics, see 532*

.015 195                  Statistical mathematics

                          Class classical statistical mechanics in 530.132

## .1     Dynamics, statics, mass and gravity, particle mechanics

                  Including pressure, mechanics of points

[.101–.109]       Standard subdivisions

                  Do not use; class in 531.01–531.09

.11               Dynamics

                          *For particle dynamics, see 531.163; for solid dynamics, see 531.3*

.112              Kinematics

                  Motion considered apart from mass and force

                  Including linear and relative motion, velocity, acceleration, vector
                  quantities; search for a moving target

.113              Kinetics

                  Including centrifugal and centripetal forces, rotational motion

                  Class comprehensive works on motion in 531.11

.113 3            Waves

                  Waves observable in matter of classical physics

                  Including shock waves

                          *See also 530.124 for waves considered as a fundamental property
                          of matter*

.113 4            Rheology (Deformation and flow)

                  Including viscosity and friction

                  Most works on deformation are limited to solids and are classed in
                  531.38; most works on flow are limited to fluids and are classed in
                  532.051

.12               Statics

                  Including graphic statics

                          *For particle statics, see 531.16; for solid statics, see 531.2*

.14       Mass and gravity

Including density, gravity of earth, specific gravity

Class geodetic gravity determinations in 526.7

*For gravity in celestial mechanics, see 521.1*

*See also 539.754 for fundamental gravitational interaction*

.16       Particle mechanics

Class here mechanics of solid particles

Class mechanics of molecular, atomic, and subatomic particles (quantum mechanics) in 530.12

*See also 620.43 for fine particle technology*

*See Manual at 530.475 vs. 530.12, 531.16*

.163       Dynamics

---

>       **531.2–531.5   Mechanics of solids**

Class here mechanics of rigid bodies

Class comprehensive works in 531

*For mechanics of solid particles, see 531.16*

**.2**       **Solid statics**

Including graphic statics

**.3**       **Solid dynamics**

Including solid kinematics

Class here solid kinetics

*For friction and viscosity, see 531.4; for ballistics, see 531.55*

.32       Vibrations

Class here oscillations

.324       Pendulum motion

.33       Waves

Including shock waves

.34       Rotational motion (Spin)

Class here gyrodynamics

*For centrifugal and centripetal forces, see 531.35*

.35       Centrifugal and centripetal forces

Standard subdivisions are added for either or both topics in heading

| | |
|---|---|
| .38 | Deformation; stresses and strains |

Standard subdivisions are added for deformation, stresses, strains together; for deformation alone

| | |
|---|---|
| .381 | Stresses and strains |

Standard subdivisions are added for either or both topics in heading

Including elastic constants, Poisson's ratio, yield point

Class application to elasticity in 531.382; class application to plasticity in 531.385

| | |
|---|---|
| .382 | Elasticity |

Variant names: elastic, temporary deformation

Including elastic limit, coefficient of restitution

Class here Hooke's law

Class elastic vibrations in 531.32

| | |
|---|---|
| .385 | Plasticity |

Variant names: permanent, plastic deformation

**.4**      **Friction and viscosity of solids**

Standard subdivisions are added for either or both topics in heading

**.5**      **Mass and gravity of solids; projectiles**

Including laws of falling bodies

| | |
|---|---|
| .54 | Density and specific gravity |

Standard subdivisions are added for either or both topics in heading

| | |
|---|---|
| .55 | Projectiles |

Class here ballistics

**.6**      **Energy**

Including momentum, work

Class comprehensive works on energy in physics in 530; class interdisciplinary works on energy in 333.79

| | |
|---|---|
| .62 | Conservation of energy |

*See also 333.7916 for programs to conserve energy, also 530.11 for conservation of mass-energy*

| | |
|---|---|
| .68 | Transformation |

Change in form of energy

*For a specific transformation, see the resultant form, e.g., transformation of light to heat 536*

## 532     Fluid mechanics

Class here hydraulics (hydromechanics), liquid mechanics

*For pneumatics, see 533*

.001–.009      Standard subdivisions

---

>        532.02–532.05   Fluid statics and dynamics

Class comprehensive works in 532

.02       Statics

Including buoyancy

*For liquid statics, see 532.2*

.05       Dynamics

Including kinematics, vibrations

Class here kinetics

*For liquid dynamics, see 532.5*

.051      Flow

Including boundary layers

Class waves and vortex motion in 532.059

*For types of flow, see 532.052; for flow properties, see 532.053*

.052      Types of flow

Class properties of specific types of flow in 532.053

*For viscous flow, see 532.0533; for rotational flow, see 532.0595*

.052 5       Laminar flow

.052 6       Transitional flow

.052 7       Turbulent flow

.053       Flow properties

.053 2        Velocity

.053 3        Viscosity and friction

Standard subdivisions are added for either or both topics in heading

Class here viscous flow

.053 5        Elasticity and compressibility

Standard subdivisions are added for either or both topics in heading

.059       Waves and vortex motion

.059 3        Waves

Including shock waves

.059 5         Vortex motion

            Including centrifugal and centripetal forces

            Class here rotational flow

---

\>      **532.2–532.5 Hydraulics**

         In sense of liquid mechanics

         Class comprehensive works in 532

**.2**       **Hydrostatics**

         In sense of liquid statics

           *See also 532.02 for hydrostatics in sense of fluid statics*

.25       Buoyancy

         Class here floating, sinking

**.4**       **Mass, density, specific gravity of liquids**

**.5**       **Hydrodynamics**

         In sense of liquid dynamics

         Including kinematics

         Class here kinetics

           *See also 532.05 for hydrodynamics in sense of fluid dynamics*

.51       Flow

         Class waves and vortex motion in 532.59

           *For flow variations, see 532.52–532.56; for flow properties, see 532.58; for rotational flow, see 532.595*

.515      Laminar flow

.516      Transitional flow

.517      Turbulent flow

---

\>      532.52–532.56   Flow variations

         Class comprehensive works in 532.51

.52       Flow through openings

.53       Flow over and around obstacles

         Standard subdivisions are added for either or both topics in heading

.54       Flow through open and closed channels

         Standard subdivisions are added for either or both topics in heading

| | |
|---|---|
| .55 | Flow through bends and irregular enclosures |

Standard subdivisions are added for either or both topics in heading

| | |
|---|---|
| .56 | Flow when pressure is variable |

Including flow over and around submerged bodies, multiphase flow

| | |
|---|---|
| .57 | Flow velocity |
| .58 | Flow properties |

Including elasticity and compressibility, viscosity and friction, viscous flow

*For flow velocity, see 532.57*

*See also 536.413 for expansion and contraction of liquids as a result of heating and cooling*

| | |
|---|---|
| .59 | Waves, vortex motion, cavitation |
| .593 | Waves |

Including shock waves

| | |
|---|---|
| .595 | Vortex motion |

Class here rotational flow

| | |
|---|---|
| .597 | Cavitation |

## 533 Pneumatics (Gas mechanics)

---

> **533.1–533.5 Specific aspects of pneumatics (gas mechanics)**

Class comprehensive works in 533

| | |
|---|---|
| **.1** | **Statics; mass, density, specific gravity** |

*For vacuums, see 533.5*

| | |
|---|---|
| .12 | Statics |

Including buoyancy

*For aerostatics, see 533.61*

| | |
|---|---|
| .15 | Mass, density, specific gravity |
| **.2** | **Dynamics** |

Including kinematics

Class here kinetics

*For aerodynamics, see 533.62; for kinetic theory of gases, see 533.7*

| | |
|---|---|
| .21 | Flow |

Class waves and vortex motion in 533.29

*For flow at specific speeds, see 533.27; for flow properties, see 533.28; for rotational flow, see 533.295*

.215 Laminar flow

.216 Transitional flow

.217 Turbulent flow

.27 Flow at specific speeds

Class here velocity

.273 Subsonic flow

.274 Transonic flow

.275 Supersonic flow

*For hypersonic flow, see 533.276*

.276 Hypersonic flow

.28 Flow properties

Including elasticity and compressibility, viscosity and friction, viscous flow

Class flow properties at specific speeds in 533.27

*See also 536.412 for expansion and contraction of gases resulting from heating and cooling*

.29 Waves and vortex motion

.293 Waves

Including shock waves

.295 Vortex motion

Class here rotational flow

**.5** **Vacuums**

**.6** **Aeromechanics**

Including mass, density, specific gravity of air

*For vacuums, see 533.5*

.61 Aerostatics

Including buoyancy

.62 Aerodynamics

**.7** **Kinetic theory of gases**

---

> **534–538 Specific forms of energy**

Class here transformation into specific forms of energy

Class specific forms of energy as properties of specific states of matter in 530.4; class comprehensive works in 530; class comprehensive works on transformation of energy in 531.68

*For mechanical energy, see 531.6*

**534        Sound and related vibrations**

> Standard subdivisions are added for sound and related vibrations together, for sound alone

> **534.1–534.3  Sound**

> Class comprehensive works in 534

**.1        Generation of sound**

**.2        Transmission of sound**

.200 1–.200 9        Standard subdivisions

.202              Velocity

.204              Reflection (Echoes)

.208              Absorption (Damping)

.22              Transmission in solids

.23              Transmission in liquids

.24              Transmission in gases

**.3        Characteristics of sound**

> Including Doppler effect

**.5        Vibrations related to sound**

> Class here vibrations that can not be heard by the human ear

.52              Subsonic vibrations

.55              Ultrasonic vibrations

**535        Light and related radiation**

> Standard subdivisions are added for light and related radiation together, for light alone

> Class here optics

> *See also 537.56 for electron and ion optics*

.01              Infrared and ultraviolet radiation; philosophy and theory of light and related radiation

> Notation 01 from Table 1 as modified below

> Class here radiation of nonvisible spectral regions

> Class a specific element of infrared and ultraviolet radiation in 535.2–535.6

.010 1–.010 9        Standard subdivisions of infrared and ultraviolet radiation

.012              Infrared radiation

> Class heat radiation in 536.3

| [.013] | Visible region |
|---|---|

Number discontinued; class in 535

| .014 | Ultraviolet radiation |
|---|---|

| .019 | Philosophy and theory of light and related radiation |
|---|---|

Add to base number 535.019 the numbers following —01 in notation 011–019 from Table 1, e.g., abbreviations, acronyms, symbols in optics 535.01948

Class theories in 535.1

| .02 | Miscellany |
|---|---|

| .028 | Auxiliary techniques and procedures; apparatus, equipment, materials |
|---|---|

Class spectroscopy in 535.84

| **.1** | **Theories** |
|---|---|

*See also 539.7217 for photons*

| .12 | Corpuscular theory |
|---|---|

| .13 | Mechanical wave theory |
|---|---|

| .14 | Electromagnetic theory |
|---|---|

| .15 | Quantum theory |
|---|---|

---

> **535.2–535.6 Specific elements of light**

Class comprehensive works in 535

*For spectroscopy, see 535.84*

| **.2** | **Physical optics** |
|---|---|

Including coherent and nonlinear optics

*For dispersion of light, see 535.4; for beams, see 535.5*

| .22 | Intensity of light |
|---|---|

| .220 287 | Testing and measurement |
|---|---|

Class here photometry

| .24 | Velocity of light |
|---|---|

| **.3** | **Transmission, absorption, emission of light** |
|---|---|

| .32 | Geometrical optics |
|---|---|

| .323 | Reflection |
|---|---|

| .324 | Refraction |
|---|---|

| .326 | Absorption |
|---|---|

| .35 | Luminescence |
|---|---|

.352      Fluorescence

Class fluorescence by source of exciting energy in 535.355–535.357

.353      Phosphorescence

Class phosphorescence by source of exciting energy in 535.355–535.357

---

>      535.355–535.357 Luminescence by source of exciting energy

Class comprehensive works in 535.35

*For chemiluminescence, see 541.35; for bioluminescence, see 572.4358*

.355      Photoluminescence

.356      Thermoluminescence

.357      Electroluminescence

**.4**      **Dispersion of light**

Including shadows

Class comprehensive works on beams and their dispersion in 535.5

*See also 774.0153 for physical properties of holography*

.42      Diffraction

.420 284      Apparatus, equipment, materials

Class here interdisciplinary works on prisms

*For a specific aspect of prisms, see the aspect, e.g., geometry of prisms 516.156*

.43      Scattering

.47      Interference

**.5**      **Beams**

.52      Polarization

**.6**      **Color**

**.8**      **Special developments of light and related radiation**

.84      Optical, infrared, ultraviolet spectroscopy

Class here comprehensive works on spectroscopy in physics

Class interdisciplinary works on spectroscopy in 543.5

*For a specific kind of spectroscopy in physics other than optical, infrared, or ultraviolet, see the kind, e.g., radiofrequency spectroscopy 537.534*

.842      Infrared spectroscopy

.843      Light spectroscopy

.844      Ultraviolet spectroscopy

.845                    Vacuum ultraviolet spectroscopy

.846                    Raman spectroscopy

                       Including Raman effect

# 536        Heat

.01                    Philosophy and theory

                       Do not use for theories; class in 536.1

**.1        Theories**

**.2        Heat transfer**

            *For radiation, see 536.3*

.200 1–.200 9          Standard subdivisions

.201                   Heat-transfer properties of matter

                       Class specific heat in 536.6

                           *For heat-transfer properties of matter at low temperatures, see*
                           *536.56; for heat-transfer properties of matter at high temperatures,*
                           *see 536.57*

                           *See also 620.11296 for thermal properties of engineering materials*

.201 2                 Thermal conductivity

.201 4                 Thermal diffusivity

.23         Conduction

            Class here heat transfer in solids

            Class thermal conductivity in 536.2012

            *For conduction in fluids, see 536.25*

.25         Convection

            Class here heat transfer in fluids

**.3        Radiation**

            Class here absorption, scattering

**.4        Effects of heat on matter**

            Class here effects of heat that can be readily observed or measured with simple
            instruments

.41         Expansion and contraction

            Class here coefficients of expansion

            Class expansion and contraction in fusion and solidification in 536.42; class
            expansion and contraction in vaporization and condensation in 536.44

.412        Gases

> *For liquefaction and solidification of gases at low temperatures, see 536.56*

.413        Liquids

.414        Solids

.42        Fusion (Melting) and solidification

> Including freezing and melting points, latent heat of fusion and solidification

> Class comprehensive works on fusion and solidification(536.42) and vaporization and condensation (536.44) in 536.4

.44        Vaporization and condensation

> Including boiling points, dew points, latent heat of evaporation and condensation, liquefaction of gases

> *For liquefaction of gases at low temperatures, see 536.56*

.5        **Temperature**

> Class here absolute temperature

.502 87        Testing and measurement

> Including resistance thermometry

> Class here thermometry

> *For measurement at a specific range of temperature, see 536.51–536.54*

---

>        536.51–536.54 Measurement at a specific range of temperature

> Class comprehensive works in 536.50287

.51        Measurement of normal-range temperatures

> Including liquid-in-glass thermometry

.52        Measurement of high temperatures (Pyrometry)

> Including thermocouples

.54        Measurement of low temperatures (Cryometry)

.56        Cryogenics and low temperatures

> Standard subdivisions are added for either or both topics in heading

> Including liquefaction and solidification of gases at low temperatures, properties of matter at low temperatures

> Class a specific property of matter at low temperature with the property, e.g., conduction of electricity at low temperatures 537.62

.560 287        Testing

> Do not use for measurement; class in 536.54

| | | |
|---|---|---|
| .57 | | High temperatures |

Including properties of matter at high temperature

Class a specific property of matter at high temperature with the property, e.g., conduction of electricity 537.62

.570 287    Testing

Do not use for measurement; class in 536.52

**.6**    **Specific heat**

Class here calorimetry, heat capacity

Class heat of transformation in fusion and solidification in 536.42; class heat of transformation in vaporization and condensation in 536.44

.63    Solids and liquids

.65    Gases

**.7**    **Thermodynamics**

.701    Philosophy and theory

Do not use for theories; class in 536.71

.71    Theories

Including Carnot cycle, Joule's law, Maxwell's thermodynamic formulas

Class here laws of thermodynamics

.73    Entropy

**537**    **Electricity and electronics**

Standard subdivisions are added for electricity and electronics together, for electricity alone

Class here electromagnetism

Class interdisciplinary works on electricity in 333.7932

*For magnetism, see 538*

.01    Philosophy and theory

Do not use for theories; class in 537.1

**.1**    **Theories**

.12    Wave theories

Class electromagnetic theory of matter in 530.141

**.2**    **Electrostatics**

.21    Electric charge and potential

Standard subdivisions are added for either or both topics in heading

Including triboelectricity

| | |
|---|---|
| .24 | Dielectrics |

Including electrets, electrocapillarity, electrostriction

| | |
|---|---|
| .243 | Dipole moments |
| .244 | Piezoelectricity and ferroelectricity |

*See also 548.85 for electrical properties of crystals*

| | |
|---|---|
| .244 6 | Piezoelectricity |
| .244 8 | Ferroelectricity |
| **.5** | **Electronics** |

Including exploding wire phenomena

Class here quantum electronics

*For semiconductors, see 537.622*

| | |
|---|---|
| .52 | Disruptive discharges |

Including coronas, electric arcs

Class discharge through rarefied gases and vacuums in 537.53

| | |
|---|---|
| .53 | Discharge through rarefied gases and vacuums |
| .532 | Ionization of gases |

Class comprehensive works on ionization of gases in 530.444

| | |
|---|---|
| .534 | Radio wave and microwave electronics |

Standard subdivisions are added for radio wave and microwave electronics together, for radio wave electronics alone

Class here spectroscopy

| | |
|---|---|
| .534 2 | Long waves |
| .534 3 | Short waves |
| .534 4 | Microwaves and ultrahigh-frequency waves |
| .535 | X-ray and gamma-ray electronics |
| .535 2 | Spectroscopy |

Including Mössbauer spectroscopy and effect

Class a specific application of spectroscopy with the application, e.g., X-ray spectroscopy in chemical analysis 543.62

| | |
|---|---|
| .54 | Photoelectric phenomena |

Including photoconductivity, photoemission, photovoltaic effect

| | |
|---|---|
| .56 | Electron and ion optics |

Standard subdivisions are added for electron and ion optics together, for electron optics alone

.6 **Electrodynamics (Electric currents) and thermoelectricity**

> Standard subdivisions are added for electrodynamics and thermoelectricity together, for electrodynamics alone
>
> *For quantum electrodynamics, see 530.1433*

.62 Electric conductivity and resistance

> *For dielectrics, see 537.24*

.622 Semiconductivity

> Class here solid-state physics of semiconductors

.622 1 Structure of semiconductors

> Class structure of specific kinds of semiconductors in 537.6223

.622 3 Kinds of semiconductors

> Class diffusion and mass transfer in specific kinds of semiconductors in 537.6225; class interactions in and specific properties of specific kinds of semiconductors in 537.6226

.622 5 Diffusion and mass transfer in semiconductors

> Standard subdivisions are added for either or both topics in heading

.622 6 Interactions in and specific properties of semiconductors

> Including effects of beams and electromagnetic fields, Hall effects; adsorption, instabilities, resistivity, tunneling

.623 Superconductivity

> Class here solid-state physics of superconductors
>
> Add to base number 537.623 the numbers following 537.622 in 537.6221–537.6226, e.g., ternary superconductors 537.6233

.624 Thermal effects of currents

.65 Thermoelectricity

# 538 Magnetism

.3 **Magnetic properties and phenomena**

> Standard subdivisions are added for either or both topics in heading
>
> Including hysteresis, magnetic moment and relaxation
>
> Class specific magnetic substances and their characteristic phenomena in 538.4

.36 Magnetic resonance

.362 Nuclear magnetic resonance (NMR)

> Including nuclear quadrupole resonance (NQR), electron-nuclear double resonance (ENDOR)

.364 Electron paramagnetic resonance (EPR)

> Variant name: electron spin resonance (ESR)

**.4**  **Magnetic substances and their characteristic phenomena**

> Standard subdivisions are added for either or both topics in heading
>
> Class here magnetic induction, natural magnets
>
> Class comprehensive works on specific magnetic phenomena in 538.3

.42  Diamagnetism

.43  Paramagnetism

.44  Ferromagnetism

.45  Ferrimagnetism

**.6**  **Magnetohydrodynamics**

**.7**  **Geomagnetism and related phenomena**

> Standard subdivisions are added for geomagnetism and related phenomena together, for geomagnetism alone

.709  History, geographic treatment, biography

> Do not use for geographic treatment of magnetic surveys; class in 538.78. Do not use for geographic treatment of magnetic observations at observatories; class in 538.79

.72  Magnetic fields of solid earth

> Class here secular variations
>
> Class transient variations in magnetism of solid earth in 538.74; class observations of magnetic fields of solid earth at observatories in 538.79
>
> *For magnetic surveys, see 538.78*

.727  Paleomagnetism

> Class here geomagnetic reversals, paleomagnetic observations at observatories, paleomagnetic surveys

.74  *Transient magnetism

> *For auroras, see 538.768*

.742  *Diurnal variations

.744  *Magnetic storms

.746  *Sunspot effects

.748  *Earth currents

.76  Magnetosphere, ionosphere, auroras

.766  Magnetosphere

> Including Van Allen radiation belts
>
> Class transient magnetism of magnetosphere in 538.74

---

*Do not use notation 09 from Table 1 for magnetic observations at permanent observatories; class in 538.79

| | |
|---|---|
| .767 | Ionosphere |

Class here atmospheric ionization

| | |
|---|---|
| .767 2 | D region |
| .767 3 | E region |

Variant name: Kennelly-Heaviside layers

| | |
|---|---|
| .767 4 | F region |

Variant name: Appleton layers

| | |
|---|---|
| .768 | Auroras |

Class here northern lights

| | |
|---|---|
| .78 | Magnetic surveys |

*For paleomagnetic surveys, see 538.727*

| | |
|---|---|
| .780 9 | History and biography |

Do not use for geographic treatment; class in 538.781–538.789

| | |
|---|---|
| .781–.789 | Geographic treatment |

Add to base number 538.78 notation 1–9 from Table 2, e.g., surveys of Ireland 538.78415

| | |
|---|---|
| .79 | Magnetic observations at observatories |

*For paleomagnetic observations at observatories, see 538.727*

| | |
|---|---|
| .790 9 | History and biography |

Do not use for geographic treatment; class in 538.791–538.799

| | |
|---|---|
| .791–.799 | Geographic treatment |

Add to base number 538.79 notation 1–9 from Table 2, e.g., findings from observatories in Russia 538.7947

# 539　　Modern physics

Class here quantum physics

*For theories of modern physics, see 530.1; for states of matter, see 530.4; for modern physics of specific forms of energy, see 534–538*

### SUMMARY

| | |
|---|---|
| 539.01 | **Philosophy and theory** |
| .1 | **Structure of matter** |
| .2 | **Radiation (Radiant energy)** |
| .6 | **Molecular physics** |
| .7 | **Atomic and nuclear physics** |

| | |
|---|---|
| .01 | Philosophy and theory |

Do not use for theories; class in 530.1

| [.015 1] | Mathematical principles |
|---|---|

Do not use; class in 530.15

**.1     Structure of matter**

*For structure of specific states of matter, see 530.4*

.12      Molecular structure

Use 539.12 only for studies of molecular structure without reference to chemical characteristics. Prefer 541.22 if there is discussion of chemical phenomena

.14      Atomic structure

*For nuclear structure, see 539.74*

**.2     Radiation (Radiant energy)**

Class here electromagnetic radiation, spectrum, waves

*For a specific kind of radiation, see the kind, e.g., ultraviolet radiation 535.014, ionizing radiation 539.722*

**.6     Molecular physics**

Atom-atom and molecule-molecule relationships

Including molecular and vibrational spectra

*For molecular structure, see 539.12*

.602 87      Testing and measurement

Class here comprehensive works on mass spectrometry in physics

Class interdisciplinary works on mass spectrometry in 543.65

*For spectrometry of a specific nonmolecular particle, see the particle, e.g., atomic spectrometry 539.7*

**.7     Atomic and nuclear physics**

Standard subdivisions are added for either or both topics in heading

*For atomic structure, see 539.14*

### SUMMARY

| 539.72 | Particle physics; ionizing radiation |
|---|---|
| .73 | Particle acceleration |
| .74 | Nuclear structure |
| .75 | Nuclear activities and interactions |
| .76 | High-energy physics |
| .77 | Detecting and measuring particles and radioactivity |

| | |
|---|---|
| .72 | Particle physics; ionizing radiation |

Standard subdivisions are added for particle physics and ionizing radiation together, for particle physics alone

Class here antiparticles, relativistic particles

*For field and wave theories accounting for fundamental particles, see 530.14; for particle acceleration, see 539.73; for nuclear activities and interactions, see 539.75; for detection and measurement of particles and radioactivity, see 539.77*

| | |
|---|---|
| [.720 287] | Testing and measurement |

Do not use; class in 539.77

| | |
|---|---|
| .721 | Specific kinds of subatomic particles |

Including bosons, fermions, Regge poles

Class subatomic particles considered as a cosmic ray in 539.7223

| | |
|---|---|
| [.721 01–.721 09] | Standard subdivisions |

Do not use; class in 539.7201–539.7209

| | |
|---|---|
| .721 1 | Leptons |

*For neutrinos, see 539.7215; for photons, see 539.7217*

| | |
|---|---|
| .721 12 | Electrons |

Including beta particles

*For beta positrons, see 539.7214*

*See also 537.5 for electronics*

| | |
|---|---|
| .721 14 | Muons (Mu-mesons) |
| .721 2 | Nucleons |

*For neutrons, see 539.7213*

| | |
|---|---|
| .721 23 | Protons |

Class here antiprotons

Class protons considered as cosmic rays in 539.7223

| | |
|---|---|
| .721 3 | Neutrons |
| .721 4 | Positrons |
| .721 5 | Neutrinos |
| .721 6 | Hadrons |

Class here strange particles and strangeness

| | |
|---|---|
| .721 62 | Mesons |

Including pions (pi-mesons), kaons (K-mesons)

*For mu-mesons, see 539.72114*

| .721 64 | Baryons |
|---|---|

Including hyperons

*For nucleons, see 539.7212*

| .721 67 | Quarks |
|---|---|

Including quantum flavor

*See also 539.7548 for quantum chromodynamics*

| .721 7 | Photons |
|---|---|

*See also 539.756 for photonuclear reactions*

| .722 | Ionizing radiation |
|---|---|

*For a specific kind of ionizing radiation not provided for here, see the kind, e.g., alpha particles 539.7232*

*See also 537.532 for ionization of gases by electron discharge*

| .722 2 | X and gamma rays |
|---|---|

Including bremsstrahlung (secondary X rays), gamma particles

*See also 537.535 for X-ray and gamma-ray electronics*

| .722 3 | Cosmic rays |
|---|---|

Class here any particle considered as a cosmic ray

| .723 | Nuclei and atoms considered as particles |
|---|---|

| .723 2 | Nuclei |
|---|---|

Including alpha particles, deuterons

Class component particles of nuclei in 539.721; class nuclei considered as cosmic rays in 539.7223; class nuclear structure in 539.74

| .723 4 | Heavy ions |
|---|---|

| .725 | Particle characteristics |
|---|---|

Including angular momentum, charge, energy levels, orbits, spin, symmetry, supersymmetry

Class characteristics of a specific particle with the particle, e.g., orbits of electrons 539.72112, strangeness of strange particles 539.7216

*For supergravity, comprehensive works on supergravity and supersymmetry, see 530.1423; for magnetic properties, see 538.3*

| .725 8 | String theory |
|---|---|

Class here superstring theory

| .73 | Particle acceleration |
|---|---|

Including bombardment, particle beams

.732　　　　　　　High-voltage accelerators

　　　　　　　　　　Including Van de Graaff electrostatic generators

.733　　　　　　　Resonance accelerators

　　　　　　　　　　Including cyclotrons, linear accelerators

.734　　　　　　　Induction accelerators

　　　　　　　　　　Including betatrons

.735　　　　　　　Synchronous accelerators

　　　　　　　　　　Including synchro-cyclotrons and synchrotrons (betatron-synchrotrons)

.736　　　　　　　Supercolliders

　　　　　　　　　　Class here superconducting supercolliders

.737　　　　　　　Acceleration of specific particles

　　　　　　　　　　Class acceleration of specific particles in specific accelerators in
　　　　　　　　　　539.732–539.736

[.737 01–.737 09]　　Standard subdivisions

　　　　　　　　　　　Do not use; class in 539.7301–539.7309

.737 1–.737 7　　Specific particles

　　　　　　　　　　Add to base number 539.737 the numbers following 539.721 in
　　　　　　　　　　539.7211–539.7217, e.g., proton acceleration 539.73723

.74　　　　　　Nuclear structure

　　　　　　　　　　Class here isotope and nuclide structure, nuclear models

.742　　　　　　Liquid-drop model

.743　　　　　　Shell model

.744　　　　　　Interpretation through spectroscopy

.75　　　　　　Nuclear activities and interactions

　　　　　　　　　　Standard subdivisions are added for either or both topics in heading

　　　　　　　　　　Including annihilation, capture, coupling, creation

　　　　　　　　　　　*For ionizations of gases, see 530.444; for high-energy physics, see*
　　　　　　　　　　　*539.76*

　　　　　　　　　　　*See Manual at 530.416 vs. 539.75*

.752　　　　　　Natural radioactivity

　　　　　　　　　　Including half-life

　　　　　　　　　　Class here decay schemes, radioactive substances (radioelements),
　　　　　　　　　　radioisotopes, radionuclides; comprehensive works on radioactivity

　　　　　　　　　　　*For artificial radioactivity, see 539.753*

[.752 028 7]　　　　　Testing and measurement

　　　　　　　　　　　Do not use; class in 539.77

| | |
|---|---|
| .752 2 | Alpha decay |
| .752 3 | Beta decay |
| .752 4 | Gamma decay |
| .753 | Artificial radioactivity |

Including radioactive fallout

*See also 363.738 for pollution from radioactive fallout*

| | |
|---|---|
| [.753 028 7] | Testing and measurement |

Do not use; class in 539.77

| | |
|---|---|
| .754 | Fundamental interactions |

Including gravitational interaction, gravitational waves

Class field theories covering fundamental interactions in 530.14

*See also 531.14 for gravity*

| | |
|---|---|
| .754 4 | Weak interaction |

*For beta decay, see 539.7523*

| | |
|---|---|
| .754 6 | Electromagnetic interaction |
| .754 8 | Strong interaction |

Including quantum chromodynamics

| | |
|---|---|
| .756 | Photonuclear reactions |
| .757 | Collision |
| .758 | Scattering |
| .76 | High-energy physics |

Class high-energy levels of particles in 539.725

| | |
|---|---|
| .762 | Nuclear fission |
| .764 | Nuclear fusion (Thermonuclear reaction) |
| .77 | Detecting and measuring particles and radioactivity |

Class here radiation measurement

| | |
|---|---|
| .772 | Ionization chambers |
| .773 | Proportional counters |
| .774 | Geiger-Müller counters |
| .775 | Scintillation counters |
| .776 | Crystal conduction counters |
| .777 | Wilson cloud chambers |
| .778 | Photography |

# 540    Chemistry and allied sciences

Standard subdivisions are added for chemistry and allied sciences together, for chemistry alone

Class cosmochemistry in 523.02

### SUMMARY

**.1**      **Philosophy and theory**

       Do not use for theoretical chemistry; class in 541.2

.11      Alchemy and systems

.112       Alchemy

.113       Systems

       Add to base number 540.113 the numbers following 003 in 003.1–003.8, e.g., computer modeling and simulation 540.1133

[.28]      Auxiliary techniques and procedures; apparatus, equipment, materials

       Do not use; class in 542

**.7**      **Education, research, related topics**

.72      Research; statistical methods

       Do not use for laboratories; class in 542.1

---

\>      ## 541–547   Chemistry

       Class comprehensive works in 540

# 541    Physical chemistry

       Inorganic and combined inorganic-organic chemistry

       Class physical crystallography in 548

       *For physical chemistry of specific kinds of inorganic chemicals, see 546; for physical chemistry of organic compounds, see 547*

       *See Manual at 541 vs. 546*

## SUMMARY

| | |
|---|---|
| **541.04** | **Special topics of physical chemistry** |
| **.2** | **Theoretical chemistry** |
| **.3** | **Miscellaneous topics in physical chemistry** |
| **.7** | **Optical activity** |

.04      Special topics of physical chemistry

.042      Chemistry of states of matter

Add to base number 541.042 the numbers following 530.4 in 530.41–530.44, e.g., solid-state chemistry 541.0421

.2      **Theoretical chemistry**

.22      Molecular structure

*For molecular structure studied without reference to chemical characteristics, see 539.12; for quantum chemistry, see 541.28*

.222      Molecular weights

.223      Stereochemistry

Class comprehensive works on stereochemistry in 547.1223

*For structural variations, see 541.225*

.224      Chemical bonds, valence, radicals

Standard subdivisions are added for chemical bonds, valence, radicals together; for chemical bonds alone; for valence alone

Class bond angles and distances in 541.223

.224 2      Coordination chemistry

Including ligands

Class chelates in 547.59044242

.225      Structural variations

.225 2      Isomers

Class here tautomerism

Class comprehensive works on isomers in 547.12252

.225 4      Polymers

Class comprehensive works on polymerization in 547.28; class comprehensive works on polymers in 547.7

.226      Intermolecular forces

Class here supramolecular chemistry

Class comprehensive works on supramolecular chemistry in 547.1226

.24      Atomic structure

*For periodic law, see 546.8*

.242          Atomic weight

> Class here atomic mass and number

.26          Stoichiometry

.28          Quantum chemistry

> Including molecular and atomic orbitals

> Class radiochemistry in 541.38

**.3**          **Miscellaneous topics in physical chemistry**

> Limited to topics named below

### SUMMARY

| | |
|---|---|
| 541.33 | **Surface chemistry** |
| .34 | **Solution chemistry** |
| .35 | **Photochemistry** |
| .36 | **Thermochemistry and thermodynamics** |
| .37 | **Electrochemistry and magnetochemistry** |
| .38 | **Radiochemistry** |
| .39 | **Chemical reactions** |

[.301–.309]          Standard subdivisions

> Do not use; class in 541.01–541.09

.33          Surface chemistry

> Including absorption, adhesion

> Class surface chemical reactions in 541.39

.335          Adsorption

> Including chemisorption

.34          Solution chemistry

> *For electrolytic solutions, see 541.372*

.341          Properties of solutions

.341 3          Mechanical properties

.341 4          Optical properties

.341 5          Colligative properties

> Including effect of osmotic pressure

.341 6          Thermal properties

.342          Solutions by type of solvent

> Class here solubility

> Class properties of specific type of solvent in 541.341

.342 2          Aqueous solutions

.342 3          Nonaqueous solutions

.345         Colloid chemistry

.345 1         Specific types of colloids

[.345 101–.345 109]         Standard subdivisions

        Do not use; class in 541.34501–541.34509

.345 13         Matter dispersed in solids

        Including gels, solid foams

.345 14         Hydrosols

        Including emulsions, foams, froths, lathers

        Class solid foams in 541.34513

.345 15         Aerosols

        Including fogs, mists, smokes

.348         Solution components

.348 2         Solvents

.348 3         Solutes

.348 5         Precipitates

        Including Liesegang rings

.35         Photochemistry

        Including chemiluminescence

        *For bioluminescence, see 572.4358*

.351         Energy transformations

.353         Photochemical reactions due to specific radiation

[.353 01–.353 09]         Standard subdivisions

        Do not use; class in 541.3501–541.3509

.353 2         Infrared radiation

.353 3         Visible light

.353 4         Ultraviolet radiation

.36         Thermochemistry and thermodynamics

        Standard subdivisions are added for thermochemistry and thermodynamics together, for thermochemistry alone

---

>         541.361–541.368   Thermochemistry

        Class comprehensive works in 541.36

.361         Combustion

        Including explosion, flame, ignition

| | | |
|---|---|---|
| .362 | | Exothermic and endothermic reactions |

> Including latent heat
>
> *For combustion, see 541.361*

| | | |
|---|---|---|
| .363 | | Changes of state (Phase transformations) |

> Including Gibbs' phase rule
>
> Class interdisciplinary works on phase transformations in 530.474
>
> *For latent heat, see 541.362*
>
> *See also 541.042 for chemistry of specific states of matter*

| | | |
|---|---|---|
| .364 | | Thermal dissociation |
| .368 | | Reactions under temperature extremes |
| .368 6 | | Low temperatures |

> Reactions below -100°C

| | | |
|---|---|---|
| .368 7 | | High temperatures |
| .369 | | Thermodynamics |
| .37 | | Electrochemistry and magnetochemistry |

> Standard subdivisions are added for electrochemistry and magnetochemistry together, for electrochemistry alone

---

>     541.372–541.377   Electrochemistry
>
> Class comprehensive works in 541.37

| | | |
|---|---|---|
| .372 | | Electrolytic solutions |

> Including electrodialysis, electrolyte conductivity, electrophoresis
>
> Class here ions
>
> *For nonelectrical properties, see 541.374*

| | | |
|---|---|---|
| .372 2 | | Ionization (Electrolytic dissociation) |
| .372 3 | | Ion exchange and ionic equilibriums |

> Standard subdivisions are added for either or both topics in heading

| | | |
|---|---|---|
| .372 4 | | Electrodes and electrode phenomena |

> Standard subdivisions are added for either or both topics in heading

| | | |
|---|---|---|
| .372 8 | | Hydrogen-ion concentration |

> Class here pH

| | | |
|---|---|---|
| .374 | | Nonelectrical properties of electrolytic solutions |

> Add to base number 541.374 the numbers following 541.341 in 541.3413–541.3416, e.g., optical properties 541.3744

| | | |
|---|---|---|
| .377 | | Semiconductors |

| .378 | Magnetochemistry |
| .38 | Radiochemistry |

Class here nuclear chemistry

Class quantum chemistry in 541.28

| .382 | Radiation chemistry |

Class here radiolysis

| .388 | Isotopes |
| .388 4 | Radioisotopes |
| .39 | Chemical reactions |

Including addition, condensation, hydrolysis, polymerization, substitution

Class here synthesis

Class thermochemistry of reactions in 541.36; class comprehensive works on polymerization in 547.28

| .392 | Chemical equilibrium |
| .393 | Oxidation-reduction reaction (Redox reaction) |

Class here oxidation, reduction

| .394 | Reaction kinetics |

Class kinetics of oxidation-reduction reaction in 541.393

*For catalysis, see 541.395*

| .395 | Catalysis |

**.7** **Optical activity**

Including optical rotation

# 542 Techniques, procedures, apparatus, equipment, materials

Of inorganic and combined inorganic-organic chemistry

Standard subdivisions are added for any or all topics in heading

Class techniques, procedures, apparatus, equipment, materials used in a specific application with the application, e.g., techniques and equipment for chemical analysis 543

**.1** **Laboratories**

Class containers and accessory equipment in 542.2; class specific techniques and procedures of laboratories in 542.3–542.8

## .2 Containers and accessory equipment

Standard subdivisions are added for containers and accessory equipment together, for containers alone

Including crucibles, test tubes

Class containers and accessory equipment for specific techniques and procedures in 542.3–542.8

---

> ## 542.3–542.8 Specific techniques and procedures

Class here apparatus, equipment, materials used in specific techniques and procedures

Class comprehensive works in 542

## .3 Testing and measuring

Standard subdivisions are added for either or both topics in heading

*For gas measuring, see 542.7; for analytical chemistry, see 543*

## .4 Heating and distilling

Standard subdivisions are added for heating and distilling together, for heating alone

Including blowpipes

## .6 Filtering and dialysis

Standard subdivisions are added for either or both topics in heading

Class dialysis in chemical analysis in 543.2

## .7 Gas production, processing, measuring

## .8 Auxiliary techniques and procedures, electrical and electronic equipment

Add to base number 542.8 the numbers following —028 in notation 0284–0289 from Table 1, e.g., electrical and electronic equipment 542.84; however, for comprehensive works on apparatus, equipment, materials, see 542; for testing and measurement, see 542.3

# 543 Analytical chemistry

Of inorganic or organic chemicals in general

Class here analytical chemistry of metals in general

Unless other instructions are given, class a subject with aspects in two or more subdivisions of 543 in the number coming last, e.g., chromatography in organic chemical analysis 543.8 (*not* 543.17)

*For analytical chemistry of specific elements, compounds, mixtures, groupings (other than metals and metallic compounds in general), see 546; for analytical chemistry of specific organic compounds, see 547*

| | | |
|---|---|---|
| .028 4 | | Materials |
| | | Including reagents |
| | | Do not use for apparatus and equipment; class in 543.19 |
| **.1** | | **General topics in analytical chemistry** |
| | | Including qualitative analysis, quantitative analysis |
| .17 | | Analytical organic chemistry |
| .19 | | Techniques of general application |
| | | Including sample preparation |
| | | Class here instrumentation |

---

> **543.2–543.8 Specific methods**

Class comprehensive works in 543

| | | |
|---|---|---|
| **.2** | | **Classical methods** |
| | | Not provided for elsewhere |
| | | Including diffusion methods, gravimetric analysis |
| .22 | | Microchemistry (Microanalysis) |
| | | Including microscopic analysis, spot tests |
| .24 | | Volumetric analysis |
| | | Class here titration |
| .26 | | Thermal analysis |
| | | Including thermogravimetry |
| **.4** | | **Electrochemical analysis** |
| | | Including coulometry, electrophoresis, polarography |
| **.5** | | **Optical spectroscopy (Spectrum analysis)** |
| | | Class here atomic and ultraviolet spectroscopy, interdisciplinary works on spectroscopy |

*For spectroscopy in physics, see 535.84; for spectroscopic interpretation of chemical structure, see 541.2; for nonoptical spectroscopy, see 543.6*

| | | |
|---|---|---|
| .52 | | Atomic emission spectroscopy |
| | | Including flame emission spectroscopy |
| .54 | | Molecular spectroscopy |
| .55 | | Spectrophotometry |
| | | Class here colorimetry |

.56         Luminescence spectroscopy

Class here fluorescence spectroscopy

.57         Infrared and Raman spectroscopy

Standard subdivisions are added for infrared and Raman spectroscopy together, for infrared spectroscopy alone

.59         Methods based on refraction, interference, scattering

Including interferometry, polariscopic analysis, refractometry

*For Raman spectroscopy, see 543.57*

**.6         Nonoptical spectroscopy**

Including gamma-ray, microwave spectroscopy

Class here nuclear spectroscopy

.62         X-ray and electron spectroscopy

Standard subdivisions are added for X-ray and electron spectroscopy together, for X-ray spectroscopy alone

.63         Radiochemical analysis

Including nuclear activation analysis

.65         Mass spectrometry (Mass spectroscopy)

.66         Nuclear magnetic resonance spectroscopy

.67         Electron paramagnetic resonance spectroscopy

Variant name: electron spin resonance spectroscopy

**.8         Chromatography**

.82         Ion-exchange chromatography

.84         Liquid chromatography

Including paper and thin-layer chromatography

.85         Gas chromatography

.86         Supercritical fluid chromatography

Variant name: supercritical gas chromatography

# [544]       [Unassigned]

Most recently used in Edition 21

# [545]       [Unassigned]

Most recently used in Edition 21

# 546    Inorganic chemistry

Class here general topics of chemistry applied to specific elements, compounds, mixtures, groupings; comprehensive works on inorganic and organic chemistry of specific elements, compounds, mixtures, groupings

Specific compounds are classed with the first element named, except that hydrogen is disregarded for acids

Add to each subdivision identified by * as follows:
>1–3    The element, compounds, mixtures
       Class theoretical, physical, analytical chemistry of the element, compounds, mixtures in 4–6; class comprehensive works in base number for the element in 546.3–546.7
  · 1    The element
    2    Compounds
       Names of compounds usually end in -ide or one of the suffixes listed in 22 and 24 below
         *For organo compounds, see 547.01–547.08*
    22    Acids and bases
       Names of acids usually end in -ic or -ous
    24    Salts
       Names of salts frequently end in -ate or -ite
    25    Complex compounds
    3    Molecular and colloidal mixtures
       Class here alloys
    4    Theoretical chemistry
       Add to 4 the numbers following 541.2 in 541.22–541.28, e.g., molecular structure 42
       Class comprehensive works on physical chemistry in 5
    5    Physical chemistry
       Add to 5 the numbers following 541.3 in 541.33–541.39, e.g., radiochemistry 58
         *For theoretical chemistry, see 4*
    6    Analytical chemistry
Class physical chemistry applied to inorganic chemistry as a whole in 541

*For organic chemistry of specific elements, compounds, mixtures, groupings, see 547*

*See Manual at 541 vs. 546; also at 549 vs. 546*

## SUMMARY

| | |
|---|---|
| 546.2 | **Hydrogen and its compounds** |
| .3 | **Metals, metallic compounds, alloys** |
| .4 | **Group 3** |
| .5 | **Groups 4, 5, 6, 7** |
| .6 | **Groups 8, 9, 10, 11, 12, 13, 14** |
| .7 | **Groups 15, 16, 17, 18** |
| .8 | **Periodic law and periodic table** |

## .2    Hydrogen and its compounds

Standard subdivisions are added for hydrogen and its compounds together, for hydrogen compounds alone

Class here hydrogen chemistry

Class the element hydrogen studied by itself in 546.21

| .21 | The element |
|---|---|
| .212 | Deuterium |
| .213 | Tritium |

---

>      **546.22–546.24 Hydrogen compounds**

Class comprehensive works in 546.2

*For bases, see 546.32*

| .22 | Water |
|---|---|

Including deuterium oxide (heavy water)

| .224 | Theoretical chemistry |
|---|---|

Class comprehensive works on physical chemistry in 546.225

| .225 | Physical chemistry |
|---|---|

*For theoretical chemistry, see 546.224*

| .226 | Analytical chemistry |
|---|---|

| .24 | Acids |
|---|---|

*For a specific acid, see the distinguishing element, plus notation 22 from table under 546, e.g., hydrochloric acid 546.73222*

| .25 | Theoretical chemistry of hydrogen |
|---|---|

Class comprehensive works on physical chemistry of hydrogen in 546.26

| .26 | Physical chemistry of hydrogen |
|---|---|

*For theoretical chemistry of hydrogen, see 546.25*

| **.3** | **Metals, metallic compounds, alloys** |
|---|---|

Standard subdivisions are added for any or all topics in heading

Class analytical chemistry of metals in general in 543; class metallic elements studied collectively in 546.31; class physical and chemical metallurgy in 669.9; class interdisciplinary works on metals in 669

*For metals of groups other than 1 and 2, see 546.4–546.7; for organometallic compounds, see 547.05*

| .31 | Metallic elements |
|---|---|

*For a specific metal treated as an element, see the metal in 546.38–546.7, plus notation 1 from table under 546, e.g., the element iron 546.6211*

| .32 | Bases |
|---|---|

*For bases of a specific metal, see the metal in 546.38–546.7, plus notation 22 from table under 546, e.g., bases of iron 546.62122*

.34       Salts

> *For salts of a specific metal, see the metal in 546.38–546.7, plus notation 24 from table under 546, e.g., salts of iron 546.62124*
>
> *See also 546.38224 for table salt*

---

>    546.38–546.39   Alkali and alkaline-earth metals
>
> Class comprehensive works in 546.38

.38       Alkali metals (Group 1)

> Class here comprehensive works on alkali and alkaline-earth metals
>
> *For alkaline-earth metals, see 546.39*

.381       *Lithium

.382       *Sodium

.383       *Potassium

.384       *Rubidium

.385       *Cesium

.386       *Francium

.39       Alkaline-earth metals (Group 2)

.391       *Beryllium

.392       *Magnesium

.393       *Calcium

.394       *Strontium

.395       *Barium

.396       *Radium

**.4**       **Group 3**

.400 1–.400 9       Standard subdivisions

.401       *Scandium

.403       *Yttrium

.41       Rare earth elements (Lanthanide series)

.411       *Lanthanum

.412       *Cerium

.413       Praseodymium and neodymium

.414       *Promethium

.415       Samarium and europium

*Add as instructed under 546

| | |
|---|---|
| .416 | Gadolinium and terbium |
| .417 | Dysprosium and holmium |
| .418 | Erbium and thulium |
| .419 | Ytterbium and lutetium |
| .42 | Actinide series |

> *For uranium, see 546.431; for transuranium elements, see 546.44*

| | |
|---|---|
| .421 | *Actinium |
| .422 | *Thorium |
| .424 | *Protactinium |
| .43 | Uranium, neptunium, plutonium |
| .431 | *Uranium |
| .432 | *Neptunium |
| .434 | *Plutonium |
| .44 | Transuranium elements |

> *For neptunium, see 546.432; for plutonium, see 546.434; for rutherfordium, see 546.51; for dubnium, see 546.52; for seaborgium, see 546.53; for bohrium, see 546.54; for darmstadtium, hassium, meitnerium, see 546.62; for roentgenium, see 546.65*

| | |
|---|---|
| .441 | Americium |
| .442 | Curium |
| .444 | Berkelium |
| .448 | Californium |
| .449 | Other transuranium elements |

> Including einsteinium, fermium, lawrencium, mendelevium, nobelium

| | |
|---|---|
| **.5** | **Groups 4, 5, 6, 7** |
| .51 | Titanium group (Group 4) |

> Including rutherfordium

| | |
|---|---|
| .512 | *Titanium |
| .513 | *Zirconium |
| .514 | *Hafnium |
| .52 | Vanadium group (Group 5) |

> Including dubnium

| | |
|---|---|
| .522 | *Vanadium |

*Add as instructed under 546

| .524 | *Niobium (Columbium) |
|------|----------------------|
| .526 | *Tantalum |
| .53 | Chromium group (Group 6) |

Including seaborgium

| .532 | *Chromium |
|------|-----------|
| .534 | *Molybdenum |
| .536 | *Tungsten |
| .54 | Manganese group (Group 7) |

Including bohrium

| .541 | *Manganese |
|------|------------|
| .543 | *Technetium |
| .545 | *Rhenium |

**.6**     **Groups 8, 9, 10, 11, 12, 13, 14**

Class here comprehensive works on transition metals

*For group 3, see 546.4; for groups 4, 5, 6, 7, see 546.5*

**.62**     Groups 8, 9, 10

Former heading: Iron, cobalt, nickel

Standard subdivisions are added for any or all topics in heading

Including darmstadtium, hassium, meitnerium

*For platinum metals, see 546.63*

| .621 | *Iron |
|------|-------|
| .623 | *Cobalt |
| .625 | *Nickel |
| .63 | Platinum metals |

*For osmium, iridium, platinum, see 546.64*

| .632 | *Ruthenium |
|------|------------|
| .634 | *Rhodium |
| .636 | *Palladium |
| .64 | Osmium, iridium, platinum |
| .641 | *Osmium |
| .643 | *Iridium |

*Add as instructed under 546

| .645 | *Platinum |
|---|---|

Class comprehensive works on platinum metals in 546.63

| .65 | Group 11 |
|---|---|

Including roentgenium

| .652 | *Copper |
|---|---|
| .654 | *Silver |
| .656 | *Gold |
| .66 | Group 12 |
| .661 | *Zinc |
| .662 | *Cadmium |
| .663 | *Mercury |
| .67 | Group 13 |
| .671 | *Boron |
| .673 | *Aluminum |
| .675 | *Gallium |
| .677 | *Indium |
| .678 | *Thallium |
| .68 | Group 14 |
| .681 | *Carbon |
| .681 2 | Carbon compounds |

Number built according to instructions under 546

Use this number for carbon oxides, carbonates, metal carbonyls, carbon halides when treated as inorganic compounds. Class other carbon compounds, comprehensive works on carbon compounds, in 547

| .683 | *Silicon |
|---|---|
| .684 | *Germanium |
| .686 | *Tin |
| .688 | *Lead |
| **.7** | **Groups 15, 16, 17, 18** |

Class here nonmetals

*For a specific nonmetallic element not provided for here, see the element, e.g., silicon 546.683*

| .71 | Group 15 |
|---|---|

*Add as instructed under 546

| | |
|---|---|
| .711 | *Nitrogen |
| .712 | *Phosphorus |
| .715 | *Arsenic |
| .716 | *Antimony |
| .718 | *Bismuth |
| .72 | Chalcogens (Group 16) |
| .721 | *Oxygen |
| .723 | *Sulfur |
| .724 | *Selenium |
| .726 | *Tellurium |
| .728 | *Polonium |
| .73 | Halogens (Group 17) |
| .731 | *Fluorine |
| .732 | *Chlorine |
| .733 | *Bromine |
| .734 | *Iodine |
| .735 | *Astatine |
| .75 | Noble gases (Group 18) |

Variant names: inert, rare gases

| | |
|---|---|
| .751 | *Helium |
| .752 | *Neon |
| .753 | *Argon |
| .754 | *Krypton |
| .755 | *Xenon |
| .756 | *Radon |

**.8** **Periodic law and periodic table**

Class here periodicity

Class comprehensive works on atomic structure in 541.24

*Add as instructed under 546

# 547    Organic chemistry

Class here biochemicals when not considered in their biological context

Add to each subdivision identified by * as follows:
| | | |
|---|---|---|
| 04 | Special topics | |
| 044 | | Theoretical chemistry |
| | | Add to 044 the numbers following 541.2 in 541.22–541.28, e.g., molecular structure 0442 |
| | | Class comprehensive works on physical chemistry in 045 |
| 045 | | Physical chemistry |
| 0453–0458 | | Specific topics of physical chemistry |
| | | Add to 045 the numbers following 541.3 in 541.33–541.38, e.g., solution chemistry 0454 |
| | | *For theoretical chemistry, see 044* |
| 046 | | Analytical chemistry |

Class interdisciplinary works on biochemicals in 572

*For biochemistry, see 572*

## SUMMARY

| | |
|---|---|
| 547.001–.009 | **Standard subdivisions** |
| .01–.08 | **Kinds of compounds identified by component elements** |
| .1 | **Physical and theoretical chemistry** |
| .2 | **Organic chemical reactions** |
| .4 | **Aliphatic compounds** |
| .5 | **Cyclic compounds** |
| .6 | **Aromatic compounds** |
| .7 | **Macromolecules and related compounds** |
| .8 | **Other organic substances** |

.001        Philosophy and theory

> Do not use for theoretical organic chemistry; class in 547.12

.002–.009        Standard subdivisions

---

>        547.01–547.08   Kinds of compounds identified by component elements

Unless other instructions are given, class a subject with aspects in two or more subdivisions of 547.01–547.08 in the number coming last, e.g., sulfonamides 547.067 (*not* 547.042)

Class chemical reactions of compounds identified by component elements in 547.2; class kinds of compounds identified by structure and function in 547.4–547.8; class comprehensive works in 547

.01        *Hydrocarbons

.02        *Halocarbons

.03        *Oxy and hydroxy compounds

.031        *Alcohols

.035        *Ethers

*Add as instructed under 547

.036          *Aldehydes and ketones

> Subdivisions are added for either or both topics in heading

.037          *Acids

.038          *Esters

.04          *Organonitrogen compounds

.041          *Nitro and nitroso compounds

.042          *Amines and amides

> Subdivisions are added for either or both topics in heading

.043          *Azo compounds

.044          *Nitriles and isonitriles

> Subdivisions are added for either or both topics in heading

.05          *Organometallic compounds

.053–.057     Specific organometallic compounds

> Add to base number 547.05 the numbers following 546 in 546.3–546.7 for the element only, e.g., organozinc compounds 547.05661; then add further as instructed under 547, e.g., analytic chemistry of organozinc compounds 547.05661046; however, for organophosphorus compounds, see 547.07; for organosilicon compounds, see 547.08

.06          *Organosulfur compounds

.061          *Sulfides

.063          *Hydrosulfides

.064          *Thio acids

.065          Oxy derivatives of sulfides

> Including sulfones, sulfoxides, thioaldehydes, thioketones

.066          *Sulfinic acids

.067          *Sulfonic acids

.07          *Organophosphorus compounds

.08          *Organosilicon compounds

**.1          Physical and theoretical chemistry**

> Add to base number 547.1 the numbers following 541 in 541.2–541.3, e.g., stereochemistry 547.1223; however, for organic chemical reactions, see 547.2

> Class physical and theoretical chemistry of specific kinds of compounds identified by component elements in 547.01–547.08; class physical and theoretical chemistry of kinds of compounds identified by structure and function in 547.4–547.8

*Add as instructed under 547

**.2** **Organic chemical reactions**

Class here chemical reactions of compounds identified by component elements, chemical reactions of compounds identified by structure and function; addition, synthesis

.21 General topics in chemical reactions

.212 Chemical equilibrium

.214 Reaction kinetics

*For catalysis, see 547.215*

.215 Catalysis

.23 Oxidation-reduction reaction (Redox reaction)

Including hydrogenation

Class here oxidation, reduction

.27 Reactions producing specific kinds of organic compounds

Including amination, aromatization, diazotization, esterification, halogenation, nitration, nitrosation, saponification, sulfonation

Class comprehensive works on a specific kind of organic compound identified by its component element and the reaction producing it with the kind in 547.01–547.08, e.g., halocarbons and halogenation 547.02; class comprehensive works on a specific kind of organic compound and the reactions producing it with the kind in 547.4–547.8, e.g., aromatic compounds and aromatization 547.6

*For polymerization, see 547.28*

.28 Polymerization

Class comprehensive works on polymers and polymerization in 547.7

.29 Fermentation

---

> **547.4–547.8 Kinds of compounds identified by structure and function**

Class comprehensive works in 547; class chemical reactions of compounds identified by structure and function in 547.2

**.4** ***Aliphatic compounds**

Unless other instructions are given, class a subject with aspects in two or more subdivisions of 547.4 in the number coming last, e.g., aliphatic sulfonamides 547.467 (*not* 547.442)

Class aliphatic macromolecular compounds in 547.7

.41 *Hydrocarbons

.411 *Paraffins (Alkanes)

*See also 547.77 for paraffin wax*

*Add as instructed under 547

.412          *Olefins (Alkenes)

.413          *Acetylenes (Alkynes)

.42–.48    Other compounds

> Add to base number 547.4 the numbers following 547.0 in 547.02–547.08, e.g., carboxylic acids 547.437

> *For proteins, see 547.7*

.5      **\*Cyclic compounds**

> Class here alicyclic compounds

> *For aromatic compounds, see 547.6*

> ─────────────

> 547.51–547.58  Alicyclic compounds

> Unless other instructions are given, class a subject with aspects in two or more subdivisions of 547.51–547.58 in the number coming last, e.g., alicyclic sulfonamides 547.567 (*not* 547.542)

> Class comprehensive works in 547.5

.51          *Alicyclic hydrocarbons

.511           *Cycloparaffins

.512           *Cycloolefins

.513           *Cycloacetylenes

.52–.58    Other alicyclic compounds

> Add to base number 547.5 the numbers following 547.0 in 547.02–547.08, e.g., alicyclic halocarbons 547.52

.59          *Heterocyclic compounds

.592           *Hetero oxygen compounds

> Including furans, oxazoles, pyrans

.593           *Hetero nitrogen compounds

> Including chlorophylls, diazines, imidazoles, porphyrins, pyrazoles, pyridines, pyrroles

.594           *Hetero sulfur compounds

> Including thiazoles, thiophenes

.595           Compounds with two or more different hetero atoms

> Including oxazines, oxdiazines, oxdiazoles

.596           *Fused heterocyclic compounds

> Including purines, quinolines

*Add as instructed under 547

| .6 | **\*Aromatic compounds** |
| | Unless other instructions are given, class a subject with aspects in two or more subdivisions of 547.6 in the number coming last, e.g., aromatic sulfonamides 547.667 (*not* 547.642) |
| .61 | \*Hydrocarbons |
| .611 | \*Benzenes |
| .613 | \*Polyphenyl hydrocarbons |
| | Including diphenyl hydrocarbons |
| .615 | \*Fused hydrocarbons |
| | Including naphthalenes |
| | *For anthracenes, see 547.616* |
| .616 | \*Anthracenes |
| .62 | \*Halogenated compounds |
| .63 | \*Oxy and hydroxy compounds |
| | Subdivisions are added for either or both topics in heading |
| .631 | \*Alcohols |
| | Class phenols in 547.632 |
| .632 | \*Phenols |
| | Including monohydric hydroxy aromatics |
| .633 | \*Polyhydroxy aromatics |
| | Including dihydroxy and trihydroxy aromatics, catechols, hydroquinones, resorcinols |
| .635 | \*Ethers |
| .636 | \*Aldehydes and ketones |
| | Subdivisions are added for either or both topics in heading |
| .637 | \*Acids |
| .638 | \*Esters |
| .64–.68 | Other aromatic compounds |
| | Add to base number 547.6 the numbers following 547.0 in 547 04  547.08, e.g., aromatic amines 547.642 |

\*Add as instructed under 547

.7 **\*Macromolecules and related compounds**

> Including alkaloids, antibiotics, hormones, nucleic acids, proteins, steroids, vitamins

> Class here macromolecules when not considered in their biological context; comprehensive works on polymers

> Subdivisions are added for macromolecules and related compounds, for macromolecules alone

> Class interdisciplinary works on macromolecules in 572

>> *For inorganic polymers, see 541.2254; for fossil substances, see 547.82; for comprehensive works on high polymers, see 547.84; for dyes and pigments, see 547.86*

>> *See also 668.9 for synthetic polymers*

.71 Terpenes and essential oils

> Including camphors

.77 **\*Lipids**

> Including waxes

> Class here fats

> Class steroids in 547.7

>> *For essential oils, see 547.71*

>> *See also 547.411 for paraffin hydrocarbons*

.78 **\*Carbohydrates**

> Including sugars, starches, gums

**.8 Other organic substances**

.82 **\*Fossil substances**

> Including coal tar

> Class a specific compound derived from a fossil substance with the compound, e.g., synthetic rubber 678.72

>> *For petroleum, see 547.83*

.83 **\*Petroleum**

.84 **\*High polymers**

> Class high polymers of a specific chemical group with the group, e.g., starches 547.78

.842 **\*Elastomers**

.842 5 **\*Latexes**

.842 6 **\*Rubber**

---

\*Add as instructed under 547

| .843 | *Flexible polymers |
| .843 4 | *Resins |
| .86 | *Dyes and pigments |

Standard subdivisions are added for dyes and pigments together, for dyes alone

| .869 | *Pigments |

# 548 Crystallography

Class crystallographic mineralogy in 549.18; class comprehensive works on solid-state physics in 530.41

*See Manual at 548 vs. 530.41; also at 549 vs. 548*

| .015 1 | Mathematical principles |

Do not use for mathematical crystallography; class in 548.7

## .3 Chemical crystallography

Relationship between structure and bonding

Including isomorphism, polymorphism, pseudomorphism

## .5 Crystallization

Class here crystal growth

## .7 Mathematical crystallography

Measurement and calculation of angles

Class geometric crystallography in 548.81

## .8 Physical and structural crystallography

Standard subdivisions are added for physical and structural crystallography together, for physical crystallography alone

| .81 | Structural crystallography |

Class here crystal lattices, geometrical crystallography

Class structural crystallography of a specific substance with the substance, e.g., structural chemistry of silicates 549.6

*For diffraction methods, see 548.83*

| .810 151 | Mathematical principles |

Do not use for mathematical crystallography; class in 548.7

| .83 | Diffraction crystallography |

Including crystallograms

Class optical methods of crystal study in 548.9

---

*Add as instructed under 547

> 548.84–548.86  Physical properties of crystals

Class comprehensive works in 548.8

*For optical properties, see 548.9*

.84 Mechanical properties

.842 Stresses, deformation, strength properties

Including elasticity, plasticity; dislocation, fracture, hardness

.85 Electrical, electronic, magnetic properties

Including conductivity, dielectricity

.86 Thermal properties

Including fusibility

## .9 Optical crystallography

Optical properties of crystals and optical methods of crystal study

# 549 Mineralogy

Occurrence, description, classification, identification of naturally occurring minerals

Class crystallography in 548; class economic geology in 553

*See Manual at 549 vs. 546; also at 549 vs. 548*

### SUMMARY

| | |
|---|---|
| 549.09 | **History, geographic treatment, biography** |
| .1 | **Determinative mineralogy** |
| .2 | **Native elements** |
| .3 | **Sulfides, antimonides, arsenides, selenides, tellurides; sulfosalts** |
| .4 | **Halides** |
| .5 | **Oxides** |
| .6 | **Silicates** |
| .7 | **Other minerals** |
| .9 | **Geographic treatment of minerals** |

.09 History, geographic treatment, biography

Do not use for geographic treatment of minerals; class in 549.9

## .1 Determinative mineralogy

Class determinative mineralogy of specific minerals in 549.2–549.7

.11 Minerals in specific kinds of formations

.112 Meteorite minerals

Class here petrology of meteorites

Class comprehensive works on meteorites in 523.51

| | |
|---|---|
| .114 | Minerals in rocks |

> Add to base number 549.114 the numbers following 552 in 552.1–552.5, e.g., determinative mineralogy in sedimentary rocks 549.1145
>
> Class comprehensive works on rocks in 552

| | |
|---|---|
| .116 | Minerals in pegmatite dikes |

> Class comprehensive works on dikes in 551.88

| | |
|---|---|
| .12 | Physical mineralogy |
| .121 | Mechanical properties |

> Including cleavage, fracture, hardness

| | |
|---|---|
| .125 | Optical properties |

> Including color, fluorescence, luminescence

| | |
|---|---|
| .127 | Electrical, electronic, magnetic properties |
| .13 | Chemical mineralogy |
| .131 | Composition, properties, reactivity |
| .133 | Analysis |
| .18 | Crystallographic mineralogy |

> Study of crystalline structure and properties of minerals

---

> **549.2–549.7  Specific minerals**
>
> Class comprehensive works in 549

| | |
|---|---|
| .2 | **Native elements** |

> Use 549.7 for mineral compounds of specific elements not provided for elsewhere in 549.3–549.6

| | |
|---|---|
| .23 | Metals |

> Native metals only
>
> Class interdisciplinary works on physico-chemical characteristics of metals in 669.9

| | |
|---|---|
| .25 | Semimetals |

> Including antimony, arsenic, bismuth, boron, selenium, tellurium

| | |
|---|---|
| .27 | Nonmetals |

> Including graphite (carbon)

| | |
|---|---|
| .3 | **Sulfides, antimonides, arsenides, selenides, tellurides; sulfosalts** |

> Class sulfates in 549.75

| | |
|---|---|
| .32 | Sulfides, antimonides, arsenides, selenides, tellurides |

> Including chalcocite, cinnabar, galena, molybdenite, pyrite, sphalerite

| | |
|---|---|
| .35 | Sulfosalts (Double sulfides) |
| | Including tetrahedrite |
| **.4** | **Halides** |
| | Including carnallite, cryolite, fluorite (fluorspar), halite, rock salt |
| **.5** | **Oxides** |
| .52 | Simple and multiple oxides |
| | Standard subdivisions are added for either or both topics in heading |
| .522 | Cuprite, ice, zincite |
| .523 | Hematite group |
| | Including corundum, ilmenite |
| .524 | Rutile group |
| | Including cassiterite |
| .525 | Goethite group |
| | Including diaspore |
| .526 | Spinel group |
| | Including chromite, magnetite |
| .528 | Other groups of oxides |
| | Including uraninite |
| .53 | Hydroxides |
| | Including bauxite, limonite |
| **.6** | **Silicates** |
| | Class here clay |
| .62 | Nesosilicates |
| | Including andalusite, cyanite, garnet, kyanite, sillimanite, staurolite, topaz, zircon |
| .63 | Sorosilicates |
| | Including epidote |
| .64 | Cyclosilicates |
| | Including beryl, chrysocolla, cordierite, tourmaline |
| .66 | Inosilicates |
| | Including amphiboles, pyroxenes, spodumene, wollastonite |
| .67 | Phyllosilicates |
| | Including chlorite, glauconite, kaolinite, mica, pyrophyllite, serpentine, talc |

.68        Tectosilicates

          Including feldspar, leucite, opal, quartz, scapolite, zeolite

**.7        Other minerals**

[.701–.709]        Standard subdivisions

          Do not use; class in 549.01–549.09

.72        Phosphates, arsenates, vanadates

          Including apatite, monazite, turquoise

.73        Nitrates and borates

.732        Nitrates

          Including saltpeter (niter), Chile saltpeter (soda niter)

.735        Borates

          Including borax, colemanite

.74        Molybdates and tungstates

          Including scheelite, wolframite

.75        Sulfates and chromates

          Standard subdivisions are added for sulfates and chromates together, for sulfates alone

.752        Chromates and anhydrous sulfates

          Including anhydrite, barite, celestite

.755        Hydrous and basic sulfates

          Including alunite, gypsum

.78        Carbonates

.782        Calcite group

          Including dolomite, magnesite, siderite

.785        Aragonite group

          Including malachite

**.9        Geographic treatment of minerals**

          Add to base number 549.9 notation 1–9 from Table 2, e.g., minerals of Greenland 549.9982

# 550    Earth sciences

Class here geophysics; phenomena of celestial bodies directly comparable to terrestrial phenomena, e.g., volcanic activity on Mars 551.21099923

Use 550 and its standard subdivisions for works that deal comprehensively with geology, hydrology, and meteorology; for works on geology in the sense of all earth sciences. Use 551 and its standard subdivisions for works on geology in the sense limited to properties and phenomena of the solid earth

> *See Manual at 523 vs. 550; also at 550 vs. 910*

### SUMMARY

| | |
|---|---|
| 551 | Geology, hydrology, meteorology |
| 552 | Petrology |
| 553 | Economic geology |
| 554–559 | Earth sciences by specific continents, countries, localities in modern world; extraterrestrial worlds |

[.154]      Chemical principles

Do not use; class in 551.9

[.94–.99]      Specific continents, countries, localities in modern world; extraterrestrial worlds

Do not use; class in 554–559

# 551    Geology, hydrology, meteorology

Geology: science that deals with properties and phenomena of the solid earth (lithosphere)

Use 550 and its standard subdivisions for works that deal comprehensively with geology, hydrology, and meteorology; for works on geology in the sense of all earth sciences. Use 551 and its standard subdivisions for works on geology in the sense limited to properties and phenomena of the solid earth

> *For astronomical geography, see 525; for geodesy, see 526.1; for petrology, see 552; for economic geology, see 553; for physical geography, see 910.02*

> *See also 363.34 for disasters; also 904.5 for history of events of natural origin*

### SUMMARY

| | |
|---|---|
| 551.01–.09 | Standard subdivisions of geology |
| .1 | Gross structure and properties of the earth |
| .2 | Volcanoes, earthquakes, thermal waters and gases |
| .3 | Surface and exogenous processes and their agents |
| .4 | Geomorphology and hydrosphere |
| .5 | Meteorology |
| .6 | Climatology and weather |
| .7 | Historical geology |
| .8 | Structural geology |
| .9 | Geochemistry |

.01      Philosophy and theory of geology

[.015 4]      Chemical principles

Do not use; class in 551.9

| | |
|---|---|
| .02–.08 | Standard subdivisions of geology |
| .09 | History, geographic treatment, biography of geology |

[.091 62–.091 68]     Treatment in oceans and seas

Do not use; class in 551.4608

[.094–.099]     Geology by specific continents, countries, localities in modern world; extraterrestrial worlds

Do not use; class in 554–559

**.1       Gross structure and properties of the earth**

*For geomagnetism, see 538.7*

.11       Interior of the earth

*For properties, see 551.12*

.112       Core

.116       Mantle

.12       Properties of interior

Including heat, temperature ranges

.13       Crust

Including magma

*For properties, see 551.14; for structural geology, see 551.8*

.136       Plate tectonics (Continental drift)

Including sea-floor spreading

Class comprehensive works on tectonics in 551.8

.14       Properties of crust

Including elasticity, heat, temperature ranges

**.2       Volcanoes, earthquakes, thermal waters and gases**

.21       Volcanoes

Class here comprehensive works on craters

Class volcanic thermal waters and gases in 551.23; class petrology of volcanic rocks in 552.2

*For meteorite craters, see 551.397*

.22       Earthquakes

Class here seismology

Class seismic sea waves in 551.463

.220 287       Testing and measurement

Class here seismography

.23       Thermal waters and gases

> Standard subdivisions are added for thermal waters and gases together, for thermal waters alone
>
> Including volcanic volatiles
>
> Class here surface manifestations, e.g., fumaroles, hot springs

**.3**       **Surface and exogenous processes and their agents**

> Standard subdivisions are added for any or all topics in heading
>
> Class here sedimentology as study of surface processes
>
> Class comprehensive works on landforms in 551.41; class comprehensive works on sedimentology in 552.5

.300 1–.300 9       Standard subdivisions

---

>       551.302–551.307 Erosion and weathering, sediments and sedimentation, soil formation, mass movement

> Class comprehensive works in 551.3
>
> *See Manual at 551.302–551.307 vs. 551.35*

.302       Erosion and weathering

> Class here soil erosion, interdisciplinary works on erosion
>
> Class role of weathering in soil formation in 551.305
>
> > *For a specific aspect of erosion, see the aspect, e.g., erosion engineering 627.5, control of agricultural soil erosion 631.45*

.303       Transporting and depositing of materials

> Standard subdivisions are added for either or both topics in heading
>
> Class here sedimentation

.304       Transported materials (Sediments)

.305       Soil formation

> Class here role of water in soil formation

.307       Mass movement (Mass wasting)

> Including avalanches, creep, mud flows, rockfalls; subsidence
>
> Class here landslides, slope failure, work of water in mass movement
>
> > *See also 363.349 for disasters resulting from avalanches and other mass movements*

.31       Glaciology

> Class here geologic work of ice; interdisciplinary works on ice
>
> > *For ice in water and other forms of ice, see 551.34; for geologic work of frost, see 551.38. For a specific aspect of ice, see the aspect, e.g., ice manufacture 621.58*

.312         Glaciers

> *For icebergs, shelf ice, growlers, see 551.342*

.313         Glacial action

> Including work of glaciers in erosion, soil formation, weathering

.314         Material transported by glaciers

> Class here glacial drift and till, moraines regarded as materials

> Class glacial drift and till, moraines regarded as landforms in 551.315

.315         Landforms created by glaciers

> Including cirques, drumlins, kames, kettles, roches moutonnées

> Class here glacial drift and till, moraines regarded as landforms

.34         Ice in water and other forms of ice

> Standard subdivisions are added for ice in water and other forms of ice together, for ice in water alone

> *For snow, see 551.5784; for hail, see 551.5787*

.342         Ice in the sea

> Including icebergs, shelf ice, growlers

> *For sea ice, see 551.343*

.343         Sea ice (Frozen seawater)

.344         Anchor and frazil ice

.345         Lake and river ice

> Class here ice cover

> *For anchor and frazil ice, see 551.344*

.35         Geologic work of water

> Work of precipitation, of surface and subsurface waters

> *For role of water in soil formation, see 551.305; for geologic work of marine waters, see 551.36*

> *See Manual at 551.302–551.307 vs. 551.35*

.352         Erosion and weathering

> Standard subdivisions are added for erosion and weathering together, for erosion alone

.353         Transporting and depositing materials

> Standard subdivisions are added for either or both topics in heading

> Class here sedimentation in water

> *For role of water in mass movement, see 551.307*

.354         Transported materials (Sediments)

.355      Landforms created by water

> *For specific landforms created by water, see 551.42–551.45*

.36      Geologic work of marine waters

Including wave action, beach erosion

> *For specific landforms created by marine waters, see 551.42–551.45*

.37      Geologic work of wind

.372      Erosion

Class here weathering

.373      Transporting and depositing materials

Standard subdivisions are added for either or both topics in heading

.374      Transported materials

.375      Landforms created by wind

Class here dunes

.38      Geologic work of frost

Class here nivation; work of frost in erosion, in soil formation, in weathering; comprehensive works on frost

> *For frost as a cold spell, see 551.5253; for condensation of frost, see 551.5744*

.382      Fragmentation of rocks

.384      Permafrost

.39      Geologic work of other agents

Including temperature changes

.397      Meteorites

Class here meteorite craters

**.4      Geomorphology and hydrosphere**

### SUMMARY

| | |
|---|---|
| **551.41** | **Geomorphology** |
| **.42** | **Islands and reefs** |
| **.43** | **Elevations** |
| **.44** | **Depressions and openings** |
| **.45** | **Plane and coastal regions** |
| **.46** | **Oceanography and submarine geology** |
| **.48** | **Hydrology** |
| **.49** | **Groundwater (Subsurface water)** |

.41        Geomorphology

Creation and modification of topographic landforms by erosional and depositional processes

Class here geomorphology of continents, comprehensive works on landforms

*For landforms created by water, see 551.355; for specific landforms, see 551.42–551.45; for submarine geomorphology, see 551.4683*

*See also 551.136 for continental drift*

[.410 916 2–.410 916 8]        Treatment in oceans and seas

Do not use; class in 551.4683

.415        Arid-land geomorphology

Class here desert geomorphology

.417        Wetland geomorphology

---

&gt;        551.42–551.45   Specific landforms

Class here specific land formations created by water; comprehensive works on specific kinds of topographical features, on present and past examples of specific landforms

Class comprehensive works in 551.41

*For a specific landform created by plutonic action, see the landform in 551.2, e.g., volcanic mountains 551.21; for a specific landform created primarily by exogenous agents other than water or living organisms, see the landform in 551.3, e.g., glacial moraines 551.315; for a specific landform created by tectonic deformations, see the landform in 551.8, e.g., rift valleys 551.872*

.42        Islands and reefs

Standard subdivisions are added for islands and reefs together, for islands alone

.423        Barrier islands

Class barrier reefs in 551.424

.424        Reefs

Including atolls

.43        Elevations

Including slopes

Class slopes of specific kinds of elevations in 551.432–551.436; class orogeny in 551.82

.432        Mountains

.434        Plateaus

.436        Hills

.44          Depressions and openings

    Including sedimentary basins

    *For craters, see 551.21*

.442         Valleys

    Including canyons, gorges, ravines; floodplains; river beds

    *For deltas, see 551.456; for rift valleys, see 551.872*

.447         Caves and related features

    Standard subdivisions are added for caves and related features together, for caves alone

    Including karst formations, sink holes

.45          Plane and coastal regions

.453         Plane regions

    Class here pampas, plains, prairies, steppes, tundras; comprehensive works on grasslands

    *For floodplains, see 551.442; for deltas, see 551.456. For a specific kind of grassland not in a plane region, see the kind, e.g., alpine meadows 551.432*

.456         Deltas

.457         Coastal regions

    Including beaches

    *For deltas, see 551.456; for shorelines, see 551.458*

.458         Shorelines

    Marine and lake

    Class here changes in sea and lake levels

.46          Oceanography and submarine geology

    Standard subdivisions are added for oceanography and submarine geology together, for oceanography alone

    Class here hydrography, hydrosphere; physical oceanography, seawater; interdisciplinary works on marine science, on oceans and seas

    Class ice in 551.31; class geologic work of water in 551.35; class ocean-atmosphere interactions in 551.5246; class interdisciplinary works on water in 553.7

    *For hydrology, see 551.48. For a specific aspect of marine science, of oceans and seas, not provided for here, see the aspect, e.g., international law of ocean and sea waters 341.45, marine biology 578.77*

    *See Manual at 578.76–578.77 vs. 551.46, 551.48*

.460 9       History, geographic treatment, biography

| | |
|---|---|
| [.460 916 3–.460 916 7] | Treatment in specific oceans and seas |
| | Do not use; class in 551.4613–551.4617 |
| [.460 916 8] | Special oceanographic forms and inland seas |
| | Do not use for coastal water saltwater bodies; class in 551.4618. Do not use for inland seas; class in 551.4829 |
| .461 | Specific oceans and seas, coastal saltwater bodies |
| | Class treatment of a specific topic in oceanography in specific oceans and seas in 551.462–551.468 |
| .461 3–.461 7 | Specific oceans and seas |
| | Add to base number 551.461 the numbers following —16 in notation 163–167 from Table 2, e.g., Atlantic Ocean 551.4613 |
| .461 8 | Coastal saltwater bodies |
| | Including fjords, saltwater lagoons |
| | Class here estuaries |
| | *For coastal saltwater bodies in a specific ocean or sea, see the ocean or sea in 551.4613–551.4617, e.g., estuaries in Atlantic Ocean 551.4613* |
| | *See also 551.4829 for salt lakes and inland seas* |

---

>        551.462–551.468 Specific topics in oceanography; submarine geology

Except for modifications shown under specific entries, add to each subdivision identified by * as follows:
- 01–09    Standard subdivisions
  - As modified under 551.46
- 1      Specific oceans and seas, coastal saltwater bodies
- 13–17    Specific oceans and seas
  - Add to 1 the numbers following —16 in notation 163–167 from Table 2, e.g., Atlantic Ocean 13
- 18      Coastal saltwater bodies
  - Including fjords, saltwater lagoons
  - Class here estuaries
    - *For coastal saltwater bodies in a specific ocean or sea, see the ocean or sea in 13–17, e.g., estuaries in Atlantic Ocean 13*

Unless other instructions are given, class a subject with aspects in two or more subdivisions of 551.462–551.468 in the number coming last, e.g., physical properties of sediments 551.4686 (*not* 551.465)

Class comprehensive works in 551.46

| | |
|---|---|
| .462 | *Ocean circulation |
| | Including eddies, mixing, turbulence, upwelling |
| | Class here dynamic oceanography, ocean currents |

*Add as instructed under 551.462–551.468

.463        *Waves

       Including seiches, storm surges

       Class here wind waves

       Class comprehensive works on ocean-atmosphere interactions in 551.5246

       *See also 551.36 for geologic work of waves*

.463 7        *Tsunamis

       Variant names: seismic sea waves, tidal waves

.464        *Tides

       Class here tidal currents

       *See also 551.36 for geologic work of tides*

.465        *Physical properties of seawater

.465 3        *Temperature

.465 4        *Acoustical properties

.465 5        *Optical properties

.466        *Chemical oceanography

.466 4        *Salinity

.466 43        *Temperature-salinity relationships

.468        *Submarine geology

       Class here ocean floor

       *For sea-floor spreading, see 551.136*

.468 3        *Submarine geomorphology

       Class here topography of ocean floor

.468 6        *Sediments

.48        Hydrology

       Class here hydrological cycle, limnology, water balance

       Class comprehensive works on oceanography and hydrology in 551.46; class water resources, interdisciplinary works on water in 553.7

       *For fumaroles, see 551.23; for groundwater, see 551.49; for hydrometeorology, see 551.57*

       *See also 551.417 for wetland geomorphology*

       *See Manual at 578.76–578.77 vs. 551.46, 551.48*

.482        Lakes and inland seas

       Class here freshwater lakes, freshwater ponds, freshwater lagoons

*Add as instructed under 551.462–551.468

| | |
|---|---|
| .482 9 | Salt lakes and inland seas |

> Standard subdivisions are added for either or both topics in heading

> Class interdisciplinary works on a specific inland sea or salt lake in 940–990, e.g., Caspian Sea 947.5

| | |
|---|---|
| .483 | Rivers and streams |

> Standard subdivisions are added for either or both topics in heading

> *For waterfalls, see 551.484; for floods, see 551.489*

| | |
|---|---|
| .484 | Waterfalls |
| .488 | Runoff |
| .489 | Floods |
| .49 | Groundwater (Subsurface water) |

> Class here aquifers

> *For thermal waters, see 551.23*

| | |
|---|---|
| .492 | Water table |
| .498 | Surface manifestations |

> Including springs, wells

> *For hot springs, see 551.23*

| | |
|---|---|
| **.5** | **Meteorology** |

> Class here atmosphere

> Class forecasting and forecasts of specific phenomena in 551.64; class forecasts of specific phenomena in specific areas in 551.65; class micrometeorology in 551.66

> *For climatology and weather, see 551.6*

> *See Manual at 551.5 vs. 551.6*

### SUMMARY

| | |
|---|---|
| **551.51** | **Composition, regions, dynamics of atmosphere** |
| **.52** | **Thermodynamics, atmosphere interactions with earth's surface, temperatures, radiation** |
| **.54** | **Atmospheric pressure** |
| **.55** | **Atmospheric disturbances and formations** |
| **.56** | **Atmospheric electricity and optics** |
| **.57** | **Hydrometeorology** |

| | |
|---|---|
| [.501 12] | Forecasting and forecasts |

> Do not use; class in 551.63

| | |
|---|---|
| .51 | Composition, regions, dynamics of atmosphere |
| .511 | Composition |

> Class here chemistry, photochemistry of atmosphere

| | |
|---|---|
| .511 2 | Gases |
| .511 3 | Aerosols and dust |
| | Class dust storms in 551.559 |

---

>      551.513–551.514   Atmospheric regions

Class comprehensive works in 551.51. Class a specific aspect with the aspect, e.g., upper-atmosphere temperatures 551.5257

| | |
|---|---|
| .513 | Troposphere |
| .514 | Upper atmosphere |

Including magnetosphere, mesosphere

Class magnetic phenomena in magnetosphere, comprehensive works on magnetosphere in 538.766

| | |
|---|---|
| .514 2 | Stratosphere |

Class here ozone layer

| | |
|---|---|
| .514 5 | Ionosphere |
| .515 | Dynamics |

Including gravity waves

Class here mechanics

*For circulation, see 551.517*

| | |
|---|---|
| .515 1 | Kinematics |
| .517 | Circulation |

*For wind, see 551.518; for atmospheric disturbances and formations, see 551.55*

| | |
|---|---|
| .518 | Wind |

Class wind in atmospheric disturbances and formations in 551.55

---

>      551.518 3–551.518 5   Wind systems in troposphere

Class comprehensive works in 551.518

| | |
|---|---|
| .518 3 | Planetary wind systems |

Including jet streams, trade winds, westerlies

| | |
|---|---|
| .518 4 | Monsoons |
| .518 5 | Local wind systems |

Including land and sea breezes; mountain and valley winds, e.g., chinooks, foehns

| | |
|---|---|
| .518 7 | Winds in upper atmosphere |

| | |
|---|---|
| .52 | Thermodynamics, atmosphere interactions with earth's surface, temperatures, radiation |
| .522 | Thermodynamics |

Class thermodynamics in microclimatology in 551.66

| | |
|---|---|
| .523 | Land-atmosphere interactions |

Class here earth temperatures affecting atmosphere

| | |
|---|---|
| .524 | Atmosphere interactions with earth's surface |

Class here water-atmosphere interactions, water temperatures affecting atmosphere

*For land-atmosphere interactions, see 551.523*

| | |
|---|---|
| [.524 091 62–.524 091 68] | Treatment in oceans and seas |

Do not use; class in 551.5246

| | |
|---|---|
| [.524 091 69] | Fresh and brackish waters |

Do not use; class in 551.5248

| | |
|---|---|
| .524 6 | Ocean-atmosphere interactions |
| [.524 609 163–.524 609 167] | Treatment in specific oceans and seas |

Do not use; class in 551.52463–551.52467

| | |
|---|---|
| .524 63–.524 67 | Specific oceans and seas |

Add to base number 551.5246 the numbers following —16 in notation 163–167 from Table 2, e.g., temperatures of Indian Ocean 551.52465

| | |
|---|---|
| .524 8 | Lake and river interactions with atmosphere |
| .525 | Temperatures |

Class here air temperatures, energy budget, energy flow

*For earth temperatures affecting atmosphere, see 551.523; for water temperatures affecting atmosphere, see 551.524; for radiant energy, see 551.527*

*See also 333.79 for economic aspects of energy budgets*

| | |
|---|---|
| .525 091 732 | Urban regions |

Class here urban heat islands

*For specific urban heat islands, see 551.525093–551.525099*

| | |
|---|---|
| .525 3 | Variations over time at earth's surface |

Including maximums, minimums, frosts

Class comprehensive works on frost in 551.38

| | |
|---|---|
| .525 4 | Vertical distribution in troposphere |
| .525 7 | Upper-atmosphere temperatures |

| | |
|---|---|
| .527 | Radiation |

*For optical phenomena, see 551.565*

| | |
|---|---|
| .527 1 | Solar radiation |
| .527 2 | Terrestrial radiation |

*For radiation originating in atmosphere, see 551.5273*

| | |
|---|---|
| .527 3 | Radiation originating in atmosphere |
| .527 6 | Cosmic radiation |

Including cosmic noise

Class here cosmic rays

| | |
|---|---|
| .54 | Atmospheric pressure |
| .543 | Variations over time at earth's surface |
| .543 09 | History and biography |

Do not use for geographic treatment; class in 551.5409

| | |
|---|---|
| .547 | Upper-atmosphere pressures |
| .55 | Atmospheric disturbances and formations |

Standard subdivisions are added for atmospheric disturbances and formations together, for atmospheric disturbances alone

Class here storms

Class precipitation from storms in 551.577

*See also 363.3492 for storms as disasters*

| | |
|---|---|
| .551 | Atmospheric formations |
| .551 2 | Air masses and fronts |
| .551 3 | Cyclones |

*See also 551.552 for hurricanes; also 551.553 for tornadoes*

| | |
|---|---|
| .551 4 | Anticyclones |

---

| | |
|---|---|
| > | 551.552–551.559 Atmospheric disturbances |

Class comprehensive works in 551.55

| | |
|---|---|
| .552 | Hurricanes |

Variant names: typhoons, baguios, tropical cyclones, willy-willies

| | |
|---|---|
| .553 | Tornadoes |

Variant names: cyclones, twisters

Including waterspouts

| .554 | Thermal convective storms |
|---|---|

Including hailstorms

Class here thunderstorms

*For tornadoes, see 551.553*

| .555 | Snowstorms |
|---|---|

Class here blizzards

| .556 | Ice storms |
|---|---|
| .559 | Dust storms |
| .56 | Atmospheric electricity and optics |
| .561 | Electricity in stable atmosphere |

Including conductivity, ionization

| .563 | Atmospheric electricity |
|---|---|

Class magnetic phenomena in 538.7

*For electricity in stable atmosphere, see 551.561*

| .563 2 | Lightning |
|---|---|

*For ball lightning, see 551.5634*

| .563 4 | Ball lightning |
|---|---|
| .565 | Atmospheric optics |

Class here optical phenomena produced by refraction, e.g., mirages, scintillation

Class visibility in 551.568

*For optical phenomena produced by absorption and scattering, see 551.566; for optical phenomena produced by condensation products, see 551.567*

| .566 | Optical phenomena produced by absorption and scattering |
|---|---|

Including sky color, twilight, night skies

| .567 | Optical phenomena produced by condensation products |
|---|---|

Including cloud colors, rainbows

| .568 | Visibility |
|---|---|
| .57 | Hydrometeorology |
| .571 | Humidity |
| .571 3 | Variations of humidity over time |
| .572 | Evapotranspiration |

Class here evaporation

| | |
|---|---|
| .574 | Condensation of moisture |

*For condensation of moisture in a specific form, see the form, e.g., clouds 551.576*

| | |
|---|---|
| .574 1 | Condensation processes |

Class here atmospheric nucleation, formation of particles on which moisture condenses

Class condensation processes on earth's surface in 551.5744; class comprehensive works on atmospheric aerosols and dust in 551.5113

| | |
|---|---|
| .574 4 | Condensations on earth's surface |

Including dew, glaze, hoarfrost

Class comprehensive work on frost in 551.38

| | |
|---|---|
| .575 | Fog and mist |

Standard subdivisions are added for fog and mist together, for fog alone

| | |
|---|---|
| .576 | Clouds |

Class cloud colors in 551.567

| | |
|---|---|
| .577 | Precipitation |

Class here liquid precipitation, rain, rainfall

Class geologic work of precipitation in 551.35

*For frozen precipitation, see 551.578*

| | |
|---|---|
| .577 09 | History and biography |

Do not use for geographic treatment; class in 551.5772

| | |
|---|---|
| .577 1 | Properties |

Including composition, temperature; meteorology of acid rain

Class interdisciplinary works on acid rain in 363.7386

| | |
|---|---|
| .577 2 | Geographic distribution of precipitation |

Add to base number 551.5772 notation 1–9 from Table 2, e.g., rainfall in Nigeria 551.5772669

Class geographic distribution of variations over time in 551.5773

| | |
|---|---|
| .577 3 | Variations over time |

Including droughts, maximums, minimums

*See also 551.489 for floods*

| | |
|---|---|
| .577 5 | Factors affecting precipitation |

Including bodies of water, cities, topography, vegetation

Class comprehensive works on atmosphere interactions with earth's surface in 551.524

| | |
|---|---|
| .578 | Frozen precipitation |

| | |
|---|---|
| .578 4 | Snow |

Class snowstorms in 551.555

| | |
|---|---|
| .578 409 | History and biography |

Do not use for geographic treatment; class in 551.57842

| | |
|---|---|
| .578 41–.578 43 | Properties, geographic distribution, variations over time |

Add to base number 551.5784 the numbers following 551.577 in 551.5771–551.5773, e.g., variations in snow and snowfall over time 551.57843

| | |
|---|---|
| .578 46 | Snow cover |

*For snow surveys, see 551.579*

| | |
|---|---|
| .578 464 | Ablation |

Class here melting

| | |
|---|---|
| .578 47 | Snow formations |

Including drifts

*For avalanches, see 551.57848*

| | |
|---|---|
| .578 48 | Avalanches |
| .578 7 | Hail and graupel |

Standard subdivisions are added for hail and graupel together, for hail alone

Class hailstorms in 551.554

| | |
|---|---|
| .579 | Snow surveys |
| .579 09 | History and biography |

Do not use for geographic treatment; class in 551.5791–551.5799

| | |
|---|---|
| .579 1–.579 9 | Geographic treatment |

Add to base number 551.579 notation 1–9 from Table 2, e.g., snow surveys in Nevada 551.579793

| | |
|---|---|
| **.6** | **Climatology and weather** |

Standard subdivisions are added for either or both topics in heading

*See Manual at 551.5 vs. 551.6*

| | |
|---|---|
| [.601 12] | Forecasting and forecasts |

Do not use; class in 551.63

| | |
|---|---|
| .609 | History, geographic treatment, biography |

Do not use for geographic treatment of weather; class in 551.65. Do not use for geographic treatment of climate, of climate and weather taken together; class in 551.69

| | |
|---|---|
| .62 | General types of climate |

| .620 9 | History and biography |
|---|---|

Do not use for geographic treatment; class in 551.69

**.63 Weather forecasting and forecasts, reporting and reports**

Standard subdivisions are added for weather forecasting and forecasts, reporting and reports together; for weather forecasting alone; for weather forecasts alone

*For forecasting and forecasts of specific phenomena, see 551.64*

| .630 284 | Materials |
|---|---|

Do not use for apparatus and equipment; class in 551.635

| .630 9 | History and biography |
|---|---|

Do not use for geographic treatment; class in 551.65

**.631 Historical methods of forecasting**

Class here weather lore

**.632 Reporting and reports**

Standard subdivisions are added for either or both topics in heading

Class reports of specific weather phenomena in 551.5

*For instrumentation in reporting, see 551.635*

| .632 09 | History, geographic treatment, biography |
|---|---|

Do not use for geographic treatment of weather reports; class in 551.65

**.633 Statistical forecasting**

**.634 Numerical forecasting**

**.635 Instrumentation in reporting and forecasting**

Standard subdivisions are added for either or both topics in heading

| .635 2 | Radiosondes |
|---|---|
| .635 3 | Radar |
| .635 4 | Weather satellites |

**.636 Short-range and long-range forecasts**

Class a specific aspect of short-range and long-range forecasts with the aspect, e.g., satellites in long-range forecasts 551.6354

| .636 2 | Short-range forecasts |
|---|---|

Forecasts for a maximum of a week

| .636 5 | Long-range forecasts |
|---|---|

Forecasts more than a week in advance

**.64 Forecasting and forecasts of specific phenomena**

[.640 1–.640 9]     Standard subdivisions

> Do not use; class in 551.6301–551.6309

.641–.647     Specific meteorological phenomena

> Class here methods of forecasting specific phenomena for specific areas

> Add to base number 551.64 the numbers following 551.5 in 551.51–551.57, e.g., hurricane warnings 551.6452

> Class flood forecasting and forecasts in 551.4890112; class forecasts of specific phenomena for specific areas in 551.65

.65     Geographic treatment of weather

> Class here geographic treatment of weather forecasts and reports, of forecasts of specific phenomena

> Class geographic treatment of climate and weather taken together in 551.69

[.650 1–.650 9]     Standard subdivisions

> Do not use; class in 551.601–551.609

.651–.659     Specific regions and areas

> Class here forecasts of specific phenomena for specific regions and areas

> Add to base number 551.65 notation 1–9 from Table 2, e.g., forecasts for South Africa 551.6568

.66     Microclimatology

> Small-scale interactions of atmosphere with land and water

> Class here micrometeorology

> Class specific meteorological phenomena other than thermodynamics in 551.5; class comprehensive works on atmosphere interactions with earth's surface in 551.524

.68     Artificial modification and control of weather

> Add to base number 551.68 the numbers following 551.5 in 551.51–551.57, e.g., cloud seeding 551.6876

> Subdivisions are added for either or both topics in heading

.69     Geographic treatment of climate

> Class here paleoclimatology of specific areas, geographic treatment of climate and weather taken together

> Add to base number 551.69 notation 1–9 from Table 2, e.g., climate of Australia 551.6994

> Class general types of climate in 551.62; class microclimatology of specific areas in 551.6609; class comprehensive works on paleoclimatology in 551.60901

> *For geographic treatment of weather, see 551.65*

[.690 1–.690 9]        Standard subdivisions

> Do not use; class in 551.601–551.609

## .7      Historical geology

Class here paleogeography, stratigraphy

Class history of a specific kind of geologic phenomenon with the kind, e.g., history of Jurassic volcanism in Pacific Northwest 551.210979509012, Devonian reefs 551.42409012, paleozoic orogeny 551.8209012

*For paleontology, see 560*

*See Manual at 551.7 vs. 560*

.700 1–.700 8        Standard subdivisions

.700 9              History, geographic treatment, biography

> Do not use for geographic treatment of historical geology during a specific geological era or period; class in 551.71–551.79

[.700 94–.700 99]       Historical geology of specific continents, countries, localities in modern world; extraterrestrial worlds

> Do not use; class in 554–559

.701             Geologic time and age measurements

> Standard subdivisions are added for either or both topics in heading

---

>           551.71–551.79   Specific geological periods

Class comprehensive works in 551.7

.71             Precambrian era

Variant name: Cryptozoic eon

.712            Archean era

Variant names: Archeozoic, Lower Precambrian era

.715            Proterozoic era

Variant names: Algonkian, Upper Precambrian era

.72             Paleozoic era

*For Ordovician and Silurian periods, see 551.73; for Devonian period, see 551.74; for Carboniferous and Permian periods, see 551.75*

.723           Cambrian period

Standard subdivisions are added for the period as a whole and for specific epochs, stages, or formations

.73            Ordovician and Silurian periods

.731 Ordovician period

> Standard subdivisions are added for the period as a whole and for specific epochs, stages, or formations

> Former name: Lower Silurian epoch

.732 Silurian period

> Standard subdivisions are added for the period as a whole and for specific epochs, stages, or formations

> Former name: Upper Silurian epoch

.74 Devonian period

> Standard subdivisions are added for the period as a whole and for specific epochs, stages, or formations

.75 Carboniferous and Permian periods

> Standard subdivisions are added for Carboniferous and Permian periods together, for Carboniferous period alone

---

> 551.751–551.752 Carboniferous period

Class comprehensive works in 551.75

.751 Mississippian period (Lower Carboniferous period)

> Standard subdivisions are added for the period as a whole and for specific epochs, stages, or formations

.752 Pennsylvanian period (Upper Carboniferous period)

> Standard subdivisions are added for the period as a whole and for specific epochs, stages, or formations

.756 Permian period

> Standard subdivisions are added for the period as a whole and for specific epochs, stages, or formations

.76 Mesozoic era

> *For Cretaceous period, see 551.77*

.762 Triassic period

> Standard subdivisions are added for the period as a whole and for specific epochs, stages, or formations

.766 Jurassic period

> Standard subdivisions are added for the period as a whole and for specific epochs, stages, or formations

.77 Cretaceous period

> Standard subdivisions are added for the period as a whole and for specific epochs, stages, or formations

| | |
|---|---|
| .78 | Cenozoic era |

Class here Tertiary period

*For Quaternary period, see 551.79*

| | |
|---|---|
| .782 | Paleogene period |

*For Paleocene epoch, see 551.783; for Eocene epoch, see 551.784; for Oligocene epoch, see 551.785*

| | |
|---|---|
| .783 | Paleocene epoch |

Standard subdivisions are added for the epoch as a whole and for specific stages or formations

| | |
|---|---|
| .784 | Eocene epoch |

Standard subdivisions are added for the epoch as a whole and for specific stages or formations

| | |
|---|---|
| .785 | Oligocene epoch |

Standard subdivisions are added for the epoch as a whole and for specific stages or formations

| | |
|---|---|
| .786 | Neogene period (Neocene period) |

Class Quaternary period in 551.79

*For Miocene epoch, see 551.787; for Pliocene epoch, see 551.788*

| | |
|---|---|
| .787 | Miocene epoch |

Standard subdivisions are added for the epoch as a whole and for specific stages or formations

| | |
|---|---|
| .788 | Pliocene epoch |

Standard subdivisions are added for the epoch as a whole and for specific stages or formations

| | |
|---|---|
| .79 | Quaternary period |
| .792 | Pleistocene epoch (Ice age) |

Standard subdivisions are added for the epoch as a whole and for specific stages or formations

| | |
|---|---|
| .793 | Holocene epoch |

Standard subdivisions are added for the epoch as a whole and for specific stages or formations

Variant names: postglacial, recent epoch

| | |
|---|---|
| **.8** | **Structural geology** |

Class here deformation, diastrophism, epeirogeny, tectonics

Class geomorphology in 551.41

*For plate tectonics, see 551.136*

| | |
|---|---|
| .81 | Stratifications |

.810 9          History, geographic treatment, biography

> Do not use for geographic treatment of stratifications during a specific geologic era or period; class in 551.71–551.79

[.810 94–.810 99]          Stratifications by specific continents, countries, localities in modern world; extraterrestrial worlds

> Do not use; class in 554–559

.82          Orogeny

> Class here lateral compression of earth's crust, specific orogenies

> Class comprehensive works on elevations (e.g., mountains, plateaus, hills) in 551.43. Class a specific aspect of orogeny with the aspect, e.g., volcanism 551.21

.84          Joints and cleavages

> Standard subdivisions are added for either or both topics in heading

.85          Dips, outcrops, strikes

.86          Anticlines and synclines

.87          Faults and folds

.872          Faults

> Including nappes, rift valleys

> Class here dislocations

> Class nappes produced by folding in 551.875

.875          Folds

> *For anticlines and synclines, see 551.86*

.88          Intrusions

> Including dikes, laccoliths, necks, sills, veins

> Class volcanoes in 551.21

**.9**          **Geochemistry**

> *For geochemistry of a specific subject in earth sciences or mineralogy, see the subject, e.g., organic geochemistry 553.2*

# 552    Petrology

Class here petrography, lithology, rocks

Class structural geology in 551.8

> *For mineralogy, see 549; for petrology of geologic materials of economic utility other than structural and sculptural stone, see 553*

.001–.008          Standard subdivisions

.009          History, geographic treatment, biography

> Do not use for geographic distribution of rocks; class in 552.09

.03        Petrogenesis

            Class here diagenesis

.06        Properties, composition, analysis, structure of rocks

            Class comprehensive works on geochemistry in 551.9

.09        Geographic distribution of rocks

            Add to base number 552.09 notation 1–9 from Table 2, e.g., rocks of Sahara Desert 552.0966

            Class rocks studied in their stratigraphic setting in 554–559

---

>        **552.1–552.5 Specific kinds of rocks**

            Class comprehensive works in 552

**.1**        **Igneous rocks**

            *For volcanic rocks, see 552.2; for plutonic rocks, see 552.3*

**.2**        **Volcanic rocks**

            Class here aphanite

            *See also 551.23 for volcanic volatiles*

.22        Lava

            Including felsite, obsidian, rhyolite

            Class pyroclastic felsite in 552.23

            *For basalt, see 552.26*

.23        Pyroclastic rocks

            Including andesite, pumice, tuff, volcanic ash

            Class andesitic lava in 552.22

.26        Basalt

            Including pillow lava

            Class basaltic pyroclastic rocks in 552.23

**.3**        **Plutonic rocks**

            Including diorite, dolerite, gabbro, granite, norite, peridotite, porphyry, syenite

            Class here phanerite

**.4**        **Metamorphic rocks**

            Including gneiss, marble, quartzite, schist, serpentinite, slate

**.5**　　　**Sedimentary rocks**

> Including gypsum, sandstone, shale, tufa; clay, diatomaceous earth, sand, silt, soil
>
> Class here comprehensive works on sedimentology
>
> Class pyroclastic tufa (tuff) in 552.23
>
> > *For sedimentology as study of surface processes, see 551.3*

**.58**　　　Carbonate rocks

> Including chalk, dolomite, limestone, oolite

**.8**　　　**Microscopic petrology**

> Class microscopic petrology of specific kinds of rocks in 552.1–552.5

**553**　　**Economic geology**

> Quantitative occurrence and distribution of geologic materials of economic utility
>
> Class here interdisciplinary works on nonmetallic geologic materials
>
> Class economic aspects other than reserves of geologic materials in 333.7; class interdisciplinary works on metals in 669
>
> > *For a specific aspect of nonmetallic geologic materials other than economic geology, see the aspect, e.g., mining 622*

### SUMMARY

| | |
|---|---|
| **553.1** | **Formation and structure of deposits** |
| **.2** | **Carbonaceous materials** |
| **.3** | **Iron** |
| **.4** | **Metals and semimetals** |
| **.5** | **Structural and sculptural stone** |
| **.6** | **Other economic materials** |
| **.7** | **Water** |
| **.8** | **Gems** |
| **.9** | **Inorganic gases** |

**.1**　　　**Formation and structure of deposits**

> Class formation and structure of deposits of specific materials in 553.2–553.9

**.13**　　　Placer deposits

**.14**　　　Stratified layers and beds

**.16**　　　Pegmatite dikes

**.19**　　　Veins and lodes

---

**>**　　　**553.2–553.9 Specific materials**

> Class comprehensive works in 553

**.2**      **Carbonaceous materials**

Class here fossil fuels, nonrenewable fuels, organic geochemistry; comprehensive works on fuels

Class interdisciplinary works on fuels in 662.6

> *For nuclear fuels, see 553.493; for diamonds, see 553.82; for jet, see 553.87; for amber, see 553.879*

---

\>      553.21–553.25   Coal

Class comprehensive works in 553.24

.21      Peat

Including peat coal

.22      Lignite (Brown coal)

.23      Cannel coal

.24      Bituminous and semibituminous coal

Standard subdivisions are added for bituminous and semibituminous coal together, for bituminous coal alone

Class here comprehensive works on coal

> *For peat, see 553.21; for lignite, see 553.22; for cannel coal, see 553.23; for anthracite, see 553.25; for jet, see 553.87*

.25      Anthracite

.26      Graphite

Variant names: black lead, plumbago

Class graphitic anthracite coal in 553.25

.27      Solid and semisolid bitumens

Standard subdivisions are added for either or both topics in heading

Including ozokerite

Class here asphalt (pitch)

Class liquid bitumens (oil) in 553.282; class rocks and sands impregnated with solid or semisolid bitumens in 553.283

.28      Oil, oil shales, tar sands, natural gas

Class here petroleum geology

Use 553.28 for petroleum covering oil and gas, use 553.282 for petroleum limited to oil

.282      Oil

.283      Oil shale and tar sands

Variant names for oil shale: bituminous shale, black shale; for tar sands: bituminous sands, oil sands

| .285 | Natural gas |
|------|-------------|
| .29 | Fossil resins and gums |

> Standard subdivisions are added for fossil resins and gums together, for fossil resins alone

> *For amber, see 553.879*

| **.3** | **Iron** |
|--------|----------|
| **.4** | **Metals and semimetals** |

> Standard subdivisions are added for metals and semimetals together, for metals alone

> *For iron, see 553.3*

| .41 | Gold |
|-----|------|
| .42 | Precious metals |

> *For gold, see 553.41*

| .421 | Silver |
|------|--------|
| .422 | Platinum |
| .43 | Copper |
| .44 | Lead |
| .45 | Zinc, tin, mercury |
| .452 | Zinc |
| .453 | Tin |
| .454 | Mercury |
| .46 | Metals used in ferroalloys |

> *For cobalt and nickel, see 553.48*

| .462 | Titanium, vanadium, manganese |
|------|-------------------------------|
| .462 3 | Titanium |
| .462 6 | Vanadium |
| .462 9 | Manganese |
| .464 | Chromium, molybdenum, tungsten |
| .464 3 | Chromium |
| .464 6 | Molybdenum |
| .464 9 | Tungsten |
| .465 | Zirconium and tantalum |
| .47 | Antimony, arsenic, bismuth |
| .48 | Cobalt and nickel |

| .483 | Cobalt |
|---|---|
| .485 | Nickel |
| .49 | Other metals |
| .492 | Light metals |
| .492 3 | Beryllium |
| .492 6 | Aluminum |
| .492 9 | Magnesium |
| .493 | Fissionable metals |

Including radium, thorium

Class here nuclear fuels

| .493 2 | Uranium |
|---|---|
| .494 | Rare-earth metals |

Class here lanthanide series

| .494 2 | Scandium |
|---|---|
| .494 3 | Cerium group |
| .494 7 | Yttrium group |
| .495 | Platinum metals |

*For platinum, see 553.422*

| .499 | Metals not provided for elsewhere |
|---|---|

Including barium, indium, lithium, niobium, sodium, tellurium

Class here semimetals

*For antimony, arsenic, bismuth, see 553.47*

**.5 Structural and sculptural stone**

Standard subdivisions are added for either or both topics in heading

Class petrology of structural and sculptural stone in 552

*For semiprecious sculptural stone, see 553.87*

| .51 | Marble and limestone |
|---|---|
| .512 | Marble |

*For verd antique and onyx marble, see 553.55*

| .516 | Limestone |
|---|---|

Including dolomite, travertine

| .52 | Granite and syenite |
|---|---|

Standard subdivisions are added for granite and syenite together, for granite alone

.53 Sandstone

Including bluestone, flagstones

*For flagstones of a specific stone other than sandstone, see the stone, e.g., slate 553.54*

.54 Slate

.55 Serpentine, soapstone (steatite), and their variants

Including verd antique and onyx marble

*See also 553.87 for onyx*

**.6 Other economic materials**

Including diatomaceous earth

Class here earthy materials, industrial minerals

*For inorganic gases, see 553.9; for soils, see 631.4*

.61 Clay

Including bentonite, diaspore clay, kaolin; fuller's earth

Class here comprehensive works on ceramic materials

*For fireclay, see 553.67. For a specific nonclay ceramic material, see the material, e.g., glass sands 553.622*

.62 Sand and gravel

Class here aggregates

.622 Sand

Including glass sand

.626 Gravel

.63 Salts

*For saltpeter, see 553.64; for mineral waters, see 553.73*

.632 Rock salt (Sodium chloride)

.633 Borates

Including borax

.635 Gypsum

Including alabaster

.636 Potash salts

Class here potassium minerals

.64 Nitrates and phosphates

Including apatites, saltpeter

Class here mineral fertilizers

| .65 | Abrasives |
|---|---|

Including corundum, flint, industrial diamonds

Class comprehensive works on abrasives that are also gems in 553.8

*For sand, see 553.622*

| .66 | Mineral pigments and sulfur |
|---|---|
| .662 | Mineral pigments |

Including barite

| .668 | Sulfur |
|---|---|
| .67 | Refractory materials |

Including alumina, fireclay

*For soapstone, see 553.55*

| .672 | Asbestos |
|---|---|
| .674 | Mica |
| .676 | Talc |
| .678 | Vermiculite |
| .68 | Cement materials |

Including chalk, lime, marl

*For gypsum, see 553.635*

| **.7** | **Water** |
|---|---|

Including ice

Class interdisciplinary works on thermal waters in 333.88; class interdisciplinary works on ice in 551.31

*For geology of thermal waters, see 551.23*

*See Manual at 363.61*

| .72 | Saline water |
|---|---|
| .73 | Mineral waters |

*For saline water, see 553.72*

| .78 | Surface water |
|---|---|
| .79 | Groundwater (Subsurface water) |
| **.8** | **Gems** |

Class here comprehensive works on stones that are both gems and abrasives

*For gemstones treated as abrasives, see 553.65*

>        553.82–553.86   Precious stones

       Class comprehensive works in 553.8

.82        Diamonds

       *For industrial diamonds, see 553.65*

.84        Rubies and sapphires

.86        Emeralds

.87        Semiprecious stones

       Including agates, amethysts, garnet, jet, tourmaline, turquoise

.873        Opals

.876        Jade

       Class here jadite, nephrite

.879        Amber

**.9**        **Inorganic gases**

.92        Hydrogen

.93        Nitrogen

.94        Oxygen

.95        Chlorine and fluorine

.97        Noble gases

       Variant name: inert, rare gases

       Including radon

.971        Helium

## 554–559   Earth sciences by specific continents, countries, localities in modern world; extraterrestrial worlds

Class here geology, geological surveys, stratifications

Add to base number 55 notation 4–9 from Table 2, e.g., geology of Japan 555.2, of moon 559.91

Class historical geology and stratifications of specific continents, countries, localities during a specific era or period in 551.71–551.79; class geological surveys of specific areas emphasizing materials of economic importance in 553.094–553.099; class comprehensive works on earth sciences in 550; class comprehensive works on geology in 551. Class a specific geologic topic (other than historical geology taken as a whole) in a specific area with the topic, e.g., volcanoes in Japan 551.210952, geomorphology of Japan 551.410952

## 554        Earth sciences of Europe

Number built according to instructions under 554–559

**555 Earth sciences of Asia**

> Number built according to instructions under 554–559

**556 Earth sciences of Africa**

> Number built according to instructions under 554–559

**557 Earth sciences of North America**

> Number built according to instructions under 554–559

**558 Earth sciences of South America**

> Number built according to instructions under 554–559

**559 Earth sciences of Australasia, Pacific Ocean islands, Atlantic Ocean islands, Arctic islands, Antarctica, extraterrestrial worlds**

> Number built according to instructions under 554–559

**.9 Earth sciences of extraterrestrial worlds**

> Number built according to instructions under 554–559
>
> > *See Manual at 523 vs. 550; also at 629.43, 629.45 vs. 559.9, 919.904*

# 560 Paleontology

> Including organisms of uncertain status as plant or animal, as chordate or invertebrate
>
> Class here paleozoology
>
> Class the analysis of paleontological evidence to determine geological time and age in 551.701; class the analysis of paleontological evidence to determine a specific geological age in 551.71–551.79; class comprehensive works on paleontology and historic geology in 551.7
>
> > *See Manual at 551.7 vs. 560; also at 576.8 vs. 560*

### SUMMARY

| | | |
|---|---|---|
| 560.1–.9 | Standard subdivisions; stratigraphic paleontology; special topics of paleontology and paleozoology | |
| 561 | Paleobotany; fossil microorganisms | |
| 562 | Fossil invertebrates | |
| 563 | Miscellaneous fossil marine and seashore invertebrates | |
| 564 | Fossil Mollusca and Molluscoidea | |
| 565 | Fossil Arthropoda | |
| 566 | Fossil Chordata | |
| 567 | Fossil cold-blooded vertebrates | |
| 568 | Fossil Aves (birds) | |
| 569 | Fossil Mammalia | |

**.1 Philosophy and theory; stratigraphic paleontology**

.17      Stratigraphic paleontology

Class here stratigraphic paleozoology

Add to base number 560.17 the numbers following 551.7 in 551.71–551.79, e.g., Precambrian paleontology 560.171

Class fossils of specific kinds of organisms in 561–569

**.4**      **Special topics of paleontology and paleozoology**

.41      Fossilization (Taphonomy)

.43      Trace fossils

Class here fossil footprints, ichnology

.45      Paleoecology and fossils of specific environment

Class here zoological paleoecology and fossil animals of specific environments

Subdivisions are added for either or both topics in heading

.450 1–.450 8      Standard subdivisions

Notation from Table 1 as modified under 578.01–578.08, e.g., microscopy 560.450282

.450 9      History, geographic treatment, biography

[.450 914–.450 919]      Areas, regions, places in general other than polar, temperate, tropical regions

Do not use; class in 560.453–560.457

.451–.457      Specific aspects of paleoecology and fossils of specific environment

Add to base number 560.45 the numbers following 577 in 577.1–577.7, e.g., marine paleoecology 560.457

.47      Micropaleontology

Class here microfossils

Class a specific kind of microfossil with the kind, e.g., fossil microorganisms 561.9

**.9**      **History, geographic treatment, biography**

Class stratigraphic paleontology and paleozoology in 560.17

[.914–.919]      Areas, regions, places in general other than polar, temperate, tropical regions

Do not use; class in 560.45

# 561     Paleobotany; fossil microorganisms

Standard subdivisions are added for paleontology and fossil microorganisms together, for paleontology alone

Including plantlike fossils of uncertain taxonomic position

Class here fossil Spermatophyta, Angiospermae; taxonomic paleobotany

Class fernlike fossils of uncertain taxonomic position in 561.597

.09         History, geographic treatment, biography

> *For geographic treatment of fossil plants, see 561.19*

[.091 4–.091 9]         Areas, regions, places in general other than polar, temperate, tropical regions

> Do not use; class in 561.1

.1         **General topics of paleobotany**

Including botanical paleoecology, plant fossils of specific environments

Class general topics of specific plants and groups of plants in 561.3–561.9

.11         Stratigraphic paleobotany

> Add to base number 561.11 the numbers following 551.7 in 551.71–551.79, e.g., Carboniferous paleobotany 561.115

.13         Fossil pollen and spores

> Standard subdivisions are added for either or both topics in heading
>
> Class here paleopalynology
>
> Class comprehensive works on palynology, comprehensive works on pollen in 571.8452; class comprehensive works on spores in 571.847

.14         Fossil fruits and seeds

> Standard subdivisions are added for either or both topics in heading

.15         Fossil leaves

.16         Trees and petrified wood

> Standard subdivisions are added for either or both topics in heading

.19         Geographic treatment of fossil plants

> Add to base number 561.19 notation 1–9 from Table 2, e.g., plant fossils of West Indies 561.19729; however, for treatment by areas, regions, places in general other than polar, temperate, tropical regions, see 561.1

---

>         **561.3–561.9 Specific plants and groups of plants**

Class comprehensive works in 561

.3         **Fossil Magnoliopsida (dicotyledons)**

.4         **Fossil Liliopsida (monocotyledons)**

.45 Arecidae

> Class here Arecales (Palmales), Arecaceae (Palmae, palm family)

.49 Poales

> Variant names: Graminales, grasses

**.5 Fossil Pinophyta and fernlike fossils of uncertain taxonomic position**

> Standard subdivisions are added for fossil Pinophyta and fernlike fossils of uncertain taxonomic position together, for fossil Pinophyta alone

> Variant name for fossil Pinophyta: fossil gymnosperms

> Class here Coniferales (conifers)

.52–.58 Pinophyta (Gymnosperms)

> Add to base number 561.5 the numbers following 585 in 585.2–585.8, e.g., fossil Pinaceae 561.52

>> *For Cycadales, Cycadeoidales, Pteridospermales, Cordaitales, see 561.59*

.59 Cycadales, Cycadeoidales, Pteridospermales, fernlike fossils of uncertain taxonomic position, Cordaitales

.591 Cycadales (True cycads)

.592 Cycadeoidales (Bennettitales)

> Including Cycadeoidaceae, Williamsoniaceae

.595 Pteridospermales

> Variant names: Cycadofilicales, seed ferns

> Including Calamopityaceae, Lyginopteridaceae, Medullosaceae

.597 Fernlike fossils of uncertain taxonomic position

> Including Archaeopteris, Callipteris, Glossopteris, Mariopteris, Megalopteris, Neuropteris, Odontopteris, Pecopteris, Sphenopteris

**.6 Fossil Cryptogamia**

> *For Pteridophyta, see 561.7; for Bryophyta, see 561.8; for microorganisms, fungi, algae, see 561.9*

**.7 Fossil Pteridophyta**

> Class fernlike fossils of uncertain taxonomic position in 561.597

.72 Sphenopsida

> Including Calamitales, Equisetales, Hyeniales, Pseudoborniales, Sphenophyllales

.73 Polypodiopsida (Filicopsida)

> Including Coenopteridales, Filicales, Marattiales, Ophioglossales

.74 Psilopsida

> Including Psilophytales, Psilotales

.79 Lycopsida (Club mosses)

> Including Isoetales, Lepidodendrales, Pleuromeiales, Protolepidodendrales

**.8 Fossil Bryophyta**

**.9 Fossil microorganisms, fungi, algae**

> Class comprehensive works on micropaleontology in 560.47

.91 Prokaryotes

> Class here bacteria

.92 Fungi

.93 Algae

> Add to base number 561.93 the numbers following 579.8 in 579.82–579.89, e.g., fossil diatoms 561.935

.99 Protozoa

.992 Zoomastigophorea

.994 Foraminifera

.995 Radiolaria

---

> **562–569 Specific taxonomic groups of animals**

> Class here taxonomic paleozoology

> Class comprehensive works in 560

**562 Fossil invertebrates**

> *For Protozoa, see 561.99; for miscellaneous marine and seashore invertebrates, see 563; for Mollusca and Molluscoidea, see 564; for Arthropoda, see 565*

**.2 Conodonts**

**.3–.7 Worms and related animals**

> Add to base number 562 the numbers following 592 in 592.3–592.7, e.g., Annelida 562.6

> Class comprehensive works in 562.3

**563 Miscellaneous fossil marine and seashore invertebrates**

[.01–.09] Standard subdivisions

> Do not use; class in 562.01–562.09

**.4**        **Porifera (Sponges) and Archaeocyatha**

Standard subdivisions are added for Porifera and Archaeocyatha together, for Porifera alone

Class here Parazoa

.47          Archaeocyatha

**.5**        **Cnidaria (Coelenterata)**

Including Scyphozoa

*For Anthozoa, see 563.6*

.55          Hydrozoa

Including Graptolitoidea

.58          Stromatoporoidea

**.6**        **Anthozoa**

Class here corals

Class Archaeocyatha in 563.47

**.8**        **Ctenophora**

**.9**        **Echinodermata and Hemichordata**

Standard subdivisions are added for Echinodermata and Hemichordata together, for Echinodermata alone

---

>            563.92–563.96  Echinodermata

Class comprehensive works in 563.9

.92          Crinozoa, Blastozoa, Homalozoa

Standard subdivisions are added for Crinozoa, Blastozoa, Homalozoa together; for Crinozoa alone

Including Camerata, Flexibilia, Inadunata; carpoids

.93          Asterozoa (Starfish)

*For Ophiuroidea, see 563.94*

.94          Ophiuroidea

.95          Echinozoa

Including Cystoidea

*For Holothurioidea, see 563.96*

.96          Holothurioidea

Including Arthrochirotida

.99     Hemichordata

> Including Enteropneusta, Planctosphaeroidea
>
> Class here Pterobranchia

# 564     Fossil Mollusca and Molluscoidea

---

>     **564.2–564.5 Mollusca (Mollusks)**
>
> Class comprehensive works in 564

**.2–.4**     **Specific Mollusca other than Cephalopoda**

> Add to base number 564 the numbers following 594 in 594.2–594.4, e.g., Bivalvia 564.4

**.5**     **Cephalopoda**

.52     Nautiloidea

.53     Ammonoidea

.56     Octopoda

.58     Decapoda

**.6**     **Molluscoidea**

> Including Entoprocta

.67     Bryozoa

.68     Brachiopoda (Lamp shells)

# 565     Fossil Arthropoda

**.3**     **Crustacea and Trilobita**

> Standard subdivisions are added for Crustacea and Trilobita together, for Crustacea alone
>
> Including Bradoriida, Phosphatocopida

.32–.38     Specific kinds of Crustacea

> Add to base number 565.3 the numbers following 595.3 in 595.32–595.38, e.g., Ostracoda 565.33

.39     Trilobita

**.4**     **Chelicerata**

> Including Architarbi
>
> Class here Arachnida

.49     Merostomata and Pycnogonida

> Standard subdivisions are added for Merostomata and Pycnogonida together, for Merostomata alone

| .492 | Xiphosura (Horseshoe crabs) |
| .493 | Eurypterida |

**.6 Myriapoda**

**.7 Insecta**

Class here Uniramia, Hexapoda, Pterygota

Add to base number 565.7 the numbers following 595.7 in 595.72–595.79, e.g., Coleoptera 565.76

*For Myriapoda, see 565.6*

# 566 Fossil Chordata

Including Cephalochordata, Urochordata (Tunicata)

Class here Vertebrata (Craniata, vertebrates), Tetrapoda (land vertebrates)

*For fossil cold-blooded vertebrates, see 567; for fossil Aves, see 568; for fossil Mammalia, see 569*

# 567 Fossil cold-blooded vertebrates

Including Leptolepis

Class here Pisces (fishes); Actinopterygii, Osteichthyes, Teleostei

Class specific kinds of Actinopterygii, Osteichthyes, Teleostei in 567.4–567.7

---

> **567.2–567.7 Fossil Pisces (fishes)**

Class comprehensive works in 567

**.2 Agnatha, Acanthodii, Placodermi**

Including Cyclostomata

**.3 Chondrichthyes and Sarcopterygii**

Standard subdivisions are added for Chondrichthyes and Sarcopterygii together, for Chondrichthyes alone

Including Bradyodonti, Cladoselachii, Pleuracanthodii

Class here Elasmobranchii, Selachii; sharks

Add to base number 567.3 the numbers following 597.3 in 597.33–597.39, e.g., Sarcopterygii 567.39

**.4–.7     Specific fossil Actinopterygii**

Class here Osteichthyes, Teleostei

Add to base number 567 the numbers following 597 in 597.4–597.7, e.g., Salmoniformes 567.5

Class fossil Actinopterygii not traceable to surviving superorders, e.g., Leptolepis; comprehensive works on Actinopterygii, Osteichthyes, Teleostei in 567

*For Sarcopterygii, see 567.39*

**.8     Amphibia**

Including Anura, Gymnophiona, Labyrinthodontia, Lepospondyli, Urodela

**.9     Reptilia**

Class here Archosauria, Diapsida, Dinosaurs

**.91     Specific dinosaurs and other Archosauria**

Including Thecodontia

*For Crocodilia, see 567.98. For a "dinosaur" of an order not assigned to Archosauria, see the order, e.g., Ichthyosauria 567.937*

**[.910 1–.910 9]     Standard subdivisions**

Do not use; class in 567.901–567.909

>     567.912–567.915   Specific dinosaurs

Class comprehensive works in 567.9

**.912     Saurischia**

Including Allosaurus, Baryonyx, Coelophysis, Deinonychus, Oviraptor

Class here Theropoda (carnivorous dinosaurs)

*For Sauropodomorpha, see 567.913*

**.912 9     Tyrannosaurus**

**.913     Sauropodomorpha (Herbivorous Saurischia)**

Including Diplodocus, Seismosaurus

**.913 8     Apatosaurus (Brontosaurus)**

**.914     Ornithischia**

Including Hadrosauridae (duck-billed dinosaurs); Anatosaurus, Corythosaurus, Hypsilophodon, Iguanodon, Maiasaura, Pachycephalosaurus, Parasaurolophus

Class here Ornithopoda

*For Stegosauria, Ankylosauria, Ceratopsia, see 567.915*

**.4**      **Porifera (Sponges) and Archaeocyatha**

> Standard subdivisions are added for Porifera and Archaeocyatha together, for Porifera alone

> Class here Parazoa

**.47**      Archaeocyatha

**.5**      **Cnidaria (Coelenterata)**

> Including Scyphozoa

> *For Anthozoa, see 563.6*

**.55**      Hydrozoa

> Including Graptolitoidea

**.58**      Stromatoporoidea

**.6**      **Anthozoa**

> Class here corals

> Class Archaeocyatha in 563.47

**.8**      **Ctenophora**

**.9**      **Echinodermata and Hemichordata**

> Standard subdivisions are added for Echinodermata and Hemichordata together, for Echinodermata alone

---

>      563.92–563.96   Echinodermata

> Class comprehensive works in 563.9

**.92**      Crinozoa, Blastozoa, Homalozoa

> Standard subdivisions are added for Crinozoa, Blastozoa, Homalozoa together; for Crinozoa alone

> Including Camerata, Flexibilia, Inadunata; carpoids

**.93**      Asterozoa (Starfish)

> *For Ophiuroidea, see 563.94*

**.94**      Ophiuroidea

**.95**      Echinozoa

> Including Cystoidea

> *For Holothurioidea, see 563.96*

**.96**      Holothurioidea

> Including Arthrochirotida

.99             Hemichordata

                Including Enteropneusta, Planctosphaeroidea

                Class here Pterobranchia

# 564        Fossil Mollusca and Molluscoidea

---

> **564.2–564.5  Mollusca (Mollusks)**

                Class comprehensive works in 564

**.2–.4      Specific Mollusca other than Cephalopoda**

                Add to base number 564 the numbers following 594 in 594.2–594.4, e.g.,
                Bivalvia 564.4

**.5          Cephalopoda**

.52             Nautiloidea

.53             Ammonoidea

.56             Octopoda

.58             Decapoda

**.6          Molluscoidea**

                Including Entoprocta

.67             Bryozoa

.68             Brachiopoda (Lamp shells)

# 565        Fossil Arthropoda

**.3          Crustacea and Trilobita**

                Standard subdivisions are added for Crustacea and Trilobita together, for
                Crustacea alone

                Including Bradoriida, Phosphatocopida

.32–.38        Specific kinds of Crustacea

                Add to base number 565.3 the numbers following 595.3 in 595.32–595.38,
                e.g., Ostracoda 565.33

.39             Trilobita

**.4          Chelicerata**

                Including Architarbi

                Class here Arachnida

.49             Merostomata and Pycnogonida

                Standard subdivisions are added for Merostomata and Pycnogonida together,
                for Merostomata alone

| .492 | Xiphosura (Horseshoe crabs) |
| .493 | Eurypterida |

**.6 Myriapoda**

**.7 Insecta**

Class here Uniramia, Hexapoda, Pterygota

Add to base number 565.7 the numbers following 595.7 in 595.72–595.79, e.g., Coleoptera 565.76

*For Myriapoda, see 565.6*

# 566 Fossil Chordata

Including Cephalochordata, Urochordata (Tunicata)

Class here Vertebrata (Craniata, vertebrates), Tetrapoda (land vertebrates)

*For fossil cold-blooded vertebrates, see 567; for fossil Aves, see 568; for fossil Mammalia, see 569*

# 567 Fossil cold-blooded vertebrates

Including Leptolepis

Class here Pisces (fishes); Actinopterygii, Osteichthyes, Teleostei

Class specific kinds of Actinopterygii, Osteichthyes, Teleostei in 567.4–567.7

---

\> **567.2–567.7 Fossil Pisces (fishes)**

Class comprehensive works in 567

**.2 Agnatha, Acanthodii, Placodermi**

Including Cyclostomata

**.3 Chondrichthyes and Sarcopterygii**

Standard subdivisions are added for Chondrichthyes and Sarcopterygii together, for Chondrichthyes alone

Including Bradyodonti, Cladoselachii, Pleuracanthodii

Class here Elasmobranchii, Selachii; sharks

Add to base number 567.3 the numbers following 597.3 in 597.33–597.39, e.g., Sarcopterygii 567.39

**.4–.7** **Specific fossil Actinopterygii**

Class here Osteichthyes, Teleostei

Add to base number 567 the numbers following 597 in 597.4–597.7, e.g., Salmoniformes 567.5

Class fossil Actinopterygii not traceable to surviving superorders, e.g., Leptolepis; comprehensive works on Actinopterygii, Osteichthyes, Teleostei in 567

*For Sarcopterygii, see 567.39*

**.8** **Amphibia**

Including Anura, Gymnophiona, Labyrinthodontia, Lepospondyli, Urodela

**.9** **Reptilia**

Class here Archosauria, Diapsida, Dinosaurs

**.91** Specific dinosaurs and other Archosauria

Including Thecodontia

*For Crocodilia, see 567.98. For a "dinosaur" of an order not assigned to Archosauria, see the order, e.g., Ichthyosauria 567.937*

**[.910 1–.910 9]** Standard subdivisions

Do not use; class in 567.901–567.909

---

> 567.912–567.915 Specific dinosaurs

Class comprehensive works in 567.9

**.912** Saurischia

Including Allosaurus, Baryonyx, Coelophysis, Deinonychus, Oviraptor

Class here Theropoda (carnivorous dinosaurs)

*For Sauropodomorpha, see 567.913*

**.912 9** Tyrannosaurus

**.913** Sauropodomorpha (Herbivorous Saurischia)

Including Diplodocus, Seismosaurus

**.913 8** Apatosaurus (Brontosaurus)

**.914** Ornithischia

Including Hadrosauridae (duck-billed dinosaurs); Anatosaurus, Corythosaurus, Hypsilophodon, Iguanodon, Maiasaura, Pachycephalosaurus, Parasaurolophus

Class here Ornithopoda

*For Stegosauria, Ankylosauria, Ceratopsia, see 567.915*

| | |
|---|---|
| .915 | Stegosauria, Ankylosauria, Ceratopsia (horned dinosaurs) |
| | Including Protoceratops |
| | Class here armored dinosaurs |
| .915 3 | Stegosaurus |
| .915 8 | Triceratops |
| .918 | Pterosauria (Flying reptiles) |
| | Including Pteranodon, Pterodactylus |
| | Class comprehensive works on flying and marine reptiles in 567.937 |
| .92 | Anapsida |
| | Including Chelonia (Testudines), Cotylosauria |
| | *For Mesosauria, see 567.937* |
| .93 | Euryapsida, Synapsida; Mesosauria |
| | Including Araeoscelidia, Pelycosauria, Placodontia, Therapsida |
| .937 | Marine reptiles |
| | Including Ichthyosauria, Mesosauria, Sauropterygia (Nothosauria and Plesiosauria) |
| | *For Mosasauridae, see 567.95* |
| .94 | Lepidosauria |
| | Including Eosuchia |
| | Class here Squamata |
| | *For Sauria, see 567.95; for Serpentes, see 567.96* |
| .945 | Rhynchocephalia |
| .95 | Sauria |
| | Including Mosasauridae (marine lizards) |
| | Class comprehensive works on Sauria and Serpentes in 567.94 |
| .96 | Serpentes |
| .98 | Crocodilia |

## 568 Fossil Aves (birds)

Class here Neornithes

| | |
|---|---|
| **.2** | **Archaeornithes, Hesperornithiformes, Ichthyornithiformes** |
| .22 | Archaeornithes |
| .23 | Hesperornithiformes and Ichthyornithiformes |
| **.3** | **Charadriiformes, Ciconiiformes, Diatrymiformes, Gruiformes, Phoenicopteriformes** |

**.4** **Water birds**

Including Anseriformes, Gaviiformes, Pelecaniformes, Podicipediformes, Procellariiformes, Sphenisciformes

*For Hesperornithiformes and Ichthyornithiformes, see 568.23; for Charadriiformes, Ciconiiformes, Diatrymiformes, Gruiformes, Phoenicopteriformes, see 568.3*

**.5** **Palaeognathae**

Including Aepyornithiformes, Apterygiformes, Caenagnathiformes, Casuariiformes, Rheiformes, Struthioniformes, Tinamiformes

Class here ratites

**.6** **Galliformes and Columbiformes**

Standard subdivisions are added for Galliformes and Columbiformes together, for Galliformes alone

**.7** **Miscellaneous land birds**

Limited to those named herein

Including Apodiformes, Coliiformes, Coraciiformes, Cuculiformes, Piciformes, Psittaciformes, Trogoniformes

Class comprehensive works on land birds in 568

[.701–.709]    Standard subdivisions

Do not use; class in 568.01–568.09

**.8** **Passeriformes**

**.9** **Falconiformes, Caprimulgiformes, Strigiformes**

Standard subdivisions are added for Falconiformes, Caprimulgiformes, Strigiformes, together; for Falconiformes alone

# 569    Fossil Mammalia

**.2** **Metatheria and Prototheria**

Standard subdivisions are added for Metatheria and Prototheria together, for Metatheria alone

Including Trituberculata

Class here Marsupialia

.29    Prototheria

Including Allotheria, Eotheria

Class here Monotremata

---

>    **569.3–569.9  Eutheria**

Class comprehensive works in 599

**.3**      **Miscellaneous orders of Eutheria**

> Limited to those named below

[.301–.309]      Standard subdivisions

> > Do not use; class in 569.01–569.09

.31      Edentata, Palaeanodonta, Pholidota, Taeniodontia, Tillodontia, Tubulidentata

.32–.37      Dermoptera, Insectivora, Lagomorpha, Macroscelidea, Rodentia, Scandentia

> > Add to base number 569.3 the numbers following 599.3 in 599.32–599.37, e.g., Insectivora 569.33

**.4**      **Chiroptera (Bats)**

> Including Megachiroptera

> Class here Microchiroptera

**.5**      **Cetacea, Desmostylia, Sirenia**

> Standard subdivisions are added for Cetacea, Desmostylia, Sirenia together; for Cetacea alone

> Including Archaeoceti

> Class here Mysticeti, Odontoceti; marine mammals, whales

> *For Pinnipedia, see 569.79*

**.6**      **Ungulates**

> Class Desmostylia, Sirenia in 569.5

.62      Extinct orders of ungulates

> > Including Astrapotheria, Condylarthra, Dinocerata, Embrithopoda, Litopterna, Notoungulata, Pantodonta, Pyrotheria, Xenungulata

> > Class extinct members of surviving orders in 569.63–569.68

.63–.68      Surviving orders of ungulates

> > Add to base number 569.6 the numbers following 599.6 in 599.63–599.68, e.g., Proboscidea 569.67

**.7**      **Carnivores**

> Including Creodonta

> Class here Fissipedia

> Add to base number 569.7 the numbers following 599.7 in 599.74–599.79, e.g., Pinnipedia 567.79

**.8**          **Primates**

Class here Anthropoidea, monkeys

Add to base number 569.8 the numbers following 599.8 in 599.83–599.88, e.g., Hominidae 569.88

Class Tupaiidae in 569.338

> *For Homo and related genera, see 569.9*

**.9**          **Homo and related genera**

Humans and forebears, including species and genera that are more closely related to the species Homo sapiens than to any other living species, e.g., Ardipithecus

Including Piltdown forgery

**.93**          Australopithecus

Including Paranthropus, Plesianthropus

Class here australopithecines

Class australopithecines not assigned to genus Australopithecus in 569.9

**.97**          Homo erectus

Including Heidelberg man, Java man, Peking man

**.98**          Homo sapiens

Including Cro-Magnon man, Kabwe (Rhodesian) man

**.986**          Homo sapiens neanderthalis (Neanderthals)

# 570          Biology

Class here life sciences

> *For paleontology, see 560; for plants, see 580; for animals, see 590; for medical sciences, see 610*
>
> *See Manual at 363 vs. 302–307, 333.7, 570–590, 600; also at 578 vs. 304.2, 508, 910*

### SUMMARY

| | |
|---|---|
| **572** | **Biochemistry** |
| .3 | General topics of biochemistry |
| .4 | Metabolism |
| .5 | Miscellaneous chemicals |
| .6 | Proteins |
| .7 | Enzymes |
| .8 | Biochemical genetics |
| | |
| **573** | **Specific physiological systems in animals, regional histology and physiology in animals** |
| .1 | Circulatory system |
| .2 | Respiratory system |
| .3 | Digestive system |
| .4 | Endocrine and excretory systems |
| .5 | Integument |
| .6 | Reproductive system |
| .7 | Musculoskeletal system |
| .8 | Nervous and sensory systems |
| .9 | Miscellaneous systems and organs in animals, regional histology and physiology in animals |
| | |
| **575** | **Specific parts of and physiological systems in plants** |
| .4 | Stems |
| .5 | Roots and leaves |
| .6 | Reproductive organs |
| .7 | Circulation, food storage, excretion |
| .8 | Transpiration |
| .9 | Animal-like physiological processes |
| | |
| **576** | **Genetics and evolution** |
| .01–.09 | Standard subdivisions |
| .5 | Genetics |
| .8 | Evolution |
| | |
| **577** | **Ecology** |
| .01–.09 | Standard subdivisions |
| .1 | Specific ecosystem processes |
| .2 | Specific factors affecting ecology |
| .3 | Forest ecology |
| .4 | Grassland ecology |
| .5 | Ecology of miscellaneous environments |
| .6 | Aquatic ecology |
| .7 | Marine ecology |
| .8 | Synecology and population biology |
| | |
| **578** | **Natural history of organisms and related subjects** |
| .01–.09 | Standard subdivisions |
| .4 | Adaptation |
| .6 | Miscellaneous nontaxonomic kinds of organisms |
| .7 | Organisms characteristic of specific kinds of environments |
| | |
| **579** | **Natural history of microorganisms, fungi, algae** |
| .01–.09 | Standard subdivisions |
| .1 | Specific topics in natural history of microorganisms, fungi, algae |
| .2 | Viruses and subviral organisms |
| .3 | Prokaryotes |
| .4 | Protozoa |
| .5 | Fungi |
| .6 | Mushrooms |
| .7 | Lichens |
| .8 | Algae |

**.1**      **Philosophy and theory**

Class here nature of life, differences between living and nonliving substances

Class origin of life, conditions needed for life to begin in 576.83

.12      Classification

Class taxonomic classification in 578.012

.15      Scientific principles

.151 95      Statistical mathematics

Class here biometrics, biostatistics

*See Manual at 519.5, T1—015195 vs. 001.422, T1—0727*

**.2**      **Miscellany**

.28      Auxiliary techniques and procedures; apparatus, equipment, procedures

Notation 028 from Table 1 as modified below

.282      Microscopy

Including photomicrography, stereology

Class here microscopes

Class interdisciplinary works on microscopy in 502.82

.282 3      Light microscopy

Including magnifying glasses (simple microscopes)

Class here compound microscopes

Class stereology with compound microscopes in 570.282

.282 5      Electron microscopy

Class stereology with electron microscopes in 570.282

.282 7      Slide preparation

Including fixation, staining; microtomy

.284      Apparatus, equipment, materials

Do not use for microscopes; class in 570.282

.288      Maintenance and repair

Do not use for preservation of biological specimens; class in 570.752

**.7**      **Education, research, related topics**

.72      Research

.724      Experimental research

Class here experimental biology

Class tissue and organ culture in 571.538; class cell culture in 571.638

.75      Museum activities and services

.752        Preserving biological specimens

**.9        History, geographic treatment, biography**

> Do not use for geographic treatment of organisms; class in 578.09

.919        Space

> Do not use for space biology; class in 571.0919

.999        Extraterrestrial worlds

> Do not use for extraterrestrial life; class in 576.839

---

> ## 571–575 Internal biological processes and structures

Class here internal biological processes and structures in plants and animals

Unless other instructions are given, class a subject with aspects in two or more subdivisions of 571–575 in the number coming last, e.g., cytology of animal circulatory system 573.136 (*not* 571.1 or 571.6)

Class comprehensive works in 571

> *See Manual at 571–575 vs. 630; also at 579–590 vs. 571–575*

---

> ## 571–572 General internal processes common to all organisms

Add to each subdivision identified by * as follows:
01–08    Standard subdivisions
       Notation from Table 1 as modified under 570.1–570.8, e.g.,
       microscopy 0282
09       History, geographic treatment, biography
       Notation from Table 1 as modified under 571.09, e.g., space
       biology 0919
1–2    Specific kinds of organisms
       Add the numbers following 571 in 571.1–571.2, e.g., the subject in
       animals 1, the subject in plants and microorganisms 2
Class comprehensive works in 571

> *See Manual at 571–573 vs. 610*

**571      Physiology and related subjects**

Standard subdivisions are added for physiology and related subjects, for physiology alone

Class here comprehensive works on internal biological processes

> *For biochemistry, see 572; for specific physiological systems in animals, regional histology and physiology in animals, see 573; for specific parts of and physiological systems in plants, see 575; for genetics, see 576.5*

> *See Manual at 571–575 vs. 630*

## SUMMARY

| | |
|---|---|
| 571.01–.09 | **Standard subdivisions** |
| .1 | **Animals** |
| .2 | **Plants and microorganisms** |
| .3 | **Anatomy and morphology** |
| .4 | **Biophysics** |
| .5 | **Tissue biology and regional physiology** |
| .6 | **Cell biology** |
| .7 | **Biological control and secretions** |
| .8 | **Reproduction, development, growth** |
| .9 | **Diseases** |

.01–.08      Standard subdivisions

> Notation from Table 1 as modified under 570.1–570.8, e.g., microscopy in physiology 571.0282

.09      History, geographic treatment, biography

.091 9      Space

> Class here space biology

.099 9      Extraterrestrial worlds

> Class extraterrestrial life in 576.839

## .1      Animals

> Class here comparative physiology

> Class comprehensive works on animals in 590

> *For comparative physiology of plants and microorganisms, see 571.2; for physiology of Protozoa, see 571.294*

.101–.109      Standard subdivisions

> Notation from Table 1 as modified under 590.1–590.9, e.g., microscopy in animal physiology 571.10282

.11–.19      Specific kinds of animals

> Add to base number 571.1 the numbers following 59 in 591–599, e.g., marine animals 571.1177, mammals 571.19; however, for physiology and related subjects in humans, see 612; for physiology and related subjects in domestic animals, see 636.0892

## .2      Plants and microorganisms

> Standard subdivisions are added for plants and microorganisms together, for plants alone

> Class here comparative physiology of plants and microorganisms, physiology of agricultural plants

> Class comprehensive works on plants in 580

.201–.209      Standard subdivisions

> Notation from Table 1 as modified under 580.1–580.9, e.g., microscopy in plant physiology 571.20282

.21–.28      Specific kinds of plants

> Add to base number 571.2 the numbers following 58 in 581–588, e.g., aquatic plants 571.2176, monocotyledons 571.24
>
> *For physiology of fungi, see 571.295; for physiology of algae, see 571.298*

.29      Microorganisms, fungi, algae

> Subdivisions are added for microorganisms, fungi, algae together, for microorganisms alone
>
> Class comprehensive works on microorganisms, fungi, algae in 579
>
> *See Manual at 571.629 vs. 571.29*

.290 1–.290 9      Standard subdivisions

> Notation from Table 1 as modified under 579.01–579.09, e.g., microscopy in microorganism physiology 571.290282

.291–.298      Specific kinds of microorganisms, fungi, algae

> Add to base number 571.29 the numbers following 579 in 579.1–579.8, e.g., marine microorganisms 571.29177, Protozoa 571.294

**.3      \*Anatomy and morphology**

> Class here comparative anatomy
>
> Subdivisions are added for either or both topics in heading
>
> *For anatomy and morphology of microorganisms, see 571.63329*

**.4      \*Biophysics**

> Class here effects of physical forces on organisms
>
> Class comprehensive works on biophysics and biochemistry in 572
>
> *For bioenergetics, physical biochemistry, see 572.43*

.43      \*Biomechanics and effects of mechanical forces

> Class here biodynamics, solid biomechanics
>
> Subdivisions are added for either or both topics in heading
>
> Class biomechanics of locomotion in 573.79343

.435      \*Gravity

.437      \*Pressure

.44      \*Effects of mechanical vibrations, sound, related vibrations

.443      \*Mechanical vibrations

> Class here subsonic vibrations

.444      \*Sound

---

\*Add as instructed under 571–572

| | |
|---|---|
| .445 | *Ultrasonic vibrations |
| .45 | *Radiobiology |
| .453 | *Radio waves and microwaves |

> Subdivisions are added for either or both topics in heading

| | |
|---|---|
| .454 | *Infrared radiation |
| .455 | *Light |
| .456 | *Ultraviolet radiation |
| .457 | *X rays |
| .459 | *Particle radiation |

> Including beta, gamma, neutron radiation; cosmic rays
>
> *For X rays, see 571.457*

| | |
|---|---|
| .46 | *Effects of temperature |
| .464 | *Low temperatures |
| .464 5 | *Cryogenic temperatures (Cryobiology) |
| .467 | *High temperatures |
| .47 | *Effects of electricity and magnetism |

> Subdivisions are added for effects of electricity and magnetism together, for effects of electricity alone, for effects of electromagnetism alone

| | |
|---|---|
| .49 | *Environmental biophysics |

> Effects of combinations of physical forces characteristic of unusual environments
>
> Including effects of climate, of high altitudes
>
> Class effects of a specific physical force with the force in 571.43–571.47

| | |
|---|---|
| .499 | *Extraterrestrial biophysics |

> Class here bioastronautics

*Add as instructed under 571–572

>        **571.5–571.9   Tissue biology, regional physiology, cell biology, biological control and secretions, reproduction, development, growth, diseases**

> Except for modifications shown under specific entries, add to each subdivision identified by † as follows:
>
> 01–08    Standard subdivisions
>> Notation from Table 1 as modified under 570.1–570.8, e.g., microscopy in physiology 0282
>
> 09         History, geographic treatment, biography
>> Notation from Table 1 as modified under 571.09, e.g., space biology 0919
>
> 1–2    Specific kinds of organisms
>> Add the numbers following 571 in 571.1–571.2, e.g., the subject in animals 1, the subject in plants 2
>
> 3       Anatomy and application of processes to other processes
>
> [301–309]    Standard subdivisions
>> Do not use; class in 01–09
>
> 33–38    Anatomy and application of specific processes to other processes
>> Add to 3 the numbers following 571 in 571.3–571.8, e.g., anatomy 33, biophysics 34, cell biology 36

> Class comprehensive works in 571.5

**.5**       **\*Tissue biology and regional physiology**

> Class here histology, histophysiology; comprehensive works on tissue and cell biology

> Subdivisions are added for tissue biology and regional physiology together, for tissue biology alone

> Class biophysics of tissues in general in 571.4; class biophysics of specific tissues in 571.55–571.58

> *For cell biology, see 571.6; for histogenesis, see 571.835*

.53       Tissue anatomy, morphology, culture

[.530 1–.530 9]     Standard subdivisions

> Do not use; class in 571.501–571.509

.533       \*Tissue anatomy and morphology

> Subdivisions are added for either or both topics in heading

.538       \*Tissue culture

> Class here organ culture, comprehensive works on tissue and cell culture

> *For cell culture, see 571.638*

\*Add as instructed under 571–572

>          571.55–571.57 Specific tissues in animals

         Class comprehensive works in 571.51

> *For tissues of a specific physiological system, see the system in 573, plus notation 35 from table under 573, e.g., tissues of circulatory system 573.135*

.55          †Epithelial tissues

.555          †Endothelium

.56          †Connective tissues

> *For adipose tissues, see 571.57*

.57          †Adipose tissues

.58          Specific tissues in plants

         Class comprehensive works in 571.52

> *For tissues of a specific part or physiological system, see the part or physiological system in 575, plus notation 35 from table under 575, e.g., tissues of leaves 575.5735*

[.580 1–.580 9]          Standard subdivisions

         Do not use; class in 571.5201–571.5209

.585          †Parenchyma

         Class here pith, sclerenchyma

.59          Regional histology and physiology

         Standard subdivisions are added for either or both topics in heading

> *For regional histology and physiology of animals, see 573.99; for regional physiology of plants, see 575.4; for regional histology of plants, see 575.4359*

.590 1–.590 9          Standard subdivisions

         Notation from Table 1 as modified under 570.1–570.9, e.g., microscopy in regional physiology 571.590282

.592          Fungi and algae

.592 9          Specific fungi and algae

         Add to base number 571.5929 the numbers following 579 in 579.5–579.8, e.g., regional physiology of mushrooms 571.59296

**.6**          **\*Cell biology**

         Class here cell physiology, cytology, eukaryotic cells, protoplasm

> *For reproduction and growth of cells, see 571.84; for cytopathology, see 571.936; for cytochemistry, see 572; for cell digestion, metabolism, nutrition, see 572.4; for cell respiration, see 572.47*

---

\*Add as instructed under 571–572
†Add as instructed under 571.5–571.9

.629              Microorganisms, fungi, algae

                  Number built according to instructions under 571–572

                  *See Manual at 571.629 vs. 571.29*

.63               Cell anatomy, morphology, biophysics, culture

[.630 1–.630 9]   Standard subdivisions

                  Do not use; class in 571.601–571.609

.633              *Cell anatomy and morphology

                  Class here ultrastructure

                  Subdivisions are added for either or both topics in heading

.634              *Cell biophysics

.634 3–.634 9     Specific topics of cell biophysics

                  Add to base number 571.634 the numbers following 571.4 in
                  571.43–571.49, e.g., effect of high temperatures on cells 571.63467

.638              *Cell culture

                  Class comprehensive works on tissue and cell culture in 571.538

.64               †Membranes

                  Class here biological transport

                  Class lipid membranes and their chemistry in 572.577; class protein
                  membranes and their chemistry in 572.696

                  *For membranes of specific cellular components, see 571.65–571.68; for
                  ion transport, see 572.3*

.65               †Cytoplasm

                  Class here endoplasmic reticulum, organelles

.654              †Cytoskeleton

                  Class here microfilaments, microtubules

.655              †Vacuoles

                  Including peroxisomes

                  Class here lysosomes, vesicles

.656              †Golgi apparatus

.657              †Mitochondria

.658              †Ribosomes

.659              †Plastids

*Add as instructed under 571–572
†Add as instructed under 571.5–571.9

.659 2        Plants and microorganisms

> Number built according to instructions under 571.5–571.9

> Class here chloroplasts

.66        †Nucleus

> Including linin network, nuclear envelope, nuclear membrane, nucleolus

> Class here nucleoplasm

> Class nucleic acids in 572.8

> *For chromosomes, see 572.87*

.67        †Cell movement

> Including basal body

> Class here cilia, flagella, irritability, pseudopoda

.68        †Cell walls

**.7**        **†Biological control and secretions**

> Biological control: control of an organism's own physiological processes

> Subdivisions are added for biological control and secretions together, for biological control alone

> *See also 632.96 for biological control of agricultural pests*

.71        Animals

> Number built according to instructions under 571.5–571.9

> Class here comprehensive works on endocrine and nervous systems

> > *For endocrine system, see 573.4; for nervous and sensory systems, see 573.8*

.72        Plants and microorganisms

> Number built according to instructions under 571.5–571.9

> > *See also 575.9 for animal-like physiological processes in plants*

.74        †Biochemistry of control

> Class here comprehensive works on hormones

> > *For animal hormones, see 573.44*

> > *See Manual at 573.44 vs. 571.74*

.75        †Homeostasis and physiological balance

> Including electrolytic balance, fluid balance

> Subdivisions are added for either or both topics in heading

†Add as instructed under 571.5–571.9

| .76 | †Body temperature |
|---|---|

Class here homoiothermy, poikilothermy

| .77 | †Periodicity |
|---|---|

Class here biorhythms, chronobiology

| .78 | †Dormancy |
|---|---|
| .785 | †Diapause |
| .786 | †Aestivation |
| .787 | †Hibernation |

Class comprehensive works on hibernation in 591.565

| .79 | †Secretion |
|---|---|

Other than hormones

Class here exocrine glands, comprehensive works on glands

Class excretory system of animals in 573.49

*For endocrine glands, see 573.4. For secretions of a specific organ or system, or ones related to a specific process, see the organ, system or process, plus notation 379 from add tables under 571.5–571.9, 573, 575, e.g., digestive secretions 573.3379*

| **.8** | **†Reproduction, development, growth** |
|---|---|

Class here physiology of life cycle, sexual reproduction

Subdivisions are added for any or all topics in heading

*See Manual at 571.8 vs. 573.6, 575.6*

| .81 | Animals |
|---|---|

Number built according to instructions under 571.5–571.9

Class comprehensive works on life cycle of animals in 591.56

*For reproduction, sexual reproduction in animals, see 573.6*

| .82 | Plants and microorganisms |
|---|---|

Number built according to instructions under 571.5–571.9

*For reproduction, sexual reproduction in plants, see 575.6*

| .829 | Fungi and algae |
|---|---|

Number built according to instructions under 571.5–571.9

Class reproduction and development of unicellular microorganisms in 571.8429; class sexual reproduction of unicellular microorganisms in 571.84529

†Add as instructed under 571.5–571.9

| .835 | Histogenesis |
|---|---|

Number built according to instructions under 571.5–571.9

Class here cell differentiation, tissue differentiation

Class cell differentiation in embryology, cell determination in 571.8636

| [.836] | Cell biology |
|---|---|

Do not use for cell differentiation; class in 571.835. Do not use for cell reproduction and growth; class in 571.84

| .84 | †Reproduction and growth of cells |
|---|---|

Subdivisions are added for reproduction and growth together, for reproduction alone

Class chromosome recombination in 572.877

*For cell differentiation, see 571.835*

| .844 | †Cell division |
|---|---|

Including centromeres, chromatids

Class here mitosis

| .845 | †Gametogenesis |
|---|---|

Including egg cells

Class here meiosis; germ, haploid, sex cells

*For maturation and fertilization of gametes, see 571.864*

| .845 2 | Plants |
|---|---|

Number built according to instructions under 571.5–571.9

Class here comprehensive works on palynology

| .847 | †Reproduction by asexual spores |
|---|---|

Class here asexual spores, sporulation

Class sexual spores (gametes) in 571.845

| .849 | †Cell growth |
|---|---|

Class cell differentiation in 571.835

*See also 571.936 for cell pathology and death*

| .85 | †Developmental genetics |
|---|---|
| .86 | †Embryology |

Class comprehensive works on developmental biology in 571.8

---

†Add as instructed under 571.5–571.9

| | | |
|---|---|---|
| .864 | †Fertilization | |

Including maturation of gametes

Class here zygotes

.864 2 Fertilization in plants and microorganisms

Number built according to instructions under 571.5–571.9

Class here pollination

*For coevolution of pollination, see 576.875*

.865 †Early cell division

Class here blastulas, gastrulation

.87 †Development after embryo

Class here maturation

Class comprehensive works on development in 571.8

.876 †Development in distinct stages

Including larvae

Class here comprehensive works on metamorphosis

*For embryo stage, see 571.86*

.878 †Aging

Class pathological aging and death in 571.939

.879 †Longevity

.88 Miscellaneous topics in reproduction

Limited to topics named below

[.880 1–.880 9] Standard subdivisions

Do not use; class in 571.801–571.809

.882 †Sex differentiation

*For gametogenesis, see 571.845*

.882 157 9 Sex differentiation in Hymenoptera

Number built according to instructions under 571.5–571.9

Class here physiology of caste differentiation among social insects

.884 †Alternation of generations (Metagenesis)

.886 †Hermaphroditism

.887 †Parthenogenesis

Class comprehensive works on asexual reproduction in 571.89

†Add as instructed under 571.5–571.9

| .889 | †Regeneration |

| .89 | †Vegetative reproduction |

Class here asexual reproduction

*For asexual reproduction of microorganisms, see 571.8429; for parthenogenesis, see 571.887*

| .892 | Microorganisms, fungi, algae |

Number built according to instructions under 571.5–571.9

Do not use for vegetative reproduction of plants; class in 575.49

| .892 9 | Specific microorganisms, fungi, algae |

Number built according to instructions under 571.5–571.9

Add to base number 571.8929 the numbers following 579 in 579.2–579.8, e.g., vegetative reproduction of fungi 571.89295

| **.9** | **\*Diseases** |

Class here pathology, histopathology, pathogenicity, pathophysiology; noncommunicable diseases

*For human diseases, results of experimental research on human diseases in animals, see 616; for comprehensive works on agricultural diseases, see 632. For diseases of a specific physiological system in animals, see the system in 573, plus notation 39 from table under 573, e.g., bone diseases 573.7639; for diseases of specific parts of and physiological systems in plants, see the part or system in 575, plus notation 39 from table under 575, e.g., diseases of leaves 575.5739*

| .91 | Animal diseases |

Number built according to instructions under 571–572

*For diseases of domestic animals, see 636.0896*

| .92 | Plant diseases |

Number built according to instructions under 571–572

*For diseases of domestic plants, see 632.3*

| .93 | Generalities of diseases |

| [.930 1–.930 9] | Standard subdivisions |

Do not use; class in 571.901–571.909

| .933–.938 | General topics of disease |

Add to base number 571.93 the numbers following 571 in 571.3–571.8, e.g., physical causes of diseases 571.934; however, for pathological aging, see 571.939

Class comprehensive works in 571.9

---

\*Add as instructed under 571–572
†Add as instructed under 571.5–571.9

.939 †Pathological aging and death

> Subdivisions are added for either or both topics in heading

> Class comprehensive works on physiology and pathology of aging in 571.878

.94 *Pathological biochemistry

.943–.948 Specific topics of pathological biochemistry

> Add to base number 571.94 the numbers following 572 in 572.3–572.8, e.g., protein deficiency 571.946

.95 †Toxicology

> Class here diseases and stress caused by pollutants, by water pollution; ecotoxicology, environmental diseases, poisons

> *For environmental diseases induced by physical stresses, see 571.934*

> *See Manual at 363.73 vs. 571.95, 577.27*

.954 Specific elements and groups of elements

[.954 01–.954 09] Standard subdivisions

> Do not use; class in 571.9501–571.9509

.954 3–.954 7 Specific elements and groups of elements

> Add to base number 571.954 the numbers following 546 in 546.3–546.7 for the element or group of elements only, e.g., metal toxicology 571.9543, mercury toxicology 571.954663

.956 †Air pollutants

> Class here toxicology of combustion gases

.957 †Organic compounds

> Including toxins

> Class organic pesticides in 571.959

.959 †Pesticides

.96 †Immunity

> Class here disease resistance, immune system, immunology, leukocytes, lymphocytes

> Class allergies in 571.972; class autoimmunity in 571.973; class immune deficiency diseases in 571.974

> *For immunity in relation to diseases in humans, see 616.079*

.964 †Immunochemistry and immune response

> Subdivisions are added for immunochemistry and immune response together, for immunochemistry alone

---

*Add as instructed under 571–572
†Add as instructed under 571.5–571.9

| .964 4 | †Interferons |
| .964 5 | †Antigens |
| | Class blood groups in 573.154 |
| | *See also 573.154 for blood groups* |
| .964 6 | †Immune response |
| | Including clonal selection |
| | Class here antigen recognition |
| | Class antigen-antibody reactions in 571.9677 |
| .964 8 | †Immunogenetics |
| | Including transduction, transfection, transformation |
| .966 | †T cells (T lymphocytes) |
| | Class here cell-mediated (cellular) immunity, cytotoxic T cells |
| | *See also 571.968 for killer cells* |
| .967 | †B cells (B lymphocytes) |
| | Class here antibodies (immunoglobulins) |
| | *For maternally acquired antibodies, see 571.9638; for antibody-dependent immune mechanisms, see 571.968* |
| .967 7 | †Antigen-antibody reactions |
| .968 | †Phagocytes and complement |
| | Including granulocytes, killer cells |
| | Class here antibody-dependent immune mechanisms |
| | Subdivisions are added for phagocytes and complement together, for phagocytes alone |
| | *See also 571.966 for cytotoxic T cells* |
| .968 5 | †Macrophages |
| .968 8 | †Complement |
| | Class activation of macrophages by complement in 571.9685 |
| .97 | Miscellaneous diseases |
| | Limited to those named below |
| [.970 1–.970 9] | Standard subdivisions |
| | Do not use; class in 571.901–571.909 |
| .972 | †Allergies |

†Add as instructed under 571.5–571.9

.973        †Autoimmunity

>   Class here autoimmune diseases

.974        †Immune deficiency diseases

.975        †Injuries and wounds

>   Subdivisions are added for either or both topics in heading

.976        †Deformities

>   Class here teratology

.978        †Tumors

>   Class here cancer

.98        †Communicable diseases

>   Class here diseases caused by living organisms, by microorganisms

>   Class poisons in 571.95; class comprehensive works on immunity to communicable diseases in 571.96

>   *For specific communicable diseases, see 571.99*

.986        †Disease vectors

.99        Specific communicable diseases

[.990 1–.990 9]        Standard subdivisions

>   Do not use; class in 571.9801–571.9809

.992–.995        Diseases caused by microorganisms and fungi

>   Add to base number 571.99 the numbers following 579 in 579.2–579.5 for the organism only, e.g., protozoan diseases 571.994; then add 1 and to the result add further the numbers following 571 in 571.1–571.2, e.g., protozoan diseases in animals 571.99411, protozoan diseases in plants 571.99412
>>   Do not add notation 12 (derived from 571.2) to 571.9928 (diseases caused by plant viruses) except for viral diseases of specific kinds of plants. Do not add notation 1293 (derived from 571.293) to 571.9926 (diseases caused by bacterial viruses) except for viral diseases of specific kinds of bacteria

>   Class comprehensive works in 571.98

.999        †Parasitic diseases

>   Class here diseases caused by animals, by endoparasites, by worms, comprehensive works on parasitism

>   *For protozoan diseases, see 571.994; for ecology of parasitism, see 577.857*

†Add as instructed under 571.5–571.9

# 572     *Biochemistry

Class here cytochemistry, histochemistry; comprehensive works on biochemistry of nonmetallic elements and their compounds; comprehensive works on biochemistry and biophysics; interdisciplinary works on biochemicals, on macromolecules

*For chemistry of biochemicals, see 547; for chemistry of macromolecules, see 547.7; for biophysics, see 571.4; for biochemistry of control processes, see 571.74; for pathological biochemistry, see 571.94; for immunochemistry, see 571.964; for biogeochemistry, see 577.14; for industrial biochemistry, see 660.63. For biochemistry of a specific physiological system in animals, see the system in 573, plus notation 4 from table under 573, e.g., chemistry of circulatory fluids in animals 573.154; for biochemistry of a reproductive organ or physiological system in plants, see the organ or system in 575.6–575.9, plus notation 4 from table under 575.6–575.9, e.g., chemistry of circulatory fluids in plants 575.754*

### SUMMARY

| | |
|---|---|
| 572.3 | General topics of biochemistry |
| .4 | Metabolism |
| .5 | Miscellaneous chemicals |
| .6 | Proteins |
| .7 | Enzymes |
| .8 | Biochemical genetics |

.3      **General topics of biochemistry**

Including ion transport

[.301–.309]      Standard subdivisions

Do not use; class in 572.01–572.09

.33      *Molecular structure

Class here bonds, conformation, sequences of polymers and other component units of large molecules, theoretical chemistry

Class structure-activity relationships in 572.4; class molecular biology (biochemical genetics) in 572.8

.36      *Analytical biochemistry

.38      *Biochemical evolution

Class comprehensive works on molecular evolution in 572.838

*For biochemistry of origin of life, see 576.83*

.39      *Nutritional requirements

Class conditions needed for life to begin in 576.83

*For a specific kind of chemical requirement, see the chemical in 572.5–572.8, plus notation 39 from table under 572.5–572.8, e.g., vitamin requirements 572.5839*

*Add as instructed under 571–572

**.4** ***Metabolism**

Class here cell digestion and metabolism, structure-activity relationships, comprehensive biological works on nutrition

Class molecular structure in 572.33; class interdisciplinary works on human nutrition in 363.8

*For metabolism of a specific chemical, see the chemical in 572.5–572.8, plus notation 4 from table under 572.5–572.8, e.g., metabolism of enzymes 572.74, enzyme kinetics 572.744; for a specific aspect of biology of nutrition, see the aspect, e.g., nutritional requirements 572.39, digestive system 573.3*

**.41** Animal metabolism

Number built according to instructions under 571–572

Class comprehensive works on animal digestion in 573.3

**.43** *Energy metabolism

Class here biochemical interactions, reactions; bioenergetics, energy phenomena in organisms, physical biochemistry

Class effects of physical agents on organisms, comprehensive works on biophysics in 571.4

*For bonds, see 572.33*

**.435** *Photobiochemistry and bioluminescence

Subdivisions are added for photobiochemistry and bioluminescence together, for photobiochemistry alone

*For photosynthesis, see 572.46*

**.435 8** *Bioluminescence

*For bioluminescent organs, see 573.95*

**.436** *Thermodynamics

Class here thermobiology, thermochemistry

**.437** *Bioelectrochemistry

*For electric organs, see 573.97*

**.44** *Reaction kinetics

**.45** *Biosynthesis (Anabolism)

*For photosynthesis, see 572.46*

**.46** *Photosynthesis

Class here chlorophylls

**.47** *Cell respiration

Class here tissue respiration, comprehensive works on respiration

*Add as instructed under 571–572

.471        Cell respiration in animals

> Number built according to instructions under 571–572
>
> Class comprehensive works on respiration in animals in 573.2

.472        Cell respiration in plants and microorganisms

> Number built according to instructions under 571–572
>
> *For gas exchange from surface tissues of plants, see 575.8*

.475        *Tricarboxylic acid cycle

> Variant names: citric acid cycle, Krebs cycle
>
> Class here adenosine triphosphate

.478        *Anaerobic respiration

.48        *Catabolism

.49        *Fermentation

---

> ## 572.5–572.8 Specific biochemicals and biochemical genetics

Except for modifications shown under specific entries, add to each subdivision identified by † as follows:

01–08    Standard subdivisions
       Notation from Table 1 as modified under 570.1–570.8, e.g., microscopy in physiology 0282

09        History, geographic treatment, biography
       Notation from Table 1 as modified under 571.09, e.g., space biology 0919

1–2    Specific kinds of organisms
       Add the numbers following 571 in 571.1–571.2, e.g., the subject in animals 1, the subject in plants 2

3        General topics in biochemistry

[301–309]    Standard subdivisions
       Do not use; class in 01–09

33–39    Anatomy and application of specific processes to other processes
       Add to 3 the numbers following 572.3 in 572.33–572.39, e.g., molecular structure 33, nutritional requirements 39

4        Metabolism and genetic aspects
       Subdivisions are added for either or both topics in heading

401–408    Standard subdivisions
       Notation from Table 1 as modified under 570.1–570.8, e.g., microscopy 40282

409        History, geographic treatment, biography
       Notation from Table 1 as modified under 571.09, e.g., space biology 40919

41–49    Specific aspects of metabolism
       Add to 4 the numbers following 572.4 in 572.41–572.49, e.g., biosynthesis 45

Class comprehensive works in 572

---

*Add as instructed under 571–572

**.5** **Miscellaneous chemicals**

Not provided for elsewhere

[.501–.509]     Standard subdivisions

Do not use; class in 572.01–572.09

.51     †Bioinorganic chemistry

Class here biomineralization, coordination biochemistry, metals in biochemistry

*For bioinorganic chemistry of metals other than calcium, iron, copper, see 572.52; for bioinorganic chemistry of nonmetallic elements, see 572.53–572.55*

.511     Animals

Number built according to instructions under 572.5–572.8

*For biomineralization in animals, see 573.76451*

.515     †Trace elements

Class here micronutrients

*For a specific trace element, see the element in 572.51–572.55, e.g., iron 572.517*

.516     †Calcium

.517     †Iron

.518     †Copper

.52     Bioinorganic chemistry of metals other than calcium, iron, copper

[.520 1–.520 9]     Standard subdivisions

Do not use; class in 572.5101–572.5109

.523–.527     Specific metals

Add to base number 572.52 the numbers following 546 in 546.38–546.72, e.g., magnesium 572.52392; however, for calcium, see 572.516; for iron, see 572.517; for copper, see 572.518

---

>     572.53–572.55 Nonmetallic elements and their compounds in biochemistry

Class comprehensive works in 572

.53     †Oxygen

*For oxygen in respiration, see 572.47*

.539     †Water

Class fluid balance in 571.75

†Add as instructed under 572.5–572.8

| | |
|---|---|
| .54 | †Nitrogen |

> *For biogeochemical nitrogen cycle, see 577.145*

| | |
|---|---|
| .545 | †Nitrogen fixation |
| .548 | †Amines |

> *For alkaloids, see 572.549; for amino acids, see 572.65*

| | |
|---|---|
| .549 | †Alkaloids |
| .55 | Other nonmetallic elements and their compounds in biochemistry |

Class carbon, hydrogen in 572

| | |
|---|---|
| [.550 1–.550 9] | Standard subdivisions |

Do not use; class in 572.01–572.09

| | |
|---|---|
| .553 | †Phosphorus |
| .554 | †Sulfur |
| .555 | †Selenium |
| .556 | †Halogens |
| .56 | †Carbohydrates |

Class here saccharides

| | |
|---|---|
| .565 | †Sugars |

Including insulin

Class here monosaccharides, oligosaccharides

| | |
|---|---|
| [.565 49] | Fermentation |

Do not use; class in 572.49

| | |
|---|---|
| .566 | †Polysaccharides |
| .566 8 | †Structural polysaccharides |

Class cellulose in 572.56682; class chitin in 573.774

| | |
|---|---|
| .567 | †Conjugated carbohydrates |

Including glycosides

| | |
|---|---|
| .567 2 | Plants and microorganisms |

Number built according to instructions under 572.5–572.8

Including gums

| | |
|---|---|
| .57 | †Lipids |

Including waxes

Class here fats, fatty acids

†Add as instructed under 572.5–572.8

| .577 | †Membrane lipids |
| | Class here bilayer lipid membranes |

| .579 | †Steroids |

| .579 5 | †Sterols |
| | Class here cholesterol |

| .58 | †Vitamins |

| .59 | †Pigments |
| | Class chlorophyll in 572.46 |

## .6       †Proteins

*For hormones, see 571.74; for antibodies, see 571.967; for enzymes, see 572.7; for nucleoproteins, see 572.84; for prions, see 579.29*

| .633 | Molecular structure |
| | Number built according to instructions under 572.5–572.8 |
| | Class here amino acid sequence |

| .645 | Biosynthesis (Anabolism) |
| | Number built according to instructions under 572.5–572.8 |
| | Class here genetic translation |

| .65 | †Components of proteins |
| | Class here amino acids, peptides, polypeptides |
| | Class amino-acid sequence in 572.633 |

| .66 | †Simple proteins |
| | Including albumins, globulins, histones |

| .67 | †Structural proteins |
| | Class here collagen, scleroproteins |

| .68 | †Conjugated proteins |
| | Including chromoproteins, glycoproteins, lipoproteins, phosphoproteins |

| .69 | †Bioactive proteins |

| .696 | †Carrier and transport proteins |
| | Including cell receptors |
| | Class here membrane proteins |
| | Subdivisions are added for either or both topics in heading |

†Add as instructed under 572.5–572.8

.7      †**Enzymes**

> Class here coenzymes, cofactors
>
> *For enzymes performing a specific physiological function, see the physiological function, e.g., enzymes in cellular respiration 572.47, digestive enzymes 573.347*

.75–.78      Enzymes catalyzing reactions of specific chemicals

> Add to base number 572.7 the numbers following 572 in 572.5–572.8, e.g., proteolytic enzymes 572.76; however, for oxidases, see 572.791
>
> Class comprehensive works on classes of enzymes named according to the reaction they catalyze in 572.79

.79      Classes of enzymes named according to specific kind of reaction they catalyze

> Including isomerases, ligases, lyases
>
> *For enzymes catalyzing specific kinds of chemicals, see 572.75–572.78*

[.790 1–.790 9]      Standard subdivisions

> Do not use; class in 572.701–572.709

.791      †Oxidoreductases

> Oxidizing and reducing enzymes
>
> Including catalases, dehydrogenases, oxidases, zymases
>
> Class cellular respiration in 572.47

.792      †Transferases

.793      †Hydrolases

.8      †**Biochemical genetics**

> Class here cytogenetics, molecular biology, molecular genetics, physiological genetics; nucleic acids
>
> Class developmental genetics in 571.85; class comprehensive works on genetics in 576.5. Class genetic aspects of a specific biochemical with the specific biochemical in 572.5–572.7, plus notation 4 from table under 572.5–572.8, e.g., genetic regulation of enzymes 572.74
>
> *See Manual at 576.5 vs. 572.8*

†Add as instructed under 572.5–572.8

.838 Molecular evolution

Number built according to instructions under 572.5–572.8

Including mutagenesis, radiogenetics

Class here evolutionary genetics, genetic evolution

Class molecular evolution of a specific biochemical with the biochemical, plus notation 38 from table under 572.5–572.8, e.g., biochemical evolution of enzymes 572.738

*For molecular evolution during origin of life, see 576.83*

.84 Metabolism

Number built according to instructions under 572.5–572.8

Class here nucleic-acid hybridization, nucleic acid-protein interactions, comprehensive works on nucleoproteins

*For nucleoproteins in a specific situation, see the situation, e.g., nucleoproteins in chromosomes 572.87*

.85 †Nucleotides

Class here nucleosides

.86 †DNA (Deoxyribonucleic acid)

Class here chromosomal DNA, codons, genes, genomes

Class genetic transfection and transformation in 571.9648; class DNA as a component of chromosomes in 572.87

.863 3 Molecular structure

Number built according to instructions under 572.5–572.8

Class here DNA topology, double helix, genetic code; chromosome, gene, genome mapping; base, gene, nucleotide sequences

Class amino acid sequence in 572.633

*For base and nucleotide sequence in RNA, see 572.8833*

.864 5 Biosynthesis

Number built according to instructions under 572.5–572.8

Class here DNA replication

Class genetic transcription in 572.8845

.864 59 *DNA repair

.865 †Gene expression

Class here genetic regulation, regulation of gene expression

*Add as instructed under 571–572
†Add as instructed under 572.5–572.8

.869      †Extrachromosomal DNA

Including plasmid DNA, plasmids, transposons

Class here chloroplastic DNA, cytoplasmic inheritance, mitochondrial DNA

Class viruses in 579.2

*For transduction, transfection, transformation, see 571.9648*

*See also 572.877 for genetic recombination*

.87      †Chromosomes

Class here chromatin, chromosome numbers, nucleosomes

.873 3      Molecular structure

Number built according to instructions under 572.5–572.8

*For chromosome mapping, nucleotide sequences in chromosomes, see 572.8633*

.877      †Genetic recombination

Including aneuploidy, crossing over, inversion, translocation

Class somatic variation resulting from genetic recombination in 576.54; class recombinant DNA in 660.65

.88      †RNA (Ribonucleic acid)

*For viroids, see 579.29*

.884 5      Biosynthesis

Number built according to instructions under 572.5–572.8

Class here genetic transcription

Class genetic translation, protein synthesis in 572.645

.886      †Transfer RNA

†Add as instructed under 572.5–572.8

# 573 Specific physiological systems in animals, regional histology and physiology in animals

Class here comprehensive works on specific physiological systems

Except for modifications shown under specific entries, add to each subdivision identified by * as follows:

01–08    Standard subdivisions
       Notation from Table 1 as modified under 570.1–570.8, e.g., microscopy 0282

09       History, geographic treatment, biography
       Notation from Table 1 as modified under 571.09, e.g., space biology 0919

1     Comparative physiology of the system
       Add to 1 the numbers following 59 in 591–599, e.g., the system in mammals 19

2     Operation of one physiological system within another system
       Class hormones in 374

21      Circulation in the system

2101–2108    Standard subdivisions
       Notation from Table 1 as modified under 570.1–570.8, e.g., microscopy 210282

2109       History, geographic treatment, biography
       Notation from Table 1 as modified under 571.09, e.g., space biology 210919

211       Comparative physiology of circulation in the system
       Add to 211 the numbers following 59 in 591–599, e.g., circulation in the system in mammals 2119

213       Anatomy and general biological processes of circulation
       Add to 213 the numbers following 571 in 571.3–571.9, e.g., anatomy of circulation 2133, development of circulation 2138

25      Integument of the system
       Class here membranes enveloping an organ even if not an integral part of the organ, e.g., pericardium 573.1725

2501–2508    Standard subdivisions
       Notation from Table 1 as modified under 570.1–570.8, e.g., microscopy 250282

2509       History, geographic treatment, biography
       Notation from Table 1 as modified under 571.09, e.g., space biology 250919

251       Comparative physiology of integument in the system
       Add to 251 the numbers following 59 in 591–599, e.g., integument of the system in mammals 2519

253       Anatomy and general biological processes of integument
       Add to 253 the numbers following 571 in 571.3–571.9, e.g., cytology of integument of an organ 2536

27      Muscles of the system

2701–2708    Standard subdivisions
       Notation from Table 1 as modified under 570.1–570.8, e.g., microscopy 270282

2709       History, geographic treatment, biography
       Notation from Table 1 as modified under 571.09, e.g., space biology 270919

(continued)

**573** **Specific physiological systems in animals, regional histology and physiology in animals (continued)**

271      Comparative physiology of muscles of the system
         Add to 271 the numbers following 59 in 591–599, e.g., muscles of the system in mammals 2719

273      Anatomy and general biological processes of muscles
         Add to 273 the numbers following 571 in 571.3–571.9, e.g., biophysics of muscles 2734

28      Innervation of the system

2801–2808      Standard subdivisions
         Notation from Table 1 as modified under 570.1–570.8, e.g., microscopy 280282

2809      History, geographic treatment, biography
         Notation from Table 1 as modified under 571.09, e.g., space biology 280919

281      Comparative physiology of innervation of the system
         Add to 281 the numbers following 59 in 592–599, e.g., innervation of the system in mammals 2819

283      Anatomy and general biological processes of innervation
         Add to 283 the numbers following 571 in 571.3–571.9, e.g., diseases of innervation of an organ 2839

3      Anatomy and general biological processes of the system or region
         Class anatomy of, or a specific biological process within, a specific physiological subsystem in 2

[301–309]      Standard subdivisions
         Do not use; class in 01–09

33–39      Anatomy and specific biological processes of the system or region
         Add to 3 the numbers following 571 in 571.3–571.9, e.g., anatomy 33, biophysics 34, cell biology 36

4      Biochemistry

401–408      Standard subdivisions
         Notation from Table 1 as modified under 570.1–570.8, e.g., microscopy 40282

409      History, geographic treatment, biography
         Notation from Table 1 as modified under 571.09, e.g., space biology 40919

41      Biochemistry of the system in specific kinds of animals
         Add to 41 the numbers following 59 in 591–599, e.g., biochemistry of the system in mammals 419

43–48      Specific topics of biochemistry
         Add to 4 the numbers following 572 in 572.3–572.8, e.g., enzymes, biochemical genetics 573

Class comprehensive works on physiological systems in 571

*For specific physiological systems in plants, see 575; for specific physiological systems in humans, see 612; for specific physiological systems in domestic animals, see 636.0892*

*See Manual at 571–573 vs. 610*

## SUMMARY

[.01–.09]     Standard subdivisions

>   Do not use; class in 571.101–571.109

.1     **\*Circulatory system**

>   Class here cardiovascular system

>   *For circulation in a specific system or organ, see the system or organ, plus notation 21 from table under 573, e.g., circulation in brain 573.8621*

.15     \*Circulatory fluids

>   Class here blood

>   *For lymph, see 573.16*

.153 6     Cell biology

>   Number built according to instructions under 573

>   Class here blood cells, erythrocytes

>   *For leukocytes, see 571.96; for platelets, see 573.159*

.154     Biochemistry

>   Number built according to instructions under 573

>   Including blood groups

.155     \*Hematopoiesis

>   Class here hematopoietic (blood-forming) system

.155 5     \*Spleen

.155 6     \*Bone marrow

.156     \*Plasma

.159     \*Blood coagulation

>   Class here blood coagulation factors, platelets (thrombocytes)

---

\*Add as instructed under 573

.16      *Lymphatic system

> Class here lymph
>
> *For role of lymphatic system in immunity, see 571.96; for spleen, see 573.1555*

.163 6      Cell biology

> Number built according to instructions under 573
>
> *For leukocytes, lymphocytes, see 571.96*

---

\>      573.17–573.18 Circulatory organs

> Class comprehensive works in 573.1

.17      *Pumping mechanisms

> Class here heart

.18      *Blood vessels

.185      *Arteries

.186      *Veins

.187      *Capillaries

**.2**      **\*Respiratory system**

> Class here aerobic respiration, comprehensive works on respiration in animals
>
> *For cell and tissue respiration in animals, see 572.471*

.25      *Lungs

.26      *Organs accessory to lungs

> Including diaphragm, nasal sinuses, nose, trachea
>
> Class olfactory nerves in 573.877; class use of accessory respiratory organs in vocal communication in 573.92
>
> *For larynx, see 573.925*

.28      *Gills

**.3**      **\*Digestive system**

> Class here digestion
>
> Class comprehensive works on biology of nutrition in 572.4; class interdisciplinary works on human nutrition in 363.8
>
> *For cell digestion, see 572.4*

.35      *Mouth and esophagus

> Class here physiology of eating, ingestion
>
> Subdivisions are added for mouth and esophagus together, for mouth alone

*Add as instructed under 573

.355         *External mouth parts

            Class here beak, bill, cheeks, lips; feeding appendages and tentacles

.356         *Teeth

            *See also 591.47 for fangs and tasks*

.357         *Tongue

.359         *Esophagus

.36         *Stomach

            Including pylorus

.37         *Intestine

.377          *Pancreas

            Including islands of Langerhans

            Class insulin in 572.565

.378          *Small intestine

            Including duodenum, ileum, jejunum

.379          *Large intestine

            Including colon, rectum

.38         *Biliary tract

            Including bile ducts, gallbladder

            Class here liver

.383 79           Bile

              Number built according to instructions under 573

              Including bile acids

**.4**       **\*Endocrine and excretory systems**

            Class here endocrinology

            Subdivisions are added for endocrine and excretory systems together, for endocrine system alone

            Class comprehensive works on animal endocrine and nervous systems in 571.71

---

*Add as instructed under 573

.44　　　　　Biochemistry

Number built according to instructions under 573

Class here comprehensive works on animal hormones

*For hormones of a specific endocrine gland, see the gland, plus notation 4 from table under 573, e.g., pituitary hormones 573.454, estrogen 573.6654; for hormones controlling a specific function in 571.5–571.9, see the function, plus notation 374 from tables under 571.5–571.9, e.g., growth hormones 571.8374; for hormones controlling a specific animal physiological system, see the function in 573, plus notation 374 from table under 573, e.g., gastrointestinal hormones 573.3374*

*See Manual at 573.44 vs. 571.74*

---

>　　　　　573.45–573.47　Specific endocrine glands

Class comprehensive works in 573.4

*For islands of Langerhans, see 573.377; for testes, see 573.655; for ovaries, see 573.665; for nervous system, see 573.8*

.45　　　　\*Pituitary gland and hypothalamus

Subdivisions are added for pituitary gland and hypothalamus together, for pituitary gland alone

Class comprehensive works on neurohormones in 573.8374

.459　　　　　\*Hypothalamus

.46　　　　\*Adrenal glands

.47　　　　\*Thyroid and parathyroid glands

Subdivisions are added for thyroid and parathyroid glands together, for thyroid gland alone

.478　　　　　\*Parathyroid glands

.49　　　　\*Excretory system

Class here excretion, urinary system

.496　　　　　\*Kidneys

**.5　　　\*Integument**

Including physiology of color

Class here skin

Class color of hair, fur, scales, feathers, horns, related topics in 573.58–573.59; class exoskeleton in 573.77; class comprehensive works on color of animals in 591.472

*For integument of a specific system or organ, see the system or organ, plus notation 25 from table under 573, e.g., pericardium 573.1725, meninges 573.8625*

---

\*Add as instructed under 573

.58          *Hair and fur

              Subdivisions are added for either or both topics in heading

.59          *Scales, feathers, horns, related topics

              Including claws, nails

.595           *Scales

.597           *Feathers

**.6          *Reproductive system**

              Class here genital organs, reproduction, sexual reproduction, comprehensive
              works on urogenital system

              Class comprehensive works on reproduction, development, growth of animals
              in 571.81

              *For urinary system, see 573.49*

              *See Manual at 571.8 vs. 573.6, 575.6*

.65          *Male reproductive system

.655           *Testes

                  Class sperm in 571.845

.656           *Penis

.658           *Prostate

.66          *Female reproductive system

              Class pregnancy and lactation in 573.67

.665           *Ovaries

                  Class egg cells in 571.845; class eggs in 573.68; class plant ovaries in
                  575.665

.667           *Uterus

.67          *Pregnancy and lactation

              Subdivisions are added for pregnancy and lactation together, for pregnancy
              alone

.679           *Lactation

                  Class here mammary glands

.68          *Eggs

                  *For embryology of animals, see 571.861*

**.7          *Musculoskeletal system**

              Class here physiology of movement

*Add as instructed under 573

.735 6      Connective tissues

Number built according to instructions under 573

*For tendons, see 573.75356; for cartilage, see 573.76356; for ligaments, see 573.78356*

.75      *Muscles

*For muscles of a specific system or organ, see the system or organ, plus notation 27 from table under 573, e.g., heart muscles 573.1727*

.76      *Bones

Class here comprehensive works on skeleton

*For bone marrow, see 573.1556; for horns, see 573.59; for exoskeleton, see 573.77*

.764 51      Bioinorganic chemistry

Number built according to instructions under 573

Class here comprehensive works on biomineralization in animals

*For biomineralization in a specific system or organ, see the system or organ, plus notation 451 from table under 573, e.g., biomineralization in teeth 573.356451*

.77      *Exoskeleton

.78      *Joints

.79      *Locomotion and related activities

Including rest

Class here crawling, running, walking, work

Subdivisions are added for locomotion and related activities together, for locomotion alone

Class behavioral aspects of locomotion in 591.57

.798      *Flying

Class here physiology of wings

Class comprehensive works on wings in 591.479

**.8      *Nervous and sensory systems**

Subdivisions are added for nervous and sensory systems together, for nervous system alone

Class comprehensive works on regulation and control in animals, on endocrine and nervous systems in 571.71

*Add as instructed under 573

.85      *Nerves and nerve fibers

         Class here irritability, peripheral nerves

         Subdivisions are added for either or both topics in heading

         Class comprehensive works on nerves, nerve fibers, central nervous system in 573.8

         *For cell irritability, see 571.67; for nerves and nerve fibers in central nervous system, see 573.86. For innervation of a specific system or organ, see the system or organ, plus notation 28 from table under 573, e.g., innervation of muscles 573.7528*

.86      *Central nervous system

         Class here brain

.868      *Physiology of sleep

         Class sleep behavior in 591.56; class interdisciplinary works on sleep in 154.6

.869      *Spinal cord

.87      *Sense organs

         Including physiology of navigation

         Class here sensation, senses

         Class migration in 591.568

         *For eyes, see 573.88; for ears, see 573.89*

.875      *Touch

.877      *Chemical senses

         Class here olfaction, olfactory nerves, smell

         *For taste, see 573.878*

.878      *Taste

         Class here taste buds

.88      *Eyes

         Including light sensing by pineal gland

         Class here sight, vision

.89      *Ears

         Class here hearing

**.9      Miscellaneous systems and organs in animals, regional histology and physiology in animals**

         Limited to topics provided for below

---

*Add as instructed under 573

| [.901–.909] | Standard subdivisions |
|---|---|

> Do not use; class in 571.101–571.109

.92    *Communication systems

Class here vocal communication

Class comprehensive works on animal communication in 591.59

> *For receiving sensory systems, see 573.87; for bioluminescent communication, see 573.95; for communication involving electric organs, see 573.97*

.925    *Larynx

Class here vocal cords

.927    *Nonvocal sound communication

Class here physiology of stridulation

.929    *Chemical communication

Production of chemicals that arouse behavioral responses

.95    *Bioluminescent organs

Class here bioluminescent communication

.97    *Electric organs

.99    *Regional histology and physiology in animals

Subdivisions are added for either or both topics in heading

.995    *Head

.996    *Thorax

.997    *Abdomen

.998    *Appendages

Class locomotor functions of appendages in 573.79

# [574]      [Unassigned]

Most recently used in Edition 20

---

*Add as instructed under 573

# 575 Specific parts of and physiological systems in plants

Except for modifications shown under specific entries, add to each subdivision identified by † as follows:

01–09    Standard subdivisions

Notation from Table 1 as modified under 570.1–570.9, e.g., microscopy 0282

2    Specific kinds of plants

Class here comparative physiology, evolution of the part or system

Add to 2 the numbers following 58 in 581–588, e.g., monocotyledons 24

*For physiological systems in fungi and algae, see 571; for specific parts of fungi and algae, see 571.5929*

3    Generalities of parts or processes

[301–309]    Standard subdivisions

Do not use; class in 01–09

33–39    Generalities of specific parts or processes

Add to 3 the numbers following 571 in 571.3–571.9, e.g., histology 35, pathology 39

*For external description of parts and organs and their configurations, see 581.4*

## SUMMARY

| | | |
|---|---|---|
| 575.4 | **Stems** | |
| .5 | **Roots and leaves** | |
| .6 | **Reproductive organs** | |
| .7 | **Circulation, food storage, excretion** | |
| .8 | **Transpiration** | |
| .9 | **Animal-like physiological processes** | |

[.01–.09]    Standard subdivisions

Do not use; class in 571.201–571.209

## .4 †Stems

Class here comprehensive works on regional physiology, on shoots

*For regional physiology of roots, see 575.54; for leaves, see 575.57*

.435 9    Regional histology

Number built according to instructions under 575

Class here comprehensive works on regional histology of plants

*For regional histology of roots, see 575.54359; for regional histology of leaves, see 575.57359*

.45    Special features of stems

Limited to those named below

[.450 1–.450 9]    Standard subdivisions

Do not use; class in 575.401–575.409

---

†Add as instructed under 575

.451 †Primary epidermis

    Including physiology of color

    Class here comprehensive works on epidermis of plants

    Class comprehensive works on color of plants in 581.47

        *For bark, see 575.452; for transpiration from primary epidermis, see 575.8. For color of a specific organ or part, see the organ or part, e.g., color of leaves 575.57*

.452 †Bark

    Class here phloem

        *For circulation in phloem, see 575.7*

.454 †Nodes

.457 †Thorns

.46 †Wood

    Class here xylem

        *For circulation in phloem, see 575.7*

.48 †Growing points and layers

    Class here meristem

    Subdivisions are added for either or both topics in heading

.485 †Apical meristem

.486 †Buds

.488 †Cambium

.49 †Stems specialized for reproduction

    Class here asexual reproduction, vegetative reproduction, underground stems

    Class food storage in specialized stems in 575.78; class comprehensive works on reproduction of plants in 575.6

.495 †Bulbs

.496 †Corms

.497 †Rhizomes

.498 †Tubers

.499 †Runners (Stolons)

**.5 Roots and leaves**

†Add as instructed under 575

.54 †Roots

> *For absorption of water and nutrients by roots, see 575.76*

> *See also 575.49 for underground stems*

.545–.548 Specific aspects of roots

> Add to base number 575.54 the numbers following 575.4 in 575.45–575.48, e.g., xylem in roots 575.546

.57 †Leaves

> *For transpiration from leaves, see 575.8*

---

> **575.6–575.9 Reproductive organs and physiological systems in plants**

> Except for modifications shown under specific entries, add to each subdivision identified by * as follows:
> 01–09    Standard subdivisions
> Notation from Table 1 as modified under 570.1–570.9, e.g., microscopy 0282
> 2–3    Specific kinds of plants; generalities of organs and systems
> Add as instructed under 575, e.g., the organ or process in monocotyledons 24, histology 35
> 4    Biochemistry
> 401–408    Standard subdivisions
> Notation from Table 1 as modified under 570.1–570.8, e.g., microscopy 40282
> 409    History, geographic treatment, biography
> Notation from Table 1 as modified under 571.09, e.g., space biology 40919
> 42    Biochemistry in specific kinds of plants
> Add to 42 the numbers following 58 in 581–588, e.g., biochemistry of the organ or process in monocotyledons 42
> 43–48    Specific topics of biochemistry
> Add to 4 the numbers following 572 in 572.3–572.8, e.g., enzymes 47, biochemical genetics 48

> Class comprehensive works in 571.2

.6    **\*Reproductive organs**

> Class here flowers, reproduction, sexual reproduction, sporangia

> Class pollination in 571.8642; class comprehensive works on reproduction, development, growth of plants in 571.82; class interdisciplinary works on flowers in 582.13

> *For asexual reproduction, vegetative reproduction, see 575.49*

> *See Manual at 571.8 vs. 573.6, 575.6*

---

\*Add as instructed under 575.6–575.9
†Add as instructed under 575

| .65 | *Male reproductive organs |
|---|---|

Class here anthers, microsporangia, stamens

Class pollen (microspores) in 571.845

| .66 | *Female reproductive organs |
|---|---|

Class here pistils

Class fruits in 575.67

| .665 | *Ovaries |
|---|---|

Class here carpels, megasporangia

Class egg cells (megaspores) in 571.845; class seeds in 575.68

| .67 | *Fruits |
|---|---|

Including nuts

*For seeds, see 575.68*

| .68 | *Seeds |
|---|---|

*For embryology of plants (including germination of seeds), see 571.862*

| .69 | *Other flower parts |
|---|---|

Class here petals, sepals

| **.7** | **\*Circulation, food storage, excretion** |
|---|---|

Subdivisions are added for circulation, food storage, excretion together; for circulation alone

Class transpiration in 575.8

*For a specific circulatory tissue, see the tissue, e.g., phloem 575.452, xylem 575.46*

| .75 | *Circulatory fluids |
|---|---|

Class here sap

| .76 | *Absorption of water and nutrients |
|---|---|

Subdivisions are added for either or both topics in heading

| .78 | *Food and water storage |
|---|---|

Subdivisions are added for food and water storage together, for food storage alone

| .79 | *Excretion |
|---|---|

Class here internal isolation of unusable substances

*Add as instructed under 575.6–575.9

**.8** **\*Transpiration**

Class here gas exchange from surface tissues

*For a specific tissue or organ of transpiration, see the tissue or organ, e.g., leaves 575.57*

**.9** **\*Animal-like physiological processes**

Class here behavior of plants

**.97** **\*Movement**

*For movement that is a direct result of growth, see 571.82*

**.98** **\*Sensitivity**

Class here irritability

**.99** **\*Physiology of predatory activity**

Trapping mobile organisms

Class comprehensive works on carnivorous plants in 583.75

---

> **576–578 General and external biological phenomena**

Class general and external biological phenomena of microorganisms, fungi, algae in 579; class general and external biological phenomena of plants in 580; class general and external biological phenomena of animals in 590; class comprehensive works in 578

**576** **Genetics and evolution**

Except for modifications shown under specific entries, add to each subdivision identified by † as follows:
01–09    Standard subdivisions
         Notation from Table 1 as modified under 570.1–570.9, e.g., microscopy 0282

**.01–.09**    **Standard subdivisions**

Notation from Table 1 as modified under 570.1–570.9, e.g., microscopy in study of genetics and evolution 576.0282

**.5** **†Genetics**

Class here heredity, experimental works on genetics of specific organisms; interdisciplinary works on genetics

*For biochemical, molecular, physiological genetics; cytogenetics, see 572.8; for genetics of microorganisms, fungi, algae, see 579.135; for genetics of plants, see 581.35; for genetics of animals, see 591.35. For a specific aspect of genetics, see the aspect, e.g., eugenics 363.92, medical genetics 616.042, genetic engineering 660.65*

*See Manual at 576.5 vs. 572.8*

---

\*Add as instructed under 575.6–575.9
†Add standard subdivisions as instructed under 576

.52 †Laws of genetics

    Class here Mendel's laws

.53 †Genetic makeup

    Class here genotypes, phenotypes

    Class biochemical aspects of genetic makeup in 572.8

.54 †Variation

    Class here factors affecting heredity and variation

    *For genetic recombination as a factor affecting heredity and variation, see 572.877*

    *See also 571.9648 for transduction, transformation; also 572.869 for transposons*

.542 †Environmental factors (Mutagens)

    Class here chemical mutagens

    Class toxic aspects of mutagens in 571.95; class mutagenesis, radiogenetics in 572.838

.544 †Breeding patterns

    Class here inbreeding

.549 †Mutation

    Class biochemistry of mutation (mutagenesis) in 572.838

.58 †Population genetics

    Class here ecological genetics, gene pools, role of populations as vehicles of evolution

    Class role of species in evolution in 576.86; class comprehensive works on population biology in 577.88

**.8 †Evolution**

    Including homoplasy

    Class creationism in 231.7652

    *For evolution of microorganisms, see 579.138; for evolution of plants, see 581.38; for evolution of animals, see 591.38. For evolution of a specific internal process or structure, see the process or structure, e.g., molecular evolution 572.838, evolution of circulatory system 573.1*

    *See Manual at 231.7652 vs. 213, 500, 576.8; also at 576.8 vs. 560*

.801 Philosophy and theory

    Do not use for theories; class in 576.82

---

†Add standard subdivisions as instructed under 576

| .82 | †Theories of evolution |
|---|---|

Including punctuated equilibrium

Class here Darwinism, natural selection

Class sexual selection in 591.562

| .827 | †Lamarckian theories |
|---|---|

Class here inheritance of acquired characteristics

| .83 | †Origin of life |
|---|---|

Including spontaneous generation

Class here conditions needed for life to begin, biochemistry of forms of life before achievement of full self-replication

Class comprehensive works on molecular evolution in 572.838

| .839 | †Extraterrestrial life |
|---|---|

Including theory of extraterrestrial origin of life on earth

Class here astrobiology

Class extraterrestrial civilization, extraterrestrial intelligence in 999

*See also 571.0919 for space biology*

| .84 | †Evolutionary cycles |
|---|---|

Class here catastrophes, extinction, radiation

| .85 | †Factors affecting evolution |
|---|---|

Including symbiosis

Class here genotype-environment interaction

Class comprehensive works on symbiosis in 577.85

*For role of genetics in evolution, see 576.5; for natural selection, see 576.82*

| .855 | †Sexual factors |
|---|---|

Class here evolution of sexes

Class sexual selection in 591.562

| .86 | †Speciation |
|---|---|

Class here role of species in evolution

Class role of populations in evolution in 576.58; class comprehensive works on species in 578.012

| .87 | †Coevolution |
|---|---|

Class symbiosis as a factor affecting evolution in 576.85

†Add standard subdivisions as instructed under 576

.875        †Coevolution of flowering plants and insects

Class here coevolution of flowering plants with insect-like pollinators

.88        †Phylogeny

# 577    Ecology

Including ecotones

Class here biomes, ecosystems, terrestrial ecology

Except for modifications shown under specific entries, add to each subdivision identified by * as follows:

    01–08     Standard subdivisions
                Notation from Table 1 as modified under 578.01–578.08, e.g., microscopy 0282
    09         History, geographic treatment, biography
    [0914–0919]    Areas, regions, places in general other than polar, temperate, tropical regions
                Do not use; class in 577.3–577.7

Unless other instructions are given, class a subject with aspects in two or more subdivisions of 577 in the number coming last, e.g., grassland swamps 577.684 (*not* 577.4)

*For paleoecology, see 560.45; for ecology of microorganisms, fungi, algae, see 579.17; for plant ecology, see 581.7; for animal ecology, see 591.7*

*See Manual at 333.7–333.9 vs. 363.1, 363.73, 577; also at 577.3–577.7 vs. 578.73–578.77*

## SUMMARY

| | |
|---|---|
| 577.01–.09 | **Standard subdivisions** |
| .1 | **Specific ecosystem processes** |
| .2 | **Specific factors affecting ecology** |
| .3 | **Forest ecology** |
| .4 | **Grassland ecology** |
| .5 | **Ecology of miscellaneous environments** |
| .6 | **Aquatic ecology** |
| .7 | **Marine ecology** |
| .8 | **Synecology and population biology** |

.01–.08      Standard subdivisions

Notation from Table 1 as modified under 578.01–578.08, e.g., microscopy 577.0282

.09         History, geographic treatment, biography

[.091 4–.091 9]    Areas, regions, places in general other than polar, temperate, tropical regions

Do not use; class in 577.3–577.7

.1       **Specific ecosystem processes**

[.101–.109]    Standard subdivisions

Do not use; class in 577.01–577.09

†Add standard subdivisions as instructed under 576

| .13 | *Ecological bioenergetics |

Class here energy budget, energy flow, physics in ecology

| .14 | *Environmental chemistry |

Class here biogeochemical cycles, biogeochemistry

Class eutrophication in 577.63158; class comprehensive works on biochemistry and biogeochemistry in 572

> *For ecological bioenergetics, see 577.13; for environmental chemistry of pollution, see 577.27*

| .144 | *Carbon cycle |

Including carbon dioxide sinks

| .145 | *Nitrogen cycle |

| .15 | *Biological productivity |

Class here primary productivity

Class eutrophication in 577.63158

| .16 | *Food chains |

Class here ecological pyramids, multitrophic reactions

| .18 | *Ecological succession |

Including biological invasions

> *See also 578.62 for nonnative species*

| **.2** | **Specific factors affecting ecology** |

> *For effect of a specific kind of microorganism, fungi, algae on the ecology, see the organism in 579.2–579.8, plus notation 17 from instructions at 579.2–579.8, e.g., effect of red algae on ecology 579.8917; for effect of a specific kind of plant on the ecology, see the plant in 583–588, plus notation 17 from instructions at 583–588, e.g., effect of grasses on ecology 589.917; for effect of a specific kind of animal on the ecology, see the animal in 592–599, plus notation 17 from instructions at 592–599, e.g., effect of wolves on ecology 599.77317*

| [.201–.209] | Standard subdivisions |

Do not use; class in 577.01–577.09

| .22 | *Biometeorology (Bioclimatology) |

Including effect of droughts, micrometeorology

Class acclimatization and temperature adaptation in 578.42

> *See also 571.95 for diseases caused by climate and weather*

| .23 | *Seasons |

Class seasonal adaptation in 578.43

---

*Add standard subdivisions as instructed under 577

.24      *Fire ecology

.26      *Autecology

> *For autecology of a specific kind of microorganism, fungi, algae, see the kind of organism in 579.2–579.8, plus notation 17 from instructions at 579.2–579.8, e.g., autecology of fungi 579.517; for autecology of a specific kind of plant, see the kind of plant in 583–588, plus notation 17 from instructions at 583–588, e.g., autecology of orchids 584.417; for autecology of a specific kind of animal, see the kind of animal in 592–599, plus notation 17 from instructions at 592–599, e.g., autecology of insects 595.717*

.27      *Effects of humans on ecology

> Class here effects of pollution on ecology

> Including fragmented landscapes

> Class comprehensive works on ecotoxicology, on environmental toxicology in 571.95; class interdisciplinary works on pollution in 363.73

>> *For soil pollution, see 577.5727; for water pollution, see 577.627*

>> *See also 304.28 for social consequences of pollution; also 577.55 for natural ecology of environments made by humans*

>> *See Manual at 363.73 vs. 571.95, 577.27*

.272      *Engineering works

> Including dams, land reclamation, roads

.272 6      *Thermal pollution

> Thermal pollution is primarily about water pollution; class comprehensive works in 577.62726

> Class interdisciplinary work on thermal pollution in 363.7394

.273      *Agricultural pollution

> Class land reclamation in 577.272

.274      *War

.275      Pollution by acids, by specific elements and groups of elements

[.275 01–.275 09]      Standard subdivisions

> Do not use; class in 577.2701–577.2709

.275 2      *Pollution by acids

> Class here acidification

*Add standard subdivisions as instructed under 577

| .275 3–.275 7 | Pollution by specific elements and groups of elements |
|---|---|

Add to base number 577.275 the numbers following 546 in 546.3–546.7 for the element or group of elements only, e.g., influence of metals on ecology 577.2753, influence of mercury 577.275663; then to the result add standard subdivision notation as modified under 577.01–577.09, e.g., microscopy in study of pollution by metals 577.27530282

Class comprehensive works in 577.27

| .276 | *Air pollution |
|---|---|

Including pollution by gases contributing to greenhouse effect (global warming), to ozone layer depletion

Class here pollution by combustion gases

| .277 | *Radioactive pollution |
|---|---|

Class here radioecology

| .278 | *Pollution by organic compounds |
|---|---|

| .279 | *Pesticide pollution |
|---|---|

---

> ### 577.3–577.6 Ecology of specific nonmarine environments

Add to each subdivision identified by † as follows:
01–08    Standard subdivisions
    Notation from Table 1 as modified under 578.01–578.08, e.g., microscopy 0282
09    History, geographic treatment, biography
[0914–0919]    Areas, regions, places in general other than polar, temperate, tropical regions
    Do not use; class in 577.3–577.7
1    Specific ecosystem processes
    Add to base number 1 the numbers following 577.1 in 577.13–577.18, e.g., food chains 16
2    Specific factors affecting ecology
    Add to base number 2 the numbers following 577.2 in 577.22–577.27, e.g., effects of pollution 27; however, do not add notation 26 derived from 577.26 for autecology; class in number for the environment in 577.3–577.6 without use of notation 26

Class terrestrial ecology, comprehensive works on ecology in 577; class comprehensive works on biology of specific environments in 578.7

*See Manual at 577.3–577.7 vs. 578.73–578.77; also at 577.3–577.7 vs. 579–590*

| .3 | †Forest ecology |
|---|---|

Class here ecology of exploited forests, of woodlands

*For forest wetland ecology, see 577.683*

---

*Add standard subdivisions as instructed under 577
†Add as instructed under 577.3–577.6

| | |
|---|---|
| .309 13 | Torrid zone (Tropics) |
| | Class tropical rain forest ecology in 577.34 |
| .34 | †Rain forest ecology |
| | Including cloud forest ecology |
| | Class here ecology of jungles, tropical rain forests |
| [.340 913] | Torrid zone (Tropics) |
| | Do not use; class in 577.34 |
| .37 | †Taiga ecology |
| | Class here ecology of boreal forests, taiga wetlands |
| .38 | †Shrubland ecology |
| | Class here chaparral, heath (dry moor) ecology, Mediterranean-type ecosystems |
| | Class bog ecology, comprehensive works on moor ecology in 577.687 |

**.4** **†Grassland ecology**

Class here ecology of agricultural grasslands, of rangelands, of temperate zone grasslands

Class alpine grassland ecology in 577.538

*See also 333.74 for management of grasslands by society*

| | |
|---|---|
| [.409 12] | Temperate zones (Middle latitude zones) |
| | Do not use; class in 577.4 |
| [.409 13] | Torrid zone (Tropics) |
| | Do not use; class in 577.48 |
| .44 | †Prairie ecology |
| [.440 912] | Temperate zones (Middle latitude zones) |
| | Do not use; class in 577.44 |
| .46 | †Meadow ecology |
| [.460 912] | Temperate zones (Middle latitude zones) |
| | Do not use; class in 577.46 |
| .48 | †Savanna ecology |
| | Class here tropical grassland ecology |
| [.480 913] | Torrid zone (Tropics) |
| | Do not use; class in 577.48 |

†Add as instructed under 577.3–577.6

.275 3–.275 7     Pollution by specific elements and groups of elements

> Add to base number 577.275 the numbers following 546 in 546.3–546.7 for the element or group of elements only, e.g., influence of metals on ecology 577.2753, influence of mercury 577.275663; then to the result add standard subdivision notation as modified under 577.01–577.09, e.g., microscopy in study of pollution by metals 577.27530282
>
> Class comprehensive works in 577.27

.276     \*Air pollution

> Including pollution by gases contributing to greenhouse effect (global warming), to ozone layer depletion
>
> Class here pollution by combustion gases

.277     \*Radioactive pollution

> Class here radioecology

.278     \*Pollution by organic compounds

.279     \*Pesticide pollution

---

>     **577.3–577.6 Ecology of specific nonmarine environments**

> Add to each subdivision identified by † as follows:
> 01–08   Standard subdivisions
>         Notation from Table 1 as modified under 578.01–578.08, e.g., microscopy 0282
> 09      History, geographic treatment, biography
> [0914–0919]   Areas, regions, places in general other than polar, temperate, tropical regions
>         Do not use; class in 577.3–577.7
> 1    Specific ecosystem processes
>      Add to base number 1 the numbers following 577.1 in 577.13–577.18, e.g., food chains 16
> 2    Specific factors affecting ecology
>      Add to base number 2 the numbers following 577.2 in 577.22–577.27, e.g., effects of pollution 27; however, do not add notation 26 derived from 577.26 for autecology; class in number for the environment in 577.3–577.6 without use of notation 26

> Class terrestrial ecology, comprehensive works on ecology in 577; class comprehensive works on biology of specific environments in 578.7

> *See Manual at 577.3–577.7 vs. 578.73–578.77; also at 577.3–577.7 vs. 579–590*

.3     **†Forest ecology**

> Class here ecology of exploited forests, of woodlands
>
> *For forest wetland ecology, see 577.683*

---

\*Add standard subdivisions as instructed under 577
†Add as instructed under 577.3–577.6

| .309 13 | Torrid zone (Tropics) |
|---|---|
| | Class tropical rain forest ecology in 577.34 |

.34 †Rain forest ecology

Including cloud forest ecology

Class here ecology of jungles, tropical rain forests

| [.340 913] | Torrid zone (Tropics) |
|---|---|
| | Do not use; class in 577.34 |

.37 †Taiga ecology

Class here ecology of boreal forests, taiga wetlands

.38 †Shrubland ecology

Class here chaparral, heath (dry moor) ecology, Mediterranean-type ecosystems

Class bog ecology, comprehensive works on moor ecology in 577.687

**.4 †Grassland ecology**

Class here ecology of agricultural grasslands, of rangelands, of temperate zone grasslands

Class alpine grassland ecology in 577.538

*See also 333.74 for management of grasslands by society*

| [.409 12] | Temperate zones (Middle latitude zones) |
|---|---|
| | Do not use; class in 577.4 |
| [.409 13] | Torrid zone (Tropics) |
| | Do not use; class in 577.48 |

.44 †Prairie ecology

| [.440 912] | Temperate zones (Middle latitude zones) |
|---|---|
| | Do not use; class in 577.44 |

.46 †Meadow ecology

| [.460 912] | Temperate zones (Middle latitude zones) |
|---|---|
| | Do not use; class in 577.46 |

.48 †Savanna ecology

Class here tropical grassland ecology

| [.480 913] | Torrid zone (Tropics) |
|---|---|
| | Do not use; class in 577.48 |

†Add as instructed under 577.3–577.6

.275 3–.275 7       Pollution by specific elements and groups of elements

> Add to base number 577.275 the numbers following 546 in 546.3–546.7 for the element or group of elements only, e.g., influence of metals on ecology 577.2753, influence of mercury 577.275663; then to the result add standard subdivision notation as modified under 577.01–577.09, e.g., microscopy in study of pollution by metals 577.27530282

> Class comprehensive works in 577.27

.276           *Air pollution

> Including pollution by gases contributing to greenhouse effect (global warming), to ozone layer depletion

> Class here pollution by combustion gases

.277           *Radioactive pollution

> Class here radioecology

.278           *Pollution by organic compounds

.279           *Pesticide pollution

---

> ### 577.3–577.6   Ecology of specific nonmarine environments

> Add to each subdivision identified by † as follows:
> 01–08     Standard subdivisions
>              Notation from Table 1 as modified under 578.01–578.08, e.g., microscopy 0282
> 09         History, geographic treatment, biography
> [0914–0919]    Areas, regions, places in general other than polar, temperate, tropical regions
>              Do not use; class in 577.3–577.7
> 1       Specific ecosystem processes
>           Add to base number 1 the numbers following 577.1 in 577.13–577.18, e.g., food chains 16
> 2       Specific factors affecting ecology
>           Add to base number 2 the numbers following 577.2 in 577.22–577.27, e.g., effects of pollution 27; however, do not add notation 26 derived from 577.26 for autecology; class in number for the environment in 577.3–577.6 without use of notation 26

> Class terrestrial ecology, comprehensive works on ecology in 577; class comprehensive works on biology of specific environments in 578.7

> *See Manual at 577.3–577.7 vs. 578.73–578.77; also at 577.3–577.7 vs. 579–590*

.3         †**Forest ecology**

> Class here ecology of exploited forests, of woodlands

> *For forest wetland ecology, see 577.683*

---

*Add standard subdivisions as instructed under 577
†Add as instructed under 577.3–577.6

| | |
|---|---|
| .309 13 | Torrid zone (Tropics) |
| | Class tropical rain forest ecology in 577.34 |
| .34 | †Rain forest ecology |
| | Including cloud forest ecology |
| | Class here ecology of jungles, tropical rain forests |
| [.340 913] | Torrid zone (Tropics) |
| | Do not use; class in 577.34 |
| .37 | †Taiga ecology |
| | Class here ecology of boreal forests, taiga wetlands |
| .38 | †Shrubland ecology |
| | Class here chaparral, heath (dry moor) ecology, Mediterranean-type ecosystems |
| | Class bog ecology, comprehensive works on moor ecology in 577.687 |
| **.4** | **†Grassland ecology** |
| | Class here ecology of agricultural grasslands, of rangelands, of temperate zone grasslands |
| | Class alpine grassland ecology in 577.538 |
| | *See also 333.74 for management of grasslands by society* |
| [.409 12] | Temperate zones (Middle latitude zones) |
| | Do not use; class in 577.4 |
| [.409 13] | Torrid zone (Tropics) |
| | Do not use; class in 577.48 |
| .44 | †Prairie ecology |
| [.440 912] | Temperate zones (Middle latitude zones) |
| | Do not use; class in 577.44 |
| .46 | †Meadow ecology |
| [.460 912] | Temperate zones (Middle latitude zones) |
| | Do not use; class in 577.46 |
| .48 | †Savanna ecology |
| | Class here tropical grassland ecology |
| [.480 913] | Torrid zone (Tropics) |
| | Do not use; class in 577.48 |

†Add as instructed under 577.3–577.6

**.5**        **Ecology of miscellaneous environments**

Only those named below

Including upland ecology

Class ecology of atmosphere in 579.175

> *For ecology of a specific upland environment, see the environment, e.g., upland forest ecology 577.3*

[.501–.509]      Standard subdivisions

> Do not use; class in 577.01–577.09

.51        †Coastal ecology

> *For ecology of a specific environment in coastal zone, see the environment, e.g., coastal forest ecology 577.3, saltwater wetland ecology 577.69, sublittoral ecology 577.78*

.52        †Island ecology

> Class island forest ecology in 577.3; class island grassland ecology in 577.4

.53        †Mountain ecology

> Class mountain forest ecology in 577.3; class mountain grassland ecology other than alpine grassland ecology in 577.4

.538       †Alpine ecology

> Ecology above timber line
>
> Including alpine grassland ecology, paramo ecology

.54        †Desert ecology

> Class here ecology in arid lands, in semiarid lands
>
> *For sand dune ecology, see 577.583*

.55        †Ecology of environments made by humans

> Including roadside ecology
>
> Class here agricultural ecology
>
> Class meadow ecology in 577.46
>
> *For ecology of exploited forests, see 577.3; for ecology of agricultural grasslands, of rangelands, see 577.4; for urban ecology, see 577.56*
>
> *See also 577.27 for effects of humans on ecology*

.554       †Garden and household ecology

> Class here backyard ecology
>
> Subdivisions are added for garden and household ecology together, for garden ecology alone

.555       †Hedgerow ecology

†Add as instructed under 577.3–577.6

.56 †Urban ecology

Class here suburban ecology

.57 †Soil ecology

Including rhizosphere

Class sand dune ecology in 577.583

.58 †Ecology of hostile land environments

Not provided for elsewhere

Including cliff ecology

Class here extreme environments

.583 †Sand dune ecology

Desert or seashore dune ecology

.584 †Cave ecology

.586 †Tundra, permafrost, glacier, snow cover ecology

Subdivisions are added for tundra, permafrost, glacier, snow cover ecology together; for tundra ecology alone; for permafrost ecology alone

**.6 †Aquatic ecology**

Class here biological limnology, freshwater ecology

Class interdisciplinary works on limnology in 551.48

*For marine ecology, see 577.7*

.63 †Lake and pond ecology

Class here ecology of freshwater lagoons, reservoirs

Subdivisions are added for lake and pond ecology together, for lake ecology alone

Class comprehensive works on ecology of lakes, ponds, rivers, streams in 577.6; class comprehensive works on lagoons in 577.78

.631 5 Biological productivity

Number built according to instructions under 577.3–577.6

.631 58 *Eutrophication

Class social measures to control eutrophication in 363.73946; class engineering measures to control eutrophication in 628.112. Class eutrophication of a specific environment with the environment in 577.6, plus notation 15 from instructions at 577.3–577.6, e.g., eutrophication of swamps 577.6815

.636 †Pond ecology

*Add standard subdivisions as instructed under 577
†Add as instructed under 577.3–577.6

.639 †Salt lake ecology

Class here ecology of inland seas

.64 †River and stream ecology

Subdivisions are added for either or both topics in heading

.66 †Floodplain ecology

Class ecology of a specific environment on a floodplain with the specific environment, e.g., ecology of floodplain grasslands 577.4

.68 †Wetland ecology

Including riparian ecology

Class here marsh, swamp ecology

*For saltwater wetland ecology, see 577.69*

.683 †Forest wetland ecology

*For taiga, see 577.37*

.684 †Grass wetland ecology

.687 †Peat bog ecology

Class here bog, peatland, wet moor ecology; comprehensive works on moor ecology

*For heath (dry moor) ecology, see 577.38*

.69 †Saltwater wetland and seashore ecology

Class here ecology of coastal wetlands, salt and tide marshes

Subdivisions are added for saltwater wetland and seashore ecology together, for saltwater wetland ecology alone

.694 †Sea grass wetland ecology

.697 †Forest saltwater wetland ecology

[.697 091 3] Torrid zone (Tropics)

Do not use; class in 577.698

.698 †Mangrove swamp ecology

Class here tropical saltwater wetland forest ecology

.699 †Seashore ecology

Including ecology of rock pools, sea caves, tidal flats, tide pools

*For sand dune ecology, see 577.583*

†Add as instructed under 577.3–577.6

.7 **Marine ecology**

Class here saltwater ecology

Class comprehensive works on marine biology in 578.77

*For salt lake ecology, see 577.639; for saltwater wetland and seashore ecology, see 577.69*

*See Manual at 577.3–577.7 vs. 578.73–578.77; also at 577.3–577.7 vs. 579–590*

.701–.708 Standard subdivisions

Notation from Table 1 as modified under 578.01–578.08, e.g., microscopy in marine ecology 577.70282

.709 History, geographic treatment, biography

[.709 162] Oceans and seas

Do not use; class in 577.7

[.709 163–.709 165] Atlantic, Pacific, Indian Oceans

Do not use; class in 577.73–577.75

.71–.72 Specific ecosystem processes; specific factors affecting marine ecology

Add to base number 577.7 the numbers following 577 in 577.1–577.2, e.g., marine food chains 577.716, marine pollution 577.727; however, for autecology, see 577.7

.73–.75 Ecology of specific oceans and seas

Add to base number 577.7 the numbers following —16 in notation 163–165 from Table 2, e.g., Atlantic Ocean ecology 577.73; then add 0 and to the result add the numbers following 577 in 577.01–577.2, e.g., food chains in Atlantic Ocean 577.73016; however, for Sargasso Sea ecology, see 577.76362

*For Antarctic Ocean, see 577.709167*

---

> 577.76–577.79 Specific kinds of marine environments

Add to each subdivision identified by ‡ as follows:
01–08 Standard subdivisions
Notation from Table 1 as modified under 578.01–578.08, e.g., microscopy 0282
09 History, geographic treatment, biography
[09162] Oceans and seas
Do not use; class in base number
[09163–09165] Atlantic, Pacific, Indian Oceans
Do not use; class in 3–5
1–5 Specific ecosystem processes; specific factors affecting marine ecology; ecology of specific oceans and seas
Add to base number the numbers following 577.7 in 577.71–577.75, e.g., food chains 16, pollution 27, the environment in Atlantic Ocean 3

Class comprehensive works in 577.7

.76 ‡Surface regions

> Class here ecology of plankton

> *For freshwater plankton ecology, see 577.6*

.763 62 Sargasso Sea

> Number built according to instructions under 577.76–577.79

.77 ‡Marine benthic ecology

> Relating to floor of oceans and seas

> Class benthic ecology of abyssal, bathyal, hadal zones in 577.79

.78 ‡Nearshore ecology

> Including saltwater lagoons, comprehensive works on lagoons

> Class here sublittoral ecology

> *For freshwater lagoons, see 577.63; for saltwater wetland and seashore ecology, see 577.69*

.786 ‡Estuarine ecology

.789 ‡Reef ecology

> Class here coral reef ecology

.79 ‡Deep sea ecology

> Including ecology of bathyal and hadal zones

> Class here ecology of abyssal zone

.799 Hydrothermal vent ecology

**.8 Synecology and population biology**

> Standard subdivisions are added for synecology and population biology together, for synecology alone

> Class here ecological aspects of sociobiology, animal-plant relationships

> Except for modifications shown under specific entries, add to each subdivision identified by † as follows:
> 01–08 Standard subdivisions
> Notation from Table 1 as modified under 578.01–578.08, e.g., microscopy 0282
> 09 History, geographic treatment, biography

> Class ecological succession in 577.18; class rhizosphere in 577.57; class behavioral aspects of sociobiology in 591.5; class predation in 591.53; class comprehensive works on synecology of a specific environment in 577.3–577.7; class interdisciplinary works on sociobiology in 304.5. Class a general relationship between a small taxonomic group and a larger taxonomic group with the smaller group, e.g., plant-microbial relationships 579.178 (*not* 581.78), relationships between mushrooms and dicotyledons 579.6178 (*not* 583.178), between ferns and flowering plants 587.3178 (*not* 581.78)

‡Add as instructed under 577.76–577.79

| .801–.808 | Standard subdivisions |
|---|---|

> Notation from Table 1 as modified under 578.01–578.08, e.g., microscopy in study of synecology 577.80282

| .809 | History, geographic treatment, biography |
|---|---|

| .82 | †Ecological communities |
|---|---|

> Including ecological niches

> Class biomes in 577. Class plant associations characteristic of a specific environment with the environment in 577.3–577.7, e.g., prairie grass associations 577.44

| .83 | †Competition |
|---|---|

| .85 | †Symbiosis |
|---|---|

> Class symbiosis as a factor affecting evolution in 576.85; class symbiosis in the sense limited to mutually beneficial relationships in 577.852

| .852 | †Mutualism |
|---|---|

> Including commensalism

| .857 | †Parasitism |
|---|---|

> Class parasites in 578.65; class pathology of parasitism, comprehensive works on parasitism in 571.999

> When classifying parasitism of specific kinds of organisms in 579 or 580–590, prefer the number for the parasite. Emphasis on the host organism usually indicates that the work should be classed as a disease in 571.999

| .88 | †Population biology |
|---|---|

> Class here population dynamics

> *See also 576.58 for population genetics*

†Add standard subdivisions as instructed under 577.8

## 578     Natural history of organisms and related subjects

Standard subdivisions are added for natural history of organisms and related subjects together, for natural history of organisms alone

Class here descriptive biology, specific nontaxonomic kinds of organisms, comprehensive works on general and external biological phenomena, comprehensive works on taxonomic biology

Except for modifications shown under specific entries, add to each subdivision identified by * as follows:

     01–08     Standard subdivisions
                Notation from Table 1 as modified under 578.01–578.08, e.g., microscopy 0282
     09        History, geographic treatment, biography

*For internal biological processes of specific kinds of organisms, see 571–575; for genetics and evolution, see 576; for ecology, see 577; for natural history of microorganisms, fungi, algae, see 579; for natural history of plants, see 580; for natural history of animals, see 590*

*See Manual at 578 vs. 304.2, 508, 910*

.012         Classification

Including chemotaxonomy, cladistic analysis, cytotaxonomy, numerical taxonomy, species

Class here systematics, taxonomy

Class speciation in 576.86; class taxonomic nomenclature in 578.014; class comprehensive works on taxonomic biology in 578

.02       Miscellany

.028      Auxiliary techniques and procedures; apparatus, equipment, materials

Notation from Table 1 as modified under 570.28, e.g., microscopy in descriptive biology 578.0282

.028 8     Maintenance and repair

Do not use for preservation of biological specimens; class in 578.0752

.07       Education, research, related topics

.073      Collections and exhibits of living organisms

Class here history and description, guidebooks; bioparks

Add to base number 578.073 notation 1–9 from Table 2 for area in which collections, exhibits are found, e.g., collections of living plants and animals in China 578.07351

.074      Museums, collections, exhibits

Do not use for collections and exhibits of living organisms; class in 578.073

.075      Museum activities and services

.075 2     Preserving biological specimens

.09       History, geographic treatment, biography

[.091 4–.091 9]     Areas, regions, places in general other than polar, temperate, tropical regions

> Do not use; class in 578.73–578.77

.099 9     Extraterrestrial worlds

> Class extraterrestrial life in 576.839

## .4     *Adaptation

> Class here organisms illustrating specific kinds of adaptation
>
> Class adaptation of miscellaneous nontaxonomic kinds of organisms in 578.6

.41     *Size, weight, shape of organisms

.42     *Acclimatization and temperature adaptation

> Standard subdivisions are added for acclimatization and temperature adaptation together, for acclimatization alone
>
> Including phenology
>
> Class climate and weather as factors influencing ecology in 577.22
>
> *For seasonal adaptation, see 578.43*

.43     *Seasonal adaptation

> Class seasonal variation as a factor influencing ecology in 577.23

.46     *Reproductive adaptation

> Class reproductive physiology in 571.8

.47     *Protective adaptation, color

> Standard subdivisions are added for protective adaptation and color together, for protective adaptation alone
>
> Including mimicry
>
> Class color of a specific adaptation with the adaptation, e.g., color of reproductive adaptation 578.46
>
> *For camouflage, see 591.472*

## .6     *Miscellaneous nontaxonomic kinds of organisms

> Not provided for elsewhere
>
> Class here economic biology

.62     *Nonnative species

> Class here alien, exotic, introduced, invasive, naturalized species

.63     *Beneficial organisms

> *See Manual at 630 vs. 579–590, 641.3*

---

*Add standard subdivisions as instructed under 578

.65      *Harmful organisms

> Including parasites
>
> When classifying parasites under a specific kind of organism in 579 or 580–590, prefer number for the parasite. Emphasis on host organism usually indicates that the work should be classed as a disease in 571.999

.68      *Rare and endangered species

> Standard subdivisions are added for either or both topics in heading
>
> Including recently extinct species

**.7**      **Organisms characteristic of specific kinds of environments**

> Class here biology of specific kinds of environments
>
> Class specific kinds of adaptation characteristic of specific kinds of environment in 578.4; class miscellaneous nontaxonomic kinds of organisms characteristic of specific kinds of environments in 578.6
>
> *For ecology of specific kinds of environments, see 577*

[.701–.709]      Standard subdivisions

> Do not use; class in 578.01–578.09

.73–.75      Specific kinds of nonaquatic environments

> Add to base number 578.7 the numbers following 577 in 577.3–577.5 for the environment only, e.g., organisms characteristic of grasslands 578.74; then to the result add standard subdivisions as instructed under 578.01–578.09, e.g., collections of living grassland plants and animals 578.74073
>
> Class comprehensive works on terrestrial environments in 578
>
> *For space biology, see 571.0919; for extraterrestrial life, see 576.839*
>
> *See Manual at 577.3–577.7 vs. 578.73–578.77*

.76–.77      Aquatic environments

> Add to base number 578.7 the numbers following 577 in 577.6–577.7 for the environment only, e.g., marine organisms, marine biology 578.77; then to the result add standard subdivisions as instructed under 578.01–578.09, e.g., collections of living marine plants and animals 578.77073
>
> *See Manual at 577.3–577.7 vs. 578.73–578.77; also at 578.76–578.77 vs. 551.46, 551.48*

*Add standard subdivisions as instructed under 578

# 579    Natural history of microorganisms, fungi, algae

Standard subdivisions are added for microorganisms, fungi, algae together; for microorganisms alone

Class here microbiology, Protista, protophytes, Thallobionta (Thallophyta); descriptive biology of microorganisms, fungi, algae; taxonomic biology of microorganisms, fungi, algae; comprehensive works on biology of microorganisms, fungi, algae; interdisciplinary works on microorganisms, fungi, algae

> *For internal biological processes of microorganisms, fungi, algae, see 571.29.*
> *For a specific aspect of microorganisms, fungi, algae, see the aspect, e.g.,*
> *cooking mushrooms 641.658*
>
> *See Manual at 577.3–577.7 vs. 579–590; also at 579–590; also at 579–590 vs.*
> *571–575; also at 630 vs. 579–590, 641.3*

### SUMMARY

| | |
|---|---|
| 579.01–.09 | **Standard subdivisions** |
| .1 | **Specific topics in natural history of microorganisms, fungi, algae** |
| .2 | **Viruses and subviral organisms** |
| .3 | **Prokaryotes** |
| .4 | **Protozoa** |
| .5 | **Fungi** |
| .6 | **Mushrooms** |
| .7 | **Lichens** |
| .8 | **Algae** |

.01–.08      Standard subdivisions

Notation from Table 1 as modified under 578.01–578.08, e.g., collections of living microorganisms 579.073

.09      History, geographic treatment, biography

> *For history, geographic treatment, biography in specific kinds of*
> *environment, see 579.17*

[.091 4–.091 9]      Areas, regions, places in general other than polar, temperate, tropical regions

Do not use; class in 579.17

**.1**      **Specific topics in natural history of microorganisms, fungi, algae**

Class here specific nontaxonomic kinds of organisms

Except for modifications shown under specific entries, add to each subdivision identified by † as follows:

01–08      Standard subdivisions
         Notation from Table 1 as modified under 578.01–578.08, e.g., microscopy 0282

09      History, geographic treatment, biography

Unless other instructions are given, observe the following table of preference, e.g., beneficial marine microorganisms 579.163 (*not* 579.177):

| | |
|---|---|
| Miscellaneous nontaxonomic kinds of organisms | 579.16 |
| Adaptation | 579.14 |
| Genetics and evolution | 579.13 |
| Organisms characteristic of specific environments, ecology | 579.17 |

Class a specific topic in natural history of microorganisms, fungi, algae with respect to a specific taxonomic group with the group, plus notation 1 as instructed under 579.2–579.8, e.g., useful fungi 579.5163

**[.101–.109]**      Standard subdivisions

Do not use; class in 579.01–579.09

**.13**      †Genetics and evolution

**.135**      †Genetics

Class here works on genetic constitution of microorganisms, fungi, algae that elucidate their total function

Class experimental works on genetics of microorganisms, fungi, algae; comprehensive works on genetics in 576.5

*For biochemical genetics in microorganisms, fungi, algae, see 572.829*

**.138**      †Evolution

Class here phylogeny

**.14**      †Adaptation

**.141–.147**      Specific kinds of adaptation

Add to base number 579.14 the numbers following 578.4 in 578.41–578.47, e.g., seasonal adaptation 579.143

**.16**      †Miscellaneous nontaxonomic kinds of organisms

Not provided for elsewhere

Including nonnative, rare, endangered species

Class here economic microbiology

Class food microbiology in 664.001579

†Add standard subdivisions as instructed under 579.1

.163      †Beneficial organisms

> Including edible organisms

.165      †Harmful organisms

> Class here pathogenic and poisonous organisms
>
> *See Manual at 579.165 vs. 616.9041*

.17      Ecology, organisms characteristic of specific environments

> Standard subdivisions are added for either or both topics in heading
>
> Class here autecology, biology of specific environments
>
> Class aerial microorganisms, ecology of atmosphere in 579.175

.170 1–.170 8      Standard subdivisions

> Notation from Table 1 as modified under 578.01–578.08, e.g., microscopy in study of ecology of microorganisms 579.170282

.170 9      History, geographic treatment, biography

[.170 914–.170 919]      Areas, regions, places in general other than polar, temperate, tropical regions

> Do not use; class in 579.173–579.177

.171–.178      Specific topics in ecology, specific environments

> Add to base number 579.17 the numbers following 577 in 577.1–577.8, e.g., effect of pollution on microorganisms 579.1727, marine microorganisms, marine botany 579.177, effect of pollution on marine microorganisms 579.17727
>
> Class comprehensive works on terrestrial microorganisms, fungi, algae in 579

.175      Ecology of miscellaneous environments

> Number built according to instructions under 579.171–579.178
>
> Including aerial microorganisms, ecology of atmosphere

---

†Add standard subdivisions as instructed under 579.1

> ### 579.2–579.8  Specific taxonomic groups of microorganisms, fungi, algae

Except for modifications shown under specific entries, add to each subdivision identified by * as follows:

01–08    Standard subdivisions
            Notation from Table 1 as modified under 578.01–578.08, e.g., collections of living organisms 073
09            History, geographic treatment, biography
[0914–0919]    Areas, regions, places in general other than polar, temperate, tropical regions
            Do not use; class in 173–176
1             General topics of natural history of microorganisms, fungi, algae
            Add to base number 1 the numbers following 579.1 in 579.13–579.17, e.g., beneficial organisms 163

Class comprehensive works in 579

*For internal biological processes of specific kinds of microorganisms, fungi, algae, see 571–575*

.2        **\*Viruses and subviral organisms**

Class here animal viruses, vertebrate viruses, virology

Subdivisions are added for viruses and subviral organisms together, for viruses alone

*See also 579.327 for rickettsias*

.23       \*Invertebrate viruses

*For specific kinds of invertebrate viruses, see 579.24–579.25*

> ### 579.24–579.25  Specific kinds of viruses

Class comprehensive works in 579.2

*For specific kinds of bacterial viruses, see 579.26; for specific kinds of fungal viruses, see 579.27; for specific kinds of plant viruses, see 579.28*

*See Manual at 579.24–579.25*

.24       \*DNA viruses

.243      \*Double-stranded, enveloped DNA viruses

.243 2       \*Poxviridae

.243 4       \*Herpesviridae

.243 6       \*Baculoviridae

.244      \*Double-stranded, nonenveloped DNA viruses

.244 3       \*Adenoviridae

\*Add as instructed under 579.2–579.8

| .244 5 | *Papoviridae |
| | Including Papillomavirus, Polyomavirus, SV40 |
| .247 | *Single-stranded, nonenveloped DNA viruses |
| | Class here Parvoviridae |
| .25 | *RNA viruses |
| .254 | *Double-stranded, nonenveloped RNA viruses |
| | Including Reoviridae |
| .256 | *Single-stranded, enveloped RNA viruses |
| | Including Arenaviridae, Filoviridae, Paramyxoviridae |
| .256 2 | *Togaviridae |
| | Class here arboviruses |
| .256 6 | *Rhabdoviridae |
| | Including Lyssavirus |
| .256 9 | *Retroviridae |
| | Class here oncoviruses, comprehensive works on oncogenic viruses |

> *For a specific nonretrovirus oncogenic virus, see the virus, e.g., oncogenic papovaviruses 579.2445*

| .257 | *Single-stranded, nonenveloped RNA viruses |
| .257 2 | *Picornaviridae |
| | Including Poliovirus |
| .26 | *Bacterial viruses (Bacteriophages) |
| .27 | *Fungal viruses |
| .28 | *Plant viruses |
| .29 | *Subviral organisms |
| | Including prions |
| | Class here viroids |

**.3 *Prokaryotes**

Variant names: Monera, Schizomycetes, Schizophyta, bacteria

Class here bacteriology, Eubacteriales, comprehensive works on bacteria and viruses

Class bacteria culture for biological research in 571.638293

> *For viruses, see 579.2*
>
> *See Manual at 579.3*

---

*Add as instructed under 579.2–579.8

| .314 | Adaptation |
|---|---|
| | Number built according to instructions under 579.2–579.8 |
| .314 9 | †Anaerobic bacteria |
| .32 | Minor kinds of bacteria |
| | Not provided for elsewhere |
| | Including chemolithotrophic bacteria, colorless sulfur bacteria, Myxobacteria, Spirochetes |
| | Class comprehensive works on minor kinds of bacteria in 579.3 |
| | *See Manual at 579.3* |
| [.320 1–.320 9] | Standard subdivisions |
| | Do not use; class in 579.301–579.309 |
| .321 | *Archaeobacteria |
| | Including methanogenic bacteria, Halobacteriaceae, halophilic bacteria |
| .323 | *Aerobic-microaerophilic, motile, helical-vibrioid gram-negative bacteria |
| | Including Aquaspirillum, Azospirillum |
| .325 | *Anaerobic gram-negative straight, curved, and helical rods |
| | Including Bacteroides |
| .327 | *Rickettsias and Chlamydias |
| .328 | *Mycoplasmas |
| | Variant names: Mollicutes, Tenericutes |
| .33 | *Gram-negative aerobic rods and cocci |
| | Including Acetobacter, Brucella, Legionella, Neisseria |
| | *For Halobacteriaceae, see 579.321* |
| .332 | *Pseudomonas |
| | Subdivisions are added for the genus as a whole and for individual species |
| .334 | *Rhizobium |
| | Subdivisions are added for the genus as a whole and for individual species |
| .34 | *Facultatively anaerobic gram-negative rods |
| | Including Erwinia, Pasteurella, Photobacterium, Shigella, Yersinia |
| | Class here Enterobacteriaceae |

*Add as instructed under 579.2–579.8
†Add standard subdivisions as instructed under 579.1

| | |
|---|---|
| .342 | *Escherichia |

> Subdivisions are added for the genus as a whole and for individual species

| | |
|---|---|
| .344 | *Salmonella |

> Subdivisions are added for the genus as a whole and for individual species

| | |
|---|---|
| .35 | *Gram-positive cocci |

> Class here lactic acid bacteria
>
> *For Lactobacillus, see 579.37*

| | |
|---|---|
| .353 | *Staphylococcus |

> Subdivisions are added for the genus as a whole and for individual species

| | |
|---|---|
| .355 | *Streptococcus |

> Class here Lactococcus (lactic acid Streptococcus)
>
> Subdivisions are added for the genus as a whole and for individual species

| | |
|---|---|
| .36 | *Endospore-forming gram-positive rods and cocci |
| .362 | *Bacillus |

> Subdivisions are added for the genus as a whole and for individual species

| | |
|---|---|
| .364 | *Clostridium |

> Subdivisions are added for the genus as a whole and for individual species

| | |
|---|---|
| .37 | *Actinomycetes and related bacteria |

> Including Frankia, Lactobacillus, Listeria, Nocardia
>
> Subdivisions are added for Actinomycetes and related bacteria together, for Actinomycetes alone
>
> *See Manual at 579.3*

| | |
|---|---|
| .373 | *Irregular, nonsporing, gram-positive rods |

> Including Arthrobacter, Bifidobacterium, Corynebacterium

| | |
|---|---|
| .374 | *Mycobacteria |
| .378 | *Streptomycetes and related genera |

> Class here Streptomyces

*Add as instructed under 579.2–579.8

.38          *Anoxygenic phototrophic bacteria

             Including green bacteria

             Class here purple bacteria; comprehensive works on photosynthetic bacteria,
             on sulfur bacteria

             *For colorless sulfur bacteria, see 579.32; for oxygenic photosynthetic
             bacteria, see 579.39*

.385         *Purple nonsulfur bacteria

             Including Rhodobacter, Rhodopseudomonas

.39      *Cyanobacteria and Prochlorales

             Oxygenic photosynthetic bacteria

             Variant name for Cyanobacteria: Cyanophyta, blue-green algae

             Including Chroococcales, Nostocales, Oscillatoriales

             Subdivisions are added for Cyanobacteria and Prochlorales together, for
             Cyanobacteria alone

**.4      *Protozoa**

             Class here Sarcomastigophora

             *For a specific group or organism that may be regarded as either protozoa or
             algae, see the group or organism in 579.8, e.g., Euglenophyta (Euglenida)
             579.84*

---

>            579.42–579.45  Sarcomastigophora

             Class comprehensive works in 579.4

.42          *Zoomastigophorea (Zooflagellates)

             Class phytoflagellates, comprehensive works on flagellates in 579.82

.43          *Rhizopodea

             Including Arcellinida

             Class here Sarcodina

             *For Foraminifera, see 579.44*

.432             *Amoebida (Amoebas)

.44          *Foraminifera

.45          *Actinopoda

             Class here Radiolaria

             The term Radiolaria is sometimes limited to one of several subtaxa of
             Actinopoda

.47          *Sporozoa

*Add as instructed under 579.2–579.8

.48      *Cnidospora

         Including Microsporida

.49      *Ciliophora (Ciliates)

         Class here Ciliatea

.495      *Hymenostomatida

         Including Paramecium

**.5**     **\*Fungi**

         Class here Eumycophyta (True fungi), filamentous fungi, mycology

         Class comprehensive works on molds, on mildew in 579.53

>             *For lichens, see 579.7; for comprehensive works on mushrooms, on macrofungi, see 579.6*

.52      *Myxomycotina

         Variant names: Mycetozoa, Myxomycetes, Myxomycophyta, Myxomycota, slime molds

         Including Acrasia (cellular slime molds), Physarales, Stemonitales, Trichiales

         Class here Myxogastromycetidae

            *For Plasmodiophoromycetes, see 579.53*

---

>         579.53–579.59   Eumycophyta (True fungi)

         Class comprehensive works in 579.5

.53      *Miscellaneous fungi

         Not provided for elsewhere

         Including Chytridiomycetes, Hyphochytridiomycetes, Plasmodiophoromycetes, Trichomycetes, Zygomycetes; Rhizopus (bread molds), uniflagellate molds

         Class here Mastigomycotina, Phycomycetes; comprehensive works on molds, on mildew

         Class slime molds in 579.52

            *For Oomycetes, see 579.54; for ascomycete molds and mildew, see 579.56*

.54      *Oomycetes

         Former name: Biflagellates

.542      *Saprolegniales

---

*Add as instructed under 579.2–579.8

.546　　　　　　**\*Peronosporales (Downy mildew)**

　　　　　　　　　Including Phytophthora

.55　　　　　　　**\*Deuteromycotina**

　　　　　　　　　Variant names: Deuteromycetes, Fungi Imperfecti

　　　　　　　　　Including Coelomycetes, Hyphomycetes; Melanconiales, Moniliales, Mycelia Sterilia, Sphaeropsidales

　　　　　　　　　When sexual reproduction of some members of a specific genus of imperfect fungi has been established with a specific kind of sexually reproducing fungi, class the genus with the kind of the sexually reproducing fungi, e.g., Penicillium 579.5654, Fusarium 579.5677. If, however, members of the genus are assigned to different families of fungi, class them here, e.g., Septoria 579.55

.56　　　　　　　**\*Ascomycotina (Ascomycetes)**

　　　　　　　　　*For Discomycetes, see 579.57*

.562　　　　　　**\*Hemiascomycetes**

　　　　　　　　　Including Protomycetales, Taphrinales; comprehensive works on Saccharomycetaceae, on yeasts

　　　　　　　　　Class here Endomycetales

　　　　　　　　　　*For Saccharomyces (common yeasts), see 579.563. For a specific kind of yeasts not in family Saccharomycetaceae, see the kind, e.g., basidiomycete yeasts 579.59*

.563　　　　　　**\*Saccharomyces (Common yeasts)**

　　　　　　　　　Subdivisions are added for the genus as a whole and for individual species

　　　　　　　　　Class comprehensive works on Saccharomycetaceae in 579.562

.564　　　　　　**\*Loculoascomycetes**

　　　　　　　　　Including Asterinales, Dothideales, Melanommatales, Mycrothyriales, Myriangiales, Pleosporales

.565　　　　　　**\*Plectomycetes**

　　　　　　　　　Including Gymnascales, Microascales, Onygenales

　　　　　　　　　Class here Eurotiales

.565 4　　　　　**\*Penicillium**

　　　　　　　　　Subdivisions are added for the genus as a whole and for individual species

.565 7　　　　　**\*Aspergillus**

　　　　　　　　　Subdivisions are added for the genus as a whole and for individual species

---

\*Add as instructed under 579.2–579.8

.567                \*Pyrenomycetes

> Including Chaetomiales, Clavicipitales, Diaporthales, Erysiphales, Laboulbeniales, Sordariales, Xylariales

.567 7            \*Hypocreales

> Including Fusarium, Nectria, Trichoderma

.57               \*Discomycetes (Cup fungi)

> Including Helotiales, Ostropales, Phacidiales, Tuberales (truffles)

.578               \*Pezizales

> Including Ascobolus, morels, saddle fungi

.59               \*Basidiomycotina (Basidiomycetes)

> Including Exobasidiales, Tremellales (jelly fungi); basidiomycete yeasts

> Class here Heterobasidiomycetes, Homobasidiomycetes

> *For Agaricales, comprehensive works on mushrooms, see 579.6*

.592               \*Uredinales (Rusts)

.593               \*Ustilaginales (Smuts)

.597               \*Polyporales

> Variant name: Aphyllophorales

> Including club, coral, pore (bracket, shelf) fungi

.599               \*Gasteromycetes

> Including Lycoperdales (puffballs), Nidulariales (bird's-nest fungi), Phallales (stinkhorns)

## .6     **\*Mushrooms**

> Including Boletaceae (boletes), Hydnaceae (spine fungi), Thelephoraceae (leather fungi)

> Class here Agaricales (Agaricaceae, gill fungi), macrofungi, toadstools

> Class comprehensive works on Basidiomycotina in 579.59

> *For mushrooms, macrofungi of a specific order other than Agaricales, see the order in 579.5, e.g., morels 579.578*

.616 3            Beneficial mushrooms

> Number built according to instructions under 579.2–579.8

.616 32           Edible mushrooms

## .7     **\*Lichens**

\*Add as instructed under 579.2–579.8

.8        **\*Algae**

>    Class here algology, phycology

>    *For blue-green algae, see 579.39; for lichens, see 579.7*

.82        \*Minor divisions of algae

>    Including Chloromonadophyta, Cryptophyta, Xanthophyta (yellow-green algae)

>    Class here Phytomastigophorea (phytoflagellates); comprehensive works on flagellates, on organisms that may be regarded as either protozoa or algae

>    *For a specific kind of flagellate, see the kind, e.g., Zoomastigophorea 579.42, Oomycetes 579.54, dinoflagellates 579.87; for a specific organism that may be regarded as either protozoa or algae, see the kind in 579.8, e.g., euglenoids 579.84*

.83        \*Chlorophyta (Green algae)

>    Including Prasinophyceae; Chaetophorales, Siphonocladales

>    Class here Chlorophyceae, green seaweeds

.832        \*Volvocales

>    Including Chlamydomonadaceae, Dunaliellaceae

.833        \*Chlorococcales

.835        \*Caulerpales

>    Variant names: Bryopodales, Codiales, Siphonales

.836        \*Dasycladales

>    Including Acetabularia

.837        \*Zygnematales

>    Variant name: Conjugales

>    Including Desmidiaceae (desmids)

.839        \*Charophyceae

>    Class here Charales, stoneworts

.84        \*Euglenophyta

>    Variant names: Euglenida, euglenoids

.85        \*Bacillariophyceae (Diatoms)

.86        \*Chrysophyta (Golden algae)

>    Including Haptophyceae

>    Class here Chrysophyceae

---

*Add as instructed under 579.2–579.8

.87        \*Pyrrophyta (Dinoflagellates)

> Including Desmophyceae, Pfiesteriaceae, red tide
>
> Class here Dinophyceae

.88        \*Phaeophyta (Brown algae)

> Class here Phaeophyceae, comprehensive works on seaweeds
>
> *For green seaweeds, see 579.83; for red seaweeds, see 579.89*

.887        \*Laminariales

> Including Macrocystis, Saccorhiza, Undaria
>
> Class here comprehensive works on kelps
>
> *For kelps of order Fucales, see 579.888*

.888        \*Fucales

> Including Ascophyllum, Fucus, Sargassum
>
> Class here rockweeds

.89        \*Rhodophyta (Red algae)

> Including Bangiophycideae, red seaweeds
>
> Class here Florideophycideae, Rhodophyceae
>
> Class red tide in 579.87

---

>       # 580–590   Natural history of plants and animals

Class comprehensive works on biology of plants and animals in 570; class comprehensive works on natural history of plants and animals in 578

*For internal biological processes of specific kinds of plants and animals, see 571–575; for natural history of microorganisms, fungi, algae, see 579*

# 580     Plants

Class here botany; Embryophyta, vascular plants (tracheophytes), Spermatophyta (seed plants), Angiospermae (flowering plants); natural history of plants; descriptive biology of plants; taxonomic biology of plants; comprehensive works on biology of plants; interdisciplinary works on plants

Class interdisciplinary works on plants of agricultural importance in 630; class interdisciplinary works on food from plants in 641.303

*For paleobotany, see 561; for internal biological processes and structures of plants, see 571.2; for fungi, see 579.5; for algae, see 579.8. For a specific aspect of plants, see the aspect, e.g., plant cultivation 631.5*

*See Manual at 363 vs. 302–307, 333.7, 570–590, 600; also at 577.3–577.7 vs. 579–590; also at 579–590; also at 579–590 vs. 571–575; also at 580 vs. 582.13; also at 630 vs. 579–590, 641.3*

\*Add as instructed under 579.2–579.8

.1–.6    **Standard subdivisions**

> Notation from Table 1 as modified under 578.01–578.06, e.g., microscopy of plants 580.282

.7    **Education, research, related topics**

.73    Collections and exhibits of living plants

> Class here botanical gardens

> Add to base number 580.73 notation 1–9 from Table 2 for area in which collections and exhibits are found, e.g., botanical gardens of Germany 580.7343

.74    Museums, collections, exhibits

> Do not use for collections and exhibits of living organisms; class in 580.73

> Class here herbariums, collections of dried plants

.75    Museum activities and services

.752    Preserving botanical specimens

.8    **Groups of people**

.9    **History, geographic treatment, biography**

[.914–.919]    Areas, regions, places in general other than polar, temperate, tropical regions

> Do not use; class in 581.73–581.76

.93–.99    Botany by specific continents, countries, localities

> Class plants by specific continents, countries, localities in 581.9

# 581     Specific topics in natural history of plants

Class here specific nontaxonomic kinds of plants

Except for modifications shown under specific entries, add to each subdivision identified by † as follows:
01–08    Standard subdivisions
> Notation from Table 1 as modified under 580.1–580.8, e.g., preservation of botanical specimens 0752

09        History, geographic treatment, biography

Unless other instructions are given, observe the following table of preference, e.g., beneficial aquatic plants 581.63 (*not* 581.76):

| | |
|---|---|
| Miscellaneous nontaxonomic kinds of plants | 581.6 |
| Adaptation | 581.4 |
| Genetics, evolution, age characteristics | 581.3 |
| Plant ecology, plants characteristic of specific environments | 581.7 |
| Plants by specific continents, countries, localities | 581.9 |

Class a specific topic in natural history of plants with respect to a specific taxonomic group with the group, plus notation 1 from table under 583–588, e.g., useful monocotyledons 584.163

*For plants noted for specific vegetative characteristics and flowers, see 582*

[.01–.09]     Standard subdivisions

Do not use; class in 580.1–580.9

## .3     †Genetics, evolution, age characteristics

Standard subdivisions are added for genetics, evolution, age characteristics together, for genetics and evolution alone

.35       †Genetics

Class here works on genetic constitution of plants that elucidate their total function

Class experimental works on plant genetics, comprehensive works on genetics in 576.5

*For biochemical genetics in plants, see 572.82*

.38       †Evolution

Class here phylogeny

.39       †Age characteristics

Class here age determination

## .4     †Adaptation

Class here plants noted for specific kinds of adaptation

.41       †Size, weight, shape

Including silhouettes

---

†Add standard subdivisions as instructed under 581

.42       †Acclimatization and temperature adaptation

> Standard subdivisions are added for acclimatization and temperature adaptation together, for acclimatization alone

> *For seasonal adaptation, see 581.43*

.43       †Seasonal adaptation

---

>       581.46–581.49   Adaptation of specific parts of plants

> Class comprehensive works in 581.4

> *For physiology of specific parts of plants, see 575*

.46       †Reproductive adaptation

> Including buds, stems specialized for reproduction

> *For comprehensive works on flowers and their adaptations, see 582.13*

.464       †Fruits

> Including nuts

> *For seeds, see 581.467*

.467       †Seeds

.47       †Protective adaptation, color

> Subdivisions are added for protective adaptation and color together, for protective adaptation alone

> Including mimicry, thorns

> Class here bark

> Class color of a specific adaptation with the adaptation, e.g., color of flowers 582.13

.48       †Leaves and fronds

> Standard subdivisions are added for either or both topics in heading

> Including tendrils

.49       †Stems and roots

.495       †Stems

> *For stems specialized for reproduction, see 581.46*

.498       †Roots

**.6**       **†Miscellaneous nontaxonomic kinds of plants**

> Not provided for elsewhere

> Class here economic botany

> Class carnivorous plants in 583.75

†Add standard subdivisions as instructed under 581

| .62 | †Nonnative plants |
| | Class here alien, exotic, introduced, invasive, naturalized plants |
| .63 | †Beneficial plants |
| | Class here herbs |
| .632 | †Edible plants |
| .634 | †Medicinal plants |
| .636 | †Plants of industrial and technological value |
| | Other than medicinal plants |
| .65 | †Harmful plants |
| .652 | †Weeds |
| | Class interdisciplinary works on weeds in 632.5 |
| .657 | †Allergenic plants |
| .659 | †Poisonous plants |
| .68 | †Rare and endangered plants |
| | Standard subdivisions are added for either or both topics in heading |
| | Including recently extinct species |

**.7  Plant ecology, plants characteristic of specific environments**

Standard subdivisions are added for either or both topics in heading

Class here autecology, botany of specific environments

Class plants characteristic of specific environments noted for specific vegetative characteristics and flowers, ecology of such plants in 582

| .701–.708 | Standard subdivisions |
| | Notation from Table 1 as modified under 580.1–580.8, e.g., microscopy 581.70282 |
| .709 | History, geographic treatment, biography |
| [.709 14–.709 19] | Areas, regions, places in general other than polar, temperate, tropical regions |
| | Do not use; class in 581.73–581.76 |
| .71–.76 | Specific topics in plant ecology, specific environments |
| | Add to base number 581.7 the numbers following 577 in 577.1–577.6, e.g., aquatic plants 581.76, aquatic gardens 581.76073 |
| | Class marine botany in 579.177 |
| | *For synecology and population biology, see 581.78* |
| .78 | †Synecology and population biology |

†Add standard subdivisions as instructed under 581

.782–.788    Specific topics of synecology and population biology

> Add to base number 581.78 the numbers following 577.8 in
> 577.82–577.88, e.g., parasitism 581.7857

**.9    Plants by specific continents, countries, localities**

> Add to base number 581.9 notation 3–9 from Table 2, e.g., plants in Argentina
> 581.982

# 582    Plants noted for specific vegetative characteristics and flowers

> Class genetics and evolution, adaptation and parts other than flowers,
> miscellaneous kinds of plants noted for vegetative characteristics and flowers in
> 581

> *For a specific taxonomic group of plants noted for either specific vegetative*
> *characteristics or flowers, see the group in 583–588, e.g., lilies noted for their*
> *flowers 584.3*

[.01–.09]    Standard subdivisions

> Do not use; class in 580.1–580.9

**.1    Herbaceous and woody plants, plants noted for their flowers**

> Except for modifications shown under specific entries, add to each subdivision
> identified by ‡ as follows:
> 01–08    Standard subdivisions
>> Notation from Table 1 as modified under 580.1–580.8, e.g.,
>> botanical gardens 073
> 09        History, geographic treatment, biography
> [0914–0919]    Areas, regions, places in general other than polar, temperate,
>> tropical regions
>>> Do not use; class in 7
> 3–7    Specific topics of natural history of plants
>> Add the numbers following 581 in 581.3–581.7, e.g., genetics 35,
>> seeds 467, rare and endangered plants 68, aquatic plants 76, aquatic
>> gardens 76073

> *See Manual at 635.9 vs. 582.1*

[.101–.109]    Standard subdivisions

> Do not use; class in 580.1–580.9

.12    ‡Herbaceous plants

> Including biennials

> Class here annuals, forbs

> Class herbaceous plants noted for their flowers in 582.13

> *For herbaceous vines, see 582.189*

‡Add as instructed under 582.1

.13         ‡Plants noted for their flowers

Class here wild flowers, interdisciplinary works on flowers

Class woody plants noted for their flowers in 582.16; class vines noted for their flowers in 582.18; class comprehensive works on Angiospermae (flowering plants) in 580

*For physiology of flowers, see 575.6. For a specific aspect of flowers, see the aspect, e.g., flower gardening 635.9, flower arrangement 745.92*

*See Manual at 580 vs. 582.13*

.16         ‡Trees

Class here dendrology; comprehensive works on perennials, on woody plants

Class forest ecology in 577.3

*For herbaceous perennials, see 582.12; for shrubs, see 582.17; for woody vines, see 582.18*

.17         ‡Shrubs

.18         ‡Vines

Class here woody vines

.189       ‡Herbaceous vines

---

>        **583–588   Specific taxonomic groups of plants**

Except for modifications shown under specific entries, add to each subdivision identified by * as follows:
01–08     Standard subdivisions
            Notation from Table 1 as modified under 580.1–580.8, e.g., collections of living plants 073
09        History, geographic treatment, biography
[0914–0919]    Areas, regions, places in general other than polar, temperate, tropical regions
            Do not use; class in 173–176
1        General topics of natural history of plants
            Add to base number 1 the numbers following 581 in 581.3–581.7, e.g., aquatic plants 176
Class comprehensive works in 580

**583      *Magnoliopsida (Dicotyledons)**

*See Manual at 583–585 vs. 600; also at 583–584*

---

*Add as instructed under 583–588
‡Add as instructed under 582.1

## SUMMARY

## .2     *Magnoliidae

Including Rafflesiales; Rafflesiaceae (Cytinaceae); monster flower

### .22     *Magnoliales

Including Magnoliaceae (magnolia family), Annonaceae (custard apple family), Myristicaceae (nutmeg family), Winteraceae (Winter's bark family)

Including cherimoya, cucumber tree, lancewoods, mace, michelias, papaws, tulip tree (yellow poplar), wild cinnamon

*See also 583.626 for papaws of family Caricaceae*

### .23     *Laurales

Including Chloranthaceae, Hernandiaceae, Monimiaceae

Including avocados, cinnamon, Oregon myrtle (California laurel), sassafras, sweet bay (bay laurel); comprehensive works on laurels

Class here Lauraceae (laurel family)

Class comprehensive works on myrtles in 583.765

*For laurels of Ericaceae family, see 583.66; for spurge laurel, see 583.67; for hedge laurels, see 583.72*

*See Manual at 579–590*

### .25     *Piperales

Including Saururaceae (lizard's-tail family); black pepper, peperomias

Class here Piperaceae (pepper family)

Class peppers of Solanaceae family, comprehensive works on peppers in 583.952

### .26     *Aristolochiales

Class here Aristolochiaceae (birthwort family)

*Add as instructed under 583–588

.29 *Nymphaeales

Including Ceratophyllaceae (hornworts)

Class here Nymphaeaceae (water lilies)

Class Nelumbo in 583.3

> *See also 588.3 for hornworts of subclass Anthocerotidae (horned liverworts)*

**.3 *Ranunculidae**

Including Illiciales, Nelumbonales (lotuses); magnolia vine, star anise

.34 *Ranunculales (Ranales)

Including Ranunculaceae (buttercup family), Berberidaceae (barberry family), Menispermaceae (moonseed family), Podophyllaceae

Including aconites, anemones, Christmas rose, clematises, columbines, delphiniums (larkspurs), hellebores, lesser celandine, mayapple (mayflower, mandrake), monkshoods (wolfsbanes)

> *See also 583.952 for mandrakes of family Solanaceae*

.35 *Papaverales (Rhoeadales)

Including Papaveraceae (poppy family), Fumariaceae (fumitory family); bleeding hearts, bloodroot, celandines, Dutchman's breeches

Class Moringaceae in 583.64

> *See also 583.34 for lesser celandine*

.36 *Sarraceniales

Class here Sarraceniaceae (New World pitcher plant family)

Class comprehensive works on carnivorous plants, on pitcher plants in 583.75

**.4 *Hamamelididae**

.43 *Minor orders of Hamamelididae

Including Balanopales (Balanopsidales), Barbeyales, Casuarinales (beefwood order), Cercidiphyllales (katsura tree), Didymelales, Eucommiales, Eupteleales, Leitneriales, Myricales (wax myrtle order), Trochodendrales

Including bayberries, candleberry, sweet gale (bog myrtle)

Class Jamaica bayberry, comprehensive works on myrtles in 583.765

> *See also 583.93 for bog myrtle (buckbean)*

*Add as instructed under 583–588

.44      \*Hamamelidales

        Including Platanaceae (sycamore family); ironwood, plane trees, sweet gums

        Class here Hamamelidaceae (witch hazel family)

        Class comprehensive works on ironwoods in 583.48

.45      \*Urticales

        Including Urticaceae (nettle family), Cannabaceae (hemp family), Moraceae (mulberry family), Ulmaceae (elm family)

        Including banyan, breadfruits, figs, hackberries, hops, marijuana, osage orange, pileas, ramie (China grass plant), rubber plant (India rubber tree), West Indian boxwood; comprehensive works on hemps

           *For hemps of a specific family other than Cannabaceae, see the family, e.g., aloe and sisil hemps 584.352*

           *See also 583.69 for boxwoods of family Buxaceae; also 583.96 for dead nettles*

.46      \*Fagales

        Including Castaneoideae (chestnuts), Fagoideae (beeches), Quercoideae (oaks); chinquapin, cork oak

        Class here Fagaceae

.48      \*Betulales

        Including alders, filberts (hazelnuts), hornbeams; comprehensive works on ironwoods

        Class here Betulaceae (birch family)

           *For ironwoods of a specific family other then Betulaceae, see the family, e.g., ironwoods of family Rhamnaceae 583.86*

.49      \*Juglandales

        Including butternuts, hickories, pecans

        Class here Juglandaceae (walnut family)

**.5**      **\*Caryophyllidae**

        Including Plumbaginales (leadwort order), Theligonales (Cynocrambales); sea lavenders, thrifts

.53      \*Caryophyllales

        Including Caryophyllaceae (pink family), Aizoaceae (carpetweed family), Amaranthaceae (amaranth family), Chenopodiaceae (goosefoot family), Nyctaginaceae, Phytolaccaceae (pokeweed family), Portulacaceae (purslane family)

        Including beets, bougainvilleas, carnations, four-o'clock, ice plants (sea figs), lithops (living stones), Madeira vine, spinach

\*Add as instructed under 583–588

.56     \*Cactales

      Class here Cactaceae (cactus family)

.57     \*Polygonales

      Including dock, rhubarbs, sorrel

      Class here Polygonaceae (buckwheat family)

**.6**     **\*Dilleniidae**

.62     \*Miscellaneous orders of Dilleniidae

      Only those orders named here and below

      Including Dilleniales, Paeoniales (peony order)

.624     \*Theales

      Including Theaceae (Ternstroemiaceae, tea family), Clusiaceae (Guttiferae), Dipterocarpaceae, Elatinaceae, Hypericaceae, Marcgraviaceae, Ochnaceae

      Including camellias, garcinias, mammee apple, mangosteen, Stewartia

.625     \*Violales

      Including Violaceae (violet family), Bixaceae (annatto tree), Cistaceae (rockrose family), Flacourtiaceae; pansies

      *See also 583.95 for African violets*

.626     \*Passiflorales

      Including Caricaceae (papaya family), Turneraceae; granadillas, maypop, papaws

      Class here Passifloraceae (passionflower family)

      *See also 583.22 for papaws of family Annonaceae*

.627     \*Begoniales

      Class here Begoniaceae, begonias

.628     \*Tamaricales

      Including Fouquieriaceae (candlewood family); alkali heath, ocotillo

      Class here Tamaricaceae (tamarisk family)

.63     \*Cucurbitales

      Including cucumbers, melons, pepos, pumpkins, squashes, watermelons

      Class here Cucurbitaceae (gourd family)

\*Add as instructed under 583–588

.64      \*Capparales

        Former name: Capparidales

        Including Capparaceae (caper family), Moringaceae, Resedaceae (mignonette family)

        Including alyssums, cabbages, candytufts, cresses, crucifixion thorns, Nasturtium genus, radishes, rapes, rutabagas, shepherd's purse, spiderflowers, stocks (Matthiola), turnips, wallflowers, watercresses

        Class here Brassicaceae (Cruciferae, mustard family)

          *See also 583.76 for Brazilian spiderflowers; also 583.79 for nasturtiums of family Tropaeolaceae*

.65      \*Salicales

        Including Populus (poplars and aspens), cottonwoods

        Class here Salicaceae (willow family), salix

          *See also 583.22 for yellow poplar*

.66      \*Ericales

        Including Clethraceae (pepperbush family), Epacridaceae, Monotropaceae (Indian pipe family), Pyrolaceae, Saurauiaceae

        Including azaleas, blueberries, cranberries, crowberries, heather, huckleberries, kalmias, kiwi (Chinese gooseberry), mountain laurel, rhododendrons, sourwood, wintergreens

        Class here Ericaceae (heath family)

        Class comprehensive works on laurels in 583.23

.67      \*Ebenales, Primulales, Diapensiales, Thymelaeales (mezereum order)

        Including daphnes, galax, spurge laurel

.674      \*Ebenales

        Including Ebenaceae (ebony family), Sapotaceae, Styracaceae (storax family), Symplocaceae (sweetleaf family)

        Including persimmons, sapodilla, star apples

.675      \*Primulales

        Including Primulaceae (primrose family), Myrsinaceae, Theophrastaceae

        Including auriculas, coralberry, cyclamens, loosestrife, primulas, shooting stars

        Class evening primroses in 583.76

          *See also 583.76 for loosestrife of family Lythraceae*

---

\*Add as instructed under 583–588

.68          *Malvales

Including Bombacaceae (silk cotton tree family), Elaeocarpaceae, Sterculiaceae (cacao family), Tiliaceae (linden family)

Including balsa, baobabs, basswood, jute, kapok, kola nuts, lime trees

.685         *Malvaceae (Mallow family)

Including cotton, hibiscuses, hollyhock, okra, rose of Sharon

.69          *Euphorbiales

Including Buxaceae (boxwood family), Dichapetalaceae

Including cassavas (maniocs), castor-oil plant, copperleaves, crotons, crown of thorns, heveas, manchineels, mercuries, poinsettias, rubber tree, snow-on-the-mountain, tallow tree, tung tree

Class here Euphorbiaceae (spurge family)

*See also 583.45 for India rubber tree, West Indian boxwood*

.7      **Rosidae**

*For orders of Rosidae not provided for below, see 583.8*

.72          *Saxifragales

Including Saxifragaceae (saxifrage family), Brunelliaceae, Bruniaceae, Byblidaceae, Cephalotaceae, Crassulaceae, Cunoniaceae, Escalloniaceae, Grossulariaceae (gooseberry family), Hydrangeaceae (hydrangea family), Parnassiaceae, Pittosporaceae (hedge laurel family)

Including brexias, currants, deutzias, escallonias, houseleeks (live-forevers), mock oranges (syringas), pickaback plants, Ribes, stonecrops (orpines, sedums), Virginia willow

Class comprehensive works on carnivorous plants in 583.75

.73          *Rosales

Including Chrysobalanaceae

Including almonds, apples, apricots, blackberries, cane fruits, cherries, chokeberries, cinquefoils, dewberries, stone fruits (drupaceous fruits), hawthorns, loquat, medlar, mountain ashes, peaches, pears, plums, pomaceous fruits, pyracanthas (fire thorns), quince, raspberries, Rubus, serviceberries, spireas, strawberries

Class here Rosaceae (rose family)

*See also 583.765 for rose apples; also 583.77 for hog plums of family Anacardiaceae*

.734         *Rosa (Roses)

Subdivisions are added for the genus as a whole and for individual species

*Add as instructed under 583–588

.74      *Fabales (Leguminales)

Including alfalfa, beans, beggar's lice, bluebonnet, carob, clovers, indigo plants, kudzu, lentils, lespedezas, locoweeds, locusts, peanuts (groundnuts), Scotch broom, shamrocks, smoke tree, soybean (soja, soya), tamarind, vetches, wisterias

Class here Fabaceae (pea family)

*See also 583.77 for smoke trees of family Anacardiaceae; also 583.79 for shamrock of family Oxalidaceae*

.748      *Mimosaceae (Mimosa family)

Including acacias, mesquite, sensitive plants, silk tree

.749      *Caesalpiniaceae (Senna family)

Including redbuds

.75      *Nepenthales

Including Nepenthaceae (Old World pitcher plant family), Droseraceae (sundew family); Venus's flytrap; comprehensive works on pitcher plants

Class here comprehensive works on carnivorous plants

*For Sarraceniaceae (New World pitcher plants), see 583.36; for Byblidaceae, Cephalotaceae, see 583.72; for Lentibulariaceae, see 583.95*

.76      *Myrtales

Including Anisophylleaceae, Combretaceae, Lecythidaceae (Brazil nut family), Lythraceae (loosestrife family), Melastomataceae (meadow beauty family), Onagraceae (evening primrose family), Trapaceae

Including Brazilian spiderflowers, cigar flower, clarkias, crape myrtle, fireweed, fuchsias, pomegranate

Class mangroves of family Combretaceae in 583.763

*See also 583.64 for spiderflowers of family Capparaceae; also 583.675 for loosestrife of family Primulaceae; also 583.99 for fireweeds of family Asteraceae*

.763      *Rhizophoraceae and Sonneratiaceae

Including mangroves of family Combretaceae, e.g., button mangrove, white mangrove

Class here comprehensive works on mangroves

Subdivisions are added for Rhizophoraceae and Sonneratiaceae together, for Rhizophoraceae alone

Class mangrove swamp ecology in 577.698

*For mangroves of family Verbenaceae, see 583.96; for mangrove of family Arecaceae (nipa palm), see 584.5*

*Add as instructed under 583–588

.765      \*Myrtaceae (Myrtle family)

Including allspice (pimento), clove, guavas, Jamaica bayberry (bay rum tree), rose apples, water chestnuts; comprehensive works on myrtles

> *For Eucalyptus, see 583.766. For myrtle of a specific family other than Myrtaceae, see the family, e.g., Oregon myrtle 583.23, wax myrtle 583.43, crape myrtle 583.76*

> *See also 583.952 for pimientos (peppers); also 584.84 for Chinese water chestnut*

.766      \*Eucalyptus (Gum trees)

Subdivisions are added for the genus as a whole and for individual species

.77      \*Rutales

Including Rutaceae (orange family), Anacardiaceae (mango family), Burseraceae (incense tree family), Coriariaceae, Meliaceae (mahogany family), Simaroubaceae (ailanthus family)

Including cashew, chinaberry tree, citrus fruits, cork trees, hog plums (Spanish plums), hop tree, orange jessamine, pistachio, poison ivies, rue, smoke trees, sumacs, tree of heaven, varnish trees; comprehensive works on balms

Class comprehensive works on ivies in 583.84

> *For balm of a specific family other than Burseraceae, see the family, e.g., bee balms 583.96*

> *See also 583.46 for cork oak; also 583.73 for hog plums of family Rosaceae; also 583.74 for smoke tree of family Fabaceae; also 583.87 for jasmines*

.78      \*Sapindales

Including Sapindaceae (soapberry family), Aceraceae (maple family), Hippocastanaceae (horse chestnut family), Sabiaceae, Staphyleaceae (bladdernut family)

Including buckeyes, honey bush, hopbushes, litchis

.79      \*Geraniales

Including Geraniaceae (geranium family), Balsaminaceae (balsam family), Erythroxylaceae (coca family), Hugoniaceae, Humiriaceae, Ixonanthaceae, Linaceae (flax family), Malpighiaceae, Oxalidaceae (wood sorrel family), Tropaeolaceae (nasturtium family), Zygophyllaceae (lignum vitae family)

Including creosote bush, erodiums, impatiens, jewelweeds (touch-me-nots), pelargoniums, shamrock, wild mango (dika)

> *See also 583.64 for Nasturtium genus in family Brassicaceae; also 583.74 for shamrocks of family Fabaceae*

**.8      Other orders of Rosidae**

\*Add as instructed under 583–588

[.801–.809]   Standard subdivisions

Do not use; class in 583.701–583.709

.82   *Minor orders of Rosidae

Including Connarales, Elaeagnales (oleaster order), Hippuridales (Haloragales), Podostemales (riverweed order), Polygalales (milkwort order); Vochysiaceae

Including gunneras, mare's tail

.84   *Cornales

Including Cornaceae (dogwood family), Araliaceae (ginseng family, ivy family)

Including Garrya, tupelos (sour gums), wild sarsaparilla; comprehensive works on ivies

*For ivies of a specific family other than Araliaceae, see the family, e.g., poison ivies 583.77*

*See also 584.356 for sarsaparilla of family Smilacaceae*

.849   *Umbelliferae

Variant names: Apiaceae, parsley family

Including anise, caraway, carrots, celery, dills, parsnips, poison hemlocks, Queen Anne's lace

.85   *Celastrales

Including Celastraceae (staff tree family), Aquifoliaceae (holly family), Hippocrateaceae, Icacinaceae; bittersweet, khat, maté

*See also 583.952 for bittersweet of family Solanaceae*

.86   *Rhamnales

Including Rhamnaceae (buckthorn family), Leeaceae, Vitaceae (grape family); Boston ivy, ironwoods, jujubes, Virginia creeper

Class comprehensive works on ironwoods in 583.48

.87   *Oleales

Including ashes, forsythias, jasmines, lilacs, privets

Class here Oleaceae (olive family)

*See also 583.77 for orange jessamine*

.88   *Santalales

Including Santalaceae (sandalwood family), Balanophoraceae, Loranthaceae (mistletoe family), Olacaceae, Opiliaceae, Viscaceae

Class Rafflesiaceae in 583.2

*Add as instructed under 583–588

.89      *Proteales

> Including banksias, grevilleas, hakeas, macadamias, Persoonia, proteas, Telopea (waratahs)
>
> Class here Proteaceae

**.9**      **\*Asteridae**

> Including Calycerales

.92      *Dipsacales

> Including Dipsacaceae (teasel family), Caprifoliaceae (honeysuckle family), Valerianaceae (valerian family)
>
> Including elders, snowballs, viburnums

.93      *Gentianales

> Including Gentianaceae (gentian family), Apocynaceae (dogbane family, Indian hemp family), Asclepiadaceae (milkweed family), Loganiaceae, Potaliaceae, Rubiaceae (madder family)
>
> Including bog myrtle (buckbean), buckbeans, buttonbushes, carrion flowers, cinchonas, coffee, gardenias, Indian sarsaparilla, oleanders, partridgeberry, periwinkles, Plumeria, rauwolfias, stephanotises
>
> > *See also 583.43 for bog myrtle (sweet gale); also 584.356 for carrion flower and sarsaprillas of family Smilacaceae*

.94      *Polemoniales

> Including Polemoniaceae (phlox family), Boraginaceae (forget-me-not family), Convolvulaceae (morning glory family), Cuscutaceae (dodder family), Hydrophyllaceae (waterleaf family), Loasaceae
>
> Including baby blue-eyes, borage, comfreys, dichondras, heliotropes, honeyworts, hound's-tongues, Jacob's ladders, sweet potatoes (yams), Virginia cowslip (bluebell)
>
> > *See also 583.98 for bluebells of bellflower family; also 584.32 for bluebells of lily family; also 584.357 for yams of family Dioscoreaceae*

.95      *Scrophulariales

> Including Scrophulariaceae (figwort family, snapdragon family), Acanthaceae (acanthus family), Bignoniaceae (catalpa family), Buddlejaceae, Gesneriaceae, Lentibulariaceae (bladderwort family), Myoporaceae, Nolanaceae, Orobanchaceae (broomrape family), Pedaliaceae (sesame family), Plantaginaceae (plantago family)
>
> Including African violets, butterfly bushes, calabash tree, foxglove, mulleins, Penstemon, plantains, trumpet creepers, unicorn plants
>
> Class here Personales
>
> Class comprehensive works on violets in 583.625; class comprehensive works on carnivorous plants in 583.75
>
> > *See also 584.39 for plantain of banana family*

*Add as instructed under 583–588

.952            *Solanaceae

Variant names: nightshade family, potato family

Including belladonna, bittersweet, butterfly flowers (schizanthuses), capsicums, daturas, eggplants, henbane, jimsonweed, mandrakes, paprika, petunias, pimientos, tobacco, tomatoes; cayenne, red, sweet peppers; comprehensive works on peppers

*For pepper of Piperaceae family, see 583.25*

*See also 583.34 for mandrake of family Podophyllaceae (mayapple); also 583.765 for pimento (allspice); also 583.85 for bittersweet of family Celastraceae*

.96       *Lamiales

Including Verbenaceae (verbena family)

Including basils, bee balms, black mangrove, catnip, Chinese artichoke, dead nettles, ground ivy, horehound, hyssop, lavenders, lopseed, marjorams, rosemary, sage, teak, thymes, vervains

Class here Lamiaceae (Labiatae, mint family)

Class comprehensive works on mangroves in 583.763; class comprehensive works on balms in 583.77

*See also 583.99 for sagebrushes*

.98       *Campanulales

Including Campanulaceae (bellflower family), Goodeniaceae, Lobeliaceae, Stylidiaceae; bluebells, Campanula, Indian tobacco

*See also 583.94 for bluebells of forget-me-not family; also 584.32 for bluebells of lily family*

.99       *Asterales

Including artichokes, asters, black-eyed Susans, chamomiles, chicory, chrysanthemums, cornflower, cosmos, dahlias, dandelions, endive, everlastings, fireweeds, fleabanes, gerberas, goldenrods, groundsels (ragworts), guayule, lettuce, marigolds, ragweeds, safflower, sagebrushes, sunflowers, thistles, wormwoods, zinnias

Class here Asteraceae (Compositae)

*See also 583.76 for fireweed of family Onagraceae; also 583.96 for Chinese artichoke*

# 584     *Liliopsida (Monocotyledons)

*See Manual at 583–585 vs. 600; also at 583–584*

---

*Add as instructed under 583–588

## SUMMARY

| | |
|---|---|
| **584.3** | **Liliidae** |
| **.4** | **Orchidales** |
| **.5** | **Arecidae** |
| **.6** | **Cyclanthales, Arales, Pandanales, Typhales** |
| **.7** | **Alismidae** |
| **.8** | **Commelinidae** |
| **.9** | **Poales** |

### .3    *Liliidae

Class here Liliales, lilies

*For Orchidales, see 584.4*

*See also 583.29 for water lilies*

---

> ### 584.32–584.35  Liliales

Class comprehensive works in 584.3

### .32    *Liliaceae (Lily family)

Including aloes, bluebells, day lilies, Easter lily, hostas (plantain lilies), hyacinths, lily of the valley, trilliums, tulips

Class comprehensive works on lilies in 584.3

*See also 583.94 for bluebells of forget-me-not family; also 583.98 for bluebells of bellflower family; also 584.72 for water hyacynths*

### .33    *Alliaceae

Including African lilies, chives, garlics, leeks, onions, shallots

### .34    *Amaryllidaceae (Amaryllis family)

Including daffodils, narcissus; atamasco, Peruvian, spider lilies

### .35    Other families of Liliales

Including Cyanastraceae, Philesiaceae, Philydraceae, Pontederiaceae, Taccaceae, Tecophilaeaceae, Xanthorrhoeaceae

Class comprehensive works in 584.3

### [.350 1–.350 9]    Standard subdivisions

Do not use; class in 584.301–584.309

### .352    *Agavaceae

Including agaves, aloe hemp, aloes (century plants), dracaenas, sansevierias (snake plants), sisal, tequila, yuccas

Class comprehensive works on hemps in 583.45

*Add as instructed under 583–588

.353      *Alstroemeriaceae

Including box lily

.354      *Haemodoraceae (Bloodwort family), Hypoxidaceae, Velloziaceae (tree lily family)

.355      *Asparagaceae

Including Ruscaceae, asparaguses

.356      *Smilacaceae

Including carrion flower, cat briers, greenbriers, sarsaparillas

*See also 583.84 for wild sarsaparilla of ginseng family; also 583.93 for carrion flowers of family Asclepiadaceae, Indian sarsaparilla*

.357      *Dioscoreaceae (Yam family)

*See also 583.94 for sweet potatoes (yams)*

.37      *Triuridales

Class here Triuridaceae

.38      *Iridales

Including Burmanniaceae

Including blackberry lily, crocuses, freesias, gladiolus (sword lilies), saffron, tigerflowers

Class here Iridaceae (iris family)

.39      *Zingiberales

Including Zingiberaceae (ginger family), Cannaceae (canna family), Costaceae, Heliconiaceae, Marantaceae (arrowroot family), Musaceae (banana family)

Including abaca (Manila hemp), cardamoms, ginger lily, heliconias, plantain, prayer plant, turmerics, zebra plant

Class comprehensive works on hemps in 583.45

*See also 583.95 for plantains of plantago family*

**.4      *Orchidales**

Including vanillas

Class here Orchidaceae (orchid family)

**.5      *Arecidae**

Including coconuts, dates, nipa palm (mangrove), palmettos, rattans

Class here Arecales (Palmales), Arecaceae (Palmae, palm family)

*For Cyclanthales, Arales, Pandanales, Typhales, see 584.6*

**.6      *Cyclanthales, Arales, Pandanales, Typhales**

*Add as instructed under 583–588

.62      *Cyclanthales

> Including jipijapa (Panama hat palm)
>
> Class here Cyclanthaceae

.64      *Arales

> Including Lemnaceae (duckweed family)
>
> Including anthuriums, caladiums, calla lilies, Chinese evergreen, dieffenbachias, elephant's ears, jack-in-the-pulpits, monsteras, philodendrons, skunk cabbages, taro, watermeals
>
> Class here Araceae (arum family)
>
> Class comprehensive works on lilies in 584.3
>
> *See also 583.64 for cabbages of Brassicaceae family*

.66      *Pandanales

> Including screw pines
>
> Class here Pandanaceae (hala family)

.68      *Typhales

> Including Sparganiaceae, Sparganium (bur reeds)
>
> Class here Typhaceae, Typha (cattails and bulrushes)
>
> Class comprehensive works on bulrushes in 584.84

**.7**      **\*Alismidae**

.72      *Alismales (Alismatales)

> Including Butomaceae (water poppy family), Limnocharitaceae; arrowheads, water hyacinths
>
> Class here Alismaceae (water plantain family)

.73      *Hydrocharitales

> Including turtle grass
>
> Class here Hydrocharitaceae (frogbit family)

.74      *Najadales (Potamogetonales)

> Including Najadaceae (naiad family), Aponogetonaceae (lattice plant family), Juncaginaceae (arrow grass family), Lilaeaceae, Posidoniaceae, Ruppiaceae (widgeon grass family), Scheuchzeriaceae, Zanichelliaceae, Zosteraceae (eelgrass family)

.742      *Potamogetonaceae (Pondweed family)

**.8**      **\*Commelinidae**

> Including Restionales
>
> *For Poales, see 584.9*

*Add as instructed under 583–588

.82      *Juncales

> Including Thurniaceae

> Class here Juncaceae (rush family), comprehensive works on rushes

> *For rushes of cattail family, see 584.68; for rushes of sedge family, see 584.84*

.84      *Cyperales

> Including Chinese water chestnut, cotton grasses, papyrus, umbrella plant; beak, spike rushes; comprehensive works on bulrushes

> Class here Cyperaceae (sedge family)

> Class comprehensive works on rushes in 584.82

> *For bulrushes of cattail family, see 584.68*

.85      *Bromeliales

> Including Spanish (black) moss

> Class here Bromeliaceae (pineapple family), bromeliads

.86      *Commelinales

> Including Rapateaceae, Xyridaceae (yellow-eyed grass family); boat lily, wandering Jews

> Class here Commelinaceae (spiderwort family)

.87      *Eriocaulales

> Class here Eriocaulaceae (pipewort family)

**.9      *Poales**

> Variant names: Graminales, grasses

> Including Agrosteae, Anomochloeae, Arundineae, Arundinelleae, Aveneae (oat tribe), Bambuseae (bamboo tribe), Chlorideae (gama grass tribe), Eragrosteae, Festuceae (fescue tribe), Hordeeae (barley tribe), Leptureae, Lygeeae, Nardeae, Olyreae, Oryzeae (rice tribe), Pappophoreae, Parianeae, Phalarideae (canary grass tribe), Phareae, Sporoboleae, Stipeae, Streptochaeteae, Thysanolaeneae, Zoysieae

> Including bent grasses, bluegrasses, bromegrasses, espartos, orchard grass (cocksfoot), pampas grass, reeds, rye, timothy, wheat

> Class here Poaceae (Gramineae), Pooideae

> Class comprehensive works on grassland ecology in 577.4; class Cyperaceae in 584.84

---

*Add as instructed under 583–588

.92          *Panicoideae

Including Paniceae (millet tribe), Andropogoneae (sugarcane tribe), Maydeae (maize tribe)

Including citronella, corn, crabgrasses, milos, panic grasses, proso, sorghums, Sudan grass, thatch grasses

# 585     *Pinophyta (Gymnosperms)

Class here Coniferales (Conifers), Pinicae

*See Manual at 583–585 vs. 600*

---

\>          **585.2–585.5  Coniferales**

Class comprehensive works in 585

.2          **\*Pinaceae (Pine family)**

Including firs, hemlocks, larches, piñons, spruces, tamaracks, true cedars; comprehensive works on cedars, on pines

*For Huon, dammar, New Zealand red pines, see 585.3; for cypress pine, cedars of the cypress family, see 585.4; for China fir, Japanese and Tasmanian cedars, see 585.5*

.3          **\*Podocarpaceae, Araucariaceae, Cephalotaxaceae (plum-yew family)**

Including Huon pine, kauris (dammar pines), New Zealand red pine, podocarpuses (yellowwoods), Prince Albert's yew

Subdivisions are added for Podocarpaceae, Araucariaceae, Cephalotaxaceae together; for Podocarpaceae alone

.4          **\*Cupressaceae (Cypress family)**

Including arborvitaes, cypress pine, junipers; Chilean, incense, red cedars

Class here comprehensive works on cypresses

*For bald cypresses, see 585.5*

.5          **\*Taxodiaceae**

Including bald cypresses, China fir, redwood, sequoias; Japanese, Tasmanian cedars

.6          **\*Taxales**

Class here Taxaceae (yew family), comprehensive works on yews

*For plum and Prince Albert's yews, see 585.3*

.7          **\*Ginkgoales**

Class here Ginkgoaceae; ginkgo (maidenhair tree)

\*Add as instructed under 583–588

.8       **Gneticae**

Including Gnetales, Ephedrales (ephedras), Welwitschiales (tumboa plant); Gnetum, Mormon tea

.9       **Cycadales (Cycads)**

Class here Cycadaceae

# 586      *Cryptogamia (Seedless plants)

*For fungi, see 579.5; for algae, see 579.8; for Pteridophyta, see 587; for Bryophyta, see 588*

# 587      *Pteridophyta

Variant names: vascular cryptogams, vascular seedless plants

.2       **Sphenopsida**

Variant names: Articulatae, horsetails

Class here Equisetales, Equisetaceae, Equisetum

.3       **Polypodiopsida**

Variant names: Filicopsida, ferns

Including Marsiliales (waterclovers), Salviniales

Including bracken, brakes, spleenworts, water spangles; maidenhair, royal, staghorn ferns

Class here Polypodiales (Filicales)

*See also 587.4 for whisk ferns*

.33      **Marattiales and Ophioglossales**

Variant name for Marattiales: giant ferns

Including adder's-tongues, moonworts; grape, rattlesnake ferns

.4       **Psilopsida (Whisk ferns)**

Class here Psilotales

.9       **Lycopsida**

Including Lycopodiales (club mosses), Isoetales (quillworts), Selaginellales (spike mosses); resurrection plants

Class here club mosses covering Lycopsida

# 588      *Bryophyta

*Add as instructed under 583–588

.2    **\*Bryopsida**

Variant names: Musci, mosses

Including Andreaeales (granite, rock mosses)

Class here Bryales (true mosses)

*See also 587.9 for club and spike mosses; also 588.3 for scale mosses*

.29    \*Sphagnales

Including Sphagnaceae (peat mosses, bog mosses)

.3    **\*Hepatopsida (Liverworts)**

Including Anthocerotidae (horned liverworts, hornworts), Marchantiales (great liverworts)

Class here Hepatidae (Hepaticae), Jungermanniales, leafy liverworts (scale mosses)

*See also 583.29 for hornworts of family Ceratophyllaceae*

## [589]    [Unassigned]

Most recently used in Edition 20

# 590    Animals

Class here natural history of animals; descriptive biology of animals; taxonomic biology of animals; zoology; comprehensive works on biology of animals, interdisciplinary works on animals

Class interdisciplinary works on food from animals in 641.306

*For paleozoology, see 560; for internal biological processes and structures in animals, see 571.1. For a specific aspect of animals, see the aspect, e.g., animal husbandry 636*

*See Manual at 363 vs. 302–307, 333.7, 570–590, 600; also at 577.3–577.7 vs. 579–590; also at 579–590; also at 579–590 vs. 571–575; also at 630 vs. 579–590, 641.3; also at 800, T3C—362 vs. 398.245, 590, 636*

### SUMMARY

| | | |
|---|---|---|
| 590.1–.9 | **Standard subdivisions** | |
| 591 | **Specific topics in natural history of animals** | |
| .3 | Genetics, evolution, age characteristics | |
| .4 | Physical adaptation | |
| .5 | Behavior | |
| .6 | Miscellaneous nontaxonomic kinds of animals | |
| .7 | Animal ecology, animals characteristic of specific environments | |
| .9 | Animals by specific continents, countries, localities | |

\*Add as instructed under 583–588

| | | |
|---|---|---|
| 592 | | Invertebrates |
| | .3 | Worms |
| | .4 | Platyhelminthes (Flatworms) |
| | .5 | Aschelminthes (Nemathelminthes) |
| | .6 | Annelida (Segmented worms) |
| | .7 | Oncopods (Pararthropoda) |
| | | |
| 593 | | Miscellaneous marine and seashore invertebrates |
| | .4 | Porifera (Sponges) |
| | .5 | Cnidaria (Coelenterata) |
| | .6 | Anthozoa |
| | .8 | Ctenophora (Comb jellies) |
| | .9 | Echinodermata and Hemichordata |
| | | |
| 594 | | Mollusca and Molluscoidea |
| | .2 | Minor classes of Mollusca |
| | .3 | Gastropoda |
| | .4 | Bivalvia |
| | .5 | Cephalopoda |
| | .6 | Molluscoidea |
| | | |
| 595 | | Arthropoda |
| | .3 | Crustacea |
| | .4 | Chelicerata |
| | .6 | Myriapoda |
| | .7 | Insecta (Insects) |
| | | |
| 596 | | Chordata |
| | .2 | Urochordata (Tunicata) |
| | .4 | Cephalochordata (Lancelets) |
| | | |
| 597 | | Cold-blooded vertebrates |
| | .073 | Collections and exhibits of living fishes |
| | .176 36 | Pond ecology |
| | .2 | Agnatha (Jawless fishes) |
| | .3 | Selachii, Holocephali, Sarcopterygii |
| | .4 | Miscellaneous superorders of Actinopterygii |
| | .5 | Protacanthopterygii |
| | .6 | Scopelomorpha, Paracanthopterygii, Acanthopterygii |
| | .7 | Perciformes |
| | .8 | Amphibia (Amphibians) |
| | .9 | Reptilia (Reptiles) |
| | | |
| 598 | | Aves (Birds) |
| | .072 3 | Descriptive research |
| | .163–.176 | [Beneficial and aquatic birds] |
| | .3 | Gruiformes, Charadriiformes, Ciconiiformes, Phoenicopteriformes |
| | .4 | Miscellaneous orders of water birds |
| | .5 | Palaeognathae |
| | .6 | Galliformes and Columbiformes |
| | .7 | Miscellaneous orders of land birds |
| | .8 | Passeriformes (Perching birds) |
| | .9 | Falconiformes, Strigiformes, Caprimulgiformes |
| | | |
| 599 | | Mammalia (Mammals) |
| | .144–.163 | [Head and beneficial mammals] |
| | .2 | Marsupialia and Monotremata |
| | .3 | Miscellaneous orders of Eutheria (placental mammals) |
| | .4 | Chiroptera (Bats) |
| | .5 | Cetacea and Sirenia |
| | .6 | Ungulates |
| | .7 | Carnivora |
| | .8 | Primates |
| | .9 | Homo sapiens (Humans) |

**.1–.6**      **Standard subdivisions**

> Notation from Table 1 as modified under 578.01–578.06, e.g., microscopy of animals 590.282

**.7**      **Education, research, related topics**

.723      Descriptive research

.723 2      Animal marking and census taking

> Standard subdivisions are added for either or both topics in heading

.723 4      Animal warching

[.723 409 4–.723 409 9]      Specific continents, countries, localities in modern world

> Do not use; class in 590.72344–590.72349

.723 44–.723 49      Specific continents, countries, localities in modern world

> Add to base number 590.7234 notation 4–9 from Table 2, e.g., animal watching in East Africa 590.7234676

.73      Collections and exhibits of living animals

> Class here general zoos; zoos limited to vertebrates in general, to land vertebrates in general, to mammals in general

> Add to base number 590.73 notation 1–9 from Table 2 for area in which collections and exhibits are found, e.g., zoos of Germany 590.7343

> Class zoos limited to other groups of animals with the group, e.g., insect zoos 595.7073, aquariums for marine vertebrates 596.177073

.74      Museums, collections, exhibits

> Do not use for collections and exhibits of living organisms; class in 590.73

.75      Museum activities and services

.752      Preserving zoological specimens

**.8**      **Groups of people**

**.9**      **History, geographic treatment, biography**

[.914–.919]      Areas, regions, places in general other than polar, temperate, tropical regions

> Do not use; class in 591.73–591.77

.93–.99      Zoology by specific continents, countries, localities

> Class animals by specific continents, countries, localities in 591.9

# 591 Specific topics in natural history of animals

Class here specific nontaxonomic kinds of animals

Except for modifications shown under specific entries, add to each subdivision identified by † as follows:
01–08   Standard subdivisions
         Notation from Table 1 as modified under 590.1–590.8, e.g.,
         preservation of zoological specimens 0752
09       History, geographic treatment, biography

Unless other instructions are given, observe the following table of preference, e.g., social behavior of beneficial animals 591.56 (*not* 591.63):

| | |
|---|---|
| Behavior | 591.5 |
| Miscellaneous nontaxonomic kinds of animals | 591.6 |
| Physical adaptation | 591.4 |
| Genetics, evolution, young animals | 591.3 |
| Animal ecology, animals characteristic of specific environments | 591.7 |
| Treatment of animals by specific continents, countries, localities | 591.9 |

Class a specific topic in natural history of animals with respect to a specific taxonomic group of animals with the group of animals, plus notation 1 from table under 592–599, e.g., beneficial mammals 599.163

### SUMMARY

| | |
|---|---|
| 591.3 | Genetics, evolution, age characteristics |
| .4 | Physical adaptation |
| .5 | Behavior |
| .6 | Miscellaneous nontaxonomic kinds of animals |
| .7 | Animal ecology, animals characteristic of specific environments |
| .9 | Animals by specific continents, countries, localities |

[.01–.09]   Standard subdivisions

Do not use; class in 590.1–590.9

.3   †Genetics, evolution, age characteristics

Standard subdivisions are added for genetics, evolution, age characteristics together, for genetics and evolution alone

.35   †Genetics

Class here works on genetic constitution of animals that elucidate their total function

Class experimental works on animal genetics, comprehensive works on genetics in 576.5

*For biochemical genetics in animals, see 572.81*

---

†Add standard subdivisions as instructed under 591

.38 †Evolution

Class here phylogeny

Class sexual selection in 591.562

.39 †Age characteristics

Class here age determination

.392 †Young animals

**.4 †Physical adaptation**

Class here animals noted for specific kinds of physical adaptation, comprehensive works on animal adaptation

*For behavioral adaptation, see 591.5*

.41 †Size, weight, shape

Including silhouettes

.42 †Acclimatization and temperature adaptation

Standard subdivisions are added for acclimatization and temperature adaptation together, for acclimatization alone

*For seasonal adaptation, see 591.43*

.43 †Seasonal adaptation

.44 †Head

Including ears, eyes, mouth

Class nose in 599.144

*For fangs, horns, tusks, see 591.47*

.46 †Reproductive adaptation

Class here sex characteristics, secondary sexual characteristics

Class reproductive physiology in 573.6

.468 †Eggs

*For physiology of eggs, see 573.68*

.47 †Protective and locomotor adaptations, color

Standard subdivisions are added for protective and locomotor adaptations, color together; for protective adaptation alone

Including animal weapons, claws, fangs, horns, tusks; integument

Class here animal defenses

Class physiology of musculoskeletal system in 573.7

*For protective behavior, see 591.566*

†Add standard subdivisions as instructed under 591

| .472 | †Camouflage and color |
| | Standard subdivisions are added for either or both topics in heading |
| | Class here protective coloration |
| | Class physiology of color in 573.5; class mimicry in 591.473 |
| .473 | †Mimicry |
| .477 | †Protective covering |
| | Class here exoskeletons, shells, armored animals |
| .479 | †Locomotor adaptation |
| | Including legs, tracks, wings |

**.5       †Behavior**

Class here animal psychology, behavioral adaptation, ethology

Class comparative psychology of humans and animals in 156; class physiology of nervous system in 573.8; class comprehensive works on animal adaptation in 591.4

*See Manual at 302–307 vs. 156*

| .51 | General topics in behavior |
| | Limited to those named below |
| | Class general topics related to specific behaviors in 591.53–591.59; class play in 591.563 |
| .512 | †Instinct |
| .513 | †Intelligence |
| .514 | †Learning |
| .518 | †Nocturnal behavior |
| | Class here nocturnal animals |
| .519 | †Sleep |
| | Class hibernation in 591.565 |
| | *For physiology of sleep, see 573.868* |

---

> 591.53–591.54  Feeding behavior

Class comprehensive works in 591.53

†Add standard subdivisions as instructed under 591

.53         †Predation

> Including food storing and hoarding

> Class here food habits, predator-prey relations; carnivorous animals, predatory animals; comprehensive works on feeding behavior

> Class physiology of eating in 573.35

>> *For herbivorous feeding, see 591.54*

.54         †Herbivorous feeding

> Class here browsing, grazing; herbivorous animals

.56         †Behavior relating to life cycle

> Class here reproductive behavior, social behavior, comprehensive works on life cycle of animals

> Class reproductive physiology in 573.6; class physical reproductive adaptation in 591.46; class interdisciplinary works on sociobiology in 304.5

>> *For physiology of life cycle of animals, see 571.81; for communication, see 591.59*

.562       †Sexual behavior

> Including sexual selection

> Class here courtship, mating

> Class grooming in 591.563

.563       †Family behavior

> Including grooming, kin recognition, play (regardless of kinship)

> Class here maternal behavior, parental behavior

.564       †Making habitations

> Class here nesting, nests

.564 8      †Burrowing

> Class here burrowing animals

> Class comprehensive works on soil animals in 591.757

.565       †Hibernation

> Class physiology of hibernation in 571.787

.566       †Territoriality

> Class here comprehensive works on fighting, on protective behavior

>> *For fighting during mating, see 591.562; for fighting, protective behaviors during parenting, see 591.563*

†Add standard subdivisions as instructed under 591

| | |
|---|---|
| .568 | †Migration |

Class here migratory animals

Class physiology of navigation in 573.87

| | |
|---|---|
| .57 | †Locomotion |

Including flying, swimming

| | |
|---|---|
| .59 | †Communication |

*For physiology of communication, see 573.92*

| | |
|---|---|
| .594 | †Acoustical communication |

Class here animal sounds

Class stridulation in 595.71594; class vocalization in 596.1594

**.6      †Miscellaneous nontaxonomic kinds of animals**

Not provided for elsewhere

Class here economic zoology

*See Manual at 630 vs. 579–590, 641.3*

| | |
|---|---|
| .62 | †Nonnative animals |

Class here alien, exotic, introduced, invasive, naturalized animals

| | |
|---|---|
| .63 | †Beneficial animals |

Including game animals

*For animals as food source, see 641.306*

| | |
|---|---|
| .65 | †Harmful animals |

Class here dangerous and poisonous animals, pests

| | |
|---|---|
| .68 | †Rare and endangered animals |

Standard subdivisions are added for either or both topics in heading

Including recently extinct, threatened, vanishing species,

**.7      Animal ecology, animals characteristic of specific environments**

Standard subdivisions are added for either or both topics in heading

Class here autecology, zoology of specific environments

| | |
|---|---|
| .701–.708 | Standard subdivisions |

Notation from Table 1 as modified under 590.1–590.8, e.g., microscopy 591.70282

| | |
|---|---|
| .709 | History, geographic treatment, biography |

†Add standard subdivisions as instructed under 591

[.709 14–.709 19]      Areas, regions, places in general other than polar, temperate, tropical regions

> Do not use; class in 591.73–591.77

.71–.78      Specific topics in animal ecology; specific environments

Add to base number 591.7 the numbers following 577 in 577.1–577.8, e.g., effect of pollution on animals 591.727, marine animals 591.77, effect of pollution on marine animals 591.7727

Class comprehensive works on terrestrial animals in 590

.788      Population biology

Number built according to instructions under 591.71–591.78

*For animal marking and census taking, see 590.7232*

**.9**      **Animals by specific continents, countries, localities**

Add to base number 591.9 notation 3–9 from Table 2, e.g., animals in Brazil 591.981

---

\>      **592–599  Specific taxonomic groups of animals**

Except for modifications shown under specific entries, add to each subdivision identified by * as follows:
01–08    Standard subdivisions
       Notation from Table 1 as modified under 590.1–590.8, e.g., collections of living animals 073
09       History, geographic treatment, biography
[0914–0919]    Areas, regions, places in general other than polar, temperate, tropical regions
       Do not use; class in 173–177
1       General topics of natural history of animals
       Add to base number 1 the numbers following 591 in 591.3–591.7, e.g., beneficial animals 163, marine animals 177
       Do not add notation from 591.3–591.7 when redundant or nearly so, e.g., marine sponges 593.4 (*not* 593.4177); however, it is not redundant to add notation to specify area, e.g., marine sponges of Atlantic Ocean 593.41773
Class comprehensive works in 590

**592**      ***Invertebrates**

*For Protozoa, see 579.4; for miscellaneous marine and seashore invertebrates, see 593; for Mollusca and Molluscoidea, see 594; for Arthropoda, see 595*

---

*Add as instructed under 592–599

**.3** **\*Worms**

> Including Echiurida (spoonworms), Phoronida (horseshoe worms), Pogonophora (beardworms), Priapulida

> Class here helminthology

>> *For Platyhelminthes, see 592.4; for Aschelminthes, see 592.5; for Annelida, see 592.6*

>> *See also 592.7 for oncopods*

**.32** **\*Nemertea**

> Variant names: Nemertina, Rhynchocoela, bootlace worms, proboscis worms, ribbon worms

**.33** **\*Acanthocephala (Spiny-headed worms)**

**.35** **\*Sipuncula (Peanut worms)**

**.38** **\*Chaetognatha (Arrowworms)**

> Class here Sagitta

**.4** **\*Platyhelminthes (Flatworms)**

> Including Aspidocotylea (Aspidobothria)

**.42** **\*Turbellaria**

> Including Acoela, Alloecoela, Rhabdocoela; planarians

**.44** **\*Monogenea**

**.46** **\*Cestoda (Tapeworms)**

> Class here Eucestoda

**.48** **\*Trematoda (Flukes)**

> Including Aspidogastrea

> Class here Digenea

**.5** **\*Aschelminthes (Nemathelminthes)**

**.52** **\*Rotifera (Rotifers)**

**.53** **\*Gastrotricha**

**.55** **\*Kinorhyncha (Echinodera)**

> *See also 593.9 for Echinodermata*

**.57** **\*Nematoda**

> Variant names: Nemata, roundworms

> Including Adenophorea, Secernentea

\*Add as instructed under 592–599

.59      *Nematomorpha

         Variant names: horsehair worms, hairworms

         Class here Gordioida

**.6**      **\*Annelida (Segmented worms)**

.62      *Polychaeta

         Including Archiannelida, Myzostomida, Phyllodocida

.64      *Oligochaeta

         Including Haplotaxia, Lumbriculida, Moniligastrida

         Class here earthworms (night crawlers)

.66      *Hirudinea (Leeches)

         Including Arhynchobdellida, Rhynchobdellida

**.7**      **\*Oncopods (Pararthropoda)**

.72      *Tardigrada (Water bears)

.74      *Onychophora

.76      *Pentastomida

         Including Linguatula

## 593      Miscellaneous marine and seashore invertebrates

     Limited to phyla provided for below

     *See also 592.3177 for marine and seashore worms; also 594 for Mollusca and Molluscoidea; also 595.3 for Crustacea*

[.01–.09]      Standard subdivisions

         Do not use; class in 592.01–592.09

**.4**      **\*Porifera (Sponges)**

     Class here Parazoa

.42      *Calcispongiae (Calcarea)

         Including Calcaronea, Calcinea

.44      *Hyalospongiae (Hexactinellida)

         Class here glass sponges

.46      *Demospongiae

         Including Haplosclerida, Spongillidae

**.5**      **\*Cnidaria (Coelenterata)**

     *For Anthozoa, see 593.6*

\*Add as instructed under 592–599

.53          *Scyphozoa

             Including Coronatae, Cubomedusae, Rhizostomeae, Semaeostomeae,
             Stauromedusae

             Class here comprehensive works on jellyfishes, medusae

             *For hydrozoan jellyfishes and medusae, see 593.55*

.55          *Hydrozoa

             Including Chondrophora, Hydroida, Milleporina, Pteromedusae,
             Siphonophora, Stylasterina, Trachylina

             Including hydras, Portuguese man-of-war

             Class here hydroids

.6       **Anthozoa**

             Including Alcyonaria, Zoantharia (Hexacorallia); sea anemones, fans, pens

             Class here corals

.8       **Ctenophora (Comb jellies)**

             Including Nuda, Tentaculata; sea walnuts

.9       **Echinodermata and Hemichordata**

             Subdivisions are added for Echinodermata and Hemichordata together, for
             Echinodermata alone

             *See also 592.55 for Echinodera*

             _____

>            593.92–593.96  Echinodermata

             Class comprehensive works in 593.9

.92          *Crinozoa

             Class here Crinoidea (sea lilies), Articulata

.93          *Asterozoa (Starfish)

             Including Concentricycloidea, Forcipulata, Phanerozonia, Spinulosa,
             Stelleroidea

             Class here Asteroidea

             *For Ophiuroidea, see 593.94*

.94          *Ophiuroidea

             Including Phrynophiurida, basket stars

             Class here Ophiurida, brittle stars

*Add as instructed under 592–599

.95 **\*Echinozoa**

Including Perischoechinoidea; sand dollars, sea urchins

Class here Echinoidea, Euechinoidea

*For Holothurioidea, see 593.96*

.96 **\*Holothurioidea (Sea cucumbers)**

Including Apodacea, Aspidochirotacea, Dendrochirotacea

.99 **\*Hemichordata**

Including Enteropneusta, Planctosphaeroidea, Pterobranchia

# 594 \*Mollusca and Molluscoidea

Class here malacology, comprehensive works on shellfish

Subdivisions are added for Mollusca and Molluscoidea together, for Mollusca alone

*For crustacean shellfish, see 595.3*

---

> ## 594.2–594.5 Mollusca (Mollusks)

Class comprehensive works in 594

.2 **\*Minor classes of Mollusca**

Including Aplacophora (Solenogastres), Caudofoveata, Monoplacophora

.27 **\*Polyplacophora**

Variant names: Amphineura, chitons

.29 **\*Scaphopoda**

Variant names: tooth shells, tusk shells

.3 **\*Gastropoda**

Including slugs

Class here snails

.32 **\*Prosobranchia**

Variant name: Streptoneura

Including Archaeogastropoda, Mesogastropoda, Neogastropoda; abalones, cowries, whelks; comprehensive works on limpets

*For pulmonate limpets, see 594.38*

\*Add as instructed under 592–599

.34      *Opisthobranchia

Including Acochlidacea, Cephalaspidea, Gymnosomata, Notaspidea, Philinoglossacea, Pyramidellacea, Thecosomata

Class here sea slugs

*For Sacoglossa, see 594.35; for Nudibranchia, sea slugs in the sense of Nudibranchia, see 594.36; for Anaspidea, see 594.37*

.35      *Sacoglossa

.36      *Nudibranchia

.37      *Anaspidea

Variant name: Tectibranchia

Including Pteropoda

Class here sea hares

.38      *Pulmonata

Including land slugs

Class here land snails

Including Basommatophora, Systellommatophora

Class here Stylommatophora

**.4      *Bivalvia**

Including Protobranchia; mussels, oysters, scallops, shipworms

Class here Lamellibranchia; clams

**.5      *Cephalopoda**

Class here Coleoidea

.52      *Nautiloidea

.55      *Vampyromorpha

.56      *Octopoda (Octopuses)

.58      *Decapoda

Including Sepioidea, cuttlefish

Class here Teuthoidea, squid

*See also 595.38 for crustacean Decapoda*

**.6      *Molluscoidea**

*See also 592.3 for Phoronida*

.66      *Entoprocta

*Add as instructed under 592–599

.67        *Bryozoa

Variant names: Ectoprocta, Polyzoa, moss animals

Including Cyclostomata, Stenolaemata

.676        *Gymnolaemata

Including Ctenostomata

Class here Cheilostomata

.68        *Brachiopoda (Lamp shells)

# 595        *Arthropoda

Class Pararthropoda in 592.7

### SUMMARY

| | |
|---|---|
| 595.3 | Crustacea |
| .4 | Chelicerata |
| .6 | Myriapoda |
| .7 | Insecta (Insects) |

## .3        *Crustacea

.32        *Branchiopoda

Including Anostraca (fairy and brine shrimps), Cladocera (water fleas), Conchostraca (clam shrimps), Notostraca (tadpole shrimps)

.33        *Ostracoda

Variant names: mussel shrimps, seed shrimps

Including Cladocopa, Myodocopa, Platycopa, Podocopa

.34        *Copepoda (Copepods)

Including Calanoida, Caligoida, Cyclopoida (cyclops), Harpacticoida, Lernaeopodoida, Monstrilloida, Notodelphyoida

.35        *Cirripedia (Barnacles)

Including Acrothoracica, Ascothoracica, Rhizocephala, Thoracica

.36        *Branchiura (Fish lice), Cephalocarida (horseshoe shrimps), Mystacocarida (mustache shrimps)

Including Arguloida

.37        *Malacostraca

Class here Peracarida

*For Eucarida, see 595.38*

*Add as instructed under 592–599

> 595.372–595.378 Peracarida

　　　　Class comprehensive works in 595.37

.372　　　*Isopoda

　　　　　Including pill and sow bugs, wood lice

.373　　　*Thermosbaenacea

.374　　　*Tanaidacea

.375　　　*Mysidacea (Opossum shrimps)

.376　　　*Cumacea

.378　　　*Amphipoda

　　　　　Including beach hoppers, sand fleas, scuds, well shrimps, whale lice

.379　　　*Phyllocarida, Hoplocarida, Syncarida

.379 2　　　*Phyllocarida

　　　　　Class here Leptostraca (Nebaliacea)

.379 6　　　*Hoplocarida

　　　　　Class here Stomatopoda (mantis shrimps)

.38　　　*Eucarida

　　　　Class here Decapoda, Reptantia

　　　　*See also 594.58 for cephalopod Decapoda*

> 595.384–595.388 Decapoda

　　　　Class comprehensive works in 595.38

.384　　　*Macrura

　　　　　Including lobsters, crayfishes

.386　　　*Brachyura (Crabs)

　　　　　*See also 595.387 for hermit and king crabs; also 595.492 for horseshoe crabs*

.387　　　*Anomura

　　　　　Including hermit and king crabs

.388　　　*Natantia (Shrimps)

　　　　　Including prawns

　　　　　Class here Caridea

.389　　　*Euphausiacea (Krill)

*Add as instructed under 592–599

**.4**  **\*Chelicerata**

> Class here Arachnida

---

> 595.42–595.48  Arachnida

Class comprehensive works in 595.4

.42  \*Acari

> Variant names: Acarida, Acarina, mites
>
> Including Opilioacariformes, chiggers
>
> Class here Acariformes

.429  \*Parasitiformes

> Including ticks

.43  \*Opiliones

> Variant names: Phalangida, harvestmen
>
> Including daddy longlegs

.44  \*Araneida

> Variant names: Araneae, spiders

.45  \*Minor orders of Arachnida

> Including Schizomida

.452  \*Palpigradi

.453  \*Uropygi and Amblypygi

.453 2  \*Uropygi (Whip scorpions)

.453 6  \*Amblypygi (Tailless whip scorpions)

.455  \*Ricinulei

.46  \*Scorpiones (Scorpions)

.47  \*Pseudoscorpiones (Book scorpions)

.48  \*Solpugida

> Variant names: Solifugae, sun spiders, weasel spiders, wind scorpions

.49  \*Xiphosura and Pycnogonida

.492  \*Xiphosura (Horseshoe crabs)

.496  \*Pycnogonida (Sea spiders)

**.6**  **\*Myriapoda**

.62  \*Chilopoda (Centipedes)

\*Add as instructed under 592–599

.63      *Symphyla

.64      *Pauropoda

.66      *Diplopoda (Millipedes)

**.7      *Insecta (Insects)**

> Class here Uniramia, Hexapoda, Pterygota, Endopterygota (Holometabola); entomology

> *For Myriapoda, see 595.6*

### SUMMARY

| | |
|---|---|
| 595.72 | **Apterygota; Orthoptera and related orders** |
| .73 | **Exopterygota (Hemimetabola)** |
| .74 | **Mecoptera, Trichoptera, Neuroptera, Megaloptera, Raphidiodea** |
| .75 | **Homoptera, Heteroptera, Anoplura, Mallophaga, Thysanoptera** |
| .76 | **Coleoptera (Beetles)** |
| .77 | **Diptera (Flies) and Siphonaptera** |
| .78 | **Lepidoptera** |
| .79 | **Hymenoptera** |

.72      *Apterygota; Orthoptera and related orders

> Subdivisions are added for Apterygota, Orthoptera and related orders together; for Apterygota alone

---

>      595.722–595.725 Apterygota

> All orders of Apterygota except Thysanura are sometimes regarded as classes coordinate with Insecta

> Class comprehensive works in 595.72

.722      *Protura

.723      *Thysanura (Bristletails)

> Including Microcoryphia, silverfish

.724      *Diplura (Entotrophi)

.725      *Collembola (Springtails)

---

>      595.726–595.729 Orthoptera and related orders

> Class comprehensive works in 595.726

*Add as instructed under 592–599

.726      *Orthoptera and Grylloblattodea (ice bugs)

         Including crickets, grasshoppers, katydids, locusts

         Class here comprehensive works on Orthoptera and related orders

         Subdivisions are added for Orthoptera and Grylloblattodea together, for Orthoptera alone

            *For Mantodea, see 595.727; for Blattaria, see 595.728; for Phasmida, see 595.729*

.727      *Mantodea (Mantises)

.728      *Blattaria (Cockroaches)

         Class here comprehensive works on Dictyoptera

         *For Mantodea, see 595.727*

.729      *Phasmida (Phasmatodea)

         Including leaf and stick insects, walkingsticks

.73      *Exopterygota (Hemimetabola)

         *For Orthoptera and related orders, see 595.726–595.729; for Homoptera, Heteroptera, Anoplura, Mallophaga, Thysanoptera, see 595.75*

.732      *Psocoptera

         Variant names: Corrodentia, book lice

.733      *Odonata

         Including damselflies

         Class here dragonflies

.734      *Ephemeroptera (Mayflies)

.735      *Plecoptera (Stone flies)

.736      *Isoptera (Termites)

.737      *Embioptera

.738      *Zoraptera

.739      *Dermaptera (Earwigs)

.74      *Mecoptera, Trichoptera, Neuroptera, Megaloptera, Raphidiodea

.744      *Mecoptera (Scorpion flies)

.745      *Trichoptera (Caddisflies)

*Add as instructed under 592–599

.747                    **\*Neuroptera (Lacewings), Megaloptera, Raphidiodea (snakeflies)**

Megaloptera consist of Corydalidae (dobsonflies) and Sialidae (alderflies)

Including ant lions

Subdivisions are added for Neuroptera, Megaloptera, Raphidiodea together; for Neuroptera alone

.75                **\*Homoptera, Heteroptera, Anoplura, Mallophaga, Thysanoptera**

.752                      **\*Homoptera**

Including aphids, cicadas, hoppers, plant lice, scale insects, whiteflies

Class comprehensive works on Homoptera and Heteroptera (sometimes regarded as a single order Hemiptera) in 595.754

.754                      **\*Heteroptera (True bugs)**

Including bedbugs, water striders

Class here Hemiptera whether regarded as a synonym of Heteroptera or as an order including Homoptera and Heteroptera

*For Homoptera, see 595.752*

.756                      **\*Anoplura**

Variant names: Siphunculata, sucking lice, true lice

Class here comprehensive works on Phthiraptera (apterous insects)

*For Mallophaga, see 595.757*

*See also 595.732 for book lice; also 595.752 for plant lice*

.757                      **\*Mallophaga**

Variant names: bird lice, biting lice, chewing lice

.758                      **\*Thysanoptera (Thrips)**

---

\>               **595.76–595.79 Endopterygota (Holometabola)**

Class comprehensive works in 595.7

*For Mecoptera, Trichoptera, Neuroptera, Megaloptera, Raphidiodea, see 595.74*

.76               **\*Coleoptera (Beetles)**

Including Strepsiptera

Class here Polyphaga

.762      \*Adephaga, Archostemata, Myxophaga

> Including Carabidae (ground beetles), Cicindelidae (tiger beetles), Cupedidae (reticulated beetles), Dytiscidae (true water beetles), Gyrinidae (whirligig beetles), Hydroscaphidae (skiff beetles)
>
> Subdivisions are added for Adephaga, Archostemata, Myxophaga together; for Adephaga alone

---

\>      595.763–595.769   Polyphaga

> Class comprehensive works in 595.76

.763      \*Minor superfamilies of Polyphaga

> Including Bostrychoidea, Buprestoidea (metallic wood-boring beetles), Byrrhoidea (pill beetles), Cleroidea, Dascilloidea, Dermestoidea, Histeroidea, Hydrophiloidea (water scavenger beetles), Lymexyloidea (ship timber beetles), Rhipiceroidea
>
> Including checkered, death watch, hister, pine, powder post, skin, soft-winged flower, spider beetles

.764      \*Staphylinoidea, Cantharoidea, Dryopoidea, Chrysomeloidea, Scarabaeoidea

.764 2      \*Staphylinoidea

> Including Pselaphidae, Silphidae (carrion beetles, burying beetles); mammal nest beetles
>
> Class here Staphylinidae (rove beetles)

.764 4      \*Cantharoidea

> Including Cantharidae (soldier beetles), Lampyridae (fireflies and glowworms), Lycidae (net-winged beetles)

.764 5      \*Dryopoidea

> Including Elminidae (riffle beetles)

.764 8      \*Chrysomeloidea

> Including Chrysomelidae (leaf beetles), Cerambycidae (wood boring beetles); Diabrotica, flea beetles

.764 9      \*Scarabaeoidea (Lamellicornia)

> Including Lucanidae (stag beetles, pinching bugs); dung, Japanese, June beetles; chafers, tumble bugs
>
> Class here Scarabaeidae

.765      \*Elateroidea

> Including wireworms
>
> Class here Elateridae (click beetles, snapping beetles)

---

\*Add as instructed under 592–599

.768          *Curculionoidea (Snout beetles)

               Including Anthribidae (fungus weevils), Scolytidae (bark beetles)

               Class here Curculionidae (weevils)

.769          *Cucujoidea

               Including Coccinellidae (ladybugs), Colydiidae (cylindrical bark beetles), Meloidea (blister beetles), Mordellidae (tumbling flower beetles), Nitidulidae (sap beetles), Tenebrionidae (darkling beetles)

               Including flour and oil beetles, mealworms

.77         *Diptera (Flies) and Siphonaptera

               Subdivisions are added for Diptera and Siphonaptera together, for Diptera alone

               Class maggots in 595.771392

---

&gt;        595.772–595.774 Diptera

            Class comprehensive works in 595.77

.772         *Nematocera (Long-horned flies)

               Including Bibionidae (March flies), Cecidomyiidae (gall gnats and midges), Chironomidae, Culicidae (mosquitoes), Psychodidae (moth flies), Sciaridae, Simuliidae (blackflies and buffalo gnats), Tipulidae (crane flies)

               Including gnats, leatherjackets, midges

               *See also 595.773 for March flies of family Tabanidae*

.773         *Brachycera

               Variant name: Brachycera-Orthorrhapha

               Including Asilidae (robber flies), Bombyliidae (bee flies), Dolichopodidae (long-legged flies), Empididae (dance flies), Rhagionidae (snipe flies), Stratiomyidae (soldier flies), Tabanidae (horseflies), Therevidae (stiletto flies)

               Including deerflies, March flies of family Tabanidae, mydas flies

               *See also 595.772 for Bibionidae (March flies)*

---

*Add as instructed under 592–599

.774          *Cyclorrhapha

Variant name: Brachycera-Cyclorrhapha

Including Agromyzidae (leaf miner flies), Braulidae (bee lice), Calliphoridae (blowflies), Chamaemyiidae (aphid flies), Chyromyiidae, Diopsidae (stalk-eyed flies), Drosophilidae (small fruit flies), Ephydridae (shore flies), Glossinidae, Hippoboscidae (louse flies), Muscidae, Oestridae (botflies and warble flies), Phoridae (humpbacked flies, coffin flies), Piophilidae (skipper flies), Sarcophagidae (flesh flies), Scatophagidae (dung flies), Sciomyzidae (marsh flies), Syrphidae (hover flies, flower flies), Tachinidae, Trypetidae (large fruit flies)

Including houseflies; bat, beach, rust, stable, tsetse, vinegar flies

.775          *Siphonaptera (Fleas)

.78           *Lepidoptera

Including Bombycoidea, Geometroidea, Noctuoidea, Pyralidoidea, Tineoidea, Tortricoidea

Including armyworms, budworms, cutworms, Heliothis

Class here moths

Class caterpillars in 595.781392

.788          *Hesperioidea (Skippers)

.789          *Papilionoidea (Butterflies)

.79           *Hymenoptera

Including Chalcidoidea, Ichneumonoidea, Scolioidea, Symphyta (sawflies)

Class here Apocrita, wasps, social insects

Class true wasps (Vespoidea) in 595.798

.796          *Formicidae (Ants)

.798          *Vespoidea and Sphecoidea

Class here true wasps

Subdivisions are added for Vespoidea and Sphecoidea together, for Vespoidea alone

Class wasps of superfamilies other than Vespoidea and Sphecoidea in 595.79

.799          *Apoidea (Bees)

# 596    *Chordata

Class here Vertebrata (Craniata, vertebrates), Tetrapoda (land vertebrates), amniotes

*For cold-blooded vertebrates, see 597; for Aves, see 598; for Mammalia, see 599*

*Add as instructed under 592–599

[.073]    Collections and exhibits of living vertebrates

> Do not use; class in 590.73

.2    **\*Urochordata (Tunicata)**

> Including Ascidiacea (sea squirts), Larvacea, Thaliacea

.4    **\*Cephalochordata (Lancelets)**

# 597    \*Cold-blooded vertebrates

Class here Pisces (Fishes), Osteichthyes (bony fishes), Actinopterygii (ray-finned fishes), Teleostei; ichthyology

Class specific kinds of Osteichthyes in 597.39 or 597.4–597.7; class specific kinds of Actinopterygii in 597.4–597.7; class specific kinds of Teleostei in 597.43–597.49 or 597.5–597.7

### SUMMARY

| | |
|---|---|
| 597.073 | **Collections and exhibits of living fishes** |
| .176 36 | **Pond ecology** |
| .2 | **Agnatha (Jawless fishes)** |
| .3 | **Selachii, Holocephali, Sarcopterygii** |
| .4 | **Miscellaneous superorders of Actinopterygii** |
| .5 | **Protacanthopterygii** |
| .6 | **Scopelomorpha, Paracanthopterygii, Acanthopterygii** |
| .7 | **Perciformes** |
| .8 | **Amphibia (Amphibians)** |
| .9 | **Reptilia (Reptiles)** |

.073    Collections and exhibits of living fishes

> Class here interdisciplinary works on aquariums

> *For fish culture in aquariums, see 639.34*

.176 36    Pond ecology

> Number built according to instructions under 592–599

> Class fishpond ecosystems in 577.636

---

>    **597.2–597.7  Pisces (Fishes)**

> Class comprehensive works in 597

.2    **\*Agnatha (Jawless fishes)**

> Class here Cyclostomata (hagfishes and lampreys)

---

\*Add as instructed under 592–599

.3 **\*Selachii, Holocephali, Sarcopterygii**

> Class here Chondrichthyes (cartilaginous fishes), Elasmobranchii, Lamniformes covering most sharks, Carcharhiniformes; sharks

> Subdivisions are added for Selachii, Holocephali, Sarcopterygii together; for Selachii alone

> Class typical sharks (family Carcharhinidae) in 597.34; class cartilaginous ganoids in 597.42

> 597.33–597.36 **Selachii**

>> Class here sharks

>> Class comprehensive works in 597.3

.33 **\*Lamnidae**

> Variant names: Isuridae, mackerel sharks

> Including mako sharks

> Class here Carcharodon carcharias (great white shark)

> Class comprehensive works on Lamniformes in 597.3

.34 **\*Carcharhinidae**

> Variant name: typical sharks

> Including Australian school, blacktip, bull, great blue, lemon, soupfin, tiger, whitetip sharks; tope

> Class comprehensive works on Carcharhiniformes in 597.3

.35 **\*Rajiformes (Batoidei)**

> Including guitarfishes, sawfishes, skates, torpedoes

> Class here rays

.36 **\*Dogfishes**

> Including Oxynotidae (Dalatiidae), Triakidae

> Class here Squaliformes, Squalidae

.38 **\*Holocephali**

> Class here Chimaerae (Chimaeriformes, chimeras, ghost sharks)

.39 **\*Sarcopterygii (Fleshy-finned fishes)**

> Including Crossopterygii (coelacanths), Dipnoi (lungfishes); barramunda

> 597.4–597.7 **Actinopterygii (Ray-finned fishes)**

>> Class comprehensive works in 597

\*Add as instructed under 592–599

**.4**     **Miscellaneous superorders of Actinopterygii**

Limited to those named below

Class comprehensive works on Actinopterygii in 597

[.401–.409]     Standard subdivisions

Do not use; class in 597.01–597.09

.41     *Holostei

Including Amiiformes (bowfins and river dogfishes), Semionotiformes (gars)

Class here bony ganoids

*See also 597.66 for garfish of order Atheriniformes*

.42     *Chondrostei

Including Polypteriformes (bichirs and reedfishes)

Class here Acipenseriformes (sturgeons and paddlefishes); cartilaginous ganoids, comprehensive works on Ganoidei

*For bony ganoids, see 597.41*

.43     *Elopomorpha

Including Elopiformes, Notacanthiformes; Saccopharyngidae (swallowers); congers, morays, tarpons

Class here Anguilliformes (eels), comprehensive works on eels

*For a specific kind of nonanguilliform eel, see the kind, e.g., electric eels 597.48, swamp eels 597.64*

*See also 597.7 for swallowers of family Chiasmodontidae*

.432     *Anguillidae (Freshwater eels)

Class here Anguilla

Subdivisions are added for the family as a whole and for individual species

.45     *Clupeomorpha

Including anchovies, menhadens, pilchards, sardines, shads

Class here Clupeiformes, Clupeidae (herring family)

Class sardines in sense of young bristling and herring in 597.452

.452     *Clupea

Class here bristling (sprat), common herring

Young bristling and common herring are often called sardines

Class true sardine in 597.45

*Add as instructed under 592–599

.47       *Osteoglossomorpha

Including Osteoglossiformes, Mormyriformes; elephant fishes, freshwater butterfly fishes

*See also 597.72 for marine butterfly fishes*

---

>       597.48–597.49 Ostariophysi

Class Gonorhynchiformes in 597.5; class comprehensive works in 597.48

.48       *Cypriniformes

Including Characidae (Characins), Citharinidae (moonfishes), Gasteropelecidae (freshwater hatchetfishes), Gymnotidae (knifefishes); electric eels, headstanders, loaches, pencil fishes, piranhas, suckers, tetras, tigerfishes

Class here Characiformes, comprehensive works on Ostariophysi

*For Siluriformes, see 597.49*

*See also 597.5 for marine hatchetfishes; also 597.66 for Cyprinodontoidei; also 597.7 for moonfishes of order Perciformes*

.482       *Cyprinidae (Carp family)

Including bighead and grass carps; barbs (barbels), bream, chubs, daces, danios, freshwater zebra fishes, roach, shiners, squawfishes, tench

Class here minnows

*For Cyprinus carpio (common carp), see 597.483; for Carassius (goldfish), see 597.484*

*See also 597.68 for marine zebra fishes*

.483       *Cyprinus carpio (Common carp)

Class koi in 639.37483; class interdisciplinary works on carp in 641.392

.484       *Carassius (Goldfish)

Class interdisciplinary works on goldfish in 639.37484

.49       *Siluriformes (Catfishes)

.492       *Ictaluridae (North American freshwater catfishes)

Including Noturus (madtoms)

Class here Ictalurus; bullheads; blue, channel catfishes

Subdivisions are added for Ictaluridae as a whole and for individual species of Ictalurus

*Add as instructed under 592–599

**.5** **\*Protacanthopterygii**

Including Gonorhynchiformes, Stomiiformes (Stomiatiformes); Sternoptychidae (marine hatchetfishes); milkfish, mudminnows, smelts, stomiatoid dragonfishes, viperfishes

Class here Salmoniformes

Class Myctophiformes in 597.61

> *See also 597.48 for freshwater hatchetfishes; also 597.64 for dragonfishes of order Pegasiformes*

---

> **597.55–597.59 Salmoniformes**

Class comprehensive works in 597.5

**.55** **\*Salmonidae**

Including Australian grayling, whitefishes (whitings)

Class brook (speckled), Dolly Varden trout, lake trout in 597.554

> *For salmon, see 597.56; for trout of genus Salmo, see 597.57*

> *See also 597.633 for whitings of genus Gadus; also 597.72 for rock whiting; also 597.725 for whiting (kingfish)*

**.554** **\*Salvelinus (Chars)**

Class here brook (speckled) trout, Dolly Varden trout, lake trout

Subdivisions are added for the genus as a whole and for individual species

**.559** **\*Thymallus (Graylings)**

Subdivisions are added for the genus as a whole and for individual species

Class Australian grayling in 597.55

**.56** **\*Salmon**

Class here Salmo salar (Atlantic salmon), Pacific salmon, comprehensive works on Oncorhynchus

Subdivisions are added for salmon as a whole and for individual species of salmon

> *For Rhabdofario, see 597.57*

> *See also 597.7 for Australian salmon*

---

\*Add as instructed under 592–599

.57      *Trout

> Species of subgenus Rhabdofario and genus Salmo other than Salmo salar

> .Class here comprehensive works on Salmo

> Subdivisions are added for trout as a whole and for individual species

>> *For Salmo salar, comprehensive works on Oncorhynchus, see 597.56*

>> *See also 597.554 for brook (speckled), Dolly Varden, lake trout*

.59      *Esocidae

> Class here Esox; muskellunge (muskie), pickerels, pikes

> Subdivisions are added for the family as a whole and for individual species

> Class comprehensive works on Esociformes in 597.5

>> *See also 597.758 for walleyed pike*

**.6      Scopelomorpha, Paracanthopterygii, Acanthopterygii**

> Class comprehensive works in 597

[.601–.609]      Standard subdivisions

> Do not use; class in 597.01–597.09

.61      *Scopelomorpha

> Including Myctophidae (lantern fishes), Synodontidae (lizard fishes); spiderfishes

> Class here Myctophiformes

.62      *Paracanthopterygii

> Including Batrachoidiformes (toadfishes), Gobiesociformes (clingfishes), Percopsiformes, Polymixiiformes (beard fishes)

> Including anglerfishes, batfishes, cavefishes, frogfishes, goosefishes, trout-perches

> Class here Lophiiformes

>> *For cave fishes of superorder Ostariophysi, see 597.48; for Gadiformes, see 597.63*

.63      *Gadiformes

> Including Carapidae (Carapodidae, pearlfishes), Macrouridae (grenadiers), Moridae (deep sea cods), Ophidiidae (brotulas and cusk eels), Zoarcidae (eelpouts)

*Add as instructed under 592–599

.632       *Gadidae, Merluciidae (Merlucciid hakes), Pycidae (Phycid hakes)

Including arctic cod, burbots, haddocks, hakes, pollocks

Class here Gadoidei

Subdivisions are added for Gadidae, Merluciidae, Pycidae together, for Gadidae alone

*For Gadus (cods), see 597.633*

.633       *Gadus (Cods)

Class here Atlantic cod, Greenland cod, Pacific cod, whitings

*See also 597.55 for whitings (whitefishes); also 597.63 for deep sea cods; also 597.632 for arctic cod; also 597.72 for rock whitings; also 597.725 for whitings (kingfish)*

.64       *Acanthopterygii (Spiny-rayed fishes)

Including Beryciformes, Channiformes (snakeheads), Dactylopteriformes, Lampridiformes, Pegasiformes (dragonfishes, seamoths), Synbranchiformes (swamp eels), Tetraodontiformes, Zeiformes

Including alfonsinos, boar fishes, boxfishes, cowfishes, filefishes, John Dories, lantern-eyed fishes, oarfishes, ocean sunfishes, opah, orange roughy, pinecone fishes, porcupine fishes, puffer fishes, squirrelfishes (soldierfishes), triggerfishes, unicorn fishes, whale fishes

*For Atheriniformes, see 597.66; for Gasterosteiformes, see 597.67; for Scorpaeniformes, see 597.68; for Pleuronectiformes, see 597.69; for Perciformes, see 597.7*

*See also 597.2 for lampreys; also 597.5 for stomiatoid dragonfishes*

.66       *Atheriniformes

Including Cyprinodontoidei, Exocoetidae (flying fishes); garfish, halfbeaks, needlefishes, silversides, topminnows

Class Cyprinodontidae and topminnows of families Cyprinodontidae and Poeciliidae in 597.665–597.667

*See also 597.41 for gars of order Semionotiformes; also 597.48 for Cypriniformes*

.665       *Cyprinodontidae (Killifishes)

.667       *Poeciliidae (Live-bearers)

Including guppies, mollies, platy, swordtail

.67       *Gasterosteiformes

Including ghost pipefishes, trumpet fishes

.672       *Gasterosteidae (Sticklebacks)

Subdivisions are added for the family as a whole and for individual genera and species

*Add as instructed under 592–599

| | | |
|---|---|---|
| .679 | | *Syngnathidae |

Class here pipefishes

Subdivisions are added for the family as a whole and for individual species of pipefishes

Class ghost pipefishes in 597.67

.679 8          *Sea horses

Class here Hippocampus

Subdivisions are added for sea horses as a whole and for individual genera and species

.68          *Scorpaeniformes

Including gurnards, marine zebra fishes, rockfishes, scorpion fishes

*See also 597.482 for freshwater zebra fishes*

.69          *Pleuronectiformes

Variant names: Heterosomata, flatfishes

Including California halibut, soles, turbots

Class here flounders

Class turbot of family Pleuronectidae in 597.694

.694          *Pleuronectidae (Right-eyed flounders)

Including Greenland halibut, plaice, winter flounder

*For Hippoglossus (halibuts), see 597.695*

.695          *Hippoglossus (Halibuts)

Subdivisions are added for the genus as a whole and for individual species

*See also 597.69 for California halibut; also 597.694 for Greenland halibut*

## .7      *Perciformes

Including Mugilidae (mullets), Chiasmodontidae (swallowers); Australian salmon, barracudas, betta (Siamese fighting fish), big game fishes, cardinal fishes, goatfishes, gobies, grunts, halfmoons, labyrinth fishes, moonfishes, parrotfishes, spiny eels, stargazers, wrasses

Class here Percoidei

*See also 597.43 for swallowers of family Saccopharyngidae; also 597.48 for moonfishes of family Citharinidae*

---

*Add as instructed under 592–599

.72     *Percoidea

      Including Centropomidae (robalos, snooks), Chaetodontidae (marine butterfly fishes), Latidae (giant perches), Lethrinidae, Lutjanidae (snappers), Pomacanthidae (angelfishes), Pomacentridae (damselfishes), Sparidae (porgies, sea breams)

      Including dolphinfishes, garibaldi, jacks, rock whiting, scups; comprehensive works on angelfishes

        *For basses and related fishes, see 597.73; for Cichlidae, angelfishes of cichlid family, see 597.74; for Percidae, see 597.75*

        *See also 597.47 for freshwater butterfly fishes*

.725     *Sciaenidae

      Variant names: drums, croakers

      Including Sciaenops, red drum (channel bass), weakfish, whiting (kingfish)

        *See also 597.55 for whitings (whitefishes); also 597.633 for whitings of genus Gadus; also 597.72 for rock whiting*

.73     *Basses and related fishes

      Including Grammatidae (basslets), Percichthyidae (temperate basses, perch trout)

      Including Australian bass; macquarie perch

      Subdivisions are added for basses and related fishes together, for basses alone

        *For channel bass, see 597.725*

.732     *Moronidae

      Class here Morone; striped, white bass; white perch

.736     *Serranidae (Sea basses)

      Including graysby, groupers

.738     *Centrarchidae

      Including crappies; calico and rock basses

      Class here sunfishes

.738 8     *Micropterus (Black basses)

      Class here largemouth, smallmouth basses

      Subdivisions are added for the genus as a whole and for individual species

.74     *Cichlidae

      Including Pterophyllum (angelfishes), Symphysodon (discus fishes); tilapias

      Class comprehensive works on angelfishes in 597.72

*Add as instructed under 592–599

.75      *Percidae

     Including perches

     Class here darters

     *See also 597.72 for giant perches; also 597.732 for white perch*

.758      *Stizostedion

     Variant names: Lucioperca, pike perches

     Class here sauger, walleye (walleyed pike), zander

.77      *Blennioidei (Blennies)

.78      *Scombroidei

     Including Gempylidae, Istiophoridae, Trichiuridae (cutlass fishes), Xiphiidae (swordfish)

     Including billfishes, marlins, sailfishes, spearfishes

.782      *Scombridae

     Class here mackerel

     *For tunas, see 597.783*

.783      *Tunas

     Class here Thunnus; albacore, bonito, skipjack

     Subdivisions are added for tunas as a whole and for individual species

**.8      *Amphibia (Amphibians)**

     Class here Anura (Salientia)

     Class herpetology, comprehensive works on Amphibia and Reptilia in 597.9

.82      *Gymnophiona

     Variant names: Apoda, Caecilians

.85      *Urodela

     Variant names: Caudata, salamanders

     Including Sirenidae (sirens); congo eels, hellbender, mud puppies, newts

.858      *Ambystomatidae (Mole salamanders)

     Class here Ambystoma, axolotl

     Subdivisions are added for the genus Ambystoma and for individual species of Ambystoma

.859      *Plethodontidae (Lungless salamanders)

.859 2      *Plethodon

     Subdivisions are added for the genus as a whole and for individual species

*Add as instructed under 592–599

>        597.86–597.89 Anura (Salientia)

       Class here frogs and toads

       Class comprehensive works in 597.8

.86        *Pipoidea, Discoglossoidea, Pelobatoidea

         Including fire-bellied and midwife toads; spadefoots

         Class comprehensive works on toads in 597.87; class comprehensive works on frogs in 597.89

.865       *Pipoidea

         Including burrowing and Surinam toads

         Class here Pipidae (tongueless frogs)

.865 4      *Xenopus

         Class here African clawed frog

         Subdivisions are added for the genus as a whole and for individual species

.87      *Bufonoidea

         Including Centrolenidae (leaf frogs), Rhinodermatidae (mouth-breeding frogs)

         Class here Bufonidae, comprehensive works on toads

         *For a specific kind of toad of a superfamily other than Bufonoidea, see the kind, e.g., midwife toads 597.86*

.872      *Bufo

         Subdivisions are added for the genus as a whole and for individual species

.875      *Leptodactylidae

.875 4      *Eleutherodactylus

         Subdivisions are added for the genus as a whole and for individual species

.877      *Dendrobatidae (Poison arrow frogs)

.878      *Hylidae (Tree frogs)

.878 2      *Hyla

         Subdivisions are added for the genus as a whole and individual species

*Add as instructed under 592–599

.89      *Ranoidea

> Including Microhylidae

> Class here Ranidae, comprehensive works on frogs

> *For a specific kind of frog of a superfamily other than Ranoidea, see the kind, e.g., tree frogs 597.878*

.892      *Rana

> Class here bullfrogs

> Subdivisions are added for the genus as a whole and for individual species

## .9      *Reptilia (Reptiles)

> Class here herpetology, comprehensive works on Amphibia and Reptilia

> *For Amphibia, see 597.8*

### SUMMARY

| | | |
|---|---|---|
| 597.92 | Chelonia | |
| .94 | Lepidosauria | |
| .95 | Sauria (Lizards) | |
| .96 | Serpentes (Snakes) | |
| .98 | Crocodilia (Crocodilians) | |

.92      *Chelonia

> Variant names: Testudines, turtles

> Class here Testudinoidea

[.921 77]      Marine turtles

> Do not use; class in 597.928

.922      *Chelydridae (Snapping turtles)

> Subdivisions are added for the family as a whole and for individual genera and species

.923      *Kinosternidae

> Including musk turtles

> Class here Kinosternon (mud turtles)

> Subdivisions are added for the genus Kinosternon as a whole and for individual species of Kinosternon

.924      *Testudinidae

> Variant names: terrestrial turtles, tortoises

.924 6      *Geochelone

> Including Galapagos tortoise

*Add as instructed under 592–599

| .925 | *Emydidae |
| | |

Including Terrapene (North American box turtles)

Class here terrapins

| .925 7 | *Clemmys |

Class here bog, spotted, wood turtles

Subdivisions are added for the genus as a whole and for individual species

| .925 9 | *Chrysemys, Pseudemys, Deirochelys (Chicken turtle), Graptemys (Map turtles), Malaclemys (Diamond-backed terrapin), Trachemys (Sliders) |

| .925 92 | *Chrysemys (Painted turtle) |

| .925 94 | *Pseudemys |

Class here cooters, red-bellied turtles

Subdivisions are added for the genus as a whole and for individual species

| .926 | *Trionychidae (Soft-shelled turtles), Carettochelyidae (New Guinea plateless turtle), Dermatemydidae, Platysternidae |

Subdivisions are added for Trionychidae, Carettochelyidae, Dermatemydidae, Platysternidae together; for Trionychidae alone

| .928 | *Chelonioidea (Sea turtles) |

Class here Cheloniidae, marine turtles

Subdivisions are added for the family Cheloniidae and for individual genera and species of Cheloniidae

| .928 9 | *Dermochelyidae (Leatherback turtle) |

| .929 | *Pleurodira (Side-necked turtles) |

Including Chelyidae (snake-necked turtles), Pelomedusidae

| .94 | *Lepidosauria |

Class here Squamata (scaly reptiles)

*For Sauria, see 597.95; for Serpentes, see 597.96*

| .945 | *Rhynchocephalia (Beaked reptiles) |

Class here Sphenodontidae (tuatara)

| .948 | *Amphisbaenia (Worm lizards) |

Class here Amphisbaenidae

| .95 | *Sauria (Lizards) |

Class comprehensive works on Sauria and Serpentes in 597.94

*Add as instructed under 592–599

| .952 | *Gekkonidea |
| | Including Anelytropsidae, Dibamidae, Pygopodidae (flap-footed lizards) |
| | Class here Gekkonidae (geckos) |
| .954 | *Iguanidae |
| | Class here Iguanioidea |
| | *For Agamidae, see 597.955* |
| .954 2 | *Iguanas |
| .954 8 | *Anolis (Anoles) |
| | Class here false or New World chameleons |
| .955 | *Agamidae |
| | Including Draco (flying lizards) |
| .956 | *Chamaeleontidae (Chameleons) |
| | Subdivisions are added for the family as a whole and for individual genera and species |
| | Class here Rhiptoglossidea |
| | *See also 597.9548 for false or New World chameleons* |
| .957 | *Scincidae (Skinks) |
| | Class here Scincomorphoidea |
| | *For Teiidae, Cordylidae, Lacertidae, see 597.958* |
| .957 3 | *Eumeces |
| .958 | *Teiidae, Cordylidae (Girdle-tailed lizards), Lacertidae (Old World runners) |
| .958 2 | *Teiidae (New World runners) |
| | Including Ameiva |
| .958 25 | *Cnemidophorus |
| | Variant names: racerunners, whiptails |
| | Subdivisions are added for the genus as a whole and for individual species |
| .959 | *Anguinomorphoidea |
| | Including Anniellidae (California legless lizards), Xenosauridae |
| .959 2 | *Anguidae |
| | Including alligator and glass lizards |

*Add as instructed under 592–599

| | |
|---|---|
| .959 5 | *Helodermatidae |
| | Including beaded lizard |
| | Class here Heloderma |
| .959 52 | *Heloderma suspectum (Gila monster) |
| .959 6 | *Varanidae (Monitor lizards) and Lanthanotidae (Earless monitor lizard) |
| | Class here Varanus |
| | Subdivisions are added for Varanidae and Lanthanotidae together, for Varanidae alone |
| .959 68 | *Varanus komodoensis (Komodo dragon) |
| .959 8 | *Xantusiidae (Night lizards) |
| .96 | *Serpentes (Snakes) |
| | Class here Colubroidea |
| [.961 77] | Marine snakes |
| | Do not use; class in 597.965 |
| .962 | *Colubridae |
| | Including egg-eating and false coral snakes |
| | Class here Colubrinae |
| | Class false coral snake of family Aniliidae in 597.967 |
| .963 | *Viperidae (Vipers) |
| | Class here adders |
| | Class death adders in 597.964 |
| .963 6 | *Vipera |
| | Class here asp; common, Lebanese, Portuguese, sand adders |
| | Subdivisions are added for the genus as a whole and for individual species |
| .963 8 | *Crotalus (Rattlesnakes) and Sistrurus (Pigmy rattlesnakes) |
| | Subdivisions are added for Crotalus and Sistrurus together, for Crotalus alone, for individual species of Crotalus |
| .964 | *Elapidae |
| | Including death adders |
| .964 2 | *Cobras |
| | Class here Naja |
| | Subdivisions are added for the genus Naja and for individual species of Naja |

*Add as instructed under 592–599

.964 4      *Coral snakes

         Class here Micrurus

         Subdivisions are added for the genus Micrurus and for individual species of Micrurus

         Class false coral snakes of family Colubridae in 597.962; class false coral snake of family Aniliidae in 597.967

.965      *Hydrophiidae (Sea snakes)

         Class here marine snakes

.967      *Booidea (Henophidia)

         Including Acrochordidae (wart snakes), Aniliidae (false coral snake), Uropeltidae (pipe and shieldtail snakes), Xenopeltidae (sunbeam snakes); anacondas, wood snakes

         Class here Boidae, Boinae (Boas)

         Class false coral snakes of family Colubridae in 597.962

.967 8      *Pythoninae (Pythons)

         Class here Python

         Subdivisions are added for the genus Python and for individual species of Python

.969      *Typhlopoidea (Scolecophidia)

         Including Leptotyphlopidae (slender blind snakes), Typhlopidae (blind or worm snakes)

.98      *Crocodilia (Crocodilians)

         Including gavial

.982      *Crocodilidae (Crocodiles)

         Class here Crocodylus

         Subdivisions are added for the genus Crocodylus and for individual species of Crocodylus

.984      *Alligatoridae

         Including caimans

         Class here alligators, Alligator mississippiensis

# 598     *Aves (Birds)

         Class here land birds, ornithology

         Class specific kinds of land birds in 598.5–598.9; class comprehensive works on warm-blooded vertebrates in 599; class interdisciplinary works on species of domestic birds in 636.5

*Add as instructed under 592–599

.072 3            Descriptive research

.072 32           Bird marking and census taking

> Number built according to instructions under 592–599

> Class here birdbanding

[.072 340 94–.072 340 99]     Specific continents, countries, localities in modern world

> Do not use; class in 598.072344–598.072349

.072 344–.072 349     Specific continents, countries, localities in modern world

> Add to base number 598.07234 notation 4–9 from Table 2, e.g., bird watching in East Africa 598.07234676

.163            Beneficial birds

> Number built according to instructions under 592–599

> Including game birds, wildfowl

> Class lowland game birds, waterfowl in 598.41; class upland game birds in 598.6

.176            Aquatic birds

> Number built according to instructions under 592–599

> Class here water birds

> Class waterfowl in 598.41

> *For specific kinds of water birds, see 598.3–598.4*

---

>        **598.3–598.4 Water birds**

> Class comprehensive works in 598.176

.3      **\*Gruiformes, Charadriiformes, Ciconiiformes, Phoenicopteriformes**

> Class here wading birds

\*Add as instructed under 592–599

.32      *Gruiformes

Including Gruidae (cranes), Otididae (bustards), Psophiidae (trumpeters), Rallidae (rail family), Turnicidae (button quails)

Including coots, gallinules

.33      *Charadriiformes

Including Charadriidae (plovers and lapwings), Alcidae, Haematopodidae (oystercatchers), Jacanidae (jacanas), Phalaropodidae (phalaropes), Scolopacidae

Including auks, murres, puffins, sandpipers, snipes, turnstones, woodcocks

Class here Charadrii, shore birds

.338      *Lari

Including Rynchopidae (skimmers), Stercorariidae (skuas and jaegers)

Class here Laridae (gulls and terns)

.34      *Ciconiiformes

Including Ciconiidae (storks), Ardeidae, Threskiornithidae (ibis and spoonbills)

Including bitterns, egrets, herons

Class Charadriiformes in 598.33

.35      *Phoenicopteriformes (Flamingos)

Class here Phoenicopteridae

Subdivisions are added for the genus Phoenicopterus and for individual species of Phoenicopterus

**.4      Miscellaneous orders of water birds**

Limited to those named below

Class comprehensive works on water birds in 598.176

[.401–.409]      Standard subdivisions

Do not use; class in 598.17601–598.17609

.41      *Anseriformes

Including Anhimidae (screamers)

Class here Anatidae (waterfowl); ducks; comprehensive works on lowland game birds

*For a specific kind of lowland game bird, see the kind, e.g., murres 598.33*

*Add as instructed under 592–599

> 598.412–598.415 Ducks

Class comprehensive works in 598.41

.412 *Aix

Including mandarin duck

.412 3 *Aix sponsa (Wood duck)

.413 *Anas

Including black duck, blue-winged teal

.413 4 *Anas platyrhynchos (Mallard)

.414 *Aythya

Including canvasback

.415 *Mergini

Including eiders, goldeneyes, mergansers

.417 *Anserini (Geese)

.417 3 *Anser

Including greylag and white-fronted geese

.417 5 *Chen

Class here snow, blue goose

.417 8 *Branta

Class here Canada goose

.418 *Cygninae (Swans)

Class here Cygnus

.418 4 *Cygnus buccinator (Trumpeter swan)

.418 7 *Cygnus olor (Mute swan)

.42 *Procellariiformes

Including Procellariidae, Diomedeidae (albatrosses), Hydrobatidae (storm petrels), Pelecanoididae (diving petrels)

Including fulmars, shearwaters

.43 *Pelecaniformes

Including Pelecanidae (pelicans), Fregatidae (frigate birds), Phaethontidae (tropic birds), Phalacrocoracidae (cormorants), Sulidae (boobies)

.44 *Gaviiformes and Podicipediformes

Class here Colymbiformes

*Add as instructed under 592–599

| .442 | *Gaviiformes (Loons) |
| .443 | *Podicipediformes (Grebes) |

Class here Podicipedidae

| .47 | *Sphenisciformes (Penguins) |

---

> ## 598.5–598.9 Land birds

Class comprehensive works in 598

### .5 *Palaeognathae

Class here ratites

| .52 | *Rheiformes and Struthioniformes |
| .522 | *Rheiformes |

Subdivisions are added for the genus Rhea as a whole and for individual species of Rhea

| .524 | *Struthioniformes (Ostrich) |
| .53 | *Casuariiformes |

Including emu

Class here Casuariidae (cassowaries)

Subdivisions are added for the genus Casuarius and for individual species of Casuarius

| .54 | *Apterygiformes (Kiwis) |

Subdivisions are added for the genus Apteryx and for individual species of Apteryx

Sometimes classed with extinct moas as Dinornithiformes

| .55 | *Tinamiformes (Tinamous) |

Class here Tinamidae

### .6 *Galliformes and Columbiformes

Class here Galli, poultry, upland game birds

Subdivisions are added for Galliformes and Columbiformes together, for Galliformes alone

Class interdisciplinary works on domestic poultry in 636.5

*For a specific kind of upland game bird, see the kind, e.g., crows 598.864*

---

> ## 598.62–598.64 Galliformes

Class comprehensive works in 598.6

---

*Add as instructed under 592–599

| | |
|---|---|
| .62 | *Phasianidae |
| .623 | *Partridges |

Including francolins

| | |
|---|---|
| .623 2 | *Perdix perdix |

Variant names: common partridge, gray partridge, Hungarian partridge

| | |
|---|---|
| .625 | *Pheasants |

Including Gallus (chickens, jungle fowl)

Class results of experimental studies in internal biological processes using chickens in 571–573, plus notation 18625 from add instructions in 571–573, e.g., embryology in domestic chickens 571.8618625; class interdisciplinary works on Gallus (chickens) in 636.5

| | |
|---|---|
| .625 2 | *Phasianus colchicus (Ring-necked pheasant) |
| .625 8 | *Pavo (Peafowl) |

Subdivisions are added for the genus as a whole, and for individual species

| | |
|---|---|
| .627 | *Quails |

Including Gambel's quail

*See also 598.32 for button quails*

| | |
|---|---|
| .627 2 | *Coturnix |

Including common and Japanese quails

*See also 598.6273 for bobwhites*

| | |
|---|---|
| .627 3 | *Colinus (Bobwhites) |

Subdivisions are added for the genus as a whole and for individual species

| | |
|---|---|
| .63 | *Tetraonidae (Grouse) |

*See also 598.65 for sand grouse*

| | |
|---|---|
| .633 | *Lagopus (Ptarmigans) |

Subdivisions are added for the genus as a whole and for individual species

| | |
|---|---|
| .634 | *Tetrao |

Including black grouse, capercaillies

| | |
|---|---|
| .635 | *Bonasa |

Class here ruffed grouse

| | |
|---|---|
| .636 | *Centrocercus (Sage grouse) |

*Add as instructed under 592–599

.637           \*Tympanuchus

> Subdivisions are added for either of both species of prairie chickens

.637 8         \*Tympanuchus phasianellus (Sharp-tailed grouse)

.64        \*Other families of Galliformes

> Including Cracidae, Megapodiidae (brush turkeys, mound builders), Numididae (Guinea fowl)

> Including chachalacas, curassows, guans

.645        \*Meleagrididae (Turkeys)

> Class here Meleagris gallopavo, wild turkeys

> Class interdisciplinary works on turkeys in 636.592

.65        \*Columbiformes

> Including Pteroclididae (sand grouse), dodos

> Class here Columbidae (doves, pigeons)

.7        **Miscellaneous orders of land birds**

> Limited to those named below

> Class comprehensive works on land birds in 598

[.701–.709]     Standard subdivisions

> Do not use; class in 598.01–598.09

.71        \*Psittaciformes

> Including budgerigars, cockatoos, kakapo, lories, macaws, parakeets, rosellas

> Class here Psittacidae, parrots

.72        \*Piciformes

> Including Picidae, Bucconidae (puffbirds), Capitonidae (barbets), Galbulidae (jacamars), Indicatoridae (honey guides), Ramphastidae (toucans); woodpeckers

> Class here Pici

.73        \*Trogoniformes (Trogons)

> Including quetzals

> Class here Trogonidae

.74        \*Cuculiformes

> Including Cuculidae, Musophagidae (touracos), Opisthocomidae (hoatzin); anis, cuckoos, roadrunners

\*Add as instructed under 592–599

.75        *Coliiformes

> Class here Coliidae (mousebirds)

.76        *Apodiformes

.762        *Apodi (Swifts)

> Including Hemiprocnidae (tree swifts)
>
> Class here Apodidae (true swifts)

.764        *Trochili (Hummingbirds)

> Class here Trochilidae

.78        *Coraciiformes

> Including Corcaciidae (rollers), Alcedinidae (kingfishers), Bucerotidae (hornbills), Meropidae (bee eaters)

**.8**        **\*Passeriformes (Perching birds)**

> Including bell magpies, cuckoo shrikes, honey eaters, magpie larks, vanga shrikes, wattled crows, wood shrikes, wood swallows
>
> Class here Oscines (Passeres, songbirds)
>
> *See Manual at 598.824–598.88*

.82        *Nonoscine Passeriformes, Paridae, Alaudidae, Hirundinidae, Certhiidae, Sittidae

> Including creepers, nuthatches

.822        *Nonoscine Passeriformes

> Including Cotingidae (cotingas), Dendrocolaptidae (woodcreepers), Eurylaimidae (broadbills), Menuridae (lyrebirds), Pipridae (manakins), Pittidae (pittas)
>
> *For Tyrannidae, see 598.823*

.822 5        *Furnariidae (Ovenbirds)

.822 6        *Formicariidae (Antbirds)

.823        *Tyrannidae

> Variant names: tyrant flycatchers, New World flycatchers
>
> *See also 598.848 for Old World flycatchers*

.824        *Paridae (Titmice)

> Including chickadees

.825        *Alaudidae (Larks)

> Class magpie larks in 598.8
>
> *See also 598.874 for meadowlarks*

---

*Add as instructed under 592–599

.826        *Hirundinidae

            Including martins

            Class here swallows

            Class wood swallows in 598.8

.83        *Cinclidae, Troglodytidae, Timaliidae, Chamaeidae

.832        *Cinclidae

            Variant names: dippers, water ouzels

.833        *Troglodytidae (Wrens)

.834        *Timaliidae (Babblers) and Chamaeidae (wren-tit)

            Subdivisions are added for Timaliidae and Chamaeidae together, for Timaliidae alone

.84        *Turdidae, Sylviidae, Mimidae, Muscicapidae

.842        *Turdidae (Thrushes)

            Including bluebirds, nightingales, Old World blackbird, robins

.843        *Sylviidae (Old World warblers)

            Including kinglets

.844        *Mimidae

            Including catbirds, mockingbirds, thrashers

.848        *Muscicapidae (Old World flycatchers)

            *See also 598.823 for New World flycatchers*

.85        *Bombycillidae, Ptilogonatidae, Motacillidae

.852        *Bombycillidae (Waxwings)

.853        *Ptilogonatidae (Silky flycatchers)

.854        *Motacillidae

            Including wagtails

            Class here pipits

.86        *Laniidae, Sturnidae, Corvidae, Paradisaeidae

.862        *Laniidae (Shrikes)

            Class cuckoo shrikes, vanga shrikes, wood shrikes in 598.8

            *See also 598.878 for pepper-shrikes and shrike-vireos*

.863        *Sturnidae (Starlings)

            Including mynas, oxpeckers

*Add as instructed under 592–599

.864          *Corvidae

          Including crows, jays, magpies, ravens, rooks

          Class bell magpies, magpie larks, wattled crows in 598.8

.865          *Paradisaeidae (Birds of paradise)

.87          *Parulidae, Icteridae, Thraupidae, Tersinidae, Vireonidae, Cyclarhidae, Vireolaniidae

.872          *Parulidae (New World warblers)

.874          *Icteridae

          Including New World blackbirds, cowbirds, grackles, meadowlarks, orioles

          *See also 598.825 for larks of family Alaudidae*

.875          *Thraupidae (Tanagers) and Tersinidae (swallow-tanager)

          Subdivisions are added for Thraupidae and Tersinidae together, for Thraupidae alone

.878          *Vireonidae (Vireos), Cyclarhidae (pepper-shrikes), Vireolaniidae (shrike-vireos)

          Including greenlets

          Subdivisions are added for Vireonidae, Cyclarhidae, Vireolaniidae together; for Vireonidae alone

.88          *Finches and related birds

          Including Catamblyrhynchidae (plush-capped finch)

          Subdivisions are added for finches and related birds together, for finches alone

.883          *Fringillidae (New World seedeaters)

          Including Emberizinae (Emberizidae); buntings, cardinals, Darwin's finches, grosbeaks, juncos, towhees, comprehensive works on sparrows

          *For sparrows of genus Passer, see 598.887*

.885          *Carduelidae

          Including bullfinches, canaries, crossbills, goldfinches, hawfinches, redpolls, rosefinches, siskins

.886          *Estrildidae (Waxbills)

          Including weaver finch

          Class comprehensive works on weaver finches in 598.887

*Add as instructed under 592–599

.887       *Ploceidae

            Variant names: weaverbirds, weavers

            Including queleas; sparrows of genus Passer, e.g., English sparrow, house sparrow

            Class here comprehensive works on weaver finches

                *For weaver finch of family Estrildidae, see 598.886*

**.9**     **\*Falconiformes, Strigiformes, Caprimulgiformes**

            Including Sagittariidae (secretary bird)

            Class here birds of prey, raptors

            Subdivisions are added for Falconiformes, Strigiformes, Caprimulgiformes together; for Falconiformes alone

                ———————

>          598.92–598.96 Falconiformes

            Class comprehensive works in 598.9

.92       *Cathartidae (New World vultures)

            Including condors, king vulture, turkey vulture (turkey buzzard)

            Class here comprehensive works on vultures

                *For Old World vultures, see 598.94*

.93       *Pandionidae (Osprey)

.94       *Accipitridae

            Including true buzzards, harriers, Old World vultures

            Class comprehensive works on vultures in 598.92

                *See also 598.92 for turkey buzzard*

.942      *Eagles

                *For Haliaeetus leucocephalus (bald eagle), see 598.943*

.942 3     *Aquila chrysaetos (Golden eagle)

.943      *Haliaeetus leucocephalus (Bald eagle)

.944      *Hawks

.945      *Kites

.96       *Falconidae (Falcons)

            Including caracaras, kestrels

*Add as instructed under 592–599

.97      *Strigiformes (Owls)

> Including Tytonidae (barn and grass owls)

> Class here Strigidae

.99      *Caprimulgiformes

> Including Nyctibiidae (potoos), Podargidae (frogmouths); oilbird, whippoorwill

> Class here Caprimulgidae (goatsuckers, nighthawks, nightjars)

# 599    *Mammalia (Mammals)

> Class here warm-blooded vertebrates, Eutheria (placental mammals)

> Class interdisciplinary works on species of domestic mammals in 636

> *For Aves, see 598*

> *See Manual at 599*

### SUMMARY

| | |
|---|---|
| 599.144–.163 | [Head and beneficial mammals] |
| .2 | Marsupialia and Monotremata |
| .3 | Miscellaneous orders of Eutheria (placental mammals) |
| .4 | Chiroptera (Bats) |
| .5 | Cetacea and Sirenia |
| .6 | Ungulates |
| .7 | Carnivora |
| .8 | Primates |
| .9 | Homo sapiens (Humans) |

[.073]      Collections of living mammals

> Do not use; class in 590.73

.144      Head

> Number built according to instructions under 592–599

> Including ears, eyes, mouth, nose

> *For fangs, horns, tusks, see 599.147*

.163      Beneficial mammals

> Number built according to instructions under 592–599

> Including game mammals

> Class big game animals in 599.6; class fur-bearing animals in 599.7

[.177]      Marine mammals

> Do not use; class in 599.5

*Add as instructed under 592–599

.2          **\*Marsupialia and Monotremata**

Class here Diprotodontia, Metatheria

Subdivisions are added for Marsupialia and Monotremata together, for Marsupialia alone

---

>          599.22–599.27  Marsupialia

Class comprehensive works in 599.2

---

>          599.22–599.25  Diprotodonta

Class comprehensive works in 599.2

.22             \*Macropodidae

Including rat and tree kangaroos

Class here wallabies

.222              \*Macropus

Including gray kangaroos, wallaroos

Class here comprehensive works on kangaroos

Class rat and tree kangaroos in 599.22

.222 3              \*Macropus rufus (Red kangaroo)

.23          \*Australasian possums

Including Burramyidae, Petauridae, Tarsipedidae

Class here Phalangeroidea

*For Macropodidae, see 599.22*

*See also 599.276 for American opossums*

.232              \*Phalangeridae

Including brush-tailed and scaly-tailed possums

Class here Phalanger (cuscuses)

.24          \*Vombatidae (Wombats)

.25          \*Phascolarctidae (Koala)

.26          \*Peramelina (Bandicoots)

Class here Peramelidae

\*Add as instructed under 592–599

.27 *Marsupicarnivora and Paucituberculata

Including Caenolestidae (shrew opossums), Dasyuridae, Microbiotheriidae (monito del monte); marsupial cats, mice, moles, rats; numbat, Tasmanian devil, thylacine (Tasmanian tiger, Tasmanian wolf)

Subdivisions are added for Marsupicarnivora and Paucituberculata together, for Marsupicarnivora alone

.276 *Didelphidae (American opossums)

*See also 599.23 for Australasian possums*

.29 *Monotremata

Including Ornithorhynchidae (platypus), Tachyglossidae (echidnas, spiny anteaters)

Class here Prototheria

---

> ### 599.3–599.9 Eutheria (Placental mammals)

Class comprehensive works in 599

.3 **Miscellaneous orders of Eutheria (placental mammals)**

Limited to those named below

### SUMMARY

| | |
|---|---|
| 599.31 | Edentata (Xenarthra), Pholidota, Tubulidentata |
| .32 | Lagomorpha |
| .33 | Insectivora and related orders |
| .35 | Rodentia (Rodents) |
| .36 | Sciuridae (Squirrel family) |
| .37 | Castoridae (Beavers) |

[.301–.309] Standard subdivisions

Do not use; class in 599.01–599.09

.31 *Edentata (Xenarthra), Pholidota, Tubulidentata

Variant names for Pholidota: pangolins, scaly anteaters; for Tubulidentata: aardvark, ant bear

Subdivisions are added for Edentata, Pholidota, Tubulidentata together; for Edentata alone

---

> ### 599.312–599.314 Edentata (Xenarthra)

Class comprehensive works in 599.31

.312 *Dasypodidae (Armadillos)

Subdivisions are added for the family as a whole and for individual genera and species

---

*Add as instructed under 592–599

.313         *Bradypodidae (Sloths)

> Subdivisions are added for the family as a whole and for individual genera and species

.314         *Myrmecophagidae

> Class here comprehensive works on anteaters

> Class ant bears, scaly anteaters in 599.31

> *For spiny anteaters, see 599.29*

.32         *Lagomorpha

> Class here Leporidae; rabbits

> Class interdisciplinary works on domestic rabbits in 636.9322

---

>      599.322–599.328   Leporidae

> Class comprehensive works in 599.32

.322         *Oryctolagus (Old World rabbit)

.324         *Sylvilagus (Cottontails)

> Subdivisions are added for the genus as a whole and for individual species

.328         *Lepus

> Class here hares, jackrabbits

> Subdivisions are added for the genus as a whole and for individual species

.329         *Ochotonidae

> Variant names: conies, pikas

> Class here Ochotona

> *See also 599.68 for conies of order Hyracoidea*

.33         *Insectivora and related orders

> Including Dermoptera (Cynocephalidae, colugos, flying lemurs); otter shrews, solenodons, tenrecs

> Class here Lipotyphla

> Subdivisions are added for Insectivora and related orders together, for Insectivora alone

---

>      599.332–599.336   Insectivora

> Class comprehensive works in 599.33

---

*Add as instructed under 592–599

| | |
|---|---|
| .332 | *Erinaceidae |

         Including wood shrews

         Class here hedgehogs

| | |
|---|---|
| .332 2 | *Erinaceus |

         Class here European hedgehog

         Subdivisions are added for the genus as a whole and for individual species

| | |
|---|---|
| .335 | *Talpidae and Chrysocloridae |

         Class here moles

         Subdivisions are added for Talpidae and Chrysocloridae together, for Talpidae alone

| | |
|---|---|
| .336 | *Soricidae |

         Class here comprehensive works on shrews

         Class otter shrews in 599.33

         *For wood shrews, see 599.332; for elephant shrews, see 599.337; for tree shrews, see 599.338*

| | |
|---|---|
| .336 2 | *Sorex (Long-tailed shrews) |

         Class here pigmy shrew

         Subdivisions are added for the genus as a whole and for individual species

| | |
|---|---|
| .337 | *Macroscelidea |

         Variant names: Macroscelididae, elephant shrews

| | |
|---|---|
| .338 | *Scandentia |

         Variant names: Tupaiidae, tree shrews

| | |
|---|---|
| .35 | *Rodentia (Rodents) |

         Including jerboas; harvest and jumping mice; mole and swamp rats

         Class here Myomorpha; Muridae covering Cricetidae, Rhizomyidae, Spalacidae; mice; rats

         Class results of experimental studies on internal biological processes using laboratory mice and rats in 571–573, plus notation 1935 from add instructions in 571–573, e.g., circulation in rats 573.11935

         *For Sciuridae, see 599.36; for Castoridae, see 599.37*

---

>        599.352–599.358   Muridae

         Class comprehensive works in 599.35

*Add as instructed under 592–599

| | |
|---|---|
| .352 | *Rattus (Common rats) |

Class here black rat, Norway (brown) rat

Subdivisions are added for the genus as a whole and for individual species

Class comprehensive works on rats in 599.35

| | |
|---|---|
| .353 | *Mus (Common mice) |

Class here house mouse

Subdivisions are added for the genus as a whole and for individual species

Class comprehensive works on mice in 599.35

| | |
|---|---|
| .354 | *Voles |

Including Arvicola (water voles)

Class here Microtus (meadow mice)

| | |
|---|---|
| .355 | *Peromyscus |

Variant names: deer mice, white-footed mice

| | |
|---|---|
| .356 | *Hamsters |

Class here Cricetus, Mesocricetus (golden hamsters)

Class interdisciplinary works on domestic species of hamsters in 636.9356

| | |
|---|---|
| .357 | Miscellaneous rats of family Muridae |

Limited to those named below

| | |
|---|---|
| [.357 01–.357 09] | Standard subdivisions |

Do not use; class in 599.3501–599.3509

| | |
|---|---|
| .357 2 | *Sigmodon (Cotton rats) |
| .357 3 | *Neotoma (Wood rats) |
| .357 9 | *Muskrats |

Class here Ondatra, Neofiber

| | |
|---|---|
| .358 | Miscellaneous Muridae |

Limited to those named below

| | |
|---|---|
| [.358 01–.358 09] | Standard subdivisions |

Do not use; class in 599.3501–599.3509

| | |
|---|---|
| .358 2 | *Lemmings |

Class here Lemmus

*Add as instructed under 592–599

.358 3            *Gerbils

                  Class interdisciplinary works on domestic species of gerbils in
                  636.93583

.358 5            *Apodemus

                  Variant names: field mice, wood mice

.359        *Rodentia other than Castoridae, Muridae, Sciuridae

                  Including agoutis (pacas), capybaras, coypu (nutria), gundis, hutias,
                  springhaas; African mole rat; cane, rock, spiny rats

                  Class here Caviomorpha, Hystricomorpha, Phiomorpha

.359 2            *Caviidae

                  Class here Cavia, cavies, guinea pigs

                  Class interdisciplinary works on Cavia porcellus (domestic guinea
                  pigs) in 636.93592

.359 3            *Chinchillidae

                  Class here chinchillas

                  Class interdisciplinary works on chinchillas in 636.93593

.359 6            *Gliridae

                  Variant names: Myoxidae, dormice

.359 7            *Porcupines

                  Including Hystricidae (Old World porcupines)

.359 74             *Erethizontidae (New World porcupines)

.359 8            *Heteromyidae

                  Including pocket and kangaroo mice

.359 87             *Dipodomys (Kangaroo rats)

.359 9            *Geomyidae (Pocket gophers)

                  *See also 599.365 for gopher of genus Spermophilus*

.36         *Sciuridae (Squirrel family)

                  Class here squirrels

.362        *Sciurus (Tree squirrels)

                  Class here Eurasian red squirrel, fox squirrel, gray squirrel

                  Subdivisions are added for the genus as a whole and for individual
                  species

*Add as instructed under 592–599

.363      *Tamiasciurus

         Variant names: North American red squirrels, chickarees

         Class here Douglas squirrel

         Subdivisions are added for the genus as a whole and for individual species

.364      *Chipmunks

         Subdivisions are added for chipmunks as a whole and for individual genera and species

.365      *Ground squirrels

         Including gopher, susliks

         Class here Spermophilus

            *See also 599.3599 for pocket gophers; also 599.364 for chipmunks*

.366      *Marmota (Marmots)

         Class here woodchuck (groundhog)

         Subdivisions are added for the genus as a whole and for individual species

.367      *Cynomys (Prairie dogs)

         Subdivisions are added for the genus as a whole and for individual species

.369      *Flying squirrels

         Class here Glaucomys; eastern flying squirrel

.37      *Castoridae (Beavers)

         Class here Castor

         Subdivisions are added for the genus as a whole and for individual species

**.4      *Chiroptera (Bats)**

         Class here Microchiroptera

.45      *Phyllostomidae

         Including neotropical fruit bats, vampire bats

.47      *Vespertilionidae

         Including big brown bats, house bats

.472      *Myotis (Little brown bats)

         Subdivisions are added for the genus as a whole and for individual species

---

*Add as instructed under 592–599

.49               *Pteropodidae (Old World fruit bats)

                  Including flying foxes

                  Class here Megachiroptera

## .5        *Cetacea and Sirenia

                  Class here marine mammals; whales, great whales; Mysticeti (baleen whales), Odontoceti (toothed whales)

                  Subdivisions are added for Cetacea and Sirenia together, for Cetacea alone

                  *For Pinnipedia, see 599.79*

---

>           599.52–599.54  Cetacea

                  Class comprehensive works in 599.5

.52               Specific Mysticeti (baleen whales)

                  Including pygmy right whale

                  Class comprehensive works on Mysticeti in 599.5

[.520 1–.520 9]        Standard subdivisions

                        Do not use; class in 599.501–599.509

.522              *Eschrichtidae (Gray whale)

.524              *Balaenopteridae (Rorquals)

                  Including Bryde's, minke, sei whales

                  Class here Balaenoptera

                  *For Megaptera, see 599.525*

.524 6            *Balaenoptera physalus

                  Variant names: fin whale, finback whale

.524 8            *Balaenoptera musculus (Blue whale)

.525              *Megaptera (Humpback whale)

.527              *Balaenidae

.527 3            *Eubalaena (Right whale)

.527 6            *Balaena

                  Variant names: bowhead whale, Greenland right whale

---

>           599.53–599.54  Odontoceti (Toothed whales)

                  Class comprehensive works in 599.5

---

*Add as instructed under 592–599

.53      *Dolphins and porpoises

Including false killer and pilot whales

Class here Delphinidae

Subdivisions are added for dolphins and porpoises together, for dolphins alone

---

>      599.532–599.536   Delphinidae

Class comprehensive works in 599.53

*For river dolphins of family Delphinidae, see 599.538*

.532      *Delphinus (Common dolphin)

.533      *Tursiops (Bottle-nosed dolphins)

Subdivisions are added for the genus as a whole and for individual species

.534      *Stenella

Including spinner, spotted, striped dolphins

.536      *Orcinus (Killer whale)

.538      *River dolphins

Including Iniidae, Platanistidae, Pontoporiidae; Orcaella and Sotalia of family Delphinidae

.539      *Phocoenidae (Porpoises)

Class here Phocoena (harbor porpoises)

Subdivisions are added for the genus Phocoena as a whole and for individual species of Phocoena

.54      *Other Odontoceti (toothed whales)

Other than dolphins and porpoises

Class comprehensive works on Odontoceti in 599.5

*For false killer, pilot whales, see 599.53; for killer whale, see 599.536*

.542      *Delphinapterus

Variant names: beluga, white whale

Class here Monodontidae

*For Monodon, see 599.543*

.543      *Monodon (Narwhal)

.545      *Ziphiidae (Beaked whales)

*Add as instructed under 592–599

.547          *Physeteridae

> Including dwarf and pygmy sperm whales

> Class here Physeter (sperm whale)

.55          *Sirenia (Sea cows)

> Class here Trichechidae (manatees)

> Subdivisions are added for the genus Trichechus and for individual species of Trichechus

.559          *Dugongidae

> Class here dugong

> Class Steller's sea cow in 599.559168

**.6          *Ungulates**

> Class here hoofed mammals, comprehensive works on big game animals

> Class Sirenia in 599.55; class big game hunting in 799.26

> *For a specific kind of nonungulate big game animal, see the kind, e.g., bears 599.78*

### SUMMARY

| | |
|---|---|
| **599.63** | **Artiodactyla (Even-toed ungulates)** |
| **.64** | **Bovidae** |
| **.65** | **Cervidae (Deer)** |
| **.66** | **Perissodactyla (Odd-toed ungulates)** |
| **.67** | **Proboscidea (Elephants)** |
| **.68** | **Hyracoidea** |

.63          *Artiodactyla (Even-toed ungulates)

> Including Tragulidae (chevrotains, mouse deer)

> Class here Ruminantia (ruminants)

> Class comprehensive works on Artiodactyla and Perissodactyla in 599.6

> *For Bovidae, see 599.64; for Cervidae, see 599.65*

.633          *Suidae

> Variant names: pigs, swine

> Including African bush pig, babirusa, giant forest hog, warthog

> Class here comprehensive works on Suiformes

> *For Tayassuidae, see 599.634; for Hippopotamidae, see 599.635*

*Add as instructed under 592–599

| .633 2 | *Sus |
|---|---|

> Including bearded and Javan pigs
>
> Class here wild boars
>
> Class interdisciplinary works on Sus scrofa (domestic swine) in 636.4

| .634 | *Tayassuidae (Peccaries) |
|---|---|

> Subdivisions are added for the family as a whole and for individual genera and species

| .635 | *Hippopotamidae (Hippopotamuses) |
|---|---|

> Including pigmy hippopotamus
>
> Class here Hippopotamus amphibius

| .636 | *Camelidae |
|---|---|

| .636 2 | *Camelus (Camels) |
|---|---|

> Subdivisions are added for the genus as a whole and for individual species
>
> Class interdisciplinary works on camels in 636.295

| .636 7 | *Lama |
|---|---|

> Class here guanaco, vicuña
>
> Class interdisciplinary works on guanaco (alpaca, llama) in 636.296

| .638 | *Giraffidae |
|---|---|

> Including okapi
>
> Class here giraffe

| .639 | *Antilocapridae (Pronghorn) |
|---|---|

| .64 | *Bovidae |
|---|---|

> Including Cephalophinae (duikers)
>
> Class here antelopes
>
> *See also 599.639 for pronghorn antelope*

| .642 | *Bovinae |
|---|---|

> Including buffalo, elands, four-horned antelopes
>
> *For American buffalo, see 599.643*

| .642 2 | *Bos (Oxen) |
|---|---|

> Including banteng, gaur, yak
>
> Class interdisciplinary works on Bos taurus (domestic cattle) in 636.2

---

*Add as instructed under 592–599

.642 3              *Tragelaphus

Including bongo, bushbuck, kudus, nyalas

.643               *Bison

Including European bison (wisent)

Class here American bison (American buffalo)

.645               *Hippotraginae

Including addax, hartebeests, oryx, reedbucks, waterbuck; roan and sable antelopes

Class here Alcelaphinae

.645 9             *Connochaetes

Variant names: gnus, wildebeests

Subdivisions are added for the genus as a whole and for individual species

.646               *Antilopinae

Including dik-diks, impala, springbok

.646 9             *Gazella (Gazelles)

Subdivisions are added for the genus as a whole and for individual species

.647               *Caprinae

Including chamois, saiga, serows

*For Capra, see 599.648; for sheep, see 599.649*

.647 5             *Oreamnos (Mountain goat)

.647 8             *Ovibos (Muskox)

.648               *Capra

Including ibexes, turs

Class here goats

Class interdisciplinary works on Capra hircus (domestic goat) in 636.39

*See also 599.6475 for mountain goat*

.649               *Sheep

Including aoudad (Barbary sheep), bharals (blue sheep)

Class here Ovis

Class interdisciplinary works on Ovis aries (domestic sheep) in 636.3

.649 7             *Ovis canadensis (Bighorn sheep)

*Add as instructed under 592–599

| | |
|---|---|
| .65 | *Cervidae (Deer) |

Including chital, muntjacs

*See also 599.63 for mouse deer*

| | |
|---|---|
| .652 | *Odocoileus |

Class here white-tailed (Virginia) deer

*For Odocoileus hemionus (mule deer), see 599.653*

| | |
|---|---|
| .653 | *Odocoileus hemionus (Mule deer) |
| .654 | *Cervus |

Including sambar

| | |
|---|---|
| .654 2 | *Cervus elaphus |

Variant names: American elk, red deer, wapiti

*See also 599.657 for elk of genus Alces*

| | |
|---|---|
| .655 | *Dama (Fallow deer) |
| .657 | *Alces |

Variant name: moose, elk

*See also 599.6542 for American elk*

| | |
|---|---|
| .658 | *Rangifer |

Variant names: caribou, reindeer

| | |
|---|---|
| .659 | *Capreolus (Roe deer) |

Subdivisions are added for the genus as a whole and for individual species

| | |
|---|---|
| .66 | *Perissodactyla (Odd-toed ungulates) |

Including Tapiridae (tapirs)

| | |
|---|---|
| .665 | *Equidae |

Including asses

Class here Equus

Class interdisciplinary works on asses in 636.18

| | |
|---|---|
| .665 5 | *Equus caballus (Horse) |

Class here mustang, Przewalski's horse, wild horse

Class interdisciplinary works on horses in 636.1

*Add as instructed under 592–599

.665 7          *Zebras

> Subdivisions are added for zebras as a whole and for individual species

> Class quagga in 599.6657168

.668          *Rhinocerotidae (Rhinoceroses)

> Subdivisions are added for the family as a whole and for individual genera and species

.67          *Proboscidea (Elephants)

.674          *Loxodonta (African elephant)

.676          *Elephas

> Variant names: Asiatic elephant, Indian elephant

.68          *Hyracoidea

> Variant names: conies, dassies, hyraxes

> *See also 599.329 for conies of order Lagomorpha*

.7      **\*Carnivora**

> Class here Fissipedia (Land carnivores), comprehensive works on fur-bearing animals

> *For a specific kind of noncarnivorous fur-bearing animal, see the kind, e.g., beavers 599.37*

### SUMMARY

| | |
|---|---|
| **599.74** | **Feloidea** |
| **.75** | **Felidae (Cat family)** |
| **.76** | **Canoidea** |
| **.77** | **Canidae (Dog family)** |
| **.78** | **Ursidae (Bears)** |
| **.79** | **Pinnipedia (Marine carnivores)** |

> 599.74–599.78  Fissipedia (Land carnivores)

> Class comprehensive works in 599.7

.74          *Feloidea

> *For Felidae, see 599.75*

.742          *Viverridae

> Including civets, fossa, genets, linsangs, meercat, mongooses

.743          *Hyaenidae

> Including aardwolf

> Class here hyenas

*Add as instructed under 592–599

| | |
|---|---|
| .75 | *Felidae (Cat family) |

Including clouded leopard

| | |
|---|---|
| .752 | *Felis |

Including margay, ocelot, serval

Class genus Lynx in 599.753; class interdisciplinary works on Felis catus (domestic cats) in 636.8

| | |
|---|---|
| .752 4 | *Felis concolor |

Variant names: cougar, mountain lion, panther, puma

| | |
|---|---|
| .752 6 | *Felis silvestris (European wildcat) |

*See also 599.7536 for bobcat (wildcat)*

| | |
|---|---|
| .753 | *Lynx |

Subdivisions are added for the genus as a whole and for individual species other than Lynx rufus

| | |
|---|---|
| .753 6 | *Lynx rufus |

Variant name: bobcat, wildcat

*See also 599.7526 for European wildcat*

| | |
|---|---|
| .755 | *Panthera (Leo) |

Including jaguar

Class here big cats

*For Panthera tigris (tiger), see 599.756; for Panthera leo (lion), see 599.757. For a specific big cat not provided for here, see the cat, e.g., mountain lion 599.7524*

| | |
|---|---|
| .755 4 | *Panthera pardus (Leopard) |

Class here comprehensive works on leopards

Class clouded leopard in 599.75

*For snow leopard, see 599.7555*

| | |
|---|---|
| .755 5 | *Panthera uncia |

Variant names: ounce, snow leopard

| | |
|---|---|
| .756 | *Panthera tigris (Tiger) |
| .757 | *Panthera leo (Lion) |
| .759 | *Acinonyx (Cheetah) |
| .76 | *Canoidea |

*For Canidae, see 599.77; for Ursidae, see 599.78*

*Add as instructed under 592–599

.763         *Procyonidae

Including coatis, kinkajou, red (lesser) panda

*See also 599.789 for giant panda*

.763 2      *Procyon (Raccoons)

Subdivisions are added for the genus as a whole and for individual species

.766         *Mustelidae

Including grisons, marbled polecat, wolverine, zorilla (striped polecat)

Class here Mustelinae

*For Melinae, see 599.767; for Mephitinae, see 599.768; for Lutrinae, see 599.769*

.766 2      *Mustela

Including ermine (stoat), comprehensive works on Old World polecats

Class here weasels

Class marbled polecat, zorilla (striped polecat) in 599.766; class European polecat in 599.76628

*For weasels in genera other than Mustela, see 599.7663*

*See also 599.768 for New world polecats (skunks)*

.766 27     *Minks

Subdivisions are added for minks as a whole and for individual species

.766 28     Mustela putorius (European polecat)

Class interdisciplinary works on ferrets (domestic European polecat) in 636.976628

.766 29     *Mustela nigripes (Black-footed ferret)

.766 3      *Weasels in genera other than Mustela

Including Patagonian and striped weasels

.766 5      *Martes

Including fisher, sable

Class here martens

.767         *Melinae and Mellivorinae

Class here badgers

Subdivisions are added for Melinae and Mellivorinae together, for Melinae alone

*Add as instructed under 592–599

| .767 2 | *Meles (Old World badger) |
|---|---|
| .768 | *Mephitinae |

> Variant names: skunks, polecats
>
> *See also 599.7662 for Old World polecats*

| .769 | *Lutrinae (Otters) |
|---|---|

> Including clawless and giant otters

| .769 2 | *Lutra (River otters) |
|---|---|

> Subdivisions are added for the genus as a whole and for individual species

| .769 5 | *Enhydra (Sea otter) |
|---|---|
| .77 | *Canidae (Dog family) |

> Including dhole; dogs and wolves of genera other than Canis

| .772 | *Canis |
|---|---|

> Including dingo, jackals
>
> Class here comprehensive scientific works on dogs
>
> Class dogs of genera other than Canis in 599.77; class interdisciplinary works on dogs in 636.7
>
> > *For Canis lupus (gray wolf, timber wolf) and Canis rufus (red wolf), see 599.773*

| .772 5 | *Canis latrans (Coyote) |
|---|---|
| .773 | *Canis lupus and Canis rufus (red wolf) |

> Variant names for Canis lupus: gray wolf, timber wolf
>
> Class here comprehensive works on wolves
>
> Subdivisions are added for either or both topics in heading
>
> Class wolves of genera other than Canis in 599.77

| .775 | *Vulpes |
|---|---|

> Class here red fox, comprehensive works on foxes
>
> Subdivisions are added for the genus as a whole and for individual species
>
> *For foxes of genera other than Vulpes, see 599.776*

| .776 | *Foxes of genera other than Vulpes |
|---|---|

> Including fennec and gray foxes

| .776 4 | *Alopex (Arctic fox) |
|---|---|

*Add as instructed under 592–599

.78      \*Ursidae (Bears)

       Class here Ursus

.784     \*Ursus arctos

       Variant name: grizzly bear, brown bear

.785     \*Ursus americanus (American black bear)

.786     \*Ursus maritimus (Polar bear)

.789     \*Ailuropoda (Giant panda)

       *See also 599.763 for lesser panda*

.79      \*Pinnipedia (Marine carnivores)

       Class here Phocidae (earless seals, hair seals, true seals); seals

       *See also 599.7695 for sea otters*

---

>        599.792–599.796 Phocidae

       Variant names: earless seals, hair seals, true seals

       Class comprehensive works in 599.79

.792     \*Phoca

       Including Baikal, Caspian, ribbon, ringed, spotted seals

.792 3    \*Phoca vitulina (Harbor seal)

.792 9    \*Phoca groenlandica (Harp seal)

.793     \*Halichoerus (Gray seal)

.794     \*Mirounga (Elephant seals)

       Subdivisions are added for the genus as a whole and for individual species

.795     \*Monachus (Monk seals)

       Subdivisions are added for the genus as a whole and for individual species

.796     \*Other Phocidae

       Including bearded, crabeater, hooded, leopard, Ross, Weddell seals

.797     \*Otariidae (Eared seals)

.797 3    \*Arctocephalinae (Fur seals)

       Class here Callorhinus (northern fur seal, Pacific fur seal)

.797 38   \*Arctocephalus (Southern fur seals)

       Subdivisions are added for the genus as a whole and for individual species

---

\*Add as instructed under 592–599

| | | |
|---|---|---|
| .797 5 | | *Otariinae (Sea lions) |

Subdivisions are added for sea lions as a whole and for individual genera and species

.799    *Odobenidae (Walrus)

**.8    *Primates**

Class here Anthropoidea, monkeys

.83    *Prosimii

Including Lemuridae (lemurs), Lorisidae, Tarsiidae (tarsiers)

Including aye-ayes, bush babies, galagos, indri, lorises, sifakas

Class Tupaiidae in 599.338

---

> 599.84–599.88  Anthropoidea

Class comprehensive works in 599.8

*For Homo sapiens, see 599.9*

---

> 599.84–599.86  Monkeys

Class comprehensive works in 599.8

.84    *Callitrichidae (Marmosets)

Including tamarins

.85    *Cebidae (New World monkeys)

Class here Platyrrhini

*For Callitrichidae, see 599.84*

.852    *Saimiri (Squirrel monkeys)

Subdivisions are added for the genus as a whole and for individual species

.855    *Alouatta (Howler monkeys)

Subdivisions are added for the genus as a whole and for individual species

.858    *Atelinae

Including spider and woolly monkeys

.86    *Cercopithecidae (Old World monkeys)

Class here Catarrhini

.862    *Cercopithecus (Guenons)

Including blue and green monkeys

*Add as instructed under 592–599

| | |
|---|---|
| .864 | *Macaca (Macaques) |
| .864 3 | *Macaca mulatta (Rhesus monkey) |
| .864 4 | *Macaca fuscata |

Variant names: Japanese macaque, snow monkey

| | |
|---|---|
| .865 | *Papio (Baboons) |

Subdivisions are added for the genus as a whole and for individual species

| | |
|---|---|
| .88 | *Hominidae and Hylobatidae |

Variant name for Hominidae: great apes

Class here apes, comprehensive works on Hominoidea

Subdivisions are added for Hominidae and Hylobatidae together, for Hominidae alone

*For Homo sapiens, see 599.9*

| | |
|---|---|
| .882 | *Hylobatidae (Gibbons) |

Including siamang

Class here Hylobates

---

> 599.883–599.885 Specific Hominidae (Great apes) other than Homo sapiens

Class comprehensive works in 599.88

| | |
|---|---|
| .883 | *Pongo (Orangutan) |
| .884 | *Gorilla |
| .885 | *Pan (Chimpanzees) |

Subdivisions are added for the genus as a whole and for individual species

| | |
|---|---|
| **.9** | **Homo sapiens (Humans)** |

Class here physical anthropology

Class social anthropology, interdisciplinary works on social and physical anthropology in 306

*For psychology, see 150; for prehistoric Homo and related genera, see 569.9; for medicine, see 610*

| | |
|---|---|
| .93 | Genetics, sex and age characteristics, evolution |
| .935 | Genetics |

Class here heredity

*For variation, see 599.94; for biochemical genetics, see 611.01816*

---

*Add as instructed under 592–599

| .936 | Sex characteristics |
| | Class here secondary sexual characteristics |
| .937 | Age characteristics |
| | Class here age determination |
| | Class longevity in 612.68 |
| .938 | Evolution |
| | *For paleontology of Homo and related genera, see 569.9* |
| .94 | Anthropometry |
| | Class here variation |
| | *See Manual at 599.94 vs. 611* |
| .943 | Teeth |
| .945 | Skin |
| | Including dermatoglyphics, fingerprints |
| | Class use of fingerprints in criminal investigation in 363.258 |
| .947 | Bones |
| | *For craniology, see 599.948* |
| .948 | Head and face |
| | Standard subdivisions are added for either or both topics in heading |
| | Class here craniology |
| .949 | Somatotypes |
| | Including people with abnormal dimensions, e.g., dwarfs, giants |
| | Class pathological aspects of abnormal dimensions in 616.043 |
| .95 | Environmental effects on physique |
| | Including effect on pigmentation |
| | Class here human biological ecology |
| | Class interdisciplinary works on human ecology in 304.2 |
| .97 | Human ethnic groups |
| | Class here physical ethnology |
| | *For specific ethnic groups, see 599.98* |
| .972 | Origins and causes of physical differences among ethnic groups |
| | Class nonethnic physical characteristics in 599.9; class origins and causes of physical differences of specific ethnic groups in 599.98 |
| .98 | Specific ethnic groups |
| | Class extinct ethnic groups in 569.9 |

| | |
|---|---|
| .980 5–.980 9 | People of mixed ancestry with ethnic origins from more than one continent; Europeans and people of European descent |

> Add to base number 599.98 notation 05–09 from Table 5, e.g., Europeans 599.9809

| | |
|---|---|
| .981–.989 | Specific ethnic groups with other origins |

> Add to base number 599.98 notation 1–9 from Table 5, e.g., Celts 599.98916

**The 23rd edition of the Dewey Decimal Classification** was produced using the fourth generation of the Editorial Support System (ESS), developed by OCLC Online Computer Library Center, Inc. ESS includes a print module developed by Pansoft GmbH, Karlsruhe, Germany, under an agreement with OCLC. Composition was done in Times Roman and Arial under the supervision of Michael Panzer. The book was printed and bound by Edwards Brothers, Inc., Ann Arbor, Michigan.